WITHDRAWN

NORTH DAKOTA
STATE UNIVERSITY
JUN 1 6 1982
SERIALS DEPT.
LIBRARY

The Bowker Annual

WITHDRAWN

THE BOWKER ANNUAL

OF LIBRARY & BOOK TRADE INFORMATION

27TH EDITION · 1982

Compiled & Edited by
JOANNE O'HARE & BETTY SUN

Consulting Editor
Frank L. Schick

Sponsored by
The Council of National Library
& Information Associations, Inc.

R. R. BOWKER COMPANY
NEW YORK & LONDON

Published by R. R. Bowker Company
1180 Avenue of the Americas, New York, N.Y. 10036
Copyright © 1982 by Xerox Corporation
All rights reserved
International Standard Book Number 0-8352-1430-3
International Standard Serial Number 0068-0540
Library of Congress Catalog Card Number 55-12434
Printed and bound in the United States of America

No copyright is claimed for articles in this volume prepared by U.S. Government employees as part of their official duties. Such articles are in the public domain and can be reproduced at will.

Contents

Preface xi

PART 1
REPORTS FROM THE FIELD

NEWS REPORTS
LJ News Report, 1981. *Karl Nyren* 3
SLJ News Report, 1981. *Bertha M. Cheatham* 25
PW News Report, 1981. *John F. Baker* 34

SPECIAL REPORTS
The State of Intellectual Freedom. *Judith F. Krug* 38
Public Library Services for the Aging in the Eighties. *Betty J. Turock* 43
Recent Developments in Health Sciences Libraries in the United States.
    Maxine K. Hanke 52
Recent Developments in Library Conservation in the United States.
    Sally Buchanan 61
The Folger Shakespeare Library. *Philip A. Knachel* 68
Copyright Clearance Center. *David P. Waite* and *Virginia Riordan* 72

RESOURCE SHARING: SELECTED REPORTS
Library Networking in the United States, 1981. *Susan K. Martin* 78
Metropolitan Washington Library Council. *Barbara M. Robinson* 82

FEDERAL AGENCIES
The National Commission on Libraries and Information Science.
    Toni Carbo Bearman and *Douglas S. Price* 88
The Copyright Office: Developments in 1981. *Victor W. Marton* 93
The Center for the Book in the Library of Congress. *John Y. Cole* 98
Federal Library Committee. *James P. Riley* 100

FEDERAL LIBRARIES
The Library of Congress. *James W. McClung* 106
National Library of Medicine. *Robert B. Mehnert* 112
National Agricultural Library. *Eugene M. Farkas* 117

NATIONAL ASSOCIATIONS

American Library Association. *Elizabeth W. Stone* 120

American Booksellers Association. *G. Royce Smith* 130

American National Standards Committee Z-39 and International Organization for Standardization Technical Committee 46. *Patricia W. Berger* and *Robert W. Frase* 133

Association of American Publishers. *Jane Lippe* 139

Association of Research Libraries. *Nicola Daval* 147

Information Industry Association. *Fred S. Rosenau* 152

National Micrographics Association. *O. Gordon Banks* 156

Society for Scholarly Publishing. *Mark Carroll* 163

Special Libraries Association. *Richard Griffin* 165

PART 2
LEGISLATION, FUNDING, AND GRANTS

Legislation Affecting Librarianship in 1981. *Eileen D. Cooke* and *Carol C. Henderson* 173

Legislation Affecting Publishing in 1981. *Washington Staff, AAP* 189

Legislation Affecting the Information Industry in 1981. *Robert S. Willard* .. 195

FUNDING PROGRAMS AND GRANT-MAKING AGENCIES

Council on Library Resources, Inc. *Jane A. Rosenberg* 204

Library Services and Construction Act. 212

Elementary and Secondary Education Act, Title IV, Part B—Instructional Materials and School Library Resources. *Beatrice Simmons Arndt* 221

Higher Education Act, Title II-A, College Library Resources. *Beth Phillips* . 225

Higher Education Act, Title II-B, Library Career Training. *Frank A. Stevens* 228

Higher Education Act, Title II-B, Library Research and Demonstration Program. *Sarah G. Bishop* 233

Higher Education Act, Title II-C, Strengthening Research Library Resources. *Patricia R. Harris* 237

National Science Foundation Support for Research in Information Science and Technology. *Sarah N. Rhodes* 242

PART 3
LIBRARY EDUCATION, PLACEMENT, AND SALARIES

Guide to Library Placement Sources. *Margaret Myers* 251

Recent Library Personnel Surveys. *Margaret Myers* 266

Placements and Salaries, 1980: Holding the Line.
    Carol L. Learmont and *Stephen Van Houten* 273
Education for Library Support Staff in the United States and Canada.
    Josephine Riss Fang 288
Accredited Library Schools. 292
Library Scholarship Sources. 295
Library Scholarship and Award Recipients, 1981. 297

PART 4
RESEARCH AND STATISTICS

LIBRARY RESEARCH AND STATISTICS
Research on Libraries and Librarianship in 1981. *Mary Jo Lynch* 305
Developments in Library Statistical Activities. *Frank L. Schick* 309
Characteristics of the U.S. Population Served by Libraries. 312
Number of Libraries in the United States and Canada. 314
Public and Academic Library Acquisition Expenditures. 316
Urban-Suburban Public Library Statistics. *Joseph Green* 321
NCES Survey of Public Libraries, 1977–1978. *Helen M. Eckard* 329
NCES Survey of Public School Library Media Centers, 1978.
    Milbrey L. Jones 338
NCES Survey of Library Networks and Cooperative Library Organizations,
    1977–1978. *Helen M. Eckard* 344
Intergovernmental Library Cooperation Project. *Alphonse F. Trezza* 356
Academic Library Buildings in 1981.
    Bette-Lee Fox and *Shiri Rosenthal* 361
Public Library Buildings in 1981. *Bette-Lee Fox* and *Shiri Rosenthal* 366
Two-Year College Learning Resource Center Buildings in 1981.
    D. Joleen Bock 376

BOOK TRADE RESEARCH AND STATISTICS
Standard Address Number. *Emery I. Koltay* 380
Book Title Output and Average Prices, 1981 Preliminary Figures.
    Chandler B. Grannis 383
Book Sales Statistics: Highlights from AAP Annual Survey, 1980.
    Chandler B. Grannis 392
U.S. Consumer Expenditures on Books in 1980. *John P. Dessauer* 394
Prices of U.S. and Foreign Published Materials. *Nelson A. Piper* 396
Number of Book Outlets in the United States and Canada. 413
Book Review Media Statistics. 414

PART 5
INTERNATIONAL REPORTS AND STATISTICS

INTERNATIONAL REPORTS
Frankfurt Book Fair, 1981. *Herbert R. Lottman* 417

IFLA Conference and Council Meeting, 1981: An American Perspective.
Jane Wilson 422

Preconference and Meetings of the IFLA Section on Statistics, 1981.
Katherine H. Packer 428

Library Services in Israel. *Shmuel Sever* 430

Network Development in Canada: An Overview. *Laurent G. Denis* 436

INTERNATIONAL STATISTICS
U.S. Book Exports and Imports and International Title Output.
Chandler B. Grannis 440

British Book Production 1981 446

PART 6
REFERENCE INFORMATION

BIBLIOGRAPHIES
The Librarian's Bookshelf. *Jo Ann Michalak* 453

Basic Publications for the Publisher and the Book Trade. *Jean R. Peters* ... 464

DISTINGUISHED BOOKS
Literary Prizes, 1981 472

Notable Books of 1981 483

Best Young Adult Books of 1981 484

Best Children's Books of 1981 486

Best Sellers of 1981: Hardcover Fiction and Nonfiction. *Daisy Maryles* 490

PART 7
DIRECTORY OF ORGANIZATIONS

DIRECTORY OF LIBRARY AND RELATED ORGANIZATIONS
National Library and Information-Industry Associations, United States and
Canada 499

State, Provincial, and Regional Library Associations 563

State Library Agencies 574

State School Library Media Associations 578

State Supervisors of School Library Media Services. 584
International Library Associations 588
Foreign Library Associations 597

DIRECTORY OF BOOK TRADE AND RELATED ORGANIZATIONS
Book Trade Associations, United States and Canada 608
International and Foreign Book Trade Associations 614

CALENDAR, 1982–1983 621

INDEX 625

DIRECTORY OF U.S. AND CANADIAN LIBRARIES 651

Preface

In the tradition of the *Bowker Annual*, the 27th edition provides comprehensive and up-to-date coverage of major events, trends, and developments in librarianship and the book trade. Additionally, coverage of the information industry has become an integral part of the *Bowker Annual*.

This year, Part 1, Reports from the Field, has been significantly expanded to include articles and reports from a variety of key associations, libraries, and organizations. These include, in the Special Reports section, "The State of Intellectual Freedom," "Public Library Services for the Aging in the Eighties," "Recent Developments in Health Sciences Libraries in the United States," "Recent Developments in Library Conservation in the United States," and reports on the Folger Shakespeare Library and the Copyright Clearance Center. A separate section on Resource Sharing features an overview of library networking in the United States in 1981 and a report on the Metropolitan Washington Library Council.

Part 1 also includes, in the Federal Agencies section, a report on the Federal Library Committee and, in the National Associations section, reports on the Information Industry Association, the National Micrographics Association, the Society for Scholarly Publishing, and the Special Libraries Association.

Opening Part 2, Legislation, Funding, and Grants, are separate reports on legislation affecting librarianship, publishing, and the information industry in 1981. These reports describe and assess the impact of the new administration on these fields and are followed by detailed reports on individual funding programs and grant-making agencies.

"Education for Library Support Staff in the United States and Canada" is a feature article in Part 3, Library Education, Placement, and Salaries. An overview of recent library personnel surveys is among the revised and updated articles rounding out this part.

Part 4, Research and Statistics, has also been greatly expanded with this edition. In the Library Research and Statistics section, "Developments in Library Statistical Activities" provides an historical overview and status report on the field. Reports on three National Center for Education Statistics (NCES) surveys summarize data collected on public libraries, public school library media centers, and library networks and cooperative library organizations. A summary report on the Intergovernmental Library Cooperation Project is also featured in this section. In addition to the annually updated articles in the Book Trade Research and Statistics section, there is an article on the Standard Address Number.

Part 5, International Reports and Statistics, is highlighted by a report on the Leipzig conference of the International Federation of Library Associations and Institutions (IFLA) and a companion report on the activities of the IFLA Section on Statistics at that conference. Reports on library services in Israel and network development in Canada provide further international coverage of librarianship, while the International Statistics section includes current information on the international book trade. (Prices of foreign published materials are included in Part 4, together with U.S. price information.)

As in the previous edition, Part 6, Reference Information, includes bibliographies of recent noteworthy books for the librarian and publisher and lists of distinguished and award-winning books in various categories. Part 7, Directory of Organizations, lists hundreds of national, foreign, and international associations and organizations relating to librarianship, the book trade, and the information industry.

The editors gratefully acknowledge and appreciate the efforts of all those who contributed articles and information to the *Bowker Annual* this year.

Part 1
Reports from the Field

News Reports

LJ NEWS REPORT, 1981

Karl Nyren
Senior Editor, *Library Journal*

There were strong doubts early in the year that the National Commission on Libraries and Information Science would survive the Reagan era, but word came in November from the White House that the president was appointing five members to the commission, four for the first time, including a new chairperson, Eleanor M. Hashim of Connecticut, currently a special librarian, but with years of public library experience, and one who served a term earlier, school librarian Julia Li Wu of California. The others include a lawyer, John E. Juergensmeyer of Illinois; a computer composition company executive, Byron Leeds of New Jersey; and a banker, Jerald Conway Newman of New York.

PRESIDENTIAL LIBRARIES

The increasing pace of turnover in the White House is making new presidential library projects come along at a dizzy rate. In April, President Ford's library opened at the University of Michigan; the site was picked in Atlanta for Jimmy Carter's library; and Duke University was debating the advantages and disadvantages of hosting the Richard Nixon Library. There was new criticism of presidential libraries heard; it was pointed out that they are expensive burdens for the taxpayer, they are frequently in places hard for people to visit, and they often function more as outlets for self-serving image building rather than as the historical fonts they are supposed to be for the scholar of history.

PRICES

The prices of library materials in this inflationary time have been drawing close examination. Early in 1981 the Association of Research Libraries (ARL) statistics for a decade confirmed the fact that libraries are in an inflationary spiral. Also confirming this was a study reported by Michael R. Kronenfeldt and James A. Thompson in the April 1 *LJ*. In "Impact of Inflation on Journal Costs," they found that prices have been rising for periodicals more rapidly than would be explained by general inflation and more rapidly than other library costs. They suggest that to maintain collections librarians should press for larger budgets for periodicals than would be justified by general inflation. The authors also express their suspicion that the publishers are to blame and state that libraries should fight back against being victimized.

In *LJ*'s July feature, "Price Increases for 1981: U.S. Periodicals and Serial Services," Norman H. Brown and Jane Phillips charted a 13.3 percent increase over 1980 prices and set the average journal price for 1981 at $34.54.

Note: Adapted from *Library Journal*, January 15, 1982.

In the February *LJ*, "Price Index for Nonprint Media" by David B. Walch had a surprise: In a reversal of a four-year trend, color film prices had dropped—although rental charges for them had not. The charts began carrying new figures this year, for videocassettes, starting off with $7.58 for an average purchase price per minute.

Agencies serving libraries did what they could to soften the blow of price increases. Among them were the South Central Kansas Library System (SCKLS) in Hutchinson, which posted remarkably low prices for central processing—50 cents to member libraries and $1.50 to school libraries—but it cost them only 89 cents per book, using Ohio College Library Center (OCLC) cataloging, said SCKLS. The state library agency of Minnesota negotiated with Baker & Taylor for a 40.6 percent discount on trade books for orders of $2,000 or more. California's California Library Authority for Systems and Services (CLASS) did a similar service for its members; it negotiated with Brodart for discounts of 15–20 percent on library supplies.

Publishers in 1981 were more inclined to announce warehouse sales for their backlist books, what with the *Thor Power Tool* ruling making large inventories more costly to maintain. And the Institute for Scientific Information (ISI) expanded its "grants" program, by means of which smaller libraries can buy at a lower price than the list price that large buyers pay.

STANDARDS

As indicated in the section under Planning Process for Public Libraries (*see* Library Operation and Maintenance), work went on around the nation on the long-drawn-out effort to create something to replace the old public library standards. In the meantime, increased interest has been expressed in "evaluation" and "measurement of service effectiveness," and the Public Library Association has taken the lead in developing concrete measurements. It is worthy of note that there was discussion of the possibility of accrediting libraries in Massachusetts, with the state library association suggested as the agent of accreditation. In November, the South Carolina Library Association's Public Library Section adopted a major revision in the state's standards; it covered three levels of library service: state library, county or multicounty, and networking.

College libraries have been trying out the 1975 *Standards for College Libraries* (Chicago: American Library Assn./Assn. of College and Research Libraries) and a 1981 report surveying users found the standards both used and valued, although they were criticized for their lack of reference to nonprint, measures of library effectiveness, and program evaluation.

PREDICTIONS—PUBLIC LIBRARIES

An article by Susan O. Lundberg in the Spring 1981 issue of *Library Research* turned up a surprisingly conservative lot of predictions made by a Delphi study group composed of library administrators and library educators. By the year 2000, they generally agreed, we will have a national library system and more unions, computers, fee-based private information services, staff development, and mergers of public and school libraries. They also see in the cards more concern for measurement and evaluation of services; more conflict between professionals and other staff; and continuing devotion to outreach to the unserved, to adult education, and to service to preschoolers.

PREDICTIONS—ACADEMIC LIBRARIES

A fertile ground for predictions about the future was the Association of College and Research Libraries (ACRL) National Conference in Minneapolis. Some of the more striking ones: New technology will lead us away from centralization and more toward autonomy; it will result in smaller staffs and better buildings, predicted Canadian Margaret Beckman of Guelph University. Academic libraries can survive the computer if they remain true to their real natures as "social systems" rather than becoming "information systems," counseled Paul A. Lacy, professor of English at Earlham College. We will build and evolve on the foundation laid down by the last 50 years of library progress as long as we make intelligent day-to-day decisions in operating our libraries—especially decisions about who we hire to run them, said Beverly Lynch, ACRL "Academic Librarian of the Year," University of Illinois, Chicago Circle. In the years to come, we are going to have more storage facilities, and it behooves us to learn how to set them up and operate them, predicted Larry Ferm and Halcyon Enssle of Colorado State University. Dark days are ahead for liberal arts colleges and their libraries, and they are unlikely to be able to lay hands on the capital necessary to buy the new technology that would help them to survive on slenderer resources, warned Daniel Sullivan, vice president for planning at Carleton College.

Predictions from a somewhat different perspective, that of men who have participated in the last 50 years of library development, were made at Eastern Illinois University. Keyes Metcalf saw an end to the growth of large academic libraries, collections, and staffs. Robert B. Downs, on the other hand, felt that libraries have won such strong institutional support that their greatest, most brilliant period of growth may be ahead of them, and though forms may change, their essential functions will not. Jesse Shera saw, for his part, a host of problems clouding the future; problems that are created or exacerbated by our lack of knowledge of the mental processes we are serving and our need for staffs with greater subject expertise. Among the problems are our fear of cooperation and the content of our library collections, which have so many books that no one wants, while there are so many patrons wanting books we do not have. David Kaser, surveying the rise of academic library architecture, expressed his belief that the evolution of the library building, as we know it, has gone as far as it can, and buildings going up today show a loss in quality from the best modular buildings of the 1960s.

AUTOMATION

Libraries embraced automation with greater fervor than ever in 1981. Despite fears that scarce funding would inhibit adoption of new technologies, the shaky economy and the certain withdrawal of federal funding seems, if anything, to have stimulated the pace of library automation. Eyeing the end of the Library Services and Construction Act (LSCA), Colorado decided to put all its Title I and III funds into an automated statewide network, starting with the major public library systems and the larger academic libraries. Wyoming had already started a statewide project, adopting the Cincinnati Electronics CLASSIC system, and early reports indicated they were making progress, but discovering problems in determining the respective roles of major participants such as the state library and the University of Wyoming, not to mention problems arising from implementing an essentially untried system.

Early in the year, the Salt Lake County Library was threatened with a sharp reduction in force, but work on its public access catalog installation went on. In Lake Oswego, Oregon, the public library went ahead with a connection to the Clackamas County Library computer even though it was reducing hours of service and cutting back on both staff and book buying. And the public library in Lawrence, Massachusetts, found that state's stringent Proposition 2½ limitation on library spending all the more reason to go ahead with its plans to install a MiniMarc system. Despite a decade of statements insisting that automation would not cut library costs, it became apparent in 1981 that automation would enable libraries to get along with smaller staffs and would, in a variety of ways, realize the original goal of the OCLC system: reducing the rate of increase in library expenditures.

There was also a growing acceptance of the changes that automation would bring to libraries; in a paper delivered at the ACRL Second National Conference in Minneapolis, David R. McDonald and Robert Hurowitz noted two trends: a merging and overlapping of functions and staff assignments (between circulation and reference, for example) and a trend away from centralization made possible by access from a multitude of points to the same store of bibliographic records.

Competition for the Market

The major vendors of circulation systems—and increasingly these systems were offering a full range of library automation—were in hot and heavy competition across the map of North America; a steady stream of reports from the major vendors announced CLSI at the Free Library of Philadelphia and at the California State University, Chico; Geac at West Point and Pasadena; DataPhase at Kansas State and Ventura County; and DOBIS at the Austin, Texas, Public Library, where it replaced a CLSI system. Cincinnati Electronics, already in use in the Wyoming statewide system, could be found in such American hinterlands as Lexington, Kentucky, and the River Bend System in Rock Island, Illinois, although it was brought up by a British firm.

But CLSI maintained a commanding lead throughout the year; in a lineup of the leaders developed by *Advanced Technology/Libraries*, CLSI led the pack, followed by DataPhase, Geac, IBM's DOBIS, Gaylord, Cincinnati Electronics, and Plessey in that order. SCICON did not make the cut, but was making minor inroads on the market.

On-line Catalogs

As reports of computer output microfilm (COM) catalogs dwindled (for lack of novelty rather than lack of new installations), on-line catalogs appeared prominently in reports from libraries. In many cases, libraries were moving on from a circulation system, but in others the on-line catalog itself was the cornerstone of librarywide automation. There were reports from Seattle of its "push button catalog" and from Iowa City on its new public access terminals. The Ohio State library announced that it was the first state library with an on-line catalog of its holdings, using the Library Circulation System (LCS) developed at Ohio State and already exported to several major libraries. At the ACRL Conference in Minneapolis, Barbara Moore gave a thorough account of the Mankato State University's on-line catalog, an installation intended as the first step in the automation of the libraries of Minnesota State University. The UNIVAC-based system, she reported, was well received by students and faculty as well as by librarians. Still another report on an on-line catalog at that conference, dealing with use of the catalog at pioneer Ohio State, was rather less enthusiastic. Sue Pease and Mary Gouke found that only 25 percent of their library patrons were finding what they wanted, and the on-line catalog was particularly unsatisfactory to new users. They concluded that better instruction at the point of use was needed.

The creation of on-line catalogs, necessitating the abandonment of the card catalog or the retrospective reformatting of its thousands of bibliographic records into a Machine Readable Cataloging (MARC) format that can be merged with new records created by the library or acquired from another agency, runs up against an immediate barrier in the costs associated with this process. Even the substantial reductions made possible by using the OCLC system for retrospective cataloging runs into costs that at $1.50–$2 a record can be prohibitive. A breakthrough by Carrollton Press with its REMARC system has been promising recataloging records for as little as 50 cents apiece. Carrollton's acquisition by International Thomson Organization will make it possible for the entire REMARC data base to be available years sooner than expected and the University of California, for one, is planning on it for its massive recataloging effort.

Finally, libraries interested in discussion of retrospective cataloging have a new Library and Information Technology Association (LITA) group, which met for the first time at American Library Association (ALA) Midwinter, 1981.

Systems for Sale

Besides the systems being marketed by vendors, whether built on a data base of circulation records or on the catalog of the library and/or other libraries (CLSI and OCLC, for example), there are a number of systems developed by individual large academic and public libraries that are offered either as systems to join or software for system replication. A bewildering array of possibilities greets the library going into the marketplace for the first time. Among the new entries, Washington University announces that it is now marketing its on-line catalog system. The Boston Public Library's on-line system developed by Inforonics offers cataloging to New England libraries at rates below those offered by OCLC or RLIN (although with a smaller data base to draw on). The National Library of Medicine's Integrated Library System (ILS), with public-domain software available at cost, is now being replicated at the University of Maryland Health Sciences Library by Online Computer Systems, Inc. The pioneering and successful Northwestern automation system's NOTIS and LUIS components are tested systems now available to other libraries.

The latest entry into this market has been Claremont Colleges, long reputed to have one of the best systems going. At year's end OCLC announced its intent to offer the Claremont complete library automation system to libraries of any size and type anywhere.

Still another avenue to automation is offered by individual libraries with a system that can be joined with minimal capital outlay. At the moment, Cleveland Heights is moving toward participation in the Cleveland Public Library's Data Research Associates (DRA) automation system; it is expected to be the first step toward use of DRA for a countywide on-line circulation system.

Still more automation opportunities and pitfalls await the library this year. Automated acquisitions offers choices between vendor (bookseller) systems such as the Brodart OLAS-II, performing admirably at the Onondago County Public Library in Syracuse, New York, and the Baker & Taylor LIBRIS system, which was picked over OLAS as the 1981 choice of the Ohio State Library. OCLC's Acquisition Subsystem got its first testing in 1981 and by early 1982 reports on its performance in a wide variety of test bed libraries will be available. But acquisitions modules will be increasingly offered by vendors of circulation and on-line catalog systems, while smaller, go-it-alone libraries will find new systems developed for mini- and microcomputers, such as INMAGIC, offered for the first time last year by Warner-Eddison Associates as a "custom acquisition and retrieval service."

Micros

Microcomputers have stirred more than a flurry of library interest, especially among small libraries, which are buying the $3,000–$10,000 machines and putting them to work at a variety of library tasks—as well as playing with them and offering the public a chance to gain "computer literacy" on an Apple or a TRS. At least two library schools, the University of Iowa and Columbia, offer opportunities to handle the micros. In the public library of Palo Alto, California, you will find one in the children's room; and at Clarion State College in Pennsylvania, you will find people exploring the use of computers in rural libraries. Briefings on the micros in a library environment are turning up at library meetings and at workshop/institutes called for the purpose; an example was the October conference on micro- and minicomputers and their applications in library automation held in Rochester, New York, an area with a great many small libraries as well as major academic and special libraries.

The small computers are also bringing within range applications such as the film booking system that King County, Washington, developed for $18,000 to serve 38 branch facilities with 1,400 films. In Providence, a directory information system for the city is being run on a North Star micro.

In Farmington, Connecticut, a $75,000 grant from the Heublein Company bought the library a unique toy: a satellite antenna that provides an immense range of access to televised programming.

Electronic Mail

Libraries are being offered a wide range of products in the electronic mail field, besides the use of OCLC and other network facilities for this purpose. The University of Idaho reported that its OnTyme system is working well and the Bibliographic Center for Research in Denver published in its network newsletter an invaluable preliminary survey of the offerings available in electronic mail, many through the network at attractive prices.

On-line Reference and Interlibrary Loan

New products depending on technology were offered to the library market or announced for future availability. The September 1 issue of *Library Journal* reported on one: "Online Encyclopedias: The Potential" was written by Stephen P. Harter and Kenneth F. Kister. Shortly after, Mead Data Central offered *Encyclopaedia Britannica* on-line. A consortium of international publishers including Pergamon, Springer, Blackwell, and Elsevier announced Article Delivery over Network Information Services (ADONIS), which plans to use digital facsimile and videodisc technology to transmit the text of periodical articles—at a price low enough ($5.50 an article) to undercut the fees now being charged by a major supplier of the American interlibrary loan market, the British Library Lending Division.

One troubling aspect of the production of on-line versions of standard library reference works—troubling both to libraries and to publishers—has been the possibility that the on-line version would usurp so much of the market for the print version that the latter would no longer be profitable to publish. This could be disastrous for many smaller libraries. Hope, however, has bloomed with an article in the September *Aslib Proceedings*, wherein Susan Childs and Michael Carmel make a case for the likelihood that the creation and sale of an on-line version may actually stimulate the sale of the print version of a reference tool.

Small Libraries and Automation

There has been a resurgence of interest in the small library, possibly propelled in the past year by an almost worldwide revulsion at centralization and a renewed belief in the autonomy of smaller units of society. A bill submitted to the California legislature proposed state aid to the small public library, which has been largely left out of direct subsidy by federal and state programs as they have developed in recent years. The Kellogg Foundation in 1981 put up $200,000 to enable small libraries to get into automated circulation. An experiment in providing small libraries access to OCLC is slated for a three-year trial by the Illinois Valley Library System. And a leading vendor of automation, DataPhase, is specifically promoting its ALIS II system as suited to the small library. Needless to say, those developments in microcomputers and satellite technology that offer the possibility of widespread library autonomy with full access to information for the smallest unit must change the way people have been thinking about cooperation and networking.

FUNDING

Libraries of all types experienced fiscal anxieties as sources of funding failed to keep up with inflation, rising prices, and rising expenses. Academic libraries faced shrinking enrollments as the main threat to their sources of funding, while public libraries were threatened by taxpayer revolts, generally aimed at government expenses in general, but some specifically hostile to libraries. Federal support for academic and public library programs dwindled still further in 1981, while state support, especially of public library programs and multitype cooperative and network efforts, grew appreciably. Local public library funding ran a broad gamut, with many libraries facing dire straits by year end—but many other libraries were surprisingly prosperous. Generally speaking, the two-year colleges appeared less afflicted by the recession and in some cases to be even benefiting by it; public libraries in areas growing in population and participating in energy profits were prospering and growing.

Research Libraries

The research library community early in 1981 received the statistics for their 1979-1980 levels of activity in acquisitions, collection growth, and salary expenditures—reported against the background of a decade of trends in these areas. According to the Association of Research Libraries. the decade just past saw expenditures for library materials increase 91 percent, while salaries jumped 106 percent. Nonprofessional staffs shrank a good 11.5 percent, while professionals kept their numbers steady. But the number of volumes added per year dropped 22.5 percent and collection growth had dropped from 7 percent to 2.9 percent.

At the Second National Conference of the Association of College and Research Libraries in Minneapolis last fall, academic libraries were told by Thomas Melady, an envoy from Reagan's Department of Education, that the federal government's idea of being helpful is limited to "getting the government off your backs," "cutting down on paperwork" and regulations and enforcement.

On the other hand, academic libraries were assured by Robert Rosenzweig of Stanford that their unique partnership with government, developed since World War II, assures them a continuing closeness with the national font of research funding.

A pair of reports cast shadows of doubt on the optimism expressed at Minneapolis by Rosenzweig and in a wrap-up speech by Beverly Lynch, University of Illinois, Chicago Circle, Librarian. Lynch saw the 50-year record of growth and evolution in academic libraries continuing in the years ahead, guided by the continuing pragmatic wisdom of academic librarians exercising their responsibilities. But in Chicago this year, a 1984 merger of the independent John Crerar Library and the science collections at the University of Chicago was announced, and economic reasons were understood to be paramount—although there is much to be said for merging an applied science collection with a pure science collection.

In 1981, the Norlin Library at the University of Colorado came under the scrutiny of the North Central Association, which recommended that university accreditation at the doctoral level be continued but that the library receive a "focused visit" in three years to examine its adequacy for supporting university programs. And at the University of Rochester in New York, a $630,000 coin collection was sold to provide money for books. On the brighter side, a little faith in the likelihood of private funding's replacing government support might have been stirred by the $1 million gift to Cornell to endow the post of university librarian. Carl Kroch of Kroch's and Brentano's was the benefactor.

Public Libraries

Exceptions to the fairly general financial straits of public libraries were in some cases spectacular. The Aurora Public Library in Colorado (David Price, Director) reported a $1 million funding increase to nearly double the library's income and make possible 40 new positions, a new main library, cable TV facilities, and automation. Baltimore County, continuing to give its patrons what they want—lots of popular, new books—posted a 13 percent budget increase, and despite inflation and price increases, kept to their rigorous priority of spending 20 percent of the budget on books. The Dallas Public Library continued its growth with a victory at the polls early in the year, credited with leading voters into support of all city services. Later in the year the library, along with other municipal services, was threatened with cuts, but it came out with a nearly $2 million increase as the April date for opening of the new main library drew near.

In De Soto, Louisiana, the library had closed its doors in December 1978, but this year the Friends organization was successful in getting a vote for a ¼-cent sales tax to operate the library; it won by a three to one margin. In Forsyth County, North Carolina, with the library moving toward opening a $3 million headquarters addition, the library won a 30 percent funding increase. That growing community supports a growing library; next for them is a new branch that will feature solar technology.

Two libraries in depressed areas also got the nod from the voters: the Genessee District Library near Flint, Michigan, and the Youngstown and Mahoning County Library in Ohio. The Michigan library, surrounded by unemployment, got a 57 percent vote that assures its next six years of funding. The library's success may have some relation to its aggressive pursuit of new and increased services and programs, with much publicity for their longer hours and their "push-button" catalog.

King County, Washington; Miami-Dade, Orlando, and Palm Beach, Florida; Quincy and Wilmette, Illinois; Orange County, California; Janesville, Wisconsin; Issaquah and Fort Vancouver, Washington, were also bright spots on the funding map. Far more characteristic of the reports received by *LJ*, however, were tales of woe from Baltimore's Enoch Pratt Library, the Boston Public Library, the Buffalo and Erie County Library, Denver Public Library, the Detroit Public Library, the Metropolitan Library System (Oklahoma County), Salt Lake County Library, and the Tucson Public Library.

Two major public library systems that were on the skids for most of the year came back with restored funding: the Free Library of Philadelphia and the branch libraries of the New York Public Library.

Two statewide reports only serve to underline the complexity of the library funding patterns dimly perceived in all these individual reports. A study sponsored by California Library Association (CLA) reported late in the year that about half of the state's public libraries expect further cutbacks in the wake of Proposition 13, but the other half expect to hold their own or even to advance next year. CLA concluded that there is "no clear pattern."

But Richard Burgin, associate director of the Forsyth County Library, claims that in his state, North Carolina, the record of the last five years shows libraries staying ahead of inflation. In the 1974–1979 period, he reports, half the state's libraries increased their budgets by over 70 percent.

PRIORITIES IN LEAN TIMES

The priorities supported by librarians, the public, and funding authorities at this time show some interesting variations. As mentioned before, Baltimore County's adherence to a 20 percent budget allocation for books, and especially for books people in its suburban area want, probably helps the Baltimore County Public Library budget keep growing. But it has other service priorities as stated this year: For the professional staff, it is provision of information, collection maintenance, and programming for preschoolers.

In New Orleans, where fiscal rigors have cut staff 30 percent and hours 20 percent in three years, and where the SEALLINC local cooperative network has been abandoned, the library is moving vigorously into automation with a DataPhase system for circulation and on-line catalog and cable TV. And although local budget support for book buying has shrunk badly, the state is providing a subsidy of $237,000 just for books.

If books are perceived as basic desiderata, this could help explain the $100,000 extra funding, just to strengthen the book collection, won by East Brunswick, New Jersey, and Denver's protection of its book budget while its branches are being relegated to book centers and all reference operations and resources are being centralized at the main library. On the other hand, there is Salt Lake County losing 20 staffers, but heavily into automation with its public access catalog. There was the observation made by Donald Sager (before he was ousted from the post of commissioner of the Chicago Public Library) that Chicago showed an inclination to spend on automation in labor-intensive areas—and also on books—but preferred not to spend for children's librarians. And then there was Washington County, Oregon, a state where, despite widespread recession, people have been voting for libraries. However, Washington County voters nixed a $1.3 million levy that would have brought countywide library automation.

CAKE SALES AND PENNY PINCHING

With tax support of public libraries threatened, librarians turned—sometimes grudgingly—to alternative ways of raising and saving money. Few empires, large or small, resist abrogation of their sovereignty more than do public libraries, but in 1981 on both coasts there were serious recommendations for the merger of libraries. One proposed that the Utica Public Library and the Mid-York Library System be placed under a single management. Another proposed the merger of the San Diego Public Library and the San Diego County, a move turned down by the city council, but likely to lead to "functional" cooperation—sharing a circulation system possibly, or joint decision making on branch location.

Many libraries strove to increase their productivity and base a claim for funding on evidence that they were doing more for less. A good example was the Public Library of Columbus and Franklin County, where a voluntary cut in the library's budget request was followed by strong publicity about how the library was doing even more with its fewer resources. Columbus got its reward this year in a 73 percent vote in favor of the renewing of the library levy.

Some libraries came out fighting at the threat of fiscal attack. In Proposition 2½-ridden Massachusetts, Librarian Janet Eagelson (North Reading) went to the floor of the town meeting and won an increase of $5,204. In neighboring Billerica, Librarian Barbara Allen gave credit to good publicity for forestalling the Proposition 2½ cuts that hit the town's schools, as well as recreation, police, and fire departments. In Geneva, New York, Librarian Robert Belvin conducted a direct-mail campaign for library funds that was a success.

Selling things to one's friends is a time-honored means of supporting a worthy cause. Buffalo, New York, tried a book sale for the first time and raked in a welcome $26,000. In Clovis, New Mexico, the Friends have set up a bookstore specializing in the sale of books by New Mexico authors and about New Mexico. Huntington Beach, California, tried an auction and made $15,000. In Norfolk, Virginia, Librarian Marcie Sims came in first in a five-kilometer road race that raised $204 for the library. And in St. Clair, Michigan, there may someday be a monument to The Drunken Driver, outside a new library built by fines he paid. It seems that the library gets the fines levied on people caught driving while intoxicated (DWI), an income source now worth $220,000 with fines set at $100. Fines have been increased to $500, however, and the library will almost surely benefit.

Among the many ways that libraries found in 1981 to save money: gas-saving minibookmobiles were put on the road in Alabama, and Kentucky penitentiary inmates built bookmobiles on step van bodies. Alert librarians took advantage of a ruling making "NOW" accounts permissible for them and other nonprofit organizations. A used-equipment exchange was set up for libraries of the region by the New England Library Board; and various programs on how to make the most of the shrinking library dollars were reported. Among the latter were a program at the New England Library Association fall meeting on "The Philosophy of Scrounge"; publication by the Oklahoma state agency of a guide to saving money (tap jails for cheap labor and services, also high school students; get banks to set up circulating collections of books for the handicapped; etc.); and a Simmons seminar on managing libraries in hard times. Early in the year it was noted that some idea of what lay in store for U.S. libraries has already hit England, where in the course of taking in sail libraries had set new and higher fees and fines and cut back on services and book buying. British libraries were running book sales too, and with staff cuts foreseen, there was a new emphasis on training staff for a wider range of duties.

Fees and Fines

Inevitably, libraries found themselves in 1981 charging new and/or higher fees and fines. Lehigh and the University of Michigan now have fee-based information services for the private sector. Nonresidents found public library borrowing cards cost more: In Arlington Heights, Illinois, for example, where the library was already charging a stiff $60, the price went up to $75. As for fines, there were reports of "fine free" libraries going back to the old way. Among other variants there was Cleveland, which just stopped sending overdue reminders, pocketed the cost of clerical help that used to do the job, and found that books still come back and fines still come in at the same rate. Although many librarians maintain that fines should not be considered a source of income because they cost as much or more to apply as they bring in, there was at least one tacit admission in 1981 that fines are an important if minor source of support:

Minimally higher staff salaries were blamed in Toledo-Lucas County for increased fines/fees. There was one real innovation in this area: The St. Paul Public Library abolished the whole overdue fine concept and instituted "service charges," which are levied on overdue books after a five-day grace period has passed.

How to finance the expensive new data base services increasingly being used by reference librarians was a big, unanswered question. ALA was reported last spring to be studying how libraries pay for on-line services. Representatives of member libraries of the Pacific Northwest Bibliographic Center agreed early in the year that some kind of fees would be inevitable—but that libraries, not patrons, should pay them.

Interlibrary loan came under new scrutiny from several quarters, both as a cost and as a possible candidate for fees. The AMIGOS network came out for a notably liberal loan policy that was the object of attention from other agencies. The Library Council of Metropolitan Milwaukee (LCOMM) heard a proposal that it manage a scheme for charging interlibrary loan fees and some libraries were looking at such fees as a new source of income. But at a Rutgers meeting on the economics of library service, Herbert White of Indiana University suggested that interlibrary loan may be too expensive a service to maintain.

PUBLIC LIBRARY PROGRAMS

Public libraries in 1981 continued to generate a host of programs whose purpose was to provide the general public, or specific segments of the public, with information and entertainment. A great many of these were outreach programs, aimed at the disabled, the aged, the institutionalized, and members of minority groups separated by linguistic and other cultural barriers from the rest of the public. There were also a great many programs dealing with local history and ethnic roots; cultural programs emphasizing the humanities, again often with a local or regional slant; programs for the provision of medical, legal, community, and job information; and programs—not many, admittedly—that found the library in the ranks of social advocacy, pressing for the humane resolution of difficult issues.

Outreach

Among the reports received on outreach activity, a sampling turns up a Brooklyn, New York, Public Library project that has senior citizens serving those less able than themselves in the SAGE program. Library educators at Syracuse University showed their interest in supporting libraries in this area with a ten-day workshop on gerontological information that carried three graduate credits. Ethnic outreach was most impressive in Spanish-language projects: Proyecto Leer, for the acquisition of Spanish-language materials, was reactivated at Texas Woman's University; bilingual Spanish-English catalogs were reported from California at the Alameda County Library; and the California Spanish Language Database is headed for on-line form; a Request for Proposal was circulated to bibliographic utilities last fall. The Department of Education early in the year presented over $2 million in grants to educational institutions (no libraries) for work on bilingual education, but from public libraries came a flood of lively programs including Mexican-American Folk Medicine at the Tucson Public Library; the festive opening of the San Bernardino Public Library's Paul Villasenor Branch, with mariachi music and Mexican refreshments; a display of some 300 Mexican toys at the Houston Public Library; and a Spanish-language version of the Chicago Public Library's Dial-Law tape service.

Handicapped people were served better than ever in 1981, with libraries of all types building in or remodeling to provide barrier-free access to book stacks, rest rooms, microform readers, and other facilities, including a bookmobile of the Miami Public Library that came with a wheelchair lift. Access for the handicapped was the subject of workshops in Indiana (several) and in Illinois (two in the Chicago area) that had the sponsorship of public and medical libraries, library associations, and allied agencies concerned with the handicapped. A videotape was made available to libraries bearing six hours of a Wisconsin Conference on Library Service to Persons with Disabilities; another, dealing with Georgia Library Services to the Handicapped, was made available by the Georgia Library for the Blind and Physically Handicapped. The range of materials available to the blind was extended by such publications as a Braille cookbook from Australia and the first recorded encyclopedia for the blind, which was announced by World Book/American Printing House for the Blind. But the most dramatic advance made in this area saw the proliferation of Kurzweil reading machines, which are not only being bought by library agencies in great numbers despite their stiff price; the Xerox Corporation, which produces the Kurzweil machines, is giving away 100 of them to college libraries where they are particularly needed. Libraries are also showing enthusiasm for service to the deaf, with many library staffers learning sign language and learning—from institutions like Gallaudet College in Washington—how to serve the large population of deaf patrons of which they have until recently been unaware.

Services to the institutionalized continue to spread; Baltimore County early in the year reported new funding ($36,000) to expand its services to jails. It operates a library at the Baltimore County Detention Center that serves inmates taking adult education courses by day, and by night provides browsing for recreational material. On the other coast, the Alameda County Library reported in March that it had been able to restore the service to jails cut off by Proposition 13, and on a new, secure basis: The county board of supervisors voted to tap the general fund as a permanent funding source for the service. But where library funding was cut, service to institutions was a frequent target.

Service to the rural patron drew more attention this year; its focal point appeared to be still at the library school of Clarion State College in Pennsylvania. The H. W. Wilson Foundation gave Clarion $10,000 last year to study reference service to a rural population—and according to the April 24 *New York Times*, 42 percent of the population is now found in rural areas and is rapidly expanding to areas that lack libraries as well as other social services.

Library Operation and Maintenance

A great deal of what librarians do is keeping the library machine running smoothly and in such a way as to best support the library's goals and program objectives. The library news in 1981 recorded many of those activities in such areas as planning, evaluation, public relations, and user education.

The Planning Process for Public Libraries was tried out by more U.S. libraries and even got its first Canadian introduction in a June 15 program put on by the (American) Public Library Association and the Canadian Association of Public Libraries; it featured presentations by librarians who had tried the Planning Process at the Illinois Valley Library System, the Louisville Free Public Library, and the Hennepin County Library. Earlier in the year, the process got a hefty boost from the Washington State Library, which backed it for statewide use with $158,912 in LSCA money along with state library staff time and talent. A regional workshop on the process was scheduled for New England by the cosponsoring Public Library Association and the New England Library Association. In Spokane, a major evaluative study of library services was set up and structured with the Planning Process adapted to local needs and used as the basis for the study's strategy. And at ALA Midwinter in Washington a new Planning Process Discussion Group had its debut.

Planning for academic libraries got attention too in 1981. A paper delivered at ACRL-Minneapolis advocated the benefits of planning for even the small academic library—benefits that include better communication and relations with the administration. A planning process designed for librarians at Northern Illinois University by a consultant firm specializing in this activity, Performax Systems International of Minneapolis, took top library officers on a two-day retreat to develop goals and learn how to work together in planning.

PUBLIC RELATIONS

Library public relations may have a serious aim, but it is often wild and wacky in pursuing increased public awareness and the esteem of libraries. In 1981 the PR antics noted in *LJ* and *LJ/SLJ Hotline* pages included two outstanding examples from Pawtucket, Rhode Island, where Larry Eaton is the director and Lee Eaton is the PR person. First was Pawtucket's Thank God It's Friday Champagne Breakfast, featuring besides champagne a large assortment of catered brunch delicacies and a chanteuse, all wrapped around a message about the library. Then there was Pawtucket's Dog Show, which drew crowds of dogs and people and climaxed with the winning dog breakfasting with the mayor and being flown to Block Island for a dinner. Media coverage, the aim of the whole thing, was superb and extensive.

A high point of 1981's National Library Week occurred at Eastern Illinois University, where the week and the opening of the newly renovated Butler Library were celebrated by four eminent speakers. Following the legendary Keyes Metcalf on the program were Robert B. Downs, David Kaser, and Jesse Shera, together providing a look back at the history of libraries in their period of greatest expansion and a cautious look into the future. The remarks of these four worthies have been published as *LJ Special Report #21: Metcalf, Downs, Kaser & Shera at Eastern Illinois.*

The only comparable happenings reported from academic libraries came from the University of Nevada-Las Vegas and from the Schlesinger Library at Harvard, where money and consciousness were both raised at a cooking demonstration that charged $30 just to watch and $50 to watch and stay afterward to eat with the chef, who was none other than Jacques Pepin, author of *A French Chef Cooks at Home* and other works. At Nevada, Chef Louis Szathmary of Chicago's The Bakery made a culinary event of the celebration of their new library addition and his gift of a library of cusine.

These two glittering academic events were matched by the Huntington Beach Library in California, where $15,000 was raised at an auction accompanied by wining and dining for 400 and such attention-getters on the block as a weekend in Nantucket, a $4,000 capuccino machine, and a diamond pendant.

Glazer & Glaser: Among the many programs, workshops, and institutes aiming to help librarians do better at PR were two workshops put on in Texas by two of the best PR people in libraries: Fred Glazer, director of the West Virginia Library Commission, and Gloria Glaser, former PR director for the Nassau County Library System in New York and now an independent PR consultant.

Besides its usual support of library public relations with National Library Week and lending of model PR materials, ALA mounted a nationwide effort in February to promote telephone reference. The "call your library" campaign, put together with the aid of state library agencies, provided TV and radio tapes and a wide range of promotional materials for use in local and regional media.

A special mention is deserved by one low-cost but very clever piece of publicity developed by the Prince George's County Memorial Library: The library's annual report, plus concise information about using the library, came out on a book jacket, which patrons were encouraged to use also to protect a library book.

NETWORKS

New in 1981 were the continued growth, occasionally shaky performance, and vigorous marketing of the two giants, OCLC and RLIN. OCLC moved into a $25 million new home in Dublin, Ohio; opened an office in Birmingham, England; reported success in its Columbus, Ohio, Channel 2000 experiment at providing information directly to the home; and pulled out of a complex partnership arrangement with SOLINET that would have ceded substantial networking responsibilities to SOLINET and, potentially, to other regional or state organizations. The action apparently thwarted for the immediate future regional network aspirations within the OCLC system and SOLINET laid off 22 staff members as it scrapped its Regional Support Services (RSS) project.

Despite the defection of many research libraries to Research Libraries Group, Inc. (RLG) and the RLIN network, OCLC still has 58 university libraries that contribute a substantial share of the cataloging done on the system. This group is emerging as a vocal and potentially powerful special-interest alliance within the network membership; at a meeting this year, they set four targets they want to see accomplished: Assignment to specific libraries of responsibility for subject-specialization cataloging; cooperative microfilm projects; an automatic search system; and computerization of information relating to the preservation of rare books and scholarly materials.

OCLC membership grew, less by large, new members like the University of Oregon than by expansion into use by small libraries. Besides examples cited above, there were further experiments in terminal sharing like the one in Milwaukee, which is giving six libraries a chance to try OCLC services in a project coordinated by the Library Council of Metropolitan Milwaukee.

Despite its great accomplishments, however, OCLC, like RLIN, remains plagued with system malfunctions, and complaints about excessive downtime are frequently heard. And as OCLC branches out into providing additional services ranging from complete library automation to piping information directly into the home, the question will legitimately be asked if more bigness is the way to go.

The news from RLIN this year is a mixture of a powerfully "reconfigured" data base, the addition of prestigious new members like the University of Minnesota and the Pierpont Morgan Library, and financial difficulties that led to staff layoffs last summer. Privately, many RLIN users talk of difficulties with the reconfiguration. Meanwhile, RLG admitted that "income not working out as planned" and "new members added not as rapidly as projected" were the reasons. Pledges of support from its members, however, assured its long-term future, said RLG. During the year, the Bibcenter at Yale, once the cornerstone of the network when its headquarters was in Branford, Connecticut, was transferred to Stanford and its name was dropped. RLIN members, like OCLC members, suffered long delays and built backlogs anew in some cases.

Regional Networks

Early in the year, AMIGOS hosted (in Dallas) a technical session, "On-line Library Systems—the Network Approach." It brought together representatives of the leading regionals: INCOLSA, SOLINET, NELINET, OHIONET, CLASS, and AMIGOS. Several themes were sounded at this gathering of organizations, which (except for CLASS) depend for their existence, let alone their future, on brokering OCLC service to their member libraries—billing them for services that go directly to each library from OCLC and providing training in the use of the system. All have been seeking ways to broaden their range of services and products. The meeting themes were independence from OCLC; expansionist ambitions; dissatisfaction with OCLC's setting of fees and its communications with the regional networks; technology transfer and planning as the ideal regional roles.

At that time, before OCLC had abruptly pulled out of the SOLINET RSS project, SOLINET spoke enthusiastically of its plans for RSS, offering a wide range of services that would be based on the software of the Washington Library Network (WLN). NELINET spoke of its plans for minicomputer-based, expanded services to its members. OHIONET paraded its homemade computerized financial system, which it claimed a better buy than the one developed by OCLC. Finally, they spoke about the need for an interutility (OCLC-RLIN) communications device.

Near the end of the year, AMIGOS announced that it would no longer confine its activities to its traditional Southwest clients and appeared to be in an expansionist mood that contrasted sharply with the retreat of SOLINET and the near disaster that struck NELINET in December and cost them their three top people—John Linford, Paula Corman, and William Basinski.

New State Networks

There was substantial movement in 1981 toward the formation of single-state networks, which, in the name of economy and autonomy, could end by taking business away from the regionals. Or they could actually strengthen the regionals by providing a more extensive membership that reaches into every hamlet in the state. Eyes are on the Michigan Library Consortium, which now has 46 members, a staff of six, and a budget of $1,222,000 after what appeared to be a somewhat shaky early history. The Missouri Network Corporation, just formed by 30 libraries, draws on two regionals for its membership: the Midwest Region Library Network (MIDLNET) and the Bibliographical Center for Research (BCR); and on the tristate Association for Library Information (AFLI), based at the Carnegie Library of Pittsburgh, saving money for members by dealing directly with OCLC rather than through a middleman regional. Other states that have formed networks include Colorado, which is out to build a network overnight; Kansas, which has created a multitype board to plan networking; South Carolina, for which a new study recommends a state network; and Iowa, for which a Becker and Hays study recommends a COM catalog-based network.

OCLC, however, professes itself alarmed at the prospect of having to deal with some 50 state networks and has recently affirmed its allegiance to regional networks.

An interesting new variant, and a possible evolutionary form of the regional network, is offered by the Midwest Region Library Network. MIDLNET was considered an unnecessary proliferation of networks when it was first launched: When he was executive director of the National Commission on Libraries and Information Science, Alphonse Trezza criticized it as unnecessary. MIDLNET then seemed to lie dormant for a long period, until it acquired James Skipper, RLG director until that network's administration was taken over by Stanford. Skipper has advanced the idea of MIDLNET as a supra-agency, a service center that would coordinate resource sharing on an interstate basis among already powerful organizations such as MINITEX, the University of Illinois, the Illinois State Library, and the Wisconsin Interlibrary Loan Service.

Two other organizations that specialize in different phases of resource sharing have shown renewed vitality in 1981. One is the Universal Serials and Book Exchange, which is experiencing a surge in demand for periodical issues in its stock and new member libraries, possibly as a result of two innovations that make their holdings much more accessible for interlibrary loan and collection development demands: a microfiche listing of their main periodical holdings and on-line access to these via the Bibliographic Retrieval Service (BRS) data base system. Another organization showing new signs of life is the Center for Research Libraries (CRL). Now under the direction of former BCR Director Donald Simpson, CRL in 1981 announced new funding, new members, and groundbreaking for a new building program.

Voluntary Cooperatives

One feature of the network landscape is the voluntary cooperative formed by two or more libraries with the aim of making all parties more effective in delivery of service. In some cases, as in Spokane this past year, a voluntary co-op is successful; in others, the lack of financial reward to overcome self-interest and the desire for autonomy is blamed for failure. The latter was described in a paper this year at ACRL's Minneapolis meeting by Kul B. Gauri, "On the Nature of Relations among Libraries." Gauri described three Cleveland area projects with high aims and low performance blamed on those reasons. On the other hand, a highly euphoric report from Spokane described the many ways in which five independent libraries sharing a ULISYS automation system have managed to cooperate in standardization of their procedures and their willingness to work together to make essentially one network, every unit of which provides full access to the user to all the holdings of the Spokane County District Library, Spokane Public Library, Eastern Washington University, Spokane Community College, and Spokane Falls Community College.

Examples of other voluntary co-ops launched in 1981 abound: In Tulsa, a project launched in 1979 as Tulsa Area Library Cooperative (TALC) was infused with new funding as its members came to see in it "a way to expand services in a time of shrinking budgets." But it took the new money to create action, as it did in the New York-New Jersey metropolitan area, where new funding added to an existing cooperative resource-sharing plan enabled a new delivery service from New York to New Jersey to be launched. If libraries can save money by leaving a voluntary co-op, they may, as they are doing in Saskatchewan, where new problems have been created by libraries' abandoning the system to save money.

The Chicago metropolitan area in this past year saw the end of the Illinois Regional Library Council, a multitype cooperative grafted uneasily onto the public library systems of the area and at last abandoned when state funding was withdrawn. Its place is being taken by a library assembly with only advisory powers, but the Illinois Library Association is reported to be preparing a new drive to win state funding for multitype library systems.

PERSONNEL

Libraries last year deployed their personnel resources in a number of ways to stretch thinning staffs and shrinking personnel budgets. Van Buren County, Iowa, reported that they were in their second year of a share-the-boss program in which one administrator was managing five libraries. And when Robert Alvarez retired from his position as director of the South San Francisco Public Library, he was replaced by a member of the staff of the San Mateo County Library, who came in on a contract basis.

In many libraries, the need was felt for staff capable of handling a wider variety of duties. At the public library in Liverpool, New York, integration of children's and adult books led to a staff realignment whereby all professionals were made responsible for service to all age groups. At the much larger Baltimore County Library, a similar realignment has been in effect.

Columbus, Ohio, was the scene for a library experiment with a system commonly used in schools to cover classes during temporary absences or vacancies: a core of "as needed" substitutes in a "rover pool" that provides an economical means of coping with emergencies and an attractive job opportunity for library workers who do not want full-time jobs.

Many libraries bade goodbye in 1981 to their Comprehensive Employment and Training Act (CETA) workers, who had in many cases saved the day for staffs decimated by ruinous budget cuts. When CETA workers first appeared on the library scene, there was serious doubt that they would prove satisfactory, but their qualifications in many cases proved to be much higher than expected. In recognition of this, last spring, the Chicago Public Library issued a report hailing their CETA experience as a success.

Workers in industry last year began to take voluntary cuts in pay or hours to save their jobs; this was seen in only one library: Staff at the Contra Costa Library in California took voluntary cuts in their work week (and pay checks), saving co-workers from dismissal in the wake of Proposition 13.

A paper delivered at the ACRL National Conference in Minneapolis stated that temporary and part-time employment is on the rise in academic libraries as it is among teaching faculties. Molly O'Hara, in "Temporary Employment and Academic Librarians," warned against the misuse of the practice.

Careers and Staff Development

Library leaders in 1981 referred often to the need for more highly qualified librarians. This may have been reflected also in the extensive qualifications seen in ads for positions, with the second master's and expertise in foreign languages as well as acquaintance with library automation frequently specified for positions that often paid no more than beginning positions at other libraries.

It was also shown in such programs as SUNY-Stony Brook's workshop "Mid-Career Assessment and Strategies for Advancement in the 90s"; and at an institute offered in Boulder, Colorado, by ALA's Reference and Adult Services Division for the upgrading of reference services.

Minnesota, in the process of launching its statewide network of library systems, was reported studying the educational requirements for systems directors. At ALA Midwinter the National Librarians Association issued a statement reporting their discussions on certification and two-year library school programs (with much disagreement) and their agreement on the need for continuing education and practicum experience. More double master's programs were announced, one a double for music librarianship announced at SUNY-Buffalo. John N. Olsgaard and Jane Kinch Olsgaard, at ACRL-Minneapolis, presented the paper "Educational Requirements for Academic Librarians in Non-Director Positions"; they found libraries setting more stringent requirements for posts in public services than for those in technical services—but all requirements, they reported, are getting stiffer, so much so that they pose a threat to the employability of the beginning librarian.

An advocate of the stiffening of requirements for academic librarians was John R. Kaiser; in another paper delivered at ACRL, "The Librarian as Scholar," Kaiser argued that the librarian should be a subject specialist and publish research. And more and more, said Kaiser, this is being asked of librarians as a response to the demand for "accountability."

An older concern in this area, for the improvement of managerial skills among librarians, found frequent expression again in 1981. Californians mulled the possibility of certifying library administrators; the Council on Library Resources awarded grants for advanced study of management and named five promising librarians as academic management interns. And library managers in 1981 had a new banner to march under: productivity. Their successes in this area were frequently advanced as arguments for further funding. Salt Lake County Library reported a 30 percent productivity gain with three fewer full-time equivalents (FTEs); Librarian Robert E. Cannon of the Kern County Library in California reported that he was providing more service although the staff was 22 percent smaller.

In the article "Increasing Library Productivity," which was run in the Practicing Librarian section of *Library Journal* on February 1, Howard Samuelson, director of the Santa Ana Public Library, California, advised on the way to go: work simplification, work analysis, better management techniques, and employee motivation.

Placement and Salaries

Two major sources of information on trends in library salaries are the *LJ* annual report and the Special Libraries Association annual survey of its members. In "Placements and Salaries 1980: Holding the Line" [*see* Part 3 of this volume.—*Ed.*], Carol L. Learmont and Stephen Van Houten reported that in 1980 starting salaries increased an average of 8.4 percent (less than inflation) to $14,223, but there was a "dramatic drop" in the number of graduates of accredited programs.

SLA's report of its annual survey, in each October issue of *Special Libraries*, found salary increases of something more than 7 percent were the rule, with salaries of its reporting members averaging around $21,000 nationwide.

Placements present a more difficult situation to assess from reports coming in. The number of library school students has dropped—some say too far—but at least two schools are saying there are plenty of jobs for their graduates. One is still producing graduating classes of over 200 a year. Last January, Simmons Associate Dean Jim Matarazzo said that there had been a 130 percent increase in positions available and over 95 percent of Simmons graduates were being placed. The University of Pittsburgh's school reports that its new Bachelor of Information Science (BIS) is thriving, with 140 now in the program and the average graduate getting over $19,000 to start—as a programmer, market researcher, systems analyst, or other information worker.

Library schools and librarians have been eyeing the possibility of earning a living with library skills outside of traditional libraries. In 1981 this interest was reflected in a number of reports: The University of Wisconsin–Madison was only the latest of many to change its name to become the School of Library and Information Science. A two-day workshop at SUNY-Albany last May examined the conversion of the librarian into an information broker, and librarians were attracted to a program in Chicago last February on careers in information management; it was cosponsored by the American Society for Information Science and the Association of Information Managers. Ex-librarian Patricia Schuman (Neal-Schuman publishers) and Betty-Carol Sellen were frequent speakers on this popular topic at library meetings.

The New England Library Board operates one of the many "job-line hotlines" found around the country; they reported last fall that their listings of available library jobs were growing—but there was a decrease in job seekers in the New England area. Still another indicator, the Positions Available pages in *LJ/SLJ Hotline*, which carry the heaviest load of job listings among library media, were steadily increasing until late in 1981, when the number of listings took their first downturn since the country started to slide into recession.

One area of library employment seems to be growing, but information on it is scarce: the library consultant, who is often a retired elder statesman, but often a leading public, academic, or special librarian who has made a name for one or more specialties—building design and automation have been usual ones. This year a new specialty reared its head: cutting back the library program. The consultant business has a vigorous competitor in the state agencies and the public library systems where, at considerably less expense than private consulting fees can amount to, a corps of hardworking specialists brings expertise free to libraries that need it. An interesting variation on this pattern was seen in 1981 at the Bibliographic Center for Research in Denver. Members of this regional network were offered a consultant brokering service to help guide them to (private) consultants likely to be of help to them.

Another new wrinkle in consulting has developed—the consulting firm established by a group of librarians who may be retired or still employed full time; it generally brings together consultants with complementary specialties so that the firm can offer to handle just about any library need for guidance. The newest member of this family has been announced by Ed Howard, who on retirement from the Vigo County Library in Terre Haute, announced that he would establish a consulting firm "specializing in public libraries."

Volunteers

Volunteers became even more of a standard fixture in public libraries this past year, and they also turned up in at least one academic library. President Reagan's support of volunteers to replace paid social service workers helped legitimize them, as did praise from Oregon Ex-Governor Tom McCall at the Annual Conference of the Pacific Northwest Library Association. ALA sent out a call for copies of forms and policies developed by libraries for the use of volunteers. And legislation introduced in New York State could lead to a $150 tax credit to a library volunteer putting in 150 hours of work. The Texas State Library gave its stamp of approval with a series of workshops around the state to help libraries make good use of volunteers.

There were still some rumblings against volunteers. The British Library Association accepted a report opposing their use while its own members are unemployed. The Pennsylvania Library Association's Executive Committee went on record in opposition to a change in the state's public library standards that would have allowed the use of volunteers to fulfill staffing requirements. The bitterness of some staff objections to volunteers was vividly expressed by a union publication, the July-October issue of the *Communicator*, published by the Librarians' Guild of the Los Angeles Public Library: "As the cost of equal pay for comparable work becomes established principle, suddenly volunteerism is the way to save the City. And what sex are most volunteers?"

Several libraries reported growing numbers of volunteer hours: Los Angeles County Library logged some 30,000; the Metropolitan Library System in Oklahoma City reported that its 561 volunteers put in 10,671 hours for a full-time-equivalent of 5.13 staffers; the Suburban Library System in Illinois reports in more general terms a high level of volunteer use by member libraries, including one outlet that is operated predominantly by volunteers.

At the University of California, San Diego, volunteers have stepped in to handle Friends of the Library activities, while at the Tennessee State Library and Archives, a corps of skilled volunteers is arranging and describing historical materials, giving some

11 working days a week to the effort. One library that values volunteers, the Janesville, Wisconsin, Public Library, was noted in 1981 for its clever ads, not just asking for volunteers, but listing specific jobs with the duties and requirements they involve.

The most unusual volunteer effort of 1981 was noted at the Finkelstein Memorial Library in Spring Valley, New York: People sentenced to community service by local courts are frequently to be found doing their time as library volunteers.

WOMEN IN LIBRARIES

Librarians won two significant victories and are eying two more in the area of equal pay for women and for workers in female-dominated employment. The November 1 *LJ* has an interview with Pat Curia, a librarian and a leader in the successful San Jose strike. The City of San Jose, after a strike lasting from July 5 to 14, agreed to municipal worker demands and will pay $1,450,000 to some 750 employees who have suffered discrimination based on sex. Earlier in the year, Canadian librarians at the Canadian National Library in Ottawa won a victory on the same issue.

Another drive is being made in Canada by 52 librarians at the National Research Council in Ottawa who have lodged a complaint of discrimination with the Canadian Human Rights Commission. And librarians in California are watching a bill, AB 129, that aims to establish state policy in support of equal pay in female-dominated jobs.

Women bosses are increasing in numbers in American research libraries, reported Betty Jo Irvine at the Minneapolis ACRL National Conference. In her paper, "ARL Academic Library Leaders of the 1980s: Men and Women of the Executive Suite," she went on to say that the new women leaders have distinctly different career profiles from those of the men they are joining. They tend more often to be internally recruited, to have more middle management experience, and to have as a mentor an in-house adviser rather than a library school dean.

The latest in an annual series of studies charting the relationship between public library income growth and the salaries of men and women directors of large public libraries appeared in the September 15 *LJ*. "Sex, Salaries, and Library Support . . . 1981" by Kathleen Heim and Carolyn Kacena made the encouraging observation that over the two years 1979 and 1980 these libraries in the United States and Canada were keeping up with inflation. They found that libraries headed by women still tended to draw lower levels of financial support than did those directed by men, but the salaries of women directors showed a small but gratifying increase. Women still are not represented in the top jobs in proportion to their numbers in the profession, however, and they still generally earn less than men. But the women directors of the systems serving the largest populations showed a 3 percent advantage over men in similar libraries.

Leadership in the profession is evidenced in other ways, including attendance at increasingly expensive national conferences and appearance on the platforms of these meetings. One informal report made to *LJ* recently counted (by sex) the attendees and panelists at the November Pittsburgh Conference "The Challenge of Change: Critical Choices for Library Decision Makers." The result: about 50/50 for men and women, in contrast, said the counter, to a ratio more like ten to one (women to men) seen at local meetings. On the platform, however, men outnumbered women as speakers and panelists by something like four to one.

PRESERVATION

The past year has been an auspicious one for the cause of preservation. The alarm—sounded for years, it is true—over the deterioration of a century of the world's heritage of print now sitting on library shelves is finally turning into programs for action and the development of strategies to counter the disaster. Columbia's School of Library Service announced the first university degree program in the country to train library conservators and preservation administrators, bringing in Paul N. Banks from the Newberry Library in Chicago to direct the program. The National Endowment on the Humanities is one of the agencies helping to fund the new program.

The Library of Congress was active in urging publishers to use acid-free paper, and it was reported that such use is growing today. In mid-November, the twenty-seventh Annual Allerton Institute at the University of Illinois took preservation as its topic for four days of programs. The New England Document Conservation Center (NEDCC) found it was time to incorporate and extend its range of activity; one of its first forays into a wider world of activity was on assignment with the Colorado State Library; NEDCC's $51,200 contract called for it to assess statewide needs for preservation and to outline a strategy for dealing with them.

The federal government cut back on support for preservation of archival records, but the Society of American Archivists was active in offering workshops to help train archivists in techniques of preservation. The University of Texas at Houston announced a major microfilming project to preserve priceless Mexican heritage materials, largely Mexican periodicals in the library's Benson Collection.

Harvard celebrated a $500,000 endowment gift from the Littauer Foundation for preservation of its Judaica collection by microfilming; it called an international conference on the use of microfilm in preservation in October, bringing together a distinguished gathering to hear representatives of Harvard, the Council on Library Resources, the National Archives, and other agencies concerned with preservation. Libraries were chided, by a representative of the Mellon Foundation, for their failure to develop a working consensus or strategy on how the problem of preservation should be approached nationally and cooperatively. Mellon funding, he indicated, would wait on signs of progress in this area.

He evidently did not have long to wait; one of the university librarians in attendance, Susan K. Martin of the Milton S. Eisenhower Library at Johns Hopkins University, announced a month later that Mellon had awarded the Eisenhower Library a grant of $185,000 to set up a broad-based preservation program for the Mid-Atlantic region and for co-members of the Research Libraries Group. The three-year program will train conservators and develop workshops and other activities and will welcome participation by other libraries.

PEOPLE

Among academic librarians moving to new positions in 1981 were William F. Birdsall, leaving the University of Manitoba to become University Librarian at Dalhousie; Joseph F. Boykin, Jr., new Director at Clemson University, South Carolina; Elizabeth M. Corbett, who moved from Acting Librarian to Librarian at Barnard College; Mary R. Magruder, who became Dean of Libraries at Kansas State University, Manhattan; Bessie K. Hahn, Director of Library Services at Brandeis; C. James Schmidt, formerly Librarian of Brown University and now Executive Vice President of the Research Libraries Group.

Among public library leaders, Linda Allmand left the Dallas Public Library to become Director of the Fort Worth Public Library System; Shelah H Bell moved up from her post as Director of the Irving, Texas, Public Library to Director of Libraries and Communications of the City of Irving; Ginnie Cooper, who was Director of the

Kenosha Public Library, Wisconsin, is now Alameda County Librarian in Hayward, California; Anna Curry is the new director of the Enoch Pratt Free Library; Marcy Litzenberg is the Director of the Santa Fe Public Library; Donald F. Meadows is Director of the Metro Toronto Library Board; Stephen M. Silberstein left the University of California–Berkeley Systems Office to become an independent automation consultant and contractor; Edward M. Szynaka left the Grace A. Dow Memorial Library in Midlands, Michigan, to become Director of the Pasadena Public Library; and Ernest Siegel, who left the Los Angeles Public Library to take over the Enoch Pratt Library in Baltimore, returned to the coast as Director of the Contra Costa County Library.

LJ noted new library school heads in 1981: Jane Robbins-Carter is the Director of the Library School at the University of Wisconsin–Madison; Evelyn H. Daniel is now the Dean of the School of Information Studies at Syracuse University; and Carl Orgren is Director, School of Library Science, University of Iowa.

Among a host of changes in federal libraries there were two outstanding ones: Karen Renninger is now Chief of the Library Division of the Veterans Administration and Benjamin C. Glidden retired as Director of the Air Force Academy Library in Colorado.

Among new faces heading the state library agencies were James A. Nelson, Kentucky State Librarian; David W. Woodburn, Director of the Mississippi Library Commission; Sharon G. Womack, Director of the Arizona State Department of Library, Archives, and Public Records; Fay Zipkowitz, Director of the Rhode Island Department of State Library Services; and New Hampshire State Librarian Shirley Adamovich. David L. Reich left one state agency, the Massachusetts Bureau of Library Commissioners, to head a supra-agency, the New England Library Board in Augusta, Maine.

A surprising amount of the important decision making in libraries today is being done or influenced strongly by a cadre of consultants, some directors of leading academic and public libraries, some who have set up shop fairly recently acting purely as library consultants, and a very important and not very public group of eminent retired librarians. This latter group comes to mind on reading that John G. Lorenz, after his career at the Library of Congress and a stint at the Association of Research Libraries, was to be found in 1981 as Consultant and Interim Director of the Learning Resources Center at Southeastern University, Washington, D.C.

The masterful hand of Emerson Greenaway was to be seen this year in the newly renovated and enlarged library at Wheaton College in Norton, Massachusetts, where a beautiful old Ralph Adams Cram library was rescued from earlier "improvements" and added to impressively.

Among the many retired library leaders who were active in 1981 were James E. "Ned" Bryant, Hoyt Galvin, Meredith Bloss, and Lowell Martin. Martin was called on to provide the generalship for the retreat of the Free Library of Philadelphia in the face of fiscal calamity to a redefinition of priorities and a more secure, down-sized mission.

Retiring in 1981, some of them possibly to join the ranks of the consultants, were Barbara Gray Boyd, County Librarian, Alameda County, California; Ella Gaines Yates-Edwards, Director, Atlanta Public Library; Estelle Brodman, Librarian and Professor of Medical History at Washington University School of Medicine; Robert G. Newman, Director of the Berkshire Athenaeum, Pittsfield, Massachusetts; and Robert S. Taylor, Dean, School of Information Studies, Syracuse University, who returned to active teaching.

Other retirements included C. Lamar Wallis, Director of Libraries, Memphis-Shelby County; Edward N. Howard, Director, Vigo County Public Library, Terre

Haute; Mary Lethbridge, Information Officer, Library of Congress; and Jean Lowrie, Director of the School of Librarianship, Western Michigan, who is also returning to full-time teaching.

Obituaries in 1981 were noted for Eugene P. Kennedy, Chief of the Management Branch, Office of Records and Information Management, GSA; he had been involved in the design of the ERIC system; James A. Leathers, Director of Libraries, Mid-Continent Public Library, Independence, Missouri; Marion Milczewski, former Director of Libraries, University of Washington; Benjamin E. Powell, University Librarian at Duke from 1946 to 1975; Louis Shores, founder and Dean Emeritus of the Florida State University School of Library Science; Daniel Reicher, Director of the School of Library Science/Ecole de bibliothéconomie, University of Montreal; and Wayne S. Yenawine, former Dean and Professor Emeritus, College of Librarianship, University of South Carolina, Columbia.

Missing at sea and the object of a suit by his wife to have him declared dead was Carl Jackson, who had once successfully crossed the Atlantic singlehanded, but was evidently run over by a larger vessel somewhere off the coast of Spain on his second attempt.

SLJ NEWS REPORT, 1981

Bertha M. Cheatham
Associate Editor, *School Library Journal*

Libraries are a mere 19 years away from the year 2000. As we begin the countdown to this fast-approaching milepost in time, it is time to review the concerns, problems, and advances made this year in terms of what has been accomplished and where the profession is headed. At a 1980 colloquium of "the wisest and best-informed" scholars and information specialists, who contributed to "An Information Agenda for the 1980s" at a New York City colloquium held in mid-1980, many concerns relating to current and future conditions of access to information in the 1980s were expressed.

For example, Douglas Cater of the Aspen Institute for Humanistic Studies claimed that "information can cause problems of glut or overload as well as of deprivation." He centered on the problems of conflicting values and the tendency of society to take its values as "absolute." "Human values are always in conflict with one another," he stated. This included First Amendment principles and regulations affecting the ownership or programming of media, which are often in conflict, and conflicts about the issues of free speech, free press, the privacy of individuals, and the citizen's right to know. Among his agenda items for the 1980s was the need to "preserve the print press with high standards of excellence," and the need to find ways to use new technologies for education, health, and other social uses.

Lewis Branscomb, vice president and chief scientist for IBM Corporation, pointed out that before getting carried away with new and future technologies, libraries must solve current problems—finding money to support libraries and ways to justify services. He stated, "Libraries must once again become teachers and innovators, and

Note: Adapted from *School Library Journal*, December 1981.

not custodians, lest the treasures in their custody be obsolesced by alternative services that fail to serve humanity as imaginatively and as profoundly as they could."

While more questions were raised than answered about the future of information services, and although librarians serving the library's largest group of users, children and youth, were not in evidence at the sessions, the agenda did touch on many aspects of library service at the beginning of the 20-year countdown to the year 2000.

In this summary of the year's news, issues, and events, one finds that the path toward the technological future has had many obstacles to slow it down to a snail's pace and that librarians have had much to agonize about and to reassess as the second year in this decade drew to a close.

The top item on the 1981 agenda of library issues and events was the effects of a taxpayers' backlash against increased property taxation coupled with cutbacks in federal funds for programs in education, social services, and libraries. When Reagan won the presidency in 1980, it was feared that his election would usher in a much stronger conservatism in municipalities across the country. In 1981 that fear became a reality as conservative groups threatened to monitor library materials, services, and the types of audiovisual and print materials available to children in the community.

In the postelection months, libraries and schools were left to manage under budget stringencies. Hardest hit were Massachusetts school systems and libraries. Voters in Massachusetts passed a restricting Proposition 2½, a property and auto-excise tax cut measure that limited property tax increases to 2½ percent of "full and fair" cash value. At year's end, schools in the state's larger cities had cut back on staff drastically, closed schools, and geared up for further cuts because supplemental funds were not forthcoming. Boston closed 27 of its 150 schools; Worcester schools dismissed 247 teachers because of budget shortfalls. The school budget for the district's libraries was cut from $128,000 to $10,000. In Worcester and other communities library and testing programs were curtailed or eliminated. To make matters worse, financially strapped school administrators see no light at the end of the tunnel as their restricted budgets continue to be eroded by inflation, increased energy costs, escalating operating expenses, higher teachers' salaries, and a reduction in state funds because of lower enrollments.

The situation at the heavily used Boston Public Library reached a minor crisis this year as the administration trimmed service hours and staff to stay in operation. Positions for 172 professional and clerical staff were eliminated. Also, as a cost-saving measure, many branch libraries became "reading rooms" serviced by clerical staff under the direction of a district supervisor. Evening hours at the central library were reduced; now the young adult department (which usually services many of its clientele on Saturdays and evenings), along with other departments, is open only from 1:00 P.M. to 5:00 P.M. Monday through Friday.

Two Massachusetts libraries, Flint Memorial Library (North Reading) and the Billerica Public Library, marshaled community support to improve their budgets when other libraries were cutting back. North Reading's Director Janet Eagleson said that "hard-hitting newspaper publicity," based on the fact that the library was to assume an unfair share of the cuts, convinced the finance committee to keep the budget intact and to allot an additional $5,204. Billerica's Public Library, in commemorating its first year, turned National Library Week into a community celebration, "a big birthday bash," that convinced voters the library had something for everyone. Registration shot up 60 percent, reference questions and circulation also increased impressively—and the library retained its budget intact.

Recalcitrant taxpayers in the Alpena school district in Northeastern Michigan turned down a renewal proposal that would have increased property tax and, in effect, shut down the schools—6,800 students could not attend classes after October 15. The district's tax had expired in June. The matter has not been resolved; the voters rejected the tax measure three times. In the wake of voters' refusal to approve funding bills in Michigan, the Taylor schools in suburban Detroit and the Pontiac schools are in serious financial straits and are expected to close unless funds are found or approved by voters to cover budget deficits. Smaller districts are operating under austerity budgets; the state will not bail them out.

The picture was no brighter in the St. Louis Public Library. The directors reluctantly closed four branches this year after fighting a losing battle against out-of-control costs. Joan Collett, librarian and executive director, said, "Personnel costs, utilities, and book costs continue to escalate, with no signs of letting up. Revenues are down, costs are steadily increasing, and we are just stretched too thin."

Most libraries facing budget crunches because of declining property taxes have watched California to see how the public libraries survived the effects of 1979's Proposition 13, a measure reducing property taxes. A survey of 80 of that state's public libraries revealed that the majority of libraries (67) reported cutbacks in programming; 52 said Proposition 13 was to blame. Children's programs suffered most: 40 libraries cut out story hours, film programs, and class visits (some libraries eliminated children's services in branch locations). Twelve libraries used volunteers or Friends to run programs that had been run by paid staff members. It was a Catch-22 situation. Many libraries, which could not afford to continue outreach programs or community programs for adults and publicity activities, became less visible in the community—just at a time when voters needed to become increasingly aware of the impact of library services. As State Librarian Gary Strong summed up the situation with implications for the future, "With fewer programs and less outreach activities, a diminished number of citizens may become involved with the library and be made aware of how it can enrich their lives. There will be fewer voices speaking up for the library at budget hearings, and this can only contribute to the downward financial spiral we are enduring in public library service in the 1980s."

In contrast to the dire budget crises of the eastern and northeastern states, Florida libraries enjoyed a balmy fiscal year—thanks to revenues from sales taxes, a healthy tourist industry, and the influx of wealthy foreign investors. Due to the lobbying efforts of Friends of Florida Libraries (FFL) and the Florida Association for Media in Education (FAME), libraries have held their own and continue to realize gains in state library aid and in revenue funds earmarked for school library materials. In fact, the state library considers FFL such a powerful, effective library lobby that it granted the group $75,000 to hire a library information officer to coordinate a statewide public-awareness campaign.

FAME is well practiced in lobbying for appropriations. The combined library and media specialists organization has a lobbyist to inform and instruct key legislators about its bills. This year, the state allocated $3.7 million for library materials and equipment.

Another exception to the 1981 budget-cut fever comes out of Vancouver, Canada, where the school board voted to adopt a new staffing formula that will result in a full-time, qualified teacher-librarian for every elementary school with 300 or more students and a half-time teacher-librarian for every school with fewer than 300 students. This formula adds more than eight full-time-equivalent staff positions to the school system and provides two teacher-librarians in the 12 largest secondary schools. According to Ken Haycock, coordinator of library services and a supervisor of instruction for the board, "The Vancouver School Board has a clear commitment to the role of the teacher-librarian." Last year, the board provided a cost-of-inflation increase to the library budget of about $200,000. An increase of 14 percent is expected to offset inflationary costs for 1982. The budget will allow all 18 secondary schools to have electronic systems installed by year's end and a quantity of microform reader/printers added to the resource centers.

This is another success story due to the teacher-librarians' efforts to publicize their programs in schools. "The teacher-librarians have gone to shopping centers and information meetings for parents, and as a result, the parents' association has pushed for strong support from the board for library services," Haycock said, stressing that the school resource centers are the "heart" of the instructional programs, "and when you start making cuts, you don't start with the heart."

INTELLECTUAL FREEDOM

The next item on the 1981 agenda was book battles in school and public libraries. As we approach the year 2000, ultraconservative political groups and religious fundamentalists such as the Moral Majority continue to attract nationwide attention as they continue efforts to ban "anti" books (anti-God, anti-Bible, anti-Creation, antidecency) from libraries serving children.

Most of the censorship issues this year centered around what was perceived as pornography or sex books that are accessible to children and young adults. Many took place when election campaigns for local officials were in full swing.

Censorship is on the rise, according to a 1980 survey of 1,800 public elementary and secondary schools. The majority of the book complaints on the local level came from individual citizens, not organized groups, the report stated; however, at the state level, where many of the challenges involved textbook adoption, 17 of 27 challenges were organized by individuals receiving group support.

But there is evidence that librarians (and directors' boards) are becoming more adept at fending off book attacks. Early in the year, an incident in the Washington State Library received widespread attention from the library world when State Librarian Roderick G. Swartz refused to hand over a list of school district employees who had checked out the film *Achieving Sexual Maturity*. Swartz said it was not library policy to disclose library circulation records. Representing the state's Moral Majority chapter, attorney Michael Farris threatened to sue the library if it did not bend. His group claimed that the 21-minute film was unacceptable because it contained explicit sex information and scenes of teenagers embracing. All came to naught when Farris dropped legal proceedings.

The American Library Association Intellectual Freedom Committee (ALA/ IFC) had Farris lead off its program "Intellectual Freedom in the '80s: The Impact of Conservatism" at the annual conference in San Francisco. The audience listened to his arguments against open-shelf access for children (he maintained that it interfered with parents' rights) and ALA's complaint procedures (he called the complaint process "a charade"). In his conclusion he issued a warning that since taxpayers' money is used for purchasing books, librarians must use restraint in placing sensitive materials within the reach of children.

A long-standing IFC case, *Pico* v. *The Island Trees* (N.Y.) *Union Free School Board*, may finally be resolved in the near future. In October, the U.S. Supreme Court agreed to review the suit to decide whether the school board members must stand trial for violating the students' First Amendment rights in removing nine books from the high school library in March 1976. The larger issue of how much authority a school board is entitled to exercise in controlling a library collection may be addressed in the court's decision. Meanwhile, authors like Kurt Vonnegut will continue to read of incidents in which their books have been removed from a classroom or library. Vonnegut, who believes he is on a list of "bad books," recently asked, "Is there no school board anywhere sufficiently inventive to come up with a new list of utterly intolerable books? My goodness, *Slaughterhouse-Five* was published in 1969!"

Scattered censorship reports came in from various parts of the country during the year, but no dramatic rise in cases was evident. One volatile controversy erupted in Tampa, Florida, where the Tampa-Hillsborough County Public Library Board became embroiled in a dispute over *Where Did I Come From?* by Peter Mayle and five other sex-education books. A former Parent-Teacher Association president wanted them removed from the children's collection, charging that their content was too explicit for young children. In addition to Mayle's book, removal was also ordered for *Where Do Babies Come From?* by Margaret Sheffield; *Love and Sex in Plain Language* by Eric W. Johnson; *The Beauty of Birth* by Colette Portal; *The Wonderful Story of How You Were Born* by Sidonie Matsner Gruenberg; and *How Babies Are Made* by Andrew C. Andry and Steven Schepp. Months after the Tampa County Library Board refused to remove the books, city council members voted five to two to order the library to move the books from the library's children's section to the adult collection. The situation is ominous since the council has formed a committee to make recommendations about the supervision and control of the library and "to study the possibility of drawing guidelines for book placement and selection." Library Director Leo H. Meirose, who has staunchly defended the library's position and selection policies, said he was disappointed in the council's decision. He told them, "To withdraw the books from the collection or to place an artificial barrier between them and the audience for which they were written by moving them to the adult collection is to practice censorship—the second action is only more subtle censorship than the first. But what is more dangerous is taking either action in response to a pressure group. This sets a dangerous precedent." Despite this urgent warning, the council, under pressure from religious and political factions, subsequently adopted a resolution to pluck the six books in question off the shelves of the children's room.

Many of the book complaints came out of high schools where concerned citizens' groups and parents are finding material they deem unsuitable for students. Ronald J. Glasser's *365 Days* was considered too explicit for students in the Baileyville (Maine) High School and the school committee ordered it off the open shelf because of the "offensive and abusive" language of soldiers who had been wounded in Vietnam.

In Montello, Wisconsin, Librarian Joyce Treml was faced with a difficult situation in her first year on the job. A Concerned Citizens group checked out 33 books (23 from the high school; 10 from the elementary school) to judge their suitability for students. A review committee decided to remove *Hard Feelings* by Don Brede from the library and to retain all of the others except *Happy Endings Are All Alike* by Sandra Scoppettone (because of a tie vote).

Author Gertrude Samuels was perplexed that her book *Run, Shelley, Run* was banned from a high school in Sully Buttes school district in Central South Dakota. The school board voted four to three to remove the book after the parent of a 12-year-old student filed a complaint about the language used.

States continue to wrestle with Child Pornography laws. A coalition of booksellers, librarians, and civil libertarians challenged the constitutionality of a Georgia censorship law (Act 785) to prohibit the sale or display of material to minors that might "arouse lust." The legislation also makes it a misdemeanor to sell magazines, films, or recordings that include "descriptions or depictions of illicit sex or sexual immorality." In October, a federal judge enjoined the law's enforcement.

A New York Child Pornography statute that could have affected the sale or distribution of sex-education books like the highly controversial *Show Me* by Dr. Helga Fleischhauer-Hardt (St. Martin's, 1975) and the movie *The Tin Drum* was overturned by a five-to-two vote in the New York Court of Appeals in May. Publishers' and booksellers' organizations and St. Martin's Press had urged that section 263.15, which outlawed the sale or distribution of nonobscene works depicting children under 16 in a sexual pose regardless of whether the work had value or merit, be eliminated.

As we move closer to the year 2000, librarians and booksellers will continue to face similar challenges as taxpayers and nationally organized groups acquire more expertise in mounting censorship campaigns. With fired-up conservative groups getting wide media exposure, book protests are bound to accelerate and we will see more court battles centering around First Amendment rights (including cases involving the circulation of R-rated videodiscs and cassettes).

TECHNOLOGY IN 1981

The biggest news this year is the San Francisco Federal Court's ruling that videotaping a TV show at home violates the producer's copyright. The news of the ruling hit the manufacturers and distributors of videotape recording devices like a bombshell. They had been operating under the assumption that the practice of off-air taping on home videocassette recorders (VCRs) fell within the "fair use" provision of the copyright law, which permits limited copying for education or research use. In 1979, a federal court in Los Angeles had sided with Sony, which introduced its Betamax in 1975 and was socked with a copyright-abuse suit brought by Universal and Walt Disney studios. The ruling (which overturned the 1979 decision) raised many questions: Are copyright laws up-to-date for new developments in communications technology? Can retailers continue to sell VCRs legally? Can home taping be monitored? Are companies that make and distribute video recorders (and their advertising agencies) liable for damages? Will they be required to pay fees to the creator networks and producers of TV programs? Many expect the questions will go to the U.S. Supreme Court.

"Thought, reflection, and care" were called for by Registrar of Copyrights David Ladd. He said the Appeals Court decision "has exploded over the entertainment world," creating confusion. Ladd believes the problem is not home taping of TV programs or sale of VCRs but compensation to producers, authors, and program creators while allowing public access. The 1980s may see legislation similar to that of foreign countries that impose levies on VCR hardware or tapes to compensate the copyright holders.

Libraries are not yet affected by the off-air taping ruling, which affects only some western states. There is ample evidence that video and cable programs are becoming commonplace in public and school libraries. A 1980 survey published by ALA's Library and Information Technology Association (LITA) shows that library programming for children, young adults, and senior citizens is the most popular. It was surmised that children are more receptive to TV and enjoy producing their own programs. Cable TV is fast becoming a medium for story hour programs and book talks. The 1980s will see more use of video by libraries to reach into homes; about 97 percent of U.S. homes have access to TV.

The use of microcomputers is proliferating in libraries throughout the country. It is estimated that 50,000 are in schools. The uses are varied; their popularity is uncontested. One story comes out of the Menlo Park (California) Public Library, which houses a branch of ComputerTown, U.S.A. The staff found that things got out of hand as boisterous youngsters forgot they were in a quiet library when they challenged their buddies in playing competitive games such as Asteroids, Space Invaders, and Cosmic Fighters. The library's solution was to remove the competitive games and those that did not require thought or interaction with the computer, and replace them with tapes requiring logic, skill, and memory. After this was done, the disruptive behavior of the young patrons vastly improved, much to the satisfaction of the library staff, parents, and regular patrons. As many other librarians serving children and young adults must do during this decade, the library is compiling criteria for the selection and use of appropriate software for the library.

A constructive approach to the use of microcomputers is taking place at the San Bernardino (California) Public Library. Through a $50,000 Library Services and Construction Act (LSCA) grant, the library has begun a project titled "Public Library Computerized Support of School Proficiency Testing Program." The program, in cooperation with the San Bernardino City Unified School District, reaches students who would otherwise be high school dropouts or ineligible for graduation because they could not pass the mandated California proficiency exam.

One library has organized a Video Cassette Exchange Program with ten institutional library members having access to a video software collection. One of the organizers is Alan Engelbert, assistant coordinator of Special Library Services, Missouri State Library, who says that the cooperative program aids institutionalized people who may be functionally illiterate, have low reading levels, or be nonreaders.

Carnegie Library of Pittsburgh celebrated the International Year of Disabled Persons by acquiring the *Talking World Book Encyclopedia*.

This year, Brooklyn Public Library joined New York Public Library and others in making computerized card catalogs available to patrons. In other large academic and public libraries patrons are beginning to use on-line public access terminals to get at library materials. The Public Library of Columbus and Franklin County, Ohio, has an electronic catalog in place. The University of Illinois at Urbana-Champaign plans to have 90 public access terminals available by 1983 and will phase out the card catalog when the new system is operational.

Online Computer Library Center (OCLC) studied a computerized home information service and claims that the experimental project, Channel 2000, proved that this information service is on the horizon for the future. OCLC is developing a Viewtel to provide a variety of information ranging from basic math for children and early reader skills for preschoolers, to home banking services, a video encyclopedia (*Academic American*), and a video catalog. There are fees involved, and one can ponder whether those who are on the low rung of the economic ladder will become the technologically deprived in the year 2000. On the other hand, futurists believe that technological advances will provide a less expensive means of teaching.

Recent advances in electronic access to information have led to the formation of a group called the Electronic Library Association. At a meeting sponsored by the Public Library of Columbus and Franklin County (Ohio) and OCLC, a small group met to discuss "libraries without walls," serving patrons through home information centers, and to organize to be at the forefront of future technological developments. Many are gearing up for a future of serving patrons completely through technology, but library schools are not turning out such technicians for this wave of the future.

EDUCATION

There is talk of a demographic revolution for the 1980s. School systems, which had built up facilities and services to accommodate the baby boom of the late 1960s, were rapidly closing buildings and cutting down on service personnel because of a decline in the birthrate in the mid-1970s. However, in the 1980s the postwar products of the baby boom will come of child-bearing age and it is predicted that another baby boom will occur when, as Professor Herbert Beinstock of CUNY noted, women in their thirties will get a "nesting instinct." He asks, "How will the public sector prepare to serve this demand when the current drift is to move resources out of this sector?"

More evidence of an increase in the birthrate comes from the National Center for Education Statistics (NCES). NCES statistics show that in the last decade the number of three-to-five-year-old children in nursery school and kindergarten classes increased 15 percent.

Everything seems to go in cycles—this will not be the first baby boom. But the second boom will probably find school systems as unprepared as they were for the first, in a time when government is cutting back on federal aid to education and on tuition tax credits. Terry Herndon, executive director of the National Education Association, blames "a cohort of chronic tax resisters, reactionaries, witch hunters, super patriots, wayward dogma peddlers, and vitriolic race haters" for many of the problems affecting public schools. He urged more teachers to get involved politically to fight back and get school support from the community. This year, Reagan's administration has given school administrators a lot with which to contend. After one year of existence, the cabinet-level Education Department headed by Secretary Terrel H. Bell is recommended for elimination and the education block grants have everyone in a quandary about how funds (including Title IV-B) will be distributed in each state—although there are provisions for this in the plan that lumps funds for all programs into one major program. This brought to an end the era when school systems could rely on their fair share of Elementary and Secondary Education Act (ESEA) funds to carry on existing programs and initiate new ones.

Despite the cuts in government spending, schools are finding ways to improve services. The St. Louis Public Schools actually improved services because of a change in the grade-level structure of the system (allowing for middle schools) and renovations in buildings. About 30 newly equipped library centers were opened this year, and 29 librarians were hired to run them.

ON TO 2000

Increasingly, librarians, library media specialists, technicians, audiovisual professionals, and teachers are looking toward their professional associations for assistance and guidance in pursuing their chosen careers. They are asking questions about their role in the associations and what each can do for them—they want something in return for rising membership dues and costly conference fees. The American Association of School Librarians (AASL), which changed the name of its journal from *School Media Quarterly* to *School Library Media Quarterly* as one means of representing all of its constituency, raised questions concerning its relationship to ALA policies and procedures related to finance, divisional membership recruitment, evaluation of divisional staff performance, services provided by the ALA offices, and the relationship of ALA staff and offices to the divisions. AASL was smarting from its inability to fully control the tidy profit realized from its first national conference, held in Louisville, Kentucky, in 1980.

Despite the threatened chill on divisional conferences posed by the ALA Executive Board's approval in October of guidelines that might, if adopted by the council, limit ALA's units to only one national conference every three years, AASL is proceeding with its plans for three ALA-approved biennial conferences. The 1982 AASL national conference will take place in Houston, October 21–24.

In 1982, the Young Adult Services Division (YASD) will complete plans for a five-year program to revitalize activities, attract membership, and increase revenues. The plan calls for an expanded publications schedule; annual leadership training sessions for YASD officers, directors, and committee chairs; and conference program development to encourage interdivisional cooperation.

This year, the Association for Library Service to Children (ALSC) continued its pattern of programs designed to provide in-service education to members. A day-long program at the ALA Annual Conference in San Francisco, "Moving the Menace Out of Management," had ten sessions on such managerial tasks as strategies for developing goals and objectives, obtaining grants, budgeting, and finding ways to get more federal and local funds.

Both YASD and ALSC are considering national conferences in the future. ALSC has established a task force to study the feasibility of a divisional conference and to make recommendations about its format.

As a result of an April discussion by division leaders at what was dubbed a "summit meeting" to review the "Operating Agreement" between ALA and its divisions, the 39,000-member association may be turning down a different road in the near future as its divisions seek greater autonomy in planning conferences away from ALA's annual meetings as well as in matters pertaining to the oversight and compensation of divisional staff at ALA headquarters.

While ALA is working to iron out its relationship with divisions, the Association for Educational Communications and Technology (ACET) is actively revamping its organizational structure to broaden its membership. AECT established the new Division of School Media Specialists (DSMS) to "promote and improve communication between school personnel who share a common concern in . . . school media programs." This was approved despite the fact that AECT's membership had declined and that some believed a new division would compete for members with AECT's Division of Educational Media Management (DEMM), which already included school media specialists. It appears that AECT members who share joint membership in AASL and in state associations may have to make choices as membership and travel expenses become prohibitive and released time for professional activities is further reduced.

Taking a cue from former ALA President Peggy Sullivan's optimistic 1981 Conference theme, "Libraries and the Pursuit of Happiness," and an ALA film of the same title that promotes public awareness of the impact of libraries, library professionals are looking for ways to pursue their own "happiness"—a goal that can be reached by 2000 only if close attention is paid to stable funding for all types of libraries, and if information specialists beef up campaigns to keep taxpayers aware of the contribution libraries make to the quality of life in our republic.

PW NEWS REPORT, 1981

John F. Baker
Editor-in-Chief, *Publishers Weekly*

The seismic changes in the book publishing and bookselling business that first began to show in 1980 continued to create a state of continual upheaval throughout 1981. Old ways of doing business were altered, new kinds of marketing philosophies began to play an ever-increasing role, and seemingly well-established relationships between hardcover and paperback publishing, between publishers and booksellers, even between publishers and authors, showed signs of permanent alteration. What's more, these processes were taking place in an atmosphere of continuing economic gloom, in which disposable income and federal funding for schools and libraries were both clearly shrinking. The *Thor Power Tool* ruling, which disallowed heavy discounting of inventory for tax purposes, remained in effect throughout the year despite efforts to line up congressional support in Washington behind some kind of amelioration for publishers, and contributed its share of malaise to questions of print orders and remainders.

COMINGS AND GOINGS

It was a year of frequent moves, many of them involving top-ranking people who had become deeply identified with their companies. A number of them seemed to to involve deep-rooted differences of approach between experienced editorial executives and officials with a strong marketing or sales orientation.

A good example of this was the departure, after 21 years, of John J. Geoghegan from the company that partly bears his name, Coward, McCann & Geoghegan, and that is now part of the Putnam group. He left with an attack of what he called the "corporate business-school mentality," claiming that trade publishing could be neither "profitable nor distinguished" when guided by such an approach. His departure followed that of Patricia Soliman, Coward, McCann president, who became one of a number of top-level people to join Simon & Schuster during the year.

Similar conflicts apparently lay behind the departure of Rollene Saal as editor-in-chief at Bantam, and Leona Nevler as publisher of Fawcett, where she had been for 26 years. Jon Gillett quit as general manager of McGraw-Hill's trade department to join Franklin Watts; immediately thereafter four editors, including Beverly Jane Loo, a veteran with the company, and Bruce Lee, were dismissed in what was described as a reorganization of the department.

Other major moves included those of Ross Claiborne from Dell/Dial to Warner; Carol Baron from Crown to Dell; Betty Prashker from Doubleday to Crown; Herman Gollob from the Literary Guild to Simon & Schuster; Richard Marek, who transferred his imprint from Putnam to St. Martin's; and Robin Smith from Dell to Publishers Clearing House. The R. R. Bowker Company acquired a new president in Joseph Riccobono.

There were perhaps fewer than the usual numbers of mergers and acquisitions among companies, but several significant ones nevertheless. The Hearst Corporation bought William Morrow from SFN Companies for $25 million; International Thom-

Note: Adapted from *Publishers Weekly,* March 12, 1982, where the article was entitled "News and Trends: A Tough Time for Publishers."

son bought the publishing group of Litton Industries, which includes Van Nostrand Reinhold; Kennett and Eleanor Rawson took their part of Rawson Wade to Scribner's, splitting from James Wade; and after being openly for sale for much of the year, E. P. Dutton was bought by John Dyson, chairman of the New York State Power Authority, to become part of a diversified investment firm, Dyson-Kissner-Moran Corporation.

On the antitrust front, the Justice Department and CBS, Inc. signed a consent decree whereby the communications giant was allowed to retain Fawcett, which had been the subject of a three-year antitrust suit, but was ordered to sell Popular Library, its other paperback operation. In an ironic aftermath, CBS sold Fawcett's list and contracts to the Random House group, which already owns Ballantine Books, early in 1982, and was reported anxious to sell Popular Library too.

An innovative plan was announced at Harper & Row in late summer, whereby the company bought back about a third of its stock, owned by the Minneapolis Star & Tribune Company, for $20 million for distribution to Harper employees. Officers and employees now own 43 percent of the company, said chief executive officer Brooks Thomas, who added that the arrangement was an alternative to selling the company altogether. In another move involving employees buying their own company, Macmillan sold the Brentano's bookstore chain to a group of its officers.

ORGANIZING AND PROTESTING

Nineteen eighty-one was a year of increased activity by District 65, affiliated with the United Auto Workers, which has been trying to organize publishing employees. Oxford University Press, St. Martin's, and Springer-Verlag were all targeted during the year, and in each case the union lost its election bid.

There was growing evidence during the year that writers, who in some cases have seen their royalties and advances cut as publishers struggle with their own cash flow problems, were becoming increasingly restive with their economic lot. A study prepared for the Authors Guild by a group of social scientists at Columbia University showed that the median income from writing of 2,239 writers of (mostly trade) books in 1979 was only $4,775, and this became a major point of discussion at a strongly antipublisher gathering of writers, the American Writers Congress, held in New York in October. The principal legacy of the congress seemed likely to be the formation of a militant National Writers Union, which is already in the organizing stages and promises to hold its first convention in 1982.

THE BOOKSELLING SCENE

The more accommodating attitude publishers had begun to show toward booksellers in 1980, in response to strong bookseller representations about alleged discrimination in discount policies in favor of the big chains, continued last year. Most of the major houses offered new discount structures and changed returns policies designed to provide higher rewards for careful buying—although wholesalers complained at their own meetings and when questioned by *PW* that they felt they had essentially been left out of the new arrangements.

Despite these new accommodations and much to the irritation of many publishers, the board of the American Booksellers Association, at its convention in Atlanta, May 23–26, agreed in principle to help pay for a class action suit "instituted for the purpose of correcting alleged violations of the Robinson-Patman Acts." A California bookseller volunteered to institute such a suit, but at year's end there had been no overt legal action. The convention itself showed a marked decline in attendance—12,581 people attended, compared to 16,495 in Chicago in 1980—and this was attributed partly to the economy, and partly to the choice of Atlanta, which was still suffering at the time from a series of unexplained murders of young blacks, as a site.

Another innovation by a number of publishers to assist booksellers was to add a small amount to the cover price of a book over the invoice price, in order to help defray freight costs. Random House, Harper, Dutton, and Simon & Schuster were among the first publishers to offer this accommodation, which authors and agents seemed to be accepting, though reluctantly, because the higher price did not mean a higher royalty.

The spread of the Crown discount chain continued to make news: it opened a number of new stores in Washington, where it began, mushroomed in California, and opened two stores in suburban Chicago. B. Dalton announced it would also get into the discount business with a chain to be called Pickwick, which will be tested initially in Columbus, Ohio; no date, however, was given. Meanwhile, Waldenbooks, in an attempt to improve distribution to its 300 stores in the northeast, opened a big regional distribution warehouse outside New York City. Walden also offered another first: it put its entire Christmas catalog as a 32-page insert in *Time* magazine, the biggest and costliest book ad ever.

THE PAPERBACK OUTLOOK

The old relationship between hardcover and paperback publishing became even more unraveled in 1981. Spurred by the success of Harlequin's, and later Silhouette's, romance lines, which involved distributing quantifiable and easily identifiable merchandise to a targeted customer, the mass paperback houses turned more and more to "originals" and genre lines of their own. As the popularity of Gothics and Regency romances declined, that of "contemporary" romance grew; nearly all the mass market publishing houses had or planned such lines by the end of the year: romances aimed at older women, more "adult" romances, a slew of new series aimed at 14- and 15-year-olds, with Dell and Bantam leading the way. (*PW* surveyed the romance publishing scene extensively in a special issue in November.)

All this concentration on "originals" meant that there was less money for or interest in the traditional solid middle-list fiction and nonfiction that had once automatically sold to paperback. Blockbuster hardcover best sellers still brought high paperback prices, but the times when auction records for paperback rights would topple every other month seemed long gone. And hardcover publishers, to make up for their lost rights income, increasingly became involved in their own paperback programs by bringing back some of their backlist hits in trade paper, and publishing promising new books simultaneously in hard and soft cover. After years of being a decidedly poor third, in fact, the lists of new trade paperbacks in *PW*'s biannual announcement issues easily overtook the mass market lists, and in terms of sheer numbers began to advance on the hardcover lists.

THE RIGHT TO READ

The coming of the Reagan administration seemed to have encouraged would-be censors in the land, and 1981 saw more than its share of cases involving the removal of books from libraries or school reading lists for a variety of reasons, usually having to do with morality or religion. The shadow of the famous Scopes trial of the 1920s fell again over textbook publishers, as a number of states, led by Arkansas, proposed that "creationism," biblical doctrine about the making of the world taught as a science, be given equal attention with Darwinism in classroom instruction. The move was defeated in Arkansas, but looms still in other staes.

An important Supreme Court ruling for publishers was promised in 1982 when the high court agreed to review the decision of a New York Apellate Court in the Island Trees case involving the removal of a number of books from a school library by the school board. The court had ruled that protesting students should receive a hearing of their contention that the school board's action infringed their First Amendment rights.

A Georgia law that would have made it an offense to exhibit books or magazines involving "illicit sex or sexual immorality" where the publicatons could be seen by minors was struck down by a federal judge as "unconstitutionally overbroad and vague."

Meanwhile, it seemed clear that recent gains in the accessibility of government material to writers and others under the Freedom of Information Act were likely to be reversed under the current administration. In an apparent counterattack against a series of books that have revealed alleged Central Intelligence Agency "dirty tricks," a former CIA agent filed a $120 million libel and invasion of privacy suit against publisher Lawrence Hill. The former is claiming he was libeled in the book *Death in Washington*, which deals with alleged CIA participation in the murder of an exiled Chilean leader.

THE YEAR'S SALES

It was not a good sales year for most categories of books. Publishers reporting to the AAP showed increases over 1980 of a little under 10 percent in adult trade hardcover sales, and 5 percent in adult trade paperbacks; mass market sales for the year were not available as this publication went to press. Children's books were up 8.6 percent and 7.6 percent, respectively, book clubs 9 percent, and mail order sales up 17.4 percent—probably a reflection of the fact that publishers are becoming more and more interested in gaining sales beyond the bookstores. The last category showed the only really notable increase, for with annual inflation running not far below 10 percent, it was clear that sales, despite higher prices, barely kept up with inflationary increases. Unit sales were not reported, but, judging from these figures, were probably either flat or slightly down.

Flat is, in fact, how most of the booksellers contacted by *PW* for comment on their Christmas sales reported them.

Special Reports

THE STATE OF INTELLECTUAL FREEDOM

Judith F. Krug
*Director, Office for Intellectual Freedom,
American Library Association*

Intellectual freedom, a concept based on the First Amendment to the United States Constitution and, in that regard, unique to this country, is being threatened. The threat is manifested in many ways, not the least of which is attempted censorship of library and educational materials.

This problem is documented in *Limiting What Students Shall Read*, a report of a study cosponsored by the American Library Association (ALA), the Association of American Publishers, and the Association for Supervision and Curriculum Development. The report, issued on July 31, 1981, provides detailed information on book selection policies and censorship pressures from 1,891 public elementary and secondary school administrators and librarians and from 21 of the 22 administrators in states that have statewide textbook adoption policies.

Of the local school officials who responded to the survey, more than one in five, or 22.4 percent, reported that library or classroom materials had been challenged in the survey period, from September 1978 through spring 1980. The challenges to books, magazines, and films occurred fairly consistently in all regions of the country and in all types and sizes of communities.

Although more than one in five administrators reported challenges during the survey period, one in three of the responding librarians reported such challenges. Among other findings were:

Nearly one respondent in four indicated that the rate of challenges had increased during the period of the study;

Nearly one respondent in three indicated that the challenges had resulted in changes in the books and materials used, or changes in the educational process; school administrators reported that library materials were affected most frequently;

Respondents indicated that the local media reported only 15 percent of the challenges identified; 85 percent of the challenges received no media attention and remained unreported;

Survey responses of local-level librarians and administrators also indicated:

In 95 percent of the reported incidents, the challengers sought to limit, rather than expand, the information and viewpoints in the materials used;

More than 75 percent of the challenges were initiated by an individual representing him or herself;

Complaints on the local level most often cited sex, sexuality, obscenity, and objectionable language;

In half of the reported challenges, the material was altered, restricted, or removed *prior* to a formal review;

In more than half of the incidents, some degree of restriction or censorship was imposed on challenged materials.

Perhaps the most significant findings of the local-level survey were that many schools not only lack or fail to follow written policies and procedures for selecting materials, but also lack or fail to follow written procedures for reviewing materials when challenges arise. Schools that follow written selection policies and review procedures appear to resolve conflicts with fewer restrictions on the instructional and library materials available to students; therefore, there is a less negative impact on the educational environment.

Responses to the state-level survey contrasted with the findings at the local level:

In 17 out of 23 responses, groups or individuals representing groups were identified as challengers;

The challenges to adoption at the state level were generally more organized than those at a local level. In 10 out of 14 state-level challenges reported, the challengers referred to arguments or viewpoints developed by individuals or groups from outside the state;

The majority of state-level challenges focused on ideological concerns, such as "secular humanism, Darwinism and evolution, and atheistic or agnostic views";

Approximately half of all state-level respondents interviewed stated that the activities of Mel and Norma Gabler's Educational Research Analysts of Longview, Texas, had influenced recent adoption proceedings in their states;

Finally, responses to the state-level survey suggested that local and national pressure groups, especially those of the political right-of-center, increasingly were attempting to exploit the controversial arena of library and school book selection for political ends.

The gathering of the data for the survey was completed in August 1980 and therefore did not reflect the large increase in censorship attempts that occurred during 1981. While the magnitude of the increase nationwide cannot be precisely formulated, some idea is apparent from the files of the ALA Office for Intellectual Freedom (OIF).

From September 1980 through June 1981, the number of censorship attempts reported to OIF was three times greater than for the comparable period in the preceding year, resulting in an increase from approximately 300 reported incidents to between 900 and 1,000. More specific information was revealed by a compilation of challenged book titles, which showed that between November 1, 1980 and March 31, 1981, attempts were made to remove, restrict, or deny access to 148 different book titles in 34 states. In most states there were several incidents and many of the challenged titles were the target of multiple censorship efforts. Among those materials most regularly attacked were the feminist health manual *Our Bodies, Ourselves* and the books of young adult author Judy Blume. The list did not include magazines, newspapers, films, exhibits, or speakers to which objections were also raised during that period.

It should be noted that although the data cited in *Limiting What Students Shall Read* shows that only 15 percent of censorship incidents were aired through the popular news media, the Office for Intellectual Freedom probably learns of approximately 20 to 25 percent of such attempts. If that rule of thumb is meaningful, the total number of censorship attempts in 1981 might have been as high as 5,000.

A review of possible factors contributing to the recent rise in censorship activity may be instructive. First, and perhaps most importantly, there is what has been called a "collapse of consensus." While some question remains as to whether "the good old days" really were characterized by a unanimity of opinions and values, today even the image of consensus is hard to support. Values have changed and major traditional institutions, including the family, religion, and education, have eroded. The nation finds itself in the midst of protracted crisis, which is exacerbated by the constant economic malaise. Other factors include an apparent loss of American prestige in the world community and weak, ineffective political leadership. The advance of technology may have contributed to the artificiality of urban society; the environment is endangered with chemicals and nuclear reactors; and communications technology modifies perceptions of space and time. Energy concerns dominate national politics and international accord hangs on a fragile nuclear arms balance.

Over the past 15 years, a growing mistrust of major institutions of leadership has been evident—the federal government, the courts, Congress, corporations, and the media. Concurrently, individuals seem to believe that they are losing control over their lives and have fewer options. Perhaps this has led to a growing collective desire to "take back" from government and other institutions some of the authority that, over time, has been delegated to them. The results of the 1980 elections on all levels represents a step to change the *modus operandi*.

Although the current increase in censorship attempts indicates a growing conservatism, the "new right" is not in fact new. A thread of conservatism weaves throughout American history and has played a major role in the development of the country and society; at this time, it is in ascendancy. There is also an anti-intellectualism that has been encouraged in the public mind by fear, frustration, and a real and perceived helplessness. This anti-intellectualism has been defined by Richard Hofstadter in *Anti-Intellectualism in American Life* (New York: Knopf, 1963) as "a resentment and a suspicion of the life of the mind and and of those who are considered to represent it; and a disposition constantly to minimize the value of that life."

This disposition toward conservatism and anti-intellectualism was manifest in reactions in the Watergate scandal, an event that might be viewed as the point at which current trends began. Public reaction to Watergate was that of disillusionment with the national government. Attention and energies were turned to that level of government and to those institutions through which people believed they might exercise more control. Specifically, they began to look toward institutions in *local* communities, such as libraries and schools—institutions identified with children, education, and tax dollars.

The denouement of Watergate occurred in August 1974. In that year another event occurred, which significantly affected the issue of intellectual freedom. A major controversy emerged in Kanawha County, West Virginia, involving 325 texts selected for the curriculum. For the first time, the hillbillies and the "crickers"—the "have nots"—dictated curriculum. They subdued the urbanities of Charleston (the seat of the state government), who had previously exercised control over education provided through the district schools.

Kanawha County, West Virginia, became the prototype. Its example showed the less powerful what could be accomplished. The tactics used by those in Kanawha County, excluding the physical violence, were emulated by small but hearty bands of vocal, concerned, and heretofore helpless citizens. They were aided by front groups of the John Birch Society, Mel and Norma Gabler of Texas, the Heritage Foundation, and by various other right-of-center organizations across the United States. But at the forefront of this movement were "regular" community residents.

By 1977, the shift to the right by the body politic was becoming visible. It was heralded by the growing number of concerned citizens' groups that devoted themselves to closely examining school curricular materials and library collections, and increasing fund-raising efforts by a greater variety of conservative causes.

In the late 1970s, there was a groundswell of people who viewed with concern and dismay the problems and complexities of the country. There was a fear of the new and different, be it life-styles or books that discuss alternative life-styles. There was also a belief that by returning to the principles that had made the country great, there would be understanding and less confusion. A "born-again" right of center had learned from and applied to their movement the grassroots organizational techniques of the civil rights and antiwar movements of the 1960s.

Champions of the "new right" appeared in many forms. Among them were the "textbook watchers," whose bywords were "back to basics." For many, "back to basics" means more than renewed emphasis on fundamental skills; it also meant the elimination from classrooms and libraries of learning materials that challenged their basic values. To textbook watchers educational programs and materials often questioned values and discussed problems that were better dealt with by the family and in the home.

Anita Bryant's 1977 campaign against gay rights in Dade County, Florida, constituted the most stunning example of grassroots response to perceived violations of deeply held traditional principles and values. Ms. Bryant developed a single-issue constituency to rival that of Phyllis Schlafly, whose goal was to "Stop ERA," which movement has proved very successful.

These and many other campaigns were fought by well-meaning, average American citizens to "protect the family." The old formulae represented in marriage, religion, and sexual roles have not yet been comfortably redefined. Meanwhile, conservative forces are convincing a large percentage of Americans that they can return to the way it was.

Campaigns conducted under the banner of "protecting the family" included support for the death penalty, laetrile, nuclear power, local police, the Panama Canal, saccarine, the FBI, the CIA, the defense budget, public prayer, "free enterprise," and real estate growth. There were also campaigns against equal rights for women and homosexuals (as mentioned earlier), busing, welfare, public employee unions, affirmative action, amnesty, marijuana, communes, gun control, pornography, the 55-mile-per-hour speed limit, day care centers, religious ecumenism, sex education, car pools, and the Environmental Protection Agency.

Proposition 13 was passed in California and numerous tax limitation statutes and advisories in the majority of other states. Gay rights ordinances were repealed every time they were brought before the public. In 1978, conservative politicians were elected both to Congress and to the leadership of the states, a trend that culminated in landslide elections for conservatives in 1980.

Liberalism, as defined by Mortimer Adler and others, is the willingness on the part of individuals, and society as a whole, to avail themselves of many points of view before reaching a decision. A turning away from liberalism and the liberal philosophy that has undergirded the nation was evident in the 1978 elections. Following the elections, single-issue constituencies sharply increased, each believing they upheld truth, morality, and principle.

The state of intellectual freedom is also being affected by the ascendancy of religious fundamentalism. Previously, religious fundamentalists supported the efforts of various single-issue constituencies. (In fact, several of the leaders of the Kanawha County controversy were fundamentalist ministers.) In 1979, however, religious fundamentalists came into their own with the emergence of three distinct groups: Christian Voice in the early months of the year; the Moral Majority in the middle months; and as the year closed, the Religious Round Table. In early 1980, the Coalition for the First Amendment was organized. This was an ad hoc group of evangelists pledged to renew the fight for prayer in public schools.

Religious fundamentalists want prayer back in the classroom and the inclusion (in the biological sciences curriculum) of the "creationist" theory on an "equal time" basis with the theory of evolution. Supporters of this view argue that since the theory of evolution is not proven, its teaching should be balanced by the theory of creationism in order to give students all points of view. Consequently, many state legislatures have considered "creationism" bills to mandate the teaching of scientific creationism in public schools whenever evolution is taught. The bills have become law in Arkansas, Louisiana, and Mississippi. The Louisiana law was signed by the governor in late July 1981. The Arkansas law, however, which specifically encompassed library materials in its provisions, was challenged by the American Civil Liberties Union and declared unconstitutional on January 5, 1982. The Mississippi legislature passed its law one hour after the Arkansas law was declared unconstitutional.

Finally, there has been a movement against "secular humanism," which has been defined by the Gablers of Texas, and by other religious fundamentalists, as "faith in man instead of faith in God." To them, humanism is a godless religion which, on the basis of separation of church and state, must be removed from classrooms.

In 1980, single-issue constituencies not only joined each other, but also joined the newly visible religious fundamentalists. The result was a coordinated effort by millions of people committed to pro-God, pro-family, and "pro-America" causes. The surging conservative movement has sought to elect leaders who would correct the perceived ills of society.

By 1982, there was little doubt that the state of intellectual freedom was seriously being threatened. This was evidenced by the report *Limiting What Students Shall Read*, as well as by the substantial increase in censorship attempts as reported to the Office for Intellectual Freedom. The attack on intellectual freedom strikes at the heart of the constitutional republic; for intellectual freedom encompasses both the democratic right to express one's opinion and to enjoy access to differing opinions. Self-government is only as effective as the electorate is enlightened, and enlightenment comes from ideas and information that are freely available and easily accessible in all forms. The role of the library and the challenge to the profession lies in aiding and defending such freedom. How this challenge is met will have a profound effect on our society.

PUBLIC LIBRARY SERVICES FOR THE AGING IN THE EIGHTIES

Betty J. Turock

Assistant Professor, Rutgers University Graduate School of Library and Information Studies, New Brunswick, New Jersey

In the decade since the last White House Conference on Aging (WHCOA), public library services designed to meet the special needs of elders have begun to receive the attention they warrant. In fact, the first White House Conference on Library and Information Services, held in 1979, named older adult programs a priority for continued development. While the view from the public library has been increasingly optimistic, maintaining the impetus in the future and even consolidating the gains made over the past ten years appear to be in jeopardy.

The proliferation of learning and information sources, data bases, technical reports, and the increased need for improvement in information management with its broad ramifications have been coupled with declining financial resources. Increasingly, information services are being sold by brokers to those organizations and individuals able to pay the price, a dismal portent for the elderly.

Funded by the diminished economic surplus, public libraries are feeling the fiscal pinch more than ever, although they have historically suffered from an imbalance between an extensive range of services and minimal funding. Traditionally the place for on-demand public information and education, public libraries do not automatically profit from greater use of services. Indeed, in the fiscal climate of the new era, diminished funding may be on the horizon for all human services.

As we enter the 1980s, long-range planning is essential to ensure that changes in funding do not lead to changes in the quality of services for the aging. This report will review professional literature on an interdisciplinary basis to provide the background for a description of current public library resources, services, and research for the aging. But first, current practice is outlined to define needs and recommend practices for the future.

Five overriding areas emerge as being crucial to the development of public library services for the aging: *access, education, information, management,* and *training.* They provide the framework for designing new directions in the emerging decade.

ACCESS

Older adults, unlabeled and unannounced, are unquestionably part of the great mass of people pursuing information and learning opportunities in the 14,000 public libraries across the United States. The basic orientation of public library services for elders is to integrate such services into those provided for the general public, rather than to set up separate programs. As special needs develop, they are dealt with specially.

The public library is a neighborhood institution based on a decentralized network of branches that serve local communities. Librarians professionally trained in

Note: Adapted from a 1981 White House Conference on the Aging background paper prepared for the United States Department of Education, Office of Educational Research and Improvement, Office of Libraries and Learning Technologies. The contents of this paper do not necessarily reflect the views or policies of the Department of Education.

the skills of selecting, organizing, and interpreting information and learning resources have the experience and ability required to serve the needs of older adults. Public libraries offer a wide range of materials, including large-print books, paperbacks and magazines, records, talking books, films, slides, videotapes, and art prints. For the in-depth pursuit of any interest, there is no substitute for these collections. But public libraries do more than make materials accessible; they provide information and referral services, sponsor literacy tutoring programs, and adapt to demands for placing their services at the disposal of elders who need stored information and knowledge.[1]

Public libraries are an integral part of the growing movement to recognize and encourage the potential of the elderly, to use them as resources, and to improve their access to services and materials so that they can stay in the mainstream of life. Older adults presently act as resources for the public library, on either a fee or voluntary basis, in numerous ways. Older adults have information exchanges for part-time employment opportunities, and they canvass neighborhoods to locate peers who are prospective candidates for library service. To assist in developing local history collections, seniors locate and gather memorabilia and offer recollections on audiotapes. To create services and collections of interest and use to other older adults, seniors develop educational programs on consumerism, legislation, housing, and other areas of import. They review materials, making recommendations on content and format, and help prepare collection-building and buying lists. They edit and write library newsletters. As program mainstays, they work as camera technicians in video productions, assist in maintaining deposit collections, keeping track of circulation, and deliver materials in nursing homes and institutions. They also act as tutors in literacy efforts.

A national survey has shown that elderly volunteers participated in 71 percent of the learning activities sponsored by the public libraries. This fact was cited as one of the most important benefits of locating programs there.[2] To help the elderly combat the psychological and social pressures of role loss, ageism, and segregation, public libraries provide advocacy training for elders who then present their views on legislation to local, state, and federal officials. Lectures, films, book talks, discussion groups on current affairs, live arts programs, and humanities forums are featured free-of-charge at public libraries. To increase awareness of the problems of aging, public libraries offer preretirement seminars and create multimedia programs and kits.

For the impaired, some libaries have equipped special centers with talking books and a myriad of devices that open access to them. To reach those who are unable to come to the library, outreach programs take information and education to bilingual and other seniors. When older adults are no longer able to leave their homes to visit the library, alternative delivery systems are arranged. Seniors who are institutionalized or homebound receive materials in the mail; mediamobiles are used for delivery, some with hydraulic lifts, which take wheelchairs and their occupants inside. Librarians also participate in bibliotherapy in clinical and developmental settings in the hope of giving aging persons insights and an increased sense of reality.

The services cited are tangible evidence that the public library is at last headed in the right direction for the older population. That doesn't imply, however, that the deficiencies discovered by the *National Survey of Library Services to the Aging*, completed for the 1971 WHCOA, have all been overcome. In fact, the absence of updated information on the status of service makes any valid comparison difficult. Certainly libraries need more programs in which seniors are resources, where intergenerational activities are part of the ongoing fare, and where widespread publicity makes the elderly aware of their own existence and needs. Studies by Kramer[3] and Ferstl,[4] both completed in the 1970s, have provided a continued indictment of the failure of the library profession to adequately absorb and integrate gerontological knowledge into service provision. Many librarians perceive the importance of services based on the developmental needs of children, young adults, and adults, but fail to realize that such a perspective is essential for older adults as well.

Monroe has provided a professional framework for building service around the developmental tasks of aging, but too few librarians know about and use this model.[5] As a result, stereotypes still feed into collection development, service provision, and programming.

Although consciousness has been raised among librarians in recognizing the importance of liaisons with community organizations, and although there have been efforts to develop more responsive services, the trend in most public libraries has been to create programs for the institutionalized and homebound elderly. In the main, services have been traditional, with major spending for large-print materials and heavy emphasis on nursing homes, where a maximum of only 5 percent of the elderly can be reached.

The "service to all" philosophy of the public library is its greatest strength and, at the same time, its enduring weakness with regard to serving the aging. This orientation leads to the inclusion of the elderly as library users with no differentiation by age, and also restrains many public libraries from defining them as a major market and targeting specific programs for them in abundance. Architectural barriers in public libraries and difficulty in identifying the diverse audiences comprising the elderly population remain important problems as well.

Reaching the ethnic groups among the aging is an even more elusive task. Too few public library professionals, like professionals in other service agencies, know, understand, and utilize ethnic traditions and value systems. Public libraries need more than ethnic and foreign language materials and large-print books—although the acquisition of these might not be a bad start. The ethnic aging need to know that the library has something to offer; the library needs to enlist these individuals as resources and volunteers.

Further service development is not a task public librarians can undertake alone. Providing the elderly with responsive service is an expensive business for libraries and other agencies, and in today's society is sometimes a duplicative proposition as well. Cooperative program development and coordinated service delivery are the best answers. Activating these on the national level and in a meaningful way will take a good deal of collaboration between institutions, whereby institutional turf becomes secondary to serving the aging. Substantive incentive programs are needed at the state and federal levels to provide widespread models that demonstrate coordinated service delivery and its benefits in action.

EDUCATION

The increase in the level of education attained by older adults has led to a predictable increase in their participation in learning activities. Since educational achievement is expected to continue its ascension in the next decade, education for the elderly should be considered a priority in the 1980s. The public library has been a traditional source of free education for the general population—a people's university. Both formal and informal learning activities for elders take place in the library. Activities range from literacy tutoring to college classes for credit.

New Learning for Older Americans, a national survey conducted by DeCrow and completed in 1974,[6] found that libraries were "increasing their service to older adults, developing innovative programs and new ways to help." The report showed that most public library learning programs for older adults are supported by the basic library budget, which is sometimes supplemented by state and federal monies. About 53 percent of the libraries surveyed reported new services to older adults in the past year. Basic education was found to be important in 26 percent of public library reading programs, and the interest in reading problems is reflected in libraries' stocking materials for individual use as well as literacy classes. A few libraries conducted reading development classes or learning laboratories, others offered tutoring activities.

Hiemstra's landmark research has demonstrated that older adults' learning activities are largely independent, self-directed, and self-paced.[7] The public library is traditionally a place of independent, self-planned, self-directed education, backed up by group learning programs and in some cases one-to-one tutorial situations. Older adults may study at their own pace;[8] they are joint planners of their learning programs with librarians; they assess their own needs and interests and set their own goals.[9] Librarians infrequently act as learners' advisors, for they associate this role with a counseling function in the therapeutic sense and perceive it as more than assisting to develop an educational plan of action with the library as a base. While education brokerage is a far more acceptable practice, it is not more widespread. Advising and brokerage require skills heretofore neglected in the education of the public librarian.

Libaries have educational materials in abundance. Brokerage and counseling emanate successfully from the library, but not as successfully as they might if they were developed in collaboration with other educational agencies. Cooperation in education for the aging has not proceeded from identification of the participants to implementation of an action plan. The cooperation that has occurred is too often an informal arrangement, with no plan for participation developed along functional lines and based on institutional strength. Such plans are necessary if older adults are to get the attention they need in the future.

Service for the aging is a new focus, which emphasizes the need to provide information and educational services for those who work with older adults. Research by Dosa at Syracuse University[10,11,12] provided a model using on-line and manual searching systems amplified by a human resource network. A new role was defined for librarians as liaisons with agencies coordinating and linking Information Referral (I&R), data, and other educational systems. Librarians provided bibliographic reference and document delivery, coordinated information exchange among members of a human resource network, supplied information directly, and developed information packages. Knowledge so provided was delivered to agencies for their own purposes, which were broadly construed as advocacy for older adults. Dosa's work became the model for the field development of Dallas Public Library's Specialized Information Service (SIS).[13]

Funded by the Department of Education, SIS included information provision coupled with education to increase information literacy, i.e., the ability to differentiate among types of information and information resources, the ability to use these and public library services. Dissemination activities combined reference services with computer-assisted searches on commercially available data bases when needed. A current-awareness service operated through a monthly newsletter sent to all participants, and through fact sheets that repackaged information on specialized subject areas in a format that allowed rapid scanning.

Document delivery was incorporated by using the mail and public library branches as pickup locations. Evaluation showed that service providers found the information and education had enhanced their capabilities to serve older adults. They felt SIS demonstrated service needs that were within the role of public libraries. The guidance of a librarian in helping service providers define and meet their information needs, and access to information from on-line computer data bases without charge were two elements of SIS that service providers indicated they did not want to lose. Without ongoing financial support, those elements cannot be maintained by the library.

The SIS Project was considered extraordinary. It was also expensive. For SIS to have any long-range implications for service, public libraries must give serious consideration to the priorities that have placed information dissemination and document delivery in the realm of customer services. At the same time, if social service agencies value such services, these should be included in agency budgets with sufficient funds designated for manual and computer searches and resources.

Together public libraries and key social service agencies should explore means through which the importance of local funding for information dissemination can be communicated to officials. Also cooperatively, public libraries and social service agencies should plan in-service training seminars on information awareness. If at all possible, such seminars could be coordinated with a School of Library and Information Science.

Two concerns represent the challenge in education that is posed for library professionals in the next decade: Data and documentary support service are needed to enable practitioners to improve service to the aging population, and relevant media and reading materials for education are desperately needed by older adults.

INFORMATION

Information is a major business for the public library and the public library is a major source of information for many older adults. Traditionally information-on-demand is disseminated by libraries to older clients in print and nonprint formats. Within the last decade some libaries have added on-line data bases to assist in this task. But several innovative services of import to the elderly have developed as well. Supplying employment and career information is increasingly emphasized. Initiated in New York State's 22 public library systems, Job and Career Information Centers offer new models for service. Operating on budgets of less than $25,000 per year per center, they contain microfiche copies of the State Employment Service's job listings, classified ads, materials on resume preparation, interview techniques, and other job-seeking skills. Use figures are high and narrative evaluations positive. Seniors are one of the targeted audiences. The concept offers a new service option for the 1980s.

Public libraries are also developing information programming on consumer issues, health, social security, and other areas, to bring topics of importance to the attention of the elderly in a cost-effective fashion. Packaged programs containing films, slides, scripts, discussion questions, and guidance manuals are brought to older groups in places where they meet. Through programming, older adults may acquire, in the context of a pleasurable group activity, information that they might not seek out otherwise.

Information and Referral (I&R) is, however, the most dramatic departure from traditional information dissemination that the last decade has brought to public libraries. Most I&R services operating out of libraries are generic, containing information for a broad range of library clients, many of whom are elderly. Separate information service for older adults is considered dysfunctional, since there is considerable overlap among the information needs of people regardless of age. Some librarians, however, have developed I&R services that emphasize older adults' needs.

The Detroit Public Library's The Information Place I&R last year served 15,000 clients per month.[14] An evaluation undertaken in the mid-1970s of a national I&R project in five cities across the country, including Detroit, determined that only 8 percent of traffic was from older library users. According to the 1977 Battle Associates evaluation of I&R services funded by the Administration on Aging,[15] such services reach about 11 percent of the older adult population in their area. The study found that the centers, funded at a substantial average of over $40,000 per service per year, were not meeting their objective of updating their files at least every six months. It is possible that library and other I&R services for older adults may reach different audiences; it is also possible that services are duplicated. A study is needed to define collaborative I&R functions that would effectuate better service. In the past, libraries have largely been overlooked in the development of I&R services by networks for the aging. This report describes five functions which public libraries are ably suited to fulfill in a collaborative effort. They include: publishing directories, supplying advice on system design and implementation, providing direct information and referral, and inaugurating computer updating and maintenance of records. Libraries can also play any of the three major roles of an I&R system: host, supplementary agency, or satellite agency. The question is not whether, but how public libraries are to be involved. Advocacy through I&R remains narrowly defined by librarians as linking persons with services, although some libraries participate in more substantive advocacy activities. Librarians can and do supply information for advocacy and to advocates.

MANAGEMENT

While public libraries have moved ahead in services for the aging during the past decade, they have not lived up to their service potential. Among the major reasons are several recurring management issues. Public library leadership has failed to project the services, resources, and professional expertise available from the public library. The network for the aging, for its part, has overlooked or ignored the potential contribution public libraries can make to the services they initiate for the elderly.

One failure attributable to the lack of manifest coalition-building is the fact that the Title IV Older Readers Service amendment to the Library Services and Construction Act (LSCA) has never been funded. The amendment, which was the result of a resolution passed at the 1971 WHCOA, provides a legislative framework which, if funded, could continue to encourage in the next decade the dramatic growth and development of public library services for the aging that have emerged over the past ten years.

Through Title I, LSCA, which supplied $1.1 million in FY 1979 to reach an estimated 2.2 million people over the age of 65, has been the primary funding source for innovative public library programs for the elderly.[16] The life of LSCA drew to a close in 1981; its future life, through renewed or modified legislation, is of major significance to services for the aging in the 1980s.

Research has shown that the primary factor in sustained library services for the aging is a highly motivated, well-trained professional staff. The cadre of library leaders committed to improved services for older adults remains too small to support a continuing effort. Leadership personnel is needed at all levels. Consultants are essential at state libraries charged with the task of acting as catalysts for a wide range of planning and program development. Large public libraries and systems require coordinators to bring services, now scattered among different task groups in many locations, into a cohesive administrative unit. Such a reorganization would result in greater political viability as well. In every library where coordinators are employed to serve other client groups, there should be someone assigned to services for the aging. Since all public library staff members serve older adults, they all need training in service to this population.

TRAINING

Activity in the education and training of librarians in service for the aging has shown progress in the past ten years. At the beginning of the 1980s, library schools at North Texas University, Wayne State University, the University of Wisconsin-Madison, Syracuse University, and Rutgers University are offering educational programs in library and information services for the elderly—five programs more than were in existence ten years ago. All five were initiated through federal funding available from the Administration on Aging under the Older Americans Act, Title IV, Training and Research. All are interdisciplinary, requiring work in gerontology. They attract students from professions and disciplines outside library service; the common denominator is a need for skill in information handling.

The programs have several running threads. They emphasize tying knowledge of gerontology closely to concepts of service; impacting practice through the translation of relevant theory and research into field action, particularly as it relates to eradicating stereotypes and assumptions that impede effective service; and encouraging and developing creative, flexible attitudes in service planning and performance.[17]

Some of the educational programs are designed to ensure that those providing service are competent to design, implement, manage, and consult on services and sources for the aging. They concentrate on developing skills in: (1) selecting and using on-line and traditional sources of information about and for the aging; (2) program planning and evaluation techniques necessary to institute an effective array of services; (3) implementation of a wide range of services specifically geared to meet the library and information needs of older adults; and (4) serving special elderly populations, including ethnic groups and the impaired.[18]

In a time of diminished resources, it is difficult for a new specialty to gain ground. Professional training needs to be broadened from its current base if it is to educate specialists competent to operate in today's public library milieu. As such, management skills rank as high as skills with resources, program design, and implementation.

To whom should education on serving older adults be offered and how? All students entering master's degree programs in library and information services should have an opportunity to learn the basics of gerontology—who the aged are, what special needs they have, and what libraries are doing to meet these needs. For those studying to become public librarians, several courses in serving older adults should definitely be encouraged, if not mandated; for specialists preparing to make a major effort in serving older adults, a core of concentrated study is essential. Continuing education must be provided at institutes, workshops, and seminars for public librarians from a network involving library schools, state library agencies, and experienced professionals in the field. While education at the master's degree level should be multidisciplinary, at the continuing level it must also be open to those from other professions who have a stake in information services for the elderly. Educational opportunity for library and information service for the aging remains deficient at all levels; library schools and state library agencies must be held accountable for this situation.

FOR THE FUTURE

To develop effective long-range plans for library and information services for the aging in the 1980s, it is necessary to have a clear picture of where we are currently. Data compiled for the 1971 WHCOA are now obsolete and useless for valid comparisons. *The National Survey of Library Services to the Aging* should be repeated with modifications to collect information on the new service thrusts that have emerged. The importance of such evaluative data cannot be minimized in making the case for fiscal support of libraries in the turbulent economic times ahead.

Coalition-building at the national, state, and local levels is essential if public libraries are to continue to receive the funding they need to supply responsive service to the elderly. The Library Services and Construction Act supplies the major impetus for innovative services, research, development, and demonstration. Funding tied to LSCA, Title IV, the Older Readers Act, or another appropriate mandate, would make that legislation more than a victory on paper. In fact, the Older Readers Act could provide the continuing stimulus for services to the aging, which will be crucial in the next decade. Perhaps in the future the focus of coalition-building should be directed toward the state. If the much discussed shift is made from a program of federal grants and funding to state programs, coalitions will need comprehensive plans capable of making optimum use of that shift. To be fiscally spare and at the same time effective, these plans will have to be directed toward coordinated service delivery.

Services offered by the public library in the next decade should focus on the use of the resources of older adults, not on the problems of aging. Older adults can be incorporated more and more into planning groups and the work force and recruited as volunteers. In fact, guidelines should be developed for recruiting, utilizing, and training older adults as paraprofessionals and volunteers to work with their peers and other public library clients. Such guidelines might grow out of a survey of present practices.

A major effort needs to be directed toward matching the strength of services for the institutionalized and homebound with programs for the mobile and healthy older adult. Incentives, which have emphasized the former in the past, are now needed for the latter to develop as they should. Access—in location, convenience, and absence of physical, psychological and social barriers—does deserve continuing attention, however. For the future, career and employment information services are worth a wider geographic girth than New York State, where these services originated. The contribution public libraries can make to I&R should receive the attention it deserves from the network for the aging and from the profession as well.

To serve the elderly better in the new era, greater knowledge of and skill in using new computer and communications technologies will be required to disseminate information and learning activities on a broader scale. Research and development are essential to defining the appropriate public library roles in such service provision. Public libraries can offer viable programs for service providers who are keeping current with change in their fields to give more effective service to older adults. Dosa at Syracuse and the Dallas Public Library's SIS Project have created models for that development. Important elements in these projects included repackaging information in a format that allows for rapid scanning, combined with well developed dissemination and delivery. Federal financing backed these projects. It is time to fund a similar demonstration to develop multiagency fiscal support for similar services.

To add momentum to services for the aging in the 1980s, the American Library Association would make its most valuable contribution to date by directing a national campaign on awareness of the aging population. Emanating from the local public library, such a program could address the issues surrounding ageism in print and nonprint media.

Since the importance of a well trained staff capable of assuming leadership roles will be another primary factor in sustaining library services for the aging, current professional leaders must recruit a larger number of librarians committed to serving older adults. Any decrease in attention to professional education could be catastrophic at this juncture. The following recommendations are made for the education of library and information specialists competent to operate in the 1980s:

1. At least one institute should be required to prepare library educators in graduate library schools to teach services to the aging at preservice and continuing education levels.
2. Graduate library schools, in cooperation with the Office of Libraries and Learning Technologies, U.S. Department of Education, should offer many short (five-day, for example) institutes in all geographic regions to prepare the trainers of trainers, i.e., those employed in state library agencies and large public library systems.
3. A few additional graduate library schools should offer joint library science-gerontology programs at the master's and post-master's degree level. Since none exist in the West and Southwest at this time, these sites would be a logical beginning.
4. Graduate library schools should combine efforts with public libraries to provide on-site training in services for the aging.
5. State library agencies, in cooperation with library schools, should take the initiative in offering continuing education to public librarians in each state. Such opportunities should include a mandate to seek out information specialists outside the public library system and in allied professions that provide information services to the elderly. These specialists should be included in the educational experience.
6. Professional training for public library service should be geared to providing the skills needed to directly serve older adults and also to train those who serve the elderly. Library service education should include development of management skills in community and market analysis; human resource networking, citizen participation, funding through grantsmanship; development of implementation skills in service design and provision; and development of knowledge about gerontological information sources. Above all, librarians should have a firm base in group processes, communications technology, and human communications.
7. A national survey should be undertaken to determine the location and number of information specialists currently serving older adults, both within and outside public libraries. A model for library service education in the future can be based on knowledge of the skills needed to serve the aging population.

NOTES

1. *Serving Citizens with Special Needs*, Background Paper for the White House Conference on Library and Information Services (New York: New York Public Library, 1980).
2. Roger DeCrow, *New Learning for Older Americans* (Washington, DC: Adult Education Association of the USA, 1974).
3. Elliott E. Kanner, "The Impact of Gerontological Concepts on the Principles of Librarianship" (Ph.D. dissertation, University of Wisconsin-Madison, 1972).

4. Kenneth Ferstl, "Public Librarians and Service to the Aging: A Study of Attitudes" (Ph.D. dissertation, Indiana University, 1977).
5. Margaret E. Monroe, "Continuing Education for Older Adults," *Drexel Library Quarterly* 15 (April 1979), pp. 71–82.
6. Roger DeCrow, *New Learning for Older Americans* (Washington, DC: Adult Education Association of the USA, 1974).
7. Roger Hiemstra, "The Older Adult's Learning Projects," *Educational Gerontology* 1 (October-December 1976), pp. 331–341.
8. Christopher Bolton, "Alternative Instruction Strategies," in *Introduction to Educational Gerontology*, Ronald H. Serron and D. Barry Lumsden, eds., (Washington, DC: Hemisphere Publishing Corporation, 1978).
9. Ruth Weinstock, *The Graying of the Campus* (New York: Educational Facilities Laboratories, 1978).
10. Marta Dosa, "The Gerontological Information Program," *Bulletin of the American Society for Information Science* 5 (October 1978), p. 18.
11. Marta Dosa and Stephanie Ardito-Kirkland, *Information in Social Gerontology* (Syracuse, New York: ERIC Clearinghouse on Information Resources, 1978).
12. Marta Dosa, *Health Information Sharing Project (HISP)* (Syracuse, New York: Syracuse University School of Information Studies, 1979).
13. *Special Information Services Final Report* (Washington, DC: U.S. Department of Education, July 1978–August 1979).
14. *U.S. News and World Report* 88 (March 31, 1980), p. 68.
15. Battle (Mark) Associates, Inc., *Evaluation of Information and Referral Services for the Elderly. Final Report. February 28, 1977* (Washington, DC: Administration on Aging (DHEW), 1977).
16. Nathan Cohen et al, "Services to the Aging," in *Bowker Annual of Library and Book Trade Information 1981* (New York: Bowker, 1981), pp. 167–168.
17. Betty J. Turock, "Training for Library and Information Professionals," Year End Report to the Administration on Aging (New Brunswick, New Jersey: Rutgers University Graduate School of Library and Information Studies, June, 1980).
18. ———. "Training for Library and Information Professionals," Year End Report to Administration on Aging (New Brunswick, New Jersey: Rutgers University Graduate School of Library and Information Studies, June, 1980).

RECENT DEVELOPMENTS IN HEALTH SCIENCES LIBRARIES IN THE UNITED STATES

Maxine K. Hanke

Director, Mid-Atlantic Regional Medical Library Program,
National Library of Medicine, Bethesda, MD 20209

Developments during the 1960s and 1970s pointed most health sciences libraries toward the same distant goal—the gradual conversion of health sciences libraries into active communications centers that disseminate biomedical information of all kinds to health professionals. These developments are discussed thoroughly in Louise Darling's 1974 article, "Changes in Information Delivery since 1960 in Health Sciences Libraries," which focused on theories of what health sciences libraries in the United States should provide to users, and on major factors contributing to the development of those concepts during the previous dozen years.[1]

This article presents an overview of the status of medical libraries in the United States with a brief review of highlights from the 1970s. Particular emphasis is placed on the development and growth of on-line systems and cooperative efforts to improve information delivery.

In the past twenty years health sciences libraries have changed enormously. What has remained constant, however, is their common goal to provide health sciences practitioners, researchers, educators, and administrators with efficient, timely, and convenient access to biomedical information resources. What is new is the approach to fulfilling the goal. Traditionally, libraries have been oriented to providing service. What has made medical libraries distinctive is interlibrary cooperation at local, regional, and national levels.

What began initially as informal cooperation has developed into a strong national network based on cooperative ventures at the local, regional, and national levels. The rapid development of this coalition can be attributed to the development and growth of on-line systems, and to the establishment of a regional library network supported by federal funding.

The emergence of a national automated bibliographic information network provided the impetus for the growth and expansion of medical library services in the 1970s.

COMPUTERIZED BIBLIOGRAPHIC RETRIEVAL

The first Medical Literature Analysis and Retrieval System (MEDLARS) developed by the National Library of Medicine (NLM) in the 1960s was designed to enlarge and improve the quality of the *Index Medicus* data base. More significantly, it opened a new world for medical librarians by facilitating responses to requests for special bibliographies, both on demand and on a recurring basis. Requests for specialized bibliographies were submitted, reformulated in "computer" language, keypunched and searched in a batch mode within the sequential file of bibliographic citations stored on magnetic tape.

After preliminary studies ascertained the requirements for an improved retrieval system, NLM developed the Abridged *Index Medicus* via the Teletypewriter Exchange Network (AIM-TWX), which clearly demonstrated the value of on-line searching. It contained a five-year file compiled from 100 of the most important English-language journals in clinical medicine. The 1970 AIM-TWX on-line experiment, using an IBM 360/67 computer at the Systems Development Corporation, was the first connection to the TWX network to be made without special software. In a short time, direct access to the NLM computer was available through a commercial network operated by TYMSHARE that provided toll-free service from 30 cities in the U.S. This processing use of a "value added" telecommunications network provided an enormous stimulus for the development of on-line services by making possible telecommunications at low cost.

It was clear by this time that a flexible and effective on-line search system that allowed for efficient and economical access to a high-quality data base could be developed. Late in 1971, NLM initiated MEDLINE, a nationwide on-line bibliographic retrieval system that permits almost instantaneous, interactive searching of over 400,000 citations. MEDLINE was the first generally accessible, interactive on-line bibliographic information service.[2] In 1973, McCarn and Leiter wrote that "the establishment of a low cost, dial-up link via TYMSHARE has made commercial development of other data bases extremely attractive. There is a real potential for extending this type of application into a national (or even international) network of science information services."[3] The following table illustrates the realization of that potential.

MEDLARS/MEDLINE SERVICE AT THE NATIONAL LIBRARY OF MEDICINE*

	1972[†]	1981[‡]
Citations in data base	400,000	4,500,000
Simultaneous users (average)	25	60
Hours per week	43	158.5
Searches per year (on-line)	140,000	1,240,000
Institutions	120	1,617
Codes	200	2,081
Foreign countries	3	13
Foreign institutions	8	365
Foreign codes	3	377

*Does not include use in non–U.S. Centers or commercial U.S. sources, e.g., Bibliographic Retrieval Services (BRS), Lockheed, etc.
†From D. B. McCarn and J. Leiter, "On-Line Services in Medicine and Beyond," *Science* 181 (July 27, 1973): 318–324.
‡MEDLARS Management Section, NLM.

The response of the biomedical community to on-line service continues to be enthusiastic. The first experiments with MEDLARS and AIM-TWX demonstrated the viability of networking and identified the need for an expanded system. Since implementing MEDLINE, NLM has added other data bases of a specialized nature: Toxicology Data Bank (TDB); Health Planning and Administration (HEALTH PLANNING & ADMIN); History of Medicine Online (HISTLINE); Cancer Research Projects (CANCERPROJ), Population Information Online (POPLINE), and others. Many other health-related data bases and services that developed during the 1970s are disseminated in the United States by such vendors as Bibliographic Retrieval Service (BRS), Lockheed, and Systems Development Corporation (SDC). A complete list of computer-readable data bases is available.[4]

The technology for on-line interactive systems had been available since the 1960s, but widespread use of this technology as applied to large bibliographic files can be traced to the initiation of MEDLINE in 1971. The impact of on-line services on a broad user population is discussed in Gloria Werner's 1978 paper on a survey of 708 U.S. and Canadian MEDLINE users and their use of NLM and non-NLM data bases.[5] Fifty-eight percent of on-line service users also offered on-line service to other files available nationwide through such vendors as BRS, Lockheed, SDC, and CAN/OLE in Canada. The impact of on-line services includes heightened user expectations of library service in general, increased pressure to subscribe to additional journals, increases in requests for interlibrary loan (ILL) borrowing, and ability to serve more users.

The use of data bases to assist in the technical processing activities of medical libraries was perceived as a valuable adjunct to library operations. Among the major data bases are CATLINE, AVLINE, and SERLINE. Catalog Online (CATLINE) contains about 210,000 references to books and serials cataloged at NLM since 1965, and gives libraries in the network immediate access to authoritative cataloging information, thus reducing redundant cataloging. It is also a useful source of information for ordering books and journals, and for providing reference and interlibrary loan services. Audiovisuals Online (AVLINE) contains citations to approximately 10,000 audiovisual teaching packages, and is in general similar to CATLINE. Serials Online (SERLINE) contains bibliographic information on nearly 34,000 serial titles. Many have locator information that enables the user to determine which U.S. medical library owns a particular journal. Medical librarians also make extensive use of other on-line networks such as Online Computer Library Center (OCLC), Research Libraries Information Network (RLIN), New England Library Information Network (NELINET), Southeastern Library Network (SOLINET), and the like.

The development of automated systems for use in the library, in the community, and across the nation played a significant role in uniting the medical library field. Federal programs fostered the feeling of unity and provided funds for the development of medical libraries.

A 1970 Carnegie Commission report considered the shortage and uneven geographic distribution of professional health manpower, especially in rural and inner-city areas. It recommended the establishment of training and continuing education centers in hospitals that were not part of university health science centers, and resulted in the formation of Area Health Education Centers (AHEC). AHEC programs vary widely, but at least six have active library components: California, Maryland, North Carolina, North Dakota, South Carolina, and Virginia. The North Carolina AHEC library program contains over 150 hospital libraries in nine consortia and is frequently cited as a model program because of the high level of expertise and service available to health professionals in all areas of the state. AHEC systems are becoming increasingly active, especially in California, Maryland, and Virginia. As AHECs pursue their goal of providing educational opportunities to health professionals in remote areas, there will be an attendant continued interest in the development of the hospital library as the basic information unit in the biomedical communications network. Similar emphasis is now being given to hospital libraries by NLM's recently restructured Regional Medical Library (RML) Program, which gives high priority to providing health professionals with access to a basic level of information services.

MEDICAL LIBRARY ASSISTANCE ACT

The Medical Library Assistance Act (MLAA) established a program administered by NLM to assist in the development of medical libraries' services. Resource grants provided funds to establish or improve library collections through acquisitions and processing, and to allow for applications of new technology, purchase of equipment, and improved service to the users. The coincidence of MLAA with the technological advances described earlier provided the basis for the phenomenal development of library resources and services during the 1970s.

In a recent paper discussing medical school libraries, Nina Matheson attributed the change and growth of these libraries over the past years directly to the stimulus provided by the passage of the MLAA in 1965.[6] The very tangible stimulus of federal grant funds for resource development, and the less tangible but equally important spirit of cooperation fostered by the RML Program, enabled the health sciences libraries of this nation to progress rapidly. With the assistance of federal funds, many hospital libraries were transformed from poorly organized collections of books into reputable libraries with some assurance of continued funding. Generally, federal funding requires commitment from the parent institution in order for the support to be continued. These grants have played an important role in assisting hospital libraries to become community health information centers.

Included in the original law and in all subsequent amendments was a program to assist the development of a national system of regional medical libraries, each of which would have resources of sufficient depth and scope to supplement the services of other medical libraries within the region served. It was determined from the outset that it was neither desirable nor necessary to build new institutions for these purposes; rather, existing facilities would be expanded.

Accordingly, NLM grants were awarded to establish 11 Regional Medical Libraries (RML). This 11-region structure will be changed to 7 regions in October 1982. The new configuration takes advantage of the strong working relationships and programs developed in the 15 years since passage of MLAA. The purpose of the reconfiguration is to provide more cost-effective regional groupings while preserving or improving present levels of service to health professionals. Some of the ongoing cooperative projects in the health sciences library community are exemplified by the Midcontinental Regional Medical Library Program's OCTANET, and the on-line regional monograph-audiovisual union catalog project of the Midwest Health Science Library Network.

In the Midcontinental Region (RML VIII), the University of Nebraska received NLM funding to develop OCTANET, a pilot project designed to test a regional, telecommunications-linked and computer-based network that provides information services to support health care delivery. OCTANET is an automated interlibrary loan locating and routing system that uses the Periodical Holdings in the Library of Schools of Medicine (PHILSOM) network. Components of OCTANET include management data collection, union list production, and electronic message switching capabilities. Eight libraries are participating in the initial development and others plan to join the project.

The Midwest Health Science Library Network (RML VII) project, also funded by NLM, represents the use of modern computer technology to improve the transfer of biomedical information among over 550 libraries. The project will compile a data base of monographs and audiovisual materials from machine-readable records originating from several different systems. Computerization of the on-line catalog, which will feature automatic routing and referral capabilities, is being accomplished with the assistance of Bibliographic Retrieval Services. The development of this file of monographic and audiovisual information will improve the ability of libraries in this region to share resources and cooperate in collection development.

TRAINING

The diverse population of medical library personnel calls for a varied yet coordinated system of postgraduate education that involves the Medical Library Association (MLA), regional medical libraries, library schools, and NLM in addition to active participation by all librarians in the health sciences field. According to MLA, there are now about 90 courses in medical librarianship at 47 accredited library schools. By comparison, only 16 library schools offered similar course work in 1966. During the 1960s and 1970s, eight internship programs were offered with the goal of providing a course of study that integrates theory with practical experience. Over 100 interns were trained at academic medical libraries, and about 81 at NLM, which has the only ongoing program.[7] Recognizing the need for experienced librarians with training in administration, NLM sponsored through the Council on Library Resources Fellowship Program a new series of internships that emphasizes administrative theory and technique.

The continuing education (CE) needs of medical librarians today are as varied as their backgrounds. Areas of responsibility in medical librarianship training were divided between MLA and NLM/RML as follows: MLA concentrates on CE for professional librarians, while RMLs emphasize training for library personnel without formal background in library and information science. Today MLA has over 40 courses and the RMLs about 50. Most present-day CE courses consist of intensive one-day sessions.

A relatively recent development that calls for extensive education efforts is on-line data base searching. For health sciences librarians, the on-line search systems of primary interest are BRS, SDC, and NLM. Most training for commercial systems consists of one- to two-day workshops, some of which are oriented to the use of a particular system, while others focus on the use of specific data bases. NLM has offered extensive on-line training both at NLM in Bethesda and in sites around the United States. NLM training consists of two one-week sessions, an introductory basic course and an advanced course. In 1976, NLM developed MEDLEARN, a computer-assisted instruction (CAI) program combining tutorial dialogue, drill and practice, and testing simulations. Additional programs in development are CAI programs for the toxicology data base, TOXLEARN, and for the chemical data base, CHEMLEARN.[8] An ongoing concern is the implementation of CE courses designed to create a current awareness of new advances. Health sciences librarians realize the value of CE in bridging the gap that comes from doing today's job with yesterday's tools and concepts.

STATISTICAL RECORD

The medical library field can be proud of its exemplary record of progress over the past years. Statistical data on budget, personnel, and collections have been recorded for all segments of medical libraries, beginning with Bloomquist's 1962 survey, "The Status and Needs of Medical School Libraries in the United States,"[9] and Giesler and Yast's 1964 "Survey of Current Hospital Library Resources."[10] Subsequent surveys compiling comparable data on academic, hospital, and special health sciences libraries have been sponsored by NLM with the cooperation of the American Medical Association (AMA) and MLA. Frank Schick of the National Center for Education Statistics (NCES) has written of this effort: "... during years of survey coordination with library groups, I never encountered a group more determined to shoulder the work to provide health science library data which [sic] are uniform among the component types comparable with the concepts developed in the American Library Association's Library Statistics Handbook."[11] Susan Crawford's subsequent efforts have provided an invaluable perspective on a 20-year data base.[12]

Medical School Libraries

During this period, a dramatic change occurred in the average size of the medical school library operating budget, which increased from $57,471 in 1961 to $718,859 in 1979. From 1966 to 1977, average collection size increased 83 percent, from 76,312 bound volumes to 139,566. Staffing also showed a remarkable increase from 7 full-time-equivalent (FTE) staff in 1961 to 29.8 in 1980, an upward change of 325 percent.[13] That this increase was long overdue is attested to by Dietrick and Berson's 1953 report, in which they wrote: "Little evidence was found by a survey of attempts to meet the libraries' increased needs during a period of tremendous expansion in research and other activities of the schools.... In a nation dependent upon medical research to a greater degree than ever before, surprisingly little is being expended on the housing of the reports of that research and on making those reports available."[14]

Ten years after Dietrick and Berson's mid-century survey, Bloomquist wrote: "As a result of chronic inattention, the medical school library is woefully inadequate to meet the demands placed upon it as an agency of biomedical communication, and ...

the major investment made by society in these libraries is in jeopardy. Financial support has not kept pace with the increased demands; indeed, there is evidence that the library's share of support is shrinking."[15]

Improved resources have since enabled medical school libraries to expand their horizons beyond their immediate facility. Their contributions have assisted in the development of a nationwide network of biomedical libraries that provides services to a widening spectrum of health professionals in remote rural communities or in large urban areas. Current services range from document delivery to on-line bibliographic searches to consultation with hospital administrators on hospital library development or consortium formation. Initially, most of these services were supported through MLAA, but increasingly they are coming to be offered on a fee-for-service basis.

Hospital Libraries

In the early 1960s the most authoritative data on the status of hospital libraries appeared in the American Hospital Association study by Geisler and Yast.[16] Of the 5,444 short-term, nonfederal general hospitals registered by the American Hospital Association in 1962, just over 3,000 were estimated to have medical libraries. The average professional library maintained a collection of 561 volumes. Hospitals with fewer than 100 beds had an average collection of only 158 volumes per library, whereas libraries serving hospitals with more than 400 beds averaged 2,657 volumes.

Crawford and Rees's data on hospital libraries reports a 28 percent decline between 1969 and 1979 in the number of hospitals, and a much greater decline in the number of libraries.[17] However, the data are not directly comparable to the 1962 survey because the latter used no qualifying standards in defining a library. Later surveys have used a definition based on collection size and number and type of staff that would automatically exclude many libraries included in earlier studies. While Geisler and Yast's 1964 data showed that libraries in 100- to 400-bed hospitals subscribed to an average of 38 serial titles, Crawford's 1979 data show that even the smallest hospitals (100 or fewer beds) subscribed to at least 42 serials; this is 10 percent more subscriptions than the larger hospitals had 20 years earlier.

The 1981 *Accreditation Manual for Hospitals*, prepared by the Joint Commission on Accreditation of Hospitals,[18] presents standards for hospital library services. These standards are intended to encourage hospitals to provide professional library services that meet the basic needs of patient care, health care management, and continuing education for health professionals. The standards require that every health care institution provide professional library services whenever feasible. It also states: "When employment of a full-time or part-time qualified medical librarian is not possible, the hospital shall secure the regular consultation assistance of such an individual." While no standards are specified for collection size, the following statement on collection resources appears: "The professional library shall have an up-to-date, authoritative collection of print and nonprint materials pertinent to the clinical, educational, and research services offered." Some hospital librarians feel the standards should be more definitive and should base collection size in some way on the number of beds in the hospital. Others feel that the judgment of professional librarians in determining the collection size appropriate for a specific institution would be preferable to using an arbitrary figure.

One of the most important directions taken by hospital libraries in recent years is toward the sharing of resources in formal or informal consortium arrangements. Resource sharing in this instance may include any or all of the following: document delivery, collection development and acquisition arrangements, on-line services, cataloging, training, consultation, and library management. In general, the most developed and successful consortium programs are located in states with active AHECs or RML programs that place emphasis on such development.

Federal Libraries

In the federal sector, a development of particular interest is the review of services now underway at many military libraries. At the Department of the Navy, for example, the Bureau of Medicine and Surgery is engaged in developing instructions for establishing a coordinated medical library program for regional medical centers and hospitals. The program's goals are to provide a central point of contact for various library functions, to establish management guidelines for library operations, and to ensure that library functions are performed in a manner that balances quality with cost-effectiveness.

In mid-1981, the Department of the Army's Health Services Command created a special staff library position with responsibility to coordinate Army Medical Department libraries in the United States. In addition, this office is to write new regulations both to establish regionalization programs and cooperative automation projects and to work toward optimal efficiency in performance and operations. Concurrently, the Army Medical Research and Development Command and the Seventh Medical Command (Europe) are reviewing and rewriting their library regulations.

The Veteran's Administration health care system is the nation's largest, comprising 172 medical centers, 219 outpatient clinics, 89 nursing home care units, and 16 domiciliaries. The Veterans Administration Library Network (VALNET) provides recreational, vocational, and general library service to patients, and technical and medical library service to medical center staff. Current services offered include automated union lists of serials and audiovisual materials, and a monographic union list. The standards of service are impressively high, as is the willingness to share resources and expertise with other emerging networks.

Federal medical libraries have also shown interest in participation in the Library Subcommittee of the Federal Health Resources Sharing Committee. Established in 1981, the subcommittee joins Army, Air Force, Navy, Public Health Service, and the Veteran's Administration together in an effort to develop recommendations and propose guidelines for sharing health information resources on an interagency basis. Their current focus is on all aspects of networking and resource sharing.

OUTLOOK FOR THE 1980s

It may seem that medical libraries are segmented and isolated into groups comprising only academic, hospital, AHEC, commercial, military, and federal libraries, but in reality these mini-networks or subregional networks are working cooperatively within the national Regional Medical Library Program. There are formal and informal agreements, cooperative union catalogs, document delivery projects, and many other joint ventures intended to improve the quality and methods of promoting the transfer of biomedical information. Advances in technology are responsible for new, improved methods of library service. AIM-TWX, as a precursor to MEDLINE, developed an information-retrieval system that could be used in a variety of settings and that, when coupled with a telecommunications network, allowed for rapid and relatively inexpensive access to a data base containing citations to the world's medical literature. MEDLINE makes on-line services possible for even the smallest libraries that have no previous experience in computer technology. The Regional Medical Library Program's continuing goal is to develop a network of health sciences libraries that will provide health sciences practitioners, investigators, educators, and administrators in the United States with timely and convenient access to health care and biomedical information resources. The program also stresses the need for the active involvement of providers and users of health information alike in the planning and implementation of regional programs. Much has been accomplished in the last decade to build and strengthen a network that provides equal access to health sciences information primarily through resource sharing, consortia development, and network interfacing. There is every indication that the next decade will further strengthen this network and utilize technological advances to provide new and expanded services to all health professionals.

NOTES

1. Louise Darling, "Changes in Information Delivery since 1960 in Health Sciences Libraries," *Library Trends*, July 1974, pp. 31–62.
2. D. B. McCarn, "National Library of Medicine—MEDLARS and MEDLINE," *Encyclopedia of Computer Science and Technology*, ed. by Belzer, Holzman, and Kent, vol. 11 (New York: Marcel Dekker, Inc., 1978), pp. 116–152.
3. D. B. McCarn and J. Leiter, "On-line Services in Medicine and Beyond," *Science* 181 (July 27, 1973): 318–324.
4. Martha E. Williams et al., *Computer-Readable Data Bases: A Directory and Data Source Book* (Washington, D.C.: American Society for Information Science, 1979).
5. Gloria Werner, "Use of On-line Bibliographic Retrieval Services in Health Sciences Libraries in the United States and Canada," *Bulletin of the Medical Library Association* 67 (January 1979): 1–14.
6. Nina W. Matheson, "Medical School Libraries in the United States, 1960–1980," speech presented at Medical Library Association 81st annual meeting, Montreal, Canada, 1981.
7. Maxine K. Hanke and M. Benzer, "Training at the Postgraduate Level for Medical Librarians," *Bulletin of the Medical Library Association* 67 (January 1979): 42–46.
8. L. J. Kassebaum and J. Leiter, "Training and Continuing Education for Online Searching," *Medical Informatics* 3 (September 1978): 165–175.
9. Harold Bloomquist, "The Status and Needs of Medical School Libraries in the United States," *Journal of Medical Education* 38 (March 1963): 145–163.
10. R. H. Giesler and Helen Yast, "A Survey of Current Hospital Library Resources," *Hospitals* 38 (June 1964): 55–57.
11. Frank L. Schick, "Introduction to Statistical Surveys of Health Science Libraries," *Bulletin of the Medical Library Association* 55 (April 1967): 176–177.
12. Medical Library Association, Committee on Surveys and Statistics, "Library Statistics of Schools in the Health Sciences," *Bulletin of the Medical Library Association* 54 (July 1966): 207–229 (Part I), 55 (April 1967): 178–190 (Part II); Frank Schick and Susan Crawford, *Directory of Health Sciences Libraries in the United States* (Chicago: American Medical Association, 1970); Susan Crawford and Alan M. Rees, *Directory of Health Sciences Libraries in the United States* (Chicago: American Medical Association, 1974); idem, *Directory of Health Sciences Libraries in the United States* (Chicago: Case Western Reserve University and American Medical Association, 1980).
13. Matheson, "Medical School Libraries in the United States."
14. J. E. Dietrick and R. C. Berson, *Survey of Medical Education: Medical Schools in the United States at Mid-Century* (New York: McGraw-Hill, 1953), p. 190.
15. Harold Bloomquist, "The Status and Needs of Medical School Libraries in the United States," *Journal of Medical Education* 38 (March 1963): 145–163.
16. Geisler and Yast, "A Survey of Current Hospital Library Resources," pp. 55–57.
17. Crawford and Rees, *Directory of Health Sciences Librarians in the United States*.
18. Joint Commission on Accreditation of Hospitals, "Professional Library Services," *Accreditation Manual for Hospitals* (Chicago: American Hospital Association, 1981), pp. 147–149.

RECENT DEVELOPMENTS IN LIBRARY CONSERVATION IN THE UNITED STATES

Sally Buchanan

Conservation Officer, Stanford University Libraries

In retrospect perhaps the single incident to precipitate, more than any other, the current growth of library conservation activity in the United States was the Florence flood in 1966. It revealed, as no warning or individual concern could, the fragility of the written word and of the creative book arts. Soon after the flood, the Library of Congress initiated its preservation program in 1967, and the beginning of formal conservation programs in U.S. libraries was established. Since then the field of library conservation has been devoted to developing awareness of need, identifying problems, and articulating policies and standards. A thorough, historical review of the years 1956-1980 by Pamela W. Darling and Sherelyn Ogden may be read in the January/March 1981 issue of *Library Resources & Technical Services*[1]. The authors point out the groundwork that laid the foundations for the current expansion and development in library conservation. An examination of the growth over the past five years will serve to indicate that conservation has survived the first slow phase to emerge as a challenging and multifaceted addition to the care and management of library collections. The next decade clearly will bring greater awareness and support, developments in training and educational opportunities, cooperation between the library conservation field and the related fields of museum conservation and conservation sciences, and continued funding to help solve the variety of problems found in library collections.

NATIONAL DEVELOPMENTS

The early mandate to the Library of Congress (LC) to head up a national preservation program has been understood in the last few years to have been hasty. In light of reorganization, budget cuts, and its own massive preservation problems, the library simply could not undertake alone the responsibility of a program that would address and solve the multiplicity of library conservation problems across the nation. Instead, the Restoration Office and Preservation Research and Testing Office of LC issued a steady flow of publications detailing techniques and test results that could be implemented in conservation programs elsewhere. Additionally, the Preservation Office staff served as informal consultants whenever possible. Because Chief Restoration Officer Peter Waters had been actively involved in the Florence flood recovery, he and LC became the major resource of libraries suffering from disasters of larger proportions.

In 1976 another effort was made to examine the feasibility of a national preservation program. The participants in a two-day planning conference agreed that one of the highest priorities was automated bibliographic control of microform masters. As more and more libraries microfilmed brittle collections to save the contents, information about what had been filmed was difficult to obtain. Concern about costly duplication was growing. But with the retirement in 1977 of Frazer Poole, LC Preservation Officer, and with Norman Shaffer acting as Preservation Officer, it was clear LC could not accept the responsibility of such a national undertaking. Instead, as will be seen later, another organization began to plan for such an eventuality. In 1981 Dr. Peter Sparks was appointed the new Preservation Officer at LC, and later the same year was given the responsibility of National Preservation Officer as well. It is apparent that LC still intends to examine and initiate suitable national preservation efforts in the coming years. Whether these will constitute an expansion of current efforts or include efforts in new directions remains to be seen.

The Research Libraries Group (RLG), a consortium of larger research libraries, has had a preservation committee for many years. After RLG's restructuring in 1978, the preservation committee recommended the addition to the RLG staff of a preservation officer to coordinate preservation activities. Accordingly, in 1980 Nancy Gwinn was named Preservation Officer and assigned the task of determining the needs and priorities for coordinated RLG preservation action. It soon became apparent that, with RLG's developing bibliographic system, it might well undertake the task that had been identified as a top concern for the national preservation program—bibliographic control of master microfilms. The planning for such control is now underway, and it is expected that the program will become a reality within the next few years.

The longstanding preservation concerns and activities of the Preservation Committee of the Association of Research Libraries (ARL), which had produced several important reports in the past, establishing needs and standards, resulted in another major undertaking. In 1979 the National Endowment for the Humanities (NEH) awarded ARL's Office of Management Studies a grant to study and develop guidelines to be used by individual libraries to implement their own conservation programs. Pamela Darling was named Preservation Specialist to head the three-year project. By mid-1981 two important SPEC (Systems and Procedures Exchange Center) Kits had been issued as a result of the examination of practices in the field. Testing was underway in three sample libraries at the University of Virginia, Dartmouth College, and the University of Washington to establish the useful application of common survey techniques, standards, and procedures in initiating programs in library conservation.

The National Conservation Advisory Council (NCAC) was founded in 1973 to "identify and offer recommendations for the solution of conservation problems." Although it is concerned with the conservation of all cultural property, its Study Committee on Libraries and Archives more specifically deals with the concerns of libraries. Chaired by Paul Banks, the Committee issued in 1978 its summary of national conservation needs for libraries and archives. Broad in scope, the report should help to provide guidance for the development of library conservation in the near future.

PROFESSIONAL ORGANIZATIONS

The American Library Association (ALA) is one of several professional organizations that are continuing to express active support for library conservation. Preservation activities within ALA expanded rapidly in the 1970s, culminating with the formation in 1979 of the Preservation of Library Materials Section (PLMS) in the Resources and Technical Services Division (RTSD). The first elected officers presided over the new section at the 1980 annual meeting in New York. The section has five committees: Physical Quality of Library Materials, Library/Binders Relations, Education, Policy and Research, and the Discussion Group, which offers a forum for exchange of news in the field and for announcements of pending projects. All these groups are charged with helping channel the conservation concerns of librarians in ALA as well as indicating future directions.

The Society of American Archivists (SAA) has greatly increased its concern with and involvement in the conservation of archival materials. With the help of an NEH grant in 1980, SAA has been presenting a series of conservation workshops and programs regionally, as well as producing a series of worksheets, manuals, and bibliographies related to preservation. Librarians and archivists are discovering mutual concerns in the field as it broadens to include many aspects and problems that overlap.

Another organization that has expanded to include the concerns and interests of book and paper conservation is the American Institute for Conservation (AIC). Under the guidance of Paul Banks, President from 1978-1980, and with the active participation of Peter Waters, Don Etherington, and others, the problems of library preservation were brought to the attention of AIC. The Book and Paper Group was officially recognized in 1980. Many librarians and archivists, as well as the traditional conservators, are now active members of AIC. It is expected that AIC will help provide guidance in the areas of ethics, standards, and training for the growing field, and that it will offer a forum for new techniques.

COOPERATIVE EFFORTS

For many years it has been recognized that one sensible way to ease the financial and staffing burdens of conservation was through cooperative or regional efforts. ARL's original publication by Gordon Williams, its second major paper by Warren Haas, various articles by such concerned individuals as Paul Banks, and the support for a national preservation program indicate there is continuing interest in and acknowledgment of the concept.

One of the first responses to the suggestion that regional efforts should be undertaken was the funding in 1973 by the Council on Library Resources (CLR) of the first regional center, the New England Document Conservation Center (NEDCC), established to meet the conservation needs of libraries. Although the concept was sound, the NEDCC still had financial trouble as it tried to serve the regional library community. In 1977 George Cunha, the first director, retired, and the center was reorganized to cope with the challenge of financial problems as well as a diversity of conservation demands. Ann Russell and Mary Todd Glaser joined the staff as Administrator and Senior Conservator, respectively. By 1980 the center added several other conservators and expanded their services to the library public. In addition to in-house conservation, the center can help with conservation surveys, environmental testing, and disaster planning and help. In 1981 the center changed its name to the Northeast Document Conservation Center to indicate its ability, now enhanced by an NEH grant, to extend membership and services to a broader community. NEDCC finances appear to be sound, and it can now serve as an example for future regional centers.

Another regional approach may be seen in the example of the Book Preservation Center, founded by the New York Botanical Garden and funded by the H. W. Wilson Company. The Book Preservation Center acts as a consultant to help small and medium-sized libraries in the New York City area to assess their conservation needs and priorities. The center provides training and small workshops to assist in efforts to provide basic-level help.

Southern Illinois University at Carbondale received in late 1981 a Library Services and Construction Act (LSCA) grant to set up regional conservation help and advisory services to libraries in a number of states. Directed by Carolyn Clark Morrow, the project will emphasize a basic and practical approach, which appears to be gaining great acceptance among libraries that cannot yet afford to fund their own conservation programs.

CLR, itself a funding body for many significant conservation projects, provides a cooperative conservation service by maintaining a collection of microfilm masters from which member libraries may draw. It will film on request certain of its own or other holdings, and through these activities the council contributes to the preservation of deteriorating collections in research libraries. Because of CLR's historically strong interest in conservation, its activities in filming and storing are expected to continue.

In the last few years there has been, particularly in the Far West and Southwest, a strong interest in cooperative conservation efforts. This interest culminated in 1979 with the funding by the National Historic Publications and Records Commission of the Western States Materials Conservation Project. This project's aim was to assess the conservation interests and needs of the western states and to make recommendations for basic cooperative services. Under the auspices of the Western Council of States Libraries, a series of state workshops and inquiry sessions were held. As a result, in 1980 the Western Conservation Congress (WCC) was convened at Snowbird, Utah, to follow through on recommendations, the first being to establish an information clearinghouse. Consequently, a cataloged library of conservation information is being assembled under the guidance of William Knott, Director of the Jefferson County (Colorado) Public Library for the use of WCC members.

Another result of the Snowbird conference was the realization by several participants that the internal conservation concerns of their own states required better understanding. Since then, in several states including Colorado, Arizona, Idaho, and Utah, organizational meetings have been held to plan cooperative conservation activities. Because of the vast differences in climate, resources, and geography in the West, the direction for regional or cooperative conservation for the immediate future appears to lie with individual organizational effort on the part of libraries, archives, and historical societies within each state.

In April, 1981, the WCC and the Bibliographic Center for Research, with grant money, brought together representatives from seven states for a two-day workshop in Denver on disaster prevention and action. The participants then returned to their states to conduct a series of similar workshops to educate the library community.

INDIVIDUAL LIBRARY EFFORTS

The preservation departments or programs established in a few libraries earlier in the last decade have, in the past few years, shared generously their expertise, staff, and experience with new programs being implemented. The Newberry Library has in fact become the parent institution for a second generation of programs. Barclay Ogden, formerly at the Newberry, is now head of the Conservation Department for the libraries of the University of California, Berkeley. Paul Banks is directing the first library conservation training program in the United States at the Columbia Library School. Gary Frost from Newberry is assisting in the same training program.

Yale Library, with NEH funding and under the direction of Gay Walker and Jane Greenfield, is training interns in a program devoted to principles of library conservation, survey techniques, administration, and workshop skills. These interns then return to their home institutions to initiate conservation programs.

The Library of Congress continues to accept interns to help fill the need for library conservators. Don Etherington, formerly Assistant Restoration Officer at LC, now heads the Conservation Department of the Humanities Research Center at the University of Texas in Austin.

Major programs and efforts in conservation have been funded by NEH recently at the New York Public Library, Southern Illinois University at Carbondale, Case Western Reserve, and Princeton University. Additionally, federal money from Title

II-C of the Higher Education Act (HEA) has funded smaller projects such as preservation microfilming of specific collections or restoration of valuable and unique materials.

Several other research libraries have accepted the financial responsibility themselves for establishing conservation departments. Formal programs have been funded at the University of Connecticut, the University of Michigan, Brigham Young University, the Humanities Research Center of the University of Texas, the University of California at Berkeley, the University of Utah, and Stanford University. As these departments become established and begin to gain experience, they can help relieve some of the burden that has been carried in the last fifteen years by older programs at LC, New York Public Library, the Newberry Library, Columbia University, Yale University, and Harvard University.

The increasing variety of reports, standards, and guidelines published by conservation or preservation departments in libraries is adding considerably to the literature in the field, providing a choice to smaller institutions that may be unable to fund a formal program, but wish to be informed or to make more modest advances. These smaller institutions often choose to initiate conservation activity by forming a committee to address problems that can be solved by in-house expertise. An example may be seen in the number of disaster preparedness documents published in the last few years by archives, historical societies, and libraries.

EDUCATION AND TRAINING

Until recently, it had been impossible to receive formal training in the United States in the field of library conservation. Conservators who served libraries came from either European training programs, the museum program in the United States, or the LC intern program. But as of the 1981 academic year, the Columbia School of Library Service, with funding from several sources, is offering education for conservation administrators and library conservators. Graduates will receive an MLS degree in addition to training in their chosen area of concentration. These graduates will help to relieve the lack of trained library conservation administrators and conservators to deal with the masses of materials requiring attention in modern libraries.

In addition to this formal program, other educational opportunities are available. In 1977 the University of California at Santa Cruz, in conjunction with the Library of Congress Preservation Office, began a series of conservation workshops in the summer institute series. These were expanded as interest increased to include other experts outside LC, such as Jane and Larry Booth and Paul Banks. This series continued in 1981 with a two-day workshop on basic library conservation concerns given by Don Etherington and Sally Buchanan.

In 1978 the Columbia School of Library Service and in 1979 the University of Maryland Library School offered in-depth summer programs dealing with conservation. Many other library schools, as a regular part of the curriculum, now offer a variety of courses dealing with conservation.

A number of conferences in the last few years have also afforded librarians an opportunity to learn about the field. In 1980 the University of Oklahoma sponsored a two-day colloquium on preservation; Stanford University Libraries held a conference on disaster prevention and action in 1980; *Microform Review* sponsored its first Annual Preservation & Conservation of Library Materials Conference in 1981, to be followed by a second conference in 1982; the Twenty-Seventh Allerton Park Institute was devoted to conserving and preserving library materials; SAA continues its series of conservation workshops; and in the fall of 1981 NEDCC cosponsored a conference on general library conservation concerns. Many state organizations held seminars, workshops, and conferences to introduce librarians to the basic concepts of the field, and to offer advice and techniques for coping with general problems in conservation.

As interest grows and the understanding of care for collections increases, demands for educational opportunities in library conservation are rising. A variety of organizations appear to be responding both on the local and national levels.

RESEARCH AND DEVELOPMENT

As the Florence flood provided impetus for the growth of library conservation in general, the funding by CLR in the 1960s of the Barrow Research Laboratory stimulated research specifically in library conservation problems. The LC Preservation Research and Testing Office, until recently directed by John C. Williams, has conducted and published results from a variety of basic research. In particular its development of a mass deacidification process, using diethyl zinc in a vacuum chamber, may prove to be one answer to the immense difficulties posed by acidic corrosion of library collections. LC is in the process of running field tests, and will consider leasing the patent for the process to interested commercial firms. Other research involving mass deacidification is being conducted by Richard D. Smith, who is testing the use of a liquified gas solution under vacuum at the Public Archives of Canada.

Further testing continues, under the auspices of the Research Corporation, into the mass morpholine deacidification process developed at the Barrow Laboratory. Any or all of these solutions may be found to be suitable for given situations or materials.

Increasingly, as a greater need was expressed for sound conservation supplies and materials, testing has been conducted by various groups, including art conservation programs, the Carnegie-Mellon Institute of Research, LC, the Smithsonian Institution, and the National Archives. The American National Standards Institute (ANSI) helped develop some standards for microfilm used in preservation filming. More literature was made available on the quality and availability of adhesives, paper, board, leather, and other supplies required for the care of collections.

The Library Binding Institute has supported research by Werner Rebsamen on book structure, bindings, and materials at the Book Testing Laboratory of the Rochester Institute of Technology.

Important information on research and development has come from two symposia held by the Cellulose, Paper, and Textile Division of the American Chemical Society. Each symposium, one held in 1976 and another in 1979, entitled "Preservation of Paper and Textiles of Historical and Artistic Value," produced significant proceedings, which were edited by John C. Williams.

Each year new developments relevant to both conservation in general and library conservation in particular are presented at the annual meeting of AIC, which is a forum for valuable state-of-the-art reports about basic research or techniques, and about ongoing work and challenges.

Twice in the past five years, CRL and the Mellon Foundation have funded a conference on the longevity of the book. These conferences brought together librarians, publishers, and paper manufacturers to discuss a major problem of concern to all of them—the quality of modern book materials, in particular of paper. These conferences brought to light problems as well as developments in modern book production, and fostered discussion among the three groups represented. The 1981 conference offered sound recommendations for solutions to the problem of the deterioration of books due to acidic paper, a major concern of library conservation.

PUBLICATIONS

There has been a proliferation recently not only of conservation articles in library professional journals and publications, but also of newsletters, bulletins, bibliographies, and proceedings.

Library Journal, College & Research Libraries, Library Trends, and *Special Libraries,* among others, actively solicit articles on new developments. *Library Scene,*[2] a publication of the Library Binding Institute, prints a large number of general interest conservation articles.

The *Abbey Newsletter, Conservation Administration News (CAN),* the *AIC Newsletter, PhotographiConservation,* and the *SAA Newsletter*[3] are devoted to publicizing information on the conservation, preservation, restoration, handling, and general care of collections. They also carry news, announcements, letters, and job openings. State organizations are publishing small newsletters to keep their internal networks informed. LC continues to publish its preservation leaflets as does the *National Preservation Report.*[4] The American Association for State and Local History publishes conservation information frequently in *History News* as well as in some of its technical leaflets. PLMS of ALA reissued in 1981 a new edition of the *Preservation Education Directory,*[5] which was formerly called the *Preservation Education Flyer.*

Encyclopedias, yearbooks and annuals that provide information for libraries and librarians are including articles on conservation and preservation as part of the regular reports in the field.

Recently a number of books have been published that contribute immensely to the literature in library conservation: Booth and Weinstein's *Collection, Use and Care of Historical Photographs;* Morrow and Schoenly's *A Conservation Bibliography for Librarians, Archivists and Administrators;* Swartzburg's *Preserving Library Material: a Manual;* and Williams' *Preservation of Paper and Textiles of Historic and Artistic Value, II.*[6] This list is not exhaustive but represents the variety and depth of publications concerned with library conservation.

FUNDING

As 1981 draws to a close, it is apparent that educational institutions, libraries, and library conservation will all suffer from budgetary cuts on both the national and state or local levels. As there are fewer funds from these sources, private foundations will have more demands placed upon their declining resources. In the past, library conservation has been supported by a number of the agencies mentioned earlier, including CLR, NEH, the Mellon Foundation, the National Historic Publications and Records Commission, and HEA Title II-C. Many other private companies and foundations have funded specific projects or restoration efforts as a one-time gift. Although more educational institutions are funding their own in-house conservation programs, they cannot carry the burden alone. The critical condition of collections deteriorating because of brittle paper alone must be met with resources for research, materials, and skilled personnel. It is apparent that the growth of library conservation will depend to some extent on continued support from the private sector as well as from government agencies.

In the past five years, the field of library conservation has grown rapidly as the physical deterioration of collections becomes more apparent. Education about the problems that concern library conservators and conservation administrators is alerting libraries to techniques and planning to provide for the responsible management of collections. Library conservation has begun to define its needs and goals, and to provide trained personnel to handle these needs. Funding has offered opportunities and resources for conservation scientists to study reliable methods to save collections, and for preserving or restoring unique materials. A variety of publications provides a small but growing body of literature in the field. The next decade should see great advances in the care and preservation of library materials.

NOTES

1. Pamela W. Darling and Sherelyn Ogden, "From Problems Perceived to Programs in Practice: The Preservation of Library Resources in the U.S., 1956–1980," *Library Resources & Technical Services* 25, no. 1 (January/March 1981), 9–29.
2. *Library Journal* (New York, N.Y.: R. R. Bowker Co.); *College & Research Libraries* (Chicago: American Library Association); *Library Trends* (Champaign, Ill.: University of Illinois); *Special Libraries* (New York: Special Libraries Association); *Library Scene* (Boston: The Library Binding Institute).
3. *Abbey Newsletter* (Rockville, Md.: Ellen McCrady); *Conservation Administration News* (Tulsa, Okla.: University of Oklahoma); *AIC Newsletter* (Washington, D.C.: American Institute for Conservation); *SAA Newsletter* (Chicago: The Society of American Archivists); *Photographic Conservation* (Rochester, N.Y.: Rochester Institute of Technology).
4. *National Preservation Report* (Washington, D.C.: Library of Congress).
5. Susan G. Swartzburg and Susan B. White, eds., *Preservation Education Directory* (Chicago: American Library Association, 1981).
6. Robert A. Weinstein and Larry Booth, *Collection, Use and Care of Historical Photographs* (Nashville: American Association for State and Local History, 1977); Carolyn Clark Morrow and Steven B. Schoenly, *A Conservation Bibliography for Librarians, Archivists, and Administrators* (Troy, N.Y.: Whitson, 1979); Susan G. Swartzburg, *Preserving Library Material: A Manual* (Metuchen, N.J.: Scarecrow, 1980); John C. Williams, ed., *Preservation of Paper and Textiles of Historic and Artistic Value, II* (Washington, D.C.: American Chemical Society, 1980).

THE FOLGER SHAKESPEARE LIBRARY

201 E. Capitol St. S.E.
Washington, DC 20003
202-544-4600

Philip A. Knachel

Associate Director

The Folger Shakespeare Library, located in Washington, D.C., is an independent research institution devoted to advanced study of the Renaissance and early modern period of Western Civilization, with special emphasis on the humanities. Its collection of editions of Shakespeare's plays, including the first folio edition of 1623, of prompt books, playbills, and commentaries on Shakespeare, his theatre, and his age, is unsurpassed by any other library. The Folger holdings of approximately 220,000 books and 40,000 manuscripts provide resources as well for research in non-Shakespearean English drama and theatre, nondramatic literature, and history from the Renaissance through the eighteenth century. The library has become a center for studies of the Continental Renaissance and for work in areas as diverse as philosophy, music, exploration, and the history of science. Most of the significant books that influenced the American colonists are likewise to be found at the Folger. Indeed, the library's location in the nation's capital, two blocks from the U.S. Capitol and next to the Library of Congress, reflects a conviction that the English-speaking tradition is fundamental to our national heritage.

HISTORY

The Folger Library came into being as a result of a passion for Shakespeare shared by Henry Clay Folger and his wife, Emily Jordan. A published address by Ralph Waldo Emerson on the "Tercentenary of Shakespeare's Birth," which Henry Folger read as an undergraduate at Amherst College in the 1870s, had filled him with an enduring appreciation of Shakespeare. His wife, a Vassar graduate, had continued on to graduate school after her marriage and wrote a master's thesis entitled "The True Text of Shakespeare." The Folgers' interest in Shakespeare found outlet in book collecting, starting in 1885 with an inexpensive facsimile of the 1623 first folio edition of Shakespeare's plays. Thanks to a highly successful business career, Henry Folger was able to indulge his collecting interests. Folger had, upon his graduation from Amherst College in 1879, obtained a position in an affiliate of Standard Oil. Promotions followed and he was eventually named president of Standard Oil of New York, a post he held until 1923. After five more years as chairman of the board, he retired from the company in 1928 with a substantial fortune.

Despite the demands of business responsibilities on his time, Henry Folger, helped by his wife Emily, carefully studied booksellers' catalogs and regularly visited book shops in England and the United States. Rare quarto editions of Shakespeare's plays and the first folio edition were their prime targets, but the Folgers also collected later editions of the plays as well as materials reflecting Shakespeare production down to modern times, including printed texts, prompt books, playbills, paintings and illustrations, costumes, and memorabilia of all kinds. The Folgers realized that Shakespeare could not be studied in isolation from his age and so they sought out books that revealed the sources of his plots and ideas, and works that depicted the society in which he and his audience lived.

As their collections grew to number thousands of books and manuscripts, the Folgers had to dispatch their purchases to bank vaults and warehouses for safekeeping. At some point after World War I, they decided to bring the entire collection together in a library dedicated to Shakespeare. They selected a site in Washington, D.C., close to the Library of Congress, whose enormous collections would make their own library still more useful to researchers.

Henry Clay Folger died only two weeks after the laying of the cornerstone of his new library on May 28, 1930; but his wife lived to see the fulfillment of their dreams when the library opened April 23, 1932, appropriately on Shakespeare's birthday. Henry Clay Folger's will vested the trustees of Amherst College, his alma mater, with responsibility for the administration of the library. Folger and his wife left the bulk of their estate as endowment for the operation of their library.

In the years following its founding, the Folger Library has increased its holdings many times over with the addition of large collections and through the painstaking acquisition of individual items.

BUILDING EXPANSION AND RENOVATION

In the late 1960s and 1970s it was clear that the Folger Library would soon exhaust its remaining stack space for both rare and modern books. Storage conditions for the collection were also not satisfactory. Climate control for the protection of the collection, adequate by the standards of 1930–1932, no longer measured up to the more exacting requirements that conservation research had determined in the decades of the 1960s and 1970s. Space was lacking for the steadily growing number of readers and for the larger staff to serve library patrons and administer the academic and public programs of the library. After preliminary studies by staff and after an architectural feasibility study, the trustees of the Folger authorized a major building expansion and renovation program to begin in 1978. The work was planned for three successive stages. Phase I included the construction of 14,000 square feet of underground stack space on two levels with specially designed climate-control equipment and a fire prevention system. When the new space was completed in 1979, the collections of the library were transferred to the new underground vaults and sealed off so that renovation of the original building, Phase II, could begin. Replacement of heating, air conditioning, and electrical equipment was a primary objective. However, considerable rearrangement of space, particularly to provide more space and more efficiently located space for the technical services departments of the library, was planned. Enlarged and modernized facilities for the conservation department and the photoduplication department were among the major improvements achieved in library facilities. For the two-year period from 1979 to 1981 it was necessary to close Folger Library to readers. Once the renovation had advanced sufficiently, the Folder reading room was reopened in April, 1981 and by the end of the year most of the renovation work had been completed.

Meanwhile, work on Phase III, construction of an additional reading room to add another 6,000 square feet for readers, began in 1981 and was scheduled for completion in the spring of 1982. The building program is intended to provide for the needs of the library through the remainder of this century and well into the next.

CURRENT LIBRARY ACTIVITIES

During the past year leading up to the reopening of the library, much staff time was required to relocate the collection in renovated stack areas and to move technical services offices into new locations. New staff had to be trained to fill positions left vacant during the period of renovation. Despite these and other distractions, the library maintained an aggressive acquisitions program and added 184 rare book titles and 8 manuscripts to its collection in 1980–1981 in addition to modern reference books and periodicals.

The catalog department began active participation, in October 1981, in the Research Library Information Network (RLIN), a computerized cataloging network, which links some of the principal research libraries in the United States. At the same time, the Folger Library was readying for publication by G. K. Hall a supplementary volume to its printed book catalog to bring its published catalog up-to-date.

All departments of the Central Library Division, including the reading room, the conservation department and the photoduplication department, were once again fully operational.

ACADEMIC PROGRAMS

The Folger Institute for Renaissance and Eighteenth Century Studies was founded in 1970 to promote advanced teaching and research in the humanities. It is a collaborative enterprise sponsored by the Folger Library and 18 universities in the Middle Atlantic region. The physical center for the institute is the Folger Library. The institute offers an interdisciplinary program of seminars, workshops, symposia, colloquia, and lectures. The collections and full facilities of the Folger Library are open for the use of institute seminar participants. The institute arranged four seminars for the fall of 1981. E. Catherine Dunn of Catholic University and O. B. Hardison, Jr., director of the Folger Library, jointly led a seminar on the "Origins of Medieval Drama." Odette de Mourgues, University of London, directed a seminar on "French Poetry from Maurice Scève to Agrippa d'Aubigné." "Space and Time: An Examination of the Growth of Materialism in Eighteenth-Century Britain" was taught by John W. Yolton of Rutgers University, and Irvin Ehrenpreis of the University of Virginia gave a seminar on "Correction or Subvention: Swift, Pope, and the Established Social Order." Six additional seminars or workshops were planned for the spring semester of 1982. Seminar and/or workshop leaders will include: Edward E. Lowinsky, emeritus professor of the University of Chicago; Laetitia Yaendle of the Folger Library; Inga-Stina Ewbank of the University of London; William Arrowsmith of Johns Hopkins University; Stanley Wells of Oxford University; Gary Taylor, Associate Editor of the *Oxford Shakespeare;* and Frank E. Manuel of Brandeis University.

The Academic Programs Division of the Folger also edits a scholarly journal, *Shakespeare Quarterly*, and oversees a publication program, which has produced numerous modern editions of rare books, monographs, and other special studies from the Folger collections.

PUBLIC AND MUSEUM PROGRAMS

The Folger Library sponsors the Folger Consort, a musical group that performs Renaissance music. In October of 1981, the consort featured a program entitled *Machaut, le Noble Rhétorique*, followed in November by *Humanismus Germanicus*. Programs planned for early 1982 will be *From the Edge of the World* in January, *Musica Mediterraneo* in February, *The Seven Teares* in April, and *Josquin Incomparabilis* in May. The Folger Consort has established its artistic stature with audiences and critics alike and has helped foster an appreciation of early music. The Folger Library sponsors other musical programs as well and organizes a series of contemporary poetry readings. Small traveling exhibitions on Shakespeare and Tudor and Stuart England are sent by the library for display at colleges and universities, public libraries, and secondary schools throughout the country.

For the past two years the library has, with the assistance of the National Endowment for the Humanities, Metropolitan Life Insurance Company, Exxon, and the Corporation for Public Broadcasting, sent a major exhibition of its rarest books, manuscripts, and artifacts throughout the country. Entitled *Shakespeare: The Globe and the World*, the exhibition has toured San Francisco, Kansas City, Pittsburgh, Dallas, Atlanta, New York City, and Los Angeles. In this last city, the exhibition was sponsored by the Los Angeles Times Mirror Foundation. The exhibition has given hundreds of thousands of visitors around the country an opportunity to view the treasures of the Folger Library.

FOLGER THEATRE GROUP

Since its founding in 1970 the Folger Theatre Group has made major strides in establishing itself as a theatre of national importance. Although in past seasons the Folger Theatre Group has alternated between productions of Shakespeare and other

Renaissance or Restoration playwrights and modern plays, in 1981–1982 the schedule is completely devoted to the sixteenth and seventeenth centuries. The season began with a production of Shakespeare's *Julius Caesar*, will continue with *The Rover* by Aphra Behn, and will finish with productions of Shakespeare's *The Tempest* and *The Comedy of Errors*. All productions for the 1981–1982 season are being staged in the Folger Library's own Elizabethan theatre.

COPYRIGHT CLEARANCE CENTER

21 Congress St., Salem, MA 01970
617-744-3350

David P. Waite
President

Virginia Riordan
Marketing Manager

BACKGROUND

The Copyright Clearance Center (CCC) was established in late 1977 in response to the Copyright Act of 1976 by a group of authors, publishers, and users of copyrighted material. The U.S. Congress suggested that a cost-effective, efficient, and centralized clearance mechanism be established so that authorizations to photocopy copyrighted material, as required by law under the act, could be obtained by users quickly and easily from copyright owners.

In operation since January 1, 1978, when the act became effective, the nonprofit CCC conveys after-the-fact authorizations to photocopy to users of copyrighted material from thousands of copyright owners. A computerized royalty fee collection and distribution system invoices photocopy users for reported copying activity on titles covered by CCC at fee rates set by the publishers. These fees, less a 25 cents per-copy-reported service charge, are then distributed to the appropriate copyright owners.

As the single source for authorizations to photocopy from thousands of copyright owners, CCC is the only service of its kind in the United States.

GROWTH

CCC continued to experience growth in key areas during 1981. Seven hundred and seventy-six titles were added, increasing the total number of publications participating in the Photocopy Permissions Service at year-end to 4,549, more than double the number of titles at the end of 1978, CCC's first year of operation. One hundred and twelve publishers registered with CCC, for a year-end total of 532, or two and one-half times the number of publishers registered at the end of 1978. The number of photocopy-user organizations to establish accounts with CCC grew by 271 during 1981, thus making the year-end total 1,322, which represents an increase of two-thirds over the total number of users registered at the end of 1978. Of the 1,322 users, 118 or 9 percent reported more than an average of ten copies per month, which qualified them for a level of full service. Full service, called Level I service, includes invoicing, remittance processing and distribution, receipt of quarterly *Publishers' Photocopy Fee Catalogs* and monthly supplements, and other updated information without a surcharge.

Another 291 lower-use accounts, which constitute 22 percent of all accounts, elected to pay a $15 semiannual fee to receive full service. The remaining user organizations received partial, or Level II, service, which provides for processing of photocopy reports only when accompanied by payment, remittance processing, and distribution of fees to appropriate publishers. New accounts receive Level I service for the initial six months, after which the volume of their photocopying activity is measured to see if they qualify for Level I or Level II service.

Close to one-quarter of a million photocopies (239,857, to be exact) were reported to CCC by its users during 1981. This represents more than three and one-half times the number of copies reported in 1978, and brought the total number of copies processed since CCC's inception to 675,726.

The average royalty fee paid in 1981 by photocopy users was $1.69 per copy. This compares favorably with the 1978 average of $1.44 per copy, and represents only a 25-cent per copy, or 17 percent, fee increase over a four-year period.

Royalty fees billed to photocopy users in 1981 totaled $405,951, a quadrupling of the monies invoiced during 1978. Since its inauguration, CCC has collected $1,094,955 in royalty fees for copyright owners.

In June of 1981, CCC distributed $124,086 to publishers, which represented 45 percent of net income earned on 1980 royalty collections. This was considerably greater than the $84,374 or 40 percent distributed from 1979 net income, and was almost 10 times the $14,575 or 30 percent distributed in 1978. In total, $223,036 in royalties has been distributed by CCC to participating publishers since 1978. Part of the balance of monies has been used by CCC to develop user awareness and the capability to handle the greatly expanded volume of activity expected in the near future. The remainder is held in escrow.

As previously mentioned, CCC continues to experience good growth rates in key service areas. However, it is important to stress that much work remains to be done to educate and inform the photocopy-user community about copyright law requirements. More publisher participation is needed as well, to broaden the coverage offered to photocopy users. CCC programs reflect a commitment to both of these tasks.

CURRENT PROGRAMS FOR PHOTOCOPY USERS

Document Delivery Awareness Program

CCC introduced a new program in 1981 to help identify information brokers and document delivery services that comply with the U.S. Copyright Law. Called the Document Delivery Awareness Program, it is designed to make users of photocopies more aware of those document delivery services that obtain authorizations from copyright owners for copies of copyrighted material that are supplied.

The program links various elements in the information chain, from publishers to document suppliers to users, in such a way that authorizations for supplied photocopies can be tracked. Publishers provide CCC with checklists to indicate firms with which they maintain photocopy license agreements. Photocopy users who participate in the program send sampling postcards once a month to CCC. Data on these cards identifies photocopies received from an outside source for a fee. By comparing the data on the cards with publishers' checklists and with photocopy reports received from document suppliers and stored on the CCC database, CCC is able to identify those services that provide authorized photocopies.

Many photocopy users expressed their concern to CCC as to whether copies they request from suppliers are lawfully provided and whether copyright owners are receiving a share of the fees paid for documents supplied. The *Guide to CCC-Participating Document Delivery Services*, a new publication updated and distributed quarterly by CCC to high-volume photocopy users, is a single, convenient source of information on services that do comply with the copyright law. When users need to order photocopies of documents or journal articles, they can consult the guide and its list of suppliers. Also, document suppliers who have accounts with CCC and provide authorized copies, either under direct photocopy license agreements with publishers or through the CCC Photocopy Permissions Service, are given free space in the guide to advertise and promote their businesses.

Through the development of the Document Delivery Awareness Program and through such publications as the guide, CCC believes its program will improve and make more effective document deliverers' services to users.

Large Industry User Assistance Program

Another new program unveiled in late 1981 provides systems and application support services to large industrial firms that seek CCC's help in meeting the photocopy authorization requirements of the copyright law.

The Large Industry User Assistance Program works with industry management by directing its attention to certain key areas bearing on copyright, such as company policy, personnel directives, and photocopy control system techniques for both supervised and unsupervised machines. These are reviewed and the means available for obtaining authorizations to photocopy, including the use of CCC permissions, direct licenses with publishers, and document suppliers, are also examined. When appropriate, copyrighted material handling aids, such as those often used in libraries, are devised. In addition, the need for establishing a corporate copyright administration unit, to which responsibility for copyright compliance would be assigned, is considered. Throughout, information regarding the efforts of other large firms to comply with copyright can be shared without divulging corporate identities.

Early contacts made with corporate officers in several large, randomly selected billion-dollar U.S. industrial corporations revealed that (1) few corporations had any policy regarding the photocopying of copyrighted materials; (2) though a few officers were vaguely aware of the new law, few had any understanding of it or its significance to their companies; and (3) all affirmed that their stated corporate policies were to abide by applicable laws. These findings confirmed earlier suspicions that the need for compliance with the Copyright Act had not been brought to the attention of more than a few corporate officers in industrial firms. It explains why more industrial accounts have not been reporting photocopying activity to CCC. Many of the corporate officers contacted have invited CCC to assist them in developing a working knowledge of what the copyright law requires of them in terms of procedures for obtaining authorizations to photocopy. The officers also requested information on methods used by other firms that are already coping with the new law.

CCC believes the Large Industry User Assistance Program will foster an awareness on the part of industry of what the copyright law means and what actions are required to comply with it.

Workshops

CCC conducted a pilot workshop for user organizations in Atlanta in 1981. The one-day workshop was held in connection with the Special Libraries Association conference, and featured speakers from the industrial sector. Representatives of two large corporations, Exxon Research and Engineering and Bell Laboratories, and two smaller photocopy-user organizations, FIND/SVP and the University of Tulsa, made presentations. The speakers described their firms' copyright compliance policy, their paths of development, and internal photocopy control systems. The small group/workshop atmosphere allowed the speakers and participants to share their experiences in coming to grips with the requirements of the copyright law.

Trade Shows

CCC exhibited at a number of trade shows during 1981: Special Libraries Association (Atlanta), National Association of Quick Printers (Anaheim), and the American Society for Information Science (Washington, D.C.). Its attractive booth has aroused increased interest in CCC on the part of librarians and information industry professionals attending these conferences.

CURRENT PROGRAMS FOR PUBLISHERS

Participating Action Program for Publisher Associations

To broaden publishers' participation in CCC, the five-point Participating Action Program for Publisher Associations was developed. Under this program, the management of CCC works directly with the leadership of publishers' associations to endorse the CCC concept and introduce it to their members. The five-point plan calls for associations to (1) identify all member publications; (2) endorse and introduce the CCC concept; (3) determine the needs of their members in order to help them decide how best to apply CCC's services; (4) consider and recommend policy for reconciling the requirements of the copyright law with the behavior of publishers that do not register; and (5) consider and recommend methods for motivating greater photocopy-user compliance. During 1981, work with the Association of American Publishers' Professional and Scientific Publishing Division, the American Business Press, and the Magazine Publishers Association was undertaken to increase the rate at which members of these associations register publications with CCC.

CCC's limited resources can be utilized most effectively by soliciting participation from publishers through their associations, rather than through individual members. Tangible results in the form of publication registrations have been achieved through relationships with these associations.

Filler-Ad Campaign

During 1981, participating publishers ran CCC-prepared advertisements in publications registered with CCC. Ad copy was directed primarily to librarians and photocopy users, and identified the benefits of using CCC to obtain on-the-spot authorization to photocopy. Camera-ready copy in five different sizes and layouts was provided; most advertisements included a coupon to be sent to CCC for more information. Both publishers and photocopy users have responded favorably to this campaign.

PROPOSED PROGRAMS FOR PUBLISHERS

Permissions by Request

Publishers that participate in CCC currently use the CCC Pre-Coded Permissions Service. Fee codes are printed at the bottom of the first page of each individual article in such scholarly publications as journals or scientific papers. A fee code is printed once in the front matter of issues of nonscholarly publications, such as trade journals, business and consumer magazines, newsletters and newspapers.

Publishers that precode their publications through CCC prefer to do so because the costs for having CCC process precoded transactions are lower than the costs for handling permissions by request themselves. The resulting benefit is a higher dollar return to the copyright owner on a fixed permissions fee charged to photocopy users. Users also prefer publishers to use the precoded method, which announces availability, indicates that permission to photocopy is required, and shows the fee amount through the use of the code.

However, if publishers wish to charge permissions fees at their discretion to user groups; if they wish to offer discounted permissions fees for multiple copying, or to modify fees that have already appeared in printed codes, use of the Pre-Coded Permissions Service may not be appropriate. Thus, CCC has developed for consideration the Permissions-by-Request service. When implemented, this service should enable CCC to readily handle permissions to photocopy from books and other materials from both current catalogs and backlists. It would allow for differentiation of publishers' permissions policies toward various categories of users; it would also allow for sliding-scale fees. Fees could be changed for backlisted and current materials. Permissions could be revoked at any time, if necessary.

This service would also permit handling permissions for duplicating published materials on which fee codes may not be printed, for example, audiovisual aids; publications in electronic form, such as videocassettes and videodiscs; and publisher-approved but uncontracted machine-readable data base records distributed by wire.

Flexibility is key to this service, but perhaps its greatest attribute is the ease with which publishers of nearly any copyrighted works could provide legal access to copy their materials. In order for the service to succeed, publishers will be asked to cooperate by (1) clearly and succinctly describing the parameters and fees that apply under their established permissions policy for the reproduction of copyrighted materials; (2) conveying this information to CCC by using one of the several flexible CCC formats now being considered; and (3) empowering CCC to act as their agent in performing through a centralized system the function of permissions, which are now administered by the individual permissions desks of participating publishers.

The Permissions-by-Request service will be transactional, much like the Pre-Coded Permissions Service. However, its operation costs will be higher, especially for urgent cases in which permissions must be conveyed on short order by telephone. Use of this service would yield a lower return on the permissions fee to the copyright owner, as compared with the rate of return on precoded permissions. The costs for operating this centralized Permissions-by-Request service would be considerably lower when requests are received by mail. CCC plans to distribute preprinted request forms to its registered users. In cases in which users need permission to photocopy immediately, a nationwide toll-free telephone number would be available to contact CCC operators, who would then access permission data files via on-line computer terminals. Such terminals are already in use at CCC's data processing center.

At present, the Association of American Publishers is considering the merits of initiating a pilot Permissions-by-Request program.

INTERNATIONAL RELATIONS

Reciprocal agreements are being established between CCC and royalty collection societies in foreign countries throughout the free world. Through these arrangements, it is expected that CCC will serve as the principal agent for U.S. copyright owners to distribute the required copyright authorizations to photocopy users in foreign countries.

Negotiations are under way with the Copyright Agency Limited (Australia) and Stichting Reprorecht (the Netherlands).

PUBLICATIONS

There are numerous CCC publications available to photocopy users and publishers, many of them at no charge.

The *Handbook for Libraries and Other Organizational Users* describes in detail the procedures that photocopy users follow as participants in CCC. A brief brochure entitled *Now You Can Photocopy and Still Comply with the Copyright Law* provides an overview of the CCC system and procedures. Of primary interest to photocopy users is the quarterly *Publisher's Photo-Copy Fee Catalog* (*PPC*) and its monthly supplements. This alphabetical list of registered publications states the years in which royalty fees are collected and the fee amount; issues of *PPC* may be purchased for $3 each. The updated *Directory of Registered User Organizations* is released semiannually. This roster identifies CCC member organizations by category, for example, corporate special library, academic research library, and the like.

New, abridged instruction booklets for publishers became available in 1981. One such booklet, *Trade Publications*, describes how publishers can use the CCC Pre-Coded Permissions service for trade journals, business and consumer magazines, newsletters and newspapers. A similar booklet, entitled *Scholarly Publications*, explains in detail how publishers of scholarly serials and separates, such as scientific journals and technical papers, may participate in CCC. Registration forms are included in both booklets. In addition, a brochure entitled *Benefits to You the Publisher* summarizes the CCC system and procedures for publishers' use. Semiannually, an updated alphabetical list of member publishers entitled *Directory of Registered Publishers* is issued.

Document suppliers that provide authorized photocopies, either under direct photocopy license agreements with publishers or through the CCC Photocopy Permissions Service, are listed in the new quarterly publication mentioned earlier, the *Guide to CCC-Participating Document Delivery Services*. The guide is issued and updated quarterly and distributed at no charge to photocopy users participating in the Document Delivery Awareness Program.

Resource Sharing: Selected Reports

LIBRARY NETWORKING IN THE UNITED STATES, 1981

Susan K. Martin
*Director, Milton S. Eisenhower Library,
Johns Hopkins University*

To trace the development of library networking is, at best, difficult. As stated in Henriette Avram's article "Library Networking in the United States, 1980," the subject is complex and is approached by various writers at various times from multiple points of view.[1] Of equal significance is the astonishing rate of change in networking activities and prospects. The rapid rate of network development results in a paucity of organized documentation; by the time a writer describes and analyzes an event or set of events, the focus of networking activities may have shifted radically. Primary sources describing networking necessarily often consist of unpublished reports, press releases, brief news items, personal correspondence, and word-of-mouth information.

NAC AND BSDP

Last year's report focused on nationwide networking efforts spearheaded by the Library of Congress (LC) and the Council on Library Resources (CLR).[2] LC's Network Advisory Committee (NAC) and CLR's Bibliographic Services Development Program (BSDP) were described in depth in that report. In 1981, NAC held three hearings about the governance of library networks and the ownership and distribution of bibliographic data. Set within the contexts of the two American Library Association (ALA) national meetings and the annual meeting of the American Society for Information Science (ASIS), the hearings provided an opportunity for librarians to discuss these issues and their implications. Although varied in size and scope, these hearings resulted in lively discussion of the issues and a determination that no action beyond definition of the issues and problems was required on the part of NAC.

BSDP pursued its goal of providing nationwide direction for bibliographic products and services.[3] National Authority systems; a link between Research Libraries Group (RLG), Washington Library Network (WLN), and LC; and on-line catalogs all continued to be in the forefront of BSDP's activities. With the assistance of BSDP, libraries such as the University of Texas Library are now contributing authority records in their particular areas of strength (for example, Latin American studies) to LC.

BIBLIOGRAPHIC UTILITIES

Under the inelegant phrase "bibliographic utility" fall the major computer systems that support library bibliographic networking in the United States. OCLC (now the OnLine Computer Library Center), RLIN (RLG's computer system, Research Libraries Information Network), and WLN remain the three networking systems. The economics of creating and operating a network are of such complexity and scope that it is unlikely that any other national utilities will emerge in the foreseeable future.

Each of these three utilities underwent major change in 1981. OCLC "flipped" its enormous data base so that available Anglo-American Cataloguing Rules (AACR 2) headings would be immediately accessible, together with the old AACR 1 headings.[4] While this task was both difficult and time-consuming, OCLC successfully completed the effort. The year also saw a physical move for OCLC to its new building. The move took place over a period of months, and, while some computer downtime resulted, this change was successfully accomplished. Approximately one hundred libraries used the new OCLC acquisitions system in its pilot mode in 1981, and most libraries expressed the intention to continue doing so on a permanent basis.[5] Finally, OCLC contracted with the Claremont colleges to market their Total Library System (TLS) in addition to OCLC's own circulation system.[6] OCLC President Rowland Brown has indicated that OCLC intends to create a for-profit subsidiary to market and service systems that do not need to be linked to its massive data base.[7] In line with this thinking, OCLC plans to revise its pricing structure, which has always been predicated on a library's full use of the cataloging module. In the future, a library would have the option to use any or all of OCLC's services, while paying for services at predesignated rates.

RLIN also experienced numerous technological and organizational changes during 1981. (Organizational changes related to RLG as a *network* are described in the section entitled "Network Organizations"). Originally designed as computer support for a single library, RLIN until 1981 consisted of separate files for each user; a cataloger could peruse other libraries' files, but the procedure was complex. Also, the overlap in holdings among member libraries could not be reflected in one record. In order to streamline the system, RLG reconfigured the data base in the summer of 1981 by clustering together those records that represented the same book. The Reconfigured Data Base (RDB), another massive effort that required several months to complete, is used with more sophisticated computer programs known as RLIN II.[8] RLIN initiated its acquisitions system in pilot mode in July, with most RLG libraries planning to move to the full system during FY 1982. Simultaneously, RLIN changed operating systems, added several magnetic drums and core storage, and is planning to move to an IBM 3081 in January 1982. As mentioned earlier, RLIN is cooperating with WLN in an effort funded by the Council on Library Resources to facilitate communication between and among the bibliographic utilities. Specifications for joint use of an authority file have been identified, and the project has moved toward linking RLIN and WLN.

The Washington Library Network did not significantly change its technological environment or capabilities during 1981. For several years, WLN has been a sophisticated system, excluding only circulation control, but limited to a specific geographic region. It offered its software for either sale or license and has received a prompt response from the University of Illinois for its on-line catalog qua network.[9] In 1981, WLN played the role of a fully developed regional system that was nonetheless willing to extend its developments to any interested users. (WLN's encounter with SOLINET is described in the section entitled "Network Organizations.") WLN has had for several years a formal link with RLG/RLIN; in 1981 it began to explore the possibility of a formal link with OCLC. WLN staff thus may perceive their system as one that will fulfill the need for a linking mechanism between two large utilities.

Financial problems have plagued all three utilities. WLN is a state institution, and the Pacific Northwest region has not fared well economically. The expansion of WLN beyond the boundaries of the state of Washington now considerably increases the utility's potential for revenues. OCLC, with a new building and two new subsystems, suffers a capitalization problem. It has a $30 million long-term debt, and a short-term debt slightly under $5 million. According to its president, OCLC has a cash-flow difficulty.[10] During the year, OCLC raised the prices of some products, and added a monthly terminal charge of $25. RLG, which also grew and developed new systems during 1981, was faced with a deficit for the year. Its board of governors revised the means by which the network was financed; loans from member institutions, together with grants from private foundations, then enabled the network to reestablish a positive financial balance.

NETWORK ORGANIZATIONS

For the purposes of this article, a network organization is defined as an organization of member libraries that have joined together to facilitate access to a bibliographic utility and to develop mutually beneficial services and products, such as regional union lists of serials. Although hundreds of library consortia exist in the United States at this time, only two dozen provide their own bibliographic utility or access to OCLC. Like the bibliographic utilities, some network organizations have also had financial, organizational, or programmatic crises, while others have experienced real progress.

SOLINET (Southeastern Library Network) continues to be a focal point of attention. In the last two years, there has been much discussion about a potential Mutual Support Corporation (MSC) to be established by SOLINET and OCLC.[11] SOLINET's lengthy and expensive agenda has included recent efforts to license WLN software, and reprogram it for SOLINET's Burroughs computers, and to establish a Regional Support System (RSS) at SOLINET. SOLINET unsuccessfully sought funding from both OCLC and private foundations for its projects. As a result, the Regional Support System became a Reference Support System with applications limited to bibliographic searches only. In October, SOLINET suddenly laid off 23 staff members, including development and operations staff. It is clear that MSC is no longer under discussion, and although it is possible that SOLINET could revive its plans for a regional bibliographic center, the financial and political wounds sustained by SOLINET apparently remain sore.

Although NELINET (New England Library Information Network) had not progressed as far as SOLINET in terms of development, its board of directors apparently took note of the barriers encountered by SOLINET in seeking expansion. In December, NELINET's board dismissed the three top administrators on its staff, thus leaving a network that functions essentially as an OCLC broker, and the future of NELINET an open question.

As previously mentioned, RLG's financial position was not stable in early 1981. RLG membership is generally by institution rather than by individual library; university administrators at RLG member institutions believed that the need to provide a network for research institutions was compelling. The partner-members of RLG contributed loans and grants totaling $4 million, thus allowing the network to complete its major development effort. Simultaneously, the board of governors restructured the pricing system to avoid a recurrence of deficits. Future RLG pricing will be in three parts: (1) The administrative/program budget will be funded from an annual partnership fee, set initially at $25,000; (2) the computer operations will be self-supporting; and (3) research and development efforts will rely strictly on external funding. The support of member institutions is significant and should now allow RLG to increase the benefits of the network for its members. RLG's program includes cooperative collection development; members have already gathered data related to existing collection strengths and current collecting priorities. During the year, several members assumed primary responsibility for collecting in specific areas, and participated in BSDP-sponsored projects such as the National Authority File System.

One of the older automated networks has become a victim of rapid network development in general. The Five Associated University Libraries (FAUL) effectively dwindled to two members after Cornell University and SUNY-Binghamton joined

RLG and the University of Rochester turned to SUNY-OCLC for its services. While an office for FAUL still exists at Syracuse University, the association is informal and has no contractual relationship with OCLC. During the year, OCLC terminals were "turned off," or disabled, by OCLC at Cornell and Binghamton. After a short period of negotiation, the terminals were reactivated. OCLC's new pricing structure has a clear bearing on this incident.

Other networks are proceeding successfully, or at least without incident. In Texas, AMIGOS is slowly building its technical capacity. Used as a computer resource for its members, AMIGOS has also begun to offer computer services to libraries outside its membership. Among the services offered are reading, error-checking, and refreshing OCLC tapes.

Also expanding beyond its geographic boundaries is the California Library Authority for Systems and Services (CLASS). With a minicomputer in-house, CLASS is managing the California data bases of periodicals and monographs. In 1981, CLASS began to offer an electronic message switching system, which was available initially only in California and then nationwide.

NETWORKING TRENDS

The year 1981 clearly indicated that networking on a large-scale and sophisticated level would be a complex and expensive undertaking. Just as libraries themselves tend to be undercapitalized, so do networks. Most networks and utilities derive their income from the unit costs of transactions performed by member libraries; some networks have state subsidies. These funds, however, can in no way be considered to be assuring. As inflation continues to rise, libraries are purchasing fewer books and, therefore, transaction levels are dropping. In the current economic climate, public funding is at best uncertain. Some attempts by networks to overcome these barriers have been mentioned, such as OCLC's formation of a for-profit subsidiary to market circulation systems, RLG's fund-raising activities, and the expanded services offered by AMIGOS and CLASS. Given the clientele of networks, it may not be possible to take a single giant step toward appropriate capitalization, but it may be feasible to achieve solid financial footing slowly and carefully by using multiple strategies. The future, however, may see networks that employ an entrepreneurial staff and seek venture capital in order to significantly advance the state of the art.

Librarians have long considered the card catalog to be obsolete, microform catalogs to be undesirable, and on-line catalogs to be underdeveloped. In 1981, work was continued on specifications for a public access catalog by BSDP and by the informal Consortium to Develop an On-line Catalog (CONDOC).[12] The use of a central computer facility, such as OCLC or RLIN, is desirable for sharing bibliographic data. However, as library users gain direct access to on-line files, the computer systems would quickly become overburdened without an intermediary. While the definition of on-line catalog specifications is pursued, the utilities are becoming involved because of the obvious need to move bibliographic records from a central computer to a local one, to keep data bases properly synchronized, and to allow for the broadening of any search from the local catalog to the network. The utilities and participating libraries will issue a report to CLR in 1982.

Authority files and authority control are critical in a discussion of on-line catalogs, but they also present vexing problems for network utilities. Once held to be vitally important in a centralized network, multi-institutional authority control now appears to be excessively expensive, both for the network and for the member libraries. WLN, with its centralized staff, provides authority control for a relatively small constituency. OCLC provides an authority file but no authority control linking the file to the bibliographic records in the data base. RLG had intended to implement full authority control, but at the end of 1981 provided this service only to the New York Public Library; other users have authority-file access. The implementation of AACR 2 has made authority control exceedingly difficult, both in manual and in machine form.

In previous years, linked bibliographic systems seemed to be a real and desirable intermediary goal on the path to creating a nationwide bibliographic network. Now, all utilities have sizable data bases, and the pressure of competition or cooperation has subsided.[13] The Battelle report of 1980 outlined the costs and benefits of linking the utilities; it appears that the library community does not believe that the benefits at this time are worth the costs.[14] The conservative mood, reflected in the library profession, is characterized by less active cooperation and more individual control of one's destiny. A declining economy will of necessity engender cooperation, but will heighten the need for critical evaluation of the benefits of cooperation and resource sharing.

NOTES

1. Henriette Avram, "Library Networking in the United States, 1980" in *The Bowker Annual of Library and Book Trade Information* (New York: R. R. Bowker, 1981), p. 46.
2. Ibid.
3. Council on Library Resources, "Two-Year Report of the Bibliographic Services Development Program" (Washington, D.C.: Council on Library Resources, 1981).
4. Georgia L. Brown, "AACR 2: OCLC's Implementation and Database," *Journal of Library Automation* 14 (September 1981): 161–173.
5. *OCLC Newsletter*, Winter 1982.
6. "OCLC and Claremont Ink Marketing Contract," *Advanced Technology/Libraries* 10, no. 11 (November 1981): 10.
7. *OCLC Newsletter*, Winter 1982.
8. "OCLC Moves into New Home; RLIN Reconfigures Database," *LJ Hotline* 10, no. 30 (September 21, 1981): 1.
9. Thomas P. Brown and Raymond DeBuse, "Replicating the Washington Library Network Computer System Software," *Journal of Library Automation* 14 (September 1981): 202–204.
10. "Economic Stresses Causing Changes in Direction at OCLC," *Advanced Technology/Libraries* 10, no. 7 (July 1981): 1, 6.
11. Avram, "Library Networking."
12. "Consortium to Develop an On-line Catalog (CONDOC)" (Grass Valley, Calif.: J. Matthews and Associates, 1981).
13. Richard De Gennaro, "Research Libraries Enter the Information Age," *Library Journal* 104 (November 15, 1979): 2405–2410.
14. Donald A. Smalley et al., *Linking the Bibliographic Utilities: Benefits and Costs* (Columbus, Ohio: Batelle Columbus Laboratories, 1980).

METROPOLITAN WASHINGTON LIBRARY COUNCIL

Metropolitan Washington Council of Governments, Suite 200,
1875 Eye St. N.W., Washington, DC 20006
202-223-6800

Barbara M. Robinson

Director

The Metropolitan Washington Library Council is a library cooperative serving 250 member libraries of all types—public, special, federal, academic, and school—in the District of Columbia, suburban Maryland, and northern Virginia. Based in the

Metropolitan Washington Council of Governments (COG), the Library Council is one of the few library cooperatives to be housed in a regional planning organization in the United States. The origin of the Library Council, its membership, its institutional relationships, and its budget are described below.

BACKGROUND

In the late 1960s the directors of the ten public library systems in the region urged COG to treat issues concerning libraries on a par with housing, transportation, air quality, and public safety problems. COG responded to their concern by establishing the Librarians' Committee within the COG committee structure.[1] The public library directors were joined on the committee by a few librarians from other types of libraries that were particularly committed to resource sharing and information exchange. The three state library agencies in the District of Columbia, Maryland, and Virginia, together with COG, provided funds to cover the cost of coordinating the committee. By the early 1970s, it became apparent to the committee that library cooperation, particularly in Washington, had to include the hundreds of special libraries in government agencies, law firms, accounting firms, membership associations, trade and labor unions, research and development (R&D) and consulting firms, and business and industry. There were also university, four- and two-year college libraries, and dozens of school libraries to be included in the dialogue.

The three state librarians favored expanding the committee to include other types of libraries for two reasons. They thought that resource sharing and information exchange had to include all types of libraries to be successful, and they hoped that the membership would help bear the cost of having an organization handle the coordination for them. Consequently, the Metropolitan Washington Library Council was founded in 1976 with bylaws, membership dues, and member privileges. The Librarians' Committee was expanded. It continued to give each public library director one seat and one vote; it also added seats for other members.

The objectives of the Library Council were to formalize information exchange among all types of libraries; coordinate projects that benefit member libraries and their staffs; initiate projects in response to member demand; and collect information needed for planning and decision making.

THE PROGRAM

To meet these objectives, the Library Council program has expanded over the years. The basic activities have been to hold workshops, forums, and lectures; arrange cooperative purchasing contracts for supplies and services to members; advise members on problems; convene meetings; coordinate 14 topical committees; publish and disseminate reports, directories, and union lists; collect statistical data on salaries; and offer a job-line service, which provides a taped telephone listing. Library Council activities may be classified under the following categories: coordination (committees, joint purchasing/mylar jackets, joint purchasing/films [explored], joint purchasing/delivery service [Library Express], areawide PR, interlibrary loan procedures, reciprocal borrowing [begun in 1969], Fine Free Week, Legislative Day/National Library Week with District of Columbia Library Association, association presidents' meeting, D.C. Online User's Group [affiliated with Library Council from 1978–1981], and statistics and data collection areawide); professional development/training (workshops, brown-bag luncheon speakers, forums, tours, professional collection, and training interns); jobline; publications program; proposal writing; and grants and contracts.

Some of the highlights of the program follow. The Library Council's training program has provided a model for other continuing education providers. More than one thousand librarians, trustees, and paraprofessionals have been trained, usually through the small-group process. Heavy emphasis has been placed on managerial skill development for librarians, which the U.S. Office of Education has supported with two grants, in 1975 and 1978, under Title II-B of the Higher Education Act (HEA) of 1965.[2] Two training workshops developed by the Library Council with the instructors have become well known nationally: "Space Planning" (Aaron Cohen and Elaine Cohen), and "Online Bibliographic Services: The Very Basics" (Sheryl Rosenthal).

One of the strengths of the program has been the emphasis on cooperative purchasing. For example, Library Express, the interlibrary delivery service provided under contract with a commercial courier, is a concrete example of group savings.[3] Originally, the state of Maryland used Library Services and Construction Act (LSCA) funds to pay Montgomery County to provide a truck and driver for the hundred-mile circle connecting the ten public library systems, six universities, and the National Library of Medicine. Then the District of Columbia picked up the service using their staff. In 1977, the Library Council invited commercial couriers to bid on providing the service. Since then, commercial couriers have been providing the service at a savings of thousands of dollars. This program demonstrates the usefulness of federal seed money to stimulate subsequent private-sector investment.

PUBLICATIONS

The Library Council publications list has expanded continuously. The current brochure lists 16 titles; 10 are Library Council publications, of which half are updated annually; 3 are union lists that the Library Council is selling for other groups in town.[4]

The following selection of Library Council titles gives some indication of the types of information collected and disseminated at the request of our members: *Directory of Online Search Services Serving Metropolitan Washington; MAGS, Metropolitan Area Guide to Serials; Statistics on Area Public Libraries; A Comparison of Public Library Job Titles and Job Descriptions; Salary Survey of Special Libraries in Metropolitan Washington; Model Management Curriculum for Special Librarians;* and *Training Needs of Hearing Impaired Library Personnel in Metropolitan Washington.*

Noticeably absent from the program is any kind of automated service offered through the Library Council. Efforts to provide a dozen members with a cluster Online Computer Library Center (OCLC) terminal failed because the libraries that most wanted to participate could not afford the front-end costs. Similarly, efforts to provide members with discounts for on-line searches have been unsuccessful because members could not commit sufficient funds to warrant discounts from the vendor.

MEMBERSHIP

Since 1976, the first membership year, the number of member libraries has risen from 94 to 250 in 1981. The majority of members are special (61 percent) and federal libraries (18 percent). Academic libraries constituted 11 percent of total membership, public libraries 5 percent, and school libraries 1 percent. Overall membership increased by 12 percent between 1980 and 1981 despite slight declines in academic and federal library participation. The original public library constituency has remained the same—ten library systems with more than one hundred branches participate from the three states.

The most dramatic increase in membership has occurred among the special and federal libraries, whose numbers tripled from 1976 to 1981. There are approximately one thousand special and federal libraries in the region; roughly a quarter belong to the Library Council.

The number of academic and school library members has fluctuated slightly between 20 and 30 over the years. The Consortium of Universities (American, Catholic, Georgetown, George Washington, and Howard universities and the University of the District of Columbia) includes longtime Library Council members.

Of the 250 member libraries, many are small with very small staffs. Indeed, nearly 90 percent of the Library Council's members are small libraries paying $75 to $100 in dues per year. The number of larger member libraries paying $200 and $250 declined by 2 percent and 1 percent, respectively, between 1980 and 1981. Only 5 percent pay the highest dues and have a combined personnel and materials budget of over $1 million.[5]

MEMBERSHIP SERVICES

All members are entitled to the same services, which includes *AXIS*, the bimonthly newsletter; free listing of job vacancies on the job-line (nonmembers pay $30 per listing); discounts on Library Express, the interlibrary courier service; member rates on Library Council publications and workshops; and participation in special member programs and committees.

Although it is gratifying to report a large membership, there is a major drawback to having so many small member libraries with small budgets: The dues collected are often disproportionally small in comparison to the services rendered. As is frequently the case, the small member libraries need more personal assistance from the Library Council staff than do the large member libraries with large staffs of their own.

There are corresponding problems in having large member libraries. It is harder to inform the staff in these large libraries of Library Council activities. Indeed, in many cases staff members have never heard of the Library Council, yet their library is a member.

GEOGRAPHIC LOCATION

Most Library Council member libraries are located within a 15-mile radius of COG's offices in downtown Washington. Many of the special and federal library members are only a few blocks away, which makes it possible for the Library Council to hold frequent brown-bag lunches, set up tours of libraries and collections in the District, and organize a professional collection of library and information science journals that are jointly purchased by two dozen downtown libraries. The collection is housed in the library at COG.[6]

Some Library Council members are much closer than they used to be, thanks to the new subway system. But others are clustered around a northern Virginia shopping area or the Dulles airport, which are accessible only by car or bus. Not surprisingly, these librarians find it inconvenient to come downtown for meetings and workshops, as do those from federal and public libraries located farther out in Gaithersburg, Maryland, and in Loudoun and Prince William counties, Virginia. In order to accommodate them, Library Council meetings are occasionally held in other locations.

One of the success stories of the Library Council is the regionwide acceptance of the concept of reciprocal borrowing. This program enables citizens of any jurisdiction in the region, whether in Maryland, Virginia, or the District of Columbia, to borrow library materials from any public library in the region and to return them to any library in the region. As increasing numbers of people commute to school and places of worship, work, and play, the probability increases that some people will stop to drop off or pick up a book at any one of the 100 library branches in the region.

INSTITUTIONAL RELATIONSHIPS

As was mentioned earlier, the Library Council is housed in the Metropolitan Washington Council of Governments. It is part of the Department of Human Resources and Public Safety. COG was created by the 16 local governments that belong to it and is run by a board of elected officials. The Library Council, like COG, is tied closely to member local governments, but it also has to be responsive to its other members in special, federal, school and academic libraries, and to its affiliates.

In 1980 a number of professional library associations showed their commitment to the Library Council by joining as affiliate members, including the D.C. Library Association, the Maryland Library Association, the Virginia Library Association, the Washington, D.C., chapter of the Special Libraries Association, and the Potomac Valley chapter of the American Society for Information Science. The Library Council convenes their presidents and editors for an annual meeting.

The 1981 meeting, held in late summer, gave each association a chance to set dates without risk of conflict with other groups and to ensure that topics selected for major meetings were not selected unwittingly by other groups. The information exchange that began with this annual meeting will be continued through the *Master Calendar* of library and information science events, which the Library Council publishes regularly. Relationships with the affiliate members also extend the Library Council's visibility. For example, Library Council events are reported in the newsletters of area professional associations as well as in the national library press.

OTHER AREA LIBRARIES

Although the principal focus of the Library Council is service to member libraries, it would be shortsighted to exclude nonmember libraries. Consequently, workshops, forums, publications, and the Jobline service are offered to nonmembers at higher prices than members pay and nonmembers are encouraged to save money by joining the Library Council.

REVENUE

The Library Council's existence, like that of so many of the cooperatives Helen Eckard describes in her article "NCES Survey of Library Networks" (*see* Part 4), depends in large part on the availability of federal funds earmarked for interlibrary cooperation under Title III of the Library Services and Construction Act. In the case of the Library Council, which is tristate, a combination of LSCA and state funds is provided by Hardy Franklin, the director of the D.C. Public Library; Nettie Taylor, Assistant State Superintendent for Libraries, State of Maryland; and Donald Haynes, State Librarian of Virginia. Nearly 50 percent of the Library Council's 1982 budget of $190,000 is covered by these funds. Without them the Library Council could not survive, despite the fact that COG has contributed 13 percent of the budget and the remaining 41 percent is covered by membership dues (12 percent), grants and contracts (10 percent), and revenues from workshops, publications and Jobline (19 percent).

CONCLUSION

There is great uncertainty among state librarians concerning the future of LSCA Title III and federal funds for libraries in general. (LSCA Title III funds are awarded to local, regional, and multistate library cooperatives and networks across the country through the state libraries.) There is also great uncertainty among the members of the Library Council. Federal libraries are feeling the impact of the current administration's across-the-board cuts, and public and school libraries are being hit by local government budget cuts. Academic libraries in the region, with the exception of Howard University, are also cutting back.

In the past, members belonged to the Library Council because they believed in cooperation and wanted to support it. Now they are rightly asking whether they are getting a good return on their rather nominal investment. This kind of thinking tests the merits of cooperation. It suggests that members may be forced to drop their membership, attend fewer Library Council workshops, buy fewer Library Council publications, and list fewer job vacancies on the Jobline. A decline in participation in workshops began to show in 1981. However, despite an increase in dues, nearly all of our members have renewed their membership.

It it ironic that at a time when librarians are talking more and more about the need for cooperation and networking among different types of libraries the Library Council and other library cooperatives across the country are struggling to survive. Although the future of the Library Council is uncertain, it is to be hoped that member libraries will continue to value interlibrary cooperation and support it through their involvement in the Library Council, and that federal support for library cooperation will be forthcoming.

NOTES

1. The ten public library systems participating from the three states are located in the cities of Alexandria and Falls Church (Arlington, Fairfax, Loudoun, and Prince William counties are contingent) in Northern Virginia; Takoma Park, Montgomery, and Prince George's County in suburban Maryland; and the District of Columbia.
2. In 1975 the Library Council received a grant under HEA Title II-B to support the development of five workshops: personnel administration, supervisory skills, communication techniques, planning and budgeting, and advertising and public relations. In 1978 the Library Council was funded a second time under HEA II-B to develop and offer a model management curriculum for special libraries that included communications, planning, human resources, management, and financial management. The final reports on both projects offer insights into the process for other continuing education providers and are available through the Library Council.
3. For three years, Purolator Courier Corporation provided the delivery service. Last year, a local courier, IGExpediting, Inc., underbid Purolator.
4. Groups for whom the Library Council is distributing publications include the Interlibrary Users Association (*Journal Holdings in the Washington-Baltimore Area*); the Consortium of Universities of the Washington, D.C., Metropolitan Area (*Consortium Union List: Serials of Eight Colleges and Universities*); and the Washington Art Library Resources Committee (*Art Serials*).
5. Library Council dues for 1981 were as follows: for libraries with combined personnel and material budgets of under $100,000, $75; for budgets between $100,000 and $500,000, $100; $500,000–$1 million, $200; and over $1 million, $250. In 1982 membership rates will be $95, $125, $250, and $310.
6. The professional collection contains a dozen professional library and information science journals that are purchased jointly by 24 member libraries. The journals are housed in the COG library, and Library Council staff provides members with a table of contents service and on-demand photocopying. Prior copyright clearance is obtained from the publisher.

Federal Agencies

THE NATIONAL COMMISSION ON LIBRARIES AND INFORMATION SCIENCE

1717 K St. N.W., Suite 601, Washington, DC 20036
202-653-6252

Toni Carbo Bearman
Executive Director

Douglas S. Price
Deputy Director

The National Commission on Libraries and Information Science (NCLIS) was established by PL 91-345 in 1970 as a permanent, independent agency in the executive branch, reporting directly to both the president and Congress. The commission has four major roles: (1) to serve as a "resident expert" for both the executive and legislative branches; (2) to be an "honest broker," bringing together agencies in both branches to focus on problems of common interest; (3) to serve as a forum for the entire library/information community, including both the public and private sectors; and (4) to be a catalyst to help get programs implemented.

WHCOLIS-RELATED ACTIVITIES

During 1981, NCLIS continued its strong emphasis on promoting implementation of the resolutions of the first White House Conference on Library and Information Services (WHCOLIS). As part of its ongoing planning process, the commission established priorities for the year. Among the major sources of ideas were the president's message to Congress transmitting the WHCOLIS report, the recommendations of the White House Conference on Library and Information Services Taskforce (WHCOLIST), the commissioners' own careful examination of the 64 WHCOLIS resolutions, and their own assessments of issues and program areas. The commissioners determined that NCLIS should emphasize three areas of activity for the next year: the development of specifications for revised library and information services legislation; improving the dissemination of federal information; and resource sharing and the application of technology.

In fulfillment of the commission's dual responsibilities of implementing the resolutions of the WHCOLIS and advising government agencies on matters pertaining to library and information services, the chairperson sent a letter to the head of each government agency, enclosing copies of the resolution(s) for which that agency was considered to have primary responsibility and requesting information on actions being taken or planned to implement the resolution(s). All agencies have responded and have provided information on their implementation of the resolutions.

The WHCOLIST held its second plenary meeting in Detroit in September, in conjunction with an oversight hearing on the Library Services and Construction Act (LSCA).

The participants received reports of activities in 40 states and 4 territories engendered by the White House Conference and the pre-conferences. A number of speakers discussed critical issues and ongoing activities. Alice Ihrig, director of Civic and Cultural Programs, Moraine Valley Community College, spoke on the need for all types of libraries and librarians to work together and present a united front. Charles Benton, chairperson of NCLIS, brought the task force up to date on NCLIS activities. Margaret Warden, former state senator of Montana and member of NCLIS (and chair of its Legislation Committee) spoke on the necessity for communicating with legislators at all levels. E. J. Josey, chief of the Bureau of Specialist Library Services, New York State Education Department (and chair of the NCLIS Task Force on Services to Cultural Minorities) urged the use of existing groups to promote the cause of libraries. Other speakers included Eileen D. Cooke, executive director of the American Library Association (ALA) Washington office, and New York state senator Major Owens.

Eleven critical areas were identified by WHCOLIST for measuring progress, including, among others, the enactment of legislation to increase library funding and to authorize multitype library cooperation, adult/user education programs, continuing education for librarians, and efforts to heighten library visibility/public awareness. The next annual meeting is tentatively scheduled for September 1982 in Atlanta, with at least one meeting of the steering committee at the ALA Midwinter meeting in Denver in January.

Specifications for Legislation

Recognizing that a fundamental element for improving library and information services is carefully constructed legislation, the commission has devoted considerable attention to developing specifications for such legislation. A first effort in this direction, the Proposed National Library and Information Services Act included in the *WHCOLIS Final Report: Summary*, was based on the 64 resolutions of the first WHCOLIS. Commission staff prepared additional documents for the commission, including an overall analysis of library/information issues and two detailed analyses in the areas of networking/resource sharing, and research, education, and training.

Beginning in September, the Subcommittee on Postsecondary Education of the House Committee on Education and Labor, under the chairmanship of Congressman Paul Simon, held a series of oversight hearings on LSCA in various cities around the country. Throughout these hearings, NCLIS assisted in identifying and scheduling witnesses to ensure input from all concerned constituencies. Additional oversight and legislative hearings are planned for 1982 and 1983. NCLIS has been asked to analyze the results of these hearings and make recommendations for specifications for legislation.

In addition to this direct assistance, the reports of two NCLIS task forces will provide valuable information for these specifications for legislation. The Task Force on Community Information and Referral Services, under the chairmanship of Robert Croneberger, director, Memphis-Shelby County Public Library and Information Center, has developed definitions and elements of information and referral, and identified the problems limiting the effectiveness of information and referral efforts to date. The task force, which has met six times, has prepared recommendations for corrective action to minimize these problems and to improve the provision of information and referral services. The final report is scheduled to be presented to the commission at its first meeting in 1982. The Task Force on Library and Information Services to Cultural Minorities, under the chairmanship of E. J. Josey, chief of the Bureau of Specialist Library Services, New York State Education Department, has met four times and held two open hearings at the annual meeting of the ALA in San Francisco in late June. A drafting subcommittee will be working on the final report for approval by the full task force at its final meeting in the spring. The report, which is expected to be submitted to the commission in mid-1982, will include recommendations for improvement in five broad areas: materials and resources; personnel; programming; funding; and needs. Elements of these recommendations will include legislative provisions; equitable distribution of available funds; programming for cultural awareness; cooperation with other service agencies; recruitment of minorities into librarianship; education (including continuing education) of library personnel; collection development, utilization and preservation; production of multimedia materials by and for minorities; and literacy programs. Recommendations from these two task forces will be incorporated into specifications for library/information legislation.

Improving Dissemination of Federal Information

In 1979, after several years of planning, NCLIS established a task force on the roles of government and private organizations with respect to the dissemination of scientific, technical, business, and other information. This task force was carefully assembled to include seven representatives from each of three sectors: public, private not-for-profit, and private for-profit. Under the chairmanship of Robert M. Hayes, dean, Graduate School of Library and Information Science, University of California–Los Angeles, the members of the task force reached nearly unanimous agreement on seven principles that should guide federal government involvement in information activities. The members of the task force also reached substantial, and in most cases nearly unanimous, agreement on 27 recommendations for steps to be taken in implementation of those principles.

The principles relate to the following major issues:

1. The need for the federal government to take a position of leadership in facilitating the development and fostering the use of information products and services. As part of that, the open dissemination of information from governmental activities should be regarded as a high priority responsibility, especially through private sector means.
2. Private sector investment in information resources, products, and services should be encouraged and not discouraged. As part of that, libraries and other information services in the private sector should be used as a means for distribution of information from the federal government, in preference to using newly created governmental agencies.
3. The government should not engage in commercial information activities unless there are compelling reasons for it to do so, and there must be well-defined procedures for determining that such reasons indeed are present. Prices for government products and services should be consistent with the actual costs for making the information available.
4. If private sector information is included in any package of governmentally distributed information, the private sector property rights should be carefully protected.

Since the members of the task force strongly emphasized that the principles and recommendations should not be taken out of the context of the complete report, interested persons are referred to the final report, *Public Sector/Private Sector Interaction in Providing Information Services*, which will be available in the spring of 1982.

The NCLIS/LC-sponsored Intergovernmental Library Cooperation Project, under the direction of Alphonse F. Trezza, examined the interactions among library and information service operations at the federal, state, and local levels of government. The purpose of this project, which was undertaken jointly with the Library of Congress and the Federal

Library Committee, was to develop ways in which government agencies at all three levels can improve cooperation to meet national and local needs and to improve the dissemination of government information. The report concludes that the federal libraries represent a microcosm of the nation's libraries as a whole, encompassing libraries of all types, including academic, scientific, technical, other special libraries, general, and school. It also recommends that a federal library network be established to (1) coordinate efforts for more effective sharing of resources and services among federal libraries and information centers at both the field and national levels; (2) improve resource sharing and cooperation between federal and nonfederal libraries at the local, state, and national levels; (3) interact with cooperatives, state, regional networks, and organizations; (4) provide improved access to collections in federal libraries and information centers through the development of a data base of federal library holdings and government publications, in cooperation with the Government Printing Office (GPO) and National Technical Information Service (NTIS), and federal agencies generally; (5) provide coordination and consultant assistance to federal libraries in the selection, installation, and use of the most efficient information technologies; (6) develop guidelines for ongoing evaluation of federal library and information activities, projects, services, programs, and plans; and (7) provide for educational programs designed to encourage and support professional development in areas related to network concerns. [For further information on the Intergovernmental Library Cooperation Project, see the report in Part 4 of this volume.]

In addition to these projects, NCLIS has been working with the Office of Information and Regulatory Affairs (OIRA) of the Office of Management and Budget (OMB) on implementation of the Paperwork Reduction Act (PL 96-511), providing material and advice on information policy, standards, and information resources management, and forwarding draft recommendations from the Task Force on Public/Private Sector Relations. In addition, the commission has brought together key decision-makers from agencies in both the executive and legislative branches—including the General Accounting Office (GAO), the NTIS, the National Archives and Records Services (NARS), the Joint Committee on Printing, and the Federal Publishers Committee—to discuss information management issues and information dissemination. The commission also continues to work closely with state and local agencies, professional and trade associations, and individuals on issues in the library/information field. One of these efforts resulted in a study of federal information centers and their relationship to the GPO Depository Library Program and existing libraries. In another effort, the commission is carrying forward its mandated responsibility to study and analyze the informational needs of rural America by working closely with the National Agricultural Library and also by giving support and guidance to the program of the Intermountain Community Learning Information Center Project (Colorado, Idaho, Montana, Utah, and Wyoming). This is a grass roots activity, essentially dependent on the state and local governments and the state extension services.

Resource Sharing and the Application of Technology

While many of its programs and activities relate to resource sharing, the commission's principal effort in this area has been the Task Force on the Role of the Special Library in Nationwide Networks and Cooperative Programs (jointly sponsored by NCLIS and the Special Libraries Association). This task force held a total of four meetings, and its final report will be completed early in 1982. Even before its final report, this task force can take credit for a significant accomplishment. One of the major factors deterring special libraries from joining networks using the services of OCLC, Inc. (Online Computer Library Center), a major on-line cataloging service, was the OCLC requirement that libraries using the service will contribute all of their current roman alphabet on-line cataloging to the OCLC data base as a condition for using that data base. This concern was expressed in a letter to Rowland C. W. Brown, president of OCLC, Inc., from the chairperson of the task force (Patricia W. Berger, National Bureau of Standards) and the president of the Special Libraries Association (James B. Dodd, Jr., Georgia Institute of Technology).

In his reply, Brown stated that the OCLC board does not intend to "require any library, including special libraries, to contribute holdings which are considered proprietary or classified and would not be available for general research, lending, etc. We understand perfectly your concern not only about divulging proprietary information itself, but even revealing the scope of special collections in a manner which would diminish competitive security." He adds,

> our Board has specifically accepted the fact that we do not interpret the intent to withhold the cataloging of such materials as being in conflict with the requirement to catalogue *all* current holdings. We accept the judgment of the library and in effect place the burden of honoring in good faith the requirement to contribute all holdings other than those that would generally create security . . . difficulties for the library. Obviously, budgetary or economic considerations or other reasons one might choose to revert to searching without the obligation of contributing must not be permitted to enter these decisions or we will severely impair the viability of the system.

This reply removes a substantial barrier to special library participation in network activities.

OTHER ACTIVITIES

The commission has continued its efforts to promote awareness of NCLIS, its activities and its goals in the library and information service community, including public, professional, and private organizations and individuals. Simultaneously, NCLIS has sought to improve its own awareness of developments in the community by scheduling both of its 1981 meetings in conjunction with meetings of major associations. The April meeting was held in Chicago, in conjunction with the National Information conference and exposition sponsored by the Information Industry Association, and the June meeting was held in Atlanta, in conjunction with the annual meeting of the Special Libraries Association.

FUTURE PLANS

During 1982, NCLIS plans to continue its work on the development of specifications for legislation and to investigate other new areas such as services to senior citizens and the changing role of the public library. NCLIS will also continue its assistance to Congress in oversight and legislative hearings on library legislation. It will be continuing its work with OMB on the implementation of PL 96-511, and the work with all agencies at all levels, as well as with professional and industry groups, on the improvement of library and information services to all citizens.

THE COPYRIGHT OFFICE: DEVELOPMENTS IN 1981

Library of Congress, Washington, DC 20559
202-287-8700

Victor W. Marton
Information Supervisor, Information and Reference Division

In 1981, the Copyright Office continued to develop new policies, regulations, and systems to carry out its responsibilities under the copyright law. On January 1, 1978, a completely new copyright statute (Title 17 of the U.S. Code) came into effect, superseding the Copyright Act of 1909 as amended, and making important changes in the copyright system.

The new law preempted virtually all state common law and statutory law that was equivalent to copyright and established a single federal system of copyright for all works, published or unpublished. Copyright protection begins from the moment a work is fixed in some tangible medium of expression, and in most instances lasts for the life of the author plus 50 years after the author's death. The existence of copyright in a work is therefore not contingent on registration in the Copyright Office, nor on the exercise of any other formalities.

However, all works protected by copyright are eligible for registration in the Copyright Office. Although registration is voluntary, it is a prerequisite to the initiation of an infringement suit. There are other advantages attached to registration; in the fiscal year ending September 30, 1981, registrations reached an all-time high of 471,178.

In spite of the fact that registration is voluntary, the law does contain a mandatory deposit requirement for all works published in the United States with a notice of copyright. In 1981, the Deposit and Acquisitions Section of the Copyright Office continued to enforce these requirements, obtaining many new acquisitions for the collections of the Library of Congress. With the severe reduction of funds available to the library for acquisitions, the enforcement of the mandatory deposit requirement is an increasingly important source of materials.

Under the new law, the Licensing Division of the Copyright Office administers the compulsory licensing systems for secondary transmissions of copyrighted material by cable television (CATV) and on jukeboxes. In calendar year 1981, the office collected and then invested in interest-bearing accounts over $1 million from jukebox license-fee receipts. This money is distributed to copyright owners by the Copyright Royalty Tribunal. The office also reported that over $24 million in cable royalty fees, collected in calendar year 1980, was available for distribution by the Copyright Royalty Tribunal. This year the operations of the Licensing Division have been affected by the fact that the new royalty rates established by the Copyright Royalty Tribunal in 1980 for both jukeboxes and CATV systems have been challenged by litigation that is still pending.

The Copyright Office also maintains a national copyright information service. The Information and Reference Division responded to an increasing work load in 1981 that included assisting a record number of visitors and replying to correspondence. Answers to questions, informational circulars and copies of the law, and regulations and application forms may be obtained free of charge by writing to the Copyright Office, Library of Congress, Washington, DC 20559, or by calling 202-287-8700 between 8:30 A.M. and 5:00 P.M. (eastern standard time) on weekdays. In 1981, the office established a 24-hour application-forms hotline [202-287-9100] that permits tape-recorded requests to be made.

SPECIAL PROJECTS

The copyright law assigns to the Copyright Office several projects that require reports to be made to Congress. The Copyright Office has already delivered two of these reports: one containing recommendations on whether the law should provide performance rights in sound recordings; the other on voluntary licensing agreements that were made concerning the use of nondramatic literary works by public broadcast stations.

In 1981 the Copyright Office submitted to Congress its report on the effect of the impending elimination of the "manufacturing clause" (section 601 of Title 17 of the U.S. Code) and the impact of this development on the U.S. book manufacturing and printing industries. This clause, which has been a feature of American copyright law since 1891, provides in its present form that certain nondramatic literary works by U.S. citizens or domiciliaries must be manufactured in the United States or Canada in order to enjoy full copyright protection. Pursuant to the terms of the present statute, this provision will expire on July 1, 1982. The Copyright Office's report concluded that the manufacturing clause is a barrier to free trade; that it should not be a condition of copyright; that it is alien to the purposes of copyright law; and that the provision should be allowed to expire. The report also expressed the view that other remedies, such as subsidies, duties, import quotas, or tax credits, would be more appropriate to provide any needed protection for the U.S. printing industry. In studying this problem, the office held meetings and hearings to solicit the views of the printing industry and the affected labor unions, as well as authors and publishers. In addition, the office was aided in its consideration of the issues by the Congressional Research Service of the Library of Congress, and by the Department of Commerce. The fiscal year closed without any further legislative action on the provision.

Work continued during 1981 in preparation for the Copyright Office report on library photocopying and related activities, to be submitted to the Congress at the beginning of 1983 as required by section 108(i) of the new copyright statute. Several meetings were held with members of the advisory committee established in 1978 to aid the Register of Copyrights in connection with plans for this review. The final in a series of regional hearings was held in New York City on January 28 and 29, 1981. Four surveys conducted by King Research, Inc., on library photocopying were largely completed by the end of FY 1981. Data from these surveys will be made available to the Copyright Office in December of 1981, and the final King report is due in March 1982. It should provide quantitative information to complement the testimony presented at the hearings. The information compiled in the regional hearings and subsequent written comments, along with the data from the surveys, should contribute substantially to the Copyright Office report.

Off-the-Air Taping for Educational Uses

In 1979, the House Judiciary Subcommittee on Courts, Civil Liberties, and the Administration of Justice formed an ad hoc committee of interested persons from among educators, copyright owners, public broadcasters, and artists' guilds to discuss possible guidelines on educational fair use of broadcast audiovisual works. Such guidelines have now been produced. Their central features are: (1) that off-the-air recordings can be made only at the request of, and can be used only by, an individual teacher but cannot be regularly recorded in anticipation of requests; (2) that there will be a fair use preview period during which there can be a limited number of actual classroom uses, with additional time for use by the teacher to evaluate whether to add the program to the curriculum; and (3) that, at the end of the preview period, the tape must be erased unless the permission of the copyright owner is obtained for longer retention.

LEGISLATIVE DEVELOPMENTS

FY 1981 was marked by substantial congressional activity in the copyright field. While several proposals involved matters that might be considered part of the unfinished business of copyright revision, others reflect new concerns emanating from experience under the new law.

Bills concerning copyright issues that were considered by Congress include proposals to establish a limited performance right in sound recordings through a compulsory license that would require payments to performers and producers of copyrighted works (H.R. 1805); establish protection for ornamental designs of useful articles (H.R. 20); secure the right of creators of pictorial, graphic, or sculptural works to prevent their distortion, mutilation, alteration, and destruction and to protect the honor and reputation of artists in relation to their work (H.R. 2908); and strengthen the laws against record, tape, and film piracy and counterfeiting (H.R. 8285 and S. 691). Several bills that would exempt certain groups from liability for public performances of music were introduced in the Senate and the House to broaden the three exemptions now found in section 110 of the copyright statute (S. 603, H.R. 2108, H.R. 2007, H.R. 3408, H.R. 2006, H.R. 3392). Other bills that were introduced proposed incentives for the arts and humanities (H.R. 148); amendment of the Internal Revenue Code of 1954 to remove certain limitations with respect to charitable donations of literary, musical, or artistic compositions (H.R. 444, S. 851, S. 852); and amendment of the copyright statute to provide a filing fee in lieu of a registration fee for original, supplementary, and renewal copyright claims.

Finally, hearings were held on three bills introduced to amend section 111 of the copyright law to provide greater protection for program suppliers while assuring continued cable access to broadcast signals through compulsory licensing (H.R. 3560); to eliminate the compulsory license for secondary transmission by CATV of distant, nonnetwork programming (H.R. 3528); and to replace the license requirement with full liability (H.R. 3844).

Copyright Protection for Computer Software

The issue of liability for computer uses of copyrighted works was not resolved before passage of the new copyright law in 1976. Because of this, Congress directed the National Commission on New Technological Uses of Copyrighted Works (CONTU) to study the emerging patterns in the computer field and to recommend, based on their findings, definitive copyright provisions to deal with the situation. In the interim, section 117 of the statute made clear that rights existing under the act of 1909 were not to be suspended, nor were there any new rights created that might have been denied under the 1909 act or under applicable common law principles. On July 31, 1978, CONTU issued its final report, which included proposals to amend the copyright law. H.R. 6934 [Ninety-sixth Congress, Second Session (1980)], entitled the "Computer Software Copyright Act of 1980" and introduced by Representative Robert W. Kastenmeier, adopted certain of CONTU's proposals. The provisions of H.R. 6934 were merged with H.R. 6933 [Ninety-sixth Congress, Second Session (1980)], section 10, prior to the former's passage by the House of Representatives and the Senate in November 1980. On December 12, 1980, President Carter signed the bill into law.

The bill amended section 101 of the act to add a specific definition of "computer programs" and amended section 117 to provide authorization for making copies or adaptations of computer programs in limited cases and under certain conditions. The bill also provided copyright protection for transfers of computer software through lease, sale, or other exchange. The House report accompanying the bill stated that the new law was not intended to restrict additional legal protection that states might provide to software against unfair competition or trade-secret laws.

COPYRIGHT REGULATIONS

FY 1981 proved to be an active one in the Copyright Office for the refinement of the office's statutory responsibilities through regulations. Many of the office's actions amended previously issued regulations to take into account added experience and changed circumstances, while other regulations were issued in final form for the first time during FY 1981.

The regulation to implement section 115, which provides for a compulsory license for making and distributing phonorecords, proved to be one of the most controversial regulations the Copyright Office was called on to prepare. The compulsory license permits the use of a nondramatic musical work without the consent of the copyright owner if certain conditions are met and royalties paid. Section 115 directs the Copyright Office to issue regulations governing the content and filing of certain notices and statements of account under the section. Interim regulations were issued during FY 1978. On December 29, 1980, the Copyright Office issued final regulations intended to make the compulsory license feasible while at the same time assuring that copyright owners receive full and prompt payment for all phonorecords that are made and distributed under the license.

Section 410 of the law provides that the Register shall determine whether or not the material deposited for registration constitutes "copyrightable subject matter" and, if it does not, registration is to be refused. The Copyright Office held a public hearing during FY 1980 to elicit comments, views, and information that would be useful in drafting regulations governing policies and practices relating to the registration of the graphic elements involved in the design of books and other printed publications. A review of the relevant written comments and oral testimony led the office to conclude that much of the protection sought for such works could be secured under current regulations and practices. Accordingly, the Copyright Office advised the public on June 10, 1981, that it was terminating its proposed rule making on the subject.

Paragraph (b) of section 411 of the copyright law provides for the service of advance notices of potential infringement of copyright for the purpose of preventing the unauthorized use of certain works that are being transmitted live at the same time that they are being fixed in tangible form for the first time. On May 29, 1981, the Copyright Office issued a final regulation governing the content and manner of service of such advance notices.

Section 601(b) (2) of the copyright law permits under certain conditions the importation of 2,000 copies of copyrighted English-language nondramatic literary works by U.S. citizens or domiciliaries manufactured outside of the United States or Canada that otherwise would be denied importation under the manufacturing clause. One of the conditions under the provision is that the importer must present to the U.S. Customs Service an import statement issued by the Copyright Office. The office published an interim regulation during FY 1978 establishing requirements governing the issuance of such import statements. A final regulation on this matter was published during FY 1981.

The Copyright Office took two actions during FY 1981 relating to registration fees. Under section 708(c) of the copyright law, the Register is authorized to deduct all or any part of the registration fee otherwise prescribed by section 708 to cover the administrative costs of processing a refusal to register a claim to copyright. The Copyright Office issued an amendment to the regulations during FY 1981 that would permit the office to retain fees submitted for registration in cases where an application is rejected. The amendment also provides that, in cases of mistaken or excess payment, refunds in the amount of $5 or less will be made only by specific request.

Finally, the Copyright Office adopted regulations during FY 1981 to remove or amend as either no longer applicable or obsolete certain portions of the Copyright Office Regulations. Thus, (1) a section stating the prices for parts of the Catalog of Copyright Entries was deleted, since that information is no longer correct; (2) a section dealing with catalog cards to be submitted in certain cases by the copyright claimant was deleted, since the requirement is not applicable under the new copyright law; (3) a provision for a fee to be charged for recording certain agreements between copyright owners and public broadcasting entities was removed, since it is no longer possible to record agreements of this kind; (4) the section dealing with recording notices of use was dropped, since the new law does not call for recording notices of use; (5) a section was amended to make clear that ad interim registrations are not possible under the new law; (6) another section was amended to specify that the copyright notice provisions based on the copyright law of 1909, as amended, apply only to works published before January 1, 1978; and (7) a section was amended to eliminate reference to certain classes of works established under the old law, since the new statute provides a new system of classification.

INTERNATIONAL ACTIVITIES

In 1981, international copyright concerns continued to center on two principal tasks: assessing the impact of new technology on the rights of authors and copyright proprietors, and facilitating access to protected works by developing countries. In the former area, action has been more tentative and exploratory; in the latter, significant developments in the implementation of the Universal Copyright Convention's preferential system for developing states took place.

In 1981, in meetings held at both nongovernmental and governmental levels, copyright specialists discussed copyright protection for computer software, the spread of home videorecording technology, the implications for copyright of storage and retrieval of protected works, and the liability for the retransmission of copyrighted broadcast programming by cable television.

In June 1981, an official U.S. delegation that included David Ladd, Register of Copyrights, visited the People's Republic of China to discuss copyright issues of concern to both countries. The purposes of the mission, which toured both Beijing and Shanghai at the request of the Publishers Association of China, were to deliver lectures on American copyright law; to assess the preparedness of the Chinese to adopt a domestic copyright law; and on the basis of such a law, to begin to develop mutual copyright relations pursuant to obligations assumed by both countries under the 1979 Bilateral Trade Agreement.

THE CENTER FOR THE BOOK IN THE LIBRARY OF CONGRESS

Washington, DC 20540

John Y. Cole

*Executive Director**

The Center for the Book in the Library of Congress is a national catalyst for promoting the book and the printed word. Drawing on the resources of the Library of Congress (LC), the center works closely with the 30 organizations represented on its national advisory board to raise the public's book "awareness," to use other media to promote reading, to stimulate the study of books, to encourage the international flow of books and printed materials, and to improve the quality of book production. It pursues these goals primarily by bringing together members of the book, educational, and business communities for symposia and projects. The center also sponsors lectures and publications concerned with reading development and promotion; the role of the book in society, past, present, and future; and the international role of the book.

The Center for the Book was established in October 1977 by PL 95-129. In creating the center, the U.S. Congress responded to Librarian of Congress Daniel J. Boorstin's concern that in the age of broadcasting the book was in danger of "being stifled, drowned, suffocated, buried, obscured, mislaid, misunderstood, ununderstood, unread—from neglect and from the rising level of the increasing flood." Thus the Center for the Book in the Library of Congress was created to help "keep the book flourishing."

The center is a grand example of cooperation between the public and private sectors. While LC provides administrative support, the center's programs and publications are supported primarily by tax-deductible contributions from individuals and organizations. True to its catalytic function, the center has a full-time staff of only two people. Principal Center for the Book projects are outlined below. Further information about the center and the publications mentioned is available from The Center for the Book, Library of Congress, Washington, DC 20540.

READING DEVELOPMENT AND PROMOTION

In October 1981 CBS Television and the Library of Congress, through the Center for the Book, launched their third season of "Read More about It," a project aimed at "linking the pleasure, power and excitement of books and television." Through 30-second messages after selected CBS network presentations, "Read More about It" urges television viewers to visit their local libraries and bookstores to obtain books about the program's subject. This year's programs included "Skokie," "Bill," "Baryshnikov in Hollywood," "Agatha Christie's Murder Is Easy," "Ivanhoe," and "The Blue and the Gray." Many libraries and bookstores around the country plan exhibits and distribute their own materials in connection with the telecasts. "Read More about It" originated with a Center for the Book symposium on "Television, the Book, and the Classroom." Proceedings from the symposium are available from the Library of Congress.

"Books Make a Difference," a project intended to help libraries and other community organizations promote books and reading, completed its first phase in 1981. With

---

*John Y. Cole is on leave of absence from September 1981 to September 1982. Judith O'Sullivan is interim executive director.

support from the center and in cooperation with Virginia Polytechnic Institute and State University in Blacksburg, Virginia, two journalists traveled over 30,000 miles throughout the United States interviewing people about books that shaped their lives. They asked two vital questions: "What book made a difference in your life?" and "What was that difference?" The thought-provoking and entertaining responses provide ample evidence of the importance of books and reading to citizens at every level of society. During the second phase of the project the center is encouraging other organizations to incorporate the "Books Make a Difference" idea into their own programs and to demonstrate the usefulness of the idea in local communities. "Books Make a Difference" was the theme for several segments of National Public Radio's "All Things Considered" and for the 1981 American Book Awards promotion and awards ceremony.

In November 1981 the center hosted a national symposium on "Reading and Successful Living: The Family-School Partnership." Speakers included Robert Andringa, executive director of the Education Commission of the States; Mrs. George Bush; and representatives from the four sponsoring organizations: the National Parent-Teacher Association, the International Reading Association, the American Association of School Administrators, and the American Association of School Librarians. Each sponsoring organization is incorporating practical ideas from the symposium into its own national, regional, and local programs.

THE BOOK IN SOCIETY—PAST, PRESENT, AND FUTURE

The Center for the Book's programs for stimulating appreciation of the crucial role of books in our society involve scholars, educators, publishers, librarians, booksellers, and many others. On the historical side, one of its most important activities is the Engelhard Lecture Series on the Book, a commissioned series of public lectures by prominent scholars. The most recent Engelhard lectures have been "From Bibliothèque du Roi to World Information Network: The National Library in Historical Perspective," by Ian Willison of the British Library, and "Work and Culture in an Eighteenth-Century Printing Shop," by historian Robert Darnton of Princeton University. Another historically oriented 1981 program was a symposium celebrating the completion of the 754-volume *National Union Catalog, Pre-1956 Imprints* and featuring an international panel of publishers, librarians, and scholars. A booklet based on this meeting is available from the Library of Congress.

A meeting in the spring of 1981 pointed up the strong relationship between oral history and the printed word and emphasized the role of the spoken word as testimony for history. "Rooted in America" was a panel discussion among three well-known personalities who have recorded their memoirs for the William E. Wiener Oral History Library of the American Jewish Committee. The panelists included novelist and playwright Jerome Weidman, lyricist Sylvia Fine Kaye, and opera and concert star Jan Peerce. Author and commentator Edwin Newman was moderator. An exhibit illustrating the tape-to-type process supplemented the program.

The role of the book in contemporary society was explored in a talk on "Video Literacy in the Computer Age" by Lewis M. Branscomb, vice-president and chief scientist of the IBM Corporation. The director of the Princeton University Press, Herbert Bailey, chaired a meeting hosted by the center that brought publishers, paper manufacturers, and research librarians together to discuss "Paper for Book Longevity." This meeting was sponsored by the Council on Library Resources, Inc. *The State of the Book World 1980*, issued by the center in 1981, contains perceptive comments by critic Alfred Kazin, publisher Dan Lacy, and educator Ernest L. Boyer. Proceedings of two other Center for the Book symposia were published in 1981 under the titles *The Textbook in American Society* and *Responsibilities of the American Book Community*.

THE INTERNATIONAL ROLE OF THE BOOK

The center's international program is carried out in the spirit of the Charter of the Book, set forth in 1972 as part of the International Book Year sponsored by the United Nations Educational, Scientific, and Cultural Organization (UNESCO). The charter stresses the importance of the free flow of books between countries and the essential role of books in promoting international understanding. At one of the center's initial organizational meetings in 1978, it was agreed that the following topics were of potential interest to the center: the free flow of book and printed materials within countries and across national boundaries; publishing in both developed and developing countries; international promotion of reading; the role of government in book development and promotion; translation; universal acceptance of domestic and international copyright laws; problems of book distribution; language training; and the development of library science and the training of librarians in foreign countries.

A booklet based on a major symposium, *The International Flow of Information: A Trans-Pacific Perspective*, was published in 1981. This meeting, sponsored in cooperation with the Graduate School of Library Studies at the University of Hawaii and the U.S. International Communication Agency, emphasized means by which the two-way flow of information between the East Asia-Pacific region and the United States could be improved. In 1982, the center will publish *U.S. International Book Programs*, a booklet describing international book programs sponsored by U.S. government agencies and selected private organizations. Other center activities include a proposed forum to explore whether the United States needs an organization devoted to promoting American books abroad and what shape that organization might take, and participation in the planning for the UNESCO World Congress on Books, to be held in London in the spring of 1982.

FEDERAL LIBRARY COMMITTEE

Adams Bldg., Rm. 1023, Library of Congress
Washington, DC 20540
202-287-6055

James P. Riley
Executive Director

In 1965, the Federal Library Committee (FLC) was established to consider federal library policy and practices of the three branches of the government, in order to provide a means to develop and coordinate cooperative federal library programs on a government-wide basis. Special attention is given to activities designed to minimize increased costs to libraries and the government. Thus, serving the collective needs of federal agencies for more efficient and effective library services to the government, the FLC has conducted studies, projects, contracts, and services to achieve better use of federal library resources and facilities, to provide more effective planning and development, and to encourage efficient economies of operation in federal libraries.

Commercial information services used by federal libraries, particularly automated information services, offer economies of scale, such as lower rates to high volume users, which are otherwise attainable to many agencies only by pooling resources and consolidating certain administrative functions. The Federal Library and Information Network (FEDLINK), a self-supporting organization of the Federal Library Committee, offers such centralized, cooperative services to all federal library and information centers. The FLC office also provides coordination and cooperation with non-federal libraries and information centers through various activities, such as contracting with network offices to assist federal libraries in the field; participating in the planning and presentation of training programs; acting on the advisory committees and councils of computerized bibliographic networks; and serving as federal representatives and consultants to networks, library organizations and associations, and the information community. Thus, through such activities, the FLC is working toward achieving better use of federal library resources and facilities, which consequently should promote more effective federal service to the nation at large.

During FY 1981, FEDLINK membership grew to 365 libraries nationwide, cooperating on 15 FLC contracts with commercial vendors for on-line data base services.

During the year, FLC/FEDLINK network members approved a Mission Statement, which is a long-range plan that prepares for increased networking activities to support automation activities for sharing resources and minimizing increased costs.

ON-LINE BIBLIOGRAPHIC DATA BASE SERVICES

An on-line shared cataloging service contract with the Online Computer Library Center (OCLC) has 328 participating federal libraries. Federal records added to the OCLC data base consist of approximately 3,153,000 logical records that are growing at a rate of 60,000 logical records a month. These federal records are available to the membership for the production of customized products such as Computer Output Microfilm/Fiche (COM), book catalogs, accessions lists, regional union catalogs, special awareness bibliographies, and members' circulation and acquisitions systems through contracts with Blackwell North America and Informatics. These output tape-processing contracts have allowed federal libraries to extract their records from the FLC/FEDLINK master tape data base for the production of customized products.

Relating to shared cataloging activity, FLC conducted fifteen three-day cataloging workshops on changes in the Anglo-American Cataloguing Rules (AACR 2) in Washington, D.C., Philadelphia, St. Louis, Knoxville, San Francisco, New Orleans, Denver, Atlanta, Boston, and Cincinnati. To further assist members in AACR 2 conversion, the office prepared an AACR 2 manual under contract with Arnold Wajenberg, University of Illinois, and assistance was received by the FLC/FEDLINK Quality Control Committee and the Library of Congress, Descriptive Cataloging Policy Office. The manual was distributed to FLC/FEDINK members and other network offices.

In addition to the AACR 2 workshops, the FLC conducted over 45 training sessions on OCLC basic cataloging, interlibrary loan, serials check-in and cataloging, acquisitions, the on-line Name Address Directory, and on-line fund accounting process. The FLC office also contracted with the Bibliographical Center for Research (BCR), the Wisconsin Library Consortium (WLC), the Midwest Region Library Network (MIDLNET), and the AMIGOS Bibliographic Council (AMIGOS) to provide OCLC training to FEDLINK members located outside of the Middle Atlantic region.

To offer members alternative or additional on-line cataloging and related services, contracts were signed with the Washington (State) Library Network (WLN) and the Research Library Group (RLG) for subject access to its Research Libraries Information Network (RLIN), and with Sigma Data Computing Corporation for acquisitions use.

On-Line Information Retrieval Services

A consolidated request for waivers from the General Services Administration (GSA) for the Teleprocessing Services Program (TSP) and Delegation of Procurement Authority (DPA) was granted for the bibliographic services mentioned above and for nine on-line retrieval services: Bibliographical Retrieval Services (BRS); Lockheed, DIALOG; System Development Corporation (SDC), ORBIT; Mead Data Central (MDC); LEXIS/NEXIS; New York Times, INFOBANK; Legislate, Inc., LEGISLATE; West Publishing Company, WESTLAW; Dow Jones News/Retrieval; and Participation Systems, Inc., POLITECHS/EIES.

Shared Retrieval Services

To support shared local retrieval services, contracts with BRS, Lockheed, MDC, and West were signed, which enable members to load their own data files to retrieve information while using the full range of the search capabilities offered by the respective vendors.

Shared Acquisitions Services

FLC continued its shared acquisitions services program with Sigma Data Computing Corporation, which operates a minicomputer system called DATALIB, thus allowing federal participants to share a common on-line data base.

The OCLC on-line Acquisitions Subsystem began operation in late FY 1981. The office presented to the membership a program on the results of the test and evaluation periods, and a series of nine demonstrations of the new subsystem before the end of the fiscal year. It is anticipated that the integration of the Acquisitions Subsystem with the OCLC on-line cataloging data base will interest members in FY 1982 and will constitute a major training activity.

AUTOMATION CONSULTATION SERVICES

Library automation/management consulting services have been established as a new activity to begin in FY 1982, and will assist members in the development of automation requirements documentation, including Request for Proposals (RFPs) and microcomputer systems; evaluation of contractors; and planning of seminars on library automation to prepare library management and staff for automation planning.

OFFICE AUTOMATION

In April, a WANG VS minicomputer system with three work-stations, an operator's station, 60 megabytes of disk storage, a 250 line per minute printer, and a daisy wheel (letter quality) printer, was installed. The system came equipped with word-processing, giving the office three word processing work-stations immediately.

Applications already developed and in operation for the system include processing, mailing lists, on-line customer file of over 1,200 names and addresses, invoice processing, call-for-estimates and interagency agreements files, customer telephone directory, and management reports including annual funding and financial cost projections by service.

SURVEY OF FEDERAL LIBRARIES

The survey of federal libraries conducted in cooperation with the Learning Resources Branch of the National Center for Education Statistics (NCES), which will update the findings of the FY 1972 survey of federal libraries and provide data to the Library General Information Survey (LIBGIS) of the NCES, will be completed in FY 1982. The LIBGIS system, of which the federal survey is an integral part, is used to collect comparable information from all of the various types of libraries.

The data collected in the survey should provide planners in the legislative and executive branches of government with an overview of the scope and diversity of library operations. The data should also assist library administrators in developing uniform reporting systems and in strengthening both the interchange of resources among federal libraries and efforts to meet national needs. Accurate data on the size of collections, staff, and budgets of individual federal libraries will assist departments and agencies that are planning library services.

INTERGOVERNMENTAL LIBRARY COOPERATION PROJECT

The Intergovernmental Library Cooperation Project (ILCP), jointly sponsored by the National Commission on Libraries and Information Science (NCLIS) and the Library of Congress, is charged with the task of determining ways to improve the coordination of resources and services among federal libraries and between federal and non-federal libraries to meet national, state and local needs. For ILCP to do so effectively, government agencies at all levels must work together to make information services available to the maximum extent.

During this past year, a number of data-gathering activities were undertaken, and an advisory committee comprised of individuals representing major government agencies was established. Visits with federal librarians in Regions V, VI, and IX of the Federal Regional Council were completed, and questionnaires were sent to over 400 field libraries in the three regions. Thirty-one parent agencies in the Washington, D.C., area were visited. Findings from both the field visits and the questionnaires indicate that federal libraries throughout the country tend to look to non-federal libraries at the local and state level for cooperation and support. One notable exception is in the case of medical libraries, where local interagency cooperation is very strong. Federal libraries throughout the country generally are prepared to share their collections and services with their non-federal counterparts. The study also documents the extent of cooperative activities among federal libraries and between federal and non-federal libraries. Although much of this activity centers on resource sharing and interlibrary loan, some involves shared processing, especially cataloging through the OCLC system, and cooperative collection development. To extend this kind of activity, which would mean improved operations and service in the face of continuing restrictions in budgets and personnel, calls for a rethinking of traditional and current practices, a search for cooperative solutions, and the provision of improved interactive and linked communications facilities. [See also the summary report of the Intergovernmental Library Cooperation Project by Alphonse F. Trezza in Part 4 of this volume.]

SLOW-SCAN TV & TELEFACSIMILE PROJECT

The experimental project to use slow-scan television and telefacsimile equipment for transmission, communications, and exchange of information was completed and an evaluation report written, of which copies were sent to the Educational Resources Information Center (ERIC), where it will be available for purchase after January 1982.

The four federal libraries participating in the experimental use of slow-scan television, as well as telefacsimile, were National Oceanic & Atmospheric Administration (NOAA), Boulder, Colorado; Corps of Engineers Libraries at Fort Belvoir and Vicksburg, Mississippi; and the National Agricultural Library. Libraries participating only in the use of telefacsimile were at the National Science Foundation and at the following Department of Energy facilities: Argonne National Laboratory, Brookhaven National Laboratory, Lawrence Berkeley Laboratory, and Oak Ridge National Laboratory.

FLC/NOAA AUTOMATED LIBRARY & INFORMATION SYSTEM

In a cooperative project funded by the National Oceanic & Atmospheric Administration (NOAA), FLC assisted in the competitive selection of a contractor to develop NOAA's Automated Library & Information System (ALIS). In December, a contract was signed with Systems Control, Inc. (SCI). The system is based on a TANDEM dual processor minicomputer and will service NOAA's catalog maintenance (interfaced with OCLC cataloging), serials control, on-line catalog searching and other functions.

CONTINUING EDUCATION

Three educational programs, namely instructional materials on chemistry for non-chemists, computer technology and information science applications, and continuing education at the para-professional level, were continued.

DEMONSTRATION PROJECT WITH ACQUISITION INSTITUTE

In July 1981, the FLC office entered into an agreement with the Acquisition Institute (AI) in Washington, D.C., regarding the latter's automated data system, Sources for Uniform Procurement Planning, Library Evaluation/Retrieval System (SUPPLIERS). Through this agreement, FLC will have access to information pertaining to private sector contractors with the resources and capacity to assure meaningful competition for the materials, products, and services required to meet the operating needs of government. Expected users of the service are government managers, planners, technologists, attorneys, librarians, and acquisition professionals such as contracting officers, contract and grant administrators, purchasing agents, and buyers employed in or supporting government uniform procurement.

FEDERAL HIGHWAY ADMINISTRATION COOPERATIVE CATALOGING PROJECT

After considerable work had been undertaken with the Federal Highway Administration (FHWA) and the Department of Transportation (DoT) to complete plans to conduct a study in cooperative cataloging with state transportation libraries during FY 1982, the project was cancelled due to budgetary cuts. The purpose of the project was to demonstrate the usefulness of a cooperative cataloging activity for state transportation libraries working with DoT and FHWA in sharing cataloging resources through the OCLC system.

OTHER ACTIVITIES

The Federal Library Committee held the following meetings: "An RFP Writer's Workshop: Contracting for Library and Information Services"; "NOAA Automated Library Information System (ALIS): A Prototype," sponsored by FLC and NOAA; and "The National Library of Medicine, Lister Hall Center Integrated Library System (ILS)."

The office cooperated with the Defense Technical Information Center (DTIC), OCLC, and LC to publish and distribute the *Preliminary Edition Summary of MARC Format Specifications for Technical Reports* (LC, October 1980), taking into consideration the respective needs of both the cataloging community that follows the AACR 2 cataloging rules and the information community that uses the COSATI (Committee on Scientific and Technical Information) rules for descriptive cataloging.

Federal Libraries

THE LIBRARY OF CONGRESS

Washington, D.C. 20540
202-287-5000

James W. McClung
Public Information Specialist

The Library of Congress, in late 1980 and in 1981, initiated activity in a number of areas. Librarian of Congress Daniel J. Boorstin announced the creation of the Council of Scholars, which held two meetings, the first of these in conjunction with a major symposium and exhibition on creativity. The library froze its existing card catalogs and adopted the second edition of the Anglo-American Cataloguing Rules (AACR 2) on January 2, 1981. Also, during that same month, the library celebrated the completion of the massive *National Union Catalog, Pre-1956 Imprints*. Moving into the new Madison Building continued to require a lot of the library staff's time and attention; Madison-related activities culminated in November with the dedication of Madison Memorial Hall by President Reagan and the opening of a major exhibition on Madison's life. The National Library Service for the Blind and Physically Handicapped celebrated its fiftieth anniversary, and the Copyright Office marked the hundred and fiftieth anniversary of music copyright with several events.

COUNCIL OF SCHOLARS

The first meeting of the Council of Scholars took place in November 1980. Held in conjunction with a symposium on creativity, it was sponsored by the library in cooperation with the Carnegie Foundation for the Advancement of Teaching, and received major support from Standard Oil Company of California (Chevron). The symposium was the first of a series planned by the council to address major topics of concern that cut across academic disciplines and specific intellectual interests.

Membership on the Council of Scholars rotates on a two-year basis. The following list identifies members initially appointed to the council, their institutions and fields of interest: Meyer H. Abrams, Cornell University, English literature; James S. Ackerman, Harvard University, fine arts; Paul Berg, Stanford University, biochemistry; Subrahmanyan Chandrasekhar, University of Chicago, astrophysics; Philip D. Curtin, Johns Hopkins University, history; Elizabeth Eisenstein, University of Michigan, history; John Hope Franklin, University of Chicago, history; Jacob W. Getzels, University of Chicago, education and behavioral sciences; Nathan Glazer, Harvard University, education and social structure; Chauncy D. Harris, University of Chicago, geography; Gerald Holton, Harvard University, physics; Henry Kissinger, former Secretary of State; Maxine Kumin, Library of Congress consultant in poetry, literature; Archibald MacLeish, former Librarian of Congress, literature; Myres S. McDougal, Yale University, law; Yehudi Menuhin, violinist, conductor, musicologist; William Meredith, former Library of Congress consultant in poetry; Jaroslav J. Pelikan, Yale University, history and religious studies (chairman of the Council of Scholars); Ernest Samuels, Northwestern University, humanities; Arthur Schlesinger, Jr., City University of New York, humanities; Carl Schorske, Princeton University, history; Theodore W. Schultz, University of Chicago, economics; and Edward G. Seidensticker, Columbia University, Japanese studies. Subsequent appointments to the council included novelist Saul Bellow and Leopold D. Ettlinger of the Center for Advanced Study in the Visual Arts. The appointment of the Inspector General of Archives of Spain, Vicenta Cortés Alonso, to the council was announced in the early fall of 1981. Loren Graham, professor of the history of science at the Massachusetts Institute of Technology and Woodrow Wilson Center fellow, and Walter Berns, resident scholar at the American Enterprise Institute, became members in November. Council membership now totals 28.

The council, which will advise the library about current intellectual and scholarly concerns and suggest directions for collection development and various library services, met again at the library in April and November. Proceedings of the symposium on creativity were published in November.

JAMES MADISON MEMORIAL BUILDING

Over the past decade and particularly during the past year, the Madison Building has been of great significance both symbolically and actually. In November, James Madison Memorial Hall, the nation's only memorial to its fourth president, was dedicated by the fortieth president of the United States before a gathering of library officials and government dignitaries, including the Chief Justice of the United States, members of the cabinet, and members of Congress. In addition, Librarian Daniel J. Boorstin escorted President and Mrs. Reagan on a tour of the new Madison Building exhibition galleries, located adjacent to the memorial hall. The inaugural exhibit, "James Madison and the Search for Nationhood," brings together manuscripts, prints, and other documents as well as many examples of the decorative arts (furnishings, paintings, and silver) that document the life and times of Madison. Over 60 American institutions and private lenders contributed to the exhibition, which includes the largest number of portraits of Madison ever assembled. An accompanying publication, *James Madison and the Search for Nationhood*, a profusely illustrated essay by Robert Rutland, editor of the Madison papers, is for sale for $18 from the Superintendent of Documents, U.S. Government Printing Office, Washington, DC 20402 (Stock No. 030-000-00133-8).

On the more practical side, the library continued to move its staff and collections into the new building. Either all or nearly all of four of the eight library departments now occupy the building: the Copyright Office, Congressional Research Service, Law Library, and Processing Services. In addition, more than 34 million items comprising the manuscript collections were moved, and plans were being made final for the last moves, in the coming year, of the some 15 million items in the collections of the music, motion picture and recorded sound, prints and photographs, and serial and government publications collections.

By the end of the fiscal year, nearly 90 percent of the staff scheduled to occupy the new building had moved. Additional office space was being readied for the relocation of the major offices of three other library departments, thus leaving room in the library's older buildings for shifting and expanding the collections and moving many units back to Capitol Hill. Having been housed temporarily in the Washington Navy Yard since the summer of 1964 with the move of the old Card Division, the library no longer has any offices in that facility.

NATIONAL LIBRARY SERVICE FOR THE BLIND AND PHYSICALLY HANDICAPPED

Marking its fiftieth year of service, the National Library Service for the Blind and Physically Handicapped (NLS/BPH) circulated more than 18 million braille and recorded books and magazines to more than 800,000 readers. Two extensive research studies were completed that confirmed the need to continue current program improvements.

The first study, a survey to determine the extent of the eligible user population not being served by or not aware of the NLS/BPH program, revealed that there are 3.1 million people in the United States eligible for the program and that awareness of the program was highest among those over 65 years of age. Another major survey, "Readership Characteristics and Attitudes: Service to Blind and Physically Handicapped Library Users," showed that approximately 50 percent of these readers are 65 years or older and that 57 percent had at least a high school education. Another finding supports the conclusion that more effort is needed to extend services to eligible institutionalized patrons.

A third study completed in 1981 revealed that volunteer contributions to the library's free reading program made up a minimum of $3 million a year. Still another study was concluded on the methods, processes, and costs of producing braille magazines and books.

STAFF, BUDGET, AND SERVICES

At the end of FY 1981, 5,183 people were in the library's employ. For FY 1982, the library is operating on an appropriation of $189,827,000, based on a continuing resolution (PL 97-51) that funds library operations through September 30, 1982. Included in this legislation was an appropriation of $4 million to the Architect of the Capitol for restoration and fire-safety work in the Thomas Jefferson Building, the original site of the library completed in 1897, and the John Adams Building, which the library annexed in 1939. The appropriation covers the design, testing, and installation of automatic sprinklers in the bookstacks of both buildings to help alleviate existing fire hazards, and the funding of a complete design package, including cost estimates, of the overall restoration project.

Other legislation affecting the library included proposed bills to restore a tax incentive for the donation of self-generated manuscripts and artwork materials to libraries, museums, and other nonprofit institutions. Another bill would change the Copyright Office's registration fee to a registration filing fee, thus helping the office reduce its administrative costs in handling claims. In testimony on a bill providing for television coverage of Senate proceedings, the library indicated its willingness to be a depository for the tapes of the proceedings.

The Copyright Office reported 471,178 registrations for fiscal year 1981, surpassing its all-time high of the preceding year. Other production figures were also high, and the Copyright Office was active in its ongoing review of certain provisions of the new copyright law and activities affected by it: the manufacturing clause, the five-year review of photocopying, and compulsory licensing regulations for cable television.

In FY 1981, more than 969,937 readers used the various public reading rooms of the library, and nearly 1,890,000 volumes and items were circulated to readers from the collections. More than 166,000 items were loaned outside the Library of Congress. The Law Library responded to some 300,000 research requests from all sources and circulated more than 740,000 items in Law Library reading rooms; more than 3,000 items were loaned from the law collections. The Congressional Research Service (CRS) responded in 1981 more than 376,000 times to the legislative, oversight, and representational needs of Congress and opened another Information Distribution Center in the James Madison Memorial Building. CRS distributed record numbers of its products to congressional staff during FY 1981.

The Chief Officers of State Library Agencies (COSLA) met at the library in April, and a week-long Cooperative Reference Exchange, funded by the Western Council of State Libraries and conducted by Library of Congress staff, was held in September for 25 senior reference staff members from 20 western states.

The American Folklife Center continued an active program of concerts, workshops, films, and publications, including *Blue Ridge Harvest: A Region's Folklife in Photographs*, available from the Superintendent of Documents for $4.75 (Stock No. 030-000-00127-3). The center coordinated an exhibit, entitled "Generation to Generation," of photographs from library collections that depict the transmission of culture from older to younger citizens. The exhibit, prepared to coincide with the White House Conference on Aging, will be a Library of Congress traveling exhibit by mid-1982. The center's Archive of Folk Song was officially renamed the Archive of Folk Culture to reflect the scope of its collections. By the fall of 1981, the Federal Cylinder Project had preserved more than 2,500 of the nearly 3,000 early cylinder recordings in the archive and prepared them for duplication.

The Center for the Book's January 1981 symposium celebrating the completion of the *National Union Catalog* opened an active year of lectures, workshops, publications, and other projects. A complete report on the center's activities appears earlier in Part 1 of this volume.

COLLECTIONS

The collections of the Library of Congress increased to 78,641,212 items in FY 1981, with especially strong growth rates in the areas of manuscripts, photographs, and microforms. Notable acquisitions augmented the library's collections of materials from the People's Republic of China, and holdings of music scores and memorabilia, personal papers of notable Americans, prints, photographs, drawings, and rare books. A major acquisition was the Eames collection, comprising the papers and working materials of Charles Eames (1907-1978). A $500,000 grant from IBM made the acquisition possible and will support projects to process and interpret the collection. The materials include original negatives and prints of each of the 106 films Eames created, business correspondence from 1944 to 1978, approximately 400,000 color slides, 31,000 black-and-white photographs, production materials from exhibits, and drawings for all the major furniture designs.

Another important acquisition in 1981 was a collection of the papers of Roy Wilkins, executive director emeritus of the NAACP, presented by the donor before his death. The papers of biologist and environmentalist Barry Commoner, Congressman John Brademas, and Defense Secretary Caspar Weinberger were also added to the library's collections. Other important pictorial acquisitions included the 60,000-item Grassl file of American magazine advertising from 1890 to 1950, and the Seagram County Court House Archives, a 1974-1976 documentary project sponsored by Joseph E. Seagram and Sons, Inc., that records more than 1,100 examples of the type of architecture exemplified by the Seagram Building. This cataloged collection includes more than 11,000 photographic negatives, 8,000 reference prints, and 2,500 master prints.

New special collections included 300 fine American and English first editions presented by Herman Finkelstein, and a substantial group of pamphlets, broadsides, and ephemera—materials frequently produced in small numbers—important in the study of American left-wing politics. Robert H. Power presented to the library for addition to the Hans P. Kraus Sir Francis Drake Collection (see *Bowker Annual 1981*, p. 85) a fine 1596 manuscript document about Drake's estate.

Access to the library's general book collections was greatly improved in 1981 by the expansion of the computer catalog center following the freezing of the library's existing card catalogs, and by concentrated efforts to inventory, weed out, or replace portions of the collections at the same time material was moved into space vacated by those divisions transferred to the Madison Building. The automated Book Paging System has significantly reduced response time for requests for books.

CATALOGING AND NETWORKING

The calendar year 1981 began with a smooth transition on day 1—January 2, 1981, the date selected by the library for the adoption of AACR 2 and for freezing the library's existing major card catalogs. In frequent discussions, interpretations of AACR 2 rules were refined, and manuals to supplement rules for the cataloging of manuscript items and cartographic and graphic materials were developed. The library's participation in AACR 2 training institutes in the United States went international in 1981, with library representatives discussing AACR 2 implementation in southern Asia, the Far East, and elsewhere.

Processing Services staff have also concentrated on planning and policymaking for increased activity in the collection, and custody and control of microforms. Internal procedures were developed for the bibliographic control of microforms via minimal level cataloging (MLC), and it was also decided to create MLC records for many seldom-requested titles of low research value that might otherwise not be cataloged for many years. A new set of cataloging priorities was instituted in midyear by which primary emphasis would be placed on the content of or need for a particular work. Previously, the library had based its cataloging priorities on the method of acquisition (e.g., by copyright, gift, or exchange), or on other internal library requirements.

Editorial work on the *Supplement* to the *National Union Catalog: Pre-1956 Imprints* (*NUC*) was completed in January 1981, bringing to a close the 14-year effort to publish, in 755 volumes, the most complete record extant of the first 500 years of the printed word. Plans to continue publishing *NUC* in a new format were assessed in light of a survey to which over 3,000 American libraries responded. The library is now reviewing its plans to publish *NUC* in a register/index format. Survey respondents stated an overwhelming preference for publication in microfiche.

The Cataloging in Publication (CIP) Division also surveyed its users in 1981 and received responses from more than 70 percent of the 2,000 U.S. libraries that received questionnaires. Respondents found the CIP program useful and valuable. As of July 1, the tenth anniversary of the program, CIP data had been provided for over 220,000 titles submitted by more than 2,500 publishers.

The Network Development Office through its Network Advisory Committee continued its involvement in the area of national network planning. Open hearings were held at both the midwinter and annual conferences of the American Library Association on two topics: governance for a nationwide network, and the ownership/distribution of bibliographic data.

The Cataloging Distribution Service (CDS) developed a new CDS Alert Service to replace the old proofsheet service. By year's end CDS had added CIP records to those available on a weekly basis to customers who order notices for any combination of over 1,800 subject categories identified in the CDS Alert Directory, or for any combination of the 22 broad subject categories representing the primary letter categories of the LC classification system. CDS also continued to work on the completion of the second phase of card service automation, the DEMAND System, which will provide on-demand printing of 5.5 million non-MARC (Machine Readable Cataloging) records in all languages. The system is to be fully operational in early 1982.

The fifth annual cooperative meeting between the Library of Congress and the National Library of Canada took place in October in Quebec, and the next annual meeting was planned for Washington, D.C., for late 1982. In addition to discussions of technical processing and networking programs, methods of preservation, especially mass deacidification of books and optical disk storage, were given considerable attention.

OTHER HIGHLIGHTS

Other exhibits in 1981 included displays of photographs from the Seagram County Court House Archives, European and American posters from the late nineteenth century to the present, photographs by the White House News Photographers Association, and memorabilia tracing the history of the Kennedy Center for the Performing Arts, which celebrated its tenth anniversary. An exhibition entitled "The World Encompassed" honored donors to the library's collections and displayed many items that had never been on view. On that occasion, numerous distinguished guests joined Librarian of Congress Daniel J. Boorstin for a dinner in the Great Hall to celebrate the exploring spirit of the collector and the civic responsibility of the donor.

Other 1981 publications of note, all of which are available from the Superintendent of Documents, included *The Openhearted Audience: Ten Authors Talk about Writing for Children* ($9; Stock No. 030-001-00089-3); *Fire Insurance Maps in the Library of Congress*, a checklist of the Sanborn Collection numbering some 700,000 individual sheets of maps ($29; Stock No. 030-004-00018-3); *Special Collections in the Library of Congress: A Selective Guide* ($12; Stock No. 030-001-00092-3); *Japanese National Government Publications in the Library of Congress: A Bibliography* ($13; Stock No. 030-001-00097-4); and *The George Kleine Collection of Early Motion Pictures in the Library of Congress: A Catalog* ($11; Stock No. 030-001-00088-5). The first publications in a new series of reports entitled Library of Congress Acquisitions: Manuscript Division, 1979 were issued last year, and a new series of guides entitled Africana Directions was inaugurated in 1981 with *Recent Afro-Libyan Relations: A Selected List of References*. Items in both series are free. Persons interested in these and other Library of Congress publications should write to the Library of Congress, Central Services Division, Washington, DC 20540, for a copy of *Library of Congress Publications in Print* or *Library of Congress Selected Publications 1981*.

Associate Librarian for National Programs Carol A. Nemeyer was elected to the American Library Association's highest office in the summer of 1981. Only the fourth Library of Congress official to become ALA president, she assumes this office at the close of the ALA annual conference in Philadelphia in July 1982.

NATIONAL LIBRARY OF MEDICINE

8600 Rockville Pike,
Bethesda, MD 20209
301-496-6308

Robert B. Mehnert
Public Information Officer

This year the National Library of Medicine (NLM) noted several anniversaries. Twenty-five years ago, on August 3, 1956, President Eisenhower signed the National Library of Medicine Act, passed by the Eighty-fourth Congress. This legislation provided for the transfer of the Armed Forces Medical Library to the U.S. Public Health Service, and renamed the resulting entity the National Library of Medicine. The library, with its military heritage, is in fact 145 years old.

The National Library of Medicine Act requires the library to acquire and preserve the literature of biomedicine, to organize the materials and publish catalogs and indexes, to make this literature available by loan and other methods, and to provide reference services and research assistance. NLM has had remarkable success over the past 25 years in fulfilling these obligations. The library has been a pioneer in introducing computer and other new technologies to assist in improving biomedical communications. An array of useful new bibliographic tools has been published, audiovisual programs have been augmented, specialized services in various disciplines such as toxicology have been instituted, grant programs have assisted in developing new information services throughout the nation, and a vigorous program of research and development has resulted in new applications of modern technology to the biomedical communications process.

Another anniversary, in October, marked the tenth year of successful operation of MEDLINE, the library's on-line bibliographic search and retrieval system. This was the first nationally available, local-call, on-line retrieval network. MEDLINE service was begun in October 1971 with a group of 25 institutions searching a file of 130,000 references to biomedical journal articles. Today, the network comprises almost 1,600 U.S. institutions with access to more than 6 million computerized records. These records are distributed over some 20 individual data bases. In addition to the recent records in MEDLINE, there are backfiles of older references and citations to the literature of specialized areas such as cancer research, toxicology, bioethics, history of medicine, population research, health planning and administration, and audiovisual materials. The network accommodated over 2 million searches in 1981.

MEDLINE is available internationally through 14 non-U.S. centers. Two new foreign centers were established this year, in Colombia and Kuwait. They join Australia, Canada, France, Italy, Japan, Mexico, Sweden, South Africa, Switzerland, the United Kingdom, the Federal Republic of Germany, and the Pan American Health Organization in Brazil. MEDLINE services, in fact, have been provided through these centers (and through NLM itself) to health professionals in more than 130 countries.

Another aspect of NLM's foreign involvement this year was the implementation of a cooperative *quid pro quo* arrangement with the Institute of Medical Information of the Chinese Academy of Sciences. In February, two physicians from the People's Republic of China began a five-month assignment at NLM to work on the library's collection of Chinese traditional medical literature. They identified, verified, and described about 800 items, and the resulting information is being entered into NLM's cataloging records and will be made available to scholars. In return for this assistance, the library will provide two Chinese with training in modern medical library management and indexing.

One of the most significant events of 1981 was the announcement of a reconfiguration of the Regional Medical Library Network, the first major change in geographical boundaries in the program's history. The network was established 14 years ago to provide rapid dissemination of biomedical information and to strengthen bibliographic services to health professionals. Through document delivery and direct access to NLM's computerized data bases, health-science libraries of all sizes share their collection resources to benefit patient care, health-science education, and research.

The network presently consists of 11 regions (each headed by a Regional Medical Library), some 125 resource libraries (at the medical schools), and more than 4,000 local institutions (such as libraries in hospitals and similar health-related institutions). NLM itself serves both as a Regional Medical Library and as the coordinator of the network. Beginning in November 1982, the present eleven regions will be reduced to seven. The change will be effected by merging the five eastern seaboard regions into two larger groupings and combining two existing regions in the Midwest. The midcontinental, northwestern, southwestern, and southcentral regions remain unchanged. The new configuration is designed to take advantage of the strong working relationship and spirit of cooperation developed in the regions, while providing a more cost-effective mechanism to meet current and anticipated budget constraints.

Several important appointments to the NLM staff were made in the last 12 months: Kenneth Carney, executive officer; Lois Ann Colaianni, deputy associate director for library operations; Betsy Humphreys, chief of the Technical Services Division; and Sheldon Kotzin, chief of the Bibliographic Services Division. Two new members were named to four-year terms on the library's Board of Regents: Dr. John Sherman, vice-president of the Association of American Medical Colleges, and Shirley Echelman, director of the Association of Research Libraries.

LIBRARY OPERATIONS

In addition to the growth of the on-line network noted previously, there were several important events in 1981 affecting the network. The first of these was to make available on-line earlier MEDLINE references for 1977 and 1978 in a file called MED77. Previously available only through off-line searching, these references now bring to five years the time span covered for on-line MEDLINE searching. The second event was the increase of on-line charges for using the system. Beginning October 1, the per-hour connect charge was $15 for non-prime time and $22 for prime time (10:00 A.M. to 5:00 P.M. eastern standard time). The charges for accessing NLM's toxicology data bases are higher and reflect royalty fees paid to the producers of the information.

MEDLARS III development continues on schedule. In general terms, the MEDLARS III automation system will improve the processes for acquiring the biomedical literature, for creating, maintaining, and distributing bibliographic records, for retrieving bibliographic information, and for providing document delivery services. Several of these areas already take advantage of some degree of computerization, ranging from the highly automated bibliographic retrieval system (MEDLINE) to the partially automated acquisitions and cataloging processes. NLM is now moving past the planning stage and into actual phased implementation of MEDLARS III. The new system will be fully operational by 1985 and should meet the library's processing requirements for the remainder of the eighties.

Excellent progress is being made in building the National Biomedical Serials Holdings Database. Through a contract, holdings statements for biomedical serials in more than 1,300 U.S. biomedical libraries are being merged into one data base. Under the MEDLARS III system, this data base will be used to produce regional and local union lists, prepare reports about cooperative acquisitions programs, and support an automated document delivery system.

This year, NLM took the historic step of closing its card catalog and announcing a new COM (Computer Output Microform) catalog for use by patrons. The imminent conversion to the *Anglo-American Cataloguing Rules* (second edition) was a factor in the decision to close the catalog. Because of changes to name headings in retrospective records, a tremendous manual effort would have been required to modify and refile cards. Although patrons must still consult the card catalog for older works, the new COM catalog, which contains records for works cataloged since 1965, is meeting most of our users' requirements. Pre-1965 records are being added to the on-line catalog file (CATLINE), and we foresee the entire catalog eventually on-line and accessible from easy-to-use terminals.

The library's outstanding historical collection was enhanced this year by the addition of two incunabula: Aristotle's *De generatione et corruptione* (Venice, 1500) and Joannes Jacobus de Manliis's *Luminare maius* (Venice, 1499). Among other rarities acquired was an item printed by Benjamin Franklin, *Every Man His Own Doctor* (Philadelphia, 1736).

In addition to *Index Medicus* and the other regularly recurring bibliographic publications of the library, 1981 saw the issuance of a revised fourth edition of the *National Library of Medicine Classification: A Scheme for the Shelf Arrangement of Books in the Field of Medicine and Its Related Sciences*. Also appearing this year is the 1,800-page *Bibliography of Medical Reviews, 1976-1980*, a subject/author listing of citations to review articles appearing in *Index Medicus* since 1976.

LISTER HILL NATIONAL CENTER FOR BIOMEDICAL COMMUNICATIONS

The Lister Hill Center, named in honor of the former senator from Alabama, was established in 1968 as the research and development arm of the library. The center explores the application of advanced computer and communications technology to improving the organization, dissemination, and utilization of biomedical information. A newly formed advisory group, the NLM Board of Scientific Counselors, met twice in 1981 to review the library's research and development programs. The board recommended that highest priorities should be assigned to the Knowledge Base Research Program, the Integrated Library System, the Electronic Document Storage and Retrieval Program, and the Video Processing Laboratory.

The Knowledge Base Research Program is a continuing research effort that addresses the need for health practitioners to have rapid access to new medical findings and research information. This information must be in an easily assimilable form so that it can be used in solving daily problems of diagnosis, prognosis, and treatment. The three subjects being addressed—viral hepatitis, peptic ulcer, and human genetics—are in different stages of development. The evaluation and field-testing of the Hepatitis Knowledge Base is now largely completed. The Peptic Ulcer Knowledge Base has been synthesized from the extant literature on that subject and is now being reviewed by a panel of experts. The Human Genetics Knowledge Base is being assembled and the text data base prepared; videodisc and magnetic disc technologies are being investigated to assist with the extensive visual (nontextual) content of this knowledge base.

The Integrated Library System (ILS), Version 2.0, was made public through the National Technical Information Service in August. The ILS is a computer-based system that automates a variety of library processing activities. In addition to the original ILS capabilities of a Master Bibliographic File (MBF), circulation system, serials check-in, and on-line catalog access, Version 2.0 features include batch loading MARC records directly to the MBF, authority file maintenance procedures to allow editing, merging records, and adding cross-references, the capability to define patron registration parameters as each ILS site, and public catalog access.

The Electronic Document Storage and Retrieval Program seeks to develop a system that will support NLM's archival mission and facilitate interlibrary lending. The first phase, already well under way, is to develop a prototype electronic system to capture, store, retrieve, and display paper documents acquired by NLM. Both magnetic and optical disc storage technologies will play an important role in the system as it develops. To this end, a Video Processing Laboratory has been established in the Lister Hill Center to support research and development in image processing and for premastering videodisc materials.

NATIONAL MEDICAL AUDIOVISUAL CENTER

The goal of the National Medical Audiovisual Center (NMAC) is to develop a national program to improve the quality and use of audiovisual learning materials in the health professions. The center's facilities were moved from Atlanta to Bethesda last year, and much of 1981 was devoted to planning for the redevelopment of NMAC physical facilities and rebuilding a drastically reduced staff.

Despite the problems attendant to redevelopment and restaffing, NMAC's training programs continued to be available to the biomedical community. More than 400 health professionals participated in 22 workshops conducted at NMAC and at the field training centers in 1981. In addition to the two existing workshops—Developing and Evaluating Audiovisual Instructional Materials and Designing Simulation Activities—a new workshop was offered on Using Videotechnology to Teach Communication Skills. Another accomplishment of the training program was the installation of a Learning Resource Laboratory that serves as a center for state-of-the-art applications of technology in health-sciences education.

In February a new interlibrary loan program was begun for videocassettes. In addition to the 1,000 titles available from NMAC, satellite collections of 300 titles have been placed in each of the 11 regions. The 16mm film loan operation was converted to a rental program this year, and a new edition of the *National Medical Audiovisual Center Catalog: Films for the Health Sciences* was published.

In collaboration with the Lister Hill Center, NMAC has an important role in exploring the potential usefulness of computer-aided videodisc technology. In addition to the Human Genetics Knowledge Base, videodisc projects were begun this year for instructional units on videomicroscopy and for transferring onto videodisc the library's historical prints and photographs collection.

The NLM Board of Regents, at its May meeting, directed that NMAC take a leadership role in establishing a National Medical Historical Film Program to serve as an archival resource for motion pictures pertinent to the history of the health sciences. Policies have been established to govern this collection, a complete inventory of the existing core collection has been carried out, and work is progressing on a cataloging system and information clearinghouse that will allow rapid identification and retrieval of historical film materials.

TOXICOLOGY INFORMATION PROGRAM

The Toxicology Information Program (TIP) was established within the library in 1967 to provide national access to information on toxicology, pharmacology, and industrial and environmental hazards. In 1981, TIP organized a symposium on Information Transfer in Toxicology which took place at the library in September. More than 200 participants from around the nation examined the technical, legislative, economic, and international aspects of current toxicology information services.

This year marked the tenth anniversary of the establishment of the Toxicology Information Response Center, a collaborative venture between the library and the Oak Ridge National Laboratory. Located in Tennessee, the center responds to requests for evaluated information about the toxic effects of pesticides, drugs, industrial chemicals, food additives, and so on. During the past ten years, the center has gained an international reputation for concise assembly and prompt delivery of pertinent information to such users as lawyers, physicians, researchers, poison control centers, and government agencies. In 1981, the center responded to more than 400 requests for comprehensive searches and also prepared for publication four annotated bibliographies—on chemical waste disposal, urea-formaldehyde compounds, vanadium compounds, and the effects of environmental chemicals on the immune system.

GRANT PROGRAMS

In FY 1981 the library awarded 147 grants and contracts totaling $9,830,000 under the Medical Library Assistance Act. These funds are used for improving library resources, research in biomedical communications, biomedical publications, training, and supporting the Regional Medical Libraries.

First passed in 1965, and renewed periodically since, the Medical Library Assistance Act was again considered for renewal by Congress in 1981. The Omnibus Reconciliation Act (PL 97-35) was passed in August. It extended NLM's grant authorities for one year at a level of $7.5 million, $2.3 million less than the previous year's appropriation.

SELECTED STATISTICS, 1981*

Collection (book and nonbook)	2,880,000
Serial titles received	23,364
Articles indexed for MEDLARS	279,105
Titles cataloged	16,541
Circulation requests filled	335,753
For interlibrary loan	177,699
For readers	158,054
Reference requests	46,070
Computerized searches (all data bases)	2,022,000
On-line	1,434,500
Off-line	587,500

*For the year ending September 30, 1981.

NATIONAL AGRICULTURAL LIBRARY

Eugene M. Farkas
Head, Educational Resources Staff

As a result of recent reorganization, the National Agricultural Library (NAL) has reemerged as an independent agency of the U.S. Department of Agriculture (USDA). For the past three years, it had been part of Technical Information Systems and the Science and Education Administration, both of which have been dissolved.

NAL, with its collection now grown to 1.7 million volumes, continues to rank as the largest agricultural library in the free world. During 1982, it will mark the hundred and twentieth anniversary of its founding as the USDA library, and the twentieth anniversary of its designation as the National Agricultural Library.

The explosive growth in modern communications technology and planned expansion of the national library and information network have led NAL to emphasize three areas of operations: (1) automated data processing, (2) service to and cooperation with state land-grant and similar institutions, and (3) broadening access to the collection by scientists, researchers, and technical-information specialists.

TECHNOLOGY AND USER FEES

The National Agricultural Library is continuing its efforts to provide better and more efficient services to its users everywhere while holding down the cost of such services. To achieve these objectives, the latest advances in technology are being adapted to appropriate library operations, expansion of user fees is being considered, and cooperating state institutions are working with NAL to hold the line on or even reduce operating costs.

The recent adoption of new technology and of more efficient marketing procedures by NAL is illustrated in two areas. New microcomputers will soon be introduced at the library for on-line data base searching and for interactive storage and retrieval of budgetary and personnel data for management purposes. NAL is now marketing its AGRICOLA on-line bibliographic data base through the federal National Technical Information Services (NTIS). NTIS sells the AGRICOLA computer tapes to commercial vendors and institutions in the United States and abroad.

DOCUMENT DELIVERY

The Regional Document Delivery System is an example of how state and federal units can work together and achieve low costs. In 1981, the system, which is jointly supported by NAL and 28 participating land-grant university libraries, filled 59,900 requests for documents, an increase of 9,000 over 1980. However, the cost per transaction stayed about the same.

Approximately 66,075 requests for information—an 18 percent increase over 1980—were answered by NAL libraries using automated literature searches and other information sources. Researchers both in this country and abroad accounted for 60 percent of all inquiries, including an increasing number from developing countries. Policymakers, consulting firms, farmers, and the general public also asked for assistance, along with a growing number of scholars and librarians. Areas in which information was most frequently requested included agricultural statistics of all kinds, pest control, wind and solar energy, alcohol fuels, agricultural machinery and equipment, and forest management and production. Special information research projects were carried out at NAL in support of USDA programs pertaining to small farms, evaluation of agricultural research, hazardous wastes, nutrition research, structures of agriculture, forest biomass, alcohol fuels, energy conservation, and aquaculture.

MICROFILMING THE COLLECTION

As part of its responsibilities, NAL provides for collection preservation. This involves microfilming and restoring important documents, unbound serial issues, newspapers, and historical materials. A nationwide project is currently underway to film the documents of all land-grant institutions, such as bulletins, circulars, reports, and other land-grant publications, before these deteriorate. The project is being conducted by NAL in conjunction with a private microfilming firm and the land-grant institutions. The result is a collection that spans the period from the late 1800s into the 1970s. The collection is both a valuable research tool for a wide variety of subjects and a practical reference resource for farmers and the lay public.

NAL conducted individual computer literature searches from nine major abstracting and indexing systems for USDA scientists and administrators under the Current Awareness Literature Service (CALS) program. In 1981 over 3,000 user-interest profiles were processed on a regular basis. CALS offers an economical and efficient means of providing USDA researchers with the most recent scientific literature appearing in journals and similar publications.

INTERNATIONAL INPUT

As part of its expanded program of cooperation with the International Information System for the Agricultural Sciences and Technology (AGRIS), NAL increased its contribution of citations from 12,000 input work sheets annually in FYs 1976 and 1977 to 50,000 machine-readable records annually since FY 1978. The United States is the most prolific of the AGRIS participants, with U.S. contributions to AGRIS through NAL constituting nearly half of all agricultural citations in the United Nations information system.

An aquaculture research project subfile was established in Current Research Information System (CRIS), an independent data base maintained by NAL. All ongoing and recently completed projects directly or indirectly related to aquaculture have been classified in subject categories. Eighty-four translations of important scientific and technical publications in foreign languages were provided by NAL to the Interagency Committee on Marine Sciences and Fisheries. Lists of the translations were distributed to key FDA (Food and Drug Administration), Commerce, Interior, and land-grant program officers in aquaculture, as well as information officers, librarians, and state experiment station directors.

ELECTRONIC MAIL NETWORK

After a one-year test, a national electronic mail network was implemented to meet the needs of the USDA Extension Service. It is accessible to both the Cooperative State Research Service (CSRS) and the entire state research and education community. The network can be accessed by a wide variety of devices, including programmable terminals, word processing equipment, and optical-character readers, by providing not only communication services, but also electronic filing and retrieval, data transmission, hard-copy production, and communication services. At the end of 1981 there were 44 state extension directors, and 22 state experiment station directors on the electronic mail system.

ON-LINE WORKSHOPS

As a major producer of a large, commercially available data base, NAL has a responsibility to train its users in the efficient retrieval of information from AGRICOLA. To accomplish this goal, NAL offered training workshops in Washington, D.C., and at land-grant universities throughout the continental United States in 1981, the program's first year. Approximately 500 people were reached by the workshops last year. To reduce the costs of this service, NAL has instituted a series of advanced classes, each designed to train instructors who could in turn train people at their own universities.

Dissemination of technical information to specific audiences was carried out through the NAL education program. One- to two-hour seminars were presented to such specialized USDA groups as soil conservation managers. Approximately 25 of these short seminars were presented in 1981, primarily at the Educational Resources Center in Washington, D.C. Demonstrations of the AGRICOLA data base were held at meetings of professional scientific societies throughout the United States. An effective tool for the dissemination of technical information to specific audiences is *Agricultural Libraries Information Notes (ALIN)*, published monthly for an estimated 25,000 readers, most of whom are cooperators in land-grant and private libraries and other educational institutions.

An estimated 1,200 visitors were guests of the National Agricultural Library in 1981. Visitors represented approximately 35 countries, including the People's Republic of China, Czechoslovakia, the Union of Soviet Socialist Republics (USSR), Great Britain, the Netherlands, Belgium, Denmark, Tunisia, and Brazil. The majority of these visitors were scientists and technical information specialists who were briefed on NAL resources and services, given tours of the facility, or met with subject specialists on the NAL staff.

A special two-month exhibition on sugar production, entitled "Green Fields: Two Hundred Years of Louisiana Sugar," was presented at the National Agricultural Library. The exhibit depicted the history of Louisiana's sugar cane industry, its people, and their distinctive culture. It included 185 photographs and a Cajun musical trio.

The primary activities of the library, in addition to acquisition of agricultural materials, are listed in Table 1.

Officers of the National Agricultural Library are Richard A. Farley, Acting Director and Acting Chief of the Information Access Division; Samuel T. Waters, Associate Director; Eugene M. Farkas, Head, Educational Resources Staff; Joseph R. Judy, Chief, Information Systems Division; Wallace C. Olsen, Chief, Field and Special Programs Division; and Leslie Kulp, Chief, Resources Development Division.

TABLE 1 ACTIVITIES OF THE NATIONAL AGRIGULTURAL LIBRARY IN 1981

Activity	1981 Volume
Additions to serial issues	188,000
Titles cataloged	15,500
Articles indexed	129,400
Volumes bound	11,800
Document requests filled	325,800
Reference requests answered	38,000
Automated searches conducted	28,000
Current Awareness (CAL) searches	518,000
Current Awareness (CALS) profiles processed by all data bases	21,500

National Associations

AMERICAN LIBRARY ASSOCIATION

50 E. Huron St., Chicago, IL 60611
312-944-6780

Elizabeth W. Stone
President

The 105-year-old American Library Association (ALA)—the oldest and largest library association in the world—entered the 1980s as a strong and vital organization. In 1981 its membership increased by 10 percent, to reach an all-time high of nearly 40,000, including librarians, libraries, library trustees, authors, publishers, information scientists, business firms, and Friends of the Library in the United States, Canada, and abroad. Nearly 2,500 of ALA's members actively participate in its 837 divisions, round tables, committees, task forces, and other voluntary units in the Association.

October 27, 1981, was a special day in the history of ALA: It was marked by the dedication of the Huron Plaza building. Six floors of the 56-story complex house offices and the remaining 50 floors accommodate 460 rental apartments. Construction was completed in the spring of 1981 at a cost of $24 million. ALA owns all six office floors and is currently leasing space in the top three. With the completion of Huron Plaza, the association expanded its executive offices beyond the 50 East Huron Street location to include three floors in the new building, thus increasing its space by 50,000 square feet; with 35,000 square feet at 50 East Huron, the total office space comes to 85,000 square feet. In addition, the building at 50 East Huron was completely refurbished and connected with Huron Plaza offices by means of extended corridors. The additional space makes it possible for ALA to undertake major programmatic initiatives that will benefit the entire library and information service field, as well as more adequately support ongoing services.

The hundredth annual conference of ALA, held in San Francisco June 26-July 1, attracted over 13,000 librarians, trustees, and exhibitors. The conference theme was featured in a speech by ALA's 1980-1981 President, Peggy Sullivan, entitled "Libraries and the Pursuit of Happiness," which was also the title of a film that premiered at the conference. The 16mm sound film or videocassette, produced by Encyclopaedia Britannica Educational Corporation in cooperation with ALA, portrays the variety of services offered by libraries across the United States and was introduced by Dr. Sullivan as the president's program. All types of libraries and many innovative services are portrayed, making the film a useful tool to stimulate library support and promote both new and traditional services. The conference program included over 1,500 meetings, featuring such speakers as Stephen King and P. D. James; programs on literacy, electronic delivery of information, the Moral Majority and intellectual freedom, and "How to Manage Your Boss," and a dazzling film extravaganza on the history of the Library Services and Construction Act (LSCA) entitled "Star Years LSCA," produced and presented by Fred Glazer. Over 700 exhibits and displays featured the latest in library materials and services.

Another special event during 1981 that has long-term implications was the meeting of ALA's executive board in a seminar November 30–December 2 to consider its structure and organization. The board endorsed the concept of greater working involvement in board responsibilities by its individual members, and agreed on a restructuring of its committees. To promote more informed decision making and adapt to increasing demands on the association as well as its more complex organization, the board approved the addition of the Administrative Committee, the Finance and Audit Committee, the Directions and Program Review Committee, and the Personnel Committee to those already in existence, namely, the Policy Monitory Committee and the Honorary Members, Special Nominations, and Assignments Committee. The board's committees are not intended to usurp the responsibilities of council committees dealing with related matters, but rather to supplement the latter. Steps were also taken at the seminar toward the development of a continuing operational strategy for the executive board.

The overarching mission of the American Library Association is to promote and improve library service and librarianship as a means to assuring the delivery of user-oriented library and information services to the public. Current priorities, as adapted by the ALA Council, for carrying out this mission are access to information, legislation/funding, intellectual freedom, public awareness, and personnel resources. The next section of this report is organized according to these priorities.

ACCESS TO INFORMATION FOR EVERYONE

Access to information for the blind and physically handicapped was a major emphasis during 1981, the International Year for Disabled Persons (IYDP). Early in the year, a four-point program was adopted in the areas of international cooperation, dissemination of information about technological advances, training for librarians, and provision of braille copies of ALA papers and agendas.

This program, which expanded as the year went on, was headed by an ad hoc committee chaired by Phyllis I. Dalton that worked closely with the Association of Specialized and Cooperative Library Agencies (ASCLA), a division of ALA. A major activity was the Symposium on Educating Library and Information Scientists to Provide Information and Library Services to the Disabled, held in San Francisco July 2–4, under the sponsorship of ALA/ASCLA; the Library of Congress's National Library Service for the Blind and Physically Handicapped; the Library of Congress (LC); the School of Library and Information Science of the Catholic University of America; and the National Rehabilitation Information Center (NARIC), in Washington, D.C. Proceedings of the symposium have been published by the Government Printing Office.

Other IYDP activities and events included, but were not limited to, presentation of recommendations from the July San Francisco symposium to the Library Service to Patients Section and the Round Table on Libraries for the Blind at the conference of the International Federation of Library Associations and Institutions (IFLA) in Leipzig, East Germany, in August; production of a tape of the San Francisco conference program, "Celebrating IYDP through Libraries," available through ALA Publishing Services; development and dissemination of the Deaf Action Kit and IYDP (kit available through ASCLA); publication of an issue of *Library Technology Reports* (November/December 1981) on disabilities and technology; and the International Book/Author Reception, which recognized books and authors concerned with disabled people and was held at the Martin Luther King Memorial Library, Washington, D.C., on October 27. In addition, the Winter and Spring 1981 issues of the ASCLA publication

Interface featured the work of groups and individuals involved in services to disabled persons.

To enhance the accessibility of libraries designed to serve special groups, ASCLA developed and published two sets of standards. *Standards for Libraries at Institutions for the Mentally Retarded* reflects the basic assumption that mentally retarded individuals are able to profit from many library services and programs. Information is also supplied that allows for the evaluation of existing library services. *Library Standards for Adult Correctional Institutions,* developed by ASCLA in cooperation with the American Correctional Association, is a part of ASCLA's continuing effort to promote quality library service in prisons and jails.

The 1981 Ralph R. Shaw Award for Library Literature was given to Ruth A. Velleman for her landmark book, *Serving Physically Disabled People: An Information Handbook for All Libraries* (R. R. Bowker).

The Reference and Adult Services Division (RASD) of ALA made a major contribution to making information accessible by revising the document "Library's Responsibility to the Aging."

During the closing months of 1981, the IYDP/ASCLA committee promoted a congressional resolution to make 1982 the National Year of Disabled Persons and the possible U.N. proposal to make the rest of the 1980s the Decade of Disabled Persons.

The ALA unit that has as its overriding objective the provision of access to information for everyone is the Office of Library Outreach Services (OLOS). A long-sought goal was achieved with the approval of an ALA proposal to the Advertising Council for the development of a multimedia campaign on national adult illiteracy. OLOS will coordinate the activities of the Coalition for Literacy, which will become a client of the Advertising Council and will be responsible for implementing the campaign. OLOS publications include *How Public Libraries Serve the Aging,* which was available at the 1981 White House Conference on Aging; and *Libraries and Literacy,* which describes an OLOS project that trained 124 state and regional librarians. At the 1981 ALA annual conference, a new council committee was approved; the Minority Concerns Committee is a policy committee representing the "interests and concerns of ethnic minority librarians." OLOS serves as the liaison office for this group. A major contribution of ALA to promoting the accessibility of information is its extensive publishing program, which will be covered in a separate section of this report.

LEGISLATION/FUNDING

During this landmark year in national politics, legislation and funding demanded close attention as one of ALA's priorities. Events moved at a fast pace and provided high drama as the Reagan administration took aim at many domestic programs, including those in the Department of Education, and proposed the elimination of the department itself. However, as the library community celebrated the twenty-fifth anniversary of LSCA, Congress reauthorized the act in the Omnibus Budget Reconciliation Act of 1981 (PL 97-35) and held a series of regional hearings in the fall that highlighted the accomplishments of this outstanding federal program. That appropriations were maintained at close to FY 1981 levels testifies to the importance of convincing the public and Congress that libraries are responsive to user needs and that they operate efficiently. Legislation Day, sponsored by the District of Columbia Library Association and ALA, once again provided an opportunity for library supporters to promote libraries to their congressional delegations.

With the pie of local, state, and federal funds shrinking in many parts of the country, Eileen Cooke, associate executive director of ALA and a registered lobbyist, has stated in speeches to audiences across the nation that libraries face serious fiscal problems in coping with the "new federalism." Indeed, the most pressing concern for many libraries is that their funding is, in real terms, either decreasing or remaining the same while demands for service increase. With school library resources programs folded into education block grants and funding for college library resources, training, and research in jeopardy, the need has never been greater to document the services that libraries provide to their user communities. Libraries that are highly responsive stand the best chance of securing adequate funding. No institution has its finger closer to the pulse of community life than does the library. It is hoped that the theme of the ALA president's program for 1981–1982, "Responsiveness and Awareness," is helping libraries across the country to respond to financial challenges.

With traditional sources of funding strained, alternative sources must be explored more imaginatively. A close look at the tax bill passed by Congress in 1981 is needed to see if there are provisions that could encourage both businesses and tax legislation to benefit libraries, such as the bill to restore a tax incentive for donations to libraries and museums of artwork and manuscripts by authors and artists. As we move into the "age of information," legislative issues like telecommunications, copyright, information policy, and adequate funding for libraries will continue to challenge us and to bring new opportunities.

INTELLECTUAL FREEDOM

Following the adoption in 1980 of the revised Library Bill of Rights, the Intellectual Freedom Committee prepared several interpretations of the bill and other intellectual-freedom policy statements that contribute substantially to an already strong body of intellectual-freedom documentation. The revised policies, which were presented and approved by the ALA Council at the annual conference in July, cover these areas: challenged materials, evaluating library collections, expurgation of library materials, free access to libraries for minors, policy on governmental intimidation, restricted access to library materials, and a statement on labeling. The committee also adopted a new document entitled *Dealing with Complaints about Resources*, which is procedural and contains suggestions on the implementation of intellectual-freedom policies; this document replaces *How Libraries Can Resist Censorship*. Also, the Intellectual Freedom Committee recommended, and the ALA Council endorsed, in June a strong statement circulated by the Campaign for Political Rights in support of the Freedom of Information Act. Released on July 4, the fifteenth anniversary of the signing of that act, the statement contained signatures representing 150 other diverse organizations. The ALA Council also passed a resolution in June reaffirming the importance of access for the physically handicapped.

During the fall of 1981, the Office of Intellectual Freedom held academic freedom group workshops in Spokane and Des Moines, which were designed to develop regional anticensorship coalitions and networks. The workshops were conducted in cooperation with the Academic Freedom Group, which is a coalition of ten educational organizations. The group's purposes are to educate teachers, librarians, school officials, and boards of education to the current restrictive climate, and to offer some suggestions for dealing with censorship attempts. The Freedom to Read Foundation received a gift of $25,000 from author Sidney Sheldon toward the establishment of an endowment fund. Sheldon also wrote to a dozen publishers, urging them to send donations to the Freedom to Read Foundation: "I urge you to send to the Freedom to Read Foundation a check to help them in *our* fight. I urge you to do it today, because tomorrow may be too late."

A significant event during the annual conference was the adoption by the ALA membership and council of a new statement on professional ethics, which revised a 1975 statement and was based on solicited written and oral comments from the ALA membership.

LIBRARY AWARENESS

The fourth current priority statement of ALA declares that ALA will promote the use of libraries and their resources and services, as well as an awareness of their importance to all segments of society. With this objective in mind, I chose as my presidential theme for the 1981-1982 presidency of ALA "Responsiveness: Key to Developing Library Awareness; Awareness: Key to Meeting Fiscal Challenges." The principal goal for the year is to enable ALA members everywhere to become more involved with this theme. A number of activities have been initiated, including (1) poster sessions, a new opportunity for members with research to report and projects to share to hold court free of charge near the exhibit area at the annual conference; (2) the Library Awareness Idea Search, an ALA-sponsored nationwide search for the best ideas, both tried and untried, to promote public awareness of libraries, which will review all ideas for possible inclusion in a library awareness idea handbook to be published by ALA and sold at the conference; and (3) the president's program at the 1982 midwinter conference, which will focus on marketing library information services and will be broadcast by satellite to some 50 receiver sites in libraries across the nation. The ALA Public Information Office lists a number of programs designed to make the public more aware of library services, including a new library promotion drive designed to create the most far-reaching national public-awareness campaign since the launching in 1900 of National Library Week (NLW). In this campaign, ALA and the chief officers of state library agencies join together to promote libraries' telephone reference service. The Call Your Library Campaign was created to help libraries market particular services to targeted audiences and to reach out to nonusers. All the materials of the campaign were developed to work together on the national, state, and local levels and to let everyone know that if they have questions, they can call the library for answers. Bob Newhart, a master of telephone conversation, donated his time and talent to serve as a campaign spokesman. On March 3, 1981, Johnny Carson had a 12-minute segment of his "Tonight Show" featuring the Call Your Library Campaign, in which 41 states participated. ALA also initiated and is presenting in cooperation with National Public Radio a new 26-week radio series, "About Books and Writers with Robert Cromie," which had its premier in October. Author and critic Robert Cromie serves as host. ALA also initiated a newspaper called *Openers*; its first issue was published in spring, 1981. It is written for people with a wide range of interests, and explores the world of books, television, films, and music as they relate to libraries. All subscribing libraries also received an 18-page marketing kit filled with ideas on how to promote *Openers* and to use it to promote their collections and services.

A third major marketing tool made available for library use in 1981 consisted of materials for National Library Week, which featured the theme "America, the Library Has Your Number." As a part of this program for the third successive year, the McDonald's Corporation encouraged McDonald's restaurants throughout the country to develop cooperative programs with libraries for a special salute to National Library Week. A kit containing public relations materials for use in teaching case histories was sent to over 3,500 McDonald's representatives in January; they in turn developed successful library tie-ins. This project provides an excellent opportunity to work with local merchants to help communities discover their libraries. April 5-11 marked the twenty-third observance of National Library Week, and President Ronald Reagan continued the tradition of issuing a presidential statement to launch this week. The president stated that the theme, "America, the Library Has Your Number," meant to him

> that there just isn't any request too big or too small for our libraries. If we are to guard against ignorance and remain free, as Jefferson cautioned, it is the responsibility of every American to be informed. During National Library Week, I urge Americans everywhere to use our nation's libraries and to take full advantage of the services which they provide.

ALA furthered its National Library Week theme throughout 1981 through public service announcements in which each spot featured a celebrity whose library endorsement ties into the National Library Week theme. The reel-to-reel tape contains nine spots.

Looking forward to 1982 National Library Week, ALA announced in October that the theme will be: "A Word to the Wise: Library." A new dimension has been added with award-winning library graphics designed to create a sensational National Library Week celebration in every community and school; the promotion of NLW will continue all year long.

PERSONNEL RESOURCES

ALA promoted the professional- and staff-development rights, interests, and obligations of library personnel, not only through its annual conference, but also through a wide array of continuing education opportunities. In addition to the usual preconference workshops, ALA divisions and offices toured the country with workshops and institutes on topics ranging from Anglo-American Cataloguing Rules 2 (AACR 2) to reference performance. The following are a few highlights from ALA divisions.

The Association for Library Service to Children (ALSC) presented its annual Arbuthnot lecture and completed a three-year series of workshops entitled "Media Evaluation: The Group Process," which grew out of a prototype ALA Goal Award project.

The Association of College and Research Libraries (ACRL) held 12 one- or two-day continuing education courses prior to both the 1981 annual conference and the second ACRL national conference. The latter, entitled "Options for the 80s," met in Minneapolis October 1-4, with 1,881 persons in attendance. Conferees attended courses on such topics as supervisory skills, library turnkey systems, bibliographic instruction, group skills, consulting, management issues in automation, and career development. ACRL was awarded a $67,293 grant from the National Endowment for the Humanities (NEH) to hold two workshops on humanities programming. The number of state ACRL chapters, incidentally, grew from 26 to 30.

The Association of Specialized and Cooperative Library Agencies developed guidelines for the cosponsorship of workshops, institutes, and conferences; authorized a needs assessment of several of its membership groups; and developed a program-planning evaluation form to be used at ASCLA programs.

A needs assessment survey of members of the Library Administration and Management Association (LAMA), Library Organization and Management Section, indicated there is interest in measurement techniques for planning and evaluating library programs.

The Library and Information Technology Association (LITA) continued its pattern of regional workshops by presenting a tutorial, "Data Processing Specifications and Contracting," in Boston and San Francisco, as well as a preconference session entitled "The Office in the Home." LITA preconference audiocassettes are available on the needs of librarians whose institutions are having automated systems installed.

Workshops on public relations were presented by the Public Information Office in Kentucky, Maryland, Michigan, and Pennsylvania.

The Public Library Association (PLA) featured "Planning Process for Public Libraries" as the focus of a series of three-day workshops for consultants, offered in Maryland and Indiana. A $35,337 grant from NEH provided PLA with the capability of presenting two workshops on library humanities projects for public libraries responsible for adult programming.

A preconference on genealogy and local history reference sources, in addition to an April workshop entitled "Improving Reference Performance," were continuing education efforts by the Reference and Adult Services Division. In addition, the RASD Machine-Assisted Reference Section developed guidelines for on-line training sessions that were later published in the Summer 1981 issue of *Research Quarterly* (*RQ*).

From May 1980 to June 1981, the Resources and Technical Services Division (RTSD) sponsored fourteen AACR 2 institutes throughout the country, attended by 2,233 registrants. An AACR 2 institute handbook summarized Library of Congress interpretations and choices of optional rules for the benefit of registrants. A pilot collection management and development institute, held at Stanford University, was attended by 175 persons as a postconference to the 1981 ALA annual conference. Partially supported by the Council on Library Resources, the institute received favorable evaluations and will be repeated in 1982 and 1983. A planner's handbook based on the experience of the 1981 program will be used by future institute staff.

The 1981 edition of the RTSD *Preservation Education Directory* provided information on educational opportunities in the preservation of library materials both within and outside the traditional academic framework.

Cheap CE—Providing Continuing Education with Limited Resources: A Practical Guide, by Linda Waddle, was published at year-end by the Young Adult Services Division.

An ongoing activity of the Office of Library Personnel Resources, under the direction of Margaret Myers, has been the development and publication of *General Concepts of Employment for Library and Information Personnel.* This much-needed publication is designed to promote mutually satisfying relationships between employees and employers, and is generally pertinent to employment in all fields of practice. It is designed to serve as a reference source against which employers can evaluate their own practices. In addition, it will be of use both to employees in evaluating both their own responsibilities and those of their employers, and to new graduates and other job seekers in obtaining a better picture of prospective employment.

ACCREDITATION

As a standing committee of ALA, the Committee on Accreditation (COA) continued its responsibility for the execution of the association's accreditation program. Its "accredited list," published in October, reported that 69 master's degrees programs were then accredited, seven of them in Canada and the rest in the United States. Although ALA does not accredit post-master's specialist certificate programs or doctoral degree programs, the accredited list indicates that schools offer such programs. In October, 39 of the 62 accredited schools in the United States (63 percent) offered post-master's certificate programs, and 25 of the total (36 percent) listed doctoral programs. Twelve site visits were made during the year, resulting in continuation of accreditation for six programs, initial accreditation for one program, denial of accreditation to one program, and conditional accreditation for three programs. Action on one program was deferred at the request of the school. COA also took action to restore continuing accredited status to one program that had previously received conditional accreditation.

During 1981, COA also completed revisions for its *Manual of Procedures for Evaluation Visits* and *Self-Study: A Guide to the Process;* copies of both were distributed to all graduate library education programs. It also reprinted the *Standards for Accreditation, 1972,* which was edited to eliminate sexist language and to include references to nondiscrimination with respect to students, faculty, and support staff.

The J. Morris Jones Award of $5,000 went to ALA's Public Library Association for use by its Goals, Guidelines, and Standards for Public Libraries Committee. The funds will be applied to the costs of a meeting to review a draft of a forthcoming publication, *Procedures for Performance Measures.*

PUBLISHING AT ALA

As income from publication contributes approximately 52 percent of ALA's overall revenues and publications reach members who do not attend national meetings, it seems appropriate at the beginning of a new decade to review in some detail the scope of the publishing unit for the first year of the 1980s.

ALA Publishing Services issued two comprehensive works in art and music. *Guide to the Literature of Art History,* by Etta Arntzen and Robert Rainwater (634 pages; $75) replaces Chamberlin's *Guide* (ALA, 1959). *Historical Sets, Collected Editions, and Monuments of Music,* by Anna Harriet Heyer (1,132 pages, 2 vols.; $175), in its third edition, provides access to information on the published scores of Western composers.

Other new titles published in 1981 were Sheila Egoff's *Thursday's Child: Trends and Patterns in Contemporary Children's Literature,* which was featured as an exemplary work of its kind in *Booklist; Doors to More Mature Reading,* second edition, by Elinor Walker (first printing: 8,000); and the third edition of *Books for Public Libraries,* edited by Constance E. Koehn. The computer program written for the author-title index of the last publication will be used for similar bibliographies.

ALA unit publications cover a wide spectrum of diverse professional and general interests. They range from ACRL's *Academic Library Survey* (340 pages, $17), to the Social Responsibilities Round Table's "Peace Information Exchange Task Force" (free). These and hundreds of other items appear in *ALA Publications Checklist,* edited by Joel Lee.

At the end of FY 1980–1981, Publishing Services earned revenues of $1,614,399 and had expenses of $1,602,171, for a margin of $12,228.

Review Journals

In addition to its regular reviews of fiction, nonfiction, books for young adults, children's books, films and filmstrips, recordings, and videocassettes, which totaled 6,210 in 1980–1981, *Booklist* continued its publication of non-English language bibliographies, "U.S. Government Publications," "Easy Reading," and other special features. "Upfront: Advance Reviews" became a useful and popular feature. "YA Reviewers' Choice" first appeared in the January 1, 1981, issue of *Booklist.* Circulation for *Booklist* averaged 36,980 in 1980–1981. Net revenue totaled $1,543,577 and expenses $1,500,484; after all indirect costs were paid and transfers for reference and subscription books expenses made, the margin was $43,093.

The Reference and Subscription Books Committee, one of ALA's largest and hardest working committees, consists of 50 volunteer members of ALA. Chaired by Robert Pierson, the committee appointed the Statistical Sources Evaluation Subcommittee. The committee's Subcommittee on Scope is exploring ways of expanding the coverage of *Reference and Subscription Books Reviews*, which is published within the covers of *Booklist*, to include nonprint media. Its Omnibus Reviews Subcommittee initiated a consumer article published in early 1981, entitled "Encyclopedia Yearbooks, Annuals, and Supplements," and worked on similar projects concerned with children's dictionaries, adult encyclopedias, children's encyclopedias, grant literature, and general atlases.

In January 1981, *American Libraries* launched its "America's Library Heritage" cover series, which featured during the year four-color illustrations of ten libraries. Among the major stories were reports on on-line public access catalogs, and a back-to-basics article entitled "More Books, Not Market Surveys," which provoked the greatest response of the year. Changes in this publication during 1981 included a new type and format design, more editorials, and increased coverage of technical services and networking in a section entitled "The Source." Circulation rose from 39,112 to 41,510, a figure that includes those who receive the magazine as part of ALA membership and 2,700 institutional subscribers who paid $25 (subscription rate will rise to $30 after January 1, 1982).

The Central Production Unit (CPU) at ALA headquarters provides journal and newsletter production services to ALA offices and divisions and to some round tables. In 1981, the unit monitored budgets that totaled $777,000. It processed 18,169 manuscript pages, which resulted in 4,238 published pages. Net revenues for the six publications produced by CPU for ALA divisions, namely, *School Media Quarterly*, *Top of the News*, *RQ*, *College & Research Libraries News*, *College & Research Libraries*, and *Library Resources and Technical Services*, totaled $88,319 from advertising and $161,722 from subscriptions. Both figures exceeded budgeted estimates.

Choice

The year at *Choice*, a program of ACRL, was primarily concerned with improving service to users of the magazine. A small computer allowed the publication to automate most housekeeping and clerical functions (subscription fulfillment, mailing lists, advertising files, reviewer files) and represents the first step toward automated typesetting at ALA. The timeliness of reviews was improved by getting materials to reviewers more promptly and by simplifying some office routines. Revenues from *Choice* in FY 1980–1981 totaled $708,814 and expenses $698,749 (margin: $10,065).

LTR

Library Technology Reports (*LTR*) is a unique customer-oriented subscription service unit within the ALA Publishing Services that provides objective information on which to base effective buying decisions about products and services offered to libraries. In the second half of 1981, *LTR* introduced a new title, *Library Systems Newsletter*. Published monthly, it reports on developments in the library automated systems market with emphasis on turnkey stand-alone systems and modules being developed by bibliographic utilities. *LTR*'s revenues totaled $273,375 and expenses $240,875 (margin: $32,500).

Other Activities

Cognotes, the ALA conference newspaper written and edited by a Junior Members Round Table staff, appeared in an expanded new format at the San Francisco annual conference. Also at the conference, the ALA Publishing Committee sponsored a publishing information forum, and Publishing Services honored recent ALA authors at a luncheon attended by the president and president-elect of ALA.

The long-awaited *Who's Who in Library and Information Services* was in the final stages of editorial preparation at year-end; publication was announced for April 1982. Joel Lee is its editor-in-chief.

INTERNATIONAL RELATIONS

The forty-seventh International Federation of Library Associations and Institutions general conference and council was held in Leipzig August 17–22, 1981. Approximately 900 delegates were in attendance from 64 countries. The largest delegation was from the Federal Republic of Germany, including West Berlin; it numbered approximately 100. As has been the custom in recent years, the second largest delegation was that of the United States, which numbered approximately 80. The American Library Association was officially represented by ALA president Elizabeth Stone, immediate past president Peggy Sullivan, executive director Robert Wedgeworth, and international relations officer Jane Wilson. At the first plenary session, Dr. Sullivan delivered the speech "Local and Regional Library Associations: Views beyond National Library Associations' Boundaries." IFLA board member and former ALA president Jean Lowrie chaired a plenary session entitled "Library Associations on the Move," at which the executive director of the National Commission on Libraries and Information Science (NCLIS), Toni Bearman, was the featured speaker. Henriette Avram was elected chair of the professional board of IFLA and is also a member of the IFLA executive board. Two showings of the film "Libraries and the Pursuit of Happiness" were presented during the IFLA meetings, and both showings were introduced by Dr. Sullivan.

ALA's executive director, Robert Wedgeworth, also visited Kenya and Nigeria for two weeks in the spring on assignment for the UNESCO/General Information Program, funded by the U.N. Interim Fund for Science and Technology Development. The purpose of the trip was to produce analytical case studies that examine the national development plans of both countries in the areas of science and technology; to assess the information requirements for support of development activities; and to make recommendations to strengthen existing capabilities. He also attended the thirty-third Frankfurt Book Fair in October. President Stone spent two weeks in August on a study tour of West German libraries, information centers, and library schools as a guest of the International Committee of the Library Association of the Federal Republic of Germany.

NOTES AND NAMES

A widely discussed issue during the year was a draft of the Operating Agreement for ALA and its divisions, which was based on the document drafted at the special meeting in the spring and reviewed by divisions at the annual conference and by department heads. The agreement identifies the general operational policies and principles that relate to ALA divisions. The agreement is restricted to ALA and its membership divisions, that is, it does not address the association's relationships with its offices, round tables, and organizational units other than divisions. The principal intent of the Operating Agreement is to define those services that divisions receive from ALA at no cost and those for which they are charged. In addition, the document seeks to establish a cooperative framework in which the inevitable question of organizational relationships can be addressed and resolved. At the San Francisco annual conference, the council voted that the agreement be published for the membership, along with pro and con position papers. It was also agreed that no part of the Operating Agreement be put into practice before it is authorized in accordance with procedures specified in the ALA constitution.

Jane Wilson, international relations officer, resigned as of November 30, 1981. By acclamation the executive board acknowledged with respect and appreciation her years of outstanding service to the association.

Officers of the association for 1981-1982 are Elizabeth W. (Betty) Stone, president; Carol Nemeyer, vice-president/president-elect; and Herbert Biblo, treasurer. Robert W. Wedgeworth is ALA's executive director.

AMERICAN BOOKSELLERS ASSOCIATION

122 East 42nd St., New York, NY 10168
212-867-9060

G. Roysce Smith
Executive Director

The American Booksellers Association (ABA), Inc., was organized in 1900 to bring together for their mutual benefit bookstores of all sizes and philosophies in one organization. On July 31, 1981, the association recorded 4,296 main stores and 819 branch stores as regular members. Publishers, wholesalers, sidelines manufacturers, and suppliers of goods and services are accepted as associate members, of which there were 683 recorded.

The ABA achieves its purpose in many ways—through publications, workshops and seminars, liaison with other segments of the industry, surveys and studies, national and regional meetings, and other related activities. It is governed by an elected board of 4 officers, 16 directors, and the immediate past president. Current officers, who will serve through May 30, 1982, are as follows: president, Joan Ripley, Second Story, Chappaqua, New York; vice president, Donald Laing, Boulder Bookstore, Boulder, Colorado; treasurer, Richard H. Noyes, The Chinook Bookshop, Colorado Springs, Colorado; and secretary, Jo Ann McGreevy, New York University Book Centers, New York, New York.

The board employs a staff of 25, including G. Roysce Smith, executive director; Robert D. Hale, associate executive director; and Victoria M. Stanley, assistant director.

PUBLICATIONS

The ABA Book Buyer's Handbook, revised annually, lists publishers' addresses, key personnel, and the terms under which publishers do business with booksellers, e.g., discounts, co-op ad policies, and returns policies. It also contains a useful collection of supplementary information in its 504 pages. Edited by Mary Ann Tennenhouse, it is an indispensable bookselling tool. It is available only to ABA bookseller members. A copy of each of ABA's other publications is sent free of cost to all bookseller members and, unless otherwise noted, to associate members. These publications are also available to nonmembers at established rates.

American Bookseller, the ABA's monthly trade magazine, began publication in September 1977. Edited by Ginger Curwen, the magazine addresses itself to the day-to-day challenges and problems of retail bookselling. Such topics as merchandising and promotion, inventory control, bookseller/publisher relations, computers, sidelines, and children's books are featured regularly in articles; media tie-ins, activities of the ABA, and those of regional bookseller associations are also covered each month in regular departments.

ABA Newswire, a weekly publication first issued in February 1973, lists advance information on author tours, book reviews, and advertising and promotion. The author listings include lectures as well as television, radio, and in-store appearances. Booksellers and librarians find this a valuable aid in ensuring that they have books on hand when demand is greatest. Also included are front page news briefs on matters of vital interest to retail booksellers. Barbara Livingston is the editor of *Newswire*.

The *ABA Basic Book List* is issued annually. A highly selective list of titles chosen by a committee of booksellers and based on actual sales records of member stores, it is intended as a guide for the neophyte bookseller or the established bookseller who may want to review what others find saleable. It is edited by Mary Ann Tennenhouse, as is the biennial *ABA Sidelines Directory*, which contains brief articles by booksellers about sidelines and lists sources for both sidelines and store supplies and fixtures.

A Manual on Bookselling, a comprehensive textbook about establishing and maintaining a bookstore, now has over 20,000 copies in print of the third revised edition, which was published in 1980. A copy is supplied free of cost by ABA to each member store, and a trade edition for resale is published by Harmony Books, an imprint of Crown Publishers. A fourth edition is tentatively planned for 1985 publication.

In response to booksellers' growing interest in computers, ABA recently published the *ABA Computer Specifications for Independent Bookstores*, which was sent free of charge to bookstore members only (but is available to nonmembers). A follow-up study evaluating computer vendors is planned for publication in the spring of 1982. Also available in reprint form is the *ABA Bookstore Financial Profile 1981*, to be published first in the January, 1982 issue of *American Bookseller*.

WORKSHOPS AND SEMINARS

A major function of ABA is promoting professional competence through continuing bookseller education. While part of this goal can be attained through publications and through national meetings, ABA is committed to a series of highly successful training sessions, which provide more intensive advice and participation for those attending. The Booksellers School, now in its sixteenth year, is sponsored jointly by ABA and the National Association of College Stores (NACS). Nearly 6,000 established and aspiring booksellers have attended the school. Five schools are scheduled for 1982, with three geared to experienced booksellers, one to prospective booksellers, and one for a combined audience. The basic schools will open in Nashville, Tennessee (February); Colorado Springs, Colorado (April); and Cambridge, Massachusetts (April). A school for prospective booksellers will open in Chicago, Illinois (March); and a combined school is tentatively scheduled for the fall in California.

BOOK PROMOTION

The Give-A-Book Certificate program, initially launched in 1978 as a joint project of NACS and ABA, gained the Association of American Publishers as a new partner in 1981, following the withdrawal of NACS from the venture. Over 6,000 stores now participate in the program, and a major promotional campaign is scheduled for 1982. The Give-A-Book Certificate program has also been enthusiastically embraced by several Friends of the Library groups, which have found the program useful as a fund-raising tool.

Along with other organizations in the book industry, ABA has also been active in its support of The American Book Awards, now entering its third year.

CONVENTIONS AND REGIONAL MEETINGS

Due in part to the dramatic growth of regional booksellers associations across the country, the ABA no longer sponsors regional meetings during the year. At the close of 1981, ABA records showed 21 regional associations; 7 sponsored regional trade shows in the previous fall. While the regional associations are not branches of nor sponsored by ABA, ABA does offer them assistance and support.

The annual ABA Convention continues to be a major event in the international book world. The 1981 Convention & Trade Exhibit was held in Atlanta, Georgia, from May 23-26. Some 13,000 booksellers, exhibitors, wholesalers, authors, and other members of the book industry were in attendance.

Authors addressing the convention included Eric Carle, Rosemary Wells, Ashley Bryan, Fannie Flagg, M. M. Kaye, Garry Trudeau, Harry Reasoner, John Irving, and Eudora Welty. Another 100 authors met booksellers in the autograph areas and at parties.

The 1982 Convention will be held in Anaheim, California, from May 29-June 1.

CRITICAL ISSUES IN BOOKSELLING

Like libraries, bookstores have also been plagued by censorship problems in the past year, particularly because of the proliferation of "minors access" legislation across the country. In conjunction with the Media Coalition, ABA has taken an active stance against censorship. ABA was one of the plaintiffs in a civil suit against Georgia's Act 785, which would have forced booksellers to either remove many books from display or bar minors from their stores. On October 23, 1981, the U.S. District Court in Georgia granted a permanent injunction against Act 785. ABA is participating in similar suits in Pennsylvania, Colorado, and three California municipalities. It is also joining other segments of the industry in filing an *amicus curiae* brief in the case of *Pico* v. *Island Trees*.

The survival of the independent bookstore has also been a major concern of ABA. Convinced that practices exist in publishing and bookselling that are truly forms of restraint of trade, ABA member booksellers passed a resolution at the 1980 ABA Convention recommending that ABA sponsor a series of regional meetings for the purpose of discussing with members "the Association's role in correcting, by any legal means, publishers' discriminatory pricing, advertising, and shipping policies." Following the well-attended "Survival Strategy" meetings in the fall of 1980, ABA created a Publisher Planning Committee whose members have visited with many heads of publishing houses over the past year and a half, explaining the financial problems of independent booksellers. As a direct consequence or not, many changes in sales terms have been announced by major publishers, ranging from a non-returns policy (Harcourt, Brace, Jovanovich) to the freight pass-through concept (Dutton, Harper & Row, Simon & Schuster, Random House). In May, 1981, the ABA Board of Directors also voted to assist the financing of any class action suit initiated by a member if the action met with the board's approval and was "instituted for the purpose of correcting alleged violations of the Robinson/Patman Acts with respect to price discrimination, returns policy discrimination, cooperative advertising policy discrimination" to the extent of $100,000 a year. ABA has stated publicly that it hopes there will be no need for antitrust litigation in order to correct alleged inequities. By the end of 1981, no further details had been announced on the matter.

AMERICAN NATIONAL STANDARDS COMMITTEE Z39: LIBRARY AND INFORMATION SCIENCES AND RELATED PUBLISHING PRACTICES AND INTERNATIONAL ORGANIZATION FOR STANDARDIZATION TECHNICAL COMMITTEE 46—DOCUMENTATION

U.S. Department of Commerce, National Bureau of Standards,
Library E-106, Washington, D.C. 20234
301-921-3402

Patricia W. Berger
Chair

Robert W. Frase
Executive Director

The American National Standards Committee Z39: Library and Information Sciences and Related Publishing Practices has the principal responsibility in the United States for developing and promoting standards for information systems, products, and services. Committee Z39 was established in 1939 by the American Standards Association, predecessor of the American National Standards Institute (ANSI). The Council of National Library and Information Associations serves as the Z39 Secretariat and is responsible to ANSI for the work of Z39.

The American National Standards, developed and promulgated by Z39 and published by ANSI, are intended to benefit both producers and consumers of information. Although compliance with Z39 standards is voluntary, Z39 encourages their adoption when appropriate in library, publishing, document delivery, information-dissemination, and information- and data-handling systems.

Z39 participates in the development of international standards for libraries, documentation and information centers, indexing and abstracting services, and publishing through its membership in the International Organization for Standardization, Technical Committee 46: Documentation.

Z39 ACTIVITIES DURING 1981

New Standards

Z39.30-1982 Order Form for Single Titles of Library Materials
Z39.32-1981 Information on Microfiche Headings

Revisions of Published Standards

Z39.22-1981 Proof Corrections
Z39.26-1981 Advertising of Micropublications

Published Standards Being Revised

Z39.1-1977 Periodicals: Format and Arrangement
Z39.4-1974 Basic Criteria for Indexes
Z39.5-1969 (R1974) Abbreviation of Titles of Periodicals
Z39.7-1974 Library Statistics
Z39.18-1974 Guidelines for Format and Production of Scientific Technical Reports
Z39.20-1974 Criteria for Price Indexes for Library Materials
Z39.25-1975 Romanization of Hebrew

Standards for Review in 1981

Z39.24-1976 System for the Romanization of Slavic Cyrillic Characters
Z39.27-1976 Structure for the Identification of Countries of the World for Information Interchange
Z39.31-1976 Format for Scientific and Technical Translations

Other Published Standards

Z39.2-1979 Bibliographic Information Interchange on Magnetic Tape
Z39.6-1965 (R1977) Trade Catalogs
Z39.8-1977 Compiling Book Publishing Statistics
Z39.10-1977 (R1977) Directories of Libraries and Information Centers
Z39.11-1972 (R1978) System for the Romanization of Japanese
Z39.12-1972 (R1978) System for the Romanization of Arabic
Z39.13-1979 Describing Books in Advertisements, Catalogs, Promotional Materials, and Book Jackets
Z39.14-1979 Writing Abstracts
Z39.16-1979 Preparation of Scientific Papers for Written or Oral Presentation
Z39.29-1977 Bibliographic References
Z39.33-1977 Development of Identification Codes for Use by the Bibliographic Community
Z39.34-1977 Synoptics
Z39.35-1979 System for the Romanization of Lao, Khmer, and Pali
Z39.37-1979 System for the Romanization of Armenian
Z39.39-1979 Compiling Newspaper and Periodical Publishing Statistics
Z39.40-1979 Compiling U.S. Microfilm Publishing Statistics

Z39.41-1979 Book Spine Formats
Z39.42-1980 Serial Holding Statements at the Summary Level
Z39.43-1980 Identification Code for the Book Industry

NEW STANDARDS IN PROCESS

New standards being prepared by Z39 subcommittees include: *Romanization of Yiddish*, by Z39/SC 5, Herbert Zafron, Hebrew Union College, chairperson; *Serials Claim Form*, by Z39/SC 42, Lois Upham, University of Southern Mississippi, chairperson; *Multiple Copy Standard Order Form*, by Z39/SC 36, Peter Jacobs, BroDart, Inc., chairperson; *Language Codes*, by Z39/SC C, Arlene Schwartz, ILLINET Bibliographic Data Base Service, chairperson; *Computer-to-Computer Protocol*, by Z39/SC D, David C. Hartmann, Network Development Office, Library of Congress, chairperson; *Serial Holdings Statements at the Detailed Level*, by Z39/SC E, Susan Brynteson, Director, University of Delaware Library, chairperson; *Terms and Symbols Used in Form Functional Areas of Interactive Retrieval Systems*, by Z39/SC G, Pauline Cochrane, Syracuse University School of Information Studies, chairperson; *Patent Data Element Identification and Application Numbering*, by Z39/SC H, Philip J. Pollick, Chemical Abstracts Service, chairperson; *Bibliographic Data Source File Identification*, by Z39/SC J, John G. Mulvihill, American Geological Institute, chairperson; *Romanization*, by Z39/SC I, Charles W. Husbands, Harvard University Library, chairperson; *Coded Character Sets for Bibliographic Information Interchange*, by Z39/SC N, Charles T. Payne, University of Chicago Library, and Sally McCallum, Library of Congress, co-chairpersons; *Environmental Conditions for Storage of Paper-Based Library Materials*, by Z39/SC R, Paul Banks, Columbia School of Library Service, chairperson; *Paper Quality for Library Books*, by Z39/SC S, Gay Walker, Yale University Library, chairperson; *Standard Format for Computerized Book Ordering*, by Z39/SC U, Ernest Muro, The Baker and Taylor Companies, chairperson; and *Standard Identification Numbers for Libraries, Library Items, and Library Patrons*, by Z39/SC V, Paul Lagueux, Council on Library Resources, Chairperson.

MEMBERSHIP

During 1981, the following organizations became full voting members: Pennsylvania Area Library Network (PALINET), Library of the University of California-Los Angeles, and the National Archives. Four members resigned their voting memberships: Shoestring Press, American Society of Mechanical Engineers, American Translators Society, and the Association for Computing Machinery. By the year's end a total of 30 academic, public, and government libraries, commercial organizations, and other agencies had become Z39 Information Members.

The Z39 Executive Council appointed the first three honorary members for outstanding contributions to national or international standards development as authorized by a new provision of the Z39 bylaws. They are Jerrold Orne, Z39 Chairman for 1965 to 1978; Anne J. Richter, who served as vice-chair of Z39 and chair of several subcommittees while with the R. R. Bowker Company; and Daniel Melcher, former president of R. R. Bowker Company, for his leadership in securing U.S. participation in the International Standard Book Numbering (ISBN) System and then providing for the administration of that system in the United States by the U.S. Standard Book Numbering Agency at the R. R. Bowker Company.

ACCESS TO Z39 STANDARDS/PUBLICITY

In 1980, Z39 published standards began to be entered into the Cataloging in Publication (CIP) program of the Library of Congress. Another major step to improve knowledge of Z39 standards and thus to increase their use was taken in 1981. Z39 standards series became a monographic serial with an assigned International Standard Serial Number: ISSN 0276-0762. Subsequently, ANSI made provision in the order form in the September 1981 edition of the catalog of Z39 published standards to enter standing orders for Z39 standards. Knowledge of Z39 standards was also promoted in a variety of other ways. There were tabletop exhibits of Z39 materials at the annual meetings of the National Federation of Abstracting and Indexing Societies (NFAIS), the Special Libraries Association (SLA), the American Library Association (ALA), and the American Society for Information Science (ASIS), all Z39 member organizations. A revised information pamphlet on Z39 programs was published in March with an index for Z39 published standards. Copies are available on request to the Z39 office. Four issues of the newsletter, the *Voice of Z39*, were published in 1981 and distributed to a mailing list of approximately 1,400. Articles on Z39 and Technical Committee 46 of the International Organization for Standardization appeared in the 1981 editions of the *ALA Yearbook* and *The Bowker Annual* (see *The Bowker Annual 1981*, p. 107).

FUNDING

Early in the year, Z39 took the first step toward becoming self-supporting through membership fees, thereby ending the former reliance on foundation and government grants and voluntary contributions. Following approval by the Z39 membership of a change in bylaws, the Z39 Executive Council adopted a sliding scale of annual participating member service fees based on the size of member organization budgets. The fees, which now range from a minimum of $200 to a maximum of $5,000, were formerly voluntary but are mandatory as of 1982. The response of the Z39 membership to the new method of financing was positive, and fees were sufficient to support the Z39 program in 1981 with some carry-over of funds into 1982.

Z39 OFFICERS AND COMMITTEES

In accordance with changes in bylaws approved by the Z39 membership in 1980, an election was held in the spring for the following Z39 officers for terms beginning on July 1, 1981: chairperson (two-year); vice-chairperson and chairperson-elect (two-year); three members of the executive council for three-year terms; and three members of the council for one-year terms. There will now be a Z39 election every year for one-third of the members of the executive council, and every other year for vice-chairperson and chairperson-elect. Following the spring election, the Z39 Executive Council on July 1, 1981, was as follows: Patricia W. Berger, Chief of the Library and Information Services Division, National Bureau of Standards, *Chpn.*; Margaret K. Park, Office of Computer and Information Services, University of Georgia, *V. Chpn/Chpn-Elect*, each for two-year terms ending on June 30, 1983; *Councillors Representing Libraries:* Linda K. Bartley, Head of the National Serials Data Program, the Library of Congress (three-year term); Carol A. Nemeyer, Associate Librarian for National Programs, the Library of Congress (two-year term); Larry X. Besant, Assistant Director of the Ohio State University Libraries (one-year term); *Councillors Representing Information Services:* James E. Rush, President, James E. Rush Associates, Inc. (three-year term); W. Theodore Brandhorst, Director of ERIC Processing and Reference Facility (two-year term); M. Lynne Neufeld, Executive Director of the National Federation of Abstracting and Indexing Services (one-year term); *Councillors Representing Publishing:* Karl F. Heumann, Director of Publications for the Federation of American Societies for Experimental Biology (three-year term); Sandra K. Paul, President, SKP Associates (two-year term); Seldon W. Terrant, Head of Research and Development, American Chemical Society (one-year term); *Ex-officio: Secretariat Rep.:* John T. Corrigan, C.F.X., Council of National Library and Information Associations; *Exec. Dir.:* Robert W. Frase.

In addition to the Z39 Executive Council, which met three times in 1981, Z39 has several operating committees. The Program Committee is chaired by Margaret K. Parks, Z39 Vice-Chairperson and Chairperson-Elect, and has the following additional members: Sally H. McCallum, Robert S. Tannehill, Jr., James E. Rush, Sandra K. Paul, and W. Theodore Brandhorst. The Finance Committee consists of Seldon W. Terrant, Chairperson; John T. Lorenz, Vice-Chairperson and Z39 Treasurer; Samuel Beatty, American Society for Information Science; David R. Bender, Special Libraries Association; Patricia W. Berger, Z39 Chairperson; John T. Corrigan, C.F.X. and Z39 Secretariat Representative; Robert W. Frase, Z39 Executive Director; H. Joanne Harrar, McKeldin Library, University of Maryland; Gerald R. Lowell, F. W. Faxon Company; Douglas Price, National Commission on Libraries and Information Science; and Robert Wedgeworth, American Library Association. The Membership Committee consists of Larry X. Besant, Chairperson, and Karl F. Heumann; the Publicity Committee consists of Sandra K. Paul, Chairperson, and Linda K. Bartley; and the International Committee is chaired by Henriette Avram, Library of Congress.

ANNUAL MEETING

The 1981 annual business meeting of Z39 was held in the Whittall Pavilion in the Library of Congress. Some 50 individuals representing member organizations, the executive council, and its committees and Z39 subcommittees were in attendance. Reports were made on the election of officers, the status of work of Z39 subcommittees, and on finances, membership, publicity, and international affairs. The minutes of the annual meeting were distributed to the Z39 members; a shorter account of the meeting appeared in the June 12, 1981, issue of the *Library of Congress Information Bulletin*. The 1982 annual business meeting, which is open to observers, will be held at the Library of Congress on April 29.

INTERNATIONAL STANDARDIZATION ACTIVITIES

Z39 participates through ANSI in the development of international standards for libraries, documentation and information centers, and indexing and abstracting services, and in publishing through its membership in the International Organization for Standardization, Technical Committee 46: Documentation (ISO/TC 46). ISO/TC 46 is one of 1,940 technical bodies within ISO engaged in developing international standards to facilitate the exchange of goods and services and to foster mutual cooperation in intellectual, scientific, technological, and economic activities. Since its establishment in 1947, TC 46 has produced 29 ISO standards.

The plenary assembly, which meets every two years, is the governing body of TC 46. Delegates to the assembly represent member bodies (national standards organizations) that participate in the work of TC 46. The secretariat of TC 46, which is held by the Deutsches Institut für Normung (DIN), is responsible to the ISO council and to the members of the technical committee for TC 46 activities. An elected steering committee, on which the United States presently serves, assists the secretariat to plan and program the work of TC 46 and its subcommittees and working groups between meetings of the plenary assembly.

TABLE 1   ISO/TC 46 SUBCOMMITTEES AND WORKING GROUPS

Subcommittees and Working Groups	Status of U.S. Participation	Secretariat
SC 2: Conversion of Written Languages	O	France
SC 3: Terminology of Documentation	O	West Germany
SC 4: Automation in Documentation	P	Sweden
WG 1: Character Sets	P (C)	
WG 3: Bibliographic Filing Principles	P	
WG 4: Format Structure	P	
WG 5: Application Level Protocols	P	
SC 5: Mono- and Multi-lingual Thesauri and Related Indexing Practices	O	West Germany
SC 6: Bibliographic Data Elements	P	Canada
WG 1: Data Element Directory	P	
WG 2: Codes and Numbering Systems	P (C)	
SC 7: Presentation of Publications	O	France

O = Observer (wants to be kept informed).
P = Participating Member (participates in work).
P (C) = Participating, holding convenership.

The program of work of TC 46 is conducted by six subcommittees, each of which is served by a secretariat in one of the national standards organizations. Most of the TC 46 subcommittees also have working groups. Table 1 lists the TC 46 subcommittees and working groups, showing the status of their U.S. participation and the national standards organization holding the secretariat of each. Henriette Avram and Patricia W. Berger are conveners of SC4/WG1 (Character Sets) and SC6/WG2 (Codes and Numbering Systems), respectively.

In 1981, the plenary assembly meeting was held in Nanjing, People's Republic of China, March 31-April 3. Because of the traveling distances involved, attendance at this meeting was more limited than is usually the case. Thirteen countries were represented by voting delegates and four international organizations were represented by observers. The Z39 Executive Director attended for the United States. Only one of the two subcommittees on which the United States serves as a participating member had meetings in Nanjing: Subcommittee 4, Automation in Documentation.

Subsequent to the Nanjing meeting, several TC 46 subcommittees and working groups held meetings in 1981, all of them in Europe. The United States was represented at two of these: a meeting of Subcommittee 6 (Bibliographic Data Elements and its two working groups) near Graz, Austria, October 13-16, at which the United States was represented by Patricia W. Berger and Henriette Avram; and a meeting of the TC 46 Steering Committee in Stockholm, Sweden, November 10-11, at which the United States was represented by Patricia W. Berger.

Z39 comments and votes on TC 46 proposals many times each year at various stages in the development or revision of ISO standards: on subcommittee drafts; on Draft Proposals (DPs), through ANSI; on Draft International Standards (DISs), through ANSI. There is frequently a close relationship between American and international standards. In important instances they are the same, as, for example, Bibliographic Information Interchange on Magnetic Tape (Z39.2 and ISO 2709); the International Standard Serial Number (Z39.9 and ISO 3297); and the International Standard Book Number (Z39.2 and ISO 2108). Several American National Standards are being used by TC 46 as a basis for developing ISO standards: Z39.20 (Criteria for Price Indexes for Library Materials), Z39.32 (Information on Microfiche Headings), and Z39.34 (Synoptics).

ISO/TC 46 published standards are sold in the United States by the American National Standards Institute, 1430 Broadway, New York, NY 10018. In addition to the individual ISO/TC 46 published standards, ANSI also has for sale a 500-page compilation of the texts of 56 ISO/TC 46 and related ISO standards covering the fields of bibliographic references and descriptions, abstracts and indexing, presentation of documents, conversion of written languages, document copying, microforms, bibliographic control, libraries and information systems, mechanization and automation in documentation, classifications and controlled language for information storage and retrieval, and terminology (principles): *ISO Standards Handbook I—Information Transfer* (1977).

ASSOCIATION OF AMERICAN PUBLISHERS

One Park Ave., New York, NY 10016
212-689-8920

1707 L St. N.W., Washington, DC 20036
202-293-2585

Jane Lippe
Public Relations

The eleventh year of the Association's existence was marked by a new economic climate in Washington, and significant accomplishments and new developments in the postal, international, and new technology areas. At the AAP annual meeting in May, incoming Chairman Martin P. Levin (Times Mirror Company) proposed action on four fronts: "(1) to restore education and books as a #1 national priority; (2) to increase the number of book readers; (3) to improve the marketing of books; (4) to keep abreast of the new technology." Reconfirming the Association's commitment to literacy, Levin announced he had written to President Reagan to suggest a meeting between a group of publishers and the President. AAP later renewed its request for a meeting, and also proposed the creation of a Business Council for Literacy to provide private sector funding and guidance for programs to improve reading efficiency and reduce functional illiteracy. Initial response from the White House was favorable.

The second annual American Book Awards were presented, honoring 110 hardcover and paperback literary nominees and 22 winners for exemplary achievement and literary excellence. The program was chaired by Esther Margolis (Newmarket Press).

In the international area, in response to a request from the People's Republic of China and in cooperation with the U.S. International Communication Agency and the China National Publications Import and Export Corporation (CNPIEC), AAP organized an exhibit of 14,500 American books, which were displayed simultaneously in six Chinese cities in May 1981.

The Thor Power Tool Company decision as rendered by the U.S. Supreme Court and subsequent IRS rulings held that publishers could no longer depreciate unsold books for tax purposes while continuing to sell them at regular prices. AAP quickly assumed leadership of a Washington initiative aimed first at delaying the application of the ruling and, eventually, at obtaining exemption from it for the publishing industry. Both initiatives failed in the Ninety-sixth Congress.

Senator Daniel Patrick Moynihan (D-N.Y.) introduced a bill early in the new Congress to amend the Internal Revenue Code by permitting taxpayers to "write down" excess inventory items to their net realizable value. Additionally, the bill included a provision that would make a switch to the more advantageous "last-in-first-out" (LIFO) accounting system available to publishers. Moynihan offered this measure as an amendment to the Reagan administration's tax measure during Senate debate. He subsequently withdrew it prior to a vote, when Senator Robert Dole (R-Kans.), chairman of the Senate Finance Committee, promised the proposal would be considered in the next tax bill.

In a somewhat unexpected move, U.S. Treasury officials, testifying during a September 25 hearing on Thor, put a cost tag of $8 billion annually on the Moynihan measure. AAP, in its submitted testimony, stated that the $8 billion estimate could only be the cost of changes in accounting procedures and not of the primary part of the bill that would allow write-downs of inventories based upon the previous five-year experience of the firm in selling the stock. AAP President Townsend Hoopes stated "we do not understand that any significant amount would be involved if the write-down section were enacted, particularly if the effect were limited to industries who demonstrate hardship." With the $8 billion estimate in lost government revenues and the generally austere mood in Washington, it is unlikely that relief from Thor Power will receive further congressional attention during the current session of the Congress.

AAP witnesses—publishers and staff—appeared before Senate and House committees as well as federal administrative bodies to testify on such matters as education, postal rates, literacy and basic skills, and testing.

ORGANIZATION

The association, whose membership comprises some 350 companies, is the major voice of the book publishing industry in the United States. AAP was founded in 1970 as the result of the merger of the American Book Publishers Council and the American Educational Publishers Institute.

AAP members publish the great majority of printed materials sold to American schools, colleges, libraries, and bookstores and by direct mail to homes. All regions of the country are represented. Member firms publish hardcover and paperback books: textbooks, general trade, reference, religious and technical, scientific and medical, professional and scholarly books, and journals. AAP members also produce a range of other educational materials including classroom periodicals, maps, globes, films and filmstrips, audio- and videotapes, records, slides, transparencies, test materials, and looseleaf services and computer software learning packages.

Association policies are established by an elected 29-member board of directors representing large and small firms from many geographic locations. Martin P. Levin (Times Mirror Company) is chairman of the board for FY 1981/82. AAP President Townsend Hoopes, chief operating officer, is responsible for managing AAP within the framework of basic policies set by the board. A staff of approximately 40 professional and nonprofessional personnel is located in two offices, New York and Washington.

The AAP operates under an organizational plan that ensures central direction of association affairs as "core" activities and gives important initiatives to the seven AAP divisions, each covering a major product line or distinct method of distribution of the industry. Each AAP division annually elects a chairperson and establishes committees to plan and implement independent projects. Marketing, promotion, research projects, and relations with other associations concerned with mutual problems are central features of divisional programs.

CORE COMMITTEES

Core activities include matters related to copyright, new technology, freedom to read, postal rates and regulations, statistical surveys, book distribution, public information, press relations, communications, international freedom to publish, and education for publishing.

The Copyright Committee safeguards and promotes the proprietary rights of authors and publishers domestically and internationally. It closely monitors copyright activity in the United States and abroad. It prepares congressional testimony for appropriate AAP spokespersons, assigns representatives to attend national and international copyright meetings, and sponsors seminars on copyright matters. Allan Wittman (John Wiley & Sons) chairs this committee. The committee plays an active role in disseminating information about the copyright law by providing speakers to address publisher, librarian, and educator groups, and by preparing and distributing printed information. Over 3,500 copies of its publication *Photocopying by Academic, Public and Non-Profit Libraries* have been distributed. The Copyright Committee maintains liaison with the U.S. Copyright Office and informs publishers of new and proposed regulations that relate to their activities. It participates in negotiations concerning copyright-related policy to be followed by users of copyrighted material.

The New Technology Committee was created in 1981 to meet the need expressed by member publishers to monitor the new technologies—the new means of distributing published information and the new products, i.e., on-line data bases, computer programming, videodiscs, videotapes, teletext and videotext. Functioning as an information clearinghouse, the committee publishes a monthly column on technologies that affect the publishing business and sponsors workshops and seminars to assist publishers in gaining the knowledge required to enter these fields. Dr. Frank Greenagel (Aretê) chairs this committee.

The Freedom to Read Committee is concerned with protecting freedoms guaranteed by the First Amendment. It analyzes individual cases of attempted censorship by Congress, state legislatures, federal, state, or municipal governments, local school boards, or any other institution. Its actions may take the form of a legal brief in support of a position against censorship, testimony before appropriate legislative committees, or public statements and communications protesting any attempt to limit freedom of communication. The committee works closely with other organizations that support its goals.

The major event of the committee's activities during the past year was the publication in July of a study resulting from a year-long research project on the challenges raised against books and other learning materials in public school classrooms and libraries. The report, entitled *Limiting What Students Shall Read*, was widely publicized and circulated after publication. Anthony M. Schulte (Random House/Knopf) served as Project Chairman and Michelle Marder Kamhi of New York City was the Project Researcher. The Freedom to Read Committee is chaired by Brooks Thomas (Harper & Row).

The Postal Committee monitors the activities of the U.S. Postal Service, the Postal Rate Commission, and congressional committees responsible for postal matters. It presents the publisher's point of view to those in policy making positions through direct testimony, by economic analyses of proposed postal programs, and through a variety of other means. Leo Albert (Prentice-Hall) chairs the committee.

The International Freedom to Publish Committee is the only body formed by a major group of publishers in any country for the specific purpose of protecting and expanding the freedom of written communication. The committee monitors the general status of freedom to publish and discusses problems of restriction with the U.S. government, other governments, and international organizations. When appropriate, it makes recommendations to these organizations and issues public statements.

During the year the committee investigated violations of free expression in Argentina, China, Czechoslovakia, Haiti, Iran, Peru, Poland, South Africa, Taiwan, Uruguay, the USSR, and Yugoslavia. Together with the Fund for Free Expression, the committee mounted a central exhibit, "America Through American Eyes," for the U.S. book exhibition in China and published catalogs in English and Chinese to accompany the exhibit. The committee also organized the Third Moscow Book Fair Reception in Exile, which was held at the New York Public Library in September 1981 and honored Soviet writers in exile as well as those silenced by prison or other forms of persecution in the USSR. John Macrae III (E. P. Dutton) is chairman.

The Book Distribution Task Force was created in 1976 to foster the development and implementation of more efficient book distribution systems for all book publishers. In April 1981 the task force conducted a seminar on voluntary industry-wide standardized forms and systems, which offer book publishers cost reductions and/or increased efficiencies in the area of distribution. The task force also conducted two major publisher surveys, one on computer hardware and software in use and the other on fulfillment costs. It also revised the glossary of terms relating to book distribution it had issued two years prior. The task force organized a second international meeting on book distribution, which took place in Frankfurt as part of the Book Fair. Reports were substantive and the British Publishers Association organized a follow-up meeting in 1981. A group from the Netherlands will plan the 1982 meeting.

The task force represents the AAP on American National Standards Institute Committee Z39, which develops standards for publishing and library information science. It also participates as a member of the Network Advisory Committee to the Library of Congress. In 1981/82 the task force plans to publicize new Book Industry Systems Advisory Committee (BISAC) formats for computer-to-computer communications that are now under development, to report on progress in SAN (Standard Address Numbering) assignment and implementation, and to consider holding a computer hardware/software fair during which vendors can discuss their offerings with interested publishers. Robert J. R. Follett (Follett Corporation) is chairman of the Book Distribution Task Force.

The Education for Publishing Program, implemented by AAP in 1978 after a three-year exploration and study of the education and training needs of the book publishing industry, works to promote and advance the continuing education of employees already in the industry; to help attract, prepare, and educate new talent to enter the industry; and to help inform the public about the book publishing industry. This mission is being carried out by informing and guiding educational and training institutions in providing authoritative and useful courses on book publishing; initiating and sponsoring professional development courses on book publishing for industry employees; encouraging and assisting in the development and improvement of in-house training programs conducted by member companies; and by creating and providing career and other information about the industry.

An Entry-Level Job Clearinghouse, started in 1980, continues to assist newcomers in entering the industry. A Publishing Education Information Service, established in 1979, acts as a research, referral, and communication resource for publishers, educators, and serious students seeking information about book publishing. A collection of over 300 books about publishing, 40 periodicals dealing with the industry, and archival material are available by appointment in the service office library, known as the Stephen Greene Memorial Library.

DIVISIONS

General Publishing Division

The General Publishing Division (GPD), chaired by Jeremiah Kaplan (Macmillan), represents 145 publishers of fiction, nonfiction, children's literature, religious, and reference books. In its interests and activities, the division frequently works cooperatively with publishers of professional and scholarly books and with mass market paperback publishers within AAP. The division's programs focus on three key objectives: broadening the audience for books, strengthening relationships with librarians and booksellers for the solution of common problems, and improving the management and marketing skills of publishers.

Among the activities the division supports are the American Book Awards and the Give-A-Book Certificate program. The American Book Awards program is a major recipient of divisional funds as well as contributed services and materials in its effort to call public attention to the best of American books. The program is also supported by authors, agents, booksellers, wholesalers, and librarians. The new Give-A-Book Certificate program, initiated by the American Booksellers Association (ABA) and cosponsored by AAP, offers an additional vehicle for longterm expansion of the audience for books. It provides a mechanism for the redemption of gift certificates at 6,000 bookstores nationwide.

With the cooperation of ABA, members of the division serve as faculty members at schools for booksellers and promote the marketing of books through special activities for booksellers. Other educational initiatives and programs designed to enhance the effectiveness of book promotion efforts are under development. Active liaison with librarians is maintained through joint committees with the American Library Association and the Special Libraries Association. An active group of smaller publishers within the GPD plans programs and publications of particular interest to the growing number of smaller publishers within all AAP divisions.

Mass Market Paperback Division

The Mass Market Paperback Division, chaired by Howard Kaminsky (Warner Books), is concerned with making the paperback book an integral part of the educational and leisure reading of Americans today. The division also works closely with the General Publishing Division in the ongoing support of the American Book Awards.

The Mass Market Paperback Division maintains close communication with booksellers through the ABA-Mass Paperback Liaison Committee, which works on programs of common interest such as the American Book Awards, a future Paperback Category Bestseller List, and a possible Mass Paperback Fiche program. This past spring, the division updated a survey it had undertaken in 1977 on the effectiveness of various advertising techniques in the publishing industry and found many attitudes unchanged since 1977: TV advertising and author appearances were still considered the most effective publicity techniques. The survey also compiled booksellers' attitudes concerning the effectiveness of various trade publications, sales representatives, telephone solicitations, mailings, and radio, magazine and newspaper advertising. (Copies of the 1981 survey are available from the Mass Market Paperback Division.)

The division is also concerned with the mass paperback industry's marketing, production, and distribution problems, focusing on issues at national and international levels. Separate divisional committees address financial planning, industry statistics, operational management, advertising and promotion, production, and freight and postal concerns. The division represents the industry at both ABA and National Association of College Stores (NACS) annual meetings.

College Division

The College Division, chaired by Howard Aksen (Harper & Row), is directly concerned with all aspects of the marketing, production, and distribution of textbooks to the postsecondary education field. It pays special attention to maintaining good relations between the publishing industry and college faculty, bookstore managers, and college students. To develop and maintain strong relations with college students, the division has established the AAP Student Service, a public relations program featuring a series of publications directed to college students. They include *How to Get the Most Out of Your Textbook*, *How to Prepare Successfully for Examinations*, *How to Improve Your Reading Skills*, *How to Build Your Writing Skills*, *How to Get the Most Out of a College Education*, and *How to Read Technical Textbooks*. A new study skills publication, *How to Succeed in College: A Guide for the Non-Traditional Student*, was recently published. The division has developed several publications directed to college faculty, including an audio-visual slide show and the pamphlet *An Author's Guide to Academic Publishing*.

The division maintains close relations with college bookstores through the NACS-College Division Liaison Committee and continues the AAP Fiche Service started by the division and NACS in 1980. College bookstores can subscribe to the service for a nominal fee; in return, they are provided with microfiches (updated monthly) of about 40,000 textbook titles available from more than two dozen leading textbook publishers. The Liaison Committee also published a booklet for college bookstore managers, on *Textbook Questions and Answers*, and each spring it cosponsors an Advanced Financial Management Seminar for college store managers.

The College Division Marketing Committee sponsored a "Rely on Your Textbook" advertising program with posters and news releases to campus newspapers and college bookstores. Another important part of the College Division's public relations program is its sponsorship of a series of panels at various academic associations' annual meetings. Past programs have dealt with such subjects as "An Author's Guide to Academic Publishing," "The Copyright Law and the College Teacher," and "How the New Technology Affects the Academic World."

Professional and Scholarly Publishing Division

The Professional and Scholarly Publishing Division (PSP), chaired by William Begell (Hemisphere), is primarily concerned with production, marketing, and distribution of technical, scientific, medical, and scholarly books and journals. Essentially, although not exclusively, many of these publications are for the practicing engineer, scientist, and businessperson. To this end the division monitors relevant government activity and policies, levels of funding, and related matters. It provides for a continuous exchange of information and experience through seminars in journal publishing, marketing, sales, new technology, and copyright, and maintains relations with other professional associations, including the International Group of Scientific, Technical and Medical Publishers, government agencies, and industrial research groups. Professional societies and university presses play an integral role in divisional activities.

In 1980, an experimental committee of looseleaf publishers was added to the division and, accordingly, the annual PSP Awards program was expanded to include their publications. The Government Relations Committee continued to monitor the courses of various pieces of legislation and participated in developing AAP's position on such issues as the Thor Power Tool ruling, Small Business Administration regulations regarding loans to publishers, Office of Management and Budget policy on dissemination of federal information, and industry representation on NCLIS/SLA Task Force on the Role of the Special Library in a National Network System. The Marketing Committee is developing a presentation on selling professional books for the American Booksellers Association and other booksellers' meetings, and a booth for the ABA Convention. The Journals Committee conducted an extensive program of seminars and workshops. Other standing committees are concerned with statistics and public relations. The division's tenth annual meeting addressed electronic publishing.

School Division

The School Division, chaired by James R. Squire (Ginn & Company), is concerned with the production, marketing, and distribution of textbooks and instructional materials for kindergarten through twelfth grade and works to improve instructional programs and to seek increased levels of funding. It also sponsors seminars and conferences on topics of interest to educators and publishers.

Activities in the 50 state legislatures relative to schools and educational publishing are very important to school publishers. The division retains legislative advocates in key states to monitor legislative activities and to represent the interests of educational publishers at educational conferences. Liaison committees have also been organized to meet with state boards of education and members of state legislatures in the 22 adoption states, as well as selected open territory states, to review laws and regulations concerning the selection and purchase of instructional materials.

The School Division sponsored an awards competition in 1981/82 to provide grants to graduate students in education for research on the relationship between the availability of instructional materials and educational performance in the classroom. The Public Relations Committee works to acquaint parents, educators, and others with some of the concerns of educational publishers through meetings and publications such as the *Parent's Guide to More Effective Schools*, *Textbook Publishers and the Censorship Controversy*, and others. Public service ads and radio spots, emphasizing the fact that "for every dollar we spend on education, less than one penny goes for school books," are also part of the grass-roots public information campaign of the division.

Other standing committees of the division include: Social Issues in Education; Research; Statistics Review; Testing; and Right to Read.

International Division

The International Division, chaired by Nicholas G. Chantiles (Times Mirror Company), was formed in recognition of the rising importance of foreign markets for U.S. books, and focuses on those issues that affect the marketing of books to other countries and the ever-growing complexities of the international marketplace. The division represents the entire spectrum of publishing in both size of firm and product line.

Among the division's priorities are improving trade relations with the third world; developing the professional skills of members through seminars and workshops; developing strong relationships with U.S. government agencies (U.S. International Communication Agency and the State and Commerce Departments) interested in promoting the book abroad through national fairs and exhibits; promoting respect for international copyright;

developing international sales statistics; and promoting attendance and active participation at international book fairs. Continuing its efforts to combat piracy around the world, the division collects and disseminates information in cooperation with the International Publishers Association and lends support to members in their individual efforts.

The division's second annual meeting included reports on major world book markets. The division also assisted in organizing a major exhibit of American books held in the People's Republic of China in May 1981.

Direct Marketing/Book Club Division

The Direct Marketing/Book Club Division, chaired by Richard Spaulding (Scholastic, Inc.), is actively concerned with the marketing and distribution of books through direct response and book clubs. It works closely with the AAP Postal Committee to study the effects of new postal rates and regulations, and monitors new developments. The division's Marketing Committee sponsored seminars during the year, including "Direct Marketing Strategy: The Eight Indispensable Steps to Selling Your Books," "List Management," and "Credit and Collection." Other issues of concern were privacy legislation, copyright, and improved statistics programs.

AWARDS

On April 13, 1981, under AAP auspices, the second American Book Awards were presented to 22 books at a ceremony in New York City's Carnegie Hall. The National Medal for Literature, endowed by the Guinzburg Fund in honor of Harold K. Guinzburg, founder of Viking Press, was presented to Kenneth Burke. The medal, administered under the Book Awards aegis, carries a $15,000 cash prize.

The Association presented the sixth annual Curtis G. Benjamin Award for Creative Publishing during the AAP Annual Meeting in May. This year's recipient, Arthur J. Rosenthal, director of Harvard University Press, was cited for his "brilliant lists, season after season" and for his success in restoring the press to a sound financial footing.

The Professional and Scholarly Publishing Division completed the fifth year of its awards program, recognizing the best books and journals in its field; the program was expanded to include looseleaf publications and other media.

LIAISON WITH OTHER ASSOCIATIONS

The AAP has effective working relations with a large number of professional associations and agencies with allied interests. These include the American Booksellers Association, American Council on Education, American Library Association, Association of American University Presses, Book Industry Study Group, Book Manufacturers Institute, Children's Book Council, Council of the Great Cities Schools, Association of Media Producers, Information Industry Association, International Publishers Association, International Reading Association, National Association of College Stores, National Council of Teachers of English, National Education Association, P.E.N. American Center, Publishers Publicity Association, Publishers Library Marketing Group, Special Libraries Association, and UNESCO.

PUBLICATIONS

Although some AAP publications are circulated to members only, many are available to nonmembers.

The *AAP Newsletter* provides a periodic report to members on issues of concern to the publishing industry. The *Capital Letter*, issued monthly, offers news of federal government actions relating to the book community. *Publishing Abstracts* provides concise summaries of book publishing information from 500 newspapers and 4,000 periodicals, plus key information from AAP-sponsored events. Newsletters are prepared by the College, International, School, General Publishing, Mass Market Paperback, and Professional and Scholarly Publishing Divisions and the Education for Publishing Program. Periodic bulletins are published by the Book Distribution Task Force.

The AAP also publishes industry statistics on sales and operating expenses and a report on compensation and personnel practices in the industry. The annual *AAP Exhibits Directory* lists more than 800 book fairs and association meetings. The International Division publishes an annual *Profiles of International Book Fairs*. A publications list is available from AAP on request.

ASSOCIATION OF RESEARCH LIBRARIES

1527 New Hampshire Ave. N.W.,
Washington, DC 20036

Nicola Daval

Information Officer

The Association of Research Libraries (ARL) is an effective advocate for research libraries in the scholarly community, the government, and the private sector. Long a coordinating force to help research libraries meet demands for their services, ARL carries out studies, develops plans, and coordinates collective actions among its member institutions as they adapt to changing library operations, to new technological developments, and to increasingly stringent economic conditions.

Membership in the association reached 113 in 1981. Twelve ARL members are Canadian; 101 are university libraries, the remainder are the national libraries of both countries, and several public and special libraries with substantial research collections. In May 1981, Shirley Echelman, formerly executive director of the Medical Library Association, became ARL's executive director. Ralph McCoy, Dean of Libraries Emeritus at Southern Illinois University, served as interim executive director from January 1980 to April 1981, following the retirement of John Lorenz in December 1979.

ARL's areas of interests are reflected in its current programs and activities.

NETWORK DEVELOPMENT

The association has a continuing commitment to cooperation among research libraries, and to those activities and programs that support such cooperation. An essential element is the development of a nationwide bibliographic network. At its meeting in May 1980, the ALR membership endorsed eight statements of principle pertaining to network development and research libraries. Drafted by the ARL Task Force on National Library Network Development, the principles articulate the particular needs and concerns of research libraries, as libraries, bibliographic utilities, publishers, and others continue to build a national network. The statements cover research library collaboration, network participation, quality and scope of bibliographic data, linkage of utilities, nonexclusive contracts with utilities, regional network development, local systems development, and description of services and products.

Many current ARL programs reflect the importance of the network principles, to which the association is committed. The association is an active member of the Network Advisory Committee of the Library of Congress, represented on that body by the chair of the ARL Task Force on National Library Network Development. At the October 1980 ARL membership meeting, the membership reiterated its support for the Conversion of Serials (CONSER) Project, an essential segment of network-building activities, and emphasized the need to pursue methods of linking the utility data bases in order to ensure widespread sharing of CONSER records.

BIBLIOGRAPHIC CONTROL

Improving bibliographic access to materials, including development and implementation of national standards and mechanisms for sharing data, has been an important goal of the association for several years. A new initiative in this area began in 1981 with the ARL Microform Project, funded by grants from the Andrew W. Mellon Foundation and the Council on Library Resources. Designed to stimulate and coordinate the work of libraries, microform publishers, bibliographic utilities, and regional networks in providing bibliographic access to millions of microform titles that are now inadequately or insufficiently cataloged, the project is based on a planning study conducted for ARL in 1980 by Information Systems Consultants, Inc. Goals for the project include (1) agreement on national standards for bibliographic records describing microforms; (2) entry of catalog records produced by microform publishers into the data bases of the major bibliographic utilities; (3) cooperative projects by libraries to create original cataloging for both new and retrospective microform sets and to convert existing catalog records to machine-readable form; (4) development of "profile-matching" by bibliographic utilities to allow libraries to retrieve and add holding codes to records for titles in microform sets on a set-by-set rather than title-by-title basis; and (5) development of standard cataloging and recording practices for preservation of microfilms and for provision of records to a national data base of microform masters.

To aid in coordinating cooperative projects, Project Coordinator Jeffrey Heynen is developing an on-line data base of information about catalog records available for microform sets. In 1981, three ARL member libraries (Stanford University, Indiana University, and the University of Utah) received grants under the Higher Education Act (HEA) Title II-C program to carry out major microform cataloging projects, and the three libraries will be coordinating their efforts through the ARL project. Several cooperative cataloging projects have been spawned by the ARL project as well.

The ARL Task Force on Bibliographic Control has been concerned for several years with ways to control cataloging costs while still adhering to national standards and maintaining an appropriate level of service to users. In 1979, with the impending implementation of the Anglo-American Cataloguing Rules (AACR) 2, the task force recommended that the association contract with a consultant to develop cost models for the adoption of AACR 2. King Research, Inc., was engaged to carry out a project designed to help libraries assess the economic effects of AACR 2 and catalog closing, which is a major consideration for ARL libraries. The computer cost model developed by King Research for the project can be used to determine and compare the costs of different library catalog alternatives for individual libraries. The project was funded by the 71 libraries that participated; King Research published the final report of the project, *Alternatives for Future Catalogs: A Cost Model*, in 1980.

Noting that the increasing complexity of bibliographic records and the demands of automated systems are having a significant impact on cataloging costs, the task force decided to address specifically the question of simplification of the Machine Readable Cataloging (MARC) formats for bibliographic records as a possible means of reducing costs. D. Kaye Gapen, Dean of Libraries at the University of Alabama, was commissioned to prepare a paper on the feasibility as well as the benefits, disadvantages, and consequences of simplifying the MARC formats. Ms. Gapen found that simplification of the formats was not necessarily feasible, that substantial costs would result from revising the formats even to simplify them, but also that, once mastered, the formats did not hamper cataloging efficiency any more than did other cataloging rules and standards. She concluded that, rather than deleting elements, the association and other interested parties should strive for consistency of the formats among various types of material, and for consistent application of the formats. An abridged version of Ms. Gapen's paper appeared in the December 1981 issue of the *Journal of Library Automation.*

ACCESS TO PERIODICALS

During 1980–1981, the association continued efforts to enhance scholars' access to periodical literature. In addition to supporting existing library programs under Title II of HEA, ARL, working with other library and higher education organizations, supported the addition of a new Part D to create the National Periodicals System during the reauthorization of the act. The final legislation, passed by both houses of Congress in September 1980, called for the establishment of the National Periodicals System Corporation to determine the feasibility and advisability of an alternative system for improving access to periodical literature and, if deemed feasible and advisable, to design and implement an effective system. Part D was not funded for FY 1981, however, and with a new administration in Washington, the prospects for federal funding for such an endeavor seemed dim. Realizing that a new approach to this problem was necessary, ARL and the Center for Research Libraries formed in November 1980 the Joint Committee on Expanded Access to Journal Collections to work with the center in developing plans to expand its program of access to journal collections to help meet the needs of researchers.

LEGISLATION

The association maintains an active interest in federal legislative matters of concern to research libraries. Title II-C of HEA, Strengthening Research Library Resources, has been a primary focus on ARL efforts, particularly in 1980, when the act was reauthorized. In 1981, the Department of Education conducted a review of the regulations for Title II-C. ARL provided a forum at the May 1981 membership meeting for the directors to discuss their concerns about the regulations and the II-C program in general, and then conducted a survey of U.S. directors about the II-C regulations specifically. ARL also monitors legislation concerning a number of agencies, including the Library of Congress, the National Endowment for the Humanities, and the National Historical Publications and Records Commission, and is concerned with issues such as postal rates, government publications, and copyright. The association has also been active in efforts to change the provisions of the Tax Reform Act of 1969, which disallowed deductions at fair market value for artists and writers who donate their manuscripts and creative works to nonprofit organizations; ARL is working with congressional staff to gather support and urge hearings on this issue. In November 1981, hearings were held by the Senate Subcommittee on Estate and Gift Taxation, and it is hoped that hearings will be held in the House in 1982.

RELATIONS WITH SCHOLARS

As an outgrowth of efforts on behalf of the National Periodicals System, ARL has begun working with other organizations to improve communications between research libraries and the scholarly community. The association is a member of the Committee on Scholarly Communication, set up in 1980 by the American Council on Learned Societies, to give continuing attention to issues raised by the National Enquiry into Scholarly Communication. ARL also assisted in the preparation of the research libraries section of the new Association of American Universities project, "The Future of the Research University."

In 1981, the association joined with the American Association for the Advancement of the Humanities to address specifically communication between scholars and librarians, especially the need to increase scholars' awareness and understanding of research library problems and resources. Supported by a grant from the Council on Library Resources, the two associations convened a small group of librarians and faculty members in Washington in April. The group agreed that scholars should be approached both through national associations and on individual campuses, and made two recommendations: (1) To stimulate faculty interest on campuses, three ARL libraries (Princeton University and the universities of Colorado and North Carolina) will participate in a one-year test distribution of *Library Issues*, a bimonthly newsletter desciribing important developments in research libraries, edited by Richard Dougherty, Director of Libraries at the University of Michigan, with appropriate follow-up and evaluation on each campus; and (2) communication through scholarly associations will be initiated by increasing library visibility at annual meetings and in publications of scholarly societies.

An additional initiative to bring libraries and university administrators together to consider the economics and financial management of research libraries in the context of higher education has been undertaken in conjunction with the Research Libraries Group (RLG). In October 1981, ARL and RLG held an exploratory meeting with librarians, economists, and university administrators to begin an examination of these issues and possible solutions to the economic dilemmas facing research libraries.

LIBRARY EDUCATION

Another area that has received particular attention from the association in the past two years is the education of new librarians. The ARL Task Force on Library Education was appointed in 1980 to develop a position outlining the preparation ARL directors consider necessary for new professionals in research libraries. The task force conducted a survey of the membership on the topic, and presented the preliminary results as part of the October 1980 ARL meeting. That meeting, "Education for the Research Library Professional," included a panel of educators and librarians who assessed current library education, offering recommendations and outlining proposed programs and reforms. The lively discussion reflected the high degree of interest in this topic among ARL directors. Based on the results of the survey and the discussion at the meeting, the task force has developed a number of specific objectives designed to improve library education. Current activities center around preparation of a brochure on careers in research libraries to help recruit outstanding students and Ph.D. candidates, developing guidelines for internships and for educational programs in research librarianship, and fostering intellectual exchange between library practitioners and library school faculty through collaborative research projects and team teaching.

STATISTICS

An important ARL program is the collection, analysis, and distribution of statistical information on member libraries. ARL's statistical publications are designed to meet the needs of administrators, researchers, and the library community for information on the growth and expenditure patterns of North America's research libraries. In 1981, the association published the *Cumulated ARL University Library Statistics, 1962-63 through 1978-79*. Compiled by Kendon Stubbs and David Buxton of the University of Virginia Libraries, this publication includes data from the annual *ARL Statistics* and *ARL Annual Salary Survey* describing collections, expenditures, interlibrary loan volume, staffing, and salaries. Also included are data from sources outside ARL on university enrollments, federal support, and Ph.D.s awarded. The data are available in machine-readable form as well.

ARL adopted new membership criteria in May 1980. For academic libraries, a major part of the new criteria is a statistical index developed to compare ARL libraries in the ten categories that best describe the characteristics ARL members have in common. A description of the index is included in the annual *ARL Statistics;* a more detailed description appears in *The ARL Library Index and Quantitative Relationships in the ARL*, prepared by Kendon Stubbs for the Committee on ARL Statistics and published by the association late in 1980. Two libraries, at the universities of Manitoba and California, Irvine, have joined ARL under the new criteria.

PUBLICATIONS

The association maintains an active publications program. In addition to the statistical compilations described above, ARL publishes two other serials: the ARL *Newsletter*, issued five times per year; and the semiannual *Minutes of the Meeting*, proceedings of ARL membership meetings (edited transcripts of both program and business sessions are included). Topics of recent program sessions include education for research library professionals, resources for research libraries (management resources and national programs that support research libraries), and scholars' access to information (implications for scholars as responsibilities for dissemination of information shift between the public and the private sectors).

The *Foreign Acquisitions Newsletter* (*FAN*) will no longer be published by the association. The ARL Board, after reviewing results of surveys on *FAN*'s readership and economic viability, concluded that while *FAN* had been a valuable tool, the association could not afford to continue subsidizing the publication given the current economic climate, and that *FAN*'s potential readership was too small to guarantee full cost recovery. *FAN* was begun in 1949 as the *Farmington Plan Newsletter*. Lloyd Griffin, who became editor in 1963, expanded its scope to include all phases of the trade and bibliographic control of foreign publications, and in 1970 the title was changed to reflect the broader coverage. Publication of *FAN* was suspended in 1980 pending the board's decision.

MANAGEMENT STUDIES AND CHINESE RESEARCH MATERIALS

The association also operates the Office of Management Studies (OMS) and the Center for Chinese Research Materials (CCRM). OMS, which helps research libraries to improve their management and service capabilities, was described in detail in the

1981 *Bowker Annual.* CCRM serves primarily as a publishing house that reproduces hard-to-find newspapers, periodicals, monographs, government documents, and research tools focusing on twentieth-century China.

SUMMARY

The programs described briefly above will form the core of the association's activities in the coming years. Planning is under way for projects in additional areas such as collection development and bibliographic control of serials. Aware of its important role in both library and research communities, the association will continue its efforts to identify and solve problems common to large research libraries so that these libraries may effectively serve the needs of students, faculty, and the research community in general, and to strengthen and extend the capacity of North American research libraries to provide the recorded information needed both now and in the future by the research community.

INFORMATION INDUSTRY ASSOCIATION

316 Pennsylvania Ave. S.E., Washington, DC 20003
202-544-1969

Fred S. Rosenau

Director, Marketing and Publications

A catalytic development for the Information Industry Association (IIA) has been the discovery by Wall Street analysts of the growth potential of information industry firms. One analyst's report depicts "the media industry as one of the most attractive areas of investment, for both total return and relative importance, among all consumer and consumer-related economic sectors." Another cites business information services as "an attractive investment vehicle for the emerging information age." Yet another depicts commercial software, the information-vending business, as "being quietly revolutionized by electronics." One reason advanced by this analysis is that there is a "perpetually strong appetite for relevant, timely information with which to make better decisions." Another reason cited is that "the coming electronic dissemination of information provides an opportunity to dramatically increase the value of information by making it more directly and specifically accessible."*

In reaching these conclusions, analysts often cite IIA's *Business of Information Report* as the source of much of their data. Clearly, its publication has contributed to establishing a firm identity for this burgeoning industry.

To further reinforce the wider recognition of the information industry, Booz, Allen & Hamilton has begun issuing a newsletter entitled *Information Industry In-*

---

*Smith, Barney, Harris, Upham & Co., *Electronic Information Services: Structure of an Emerging Industry,* July 29, 1981; Paine, Webber, Mitchell, Hutchins, Inc., "Ten New Growth Industries for 1982," *Viewpoint,* September 24, 1981; Lehman Brothers Kuhn Loeb, Inc., *Business Information Services,* November 12, 1981; F. Eberstadt & Co., *Industry Report: Diversified Media Companies,* April 13, 1981.

sights for its clients. In the inaugural issue, the firm defines the information industry quite simply: It "produces information and facilities with which to handle it . . . the fusion of numerous businesses—the media, office equipment and telecommunications, for example—related casually, if at all, until now."

The Information Industry Association represents the many business organizations that package and sell *information content* through new technologies alone or in combination with traditional media. IIA estimates that the industry generates over $10 billion in revenues per year, with a growth rate of 20 percent to 30 percent annually.

This growth was reflected in registration figures for IIA's thirteenth annual conference, held in Boston, Massachusetts. Four weeks before the conference, advance registration exceeded previous record attendance levels by 20 percent. Between 400 and 500 executives attended that conference in November 1981. At that time the leaders of this complex growth industry explored the strategic outlook for the years just ahead. For the first time, all major components of the information industry conferred at a single, carefully planned meeting. There is not a business in the nation that is not sharply affected by the issues explored during the two-and-one-half-day conference.

Publishers, hardware technologists, and communications experts intermingled in tightly focused workshops on electronic distribution, deregulation, videodisc technologies, information delivery, opportunities in European markets, ways in which the mind processes information, strategic planning, and more.

The central focus of the meeting was the delivery of information content and its strategic effect on the U.S. economy. This $10 billion industry has impact well beyond that simple dollar volume measure, since the key decisions its products affect propel the entire U.S. economy. The new information technologies on which this industry is based are significant. But this meeting demonstrated that repeated use of these technologies in the creative delivery of information content in new ways to new audiences requires development of not just an information industry strategy, but of a *national* strategy that would capitalize on the United States' lead in this business domain.

Within IIA, member organizations serving specific markets work closely with other organizations that provide similar services to comparable, but different, market segments. In 1979, the industry employed some 389,000 information workers, according to *The Business of Information Report*. The total market and representative suppliers can be broken down as follows:

Primary information services (credit data, economic modeling, business information services, market research, scientific and technical information): McGraw-Hill, Dun and Bradstreet, Chase Econometrics, Nielsen Survey

Secondary information services (business, scientific, technical, and government data bases): Congressional Information Service, Predicasts, Environment Information Center (EIC), Ziff-Davis

Computer-Based information distribution services (on-line distribution of hundreds of machine-readable data bases): DIALOG, SDC Search Service, Bibliographic Retrieval Services (BRS), Interactive Data

Retail information services (custom searching of computerized data bases, document delivery, other retail information services): FIND/SVP, Information Store, Information for Business, and hundreds of small retail operations across the nation.

Seminars and meetings: Aspen Systems, Frost & Sullivan

Information support services (facility management, turnkey systems design): Informatics, Inforonics, Warner-Eddison, Herner & Co.

The Business of Information Report (1980) also showed that the universe of U.S.-based information companies ran to more than 1,000. More than half had revenues under $1 million, about a third had revenues between $1 and $10 million, and 146 firms had revenues in excess of $10 million. Overall, this 14 percent of the firms produced 89 percent of total U.S. domestic revenues. Most information is still delivered in traditional non-machine-readable form. But ink-print revenues showed below-average growth rates, whereas on-line revenues grew at twice the ink-print growth rate. The principal markets for information were identified as manufacturing, government, finance, insurance/real estate, construction, transportation/communications/electricity and gas/sanitary services, services, wholesale trade, academic libraries, mining, retail trade, and agriculture. A new full-scale industry survey conducted early in 1982 is scheduled for publication by IIA later in the year.

Another key IIA publication is its annual directory, *Information Sources 1982-83*, which describes the functions, services, and products of each member operating entity. Included in the directory are the names, addresses, phone numbers, and responsibilities of key management personnel in each firm, along with various indexes to make the reference work especially useful to librarians and clients/users of IIA member services.

Yet another major IIA publication scheduled to appear in 1982 is *Understanding U.S. Information Policy*, the second edition of a significant information resource that analyzes such issues as productivity, information technologies, the role of government, proprietary rights, public interest, knowledge centers, international challenges, information management, and the future. Each section of this large reference work investigates these issues from legislative, executive, judicial, private-sector, and international viewpoints and provides the user with an array of listings and references. For example, in "Restructuring the Telecommunications and Computer Industries" in the first edition of this work, there were explanations of component issues (e.g., paperless society), a list of key statutes (e.g., PL 95-602, which requires state plans for information and referral programs for the handicapped), congressional initiatives (e.g., communications act rewrite), Senate and House committees that deal with these issues, administration initiatives (e.g., presidential statements), federal regulatory agencies (their policies and programs in this domain), landmark litigation (e.g., *U.S.* v. *AT&T*), citizen and consumer groups, U.S. trade and business groups (including lobbies), U.S. academic and research institutions, U.S. professional and scholarly societies, U.S. conferences and symposia, U.S. journals and other publications, selected literature and documents, and so on.

At its annual business meeting, the membership of IIA adopted a new council structure recommended by the Board of Directors Long-Range Planning Committee. Three councils have been formed: Business Operations, Policy and External Affairs, and Future Technology and Innovation. Each now provides oversight, guidance, and direction for all IIA programs and activities in its area of responsibility.

The Business Operations Council, chaired by William Beltz of the Bureau of National Affairs, Inc., attends to activities that help members perform their current business operations more expertly and efficiently. The Policy and External Affairs Council, chaired by James Kollegger of Environment Information Center, Inc., focuses on government relations activities (e.g., proprietary rights, international issues) and public relations. The Future Technology and Innovation Council, chaired by Daniel Sullivan of Frost & Sullivan, Inc., helps members meet the challenges posed by technology and innovative information-handling developments (e.g., electronic media publishing, videotext, etc.). Each council is responsible for making annual budget and program recommendations to the IIA Board of Directors, which is chaired by Thomas Grogan of McGraw-Hill, Inc.

As recommended by the Long-Range Planning Committee, the IIA membership established three classes of membership. Class I (voting) membership is available now to publishers and information service organizations offering information products and services through new technologies or innovative information-handling methods. Class II (associate) members are suppliers of equipment, supplies, and services to present and potential members; foreign companies that, if based in the United States, would be entitled to voting or supplier membership; or individual members employed by firms not otherwise eligible who, as lawyers, librarians, investment analysts, information managers, or other professionals have a special interest in IIA's work. (Class II membership is nonvoting.) Class III (affiliate) membership is available to businesses in closely related industries (e.g., book, magazine, newsletter, or newspaper publishing; data processing; broadcasting; cable or movie production) considering the application of new technologies or innovative information-handling systems to their businesses. (Class III membership is also nonvoting).

The most significant change adopted at the annual meeting was the opening of separate voting membership to entities owned or operated by, or operating within, a single company. An eligible entity may be no smaller than a profit center with a unique commercial identity and management. It may be a subsidiary, division, or group, or the holding company itself. A new dues structure for members was also established for 1982.

IIA has also reconfigured and strengthened its headquarters staff. Paul Zurkowski continues as president and Robert Willard as vice president. Karen MacArthur has become meetings coordinator, Frank Martins manages administration and finance, and Fred Rosenau is responsible for marketing and publications.

The association awarded, through Associated Information Managers (AIM), its second annual William T. Knox Award to Craig M. Cook of Arthur Young & Company. AIM was spun off January 1, 1982, to become an independent organization. AIM, directed by Rita Lombardo, published its own membership directory, *Who's Who in Information Management: 1981–82*.

In April 1981, IIA sponsored the fifth National Information Conference and Exposition (NICE V) in Chicago. There were 1,400 registrants. No NICE conference was scheduled for 1982; however, IIA has scheduled a number of workshops that will be open to both members and nonmembers in 1982–1983. A successful "Electronic Business Publications Workshop," piloted in New Jersey late in 1981, will lead to other offerings throughout 1982 in the East, Midwest, and West Coast areas. Other workshop topics include managing the information worker, training and staff development, marketing, proprietary rights, and hardware/communications interface.

Those who are not members of IIA are now permitted for the first time to subscribe to its newly launched external newsletter, *Friday Memo Special Report*, which complements the association's newsletter for members, *Friday Memo*. Only 18 issues per year are offered, on a subscription basis, to nonmembers, but each of those is enlarged in format and features a special report on a topic deemed both important and timely to the information industry.

IIA's fourteenth annual conference is being held at Walt Disney World November 8-11, 1982, in conjunction with the opening of Experimental Prototype Community of Tomorrow (EPCOT). The 1983 conference is scheduled for New York City.

[A listing of IIA staff members, board members, and board committee chairpersons is included in Part 7 under "National Library and Information Associations, U.S. and Canada"—*Ed.*]

NATIONAL MICROGRAPHICS ASSOCIATION

8719 Colesville Rd., Silver Spring, MD 20910
301-587-8202

O. Gordon Banks
Executive Director

In 1943, a group of individuals who had their first experience using microfilm during World War II and others who earlier appreciated its potential formed the National Microfilm Association (NMA). Eugene B. Power, University Microfilms, Ann Arbor, Michigan, became its first president.

The stated purpose of the new association was "to promote the lawful interests of the Microfilm Industry in the direction of good business principles by: (1) the discussion of subjects pertaining to improvement of industry manufacturing and marketing; (2) establishment of standards for equipment and material; (3) the education of the consumer in the use of the microfilm technique."

NMA struggled for several years to decide whether it should be a trade association or a technical society, and attempted to collect information and news and to make its influence felt. This struggle came to a head in 1952, when a meeting was held in conjunction with a meeting of the American Documentation Institute, now the American Society for Information Science (ASIS). This meeting included a small display of microfilm equipment, and four papers were presented. At a business session, it was decided to revitalize the association, making any necessary changes in the constitution and bylaws to make the association viable. From that point on, the association flourished. The second of what was to become an annual convention took place in New York City in 1953, where the association had its own exhibits, its own program, and its own speakers. It was attended by about 225 people. There were nine exhibitors and eight papers were presented.

The middle years of NMA's development (1954–1958) saw continuing growth in membership and programs and in the convention, too. A highlight of the 1954 convention in Cleveland, and an important milestone for the association, was the presentation of the first NMA Award of Merit to George McCarthy, chairman of the board of Recordak Corporation and inventor of modern bank check microphotography. During this middle period, several other milestones also stand out. Notable among them was inauguration of a commonly accepted nomenclature for the industry, achieved by preparation of the *Glossary of Terms Used in Microreproduction.*

During these years, the concept of NMA as an association of small service companies began to change. Larger manufacturers of equipment were encouraged to participate in NMA programs and leadership, a move that was to have far-reaching consequences for the association in later years and that formed the basis for the present concept of NMA as both a professional society and a trade association.

During the period 1959-1976, the association's programs grew to become closer to what they are today. In 1958, in New Orleans, the annual convention drew about 200 people and 14 exhibitors. In 1959, in Washington, D.C., there were 29 exhibitors and over 1,000 attendees. The technical program grew as well, with more speakers sharing their experiences in applications. By 1961, the program committee had planned a program of application-oriented papers, the precursor of today's multitrack programs. Automatic files, micropublishing, and computer output microfilm (COM) were topics in the programs of 1962 and 1963, with microfiche, facsimile, and other topics to follow through the mid-1960s.

Standards had been an area targeted for NMA involvement since the association was founded. However, it was not until 1953 that the American Standards Association (ASA), now the American National Standards Institute (ANSI), established a standards committee to include microfilm. By 1956, one-third of the ASA committees working on microfilm standards were composed of NMA members.

A turning point in the NMA standards program came in 1959, when association members took part in an intensive review of Department of Defense microfilming specifications. The standards and specifications that emerged from the meeting, backed by the influence of the government, carried sufficient weight to gain immediate acceptance; the broad representation that produced them ensured workable and optimum documents. NMA became the established center for working with the government, expanding NMA's stature in the standards field. In 1964, NMA's first standards committee was formed and by 1967, twelve standards subcommittees had been organized. The NMA Standards Board was created to review and recommend action on standards proposed by the various subcommittees. Today, there are twenty standards committees with a constituency of more than 500 individuals working on the creation of standards.

NMA's publications program has followed the development of the association itself. In 1949, a small newspaper-format publication, the *National Micro News*, was born. It was issued irregularly over several years until in 1957 it became a small magazine, published six times a year. In 1967, the publication was superseded by two publications, the *NMA Journal* and a newsletter, the *Micro-News Bulletin*. The bulletin continued to present news, announcements, information briefs, and conference programs from 1975, when the association changed its name to the National Micrographics Association and the publication became *Micrographics Today*. In 1979 it began monthly publication, and in 1980 was incorporated into the *Journal of Micrographics* (*JM*) as a regular news section.

The *NMA Journal* was originally a quarterly publication devoted to the science, technology, art, and applications of microphotography. It became the *Journal of Micrographics* in 1969, began publishing six times a year in 1971, and, in 1981, became a monthly publication. The journal has continued to cover the science, technology, art, and applications of micrographics, but has expanded its coverage to include the interfaces of micrographics with other information-handling technologies, to more closely represent the interests of the association's membership.

A major undertaking was publication in 1959 of the first *Guide to Microreproduction Equipment*, edited by Hubbard Ballou. This volume contained announcements of equipment manufactured in the United States. Seven editions, with modifications to fit the changing needs of the membership, have been published to date.

NMA also developed publications in a number of other categories. The Consumer Series was inaugurated in 1973 with the booklet "Introduction to Micrographics," one of NMA's all-time best-sellers. There are now six booklets in the series. The Reference Series contains publications of greater coverage and depth, including several full-length textbooks. Numerous other publications are produced and distributed worldwide by NMA, overseen by an active publications committee that, over the years, has consisted of some of the best and most knowledgeable people in the industry.

The first NMA chapter was established in the Minneapolis–St. Paul area in 1968. Today there are 47 chapters throughout the country, actively participating in NMA programs. In its 38-year history, NMA has moved from an organization with 18 professional and 3 affiliate members to one with over 8,000 professional members and nearly 300 company members. It has moved from an annual convention with 225 attendees, nine exhibitors, and eight papers to an annual conference and exposition drawing over 9,000 attendees, over 130 exhibitors, and nearly 50 papers. It has grown from a publications program offering a sporadic magazine and one publication to one offering an annual list of over 100 titles, including a monthly journal. It has expanded from one chapter to 47 nationwide. Its headquarters has moved from a small house in Annapolis, Maryland, to the entire floor of a large building in downtown Silver Spring, Maryland, adjacent to the nation's capital. Its operating budget has increased from about $300 to over $2 million annually. Its staff has grown from one person to about 25. Its name has changed from National Microfilm Association to National Micrographics Association, and its logo carries the tag line "The Image Processing People": all changes that reflect the expanding horizons of its diversified membership.

PUBLICATIONS AND TECHNICAL SERVICES

In 1980, publishing activity increased greatly with publication of two new hardcover books and three Consumer Series publications. Making their debut in September 1980 were updates and revisions of three of NMA's most popular Consumer Series booklets, *An Introduction to Micrographics* (CS101), *An Introduction to Computer-Output Microfilm* (CS103), and *An Introduction to Microform Indexing and Retrieval Systems* (CS104). Also in September, a new hardcover book, *A History of Micrographics: In the First Person*, by NMA historian Jack Rubin, appeared. Following closely in October was the second edition of Daniel Costigan's best-selling *Micrographics Systems*.

Several major standards were produced during 1980, including MS1, *Practice for Operational Practices/Inspection and Quality Control for Alphanumeric Computer-Output Microforms*, and MS24, *Test Target for Use in Microrecording Engineering Graphics on 35mm Microfilm*. An important achievement during 1980 was publication of an entirely new, up-to-date version of the popular NMA *Glossary of Terms* (TR2). This publication appeared first in the 1950s, was updated several times, and has now been completely revised, including changing a number of definitions.

In July 1980, in the midst of a budget crunch, NMA's monthly newsletter, *Micrographics Today*, was incorporated into the *Journal of Micrographics* as a regular news section. The journal itself was completely redesigned, and several new standing columns were introduced: "In the Marketplace" (new product announcements), "Calendar of Events," "People on the Move," "Capital Comment" (government affairs), and "Speak Out," a column of opinion. The acronym "JM" was added to the journal along with a distinctive logo.

A significant development occurred in January 1981, when *JM*, first a quarterly, then a bimonthly for many years, began monthly publication. Incorporation of papers presented at NMA's annual conference made this big step possible. Theme issues were introduced in 1981 and each issue carried an applications theme (Micrographics and Banking, Micrographics and Records Management, Micrographics and Industry Applications, etc.). In 1982, this theme concept will continue, with more themes on the interfaces of micrographics with other information-handling technologies (Micrographics and Optical Disk, Micrographics and On-Line Access, Micrographics and Word Processing).

During 1981, a 25-percent member discount was initiated on sales of publications to NMA members. The entire pricing policy for publications was also reviewed and revamped, making pricing more realistic in view of the costs involved in printing, promotion, and fulfillment.

The highlight of the 1981 publishing year was release in April of a new hardcover book, *The Automated Office: An Introduction to the Technology*, by well-known author and lecturer William Saffady. This book represented NMA's first real step outside the area of pure micrographics into the interface of micrographics with other information-handling technologies, and the book has become a leader in NMA's sales program.

At the urging of its publications committee, NMA sponsored a publications and information booth at the annual conference of the Association of Records Managers and Administrators (ARMA) in October 1980, in Boston, and again in October 1981, in St. Paul. While the total publications sales were low, the goodwill generated was invaluable.

Advertising in NMA serial publications has shown a steady increase in the past two years. There is more use of color advertising (both two-color and four-color) in *JM*, which has allowed the incorporation of color into more areas of the magazine.

During 1982, the Publications and Technical Services Department will continue its momentum in publishing. Manuscripts are already in the works for a major new book on optical data disk, a textbook on micrographic retrieval systems, an update of the Consumer Series publication *How to Select a Microform Reader or Reader-Printer*, and several others. Standards are also underway in several vital areas.

MEMBERSHIP

The association has approximately 9,000 members, consisting of 260 trade member companies and about 8,800 individual-type members. The membership is diverse, coming from such groups as government, insurance, banking, engineering, public utilities, manufacturing, organizations, libraries, transportation, and the retail business. The members work in such job classifications as sales, marketing, systems analysis, records management, and data processing and management, with a large percentage (30 percent) of the members carrying the title "Department Head" or "Manager."

The membership generates dues income to the organization of approximately $550,000 per year. Of this amount, approximately one-quarter comes from the trade-member segment and the balance from the individual-member segments. It is anticipated that the current economic situation will cause the size of the association to remain relatively unchanged in the immediate future.

CHAPTERS

At present there are 47 active local chapters in major metropolitan areas throughout the United States. These chapters provide each member with the means of periodically meeting and exchanging ideas with peers. The chapters are recognized as a vibrant element in NMA and they are the most direct and valuable source of input to the national organization. Through chapters, NMA has consistently determined the needs, desires, problems, and potential of the membership. As a means of helping support the chapters financially, the NMA Board of Directors has stipulated that a grant be made to the chapter in the name of each professional member who chooses a chapter. It is estimated that approximately 6,000 of NMA's individual members have chosen to affiliate with a chapter.

The NMA Chapter Presidents' Council is a body comprised of all chapter presidents and is structured to recommend policy regarding chapters to the NMA Board. In recent years, chapter presidents have been invited to attend the annual Leadership Conference. Generally a two-day meeting, the Leadership Conference is designed to assist the newly elected chapter presidents and maximize their effectiveness.

NMA has implemented its Regional Coordinator Program to help improve communications between the chapters and the national association and among the coordinators. Each coordinator is responsible for at least four chapters in a certain geographic region.

A chapter's function is to emulate locally the programs and services that the association provides nationally. In recent years the chapters have been successful in conducting mini-equipment expositions, seminars, workshops, and various other activities that are valuable to the members educationally. The chapters have also kept pace with the association's objectives in reaching out to embrace certain interfacing technologies. They have been busy conducting joint meetings with other industry information associations such as ARMA, the International Word Processing Association (IWPA), the Data Processing Management Association (DPMA), the Association for Systems Management (ASM), and the Administrative Management Society (AMS).

PUBLIC RELATIONS

The association engages in a modest public relations program designed to position micrographics as a viable information storage and retrieval tool. Highlighting this activity are the "white papers" (advertising supplements) the association has managed to place in *Fortune* and *Business Week* magazines. These white papers focus on how integrating micrographics with other technologies will significantly improve office-worker productivity. The sections have carried heavy assortments of micrographic and related technology case histories, which have been beneficial to the industry. Studies show that these special sections generate thousands of inquiries for the advertisers and the association.

In addition to the special white papers appearing in national magazines, the association works through its public relations committee to promote the acceptance and use of micrographics via news releases, product releases, and service to the media in general.

ASSOCIATION INTERFACE

The association has participated in a group of several associations that aim to share services and resources and work as a group on information-processing considerations. Associations represented along with NMA in this activity are ASIS, AMS, ARMA, DPMA, IWPA, ASM, the Association of Data Processing Service Organizations (ADAPSO), the National Business Forms Association (NBFA), and the Information Industry Association (IIA). The group is currently developing an audiovisual presentation on the general subject of information-resource management and how the various technologies come together to make the whole.

ANNUAL CONFERENCE, EXPOSITION, AND INSTITUTES

The single most important week in NMA's year is conference week. The site is selected eight years in advance and it takes 18 months to plan and prepare for this exciting event.

Approximately 130 exhibiting companies and organizations come together for the largest display of micrographics equipment, products, and services in the world. In the exposition business, the NMA show has a reputation for being one of the most visually attractive. NMA exhibitors have received design awards for their individual exhibits. An extra effort is being made to invite and welcome persons from foreign micrographics communities. The U.S. Department of Commerce (DOC) has included the exposition in its annual Foreign Buyers Program. This is quite an honor and an achievement, since DOC selects only 15 out of approximately 10,000 trade shows held annually to be included in this program.

NMA staff and a volunteer committee develop and design an educational program that best suits the needs of NMA members and others interested in micrographics and related information technologies. The popular NMA Institute seminar program provides professionally taught, in-depth training on a variety of topics. The numerous conference sessions provide a forum for over 50 speakers, both users and vendors of micrographics, to share their experience and knowledge with an audience always eager to learn. Frequently the most learning takes place during the ample time allowed for informal discussions during the week.

NMA's thirty-first annual conference and exposition will take place May 3-6, 1982, in St. Louis, Missouri. There are several special events planned in addition to social events such as receptions, luncheons, and banquets. Plant tours are scheduled as well as a "meet the press" session and a forum for new and featured products.

OTHER MEETINGS

The association also sponsors several specialized meetings for different segments of its membership. One of the most popular and enthusiastically attended is the Service Company Presidents' Forum. This meeting, held each spring, offers service company executives the opportunity to meet and exchange information on the state of the art and contemporary business practices.

Another meeting held each year is the prestigious Executive Conference, providing an open atmosphere for top micrographics industry leaders to discuss major issues affecting the industry and the association and to offer guidance to the board of directors.

RESOURCE CENTER

The Resource Center, created in 1974 at NMA headquarters, is a vital part of the association. It is designed to provide both NMA members and nonmembers with complete information on the micrographics industry. The Resource Center is constantly expanding to include information not only on micrographics, but also on other interfacing technologies such as optical disk, computer-assisted retrieval, and word processing. Since its inception, the Resource Center has indexed over 6,000 items, providing instant access to micrographics applications, case histories, standards, directories, technical processes, research reports, equipment evaluations, "how to" guides, state-of-the-art reports, market studies, and industry surveys.

The Resource Center has experienced growth of approximately 20 percent in the number of inquiries by mail, phone, and in-house visitors over the past two years. Various services are provided both for NMA members and for nonmembers, including a Current Awareness Service, the Micrographics Index, and Publications and Market Study Research.

A subscription to the Current Awareness Service provides 12 monthly listings of current additions to the Resource Center, as well as two fiche indexes per year. By scanning these listings, subscribers keep abreast of important industry publications and articles from journals and magazines received and indexed by the NMA Resource Center.

The Micrographics Index is the key to the Resource Center's data base. This index, which is updated biannually, consists of 5 parts: Main Entry, Journal Index, Author Index, Key-Word Index (KWIC), and Subject Index. The index serves as a current-awareness tool for micrographics professionals and it allows one to do research in as much depth as one wishes and at one's own pace. For a small fee, reprints of most items listed in the index may be ordered from the Resource Center in paper copy or on microfiche.

Another valuable service of the Resource Center is the compilation of Special Interest Packages (SIPS) and Resource Reports. Through these publications, one can obtain valuable information on specific topics. SIPS, of which there are presently 18, are compilations of current articles from journals and magazines indexed in the Resource Center. Some of the most popular are "Libraries and Micrographics," "Human Factors and Acceptance of Microforms," and "Micrographic Systems Design." There are presently five publications that form the Resource Report Series. Resource reports consist of brief lists and summaries on key topics in the micrographics industry.

Computerized data base searches provide printouts on topics, authors, or journals in the data base. Nonmembers pay a nominal fee for the search while members receive this service free. Market Study Research ($20/hour) provides statistical information on the micrographics industry. Telephone and written inquiries about micrographics processes, applications, and other topics are handled both for NMA members and for nonmembers. Also available are free brochures and flyers describing the association and the field of micrographics.

The Resource Center is considered the clearinghouse for all information on micrographics. This is borne out by the users of the center. Each year, the Resource Center welcomes visitors from all parts of the country and from around the world. Their needs range from general questions on micrographics to an interest in microfilm equipment, marketing, legal aspects, indexing, and retrieval. Inquiries have come from federal and military agencies, many Fortune 500 companies, consultants, and foreign corporations and governments, along with university and high-school institutions and students.

SOCIETY FOR SCHOLARLY PUBLISHING

2000 Florida Ave. N.W., Washington, DC 20002
202-638-5970

Mark Carroll
President

In a deliberative document prepared by its long-range planning committee, the Society for Scholarly Publishing (SSP) describes its purpose as follows:

> The scholarly communication system as a whole depends on a variety of components which interface with one another interactively and in changing patterns. These interfaces need to be better understood by those within each affected component in order that the system can be improved.
>
> SSP's mission is to enable and encourage participants in the system to improve their understanding of these interfaces and to act accordingly to help optimize the system. As a corollary, it is not SSP's mission to improve the participants' understanding of their own isolated components since this need is already served by many specialty associations.

The Society was formed in June 1978 to carry out this purpose. Its clear antecedents were the Association for Scientific Journals (ASJ), and the Innovation Guide Project of the National Science Foundation (NSF).

The Association, a very informal group, held three meetings between 1973 and 1977, organized under the auspices of the Professional Communication Group of the Institute of Electrical and Electronic Engineers (IEEE). The conference proceedings were published in the IEEE *Transactions on Professional Communication*. In his preface to the record of the first conference, editor J. M. Lufkin, who was a prime mover in founding ASJ, wrote:

> The conference represented by this Record was remarkable in at least two respects. It brought together editors and publishers from engineering and engineering-related sciences on one hand, and those from the biological and social sciences on the other. It also joined in discussion the editors and publishers on one hand, and the users—librarians and information scientists—on the other. The informal exchanges alone from these unusual encounters were enough to justify the conference for many of those who attended.
>
> If the bridges we have built in this way between these quite different "subcultures" of science are strong enough to last, we may look forward to some important new traffic in ideas.

Editor Lufkin's remarks foreshadowed the role that SSP was to assume in bringing together those engaged in all facets of scholarly publishing, in whatever medium, in whatever discipline, and in whatever context or country.

After the third ASJ meeting, Lufkin undertook new duties for his employer, and was unable to continue his association duties. While there had been talk of a fourth meeting, there was also consultation and discussion about a permanent, larger, and more broadly based formal organization to carry on the work of ASJ.

Concurrently, NSF's Innovation Guide Project, the second antecedent of SSP, had been well under way. It was designed for the scientific and technical journal community, and its purpose was to help editors and publishers "to adopt innovative concepts and techniques to enhance the services they provide, reduce the costs of their operation, or both." A private contractor, assisted by user and advisory committees, prepared a planning guide to make available to that journal community a range of up-to-date infor mation on such diverse topics as videodiscs, automated refereeing of journal articles, miniprint, cooperative promotion, and micropublishing.

By the time the final version of the inquiry was ready for publication, SSP had been formally organized, incorporated, classified as tax exempt, toasted, and prepared to carry on the work of its predecessors.

The Innovation Project's *Guide* was issued in 1978. Its front matter announced the end of the project, and called the attention of the recipients to the formation of SSP, adding that "it will deal with the concerns of all individuals interested in scholarly publishing, regardless of discipline, institutional setting, or professional identity."

SSP's first annual meeting was held in Boston in June 1979, and the two-day program considered such matters as the changing library market for scholarly works, the review process, impacts of technology on the future of scholarly communication, and book composition by authors. At this meeting, a slate of member-elected officers and board members succeeded the self-elected pro tem officials who had founded the society.

The second annual meeting was held in Minneapolis the following June, flying the banner of "Scholarly Publishing in an Era of Change," and grappling *inter alia* with the electronic journal, graphic design for scholarly publications, processing and distribution of direct mail, and the human side of change.

To assert its role as a national and, indeed, international organization SSP held its third annual meeting in San Francisco in June 1980. The theme, "Bridging the Gaps," was appropriate both for the Bay Area and for the interacting role that SSP emphasized. Participants wrestled with issues such as desirable levels of editing, cooperative publishing, publishing in the Third World, and, as always, economics in publishing.

Each of the three meetings attracted more than 250 registrants, and each was followed by a set of proceedings published by SSP for members and non-members alike.

The fourth annual meeting will take place in June 1982, just outside of Washington, D.C. As before, proceedings will be published.

To complete the summary of meetings past and future, SSP is joining with two other organizations, the International Federation of Scientific Editors' Association and the Council of Biology Editors, to mount a joint meeting in May 1983. The advance announcement states the theme as "Scholarly Communication Around the World: A Joint Program for Authors, Editors, Publishers, Librarians, Printers, Computer Scientists, Users, et al." Philadelphia will be the site.

The following listing of the officers and directors of the society is indicative of the breadth of interest in its programs, and of the wide audience it is designed to serve: President, Mark Carroll, National Park Services; Vice-President/President-Elect, Robert A. Day, Institute for Scientific Information Press; Secretary-Treasurer, Judy Holoviak, American Geophysical Union; Directors: Harald Bohne, University of Toronto Press; Constance Greaser, The Rand Corporation; Marjorie Laflin, independent copyright consultant; Ethel G. Langlois, Elsevier North Holland, Inc.; James M. Lufkin, Honeywell, Inc.; Barbara E. Meyers, American Chemical Society; G. William Teare, Byrd Press; George L. Trigg, American Physical Society; Herbert S. White, Indiana University; and Allen Wittman, John Wiley and Sons.

There are now some 1,200 SSP members in the United States, Canada, England, Europe, Israel, Australia, and points in between. The society publishes, in addition to the meeting proceedings, a newsletter and directory. It has sponsored workshops on word processing and the marketing of books and journals, and plans other workshops for the future.

In the few short years of its existence, SSP has defined a need and filled a niche within the several worlds of scholarly publishing. It deals creatively with other older, existing organizations, and through its particular emphases, provides programs that complement existing ones. "The need to communicate" in a communications-oriented society may be a cliché, just as "capturing key strokes" is an obligatory cliché in any discussion of new and maturing technologies, but the need is there, and SSP is dedicated to adding its voice to produce new harmonies.

SPECIAL LIBRARIES ASSOCIATION

235 Park Ave. S., New York, NY 10003
212-477-9250

Richard Griffin
Assistant Executive Director

In 1981 the Special Libraries Association (SLA) displayed all the hallmarks of a vigorous and healthy professional membership society. The year began with the good news that a modest but unanticipated budget surplus would be carried over from 1980, due largely to the success of the seventy-first annual conference in Washington, D.C., record enrollment in continuing education courses, and careful monitoring of all association expenditures.

The fiscal good tidings were heard also as 1981 drew to a close. Once again the association staff announced that the annual conference and the continuing education program came in over budget. Furthermore, in spite of the dues increase effective January 1, 1981, total membership, at approximately 11,200, had remained stable. Consequently, SLA finds itself in the fortunate position of being able to support needed programs and services, while simultaneously bolstering its reserve fund.

GOVERNMENT RELATIONS

Government relations continues to be a high-priority concern of SLA members. Since the majority of members are employed by organizations in the private sector, they can be and frequently are affected by laws and regulations that have little or no effect on information professionals in publicly supported institutions. Conversely, government actions that affect libraries in the public sector do not always apply, or may apply differently, to privately supported libraries. There is a need, then, for SLA to be particularly vigilant toward federal, state, and local legislation and regulatory actions. To this end, the SLA Board of Directors approved in January 1981 the formation of a new standing committee on government relations.

Ten percent of the association's membership is Canadian. Therefore, the membership of the Government Relations Committee includes both a U.S. coordinator, who also serves as chairman, and a Canadian coordinator. The committee is charged with supporting SLA's president and executive director in carrying out the association's government relations policy, which was adopted in January 1980.

The executive director keeps the Government Relations Committee, SLA officers, members, and staff informed of issues of national concern, and represents the interests of SLA in the seat of U.S. government through bimonthly visits to Washington, D.C., to meet with congressional staff members and representatives of various federal departments and agencies. He also coordinates SLA's activities as appropriate with the government relations programs of the American Library Association (ALA), the Association of Research Libraries, and other library/information organizations.

NETWORKING

In January 1980, the board of directors authorized the SLA staff to solicit the assistance of the National Commission on Libraries and Information Science (NCLIS) in establishing a task force to study the benefits and constraints that would result from the inclusion of special libraries and technical information centers in networks and other cooperative activities. At its March 1980 meeting, NCLIS agreed to establish the NCLIS/SLA Task Force on the Role of the Special Library in Nationwide Networks and Cooperative Programs. The Task Force, which is funded solely by SLA, has 17 months from October 1980 to complete its mission. The final report is due in April 1982.

The composition of the task force is representative of SLA's diverse membership. It consists of 14 SLA members from both the profit and nonprofit sectors, two NCLIS commissioners, one NCLIS staff member, and SLA's executive director. The task force is under the capable leadership of chairperson Patricia Berger, who is chief of the Library and Information Services Division at the National Bureau of Standards.

The mission statement of the task force, adopted in October 1980, reads:

> Given the present state of access to information (including access via networks) the Task Force will describe, delineate and clarify the benefits from and to special library participation, and constraints which [sic] inhibit such participation in nationwide programs of library and information services. The Task Force will develop a plan of action for appropriate institutions and agencies.

An important undertaking of the task force in the spring of 1981 was a survey of special libraries and technical information centers to determine their involvement in national, regional, and local networks. Such data, which had never before been collected, is essential to the completion of the task force's mission. Of the libraries and information centers surveyed, responses from more than 54 percent (2,500) were received. Analysis of the data collected provides valuable insight into the present state of networking in the special library community, and gives the task force a solid basis for projecting what kinds of national programs might attract special library participation and support.

A successful electronic mail experiment, begun in March 1981, has given the board of directors, SLA staff, and two key committees hands-on practical experience with a networking system for the transaction of association business. Participating committees include the 1983 Annual Conference Program Planning Committee and the Special Committee on Long-Range Planning. The Networking Committee will begin participation in 1982.

The electronic mail system selected, On-Tyme II (a service of Tymnet), is an electronic communications alternative to the U.S. mail, telephone, telex, and TWX. SLA's participation was arranged through the California Library Authority for Systems and Services. SLA members and other persons who have access to On-Tyme II terminals are encouraged to use the system to communicate with the association office.

INFORMATION DISSEMINATION

An association's journal is its most visible membership benefit and its most important means of direct communication with members. In response to criticism that *Special Libraries*, SLA's official journal, is not the medium for publishing association news and placement listings, a monthly newsletter, the *SpeciaList*, began publication in July 1980.

The *SpeciaList* is produced on a shortened production schedule to ensure the timeliness of its contents. The newsletter includes new columns not previously included in *Special Libraries*, profiles of special libraries, and current news items on library-related activities inside and outside the association.

With the advent of *SpeciaList*, *Special Libraries* has changed in frequency of publication and in appearance. In January 1981, it became a quarterly publication. The changed format allows for new graphics and an average issue size of 128 pages, 75 percent of which is devoted to scholarly papers and reports. Member response to the new *Special Libraries* has been positive. Particular praise has been given to the April 1981 special issue on information technology.

During 1980–1981, SLA published ten new books, including *The Special Library Role in Networks* and a revised edition of *Equal Pay for Equal Work: Women in Special Libraries*. The association expects to publish ten new books in 1981–1982 also, including a newly revised edition of *Special Libraries: A Guide for Management*.

SLA's Information Services Department continues to be consulted frequently by members, students, and other persons who require accurate, up-to-date information on special librarianship, information management, and information technology. The management documents collection, in particular, receives heavy use. Currently, the department's print collection is being reorganized, and microfilming of the association's archives is underway.

PROFESSIONAL DEVELOPMENT

SLA's concern with the professional development of its members is apparent in the rapid growth and development of the continuing education program since its inception in 1977. In 1981, there was a record attendance of 853 at the 12 continuing education courses and two workshops offered at the seventy-second annual conference of SLA, held in Atlanta. In addition, there were 10 courses presented in various regions of the country throughout 1981 as part of the Regional Continuing Education Program.

Management courses have frequently been among the most popular SLA continuing education course offerings. Therefore, plans are underway to establish a middle management certificate program that would provide a course of study for librarians who are middle managers. The program will be analogous to an organization's management training program, focusing on developing skills, decision-making aptitudes, and practical training experience. Participants who complete the 75-hour program during an 18-month period will earn an SLA Management Certificate and 7.5 Continuing Education Units (CEU's). Unit I, Management Skills, will be offered for the first time at the association's June 3–5 1982 annual conference in Detroit.

The experience of an SLA annual conference is, in its own right, a valuable professional development activity for members. The 1981 conference in Atlanta attracted more than 2,900 registrants, the highest attendance SLA has had for a conference outside of New York City or Washington, D.C. The theme of the meeting, "Beyond Efficiency to Effectiveness," encouraged the presentation of papers and programs on management and management techniques and the effective utilization of new and emerging information technologies. There were more than 250 programs scheduled on these and other information-related topics.

Conference exhibits are another form of continuing education for special librarians. Exhibit space was completely sold out in Atlanta, and several potential exhibitors could not be accommodated. All told, there were 176 exhibiting firms in 203 booths.

In an effort to assist special librarians and the supervisors of special librarians in salary negotiations, SLA conducts an in-depth salary survey every three years. In the intervening years the association, using a sampling technique, polls 25 percent of the membership in an effort to provide an overview of the salaries of special librarians and to measure annual salary increases since the last survey.

The 1981 poll, which updates the 1979 salary survey, elicited responses from 62 percent of the polled membership. Analysis of the data revealed the 1981 median salary to be $21,100 (17 percent higher than the 1979 median), while the 1981 mean salary increased to $22,800 (18 percent higher than the 1979 mean).

The SLA Employment Clearinghouse provides a service to members who are contemplating a job change to advance their careers. At the 1981 annual conference, the clearinghouse posted 99 positions open for 122 job seekers. Salaries posted ranged from $12,000-$35,000. The median starting salary was $17,100; the mean was $18,200.

For the first time ever, a career advisory service was provided by SLA at the Atlanta conference. Seventeen experienced SLA members served as advisors to members beginning their careers or in career transition. The service was well received and will be repeated at the 1982 annual conference in Detroit.

INTERASSOCIATION COOPERATION

Whenever possible, the association seeks to participate in mutually beneficial cooperative programs with other organizations whose purposes and objectives are consistent with those of SLA.

SLA's most ambitious cooperative endeavor in 1981 was a library/information association staff leadership institute on membership services. The program was organized and funded by SLA. Enrollment included 17 participants, representing seven library and information associations. The membership director of the American Society of Association Executives served as program leader and resource person. The institute was rated a success by all participants; it was therefore unfortunate that several associations did not participate. Another leadership institute is planned for 1983.

Several cooperative programs involving SLA and other library and information associations have been implemented. The first to be established was the exchange of continuing education courses with the Medical Library Association (MLA) at SLA and MLA annual conferences. Members of both associations can register for the exchange courses at the lower member rates. A similar continuing education course exchange takes place between SLA and the American Society for Information Science (ASIS).

Other SLA cooperative ventures have been (1) the negotiation of reciprocal reductions of annual conference registration fees with ASIS, the Art Libraries Society of North America (ARLIS/NA), and the American Association of Law Libraries (AALL); and (2) the establishment of an SLA/MLA joint committee for the exploration and recommendation of mutually beneficial cooperative programs for the two associations.

MEMBERSHIP SERVICES

An organization such as SLA exists primarily to provide services to its members. It is not surprising, then, that the SLA board of directors and staff consider foremost among their responsibilities the provision of membership services.

In 1981, the SLA staff presented the board of directors with several proposals for new or improved services. Those approved by the board for implementation by the staff in 1981 and 1982 are:

1. Group insurance plans
2. 50 percent dues discount for unemployed members
3. Lower member prices for SLA publications
4. Substantial increases in annual allotments to chapters (40 percent), divisions (80 percent), and student groups (60 percent)
5. Reinstatement of a printed membership directory
6. Career advisory service
7. A subscription discount to a prominent national business periodical
8. A discount on the products of a data terminal manufacturer
9. Increased funding of government relations activities
10. Increased funding of committee expenses
11. A national jobline
12. The establishment of a doctoral scholarship program
13. Increased funding for association publications
14. Installation of an electronic mail system

SLA sustaining members, sponsors, and patrons had several new services added in 1981. Services to these institutional categories now include (1) complimentary personal membership for a qualified staff member (patrons only); (2) a 50 percent discount on SLA publications and employment clearinghouse listings; (3) preferred exhibit booth selection at annual conferences (patrons only); and (4) member registration rate for continuing education courses and annual conferences.

As the new year begins, SLA members, board of directors, and staff are anticipating discussions and preparing for decisions on several proposals that could profoundly affect SLA's organization and future direction. Among the matters to be brought to the board in 1982 are (1) the selection of a long-range planning model and the establishment of a long-range planning committee; (2) the purchase of property and subsequent relocation of the association office; (3) the purchase of a new computer system; and (4) a controversial proposal for the selection of a new name for SLA that would reflect the substantial and steadily increasing involvement of SLA members in both information management and the evolving information technologies.

Part 2
Legislation, Funding, and Grants

LEGISLATION AFFECTING LIBRARIANSHIP IN 1981

Eileen D. Cooke

Director, Washington Office, American Library Association

Carol C. Henderson

Deputy Director, Washington Office, American Library Association

President Reagan's clean sweep in the 1980 election was followed in 1981 by extraordinary success in Congress as the president used Congress' own budget procedures, designed to increase congressional independence from the administration, to his advantage. The Reagan administration and a bipartisan coalition in Congress fashioned huge omnibus budget, reconciliation, tax, and funding measures. Many members, although uncomfortable or unfamiliar with details of these massive packages, found them irresistible due to the president's real or perceived popularity, and the major part of the administration's economic recovery program was passed.

The results, in a few months' time, included astounding and far-reaching changes in hundreds of basic laws; a major increase in the defense budget; reductions in both authorized and appropriated levels in the domestic area (including library and education programs); and reductions in tax revenues, including almost total elimination of the corporate income tax. Despite the "supply-side-economics" emphasis on the business and defense sectors, inflation, interest rates, and unemployment remained high as the year ended.

Another result of the Reagan program was a "new federalism," in which many federal domestic responsibilities were to be returned to state and local governments or the private sector, despite the fact that most federal programs were enacted precisely because of inaction in these other sectors. Although in some areas, such as the arts and humanities, this philosophy was substantially rejected by Congress, in other areas federal programs were combined into block grants to the states with reduced funding and fewer federal "strings" attached. The school library program was eliminated in favor of an elementary and secondary education block grant in which school library resources are but one of over 30 items for which the reduced funds may be spent. Some state and local officials felt the cuts were too much too fast, and returned neither additional revenue sources nor full authority to state and local governments.

Other library grant programs were affected mainly by reductions in authorized or maximum levels, although cuts in actual funding were in most cases less severe than the administration requested. However, Congress had provided FY 1982 funding for only half the year, and the final outcome is still unknown. Libraries were suffering at year's end from the administration's reluctance to release figures on congressional funding levels for the Library Services and Construction Act (LSCA); from elimination of CETA (Comprehensive Service and Training Act) public service jobs; from postal rate increases due to cuts in postal subsidies; and from cuts in related grant programs. Finally, libraries were affected by cuts in many non-library-related programs of assistance to state and local governments that made it all but impossible to restore losses in federal library and related programs at the state or local level.

CONGRESSIONAL BUDGET AND RECONCILIATION MEASURES

Ironically, President Reagan's first major victory was achieved through Congress' own budget process. The House and Senate gave final approval in May to recommended congressional budget levels and to binding reconciliation instructions that affect FYs 1981 through 1984. The Senate-passed version, which closely followed the president's recommendations, encompassed S. Con. Res. 9, budget reconciliation requirements, and S. Con. Res. 19, the first budget resolution for FY 1982. The House put both subjects in one resolution, H. Con. Res. 115, and passed it with a substitute amendment developed by Phil Gramm (D-Tex.) and Delbert Latta (R-Ohio) that made reductions greater than those outlined in the Reagan budget. House-Senate conferees then split the difference between the two versions. Congressional budget resolutions do not require the president's signature.

Although budget resolutions do not mention library programs specifically, they do set spending levels for various budget functions. One of these, function 500, covers education (including libraries, arts, and humanities), training, employment, and social service programs. Function 500 was cut from the $36.6 billion needed to maintain current programs to $26.2 billion.

The budget resolutions also invoked a complex process called "reconciliation," which sets ceilings and requires committees to make legislative adjustments to programs to stay within the budget resolution. These adjustments usually involve appropriations committee savings and perhaps changes in eligibility for entitlement programs. In 1981, for the first time ever, authorizing committees were directed to recommend legislative changes to reduce the authorized levels of funding for direct and discretionary grant programs for FYs 1982 through 1984. In just two weeks each committee had to review all the programs under its jurisdiction and make recommendations to the budget committees, which then combined the recommendations into two comprehensive bills (H.R. 3982 and S. 1377). House Education and Labor Committee chairman Carl Perkins (D-Ky.) compared the situation to working "with a gun pointed at our heads."

In June, the House and Senate passed these measures, mandating approximately 1,000 changes in 250 disparate programs and 100 laws all at once. The scope of the legislation was truly unprecedented; it took Congress itself (and those who follow its activities) some time to figure out exactly what had been done. This was especially true in the House, where a Republican draft of the Budget Committee's bill was still being prepared the night before it was passed. By the end of July, a conference report (H. Report 97-208)

TABLE 1   AUTHORIZATION LEVELS SET BY RECONCILIATION (PL 97-35)

	Previous FY 1982 Authorization	FY 1982	FY 1983	FY 1984
Elementary & Secondary Education Act (ESEA)				
IV-B School Libraries	Necessary sums	$161,000,000	—	—
LSCA				
I Public Library Services	150,000,000	65,000,000	65,000,000	65,000,000
II Library Construction	97,000,000	0	0	0
III Interlibrary Cooperation	20,000,000	15,000,000	15,000,000	15,000,000
Higher Education Act (HEA)				
II-A College Libraries	30,000,000	5,000,000	5,000,000	5,000,000
II-B Training, Research	30,000,000	1,200,000	1,200,000	1,200,000
II-C Research Libraries	15,000,000	6,000,000	6,000,000	6,000,000
II-D Nat'l Periodical Sys.	750,000	0	0	0
Medical Library Assistance Act	Pending	7,500,000	—	—
National Commission on Libraries & Information Science (NCLIS)	750,000	700,000	700,000	700,000

of over 1,000 pages was worked out by 256 House and Senate conferees who met in 58 separate conferences, and Congress gave final approval to the Omnibus Budget Reconciliation Act of 1981 (PL 97-35).

The measure set new and lower authorization levels for major library programs as shown in Table 1.

The Omnibus Budget Reconciliation Act went far beyond budget adjustments. It reauthorized some programs, amended others, eliminated still others, and established several block grants. Regulation writers for block grants and other revised programs were given little legislative history to guide them, since many of the provisions were enacted without public hearings, committee reports, or extensive floor debate. Library-related reconciliation changes include a two-year reauthorization of LSCA, a one-year extension of the expiring Medical Library Assistance Act, consolidation of the ESEA IV-B school library program in one elementary and secondary education block grant comprising over 30 other programs [Education Consolidation and Improvement Act (ECIA), Chapter 2], and several substantive changes in communications law.

FUNDING, FY 1981

President Reagan's March 10 budget message to Congress not only laid out his FY 1982 budget, but requested cutbacks in FY 1981 funding, including a 25 percent cut in the school library program. The congressional response took shape in H.R. 3512, the FY 1981 supplemental and rescission bill, which also extended the previous year's continuing resolution. H.R. 3512 was signed into law (PL 97-12) by the president on June 5, the day the previous continuing resolution expired; amounts for FY 1982 appropriations for library and related programs are given in Table 2.

The early June 5 expiration date of the previous continuing resolution was most critical for LSCA, which is not advance funded. (Most federal library and education programs are either advance funded or, after grant applications are solicited, received, and processed, funds are released late in the fiscal year for use the following academic year.) For LSCA, where immediate allocations are made to the states, the Education Department withheld 28 percent of the funds until Congress made a decision on funding for the rest of the year. The remaining funds were finally released after H.R. 3512 was passed.

Congress rescinded only $10 million from the school library program, compared with the $42,750,000 cut requested, leaving $161 million for ESEA Title IV-B. Although not requested, all funding for the HEA II-A college library program ($4,988,000) was removed by the Senate, along with $500,000 of the $1,167,000 appropriated for the HEA II-B library training and research program. As finally approved, the bill cut $2 million from HEA II-A, leaving $2,988,000 for college library resources, and $250,000 from HEA II-B, leaving $917,000 for training and research.

A supplemental amount of $2,562,000 had been requested by the Government Printing Office (GPO) to meet the increased costs of the depository library program, including distribution of the General Accounting Office's (GAO) Legislative History File. Congress provided only $400,000 of this amount, a decision that delayed the distribution of the GAO file and hastened the conversion of many government documents to microfiche.

FUNDING, FY 1982

President Carter submitted his last budget to Congress on January 15, proposing increases in library training and research, research libraries, and interlibrary cooperation. President Reagan's revisions, submitted March 10, called for the elimination of

TABLE 2 FY 1982 APPROPRIATIONS FOR LIBRARY AND RELATED PROGRAMS*

Programs	FY 1981 Appropriations	FY 1982 Authorization	Sept. FY 1982 Reagan Budget	FY 1982 House Bill	FY 1982 Senate Bill	FY 1982 Appropriations or Continuing Resolution
Library Programs						
ECIA Chapter 2 (including school libraries)	$535,485	$589,368	$518,643	$535,485	$350,000	$483,840†
GPO Superintendent of Documents	23,800	44 USC 301	29,279	27,120	—	27,120
Higher Education Act Title II	9,905	12,200	6,307	9,167	6,000	8,560†
Title II-A: College Libraries	2,988	5,000	0	2,000	0	1,920†
Title II-B: Training & Research	917	1,200	1,027	1,167	0	880†
Title II-C: Research Libraries	6,000	6,000	5,280	6,000	6,000	5,760†
Library of Congress	184,872	2 USC 131	197,611	192,585	188,827	189,827
Library Services & Construction Act	74,500	80,000	51,810	74,500	74,500	71,520†
Title I: Public Library Services	62,500	65,000	41,250	62,500	62,500	60,000†
Title III: Interlibrary Cooperation	12,000	15,000	10,560	12,000	12,000	11,520†
Medical Library Assistance Act	9,831	7,500	8,925	7,500	8,925	7,500†
National Agricultural Library	8,822	7 USC 2204	8,158	9,271	8,500	8,750
National Commission on Libraries and Information Science	691	700	618	702	702	674†
National Library of Medicine	34,899	40 USC 275	38,752	38,752	38,752	36,902†
Library Related Programs						
Adult Education Act	100,000	100,000	84,480	100,000	90,000	86,400†
Bilingual Education	161,427	143,810	126,553	143,810	143,810	138,057†
Corporation for Public Broadcasting	137,000	130,000	93,500	110,000	130,000	105,600†
ECIA Chapter 1 (ESEA I Disadvantaged Children)	2,965,614	Formula-based	2,363,564	3,164,387	2,966,287	2,847,636†

Education for Handicapped Children (state grants)	874,500	969,850	649,088	914,500	900,000	931,008†
HEA Title I-B: Education Outreach	2,200	8,000	0	0	0	0
Title III: Developing Institutions	120,000	129,600	129,600	129,600	129,600	124,416†
Title IV-C: College Work Study	550,000	550,000	484,000	550,000	550,000	528,000†
Title VI: International Education	21,800	30,600	14,960	21,800	20,000	19,200†
Indian Education Act	81,680	81,700	71,364	82,096	81,096	77,853
National Archives & Records Service	84,941	44 USC 21-33	79,294	88,999	76,294	74,138†
National Center for Educational Statistics	8,947	8,947	8,747	8,947	8,947	8,589†
National Endowment for the Arts	158,795	119,300	77,440	157,500	119,300	143,040
National Historical Publications and Records Committee	151,299	113,700	74,800	144,061	113,700	130,560
	4,000	Needs new authorization	0	1,000	3,000	1,000†
National Institute of Education	65,614	55,614	53,645	55,614	55,614	53,389†
Postsecondary Education Improvement Fund	13,500	13,500	11,880	13,500	12,000	11,520†
Public Telecommunications Facilities	19,717	20,000	0	16,000	20,000	18,000†
Women's Education Equity	8,125	6,000	0	6,000	6,000	5,760†

*Figures are rounded to thousands.
†Funded only through 3/31/82 by a further continuing resolution, PL 97-92.

college library funds, a cutback in public library services of 25 percent, and inclusion of school library funding into one block grant to be reduced by 20 percent. The House passed most of the regular appropriations bills based on the March budget, as did the Senate Appropriations Committee. In September, however, the President asked for an additional 12 percent reduction below his March figures. At that point the Republican Senate held up action on all appropriations bills until details of the new budget cuts were received. The Senate Appropriations Committee then went back and revised downward many of the figures previously agreed upon.

Few of the appropriations bills reached a Senate vote or final passage, so Congress resorted to temporary continuing resolutions (four of them) to keep the government functioning once FY 1982 began on October 1. The resolution in place as the year ended provided funding only through March 31, 1982 (PL 97-92), and cut the lower of the House-passed or Senate committee amounts by 4 percent. LSCA Title I public library services wound up with $60 million; LSCA III interlibrary cooperation with $11,520,000; HEA II-A college libraries with $1,920,000; HEA II-B library training and research with $880,000; and HEA II-C research libraries with $5,760,000. The National Commission on Libraries and Information Science (NCLIS) was cut to $674,000. All these figures were much higher than the president's September budget recommendations. Details are shown in Table 2.

Once FY 1982 began, a problem again arose over release of LSCA funds. Under the earlier shorter-term continuing resolution, the Education Department was releasing only 21 percent of the September requested budget levels. Once Congress provided funding for half the fiscal year at higher levels, the Office of Management and Budget was still not allowing release of any additional funds, apparently because rescissions were to be proposed for LSCA. The normal procedure is for states to receive full allotments immediately because LSCA is not advance funded. Because LSCA funds are used to strengthen state library agencies, provide statewide services, and support a variety of projects involving individual libraries and library systems and networks, the effects of withholding funds were immediate and severe. At year's end some states were on the verge of letting staff go because congressional intent was being thwarted.

For the new state block grant for elementary and secondary education [Education Consolidation and Improvement Act (ECIA), Chapter 2], which includes school library resources and instructional equipment formerly covered by ESEA IV-B as one of over 30 purposes, the outlook for funding was bleak even though the program does not take effect until the 1982–1983 school year. The combined programs received $760,896,000 in FY 1980 and $535,485,000 in FY 1981 after rescissions. The September budget request was $518,643,000; the amount in the continuing resolution through March 31, 1982 was $483,840,000. Table 3 shows ECIA Chapter 2 funding levels.

Congress used the first continuing resolution as an opportunity to provide funding for its own arm of government for the entire FY 1982. PL 97-51 included $189,827,000 for the Library of Congress (LC), a funding level higher than that of the previous year but lower than the level requested. Attempts to prohibit LC's National Library Service for the Blind and Physically Handicapped from continuing a braille edition of selected print material from *Playboy* were successfully defeated. The Government Printing Office received $2 million less than requested for the Superintendent of Documents, thus hastening the conversion to microfiche of documents distributed to depository libraries. The National Agricultural Library (NAL) received marginally less than the previous year. The National Library of Medicine (NLM) also received less funding due mainly to a congressional cut in its Medical Library Assistance Act of 24 percent. NAL's funds were allocated for the entire fiscal year, while NLM funding extended only through March 31, 1982.

The National Archives and Records Service had its budget cut 16 percent from the previous year in the continuing resolution effective through March 31, 1982, and as a result had to discontinue interlibrary loan of microfilm publications from its Fort Worth Federal Archives and Records Center. About 400,000 reels of census, diplomatic, pension, and other records used heavily by genealogists had been lent to libraries annually. Out of the National Archives' budget, the National Historical Publications and Records Commission was to receive $1 million, compared with $4 million the previous year.

For FY 1982, the National Endowment for the Humanities (NEH) received $130,560,000, the National Endowment for the Arts (NEA) $143,040,000. These amounts represent a reduction of about 14 percent for NEH and 10 percent for NEA, considerably less than the 50 percent cuts requested by the Administration. Thanks to Congressman Sidney Yates (D–Ill.), these figures are higher than the new authorizations set by congressional reconciliation, a technicality against which no point of order was raised.

Library Services and Construction Act

The Omnibus Budget Reconciliation Act extended the authorization for LSCA for two years, through FY 1984, subject to an automatic one-year extension through FY 1985. Meanwhile, the National Library and Information Services Act, S. 1431, was reintroduced June 25 by Senate Education Subcommittee chairman Robert Stafford (R–Vt.) with only minor changes from the previous year's S. 2859. No Senate hearings were held on this bill in 1981.

The House Postsecondary Education Subcommittee held a series of oversight hearings on LSCA during which almost 200 persons gave testimony either in person or for the record. All testimony will be published in a multi-volume hearing record. The subcommittee, chaired by Representative Paul Simon (D–Ill.), held hearings in Washington on September 15, in Detroit on September 17, in New Haven on September 25, in Cleveland on October 19, in Kansas City, Missouri, on November 9, and in San Francisco on December 7.

Preceding the September 15 hearing, the American Library Association arranged for multiple showings of the slide-tape presentation, "Star Years LSCA," produced by West Virginia State Librarian Fred Glazer to celebrate the 25th anniversary of LSCA and its predecessor, the Library Services Act. The September 17 hearing was arranged to coincide with the Detroit meeting of the White House Conference on Library and Information Services Task Force.

Education Consolidation and Improvement Act (ECIA)

The nature of federal assistance to elementary and secondary education was changed significantly with passage through the Omnibus Budget Reconciliation Act (PL 97-35) of a block grant for FYs 1982 through 1987 that combines 33 programs, including ESEA Title IV-B school library resources and instructional equipment program. Although ECIA has two titles or chapters in PL 97-35, the first part consists of one program, the former ESEA I aid for disadvantaged children. In effect, there is only one block grant, the second part or Chapter 2 of ECIA, that covers school library media centers, which will be competing with 32 other programs for funding. The authorized level for Chapter 2 is $589,368,000, but actual funding for FY 1982 was only $483,840,000. The consolidation is to begin with the 1982–1983 school year.

Block grant funds are divided as follows: 1 percent for insular areas; 6 percent for the Secretary of Education's discretionary fund, from which the Inexpensive Book Distribution Program, as carried out through "Reading Is Fundamental," is to be funded at FY 1981 levels; and the remainder to states on a school-age population basis. From the

TABLE 3 ECIA CHAPTER 2 FUNDING FOR FY 1982 (1982/1983 SCHOOL YEAR)*
(State block grant for elementary & secondary education, estimated, by Omnibus Budget Reconciliation Act (PL 97-35))

Programs combined in ECIA Chapter 2	FY 1980 Appropriations	FY 1981 Appropriations	Sept. FY 1982 Reagan Budget	HR 4560, FY 1982 House-passed bill	Senate Committee	PL 97-92 Continuing Resolution thru 3/31/82
State block grants	—	—	$487,525	$490,195	$329,000	$442,176
School libraries (ESEA IV-B)	171,000	161,000	—	—	—	—
Emergency school aid (ESAA)						
Basic grants to schools	107,800	33,400	—	—	—	—
Special programs & projects	92,019	75,859	—	—	—	—
Magnet schools, etc.	36,302	30,000	—	—	—	—
Grants to nonprofit organizations	5,000	5,000	—	—	—	—
Educational TV & radio	6,450	4,450	—	—	—	—
Evaluation	1,000	500	—	—	—	—
Educational innovation and support (ESEA IV-C)	146,400	66,130	—	—	—	—
Guidance, couns. (ESEA IV-D)	0	0	—	—	—	—
State educ. agency mgt. (ESEA V-B)	51,000	42,075	—	—	—	—
Basic skills (ESEA II)	28,500	25,650	—	—	—	—
Community schools (ESEA VIII)	3,138	3,138	—	—	—	—
Consumers education (ESEA III-E)	3,617	1,356	—	—	—	—
Gifted & talented (ESEA IX-A)	6,280	5,652	—	—	—	—
Metric education (ESEA III-B)	1,840	1,380	—	—	—	—
Ethnic heritage (ESEA IX)	3,000	2,250	—	—	—	—
Law-related education (ESEA III-G)	1,000	1,000	—	1,000	—	960
Cities in schools (ESEA III-A 303)	3,050	2,745	—	—	—	—
PUSH for excellence (ESEA III-A 303)	1,000	825	—	—	—	—
Teacher corps (HEA V-A)	30,000	22,500	—	—	—	—
Teacher centers (HEA V-B 532)	13,000	9,100	—	—	—	—

Pre-college science teacher training (NSF Act)	2,500	1,875	—	—	—
Biomedical science (ESEA III-L)	3,000	3,000	—	3,000	2,880
Career education incentive	15,000	10,000	—	10,000	9,600
Subtotal to states	731,896	508,885	487,525	504,195	329,000	455,616
Secretary's discretionary fund					
Inexpensive book distribution (RIF)	6,500	5,850	5,850	5,850	—
Arts in education (ESEA III-C)	3,500	3,150	2,025	3,150	—
Alcohol & drug abuse education	3,000	2,850	2,850	2,850	—
National diffusion program	10,000	8,750	—	10,750	—
Educational TV programming	6,000	6,000	—	6,000	—
Special initiatives	—	—	20,393	2,690	—
Subtotal for secretary	29,000	26,600	31,118	31,290	21,000	28,224
Total, block grant	$760,896	$535,485	$518,643	$535,485	$350,000	$483,840

*Figures are rounded to thousands.

allocation to states, each state educational agency must distribute 80 percent to local educational agencies on an enrollment basis, with higher allocations to go to those with the greatest concentrations of high-cost children. Funds may be used for any or all of the previous program purposes; the predecessor programs have been repealed. Requirements for applications, consultation, reporting, and maintenance of effort have been loosened considerably.

President Reagan's March budget indicated his intention to consolidate elementary and secondary education programs; a detailed consolidation proposal was sent to Congress in late April, and education subcommittees had begun hearings on the block grants. However, block grant provisions included at the last minute in the budget reconciliation measures received little committee consideration. Both House and Senate versions were based on H.R. 3941, a consolidation bill introduced on June 17 by Representative John Ashbrook (R-Ohio) which was a definite improvement on the block grant proposed by the Reagan administration.

National Historical Publications and Records Commission

The $4 million provided in FY 1981 for the National Historical Publications and Records Commission (NHPRC) supported the publication of the papers of numerous American historical figures and assisted a variety of preservation projects, including many in libraries, historical societies, universities, and state and local governments. Attempts to extend the authorization for NHPRC grant programs form a strange tale that testifies to the unusualness of this legislative year.

Bills were introduced in both the House and Senate to extend NHPRC for two years at an authorization level of $3 million, down from the FY 1981 level of $4 million, and hearings were held. The House bill, H.R. 2979, was the first reauthorization measure to come to the House floor for a program eliminated by the Reagan budget. H.R. 2979 was attacked by Representative William Dannemeyer (R-Calif.) as a budget-busting measure; he sent out a "Dear Colleague" letter urging its defeat. The proposed bill was brought up under suspension of the rules, a procedure used for noncontroversial legislation allowing no amendments and requiring a two-thirds majority for passage. It was defeated by a vote of 165 to 231 on May 19. The "nays" included strong supporters of education and library assistance who apparently knew little about the program because it originated in the Government Operations Committee, which has jurisdiction over the General Services Administration and the National Archives and Records Service, NHPRC's parent organizations.

The Senate bill, S. 1050, was passed by voice vote on June 2. Senator Charles Mathias (R-Md.), who introduced the bill, submitted to the *Congressional Record* a letter from the Coalition to Save Our Documentary Heritage explaining the NHPRC grant programs and refuting Representative Dannemeyer's arguments. The Coalition is a group of over 40 organizations that had been working for months for continuation of NHPRC and adequate funding of both NHPRC and the National Archives. The Senate-passed bill was sent to the House in expectation of another House vote. By the end of the summer, however, House supporters of NHPRC decided against a second vote because the political climate was so uncertain and because House action on NHPRC funding had already taken place. Technically, this left the grant programs without authorization, although the commission does retain separate authority for limited activities.

Medical Libraries

In an unusual situation, tie votes in both House and Senate committees stymied the extension of the Medical Library Assistance Act (MLAA). Therefore, Congress took advantage of the Omnibus Budget Reconciliation Act (PL 97-35) as a vehicle to keep the expiring MLAA alive. However, it was extended for only one year, FY 1982, at an authorization level of $7.5 million, lower than the budget recommendation of $8.9 million and considerably less than the FY 1981 funding of $9.8 million.

Senator Orrin Hatch (R-Utah), Chairman of the Senate Labor and Human Resources Committee, proposed an amendment to the Senate extension bill, S. 800, to require the National Library of Medicine (NLM) to charge fees for the information products and services it supplies to commercial organizations at rates designed to recover their full cost. This amendment was not included in the reconciliation bill, but at Senator Hatch's request, various studies are being conducted of NLM's pricing policies.

COPYRIGHT

After two years of negotiating, an ad hoc committee of educational users and copyright proprietors reached agreement on guidelines for off-air recording of broadcast programming for educational purposes. The guidelines reflect the Negotiating Committee's consensus on the application of "fair use" to the recording, retention, and use of television broadcast programs for use in classrooms and other places of instruction.

The Negotiating Committee was established in April, 1979 by Representative Robert Kastenmeier (D-Wis.), chairman of the House Judiciary Subcommittee on Courts, Civil Liberties, and the Administration of Justice, with the cooperation of the Register of Copyrights. On September 28, 1981, the guidelines were transmitted to Representative Kastenmeier, who intends to include them in a later House Judiciary Committee report on other copyright-related issues. Although the guidelines do not have the force of law, judges are expected to consider them in arriving at rulings in copyright violation suits. The guidelines are best considered in the context of explanatory material that accompanied the publication of the guidelines in the October 14 *Congressional Record* (pp. E4750-52, daily edition). The main points are as follows:

1. Off-air recordings may be retained by the institution for up to 45 days, after which they must be erased or destroyed.
2. The recordings may be used no more than twice during the first 10 school days of the 45-day period.
3. After the initial 10-day period, the recordings may be used only for evaluation.
4. The recordings may be made only when specifically requested by a teacher, cannot be regularly taped in anticipation of requests and can be recorded only once, regardless of rebroadcasts by the station.
5. A limited number of reproductions of the recordings may be made to meet the legitimate needs of teachers.
6. The original content of the program may not be altered but also need not be used in its entirety; the recordings may not be included in anthologies or compilations.
7. Copies must include a copyright notice on the broadcast program as recorded.
8. The institutions are expected to establish proper controls to assure conformity with the guidelines.

Subsequently, on October 19, the 9th U.S. Circuit Court of Appeals in San Francisco overturned the December 1979 court decision in the controversial *Betamax* case and ruled that taping a television show in the home violates a producer's copyright, and that manufacturers of recording equipment are liable for such infringement. Immediately several bills were introduced in Congress to exempt home taping from copyright infringement. Hearings were held in the Senate and further action can be expected in 1982. The broad implications of the court's decision could include a narrower application of fair use and restrictions on the copyright law's flexibility in dealing with new technologies.

In December, the Senate passed a bill (S. 691) to increase the penalties for trafficking in counterfeit labels for copyrighted records, tapes, and audiovisual works, and for copyright infringements caused by the illicit reproduction and distribution of these products. Also in December, hearings were held in the House on whether the manufacturing clause, a non-tariff protective device for the U.S. printing industry, should be extended or allowed to expire on July 1, 1982, as current copyright law provides.

The fifth and last Copyright Office hearing in preparation for the five-year review of the library photocopying provisions of the 1976 Copyright Law (PL 94-553) was held in New York City January 28-29, 1981. A survey of libraries, publishers, and users in preparation for the five-year review was conducted by King Research, Inc. The Register of Copyrights established a national Copyright Advisory Committee and also initiated discussions between producers and users of copyrighted material on unresolved issues. The Copyright Office also published final regulations on the affixation of copyright notices on various types of works, and concluded that copyright regulations were not needed in graphic elements of printed publications [see report of the Copyright Office in Part I of this volume-*Ed.*].

FLORENCE PROTOCOL

At a Senate Foreign Relations Committee hearing on October 20, 1981, a State Department spokesman urged the Senate to ratify the protocol to the Florence Agreement on the Importation of Educational, Scientific and Cultural Materials. The protocol or supplement to the 1950 Florence Agreement would extend duty-free status to audio, visual, and microform materials for both educational and noneducational uses, and to products for the blind and other handicapped persons. At year's end the Senate committee was awaiting receipt of the draft to implement legislation from the Commerce Department before taking up the protocol for approval. Before leaving office in January, President Carter had transmitted the protocol to Congress (Treaty Doc. 97-2) with a recommendation for ratification.

INFORMATION POLICY AND TELECOMMUNICATIONS

Significant attention was devoted to information policy and telecommunications issues during the first session of the 97th Congress, although very little of the proposed legislation reached final passage. In April, 1981, Representative George Brown (D-Calif.) introduced the Information Science and Technology Act (H.R. 3137) based on the previous year's "Brown Bill" (H.R. 8395). Representatives of several library and information organizations, including ALA and NCLIS, testified at hearings in May and June. H.R. 3137's proposal to establish an Institute for Information Policy and Research is similar to the 1968 recommendations of the National Advisory Commission on Libraries for the establishment of both a permanent National Commission on Libraries and Information Science and a federal Institute of Library and Information Science. Although no action was taken on H.R. 3137, it did achieve one of Representative Brown's objectives—to help educate Congress about the importance of information technology issues.

Congressional concern that the United States was organizationally unprepared to meet the expanding set of problems in international communications and information prompted the introduction of international communications reorganization legislation in both the House (H.R. 1957) and the Senate (S. 821). However, lack of agreement on how to reorganize and other problems stalled the measures. Other provisions of S. 821 were enacted through budget reconciliation. One of the committees to which H.R. 1957 was referred reported unfavorably on the proposed measure.

A reduction in the role of federal government in public broadcasting and facilities, and some deregulation of commercial broadcasting were achieved through the Omnibus Budget Reconciliation Act (PL 97-35). In October, the Senate overwhelmingly passed S. 898, the Telecommunications Competition and Deregulation Act, which introduced major revisions to the common carrier provisions of the Communications Act of 1934. The title of S. 898 accurately describes its thrust. Several provisions that would prohibit regulation of cable rates, instruct the FCC to set ceilings on franchise fees for cable communications, and regulate access to utility pole attachments were added at the last minute during committee markup, but then later removed on the Senate floor.

The House Telecommunications Subcommittee held a series of hearings during 1981 on competition and deregulation and on protecting diversity of information sources. In December subcommittee chairman Timothy Wirth (D-Colo.) introduced H.R. 5158, the Telecommunications Act of 1981. Although strongly pro-competition, it also aims to protect rate-payers and users and to prevent major carriers from controlling information content. Hearings on the bill are scheduled for early 1982. Because of the growth in use by libraries of telecommunications technologies to provide library and information services, the outcome of common carrier legislation could profoundly affect libraries for decades to come.

NCLIS APPOINTMENTS

According to the White House Office for Presidential Personnel, President Reagan has taken the unprecedented step of removing three members of NCLIS before the expiration of their terms. Although by law their terms do not expire until July 19, 1982, Joan Gross, Clara Jones, and Frances Naftalin received notification last fall that their service on the commission was terminated.

On November 9, the president nominated John Juergensmeyer, a lawyer with Smith and Leahy in Elgin, Illinois; Jerald Newman, executive vice president of Bank Leumi Trust Co. of New York; and Julia Li Wu, head librarian at Virgil Junior High School in Los Angeles, for the remainder of the terms expiring July 19, 1982. Also nominated, but for full five-year terms, were Byron Leeds of Publishers Phototype in Secaucus, New Jersey, and Elinor Hashim, assistant manager of the Perkin-Elmer Corporation Library in Norwalk, Connecticut. Hashim would be designated NCLIS chairperson upon confirmation.

PL 91-345, which established NCLIS in 1970, states that commissioners are to be appointed by the president with the advice and consent of the Senate for five-year terms. Until 1981, no president of either party had attempted to remove commissioners before the normal expiration of their terms. The statute directs NCLIS to advise and report to both the president and Congress. The Senate Labor and Human Resources Committee had not acted on the nominations at year's end. The House Postsecondary Education Subcommittee may hold hearings on the legality of the president's actions.

OVERSIGHT HEARING

"What are you doing to motivate people who use libraries to get in touch with their members of congress?" asked Congressman Peter Peyser (D-N.Y.) at an April 7 oversight hearing on federal library programs. "You had better take those gloves off and let people know what is happening, get them fighting," Peyser continued. Representative Dale Kildee (D-Mich.) agreed: "It's true there is greater use of libraries when the economy is bad. There is a tremendous group of people out there who could influence Congress."

Cosponsored by the House Elementary, Secondary, and Vocational Education Subcommittees and the Postsecondary Education Subcommittee, the hearing was held

186 / LEGISLATION, FUNDING, AND GRANTS

TABLE 4 STATUS OF LEGISLATION OF INTEREST TO LIBRARIANS

(97th Congress, 1st Session Convened January 5, 1981 Adjourned December 16, 1981 Chart Date: December 31, 1981)

Legislation	House Introduced	House Hearings	House Reported by Subcommittee	House Committee Report Number	House Floor Action	Senate Introduced	Senate Hearings	Senate Reported by Subcommittee	Senate Committee Report Number	Senate Floor Action	Final Action Conference Report	Final Action Final Passage	Final Action Public Law
Copyright—home video taping	HR 4783, etc.					S 1758	X						
Copyright manufacturing clause	HR 3940	X				S 1880			274	X			
Copyright Piracy Act						S 691							
Department of Education termination						S 1821							
Disaster Relief Act extension	HR 3537			96		S 1212, 1217	X		118	X			PL 97-34
Economic Recovery Tax Act	HR 4242	X		201	X	HJRes 266	X		144	X	215	X	
Elementary & Secondary Education Consolidation	HR 3645, 3941	X				S 1103	X						(PL 97-35)
Foreign Language program assistance	HR 3231	X	X			S 1817							
Freedom of Information Act Amendments	HR 4805	X				S 1730	X	X					
Information Science & Technology Act	HR 3137												
International Communications Reorganization	HR 1957	X	X	100		(S 821)	X		73				(PL 97-35)
Medical Library Assistance Act	HR 2562	X				S 800	X						
National Archives—Independent Agency						S 1421	X						
NHPRC Extension	HR 2979			39	X	S 1050	X		85	X			
National Library and Information Services Act						S 1431							
National Science Foundation Authorization	HR 1520	X		34	X	S 1194			72				

Older Americans Act extension	HR 3046	X	70	X	S 1086	159	X	PL 97-115
Omnibus Budget Reconciliation Act	HR 3982	X	158	X	S 1377	139	X	PL 97-35
Public Telecommunications	HR 3238	X	82	X	S 720	98		(PL 97-35)
Taxation—Independent Research Libraries					S 696			
Taxation—Manuscript donations	HR 2823, 2835, etc.				S 649, 851-2			
Taxation (*Thor Power Tool v. IRS*)	HR 1016, 1936				S 578			
Telecommunications Competition & Deregulation	HR 5158			X	S 898	170	X	
Appropriations								
Suppl., Rescission, Ext. Continuing Resolution, FY 1981	HR 3512	X	29	X	HR 3512	67	X	PL 97-12
Continuing Resolution, FY 1982	HJRes 325		223	X	HJRes 325	none	X	PL 97-51
Further Continuing Resolution, FY 1982	HJRes 357		319	X	HJRes 357	none	X	Vetoed
Further Continuing Resolution, FY 1982 thru 3/31/82	HJRes 370		372	X				
Agriculture, FY 1982	HR 4119	X	172	X	HR 4119	248	X	PL 97-92
HUD & Independent Agencies, FY 1982	HR 4034	X	162	X	HR 4034	163	X	PL 97-103
Interior & Related Agencies, FY 1982	HR 4035	X	163	X	HR 4035	166	X	PL 97-101
Labor-HHS-Education, FY 1982	HR 4560	X	251	X	HR 4120	268	X	PL 97-100
Legislative Branch, FY 1982	HR 4120	X	170	X				
State, Justice, Commerce, FY 1982	HR 4169	X	180	X	HR 4169	265		
Treasury, Postal Service, FY 1982	HR 4121	X	171	X	HR 4121	192		

For bills, reports & laws write: House and Senate Documents Rooms, U.S. Capitol, Washington, D.C. 20515 and 20510, respectively.

on National Library Week Legislative Day for the third year in a row. In 1981, the focus of the hearing was the impact of proposed budget cuts on libraries. Testimony covered not only the effect of cuts in Education Department library programs, but also the added impact of cuts in postal subsidies, CETA public service jobs, and other federal programs.

POSTAL RATES AND SUBSIDIES

The fourth class library postal rate increased 68 percent over the past year. Library mailers had to keep track of four different rates as the year progressed, from 19 cents for the first pound in January, 1981, to 32 cents as of January 10, 1982. A combination of factors, including cuts in postal subsidies, increased postal costs, and regularly scheduled phased rate increases, accounted for the diverse rates.

Both the administration's budget and the first congressional budget resolution assumed deep cuts in the revenue foregone appropriation to the postal service. The revenue foregone subsidy pays the difference between attributable costs and total costs for certain types of nonprofit mailers, and also pays for the phasing in of attributable costs for certain rates over a period of years. Thus the reconciliation measures, which put teeth in those cuts, threatened both the continued phasing in of full subsidy for the library postal rate, and free postal matter for the blind. Skillful negotiating by House Post Office and Civil Service Committee chairman William Ford (D-Mich.) made it possible to retain full phasing for the library rate postage until 1987, and to retain free matter for the blind intact.

Actual appropriations, however, fell short. Despite valiant efforts by Senators Ted Stevens (R-Ark.) and Robert Kasten (R-Wis.), postal subsidies in the continuing resolution through March 31, 1982 totaled $836 million, compared with the $946 million needed and authorized by the Omnibus Budget Reconciliation Act. Although the library rate increased less than other preferred rates, it did go up due to the appropriations shortage.

TAXATION

In early August, Congress completed work on the administration's tax cut measure, the Economic Recovery Tax Act of 1981 (PL 97-34). It extended the allowable deduction from federal income tax of charitable contributions for those who do not itemize their deductions. Non-itemizers are now allowed to deduct a percentage of their contributions that will rise from 25 percent (up to $100) in 1982 to 100 percent in 1986. The tax bill also provided for an increase in the limit on corporate deductions for charitable contributions from 5 to 10 percent of taxable income. It had been estimated that, without increasing their charitable contributions, many corporations would exceed the 5 percent limit because the tax measure made such a large reduction in taxable corporate income.

During consideration of PL 97-34 on the Senate floor, Senator Daniel Moynihan (D-N.Y.) offered as an amendment his bill to remedy the effects of the *Thor Power Tool Company v. The Commissioner of Internal Revenue* ruling on publishers' backlists. The amendment would have allowed a taxpayer to write down the value of excess inventory for its net realizable value. When promised the Senate Finance Committee would address the issue, Moynihan withdrew his amendment. And indeed, Senate hearings were held on the Thor problem in September. A Treasury Department spokesman testified against remedial legislation, and no further action was taken in 1981.

Senate hearings were also held in November on three bills to restore a tax incentive for donations of artwork and manuscripts by authors and artists to libraries and museums. The hearing followed closely on the heels of a recommendation by the Presidential Task Force on the Arts and Humanities to restore the pre-1969 tax deduction. Co-chaired by the actor Charlton Heston, University of Chicago president Hannah Gray, and Ambassador-at-Large for Cultural Affairs Daniel Terra, the task force was established earlier in 1981 to examine endowments to the arts and humanities and to suggest ways to increase private sector support. Similar legislation involving several bills with over 30 cosponsors was introduced in the House during the year, but no hearings were held and the issue is still pending.

Shortly before Congress adjourned in December, there was yet another Senate hearing on a library-related tax issue, but no final action resulted. Legislation pending in both the House and the Senate would assist certain organizations that operate independent research libraries as their sole activity if the libraries are open to the public at no charge. For federal income tax purposes, the legislation would treat such organizations like other educational institutions as a public charity without regard to the source of their funds, thus exempting them from general private foundation restrictions and from the 2 percent excise tax on net investment income.

OTHER LEGISLATIVE AND REGULATORY ACTIVITY

Hearings were held on legislation to extend the Disaster Relief Act of 1974; the House version (H.R. 3527) would extend the list of eligible institutions to include privately owned nonprofit libraries. In another area, the Reagan Administration proposed to limit the applicability of the Freedom of Information Act (FOIA). A less limiting but still restrictive FOIA bill, S. 1730, was approved by a Senate subcommittee.

A bill (H.R. 3727) to assist counties in providing public library services to small communities was reintroduced by Representative Leon Panetta (D–Calif.), but no action was taken. Final regulations for the HEA Title II-A college library resources program were published in June. The White House Conference on Aging, held November 30 through December 3 in Washington, D.C., passed a resolution supporting LSCA. Finally, the year ended on a worrisome note. New classification standards for federal library/information positions proposed by the Office of Personnel Management appeared to downgrade the library profession, and the Reagan administration seemed about to propose a plan for the abolition of the Department of Education that would eliminate all library support programs. Table 4 shows the status of legislation of interest to librarians.

LEGISLATION AFFECTING PUBLISHING IN 1981

Washington Staff, AAP*

Assuredly 1981 was not the best of times for book publishing in the halls of Congress; whether or not it was the worst of times, only more time will tell, but there was ample foreboding that things will get appreciably worse before they get better—if indeed they ever do.

*The Association of American Publishers's (AAP) general Washington staff includes Richard P. Kleeman, Roy H. Millenson, Judith Platt, Diane Rennert, and Carol A. Risher, all of whom contributed to this article.

With the single exception of postal rates and classification, where publishers and librarians could draw a modicum of comfort from the ultimate outcome of lengthy proceedings (i.e., a modest increase in book mailing rates, a slight decrease in the Library Rate, and a broadened rule on enclosures), the news was almost uniformly dismal. Appropriations were cut severely and in some cases impounded; programs were eliminated or threatened with elimination by being combined into "block grants" with reduced funding; the free flow of information about government seemed on the verge of becoming less free; and the general ethos of Washington in this first year of the Reagan Administration was not one to inspire great hope for early improvement in the outlook for untrammeled publishing.

EDUCATION AND LIBRARY AFFAIRS

The year 1981 was a banner year for federal education and library programs. But the banner was at half-mast.

Events to come were foreshadowed on March 10 when President Reagan submitted his budget to Congress and to the nation. The president not only asked Congress to approve more than $1.2 billion in impoundments of fiscal 1981 funds, but his $12.354 billion FY 1982 budget request for the Department of Education was less than the $14.776 billion that had been appropriated the previous year.

The Republican-controlled Senate and the Democrat-controlled House did not hesitate for long in registering their support for the president. In late May the First Budget Resolution reflected many of the cuts the president had requested. A few weeks later, in early June, as part of a FY 1981 stopgap funding bill (the so-called continuing resolution), PL 97-12, most of the education impoundment requests of the president were granted. A few months later, on July 31, Congress sent to the president the Omnibus Budget Reconciliation Act of 1981, which became PL 97-35 when it was signed on August 13.

Some features of the new law merit mention. Section 520 extended Title I (Library Services) of the Library Services and Construction Act (LSCA) for three years through FY 1984 with an authorization of $65 million annually; it specifically barred appropriations for Title II (Public Library Construction) for those years; and it extended Title III (Interlibrary Cooperation) through FY 1984 with an allocation of $15 million annually.

Section 516(b) extended the first three parts of Title II (College and Research Library Assistance and Library Training and Research) of the Higher Education Act (HEA) for three years through FY 1984, but specifically barred appropriations for Part D (National Periodicals System) for those years. College Library Resources (Part A) was authorized at $5 million for each of the three years; Library Training, Research and Development (Part B) was authorized at $1.2 million annually for those years; and Strengthening Research Library Resources (Part C) received a $6 million annual authorization for the period.

Title V-D-2 of the new law consolidated some 28 elementary and secondary school programs into a single block grant, including Elementary and Secondary Education Act (ESEA) Title IV-B (Instructional Materials and School Libraries Resources). The statute authorizes $589 million annually for each of three years beginning with the 1982–1983 school year and then continues for three more years with no specified allocation. States would receive 20 percent of any money appropriated and local educational agencies would receive 80 percent. Requirements for states and localities to maintain levels of spending for education were relaxed.

Section 925 extended the program of assistance to medical libraries through the current fiscal year at $7.5 million.

It should be emphasized that the authorization set out in PL 97-35 are only upper limits and do not guarantee the amount of funds, if any, that will be appropriated.

The next blow came in November 1981, when the text of the "Decision Memorandum to the President from the Task Force on the Education Department" was revealed. This plan to dismantle the Department of Education called for the elimination of federal programs to support public and college libraries. The plan, including termination of the two library programs, would have to receive Congressional approval to become effective.

At the end of the calendar year, Congress will have failed for the third consecutive year to enact the routine appropriation bill for the departments of Labor, Health and Human Services, and Education. Thus, once again, education and library programs are being funded on the basis of a "continuing resolution."

POSTAL RATE INCREASE

AAP, in cooperation with the Recording Industry Association of America (RIAA), intervened before the Postal Rate Commission (PRC) in the rate case filed by the U.S. Postal Service (USPS) in April 1980.

The Postal Service proposed raising the first-class stamp from 15 to 20 cents for the first ounce, and from 13 to 17 cents for each additional ounce. Based on the revenue that this would bring to the Postal Service, an increase was proposed in Special Rate–Fourth Class mail (book rate), from 59 cents for the first pound to 61 cents, with 22 cents for additional weight through the seventh pound and 13 cents for additional pounds in excess of seven. The Officer of the Commission, required by law to represent the public before the Postal Rate Commission, proposed to raise the first-pound rate to 65 cents, with a 27-cent-per-pound rate through the seventh pound and 17 cents for each pound over the seventh. This proposed 16 percent increase in the book rate became the focal point of the AAP-RIAA case.

The Postal Rate Commission rejected the Postal Service request for a 20-cent first-class mail rate and adopted the Officer of the Commission's proposal to accept an 18-cent stamp. The Postal Service then redistributed rate increases over other classes to make up for the revenue loss. In Special Rate–Fourth Class this meant setting a first-pound rate of 63 cents, and raising the subsequent pound rates one cent in each category to 23 cents for each additional pound through the seventh and 14 cents for all pounds over seven.

The board of governors of USPS rejected the recommended decision issued by the Postal Rate Commission and ordered the entire rate decision back to the Rate Commission for reconsideration. Meanwhile the recommended rates of PRC were adopted temporarily, under protest. PRC held firm in its recommendations and finally, in October, the board *overturned* PRC and increased the rate of the first-class stamp from 18 cents to 20 cents, which became effective November 1, 1981. The rates for Special Rate–Fourth Class remained at the original PRC recommendation of 63 cents for the first pound. However, the Library Rate was *reduced* by one cent—from 25 cents to 24 cents for the first pound. Overall, the decision was considered good news by book publishers.

Several mail-user groups whose rates were increased under the decision went to court to challenge the increases.

POSTAL CLASSIFICATION

AAP achieved a long-standing goal in February 1981, when the Postal Service adopted a ruling that allows unlimited enclosures with Special Rate–Fourth Class parcels; under the new liberalized rules, enclosures may include advertising and announcement of products other than books.

In another classification breakthrough, the Attached Mail proceeding pending before the Postal Rate Commission was resolved and implemented as of December 6. The Attached Mail decision will permit most first-class attachments or enclosures that are "incidental" to the non–first class items to be mailed at less than first-class postage. Incidental enclosures include such items as bills, invoices, and account statements. This new ruling should produce substantial savings for publishers, who will be able to enclose statements of account without additional postage.

NINE-DIGIT ZIP

USPS had planned to begin implementation of the new ZIP-plus-4 Code (nine-digit ZIP) in mid-1981. However, as part of the Omnibus Budget Reconciliation Act, Congress prohibited implementation of the new system for the public before October 1, 1983, and additionally prohibited any agency of the executive branch from taking action "to conform its mailing procedures to those appropriate for use under any ZIP Code system using more than five digits" through December 31, 1982.

POSTAL LEGISLATION

The major postal bill in the Ninety-sixth Congress never made it to the Senate floor for consideration. H.R. 79, the Postal Service Act of 1979, was introduced on the first day of the Ninety-sixth Congress and passed the House in early spring of 1979 by an overwhelming vote of 350 to 14. It contained several major provisions of special import to publishers, including a substantial increase in public service appropriations, and the extension of the phasing of postal rates for an additional two years beyond July 1979. Due to lack of Senate consideration, the bill died in the Ninety-sixth Congress.

No comparable legislative efforts were undertaken in 1981. However, the Postal Service did not survive the budget-cutting of the Reagan Administration. In his first budget address to the nation in February, President Reagan recommended that all public service funding (payments to offset costs of maintaining services that are not self-sustaining, such as keeping open small rural post offices and Saturday mail delivery) be eliminated by 1984, and that the revenue-foregone provisions (which cover the Library Rate and other phased rates) be reduced from $789 million to $500 million.

These figures kept changing throughout the complicated budget process and finally the public service appropriation settled at $230 million and $639 million for revenue foregone. This was incorporated into the continuing resolution passed by Congress in the closing days of 1981, effective through March 31, 1982.

In December 1981, two subcommittees of the House Post Office and Civil Service Commission began a series of joint hearings examining the USPS performance a decade after it was created as a quasi-independent corporation with broad powers of self-government. The subcommittee believed that they would obtain from expert witnesses a broad cross section of informed opinion on a variety of postal matters, including accountability of the Postal Service, rate-making procedures, accelerating costs, research and development, postal finances, and labor relations. The hearings were to continue in early 1982, at which time AAP, along with other mail users, is to testify.

THOR POWER TOOL DECISION

A major effort during 1981 was to find a solution to the problem of inventory accounting created by the Supreme Court decision in January 1979 in the *Thor Power Tool* case and by subsequent IRS rulings.

Early in 1981, Senator Daniel Patrick Moynihan (D-N.Y.) introduced a bill to allow industries to write down the value of inventory based on past sales experience with warehouse goods, and also to liberalize accounting methods.

Moynihan offered his bill as an amendment to the administration's tax measure when the latter was being debated by the Senate in the spring, but subsequently withdrew it prior to a vote, when Senator Robert Dole (R-Kan.), chairman of the Senate Finance Committee, promised that the proposal would be considered in the next tax bill. Moynihan also received assurances at the time from treasury officials that they would work with him toward resolution of the *Thor* issue.

A hearing was scheduled on *Thor* and other miscellaneous tax bills in mid-September, whereupon, in a somewhat unexpected move, U.S. Treasury officials attached an $8 billion annual price tag to the Moynihan measure. AAP refuted this in its testimony, contending that the $8 billion estimate could relate only to the cost of accounting procedure changes, and not to the bill's primary portion pertaining to inventory writedowns.

In view of the $8 billion estimate of lost government revenue and the prevailing mood of general austerity in Washington, relief from the *Thor Power Tool* ruling was thought unlikely to receive further legislative attention until the second session of Congress, beginning in 1982.

FREEDOM OF INFORMATION ACT

The past year was hardly a vintage year for open government and the free exchange of information. The 15-year-old Freedom of Information Act (FoIA), which has provided invaluable access to government documents for authors and journalists, came under the administration's guns. Under the laudable guise of cutting costs and government waste and of strengthening national security, an effort was made to sharply curtail the flow of government information.

The first concrete sign of this official intent surfaced last spring in a memorandum from Attorney General William French Smith to agency heads, which indicated that the Justice Department would henceforth fight court challenges arising out of an agency's refusal to release information under FoIA. The Smith memorandum repealed a standard established by the former attorney general, Griffin Bell, which directed government agencies to release information under FoIA unless the result would be "demonstrably harmful."

With administration blessings, Congress also executed several "back-door" maneuvers to weaken FoIA by exempting large numbers of documents held by the Consumer Products Safety Commission and the Department of Energy. Provisions adversely affecting FoIA were even made part of the Omnibus Tax Bill, that is, IRS auditing standards and procedures were exempted from FoIA disclosure requirements. Added to exemptions already granted by the last Congress for Federal Trade Commission and Nuclear Regulatory Commission documents, these provisions create a major threat to the integrity of the act.

In October 1981, the administration finally unveiled its legislative proposals under the deceptively benign title "The Freedom of Information Improvements Act of 1981." Its title notwithstanding, the bill would severely limit the reach of FoIA and would curtail public access to government records by: (1) increasing costs to requesters; (2) excluding records "created for the personal convenience of any government employee"; (3) expanding the time limits within which the FoIA request must be answered; (4) denying use of the FoIA to parties engaged in litigation or adjudicatory administrative proceedings; (5) drastically reducing access to the records of the FBI, CIA, and other investigative agencies; and (6) dramatically curtailing the scope of permissible judicial review with respect to the government's withholding of information for reasons of national security.

The proposed administration bill and related legislation submitted by Senator Orrin Hatch (R-Utah), who chairs the Senate subcommittee dealing with FoIA matters, alarmed AAP and a coalition of media groups sufficiently to prompt the formation of an ad hoc task force to monitor developments and to resist all efforts to eviscerate FoIA. In a strongly worded statement submitted to the Hatch subcommittee, AAP cited an impressive list of important books, on a wide range of subjects, that could not have been written or published without documents obtained under FoIA. On November 12, AAP issued two further statements asserting that the administration's proposed amendments would "significantly contract the opportunity for . . . authors and their publishers to obtain access to information which will foster informed public debate." AAP further expressed its belief that the administration's purpose is clearly to undermine the premise for the availability of information to the public and "replace it with a presumption in favor of secrecy concerning a range of government activities."

AAP criticized the Hatch bill (S. 1730) less severely, but said that book publishers "remain disquieted by its restrictions . . . and the consequent negative impact that such restrictions would have upon the creation and vitality of works of contemporary and historical value."

MANUFACTURING CLAUSE OF COPYRIGHT LAW

Congressman Ashbrook (R-Ohio) and Senator Thurmond (R-S.C.) introduced H.R. 3940 and S. 1880 respectively, to amend the U.S. copyright law for the purpose of retaining the manufacturing requirement scheduled to end July 1, 1982. Hearings were held on December 2, 1981, before the House Judiciary Subcommittee on Courts, Civil Liberties, and the Administration of Justice. Testimony presented by all parties affected dramatically highlighted their concerns. The Authors League of America and AAP testified in opposition to the bill, as did the U.S. Copyright Office. The Printing Industries of America, the Book Manufacturing Institute, and the Graphic Arts International Union testified in support of the bill, as did the AFL-CIO's Industrial Union Department. If the bills as proposed are enacted into law, it will become a condition of copyright protection in the United States that works consisting preponderantly of nondramatic literary material in the English language will have to be manufactured in the United States or Canada. There will be few exceptions to this rule.

U.S. CRIMINAL CODE

A hardy perennial, recodification of federal criminal statutes, had been expected to be dormant in the Ninety-seventh Congress, in part because its one-time champion, Senator Edward M. Kennedy (D-Mass.), was in the minority, and in part because the conservative Republican leadership of the Senate had been expected to seek piecemeal criminal statutory reform without pushing for the long-deferred sweeping recodification. But in November 1981, the Senate Judiciary Committee approved by an 11-5 vote an omnibus revision bill, which was amended from its earlier versions to reflect greater stringency, in part at the behest of the Moral Majority. Most of the committee minority opposing the bill considered even the amended version "too liberal." Among the revisions affecting book publishers in the more than 100 committee amendments were a broadening of the definition of "obscenity," and a relaxing of restrictions on the jurisdictions in which prosecutions for disseminating "obscene" materials could be undertaken. Full Senate debate on the proposed criminal code is expected in the early months of the second (1982) session of the Ninety-seventh Congress.

In the House, meanwhile, a Judiciary subcommittee with little stomach for omnibus revision was under full committee instructions to report progress on the measure by January 31, 1982. The different approaches of House and Senate, combined with the controversy that has dogged the criminal recodification process since the days of the notorious "S. 1" nearly a decade ago, combined to make the outlook for ultimate enactment of a full-scale code revision uncertain.

AGENTS' IDENTITY LEGISLATION

Two versions of a bill to make it a crime to expose the identity of intelligence agents clashed at the close of the first session of the Ninety-seventh Congress, and the threat of a Senate filibuster led by Senator Bill Bradley (D-N.J.) resulted in postponement of the debate until 1982. Although both versions were termed unconstitutional and were opposed by the press and by media and civil liberties groups, the version proposed by Representative John Ashbrook (R-Ohio), passed by the House and supported by the Reagan Administration, would have made the identification of agents a crime if the identifier had "reason to believe" that this would impair or impede intelligence activities. As approved by the Senate Judiciary Committee and pending full Senate action at the close of the last session in December, the bill would make the identifier of an intelligence agent subject to prosecution if he or she had "intent to impair or impede" intelligence activities. The latter version was deemed to be less offensive to the First Amendment by media groups, but the bill was expected to be enacted in some form during 1982.

LEGISLATION AFFECTING THE INFORMATION INDUSTRY IN 1981

Robert S. Willard

Vice President, Government Relations, Information Industry Association

The quiet revolution of the ballot box in November 1980 brought a windstorm of change in the Congress and the administration in January 1981. When Ronald Reagan became the fortieth president (an event the media shared with scenes of newly freed hostages from Iran), he was cheered by his fellow Republican party members who now constituted the majority in the Senate and had significantly narrowed their minority status in the House of Representatives. These profound changes in the structure of government (along with the grisly horror of the March 30 assassination attempt on the president) contributed to an environment in which the First Session of the Ninety-seventh Congress was able to enact sweeping legislation designed to implement much of the president's economic program; even the Democrat-controlled House was unable to slow the momentum of "Reaganomics," as the old Southern Democrat-Republican coalition rose to prominence once more.

Much of the early energy of Congress, however, at least on the Senate side, was devoted to the constitutional responsibility to advise on and consent to the president's nominees for various leadership roles in the new administration. While the Democrats

Note: The opinions expressed in this article are those of the author and do not necessarily represent those of the Information Industry Association.

complained of the slow pace of appointments and the White House issued statistics demonstrating that President Reagan had made more appointments earlier than any prior president, the process lumbered along. A few nominees (such as Ernest Lefever and Warren Richardson) encountered the Senate's political buzz saw and were confined to be footnotes in future history books as "appointed but not confirmed." Most, if not all, of the president's men and women (very few of the latter) were approved and a new cast of players took the responsibility for running the governmental machinery.

In the area of communications and information, the Senate approved the nominations of former senator James L. Buckley (whose name is linked to privacy legislation in the educational arena) as Under Secretary of State whose responsibilities include international information flows; Danford L. Sawyer, to become Public Printer and manage one of the largest printing operations in the world, the Government Printing Office; Charles Z. Wick, a close personal friend of the president and former Hollywood executive, to run the International Communications Agency; and Bernard J. Wunder, Jr., as Assistant Secretary of Commerce and head of the National Telecommunications and Information Administration. Also, in the first year of his administration, the president had the opportunity to appoint, and the Senate confirmed, a majority of seats on the Federal Communications Commission. Mark Fowler, a communications lawyer active in the Reagan campaign, was appointed chairman of the commission.

The productivity of the First Session of the Ninety-seventh Congress, by conventional measures, was not significant and was in fact low compared to prior Congresses. Very disappointing was the fact that Congress did not pass even one of the required appropriations acts providing funding for the government before the new fiscal year began on October 1; when the First Session concluded, only a handful of the required funding bills had been passed. In both cases, Congress met the situation by using a legislative contrivance, called a "continuing resolution," to provide funding at the last minute, although the lateness of the legislation made the government go through the charade of "closing down." The current resolution expires March 31, 1982, when the same midnight anguish can be expected again.

In terms of numbers, President Reagan signed 111 Public Laws in 1981, more than 100 fewer than the average output of the five prior Congresses. (First sessions typically account for only 25–35 percent of the output of a normal two-session Congress.) However, two of these laws were of monumental significance and absorbed the attention of Congress for much of the entire year; these laws were the Economic Recovery Tax Act (PL 97-34) and the Omnibus Budget Reconciliation Act (PL 97-35). In sheer bulk, these laws, which comprise more than 750 pages, must set some productivity record for Congress!

Of the two, the budget act is of greater importance from the point of view of public policy. Some critics, including this author, view the Budget Reconciliation Act as a dangerous undermining of the legislative process. The reconciliation process, as originally conceived, is part of a much bigger budgeting process that was adopted in the mid-1970s to force some discipline on the spending proclivities of the legislators; reconciliation is used to make changes in the spending authority in order to keep the total expenditures below an agreed-on ceiling. In the 1981 act, the process was used to effect wholesale program reductions with minimal public comment. The bill also became a vehicle for major substantive legislative initiatives. At times, the texts of complete bills that had not been formally considered at committee level were included in the Budget Reconciliation Act; some of these successfully remained in the act and became law with the president's signature on August 13. (Examples of such proposals in the information area will be mentioned below.)

In this maelstrom of economic legislation, little attention was paid to information-policy law. No major piece of legislation affecting information became law during the First Session of the Ninety-seventh Congress (except those proposals in the Budget Reconciliation Act), but both houses did consider some important bills and they will be highlighted below. Such legislation can be analyzed in five categories. First, there are those proposals that mandate or encourage the government to become involved in the information marketplace, thus possibly competing with other providers in that marketplace. Second, there are measures aimed at protecting the economic value of information resources. Comprising the third category are government rules affecting the transport of information, or communications. Fourth are those legislative items that address civil liberty issues in the information arena, specifically privacy and First Amendment rights. Finally, the fifth category contains those proposals that assign a regulatory role to the government that may be an incentive or an impediment to flows of information.

GOVERNMENT COMPETITION

The Information Industry Association, numerous times in the past, has voiced concern over one government information enterprise or another that threatened to have serious effects on competitive private-sector activities. The general philosophy has been and remains a belief that a government information activity, unless undertaken with an exceptional sensitivity to its marketplace impact, can operate with institutional advantages that will drive its private-sector competitors out of the market, thus discouraging diversity of information sources. In the past, this argument has been addressed to case-by-case situations, but in 1981 some legislative activity was focused on a generic approach to the issue.

Two of the former case situations were addressed by Congress in 1981. The Worldwide Information and Trade System (WITS), a Department of Commerce-sponsored data base of international trade opportunities and capabilities, was still perceived by the information industry as a threat. As originally proposed, it would have contained much of the same data as is held in private-sector data bases; moreover, the industry could see little movement in the direction of the compromise that had been worked out the year before between the industry and Jimmy Carter's Department of Commerce and had been endorsed by Congress. The industry voiced this concern to Congress, and Congress reemphasized its directive to the Commerce Department to work with and not compete against the private sector. This endorsement was contained in language accompanying the appropriations bill for the department. (However, as noted earlier, Congress passed a continuing resolution, in lieu of this and a number of other departments' appropriations.)

The second government competition issue is the proposed National Periodicals Center, a centralized lending library that the information industry argues would compete on a subsidized basis with private-sector document fulfillment services and that publishers see as a threat to their circulation base and their copyright holdings. Congress, in 1980, had deferred implementation of such a proposal until a government feasibility and, if necessary, design project could be completed. However, in the Budget Reconciliation Act, the funds for the study were deleted completely, and prospects for proponents of the project do not seem bright in the near future.

The Senate version of the Budget Reconciliation Act contained a proposal that was aimed at a specific case of government competition, but that, some observers felt, could be applied generically to many government information activities. Senator Orrin

Hatch (R-Utah) proposed that the National Library of Medicine charge the full cost of providing its information products; that is, users of the on-line index would not only pay for the connect time during which they were using the data base, but would also have to pay an equitable share of the intellectual cost of building the data base. (Recognizing the public-interest aspect of this data base, the Hatch proposal allowed for exemptions to the requirement to pay full costs; educational institutions and hospitals, other government entities, and certain international organizations might continue to have access to the data base on a subsidized basis, providing they did not further disseminate the information to nonexempt entities.) Because of complex political difficulties, the House of Representatives did not accept this proposal and the final Budget Reconciliation Act compromise did not contain the Hatch amendment. However, Senator Hatch, on the floor of the Senate, expressed his commitment to the philosophy of charging full cost for government-provided information products and services.

Taking this concept even further was a bill introduced in October by Congressman Glenn English (D-Okla.). His bill, H.R. 4758, would prohibit the government from offering information services to the public; English said that "the object is to insure that the Government does not stifle the development of innovative and competitive information services by private enterprise." The bill is principally concerned with the issues of federal agencies' offering electronic funds transfer or electronic mail services, but it also applies to competition in the information content area. The bill also recognizes that there are exceptional circumstances and it establishes mechanisms for allowing the government to provide information services when necessary. Some hearings were held on the bill in 1981, and additional hearings are expected in early 1982.

The proposals to eliminate or restrict government information activities go hand in hand with the pronounced emphasis on budget cutting that characterized Congress in 1981. Only a small amount of attention was given to possible negative effects of a reduced level of government information activities. The Joint Economic Committee, for example, published a report on the decreasing quality of economic data. One major study of the overall question of proper roles for public- and private-sector organizations in the information area also fell victim, at least temporarily, to the budget-cutting fever. The National Commission on Libraries and Information Science, in the name of saving money, had to delay a scheduled meeting at which it would have received the report from its special task force on the subject of public-sector and private-sector responsibilities.

PROPRIETARY RIGHTS

No significant piece of legislation dealing with copyright or patents moved very far during the First Session of the Ninety-seventh Congress. In early 1981, the Register of Copyrights concluded a series of hearings throughout the country on the effectiveness of Section 108 of the Copyright Act of 1976. This section deals with library photocopying, and the Register is required by the law to report to the Congress every five years how the law is working and to provide suggestions for legislative remedies to any shortcomings in the law that have been observed. The first report is due in January 1983.

Proprietary rights issues received some attention in the courtroom in 1981, and some of this attention led to legislative proposals. The Supreme Court decided that in some narrowly defined circumstances a computer program could enjoy patent protection. In a federal district court, a case dealing with some of the esoteric features of new electronic media was being argued; the issue: Is it a copyright infringement to remove teletext (data) signals from a television broadcast and replace them with other data before retransmitting the signal via satellite to cable distributors throughout the country?

Receiving a great deal of attention in the media was the appeals court decision in late October reversing the lower court decision on the probity of recording television broadcasts off the air on home video recorders. A three-judge panel ruled such activity was a copyright infringement and sent the case back to the lower court for further consideration. Almost immediately, bills were introduced in both Houses (S. 1758 by Senator Dennis DeConcini [D–Ariz.], H.R. 4783 by Congressman John J. Duncan [R–Tenn.], and H.R. 4794 and H.R. 4808 by Congressman Stan Parris [R–Va.]) to reverse the court's decision legislatively. However, each of these bills goes further than the original lower court decision and would seem to allow copying from other videotapes and cable services, as well as from over-the-air transmissions. Hearings were held in the Senate just before Congress adjourned.

Similar legislation dealing with criminal penalties for copyright infringement moved in both House and Senate. The bills, H.R. 3530 and S. 691, provide stiff prison sentences and large monetary fines for counterfeiting and piracy of phonorecords and audiovisual works. The information industry sought expansion of this legislation to also embrace computer programs and data bases; however, members of Congress were unwilling to include such provisions in the present legislation. Instead, legislation dealing directly with criminal penalties for software piracy may be dealt with by Congress in 1982.

One final copyright issue that Congress began to address in the final days of the First Session relates to the manner in which cable systems redistribute copyrighted works that were originally broadcast over the air. There is a fragile compromise between broadcast and cable interests that has been incorporated in H.R. 3560. Action has taken place at the subcommittee level, and further action is expected in 1982.

COMMUNICATIONS

Major communications legislation has been before Congress since at least the Ninety-fourth Congress, but has never been able to move very far. The enormous implications of such legislation are mind-numbing; the computer and communications industries constitute a significant proportion of the gross national product (GNP) and any attempt to change the 1934 Communications Act is going to affect who gets what part of that massive amount of money. However, during the First Session of the Ninety-seventh Congress, legislation moved further than ever before and some optimistic seers predict that the president will sign a major communications law revision in 1982.

Some legislation amending the 1934 act was approved by both houses in the waning days of the First Session; Section 222, which prescribes the ground rules for participation in the domestic or international marketplaces, was amended to allow greater competition. Also, the Budget Reconciliation Act was used as a vehicle to change the length of broadcast licenses, to authorize a lottery selection for competing applications for a broadcast license, to authorize a managing director for the Federal Communications Commission (FCC), and to prod the FCC into moving more quickly on a particular ruling having to do with how telephone companies keep their financial records. (One might rightfully ask what such issues have to do with reconciling the national budget!)

However, the major honors for accomplishment in terms of communications legislation in 1981 belong to the Senate. Senator Robert Packwood (R–Oreg.), who became chairman of the Commerce, Science, and Transportation Committee when the Republicans became the majority party, tackled common carrier (i.e., telephone) legislation as one of his highest priorities, and introduced S. 898, the Telecommunications Competition and Deregulation Act. Legislation is believed necessary because of recent technological advances involving the use of computers and communications systems in such an intermixed way that the old legal boundaries defining what a telephone company can and cannot do no longer work. Complicating any legislative development is the 1980 FCC decision known as *Computer Inquiry II*, which attempts to draw new boundaries and which is now under legal attack from a number of quarters. Furthermore, developments in early 1982 affecting the *U.S.* v. *AT&T* antitrust case clouded the legislative scene. The case, which began January 1981, sought to break up AT&T into a number of smaller companies. In a dramatic move on January 8, 1982, the government announced it would drop the case and AT&T agreed to divest itself of its 22 local telephone companies. This step led to a wide divergence of opinion on whether legislation was now needed or not, and whether it had a greater or lesser chance of passage.

A description of the Byzantine politics surrounding S. 898 is beyond the scope of this article. One issue worth reviewing, however, is the information-services question. While the general direction of the legislation is to promote competition, the bill recognizes that AT&T occupies such a dominant position in the marketplace that special rules of operation must be imposed on the Bell System at the current time. Many of these rules are implemented by requiring that AT&T provide competitive services only through a fully separated affiliate. When it comes to offering information content, AT&T is even further restricted. It may not offer certain "mass media" types of information electronically over the communications facilities it owns. Other information, such as directory listings, time, weather, and Yellow Pages–like information, may be provided by Bell but only through another fully separated affiliate that is restricted from providing any other service. The theory behind these strictures is that competition in the provision of information content will be seriously hampered if one of the competitors owns the communications link that all the competitors must use to service their customers.

The Senate passed S. 898 on October 7, by the lopsided vote of 90 to 4. Attention then turned to the House of Representatives. No legislation had been introduced on the House side. Instead, Congressman Timothy E. Wirth (D–Colo.), chairman of the House Subcommittee on Telecommunications, Finance, and Consumer Affairs, had been holding a series of hearings on the subject of market structure and status of competition within the telecommunications industry. Two months after the passage of the Senate bill, Wirth introduced his own bill in the House (H.R. 5158). Wirth (whose name was linked with a Communications Act Rewrite amendment in the Ninety-sixth Congress that restricted AT&T in the area of electronic information services) included a section in H.R. 5158 aimed at protecting "Diversity of Information Services"; his requirements in this area go further than the Senate-passed bill. Wirth promises early hearings in 1982 and hopes the House will act fast enough for conferees from the House and Senate to meet to iron out the differences in the two bills before summer. If he is successful, it would be difficult to identify any legislation that more significantly affects the information industry coming out of the Ninety-seventh Congress.

CIVIL LIBERTIES

The new administration did not include among its high priorities any legislative treatment of issues of personal privacy. While Congressman Barry Goldwater, Jr. (R–Calif.), a former member of the Privacy Protection Study Commission, introduced a host of bills growing out of the commission recommendations (as he has done in each of the past three Congresses), no movement occurred to bring about the enactment of any privacy legislation.

Internationally, however, the new administration was very active in supporting the "Guidelines Governing the Protection of Privacy and Transborder Flows of Personal Data," which had been developed by the Organization for Economic Cooperation and Development. These guidelines included provision for voluntary compliance with their principles as an alternative to mandatory legislation. The administration sought the commitment of major U.S. industrial firms during the summer of 1981. Congressman Goldwater introduced a resolution (H.Con.Res. 307) indicating congressional support for the guidelines, although no further action was taken on this measure.

One element of personal privacy the administration strongly supported was the protection of identities of intelligence agents. Congress had struggled with this issue the year before but reached no conclusion before adjourning. The legislation pits two conflicting principles against one another: The need for a strong defense requires effective intelligence activities that are seriously hampered by disclosure of agents' identities, but the First Amendment freedoms of speech and of the press rule against any proscription of publication. On the first day of the Ninety-seventh Congress, H.R. 4 was introduced by Congressman Edward Boland (D-Mass.), the chairman of the Permanent Select Committee on Intelligence. When the full House took up the bill, however, it was amended on the floor in such a way that the original sponsor no longer felt it could meet a constitutional challenge and he ended up voting against passage of the bill. Nevertheless, the House approved the bill and sent it to the Senate, which was already considering similar legislation (S. 391) introduced by Senator John Chafee (R-R.I.). Final action on this measure is expected in early 1982.

Another controversial information law that Congress began to address also dealt with the right of citizens to have access to information about the workings of their government. The Freedom of Information Act (FOIA), first enacted in the mid-1960s, allows individuals to request information from any agency subject to certain legislative exemptions. The Justice Department has listed this law as one of its high priorities for amendment. Basically, Justice wants to stem the flow of information that it feels weakens its criminal prosecution efforts; examples are information that might reveal identities of informants or strategies for criminal apprehension (such as "sting" operations). Another concern is that business information submitted to the government in confidence cannot be protected from release to competition. One Senate subcommittee has already amended and approved S. 1751, a bill introduced by Senator Orrin Hatch (R-Utah); the amendments include a number of administration proposals. It is likely the Senate will approve this legislation, but the House is more reluctant to tamper with FOIA, and it is not clear whether 1982 will see any changes in this law.

REGULATION OF INFORMATION FLOWS

The overall role of the government in terms of action it takes to encourage or impede flows of information is the final category of 1981 legislation affecting the information industry. The major aspect of this category is how the government organizes itself to deal with information-flow issues.

On April 1, 1981, a new statutory office assumed a responsibility for policy concerning how the government manages its information. The Office of Information and Regulatory Affairs (OIRA), created by PL 96-511, the Paperwork Reduction Act, is assigned principal responsibility for all federal government collection, use, storage, and distribution of information. The office has had difficulties in its first year of operation and congressional hearings were held in the House to oversee the early accomplishments of OIRA.

A major difficulty, in the view of many observers, is the attention the new office has paid to regulatory matters. By executive order, President Reagan tasked the office with review of all proposed regulations. Also, the requirement to approve any agency's request to send forms to the public to gather information (including some agencies like the independent regulatory bodies and the Internal Revenue Service) has created a tremendous paperwork logjam in OIRA. Finally, there has been some turnover in the leadership; James C. Miller III, the first head of OIRA, was named to head the Federal Trade Commission and, following Miller's Senate confirmation, Christopher DeMuth took his place. (Both men had come from a background emphasizing regulatory economics.)

One major information policy that emanated from OIRA during the year reflected a concern both for decreasing expenditures and for considering marketplace effects when government provides information products and services. David Stockman, director of the Office of Management and Budget (OIRA's parent agency), issued a directive to all federal agencies asking for a review of all government information centers. This September 11 memorandum requested that the review include a consideration of whether the service is duplicative of other services, whether the private sector could provide the same or similar services, and whether the services are provided on a full cost-recovery basis.

Congress additionally considered other proposals to establish government mechanisms to deal with information issues during 1981. One of these proposals focused exclusively on international information issues. H.R. 1957, sponsored by Glenn English (D–Okla.), was meant to provide a coordinated approach in this area by establishing an interagency committee to formulate international information policy and an advisory committee to provide private-sector input. The bill was approved by the House Government Operations Committee but ran into some roadblocks in the Foreign Affairs Committee, which recommended it not be passed. The bill is currently stalled, waiting for a resolution of the differences between the two committees, but the sponsor of the bill is optimistic that the House will take action in 1982. (There is no similar bill in the Senate, but during the consideration of the Budget Reconciliation Act in the Senate, text similar to the English bill was part of the Reconciliation bill. It was deleted before final passage.)

Another proposal for a new government mechanism was contained in Congressman George Brown's Information Science and Technology Act (H.R. 3137). The California Democrat proposed the establishment of an Institute for Information Policy and Science that would provide a U.S. counterpart to agencies in countries such as England, France, West Germany, and Japan, which are aggressively addressing the issues brought about by the new information economy. Proposals to establish new government activities during a period of government retrenchment have little hope for enactment and H.R. 3137 is no exception. Representatives of the National Telecommunications and Information Administration, the National Science Foundation, the Office of Science and Technology Policy, and other government agencies testified in support of the philosophy of the bill (i.e., heightened attention to information issues) but also averred that there was no need for any new government structure. Meanwhile, a number of witnesses testifying on behalf of private-sector activities urged the enactment of the bill. It is difficult to imagine, however, any set of circumstances that would lead to the passage of this legislation in the current political and economic climate.

CONCLUSION

Information issues continue to absorb much of the attention of U.S. legislators, but generally in an ad hoc, fragmented fashion. Such issues crop up across the congressional committee landscape and no attempt to centralize information-policy issues in a single committee is currently being discussed, nor would it meet with much success.

The First Session of the Ninety-seventh Congress, like most first sessions, leaves undone far more than it has accomplished. The Second Session, faced with both the early signs of whether the Reagan economic program is working and the pressure of elections in early November, will move a great deal of legislation. The outcome of some bills will remain undiscernible, perhaps until Congress's final hours when dozens, maybe hundreds, of measures will be herded through in the traditional legislative stampede at the end of each Congress. For the followers of legislation in the information area, the times will do nothing if not get more interesting and exciting.

Funding Programs and Grant-Making Agencies

COUNCIL ON LIBRARY RESOURCES, INC.

One Dupont Circle, Suite 620, Washington, D.C. 20036
202-296-4757

Jane A. Rosenberg
Program Associate

September 18, 1981, marked the twenty-fifth anniversary of the Council on Library Resources, Inc. (CLR), a privately operated foundation that funds and undertakes activities designed to assist in the solution of library problems, especially those of academic and research libraries. The council awards grants to institutions and individuals to carry out projects that relate to its areas of interest: bibliographic services; library management, operations, and services; library resources and their preservation; and professional education and training. CLR also establishes and administers its own programs, contracting with and granting funding to individuals and organizations to perform research or carry out specific projects. Because it is the council's aim to support activities pertinent to the generic problems of libraries, proposals that will benefit only the host institution normally are not funded.

The board of directors of the council consists of 18 representatives from the academic, business, and research library communities. Warren J. Haas is president of the council. Mary Agnes Thompson is secretary and treasurer. In addition to the board, the officers, and the staff, the council frequently calls on qualified persons to aid in its task force and committee work, and to provide advice and counsel.

The fiscal year that ended on June 30, 1981, witnessed a range of activities that represent both continuing and changing council interests. Eighty-two grants and contracts were active during the year, as well as internships and fellowships. Projects related to the Bibliographic Service Development Program (BSDP) and the new Professional Education and Training for Research Librarianship program (PETREL) account for much of the funding.

In April 1981, a CLR-funded meeting convened by the Association of Research Libraries (ARL) and the American Association for the Advancement of the Humanities (AAAH) brought together scholars, librarians, and association officials to discuss improvements in communication between libraries and the scholarly community. Another recent initiative in sharing library concerns was the CLR–Association of American Universities examination of major issues facing U.S. research libraries. During a meeting of 12 university officials, librarians, and foundation executives convened for this purpose, five major issues were discussed: access to bibliographical information; resource sharing, collection building, and making collections available; preservation of materials; technological applications; and professional education. Five task forces were formed to address the issues and to produce reports for a later conference of library directors, university administrators, scholars, and others.

BIBLIOGRAPHIC SERVICES

In 1978, the council established the Bibliographic Service Development Program to assist coordination and cooperation among bibliographic efforts already underway, and to channel funding for new projects. The program's goals are to provide effective bibliographic services for all who need them; to improve bibliographic products; and to stabilize costs (in constant dollars) of many bibliographic processes in individual libraries. A seven-member program committee advises the council on ongoing projects and new initiatives.

During FY 1981, BSDP awarded more grants than in any previous year and undertook major program initiatives. Thirty-eight grants and contracts were active, and new awards totaled over $1,000,000.

Much of the BSDP program activity relates to the structure and functions of parts of a planned comprehensive nationwide bibliographic record service, which is most likely to be composed of existing major data bases. An important component of such a service is standardized bibliographic records that can be shared among data bases. To assist the standardization effort, the BSDP Joint Committee on Bibliographic Standards continues in its role of advising the Library of Congress on the interpretation of the Anglo-American Cataloguing Rules, on the impact of these decisions on shared cataloging activities, and on applications to specialized materials such as archives and maps.

Also in the standards area, Sue A. Dodd, data librarian at the University of North Carolina, has completed *Cataloging Machine-Readable Data Files: An Interpretive Manual* with the aid of a CLR grant. Papers have been produced on standardization of holdings statements and on institution identification codes, by Richard Anable, and Howard Harris and Patricia Harris, respectively. The Pittsburgh Regional Library Center received funds for a project to improve the sharing of information on serials holdings. The center is developing a system for recording and communicating cancellations so that the last copy of a serial title within a given region can be identified.

BSDP maintains a strong interest in network services and the networks' role in the evolving bibliographic framework. In late 1980, the council contracted with James E. Rush and Norman Stevens to produce a report on current network configuration. In addition, BSDP has pursued its interest in linking the major bibliographic data bases, as recommended in the 1980 Battelle-Columbus Laboratories report, *Linking the Bibliographic Utilities: Benefits and Costs*.

During the process of evaluating the benefits of linking, Battelle developed an interactive computer model called BIBLINK. Using BSDP funds, Battelle augmented the model and prepared a user guide for those who might wish to employ it for research on network links.

Two essential elements in linking data bases—providing technical linkage capability and standardizing the content of data bases—are the subjects of current BSDP projects. In the technical applications area, the council funded a two-year investigation by the Research Libraries Group (RLG) and the Washington Library Network for the purpose of investigating the technical capability required to link their authority file systems. The Library of Congress also joined in the project, now known as the Linked Systems Project. Another BSDP grant went to Northwestern University to develop a means of computer-to-computer interchange of information, including textual messages, record transmission, and individual search and retrieval of records among systems.

To promote integration of existing files and to secure cooperation in establishing the basis for nationwide authority control, the council formed a task force on a

Name Authority File Service (NAFS). The nine-member group, which includes the participants in the Linked Systems Project, is formulating guidelines for a national Name Authority File Service. The task force has produced a report entitled *Requirements Statement for a Name Authority File Service.*

In the related field of subject authority work, two projects have been completed. Dora Crouch, Pat Molholt, and Toni Peterson's *Indexing in Art and Architecture: An Investigation* identifies eleven projects that provide a beginning for establishing a standard indexing vocabulary for the two fields. In order to encourage examination of the more generalized problems attending subject access, BSDP awarded a contract to Carol Mandel and Judith Herschman to produce a paper evaluating subject access systems in relation to the needs of researchers and scholars. An ongoing effort to help shared cataloging services identify growth trends within specific areas is underway as well. Martha Williams of the University of Illinois Coordinated Science Laboratory is compiling statistics to determine trends and statistical relationships among elements in the Machine Readable Cataloging (MARC) data base.

A major new project within BSDP is the multiphase effort to evaluate on-line catalogs. CLR has made grants and contracts to the following six groups to collaborate in a project to evaluate on-line public access catalogs: J. Matthews & Associates; OCLC, Inc.; the Research Libraries Group; the University of California, Division of Library Automation; the Library of Congress; and the University of Toronto Library Automated System. The major objectives of the project are to produce comparative data on existing systems and to provide information for use in guiding future on-line catalog development.

A BSDP grant of $20,000 was awarded in March 1981 to ARL for a two-year project designed to improve bibliographic access to microform collections in American and Canadian libraries. The project emphasizes making available a number of records for items included in microform projects but not previously cataloged, and promoting cooperative projects directed to this goal.

The council has long been interested in Conversion of Serials (CONSER), a cooperative file-building effort that has resulted in a national serials data base. CLR supports telecommunications costs for some CONSER participants. In additoin, BSDP funding supported a Boston Theological Institute project to catalog over 7,000 serial titles. Completed this year, the project relied on CONSER data in the conversion of the union list of serials.

Disseminating bibliographic information through cataloging in publication is another long-standing council interest. In 1971, the council, in cooperation with the National Endowment for the Humanities, provided support for the Library of Congress's Cataloging in Publication (CIP) program, which has prepared data for over 200,000 titles. A current grant enables the library to evaluate the effectiveness and impact of the program.

LIBRARY OPERATIONS AND SERVICES

Central to the assessment of the current status of research libraries is an awareness of their increasingly varied array of programs and services. Due to technological advancements and financial strictures, the services sector is characterized by the paradox of opportunity and the inability to take advantage of what is available. Managing this changing environment is in itself a complicated task that involves every level of operations and services from the relationship between the library and its parent institution to assistance to users and staff training needs.

The primary channel for council assistance in improving library management continues to be the Office of Management Studies (OMS) of ARL. OMS programs include a variety of training, publication, and research activities, with major efforts devoted to the Academic Library Program. Within this program, the OMS staff aids individual libraries with planning and problem-solving through the assisted self-study method. The program includes eight major study areas, ranging from the original Management Review and Analysis Program (MRAP) to the new Preservation Program.

The council grant also provides support for the office's Consultant Training Program, which gives selected individuals the opportunity to develop skills in consulting and to obtain an understanding of OMS self-study procedures and their application. Two classes of 20 consultants have been selected and trained since the program began in 1979.

Related to the council's interest in furthering communication among librarians, faculty, and administrators is a CLR project to explore research library economics and financing. ARL and the Research Libraries Group, Inc., received CLR funds to hold a meeting of 18 invited participants to provide guidance for future efforts to improve information on library costs, the relationship between library operations and the academic and financial structures of their parent institutions, and the economics of scholarly communication in general.

Additional projects in the services and operations area during the year included support for the fifth Earlham College conference on bibliographic instruction, and the Society of American Archivists program to formulate and implement procedures for institutional evaluation of archival agencies. The council also made a grant to the American Library Association (ALA) to support research on the methods libraries use to cover the costs of on-line bibliographic search services. The data is expected to be helpful to libraries that may introduce on-line services; it may also encourage improvement and expansion of existing services and help in planning other technological innovations in the services area.

LIBRARY RESOURCES AND THEIR PRESERVATION

In recent years, there has been an increase in professional interest in preservation. Much of the attention now given to this topic is a result of losses in library buying power, and of the desire to avoid duplication of needed resources. Assuring the future availability of materials has consequently drawn more and more attention.

During a quarter century of research on preservation, the council has supported a laboratory for chemical research on paper deterioration and the means to prevent it; sponsored efforts to develop specifications for selecting paper and bindings; and provided assistance for other preservation activities. A modest grant supports production of a newsletter, *Conservation Administration News*, at the University of Wyoming. In 1979, with the assistance of the Andrew W. Mellon Foundation, CLR established the Committee on Production Guidelines for Book Longevity. Composed of publishers and librarians, the committee has studied the book paper problem as a first step toward its goal of considering all aspects of book longevity. In February 1981, the group held an all-day meeting at the Library of Congress under the auspices of the Center for the Book. Two months later, the committee issued its interim report on book paper.

The report of the committee has a dual purpose: to increase awareness of the problem and to establish guidelines to assure permanence and durability. It contains statements regarding the present status of acid-free paper manufacture, and a set of guidelines for paper to be used in book production. The committee urges publishers to use acid-free paper and to identify acid-free books with appropriate statements in each book. Librarians are asked to make publishers aware of their preservation needs.

Collection management initiatives have also increased as a result of the austerity problem. A CLR grant went to ALA to conduct a pilot collection management and development institute, designed to introduce academic collection development officers and acquisitions librarians to concepts and techniques in the area. Also, reductions in funding for the Library of Congress field office in New Delhi prompted council support for a workshop to review alternative ways to maintain the South Asian acquisitions program.

Providing a means of collection analysis and review that can be employed by individual libraries has been the objective of the Associated Colleges of the Midwest (ACM) project, which received CLR funding in 1980. The project concluded with a test of the methodology in three ACM libraries, and the production of a manual for performing similar studies. In 1981, the council awarded a grant to ARL to review and test the study manual. ARL's Office of Management Studies will carry out the test in four member libraries of the Cooperative College Library Center.

Previously awarded council grants resulted in several major research studies and guides. *Essays from the New England Academic Librarians' Writing Seminar* was published in 1980, and essays from the University of Kentucky Research Foundation project on researching the careers of prominent academic library readers will appear in the *Journal of Academic Librarianship*. In addition, Etta Arntzen and Robert Rainwater's *Guide to the Literature of Art History*, an updated and revised version of Mary W. Chamberlain's *Guide to Art Reference Books*, appeared during 1980 (Chicago: American Library Association, 1980).

PROFESSIONAL EDUCATION AND TRAINING

The council has expanded considerably its program efforts in the area of professional education during the past year. The new program is based, in part, on past CLR activities and interests in this field. The most recent result of council encouragement of projects to assess librarians' status, for example, is the ALA's Office for Library Personnel Resources survey entitled *The Racial, Ethnic and Sexual Composition of Library Staff in Academic and Public Libraries* (Chicago, 1981).

In 1980 the board of directors approved the council's plans for library education projects. Funds for the proposed Professional Education and Training for Research Librarianship program were granted by the Andrew W. Mellon Foundation and the Carnegie Corporation of New York. An advisory committee has been established to assist program planning.

Three library schools have been granted funds to carry out specific aspects of the PETREL program. At the University of Chicago, the Graduate Library School, in cooperation with the Graduate School of Business, has established a special postgraduate program leading to a certificate of advanced study in library management. The University of Michigan's School of Library Science has begun a recruiting program designed to attract highly qualified candidates to specialize in research librarianship.

The Graduate School of Library and Information Science at the University of California, Los Angeles (UCLA) has assumed responsibility for two projects. The first, the Senior Fellows Program, is designed to provide an opportunity for specialized training for individuals who have recently assumed major management posts. UCLA also will organize a conference to explore the frontiers of research librarianship. The objective of the initial week-long conference is to relate research library development and operations to the economic, technological, political, and intellectual factors that promise to dominate policymaking for the next decade. The conferences will be attended by librarians, university administrators, and others.

The council's professional development program, the Academic Library Management Intern Program, continued with the selection of five interns for 1981-1982. This brings to 35 the total number of participants in this program for midcareer librarians. Those chosen for the program work closely with the directors and staff at large university libraries. This year, for the first time, two interns were assigned to one institution.

Anne W. LeClercq, associate professor and head of the undergraduate library at the University of Tennessee, will work with Russell Shank, University of California at Los Angeles. Patricia McClung, North American bibliographer at the University of Virginia, will also work at UCLA with Russell Shank. James G. Neal, head of the collection management department at the University of Notre Dame, has been assigned to work with Stuart Forth at Pennsylvania State University. Virginia F. Toliver, coordinator of computer-assisted retrieval services at the University of Southern Mississippi, will work with Charles Churchwell, Washington University. Karen Wittenborg, social sciences bibliographer and reference librarian at Stanford University, will intern with Jay Lucker, Massachusetts Institute of Technology.

As the year ended, the council decided not to select a class of interns for 1982-1983. Rather, the program will be suspended for a year to allow for an evaluation of its results and to assess future prospects in the context of PETREL projects.

Additional projects in the area of education and training include a grant to the Medical Library Association (MLA) to support a study group assigned to investigate MLA's role in the educational process for health science librarianship. To assist students in the specialized area of archival administration, CLR has granted funding to Wright State University to provide internships in national agencies or institutions. Also, C. W. Post Center of Long Island University received support for its faculty development program. Rutgers Graduate School of Library and Information Studies faculty members conducted course work in basic information science for five C. W. Post Center faculty members during 1980-1981. The program will enable Long Island University to offer course work in information science.

INTERNATIONAL PROGRAMS

Since the early 1970s, the major channel of CLR support for international library activities has been the International Federation of Library Associations and Institutions (IFLA). Ongoing council grants have supported the work of its secretariat and the International Office for Universal Bibliographic Control. New grants are made primarily for special projects.

In 1981, the council granted funding to IFLA to cover travel and related costs for IFLA delegates to visit China to establish an active relationship with the People's Republic, especially in bibliographic matters. IFLA delegates reported that their hosts were interested in becoming involved in international library cooperation. Additional grants support IFLA special projects in the area of copyright of bibliographic records and files, and conversion of copyrighted materials for use by handicapped readers.

The International Council on Archives (ICA) has received CLR funds to aid its activities in the worldwide preservation and use of archival sources. During the past year, ICA held a symposium on advancing the status and professional development of archivists in Latin America. Also, three model curricula for the in-service training of archival personnel were developed, and a records-management manual designed for use in newly independent countries was published. This manual will be tested at a regional seminar, and an additional manual dealing with the management of archival institutions will be prepared.

CLR-SUPPORTED PROJECTS, 1980–1981

NEW GRANTS AND CONTRACTS

American Association for the Advancement of the Humanities	
AAAH/ARL meeting of research librarians and scholars	$ 1,500
American Library Association	
Collection Management Institute	$ 5,150
Financing on-line search services	$ 7,110
Association of Research Libraries	
Collection assessment for small academic libraries	$ 11,200
ARL/RLG project on decision support systems for libraries	$ 30,000
Association for Asian Studies	
South Asia Library Workshop	$ 4,500
Earlham College	
Fifth Conference on Bibliographic Instruction	$ 5,900
Forest Press	
Investigation of the need for an Arabic edition of the Dewey Decimal classification	$ 6,000
International Council on Archives	
Projects	$ 20,000
International Federation of Library Associations and Institutions	
IFLA/People's Republic Liaison	$ 5,000
Lesotho Library Association	
Workshop for training school librarians	$ 5,500
Library of Congress	
Travel grant for LC representative–British conference on resource sharing	$ 1,000
Evaluation of Cataloging in Publication program	$ 11,000
C. W. Post Center, Long Island University	
Faculty development in information science	$ 10,000
Rutherford D. Rogers	
Travel grant to chair IFLA Program Management Committee	$ 6,500
Total	$130,360

NEW COUNCIL-ADMINISTERED PROGRAM GRANTS AND CONTRACTS

Bibliographic Service Development Program	
Richard Anable	
Position paper on holdings statements	$ 2,600
Association of Research Libraries	
ARL microform project	$ 20,000
Battelle Institute–Columbus Laboratories	
Training in use of BIBLINK model	$ 15,068
Augmentation of BIBLINK; preparation of user guide	$ 16,500

Dartmouth College Library
   Participation in on-line catalog project (Phase 2) $ 12,919
Library of Congress
   Travel costs for Linked Systems Project $ 21,000
   Participation in on-line public access catalog project (Phase 2) $ 16,351
Carol Mandel and Judith Herschman
   Paper on subject access $ 2,500
J. Matthews & Associates
   Participation in project to define data elements and collection methods–on-line public access catalog project $ 9,500
   Participation in on-line public access catalog project (Phase 2) $ 99,500
Northwestern University
   Development of an application level protocol $ 36,000
   Participation in on-line public access catalog project (Phase 2) $ 25,260
OCLC, Inc.
   Participation in project to define data elements and collection methods–on-line public access catalog project $ 25,000
Pittsburgh Regional Library Center
   Serials cancellation project $ 24,000
Research Libraries Group, Inc.
   RLG/WLN/LC project: authority file service $165,542
   Preliminary work for on-line public access catalog project $ 19,892
   Participation in project to define data elements and collection methods–on-line public access catalog project $ 26,850
   Participation in on-line public access catalog project (Phase 2) $116,614
James E. Rush Associates
   Preparation of paper on the role of regional networks $ 10,425
Stanford University Libraries
   Participation in on-line public access catalog project $ 20,960
Norman B. Stevens
   Preparation of paper on the role of regional networks $ 3,000
University of California
   Participation in project to define data elements and collection methods–on-line public access catalog project $ 5,650
   Participation in on-line public access catalog project (Phase 2) $ 22,000
   Analysis of data collected in on-line public access catalog project (Phase 3) $113,000
H. D. L. Vervliet, University of Antwerp
   Travel grant for study trip to U.S. research libraries $ 2,500
Washington Library Network
   WLN/RLG/LC project-authority file service (Phase 2) $182,197
   Total $1,014,828

PROFESSIONAL EDUCATION AND TRAINING FOR RESEARCH

Librarianship Program (PETREL)
   Medical Library Association
      Study group in education for health sciences librarianship $ 2,000

University of California	
Senior Fellows Program	$125,000
Frontiers Conference	$ 90,000
University of Chicago	
Program for advanced study in library management	$250,000
University of Michigan	
Program for basic education for research librarianship	$275,000
Total	$742,000

COUNCIL ON LIBRARY RESOURCES PUBLICATIONS

(Free on request)
Twenty-fifth Annual Report (Washington, D.C., 1981)
CLR Recent Developments (Washington, D.C., 1973-   )
CLR Program Guidelines (brochure)

LIBRARY SERVICES AND CONSTRUCTION ACT

State and Public Library Services Branch Staff
Division of Library Programs, Office of Libraries and Learning Technologies, ED

The Library Services and Construction Act (LSCA) celebrated its twenty-fifth year of operations in 1981. Originally enacted in 1956, it was intended to assist states in extending library services to rural areas. At that time there were 940 counties without any public library service and only six states offered state aid for public library support. Statewide library planning was just beginning. Today 46 states have public library state-aid programs and only 4 percent of the nation's population is without access to public libraries.

With the broadening amendments and relatively modest federal funding, LSCA has extended library services in many new and innovative directions affecting virtually all of the nation's 14,000 public libraries and many more thousands through the interlibrary cooperation program. The recent program evaluations of Title I (Public Library Services) and Title III (Interlibrary Cooperation) by Applied Management Sciences noted specific LSCA successes in (1) increasing citizen access to resources, (2) improving services for the blind and physically handicapped, (3) improving the capacity of public libraries to provide services to new users; and (4) introducing users to many nontraditional information resources, for example, on-line data bases, nonbook materials, and so forth. The Title III evaluation study noted that Title III was the major force behind the initial development of multitype library cooperation and networking in the country. It was also credited with being the major influence on state legislatures in initiating their own efforts in interlibrary cooperation and networking.

In 1981, congressional budgetary action culminated in the reauthorization of LSCA through FY 1984. The act still has four titles with only Title I and Title III presently funded. Title II (Public Library Construction) continues to receive funds through

Note: Written by Adrienne Chute, Nathan Cohen, Clarence Fogelstrom, Dorothy Kittel, Evaline Neff, Trish Skaptason, and Robert Klassen, Acting Branch Chief.

transfer from other federal agencies, such as the Appalachian Regional Commission. Funding in FY 1981 for Public Library Services was $62.5 million; for Interlibrary Cooperation, $12 million. To qualify for Title I funding, states and communities must match the federal contribution. The matching ratio, which is set on the basis of the state's per capita income, must be at least 34 percent and can go as high as 66 percent of the program costs.

To participate in both programs, states must have a basic state plan and a comprehensive program setting forth the state's priorities, procedures, and specific activities to meet the library and information needs of the people on a three-to-five-year basis. In addition, an annual program that describes all projects must be submitted to the U.S. Department of Education. All these qualifying documents are developed by the state in consultation with the branch program officers. A statewide advisory council assists the state library administrative agencies in developing and reviewing the documents. At the end of the year, the states' annual reports submitted to the branch provide the data from which the following analyses and descriptions are made. More detailed reports for these areas have been compiled by the branch, and are available to readers on request.

TITLE I—PUBLIC LIBRARY SERVICES

By legislative mandate the Public Library Services Program operates to:

Extend public library services to geographical areas and groups of persons without library services and to improve such services in such areas and for groups that may have inadequate public library services;

Establish, expand, and operate programs and projects to provide library services to the disadvantaged, state institutionalized, physically handicapped, and to those who have limited English-speaking ability;

Improve and strengthen state library administrative agencies;

Strengthen metropolitan public libraries that serve as national or regional resource centers;

Support and expand services of Major Urban Resource Libraries (MURLs) (the Major Urban Resource Library provision is effective when the appropriation exceeds $60 million).

The breakdown of FY 1980 LSCA expenditures (including carry-over funds from the previous year) is noted in Table 1.

Services to Persons of Limited English-Speaking Ability

The Education Amendments of 1974 required the states under Title I of LSCA to add criteria in their needs assessments and state plans to ensure that priority would be given to programs and projects serving areas with high concentrations of persons of limited English-speaking ability. In FY 1980 nearly $1.8 million in LSCA funds was augmented by $3.7 million of state and local funds supporting 45 projects in 25 states and territories, serving an estimated 3.2 million persons of limited English-speaking ability. Eighty-eight percent of the funds was used to provide cultural and library services to the Hispanic population. The services are varied but include:

Provision of books, magazines, and audiovisual materials in foreign languages, with some in both the foreign language and English;

Storytelling for children in foreign languages, both live and recorded for telephone Dial-a-Story programs;

TABLE 1 LSCA TITLE I, PUBLIC LIBRARY SERVICES, FUNDS SPENT ON PRIORITIES, FY 1980

	Federal	State and Local	Total
Disadvantaged	$ 8,581,312	$ 22,567,799	$ 31,149,111
Limited English-speaking	$ 1,802,899	$ 1,830,925	$ 3,633,824
Institutionalized	$ 3,002,026	$ 9,226,902	$ 12,228,928
Physically handicapped	$ 3,729,426	$ 7,955,688	$ 11,685,114
Major Urban Resource Libraries	$ 1,764,983	$ 516,021	$ 2,281,004
Aging	$ 816,445	$ 222,289	$ 1,038,734
Subtotal	$19,697,091	$ 42,319,624	$ 62,016,715
Without services, inadequate service, administering LSCA, strengthening the state library agency, Title III-type projects	$44,479,904	$571,853,451	$616,333,355
Total	$64,176,995	$614,173,075	$678,350,070

Cultural programs featuring non-English-speaking authors and artists whose works are available for loan, or are on exhibit at libraries;

Outreach programs to deliver library materials and information to penal institutions, migrant camps, and nursing homes;

Training library personnel in providing services to bilingual communities;

English-as-a-second-language classes;

Information programs featuring specialists and community leaders on topics of practical nature such as securing employment;

Publications such as directories, brochures, and pamphlets in a foreign language and English dealing with sources of information useful to ethnic groups.

Services to the State Institutionalized

One of the priorities specifically cited in the act for special attention is service to those persons residing in state-supported institutions. These include inmates, patients, or residents of penal institutions, reformatories, residential training schools, orphanages, residential schools for handicapped persons, and other institutions or hospitals operated or substantially supported by the state. In FY 1980, $3.1 million in LSCA funds was used in projects representing $15.8 million of combined state and local funds to reach persons living in state institutions with library services.

Although there have been some problems in maintaining old levels of service with basic budget cutbacks, there have also been some improvements in services. The typical FY 1980 expenditure is a grant to add more basic materials to a state institution's collection. The reports note some of the following efforts:

Paperback collections still comprise a large portion of any typical LSCA grant. Recreational reading in many of the institutions is severely limited.

Greater awareness of limited reading skills and the need for more multimedia materials is recognized in mental health and rehabilitation institutions where projects involved toys, realia, games, prints, etc.

Public libraries are also extending services to mental health and rehabilitation institutions.

Training for institutional librarians in correctional institutions is increasing in a field in which there is a high turnover.

Educational courses such as preparation for Graduate Equivalency Diplomas (GEDs) are a high priority in juvenile correctional facilities, but not as high in adult correctional programs.

Services to the Physically Handicapped

LSCA defines services to the physically handicapped as "the providing of library services, through public or other nonprofit libraries, agencies, or organizations, to physically handicapped persons (including the blind and other visually handicapped) certified by competent authorities as unable to read or to use conventional printed materials as a result of physical limitations." In practice, library services to the disabled are of a broader nature and encompass the entire handicapped community, including parents, relatives, teachers, and others who are involved with the handicapped. One of the most significant outcomes of this LSCA priority is increased public awareness of needs and problems of the disabled and fostering some new approaches to service.

According to FY 1980 reports, $3.7 million in LSCA funds was used in conjunction with $11.9 million in state and local funds to support library projects serving 1.4 million handicapped persons, of whom approximately 400,000 were legally blind.

The types of services that are offered on a statewide basis from the regional libraries include primarily books and magazines recorded on disc, cassette, and magnetic tape along with the appropriate playback equipment, and books in braille. Large-type print books are purchased for those persons who are visually impaired, but not blind. Custom recordings of textbooks and specialized information publications are made for blind students and researchers (these tapings are usually narrated by volunteers). Also provided are summer "reading" programs for children and newsletters to inform people of the status of services and the choice of available materials. Projects at the area and community levels focus on outreach activities such as visits to shut-ins, programs for the deaf and hearing-impaired, and radio reading services.

States also provide services on a statewide basis through a "regional" library for the blind and physically handicapped, which serves as a distribution center for audio recorded materials and playback equipment available from the National Library Services (NLS) of the Library of Congress. Since NLS makes no cash grants to the states, operating funds for the regional libraries come from LSCA, state, and, occasionally, local resources. Several states contract with a neighboring state to provide all or some of the services to their residents. In addition to statewide approaches, many states use LSCA funds to reach persons whose disabilities prevent them from coming to a library. Some of the trends that are represented in the FY 1980 projects are:

Number of readers and circulation of materials are increasing.

More user surveys are being conducted to evaluate services.

Several states are beginning to review the desirability and effectiveness of subregional libraries.

More and greater efforts are being made to publicize services.

Several attempts at providing bibliotherapy were made.

More Friends of Libraries' groups are being established.

More libraries are providing services to the deaf (25 projects in 14 states) and installing teletypewriters.

More Kurzweil Reading Machines are being purchased (1-25 machines per state in 10 states), some of them with LSCA funds.

Radio reading services are provided by 16 states.

Services to the Aging

In 1971 the White House Conference on Aging was responsible for an amendment to LSCA that authorized funding for library services to the aging under Title IV of the act. This title was never funded; however, public libraries have supported programs for the aging under Title I. In FY 1980 an estimated $816,000 in LSCA funds was used and combined with over $200,000 of nonfederal funds to reach an estimated 2.2 million persons over age 65 with special library services. Some trends in these services are noted here:

Programs funded a few years back tended to have a single focus and would disappear after a fiscal crunch.

The most common project provides library services to shut-ins.

Present projects tend to emphasize the delivery of regular reading materials and the development of programs on topics of interest to the older citizen such as crime prevention, cooking for one or two, etc.

With cutbacks in funds, more LSCA projects are "piggybacking" existing delivery systems such as Meals-on-Wheels, using volunteers, and forming Information and Referral Centers with strong components for services to the aging.

Services to the Disadvantaged

Public Library service to disadvantaged persons is one of the general priorities for which a significant amount of LSCA funds has been committed in the past. But there is also an identifiable trend that indicates decreasing investments in projects for the disadvantaged as generally defined in LSCA. A breakdown or these categories appears in Table 2. Total federal dollars spent in FY 1981 for the disadvantaged were $8.6 million or approximately 13 percent of the total LSCA funds. These funds impacted over 7 million persons.

Major Urban Resource Libraries

MURL program activity concluded its third year of operation in FY 1981 with the $2.5 million designated amount above the $60 million LSCA Title I appropriation. For all three years, 169 cities with populations over 100,000 were eligible to share in some of these funds if the libraries in these cities met the state library's criteria for assessing the value of their collections, were able to demonstrate the extent to which the needs of users were being met, and showed that their library collections served a defined region in the state.

The MURL formula divides the $2.5 million in each state based on the ratio of the population in these cities to the total state population. If that population is under 50 percent (as it is in every case except Hawaii), half of the state's allotment must go to the designated MURLs. Seventeen states and territories alloted more than the minimum required under the law. The total amount paid to MURLs from federal, state, and local funds appears in Table 3.

One hundred and fifty-one city libraries received these funds. The funds were used to strengthen interlibrary loan capabilities in the state. Some of the uses of these funds include:

The purchase of reference and audiovisual materials, periodicals, microfilm and microfiche readers and printers;

TABLE 2 LSCA TITLE I, PUBLIC LIBRARY SERVICES, DOLLARS SPENT ON DISADVANTAGED TARGET GROUPS AND CATEGORIES, FY 1980

Target Group/Category	Federal $	State and/or Local $	Total $	% of All Disadvantaged $	Average $/Project	Number of Projects	% of All Disadvantaged Projects	Number of States with Projects
Socioeconomically disadv.								—
All disadvantaged	6,079,208	17,460,783	23,539,991	76	148,987	158	54	35
Migrant workers	3,411,292	15,631,690	19,042,982	61	244,141	78	27	3
Appalachian whites	17,728	30,956	48,684	0	12,171	4	1	1
American Indians	103,144	370,826	473,970	2	413,970	1	.343	10
Spanish-speaking	405,304	89,015	494,319	1	17,654	28	10	9
Alaskan natives	1,153,769	1,184,165	2,337,934	8	137,526	17	6	1
Unemployed	12,849	0	12,849	0	12,849	1	.343	8
Displaced homemakers	975,122	154,131	1,129,253	4	38,940	29	10	0
Women	0	0	0	0		0	0	0
Educationally disadv.	0	0	0	0		0	0	—
Children of socioeconomically disadv. adults	1,818,969	4,975,895	6,794,864	22	80,891	84	29	
Preschoolers and parents of preschoolers	240,135	74,790	315,759	1	20,995	15	5	8
Adult basic education	663,739	4,163,269	4,827,008	15	219,409	22	8	12
Developmentally disabled (not institutionalized)	87,276	22,481	109,757	0	15,680	7	2	5
Literacy	106,858	300	107,158	0	13,395	8	2	6
Culturally disadvantaged	720,961	715,055	1,436,016	5	44,876	32	11	16
Young adults	683,135	131,121	814,256	2	16,617	49	17	—
New Americans	375,583	46,173	421,756	1	17,573	24	8	11
Institutionalized (nonstate)	50,062	3,330	53,392	0	8,899	6	2	5
Mentally ill (noninstitutionalized)	103,006	76,586	179,592	1	19,955	9	3	5
Ethnic cultures	1,000	0	1,000	0	1,000	1	.343	1
	153,484	5,032	158,516	1	17,613	9	3	8

TABLE 3 LSCA TITLE I, PUBLIC LIBRARY
SERVICES, *TOTAL AMOUNT PAID TO
MAJOR URBAN RESOURCE LIBRARIES*
(MURLs)

Fiscal Year	Federal	State	Local
1979	$1,679,849	$ 15,523	$ 187,197
1980	1,764,983	18,138	497,883
1981	1,783,084	678,114	502,393
Total	$5,227,916	$711,775	$1,187,473

Salaries for interlibrary loan personnel, including travel and training funds; Preservation of materials.

TITLE II—PUBLIC LIBRARY CONSTRUCTION

LSCA Title II funds for public library construction were last appropriated in FY 1973. These funds were obligated in FY 1974 and FY 1975.

During the six-year period from FY 1976 to FY 1981, when there were no appropriations, 55 construction projects were administered under the Title II authority, utilizing $10.1 million of transfer funds from other federal programs. Federal funds for the 55 projects represented 40 percent of the total cost of the projects and state/local funds 60 percent. Of the 55 projects, 46 were funded from the Appalachian Regional Development Act program in the amount of $8.6 million. In FY 1981, ten projects were funded under the Title II authority receiving $1,653,963 in federal funds. All of these funds were from the Appalachian Regional Development Act program.

During the 17-year period that public library construction was administered under LSCA (FY 1965-FY 1981), 2,081 projects were approved by the states for a total obligation of $695.9 million. The federal share of the obligation was $199 million, of which $174.5 million was provided by LSCA and $24.4 million from other federal sources. Approximately $497 million came from state and local sources, representing 71.4 percent of the total. The high level of state and local support testifies to the effectiveness of federal funds in stimulating matching support.

TITLE III—INTERLIBRARY COOPERATION

When Congress added Title III to LSCA in 1966, it noted that "no part of this bill is more likely to stimulate new ideas and imaginative or innovative programs than is this provision for interlibrary cooperation. It will make possible the establishment of regional retrieval centers and make available to the individual vastly expanded library services in his particular community. It is this title also that provides the greatest assurance that all funds, state, local, and federal, will be invested in the most productive manner possible."* The Congress expected that in the development of coordinated services, the special purposes and functions of the various existing types of libraries would be recognized as essential, but that Title III would be the catalyst to encourage planning for coordination of total library services within the state and across state lines.

*House of Representatives, 89th Congress, 2d Session, Report No. 1474, *Library Services and Construction Act Amendments of 1966* (to accompany H.R. 14050).

The FY 1980 reports for Title III indicate that 49 states and two outlying territories had actual expenditures of $4.8 million from FY 1979 carry-over funds and FY 1980 funds. Although no state or local matching funds are required, 14 states reported spending $11.2 million ranging from $8,010 by Vermont to $7.5 million by California. Total expenditures for interlibrary cooperation under the LSCA Title III program in FY 1980 were nearly $16 million.

It should be noted that in many projects, especially statewide projects such as the interlibrary loan and reference networks, and the development of computerized union catalogs and serials lists, the public library participation is supported with LSCA Title I funds. The types of activities supported by Title III are rarely discrete projects, but are elements of one project that may itself be an element of a more comprehensive activity (see Table 4).

The numbers of different types of libraries participating in activities have become a meaningless measure since some states report "all" libraries; some report only the major participating libraries; and some report the total number of libraries of each type receiving services. Perhaps more meaningful is the fact that, for example, a public library and a community college library have been engaged in a joint acquisition program and that in FY 1980 the education service center of the school system joined the program. Selected highlights are noted below:

Arizona. Continued building on the concept of the development of the Regional Library Systems for interlibrary loan, with Arizona State University and the University of Arizona as the libraries of last resort. Its interlibrary loan and reference service is the Channeled Arizona Information Network (CHAIN). The Regional Library Systems support such services as in-service training and continuing education, correspondence courses, training in technical processing, acquisition, and program consultants.

Florida. Supported the Florida Interlibrary Loan Improvement Project (FILIP), designed to study interlibrary loan patterns and problems, particularly as they relate to Florida Library Information Network (FLIN), and to make recommendations for improvements. Recommendations of the FILIP Report have been the focus of extensive discussion and are in the process of being tested and evaluated.

TABLE 4 LSCA TITLE III, INTERLIBRARY COOPERATION, TYPES OF ACTIVITIES

Type of Activity	Number of States Reporting
Interlibrary loan and reference networks	36
Use of computers and automation	28
Computerized union catalogs and serials lists	24
Participation in multistate organizations	20
Automated circulation systems	15
Continuing education for interlibrary cooperation	14
Within-state multitype regional system	11
Continuing planning for interlibrary cooperation	10
Access to data base services	9
Preparation of special bibliographies, directories, etc.	6
Delivery systems	5
Processing centers	3
Other interlibrary delivery systems	13

Maine. Dropped the teletype element of the Maine network in favor of the new OCLC/NELINET interlibrary loan subsystem. Formally established the TALI-MAINE search service at the state library in Spring 1979 with access to the Lockheed (DIALOG) on-line data bases. Later three additional data base brokers were added: SDC, Department of Energy RECON, and OL Systems (Canada), bringing the total of accessible data base systems to around 180. Document delivery services were used for the first time to supplement regular interlibrary loan channels, particularly for obscure technical documents.

Oklahoma. The Oklahoma Telecommunications Interlibrary Systems (OTIS) changed over from teletype to computer, using the OCLC interlibrary loan subsystem as a basis. Completion of installation of terminals and printers in all transmission site libraries was accomplished in FY 1980, and a new reimbursement formula was adopted. Increases in both speed and efficiency of interlibrary loan transactions were realized.

Oregon. Supported the Resource Library Network that provides library resources available in Oregon to Oregon residents through interlibrary loan. The state library serves as a clearinghouse for most monographic requests from Oregon libraries to the Resource Library Network libraries (University of Oregon, Oregon State University, Portland State University, and the University of Oregon Health Sciences Center) through contract with the state library. Requests for serials listed in the Oregon Union List of Serials are sent directly to the holding libraries. Requests that cannot be filled through this network may be sent to the Pacific Northwest Bibliographic Center to identify a Pacific Northwest library able to fulfill them.

South Carolina. Continued the support of demonstrations involving groups of libraries participating in SOLINET. To make it possible for small libraries to share a computer terminal and benefit from participation in an automated bibliographic control system, the state library has supported the hardware, membership costs, and communication charges on a decreasing scale over three years. The libraries in the cluster have to absorb all actual cataloging charges and a portion of the communication charges. One cluster is composed of the Spartanburg County Public Library, the Converse College Library, and the Wofford College Library. The second cluster is composed of the Florence County Library, the Darlington County Library, and the Florence—Darlington Technical Education College Library. The two clusters began operation in April 1980. While only a small portion of their holdings are, as yet, in the SOLINET data base, use has already been made of their data for determining locations of unique materials. In all cases, participating libraries have reduced cataloging backlogs and found SOLINET useful in the verification of materials needed for interlibrary loan.

Wisconsin. A grant to the Council of Wisconsin Libraries to establish a reference service as an extension of the present interlibrary loan service provided by the Council of Wisconsin Library System. Access will be to the collections of the University of Wisconsin–Madison Libraries.

ELEMENTARY AND SECONDARY EDUCATION ACT, TITLE IV, PART B—INSTRUCTIONAL MATERIALS AND SCHOOL LIBRARY RESOURCES

Beatrice Simmons Arndt

*Education Program Specialist, School Media Resources Branch,
Division of Library Programs,
Office of Libraries and Learning Technologies,
Office of Educational Research and Improvement, Department of Education*

The passage of the Omnibus Budget Reconciliation Act of 1981 (PL 97-35), signed into law on August 13, 1981, repealed Titles II, III, IV, V, VI, VIII, and IX (except Part C) of the Elementary and Secondary Education Act (ESEA), and folded into Chapter 2 Title V (Omnibus Education Reconciliation Act of 1981) most of the ESEA programs, including Title IV, Part B. Since ESEA Title IV-B, as it now exists, will disappear on June 30, 1982, it seems to be an appropriate moment to look at the history of the program and to summarize some of its accomplishments and its impact.

BACKGROUND

Title IV of ESEA, created by the Education Amendments of 1974 (PL 93-380), was the first major attempt at consolidation of various elementary and secondary education programs. The purpose of consolidation was to reduce paperwork for state and local administrators in applying for, and reporting use of, federal programs and to increase local flexibility in the use of federal funds. Title IV consisted of two parts, B and C. Part B included the former program purposes of ESEA Title II (school library resources, textbooks, and other instructional materials), ESEA Title III (related to testing, counseling, and guidance), and Title III of the National Defense Education Act (NDEA) of 1958 (financial assistance for strengthening instruction in academic subjects). Part B, known as Libraries and Learning Resources, provided grants to states for the acquisition by local educational agencies (LEAs) of instructional materials; for instructional equipment suitable for use in providing education in academic subjects; for minor remodeling to accommodate the equipment; and for counseling and guidance. LEAs were given complete discretion in the use of ESEA Title IV-B funds for the various program purposes, subject to the equitable treatment of private-school children.

The Education Amendments of 1978 (PL 95-561) amended Title IV by adding a new Part D. Testing, guidance, and counseling were removed from Part B and placed in Part D. Other major changes made at that time in Part B of Title IV included changing the program title to Instructional Materials and School Library Resources; adding the requirement that materials and equipment be used for instructional purposes only; providing for consultation among local school personnel to ensure coordination of selection of equipment and materials with school curricula; tightening of method for allocating higher per-pupil amounts because of high tax effort or large numbers or percentages of high-cost children; and allowing participation of private-school children in nonparticipating LEAs. A chronology of Title IV of the ESEA and the Title IV regulations appears at the end of this article.

ACCOMPLISHMENTS AND IMPACT

Funds for the benefit of public and private elementary and secondary school pupils under ESEA Title IV-B programs have made possible substantial improvement in educational practices and have had a significant impact on the quality of education. New instructional programs have been initiated because these funds were available to acquire instructional equipment and materials necessary to support programs. Officials of many LEAs have stated that such programs would not have been possible without ESEA IV-B funds as "seed money" to develop programs identified as basic to acquiring skills required to compete in the changing job market. The widespread use of microcomputers to teach in the curricular areas, as well as the furtherance of computer literacy, has been greatly influenced by the availability of IV-B funds for the acquisition of this type of instructional equipment.

Possibly the greatest impact of this program over the years has resulted from the use of funds for purchasing printed and audiovisual materials necessary for establishing and improving school library media centers. As of 1978, nearly all public secondary schools and over 80 percent of public elementary schools had library media centers. The need for maintaining printed and audiovisual collections of high quality in school library media centers was highlighted by a national survey conducted by the National Center for Education Statistics. The survey indicated that, in 1978, more than 85 percent of school library media centers were in some need of library books, audiovisual materials, and equipment. Of the 85 percent, over one-half had a strong or very strong need for audiovisual materials; well over one-half (47.2 percent) had a strong or very stong need for audiovisual equipment; and well over one-third (43 percent) had a strong need for library books. [See NCES Survey in Part 4 of this volume.—*Ed.*]

Table 1 shows the expenditure of funds by LEAs for various program purposes. Table 2 provides data on expenditures for the benefit of public and private school children. Although 5 percent of the total allotment for Part B and Part C, or $225,000, whichever is greater, has been available for administration of the state plan, Table 1 shows conservative use of Part B funds for program administration. Expenditures for testing, counseling, and guidance services have remained consistently lower than expenditures for equipment and materials; however, a total of $65.5 million was spent for testing, counseling, and guidance during the years these services were eligible.

Title IV, Part B, of ESEA is regarded as the foremost Department of Education program serving private-school children. The U.S. Catholic Conference has testified that parochial school officials regard it as the fairest and most equitable program for providing services and benefits to private-school children. Participation of private-school children in ESEA IV-B benefits has increased slightly through the years, principally because of cooperative planning by public and private representatives and because technical assistance from state education agencies encouraged greater participation. In FY 1981, about 88 percent of enrolled private-school children participated in the program.

Two national studies conducted by professional evaluators provide objective assessments of the impact of ESEA Title IV-B. "Program Consolidation and the State Role in ESEA Title IV," an evaluation by the Rand Corporation (1980), concludes that:

> Title IV-B is a popular, well-run program that is praised for its flexibility and ease of administration.
>
> Title IV-B did not result in the consolidated management of former categorical programs.

TABLE 1 FUNDS EXPENDED FOR ESEA TITLE IV-B PROGRAM PURPOSES AND FOR STATE ADMINISTRATION: FY 1976–1982

Item	FY 1976	FY 1977	FY 1978	FY 1979[1]	FY 1980[2]	FY 1981[3]	FY 1982[3]	Total
School Library Resources & Other Instructional Materials	$29,885,331 (52.4%)[4]	$66,004,262 (50.5%)	$76,540,387 (52.5%)	$79,136,110 (52.6%)	$87,149,984 (54.6%)	$97,000,000 (56.7%)	$75,000,000 (46.6%)	$510,716,074 (52.3%)
Textbooks	1,201,001 (2.1%)	4,983,354 (3.8%)	4,103,489 (2.8%)	4,330,501 (2.9%)	5,822,640 (3.6%)	5,000,000 (3.0%)	4,000,000 (2.5%)	29,440,985 (3.0%)
Equipment	16,036,114 (28.1%)	40,428,691 (30.9%)	39,417,908 (27.1%)	45,567,710 (30.3%)	51,058,023 (32.0%)	62,000,000 (36.2%)	75,000,000 (46.6%)	329,508,446 (33.8%)
Minor Remodeling[1]	292,065 (0.5%)	608,992 (0.5%)	1,125,129 (0.8%)	447,673 (0.3%)	—	—	—	2,473,859 (0.2%)
Testing[2]	1,285,604 (2.3%)	2,540,286 (1.9%)	3,166,287 (2.2%)	3,968,910 (2.6%)	2,623,806 (1.6%)	—	—	13,584,893 (1.4%)
Counseling and Guidance[3]	4,758,305 (8.3%)	11,678,142 (8.9%)	14,312,753 (9.8%)	10,290,331 (6.8%)	6,925,984 (4.3%)	—	—	47,965,515 (5.0%)
State Administration	3,576,662 (6.3%)	4,513,772 (3.5%)	6,919,216 (4.8%)	6,708,062 (4.5%)	6,167,368 (3.9%)	7,000,000 (4.1%)	7,000,000 (4.3%)	41,885,080 (4.3%)
Total	$57,035,082 (100.0%)	$130,757,499 (100.0%)	$145,585,169 (100.0%)	$150,449,297 (100.0%)	$159,747,805 (100.0%)	$171,000,000 (100.0%)	$161,000,000 (100.0%)	$975,574,852 (100.0%)
Appropriation Expenditures	$68,665,000	$147,330,000	$154,497,324	$167,500,000	$180,000,000	$171,000,000	$161,000,000	$1,049,992,324

[1] The authority for LEAs to spend ESEA Title IV-B funds for minor remodeling terminated 9/30/79.
[2] The authority for LEAs to spend ESEA Title IV-B funds for testing, counseling, and guidance terminated 9/30/80.
[3] Estimated.
[4] Each percentage corresponds with the figure above it.

TABLE 2 FUNDS EXPENDED FOR BENEFIT OF PUBLIC AND PRIVATE ELEMENTARY AND SECONDARY SCHOOL PUPILS UNDER ESEA TITLE IV-B PROGRAMS: FY 1976–1982

FY	Public Amount	Public Percent	Private Amount	Private Percent	Total Amount	Total Percent
1976	49,614,828	92.8	3,843,592	7.2	53,458,420	100.0
1977	117,029,392	92.7	9,214,335	7.3	126,243,727	100.0
1978	112,137,312	92.5	9,066,161	7.5	121,203,473	100.0
1979	131,374,617	91.4	12,366,618	8.6	143,741,235	100.0
1980	141,377,918	92.1	12,202,519	7.9	153,580,437	100.0
1981*	151,000,000	92.0	13,000,000	8.0	164,000,000	100.0
1982*	140,000,000	90.9	14,000,000	9.1	154,000,000	100.0
Total	$842,534,067	92.0	$73,693,225	8.0	$916,227,292	100.0

*Estimated.

State educational agencies (SEAs) and LEAs vary in the substance, management, and quality of their IV-B activities.

Small IV-B grants can induce substantial improvement in local practices.

The majority of eligible private-school children receive IV-B services and find them useful.

"Federal Aid to Rural Schools: Current Patterns and Unmet Needs," the Rand Corporation's 1979 assessment, found that "Title IV-B funding formulas are operating to provide rural school districts in sampled States with at least a proportional share of Federal funds and in some cases, somewhat more."

The Indiana Department of Public Instruction funded an assessment of the impact of ESEA Title IV-B on local schools with the following results:

Materials and equipment contributed heavily to pupil motivation and interest.

More than half of the projects oriented toward curricular areas showed remarkable success.

ESEA IV-B was used frequently to try new approaches to teaching.

93 percent of schools were satisfied with materials purchased and 12 percent reported more use than expected.

63 percent indicated that purchases were essential items and not frills.

Other indicators of the effectiveness of this national program in 1980–1981 include media per pupil expenditure of $2.36; use by LEAs of program funds to install new technologies such as microcomputers, videotaping systems, and videodiscs; allocations of $33.2 million for 9.4 million children whose education imposes a higher than average cost; a median amount of $2.55 to 6.5 million children in 1,861 needy LEAs; and allocation of more than $1.3 million for the benefit of rural children.

BLOCK GRANTS

Implementation of Chapter 2, Consolidation of Federal Programs for Elementary and Secondary Education, will begin officially on July 1, 1982. Chapter 2 consolidates about 33 program purposes (including those of ESEA IV-B) into a single authorization of grants to state educational agencies for the same purposes as the categorical programs, but to be used in accordance with the educational needs and priorities of state and local educational agencies as determined by these agencies. Members of the school library media and education community who have an interest in developing programs for the acquisition and use of high-quality instructional materials and equipment with block grant (Chapter 2) funds should consider the following: becoming familiar with the provisions of Chapter 2, Title V of PL 97-35; seeking strong representation of school library media interests on governors' advisory committees; and pursuing involvement in local design, planning, and implementation of applications under the block grant.

CHRONOLOGY OF TITLE IV OF THE ESEA AND THE TITLE IV REGULATIONS, 1974-1980

August 21, 1974	The Education Amendments of 1974 became law and created Title IV of ESEA (PL 93-380).
March 12, 1975	Proposed rules published in *Federal Register* (40 FR 11686).
November 18, 1975	Final Title IV Regulations published in *Federal Register* (40 FR 53482).
October 12, 1976	The Education Amendments of 1976 (PL 94-482) became law and made technical amendments to the Title IV statute, revising the Title IV maintenance-of-effort requirements.
November 22, 1976	Notice of intent to issue regulations on Title IV maintenance-of-effort requirement published in *Federal Register* (41 FR 44961).
September 7, 1977	Amendments to existing Title IV Regulations published in *Federal Register* (42 FR 44961).
November 1, 1978	The Education Amendments of 1978 (PL 95-561) became law and amended Title IV of ESEA.
May 14, 1979	Proposed rules published in *Federal Register* (44 FR 28238).
February 1, 1980	Notice of Interpretation for funding guidance, counseling, and testing activities during FY 1980 published in *Federal Register* (45 FR 7261).
April 7, 1980	Final Title IV Regulations published in *Federal Register* (45 FR 23602).
September 3, 1980	Amended existing Title IV Regulations to prohibit use by local educational agencies of ESEA IV-B funds to acquire physical education equipment.

HIGHER EDUCATION ACT, TITLE II-A, COLLEGE LIBRARY RESOURCES

Beth Phillips

*Education Program Specialist, Division of Library Programs,
Office of Libraries and Learning Technologies,
Office of Educational Research and Improvement, Department of Education*

The College Library Resources Program under Title II-A of the Higher Education Act of 1965 (HEA), as amended, supports the improvement of library resources in eligible institutions of higher education and certain other eligible library agencies.

Since the beginning of the program in 1966, over 2,500 institutions of higher education have participated annually, and over 40,000 awards for basic, supplemental, and special purpose grants exceeding $193 million have been made.

In FY 1981, Congress reauthorized the Title II-A program until FY 1985 by enacting the "Education Amendments of 1980." This recent legislation established a "Resource Development Grant," which is designed to assist in the institution's acquisition of library materials, including books, periodicals, documents, magnetic tapes, phonograph records, and audiovisual and other related library materials. Institutions are also encouraged to use grant funds to pursue eligible networking activities for the purpose of resource sharing. Eligible networking activities include, but are not limited to, user fees, membership fees, and transaction expenses.

Funding is based on eligibility and fulfillment of the maintenance-of-effort requirement. Eligible applicants include public and nonprofit institutions of higher education, as well as nonprofit library institutions whose primary function is to provide library and information services to students, faculty, and researchers in higher education on a formal cooperative basis. The maintenance-of-effort requirement asks for consistency in the institution's history of library materials expenditures, and may be calculated through actual expenditures or average annual expenditure per full-time-

TABLE 1 HIGHER EDUCATION ACT, TITLE II-A, COLLEGE LIBRARY RESOURCES, FY 1981

State or Area	No. of Grants	1981 Obligations	State or Area	No. of Grants	1981 Obligations
Alabama	52	$62,400	Nevada	7	$ 8,400
Alaska	11	13,200	New Hampshire	24	28,800
Arizona	27	32,400	New Jersey	40	48,000
Arkansas	23	27,600	New Mexico	18	21,600
California	183	219,600	New York	196	235,200
Colorado	28	36,000	North Carolina	97	116,400
Connecticut	41	49,200	North Dakota	12	14,400
Delaware	11	13,200	Ohio	97	116,400
District of Columbia	16	19,200	Oklahoma	34	40,800
Florida	74	88,800	Oregon	35	42,000
Georgia	62	74,400	Pennsylvania	139	166,800
Hawaii	11	13,200	Rhode Island	14	16,800
Idaho	8	9,600	South Carolina	50	60,000
Illinois	111	133,200	South Dakota	19	22,800
Indiana	50	60,000	Tennessee	44	52,800
Iowa	51	61,200	Texas	101	121,200
Kansas	37	51,600	Utah	8	9,600
Kentucky	34	40,800	Vermont	23	27,600
Louisiana	24	28,800	Virginia	60	72,000
Maine	23	27,600	Washington	43	51,600
Maryland	43	52,800	West Virginia	25	30,700
Massachusetts	97	116,400	Wisconsin	71	85,200
Michigan	75	90,000	Wyoming	6	7,200
Minnesota	49	58,800	American Samoa	1	1,200
Mississippi	44	52,800	Guam	1	1,200
Missouri	52	62,400	Puerto Rico	28	34,300
Montana	16	19,200	Trust Territories	2	2,400
Nebraska	21	25,200	Virgin Islands	2	2,400
			Total	2,471	$2,977,400

TABLE 2 HIGHER EDUCATION ACT, TITLE II-A,
COLLEGE LIBRARY RESOURCES, FY 1981

FY	Appropriation	Basic	Supplemental	Special Purpose	Obligations
1966	$10,000,000	1,830	—	—	$ 8,400,000
1967	25,000,000	1,983	1,266	132	24,500,000
1968	25,000,000	2,111	1,524	60	24,900,000
1969	25,000,000	2,224	1,747	77	24,900,000
1970	12,500,000	2,201	1,783	—	9,816,000
1971	9,900,000	548	531	115	9,900,000
1972	11,000,000	504	494	21	10,993,000
1973	12,500,000	2,061	—	65	12,500,000
1974	9,975,000	2,377	—	—	9,960,000
1975	9,975,000	2,569	—	—	9,957,416
1976	9,975,000	2,560	—	—	9,958,754
1977	9,975,000	2,600	—	—	9,946,484
1978	9,975,000	2,568	—	—	9,963,611
1979	9,975,000	2,520	—	—	9,903,201
1980	4,988,000	2,595	—	—	4,926,970
1981	2,988,000	2,471	—	—	2,977,400

equivalent student. Waiver of the maintenance-of-effort requirement is exercised under "very unusual circumstances."

Title II-C of HEA, the Strengthening Research Library Resources Program, assists major research libraries in the collection, preservation, and dissemination of research materials. The legislation prohibits an institution from receiving funding from both Title II-A and II-C in the same fiscal year.

Funding in FY 1981 provided a grant of $1,200 for each successful applicant. Grantees are found in every state, the District of Columbia, Puerto Rico, the Virgin Islands, and the Trust Territories. In FY 1981, $2.9 million was awarded to a total of 2,471 institutions of higher education, including 38 nonprofit library institutions and 26 combinations of higher education institutions.

Notification of grant awards was made on August 31, 1981, and the monies are to be used during the grant period of October 1, 1981, through September 30, 1982. Table 1 outlines the number of awards and funding by state. Table 2 traces the funding history of Title II-A from FY 1966 to date.

HIGHER EDUCATION ACT, TITLE II-B, LIBRARY CAREER TRAINING

Frank A. Stevens
Chief, Library Education, Research, and Resources Branch,
Division of Library Programs,
Office of Libraries and Learning Technologies,
Office of Educational Research and Improvement, Department of Education

Janice Owens
Education Technician, Library Education, Research, and Resources Branch

Title II-B (Library Career Training) of the Higher Education Act of 1965 (HEA), as amended (20 U.S.C. 1021, 1032), authorizes a program of federal financial assistance to institutions of higher education and other library organizations and agencies to assist in training programs of library and information science, including new techniques of information transfer and communication technology. Grants are made for fellowships and traineeships at the associate, bachelor, master, post-master, and doctoral levels for training in librarianship. Grants may also be used to assist in covering the costs of institutes or courses of training or study to upgrade the competencies of those persons serving in all types of libraries, information centers, or instructional materials centers offering library information services, and of those serving as educators.

Title II-B was reauthorized by the Education Amendments of 1980 (PL 96-374), with no major changes other than to introduce a new program goal: "new techniques of information transfer and communication technology." However, it was incumbent on the Department of Education to revise program regulations at that time to reflect both the statutory change and general selection criteria of the Education Division General Administrative Requirements (EDGAR). This led to the publication on December 24, 1980, of a new set of program regulations in the *Federal Register* (pp. 85422–85428). While these regulations were termed "final," the preamble noted that they were not offered for public comment, as is normally the case, because of the need to make grant awards in a timely manner in FY 1981. The preamble further noted: ". . . it is intended that these regulations will undergo a more thorough and exhaustive revision at a later date for implementation in FY 1982, at which time these regulations will be made available for public comment." This revision was published as a Notice of Proposed Rulemaking in the *Federal Register* on October 28, 1981 (pp. 53362–53367), with a deadline for public comment of December 14, 1981. Subject to the merits of the public comment, the proposed rule is targeted for final publication—with or without major revisions—in the spring of 1982. Program regulations are a part of the application package that is provided on request to all interested parties at the time of the annual program announcement.

FELLOWSHIP PROGRAM

The entire FY 1981 appropriation of $667,000 was awarded for fellowships. Thirty-four library and information science education programs received 79 (13 doctoral, 2 post-master, 59 master, and 5 associate) fellowship awards. The order of priorities for fellowship training levels in FY 1981 was as follows: master's, doctoral, associ-

TABLE 1 LIBRARY EDUCATION FELLOWSHIP/TRAINEESHIP PROGRAM FY 1966–1981

Academic Year	Institutions	Doctoral	Post-master	Master	Bachelor	Associate	Total	FY
1966/67	24	52	25	62	—	—	139	1966
1967/68	38	116	58	327	—	—	501	1967
1968/69	51	168	47	494	—	—	709	1968
1969/70	56	193	30	379	—	—	602	1969
1970/71	48	171	15	200	+ 20[a]	—	406	1970
1971/72	20	116	6	—	+ 20[a]	—	142	1971
1972/73	15	39	3	+ 20[a]	—	—	62	1972
1973/74	34	21	4	145 + 14[a]	—	20	204	1973
1974/75	50	21	3	168 + 3[a]	—	5	200	1974
1975/76	22	27	6	94	—	—	127	1975
1976/77	12	5	3	43	—	—	51	1976
1977/78	37	18	3	134	—	5	160	1977
1978/79	33	25	9	139	10	5	188	1978
1979/80	36	19	4	134	2	3	162	1979
1980/81	32	17	5	72	—	7	101	1980
1981/82	34	13	2	59	—	5	79	1981
Total	542	1021	223	2,450 + 37[a]	52 + 40[a]	50	3,883	

[a]Indicates traineeships.

ate of arts, post-master's, and baccalaureate. Stipend levels varied, depending on level of study and length of program, within a range of $1,500 to $6,000 per fellow plus dependency allowance as permitted. Additionally, grantee institutions receive an institutional allowance equal to the amount of stipend per fellow.

The selection of persons to be fellowship recipients was, for FY 1981 awards and throughout the history of the program, the responsibility of the grantee institution. This selection and program operation must be consistent with the plan stipulated in the grant application on which award of funds was based.

Key factors given substantial consideration in the review process were the extent to which the fellowship program award would increase opportunities for minority groups and/or economically disadvantaged persons to enter the library profession, and the extent to which the fellowship program award could prepare librarians to work more responsively with the disadvantaged and to develop viable alternatives to traditional library service patterns. Table 1 represents a review of the fellowship program since it began in 1966.

Fellowship grants were awarded in FY 1981 to the institutions shown in Table 2. A more detailed analysis of these awards is contained in a booklet available on request from the Library Education, Research, and Resources Branch, Division of Library Programs, Office of Libraries and Learning Technologies, 400 Maryland Avenue S.W., Washington, D.C. 20202.

INSTITUTE PROGRAM

The institute program provides long- and short-term training and retraining opportunities for librarians, media specialists, information scientists, and persons desiring to enter these professions. Many institutes have given experienced practitioners

TABLE 2 FELLOWSHIPS FOR TRAINING IN LIBRARY AND INFORMATION SCIENCE, ACADEMIC YEAR 1981–1982

Institution	Project Director	No.	Level*	Amount
Alabama				
Alabama A & M University, Normal 35762	Howard G. Ball	1	M	$8,000
Arizona				
University of Arizona, Tucson 85719	Ellen Altman	2	M	16,000
California				
University of California, Berkeley, Berkeley 94720	Michael K. Buckland	3	M	24,000
University of California, Los Angeles, Los Angeles 90024	Robert M. Hayes	2	M	16,000
Colorado				
University of Denver, Denver 80208	Travis White	1	M	8,000
D.C.				
Catholic University of America, Washington 20064	Elizabeth W. Stone	3	M	24,000
University of D.C., Washington 20001	Edith Griffin	3	AA	10,500
Florida				
Florida State University, Tallahassee 32306	Harold Goldstein	4	M (2) D (2)	40,000
Georgia				
Atlanta University, 223 Chestnut St. S.W., Atlanta 30314	Penelope L. Bullock	3	M	24,000
Illinois				
Northern Illinois University, DeKalb 60115	Henry C. Dequin	1	PM	12,000
University of Chicago, Chicago 60637	W. Boyd Rayward	1	M	8,000
University of Illinois, 410 David Kinley Hall, Urbana 61801	Charles H. Davis	1	D	12,000
Indiana				
Indiana University, Bloomington 47402	Herbert S. White	2	M (1) D (1)	20,000
Iowa				
University of Iowa, Iowa City 52242	Carl F. Orgren	2	M	16,000
Massachusetts				
Simmons College, 300 The Fenway, Boston 02115	Ching-chih Chen	3	D	36,000
Michigan				
University of Michigan, 580 Union Dr., Ann Arbor 48109	Russell E. Bidlack	6	M (4) D (2)	56,000
Mississippi				
Coahoma Junior College, Rte. 1, Box 616, Clarksdale 38614	Joel Davis	2	AA	7,500
University of Southern Mississippi, Southern Sta., Box 5146, Hattiesburg 39401	Onva K. Boshears, Jr.	3	M	24,000
Missouri				
University of Missouri, Columbia 65211	Mary F. Lenox	2	M	16,000

TABLE 2   FELLOWSHIPS FOR TRAINING IN LIBRARY AND INFORMATION SCIENCE, ACADEMIC YEAR 1981-1982   (cont.)

Institution	Project Director	No.	Level*	Amount
New York				
CUNY, Queens College, 65-30 Kissena Blvd., Flushing 11367	Richard J. Hyman	2	M	$16,000
Pratt Institute, DeKalb Ave. & Hall St., Brooklyn 11205	Rhoda Garoogian	2	M	16,000
St. John's University, Grand Central & Utopia Pkwys., Jamaica 11439	Fr. Jovian P. Lang	2	M	16,000
SUNY at Albany, 135 Western Ave., Albany 12222	Richard S. Halsey	1	PM	12,000
SUNY at Buffalo, 201 Bell Hall, Buffalo 14260	George S. Bobinski	2	M	16,000
North Carolina				
Appalachian State University, Boone 28608	Alice P. Naylor	3	M	24,000
North Carolina Central University, 1801 Fayetteville St., Durham 27707	Annette L. Phinazee	3	M	24,000
Ohio				
Case Western Reserve University, Cleveland 44106	James E. Rogers	3	M (1) D (2)	32,000
Oklahoma				
University of Oklahoma, 1000 Asp Ave., Norman 73019	Taylor C. Anthony	1	M	8,000
Pennsylvania				
University of Pittsburgh, 1028 Cathedral of Learning, Pittsburgh 15260	Patricia B. Pond	3	M (2) D (1)	28,000
Texas				
North Texas State University, N.T. Box 13796, Denton 76203	Kenneth L. Ferstl	2	M	16,000
Texas Woman's University, Box 22905, T.W.U. Sta., Denton 76204	Brooke E. Sheldon	2	M (1) D (1)	20,000
University of Texas, Box 7576, University Sta., Austin 78712	C. G. Sparks	3	M	24,000
Washington				
University of Washington, Seattle 98195	Peter Hiatt	3	M	21,000
Wisconsin				
University of Wisconsin, Box 413, Milwaukee 53202	Mohammed M. Aman	2	M	16,000

*D = doctoral, PM = post-master, M = master, AA = associate of arts.

the opportunity to update and advance their skills in a specific subject area. Institute programs have been supported since FY 1968 under HEA and since FY 1973 under further amendments included in the Education Amendments of 1972. However, due to the limited appropriation in FY 1981, no institute or traineeship applications were requested.

In FY 1971, the program was redirected to allow it to focus on certain critical and priority areas. The priorities through FY 1981 were:

TABLE 3   LIBRARY TRAINING INSTITUTE PROGRAM
ENROLLMENT DATA, FY 1968–1979

Academic Year	Participants	Institutes	FY
1968/69	2,084	66	1968
1969/70	3,101	91	1969
1970/71	1,347	46	1970
1971/72	1,557	38	1971
1972/73	684	17	1972
1973/74	1,301 + 45[a]	26 + 3[a]	1973
1974/75	1,339 + 35[a]	30 + 2[a]	1974
1975/76	1,244 + 35[a]	26 + 2[a]	1975
1976/77	120	5	1976
1977/78	802 + 112[a]	22 + 3[a]	1977
1978/79	1,101 + 100[a]	24 + 1[a]	1978
1979/80	1,081	24	1979
Total	16,088	426	

[a]Traineeship program.

1. To attract minority and/or economically deprived persons to librarianship as professionals and paraprofessionals.
2. To train professionals in service to the disadvantaged, including the aged and the handicapped.
3. To present alternatives for recruitment, training, and utilization of library personnel and manpower.
4. To foster and develop innovative practice to reform and revitalize the traditional system of library and information service.
5. To retrain librarians to master new skills needed to support key areas, such as the Right to Read campaign, drug abuse education, environmental and ecological education, early childhood education, career education, management (planning, evaluation, and needs assessment), human relations and social interaction, service to the institutionalized, community learning center programs, service to foster the quality of life, intellectual freedom, and institute planning.
6. To train those who teach other trainers.
7. To train library trustees, school administrators, and other persons with administrative, supervisory, and advisory responsibility for library, media, and information services, such as boards of education, state advisory councils, and so forth.
8. To train and retrain persons in law librarianship.

Table 3 outlines the history of the institute awards.

PROGRAM REDIRECTION

As indicated earlier, the program regulations have been revised and were published as a Notice of Proposed Rulemaking in the *Federal Register* on October 28, 1981. These proposed rules contain some important changes. Program priorities have been eliminated and program objectives have been more carefully defined to include the statutorily mandated emphasis on information acquisition and transfer, and communication technology. The program selection criteria have been revised to conform with EDGAR and to simplify special program criteria. The point system has been standardized for all three categories of training; several new definitions appear for the first time, and several old definitions have been redefined; participant eligibility has been simplified; and burdensome selection criteria dealing with institutional growth have been eliminated. After public comment is received, the new rules will be finalized and will govern the selection of grant proposals for FY 1982, subject to the availability of program funds.

HOW TO APPLY

Announcement of the closing date for receipt of applications is published each year in the *Federal Register*. Application packages are available on request. For further information on the Title II-B Library Career Training Program or to request an application package, contact Frank A. Stevens at the office of Libraries and Learning Technologies, 400 Maryland Avenue S.W., Washington, DC 20202, or by calling 202-245-9530.

HIGHER EDUCATION ACT, TITLE II-B, LIBRARY RESEARCH AND DEMONSTRATION PROGRAM

Sarah G. Bishop

Program Officer, Division of Library Programs,
Office of Libraries and Learning Technologies,
Office of Educational Research and Improvement,
Department of Education

The Library Research and Demonstration Program of the Office of Libraries and Learning Technologies (OLLT) is authorized to award and administer grants and contracts for research and demonstration projects related to the improvement of libraries, training in librarianship, and information technology, and for the dissemination of information derived from these projects. On July 20, 1981, new grant regulations were published for this program in the *Federal Register* (p. 37484). Some significant changes from the former regulations include the purpose of the program, which has been expanded to include the promotion of economic and efficient information delivery and of cooperative efforts related to librarianship, the support of developmental projects, and the improvement of information technology. The grant regulations also expand program eligibility to include profit-making organizations, agencies, and institutions. However, since late 1980 this program has awarded only contracts, and will continue to do so during FY 1982.

The projects described below include those funded or completed in 1981 as well as several projects that were funded in previous years. Tables 1 and 2 provide additional information on these projects.

TABLE 1 FUNDED PROJECTS, FY 1981, HEA TITLE II-B, LIBRARY RESEARCH AND DEMONSTRATION

Institution/Organization/ Contractor & Principal Investigator	Project Title	Funds Awarded
Cuadra Associates 1523 Sixth St., Suite 12, Santa Monica, CA 90401 Carlos Cuadra	National Research Agenda for the 1980s	$127,354
Simmons College, Graduate School of Library and Information Science 300 The Fenway, Boston, MA 02115	Citizens' Information Needs	56,888
Commissioned Papers		
Mary Tochim	The Effect of Membership in Bibliographic Utilities on Interlibrary Loan Trends	4,850
Dr. Nina Martin	State Educational Agency Responsibilities and Services for School Media Programs	7,500
Abigail Studdiford	History of HEA Title II-C, Strengthening Research Library Resources Projects	9,420
Dr. Blanche Woolls	The Use of Technology in School Library Media Administration	3,449
Donald King, King Research, Inc.	New Technology and the Public Library	5,500
Dr. Donald Foos	The Changing Institutional Role of the Public Library	5,000
Marilyn Mason	Public Library Finance	5,000
Marilyn Mason	Federal Role in Library Networking	5,000
Virginia Mathews	Libraries: Aids to Life Satisfaction for Older Women	5,000
Betty Turock	Public Library Services for the Aging in the Eighties	4,993

PROJECTS FUNDED IN FY 1981

"The Library and Information Science Research Agenda for the 1980s" project, being conducted by Cuadra Associates, is coming to a close. A major activity of the project was a colloquium convened by the Department of Education on December 2, 1981. The presidents of 15 major library and information science organizations were invited to review the project results and to help develop a means of disseminating the research agenda and translating it into action. There has been significant national interest in this project and the results could form the beginning of an ongoing dialogue between the funders of research and the researchers themselves concerning important issues in library and information science to be addressed during the next decade. Project results should be available in February 1982.

A contract was awarded to Simmons College to conduct Phase II of a project concerned with consumer information needs. During Phase I, researchers determined the information needs and searching patterns of New England households. Phase II will determine criteria of effectiveness for network delivery of consumer information

TABLE 2 TOTAL OBLIGATIONS AND NUMBER OF PROJECTS FUNDED, HEA TITLE II-B, LIBRARY RESEARCH AND DEMONSTRATION, FY 1967–1981

FY	Obligation	No. of Projects
1967	$ 3,381,052	38
1968	2,020,942	21
1969	2,986,264	39
1970	2,160,622	30
1971	2,170,274	18
1972	2,748,953	31
1973	1,784,741	24
1974	1,418,433	20
1975	999,338	19
1976	999,918	19
1977	995,193	18
1978	998,904	17
1979	980,563	12
1980	319,877	4
1981	235,826	12
Total	$24,200,900	322

through libraries. Existing library and nonlibrary networks have been surveyed and the results analyzed. An assessment model is being developed to determine the optimum design and performance of library consumer information networks. This will be the first comprehensive study to link consumer information needs with networks. Project results should be available by early summer.

Between July and October 1981, contracts were awarded for ten commissioned papers to discuss relevant library issues. Two papers were prepared for the White House Conference on Aging: "Libraries: Aids to Life Satisfaction for Older Women" and "Public Library Services for the Aging in the Eighties." Two papers concern school library media programs and administration; two papers will review the federal role in library networking and the impact of network relationships on interlibrary loans. Three papers will discuss various aspects of the role and financing of public libraries, and a study has been commissioned to review the Higher Education Act (HEA) II-C (Strengthening Research Library Resources) project history. The two White House Conference papers are available now; the others should be available by early spring.

OLLT, in cooperation with the Fund for the Improvement of Postsecondary Education, sponsored the project "Develop New Methods of Teaching On-Line Searching of Computerized Data Bases." This project is studying the effectiveness and cost of Computer Assisted Learning Packages (CALPs) and is comparing them with traditional workshop training for librarians and other information workers who perform computerized literature searches. One finding of the project has been that participants who used the CALP method of learning experienced a feeling of isolation since they worked alone, something that was not felt by participants who attended the workshops. The project also found that CALP participants had a higher failure rate on tests than did workshop participants. The second half of this project will study the cost-effectiveness of CALP and try to make it more economical. (Comparative studies so far indicate very little difference between the cost of CALP and that of workshops.)

PROJECTS COMPLETED IN 1979-1980

In 1979 a contract was awarded to Contract Research Corporation to examine library involvement in literacy education. The results of that study have been published in two volumes. Among other things, the study found that most literacy projects have been initiated through federal funding, the uses of which are planned by local school and library officials; that state school and library officials function in a capacity to help develop cooperative arrangements among several localities; that a large number of facilities—73,000 school libraries, 8,300 public libraries, 1,000 community college libraries, and associated community and civic associations—have the potential for sustaining literacy education; that generally libraries become aware of the need for literacy education through information from library educators and community groups; and that 75 percent of community agencies involved in literacy education cooperate with public libraries in sustaining the projects.

In 1979, Temple University received a grant to produce "Alternative Publications in College Libraries: An Evaluative Model." James P. Dandy and Elliott Shore are the editors of *Alternative Materials in Libraries*, which will be published by Scarecrow Press and should be available by early 1982.

A 1979 grant to the American Library Association assisted the development of a project entitled "Improving Jail Library Service." A major product of this project is *Jail Library Service: A Guide for Librarians and Jail Administrators*. The 1981 publication is a step-by-step guide for prison and library staff on how to initiate or improve local jail library services. It also provides guidelines for workshops on jail library services.

The second phase of a grant awarded to Elgin Community College to prepare a package of computer programs to serve community college learning resource centers was completed in 1980. *A Comprehensive Automated Learning System* (CALS), a product of this project, is being used in several libraries in the Northern Illinois Learning Resources Cooperative. Further marketing prospects are being explored.

ADDITIONAL INFORMATION

The Directory of Library Research and Demonstration Projects, 1966-1975, and abstracts for FY 1976 through FY 1979 are available on request from the Department of Education, Office of Libraries and Learning Technologies, Library Education, Research, and Resources Branch, 400 Maryland Avenue S.W., ROB3, Room 3622, Washington, D.C. 20202, or by calling 202-245-2993.

All project reports are generally made available to the Education Resources Information Center (ERIC). As the material becomes available, it is announced in ERIC's monthly *Resources in Education* (Washington, D.C.: Superintendent of Documents, U.S. Government Printing Office). The announcement includes an abstract, price of the report in hard copy or microfiche, and order instructions.

HOW FUNDS ARE DISTRIBUTED

During FY 1982 OLLT will conduct directed contract research in the area of library and information science research and demonstration. Requests for Proposals (RFPs) that describe the work to be done will be prepared for public response. Announcements of opportunities to offer proposals are published in *Commerce Business Daily*, the publication in which all U.S. Government solicitations are advertised. Forty-five to 60 days are usually allowed for responses to an RFP. *Commerce Business Daily* provides information on how to obtain the RFP, which in turn provides all the information an offerer needs to prepare a proposal for consideration by OLLT and the Department of Education.

HIGHER EDUCATION ACT, TITLE II-C, STRENGTHENING RESEARCH LIBRARY RESOURCES

Patricia R. Harris

*OERI Associate,
Office of Libraries and Learning Technologies,
Division of Library Programs,
Library Education, Research, and Resources Branch,
Office of Educational Research and Improvement,
Department of Education*

PROGRAM HISTORY AND PURPOSE

The Strengthening Research Library Resources Program is one of the major federal discretionary grant programs focused on improving the services and collections of research libraries in the United States. The program is authorized under Title II, Part C, of the Higher Education Act of 1965 (HEA) as amended by Section 201 of the Education Amendments of 1980. First enacted in 1976, the program has awarded almost $23 million to 57 major research institutions in four years of operation.

The purpose of the grant awards is to make available to researchers and scholars the basic tools of research: the books, serials, manuscripts, and other library materials that trained librarians and bibliographers are expert in collecting and organizing for use. In the past decade, research libraries have been particularly hard hit by continued high inflation; this erosion in buying power has been coupled with more intense demands on research collections. *ARL Statistics*, compiled by the Association of Research Libraries (ARL), reports that in the period 1970–1980 expenditures for library materials increased 91 percent; in the same period, however, the gross number of volumes added each year decreased by 22.5 percent. The Title II-C grant program is one response to alleviating this pressure.

According to the law, this program is intended to support major research libraries. An eligible applicant is defined as a public or private nonprofit institution of higher education, an independent research library, or a state or other public library, which has a collection that makes a significant contribution to higher education and research, is broadly based and recognized as having national or international significance for research, and contains unique materials that are in demand by scholars not connected with that institution. Each year approximately 100 institutions submit grant applications.

The authorizing legislation prohibits any institution from receiving a grant under HEA Title II-A, College Library Resources Program, and Title II-C during the same fiscal year.

FY 1981 GRANTS PROGRAM

In FY 1981, 30 grant awards were made to support project activities at 41 major research libraries. Table 1 is a list of FY 1981 recipients, giving the amount of the grant award, listing joint grant recipients, and providing a brief project description. In re-

TABLE 1   PROJECTS FUNDED UNDER HEA II-C, STRENGTHENING RESEARCH LIBRARY RESOURCES PROGRAM, FY 1981

Institution & Project Director	Grant Award	Project Description
Academy of Natural Sciences of Philadelphia Sylva Baker	$ 43,680	To begin a retrospective conversion of the Academy of Natural Sciences collection to OCLC.
American Museum of Natural History Nina J. Root	166,539	To begin the preservation and cataloging of the photographic collection.
University of Arizona David Laird	184,785	To continue for a second year the collection of materials on arid lands and publish a comprehensive guide to the literature.
*Boston Public Library Philip J. McNiff	187,069	To undertake the preservation of rare and fragile materials in the research collections.
Brown University C. James Schmidt	165,000	To support the John Carter Brown–John Hay libraries rare book cataloging project and John Hay sheet music cataloging project.
Center for Research Libraries Donald B. Simpson	122,809	To produce a microfiche catalog of the CRL collections.
University of Chicago Martin Runkle	55,820	To continue for a third year the acquisition, processing, and preservation of South Asia materials and editing the publication of the South Asia Reference Center Catalog.
Cleveland Public Library Ervin J. Gaines	80,306	To undertake retrospective cataloging of serial titles.
Cornell University Louis Martin	284,639	To continue the acquisition and cataloging of serials, dissertations, and archives and monographs for Southeast Asia and East Asia.
Dartmouth College Jutta Reed-Scott	150,000	To preserve through microfilming and treatment the collection on polar studies.
University of Florida Gustave Harrer	800,000	A cooperative project involving the University of Florida, Emory University, Florida State University, University of Georgia, University of Kentucky, University of Miami, University of Tennessee, and Virginia Polytechnic Institute to create an on-line serials data base.
Harvard College Oscar Handlin	167,747	To continue the microfilming and preservation of materials on Slavic studies.
University of Hawaii Don Bosseau	150,000	To undertake the retrospective conversion of the Pacific Collection to OCLC.
*University of Illinois Nancy D. Anderson	120,000	To create an on-line mathematics delivery and reference system.
Indiana University Elaine Sloan	145,000	To catalog the microform set *English & American Plays of the 19th Century*.

TABLE 1 PROJECTS FUNDED UNDER HEA II-C, STRENGTHENING RESEARCH LIBRARY RESOURCES PROGRAM, FY 1981 (cont.)

Institution & Project Director	Grant Award	Project Description
Iowa State University Stanley Yates and Richard H. Kraemer	$127,975	To both preserve and provide access to the American Archives of the Factual Film.
University of Michigan Richard Dougherty	300,000	A joint project with Michigan State University and Wayne State University to create a serials data base on OCLC and RLIN.
Newberry Library Joel Samuels	131,658	To replace and preserve rare materials on British history and family history, reference works, and scholarly journals.
New York Public Library David H. Stam	662,816	A cooperative project with Columbia University and New York University to improve access and preserve materials in the field of art and architecture.
University of North Carolina–Chapel Hill James Govan	270,937	To develop an on-line catalog to provide access to the research collections of the University of North Carolina, North Carolina State University, and Duke University.
Ohio State University William J. Studer	179,000	To preserve and strengthen the agriculture, education, and engineering/technology collections and enter the bibliographic records for these collections in OCLC.
University of South Carolina Kenneth Toombs	172,000	To produce an on-line catalog of the complete collection of the "Fox Movietonews" newsfilm collection.
University of Southern California Jean E. Mueller	126,695	To strengthen the resources of the Andrus Gerontology Center Research Library.
*Southern Illinois University Kenneth G. Peterson	180,000	To acquire the Library of Living Philosophers Archives and publish a guide to the Philosophy Collections.
Stanford University David C. Weber	209,013	To catalog the microform set *Early American Imprints, 1801-1819*.
University of Texas Harold Billings	174,000	To continue the preservation of Mexican research materials.
*University of Utah Roger K. Hanson	110,883	To catalog the microform set *Landmarks of Science*.
University of Washington Gary L. Menges	175,025	To preserve and provide access to rare materials in the Native Americans of the Pacific Northwest collection including explorer journals, photographs, and pictorial materials and archival recordings of Indian languages.
University of Wisconsin–Madison Joseph H. Treyz	128,604	To preserve and develop the Germanic collection.
Yale University Lawrence Dowler	228,000	To support the organization, preservation, and automated cataloging of the manuscript and Latin American collections.

*Projects to be funded for 24 months.

TABLE 2   NUMBER OF APPLICATIONS AND AWARDS BY REGION,
HEA, TITLE II-C, FY 1981

Region	No. of Applications	No. of Awards
I: New England (Connecticut, Maine, Massachusetts, New Hampshire, Rhode Island, Vermont)	9	5
II: New York, Puerto Rico, Virgin Islands	9	3
III: Middle Atlantic states (Delaware, District of Columbia, Maryland, New Jersey, Pennsylvania, West Virginia)	9	1
IV: Southeastern states (Alabama, Florida, Georgia, Kentucky, Mississippi, North Carolina, South Carolina, Tennessee, Virginia)	10	3
V: Great Lakes states (Indiana, Michigan, Ohio)	10	4
VI: Midwest (Illinois, Iowa, Minnesota, Missouri, Wisconsin)	17	7
VII: Southwestern states (Arizona, Arkansas, Louisiana, New Mexico, Oklahoma, Texas)	13	2
VIII: Mountain Plains states (Colorado, Kansas, Montana, Nebraska, Nevada, North Dakota, South Dakota, Utah, Wyoming)	3	1
IX: Pacific Northwest states (Alaska, Idaho, Oregon, Washington)	3	1
X: California, Hawaii, American Samoa, Guam	8	3

sponse to both congressional advice and concerns voiced by the library constituency, the program has endeavored to broaden and increase the number of grant recipients under Title II-C. In FY 1981 the number of participating institutions was increased to 41; one-half of these libraries were first-time grantees. This is likely to be a trend that will be maintained in FY 1982.

The selection criteria used to evaluate applications for grants are established by regulation; the criteria for the FY 1981 competition were published in the *Federal Register* of December 24, 1980. These criteria are designed to measure an applicant's

TABLE 3   ANALYSIS OF APPLICATIONS,
HEA, TITLE II-C, FY 1981

Category	Amounts
Number of proposals received	91
Amount of funds requested	$19,167,195
Number of proposals supported	30*
Applicants by type of library	
Institutions of higher education	62
Independent research libraries	10
Public libraries	5
State libraries	4
Museums	3
Other	6

*Three of these proposals were jointly sponsored, directly benefiting eleven additional institutions.

TABLE 4   HEA II-C, STRENGTHENING RESEARCH LIBRARY RESOURCES PROGRAM, PROGRAM ACTIVITIES FY 1978-1981

Fiscal Year	Collection Development	Preservation	Bibliographic Control	Total Funding
1978	$ 795,103	$1,340,554	$ 2,864,339	$ 4,999,996
1979	628,433	1,393,201	3,978,366	6,000,000
1980	841,120	805,383	4,345,765	5,992,268
1981	427,253	1,298,542	4,274,205	6,000,000
Total	2,691,909	4,837,680	15,462,675	22,992,264

significance as a major research library and the plan and appropriateness of the project. All of the applications are reviewed and scored by a three-member panel of experts representing the research library community. After the panel review, a geographical analysis is made of the highest scoring applications to determine if this group of prospective grant recipients represents the "broad and equitable geographical distribution" required by law. The regulations specify that up to 15 points may be added to an applicant's score to achieve a geographical balance among the grantees. Table 2 indicates Title II-C-designated regional areas and the number of applications and awards for each region in FY 1981. Table 3 is an analysis of all FY 1981 applications.

As in the past, II-C grant awards in FY 1981 supported collection development efforts, preservation microfilming, and other techniques to extend the life of research materials, and promoted greater resource sharing by coordinated bibliographic control of scholarly resources. Table 4 provides an analysis of funding support for FY 1981 and all previous grant years.

DEVELOPMENT OF NEW REGULATIONS

It was announced in late 1980 that a complete and thorough revision of Title II-C program regulations would be carried out in FY 1981. This process was begun. On October 28, 1981, a Notice of Proposed Rule-making was published in the *Federal Register* requesting public comment on the revised and streamlined regulations. It is expected that the new regulations will be finalized in FY 1982. However, time constraints will not permit their use in the FY 1982 grant cycle. It is expected that these new regulations will be used for the FY 1983 grant cycle.

ADDITIONAL INFORMATION

Abstracts giving brief project descriptions of activities funded in FY 1981 and abstracts for FY 1978, FY 1979, and FY 1980 are available on request from the Department of Education, Office of Libraries and Learning Technologies, Division of Library Programs, Library Education, Research, and Resources Branch, 400 Maryland Avenue S.W., ROB-3, Room 3622, Washington, D.C. 20202.

HOW TO APPLY

Announcement of the closing date for receipt of applications is published each year in the *Federal Register*. Application packages are available on request. For further information on the Title II-C Program or to request an application package, contact Frank A. Stevens at the address given above or by calling 202-245-9530.

… / FUNDING PROGRAMS AND GRANT-MAKING AGENCIES

NATIONAL SCIENCE FOUNDATION SUPPORT FOR RESEARCH IN INFORMATION SCIENCE AND TECHNOLOGY

1800 G St. N.W., Washington, DC 20550
202-357-9554

Sarah N. Rhodes

Division of Information Science and Technology

The National Science Foundation (NSF), an independent agency of the federal government, was established by Congress in 1950 to promote the progress of science. Through its Division of Information Science and Technology (IST), NSF supports basic and applied research in information science under three related programs. The objectives of the division are to increase understanding of the properties and structure of information and information transfer; to contribute to the body of scientific and technical knowledge that can be applied in the design of information systems; and to improve understanding of the economic impact and other effects of information science and technology.

The Information Science Program is concerned with increasing the fundamental knowledge necessary for understanding information processes. Information science deals with the study of information as idealized organization or structure, as well as with its many facets, such as measures, storage, manipulation, retrieval, coding, and interpretation. Research is also directed toward biological systems because these are capable of complex information processing that contemporary artificial systems cannot accomplish. Human information processes, such as the extraction of meaning from text, complex object identification, language processing, and associative memory, are being investigated.

The Information Technology Program supports research to expand the scientific base for information system design. It provides a vehicle for translating the results of basic research into useful applications, as well as for the refinement and testing of theory. Information technology is usually understood to include the technologies of information storage, processing, transmission, input, and output. This program is not directly concerned with the development of such technologies, but focuses instead on the application of technologies to systems capable of augmenting human intellectual activities, and on research on the relationship of system design parameters to the abilities, limitations, and purposes of human users.

The Information Impact Program supports research that contributes to understanding both the impact of information production, distribution, and use, and the increasingly pervasive applications of advanced information technology. Information is a major consumer good and an element in the production of all goods and services. Much interest centers on its unusual economic properties as a commodity, on its exchange, and on the complex phenomena to which it gives rise. There is interest also in how the accessibility and availability of information channels affect patterns of communication, processes of decision making, and interpersonal transactions.

In order to enhance the development of information science and contribute to the scientific vitality of the field, IST has established Special Research Initiation Awards for New Investigators as part of its program of research support. These awards are offered only to principal investigators who have earned a doctoral degree within the

TABLE 1 INFORMATION SCIENCE AND TECHNOLOGY—FY 1981 AWARDS

Principal Investigator	Organization/Title	Amount ($)/Duration
C. E. Agnew	Stanford University Innovation and Efficiency in Spectrum Management Theoretical Analysis	132,436 14 mos.
B. E. Allen	University of Pennsylvania Alternative Representations of Information in Microeconomic Systems	125,959 24 mos.
J. R. Anderson	Carnegie-Mellon University An Information Processing Analysis of Learning Geometry	134,742 36 mos.
M. A. Arbib & D. D. McDonald	University of Massachusetts Dynamic Interaction of Multiple Representations: Vision and Language	174,416 36 mos.
A. Bookstein	University of Chicago Robustness Properties of Bibliometric Laws	23,810 12 mos.
L. R. Caporael*	Rensselaer Polytechnic Attribution of Human Characteristics to Machine Intelligence	34,785 12 mos.
G. C. Carter	National Academy of Sciences Partial Support of the Numerical Data Advisory Board (NDAB)	15,139 12 mos.
G. C. Carter	National Academy of Sciences Partial Payment of Dues from the USA for the Committee on Data for Science and Technology of the International Council of Scientific Unions	12,000 12 mos.
W. S. Cooper	University of California, Berkeley Nonstandard Decision Rules and Information Representations	75,046 24 mos.
J. R. Corsi & J. V. Scaletti	University of New Mexico The Use of Teleconferencing in Administrative Hearings	31,971 4 mos.
W. H. Dutton	University of Southern California Organizational Impact of Video-Teleconferencing: Pilot Study	34,754 7 mos.
J. H. Flowers	University of Nebraska Research on Human Information Processing of Visual Displays	60,429 24 mos.
J. B. Friedman	University of Michigan Computational Studies of the Representation of Information in Logic and in Natural Language	123,541 24 mos.
O. H. Gandy, Jr.	Howard University Tenth Annual Telecommunications Policy Research Conference	17,000 14 mos.
Z. S. Harris	Columbia University Information Correlates of Basic Language Structures	115,471 †
R. J. Herrnstein	Harvard University Studies on Natural and Artificial Visual Categories	218,785 24 mos.
J. H. Holland	University of Michigan Research on Adaptive Knowledge Acquisition Systems	118,437 24 mos.
G. P. Huber	University of Wisconsin A Study of the Distribution, Processing and Use of Scientific and Technical Information in Research Organizations	95,353 14 mos.
R. B. Hull	University of Southern California Theoretical Investigation of Database Constraints and Semantic Constructs	28,949 24 mos.

TABLE 1   INFORMATION SCIENCE AND TECHNOLOGY—FY 1981 AWARDS (cont.)

Principal Investigator	Organization/Title	Amount ($)/ Duration
T. Indow	University of California, Irvine Geometrical Structure in Perceptual Systems	90,075 24 mos.
P. B. Kantor	Tantalus, Inc. Study of the Cost Function for Academic Libraries	99,957 24 mos.
S. J. Kaplan*	Stanford University Theory and Computation for Natural-Language Question-Answering	50,209 24 mos.
H. G. Kaufman	Polytechnic Institute Factors Related to Use of Scientific and Technical Information and Effectiveness of Engineers: A Longitudinal Study	10,000 8 mos.
S. Kemper*	University of Kansas An Information Theoretic Approach to Reading	76,989 24 mos.
D. H. Klatt	Massachusetts Institute of Technology Auditory Information Processing and Speech Perception	142,000 18 mos.
J. L. Kolodner	Georgia Institute of Technology Computer Memory for Current Events	132,664 24 mos.
D. H. Kraft	Louisiana State University Modeling of Generalizations of Boolean Query Processing in Retrieval Systems	34,722 12 mos.
D. M. Liston	King Research Research into the Structure, Accessing, and Manipulation of Numeric Databases: Phase I	29,970 6 mos.
P. R. McAllister	Computer Horizons Interrelationships between Federal Funding and Production of Scientific Papers	95,163 12 mos.
F. Machlup	New York University Knowledge: Its Creation, Distribution, and Economic Significance	173,493 24 mos.
B. Mahoney	Institute for Court Management Evaluation of Telephone Conferencing to Conduct Civil Motion Hearings	186,415 24 mos.
C. A. Montgomery	Logicon, Inc. Workshop on Logic Programming for Intelligent Systems	34,729 4 mos.
M. G. Morgan	Carnegie-Mellon University Experimental Analysis of Factors in the Design of Information Systems for Modeling Engineering/Economic Decisions	225,934 18 mos.
D. E. Payne	University of North Dakota Effects of Mass Media Interpersonal, Contact and Social Background in a Rural Cross National Setting: A Longitudinal Study	59,811 36 mos.
A. Peters	Franklin Research Institute Support for Coordination of Scientific and Technical Information Activities	120,000 †
E. L. Rissland	University of Massachusetts The Structure of Examples	147,848 24 mos.
J. J. Robinson	SRI International Computational Efficiency of Formal Grammars	169,826 24 mos.

TABLE 1 INFORMATION SCIENCE AND TECHNOLOGY—FY 1981
AWARDS (cont.)

Principal Investigator	Organization/Title	Amount ($)/ Duration
N. Sager	State University of New York Computable Models of Time and Quantity in Natural Language Data	184,451 24 mos.
G. Salton	Cornell University Automatic Indexing and Clustered File Search Methodologies Applied to Business Correspondence	147,435 24 mos.
G. Salton	Cornell University Mathematical Models in Automatic Information Retrieval	132,054 24 mos.
T. Saracevic	Case Western Reserve University Classification and Structure of Questions in Information Retrieval	101,782 12 mos.
R. C. Schank	Yale University Theoretical Foundations of Natural Language Processing	16,215 †
R. J. Schweickert*	Purdue University Analysis of Reaction Times Using Scheduling Theory	66,686 24 mos.
E. Sciore*	SUNY, Stony Brook Incorporating Structure and Semantics into Relational Databases	53,821 24 mos.
E. M. Soloway	Yale University Information Processing in Algebra and Computer Programming	125,489 24 mos.
H. R. Swearer	Brown University Research on Natural Language Processing (Frame Selection)	131,920 24 mos.
R. S. Taylor	Syracuse University Value Added Processes in the Information Life Cycle	166,612 18 mos.
A. M. Tenenbaum	CUNY, Brooklyn College Efficiency of Sequential Search Algorithms	84,646 24 mos.
D. S. Warren	SUNY, Stony Brook Representing Semantic Information within Databases	183,755 24 mos.
S. B. Weiner	Center for Policy Research Partial Support for a Workshop on Information Retrieval	6,538 6 mos.
A. B. Whinston	Purdue University Development of a Computerized Decision Support System	240,138 24 mos.
R. Wilensky	University of California, Berkeley Modeling Contextual Language Understanding	124,433 24 mos.
R. L. Winkler	Indiana University Research on Information Aggregation and Value	46,793 24 mos.
L. A. Zadeh	University of California, Berkeley Analysis of Imprecise Information	195,825 36 mos.

*Special Research Initiation Award
†Second increment for 24-month continuing grant

last five years in a field related to information science, including the information, computer, cognitive, and mathematical sciences, linguistics, and electrical engineering.

SUBMISSION AND REVIEW OF PROPOSALS

Proposals may be submitted by academic institutions, by nonprofit and profit-making organizations, or by groups of such organizations. Joint proposals that bring a coordinated range of expertise and research skills to bear on complex problems are particularly encouraged. In the selection of projects to be supported, preference is given to research that is fundamental and general, and to applied research concerned with scientific and technical information rather than, for example, business information or mass communication. The development of hardware is beyond the scope of this program, as are projects to develop, implement, or evaluate information systems except for the purpose of generalizations beyond the particular information systems involved.

A program announcement, *Research in Information Science*, NSF-81-34, which also provides information on how to submit a proposal, is available from the Division of Information Science and Technology. Potential applicants are encouraged to discuss their research ideas with IST staff, either in person or by letter or telephone.

Except for proposals for Special Research Initiation Awards, for which deadlines are announced, research proposals may be submitted at any time. Review generally requires six to eight months, and proposed activities should be scheduled with that in mind. Proposals are reviewed by NSF staff and outside reviewers selected for their knowledge and expertise in topics addressed by the proposals. The award of NSF grants is discretionary. In general, projects are supported in order of merit to the extent permitted by available funds. The principal criteria by which a research proposal is evaluated are (1) the technical adequacy of the investigators and their institutional base; (2) the adequacy of the research design; (3) the scientific significance of the proposed proj-

TABLE 2   INFORMATION-RELATED AWARDS BY OTHER NSF DIVISIONS WITH PARTIAL SUPPORT FROM IST, FY 1981

Principal Investigator	Organization (NSF Division)/Title	Amount ($)/Duration
J. A. Anderson	Brown University (BNS) Cognitive Applications of Matrix Memory Models	31,670 12 mos.
B. W. Ballard	Duke University (MCS) Natural Language Interfaces to "Layered" Domains: A Multiple-Prototype Approach	62,598 24 mos.
R. B. Banerji	Temple University (MCS) Flexibility and Efficiency of Knowledge Representation in Intelligent Information Systems	79,298 24 mos.
L. Hurwicz	University of Minnesota (SES) Comparison and Analysis of Systems and Techniques of Economic Organizations	55,999 12 mos.
S. Pinker	Stanford University (BNS) The Mental Representation of 3-D Space	84,883 24 mos.
W. A. Richards	Massachusetts Institute of Technology (MCS) Natural Computation and Control	411,972 12 mos.
H. W. Slotkin	Massachusetts Institute of Technology (SES) Appraisal and Records Management Guidelines for Scientific and Technological Records	60,000 24 mos.
L. A. Zadeh	University of California, Berkeley (MCS) A Theory of Approximate Reasoning	31,500 12 mos.

ect; (4) its utility or relevance; and (5) its implications for the scientific potential of the field.

The foundation plans to award approximately $5.2 million for information science research in FY 1982.

DISSEMINATION OF RESULTS

NSF encourages grantees and contractors to present their research results at appropriate professional meetings and to publish in scientific journals. Copies of final technical reports are made available through the National Technical Information Service of the U.S. Department of Commerce. In addition, summaries of awards are available through the Smithsonian Science Information Exchange. Annual lists of awards and bibliographies of reports from completed projects are available from IST.

Table 1 lists the research grants awarded by IST in FY 1981. Table 2 lists those awards funded jointly by IST and other NSF divisions, including the Division of Behavioral and Neural Sciences (BNS), the Division of Mathematical and Computer Sciences (MCS), and the Division of Social and Economic Sciences (SES).

Part 3
Library Education, Placement, and Salaries

GUIDE TO LIBRARY PLACEMENT SOURCES

Margaret Myers
*Director, Office for Library Personnel Resources,
American Library Association*

This year's guide updates the listing in the 1981 *Bowker Annual* with information on new job-lines, new services, and changes in contacts and groups listed previously. The sources listed give assistance primarily in obtaining professional positions, although a few indicate assistance for paraprofessionals. The latter, however, tend to be recruited through local sources.

GENERAL SOURCES OF LIBRARY JOBS

Library Literature: Classified ads of library vacancies and positions wanted are carried in many of the national, regional, and state library journals and newsletters. Members of associations can sometimes list "position wanted" ads free of charge in their membership publications. Listings of positions available are regularly found in *American Libraries, Catholic Library World, Chronicle of Higher Education, College & Research Libraries Newsletter, Journal of Academic Librarianship, Library Journal, LJ/SLJ Hotline,* and *Wilson Library Bulletin.* State and regional library association newsletters, state library journals, foreign library periodicals, and other types of periodicals carrying such ads are listed in later sections.

Newspapers: The *New York Times* Sunday Week in Review carries a special section of ads for librarian jobs in addition to the regular classifieds. Local newspapers, particularly the larger city Sunday editions, often carry job vacancy listings in libraries for both professionals and paraprofessionals.

LIBRARY JOB-LINES

New job-lines were added during 1981 in Oklahoma and by the Mountain Plains Library Association. Library job-lines or job "hotlines" give recorded telephone messages of job openings in a specific geographical area. Most tapes are changed once a week on Friday afternoon, although individual listings may sometimes be carried for several weeks. Although the information is fairly brief and the cost of calling is borne by the individual job seeker, a job-line provides a quick and up-to-date listing of vacancies that is not usually available in printed listings or journal ads.

Most job-lines carry listings for their state or region only, although some will occasionally accept out-of-state positions if there is room on the tape. While a few will list technical and other paraprofessional positions, the majority of job-lines refer professional jobs only. When calling the job-lines, one might occasionally find that the telephone keeps ringing without any answer; this will usually mean that the tape is being changed or that there are no new jobs for that period. The classified section of *American Libraries* carries job-line numbers in each issue.

The following are in operation: *American Society for Information Science* (ASIS), 202-659-1737; *Arizona State Library/JAM,* 602-278-1327; *Association of*

Note: The author wishes to acknowledge the assistance of Sandra Raeside, OLPR Administrative Assistant, in compiling the information for this article.

College and Research Libraries (ACRL), 312-944-6795; *British Columbia Library Association*, 604-263-0014 (British Columbia listings only); *California Library Association*, 916-443-1222 for northern California, 213-629-5627 for southern California (identical lists); *California Media and Library Educators Association*, 415-697-8832; *Colorado State Library*, 303-866-2210 (Colorado listings only, includes paraprofessional); *Florida State Library*, 904-488-5232 (in-state listings only); *Georgia Library Association/JMRT*, 404-634-5726 (5:00 P.M. to 8:00 A.M. Monday thru Friday; 12 noon Saturday thru 8:00 A.M. Monday); *Illinois Library Job Hotline*, 312-828-0930 (cosponsored by the Special Libraries Association Illinois Chapter and Illinois Library Association, all types of jobs listed); *Maryland Library Association*, 301-685-5760; *Metropolitan Washington Council of Governments* (D.C.), 202-223-2272; *Midwest Federation of Library Associations*, 517-487-5617 (also includes paraprofessional and out-of-state if room on tape; cosponsored by six state library associations—Illinois, Indiana, Michigan, Minnesota, Ohio, and Wisconsin); *Mountain Plains Library Association*, 605-624-2511 (includes listings for the states of Kansas, Nebraska, Nevada, North and South Dakota, Utah, and Wyoming); *New England Library Board*, 207-623-2286 (New England jobs only); *New Jersey Library Association/State Library*, 609-695-2121; *New York Library Association*, 212-227-8483; *North Carolina State Library*, 919-733-6410 (professional jobs in North Carolina only); *Oklahoma Jobline*, 405-521-2502 (cosponsored by Oklahoma Library Association and Oklahoma Department of Libraries; 5:00 P.M. to 8:00 A.M. Monday thru Friday and all weekend);*Oregon Library Association*, 503-585-2232 (cosponsored by Oregon Educational Media Association); *Pacific Northwest Library Association*, 206-543-2890 (Alaska, Alberta, British Columbia, Idaho, Montana, Oregon, and Washington; includes both professional and paraprofessional and other library-related jobs); *Pennsylvania Cooperative Jobline*, 412-362-5627 (cosponsored by Pennsylvania Library Association; Pennsylvania Learning Resources Association; Pittsburgh Regional Library Center; *Special Libraries Association*, Philadelphia Chapter; *Medical Library Association*, Philadelphia and Pittsburgh groups; *American Society for Information Science*, Delaware Valley Chapter; *Pennsylvania School Librarians Association;* and *West Virginia Library Association;* also accepts paraprofessional out-of-state listings); *Special Library Association* (SLA), New York Chapter, 212-753-7247; *Special Libraries Association*, San Francisco Bay Chapter, 415-968-9748; *Special Libraries Association*, Southern California Chapter, 213-795-2145; *Texas State Library Jobline*, 512-475-0408 (Texas listings only); *University of South Carolina College of Librarianship*, 803-777-8443; *Virginia Library Association Jobline*, 804-355-0384. Delaware jobs are listed on the New Jersey, Pennsylvania, and Maryland job-lines.

Employers who wish to place vacancy listings on the job-line recordings can call the following numbers: *ACRL*, 312-944-6780; *ASIS*, 202-659-3644; *Arizona*, 602-269-2535; *California*, 916-447-8541; *Colorado*, 303-866-2175; *District of Columbia*, 202-223-6800, ext. 458; *Florida*, 904-487-2651; *Georgia*, 404-329-6840; *Illinois*, 312-644-1896; *New England*, 207-622-4733; *New Jersey*, 609-292-6237; *New York*, 212-227-8032; *New York/SLA*, 212-790-0639; *North Carolina*, 919-733-2570; *Oklahoma*, 405-521-2502; *Pennsylvania*, 412-362-6400; *San Francisco/SLA*, 408-277-3784; *Southern California/SLA*, 213-446-8251, ext. 32; *Texas*, 512-475-4110; *Virginia*, 804-770-5572.

Listings can be placed by writing to: *British Columbia Library Association*, Box 46378, Station G, Vancouver, B.C. V6R 4G6, Canada; *California Media and Library Educators Association*, 1575 Old Bayshore Hwy., Suite 204, Burlingame, CA 94010; *Colorado State Library Jobline*, 1362 Lincoln, Denver, CO 80203; *Illinois Library Job Hotline*, Illinois Library Association, 425 N. Michigan Ave., Suite 1304, Chicago,

IL 60611 ($20 fee/2 weeks); *Maryland Library Association*, 115 W. Franklin St., Baltimore, MD 21201; *Mountain Plains Library Association*, c/o I. D. Weeks Library, University of South Dakota, Vermillion, SD 57069; *Oregon Library Association JOBLINE*, Oregon State Library, Salem, OR 97310; *PNLA Jobline*, c/o Pacific Northwest Bibliographic Center, University of Washington, 253 Suzzalo Library FM-25, Seattle, WA 98195; *University of South Carolina, College of Librarianship Placement*, Columbia, SC 29208 (no geographical restrictions). For the *Midwest Federation* jobline, employers should send listings to the executive secretary of their own state association, who will refer these to the Michigan Library Association where the recording equipment is housed. There is a $5 fee to be paid by the employer for each listing. Paraprofessional positions are also accepted.

SPECIALIZED LIBRARY ASSOCIATIONS AND GROUPS

American Association of Law Libraries, 53 W. Jackson Blvd., Chicago, IL 60604; 312-939-4764. Placement service is available without charge. Lists of openings and personnel available are published several times per year in a newsletter distributed to membership. Applicants are referred to placement officers for employment counseling.

American Libraries (AL), c/o J. W. Grey, 50 E. Huron St., Chicago, IL 60611. "Career LEADS EXPRESS": advance galleys (3–4 weeks) of job listings to be published in the next issue of *American Libraries*. Early notice of some 40–60 "Positions Open" sent about the fourteenth of each month; does not include editorial corrections, late changes, and the majority of "Late Job Notices" as they appear in the regular *AL* "LEADS" section. For each month, send $2 check made out to *AL* EXPRESS; self-addressed, stamped, standard business-size envelope.

American Libraries, Consultants Keyword Clearinghouse (CKC), an *AL* service that helps match professionals offering library/information expertise with institutions seeking it. Published quarterly, *CKC* appears in the "Career LEADS" section of the January, April, June, and October issues of *AL*. Rates: $3/line—classified; $30/inch—display. Inquiries should be made to J. W. Grey, LEADS Editor, American Libraries, 50 E. Huron St., Chicago, IL 60611; 312-944-6780, ext. 326.

American Library Association (ALA), 50 E. Huron St., Chicago, IL 60611; 312-944-6780. A placement service is provided at each annual conference (June or July) and midwinter meeting (January). Handouts on interviewing, preparing a résumé, and other job-seeking information are available from the ALA Office for Library Personnel Resources.

American Library Association, American Indian Libraries Newsletter, 50 E. Huron St., Chicago, IL 60611; 312-944-6780. Periodic newsletter will list job openings, especially those oriented toward library services to American Indians and minority librarian recruitment.

American Library Association, Association of College and Research Libraries, Fast Job Listing Service, 50 E. Huron St., Chicago, IL 60611; 312-944-6780. Monthly circular listing job openings received in ACRL office during previous four weeks (supplements listings that will continue to appear in *C&RL News*); $10 to ACRL members requesting service (indicate ALA/ACRL membership number); $15 to nonmembers. Renewable each six months. Job-line recorded telephone message updated each Friday lists current job openings; phone 312-944-6795 for listing. Employers who wish to have a listing for two weeks should send check for $30 (ACRL members) or $35 (non-ACRL members).

American Library Association Black Caucus, c/o Dean Virginia Lacy Jones, Atlanta University School of Library Service, Atlanta, GA 30314. Although this is not a placement service, a data bank of black librarians is maintained, and employers do request information on possible candidates. The *Black Caucus Newsletter* publishes some job openings ($10 membership fee). Contact Edna F. Reid, Box 2145, Capitol Plaza Branch, Hyattsville, MD 20784.

ALA Social Responsibilities Round Table, Rhode Island Affiliate, c/o Mary Frances Cooper, Providence Public Library, 150 Empire St., Providence, RI 02903. "SRRT Jobline" appears monthly in the *Rhode Island Library Association Bulletin,* listing positions in southeast New England, including paraprofessional and part-time jobs. Job seekers desiring a copy of the most recent monthly job-line, send self-addressed, stamped envelope. Groups of envelopes may also be sent. To post a notice, contact Elizabeth Rogers, 150 Empire Street, Providence, RI 02903.

American Society for Information Science, 1010 16th St. N.W., 2nd Floor, Washington, DC 20036; 202-659-3644. There is an active placement service operated at ASIS annual meetings (usually October) and mid-year meetings (usually May) (locales change). All conference attendees (both members and nonmembers), as well as ASIS members who cannot attend the conference, are eligible to use the service to list or find jobs. Job listings are also accepted from employers who cannot attend the conference; interviews are arranged and special seminars are given. During the rest of the year, current job openings are listed on the ASIS job-line, 202-659-1737. Seventeen of the ASIS chapters have placement officers who further assist members in finding jobs.

The ASIS job-line operates 24 hours a day, 7 days a week. Brief descriptions, including contact information, of current job openings around the country are recorded biweekly. New jobs are listed first, starting with overseas or West Coast jobs and working eastward toward jobs in the Washington, D.C., area. Thereafter, jobs still available from the preceding recording are listed. The number to call is 202-659-1737.

American Theological Library Association, c/o Office of the Executive Secretary, 1421 Ramblewood Dr., East Lansing, MI 48823. Free to members; $5 filing fee for nonmembers for listing up to two years or until employment is secured. Application forms should be requested. Referrals are made throughout the year. Although not large in numbers, openings are representative of the size of the association.

Art Libraries Society/North America (ARLIS/NA), c/o Executive Secretary, 3775 Bear Creek Circle, Tucson, AZ 85715. Art librarian and slide curator jobs are listed in the newsletter *Art Documentation* (5 times a year).

Associated Information Managers (AIM), 316 Pennsylvania Avenue S.E., Suite 502, Washington, DC 20003; 202-544-1969. AIM Career Clearinghouse lists positions open on a biweekly basis in conjunction with the AIM Network. Position applicants send résumé and cover letter to AIM, which forwards materials to employers. Open to AIM members only. Employers may list positions free of charge.

Association for Educational Communication and Technology (AECT), Placement Service, 1126 16 St. N.W., Washington, DC 20036; 202-833-4180. Positions available are listed in the bimonthly member newsletter, *Ect Network,* and the association publication, *Instructional Innovator,* by code number and state. Responses to ads are forwarded by the association to the appropriate employer. A referral service is also available at no charge to AECT members only. A placement center operates at the annual conference, free to members and for a fee to nonmembers.

Catholic Library Association (CLA), 461 W. Lancaster Ave., Haverford, PA 19041; 215-649-5250. Personal and institutional members of CLA are given free space (35 words) to advertise for jobs or to list job openings in *Catholic Library World* (10/ year). Others may advertise at $1 per printed line.

GUIDE TO LIBRARY PLACEMENT SOURCES / 255

Council on Library/Media Technical Assistants, c/o Cynthia Clark, 3841 N. Calle Barranco, Tucson, AZ 85715. *COLT Newsletter* appears 11 times a year and will accept listings for library/media technical assistant positions. However, correspondence relating to jobs cannot be handled.

Information Exchange System for Minority Personnel (IESMP, Inc.), Box 668, Fort Valley, GA 31030. Nonprofit organization designed to recruit minority librarians for EEO/AA employers. *Informer*, quarterly newsletter. Write for membership categories, services, and fees.

Medical Library Association (MLA), 919 N. Michigan Ave., Suite 3208, Chicago, IL 60611; 312-266-2456. Monthly *MLA News* lists positions wanted and positions available in its "Employment Opportunities" column (up to 20 free lines for MLA members plus $2 per line over this, or $3 per line for nonmembers). MLA members may request advance mailings of "Employment Opportunities" at no charge for six months; this service is available to nonmembers for a prepaid fee of $25. Placement service is offered at annual conference each summer.

Music Library Association (MLA), Placement Director, Karen K. Griffith, The Cleveland Institute of Music, 11021 E. Boulevard, Cleveland, OH 44106. Registration fee of $7 per year (September thru August). MLA members who register receive the *Job List*.

National Registry for Librarians, 40 West Adams Street, Chicago, IL 60603; 312-793-4904. Established as a professional placement service in 1965, the registry is a centralized nationwide clearinghouse for professional librarians and employers. There are no registration, referral, or placement fees for this service. Librarians seeking professional employment complete an application form. Employers also complete job order forms that describe their vacancies. Copies of all applications meeting the employer's selection criteria are forwarded to allow the employer to contact the applicant directly. The registry does not maintain a file of school credits or personal references, nor does it make any recommendations; it does not maintain or distribute vacancy lists.

Online, Inc., c/o John Edward Evans, Head of Reference, Memphis State University Libraries, Memphis State University, Memphis, TN 38152; 901-454-2208. "Jobline" column in *Online* and *Database* lists positions in the field of on-line searching. "Jobline" also distributes biweekly placement lists. Applicants must provide stamped, self-addressed business-size envelopes. Several envelopes may be sent at one time to ensure continuing service. Due to deadlines, not all jobs appear in the journals but all announcements are reported in the biweekly lists. Some newsletters of local or state on-line user groups list positions for searchers. (For "User Group Directory," see latest January or July issue of *Online*.)

Reforma, National Association of Spanish-Speaking Librarians in the U.S. Editor, Luis Herrera, El Paso Public Library, 501 N. Oregon, El Paso, TX 79901. Quarterly newsletter lists and invites listings, especially for bilingual and minority librarians. In addition, job descriptions will be matched and sent to those who submit résumé and job qualifications to Reforma Jobline at the above address (members free; nonmember fee $10/year for job-matching service). For listing of Spanish-speaking/Spanish-surnamed professionals, request: "Quien es Quien: A Who's Who of Spanish-Heritage Librarians in the U. S." (rev. ed. 1981) for $5.50 from Mexican American Studies, College of Liberal Arts, University of Arizona, Tucson, AZ 85721. The *Amoxcalli* quarterly newsletter of the Reforma El Paso Chapter also lists job openings. Contact chapter at Box 2064, El Paso, TX 79951.

Society of American Archivists, 330 S. Wells, Suite 810, Chicago, IL 60606; 312-922-0140. The *SAA Newsletter* is sent to members only six times annually and lists jobs and applicants, as well as details of professional meetings and courses in archival administration. The "Employment Bulletin" is sent to members who pay a $10 subscription fee and alternates with the *Newsletter*.

Special Libraries Association, 235 Park Ave. S., New York, NY 10003; 212-477-9250. In addition to the Conference Employment Clearing House, a monthly listing of positions wanted and available, *Employment Opportunities*, is available free for six months to SLA members who request this in writing. Most SLA chapters also have employment chairpersons who act as referral persons for employers and job seekers. The official newsletter of the association, *SpeciaList*, carries classified advertising 12 times a year.

Theresa M. Burke Employment Agency, 25 W. 39 St., New York, NY 10018; 212-398-9250. A licensed professional employment agency that has specialized for over 30 years in the recruitment of library and information personnel for academic, public, and special libraries, this agency is staffed by employment counselors who have training and experience in both library service and personnel recruitment. Presently the majority of openings are in special libraries in the Northeast and require subject backgrounds and/or specific kinds of experience. Fees are paid by the employer.

STATE LIBRARY AGENCIES

In addition to the job-lines mentioned previously, some of the state library agencies issue lists of job openings within their areas. These include Indiana (on request); Iowa (job-line, monthly); Kentucky (monthly, on request); Maine (on request); Minnesota (*Position Openings in Minnesota and Adjoining States*, semimonthly, sent to public and academic libraries); Mississippi (job vacancy list, monthly); Ohio (*Library Opportunities in Ohio*, monthly, sent to accredited library education programs and interested individuals on request); Pennsylvania ("Positions Open"); and Texas (*Texas Placement News*, bimonthly, free).

On occasion, when vacancy postings are available, state library newsletters or journals will list these, such as Alabama (*Cottonboll*, bimonthly); Indiana (*Focus on Indiana Libraries*); Louisiana (*Library Communique*, monthly); Massachusetts (*Massachusetts Position Vacancies*, monthly, sent to all public libraries in state and to interested individuals on a one-time basis); Missouri (*Show-Me Libraries*, monthly); Nebraska (*Overtones*, 13 times/year); New Hampshire (*Granite State Libraries*, bimonthly); New Mexico (*Hitchhiker*, weekly newsletter); Oklahoma (*ODL Source*, monthly); Utah (*Horsefeathers*, monthly); Virginia (*News*, bimonthly); and Wyoming (*Outrider*, monthly).

Many state library agencies will refer applicants informally when vacancies are known to exist, but do not have formal placement services. The following states primarily make referrals to public libraries only: Alabama, Georgia, Idaho, Louisiana, South Carolina (institutional also), Tennessee, Vermont, and Virginia. Those that refer applicants to all types of libraries are Delaware, Florida, Maine, Maryland, Massachusetts, Mississippi, Missouri, Montana, Nebraska, Nevada (largely public and academic), New Hampshire, New Mexico, North Dakota, Ohio, Oklahoma, Rhode Island, South Dakota, Utah, West Virginia (public, academic, special), and Wyoming. A bulletin board in the Connecticut State Library posts library vacancies for all types of libraries.

The Missouri State Library offers a formal placement service, matching interests and qualifications of registered job applicants with positions available in Missouri libraries. Addresses of the state agencies are found in the *Bowker Annual* or *American Library Directory*.

STATE AND REGIONAL LIBRARY ASSOCIATIONS

State and regional library associations will often make referrals, run ads in association newsletters, or operate a placement service at annual conferences, in addition to the job-lines sponsored by some groups. Referral of applicants when jobs are known is done by the following associations: Arkansas, Delaware (also for Delaware listings, call the Maryland, New Jersey, or Pennsylvania job-lines), Hawaii, Louisiana, Michigan, Nevada, Pennsylvania, South Dakota, Tennessee, Texas, and Wisconsin. Although listings are infrequent, job vacancies are placed in the following association newsletters or journals when available: Alabama (*Alabama Librarian*, 10 times a year); Alaska (*Sourdough*, 4 times a year); Arkansas (*Arkansas LA Newsletter*, 8 times a year); Connecticut (*Newsletter of the CLA*, 10 times a year); Georgia (*Georgia Librarian*, 4 times a year); Indiana (*Focus on Indiana Libraries*, 6 times a year; *Indiana Libraries: A Quarterly Journal*); Iowa (*Catalyst*, 6 times a year); Kansas (*KLA Newsletter*, 3 times a year); Minnesota (*MLA Newsletter*, 10 times a year); Mountain Plains (*MPLA Newsletter*, bimonthly, lists vacancies and position-wanted ads for individual and institutional members or area library school students); Nevada (*Highroller*, 6 times a year); New Hampshire (*NHLA Newsletter*, 6 times a year; *Granite State Libraries*); New Jersey (*New Jersey Libraries*, 4 times per year); New Mexico (shares notices via state library's *Hitchhiker*, weekly); New York (*NYLA Bulletin*, 10 times a year); Oklahoma (*The Oklahoma Librarian; President's Newsletter*); Oregon (*Oregon Library News*, monthly); Pennsylvania (*PLA Bulletin*, monthly); Rhode Island (*Bulletin*, monthly); South Dakota (*Bookmarks*, bimonthly); Vermont (*VLA News*, Box 803, Burlington, VT 05402, 10 times a year); Virginia (*Virginia Librarian*, bimonthly); and Wyoming (*Roundup*, quarterly). The *Southeastern Librarian* lists jobs in that geographical area.

The following associations have indicated some type of placement service at the annual conference, although it may consist only of bulletin board postings: Alabama, Illinois, Indiana, Kansas, Louisiana, Maryland, Missouri, Mountain Plains, New Jersey, New York, Pennsylvania, South Dakota, Texas, and Vermont.

The following associations have indicated they have no placement service at this time: Minnesota, Mississippi, Montana, New Mexico, North Dakota, Oklahoma, Pacific Northwest, Tennessee, and Wyoming. State and regional association addresses are found in Part 7.

LIBRARY EDUCATION PROGRAMS

Library education programs offer some type of service for their current students as well as for alumni. Of the ALA-accredited programs, the following handle placement activities through the library school: Alberta, British Columbia, Columbia, Dalhousie, Denver, Drexel, Emory, Geneseo, Hawaii, Illinois, Long Island, Louisiana, McGill, Michigan, Minnesota, Missouri, Pittsburgh, Pratt, Rosary, Queens, Rutgers, Tennessee, Texas-Austin, Toronto, Western Ontario, and Wisconsin-Madison.

The central university placement center handles activities for the following schools: Brigham Young, Case Western, North Carolina, Peabody/Vanderbilt, Southern California, and UCLA. However, in most cases, faculty in the library school will still do informal counseling regarding job seeking.

In some schools, the placement services are handled in a cooperative manner; in most cases, the university placement center sends out credentials while the library school posts or compiles the job listings. Schools utilizing both sources include Alabama, Albany, Arizona, Ball State, Buffalo, Catholic, Chicago, Clarion State, Denver,

Emporia, Florida State, Geneseo, Indiana, Iowa, Kent, Kentucky, Maryland, Mississippi, Montreal, North Carolina Central, North Texas, Northern Illinois, Oklahoma, Peabody/Vanderbilt, Pratt, Queens, St. John's, Rhode Island, San Jose, Simmons, South Carolina, South Florida, Southern Connecticut, Southern Mississippi, Syracuse, Tennessee, Texas Woman's, UCLA, Washington, Wayne State, Western Michigan, and Wisconsin-Milwaukee.

In sending out placement credentials, schools vary as to whether they distribute these free, charge a general registration fee, or request a fee for each file of credentials sent out.

Those schools that have indicated that they post job vacancy notices for review but do not issue printed lists are Alabama, Albany, Alberta, Arizona, Ball State, British Columbia, Catholic, Chicago, Emory, Emporia, Florida State, Hawaii, Kent, Louisiana, Maryland, North Carolina Central, Northern Illinois, Peabody/Vanderbilt, Queens, St. John's, San Jose, Simmons, South Carolina, South Florida, Southern California, Southern Mississippi, Syracuse, Tennessee, Texas Woman's, Toronto, Washington, Wayne State, and Western Michigan.

In addition to job vacancy postings, some schools issue a printed listing of open positions that is distributed primarily to students and alumni, and is only occasionally available to others. The following schools issue listings free to students and alumni *only* unless indicated otherwise: Albany (weekly to SLIS graduates registered with placement office); Brigham Young; Buffalo (monthly newsletter; service to all area professionals on request for academic year); California-Berkeley (alumni receive 10/year out-of-state listings if registered, $35 fee for service; also a job-line, call 415-642-1716 to list positions); Case Western (alumni $10 for 6 lists); Clarion State (free to students and alumni); Columbia (alumni $2 for 6 issues); Dalhousie ($5/year for students, alumni, and others); Denver (alumni $8/year, biweekly); Drexel (free in office; by mail to students and alumni who supply self-addressed stamped envelopes—12 for 6 months); Geneseo (free in office; by mail only to students and alumni who send self-addressed stamped envelopes); Illinois (free in office; by mail to anyone who sends self-addressed stamped business-size envelopes); Indiana (others may send self-addressed stamped envelopes); Iowa (weekly, $5 for 4 months for registered students and alumni); Long Island (no charge); Michigan (free for one year following graduation, all other alumni $10/year for 24 issues); Minnesota (37-cent self-addressed envelopes are to be supplied); Missouri (Library Vacancy Roster, triweekly printout, 50 cents/issue, with minimum of 5 issues, to anyone); North Carolina (available by mail to alumni and students who pay $15 referral fee); North Texas State ($5 for 6 months, students and alumni); Peabody/Vanderbilt (students and alumni if registered, for fee); Pittsburgh (others $3 for 6 months); Pratt (alumni–weekly during spring, fall, and summer sessions; others renew every 3 months); Rhode Island (monthly, $21/year); Rosary (every 2 weeks, $15/year for alumni); Rutgers (subscription $4 for 6 months, $8/year; twice a month to anyone); Southern Connecticut; Texas-Austin (biweekly placement bulletin free to alumni and students); UCLA (alumni, every 2 weeks by request, renew every 3 months); Western Michigan ($7.50 for 26 weeks to anyone; issued by University Placement Services); Wisconsin-Madison (subscription $6/year for 12 issues, to anyone); Wisconsin-Milwaukee (monthly to SLS graduates registering with Department of Placement and Career Development); and Western Ontario (sends notices of positions open reported to school as they are received to graduates on the school's placement mailing list).

As the job market has tightened, a number of schools are providing job-hunting seminars and short courses, or are more actively trying to help graduates obtain positions. Most schools will offer at least an annual or semiannual discussion on job placement, often with outside speakers representing different types of libraries or recent graduates relating experiences. Some additional programs offered by schools include Albany (alumni/student career day, career possibilities colloquium series; sessions on résumé writing, interviewing, job counseling, computer-based placement file); Arizona (job hunting, résumé-writing workshops); Ball State (job hunting, résumé writing, videotaped job interview role-playing sessions); Brigham Young (students write résumé, which is critiqued in basic administration class); British Columbia ("Employment Week" in spring term with employers invited to interview); Buffalo (assists laid-off local employees, sends list of graduates to major libraries in the United States, operates selective dissemination of information (SDI) service, résumé seminar, and follow-up critique, strategy sessions for conference job seeking, "Put a Buffalo in Your Library" buttons); California-Berkeley (career-awareness workshops on résumés, interview, and job search); Chicago (workshop on career opportunities, résumé writing, and interviewing skills); Columbia (alumni/student career day; sessions on résumé writing, interviewing; individual and group job counseling during the spring); Dalhousie (sessions on job searching with critiquing of résumés); Denver (résumé writing in administration course, interview workshop, student profiles to match job listings, Career Day for students/alumni, career-awareness workshop with university placement personnel, individual counseling, postings); Drexel (job-search workshops, résumés, cover letters, interviewing, individual job counseling by appointment available to students and alumni); Emory (job-strategy meeting each term, résumé assistance, job counseling); Hawaii (workshop each semester, computer-based placement file); Illinois (résumé writing, interview role playing in library administration class, counseling/critiquing for individuals in library school placement office, computer-based placement profiles for students and alumni, job-search workshops by university-wide placement service); Indiana (convocation on job search, seminar on résumé writing, interview role playing in course work, critique of individual résumés and letters); Iowa (job-strategy and résumé-writing session each term, individual counseling); Kent (annual placement workshops, résumé writing, interviewing strategies); Long Island (job-hunting workshops); McGill (résumé writing, interview techniques, counseling for job hunting, reception for employers); Maryland (several placement colloquia held each academic year); Michigan (seminar sessions on job hunting, résumé writing, interviewing, and search strategies); Minnesota (résumé writing, individual counseling, interview techniques); Mississippi (résumé writing, letters, and interviewing); and Missouri (student seminars, individual counseling).

The following schools also offer additional programs: North Carolina (workshop on résumé preparation, job-seeking strategy, interview techniques; students may do mock interview on videotape with critique); North Carolina Central (seminars, counseling); Peabody/Vanderbilt (regular seminars on library marketplace, résumé preparation, interviews); Pittsburgh (individual counseling, preconference strategy sessions, placement colloquium sessions, day-long workshops covering such strategy, résumés and other means of access, interview techniques); Pratt (job clinics throughout the year, book of résumés sent to employers); Rhode Island (résumés critiqued in library administration course, jobs seminar annually); Rutgers (seminars on job search and résumé writing, individual counseling, interview role playing by video in Contemporary Issues class, paper-bag lunchtime panel discussions, postings); San Jose (two-day workshops on alternative careers, twice a year; one-day session on résumé writing, interviews, and strategies); Simmons (series of four programs each semester); South Carolina (seminars on job search and résumé writing offered as part of curriculum);

South Florida (résumé writing and interview sessions); Southern Connecticut (ETP Annual Job Workshop); Southern Mississippi (placement seminar); Syracuse (job-search strategy workshops, career possibilities colloquium series, résumé critiques, career counseling); Texas-Austin (job postings, individual counseling, and job leads for students and alumni; seminars on job hunting; résumé writing and critiquing; interview strategies); Toronto (publishes annual placement and salary survey in Canadian Library Association's *Feliciter;* conducts periodic career-awareness workshops involving outside speakers; job counseling); UCLA (compiles "Job Hunting Handbook"; colloquia on job-search strategy, résumé writing, and interviewing); Washington (job-search strategy and interviewing discussions, postings); Western Michigan (résumé writing, individual counseling, interview techniques); Western Ontario (job-search strategy workshops); Wisconsin-Madison (job-finding programs, résumé writing); and Wisconsin-Milwaukee (Job Fair with interview role playing and résumé writing).

Employers will often list jobs with schools only in their particular geographical area; some library schools will give information to nonalumni regarding their specific locale, but are *not* staffed to handle mail requests and advice is usually given in person. Schools that have indicated they will allow librarians in their areas to view listings are Alabama, Albany, Alberta, Arizona, Ball State, Brigham Young, British Columbia, Buffalo, Case Western, Catholic, Chicago, Dalhousie, Denver, Drexel, Emory, Emporia, Florida State, Geneseo, Illinois, Indiana, Iowa, Kent, Kentucky, Louisiana, McGill, Maryland, Michigan, Minnesota, Missouri, North Carolina, North Texas, Peabody/Vanderbilt, Pittsburgh, Pratt, Queens, Rhode Island, Rutgers, St. John's, San Jose, South Carolina, Southern California, Southern Connecticut, Southern Mississippi, Syracuse, Tennessee, Texas-Austin, Texas Woman's, Toronto, UCLA, Washington, Wayne State, Western Michigan, Western Ontario, Wisconsin-Madison, and Wisconsin-Milwaukee.

A list of accredited program addresses can be requested from ALA or found in the *Bowker Annual*. Individuals interested in placement services of other library education programs should contact the schools directly.

FEDERAL LIBRARY JOBS

The first step in obtaining employment in a federal library is to become listed in the Librarian's Register, which is a subset of files maintained by the U.S. Office of Personnel Management (OPM), in order to match federal job applicants with federal job vacancies (Washington Area Office [SSS], Box 52, Washington, DC 20044). Applicants may obtain a Qualifications Information Statement for Professional Librarian Positions (QI-1410), a Federal Employment Application Instructions and Forms Pamphlet (OPM Form 1282), and an Occupational Supplement for Professional Librarian Positions (OPM Form 1203-B) from any Federal Job Information Center. (Federal Job Centers are located in many cities across the country. They are listed under "U.S. Government" in major metropolitan area telephone directories. The *Federal Job Information Centers Directory* is available from OPM.)

One is considered for all grades for which one is qualified and indicates one will accept. As vacancies occur, applications will be evaluated in relation to an agency's specific requirements, and the most qualified candidates are referred for consideration. Eligibility will remain in effect for one year; updated information must be submitted to remain eligible after this time.

Federal job examiners do not select those to be hired, but play a crucial role in weighing the relative experience of those on the register. When selecting the most qualified candidates (whose forms are then forwarded to the hiring agency), the examiner must consider many factors simultaneously: work experience, education (formal and informal), geographical preference, and the like. Any information that should be considered must be on these forms and must not be left for someone to discover during the interview stage. Chances are that the applicant may never reach the interview stage if pertinent experience or education is not explained at the outset.

Applications are accepted only when the register is "open." The frequency with which the register is open and the duration of that period depend on the size of the inventory. The inventory is judged to be too low when a significant proportion of applicants who are qualified for positions decline them. This so-called declination rate is reversed by opening the register, thereby expanding the applicant pool.

In recent years, the register has been opened once each year, generally only for several weeks at a time. Advance notice goes to all local Federal Job Information Centers, so it is important to check frequently in order to be alerted to the registration period. During 1981, the register was not open at all for general librarian positions. It may open in early 1982 for a short period. The Librarian's Register is open, however, on a continuing basis at this time for persons with training and experience in the fields of medical and law librarianship, engineering, the sciences, audiovisual materials, and computerized library systems.

In addition to filing the appropriate forms, applicants can attempt to make personal contact directly with federal agencies in which they are interested. Over half the vacancies occur in the Washington area. Most librarian positions are in three agencies—Army, Navy, and Veterans Administration. The *Federal Times* and the Sunday *Washington Post* sometimes list federal library openings. There are some "expected" agencies that are not required to hire through the usual OPM channels. While these agencies may require the standard forms, they maintain their own employee selection policies and procedures. Government establishments with positions outside the competitive civil service include Energy Research and Development Administration; Board of Governors of the Federal Reserve System; Central Intelligence Agency; Department of Medicine and Surgery; Federal Bureau of Investigation; Foreign Service of the United States; National Science Foundation; National Security Agency; Central Examining Office; Tennessee Valley Authority; U.S. Nuclear Regulatory Commission; U.S. Postal Service; judicial branch of the government; legislative branch of the government; U.S. Mission to the United Nations; World Bank and IFC; International Monetary Fund; Organization of American States; Pan American Health Organization; and United Nations Secretariat.

In addition, the Library of Congress operates its own independent merit selection system. Thus, applicants for positions at the library should submit an SF-171, Personal Qualifications Statement, to the Recruitment and Placement Officer, Library of Congress, 10 First St. S.E., G-114, Washington, DC 20540. Persons who apply for specific vacancies by Posting Number enhance their prospects for consideration.

ADDITIONAL GENERAL AND SPECIALIZED JOB SOURCES

Affirmative Action Register, 8356 Olive Blvd., St. Louis, MO 63132. The goal is to "provide female, minority, and handicapped candidates with an opportunity to learn of professional and managerial positions throughout the nation and to assist employers in implementing their Affirmative Action Programs." Free distribution of monthly bulletin is made to leading businesses, industrial and academic institutions, and over 4,000 agencies that recruit qualified minorities and women, as well as to all known female, minority, and handicapped professional organizations, placement offices, newspapers, magazines, rehabilitation facilities, and over 8,000 federal, state, and local governmental employment units. Individual mail subscriptions are available for $15 per year. Librarian listings are in most every issue. It is sent free to libraries on request.

The Chronicle of Higher Education (published weekly during the academic year, 1333 New Hampshire Ave. N.W., Washington, DC 20036) is receiving more classified ads for library openings than previously, although many are at the administrative level; *Academe* (Bulletin of the American Association of University Professors, One DuPont Circle, Washington, DC 20036) also lists library jobs at times.

Education Information Service (EIS), Box 662, Newton Lower Falls, MA 02162. Instant Alert service for $29 sends individual 12 notices of openings in field and location of interest on same day EIS hears of job. Publishes lists of faculty and administrative education openings (library jobs only a small portion, however). Service is renewable. Send for lists of other services and fees.

Federal Research Service, Box 1059, Vienna, VA 22180; 703-281-0200. Published every other Wednesday, "Federal Career Opportunities" (FCO) report is a compilation of current vacancies in federal government agencies. Subscription rates are $28 for six biweekly reports; send for information on rates for longer periods. Since this includes all types of government positions, it is likely that only a small percentage are librarian vacancies.

School Libraries. School librarians often find that the channels for locating positions in education are of more value than the usual library ones, for example, contacting county or city school superintendent offices. The National Center for Information on Careers in Education is no longer in operation. A list of commercial teacher agencies may be obtained from the National Association of Teacher Agencies, c/o Elwood Q. Taylor, 1825 K St. N.W., Suite 706, Washington, DC 20006.

OVERSEAS

Opportunities for employment in foreign countries are limited and immigration policies of individual countries should be investigated. Employment for Americans is virtually limited to U.S. government libraries, libraries of U.S. firms doing worldwide business, and American schools abroad. Library journals from other countries will sometimes list vacancy notices (e.g., *Quidunc* [Australia], *British Columbia Library Association Reporter, Canadian Library Journal, Feliciter,* and *Library Association Record; Times Literary Supplement, Ontario Library Review,* and *Times Higher Education Supplement*). Some persons have obtained jobs by contacting foreign publishers or vendors directly. Non–U.S. government jobs usually call for foreign-language fluency.

Although they do not specifically discuss librarian positions, several general brochures may be of help in providing further addresses. *American Students and Teachers Abroad: Sources of Information about Overseas Study, Teaching, Work, Travel* and *Federal Jobs Overseas* may be obtained from the Superintendent of Documents, U.S. Government Printing Office, Washington, DC 20402, for $1 and 30 cents respectively.

Action, P305, Washington, DC 20525. An umbrella agency that includes the Peace Corps and Vista. Will sometimes need librarians in developing nations and host communities in the United States. For further information, call 800-424-8580 and ask for Recruitment. Recruiting offices are in many large cities.

Council for International Exchange of Scholars, Suite 300, 11 DuPont Circle, Washington, DC 20036; 202-833-4950. Administers U.S. government Fulbright awards for university lecturing and advanced research abroad; usually six to eight awards per year are made to specialists in library science. Open to U.S. citizens with university or college teaching experience. Request registration forms to receive spring announcement for academic year to start 12–18 months later.

Department of Defense (DOD), c/o Director, Department of Defense Dependent Schools, OAS (M&RA), Room 152, Hoffman I, 2461 Eisenhower Avenue, Alexandria, VA 22331. Overall management and operational responsibilities for the education of dependents of active duty military personnel and DOD civilians who are stationed overseas, including recuitment of teaching personnel, are assigned to this agency. For application brochures, write to above address specifying "Attention: Recruitment."

Education Information Service, Box 662, Newton Lower Falls, MA 02162. Instant Alert service for $29 will send individual 12 notices of overseas openings on same day EIS learns of opening (library jobs small portion, however). Send for free details of other services.

Home Country Employment Registry, National Association for Foreign Student Affairs, 1860 19 St. N.W., Washington, DC 20009. Services are offered to U.S.-educated foreign students to assist them in locating employment in their home countries following completion of their studies.

International Association of School Librarianship, c/o School of Librarianship, Western Michigan University, Kalamazoo, MI 49008. Informal contacts might be established through this group.

International School Services (ISS), Box 5910, Princeton, NJ 08540. Private, nonprofit organization established to provide educational services for American schools overseas, other than Department of Defense schools. These are American elementary and secondary schools enrolling children of business and diplomatic families living away from their homeland. ISS seeks to register men and women interested in working abroad in education who meet basic professional standards of training and experience. Specialists, guidance counselors, department heads, librarians, supervisors, and administrators normally will need one or more advanced degrees in the appropriate field, as well as professional experience commensurate with positions sought.

U.S. International Communication Agency (USICA) (formerly USIA) will occasionally seek librarians with MLS and four years' experience for regional library consultant positions. Candidates must have proven administrative ability and skills to coordinate the overseas USICA library program with other information functions of USICA in various cities worldwide. Relevant experience might include cooperative library program development, community outreach, public affairs, project management, and personnel training. USICA maintains more than 125 libraries in more than 76 countries, one million books, and 400 local library staff worldwide. Libraries provide reference service and material about the United States for foreign audiences. Five years U.S. citizenship are required. Overseas allowances and differentials where applicable, vacation leave, term life insurance, medical and retirement programs. Send standard U.S. Government Form 171 to Employment Branch, ICA, Washington, DC 20547. All types of jobs within USICA are announced through a recording (202-724-9864, 9865). However, chances of librarian positions being announced are slim.

OVERSEAS—SPECIAL PROGRAMS

International Exchanges. Most exchanges are handled by direct negotiation between interested parties. A few libraries, such as the Chicago Public Library, have established exchange programs for their own staff. In order to facilitate exchange arrangements, the *IFLA Journal* (issued February, May, August, and November) provides a listing of persons wishing to exchange positions *outside* their own country. All listings must include the following information: full name, address, present position, academic qualifications (with year of obtaining), language(s), abilities, preferred country/city/library, and type of position. Send to International Federation of Library Associations and Institutions (IFLA) Secretariat, Netherlands Congress Building, Box 82128, 2508 EC, The Hague, Netherlands.

USING INFORMATION SKILLS IN NONLIBRARY SETTINGS

A great deal of interest has been shown in "alternative careers" or in using information skills in a variety of ways in nonlibrary settings. These jobs are not usually found through the regular library placement sources, although many library schools are trying to generate such listings for their students and alumni. Job listings that do exist may not call specifically for "librarians" by that title, so ingenuity may be needed to search out jobs where information-management skills are needed. Some librarians are working on a free-lance basis by offering services to businesses, alternative schools, community agencies, and legislators; these opportunities are usually not found in advertisements but are created by developing contacts and publicity over a period of time. A number of information brokerage firms have developed from individual free-lance experiences. Small companies or other organizations often need "one-time" service for organizing files or collections, bibliographic research for special projects, indexing or abstracting, compilation of directories, and consulting services. Bibliographic networks and on-line data base companies are using librarians as information managers, trainers, researchers, systems and data-base analysts, and on-line services managers. Jobs in this area are sometimes found in library network newsletters or other data-processing journals. Classifieds in *Publisher's Weekly* may lead to information-related positions.

Librarians can be found working in law firms as litigation case supervisors, organizing and analyzing records needed for specific legal cases; with publishers as sales representatives, marketing directors, editors, and computer services experts; with community agencies as adult education coordinators, volunteer administrators, and grants writers.

Information on existing information services or methods for using information skills in nonlibrary settings can be found in *Wilson Library Bulletin* 49: 440–445, February 1975; *Special Libraries* 67:243–250, May/June 1976; *ASIS Bulletin* 2: 10–20, February 1976; *RQ* 18: 177–179, Winter 1978; *New York Times*, December 12, 1979, "Careers" section; *Show-Me Libraries* 31: 5–8, May 1980; *Bay State Librarian* 69: 9–11, Winter 1980; and *Savvy*, January 1981, pp. 20–23. *Canadian Library Journal* 34, no. 2, April 1977, is a whole issue on alternative librarianship. Syracuse University School of Information Studies, 113 Euclid Avenue, Syracuse, NY 13210, has available *Proceedings of the Information Broker/Free-Lance Librarian Workshop* (April 1976) for $5.00, and *Alternative Careers in Information/Library Services: Summary of Proceedings of a Workshop* (July 1977) for $5.50.

The Directory of Fee-Based Information Services lists information brokers, free-lance librarians, independent information specialists, and institutions that provide services for a fee. Individuals do not need to pay to have listings; the directory is available for $6.95 prepaid from Information Alternative, Box 5571, Chicago, IL 60680. It is supplemented by *The Journal of Fee-Based Information Services*, bimonthly ($11/one-year subscription to institutions, $9 to others). Issues include new listings, changes of address, announcements, feature articles, and exchange column. Another Information Alternative publication is *So You Want to Be an Information Broker?* (proceedings of a workshop May 1-2, 1981, at SUNY-Albany School of Library and Information Sciences; $29.50 plus $1.50 postage).

A selected bibliography, "The Changing Role of the Information Professional," prepared for a 1980 workshop of the D.C. Law Librarians' Society is available for $1.50 from Sheryl Segal, 2144 California St. N.W., Washington, DC 20008. *What Else You Can Do with a Library Degree*, edited by Betty-Carol Sellen, is published by Neal-Schuman Publishers and Gaylord Brothers, Inc. (Box 4901, Syracuse, NY 13221) and is available for $14.95 plus 25 cents postage. Other publications include *Fee-Based Information Services: A Study of a Growing Industry* by Lorig Maranjian and Richard W. Boss (New York: R. R. Bowker, 1980, $24.95); *The Information Brokers: How to Start and Operate Your Own Fee-Based Service* by Kelly Warnken (New York: R. R. Bowker, 1981, $24.95); and *Information Brokering: A State-of-the-Art Report* by Gary M. Kaplan (Emerald Valley Publishing Company, 2715 Terrace View Dr., Eugene, OR 97405; write for a current list of other titles in the series, The Business of Information). Directories such as *Information Sources: The Membership Directory of the Information Industry Association* (Washington, D.C.: Information Industry Association, 1981, $21), *Library Resources Market Place* (New York: R. R. Bowker, 1981, $35), and *Information Industry Market Place* (New York: R. R. Bowker, $37.50) might provide leads to possible organizations in which information skills can be applied.

"A National Profile of Information Professionals" by Donald W. King et al. (*Bulletin of the American Society for Information Science* 6: 18-22, August 1980) gives the results of a 1980 study funded by the National Science Foundation and carried out by the University of Pittsburgh School of Library and Information Science and King Research, Inc. The book *The Information Professional: Survey of an Emerging Field* is based on the study and was published in 1981 by Marcel Dekker.

New books scheduled for publication in 1982 include *New Career Options for Librarians*, edited by Dimi Berkner (New York: Neal-Schuman), and *Careers in Information*, edited by Jane Spivack (White Plains, N.Y.; Knowledge Industry Publications).

JOB HUNTING IN GENERAL

Wherever information needs to be organized and presented to patrons in an effective, efficient, and service-oriented fashion, the skills of professional librarians can be applied whether or not they are used in traditional library settings. However, it will take a considerable investment of time, energy, imagination, and money on the part of an individual before a satisfying position is created or obtained, in the conventional library or other information service. Usually, no one method or source of job hunting can be used alone. Public and school library certification requirements often vary from state to state; contact the state library agency for such information in a particular state. Certification requirements are summarized in *Certification of Public Libraries in the U.S.* (3rd. ed., 1979) and may be obtained from the ALA Library Administration and Management Association ($3). A summary of school library/media certification requirements by state appears in *School Library Journal* 24: 38-50, April 1978, and in *Requirements for Certification 1981* (46th ed.), by Elizabeth H. Woellner (University of Chicago Press, 1981, $18.00). Civil service requirements on a local, county, or state level often add another layer of procedures to the job search. Some civil service jurisdictions require written and/or oral examinations; others assign a ranking based on a review of credentials. Jobs are usually filled from the top candidates on a qualified list of applicants. Since the exams are held only at certain time periods and a variety of jobs can be filled from a single list of applicants (e.g., all Librarian I positions regardless of type of function), it is important to check whether a library in which one is interested falls under civil service procedures.

If one wishes a position in a specific subject area or in a particular geographical location, reference skills should be employed to ferret information from directories and other tools regarding local industries, schools, and subject collections. Directories such as the *American Library Directory, Subject Collections, Directory of Special Libraries and Information Centers,* and *Directory of Health Sciences Libraries,* as well as state directories on other special subject areas, can provide a wealth of information for job seekers. Some students have pooled resources to hire a clipping service for a specific time period in order to get classified librarian ads for a particular geographical area. Working as a substitute librarian or in temporary positions while looking for a regular job can provide valuable contacts and experience. A description of a corps of temporary library workers who tackle all types of jobs through a business called Pro Libra can be found in *American Libraries* 12: 540–541, October 1981. Part-time jobs are not always advertised, but are often found by canvassing local libraries and leaving applications.

For information on other job-hunting and personnel matters, request a checklist of personnel materials available from the ALA Office for Library Personnel Resources, 50 East Huron Street, Chicago, IL 60611.

RECENT LIBRARY PERSONNEL SURVEYS

Margaret Myers
Director, Office for Library Personnel Resources, American Library Association

Library personnel statistics are often collected for specific types of libraries or positions, for particular geographical areas, or at different time periods and by a variety of organizations or associations. Therefore, administrators, staff members, and others who seek comparative data for setting compensation structures or negotiating salaries, establishing affirmative-action goals, determining staffing patterns, or other purposes often have difficulty knowing where to turn for current statistical data on library personnel. This article updates last year's report [see *Bowker Annual 1981*, p. 223—*Ed.*], summarizing selected sources of current data, particularly for salaries.

In using salary data for comparative purposes, it is important to ascertain when the information was collected, what constituted the sample, and whether the positions surveyed match those with which one wishes to make comparisons. Geographic location, size of organization, job scope, or type of library will often influence the pay level of a particular job.

ACADEMIC LIBRARY SURVEYS

The only regularly updated salary data for academic libraries is compiled from the annual survey of the Association of Research Libraries (ARL). This provides information on the average, median, and beginning professional salaries in ARL libraries. In addition, tables cite the numbers of staff and average salaries for 19 positions in ARL libraries, from directors to professionals with under five years of experience. Tables also display the distribution of these positions by sex, minority group, geographical location, and size and type of institution. Table 1 shows average salaries of ARL university librarians by region from the *ARL Annual Salary Survey 1981*. In 1981, ARL published *Cumulated ARL Statistics, 1962/63 through 1978/79*. Both publications are available from the Association of Research Libraries, 1527 New Hampshire Avenue N.W., Washington, DC 20036. The 1981 annual survey is $8 to members and $10 to nonmembers; the cumulated statistics report, $10 to members and $15 to nonmembers.

Salaries of directors of library schools and academic libraries are included with other college and university administrators in the *1980-81 Administrative Compensation Survey Report* by the College and University Personnel Association and summarized in the *Chronicle of Higher Education* (22 [March 23, 1981]: 8-10). Salaries are reported by type of institution and include comparisons of salaries for male, female, minority, and nonminority personnel. See Table 2 for data on library administrators. The full survey is available for $25 to members and $75 to nonmembers from the College and University Personnel Association, 11 Dupont Circle, Suite 120, Washington, DC 20036.

PUBLIC LIBRARY SURVEYS

The most recent biennial *Statistics of Public Libraries in the U.S. and Canada Serving 100,000 Population or More* was published in 1981 by the Fort Wayne and Allen County (Indiana) Public Library. It gives salary information for director, assistant director, and beginning professional positions in large public libraries. This data is then further analyzed to show relationships between the sex of the director, geographic area, population served, per capita support, and beginning librarian salaries (*see* "Sex, Salaries, & Library Support—1981," by Kathleen M. Heim and Carolyn Kacena, *Library Journal* 106 [September 15, 1981]: 1692-1699).

A compilation of salary data for public libraries, systems, and state agencies in West-North Central states (North Dakota, South Dakota, Nebraska, Kansas, Minnesota, Iowa, Missouri) has been conducted by Carl Sandstedt, Director, St. Charles City-County Library (425 Spencer Road, Box 529, St. Peters, MO 63376; send a self-addressed stamped envelope if requesting survey results). The "1982 Salary Survey" gives data for directors, assistant directors, department heads, starting master of library science (MLS), and several support positions by size of library.

The Memphis Public Library compiles an annual salary survey for public libraries in the southeastern and southwestern states, which gives information for a variety of positions in individual libraries as well as low and high ranges and the average and median salaries by size of institution. Individual copies of the 1982 survey can be obtained by sending a self-addressed, stamped envelope to Robert Croneberger, Memphis-Shelby County Public Library and Information Center, 1850 Peabody Street, Memphis, TN 38104. In 1981, head librarian salaries ranged from $20,958 to $62,642 and assistant librarian salaries ranged from $15,000 to $43,788. Top department-head salaries went from $10,500 to $36,985, while beginning professionals received salaries from $9,000 to $16,484.

"Salaries of Municipal Officials for 1980" are included in the *Municipal Yearbook 1981*, published by the International City Management Association (Washing-

268 / LIBRARY EDUCATION, PLACEMENT, AND SALARIES

TABLE 1 AVERAGE SALARIES OF ARL UNIVERSITY LIBRARIANS BY REGION, 1981*

	Northeast		North Central		South			West	
	New England (8)**	Middle Atlantic (14)	East N. Central (14)	West N. Central (7)	South Atlantic (14)	East S. Central (4)	West S. Central (8)	Mountain (7)	Pacific (13)
Position									
Director	$51,322	$55,700	$53,821	$52,571	$50,079	$45,833	$48,443	$52,145	$54,001
Associate director	37,685	40,871	39,288	35,927	38,438	30,976	29,891	35,493	44,185
Assistant director	33,264	33,674	34,332	32,928	29,911	25,709	32,803	32,046	37,560
Medical/law head	43,496	46,254	41,073	38,470	44,057	37,341	28,500	41,551	42,684
Branch head	27,103	25,472	24,540	20,607	23,269	21,891	20,733	23,217	28,375
Subject specialist	23,381	22,107	22,198	22,149	19,756	18,751	19,601	22,521	27,995
Functional specialist	22,625	23,707	21,583	23,682	20,977	18,611	21,978	22,875	26,957
Department head									
Reference	25,890	25,382	22,082	24,080	25,803	23,883	26,318	23,677	30,332
Cataloging	26,628	24,782	25,584	23,432	25,445	20,229	25,900	26,690	31,051
Acquisitions	24,708	22,485	25,816	24,166	23,812	21,340	25,943	25,380	31,910
Serials	22,353	22,050	23,794	22,779	24,508	24,068	21,660	24,250	29,231
Documents/maps	25,789	21,637	22,461	21,405	21,088	17,001	23,670	23,083	30,142
Circulation	21,745	21,571	22,079	22,350	21,457	19,083	23,327	22,954	27,036
Special Collection	32,206	26,525	24,299	25,916	28,484	24,659	23,557	26,826	31,836
Other	24,535	24,301	24,883	22,290	24,227	20,867	23,660	22,179	28,143
Yrs. exper.									
Over 15 yrs. exper.	22,051	23,150	22,214	21,314	21,386	19,551	22,104	22,865	28,244
10–15 yrs. exper.	20,635	20,803	19,935	20,555	20,041	17,370	21,029	20,880	24,266
5–10 yrs. exper.	18,877	18,528	18,008	18,075	18,406	16,352	19,861	18,919	20,914
Under 5 yrs. exper.	16,197	15,656	15,569	14,900	15,799	14,525	15,568	16,434	18,858

*Canadian ARL libraries not included.
**The number in parentheses below each of the column heads indicates the number of ARL libraries included.
Source: *ARL Salary Survey, 1981* (Washington, D.C.: Association of Research Libraries, 1982), preliminary data.

TABLE 2 MEDIAN SALARIES FOR LIBRARY
ADMINISTRATORS IN ACADEMIC
INSTITUTIONS, 1980

	Director, Library Services	Dean, Library and Information Sciences
All institutions	$26,035	$38,494
Public institutions	30,525	38,500
Private institutions	21,497	33,000
Universities	35,692	41,275
4-year institutions	22,600	27,500
2-year institutions	23,903	31,839

Source: *1980–81 Administrative Compensation Survey Report* (Washington, D.C.: College and University Personnel Association, 1981). Also reported in *Chronicle of Higher Education* 22 (March 23, 1981): 9.

ton, D.C., 1981, pp. 59–84). Chief librarian salaries for public libraries are included with other head city officials' earnings. These are reported by geographic region, population size, city type (i.e., central, suburban, independent), and form of government. The mean, median, and first and third quartiles are included. See Table 3 for summary of average salaries for chief librarians of public libraries. Although the data are for 1980 and thus somewhat out of date, they are included to show the increase in head librarian salaries as the city population size grows larger.

Some state library associations or agencies collect salary data for their individual states or provide recommended guidelines based on studying existing salaries. Some examples are "Salary and Fringe Benefit Survey of Wisconsin Public Libraries, 1981" (Wisconsin Association of Public Libraries); "New Jersey Library Association 1982 Minimum Starting Salaries Recommendations" (*New Jersey Libraries* 14 [Oc-

TABLE 3 AVERAGE SALARIES OF HEADS OF
PUBLIC LIBRARIES, JANUARY 1, 1980

No. of Cities Reporting	Salary	Population
5	$50,689	Cities over 1,000,000
12	37,829	500,000–1,000,000
21	34,855	250,000–499,999
51	29,556	100,000–249,999
119	26,483	50,000–99,999
210	21,847	25,000–49,999
430	16,701	10,000–24,999
367	12,449	5,000–9,999
262	9,789	2,500–4,999
27	10,357	Under 2,500

Source: "Salaries of Municipal Officials for 1980," in *The Municipal Yearbook 1981* (Washington, D.C.: International City Management Association, 1981), pp. 59–84.

tober 1981]: 2–3); "Comparative Salary Data for Florida Public Library Personnel" (State Library of Florida); "Michigan Library Association Salary and Fringe Benefits" (*Michigan Librarian* 46 [Winter 1980]: 36); and "RILA Annual Salary Survey—1980" (*Rhode Island Library Association Bulletin* 53 [April 1981]: 11–20).

SCHOOL LIBRARY SURVEYS

"Toward a Work-Force Analysis of the School Library Media Professional" by Kathleen M. Heim (*School Media Quarterly* 9 [Summer 1981]: 235–249) summarizes data from a variety of sources on entry-level school librarians, actual and projected figures on the school library media universe, and current salary information. In particular, Heim analyzes school librarian salary information for 1979–1980 culled from the *National Survey of Salaries and Wages in Public Schools* of the Educational Research Service, Inc. (ERS). The 1980–1981 ERS report was published in March 1981 and sells for $24 for each of the three volumes. Charts comparing librarian and teacher data from the 1980–1981 report will be published in the Spring 1982 *School Library Media Quarterly*. See Table 4 for some of this data.

SPECIAL LIBRARY SURVEYS

The Special Libraries Association "1981 Salary Survey Update" (*Special Libraries* 72 [October 1981]: 399–400) updated the overall national and regional salary data reported in the 1979 in-depth triennial salary survey. The overall mean salary for 1981 was $22,800, a 7.5 percent increase over the 1980 $21,200 figure.

The Salary Survey of Special Libraries in Metropolitan Washington: 1981 is the first such survey compiled by the Metropolitan Washington Library Council. It provides data on 180 special libraries in the Washington, D.C., area for 1980. The council hopes to update the data every two or three years. Salary variables reported include organization size and type for head librarians, other library professionals, paraprofessionals, and clerical staff. Head librarians in metropolitan Washington earned an overall mean salary of $20,700, while other professional librarians averaged $17,900. Federal librarians were excluded from the survey, although several charts in the report provide February 1981 data from the U.S. Office of Personnel Management. These show an average of $28,200 for persons in the Professional Librarian 1410 Series of the federal government. Library technicians in the 1411 series averaged $15,400. Professional librarians who enter at either the GS7 or GS9 level had average salaries of

TABLE 4 SALARIES PAID SCHOOL LIBRARIANS BY ENROLLMENT GROUP, 1980–1981

	25,000 or more	10,000 to 24,999	2,500 to 9,999	300 to 2,499	Total All Reporting Systems
Mean of Lowest	$13,101	$14,657	$15,612	$15,880	$15,118
Mean of Mean	19,214	19,742	18,964	17,006	18,689
Mean of Highest	23,042	23,113	21,882	18,064	21,426

Source: *National Survey of Salaries and Wages in Public Schools, 1980–81* (Arlington, Va.: Educational Research Service, 1981), Part 2, Tables 1–3, pp. 11–13. Also to be reported in *School Library Media Quarterly*, Spring 1982.

$15,970 and $19,800, respectively. The report is available from the Metropolitan Washington Library Council, 1875 Eye St. N.W., Suite 200, Washington, DC 20006, for $15.

STATE LIBRARY AGENCY SALARY SURVEYS

The Association of Specialized and Cooperative Library Agencies (ASCLA) of the American Library Association (ALA) compiles an annual survey of state library agency salaries for the chief officers of state library agencies. This gives the minimum and maximum for a variety of positions: state librarian, assistant director, director of reference services or reader services, consultants, specialists, and beginning professionals. The latest report, dated November 1981, is available from ALA/ASCLA, 50 East Huron Street, Chicago, IL 60611.

The *State Salary Survey*, which had been published annually since 1973 by the U.S. Office of Personnel Management, ceased publication with the 1980 survey. Beginning librarian, senior librarian, and director salary ranges had been included for each state and provided a useful comparison to the 30 other occupational groups surveyed. Cutbacks in federal government expenditures probably caused this publication to be discontinued.

Similar data can be found, however, in an annual survey of 62 jobs in a variety of occupations found in jurisdictions of the federal, state, county, and municipal government conducted by the International Personnel Management Association (IMPA). *Pay Rates in the Public Sector* includes minimum, middle, and maximum average salaries for various geographical regions and types of government. Two pages are included for librarian positions: junior librarian and librarian at the second level of responsibility. Librarians in the IMPA survey had a median of $18,060 while the junior librarian median was $15,564, as of January 1, 1981. The full report is available from the International Personnel Management Association, 1850 K Street N.W., Suite 870, Washington, DC 20006, for $10 to members; $25, nonmembers.

OTHER POSITIONS

The annual survey of placements and salaries of new MLS graduates from ALA-accredited library education programs has been published in *Library Journal* since 1951 and is reprinted each year in the *Bowker Annual*. [The 1980 survey report immediately follows this article—*Ed.*] Graduates in 1980 showed an average beginning level salary of $14,223.

Since 1973, Russell E. Bidlack has been reporting on library school faculty salaries. The second annual report of library education statistics, *Association of American Library Schools Library Education Statistical Report 1981*, includes a section on faculty salaries compiled by Bidlack. (See Table 5 for some of the 1980–1981 data.) The report also provides data on students, curriculum, income and expenditures, and continuing professional education for member and associate-member schools. Copies are available for $15 from the Association of American Library Schools, 471 Park Lane, State College, PA 16801.

In July 1982, the American Library Association will publish a survey of academic and public library salaries conducted by the ALA Office for Research and the Office for Library Personnel Resources (OLPR). Results will be available by type of library, geographical area, and selected positions, such as director, deputy and assistant directors, department and branch heads, and various functional specialties (e.g., reference, cataloging, serials). Contact the ALA Order Department, 50 East Huron, Chicago, IL 60611 for order information.

TABLE 5 FACULTY SALARIES, ALA ACCREDITED PROGRAMS, 1980-1981

Rank & Term of Appointment	1980-1981 Average	1980-1981 Median
Deans & directors (fiscal year)	$42,628	$41,850
Deans & directors (academic year)	29,000	29,756
Professors (fiscal year)	39,758	40,909
Professors (academic year)	31,655	31,100
Assoc. profs. (fiscal year)	32,253	32,453
Assoc. profs. (academic year)	24,677	24,400
Asst. profs. (fiscal year)	25,851	25,835
Asst. profs. (academic year)	20,480	20,002
Instructors (fiscal year)	18,000	18,000
Instructors (academic year)	17,019	17,080
Lecturers (fiscal year)	22,684	20,766
Lecturers (academic year)	24,943	25,461

Source: *Association of American Library Schools Library Education Statistical Report 1981* (State College, Pa.: AALS, July 1981), p. F-12.

ADDITIONAL PERSONNEL DATA

Published in 1981 by the ALA Office for Library Personnel Resources, *Racial, Ethnic, and Sexual Composition of Library Staff in Public and Academic Libraries* provides information on the numbers and percentages of women and minorities in libraries. The data are useful for affirmative-action planning and for monitoring the status of women and minorities within the profession. Order for $5 prepaid from ALA/OLPR, 50 East Huron, Chicago, IL 60611. OLPR expects to publish the 1979-1981 *Degrees and Certificates Awarded by U.S. Library Education Programs* in 1982.

Many librarians have joined the growing coalition of women's groups, professional associations in predominantly female occupations, unions, and other organizations attempting to achieve "equal pay for work of equal value" or "comparable worth." Discrepancies in pay for library workers have been documented in comparison with predominantly male occupations that have similar requirements, such as level of education, experience, and responsibilities. In some cases, salary upgradings have been achieved. Case summaries of library-related actions are included in a resource packet called *Pay Equity: Comparable Worth Action Guide* available for $10 prepaid from the ALA Office for Library Personnel Resources, 50 East Huron, Chicago, IL 60611.

Fringe-benefit data are included in some of the state salary surveys mentioned previously. The summary of the 1980 Orlando Public Library's annual work-benefits survey of public libraries with annual budgets of $1 million or over was published in *Public Libraries* 20 (Summer 1981): 37-43. Limited benefits data will be included in the 1982 salary survey.

The National Center for Education Statistics (NCES) regularly provides staffing statistics, although the information is usually published several years after the surveys are conducted. Summary reports of several recent published and unpublished NCES surveys have appeared in the *Bowker Annual*. [*See* "NCES Survey of College and University Libraries, 1978-1979," *Bowker Annual 1981*, p. 287; and, in Part 4 of this volume, "NCES Survey of Public Libraries, 1977–1978," "NCES Survey of Public School Library Media Centers, 1978," and "NCES Survey of Library Networks and Cooperative Library Organizations"—*Ed.*]

The "1981–82 Library Human Resources: Study of Supply and Demand" by King Research, Inc., is anticipated by the end of 1982 and will project the supply and demand for professional librarians through 1990.

The author welcomes information on additional personnel surveys that readers have identified and are not included here.

PLACEMENTS AND SALARIES, 1980: HOLDING THE LINE

Carol L. Learmont
Associate Dean, School of Library Service, Columbia University, New York

Stephen Van Houten
PHILSOM Librarian, Medical Library Center of New York

This is the 30th annual report on placements and salaries of graduates of ALA-accredited library school programs. For the 1980 report, 63 of the 69 eligible schools completed the questionnaire in whole or in part. All of the Midwestern and Canadian schools responded, and the other geographical areas are well represented. This year, for the first time, the burden of calculating averages and means was totally on the computer, and these were computed from the raw data sent for each individual graduate from each school. In the past, the process of gathering data and completing the questionnaire was done at each school. The figures produced were then put together with those from all the other schools, and the placement survey resulted. Special thanks to Stephen Van Houten, who redeveloped the questionnaire so that the most tedious aspects of manipulating the data can now be done by the computer. Thanks also to those people who participated in the practice tests of the new questionnaire.

Please note some changes which are new to this survey. Canadian salaries are reported here in U.S. dollars for the first time. In recent years as the ratio changed this was not taken into consideration, but since the trend continues some adjustment was needed. At the request of numerous people two categories, "Special Libraries" and "Other Information Specialties," replace the category "Other Libraries and Library Agencies." The category "Other Information Specialties" provides a category in which to place positions that are becoming increasingly difficult to define in the more traditional terms.

This year the information gathered is probably more accurate than ever before since the averages and medians were computed on the basis of almost 4,400 individual reports rather than on 63 aggregate reports from responding schools. The results were awaited with some trepidation. However, no startling revelations appeared, which is a measure of the careful work done by all the participating schools over the years. Thank you for your continuing cooperation.

Note: Adapted from *Library Journal*, October 1, 1981.

TABLE 1   SALARY DATA SUMMARIZED

	Women	Men	Total
Average (Mean) Salary	$14,071	$14,917	$14,223
Median Salary	13,500	14,112	13,685
Individual Salary Range	5,700–32,000	5,640–32,500	5,640–32,500

In 1980 the average beginning level salary was $14,223, based on 1,737 known full-time professional salaries of men and women. Salaries and opportunities remained constant in 1980 compared with 1979 in terms of the percentages of people entering the various parts of the field. There was a dramatic drop in the number of graduates of accredited programs: 743 fewer graduates than in 1979. Fewer graduates are seeking work, and placement officers in many schools are making special efforts to develop new information-related job sources. The 1980 job market clearly reflected the "wait and see" election year spirit.

Forty-five schools reported no major difficulties placing graduates in 1980, four schools reported major difficulties, and four schools reported some difficulty. This was about the same as in 1979. Placement overall in 1980 was considered less difficult than in 1979 at 17 schools, more difficult at 9 schools, and about the same at 28 schools. There is still a scarcity of people with math, science, business, and language backgrounds. There is a need for people with interests in cataloging and children's work. There were very few comments on trends or employer practices this year. There were at least 201 temporary professional placements in 1980, compared with 189 in 1979 and 169 in both 1977 and 1978. It does seem that temporary appointments are on the increase.

Salaries for 1980 improved over those for 1979, but again fell well below the increase in the cost of living. The 1980 salaries increased at the rate of 8.4 percent, compared to 4.8 percent in 1979, 5.3 percent in 1978, and 6.5 percent in 1977. In 1980 the average (mean) beginning salary for all graduates was $14,223; for women, $14,071 (increased by eight percent from 1979); and for men, $14,917 (a nine percent increase). Median salaries were $13,685 for all graduates, $13,500 for women, and $14,112 for men (Table 1). Table 2 shows that, for new graduates with prior experience in a form relevant for salary purposes, the average beginning salary was $15,570 (up from $13,071 in 1979); without experience, $13,310 (up from $12,127 in 1979). Figures in Table 2 were run twice to insure accuracy.

PLACEMENTS

The 63 reporting schools awarded first professional degrees to 4,396 graduates in 1980 (Table 3). This was 743 fewer than the 5,139 degrees awarded by 61 responding schools in 1979. The drop in total number of graduates continues the trend noted in previous years. In 1977 the average number of graduates of schools reporting was 103; in 1978 it was 88; in 1979, 84; in 1980, 70.

Table 3 shows permanent and temporary professional placements, as well as nonprofessional library placements and totals for the three. These are library or information-related positions. Table 3 also shows the number of graduates reported who were not in library positions or whose employment status was unknown at the beginning of April 1981. Fifteen percent were known not to be in library positions compared to 13 percent reported for 1979 graduates. In April 1981 the whereabouts of 19 percent were unknown, compared to 21 percent in April 1980. Sixty-six percent of the 1980 graduates were known to be

TABLE 2 EFFECTS OF EXPERIENCE ON SALARIES

	Salaries without Previous Experience (51 Schools)			Salaries with Previous Experience (53 Schools)		
	Women	Men	Total	Women	Men	Total
Number of Positions	603	121	724	483	96	580
Range of Low Salaries	$6,800–16,000	$5,640–14,500	$5,640–16,000	$6,000–19,296	$10,500–24,000	$6,000–22,238
Mean (Average)	11,083	12,299	10,850	11,897	15,405	12,061
Median	10,000	14,500	10,000	12,600	12,000	12,300
Range of High Salaries	11,300–26,000	12,000–30,000	11,300–30,000	12,605–32,000	11,715–32,500	13,894–32,500
Mean (Average)	16,623	15,834	17,473	20,775	18,898	21,696
Median	18,585	14,500	18,585	27,000	24,600	20,000
Range of Average Salaries	11,085–16,000	11,820–13,471	11,212–16,000	11,500–15,000	11,715–13,500	11,500–14,700
Mean (Average)	13,184	13,937	13,310	15,273	17,100	15,570
Median	13,478	14,500	13,563	16,661	18,300	15,000

TABLE 3 STATUS OF 1980 GRADUATES, SPRING 1981

	No. of Graduates			Not in Lib. Positions			Empl. Not Known			Permanent Prof. Placements			Temp. Prof. Placements			Nonprof. Library Placements			Total in Lib. Positions		
	Women	Men	Total	Women	Men	Total	Women	Men	Total	Women	Men	Total	Women	Men	Total	Women	Men	Total	Women	Men	Total
United States	3,145	723	3,912	467	107	604	596	150	752	1,845	398	2,246	107	23	133	130	45	177	2,082	466	2,556
Northeast	1,160	258	1,449	158	39	223	297	77	377	612	114	727	46	13	60	47	15	62	705	142	849
Southeast	478	111	590	56	13	70	91	14	105	311	77	388	8	1	9	12	6	18	331	84	415
Midwest	998	220	1,224	153	38	192	124	29	155	641	135	777	30	6	36	50	12	64	721	153	877
Southwest	308	55	369	49	7	58	46	9	56	198	38	237	8	1	11	7	0	7	213	39	255
West	201	79	280	51	10	61	38	21	59	83	34	117	15	2	17	14	12	26	112	48	160
Canada	350	109	484	57	20	77	34	6	65	196	67	263	54	14	68	9	2	11	259	83	342
All Schools	3,495	832	4,396	524	127	681	630	156	817	2,041	465	2,509	161	37	201	139	47	188	2,341	549	2,898

TABLE 4 PLACEMENTS BY TYPE OF LIBRARY*

Schools	Public Women	Public Men	Public Total	Elementary & Secondary Women	Elementary & Secondary Men	Elementary & Secondary Total	College & University Women	College & University Men	College & University Total	Special Women	Special Men	Special Total	Other Info. Specialties Women	Other Info. Specialties Men	Other Info. Specialties Total	Total Women	Total Men	Total
Alabama	7	3	10	9	3	12	8	1	9	5	0	5	0	0	0	29	7	36
Albany	5	0	5	3	0	3	8	2	10	9	2	11	2	0	2	27	4	31
Alberta	2	1	3	1	0	1	4	5	9	3	1	4	1	0	1	11	7	18
Arizona	6	2	8	4	1	5	6	3	9	3	1	4	0	0	0	20	7	27
Atlanta	3	3	6	4	0	4	5	2	7	4	0	4	1	0	1	13	5	18
Ball	4	0	4	8	0	8	3	0	3	0	0	0	0	0	0	12	1	13
Brigham Young	4	5	9	2	1	3	3	2	5	0	3	3	2	0	2	11	11	22
British Columbia	10	3	13	1	2	3	5	3	8	6	1	7	1	0	1	23	9	32
Buffalo	3	2	5	3	0	3	4	0	4	1	1	2	1	0	1	12	5	17
California (Berk.)	8	3	11	0	0	0	5	6	11	11	2	13	0	0	0	24	11	35
California (LA)	6	1	7	0	0	0	0	5	5	4	1	5	0	0	0	15	2	17
Case Western	13	2	15	6	0	6	10	5	15	7	5	12	0	1	1	36	13	49
Catholic	2	0	2	0	0	0	4	1	5	11	3	14	5	0	5	22	4	26
Chicago	2	1	3	0	0	0	3	2	5	4	0	4	0	1	1	9	5	14
Clarion	1	0	1	4	1	5	1	0	1	0	0	0	0	0	0	6	1	7
Columbia	6	1	7	1	0	1	5	4	9	19	2	21	3	3	6	34	10	44
Dalhousie	6	1	7	1	0	1	5	1	6	4	1	5	1	0	1	17	3	20
Denver	7	3	10	4	2	6	10	5	15	12	3	15	4	1	5	37	14	51
Drexel	7	2	9	5	0	5	12	0	12	10	1	11	9	6	15	43	9	52
Emory	8	1	9	5	0	5	8	3	11	9	0	9	0	0	0	30	4	34
Emporia	5	1	6	27	3	30	10	4	14	2	2	4	0	1	1	44	7	51
Florida State	4	5	9	9	1	10	16	4	20	13	2	15	0	0	0	42	12	54
Hawaii	3	1	4	3	0	3	3	0	3	7	4	11	2	0	2	18	6	24
Illinois	17	6	23	4	1	5	11	4	15	5	0	5	3	0	3	38	11	49
Indiana	34	0	34	5	1	6	16	5	21	12	1	13	0	0	0	76	6	83
Iowa	10	2	12	14	1	15	8	5	13	4	1	5	0	2	2	36	8	44
Kent State	20	7	27	12	0	12	8	3	11	12	2	14	1	0	1	56	14	70
Kentucky	10	5	15	18	2	20	5	3	8	0	0	0	2	0	2	33	6	39
Long Island	14	2	16	6	0	6	7	1	8	8	0	8	0	0	0	33	7	40
Louisiana State	3	0	8	13	0	13	8	3	11	11	1	12	0	0	0	40	4	44

School													
Maryland	6	1	7	9	0	2	0	2	6	0	7	3	0	3	26	1	28
McGill	5	3	8	3	0	11	3	14	11	4	15	3	0	3	30	10	40
Michigan	26	4	30	12	1	28	6	34	31	5	36	2	0	2	99	16	115
Minnesota	5	0	5	3	0	2	2	4	9	0	9	1	0	1	20	2	22
Missouri	7	3	10	3	0	8	1	9	0	1	1	0	0	0	17	6	23
Montana	4	3	7	3	1	1	3	4	13	4	17	0	0	0	18	11	29
North Carolina	8	5	13	1	1	14	8	22	4	2	6	3	0	3	30	15	45
North Carolina Central	2	0	2	8	0	8	2	10	0	0	0	0	0	0	18	2	20
Northern Illinois	5	1	6	6	1	4	0	4	0	2	2	1	0	1	15	2	17
North Texas State	12	3	15	11	2	9	2	11	6	0	8	0	0	0	39	9	48
Peabody	3	2	5	10	0	9	3	12	5	1	11	1	0	1	27	5	32
Pittsburgh	15	1	16	9	1	12	1	13	10	2	9	5	0	5	51	4	55
Pratt	2	1	3	1	1	6	2	8	7	0	5	0	0	0	17	6	23
Queens	1	3	3	0	0	0	1	1	0	1	4	1	0	1	10	4	14
Rhode Island	9	2	11	3	0	3	7	10	5	2	15	0	0	0	25	10	35
Rosary	22	2	24	9	0	7	3	10	13	0	13	1	0	1	51	7	58
Rutgers	30	6	36	12	1	20	7	27	12	2	10	0	0	0	74	15	89
St. Johns	4	1	5	6	1	1	2	2	9	1	5	0	0	0	20	4	24
Simmons	31	3	34	8	1	32	10	42	58	3	61	0	0	0	129	17	146
South Carolina	5	1	6	8	0	4	2	6	3	2	5	0	1	1	20	6	26
Southern Connecticut	16	0	16	11	2	3	1	4	6	0	6	3	0	3	38	4	42
South Florida	4	4	4	9	0	1	0	1	0	0	2	0	0	0	14	2	16
Southern Mississippi	2	0	2	2	2	1	0	1	4	0	4	1	0	1	24	2	27 (?)
Syracuse	2	1	3	17	0	4	3	7	5	2	6	0	1	1	28	6	34
Tennessee	5	0	5	10	0	6	3	9	9	0	12	8	0	8	24	7	31
Texas Woman's	10	0	10	3	0	10	0	10	6	3	6	2	0	2	43	1	44
Toronto	14	1	15	17	0	8	0	8	16	4	20	0	0	0	41	7	48
Washington	1	0	1	0	2	6	2	8	0	0	0	5	0	5	12	4	16
Wayne	5	2	7	8	2	3	2	5	9	2	11	3	0	3	45	10	55
Western Michigan	8	3	11	22	2	6	2	8	2	1	3	0	2	2	28	10	38
Western Ontario	22	6	28	14	3	4	5	8	12	2	14	4	4	8	53	19	72
Wisconsin (Madison)	9	3	12	5	2	10	5	15	9	1	10	1	1	2	38	13	51
Wisconsin (Milwaukee)	0	0	0	3	0	0	1	1	0	1	0	0	0	0	4	1	5
Total	**535**	**124**	**659**	**427**	**45**	**473**	**444**	**165**	**610**	**492**	**90**	**583**	**77**	**27**	**104**	**1,975**	**451**	**2,429**

*Totals may include individuals undifferentiated by sex.

278 / LIBRARY EDUCATION, PLACEMENT, AND SALARIES

TABLE 5 COMPARISON OF SALARIES BY TYPE OF LIBRARY

	Place-ments	Salaries Known Women	Salaries Known Men	Salaries Known Total	Low Salary Women	Low Salary Men	Low Salary Total	High Salary Women	High Salary Men	High Salary Total	Average Salary Women	Average Salary Men	Average Salary Total	Median Salary Women	Median Salary Men	Median Salary Total
Public Libraries																
United States	578	357	75	432	5,700	10,000	5,700	21,500	30,000	30,000	12,931	13,767	13,076	12,960	13,684	13,000
Northeast	180	126	21	147	5,700	10,500	5,700	19,200	17,500	19,200	12,607	13,566	12,744	12,513	13,700	12,900
Southeast	86	40	17	57	7,200	10,356	7,500	16,900	18,470	18,470	12,641	13,483	12,892	12,900	13,500	12,957
Midwest	229	141	25	166	7,500	10,000	7,500	21,500	16,000	21,500	13,039	12,748	12,995	13,000	12,696	12,996
Southwest	51	31	4	35	9,428	14,832	9,428	18,500	15,900	18,500	12,949	15,333	13,222	12,500	15,000	13,200
West	32	19	8	27	9,000	10,440	9,000	20,472	30,000	30,000	14,854	15,578	15,578	14,700	16,428	14,964
Canada	81	37	9	46	9,408	11,974	9,408	16,678	17,106	17,106	13,979	14,381	14,057	14,540	14,373	14,540
All	659	394	84	478	5,700	10,000	5,700	21,500	30,000	30,000	13,029	13,833	13,170	13,000	13,700	13,080
School Libraries																
United States	457	299	33	333	6,000	10,000	6,000	28,800	26,484	28,800	14,349	16,169	14,523	13,500	16,000	13,800
Northeast	107	73	8	81	6,000	12,000	6,000	28,800	23,000	28,800	14,092	16,738	14,353	13,100	17,000	13,385
Southeast	91	68	5	73	6,800	11,715	6,800	23,000	18,700	23,000	13,241	14,503	13,327	12,900	12,500	12,900
Midwest	188	108	13	121	10,000	10,000	10,000	26,000	26,484	26,484	14,996	16,390	15,146	14,200	15,582	14,417
Southwest	55	39	5	44	9,000	11,000	9,000	22,600	19,500	22,600	13,699	16,198	13,888	13,000	15,000	13,000
West	16	11	3	14	12,000	13,800	12,000	28,000	29,936	28,000	18,863	16,433	18,342	19,000	16,000	18,000
Canada	16	5	2	7	12,830	21,383	12,830	31,646	29,936	31,646	21,016	25,660	22,343	21,383	21,383	21,383
All	473	304	35	340	6,000	10,000	6,000	31,646	29,936	31,646	14,459	16,711	14,684	13,500	16,000	13,850
College/Univ. Libs.																
United States	546	294	101	395	9,000	6,000	6,000	29,285	32,500	32,500	13,747	14,692	13,989	13,650	14,000	13,500
Northeast	165	101	35	136	9,256	6,000	6,000	29,285	32,500	32,500	14,102	15,396	14,435	13,650	14,000	13,800
Southeast	116	59	21	80	9,000	11,400	9,000	24,000	18,600	24,000	13,626	13,831	13,680	13,000	13,500	13,000
Midwest	180	87	28	115	10,000	10,500	10,000	25,000	18,500	25,000	13,569	14,313	13,750	13,000	14,500	13,400
Southwest	56	34	7	41	9,000	10,800	9,000	20,000	16,400	20,000	13,171	13,546	13,235	13,000	13,000	13,000
West	29	13	10	23	10,000	12,000	10,264	18,672	19,500	19,500	14,242	15,902	14,963	14,796	16,008	15,000
Canada	64	14	12	26	10,264	11,974	10,264	17,961	27,370	27,370	13,818	15,771	14,719	14,086	14,112	13,685
All	610	308	113	421	9,000	6,000	6,000	29,285	32,500	32,500	13,750	14,807	14,034	13,086	14,000	13,500
Special Libraries																
United States	501	305	50	355	8,500	5,640	5,640	32,000	24,000	32,000	15,062	14,810	15,026	14,498	14,700	14,500
Northeast	205	147	15	162	9,500	11,000	9,500	32,000	20,000	32,000	15,499	15,218	15,473	15,000	15,177	15,000
Southeast	75	44	8	52	10,027	13,200	10,027	28,800	21,000	28,800	15,284	14,945	15,231	14,498	13,925	14,040
Midwest	143	83	16	99	8,500	8,100	8,100	27,000	27,050	27,000	14,530	15,014	14,608	14,000	14,500	14,000
Southwest	46	20	5	25	9,500	10,500	9,500	20,000	17,050	20,000	14,441	13,490	14,251	14,000	13,200	14,000
West	32	11	6	17	11,000	5,640	5,640	16,200	18,000	18,000	13,468	14,164	13,714	14,000	14,760	14,000
Canada	82	36	12	48	11,974	12,830	11,974	18,389	22,238	22,238	14,313	15,613	14,638	14,012	14,968	14,224
All	583	341	62	403	8,500	5,640	5,640	32,000	24,000	32,000	14,982	14,965	14,980	14,400	14,760	14,500
Other Information Specialties																
United States	88	47	16	63	10,400	12,000	10,400	26,000	29,540	29,540	16,028	17,270	16,344	15,000	16,400	15,500
Northeast	50	27	10	37	11,700	12,500	11,700	21,000	29,540	29,540	15,686	18,030	16,319	14,500	16,000	15,000
Southeast	10	3	3	6	10,400	12,000	10,400	15,000	16,400	16,400	12,300	14,300	13,300	11,500	14,500	12,000
Midwest	17	8	1	9	12,000	17,014	12,000	20,500	17,014	20,500	16,475	17,014	16,534	16,000	17,014	17,014
Southwest	6	5	1	6	15,500	18,000	15,500	26,000	18,000	26,000	19,900	18,000	19,583	20,000	18,000	18,000
West	5	4	1	5	13,520	18,100	13,520	19,200	18,100	19,200	15,405	18,100	15,944	13,900	14,760	15,000
Canada	16	9	3	12	11,974	13,685	11,974	17,106	17,534	17,534	14,160	15,253	14,433	14,000	14,540	14,000
All	104	56	19	75	10,400	12,000	10,400	26,000	29,540	29,540	15,728	16,951	16,038	15,000	16,400	15,000

employed either in professional or nonprofessional positions in libraries or information-related work, as were 66 percent of the 1979 graduates. Fifty-seven percent of the 1980 graduates were employed in permanent professional positions, compared with 58 percent of the 1979 graduates. Employment distribution for 2,429 of the 4,396 graduates is shown in Tables 4 and 5. These are full-time professional placements and exclude part-time placements.

Based on the individual reports, there is now more accurate information about how long graduates actively sought employment, and, presumably, found it. Of 2,710 people reporting in this category, 1,741 (64 percent) reported searching for less than 90 days. This included people who had jobs in which they remained. There were 183 people (6.7 percent) who looked for three to four months; 85 (3.1 percent) searched for more than six months.

In 1980 four percent of all known library and related placements were in the nonprofessional positions (Table 3). In 1979 four percent were also in nonprofessional positions; in 1978 it was five percent. About four percent of the women and six percent of the men were in nonprofessional positions in 1980 compared to four percent of the women and four percent of the men in 1979. (These figures are revised from the 1979 report, which incorrectly gave the percentage as six for both men and women.) The percentage of graduates who have nonprofessional library positions has changed by only a percentage point or two in recent years.

The percentage of placements in 1980 in both public and college and university libraries stayed remarkably the same as the percentage for 1979, but the number of people involved dropped by more than 100 in each category. School library placement was up by two percent, but 35 fewer people were reported employed. The category "Other Library Agencies" shows a one percent drop, but a drop of 148 placements. This category was revised this year and reflects the sum of responses to placements in special libraries and in other information specialties. There is a leveling off in this category after a number of years of growth (Table 6).

Comparisons of U.S. and Canadian placements appear in Table 7. Table 8, showing special placements, is self-explanatory.

TABLE 6   PLACEMENTS BY TYPE OF LIBRARY, 1951–1980

Year	Public	School	College & Universities	Other Library Agencies*	Total
1951–1955**	2,076 (33%)	1,424 (23%)	1,774 (28%)	1,000 (16%)	6,264
1956–1960**	2,057 (33)	1,287 (20)	1,878 (30)	1,105 (17)	6,327
1961–1965	2,876 (30)	1,979 (20)	3,167 (33)	1,600 (17)	9,622
1966–1970	4,773 (28)	3,969 (23)	5,834 (34)	2,456 (15)	17,032
1971	999 (29)	924 (26)	1,067 (30)	513 (15)	3,503
1972	1,117 (30)	987 (26)	1,073 (29)	574 (15)	3,751
1973	1,180 (31)	969 (25)	1,017 (26)	712 (18)	3,878
1974	1,132 (31)	893 (24)	952 (26)	691 (19)	3,668
1975	994 (30)	813 (24)	847 (25)	714 (21)	3,368
1976	764 (27.1)	655 (23.2)	741 (26.3)	657 (23.2)	2,817
1977	846 (28.4)	673 (22.6)	771 (25.9)	687 (23.1)	2,977
1978	779 (26.1)	590 (19.8)	819 (27.4)	798 (26.7)	2,986
1979	778 (27.4)	508 (17.9)	716 (25.3)	835 (29.4)	2,837
1980	659 (27.1)	473 (19.5)	610 (25.1)	687 (28.3)	2,429

*From 1951 through 1966 these tabulations were for "special and other placements" in all kinds of libraries. From 1967 to 1979 these figures include only placements in library agencies that do not clearly belong to one of the other three groups; in the 1980 report these figures include the sum of responses to placements in special libraries and in other information specialties.

**Figures for individual years are reported in preceding articles in this series.

TABLE 7 U.S. AND CANADIAN PLACEMENTS COMPARED*

	Placements	Public Libraries	School Libraries	College & University Libraries	Special Libraries	Other Info. Specialties
All Schools	2429	659 (27.1%)	473 (19.5%)	610 (25.1%)	583 (24.0%)	104 (4.3%)
Women	1975	535 (27.1)	427 (21.6)	444 (22.5)	492 (24.9)	77 (3.9)
Men	451	124 (27.5)	45 (10.0)	165 (36.6)	90 (20.0)	27 (6.0)
U.S. Schools	2170	578 (26.6)	457 (21.1)	546 (25.2)	501 (23.1)	88 (4.1)
Women	1782	472 (26.5)	416 (23.3)	402 (22.6)	427 (24.0)	65 (3.6)
Men	385	106 (27.5)	40 (10.4)	143 (37.1)	73 (19.0)	23 (6.0)
Canadian Schools	259	81 (31.3)	16 (6.2)	64 (24.7)	82 (31.7)	16 (6.2)
Women	193	63 (32.6)	11 (5.7)	42 (21.8)	65 (33.7)	12 (6.2)
Men	66	18 (27.2)	5 (7.6)	22 (33.3)	17 (25.8)	4 (6.1)

*Percents may not total 100 because of rounding.

DEMAND AND SUPPLY

Fifty schools indicated that a total of 51,617 vacant positions were reported to them. These were listings for posts at all levels, and many of the same positions were listed in more than one place. In 1979, 50 schools reported a total of 48,230 vacancies. The average number per school reported in 1980 was 1,032 compared to 965 in 1979 and 820 in 1978.

Twenty-three schools reported increases in vacancy listings ranging from 6 to 45 percent; the median was 12 percent. Seventeen schools reported no significant changes from 1979. Three schools reported a decline, ranging from 14 to 50 percent. Four placement officers reported major difficulty in placing 1980 graduates; 4 reported some difficulty; and 44 reported no major difficulty. Nine placement officers felt they had more difficulty placing graduates in 1980 than in 1979; 17 felt they had less difficulty; and 28 felt they had about the same amount of difficulty both years.

While it appears that growth has stabilized in terms of the percentage of graduates going into various types of libraries and information-related activities, it is certain that there is a remarkably smaller pool of new graduates to draw from. This probably means that beginning level jobs are being more widely advertised and helps to account for the increased number of reported vacancies.

SALARIES

The salary statistics reported here include only full-time annual salaries and exclude such variables as vacations and other fringe benefits, which may be part of the total compensation. They do not reflect differences in hours worked per week. Such information might provide more precise comparison, but such data are probably beyond the needs of most library schools and of the profession. In any case, the validity of this analysis rests on comparable statistics collected since 1951.

Of the 63 schools reporting, 61 supplied some salary data. Not every school could provide all the information requested, nor could they supply it for all employed graduates. Schools were asked to exclude data for graduates in irregular placements such as those for graduates from abroad returning to posts in their native countries; appointments in religious orders or elsewhere where remuneration is in the form of some combination of salary plus living; and all salaries for part-time employment. With these exclusions added to the number of salaries not known or not reported, there is known salary information for 1,737 of the 1980 graduates (1,422 women, 314 men, and one undifferentiated by sex). This represents 69 percent of the known placements and 40 percent of all graduates reported, a smaller

TABLE 8 SPECIAL PLACEMENTS*

	Women	Men	Total
Government jurisdiction (U.S. and Canada)			
Other government agencies (except USVA hospitals)	40	17	57
State and provincial libraries	35	18	53
National libraries	21	6	27
Armed Services libraries (domestic)	6	1	7
Overseas agencies (incl. Armed Services)	3	1	4
Total government jurisdiction	105	43	148
Library science			
Advanced study	43	6	49
Teaching	19	7	26
Total library science	62	13	75
Children's services—school libraries	190	8	198
Youth services—school libraries	110	10	120
Children's services—public libraries	111	5	116
Business, finance, industrial	98	13	111
Science and technology	82	23	105
Law	73	19	92
Medicine (incl. nursing schools)	69	9	78
Audiovisual and media centers	51	15	66
Youth services—public libraries	64	2	66
Rare books, manuscripts, archives	31	14	45
Hospital (incl. USVA hospitals)	40	4	44
Research and development	32	5	37
Art and museum	24	5	29
Communications industry (advertising, newspaper, publishing, radio and TV, etc.)	25	4	29
Social sciences	22	7	29
Information services (nonlibrary)	23	3	26
Network consortia	16	9	25
Outreach activities and services	16	5	21
Music	13	7	20
Systems analysis, automation	17	2	19
Free lance	14	2	16
Religion (seminaries, theological schools)	9	4	13
Professional associations	10	2	12
Correctional institutions	7	4	11
Historical agencies	6	5	11
Records management	10	—	10
Bookstore	5	3	8
Youth services—other	8	—	8
Data bases	5	2	7
Geneological	5	2	7
Maps	2	5	7
Information specialists/systems	6	—	6
Library services to the blind	6	—	6
Pharmaceutical	5	1	6
Spanish-speaking centers	6	—	6
Career resources	5	—	5
International relations	5	0	5
Children's services—other	4	—	4
International agencies	3	1	4
Architecture	3	—	3
Documents	2	1	3
Archaeology	1	—	1
Computer center	—	1	1
Fashion institute	1	—	1
Mentally retarded	—	1	1
Oral history	1	—	1
Research on aging	1	—	1
Theater and motion pictures	1	—	1
Total Special Placements	**1,405**	**259**	**1,664**

*Includes special placements in all types of libraries, not limited to the "Special" or "Other Information Specialties" categories shown in Table 4.

282 / LIBRARY EDUCATION, PLACEMENT, AND SALARIES

TABLE 9 PLACEMENTS AND SALARIES OF 1980 GRADUATES—SUMMARY BY REGION

	Place-ments	Salaries**			Low Salary			High Salary			Average Salary			Median Salary		
		Women	Men	Total	Women	Men	Total	Women	Men	Total	Women	Men	Total	Women	Men	Total
United States	2,246	1,321	276	1,598	5,700	5,640	5,640	32,000	32,500	32,500	14,043	14,786	14,170	13,500	14,000	13,596
Northeast	727	482	90	572	5,700	6,000	5,700	32,000	32,500	32,500	14,206	15,336	14,384	13,500	14,000	13,787
Southeast	388	215	54	269	6,800	10,356	6,800	28,800	21,000	28,800	13,637	13,975	13,705	13,000	13,600	13,200
Midwest	777	430	83	513	7,500	8,100	7,500	27,000	26,484	27,000	13,996	14,335	14,050	13,500	13,872	13,500
Southwest	237	134	21	156	10,500	9,000	9,000	26,000	20,000	26,000	13,761	14,590	13,862	13,000	14,832	13,200
West	117	60	28	88	9,000	5,640	5,640	28,000	30,000	30,000	15,158	16,064	15,446	14,700	16,056	15,000
Canada	263	101	38	139	9,408	11,974	9,408	31,646	29,936	31,646	15,872	15,872	14,831	14,112	16,540	14,327
All Schools	**2,509**	**1,422**	**314**	**1,737**	**5,700**	**5,640**	**5,640**	**32,000**	**32,500**	**32,500**	**14,071**	**14,917**	**14,223**	**13,500**	**14,112**	**13,685**

*Includes 80 placements undifferentiated by type of library.
**Includes 20 salaries undifferentiated by type of library and one by sex.

TABLE 10 PLACEMENTS AND SALARIES OF 1980 GRADUATES

Schools	Place-ments	Salaries**			Low Salary			High Salary			Average Salary			Median Salary		
		Women	Men	Total	Women	Men	Total	Women	Men	Total	Women	Men	Total	Women	Men	Total
Alabama	36	24	5	29	10,500	12,000	10,500	24,000	17,100	24,000	13,988	14,060	14,000	13,000	13,500	13,280
Albany	32	25	4	29	11,000	12,800	11,000	22,048	17,500	22,048	14,560	14,725	14,582	13,200	14,000	13,500
Alberta	18	10	7	17	10,264	11,974	10,264	25,544	20,527	25,544	15,475	15,548	15,505	14,968	14,112	14,327
Arizona	29	15	4	19	11,410	10,800	10,800	18,306	16,400	18,306	14,042	14,450	14,128	13,500	15,000	13,500
Atlanta	18	11	4	15	10,027	12,300	10,027	15,900	18,470	18,470	14,673	15,993	13,559	12,600	15,000	12,605
Ball	13	10	1	11	11,000	8,100	8,100	14,100	8,100	14,100	12,922	8,100	12,484	12,800	8,100	12,800
Brigham Young	22	6	9	15	9,000	13,589	9,000	20,472	30,000	30,000	15,465	17,258	16,541	13,520	16,000	16,000
British Columbia	32	0	0	0			0			0			0			
Buffalo	19	12	4	16	12,900	14,500	12,900	18,585	20,000	20,000	14,684	16,800	15,213	14,600	15,200	14,600
California (Berk.)	35	11	8	19	12,000	10,440	10,440	18,672	16,512	18,672	14,390	14,298	14,351	14,304	13,992	14,304
California (LA)	18	15	2	17	12,000	16,529	12,000	18,300	19,000	19,000	15,264	17,765	15,559	15,700	16,529	15,800
Case Western	49	18	1	19	10,416	24,000	10,416	20,000	24,000	24,000	13,671	24,000	14,215	12,492	24,000	12,996
Catholic	26	21	3	24	12,900	13,900	12,900	29,285	21,500	29,285	18,304	18,200	18,291	17,500	19,200	17,500
Chicago	14	0	0	0			0			0			0			
Clarion	7	5	1	6	8,600	13,800	8,600	14,900	13,800	14,900	12,160	13,800	12,433	12,900	13,800	12,900
Columbia	45	28	7	35	10,863	11,500	10,863	32,000	16,800	32,000	15,301	14,391	15,119	13,664	15,000	13,700
Dalhousie	22	3	1	4	12,355	12,355	12,355	15,866	12,355	15,866	13,966	12,355	13,563	13,676	12,355	12,355
Denver	69	22	8	30	9,428	12,800	9,428	26,000	20,000	26,000	15,614	15,494	15,582	14,200	14,700	14,700

PLACEMENTS AND SALARIES, 1980: HOLDING THE LINE / 283

School																	
Drexel	52	31	9	40	9,245	12,500	9,245	24,000	29,540	29,540	14,666	16,580	15,097	14,000	15,000	14,000
Emory	34	28	4	32	10,350	12,500	10,350	22,500	13,750	22,500	13,767	13,075	13,681	12,957	12,710	12,957
Emporia	52	26	6	32	10,000	10,500	10,000	18,939	16,000	18,939	12,988	13,430	13,071	12,500	13,305	12,600
Florida State	55	28	10	38	10,000	10,500	10,000	28,800	18,700	28,800	14,123	14,653	14,262	13,000	14,000	13,925
Hawaii	26	17	5	22	10,000	5,640	5,640	17,616	18,100	17,616	13,162	14,748	13,522	13,000	18,000	13,000
Illinois	50	35	10	45	9,800	11,500	9,800	20,000	15,120	20,000	14,052	13,542	13,939	14,000	13,596	14,000
Indiana	83	45	4	49	9,500	13,500	9,500	19,000	18,585	19,000	13,171	16,446	13,438	13,000	15,200	13,000
Iowa	44	28	6	34	10,100	11,000	10,100	21,000	15,500	21,000	13,597	12,833	13,462	12,600	12,000	12,600
Kent State	74	47	12	59	8,800	11,770	8,800	22,425	26,484	22,425	14,604	14,827	13,462	14,250	13,200	14,084
Kentucky	39	14	0	14	7,200		7,200	19,760		19,760	14,761		14,649	14,500		14,500
Long Island	42	18	3	21	5,700	6,000	5,700	21,000	13,800	21,000	12,476	10,733	14,761	12,250	12,400	12,400
Louisiana State	44	21	1	22	9,000	13,200	9,000	19,997	13,200	19,997	12,472	13,200	12,227	12,000	13,200	12,000
Maryland	29	23	1	24	9,500	13,000	9,500	17,888	13,000	17,888	14,179	13,000	12,505	12,000	13,000	12,000
McGill	40	1	3	4	11,974	11,974	11,974	15,395	14,968	15,395	15,395	13,772	14,130	15,395	14,373	14,500
Michigan	115	77	10	87	15,395	11,974	15,395	27,000	20,000	27,000	14,111	13,885	14,178	15,395	14,373	14,373
Minnesota	26	19	2	21	10,000	14,500	10,000	20,000	14,500	20,000	14,040	14,500	14,085	13,600	12,750	13,600
Missouri	24	11	4	15	10,000	12,000	10,000	25,000	24,600	25,000	13,504	15,926	14,084	14,000	14,500	14,100
Montreal	29	10	8	18	10,320	12,855	10,320	16,271	27,370	16,271	15,307	17,192	14,150	12,210	13,000	12,500
North Carolina	47	26	15	41	14,012	10,356	9,000	24,000	15,000	27,370	13,350	13,364	16,145	15,284	15,395	15,395
North Carolina Central	20	15	2	17	9,000	13,000	9,000	16,500	13,600	24,000	13,350	13,390	13,364	13,200	14,000	13,500
Northern Illinois	20	13	2	15	9,000	12,500	9,000	17,000	15,000	16,500	12,386	13,300	11,800	11,800	13,000	12,000
North Texas State	49	33	8	41	10,200	10,500	10,200	18,500	17,000	25,000	15,065	14,750	12,494	14,450	12,500	14,450
Peabody	35	17	4	21	10,000	11,000	10,000	23,000	18,790	18,790	13,705	13,930	15,023	13,200	12,000	13,200
Pittsburgh	55	23	3	26	8,100	12,000	8,100	19,000	16,000	23,000	13,576	12,900	13,749	13,800	12,000	12,600
Pratt	28	19	6	25	10,000	14,000	10,000	21,000	18,100	23,000	13,014	17,318	13,448	12,300	16,953	12,300
Queens	16	7	2	9	10,000	13,500	10,000	17,000	17,084	21,000	14,376	15,183	13,511	14,000	14,000	14,000
Rhode Island	35	22	8	30	9,900	10,500	9,900	21,800	26,983	17,084	13,516	15,292	14,570	13,500	13,500	13,500
Rosary	59	41	6	47	8,500	11,500	8,500	25,000	20,500	26,983	13,139	15,623	13,910	12,900	14,700	13,000
Rutgers	90	57	12	69	10,000	11,000	10,000	25,000	17,000	25,000	14,024	14,850	13,801	13,500	14,500	13,500
St. Johns	26	19	4	23	6,000	13,500	6,000	21,000	17,000	20,000	13,655	13,792	14,129	13,310	14,000	13,500
Simmons	148	123	15	138	9,000	8,000	8,000	26,000	32,500	21,000	14,944	15,625	13,679	15,400	14,000	15,000
South Carolina	28	11	4	15	12,000	12,000	12,000	18,000	21,000	32,500	13,953	15,773	15,063	13,500	13,800	13,500
Southern Connecticut	43	38	4	42	9,145	13,894	9,145	29,300	27,658	21,000	13,793	15,725	14,151	13,500	13,500	13,500
South Florida	18	13	2	15	8,300	12,000	8,300	23,000	15,000	29,300	14,045	17,415	14,308	13,500	13,000	13,500
Southern Mississippi	27	23	3	26	6,800	13,894	6,800	26,986	12,500	23,000	12,997	14,447	14,366	13,894	13,894	12,380
Syracuse	34	11	4	15	10,000	11,715	10,000	18,000	15,000	26,986	13,642	14,072	13,191	12,092	12,000	12,150
Tennessee	31	5	1	6	12,800	13,700	12,800	15,126	15,127	18,000	14,526	14,497	13,460	12,365	14,000	14,500
Texas Woman's	46	43	0	44	0	14,500	9,500	20,000	14,500	15,126	14,245	14,500	14,288	15,200	14,500	13,000
Toronto	48	38	7	45	12,402	13,685	12,402	18,389	16,250	20,000	13,389	14,925	14,357	14,800	14,564	14,326
Washington	16	11	4	15	11,100	13,800	11,100	28,000	19,500	18,389	14,264	17,700	14,367	14,027	18,000	19,000
Wayne	55	16	2	18	10,000	12,600	10,000	26,000	14,000	28,000	14,697	13,300	16,229	19,000	12,600	15,600
Western Michigan	42	15	5	20	7,500	13,560	7,500	19,000	18,000	26,000	14,057	15,968	14,535	14,200	15,582	14,300
Western Ontario	74	39	12	51	9,408	12,830	9,408	31,646	29,936	19,000	14,135	16,551	14,703	13,685	14,540	14,000
Wisconsin (Madison)	51	25	11	36	10,700	10,000	10,000	23,000	17,400	31,646	13,779	13,717	13,760	13,200	13,872	13,500
Wisconsin (Milwaukee)	6	4	1	5	12,500	13,500	12,500	20,500	13,500	23,000	15,000	13,500	14,700	12,500	13,500	13,500

*Includes 80 placements undifferentiated by type of library.
**Includes 20 salaries undifferentiated by type of library.

Average (Mean) Salaries

The 1980 average salary for all graduates was $14,223, an increase of $1,096 (8.3 percent) over the 1979 average of $13,127. For women the average was $14,071, and for men the average was $14,917. Annual changes in average salaries since 1967 are shown in Table 11, which also includes a beginning salary index figure that may be compared with the Annual Cost of Living Index (COL) reports issued by the Government.

The COL index for 1980 was 247, an increase of 29.3 points over the 1979 figure of 217.7, a gain of 13.5 percent. The comparable increase in the beginning salary index is 15 points, 14.3 points below the increase in the cost of living.

In 1980 the range in the category of average salaries is from a low of $12,227 to a high of $18,431, a difference of $6,204. For women the range in average salaries was from $12,160 to $18,697, with a difference of $6,537; for men the range was $8,100 to $24,000, a $15,900 difference. In the 59 schools which reported average salaries for both men and women, the women's average was highest in 21 schools, while the men's average was highest in 38 schools.

Table 5 summarizes the salaries offered to men and women in different types of libraries and in other information specialties. In previous years the category that included special libraries was called "Other Libraries/Library Agencies." The average male salary is higher in every category except "Special Libraries," where the average female salary is only $17 higher.

Median Salaries

In 1980 the median salary for all graduates was $13,685, an increase of $802 over the 1979 median of $12,883. The median for women was $13,500; for men $14,112. In the past, information in this category was skimpy, but this year it is as full as it can be because the computer used individual returns as the basis for its calculations. In 21 of the 59 schools reporting both men and women, the median salary for women was higher than the median for men; in 37 schools it was lower; in one it was the same.

TABLE 11   AVERAGE SALARY INDEX FOR STARTING LIBRARY POSITIONS, 1967–1980

Year	Library Schools	Fifth-Year Graduates	Average Beginning Salary	Increase in Average	Beginning Index
1967	40	4,030	$ 7,305	—	—
1968	42	4,625	7,650	$ 355	105
1969	45	4,970	8,161	501	112
1970	48	5,569	8,611	450	118
1971	47	5,670	8,846	235	121
1972	48	6,079	9,248	402	127
1973	53	6,336	9,423	175	129
1974	52	6,370	10,000	617	137
1975	51	6,010	10,594	554	145
1976	53	5,415	11,149	555	153
1977	53	5,467	11,894	745	163
1978	62	5,442	12,527	633	171
1979	61	5,139	13,127	600	180
1980	63	4,396	14,223	1,096	195

Salary Range

The 1980 range of individual salaries again shows a wide range between the low and high salaries, differences attributed to such variables as education, experience, geographical location, and probably a little luck. Table 2 shows the effects of experience and of no experience on salary levels. For the survey purposes, prior experience, if known, consisted of work of a professional and/or subject nature of a year or more, or a civil service rating. The range in 1980 (Table 1) was from a low of $5,640 to a high of $32,500, a difference of $26,860. The low salary was received by a man in an academic library in New England.

High Salaries

In 1980 the range of high salaries was from $20,000 to $32,500, a difference of $12,500. Fifty-five salaries were $20,000 or more (36 women, 19 men). The median high salary for all graduates was $21,000; for women it was $20,472; for men, $17,400. For the seventh consecutive year women show the highest median. The median high salary was $19,992 in 1979, with a range of salary from $12,950 to $40,000. Forty-two salaries were over $20,000 in 1979 (25 women, 17 men). Distribution of high salaries by type of library is outlined in Table 12 and, in a different context, Table 5.

In 1980 the new category "Special Libraries" accounted for 28 percent of the 61 high salaries reported, while the new category "Other Information Specialties" accounted for eight percent. Taken together (36 percent), this is down from the 44 percent reported in 1979 for the category "Other Libraries and Library Agencies," which presumably included positions that are now in the new categories. School libraries accounted for 30 percent, up from 28 percent in 1979. Academic libraries accounted for 26 percent of the high salaries, a gain of 18 percent of the total in 1979. Public libraries had an 8 percent share, a drop from the 10 percent share of 1979. Forty salaries were said to have been affected significantly by prior experience. The

TABLE 12 HIGH SALARIES BY TYPE OF LIBRARY

	Public			School			College & Univ.			Special			Other		
	Women	Men	Total	Women	Men	Total	Women	Men	Total	Women	Men	Total	Women	Men	Total
$ 8,000										1		1			
9,000															
10,000	2	1	3	1		1	1		1	1		1			
11,000	1	2	3										1		1
12,000	4	4	8	2	3	5	8	5	13		5	5	2	1	3
13,000	11	6	17	4	2	6	4	6	10	2	3	5	1		1
14,000	9	11	20	3		3	7	4	11	4	4	8	2	1	3
15,000	11	6	17	4	2	6	9	10	19	9	6	15	4		4
16,000	7	5	12	5	2	7	9	3	12	2	5	7	1	3	4
17,000	4	2	6	4	4	8	1	2	3	6	4	10	3	2	5
18,000	4	2	6	7	4	11	4	4	8	8	2	10	2	2	4
19,000	1	1	2	6	1	7	1	2	3	2	1	3	2		2
20,000	1		1	1	2	3	5	1	6	4	4	8	3		3
21,000	1		1			4	2	1	3	4	1	5	1		1
22,000				3		3	1		1	1	1	2			
23,000				2	1	3	1		1						
24,000				1	1	2	1		1	1	1	2			
25,000				3		3	1		1						
26,000				1	1	2		1	1	2		2	1		1
27,000							1	1		1		1		1	1
28,000				2		2				1		1			
29,000				1	1	1		1	2		2	1	1		
30,000		1	1												
31,000				1		1									
32,000							1	1	1		1				

TABLE 13 LOW SALARIES BY TYPE OF LIBRARY

	Public			School			College & Univ.			Special			Other		
	Women	Men	Total	Women	Men	Total	Women	Men	Total	Women	Men	Total	Women	Men	Total
$ 5,000	1		1							1		1			
6,000				2		2	1		1						
7,000	2		2												
8,000	1		1	3		3	1		1	1	1	2			
9,000	10		10	5		5	3		3	3		3			
10,000	17	6	23	11	1	12	12	2	14	9	1	10	1		1
11,000	8	7	15	10	3	13	11	5	16	14	4	18	2		2
12,000	6	6	12	12	2	14	19	12	31	8	6	14	4	2	6
13,000	4	9	13	5	4	9	3	8	11	6	8	14	4	1	5
14,000	5	7	12	2		2	4	7	11	5	5	10	4	1	5
15,000	2	4	6	3		3	3	3	6	3	4	7	3	1	4
16,000				1		1				1	3	4	1	2	3
17,000				2		2	1		1	2	2		1	1	2
18,000		1	1	2		2	1		1	1	1	2	2	2	4
19,000		1	1	1		1									
20,000				2		2				1		1	1		1
21,000				1		1	1		1						
22,000				1		1									
23,000				1		1									
24,000				1		1				1		1			
25,000				2		2									
26,000															
27,000													1		1
28,000				1		1									

positions were scattered geographically and included 24 states and the District of Columbia, 4 Canadian provinces, and Germany, England, Saudi Arabia, Mexico, and Brazil. These last 5 countries apparently represent Americans going overseas to work in schools and special libraries. New York provided eight of the highest paid positions, and Alaska, Ohio, Texas, Illinois, and California provided three each.

Low Salaries

The lowest beginning level salaries offered to 1980 graduates ranged from $5,640 to $11,974 with the median low salary of $10,000, for all graduates. Of the 59 schools reporting low salaries for both men and women, 8 reported higher low salaries for women, 48 reported higher low salaries for men, and 3 reported the same.

Public libraries again accounted for the majority of low salaries; 33 percent, down from 40 percent in 1979. Academic libraries accounted for 25 percent, the same percentage as 1979. School libraries accounted for 23 percent, an increase from 14 percent last year. "Special Libraries" and "Other Information Specialties" accounted for about 20 percent, slightly lower than 21 percent in 1979.

There was no significant pattern in the geographical location of the low salaried positions. Thirty-one states, Puerto Rico, and four Canadian provinces were represented. New York had seven of the positions, New Jersey had four, and Texas and Illinois had three each.

Distribution of low salaries is shown in Tables 13 and 5.

NEXT YEAR?

Twenty-six placement officers see no change in the number of job vacancies reported so far in 1981 compared with those reported in 1980; 15 predict an increase; only

7 think that there will be a decrease. Thirty-four schools expect that 1981 graduates will have the same difficulty in finding professional positions as the 1980 graduates; 14 expect less difficulty; and 7 expect more difficulty. Only one reference was made to the effect of the economy and cutbacks on the future number of vacancies.

The responses to a question about types of libraries that are noticeably increasing or decreasing in the number of vacancies reported are summarized as follows:

	Increasing	*Decreasing*
Public libraries	6	11
School libraries	4	14
Academic libraries	13	4
Special libraries	24	3

Placement officers mentioned that not enough students are specializing in children's work, resulting in a shortage of school and children's librarians, especially in some of the Southern states where the school population is growing. There may also be an increase in the number of teacher/librarian retirements. Almost all who commented mentioned an increase in demand for special libraries as corporations become more aware of the value of information centers. Specific mention was made of expansion in the air industry and of the promotion of big business in the Southwest. Decreases are, once again, attributed to severe budget tightening, hiring freezes, reduced enrollments, the impact of tax cutbacks, and the overall high unemployment rate in some of the Northern industrial states. Turnover in academic libraries, especially in large cities, seems to be small.

Twenty-nine schools reported that salaries seem stronger for the 1981 graduate. Estimates ranged from $150 to $3,000, with most guesses in the $600 to $1,200 range. Twenty-one schools think there will be no change, and two think salaries will remain about the same.

It is still hard to fill positions that require specialized undergraduate degrees such as the sciences (23 mentions): biology, physics, geology, and chemistry were given special mention. Other degrees mentioned several times were computer science, math, engineering, business, languages, and education. Most of these have been in short supply for several years. There seems also to be a short supply of qualified applicants for positions requiring library school specializations in children's work, cataloging, medical librarianship, and anything to do with computers.

More and more schools are paying particular attention to nontraditional placements. Many schools are making special efforts to point out to students where and how to penetrate new markets. Placement officers are contacting business and industry, management consultant firms, and marketing departments in an effort to create job opportunities for new library school graduates. Once such organizations hire these recent graduates, they often seek others equally well-educated and trained.

Prospects for the future can be bright indeed for creative and well-prepared new graduates guided by creative placement and faculty advisors.

EDUCATION FOR LIBRARY SUPPORT STAFF IN THE UNITED STATES AND CANADA

Josephine Riss Fang

*Professor, Graduate School of Library and Information Science,
Simmons College, Boston, MA 02115*

Significant developments in paraprofessional training in the library/media field in the United States and Canada are highlighted in this article.

EDUCATION FOR SUPPORTIVE STAFF IN THE UNITED STATES

The Office of Library Personnel Resources of the American Library Association (ALA) has been intensively involved in setting criteria for training programs and assisting with definitions. The professional literature abounds with this topic and terminology extends over a wide spectrum of names.

The concept of paraprofessional education in the United States was advanced by a landmark official policy statement adopted by the council of the American Library Association in 1970 and revised in 1976, and known as "Library Education and Personnel Utilization."[1] This document clarified issues and represented a significant change in professional thinking by establishing categories of library personnel. The following statement is included: "To meet the goals of library service, both professional and supportive staff are needed in libraries. Thus, the library occupation is much broader than that segment of it, which is the library profession, but the library profession has responsibility for defining the training and education required for the preparation of personnel who work in libraries at any level, supportive or professional."

The categories listed in this policy statement are now officially recognized by ALA. They specify professional and supportive groups. The supportive group consists of three categories: the *library associate* and *associate specialist*, for which a four-year bachelor's degree is required; the *library technical assistant* and the *technical assistant*, for which "at least two years of college-level study" is required; and the *clerk*, for which some business or commercial courses are required.

On June 28, 1979, the American Library Association Council adopted a revision of its "Criteria for Programs to Prepare Library/Media Technical Assistants," originally approved in 1971.[2] In this document, the position has been defined as follows: "A "Library/Media Technical Assistant (referred to as LMTA) is a person with certain specifically library/media related skills—in preliminary bibliographic searching for example, or utilization of media equipment." This category assumes certain kinds of specific "technical" skills.

In 1977, the board of directors of the Association of American Library Schools (AALS) authorized "a study of the training of library assistants, library associates, library technical staff and the future direction in the training and use of these staff persons." The chairperson of this group, Doris Pagel, summarized the findings in a report published in 1980 under the title "Report of the AALS Task Force on Education of Non-clerical Support Staff."[3] This task force concluded "that the data needed to

Note: Adapted from a paper presented at the forty-seventh General Conference and Council Meeting of the International Federation of Library Associations and Institutions (IFLA), Leipzig, German Democratic Republic, August 18, 1981.

make recommendations regarding the developing of training and utilization programs by the schools and to delineate recommendations for AALS action are not available at this time" and that extensive research would first be needed. However, the findings of this group give some interesting insights; some of the important points should be mentioned here.

The library technical assistant category has been quite well defined in the literature, but there is very little information available on the library associate category. Thus the ambiguity of titles utilized and lack of unique functions of the two categories present a problem. Some studies even found 21 different titles assigned to 91 employed graduates of two-year library technician programs.[4] There is a general consensus that the number of library workers at the paraprofessional level will continue to grow.

The U.S. Bureau of Labor Statistics predicts that the number of library technicians and assistants will grow faster than the average of all occupations through the mid-1980s. In order to help libraries define the unique functions of paraprofessionals, professional associations have begun to establish detailed guidelines. In the educational sector, community colleges have become the institutions that train library technical assistants, usually under a two-year program, and following the guidelines set by the U.S. Office of Education.[5]

The Subcommittee on the Training of Library Supportive Staff of the Standing Committee on Library Education (SCOLE) of the American Library Association is currently compiling a directory of all institutions offering undergraduate programs in library science, including two-year colleges.

In its conclusion, the task force quotes Lester Asheim: "The primary objective in identifying subprofessional and preprofessional tasks in the library operation is to upgrade the authority and responsibility of the professional person and the education he/she requires, because the library professional needs to be educated for more than the day-to-day operation of the library, which paraprofessionals are increasingly doing."[6]

Paraprofessionals in the United States have an articulate voice through their national association, the Council on Library/Media Technical Assistants (COLT). The association adopted the new name and new constitution and bylaws in 1976 to reflect the changing scene in the library/information field. With its 400 members (300 individual and 100 institutional), COLT is actively recruiting for increased participation. Its very useful publication program includes the *COLT Newsletter*, bibliographies, and a directory of training programs published as the *Directory of Institutions Offering or Planning Programs for the Training of Library Technical Assistants* in 1976 and revised in 1981 under the new title *Directory of Institutions Offering Programs for the Training of Library/Media Technical Assistants*.[7] Suzanne Gill, longtime editor of the newsletter, shared some of her thoughts in a recent article in the *Wilson Library Bulletin*,[8] in which she says: "Paraprofessionals, like professionals, want recognition and acceptance. They want career advancement and the continuing education to make that possible. They want standardization of job titles and duties. They want salaries befitting their training." As in the library field, library/media paraprofessionals are also moving into fields other than librarianship, particularly those related to information technology, which affects the training and skills they need, so that courses in library technology, word processing, records and file management, and micrographics are now in additional demand. In some cases this involves a change in their title to "information technicians."

The basic document for the training of library/media technicians is entitled "Criteria for Programs to Prepare Library/Media Technical Assistants." First adopted by the American Library Association Council in June 1971, it was revised on June 28, 1979. Suzanne Gill compares both versions in the *COLT Newsletter*.[9] She finds that a section-by-section comparison reveals no major changes, but mainly clarifying statements. This document offers an excellent basis for evaluating paraprofessional LMTA programs as they currently exist, particularly if an accreditation process should develop. Not included in these criteria, however, is the rapidly developing area of information technology and other interdisciplinary fields. This document, however, still serves as an important tool in the development of LMTA programs and the formalization of paraprofessional training.

Library technology training programs developed rapidly during the 1960s to fill a manpower need, until they outnumbered the accredited graduate library schools. The 1976 directory lists programs in 39 states plus the District of Columbia, American Samoa, Canal Zone, and Puerto Rico, as well as 23 programs in Canada. In the United States, 130 paraprofessional programs have been identified. Currently, enrollment has leveled off and the state of the economy has apparently brought about the discontinuation of some programs. During this time, roughly 7,000 students were enrolled in library technology programs; three-fifths of them were part-time students, with the majority being women. Richard Taylor, the editor of the 1976 directory, observes that "training for Library Technical Assistants is not at a stalemate. There are new programs being offered and planned ranging all the way from self-instruction courses to the various subjects of specialization. Many programs offer options whereby students may choose what particular aspect of library work is of interest to them. Curriculum is being changed, also, to allow for such options and to remain current in outlook." The 1981 directory contains information on 115 programs in the United States and Canada. Institutions offering the bachelor's degree or beyond were omitted. The data provided on objectives, enrollment, and courses reflect the most current trends and practices in effect today.

Another trend is toward coordination in instruction with other disciplines so that the preparation of students is broadened without adding staff. There is also evidence that programs will be organized on a state- or provincewide basis. Increasing uniformity in courses, names, and even complete programs and thus a trend toward standardization in training had been predicted in the 1976 edition of the directory, although there is still evidence of a great variety of course offerings and terminology in 1981.

Charles Evans states in his very informative study that "the evolution of paraprofessionals will continue to be correlated to the evolution of librarians, and both will continue to evolve, inevitably, as libraries continue to change. At the moment, however, they have reached a plateau, consolidating and reinforcing past gains rather than pushing for further progress."[10] However, associations such as COLT and ALA promise to work toward progress.

EDUCATION AND TRAINING OF LIBRARY TECHNICIANS IN CANADA

Canadian literature uses the term *library technician* rather consistently. Periodic in-depth surveys of library technician programs have been carried out for a number of years and are published in the *Canadian Library Journal*. In the eighth such survey, in 1979, Jean Weihs, who is course director for the Library Techniques Program at Seneca College of Applied Arts and Technology in Ontario, summarizes her findings and gives detailed tabulations on the 23 programs listed.[11] Most of the Canadian programs are offered at community colleges or colleges of applied arts and sciences, and range in duration from ten months to, usually, two years.

In the article "Library Technicians in Ontario," Dorothy Kew cites the accepted definition of a library technician as "a graduate of a two-year diploma of library techniques, who fills the need for a paraprofessional level between the library clerk and the librarian."[12] To train library staff on the job was found to be too costly and time-consuming, so formal programs to prepare library workers were needed. The emerging community colleges were able to fill this need and the first library techniques course in Canada was established in Manitoba in 1962. Others followed soon, and about two thousand library technicians have been graduated in Ontario since then.

Educational programs are based on the "Guidelines for the Training of Library Technicians," developed by the Committee on Education for Library Personnel: Library Technicians and passed by the Canadian Library Association Council in 1973. These guidelines are being reviewed for any changes to meet new needs.

Under the term "basic courses" for such programs, the following subject areas are defined: introduction to libraries, acquisition procedures, cataloging and classification, circulation routines and library publicity, and reference work (reader services and children's literature). Additional requirements are developed according to regional needs. For instance, in Ontario the program of instruction combines academic courses (50 percent) with 25-30 percent library-technical and 20-25 percent technical-related courses. Field practice in different types of libraries is also part of the curriculum, and there is usually a broad range of electives; in some instances, specialization is possible, such as for the health sciences.

An interesting phenomenon in Canada is that library technicians have formed five strong provincial associations, but no national organization as yet, except for the previously mentioned committee of the Canadian Library Association. These associations work toward a clearer definition of the role of library technicians and toward promotion of their status.

Thus one can say that the professional training of library technicians is well established in Canada and detailed information is readily available through ongoing surveys.

NOTES

1. American Library Association, Office for Library Personnel Resources, "Library Education and Personnel Utilization: A Statement of Policy Adopted by the Council of the American Library Association, June 30, 1970," rev. Spring 1976 (Chicago: American Library Association, 1977).
2. "Criteria for Programs to Prepare Library/Media Technical Assistants," rev. from 1971 statement (Chicago: American Library Association, 1979).
3. Doris Pagel, "Report of the AALS Task Force on Education of Non-clerical Support Staff," *Journal of Education for Librarianship* 21 (Summer 1980): 65-70.
4. John E. James, "Library Technician Program: The Library Technician Graduates' Point of View," in *Reader in Library Technology*, ed. by Shirly Gray Adamovich (Englewood, Colo.: Microcard Editions Books, 1975), pp. 173-183; reprinted from *Special Libraries* 62 (July/August 1971): 268-278.
5. U.S. Office of Education, Manpower Development and Training Program, "A Suggested Two-Year Post High School Curriculum: Library Technical Assistant" (Washington, D.C.: U.S. Government Printing Office, 1973).
6. Pagel, "Report of the AALS Task Force on Education of Non-clerical Support Staff," *Journal of Education for Librarianship* 21 (Summer 1980): 65 70.
7. Richard L. Taylor, ed., *Directory of Institutions Offering or Planning Programs for the Train-*

ing of Library Technical Assistants, 4th ed. (Chicago: Council on Library Technical Assistants, 1976); Raymond G. Roney and Audrey V. Jones, eds., *Directory of Institutions Offering Programs for the Training of Library/Media Technical Assistants*, 5th ed. (Chicago: Council on Library/Media Technical Assistants, 1981).
8. Suzanne Gill, "New Directions for Library Professionals," *Wilson Library Bulletin* 55 (January 1981): 368–369.
9. Suzanne Gill, "Comparing Two *Criteria*," *COLT Newsletter* 12 (December 1979): 1–20.
10. Charles W. Evans, "The Evolution of Paraprofessional Library Employees," in *Advances in Librarianship*, vol. 9 (New York: Academic, 1979), pp. 63–101.
11. Jean Riddle Weihs, "Survey of Library Technician Programs in Canada," *Canadian Library Journal* 36 (December 1979): 354–362.
12. Dorothy Kew, "Library Technicians in Ontario: They've Come A Long Way," *Ontario Library Review* 64 (March 1980): 38–43.

ACCREDITED LIBRARY SCHOOLS

This list of graduate schools accredited by the American Library Association was issued in October 1981. A list of more than 400 institutions offering both accredited and nonaccredited programs in librarianship appears in the thirty-fourth edition of the *American Library Directory* (Bowker, 1981).

NORTHEAST: CONN., D.C., MASS., MD., N.J., N.Y., PA., R.I.

Catholic University of America, School of Lib. and Info. Science, Washington, DC 20064. Elizabeth W. Stone, Dean. 202-635-5085.

Clarion State College, School of Lib. Science, Clarion, PA 16214. Elizabeth A. Rupert, Dean. 814-226-2271.

Columbia University, School of Lib. Service, New York, NY 10027. Richard L. Darling, Dean. 212-280-2291.

Drexel University, School of Lib. and Info. Science, Philadelphia, PA 19104. Guy Garrison, Dean. 215-895-2474.

Long Island University, C. W. Post Center, Palmer Grad. Lib. School, Greenvale, NY 11548. John T. Gillespie, Acting Dean. 516-299-2855, 2856.

Pratt Institute, Grad. School of Lib. and Info. Science, Brooklyn, NY 11205. Nasser Sharify, Dean. 212-636-3702.

Queens College, City University of New York, Grad. School of Lib. and Info. Studies, Flushing, NY 11367. Richard J. Hyman, Dir. 212-520-7194.

Rutgers University, Grad. School of Lib. and Info. Studies, New Brunswick, NJ 08903. Thomas H. Mott, Jr., Dean. 201-932-7500.

St. John's University, Div. of Lib. and Info. Science, Jamaica, NY 11439. Mildred Lowe, Acting Dir. 212-990-6161, ext. 6200.

Simmons College, Grad. School of Lib. and Info. Science, Boston, MA 02115. Robert D. Stueart, Dean. 617-738-2225.

Southern Connecticut State College, Div. of Lib. Science and Instructional Technology, New Haven, CT 06515. Emanuel T. Prostano, Dir. 203-397-4532.

State University of New York at Albany, School of Lib. and Info. Science, Albany, NY 12222. Richard S. Halsey, Dean. 518-455-6288.

State University of New York at Buffalo, School of Info. and Lib. Studies, Buffalo, NY 14260. George S. Bobinski, Dean. 716-636-2411.

State University of New York, College of Arts and Science, Geneseo, School of Lib. and Info. Science, Geneseo, NY

14454. John E. Kephart, Dean. 716-245-5322.

Syracuse University, School of Info. Studies, Syracuse, NY 13210. Evelyn H. Daniel, Dean. 315-423-2911.

University of Maryland, College of Lib. and Info. Services, College Park, MD 20742. Michael M. Reynolds, Acting Dean. 301-454-5441.

University of Pittsburgh, School of Lib. and Info. Science, Pittsburgh, PA 15260. Thomas J. Galvin, Dean. 412-624-5230.

University of Rhode Island, Grad. Lib. School, Kingston, RI 02881. Bernard S. Schlessinger, Dean. 401-792-2878, 2947.

SOUTHEAST: ALA., FLA., GA., KY., MISS., N.C., S.C., TENN.

Atlanta University, School of Lib. and Info. Studies, Atlanta, GA 30314. Virginia Lacy Jones, Dean. 404-681-0251, ext. 230.

Emory University, Div. of Lib. and Info. Management, Atlanta, GA 30322. A. Venable Lawson, Dir. 404-329-6840.

Florida State University, School of Lib. Science, Tallahassee, FL 32306. Harold Goldstein, Dean. 904-644-5775.

North Carolina Central University, School of Lib. Science, Durham, NC 27707. Annette L. Phinazee, Dean. 919-683-6485.

University of Alabama, Grad. School of Lib. Service, University, AL 35486. James D. Ramer, Dean. 205-348-4610.

University of Kentucky, College of Lib. Science, Lexington, KY 40506. Timothy W. Sineath, Dean. 606-258-8876.

University of Mississippi, Grad. School of Lib. and Info. Science, University, MS 38677. Ellis E. Tucker, Dir. 601-232-7440.

University of North Carolina, School of Lib. Science, Chapel Hill, NC 27514. Edward G. Holley, Dean. 919-962-8366.

University of South Carolina, College of Libnshp., Columbia, SC 29208. F. William Summers, Dean. 803-777-3858.

University of South Florida, Grad. Dept. of Lib., Media and Info. Studies, Tampa, FL 33620. John A. McCrossan, Chpn. 813-974-2557, 2100.

University of Southern Mississippi, School of Lib. Service, Hattiesburg, MS 39401. Onva K. Boshears, Jr., Dean. 601-266-7168.

University of Tennessee, Knoxville, Grad. School of Lib. and Info. Science, Knoxville, TN 37916. Ann E. Prentice, Dir. 615-974-2148.

Vanderbilt University, George Peabody College for Teachers, Dept. of Lib. and Info. Science, Nashville, TN 37203. Edwin S. Gleaves, Chpn. 615-327-8037.

MIDWEST: IOWA, ILL., IND., KANS., MICH., MINN., MO., OHIO, WIS.

Ball State University, Dept. of Lib. Science, Muncie, IN 47306. Doris W. Cox, Chpn. 317-285-7180, 7189.

Case Western Reserve University, Matthew A. Baxter School of Info. and Lib. Science, Cleveland, OH 44106. Edward T. O'Neill, Dean. 216-368-3500.

Emporia State University, School of Lib. Science, Emporia, KS 66801. Robert Grover, Dean. 316-343-1200, ext. 203, 204.

Indiana University, School of Lib. and Info. Science, Bloomington, IN 47405. Herbert S. White, Dean. 812-337-2848.

Kent State University, School of Lib. Science, Kent, OH 44242. A. Robert Rogers, Dean. 216-672-2782.

Northern Illinois University, Dept. of Lib. Science, DeKalb, IL 60115. Sylvia G. Faibisoff, Chpn. 815-753-1733.

Rosary College, Grad. School of Lib. Science, River Forest, IL 60305. Sister M. Lauretta McCusker, O.P., Dean. 312-366-2490.

University of Chicago, Grad. Lib. School, Chicago, IL 60637. W. Boyd Rayward, Dean. 312-753-3482.

University of Illinois, Grad. School of Lib. and Info. Science, 410 David Kinley Hall, 1407 W. Gregory, Urbana, IL 61801. Charles H. Davis, Dean. 217-333-3280.

University of Iowa, School of Lib. Science, Iowa City, IA 52242. Carl F. Orgren, Dir. 319-353-3644.

University of Michigan, School of Lib. Science, Ann Arbor, MI 48109. Russell E. Bidlack, Dean. 313-764-9376.

University of Minnesota, Lib. School, 117 Pleasant St. S.E., Minneapolis, MN 55455. Wesley Simonton, Dir. 612-373-3100.

University of Missouri, Columbia, School of Lib. and Info. Science, Columbia, MO 65211. Edward P. Miller, Dean. 314-882-4546.

University of Wisconsin–Madison, Lib. School, Madison, WI 53706. Jane B. Robbins-Carter, Dir. 608-263-2900.

University of Wisconsin–Milwaukee, School of Lib. Science, Milwaukee, WI 53201. Mohammed M. Aman, Dean. 414-963-4707.

Wayne State University, Div. of Lib. Science, Detroit, MI 48202. Robert E. Booth, Dir. 313-577-1825.

Western Michigan University, School of Libnshp., Kalamazoo, MI 49008. Hardy Carroll, Interim Dir. 616-383-1849.

SOUTHWEST: ARIZ., LA., OKLA., TEX.

Louisiana State University, School of Lib. and Info. Science, Baton Rouge, LA 70803. Sr. Marie L. Cairns, Acting Dean. 504-388-3158.

North Texas State University, School of Lib. and Info. Sciences, Denton, TX 76203. Dewey E. Carroll, Dean. 817-788-2445.

Texas Woman's University, School of Lib. Science, Denton, TX 76204. Brooke E. Sheldon, Dean. 817-387-2418.

University of Arizona, Grad. Lib. School, Tucson, AZ 85721. Ellen Altman, Dir. 602-626-3565.

University of Oklahoma, School of Lib. Science, Norman, OK 73019. James S. Healey, Dir. 405-325-3921.

University of Texas at Austin, Grad. School of Lib. and Info. Science, Austin, TX 78712. C. Glenn Sparks, Dean. 512-471-3821.

WEST: CALIF., COLO., HAWAII, UTAH, WASH.

Brigham Young University, School of Lib. and Info. Sciences, Provo, UT 84602. Maurice P. Marchant, Dir. 801-378-2976.

San Jose State University, Div. of Lib. Science, San Jose, CA 95192. Guy A. Marco, Dir. 408-277-2292.

University of California–Berkeley, School of Lib. and Info. Studies, Berkeley, CA 94720. Michael K. Buckland, Dean. 415-642-1464.

University of California–Los Angeles, Grad. School of Lib. and Info. Science, Los Angeles, CA 90024. Robert M. Hayes, Dean. 213-825-4351.

University of Denver, Grad. School of Libnshp. and Info. Management, Denver, CO 80208. Bernard M. Franckowiak, Dean. 303-753-2557.

University of Hawaii, Grad. School of Lib. Studies, Honolulu, HI 96822. Ira W. Harris, Dean. 808-948-7321.

University of Southern California, School of Lib. and Info. Management, University Park, Los Angeles, CA 90007. Roger C. Greer, Dean. 213-743-2548.

University of Washington, School of Libnshp., Seattle, WA 98195. Margaret Chisholm, Acting Dir. 206-543-1794.

CANADA

Dalhousie University, School of Lib. Service, Halifax, N.S. B3H 4H8. Norman Horrocks, Dir. 902-424-3656.

McGill University, Grad. School of Lib. Science, Montreal, P.Q. H3A 1Y1. Hans Möller, Dir. 514-392-5947.

Université de Montréal, Ecole de bibliothéconomie, Montréal, P.Q. H3C 3J7. Suzanne Bertrand-Gastaldy, Interim Dir. 514-343-6044.

University of Alberta, Faculty of Lib. Science, Edmonton, Alta. T6G 2J4. William Kurmey, Dean. 403-432-4578.

University of British Columbia, School of Libnshp., Vancouver, B.C. V6T 1W5. Basil Stuart-Stubbs, Dir. 604-228-2404.

University of Toronto, Faculty of Lib. Science, Toronto, Ont. M5S 1A1. Katherine H. Packer, Dean. 416-978-3234.

University of Western Ontario, School of Lib. and Info. Science, London, Ont. N6A 5B9. William J. Cameron, Dean. 519-679-3542.

LIBRARY SCHOLARSHIP SOURCES

For a more complete list of the scholarships, fellowships, and assistantships offered for library study, see *Financial Assistance for Library Education* published annually by the American Library Association.

American Library Association. Three scholarships of $3,000. The David H. Clift Scholarship is given to a varying number of U.S. or Canadian citizens who have been admitted to accredited library schools. For information, write to: Staff Liaison, David H. Clift Scholarship Jury, ALA, 50 E. Huron St., Chicago, IL 60611; the Louise Giles Minority Scholarship is given to a varying number of minority students who are U.S. or Canadian citizens and have been admitted to accredited library schools. For information, write to: Staff Liaison, Louise Giles Minority Scholarship Jury, ALA, 50 E. Huron St., Chicago, IL 60611; the F. W. Faxon Scholarship is given to a U.S., Canadian, or foreign student who has been admitted to an accredited library school. Scholarship includes ten-week expenses-paid internship at F. W. Faxon in Westwood, Massachusetts. For information, write to: Staff Liasion, F. W. Faxon Scholarship, ALA, 50 E. Huron St., Chicago, IL 60611.

American-Scandinavian Foundation. Fellowships and grants for 25 to 30 students, in amounts from $500 to $6,000, for advanced study in Denmark, Finland, Iceland, Norway, or Sweden. For information, write to: Exchange Div., American-Scandinavian Foundation, 127 E. 73 St., New York, NY 10021.

Beta Phi Mu. Three scholarships: (1) $1,500 each for a varying number of persons accepted in an ALA-accredited library program; (2) $750 each for a varying number of Beta Phi Mu members for continuing education; (3) the Harold Lancour Scholarship for Foreign Study, $750 each for a varying number of students for graduate study in a foreign country related to the applicant's work or schooling. For information, write to: Exec. Secy., Beta Phi Mu, Grad. School of Lib. and Info.

Science, Univ. of Pittsburgh, Pittsburgh, PA 15260.

Canadian Library Association. Howard V. Phalin-World Book Graduate Scholarship in Library Science. A $2,500 (maximum) scholarship for a Canadian citizen or landed immigrant to attend an accredited library school in Canada or the United States. H. W. Wilson Scholarship of $2,000 and Elizabeth Dafoe Scholarship of $1,750 for a Canadian citizen or landed immigrant to attend an accredited Canadian library school. For information, write to: Scholarships and Awards Committee, Canadian Lib. Assn., 151 Sparks St., Ottawa, Ont. K1P 5E3, Canada.

Catholic Library Association, Rev. Andrew L. Bouwhuis Scholarship of $1,500 for a person with a B.A. degree who has been accepted in an accredited library school. (Award based on financial need and proficiency.) World Book-Childcraft Awards: one scholarship of a total of $1,000 to be distributed among no more than four recipients for a program of continuing education. Open to CLA members only. For information, write to: Scholarship Committee, Catholic Lib. Assn., 461 W. Lancaster Ave., Haverford, PA 19401.

Fulbright Awards. Fellowships and grants of varying amounts for university lecturing or advanced research abroad to candidates with a Ph.D. and library and teaching or research experience. Foreign-language proficiency required in some instances. For information, write to: Council for International Exchange of Scholars, Suite 300, 11 Dupont Circle, Washington, DC 20036.

Information Exchange System for Minority Personnel. Scholarship of $500, intended for minority students, for graduate study. For information, write to: Dorothy M. Haith, Chpn., Clara Stanton Jones School, Box 668, Fort Valley, GA 31030.

Medical Library Association. (1) Varying number of scholarships of $2,000 each for minority students, for graduate study in medical librarianship. (2) Grants of varying amounts for continuing education for medical librarians with an MLS and two years' professional experience. Open to MLA members only. For information, write to: Scholarship Committee, Medical Lib. Assn., Suite 3208, 919 N. Michigan Ave., Chicago, IL 60611.

The Frederic G. Melcher Scholarship (administered by Association of Library Service to Children, ALA). Scholarship of $4,000 for a U.S. or Canadian citizen admitted to an accredited library school who plans to work with children in school or public libraries. For information, write to: Exec. Secy., Assn. of Lib. Service to Children, ALA, 50 E. Huron St., Chicago, IL 60611.

Mountain Plains Library Association. Seven grants of $500 each for residents of the association area. Open only to MPLA members with at least two years of membership. For information, write to: Joseph R. Edelen, Jr., MPLA Exec. Secy., Univ. of South Dakota Lib., Vermillion, SD 57069.

Natural Sciences and Engineering Research Council. A varying number of scholarships of $9,350 each for postgraduate study in science librarianship and documentation for a Canadian citizen or landed immigrant with a bachelor's degree in science or engineering. For information, write to: J. H. Danis, Scholarships Officer, Natural Sciences and Engineering Research Council, Ottawa, Ont. K1A OR6, Canada.

New England Library Association. A varying number of scholarships in varying amounts. For information, write to: NELA Scholarship Chair, NELA, Upper Walpole Rd., Walpole, NH 03608.

Special Libraries Association. Two $5,000 scholarships for U.S. or Canadian citizens, accepted by an ALA-accredited library education program, who show an aptitude for and interest in special libraries. One $1,000 scholarship for a

U.S. or Canadian citizen with an MLS and an interest in special libraries who has been accepted in an ALA-accredited Ph.D. program. For information, write to: Scholarship Committee, SLA, 235 Park Ave. S., New York, NY 10003.

Three scholarships of $2,000 each for minority students with an interest in special libraries. Open to U.S. or Canadian citizens only. For information, write to: Positive Action Program for Minority Groups, c/o SLA.

LIBRARY SCHOLARSHIP AND AWARD RECIPIENTS, 1981

AALS Research Grant Award—$1,500–$2,500. For a project that reflects the goals and objectives of the Association of American Library Schools (AALS). *Offered by:* AALS. *Winners:* Trudy Gardner and Thomas Kochtanek, Univ. of Missouri.

AASL Distinguished Library Service Award for School Administrators. For a unique and sustained contribution toward furthering the role of the library and its development in elementary and/or secondary education. *Offered by:* ALA American Association of School Librarians. *Winner:* Joyce Jackson, Pres., Central High School, Minneapolis, Minn.

AASL/Encyclopaedia Britannica School Library Media Program of the Year Award—$5,000. For outstanding school media programs. *Offered by:* ALA American Association of School Librarians and the Encyclopaedia Britannica Co. *Winner:* Blue Valley Unified School District, Stanley, Kans.

AASL President's Award—$2,000. For demonstrating excellence and providing an outstanding national or international contribution to school librarianship and school library development. *Offered by:* ALA, American Association of School Librarians. *Donor:* Baker & Taylor. *Winner:* Mary Helen Mahar.

ACRL Academic/Research Librarian of the Year Award—$2,000 (equally divided). For an outstanding national or international contribution to academic and research librarianship and library development. *Offered by:* ALA, Association of College and Research Libraries. *Donor:* Baker & Taylor. *Winner:* Beverly P. Lynch, Univ. Libn., Univ. of Illinois Circle Campus, Chicago.

ALA Honorary Life Membership Award. *Offered by:* American Library Association. *Winners:* John Brademas, Jacob Javits, and Lawrence Clark Powell.

ASCLA Exceptional Achievement Award. For recognition of leadership and achievement in the areas of library cooperation and state library development. *Offered by:* Association of Specialized & Cooperative Library Agencies. *Winner:* Alphonse F. Trezza, Dir., Intergovernmental Library Cooperation Project, Federal Library Committee, Library of Congress.

ASCLA Exceptional Service Award. For exceptional service to ASCLA or any of its component areas of service, namely, services to patients, the homebound, medical, nursing, and other professional staff in hospitals, and inmates; demonstrating professional leadership, effective interpretation of program, pioneering activity, or significant research or experimental projects. *Offered by:* Association of Specialized & Cooperative Library Agencies. *Winner:* Phyllis Dalton, Library Consultant, Las Vegas, Nev.

Armed Forces Librarians Achievement Citation. For significant contributions to the development of armed forces library service and to organizations encouraging an interest in libraries and reading. *Offered by:* Armed Forces Librarians Section, ALA Public Library Association. *Winner:* Not awarded in 1981.

Beta Phi Mu Award—$500. For distinguished service to education for librarianship. *Offered by:* ALA Awards Committee. *Donor:* Beta Phi Mu Library Science Honorary Association. *Winner:* Haynes McMullen, professor of library history, Univ. of North Carolina.

Blackwell North America Resources Section Scholarship Award (formerly National Library Service Resources Section Publication Award). Presented to the author/authors of an outstanding monograph, published article, or original paper on acquisitions pertaining to college or university libraries. *Offered by:* ALA Resources and Technical Services Division, Resources Section. *Donor:* Blackwell North America. *Winners:* Robert D. Stueart and George B. Miller, Jr.

Rev. Andrew L. Bouwhuis Scholarship—$1,500. For a person with a B.A. degree who has been accepted in an accredited library school. (Award is based on financial need and proficiency.) *Offered by:* Catholic Library Association. *Winner:* Julia B. Davis.

CASLIS Award for Special Librarianship in Canada. *Offered by:* Canadian Assn. of Special Libraries and Information Services. *Winner:* Dr. Olga Bishop, London, Ont., Canada.

CIS/GODORT/ALA Documents to the People Award—$1,000. For effectively encouraging the use of federal documents in support of library services. *Offered by:* ALA Government Documents Round Table. *Donor:* Congressional Information Service, Inc. *Winner:* LeRoy C. Schwarzkopf.

CLA Outstanding Service to Librarianship Award. *Offered by:* Canadian Library Association. *Winner:* Francis Morrison, former chief, Saskatoon Public Library, Saskatoon, Sask., Canada.

CLR Fellowships. For a list of the recipients for the 1980–1981 academic year, see the report from the Council on Library Resources, Inc., in Part 2 of this *Bowker Annual.*

CSLA Award for Outstanding Congregational Librarian. For distinguished service to the congregation and/or community through devotion to the congregational library. *Offered by:* Church and Synagogue Library Association. *Winner:* Margaret Wade Taylor, Libn., First Baptist Church, Warren, Ohio.

CSLA Award for Outstanding Congregational Library. For responding in creative and innovative ways to the library's mission of reaching and serving the congregation and/or the wider community. *Offered by:* Church and Synagogue Library Association. *Winner:* Lutheran Church of the Holy Comforter, Baltimore, Md.

CSLA Award for Outstanding Contribution to Librarianship. For providing inspiration, guidance, leadership, or resources to enrich the field of church or synagogue librarianship. *Offered by:* Church and Synagogue Library Association. *Winner:* Library Committee, Central Presbyterian Church, Terre Haute, Ind.

CSLA Distinguished Service Award. *Offered by:* Canadian School Librarians Association. *Winner:* Not awarded in 1981.

Francis Joseph Campbell Citation. For an outstanding contribution to the advancement of library service to the blind. *Offered by:* Section on Library Service to the Blind and Physically Handicapped of the Association of Specialized and Cooperative Library Agencies. *Winners:* Blanca Judy Lastropes, former head of Louisiana State Library Service for the Blind and Physically Handicapped.

David H. Clift Scholarship—$3,000. For a worthy student to begin a program of library education at the graduate level. *Offered by:* ALA Awards Committee, Standing Committee on Library Education. *Winners:* Margaret A. Coval and Donna K. Smith.

Elizabeth Dafoe Scholarship—$1,750. For a Canadian citizen or landed immigrant to attend an accredited Canadian library school. *Offered by:* Canadian Library Association. *Winner:* Kathleen Esdaile, Montreal, P.Q., Canada.

John Cotton Dana Award. For exceptional support and encouragement of special librarianship. *Offered by:* Special Libraries Association. *Winner:* Dr. Estelle Brodman.

Melvil Dewey Medal. For recent creative professional achievement of a high order, particularly in library management, library training, cataloging and classification, and the tools and techniques of librarianship. *Offered by:* ALA Awards Committee. *Donor:* Forest Press. *Winner:* Henriette D. Avram, Director for Processing Systems, Networks, and Automation Planning, Library of Congress.

Ida and George Eliot Prize—$100. For an essay published in any journal in the preceding calendar year that has been judged most effective in furthering medical librarianship. *Offered by:* Medical Library Association. *Winner:* Judith M. Topper, Lawrence Hospital Library, Bronxville, N.Y.

Facts on File Award—$1,000. For an individual who has made current affairs more meaningful to adults. *Winners:* U. Patricia Machin and Anne M. Patterson, Westmoreland County Library Board, Greensburg, Pa.

George Freedley Memorial Award. For a publication about live performance theater that is not a compilation of published plays. *Offered by:* Theatre Library Association. *Winner:* Margot Peters, for *Bernard Shaw and the Actresses.*

Muriel E. Fuller Scholarships—$42. Awarded to three persons who show promise in the field of church or synagogue librarianship for a correspondence course in church and synagogue librarianship given by the Division of Continuing Education, Univ. of Utah. *Offered by:* Church & Synagogue Library Association. *Winners:* Betty MacNaughten, Dover, N.J.; Lois A. Laskowski, Greensburg, Ind.; and Laura Machetti, Peoria, Ill.

Louise Giles Minority Scholarship—$3,000. For a worthy student who is a U.S. or Canadian citizen and is also a member of a principal minority group. *Offered by:* ALA Awards Committee, Office for Library Personnel Resources Advisory Committee. *Winners:* Arie Dell Johnson and Cecelia A. Mestas.

Murray Gottlieb Prize—$100. For the best unpublished essay submitted by a medical librarian on the history of some aspect of health sciences or a detailed description of a library exhibit. *Offered by:* Medical Library Association. *Winner:* Not awarded in 1981.

Grolier Foundation Award—$1,000. For an unusual contribution to the stimulation and guidance of reading by children and young people through high school age, for continuing service, or one particular contribution of lasting value. *Offered by:* ALA Awards Committee. *Donor:* Grolier Foundation. *Winner:* Jane Ann McGregor.

Grolier National Library Week Award—$1,000. For the best plan for a public relations program. *Awarded by:* National Library Week Committee of the American Library Association. *Donor:* Grolier Educational Corp. *Winner:* New York Library Association, for a telephone reference service campaign entitled "For Fast Facts, Call Your Library."

Bailey K. Howard-World Book Encyclopaedia-ALA Goal Award—$5,000. To support programs that recognize, advance, and implement the goals and objectives of the American Library Association. *Donor:* World Book-Childcraft International, Inc. *Winner:* ALA Library Administration and Management Association, Statistics Section, for ANSI Z39.7 Field Test Planning Project.

John Phillip Imroth Memorial Award for Intellectual Freedom—$500. For a notable contribution to intellectual freedom and remarkable personal courage. *Offered by:* ALA Intellectual Freedom Round Table. *Donor:* Intellectual Freedom Round Table. *Winner:* Not awarded in 1981.

Information Industry Association Hall of Fame Award. For leadership and innovation in furthering the progress of the information industry. *Offered by:* Information Industry Association. *Winner:* Not awarded in 1981.

Information Product of the Year Award. For excellence in product innovations and development of a product introduced within the past five years. *Offered by:* Information Industry Association. *Winner:* Not awarded in 1981.

Information Technology of the Year Award. For a technology that impacted the information industry. *Offered by:* Information Industry Association. *Winner:* Not awarded in 1981.

JMRT Professional Development Grant. *See* 3M Company Professional Development Grant.

J. Morris Jones-World Book Encyclopaedia-ALA Goal Award—$5,000. To support programs that recognize, advance, and implement the goals and objectives of the American Library Association. *Donor:* World Book-Childcraft International, Inc. *Winner:* ALA Public Library Association's Goals, Guidelines, and Standards for Public Libraries Committee.

William T. Knox Outstanding Information Manager Award. For excellence in managing information resources or for a distinctive contribution to the information management field. *Offered by:* Associated Information Managers. *Winner:* Dr. Craig M. Cook, former principal, Arthur Young & Co., Washington, D.C.

LITA Award for Achievement in Library and Information Technology. For distinguished leadership, notable development or application of technology, superior accomplishments in research or education or original contributions to the literature of the field. *Offered by:* Library and Information Technology Association. *Winner:* Maurice J. Freedman, Associate Professor, School of Library Service, Columbia Univ.

LRRT Research Award—$500. To encourage excellence in library research. *Offered by:* ALA Library Research Round Table. *Winner:* Not awarded in 1981.

Joseph W. Lippincott Award—$1,000. For distinguished service to the profession of librarianship, such service to include outstanding participation in the activities of professional library associations, notable published professional writing, or other significant activity on behalf of the profession and its aims. *Offered by:* ALA Awards Committee. *Donor:* Joseph W. Lippincott. *Winner:* Eric Moon, former president of ALA, 1978–1979.

Margaret Mann Citation. For outstanding professional achievement in the area of cataloging and classification. *Offered by:* ALA Resources and Technical Services Division/Cataloging and Classification Section. *Winner:* Sanford J. Berman, Hennepin County Lib., Edina, Minn.

Allie Beth Martin Award—$2,000. For an outstanding librarian. *Offered by:* ALA

Public Library Association. *Donor:* Baker & Taylor. *Winner:* Birdie Law, Children's Libn., Prince George's County Memorial Lib., Oxon Hill Branch, Md.

Frederic G. Melcher Scholarship—$4,000. For young people who wish to enter the field of library service to children. *Offered by:* ALA Association for Library Service to Children. *Winners:* Yvonne Kathleen Hardy, Santa Rosa, Calif.; Kristi Larane Thomas, Montpelier, Vt.

Isadore Gilbert Mudge Citation. For a distinguished contribution to reference librarianship. *Offered by:* Reference and Adult Services Division of American Library Association. *Winner:* Eugene P. Sheehy, head, Reference Dept., Columbia Univ. Libs.

Gerd Muehsam Award—$50. For the best paper by a graduate student in library or information science on a topic dealing with art librarianship or visual resource curatorship. *Offered by:* Art Libraries Society of North America. *Winner:* Matthew Hogan.

Music Library Association Prizes—$50. For the best book-length bibliography or research tool, for the best article-length bibliography or article on music librarianship by an author not beyond the age of 40, and for the best review of a book or score published in *Notes*. *Offered by:* Music Library Association. *Winners:* Martin Marks (best article) and David Hamilton (best review) (no award in 1981 for best book.)

Shirley Olofson Memorial Award. For individuals to attend their second annual conference of ALA. *Offered by:* ALA Junior Members Round Table. *Winners:* Gale Keresey, James Deutsch, and Barbara F. Greer.

Helen Keating Ott Award. Presented to an individual or institution for a significant contribution to children's literature. *Offered by:* Church and Synagogue Library Association. *Winner:* Phyllis Anderson Wood, South San Francisco, Calif.

Howard V. Phalin-World Book Graduate Scholarship in Library Science—$2,500 (maximum). For a Canadian citizen or landed immigrant to attend an accredited library school in Canada or the United States. *Offered by:* Canadian Library Association. *Winner:* Judith Saltman, Vancouver, B.C., Canada.

Esther J. Piercy Award. For contribution to librarianship in the field of technical services by younger members of the profession. *Offered by:* ALA Resources and Technical Services Division. *Winner:* Sally McCallum, Network Resource Analyst, Library of Congress.

Plenum Scholarship Award—$1,000. For graduate study leading to a doctorate in library or information science. *Offered by:* Special Libraries Association. *Winner:* Ruth Fenske.

Rittenhouse Award—$200. For the best unpublished paper on medical librarianship submitted by a student enrolled in, or having been enrolled in, a course for credit in an ALA-accredited library school, or a trainee in an internship program in medical librarianship. *Offered by:* Medical Library Association. *Winner:* Kathleen Savoy, Louisiana State Univ., Baton Rouge, La.

SLA Hall of Fame. For an extended and sustained period of distinguished service to the Special Libraries Association in all spheres of its activities. *Offered by:* Special Libraries Association. *Winner:* Helen Waldron.

SLA Minority Stipends—$1,500. For students with financial need who show potential for special librarianship. *Offered by:* Special Libraries Association. *Winners:* Arlene Means, Carolyn J. Stephens, and Blaise G. Turney.

SLA Professional Award. For a significant achievement or contribution to librarianship that advances the stated objectives of the Special Libraries Association. *Offered by:* Special Libraries Association. *Winner:* Not awarded in 1981.

SLA Scholarships—$3,000. For students with financial need who show potential for special librarianship. *Offered by:* Special Libraries Association. *Winners:* Elizabeth A. Crosswhite, Deborah C. Osburn, and Patricia Zang.

Charles Scribner's Sons Award—$3,250. To attend ALA's annual conference. *Offered by:* ALA Association for Library Service to Children. *Donor:* Charles Scribner's Sons. *Winners:* Margaret A. Bauer, Janice M. Kellman, Mary E. Michener, and Linda Osburn.

Ralph R. Shaw Award for Library Literature—$500. For an outstanding contribution to library literature issued during the three years preceding the presentation. *Offered by:* ALA Awards Committee. *Donor:* Scarecrow Press. *Winner:* Ruth A. Velleman, for *Serving Physically Disabled People: An Information Handbook* (Bowker).

3M Company Professional Development Grant—$5,000. To encourage professional development and participation of new librarians in ALA and JMRT activities. To cover expenses for recipients to attend ALA conference. *Offered by:* ALA Junior Members Round Table. *Winners:* Marilyn E. Hawkins, Dona J. Helmer, Bennette Pizzimenti, and Linda Williams.

Trustee Citations. For distinguished service to library development whether on the local, state, or national level. *Offered by:* ALA American Library Trustee Association. *Donor:* ALA. *Winners:* Kay L. Vowvalidis, Ozark, Ala; Marie Austin Clarke Goss, Minneapolis, Minn.

H. W. Wilson Co. Award—$500. For the best paper published in *Special Libraries* in 1981. *Offered by:* Special Libraries Association. *Winner:* Patricia Wilson Berger, for "Managing Revolutions."

H. W. Wilson Foundation Award—$2,000. Available to Canadian citizen or landed immigrant for pursuit of studies at an accredited Canadian library school. *Offered by:* Canadian Library Association. *Winner:* Jocelyn Ayers, Williamstown, Ont., Canada.

H. W. Wilson Library Periodical Award—$500. To a periodical published by a local, state, or regional library, library group, or library association in the United States or Canada that has made an outstanding contribution to librarianship. *Offered by:* ALA Awards Committee. *Donor:* H. W. Wilson Co. *Winner:* North Carolina Libraries (North Carolina Lib. Assn.).

H. W. Wilson Library Staff Development Grant—$250. *Offered by:* ALA Awards Committee. *Winner:* Library Personnel Office, Indiana Univ., Bloomington, Ind.

George Wittenborn Memorial Award. For excellence of content and physical design of an art book, exhibition catalog, and/or periodical published in North America. *Offered by:* Art Libraries Society of North America. *Winners:* Yale Univ. Press; Abbeville Press; National Gallery of Art and Yale Univ. Gallery; and Brown Univ. Department of Art.

World Book-Childcraft Awards—$1,000. For continuing education program, distributed to no more than four recipients (candidates must be members of Catholic Library Association). *Offered by:* Catholic Library Association. *Winner:* American Friends of the Vatican Library.

Part 4
Research and Statistics

Library Research and Statistics

RESEARCH ON LIBRARIES AND LIBRARIANSHIP IN 1981

Mary Jo Lynch
Director, Office for Research, American Library Association

It can be said that 1981 was a year of major importance for research on libraries and librarianship, not so much because of specific projects completed or funded during the year but because of an attempt to decide what research ought to be done during the rest of the decade. Late in 1980, the Office of Libraries and Learning Technologies, now in the U.S. Department of Education, awarded a contract to Cuadra Associates "to assist the Department and the wider community it serves, in establishing research priorities for the 1980's in the field of library and information science." After searching the literature and conducting phone interviews with persons considered to be "gatekeepers" in the field, Cuadra Associates developed a preliminary outline of important topics and invited 15 "researchers" to prepare brief proposals for research in one or more of these areas.

One hundred and one proposals were prepared and in July 1981 the 15 researchers plus 11 "practitioners" were invited to a three and one-half day meeting at Airlie House, 50 miles outside Washington, D.C., to consider them. Prior to the meeting, all had given the proposals a preliminary rating. At Airlie House the proposals were discussed and rated and rated again until a consensus was reached on a final list of 20. The participants were uneasy with the requirement that they choose 20 from a collection of admittedly rough proposals. They did so, but insisted that anyone using the top 20 should understand them to be thought-provoking descriptions of what might be done in major problem areas, not specifications for Requests for Proposals (RFPs). The 101 proposals considered in the project were grouped into six areas that indicate how participants viewed the major problems of the field: (1) information generation and provision of library and information services; (2) information users and uses; (3) planning and evaluation of library and information services/systems; (4) economics of library and information services; (5) education and professional issues; and (6) intellectual freedom.

Early in December presidents of 15 major library and information science organizations met in Washington, D.C., to discuss the implications and potential uses of the agenda and methods of disseminating project results. Both T. H. Bell, secretary of the Department of Education, and Donald Senese, assistant secretary for Research and Improvement, spoke to the group about the importance of the agenda project.

From one perspective their remarks are empty because it appears that the national economy will support very little research. On the other hand, the scarcity of resources makes it even more important that they be well spent. What funds are available will most likely go to those who have a clearly articulated plan for spending them. The library and information science community is now ready with such a plan.

TECHNOLOGY

Several proposals prepared for the Airlie House meeting focused on the appropriate role of libraries in the development and dissemination of videotext information services. Libraries in Great Britain are somewhat ahead of those in the United States in this area and the British Library has already awarded grants to the London and South Eastern Library Region (LASER) to investigate a series of issues associated with the creation of a community information data base on Prestel (the British videotext system) and with the use of Prestel in public libraries. In the United States research on the use of videotext is being done primarily by entrepreneurs eager to find out how potential customers will react to the availability of home information systems. For example, the November 1981 issue of *Information Hotline* reported on a nationwide study of this nature to be conducted by Booz, Allen & Hamilton for a number of large corporations including AT&T and IBM.

How people interact with information available on-line was of major concern to participants in the Airlie House meeting. It is also the focus of a current project sponsored by the Council on Library Resources and conducted by J. Mathews and Associates, Online Computer Library Center (OCLC), and the Research Libraries Group. The major objectives of the on-line public access catalog project are "to gather comparable data on existing systems and to provide information that will be useful in guiding the development of future online catalogs." Phase I of the project, which involved development and testing of data-collection instruments and procedures, was completed in 1981. The entire project will assess "the requirements of those who use online catalogs, the influence of the catalogs on user behavior, and the performance of existing catalogs relative to user expectations and needs."

The Council on Library Resources also provided support to the American Library Association (ALA) for a survey of how publicly supported libraries finance on-line search services. A questionnaire prepared by ALA's Office for Research was mailed by three vendors of on-line search services—Bibliographic Retrieval Services (BRS), Lockheed, and Systems Development Corporation (SDC)—to their subscribers in the population of interest. Nine hundred and eighty-five responses have been analyzed in a report published by ALA entitled *Financing Online Search Services in Publicly Supported Libraries*.

RESEARCH LIBRARIES

Research related to one component of the library community will certainly receive special emphasis in the near future through the Professional Education and Training for Research Librarianship (PETREL) project sponsored by the Council on Library Resources (CLR). In April 1981, CLR announced grants totaling up to $740,000 to three library schools—Michigan, Chicago, and UCLA—"to establish professional education and supplementary training programs that relate specifically to college and research librarianship." Objectives of the PETREL project also include "support for research on major issues pertinent to research library management and operations." PETREL will "establish and help carry out a research agenda pertinent to the functions of research libraries."

PUBLIC LIBRARIES

The financing of public libraries was another topic that received attention from the participants in the Airlie House meeting. Two state library agencies also demonstrated their concern by funding studies on the topic in 1981. In June the state of Indiana issued an RFP "to undertake an investigation of the funding of public libraries in Indiana and to document funding alternatives facing libraries, including a mix of federal, state, and local funds." The contract was awarded to a proposal submitted by the University City Science Center of Philadelphia in collaboration with the Center for Information Research at the School of Library and Information Science at Drexel University. Several months later the state of Wisconsin issued an RFP for a "Public Library Development and Funding Study," which will examine some of the same problems in that state. The results of these two investigations should prove to be useful far beyond the states where they will be conducted.

LIBRARY EFFECTIVENESS

Substantial progress was made during 1981 in the measurement of library output, long an activity more talked about than practiced. Paul Kantor's 1980 technical report "Levels of Output Related to Cost of Operation of Scientific and Technical Libraries" (the LORCOST project) was made available to a wider audience through articles in two consecutive issues of *Library Research*. In October it was announced that the National Science Foundation will support a similar study of academic libraries, including both large and small colleges and universities. The C-FAL project (Cost-Function for Academic Libraries) will apply nonlinear econometric models to data from 100 participating libraries "to uncover the average ('normal') relations between costs and services rendered."

Meanwhile, a related though very different effort was being made in the public library field. The Public Library Association's Goals, Guidelines, and Standards Committee received a J. Morris Jones–World Book Encyclopaedia–ALA Goal Award to produce a manual of output measurement. After the committee had done preliminary work on the project, a subcommittee was appointed to complete it. Through the efforts of this subcommittee a consortium consisting of two Maryland public libraries (Baltimore County Public Library and Montgomery County Public Library) and two state library agencies (Maryland and Pennsylvania) funded work done by King Research, Inc. (Douglas Zweizig and Eleanor Jo Dorsey) to develop the desired manual and test it in five libraries. Once tested and revised, the draft was turned over to the full committee, which met for two days in December to review the draft and make plans for its dissemination. Publication of *Output Measures for Public Libraries: A Manual of Standardized Procedures* is expected in the spring of 1982.

An important tool for establishing consistency in measurement of library activities was provided to the library community in May when ALA published the *Library Data Collection Handbook* (*LDCH*). This volume was produced from the manuscript of a report prepared by ALA under contract to the National Center for Education Statistics (NCES). It is a revision of the draft "Handbook of Standard Terminology for Recording and Reporting Information about Libraries" submitted to NCES by another contractor. Both researchers and managers in the library community will find *LDCH* useful.

SALARIES

Plans were made in 1981 for a survey of library salaries to be conducted by ALA's Office for Research and Office for Library Personnel Resources. A sample of academic and public libraries will be surveyed to find out what salaries are paid for a number of specific positions in U.S. libraries. The Library Research Center at the University of Illinois Graduate School of Library and Information Science will conduct the survey in January 1982 under contract to ALA. The results of this survey will tell what salary might be paid to someone in a particular library position, in a particular geographic area. Librarians applying for positions, librarians setting salaries, and others in and outside the library community interested in the compensation of librarians will find the results useful. ALA intends to collect, analyze, and publish this information regularly. [*See also* the article "Recent Library Personnel Surveys" in Part 3 of this volume.—*Ed.*]

RESEARCH REPORTING

Two library publications recently began columns devoted to research. In October 1980, *American Libraries* announced that it would carry commentary on the subject four times a year by Herbert White, dean of the School of Library and Information Science at Indiana University and 1981 winner of the Award of Merit presented annually by the American Society for Information Science (ASIS) to a person who has "made a noteworthy contribution to the field of information science." The September/October 1981 issue of the *RTSD Newsletter* announced the inauguration of the column "Library Research" to be edited by Daniel O'Connor of the Graduate School of Library and Information Studies at Rutgers. "The scope of the column is to highlight ongoing or recently completed research relating to any aspect of technical services." In its Spring 1981 issue, the three-year old journal *Library Research* announced a change of personnel. Jane Robbins Carter, director of the Library School at the University of Wisconsin-Madison was appointed associate editor and will become editor in 1982. Mel Voigt, the first editor of *Library Research*, will then become associate editor.

THE CONTEXT OF LIBRARY SCIENCE

Professor Fritz Machlup, whose earlier work *The Production and Distribution of Knowledge in the United States* (Princeton University Press, 1962) is now being expanded and updated in what is to be a ten-volume work entitled *Knowledge: Its Creation, Distribution and Economic Significance* (Princeton University Press, 1980–), spoke at the October 1981 ASIS conference on the research leading to Volume 4 of the work, *The Disciplines of Information*. Since library science is one of these disciplines, scholars and researchers in the field will be especially interested in this volume. Research is currently being done under Machlup's direction "to analyze the logical and methodological relationships among the disciplines and subject areas that contribute to the scientific study of information." Fields involved have been organized as follows:

1. The Systems Group "concerned with the study of structure and relations, and with the role of information in the processes of feedback and control"
2. The Cognitive Group "concerned with the study of the processing and communication of information by intelligent entities"
3. The Processing Group "concerned with the processing of data and information, and/or the delivery of information products and services"
4. The Foundations Group "consisting of traditional disciplines recognized as organizational units in the structure of our universities"

Library Science falls into the third group, along with "Telecommunications, Computer Science, Informatics, Robotics, Information Systems and Services, and Decision Science(s)."

DEVELOPMENTS IN LIBRARY STATISTICAL ACTIVITIES

Frank L. Schick
Consulting Editor, *Bowker Annual*

Library statistics compiled prior to 1870 were of limited scope; the first continuing series of official library data can be traced to the "Report of the Commissioner of Education—for the year 1870." The last 111 years can be divided into three distinct periods.

1870–1937

During this period, combined statistical research on public, society, and school libraries was conducted either annually or less frequently. College and university library surveys were conducted infrequently. Because the Office of Education (OE) had no separate library unit, library surveys were conducted by statistical staff who requested advice when needed from the American Library Association and other related organizations.

1938–1965

A separate library unit of OE was established to oversee all library activities, including statistical research. Surveys for the different types of libraries were published separately on a cycle of four to six years. Between 1958 and the mid-1960s, academic libraries were surveyed annually; other types of surveys were conducted every two to four years. During this period, both financial support and the professional and statistical staff for library development at OE increased substantially, and library statistics were used to support the then developing federal legislation concerning public, academic, and school libraries and library education.

1965–1980

In 1965, the responsibility for all statistical surveys, including those relating to libraries, was transferred from various parts of OE to the newly created National Center for Education Statistics (NCES).

NCES and LIBGIS Developments

In 1968 library surveys were made the responsibility of a newly established Library Surveys Branch of NCES. Shortly after NCES was created in 1965, it was decided that surveys would be conducted differently. Separate but partly overlapping surveys were discontinued in favor of surveys that combine related statistical surveys into two data systems: Higher Education General Information Survey (HEGIS) and Elementary and Secondary Education General Information Survey (ELSEGIS). In the late 1960s and early 1970s, preparation for the Library General Information Survey (LIBGIS), a library data system similar to HEGIS and ELSEGIS, was started without interrupting ongoing surveys. NCES contracted with the American Library Association (ALA) for the development of an overall program for this purpose, and published *Planning for a Nationwide System of Library Statistics* in 1971. LIBGIS development was carried out through several studies and surveys. During 1971–1972, a study of library and information center statistics and data practices was conducted at the national, state, and local levels. In 1972-1973, a LIBGIS Demonstration Project was undertaken in six states, and a LIBGIS State Participation Project was held in fifteen states to develop and test LIBGIS survey instruments for all types of libraries. Results of these preliminary studies and the national plan both contributed to the development of the LIBGIS system.

The LIBGIS system provides three major features: (1) simultaneous collection of comparable items of basic data from the three key types of libraries (public, college and university, and public elementary and secondary school/media centers) on a biennial basis, as well as from other special libraries affiliated with federal, state, commercial, industrial, and national associations, on a four- to six-year basis; (2) cooperation with state agencies in the areas of survey development, data collection, and manual editing; and (3) sharing of collected and edited data with relevant state agencies to provide uniform statistics to users at the local, state, and national levels in both the public and private sectors.

LIBGIS I, funded in FY 1975, included surveys of public libraries in FY 1974, public school library media centers (fall 1974), and academic (college and university) libraries (fall 1975). This last survey was also a component of HEGIS X. LIBGIS II, funded in FY 1976, covered the following surveys: library cooperatives, consortia, and networks (a survey funded in phases over several years); academic libraries (fall 1976); state library agencies (fall 1976); state libraries serving state governments (fall 1976); and special libraries in commerce and industry (a survey that was not completed). LIBGIS III included surveys of college and university libraries (1977), public libraries (FY 1977-1978), public school libraries/media centers (fall 1978), and federal libraries (1978). LIBGIS IV, funded in FY 1978, consisted of the Library Data Base Handbook project, the survey of library cooperatives and networks, a feasibility study on a public library user survey that was not intended for publication, and a college and university library survey. LIBGIS V, funded in FY 1979, saw the completion of the cooperative and library network survey and the handbook study, as well as the initiation of the first private school library survey and the library human resources survey, which was to be conducted over a few years and was previously known as the Library Manpower Survey.

The following table gives a breakdown by category of surveys initiated under LIBGIS during the period 1960-1980.

LIBRARY SURVEY INITIATIONS
1960–1969 and 1970–1979

	1960–1969	*1970–1979*	*Total*
College & university libraries	9	7	16
Public libraries	5	3	8
Public & private school libraries	3	3	6
Special libraries	2	5	7
Library education & human resources	3	1	4
General surveys and networks	1	5	6

Computerization and Contracting

During the late 1960s and early 1970s, two innovations occurred that are responsible for the restructuring of statistical surveys. First, the editing of survey forms, tabulation of data, and related tasks were changed from hand to machine operations. The use of computers required support staff with different skills. While some data-processing staff were employed to handle this work, additional expertise was needed to cope with new demands. This need, along with other considerations, led to the second change: the gradual transferral of many in-house operations on statistical surveys to outside contracts. This shift placed the Office of Education at midpoint between NCES and potential contractors. The new mode of operation substantially changed the function of program specialists. In keeping with this new environment, the Library Surveys Branch was reorganized in 1977 under a new name, the Learning Resources Branch. This name indicates the widened scope of responsibilities of the branch, which also oversees surveys of museums and educational technology programs.

Finances and Publications

Since extramural contracts entail increased costs, it was fortunate that the Department of Education's Office of Libraries and Learning Technologies provided substantial support for such NCES library surveys as the Library Human Resources Surveys of 1970 and 1980, the Library Statistics Operations Handbook, and other projects. The Federal Library Committee of the Library of Congress partly supported all federal library surveys; some limited financial assistance for inclusion of data items was given by the National Library of Medicine, the National Agricultural Library, and a temporary commission that assisted the U.S. Copyright Office. Between 1960 and 1980, 47 surveys and studies were initiated (see table). During the first decade 24 publications were issued and during the second decade 22 publications. With few exceptions, these publications were produced by the Government Printing Office with assistance from two government agencies, two contractors, three academic institutions, and one library association. During the first decade, publications appeared within two years of the initiation of a survey. This average period nearly doubled during the second decade. The reasons for these delays include such factors as the preparation of Requests for Proposals (RFPs), increased forms-clearance requirements for work delegated by the contract office, emphasis on longer response returns, and additional manuscript reviews.

1980 AND BEYOND

The initiation of new projects and publication of completed projects have slowed down substantially. The following list indicates surveys either already conducted or projected in the last six years.

College and university libraries: 1976, 1977, 1979, 1983

Public libraries: 1974, 1977–1978, 1981

Public school libraries: 1974, 1978

Non–public school libraries: 1980

Library human resources: 1981

Research libraries: 1982

Dates for surveys in other categories had not been established yet at this writing.

Since 1980, the following publications have been issued: *Directory of Library Cooperatives and Networks, 1980; Survey of Special Libraries Serving State Governments, 1981; Library Data Collection Handbook 1981* (out of print, but available from ALA as a reprint); *College and University Libraries, 1966–1977;* and *Public School Library Survey, 1978.* The following publications are expected for 1982: *Final*

Report of the Survey of Library Cooperatives and Networks; Public Library Survey, 1978; and College and University Library Survey, 1979. Two other surveys have not been released: the Federal Library Survey of 1978 and the Nonpublic School Library Survey of 1980.

In times of nearly double-digit inflation and reductions in federal funding for all library programs in the Department of Education from over $245 million in FY 1981 to less than $60 million in FY 1982, projections about future surveys would be difficult to make. As solutions to combat inflation are found, however, new ideas will surface to cope with the cost of surveys and particularly of their publication.

CHARACTERISTICS OF THE U.S. POPULATION SERVED BY LIBRARIES

	Number	Percent
Total U.S. population (July 1, 1981)[a]	229,805,000	100.0
Resident population of 50 states and D.C.	229,304,000	99.8
Armed forces overseas	501,000	0.2
Resident population of U.S. outlying areas (April 1, 1980)[b]	3,555,000	—
U.S. population, five years and over, including armed forces abroad (April 1, 1980)[c]	210,676,000	100.0
5–9 years	16,697,000	7.9
10–14 years	18,241,000	8.6
15–19 years	21,220,000	10.1
20–24 years	21,523,000	10.2
25–64 years	107,451,000	51.0
Age 65 and over	25,544,000	12.1
Public and nonpublic school enrollment (fall 1981)[d]	73,065,000	100.0
Kindergarten through grade 8	31,035,000	42.5
Grades 9–12	14,395,000	19.7
Higher education, total enrollment	12,135,000	16.6
Nonpublic school enrollment[e]	7,750,000	10.6
Kindergarten through grade 8	3,595,000	4.9
Grades 9–12	1,515,000	2.1
Higher education, total enrollment	2,640,000	3.6
Educational status of population aged 25 and over		
Total aged 25 and over (March 1980)[f]	125,295,000	—
With four or more years of college	20,579,000	16.4
With one to three years of college	18,392,000	14.6
With four years of high school or more	84,886,000	67.7
With less than four years of high school	40,408,000	32.2
Residence in and outside metropolitan areas		
Total noninstitutional population (April 1, 1980)[g]	226,505,000	100.0
Nonmetropolitan areas	61,458,000	27.1
Metropolitan areas	165,047,000	72.9
In central cities	66,695,000	29.4
Outside central cities	98,352,000	43.5

CHARACTERISTICS OF THE U.S. POPULATION SERVED BY LIBRARIES (cont.)

	Number	Percent
Employment status		
Total civilian noninstitutional population 16 years old and over (October 1981)[h]	169,252,000	—
Civilian labor force, total	106,736,000	100.0
Employed	98,217,000	92.0
Unemployed	8,520,000	8.0
Occupational groups		
Employed persons, 16 years old and over (December 1981)[i]	97,188,000	100.0
Professional and technical works	16,414,000	16.9
Managers and administrators, except farm	11,074,000	11.3
Clerical workers	18,001,000	18.5
Staff workers	6,302,000	6.5
Craft and kindred workers	12,154,000	12.5
Operatives	13,154,000	13.5
Service workers	13,358,000	13.7
Farm workers	6,773,000	6.9
Total faculty and students served by college and university libraries (fall 1981)[j]	12,975,000	100.0
Faculty	840,000	6.4
Students	12,135,000	93.6

[a] As of July 1, 1981, estimates of the Bureau of the Census, U.S. Department of Commerce. Armed forces overseas include forces stationed in outlying areas of the United States. *Current Population Reports*, Series P-25, no. 906, December, 1981.

[b] As of April 1, 1980, Puerto Rico, Guam, Virgin Islands, American Samoa, and the Trust Territory of the Pacific Islands. Includes members of the armed forces overseas stationed in these outlying areas. 1980 Census of Population and Housing Preliminary Reports PHC 80-P-54, 55, 56; information also derived from press releases.

[c] As of July 1, 1978, age data are Series II estimates by the Bureau of the Census, U.S. Department of Commerce. 1980 Census of the Population, Supplementary Report PC80-S1-1.

[d] As of fall 1981, estimates of the U.S. Department of Education, National Center for Education Statistics, Back-to-School press release, September 6, 1981.

[e] A segment of public and nonpublic school enrollment reported above. Percentages for nonpublic school enrollment are based on the total figure for public and nonpublic school enrollment.

[f] Educational Attainment in the United States (March 1979 and 1978), published by the U.S. Bureau of the Census in *Current Population Reports*, Series P-20, no. 356.

[g] *Advance Reports*, 1980 Census of the Population. U.S. Bureau of the Census, PHC-80-V, 1-52.

[h] U.S. Department of Labor, Bureau of Labor Statistics. From *Employment and Earnings*, Table I: "Employment Status of Noninstitutional Population 16 Years and Over, 1947 to Date."

[i] U.S. Department of Labor, Bureau of Labor Statistics, "The Employment Situation: December 1981" (press release), issued January 8, 1982. Subject to revisions.

[j] As of fall 1981, estimates of the U.S. Department of Education, National Center for Education Statistics, Back-to-School press release, Sept. 6, 1981. Faculty includes full-time and part-time staff with the rank of instructor or above and junior staff, such as graduate assistants, who provide instruction in colleges, universities, and professional schools.

NUMBER OF LIBRARIES IN THE UNITED STATES AND CANADA

Statistics are from the thirty-fourth edition of the *American Library Directory* (*ALD*) edited by Jaques Cattell Press (R. R. Bowker, 1981). Data are exclusive of elementary and secondary school libraries. The directory does not list small public libraries. Law libraries with fewer than 10,000 volumes are included only if they specialize in a specific field. The count of the libraries listed, shown separately under the Summary section below, is from the R. R. Bowker Company's mailing lists. In addition to listing and describing some 32,400 individual libraries, the thirty-fourth edition of *ALD* lists over 350 library consortia, including processing and purchasing centers and other specialized organizations.

LIBRARIES IN THE UNITED STATES

A. Public libraries 8,782
   Public libraries with branches 1,284
   Public library branches .. 6,049
   Total public libraries (including branches) 14,831*
B. Junior college libraries ... 1,198
   Departmental 37
   Departmental religious 2
   University and college ... 1,892
   Departmental 1,669
   Departmental law ... 138
   Departmental medicine 139
   Departmental religious 20
   Total academic libraries .. 4,796
C. Armed forces
   Air Force 132
   Medical 17
   Army 186
   Law 3
   Medical 26
   Navy 167
   Law 1
   Medical 17
   Total armed forces libraries 485*
D. Government libraries 1,615
   Law 403
   Medical 254
   Total government libraries 1,615*
E. Special libraries 4,637*
F. Law libraries 404*
G. Medical libraries 1,640*
H. Religious libraries 870*
   Total law (including academic, armed forces and government) 949
   Total medical (including academic, armed forces and government) 2,095
   Total religious (including academic) 890
   Total special (including all law, medical and religious) 8,571
   Total libraries counted (*) 29,278

LIBRARIES IN REGIONS ADMINISTERED BY THE UNITED STATES

A. Public libraries 12
   Public libraries with branches 4
   Public library branches .. 18
   Total public libraries (including branches) ... 30*
B. Junior college libraries ... 8
   University and college libraries 27
   Departmental 13
   Departmental law ... 2
   Total academic libraries .. 48*

C. Armed forces
   Air Force 1
   Army 1
   Navy 4
   Total armed forces 6*
D. Government libraries 13
   Law 6
   Medical 2
   Total government libraries 13*
E. Special libraries 13*
F. Medical libraries 4
   Total libraries counted (*) 114

LIBRARIES IN CANADA

A. Public libraries 727
   Public libraries with branches 125
   Public library branches .. 853
   Total public libraries (including branches) ... 1,580*
B. Junior college libraries ... 99
   Departmental 11

   Departmental medicine 2
   University and college ... 148
   Departmental 225
   Departmental law ... 18
   Departmental medicine 27
   Departmental religious 9
   Total academic libraries .. 483*
C. Government libraries 254*
D. Special libraries 478*
E. Law libraries 23*
F. Medical libraries 127*
G. Religious libraries 50*
   Total libraries counted (*) 2,995

SUMMARY

Total U.S. libraries 29,278
Total libraries administered by the United States 114
Total Canadian libraries 2,995
Grand total libraries listed ... 32,387

Note: Numbers followed by an asterisk are added to find "Total libraries counted" for each of the three geographic areas (United States, U.S.-administered regions, and Canada). The sum of the three totals is the "Grant total libraries listed" in the *ALD* (shown in the Summary). For details on the count of libraries, see the preface to the thirty-fourth edition of the *ALD—Ed.*

PUBLIC AND ACADEMIC LIBRARY ACQUISITION EXPENDITURES

Every two years the R. R. Bowker Company compiles statistics on library acquisition expenditures from information reported in the *American Library Directory*. The statistics given here are based on information from the 33rd edition of the directory (1980), which was compiled from questionnaire responses received between fall 1979 and spring 1980. In most cases the statistics reflect expenditures for the 1978–1979 period.

The total number of public libraries listed in the 33rd edition of the *ALD* is 8,717, while the total for academic libraries is 4,618. Not included in the *ALD* are public libraries with annual incomes of less than $2,000 or book funds of less than $500 (of which there are an estimated 2,500 libraries) or law libraries of less than 10,000 volumes (of which there are approximately 330).

UNDERSTANDING THE TABLES

Number of Libraries includes only those libraries in the *ALD* that reported either annual income or acquisition expenditures (8,037 public libraries; 2,413 academic libraries). Those libraries that did not report acquisition expenditures but did report annual income are included in the count, although they are not reflected in the columns of acquisition expenditure figures.

Total Acquisition Expenditures for a given state is almost always greater than (in a few cases equal to) the sum of the Categories of Expenditure. This is because the Total Acquisition Expenditures amount also includes the expenditures of libraries that did not itemize by category.

Categories of Expenditure. Figures in these columns represent only those libraries that itemized expenditures. Libraries that reported a total acquisition expenditure amount but did not itemize are only represented in the Total Acquisition Expenditures column.

Unspecified includes monies reported as not specifically books, periodicals, AV, microform, or binding (e.g., library materials) or any of the categories in combination. When libraries report only Total Acquisition Expenditures without itemizing by category, the total amount is *not* reflected as unspecified.

Estimated Percent of Acquisitions is based on a comparison of the total expenditures for each of the categories and the total of all of the categories, i.e., the total amount spent on books in the United States was compared with the sum of all of the categories of expenditure. The reader should note, therefore, that the percentages are not based on the figures in the Total Acquisition Expenditures column.

Note: This is a reprint of the article that appeared in the 1981 *Bowker Annual*.

PUBLIC AND ACADEMIC LIBRARY ACQUISITION EXPENDITURES / 317

TABLE 1 PUBLIC LIBRARY ACQUISITION EXPENDITURES

State	Number of Libraries	Total Acquisition Expenditures	Books	Periodicals	Audiovisual	Microform	Binding	Unspecified
Alabama	138	$ 4,469,065	$ 1,474,580	$ 173,030	$ 148,940	$ 254,930	$ 36,327	$ 164,140
Alaska	22	992,272	329,142	119,060	75,100	160,100	14,590	—
Arizona	74	3,647,604	1,741,673	165,143	122,483	42,320	55,615	110,737
Arkansas	46	1,930,732	459,130	38,216	6,141	1,459	8,971	13,569
California	184	38,533,254	25,893,505	2,192,879	952,139	213,425	303,210	179,954
Colorado	122	9,971,430	2,448,254	259,957	98,755	20,967	62,992	353,559
Connecticut	165	6,321,715	2,052,596	247,503	192,579	12,629	54,504	95,169
Delaware	24	618,270	416,798	117,432	52,395	2,000	—	—
District of Columbia	1	815,100	647,600	114,500	53,000	—	—	—
Florida	129	5,338,591	2,354,010	273,307	294,081	57,296	50,362	43,400
Georgia	52	5,059,864	2,343,433	271,995	264,105	120,423	98,580	5,918
Hawaii	1	1,327,145	—	—	—	—	—	—
Idaho	100	1,454,696	617,833	67,584	51,726	7,212	4,844	4,591
Illinois	563	37,131,537	8,859,953	1,549,606	1,288,801	653,710	245,164	454,963
Indiana	223	7,290,287	4,160,173	482,881	513,351	67,280	137,781	80,757
Iowa	489	5,850,787	1,705,158	223,468	193,034	49,757	21,826	4,160
Kansas	304	6,192,208	2,026,345	273,025	92,285	32,899	33,358	—
Kentucky	107	15,277,741	2,452,090	148,558	328,591	15,807	36,441	21,349
Louisiana	68	5,509,053	1,559,188	261,814	164,030	15,479	58,721	534,435
Maine	164	2,765,996	744,037	101,638	30,925	16,103	11,852	10,723
Maryland	31	14,670,292	3,772,413	259,892	436,632	18,048	79,600	988,117
Massachusetts	346	11,291,409	5,421,566	537,933	441,784	132,348	128,000	2,181,139
Michigan	367	15,876,598	6,140,375	727,819	684,563	121,384	138,568	76,245
Minnesota	134	9,677,799	3,593,396	425,381	516,364	55,712	89,142	29
Mississippi	51	1,968,952	1,128,860	124,388	94,182	25,668	18,016	31,000
Missouri	122	12,139,967	3,279,023	313,410	237,140	272,064	93,505	298,800
Montana	75	894,614	500,700	40,840	27,534	400	3,230	102,662
Nebraska	241	4,789,573	786,137	82,869	138,472	32,005	21,268	17,473
Nevada	23	1,143,777	275,923	34,089	20,750	13,673	6,007	402,696
New Hampshire	216	3,232,829	1,060,242	35,548	88,732	4,692	6,750	12,712
New Jersey	309	19,596,090	6,984,922	947,302	616,501	160,922	83,298	208,846
New Mexico	46	1,405,975	535,452	63,259	13,129	1,104	4,540	—

TABLE 1 PUBLIC LIBRARY ACQUISITION EXPENDITURES (cont.)

State	Number of Libraries	Total Acquisition Expenditures	Books	Periodicals	Categories of Expenditure Audiovisual	Microform	Binding	Unspecified
New York	719	23,531,673	17,760,718	1,968,985	811,116	197,036	309,021	2,533,503
North Carolina	131	4,382,827	1,636,940	266,197	185,505	21,253	33,174	93,418
North Dakota	55	640,718	396,683	27,436	71,483	7,800	1,800	
Ohio	250	28,080,847	10,403,314	1,250,985	1,367,491	87,823	307,792	161,311
Oklahoma	84	3,526,875	1,243,423	229,511	184,568	37,734	36,003	6,468
Oregon	97	2,551,534	1,559,336	147,899	64,012	5,700	7,815	54,804
Pennsylvania	424	8,647,110	4,242,096	886,860	282,175	154,115	73,261	2,909,634
Rhode Island	47	856,204	492,920	55,586	18,598	12,021	16,274	17,659
South Carolina	40	1,904,883	970,666	64,285	80,734	5,767	25,514	265,268
South Dakota	70	858,677	401,756	75,848	95,548	28,184	10,123	4,679
Tennessee	94	2,770,329	1,827,978	229,935	298,098	31,295	25,994	306,005
Texas	359	11,411,398	17,342,085	1,467,427	802,460	50,196	331,377	2,013,904
Utah	46	2,253,563	659,580	32,646	74,860	2,500	42,675	
Vermont	175	793,074	336,562	36,945	18,018	4,951	3,309	11,787
Virginia	81	7,769,895	3,636,466	455,707	274,922	117,513	90,206	227,811
Washington	65	11,218,946	3,161,732	464,851	459,786	28,447	23,943	204,416
West Virginia	77	1,488,594	787,882	58,354	212,123	2,850	13,251	116,750
Wisconsin	320	9,752,421	2,877,886	405,577	372,025	30,796	40,918	100,635
Wyoming	22	642,073	328,115	35,196	36,098	3,000	9,900	
Pacific Islands	2	100,715	127,323	34,926	65,085	1,000	2,000	
Puerto Rico	1	2,278,660						
Virgin Islands	1	90,000						
Total U.S.	8,037	$382,736,238	$165,957,968	$18,869,482	$14,012,949	$3,411,797	$3,311,412	$15,424,195
Estimated % of Acquisitions			75	8.5	6.3	1.5	1.5	7

PUBLIC AND ACADEMIC LIBRARY ACQUISITION EXPENDITURES / 319

TABLE 2 COLLEGE AND UNIVERSITY LIBRARY ACQUISITION EXPENDITURES

State	Number of Libraries	Total Acquisition Expenditures	Books	Periodicals	Audiovisual	Microform	Binding	Unspecified
Alabama	44	$ 5,474,871	$ 1,973,280	$ 1,035,309	$ 119,163	$ 121,017	$ 159,979	$ 1,190,026
Alaska	7	1,782,694	486,326	173,012	23,445	34,703	16,418	—
Arizona	17	4,680,822	1,244,157	734,686	74,408	27,700	100,317	—
Arkansas	24	3,115,641	1,140,399	531,236	47,000	77,584	76,051	463,271
California	178	44,943,094	15,995,522	10,416,914	1,036,233	928,988	2,609,933	5,164,731
Colorado	29	4,636,719	2,219,750	2,416,507	285,990	132,132	240,659	403,544
Connecticut	36	5,746,848	1,930,984	1,283,940	35,629	86,320	371,533	—
Delaware	8	3,159,077	891,755	543,760	5,800	5,242	98,187	—
District of Columbia	12	1,368,518	1,767,648	1,103,853	28,006	100,340	193,934	606,274
Florida	74	16,429,666	11,847,182	4,530,412	856,257	1,006,627	969,164	901,601
Georgia	59	8,950,621	3,442,884	3,056,031	126,143	165,731	497,434	257,350
Hawaii	13	1,928,695	1,040,103	131,950	67,717	72,951	154,400	649,100
Idaho	8	418,581	834,213	594,264	71,388	30,971	39,708	—
Illinois	104	19,088,862	6,262,327	4,503,533	579,824	201,561	988,291	1,529,668
Indiana	47	13,555,190	3,619,526	2,957,744	119,284	51,458	539,289	2,002,806
Iowa	46	5,496,000	1,528,724	2,501,012	68,924	163,930	355,378	189,240
Kansas	47	3,284,520	2,448,944	2,040,305	132,903	313,419	228,182	3,000
Kentucky	38	5,087,353	2,469,641	1,732,023	76,750	53,517	249,662	76,590
Louisiana	25	3,388,941	2,273,571	1,836,452	56,411	161,837	351,635	915,680
Maine	26	1,958,957	606,028	359,334	21,730	19,175	47,120	17,000
Maryland	41	3,043,121	33,752	1,287,873	107,548	122,754	262,240	32,309
Massachusetts	84	9,065,191	5,122,610	3,935,042	275,816	201,338	1,212,973	4,267,974
Michigan	75	19,527,904	3,774,158	2,666,912	266,418	194,566	633,098	3,433,210
Minnesota	47	3,818,177	2,694,977	1,996,127	119,954	55,100	296,977	207,194
Mississippi	41	3,536,352	1,051,880	912,515	104,714	174,709	178,436	11,800
Missouri	57	7,635,330	2,901,168	3,308,946	239,164	283,520	372,811	16,442
Montana	11	591,859	247,791	359,295	9,593	1,540	17,000	—
Nebraska	22	2,915,002	1,720,610	1,382,116	122,832	79,132	140,339	175,290
Nevada	6	2,231,873	411,004	356,142	9,855	800	59,999	—
New Hampshire	20	2,518,122	948,471	541,285	44,278	133,813	75,192	628,923
New Jersey	51	4,720,226	4,154,255	2,431,823	362,927	254,364	378,248	4,373,884
New Mexico	21	2,291,258	1,011,051	471,760	36,318	13,922	137,854	80,321

TABLE 2 COLLEGE AND UNIVERSITY LIBRARY ACQUISITION EXPENDITURES (cont.)

State	Number of Libraries	Total Acquisition Expenditures	Books	Periodicals	Audiovisual	Microform	Binding	Unspecified
New York	169	27,655,358	11,914,842	7,078,700	501,747	635,948	1,323,018	2,882,630
North Carolina	103	17,353,428	4,116,954	3,536,736	255,919	111,215	561,683	2,226,365
North Dakota	14	840,284	680,126	533,613	33,771	13,092	36,463	150,000
Ohio	96	11,802,055	6,031,988	4,786,889	246,640	285,043	838,678	1,513,249
Oklahoma	43	3,151,402	1,021,867	1,293,887	54,527	83,803	141,729	1,040,084
Oregon	35	6,337,957	1,989,362	2,250,307	112,628	145,228	219,279	—
Pennsylvania	137	19,489,719	6,897,438	6,443,622	301,010	625,895	970,636	514,140
Rhode Island	14	2,721,536	893,060	925,046	12,282	25,562	152,006	44,626
South Carolina	49	4,221,632	2,123,830	1,687,066	87,208	72,939	227,696	113,101
South Dakota	15	1,074,975	420,872	326,908	33,738	14,950	38,541	—
Tennessee	51	12,416,235	2,832,498	3,000,061	192,027	208,765	427,828	728,587
Texas	126	20,754,939	11,763,810	6,527,831	817,557	376,135	954,660	3,184,625
Utah	10	1,587,577	1,114,919	492,900	70,273	5,500	121,735	5,000
Vermont	17	473,882	935,982	661,185	25,258	31,415	86,816	1,252
Virginia	68	8,988,067	3,964,052	2,464,810	245,865	175,452	341,649	15,000
Washington	40	7,695,761	3,521,050	3,508,331	343,292	43,793	506,021	13,039
West Virginia	19	1,328,793	537,611	386,293	63,816	62,603	32,930	26,611
Wisconsin	62	6,831,560	4,080,033	3,649,887	253,663	92,920	402,288	71,024
Wyoming	7	972,778	418,895	479,475	31,036	2,706	40,224	6,812
Pacific Islands	3	76,800	19,666	3,480	3,299	—	—	—
Puerto Rico	17	830,971	574,341	323,980	123,555	5,097	44,994	112,500
Total U.S.	2,413	$372,995,794	$153,947,797	$122,493,120	$9,341,548	$8,288,822	$19,521,315	$40,230,873
Estimated % of Acquisitions			43.5	34.6	2.6	2.3	5.5	11.4

URBAN-SUBURBAN PUBLIC LIBRARY STATISTICS

Joseph Green

Atlantic County Library, Egg Harbor City, NJ

Since 1972 (with the exception of 1980), data have been collected from several urban and suburban public library systems around the United States. The collection of pertinent data about comparative use between urban libraries and the suburban libraries around those urban agencies is our primary goal. However, comparisons between urban libraries on a national basis can also be made.

A library system is defined as one that is centrally funded and uses a common policy for controlling the basic operation of public libraries within a particular jurisdiction. This strict definition makes it difficult to survey many suburban libraries that are either cooperatives or federations, among them those in the suburbs of New York, Chicago, and Philadelphia.

Of the 50 libraries questioned, 36 answered the survey for a 72 percent response rate. Some earlier respondents did not participate this year while earlier nonparticipants chose this year to send information. This situation, of course, causes inconsistency in the survey.

Figures dating from 1969 to 1979 can be found in various editions of the *Bowker Annual*.

In Tables 1 through 6, the libraries are arranged by reported population, largest to smallest. The following abbreviations are used in the tables: "C" for calendar year, "F" for fiscal year, "U" for urban libraries, "S" for suburban libraries, and "U/S" for urban-suburban libraries.

Once again, we issue our annual caveat to anyone using the data in budget work. Because the survey participants use the statistics to meet their own local priorities, it is difficult to draw anything greater than informal comparisons between libraries.

TABLE 1 TOTAL LIBRARY SERVICE AREA POPULATION AND TOTAL OPERATING EXPENSES, 1980-1981

Library	Population 1980	Population 1981	Total Operating Expenses 1980	Total Operating Expenses 1981
Chicago Public Lib., IL (U) (C)	3,369,359	3,005,072	$27,273,792	$25,273,441
Los Angeles Public Lib., CA (U) (F)	2,817,800	2,966,763	15,110,324	16,587,592
Brooklyn Public Lib., NY (U) (F)	2,230,936	2,230,936	16,013,365	19,141,636
Philadelphia Public Lib., PA (U) (C)	1,950,098	1,950,098	17,255,960	17,070,653
Houston Public Lib., TX (U) (C)	1,232,802	1,573,847	1,935,414	10,781,107
Detroit Public Lib., MI (U) (C)	1,203,339	1,203,339	14,138,129	14,012,771
Buffalo/Erie County Public Lib., NY (U/S) (C)	1,113,491	1,113,491	11,680,265	11,945,950
Orange County Public Lib., CA (S) (F)	940,025	972,625	8,219,793	11,336,135
Milwaukee Public Lib., WI (U) (C)	981,362	971,646	9,291,000	9,923,000
San Antonio Public Lib., TX (U) (F)	926,000	924,207	2,770,203	3,294,691
San Diego Public Lib., CA (U) (F)	842,200	887,700	5,528,336	5,836,437
Cincinnati/Hamilton County Public Lib., OH (U/S) (C)	924,000	873,000	8,763,052	9,619,890
St. Louis County Public Lib., MO (S) (C)	767,937	816,672	5,890,779	6,779,443
Enoch Pratt Free Lib., Baltimore, MD (U) (F)	783,320	783,320	9,621,808	10,240,185
Memphis/Shelby County Public Lib., TX (U/S) (F)	756,800	777,113	6,196,212	6,871,578
King County Lib. System, WA (S) (C)	712,000	751,680	5,697,821	6,610,612
Columbus/Franklin County Public Lib., OH (U/S) (C)	700,000	700,000	6,677,029	7,575,804
Louisville Public Lib., KY (U/S) (F)	695,055	684,793	5,196,670	5,055,587
San Francisco Public Lib., CA (U) (F)	642,900	680,700	8,207,207	8,041,271
Prince George's County Memorial Lib., MD (S) (F)	666,603	665,071	8,301,104	8,657,185
Baltimore County Public Lib., MD (S) (F)	655,615	655,615	9,683,882	10,395,986
Fairfax County Public Lib., VA (S) (F)	614,800	641,800	6,256,526	7,172,821
Cuyahoga County Public Lib., OH (S) (C)	620,000	620,000	11,371,272	11,715,339
Jacksonville Public Lib. System, FL (U/S) (F)	598,218	603,785	3,574,660	3,717,883
Contra Costa County Lib. System, CA (S) (F)	574,500	590,500	5,016,178	5,134,318
Hennepin County Lib. System, MN (S) (C)	573,246	576,508	7,828,431	8,909,656
Cleveland Public Lib., OH (U) (C)	625,000	572,000	12,153,389	13,827,652
New Orleans Public Lib., LA (U) (C)	599,129	569,125	3,061,308	3,361,246
Dayton/Montgomery County Public Lib., OH (U/S) (C)	568,353	568,353	4,293,040	5,147,457
Denver Public Lib., CO (U) (C)	515,000	515,000	7,499,200	8,682,400
Fresno County Public Lib., CA (U/S) (F)	479,850	507,875	3,492,871	3,682,375
St. Louis Public Lib., MO (U) (C)	525,000	465,000	4,868,085	4,938,720
Tulsa City/County Lib., OK (U/S) (F)	450,000	460,000	4,068,354	4,304,875
Pittsburgh Public Lib., PA (U) (C)	520,117	423,960	6,930,578	7,370,093
Annapolis/Anne Arundel County Public Lib., MD (U/S) (F)	368,000	372,800	3,531,312	4,062,803
Omaha Public Lib., NE (U) (C)	314,255	314,255	2,435,953	2,576,101

TABLE 2   TOTAL PUBLIC LIBRARY STATE AND FEDERAL AID, 1980–1981

Library	Total State Aid 1980	Total State Aid 1981	Total Federal Aid 1980	Total Federal Aid 1981
Chicago Public Lib., IL (U) (C)	$4,875,876	$4,463,387	$401,723	$508,241
Los Angeles Public Lib., CA (U) (F)	92,053	11,995	0	0
Brooklyn Public Lib., NY (U) (F)	2,227,495	2,181,761	1,511,875	1,121,017
Philadelphia Public Lib., PA (U) (C)	2,341,147	2,458,262	242,673	136,351
Houston Public Lib., TX (U) (C)	0	0	0	0
Detroit Public Lib., MI (U) (C)	1,047,995	1,017,796	58,075	88,538
Buffalo/Erie County Public Lib., NY (U/S) (C)	1,768,428	1,549,462	254,802	313,091
Orange County Public Lib., CA (S)(F)	3,070,451	2,734,407	0	0
Milwaukee Public Lib., WI (U) (C)	0	0	0	0
San Antonio Public Lib., TX (U) (F)	72,913	91,063	155,495	72,913
San Diego Public Lib., CA (U) (F)	1,153	492	607,900	624,914
Cincinnati/Hamilton County Public Lib., OH (U/S) (C)	243,414	181,286	0	0
St. Louis County Public Lib., MO (S) (C)	271,112	291,183	50,000	50,000
Enoch Pratt Free Lib., Baltimore, MD (U) (F)	4,920,039	5,253,277	772,960	879,552
Memphis/Shelby County Public Lib., TX (U/S) (F)	376,592	333,815	257,957	212,197
King County Lib. System, WA (S) (C)	0	0	0	0
Columbus/Franklin County Public Lib., OH (U/S) (C)	0	0	0	0
Louisville Public Lib., KY (U/S) (F)	125,230	106,523	138,257	168,934
San Francisco Public Lib., CA (U) (F)	28,636	23,987	995,057	338,742
Prince George's County Memorial Lib., MD (S) (F)	1,350,982	1,350,697	156,031	190,184
Baltimore County Public Lib., MD (S) (F)	1,026,853	1,020,965	0	0
Fairfax County Public Lib., VA (S)(F)	148,911	249,673	2,538	0
Cuyahoga County Public Lib., OH (S) (C)	0	0	0	0
Jacksonville Public Lib. System, FL (U/S) (F)	248,398	298,057	211,423	219,643
Contra Costa County Lib. System, CA (S) (F)	13,849	12,759	19,471	22,520
Hennepin County Lib. System, MN (S) (C)	258,083	326,996	n/a	n/a
Cleveland Public Lib., OH (U) (C)	551,747	255,445	0	0
New Orleans Public Lib., LA (U) (C)	232,275	233,043	116,102	113,558
Dayton/Montgomery County Public Lib., OH (U/S) (C)	3,006	2,139	40,910	9,405
Denver Public Lib., CO (U) (C)	488,000	492,000	0	0
Fresno County Public Lib., CA (U/S) (F)	672,771	1,061	574,525	703,610
St. Louis Public Lib., MO (U) (C)	223,251	179,230	138,923	169,606
Tulsa City-County Lib., OK (U/S)(F)	124,671	158,942	0	0
Pittsburgh Public Lib., PA (U) (C)	1,491,280	1,530,762	2,333,463	2,864,370
Annapolis/Anne Arundel County Public Lib., MD (U/S) (F)	734,931	762,680	66,548	52,192
Omaha Public Lib., NE (U) (C)	34,474	35,839	12,000	12,000

TABLE 3   PUBLIC LIBRARY SALARY AND OTHER EXPENDITURES, 1980–1981

Library	Salary Expenditures 1980	Salary Expenditures 1981	Other Expenditures 1980	Other Expenditures 1981
Chicago Public Lib., IL (U)(C)	$17,062,903	$17,366,636	$8,027,320	$11,354,360
Los Angeles Public Lib., CA (U) (F)	14,482,057	16,587,306	628,267	843,286
Brooklyn Public Lib., NY (U) (F)	12,899,693	13,768,676	5,439,846	7,855,836
Philadelphia Public Lib., PA (U) (C)	14,116,551	13,979,575	555,589	496,465
Houston Public Lib., TX (U) (C)	5,744,271	6,819,894	340,863	498,838
Detroit Public Lib., MI (U) (C)	10,950,300	10,691,314	3,547,829	3,321,457
Buffalo/Erie County Public Lib., NY (U/S) (C)	8,992,079	9,393,914	2,688,187	2,552,035
Orange County Public Lib., CA (S) (F)	3,937,773	4,397,878	4,282,020	6,938,257
Milwaukee Public Lib., WI (U) (C)	7,532,000	8,082,000	1,759,000	1,841,000
San Antonio Public Lib., TX (U) (F)	1,597,210	1,842,536	1,172,993	2,201,155
San Diego Public Lib., CA (U) (F)	3,546,220	3,909,840	1,982,116	1,926,597
Cincinnati/Hamilton County Public Lib., OH (U/S) (C)	5,489,130	5,897,909	3,273,922	3,721,981
St. Louis County Public Lib., MO (S) (C)	3,850,086	4,676,222	2,040,693	2,103,191
Enoch Pratt Free Lib., Baltimore, MD (U) (F)	6,619,495	7,280,083	1,866,279	1,681,389
Memphis/Shelby County Public Lib., TX (U/S) (F)	4,522,677	5,109,609	1,673,535	1,761,969
King County Lib. System, WA (S) (C)	3,627,834	4,299,032	2,069,987	2,311,580
Columbus/Franklin County Public Lib., OH (U/S) (C)	3,593,338	4,035,732	3,083,691	3,538,072
Louisville Public Lib., KY (U/S) (F)	2,712,405	2,823,957	2,484,266	2,231,630
San Francisco Public Lib., CA (U) (F)	6,823,769	6,387,424	1,374,931	1,624,972
Prince George's County Memorial Lib., MD (S) (F)	5,713,921	5,882,765	2,460,199	2,626,060
Baltimore County Public Lib., MD (S) (F)	6,278,418	6,870,533	3,405,464	3,525,453
Fairfax County Public Lib., VA (S) (F)	4,501,449	5,060,212	1,755,077	2,112,609
Cuyahoga County Public Lib., OH (S) (C)	6,096,497	6,025,185	4,932,017	5,421,233
Jacksonville Public Lib. System, FL (U/S) (F)	2,323,467	2,509,071	1,251,193	1,208,811
Contra Costa County Lib. System, CA (S) (F)	3,308,041	3,513,536	1,629,973	1,595,973
Hennepin County Lib. System, MN (S) (C)	5,370,392	6,044,254	2,458,039	2,865,402
Cleveland Public Lib., OH (U) (C)	7,608,107	8,380,545	4,545,282	5,447,107
New Orleans Public Lib., LA (U) (C)	1,614,544	1,588,516	1,446,764	1,772,730

TABLE 3   PUBLIC LIBRARY SALARY AND OTHER EXPENDITURES, 1980–1981
(cont.)

Library	Salary Expenditures 1980	Salary Expenditures 1981	Other Expenditures 1980	Other Expenditures 1981
Dayton/Montgomery County Public Lib., OH (U/S) (C)	2,548,011	2,758,391	1,745,029	1,839,943
Denver Public Lib., CO (U) (C)	5,959,025	6,243,300	1,540,175	2,439,200
Fresno County Public Lib., CA (U/S) (F)	2,565,710	2,699,751	927,161	982,624
St. Louis Public Lib., MO (U) (C)	3,649,087	3,579,273	1,218,998	1,359,447
Tulsa City-County Lib., OK (U/S) (F)	2,381,942	2,762,783	1,090,138	1,273,940
Pittsburgh Public Lib., PA (U) (C)	5,121,149	5,619,078	1,809,429	1,751,015
Annapolis/Anne Arundel County Public Lib., MD (U/S) (F)	2,327,085	2,563,607	1,204,228	1,499,197
Omaha Public Lib., NE (U) (C)	1,626,753	1,864,604	809,201	711,497

TABLE 4 PUBLIC LIBRARY CIRCULATION, REFERENCE FIGURES, AND SERVICE OUTLETS, 1980–1981

Library	Circulation 1980	Circulation 1981	Reference Figures 1980	Reference Figures 1981	Service Outlets 1980	Service Outlets 1981
Chicago Public Lib., IL (U) (C)	6,608,290	7,229,063	4,007,780	5,257,749	88	88
Los Angeles Public Lib., CA (U) (F)	10,836,108	10,842,753	16,872,038	12,314,960	141	141
Brooklyn Public Lib., NY (U) (F)	6,983,217	6,667,318	2,706,754	2,534,443	59	59
Philadelphia Public Lib., PA (U) (C)	4,903,301	5,003,398	1,457,908	2,016,733	52	52
Houston Public Lib., TX (U) (C)	5,503,313	5,753,205	2,086,893	2,222,110	30	30
Detroit Public Lib., MI (U) (C)	1,921,921	1,719,039	2,508,367	2,345,429	32	32
Buffalo/Erie County Public Lib., NY (U/S) (C)	5,454,117	5,671,596	—	—	63	63
Orange County Public Lib., CA (S) (F)	5,821,330	6,604,297	634,210	826,358	116	79
Milwaukee Public Lib., WI (U) (C)	3,287,607	3,073,243	1,300,142	1,385,533	13	13
San Antonio Public Lib., TX (U) (F)	2,244,943	2,197,592	—	—	16	16
San Diego Public Lib., CA (U) (F)	4,102,386	4,235,888	1,149,268	1,237,632	31	31
Cincinnati/Hamilton County Public Lib., OH (U/S) (C)	5,654,005	5,845,093	1,750,047	1,826,696	92	88
St. Louis County Public Lib., MO (S) (C)	7,269,432	7,521,921	91,944	93,455	337	323
Enoch Pratt Free Lib., Baltimore, MD (U) (F)	2,214,845	2,318,562	371,907	373,036	36	36
Memphis/Shelby County Public Lib., TX (U/S) (F)	2,575,171	2,572,297	315,155	349,252	34	34
King County Lib. System, WA (S) (C)	3,833,681	4,150,036	96,000	103,000	44	44
Columbus/Franklin County Public Lib., OH (U/S) (C)	3,084,857	3,307,731	680,838	721,233	24	23
Louisville Public Lib., KY (U/S) (F)	2,214,707	2,371,199	418,665	548,195	28	24
San Francisco Public Lib., CA (U) (F)	2,304,102	2,435,234	987,795	929,950	29	29
Prince George's County Memorial Lib., MD (S) (F)	3,706,766	3,794,615	946,562	1,059,190	21	21
Baltimore County Public Lib., MD (S) (F)	8,141,262	8,418,223	373,162	431,491	22	22
Fairfax County Public Lib., VA (S) (F)	5,080,099	5,333,638	1,660,625	1,886,625	21	22
Cuyahoga County Public Lib., OH (S) (C)	4,196,055	4,543,226	n/a	1,525,125	26	26
Jacksonville Public Lib. System, FL (U/S) (F)	2,177,556	2,157,906	520,902	514,517	12	12
Contra Costa County Lib. System, CA (S) (F)	2,986,812	3,016,631	362,781	363,781	21	21
Hennepin County Lib. System, MN (S) (C)	4,528,641	4,612,062	646,864	665,467	25	25
Cleveland Public Lib., OH (U) (C)	2,929,777	3,118,006	2,347,053	2,555,435	35	34
New Orleans Public Lib., LA (U) (C)	1,099,425	1,143,420	816,183	393,177	12	12
Dayton/Montgomery County Public Lib., OH (U/S) (C)	4,441,967	4,598,334	517,097	523,494	21	21
Denver Public Lib., CO (U) (C)	2,862,488	2,922,046	806,904	839,051	23	23
Fresno County Public Lib., CA (U/S) (F)	2,021,585	2,028,773	510,179	535,536	72	72
St. Louis Public Lib., MO (C)	1,540,820	1,429,294	448,677	458,384	26	23
Tulsa City-County Lib., OK (U/S) (F)	1,695,892	1,753,570	617,251	674,380	21	21
Pittsburgh Public Lib., PA (U) (C)	2,942,141	2,908,157	513,679	536,616	28	28
Annapolis/Anne Arundel County Public Lib., MD (U/S) (F)	3,420,672	3,605,009	125,702	129,469	14	14
Omaha Public Lib., NE (U) (C)	1,651,365	1,735,235	243,545	268,857	11	10

TABLE 5 PUBLIC LIBRARY TOTAL FULL-TIME EQUIVALENT (FTE) PROFESSIONAL AND NONPROFESSIONAL STAFF, 1980–1981

Library	Total Staff 1980	Total Staff 1981	Professional Staff 1980	Professional Staff 1981
Chicago Public Lib., IL (U) (C)	1,885	1,457	717	572
Los Angeles Public Lib., CA (U) (F)	1,126.5	1,141.5	392.5	399
Brooklyn Public Lib., NY (U) (F)	663	638	252	261
Philadelphia Public Lib., PA (U) (C)	—	—	247	245
Houston Public Lib., TX (U) (C)	550	552	154	154
Detroit Public Lib., MI (U) (C)	450	434	214	200
Buffalo/Erie County Public Lib., NY (U/S) (C)	528.31	548.96	171.5	176.5
Orange County Public Lib., CA (S) (F)	288	292	79	82
Milwaukee Public Lib., WI (U) (C)	335	345.5	13	13
San Antonio Public Lib., TX (U) (F)	185	185	22	22
San Diego Public Lib., CA (U) (F)	220.77	235.19	84.38	84.88
Cincinnati/Hamilton County Public Lib., OH (U/S) (C)	389.8	386	126.5	121
St. Louis County Public Lib., MO (S) (C)	376	370	45	38
Enoch Pratt Free Lib., Baltimore, MD (U) (F)	425.5	447	148.5	160
Memphis/Shelby County Public Lib., TX (U/S) (F)	258.8	258.8	141	141
King County Lib. System, WA (S) (C)	228	241	68	69.5
Columbus/Franklin County Public Lib., OH (U/S) (C)	233.5	251.5	100	100
Louisville Public Lib., KY (U/S) (F)	199.41	192.80	41.57	41
San Francisco Public Lib., CA (U) (F)	284.5	292	143	140
Prince George's County Memorial Lib., MD (S) (F)	353	344	104	98
Baltimore County Public Lib., MD (S) (F)	478	479	93	93
Fairfax County Public Lib., VA (S) (F)	320	323	89.5	89.5
Cuyahoga County Public Lib., OH (S) (C)	491	478	177	170
Jacksonville Public Lib. System, FL (U/S) (F)	181	157	53	51
Contra Costa County Lib. System, CA (S) (F)	183.6	151.8	63	53.2
Hennepin County Lib. System, MN (S) (C)	312.9	347.8	102.7	112.4
Cleveland Public Lib., OH (U) (C)	417	395	35	34
New Orleans Public Lib., LA (U) (C)	169.41	161.44	41.75	37.75
Dayton/Montgomery County Public Lib., OH (U/S) (C)	216	218	43.7	43.3
Denver Public Lib., CO (U) (C)	355	345	120	110
Fresno County Public Lib., CA (U/S) (F)	136.6	136.6	38.8	38.8
St. Louis Public Lib., MO (U) (C)	240.70	226.5	61	54
Tulsa City-County Lib., OK (U/S) (F)	181.5	184.5	48	48
Pittsburgh Public Lib., PA (U) (C)	362	368	103	110
Annapolis/Anne Arundel County Public Lib., MD (U/S) (F)	223	204.5	45	41
Omaha Public Lib., NE (U) (C)	117.74	113.72	37	35

TABLE 6   PUBLIC LIBRARY PER CAPITA SUPPORT AND CIRCULATION, AND WORKLOAD PER STAFF MEMBER (RANK BY VOLUME), 1980–1981

Library	Per capita support 1980	Per capita support 1981	Per capita circulation 1980	Per capita circulation 1981	Workload per staff member 1980	Workload per staff member 1981
Chicago Public Lib., IL (U)(C)	$ 8.09 (23)	$ 8.41 (26)	1.9 (31)	2.4 (26a)	3506 (35)	4962 (34)
Los Angeles Public Lib., CA (U)(F)	5.14 (34)	5.59 (35)	3.8 (20)	3.6 (20b)	9619 (24)	9499 (25)
Brooklyn Public Lib., NY (U)(F)	7.18 (31)	8.58 (25)	3.1 (26)	3.0 (24a)	10533 (19)	10450 (20)
Philadelphia Public Lib., PA (U)(C)	8.85 (19)	8.75 (23)	2.5 (29)	2.6 (27)	—	—
Houston Public Lib., TX (U)(C)	7.25 (30)	6.85 (31)	4.5 (17)	3.7 (19)	10006 (21)	10422 (21)
Detroit Public Lib., MI (U)(C)	11.75 (10)	11.64 (11)	1.6 (33)	1.4 (29)	4271 (34)	3961 (35)
Buffalo/Erie County Public Lib., NY (U/S)(C)	10.49 (11)	10.73 (16)	4.9 (15a)	5.1 (14a)	10326 (20)	10332 (19)
Orange County Public Lib., CA (S)(F)	8.74 (20)	11.66 (10)	6.2 (8)	6.8 (19)	20213 (23)	22617 (1)
Milwaukee Public Lib., WI (U)(C)	9.47 (16)	9.50 (18)	3.3 (24)	3.2 (23)	9814 (23)	8895 (26)
San Antonio Public Lib., TX (U)(F)	2.99 (36)	3.56 (36)	2.4 (30)	2.4 (26)	12135 (15)	11879 (17)
San Diego Public Lib., CA (U)(F)	6.56 (32)	6.57 (32)	4.9 (15b)	4.8 (15)	18582 (4)	18010 (5)
Cincinnati/Hamilton County Public Lib., OH (U/S)(C)	9.48 (15)	11.02 (13)	6.1 (9)	6.7 (10)	14505 (11)	15143 (11)
St. Louis County Public Lib., MO (S)(C)	7.67 (26)	8.30 (27)	9.5 (2)	9.2 (3)	19334 (3)	20330 (3)
Enoch Pratt Free Lib., Baltimore, MD (U)(F)	12.28 (9)	13.07 (7)	2.8 (28)	3.0 (24)	5205 (33)	5187 (33)
Memphis/Shelby County Public Lib., TX (U/S)(F)	8.19 (22)	8.84 (21)	3.4 (23)	3.3 (22)	9950 (22)	9939 (22)
King County Lib. System, WA (S)(C)	8.00 (24)	8.79 (22)	5.4 (12)	5.5 (13)	16814 (6)	17220 (8)
Columbus/Franklin County Public Lib., OH (U/S)(C)	9.54 (14)	10.82 (15)	4.4 (18)	4.7 (16)	13211 (14)	13152 (15)
Louisville Public Lib., KY (U/S)(F)	7.48 (28)	7.38 (29)	3.2 (25)	3.5 (21)	11106 (17)	12299 (16)
San Francisco Public Lib., CA (U)(F)	12.77 (7)	11.81 (9)	3.6 (22a)	3.6 (20a)	8099 (28)	8340 (28)
Prince George's County Memorial Lib., MD (S)(F)	12.45 (8)	13.02 (8)	5.6 (11a)	5.6 (12)	10501 (18)	10769 (18)
Baltimore County Public Lib., MD (S)(F)	14.77 (3)	15.86 (5)	12.4 (1)	12.8 (1)	17032 (5)	17575 (7)
Fairfax County Public Lib., VA (S)(F)	10.18 (12)	11.18 (12)	8.3 (4)	8.3 (4)	15875 (8)	16513 (9)
Cuyahoga County Public Lib., OH (S)(C)	18.34 (2)	18.90 (2)	6.8 (7)	7.3 (7)	8546 (26)	9505 (23)
Jacksonville Public Lib. System, FL (U/S)(F)	5.98 (33)	6.16 (34)	3.6 (22b)	3.6 (20a)	12031 (16)	13745 (13)
Contra Costa County Lib. System, CA (S)(F)	8.73 (21)	8.69 (24)	5.2 (14)	5.1 (14)	16268 (7)	19872 (4)
Hennepin County Lib. System, MN (S)(C)	13.66 (5)	15.45 (6)	7.9 (5)	8.0 (6)	14473 (12)	13261 (14)
Cleveland Public Lib., OH (U)(C)	19.45 (1)	24.17 (1)	4.7 (16)	5.5 (13a)	7026 (30)	7894 (30)
New Orleans Public Lib., LA (U)(C)	5.11 (35)	5.91 (33)	1.8 (32)	2.0 (28)	6490 (31)	7083 (31)
Dayton/Montgomery County Public Lib., OH (U/S)(C)	7.55 (27)	9.06 (20)	7.8 (6)	8.1 (5)	20565 (1)	21093 (2)
Denver Public Lib., CO (U)(C)	14.56 (4)	16.86 (4)	5.6 (11b)	5.7 (11)	8063 (29)	8470 (27)
Fresno County Public Lib., CA (U/S)(F)	7.28 (29)	7.25 (30)	4.2 (19)	4.0 (17)	14799 (10)	14852 (12)
St. Louis Public Lib., MO (U)(C)	9.27 (17)	10.62 (17)	2.9 (27)	3.1 (25)	6401 (32)	6310 (33)
Tulsa City-County Lib., OK (U/S)(F)	9.04 (18)	9.36 (19)	3.8 (21)	3.8 (18)	9344 (25)	9504 (24)
Pittsburgh Public Lib., PA (U)(C)	13.33 (6)	17.38 (3)	5.7 (10)	6.9 (8)	8127 (27)	7903 (29)
Annapolis/Anne Arundel County Public Lib., MD(U/S)(F)	9.60 (13)	10.90 (14)	9.3 (3)	9.7 (2)	15339 (9)	17628 (6)
Omaha Public Lib., NE (U)(C)	7.75 (25)	8.20 (28)	5.3 (13)	5.5 (13a)	14026 (13)	15259 (10)

NCES SURVEY OF PUBLIC LIBRARIES, 1977-1978

Helen M. Eckard

*U.S. Department of Education, National Center for Education Statistics,
Division of Multilevel Education Statistics*

The National Center for Education Statistics (NCES) collected data on public libraries during calendar year 1979 to generate the second Library General Information Survey (LIBGIS) of the 1970s. The public libraries surveyed serve all residents of a given community, district, or region free of cost, and receive financial support in whole or in part from public funds. These public libraries are defined as being governed by a single board of trustees or authority and administered by a single director.

PUBLIC SERVICE OUTLETS

The public libraries described above are central or main libraries. In the period between 1974 and 1978, 149 central libraries and 640 branch libraries were added to the category of libraries nationwide that serve populations under 250,000. This increase brings the number of such libraries to 14,983. Central libraries often have other outlets such as branches and bookmobiles or other mobile units that transport and rotate collections from the main library; still other outlets may be found in hospitals, nursing homes, shopping malls, and the like. For the purposes of this survey, all of the above were considered public service outlets. The total number of public service outlets for all public libraries in 1978 was 70,956, indicating a decrease of 18,186 since 1974. Bookmobiles and other mobile units accounted for 69.5 percent of the total number of service outlets, with the remaining divided among central libraries (11.9 percent), branch libraries (9.2 percent), and other service outlets (9.3 percent). Table 1 provides detailed data on the distribution of public service outlets within the various population groups served.

Economic and energy constraints undoubtedly have contributed to the substantial decline in the number of mobile-unit stops and other service outlets. Since 1974 mobile-unit stops have decreased by 25 percent, and the number of libraries serving populations under 100,000 fell by 31 percent. The number of other service outlets of libraries serving 500,000 or more persons decreased by 62 percent.

LIBRARY STAFF

Library staff accounted for the largest expenditure for all public libraries. The steady increase since 1974 in the number of trained library personnel has resulted in a total of 93,335 full-time-equivalent (FTE) staff reported in the following three categories: professionals; technical, clerical, and other staff; and plant operations and maintenance. Table 2 presents data on the number and distribution of library staff, as a whole and by individual category, by population and area served.

In comparison with the fall 1974 survey of library staff, the number of total FTE staff increased 8.5 percent overall. By individual categories, the number of professional staff rose 7.1 percent; technical, clerical, and other staff 10.7 percent; and plant operation and maintenance staff 1.4 percent. Although the absolute numbers indicate an increase since 1974, the average number of FTE staff per library has grown only marginally, from 10.4 in 1974 to 11.0 in 1978. In effect, the change translates into less than one additional professional and less than one additional technician per library. The

TABLE 1 NUMBER AND PERCENT DISTRIBUTION OF PUBLIC SERVICE OUTLETS, BY TYPE AND BY METROPOLITAN STATUS AND POPULATION OF AREA SERVED, FALL 1978

Metropolitan Status & Population	Total Outlets	Central Libraries No.	Central Libraries % of Total	Branch Libraries No.	Branch Libraries % of Total	Stops by Bookmobiles & Other Mobile Units No.	Stops by Bookmobiles & Other Mobile Units % of Total	Other No.	Other % of Total
All public libraries	70,956	8,456	11.9	6,527	9.2	49,343	69.5	6,630	9.3
500,000 and over	6,149	54	0.9	1,517	24.7	3,769	61.3	809	13.2
250,000 to 499,999	4,663	61	1.3	746	16.0	3,278	70.3	578	12.4
100,000 to 249,999	13,310	219	1.6	1,346	10.1	10,506	78.9	1,239	9.3
50,000 to 99,999	14,525	444	3.1	1,009	6.9	12,072	83.1	1,000	6.9
10,000 to 49,999	23,100	2,176	9.4	1,371	5.9	17,255	74.7	2,298	9.9
under 10,000	9,209	5,502	59.7	538	5.8	2,463	26.7	706	7.7
Within SMSA,* central	18,403	608	3.3	2,928	15.9	12,661	68.8	2,206	12.0
500,000 and over	5,654	48	0.8	1,392	24.6	3,494	61.8	720	12.7
250,000 to 499,999	3,296	48	1.5	592	18.0	2,259	68.5	397	12.0
100,000 to 249,999	6,579	123	1.9	694	10.5	4,941	75.1	821	12.5
50,000 to 99,999	2,367	136	5.7	183	7.7	1,819	76.8	229	9.7
10,000 to 49,999	418	182	43.5	67	16.0	148	35.4	21	5.0
under 10,000	89	71	79.8	—	—	—	—	18	20.2
Within SMSA, other	12,981	2,349	18.1	1,315	10.1	7,827	60.3	1,490	11.5
500,000 and over	495	6	1.2	125	25.3	275	55.6	89	18.0
250,000 to 499,999	1,282	12	0.9	148	11.5	943	73.6	179	14.0
100,000 to 249,999	2,232	51	2.3	281	12.6	1,661	74.4	239	10.7
50,000 to 99,999	2,394	151	6.3	326	13.6	1,789	74.7	128	5.3
10,000 to 49,999	4,938	934	18.9	347	7.0	3,125	63.3	532	10.8
under 10,000	1,640	1,195	72.9	88	5.4	34	2.1	323	19.7
Other than SMSA	39,572	5,499	13.9	2,284	5.8	28,855	72.9	2,934	7.4
500,000 and over	85	No respondents this category							
250,000 to 499,999	85	1	1.2	6	7.1	76	89.4	2	2.4
100,000 to 499,999	4,499	45	1.0	371	8.2	3,904	86.8	179	4.0
50,000 to 99,999	9,764	157	1.6	500	5.1	8,464	86.7	643	6.6
10,000 to 49,999	17,744	1,060	6.0	957	5.4	13,982	78.8	1,745	9.8
under 10,000	7,480	4,236	56.6	450	6.0	2,429	32.5	365	4.9

Source: National Center for Education Statistics, Department of Education. Unpublished data from the Survey of Public Libraries (LIBGIS III), 1977–1978.

*SMSA = Standard Metropolitan Statistical Area.

NUMBER AND PERCENT DISTRIBUTION OF PUBLIC LIBRARY STAFF IN FTEs, BY MAJOR STAFF CATEGORY AND BY METROPOLITAN STATUS AND POPULATION OF AREA SERVED, FALL 1978

Metropolitan Status & Population	No. of Libraries	Total Staff	Total Professional Staff No.	% of Total	Technical, Clerical, & Other Staff No.	% of Total	Plant Operation & Maintenance Staff No.	% of Total
All public libraries	8,456	93,335.1	38,702.1	41.5	48,208.9	51.7	6,424.1	6.9
500,000 and over	54	25,277.8	8,828.3	34.9	14,043.6	55.6	2,405.9	9.5
250,000 to 499,999	61	8,758.5	3,468.5	39.6	4,780.1	54.6	509.9	5.8
100,000 to 249,999	219	13,200.7	5,087.6	38.5	7,403.0	56.1	710.1	5.4
50,000 to 99,999	444	12,862.0	5,196.0	40.4	7,006.0	54.5	660.0	5.1
10,000 to 49,999	2,176	23,663.8	9,936.0	42.0	12,295.5	52.0	1,432.3	6.1
under 10,000	5,502	9,572.3	6,185.7	64.6	2,680.7	28.0	705.9	7.4
Within SMSA,* central	608	46,253.6	17,620.6	38.1	24,976.3	54.0	3,656.7	7.9
500,000 and over	48	23,816.2	8,284.8	34.8	13,229.1	55.5	2,302.3	9.7
250,000 to 499,999	48	6,875.4	2,851.9	41.5	3,583.2	52.1	440.3	6.4
100,000 to 249,999	123	8,215.3	3,288.3	40.0	4,423.7	53.8	503.3	6.1
50,000 to 99,999	136	4,798.0	2,054.1	42.8	2,491.9	51.9	252.0	5.3
10,000 to 49,999	182	2,309.2	989.5	42.9	1,164.6	50.4	155.1	6.7
under 10,000	71	239.5	152.0	63.5	83.8	35.0	3.7	1.5
Within SMSA, other	2,349	26,275.9	10,776.7	41.0	14,044.0	53.4	1,455.2	5.5
500,000 and over	6	1,461.6	543.5	37.2	814.5	55.7	103.6	7.1
250,000 to 499,999	12	1,829.5	602.8	32.9	1,161.3	63.5	65.4	3.6
100,000 to 249,999	51	3,014.5	1,069.2	35.5	1,811.5	60.1	133.8	4.4
50,000 to 99,999	151	4,566.8	1,785.8	39.1	2,565.5	56.2	215.5	4.7
10,000 to 49,999	934	12,343.2	4,996.1	40.5	6,631.9	53.7	715.2	5.8
under 10,000	1,195	3,060.3	1,779.3	58.1	1,059.3	34.6	221.7	7.2
Other than SMSA	5,499	20,805.6	10,304.8	49.5	9,188.6	44.2	1,312.2	6.3
500,000 and over	No respondents this category							
250,000 to 499,999	1	53.6	13.8	25.7	35.6	66.4	4.2	7.8
100,000 to 249,999	45	1,970.9	730.1	37.0	1,167.8	59.3	73.0	3.7
50,000 to 99,999	157	3,497.2	1,356.1	38.8	1,948.6	55.7	192.5	5.5
10,000 to 49,999	1,060	9,011.4	3,950.4	43.8	4,499.0	49.9	562.0	6.2
under 10,000	4,236	6,272.5	4,254.4	67.8	1,537.6	24.5	480.5	7.7

Source: National Center for Education Statistics, Department of Education. Unpublished data from the Survey of Public Libraries (LIBGIS III), 1977–1978.
*SMSA = Standard Metropolitan Statistical Area.

slight increase in the number of plant operation and maintenance staff actually reflects a decrease of .003 persons per library. Nationally, public library staffing patterns changed only slightly.

LIBRARY RECEIPTS

The $1.5 billion received by public libraries in FY 1977 represented an increase of nearly 35 percent since 1974. Public libraries received their funds from four major sources: local, which accounted for 74.9 percent of library receipts; state, which contributed 6.6 percent; federal, 7.9 percent; and other sources, including gifts and donations, 10.6 percent. Urban central city libraries were the recipients of 33 percent more funds in 1977 than in FY 1974. In the same period of time, suburban public libraries had a 36 percent increase in income, while rural libraries enjoyed a 39 percent increase.

According to the FY 1977 distribution of total library receipts by size of population served (Table 3), public libraries serving 100,000 or more received approximately 31 percent more dollars in 1977 than in 1974. However, the actual percentage of total receipts distributed to this category of libraries was 1.57 points lower than in 1974. Libraries serving populations of 100,000 to 249,999 increased their income by 40.3 percent, while those serving 10,000 to 49,999 persons increased receipts by 45.3 percent. An increase in receipts of 35.7 percent and 39.8 percent was realized by libraries serving under 10,000 and under 100,000 persons, respectively.

LIBRARY EXPENDITURES

Total public library expenditures for FY 1977 were $1.4 billion, some $95 million less than total receipts. Operating expenditures accounted for over $1.3 billion or 92.6 percent of total expenditures reported. Fifty-four percent of all operating expenditures was distributed for salaries and wages, with the remaining percentage divided among supplies and materials (15 percent), equipment (1 percent), plant and operations (11 percent), capital outlays (7 percent), and other expenditures (12 percent). Table 4 shows the distribution of expenditures in all categories according to area and population served. Overall expenditures for public libraries were approximately 32 percent higher in 1977 than the spending levels reported in the 1974 survey. Nearly 64 percent of all public libraries had expenditures of less than $50,000, in contrast to the 71 percent reported for the same category in FY 1974.

Twenty-six percent of all public libraries had a per capita expenditure of less than $3, while 50 percent of the libraries had a per capita outlay of less than $5 and 70 percent of all libraries spent less than $7 per capita (Table 5). Compared with the 1974 survey, there was a 34 percent decrease in the number of libraries with a per capita expense of less than $3 in FY 1977, a 25.3 percent decline in libraries with a per capita expenditure of less than $5, and an 11 percent decrease in libraries with per capita costs lower than $7.

LIBRARY COLLECTIONS

Library collections were surveyed both for items held at the end of the year and for those added during the year. At the end of 1977, there were 439 million volumes of books held, compared with 387 million volumes in 1974. Periodical subscriptions came to a total of just under 1 million, compared to 1.180 million in 1974; and audiovisual material titles held at the end of the year numbered 39 million, compared with the 1974 figure of 8.3 million. The number of bound periodicals titles held at the end of the year decreased by approximately 91,000 titles since 1974, for a 1977 total of

TABLE 3 AMOUNT AND PERCENT OF PUBLIC LIBRARY RECEIPTS, BY SOURCE AND BY METROPOLITAN STATUS AND POPULATION OF AREA SERVED: FY 1977

Metropolitan Status & Population	No. of Libraries	Total Receipts	Local Amount	% of Total	State (excluding Federal Funds Distributed by the State) Amount	% of Total	Federal (including Federal Funds Distributed by the State) Amount	% of Total	Other (including Gifts & Donations) Amount	% of Total
All public libraries	8,456	$1,563,307,041	$1,170,860,993	74.9	$103,527,246	6.6	$122,816,975	7.9	$166,101,827	10.6
500,000 and over	54	485,433,645	326,026,669	67.2	47,386,792	9.8	43,493,358	9.0	68,526,826	14.1
250,000 to 499,999	61	151,053,039	128,546,033	85.1	8,289,423	5.5	7,342,621	4.9	6,874,962	4.6
100,000 to 249,999	219	224,641,340	178,057,830	79.3	12,702,532	5.7	23,407,521	10.4	10,473,457	4.7
50,000 to 99,999	444	208,906,126	157,918,604	75.6	11,250,225	5.4	14,254,042	6.8	25,483,255	12.2
10,000 to 49,999	2,176	369,055,284	289,468,186	78.4	14,247,088	3.9	26,196,275	7.1	39,143,735	10.6
under 10,000	5,502	124,217,607	90,843,671	73.1	9,651,186	7.8	8,123,158	6.5	15,599,592	12.6
Within SMSA,* central	608	842,384,686	620,368,567	73.6	60,778,762	7.2	70,087,183	8.3	91,150,174	10.8
500,000 and over	48	457,869,938	305,379,044	66.7	44,493,021	9.7	40,141,237	8.8	67,856,636	14.8
250,000 to 499,999	48	120,670,731	102,620,519	85.0	6,324,697	5.2	5,937,286	4.9	5,788,229	4.8
100,000 to 249,999	123	142,030,413	114,015,310	80.3	6,952,654	4.9	14,438,677	10.2	6,623,772	4.7
50,000 to 99,999	136	79,179,921	64,441,378	81.4	2,006,087	2.5	5,954,680	7.5	6,777,776	8.6
10,000 to 49,999	182	39,508,944	31,073,848	78.7	894,566	2.3	3,615,303	9.2	3,925,227	9.9
under 10,000	71	3,124,739	2,838,468	90.8	107,737	3.4	—	—	178,534	5.7
Within SMSA, other	2,349	436,760,305	346,845,288	79.4	18,274,096	4.2	23,399,995	5.4	48,240,926	11.0
500,000 and over	6	27,563,707	20,647,625	74.9	2,893,771	10.5	3,352,121	12.2	670,190	2.4
250,000 to 499,999	12	29,620,195	25,327,116	85.5	1,895,672	6.4	1,356,277	4.6	1,041,130	3.5
100,000 to 249,999	51	49,709,409	43,059,945	86.6	2,490,767	5.0	1,678,322	3.4	2,480,375	5.0
50,000 to 99,999	151	78,220,156	56,597,087	72.4	2,916,996	3.7	2,908,024	3.7	15,798,049	20.2
10,000 to 49,999	934	204,758,839	162,561,719	79.4	6,611,363	3.2	12,064,324	5.9	23,521,433	11.5
under 10,000	1,195	46,887,999	38,651,796	82.4	1,465,527	3.1	2,040,927	4.4	4,729,749	10.1
Other than SMSA	5,499	284,162,050	203,647,138	71.7	24,474,388	8.6	29,329,797	10.3	26,710,727	9.4
500,000 and over	No respondents this category									
250,000 to 499,999	1	762,113	598,398	78.5	69,054	9.1	49,058	6.4	45,603	6.0
100,000 to 249,999	45	32,901,518	20,982,575	63.8	3,259,111	9.9	7,290,522	22.2	1,369,310	4.2
50,000 to 99,999	157	51,506,049	36,880,139	71.6	6,327,142	12.3	5,391,338	10.5	2,907,430	5.6
10,000 to 49,999	1,060	124,787,501	95,832,619	76.8	6,741,159	5.4	10,516,648	8.4	11,697,075	9.4
under 10,000	4,236	74,204,869	49,353,407	66.5	8,077,922	10.9	6,082,231	8.2	10,691,309	14.4

Source: National Center for Education Statistics, Department of Education. Unpublished data from the Survey of Public Libraries (LIBGIS III), 1977–1978.
*SMSA = Standard Metropolitan Statistical Area.

TABLE 4 EXPENDITURES OF PUBLIC LIBRARIES, BY MAJOR CATEGORY AND

Metropolitan Status & Population	Total Expenditures	Total Operating Expenditures	Operating Expenditures Salaries & Wages	Materials
All public libraries	$1,467,891,458	$1,359,630,867	$787,424,199	$214,011,302
500,000 and over	442,911,814	425,760,353	251,559,910	60,256,136
250,000 to 499,999	146,444,815	139,074,045	84,652,299	20,353,044
100,000 to 249,999	215,350,279	195,928,153	117,700,693	29,821,511
50,000 to 99,999	189,341,984	176,431,271	102,371,212	27,595,176
10,000 to 49,999	359,941,228	323,115,159	181,092,344	55,388,124
under 10,000	113,901,338	99,321,886	50,047,741	20,597,311
Within SMSA* central	779,380,719	735,238,689	434,281,469	107,582,801
500,000 and over	414,916,147	398,697,613	234,346,204	57,091,233
250,000 to 499,999	116,533,789	109,803,365	66,687,953	15,826,766
100,000 to 249,999	135,227,741	122,376,318	73,195,154	18,537,797
50,000 to 99,999	73,176,165	67,206,614	39,185,909	10,022,345
10,000 to 49,999	36,459,894	34,102,136	19,225,449	5,572,844
under 10,000	3,066,983	3,052,643	1,640,800	531,816
Within SMSA, other	412,745,264	384,513,881	222,120,653	62,344,221
500,000 and over	27,995,667	27,062,740	17,213,706	3,164,903
250,000 to 499,999	29,176,621	28,549,413	17,553,602	4,409,773
100,000 to 249,999	48,431,016	47,924,642	28,819,386	7,004,341
50,000 to 99,999	66,823,532	64,344,377	39,001,461	9,944,043
10,000 to 49,999	199,555,073	180,298,917	101,745,788	30,341,933
under 10,000	40,763,355	36,333,792	17,786,710	7,479,228
Other than SMSA	275,765,475	239,878,297	131,022,077	44,084,280
500,000 and over	No respondents this category			
250,000 to 499,999	734,405	721,267	410,744	116,505
100,000 to 249,999	31,691,522	25,627,193	15,686,153	4,279,373
50,000 to 99,999	49,342,287	44,880,280	24,183,842	7,628,788
10,000 to 49,999	123,926,261	108,714,106	60,121,107	19,473,347
under 10,000	70,071,000	59,935,451	30,620,231	12,586,267

Source: National Center for Education Statistics, Department of Education. Unpublished
*SMSA = Standard Metropolitan Statistical Area.

over 265,000. The total number of volumes of bound periodicals held at the end of 1977 was over 6 million, 1.4 million less than in 1974. Approximately 15.2 million physical units of microforms, 9 million sound recordings, 430,000 films, 29.6 million other materials, and 998,000 magazine subscriptions were counted.

LIBRARY LOAN TRANSACTIONS

An estimated 986 million direct circulations were made of all types of library materials to users in 1977, representing an increase of 93.8 million or over 10 percent since 1974. The average number of direct circulations of all library materials to users in FY 1977 was 116,688 for all public libraries; 1,322,609 for libraries serving a population of 100,000 or more; and 67,097 for libraries that serve populations under 100,000.

There were approximately 8.8 million interlibrary loans, of which 3.9 million

BY METROPOLITAN STATUS AND POPULATION OF AREA SERVED: FY 1977

Operating Expenditures (Cont.)				
Binding & Rebinding	Equipment	Plant Operation & Maintenance	All Other Expenditures	Capital Outlay
$5,626,327	$20,155,636	$159,292,127	$173,121,276	$108,260,591
1,992,082	4,595,058	53,662,185	53,694,982	17,151,461
631,487	1,473,529	16,112,865	15,850,821	7,370,770
678,954	2,912,411	19,270,568	25,544,016	19,422,126
636,776	2,466,892	18,831,522	24,529,693	12,910,713
999,222	6,007,895	37,968,953	41,658,621	36,826,069
687,806	2,699,851	13,446,034	11,843,143	14,579,452
3,188,900	8,631,705	87,194,555	94,359,259	44,142,030
1,900,846	4,449,718	50,485,027	50,424,585	16,218,534
477,569	979,353	13,094,036	12,737,688	6,730,424
475,183	1,967,576	12,224,543	15,976,065	12,851,423
212,639	682,686	7,299,398	9,803,637	5,969,551
116,408	530,746	3,725,675	4,931,014	2,357,758
6,255	21,626	365,876	486,270	14,340
1,293,062	6,250,408	43,592,402	48,913,135	28,231,383
91,236	145,340	3,177,158	3,270,397	932,927
150,100	492,417	2,925,864	3,017,657	627,208
134,197	592,885	4,778,714	6,595,119	506,374
304,368	625,803	7,019,893	7,448,809	2,479,155
565,170	3,246,962	20,946,102	23,452,962	19,256,156
47,991	1,147,001	4,744,671	5,128,191	4,429,563
1,144,365	5,273,523	28,505,170	29,848,882	35,887,178
3,818	1,759	92,965	95,476	13,138
69,574	351,950	2,267,311	2,972,832	6,064,329
119,769	1,158,403	4,512,231	7,277,247	4,462,007
317,644	2,230,187	13,297,176	13,274,645	15,212,155
633,560	1,531,224	8,335,487	6,228,682	10,135,549

data from the Survey of Public Libraries (LIBGIS III), 1977-1978.

were outgoing loans to other libraries and the balance, or 4.9 million, incoming from other libraries. Overall, interlibrary loans increased by about 3.4 million. Outgoing loans to libraries increased by 1.4 million or 60 percent since 1974, while incoming loans from other libraries increased by 1.9 million or 63.8 percent. The average number of outgoing interlibrary loans per library in FY 1977 was 462 for all public libraries; 3,801 for libraries serving populations of 100,000 and over; and 325 for libraries serving populations less than 100,000. The average number of incoming interlibrary loans per library in FY 1977 was 581 for all public libraries; 1,824 for libraries serving populations of 100,000 or more; and 530 for libraries that serve populations under 100,000.

Bulk loans totaled 10.7 million, some 2.1 million or 24.7 percent more than in 1974.

For comprehensive data on direct circulations, interlibrary loans, and bulk loans according to areas and population sizes served in FY 1977, see Table 6.

TABLE 5   NUMBER AND PERCENT DISTRIBUTION OF PUBLIC LIBRARIES, BY TOTAL OPERATING EXPENDITURES PER CAPITA AND BY METROPOLITAN STATUS AND POPULATION OF AREA SERVED: FY 1977

Number and Percent of Total Operating Expenditures Per Capita

Metropolitan Status & Population	No. of Libraries	Less than $1.00	$1.00 to $2.99	$3.00 to $4.99	$5.00 to $6.99	$7.00 to $8.99	$9.00 to $11.99	$12.00 to $14.99	$15.00 or More
All public libraries	8,456	520 (6.1%)	1,711 (20.2%)	1,996 (23.6%)	1,681 (19.9%)	900 (10.6%)	797 (9.4%)	378 (4.5%)	473 (5.6%)
500,000 and over	54	1 (1.9)	1 (1.9)	7 (13.0)	17 (13.0)	12 (22.2)	6 (11.1)	7 (13.0)	3 (5.6)
250,000 to 499,999	61	—	5 (8.2)	12 (19.7)	20 (32.8)	11 (18.0)	10 (16.4)	3 (4.9)	—
100,000 to 249,999	219	9 (4.1)	24 (11.0)	70 (32.0)	42 (19.2)	36 (16.4)	26 (11.9)	8 (3.7)	4 (1.8)
50,000 to 99,999	444	13 (2.9)	93 (20.9)	123 (27.7)	76 (17.1)	61 (13.7)	41 (9.2)	23 (5.2)	14 (3.2)
10,000 to 49,999	2,176	103 (4.7)	324 (14.9)	549 (25.2)	475 (21.8)	192 (8.8)	270 (12.4)	137 (6.3)	126 (5.8)
under 10,000	5,502	394 (7.2)	1,264 (23.0)	1,235 (22.4)	1,051 (19.1)	588 (10.7)	444 (8.1)	200 (3.6)	326 (5.9)
Within SMSA,* central	608	6 (1.0)	58 (9.5)	155 (25.5)	141 (23.2)	104 (17.1)	80 (13.2)	36 (5.9)	28 (4.6)
500,000 and over	48	—	—	7 (14.6)	16 (33.3)	11 (22.9)	4 (8.3)	7 (14.6)	3 (6.3)
250,000 to 499,999	48	—	4 (8.3)	10 (20.8)	15 (31.3)	8 (16.7)	8 (16.7)	3 (6.3)	—
100,000 to 249,999	123	1 (0.8)	6 (4.9)	44 (35.8)	25 (20.3)	28 (22.8)	13 (10.6)	4 (3.3)	2 (1.6)
50,000 to 99,999	136	2 (1.5)	13 (9.6)	32 (23.5)	29 (21.3)	23 (16.9)	29 (21.3)	6 (4.4)	2 (1.5)
10,000 to 49,999	182	3 (1.6)	17 (9.3)	50 (27.5)	37 (20.3)	27 (14.8)	17 (9.3)	12 (6.6)	19 (10.4)
under 10,000	71	—	18 (25.4)	12 (16.9)	19 (26.8)	7 (9.9)	9 (12.7)	4 (5.6)	2 (2.8)
Within SMSA, other	2,349	22 (0.9)	432 (18.4)	358 (15.2)	489 (20.8)	262 (11.2)	357 (15.2)	184 (7.8)	245 (10.4)
500,000 and over	6	1 (16.7)	1 (16.7)	—	1 (16.7)	1 (16.7)	2 (33.3)	—	—
250,000 to 499,999	12	—	—	2 (16.7)	5 (41.7)	3 (25.0)	2 (16.7)	—	—
100,000 to 249,999	51	2 (3.9)	5 (9.8)	15 (29.4)	11 (21.6)	4 (7.8)	9 (17.6)	4 (7.8)	1 (2.0)
50,000 to 99,999	151	3 (2.0)	28 (18.5)	35 (23.2)	27 (17.9)	23 (15.2)	12 (7.9)	15 (9.9)	8 (5.3)
10,000 to 49,999	934	16 (1.7)	91 (9.7)	153 (16.4)	202 (21.6)	83 (8.9)	177 (19.0)	112 (12.0)	100 (10.7)
under 10,000	1,195	—	307 (25.7)	153 (12.8)	243 (20.3)	148 (12.4)	155 (13.0)	53 (4.4)	136 (11.4)
Other than SMSA	5,499	492 (8.9)	1,221 (22.2)	1,483 (27.0)	1,051 (19.1)	534 (9.7)	360 (6.5)	158 (2.9)	200 (3.6)
500,000 and over	No respondents this category								
250,000 to 499,999	1	—	1 (100.0)	—	—	—	—	—	—
100,000 to 249,999	45	6 (13.3)	13 (28.9)	11 (24.4)	6 (13.3)	4 (8.9)	4 (8.9)	—	1 (2.2)
50,000 to 99,999	157	8 (5.1)	52 (33.1)	56 (35.7)	20 (12.7)	15 (9.6)	—	2 (1.3)	4 (2.5)
10,000 to 49,999	1,060	84 (7.9)	216 (20.4)	346 (32.6)	236 (22.3)	82 (7.7)	76 (7.2)	13 (1.2)	7 (0.7)
under 10,000	4,236	394 (9.3)	939 (22.2)	1,070 (25.3)	789 (18.6)	433 (10.2)	280 (6.6)	143 (3.4)	188 (4.4)

Source: National Center for Education Statistics, Department of Education. Unpublished data from the Survey of Public Libraries (LIBGIS III), 1977–1978.
*SMSA = Standard Metropolitan Statistical Area.

TABLE 8. DIRECT CIRCULATION OF LIBRARY MATERIALS TO USERS, INTERLIBRARY LOANS PROVIDED TO AND RECEIVED FROM OTHER LIBRARIES, AND BULK LOANS RECEIVED FROM OTHER LIBRARIES, BY METROPOLITAN STATUS AND POPULATION OF AREA SERVED: FY 1977

Metropolitan Status & Population	No. of Libraries	Direct Circulation of Materials to Users			Number of Interlibrary Loans						No. of Bulk Loans Received from Other Libraries
					Provided to Other Libraries			Received from Other Libraries			
		Total	Median	Mean	Total	Median	Mean	Total	Median	Mean	
All public libraries	8,456	986,714,576	30,636	116,688	3,911,720	3	462	4,915,729	182	581	10,749,559
500,000 and over	54	207,282,331	3,060,278	3,838,561	470,378	4,246	8,710	129,766	1,124	2,403	194,508
250,000 to 499,999	61	94,212,821	1,485,642	1,544,472	338,547	2,599	5,549	153,561	1,762	2,517	186,489
100,000 to 249,999	219	140,256,132	612,126	640,438	460,622	486	2,103	326,040	841	1,488	312,239
50,000 to 99,999	444	142,948,293	289,307	321,955	1,125,397	100	2,534	1,112,327	514	2,505	2,425,960
10,000 to 49,999	2,176	276,413,613	108,453	127,028	1,220,194	30	560	1,805,113	367	829	3,931,800
under 10,000	5,502	125,601,386	14,418	22,828	296,582	—	53	1,388,922	104	252	3,698,563
Within SMSA,* central	608	432,216,667	320,894	10,882	1,993,419	254	3,278	1,407,309	514	2,314	481,100
500,000 and over	48	189,533,040	3,044,870	3,948,605	292,085	4,511	6,085	103,354	1,112	2,153	194,468
250,000 to 499,999	48	71,321,614	1,461,225	1,485,866	292,224	2,599	6,088	119,450	1,589	2,488	89,739
100,000 to 249,999	123	84,163,818	668,696	684,258	275,541	892	2,240	174,793	839	1,421	107,946
50,000 to 99,999	136	52,465,413	339,072	385,775	958,919	325	7,050	828,928	514	6,095	60,164
10,000 to 49,999	182	31,168,910	157,152	171,257	170,752	25	938	159,771	325	877	10,272
under 10,000	71	3,563,872			3,898	†	†	21,013		†	18,511
Within SMSA, other	2,349	291,314,367	56,040	124,016	1,235,537	13	525	1,858,216	323	791	2,796,878
500,000 and over	6	17,749,291	†	†	178,293	†	†	26,412	†	†	40
250,000 to 499,999	12	22,218,968			46,080			33,774			96,750
100,000 to 249,999	51	30,900,661	582,046	605,895	138,888	330	2,723	76,287	1,174	1,495	124,584
50,000 to 99,999	151	49,052,396	300,031	324,850	42,793	84	283	149,110	436	987	487,459
10,000 to 49,999	934	133,517,863	123,094	142,952	665,295	48	712	1,080,863	484	1,157	1,836,061
under 10,000	1,195	37,875,188	22,619	31,694	164,188	3	137	491,770	205	411	251,984
Other than SMSA	5,499	263,183,542	17,937	47,860	682,764		124	1,650,204	129	300	7,471,581
500,000 and over	No respondents this category										
250,000 to 499,999	1	672,239			243	†	†	337	†	†	†
100,000 to 249,999	45	25,191,653	478,298	559,814	46,193	98	1,026	74,960	787	1,665	79,709
50,000 to 99,999	157	41,430,484	241,019	263,888	123,685	31	787	134,289	622	855	1,878,337
10,000 to 49,999	1,060	111,725,840	86,343	105,402	384,147	18	362	564,479	305	532	2,085,467
under 10,000	4,236	84,162,326	11,807	19,868	128,496		30	876,139	94	206	3,428,068

Source: National Center for Education Statistics, Department of Education. Unpublished data from the Survey of Public Libraries (LIBGIS III), 1977–1978.
*SMSA = Standard Metropolitan Statistical Area.
†Not calculated because of too few respondents in the sample in this category.

LIBRARY HOURS AND DAYS OPEN

Of the total number of public libraries, 53 percent were open fewer than 40 hours per week. This group consisted of 4,481 libraries, with all but 7 in the category of libraries serving fewer than 100,000 persons. Of the 334 larger libraries serving over 100,000 persons, 327 or 98 percent were open 40 hours or more per week, and 262 or 78 percent were open 60 hours or more per week.

Over half of all public libraries were open six days per week, with 61 percent open fewer than eight hours per day and 34 percent open from eight to ten hours per day. Approximately 60 percent of the libraries in the population category of 500,000 and over were open six days per week, and 74 percent were open eight to ten hours per day. Over 60 percent of all public libraries were open fewer than eight hours per day per typical week.

LIBRARY PHYSICAL FACILITIES

The total net area assigned for library purposes in FY 1977 was approximately 79.9 million square feet for all public libraries, an average of 9,450 square feet per library. The total length of shelving space available for library materials was over 54.4 million linear feet. A total of over 713,000 seats were available to library users.

NCES SURVEY OF PUBLIC SCHOOL LIBRARY MEDIA CENTERS, 1978

Milbrey L. Jones
Chief, School Media Resources Branch,
Division of Library Programs,
Office of Libraries and Learning Technologies,
U.S. Department of Education

Nationwide data on public school libraries or school library media centers have been collected and reported since 1876. The methodology of the public school library media center survey that covered data for the school year ending June 30, 1978, was discussed in the 1979 *Bowker Annual* (Robert David Little, "NCES Survey of School Library Media Centers," pp. 288–289). Results of the 1978 survey of public school library media centers became available in January, 1982.[1] Analysis of data assembled for a survey of private school library media centers is in progress.

The 1978 survey collected data on the school library media center universe, and on expenditures, collections, personnel, users, and needs of these centers. Data are provided for these schools: elementary; combined, that is, those administered as a single unit serving both elementary and secondary school children; and secondary. The schools are further classified by metropolitan status (i.e., urban, suburban, and rural) and enrollment size. The following brief overview is presented to facilitate some interpretation of this information as early as possible. Statistics included in the published report but not discussed in this article include data on users, facilities, satellite media centers, interlibrary loans, and reference transactions. The published report also contains comprehensive tables on topics covered in this overview.

TABLE 1 PERCENT OF PUBLIC SCHOOLS WITH LIBRARY MEDIA CENTERS, BY GRADE LEVEL OF SCHOOL 1960-1961, 1962, 1968, 1974, AND 1978

Grade Level of School	1960-1961	1962-1963*	1968†	1974	1978
Total	46.3	58.9	84.6	85.3	85.3
Secondary only	92.1	97.4	93.9	97.1	93.3
Combined elementary and secondary	82.3	89.6	—	—	—
Elementary only	31.2	44.4	81.1	—	—
Elementary and combined elementary and secondary	—	—	—	81.1	82.7

Source: *Statistics of Public School Libraries/Media Centers, Fall 1978* (Washington, D.C.: National Center for Education Statistics, January, 1982).
*Excluded schools with fewer than 150 pupils.
†Excluded schools with fewer than 300 pupils.

SCHOOL LIBRARY MEDIA CENTER UNIVERSE

The National Center for Education Statistics (NCES) estimates that approximately 15 percent of the nation's public schools, serving about 3,000,000 or 7 percent of American public school children, were without a library media center in 1978 (Table 1). Among schools of all enrollment sizes in 1978, rural elementary or combined schools were *least likely* to have a library media center (Table 2). All elementary and combined schools in the largest enrollment category had library media centers. When the remaining public schools were categorized by metropolitan status, size, and grade level, these groups reported having library media centers in *all* schools: urban secondary schools enrolling from 300-499 pupils, and rural secondary schools enrolling from 1,000-1,999 pupils.

TABLE 2 NUMBER AND PERCENT OF PUBLIC SCHOOLS WITH BUILDING-LEVEL LIBRARY MEDIA CENTERS; NUMBERS AND PERCENTS OF BUILDING-LEVEL LIBRARY MEDIA CENTERS SERVED BY DISTRICT LIBRARY MEDIA CENTER; BY METROPOLITAN STATUS AND GRADE LEVEL, FALL 1978

Metropolitan Status & Grade Level of School	Total No.	With Library Media Center No.	% of Total	Building-level Media Centers Served by District Media Centers No.	% of Total
Urban	15,153	13,711	(90.5)	11,741	(85.6)
Secondary	3,107	2,975	(95.7)	2,360	(79.3)
Elementary and combined	12,046	10,736	(89.1)	9,382	(87.4)
Suburban	33,445	29,375	(87.8)	20,377	(69.4)
Secondary	7,634	7,078	(92.7)	4,323	(61.0)
Elementary and combined	25,812	22,297	(86.3)	16,054	(72.0)
Rural	34,445	27,768	(80.6)	17,025	(61.3)
Secondary	9,373	8,714	(92.6)	3,988	(45.7)
Elementary and combined	25,072	19,054	(75.9)	13,030	(68.4)

Source: *Statistics of Public School Libraries/Media Centers, Fall 1978* (Washington, D.C.: National Center for Education Statistics, January, 1982).

TABLE 3 NUMBER OF PUBLIC SCHOOL LIBRARY MEDIA CENTER EMPLOYEES, BY SEX AND EMPLOYMENT STATUS, AND BY SCHOOL LEVEL: UNITED STATES, FALL 1978

School Level & Membership	No. of Schools with L/MC	Men Full-time	Men Part-time	Women Full-time	Women Part-time
Total (all levels) all sizes	70,854	5,970	2,832	64,765	31,339
Secondary schools all sizes	18,767	3,774	1,173	25,637	5,961
Elementary and combined schools all sizes	52,087	2,196	1,659	39,128	25,378

Source: *Statistics of Public School Libraries/Media Centers, Fall 1978* (Washington, D.C.: National Center for Education Statistics, January, 1982).

The overall percentage of American public schools with library media centers in 1978 had not changed since 1974. The percentage of elementary and combined schools with library media centers rose slightly during the four-year period. The decline by nearly 4 percent in the number of public secondary schools with library media centers during this period may have resulted from the inclusion in the 1978 survey of a large number of vocational/technical secondary schools, some of which apparently do not have library media centers. Secondary school pupils who attend such schools may have dual enrollment in an academic or comprehensive high school that has a library media center; these students may thus have access to a library media center for part of the school day. Data on library media center staff are provided in Table 3.

DISTRICT SCHOOL MEDIA CENTERS SERVING BUILDING-LEVEL LIBRARY MEDIA CENTERS

The number and percentage of building-level school library media centers that are serviced by a district library media center should be examined in relation to expenditures for audiovisual materials and equipment and to size of collections (Table 2). Elementary and combined school library media centers in urban areas are most likely to have district library media center service. This probably reflects the practice in some large urban school districts of administering audiovisual materials in a separate department.

EXPENDITURES

In 1978, the per-pupil mean expenditures by public school library media centers were generally higher in absolute dollar amounts than in 1974, but of course inflation has considerably eroded buying power. The mean per-pupil expenditure for books in secondary schools, for example, would not add many books to a library media center's collection. An actual expenditure of $4.25 per pupil for 1,000 students results in a total expenditure of $4,250, which would buy about 212 books.

The figures shown in Table 4 should be considered in relation to size of collections (Tables 5 and 6) and the needs expressed by media centers for financial assistance to acquire library resources (Table 7).

TABLE 4 TOTAL EXPENDITURES FOR PUBLIC SCHOOL LIBRARY MEDIA CENTERS AND MEAN EXPENDITURES PER PUPIL, BY PURPOSE AND LEVEL OF SCHOOL, FALL 1978

	All Schools		Expenditures Secondary		Elementary	
Item	Total	Mean Per Pupil	Total	Mean Per Pupil	Total	Mean Per Pupil
Total	$1,385,607,951	$34.12	$550,864,372	$33.37	$834,743,580	$34.64
Salaries and wages	1,000,549,515	24.64	389,302,968	23.58	611,246,546	25.37
Books	172,472,925	4.25	66,273,695	4.01	106,199,231	4.41
Periodicals	30,011,594	0.74	15,958,068	0.97	14,053,527	0.58
Microforms	3,256,031	0.08	2,379,787	0.04	876,243	0.04
Audiovisual supplies and materials	68,421,436	1.69	28,011,985	1.70	40,409,451	1.68
Audiovisual equipment	18,755,554	0.46	8,262,555	0.50	10,492,999	0.44
All other equipment	56,634,206	1.39	23,502,246	1.42	33,131,960	1.37
All other expenditures	22,553,951	5.56	11,574,541	7.01	10,979,412	4.56

Source: *Statistics of Public School Libraries/Media Centers, Fall 1978* (Washington, D.C.: National Center for Education Statistics, January, 1982).

TABLE 5   COMPARISON OF 1974 AND 1978 COLLECTIONS IN PUBLIC SCHOOL LIBRARY MEDIA CENTERS, FALL 1978

Average Collections	1974	1978	Percent Change
Number of books per school	6,800	7,500	+ 10.3
Number of books per pupil	12.2	13.09	+ 7.3
Number of periodical subscriptions per school	39	57	+ 46.2
Number of audiovisual titles per school	912	1,072	+ 17.5

Source: *Statistics of Public School Libraries/Media Centers, Fall 1978* (Washington, D.C.: National Center for Education Statistics, January, 1982).

Expenditures for salaries were highest, with expenditures for books ranking significantly higher than the remaining categories.

COLLECTIONS

The number of books per pupil added to school library media center collections indicates that for all grade levels and in all localities, an average of less than one book per pupil was added. The fact that schools have maintained collections with only marginal additions in four years (see Table 5) may indicate both problems related to the age of collections and a need for reevaluation of book collections to ensure that these are current and responsive to curriculum needs.

Urban schools have a slightly lower number of library books per pupil than do rural and suburban schools, though the difference is less than two or three books in each case (see Table 6). Small schools average from 15 to 19 books per pupil, but the total number of books per pupil actually available results in collections of fewer than 8,000–12,000 or 16 to 24 per user, which is the standard recommended by the American Association of School Librarians and the Association for Educational Communications and Technology (AECT).[2]

There was a moderate increase in the number of periodical subscriptions per

TABLE 6   MEAN VOLUMES OF BOOKS PER PUPIL IN PUBLIC SCHOOL LIBRARY MEDIA CENTERS, IN SCHOOLS OF ALL GRADE LEVELS BY METROPOLITAN STATUS AND ENROLLMENT SIZE, FALL 1978

Metropolitan Status & Enrollment Size	Mean Volumes per Pupil — All Schools	Secondary	Elementary & Combined
United States total	13.09	11.41	14.24
Urban	11.41	9.37	12.94
Suburban	13.30	11.27	14.66
Rural	14.12	13.40	14.59
Enrollment Size of School			
2,000 or more	8.56	8.57	8.41
1,000–1,999	10.45	10.54	10.20
700–999	11.72	12.11	11.50
500–699	13.88	13.73	13.92
300–499	15.09	13.15	15.43
Under 300	19.37	18.93	19.51

Source: *Statistics of Public School Libraries/Media Centers, Fall 1978* (Washington, D.C.: National Center for Education Statistics, January, 1982).

TABLE 7 TOTAL NUMBER AND PERCENTAGE OF SCHOOLS EXPRESSING VARIOUS DEGREES OF NEED FOR FINANCIAL ASSISTANCE TO ACQUIRE LIBRARY RESOURCES, BY TYPE OF RESOURCE, FALL 1978

	Schools Expressing Need							
	Library Books		Periodicals		Audiovisual		Audiovisual Equipment	
Degree of Need	No.	%	No.	%	No.	%	No.	%
No need	9,968	14.1	20,180	28.5	6,568	9.2	9,460	13.4
Moderate need	30,366	42.8	32,946	46.5	24,984	35.3	27,866	39.3
Strong need	17,295	24.4	11,198	15.8	22,398	31.6	17,217	24.3
Very strong need	13,225	18.7	6,530	9.2	16,904	23.9	16,311	23.0

Source: *Statistics of Public School Libraries/Media Centers, Fall 1978* (Washington, D.C.: National Center for Education Statistics, January, 1982).

school, and a substantial increase in audiovisual titles per school (see Table 5). The recommended base collection for periodicals and newspapers ranges from 50–175 titles.[3]

The standard recommended for visual materials (moving images) at public schools calls for access to 3,000 titles with sufficient duplicate prints to satisfy 90 percent of all requests.[4]

NEEDS

The reports provided by public school library media centers on their degree of need for financial assistance in buying books, periodicals, audiovisual materials, and audiovisual equipment evidenced a rather high level of need in three of the four areas surveyed (see Table 6). Only one-fourth of all schools reported strong or very strong need for assistance in acquiring periodicals, while well over one-half reported strong or very strong need for assistance in acquiring audiovisual materials. The needs of schools appeared to be quite consistent, whether schools were compared by grade level, size, or metropolitan status.

NOTES

1. Robert A. Heintze and Lance Hodes, *Statistics of Public School Libraries/Media Centers, Fall 1978* (Washington, D.C.: U.S. Department of Education, National Center for Education Statistics, 1982) (NCES 81-254). Further information on this and other studies is available from the Statistical Information Office, National Center for Education Statistics, Presidential Building, U.S. Department of Education, 400 Maryland Avenue S.W., Washington, DC 20202; 301-436-7900.
2. American Association of School Librarians and Association for Educational Communications and Technology, *Media Programs: District and School* (Chicago and Washington, D.C.: American Library Association and AECT, 1975), p. 70.
3. Ibid., p. 71.
4. Ibid., p. 76.

NCES SURVEY OF LIBRARY NETWORKS AND COOPERATIVE LIBRARY ORGANIZATIONS, 1977–1978

Helen M. Eckard

U.S. Department of Education,
National Center for Education Statistics,
Division of Multilevel Education Statistics

Recognizing the growing interest within the library community in cooperative library organizations, the National Center for Education Statistics (NCES) conducted the first national survey of library networks for the period 1977–1978. The survey was designed to identify existing networks and to determine the general characteristics, participants, expenditures, funds, staff, services, and extent of computerization of these organizations. A planning committee of experts was formed to provide guidance throughout the three phases of this survey. The committee consisted of representatives from the following organizations: the National Commission on Libraries and Information Science (NCLIS), the American Library Association (ALA), the Special Libraries Association (SLA), the Association of Research Libraries (ARL), the Association of College and Research Libraries (ACRL), the National Library of Medicine (NLM), the Federal Library Committee, the chief officers of state library agencies, the Council for Computerized Library Networks (CCLN), the Consortium of Universities of the Washington Metropolitan Area, the Smithsonian Institution, the Office of Libraries and Learning Technologies (Department of Education), NCES, and the VSE Corporation, which was contracted to conduct the survey.

The planning committee established a set of criteria for the selection of organizations to participate in the survey. The criteria were that (1) participants in networks or cooperative organizations be primarily or exclusively libraries; (2) the organizations engage in cooperative activities that are beyond the scope of traditional interlibrary loan services as defined by the ALA code; (3) the activities of the organization extend beyond reciprocal borrowing; (4) the networks or cooperative organizations operate for the mutual benefit of participating libraries; and (5) the scope of the organizations be interinstitutional.

ORGANIZATIONAL TYPES

Most of the tables prepared for this survey show library networks by organizational type and by number of participants. A breakdown of all organizations is given according to these types: (1) public, which are those organizations under the control of federal, state, or local government agencies; (2) private, which are either independent nonprofit or proprietary profit-making organizations; and (3) other, which are those networks having no formal administration. The number of participants refers to the number of libraries that directly participate in the activities of each cooperative library organization.

GENERAL CHARACTERISTICS

Approximately 60 percent of the 608 library networks were administered by public agencies, while 71 percent had a headquarters and 55 percent were independent of a parent agency. Almost 80 percent operated under a written agreement or charter, and over 67 percent had membership consisting of more than one type of organization. Almost 59 percent had computer support and of these almost 73 percent had daily operations.

Table 1 indicates that 71 percent of library cooperative organizations were regional, with an area of service less than statewide. Seventeen percent did provide service statewide to most of the libraries in the respective states. Nine percent served more than one state, but not all 50 states. Networks in the national and international categories represented each only 1.2 percent of the 608 reporting organizations. Sixteen percent reported that their activities were limited to holding meetings.

CATEGORIES OF PARTICIPANTS

The 608 existing library networks comprise 32,148 participating members. The categories of participating libraries, along with the distribution of participants in terms of percentage, are college and university libraries (22 percent); school libraries (11 percent); public libraries: central (25 percent), branch (9 percent); special libraries (25 percent); state library agencies (1 percent); and other (7 percent). Further details are provided in Table 2.

Many participants were members of more than one library network. State library agencies averaged eight memberships in library networks per agency. To some extent, multiple memberships occurred in all categories. On the average, there were approximately 53 participants of all types per network.

NETWORK STAFF

Total full-time-equivalent (FTE) paid network staff numbered 5,100 persons, of which 8.8 percent were administrators, 23 percent professional librarians, 3.1 percent computer-related staff, 3.3 percent other professionals, 18 percent library technicians and paraprofessionals, and 44 percent clerical and support staff (see Table 3). Thirty-one percent of the professional staff at privately administered networks was computer-oriented, whereas in public networks this group made up only 2 percent. The professional staff in private networks was divided almost equally between librarians and computer-related professionals.

There were approximately 768 volunteers (nonpaid staff) working in networks in 1978 (see Table 4). Within this group, 65 percent or approximately 500 professionals were librarians.

NETWORK FUNDS

The $193.6 million received by networks during 1978 resulted from grants from state and local government (29 percent), federal grants (27 percent), sale of products and services (13 percent), and state and local taxes (10 percent).

Almost 73 percent of total network funds was for public networks, 22 percent for private networks, and 5 percent for those networks with no formal administrative ties. The major source of funds for public networks was federal, state, and local grants, while private networks were supported primarily through the sale of products and services, and dues and fees. Networks having no formal administration received the major part of their funding (47 percent) from state and local grants. In 1977–1978, public networks received $140.9 million, private networks $43.4 million, and other networks $9.2 million. A comparison of funding levels by source for all three types of networks can be made by consulting Table 5.

TABLE 1 COOPERATIVE LIBRARY ORGANIZATIONS BY GENERAL OF PARTICIPANTS:

Organizational Type & No. of Participants	Total No. of Organizations	Administration* Public	Administration* Private	Has Headquarters Yes	Has Headquarters No	Has Parent Agency Yes	Has Parent Agency No	Has Written Agreement Yes	Has Written Agreement No
All organizations	608	362	155	432	176	275	333	484	124
40 and over	189	131	40	171	18	93	96	158	31
30–39	46	25	9	31	15	19	27	38	8
20–29	71	37	17	45	26	30	41	55	16
10–19	172	105	44	108	64	69	103	136	36
2–9	130	64	45	77	53	64	66	97	33
Public	362	362	—	309	53	184	178	291	71
40 and over	131	131	—	125	6	70	61	104	27
30–39	25	25	—	23	2	11	14	22	3
20–29	37	37	—	34	3	20	17	31	6
10–19	105	105	—	82	23	51	54	84	21
2–9	64	64	—	45	19	32	32	50	14
Private	155	—	155	92	63	54	101	126	29
40 and over	40	—	40	33	7	12	28	39	1
30–39	9	—	9	4	5	3	6	8	1
20–29	17	—	17	8	9	5	12	12	5
10–19	44	—	44	20	24	11	33	32	12
2–9	45	—	45	27	18	23	22	35	10
Other	91	—	—	31	60	37	54	67	24
40 and over	18	—	—	13	5	11	7	15	3
30–39	12	—	—	4	8	5	7	8	4
20–29	17	—	—	3	14	5	12	12	5
10–19	23	—	—	6	17	7	16	20	3
2–9	21	—	—	5	16	9	12	12	9

Source: National Center for Education Statistics, Department of Education. Unpublished data from the Sur-
*Excludes those organizations that reported administration as "other."

All grants awarded directly to library networks by the federal government, including federal funds distributed by the state such as Library Services and Construction Act (LSCA) Title III funds, totaled $51.6 million. Over 95 percent of these funds or $49.2 million was received by public networks. Grants awarded by state and local governments excluding federal funds distributed by the state exceeded $56.4 million. Ninety-one percent of these funds was awarded to public library networks. Over 10 percent of total network funds, or $20.3 million, was received from state and local taxes, of which 85 percent went to public networks and only 11 percent to private networks.

"Pass-through" funds amounted to 6.3 percent or $12.2 million of all funding received by library networks nationally. These funds are received from participants and passed on to other library organizations for services rendered by the latter on the former's behalf. Forty-five percent of these funds was passed on to public networks, 53 percent to private networks, and 2 percent to other networks.

A gross investment income of $1.8 million was received by networks in 1977–1978. This represented income from assets, such as bank interest and dividends, and income from stocks, bonds, and endowments. Forty-nine percent of investment income was received by public networks and 42 percent by private. Funds collected from participants by networks in the form of assessments, for example, special payments to

CHARACTERISTICS, ORGANIZATIONAL TYPE AND NUMBER
1977–1978

No. of Organizations, By General Characteristics (cont.)

Membership Type		Computer Support		Frequency of Operations				Area Served			
Single Type	Multi-type	Yes	No	Daily	On-going	Meetings, etc., Only	Re-gional	State-wide	Multi-state	Nation-wide	Inter-national
195	413	356	252	442	68	98	437	103	54	7	7
22	167	131	58	166	13	10	119	40	24	3	3
9	37	27	19	28	6	12	35	7	4	—	—
20	51	37	34	45	7	19	54	8	6	2	1
70	102	95	77	108	27	37	131	27	12	1	1
74	56	66	64	95	15	20	98	21	8	1	2
109	253	211	151	311	25	26	259	77	18	5	3
16	115	92	39	125	3	3	90	32	7	2	—
4	21	16	9	21	2	2	19	5	1	—	—
13	24	20	17	31	4	2	27	7	1	2	—
45	60	56	49	82	10	13	83	16	4	1	1
31	33	27	37	52	6	6	40	17	5	—	2
62	93	96	59	94	26	35	102	15	32	2	4
5	35	28	12	31	6	3	16	5	15	1	3
2	7	6	3	4	2	3	6	1	2	—	—
5	12	8	9	10	1	6	11	—	5	—	1
19	25	26	18	15	11	18	29	7	8	—	—
31	14	28	17	34	6	5	40	2	2	1	—
24	67	49	42	37	17	37	76	11	4	—	—
1	17	11	7	10	4	4	13	3	2	—	—
3	9	5	7	3	2	7	10	1	1	—	—
2	15	9	8	4	2	11	16	1	—	—	—
6	17	13	10	11	6	6	19	4	—	—	—
12	9	11	10	9	3	9	18	2	1	—	—

vey of Library Networks and Cooperative Library Organizations, 1977–1978.

cover the costs of specific projects or to cover specific losses, came to $2.2 million. Over 63 percent of these assessments occurred in public networks and 32 percent in privately administered networks.

NETWORK EXPENDITURES

Library networks expended over $141 million between July 1, 1977, and June 30, 1978. These expenditures include only money paid out directly by network organizations from their budgets. Of the 53 library networks with operating expenditures of $500,000 or more, 74 percent were public. Of the 349 networks that spent $25,000 or more per year, 71 percent were public. Over half of all library networks spend over $25,000 per year.

The largest network expense was salaries and wages, which accounted for over $51.9 million or 36.8 percent of total expenditures. Public networks spent $38.5 million or 74 percent of all network expenditures for salaries, while private networks spent $9.9 million or 19 percent, and other networks spent $3.5 million or 7 percent. These figures do not include fringe benefits or salaries and wages paid by other organizations. Fringe benefits amounted to $6.6 million.

TABLE 2 PARTICIPANTS IN COOPERATIVE LIBRARY ORGANIZATIONS BY CATEGORY, 1977–1978

Organizational Type & No. of Participants	Total No. of Participants	College or University Library	School Library	Public Library Central	Public Library Branch	Special Library	State Library Agency	Other
All organizations	32,148	6,999	3,395	8,191	2,778	8,088	405	2,292
40 and over	25,810	5,364	3,094	6,223	2,442	6,829	284	1,574
30–39	1,551	257	126	474	97	356	34	207
20–29	1,688	417	72	552	78	373	17	179
10–19	2,353	652	78	801	130	402	47	243
2–9	746	309	25	141	31	128	23	89
Public	19,239	2,541	2,558	6,552	2,259	3,749	228	1,352
40 and over	15,708	1,900	2,360	4,961	2,007	3,361	173	946
30–39	844	84	89	342	84	95	4	146
20–29	890	174	34	454	38	93	9	88
10–19	1,437	264	62	693	100	165	23	130
2–9	360	119	13	102	30	35	19	42
Private	10,222	3,965	301	974	451	3,735	144	652
40 and over	8,656	3,301	267	801	416	3,284	87	500
30–39	306	73	11	75	1	111	30	5
20–29	398	176	10	9	7	145	6	45
10–19	598	275	6	58	26	138	19	76
2–9	264	140	7	31	1	57	2	26
Other	2,687	493	536	665	68	604	33	288
40 and over	1,446	163	467	461	19	184	24	128
30–39	401	100	26	57	12	150	—	56
20–29	400	67	28	89	33	135	2	46
10–19	318	113	10	50	4	99	5	37
2–9	122	50	5	8	—	36	2	21

Source: National Center for Education Statistics, Department of Education. Unpublished data from the Survey of Libary Networks and Cooperative Library Organizations, 1977–1978.

Table 6 shows in detail the distribution of expenditures among the different types of networks and among the different categories of expenditures. Proportionally the largest expenditures for public networks occurred in the categories of staff, office supplies, equipment, services, travel, computer software, and other expenses. For private networks, the primary expenditures were in the areas of computer hardware and telecommunications. Overall computer costs (for both hardware and software) for all networks came to over $4.2 million.

COMPUTER SUPPORT AND SERVICES

For the purposes of this survey, a computer was defined as any central processing unit with either on-line or off-line operations and its related peripheral equipment (e.g., terminals, printers, and the like). If the library network surveyed used a computer for library services, it was considered to be computerized regardless of the location of the computer. However, if the computer was used only for administrative purposes such as bookkeeping, billing, or payroll, then the network was not categorized as being computerized.

Three hundred and nine library networks reported using computers, representing over half of all library networks surveyed (see Table 7). Approximately 290 networks reported that computer terminals were used for organizational business by participants in their network organizations. Two hundred and sixty-two library networks reported use of computers to access a total of 2,246 data bases containing over 144 million titles (see Table 8).

TABLE 3 NUMBER AND PERCENT DISTRIBUTION OF PAID STAFF IN COOPERATIVE LIBRARY ORGANIZATIONS IN FTEs BY POSITION: 1977–1978

		Administrators		Professional						Library Technicians & Paraprofessionals		Clerical & Support Staff	
				Librarians		Computer-Related Staff		Other Professionals					
Organizational Type & No. of Participants	Total Paid Staff	Total	%	Total	%	Total	%	Total	%	Total	%	Total	%
All organizations	5,100.1	448.4	8.8	1,152.7	22.6	158.8	3.1	170.1	3.3	935.1	18.3	2,235.0	43.8
40 and over	2,947.4	260.0	8.8	606.9	20.6	147.3	5.0	109.2	3.7	599.7	20.3	1,224.3	41.5
30–39	318.6	28.7	9.0	57.4	18.0	0.3	0.1	—	—	32.4	10.2	199.8	62.7
20–29	331.5	41.0	12.4	85.1	25.7	2.0	0.6	9.5	2.9	46.2	13.9	147.7	44.6
10–19	900.3	80.1	8.9	248.5	27.6	4.2	0.5	29.4	3.3	123.9	13.8	414.2	46.0
2–9	602.3	38.6	6.4	154.8	25.7	5.0	0.8	22.0	3.7	132.9	22.1	249.0	41.3
Public	3,868.7	328.5	8.5	970.3	25.1	24.9	0.6	83.2	2.2	786.4	20.3	1,675.4	43.3
40 and over	1,973.9	180.1	9.1	474.6	24.0	15.3	0.8	27.5	1.4	491.1	24.9	785.3	39.8
30–39	269.2	21.7	8.1	50.9	18.9	0.3	0.1	—	—	23.9	8.9	172.4	64.0
20–29	301.7	33.9	11.2	80.3	26.6	2.0	0.7	6.5	2.2	45.2	15.0	133.8	44.3
10–19	803.1	67.0	8.3	232.5	29.0	2.4	0.3	29.3	3.6	111.1	13.8	360.8	44.9
2–9	520.8	25.8	5.0	132.0	25.3	4.9	0.9	19.9	3.8	115.1	22.1	223.1	42.8
Private	869.9	84.4	9.7	121.0	13.9	131.3	15.1	83.4	9.6	116.6	13.4	333.2	38.3
40 and over	722.9	58.8	8.1	93.0	12.9	131.0	18.1	79.2	11.0	86.0	11.9	274.9	38.0
30–39	15.5	3.0	19.4	2.0	12.9	—	—	—	—	8.0	51.6	2.5	16.1
20–29	17.0	5.1	30.0	2.0	11.8	—	—	3.0	17.6	1.0	5.9	5.9	34.7
10–19	53.5	7.9	14.8	6.7	12.5	0.2	0.4	0.1	0.2	4.8	9.0	33.8	63.2
2–9	61.0	9.6	15.7	17.3	28.4	0.1	0.2	1.1	1.8	16.8	27.5	16.1	26.4
Other	361.5	35.5	9.8	61.4	17.0	2.6	0.7	3.5	1.0	32.1	8.9	226.4	62.6
40 and over	250.6	21.1	8.4	39.3	15.7	1.0	0.4	2.5	1.0	22.6	9.0	164.1	65.5
30–39	33.9	4.0	11.8	4.5	13.3	—	—	—	—	0.5	1.5	24.9	73.5
20–29	12.8	2.0	15.6	2.8	21.9	—	—	—	—	—	—	8.0	62.5
10–19	43.7	5.2	11.9	9.3	21.3	1.6	3.7	—	—	8.0	18.3	19.6	44.9
2–9	20.5	3.2	15.6	5.5	26.8	—	—	1.0	4.9	1.0	4.9	9.8	47.8

Source: National Center for Education Statistics, Department of Education. Unpublished data from the Survey of Library Networks and Cooperative Library Organizations, 1977–1978.

TABLE 4 NUMBER AND PERCENT DISTRIBUTION OF NONPAID STAFF IN COOPERATIVE LIBRARY ORGANIZATIONS IN FTEs BY POSITION: 1977–1978

Organizational Type & No. of Participants	Total Nonpaid Staff	Professional — Administrators Total	%	Librarians Total	%	Computer-Related Staff Total	%	Other Professionals Total	%	Library Technicians & Paraprofessionals Total	%	Clerical & Support Staff Total	%
All organizations	768.4	97.9	12.7	499.6	65.0	11.1	1.4	11.2	1.5	78.9	10.3	69.7	9.1
40 and over	308.7	16.9	5.5	280.2	90.8	1.0	0.3	0.2	0.1	1.1	0.4	9.3	3.0
30–39	23.2	2.0	8.6	13.9	59.9	0.2	0.9	0.1	0.4	0.8	3.4	6.2	26.7
20–29	74.5	21.3	28.6	31.7	42.6	0.3	0.4	3.6	4.8	15.8	21.2	1.8	2.4
10–19	232.7	42.9	18.4	112.1	48.2	4.4	1.9	2.1	0.9	37.8	16.2	33.4	14.4
2–9	129.3	14.8	11.4	61.7	47.7	5.2	4.0	5.2	4.0	23.4	18.1	19.0	14.7
Public	444.0	44.7	10.1	318.9	71.8	2.3	0.5	5.0	1.1	25.6	5.8	47.5	10.7
40 and over	248.8	5.5	2.2	236.0	94.9	1.0	0.4	0.2	0.1	1.0	0.4	5.1	2.0
30–39	6.8	0.6	8.8	2.4	35.3	0.1	1.5	—	—	0.3	4.4	3.4	50.0
20–29	16.9	1.9	11.2	7.6	45.0	—	—	—	—	6.2	36.7	1.2	7.1
10–19	117.4	31.2	26.6	48.8	41.6	0.9	0.8	1.2	1.0	13.1	11.2	22.2	18.9
2–9	54.1	5.5	10.2	24.1	44.5	0.3	0.6	3.6	6.7	5.0	9.2	15.6	28.8
Private	231.8	35.1	15.1	131.6	56.8	7.9	3.4	4.1	1.8	43.6	18.8	9.5	4.1
40 and over	55.6	10.2	18.3	43.1	77.5	—	—	—	—	0.1	0.2	2.2	4.0
30–39	12.0	0.6	5.0	8.8	73.3	—	—	0.1	0.8	—	—	2.5	20.8
20–29	37.6	6.7	17.8	18.5	49.2	0.3	0.8	2.1	5.6	9.5	25.3	0.5	1.3
10–19	73.2	10.6	14.5	41.3	56.4	2.7	3.7	0.5	0.7	16.7	22.8	1.4	1.9
2–9	53.4	7.0	13.1	19.9	37.3	4.9	9.2	1.4	2.6	17.3	32.4	2.9	5.4
Other	92.6	18.1	19.5	49.1	53.0	0.9	1.0	2.1	2.3	9.7	10.5	12.7	13.7
40 and over	4.3	1.2	27.9	1.1	25.6	—	—	—	—	0.5	11.4	2.0	46.5
30–39	4.4	0.8	18.2	2.7	61.4	0.1	2.3	1.5	7.5	0.1	0.5	0.3	6.8
20–29	20.0	12.7	63.5	5.6	28.0	—	—	—	—	—	—	0.1	0.5
10–19	42.1	1.1	2.6	22.0	52.3	0.8	1.9	0.4	1.0	8.0	19.0	9.8	23.3
2–9	21.8	2.3	10.6	17.7	81.2	—	—	0.2	0.9	1.1	5.0	0.5	2.3

Source: National Center for Education Statistics, Department of Education. Unpublished data from the Survey of Library Networks and Cooperative Library Organizations, 1977–1978.

Library networks devote 75 percent of their automated service to such items as authority control, books for the blind, literature searches, copy selection, label production, computer output microfilm (COM) production, on-line cataloging, community user data, information file service, talking books, publications, business services, periodical claims, film booking, needs assessment, and printout indexes. Sixty percent of the total automated services was provided by public networks, 26 percent by private, and 14 percent by other. Twenty-four percent of the automated support activity was on standard on-line computers.

TABLE 5 AMOUNT AND PERCENT DISTRIBUTION OF COOPERATIVE

Organizational Type & No. of Participants	Total Funds (including Pass-through)	Total Funds (excluding Pass-through)	Pass-through Funds	Dues & Fees	Assessments	Sale of Products & Services
All organizations	$193,697,176	$181,490,854	$12,206,322	$6,492,931	$2,235,464	$24,733,152
40 and over	141,783,610	131,406,170	10,377,440	4,538,240	993,997	23,576,834
30-39	8,977,635	8,789,904	187,731	149,322	108,308	373,986
20-29	8,087,423	7,735,088	352,335	335,360	60,551	152,248
10-19	23,286,104	22,430,153	855,951	803,718	488,445	402,537
2-9	11,562,404	11,129,539	432,865	666,291	584,163	227,547
Public	140,991,434	135,481,371	5,510,063	1,888,327	1,402,107	2,259,913
40 and over	96,081,459	91,863,363	4,218,096	1,114,173	719,826	1,478,291
30-39	7,430,023	7,242,292	187,731	49,646	107,708	225,418
20-29	7,003,305	6,859,786	143,519	147,728	60,551	38,388
10-19	21,309,687	20,475,884	833,803	507,013	395,852	295,604
2-9	9,166,960	9,040,046	126,914	69,767	118,170	222,212
Private	43,469,092	37,030,595	6,438,497	4,302,153	718,675	22,140,784
40 and over	38,774,744	32,845,563	5,929,181	3,355,707	226,100	21,851,421
30-39	736,444	736,444	—	43,672	—	148,218
20-29	598,297	389,481	208,816	186,326	—	33,527
10-19	1,443,412	1,434,312	9,100	193,770	81,493	102,283
2-9	1,916,195	1,624,795	291,400	522,678	411,082	5,335
Other	9,236,650	8,978,888	257,762	302,451	114,682	332,455
40 and over	6,927,407	6,697,244	230,163	68,360	48,071	247,122
30-39	811,168	811,168	—	56,004	600	350
20-29	485,821	485,821	—	1,306	—	80,333
10-19	533,005	519,957	13,048	102,935	11,100	4,650
2-9	479,249	464,698	14,551	73,846	54,911	—

Source: National Center for Education Statistics, Department of Education. Unpublished data from the Survey of Library Net-

TABLE 6 AMOUNT AND PERCENT DISTRIBUTION OF COOPERATIVE LIBRARY

Organizational Type & No. of Participants	Total Expenditures (including Pass-through)	Total Expenditures (excluding Pass-through)	Expenditure of Pass-through Funds	Salaries & Wages	Fringe Benefits	Supplies & Materials	Reproduction Services
All organizations	$141,153,201	$129,284,473	$11,868,728	$51,998,320	$6,602,004	$15,996,836	$1,293,491
40 and over	98,272,287	88,892,270	9,380,017	32,345,120	4,264,978	9,161,767	792,051
30-39	6,590,057	6,317,134	272,923	2,721,925	533,957	1,377,526	24,578
20-29	7,148,512	6,712,035	436,477	3,202,851	495,010	952,726	92,707
10-19	18,547,263	17,185,505	1,361,758	8,154,785	909,266	2,812,947	265,585
2-9	10,595,082	10,177,529	417,553	5,573,639	398,793	1,691,870	118,570
Public	98,072,779	91,448,445	6,624,334	38,547,666	4,396,641	12,128,671	762,908
40 and over	60,886,035	56,182,922	4,703,113	21,217,108	2,362,518	6,155,563	299,450
30-39	5,516,600	5,291,145	225,455	2,300,442	441,659	1,220,619	23,185
20-29	6,253,205	6,025,544	227,661	2,898,685	458,984	923,883	83,801
10-19	16,954,075	15,601,417	1,352,658	7,382,911	811,078	2,528,955	253,608
2-9	8,462,864	8,347,417	115,447	4,748,520	322,402	1,299,651	102,864
Private	35,235,895	30,300,539	4,935,356	9,914,612	1,696,969	2,806,511	493,182
40 and over	31,703,287	27,324,870	4,378,417	8,515,579	1,494,411	2,328,898	463,472
30-39	452,273	404,805	47,468	143,473	21,421	22,045	535
20-29	518,810	309,994	208,816	148,447	21,115	21,339	7,906
10-19	1,135,695	1,126,595	9,100	550,566	89,027	184,768	5,605
2-9	1,425,830	1,134,275	291,555	556,547	70,995	249,461	15,664
Other	7,844,527	7,535,489	309,038	3,536,042	508,394	1,061,654	37,401
40 and over	5,682,965	5,384,478	298,487	2,612,433	408,049	677,306	29,129
30-39	621,184	621,184	—	278,010	70,877	134,862	858
20-29	376,497	376,497	—	155,719	14,911	7,504	1,000
10-19	457,493	457,493	—	221,308	9,161	99,224	6,372
2-9	706,388	695,837	10,551	268,572	5,396	142,758	42

Source: National Center for Education Statistics, Department of Education. Unpublished data from the Survey of Library Net-

LIBRARY ORGANIZATION FUNDS BY SOURCE: 1977-1978

Federal Government	State & Local Governments	Grants Foundations	Other Grants & Contracts	Income from State & Local Taxes	Investment Income	Carryover Funds	Other Funds
$51,649,154	$56,420,246	$982,019	$714,393	$20,306,822	$1,893,709	$11,856,321	$4,206,643
42,112,655	40,099,081	557,283	559,751	7,538,663	1,256,183	7,851,976	2,321,507
1,311,720	4,146,247	—	25,055	822,949	115,750	1,385,972	350,595
2,522,945	1,904,320	10,000	22,326	2,062,981	53,329	449,957	161,071
4,046,087	5,776,656	43,898	38,945	8,019,633	428,623	1,842,864	538,747
1,655,747	4,493,942	370,838	68,316	1,862,596	39,824	325,552	834,723
49,265,461	51,208,275	250,207	254,658	17,296,943	925,699	7,692,020	3,037,761
40,498,693	35,386,901	220,450	112,495	5,773,129	358,368	4,749,945	1,451,092
1,120,803	3,940,241	—	25,055	431,191	98,382	958,697	285,151
2,306,840	1,753,430	—	14,826	2,062,981	40,510	277,891	156,641
3,842,904	5,654,835	29,688	38,945	7,456,454	404,445	1,445,671	404,473
1,496,221	4,472,868	69	63,337	1,573,188	23,994	259,816	740,404
1,356,021	864,442	634,812	429,735	2,268,236	799,287	2,566,088	950,362
919,080	636,904	241,833	417,256	1,765,534	750,441	1,846,957	834,330
122,564	149,000	—	—	—	7,000	263,462	2,528
91,205	—	10,000	7,500	—	3,794	52,699	4,430
105,615	57,464	12,210	—	500,665	22,222	337,835	20,755
117,557	21,074	370,769	4,979	2,037	15,830	65,135	88,319
1,027,672	4,347,529	97,000	30,000	741,643	168,723	1,598,213	218,520
694,882	4,075,276	95,000	30,000	—	147,374	1,255,074	36,085
68,353	57,006	—	—	391,758	10,368	163,813	62,916
124,900	150,890	—	—	—	9,025	119,367	—
97,568	64,357	2,000	—	62,514	1,956	59,358	113,519
41,969	—	—	—	287,371	—	601	6,000

works and Cooperative Library Organizations, 1977-1978.

ORGANIZATION EXPENDITURES BY CATEGORY: 1977-1978

Equipment Other than Computers	Computer Costs Hardware	Software	Tele-communi-cations	Plant & Vehicles Operation & Maintenance	Staff Travel Expenses	Other Expenditures	Capital Outlay
$3,965,505	$3,722,299	$534,009	$5,234,921	$4,864,996	$14,859,206	$17,319,973	$2,892,913
2,493,949	3,297,784	274,996	4,215,302	3,633,209	14,405,283	11,654,279	2,353,552
275,314	114,442	48,081	107,533	268,823	56,576	675,896	112,483
162,276	48,653	57,466	286,449	215,401	95,118	1,039,673	63,705
572,188	210,436	125,999	449,896	488,537	173,729	2,910,704	111,433
461,778	50,984	27,467	175,741	259,026	128,500	1,039,421	251,740
2,702,181	728,437	249,927	1,813,063	3,448,623	14,173,779	11,148,201	1,348,348
1,621,158	430,114	83,665	946,902	2,426,124	13,793,252	6,003,166	843,902
214,661	55,442	48,081	69,970	174,839	42,806	600,203	99,238
151,118	44,727	29,280	259,709	193,095	74,947	853,667	53,648
530,431	168,809	63,909	396,175	419,255	155,988	2,790,478	99,820
184,813	29,345	24,992	140,307	235,310	106,786	900,687	251,740
709,444	2,983,216	114,628	3,296,010	959,314	617,547	5,380,059	1,329,047
629,873	2,863,890	89,831	3,197,414	862,478	576,772	4,992,396	1,309,856
45,180	59,000	—	16,503	14,373	4,572	70,124	7,578
4,847	560	—	13,808	6,404	7,332	78,236	—
17,014	40,127	22,622	33,351	52,343	11,990	107,569	11,613
12,530	19,639	2,175	34,934	23,716	16,880	131,734	—
553,880	10,646	169,454	125,848	457,059	67,880	791,713	215,518
242,918	3,780	101,500	70,986	344,607	35,259	658,717	199,794
15,473	—	—	21,060	79,611	9,197	5,569	5,667
6,311	3,366	28,186	12,932	15,902	12,839	107,770	10,057
24,743	1,500	39,468	20,370	16,939	5,751	12,657	—
264,435	2,000	300	500	—	4,834	7,000	—

works and Cooperative Library Organizations, 1977-1978.

TABLE 7 NUMBER AND PERCENT DISTRIBUTION OF COOPERATIVE LIBRARY ORGANIZATIONS USING COMPUTER AND OTHER AUTOMATED SUPPORT BY TYPE OF SUPPORT AND ACTIVITY: 1977–1978

Organizational Type & Activity	Total No. of Services Provided	Computers On-line Standard	Computers On-line Mini	Computers Off-line Standard	Computers Off-line Mini	Telecommunications Teletype	Telecommunications Telefacsimile	Micrographics
All organizations	4,189	1,009	557	646	102	801	391	683
Acquisitions	51	27	4	9	3	5	1	2
Cataloging	185	136	4	26	2	—	2	15
Union list production	209	59	6	95	4	3	—	42
Reference	242	106	5	37	4	63	20	7
Interlibrary loan	335	101	10	16	3	155	34	16
Circulation	45	11	8	15	3	6	—	1
Other	3,122	569	520	448	83	569	333	600
Public	2,503	602	326	357	55	510	239	414
Acquisitions	38	19	3	6	2	5	—	2
Cataloging	112	84	2	13	1	—	1	11
Union list production	114	33	4	44	4	2	—	27
Reference	150	62	4	14	2	47	15	6
Interlibrary loan	251	69	8	11	3	123	26	11
Circulation	31	7	6	10	2	5	—	1
Other	1,807	328	299	259	41	328	196	356
Private	1,082	273	143	195	23	184	93	171
Acquisitions	11	7	—	3	1	—	—	—
Cataloging	55	40	2	9	—	—	—	3
Union list production	70	19	1	38	—	2	—	12
Reference	59	29	—	16	2	9	2	—
Interlibrary loan	56	23	1	4	—	22	4	2
Circulation	9	2	—	4	1	5	—	—
Other	822	153	138	121	18	153	86	153
Other	604	134	88	94	24	107	59	98
Acquisitions	2	1	—	—	—	—	—	—
Cataloging	18	12	—	4	—	1	1	1
Union list production	25	7	1	13	—	7	—	3
Reference	33	15	1	7	—	7	3	—
Interlibrary loan	28	9	1	—	—	10	4	3
Circulation	5	2	1	1	—	1	—	—
Other	493	88	83	68	24	88	51	91

Source: National Center for Education Statistics, Department of Education. Unpublished data from the Survey of Library Networks and Cooperative Library Organizations, 1977–1978.

TABLE 8 NUMBER AND PERCENT DISTRIBUTION OF COOPERATIVE LIBRARY ORGANIZATIONS USING COMPUTERS, COMPUTER TERMINALS, AND DATA BASES, AND NUMBER OF DATA BASES AND DATA BASE TITLES REPORTED: 1977–1978

Organizational Type & No. of Participants	Total No. of Organizations	Computers — No. of Organizations Reporting	Computers — % of Total	Computer Terminals — No. of Organizations Reporting	Computer Terminals — % of Total	Data Bases — No. of Organizations Reporting	Data Bases — % of Total	Total No. of Data Bases Reported	Total No. of Titles in Data Bases
All organizations	608	309	50.8	291	47.9	262	43.1	2,246	144,279,540
40 and over	189	114	60.3	111	58.7	95	50.3	968	55,968,832
30–39	46	23	50.0	23	50.0	21	45.7	289	8,285,401
20–29	71	35	49.3	29	40.8	28	39.4	91	13,534,680
10–19	172	79	45.9	73	42.4	69	40.1	589	37,111,477
2–9	130	58	44.6	55	42.3	49	37.7	309	29,379,150
Public	362	183	50.6	180	49.7	160	44.2	1,459	95,478,660
40 and over	131	78	59.5	80	61.1	69	52.7	695	34,935,526
30–39	25	15	60.0	13	52.0	13	52.0	121	8,145,295
20–29	37	19	51.4	18	48.6	14	37.8	41	9,528,619
10–19	105	47	44.8	47	44.8	43	41.0	453	22,396,117
2–9	64	24	37.5	22	34.4	21	32.8	149	20,473,103
Private	155	87	56.1	77	49.7	68	43.9	607	26,610,915
40 and over	40	27	67.5	23	57.5	19	47.5	142	8,879,234
30–39	9	4	44.4	5	55.6	4	44.4	163	140,002
20–29	17	8	47.1	7	41.2	7	41.2	42	4,000,045
10–19	44	22	50.0	19	43.2	18	40.9	126	4,692,397
2–9	45	26	57.8	23	51.1	20	44.4	134	8,899,237
Other	91	39	42.9	34	37.4	34	37.4	180	22,189,965
40 and over	18	9	50.0	8	44.4	7	38.9	131	12,154,072
30–39	12	4	33.3	5	41.7	4	33.3	5	104
20–29	17	8	47.1	4	23.5	7	41.2	8	6,016
10–19	23	10	43.5	7	30.4	8	34.8	10	10,022,963
2–9	21	8	38.1	10	47.6	8	38.1	26	6,810

Source: National Center for Education Statistics, Department of Education. Unpublished data from the Survey of Library Networks and Cooperative Library Organizations, 1977–1978.

INTERGOVERNMENTAL LIBRARY COOPERATION PROJECT: A SUMMARY REPORT

Alphonse F. Trezza

*Director, Intergovernmental Library Cooperation Project,
Federal Library Committee, Library of Congress*

In the spring of 1980 the National Commission on Libraries and Information Science (NCLIS) and the Library of Congress (LC) agreed to a joint undertaking—a study of existing governmental library resources and services throughout the country. The purpose of the study was to determine ways to improve the coordination of resources and services among federal libraries and between federal and nonfederal libraries to meet national, state, and local needs. The Federal Library Committee (FLC) assumed the responsibility for overseeing the study and Alphonse F. Trezza, former executive director of NCLIS, agreed to serve as director.

The NCLIS national program document, *Toward a National Program for Library and Information Services: Goals for Action*, calls for the planning, development, and implementation of a nationwide network for the purpose of providing equal opportunity of access to information. A major component of such a network is the community of federal libraries and information centers, which comprise extensive collections of materials distributed among 2,000 libraries and information centers across the country. The issue of the role of federal libraries and information centers in a nationwide network was addressed in a number of resolutions adopted by the delegates to the White House Conference on Library and Information Services in 1979. The important contribution federal libraries and information centers could make was strongly emphasized. Both the need to avoid overlapping and duplication of collections and services and the need to remove barriers to access were identified. In their discussion of national information policy, the delegates at the White House conference stated that government agencies at all levels must work together to make information services available to the maximum extent possible.

The coordination of federal library resources and services, not only within the federal structure (as called for in the NCLIS national program document) but with the public at large at the local, state, and regional levels, is essential if a nationwide program is to be effective. In order to provide services to all segments of society and guarantee a right of access to publicly held information for all citizens, effective coordination of the resources and services available through federal library and information centers is critical.

The long-range national goals described in the National Commission's program document and expressed at the Federal Libraries and Information Services Pre–White House Conference are (1) to achieve, through careful planning and coordination, the integration of federal libraries and information centers in the developing nationwide library and information network, and (2) to work toward ensuring, through cooperative activity, the sharing of resources and services of federal and nonfederal libraries and information centers to meet the information and educational needs of the community.

The study officially started July 7, 1980. Early activities included a review of the study goals and objectives, the determination of the initial steps, and an assessment of the data already available. A number of visits with federal librarians in federal regions V, VI, and IX were completed and questionnaires were sent to over 400 field libraries in the three regions. Forty percent of the libraries responded. Thirty-one parent agencies in the Washington area were visited. Findings from both the field visits and the questionnaires indicate that federal libraries throughout the country tend to look to nonfederal libraries at the local and state level for cooperation and support. One notable exception is the case of medical libraries where interagency cooperation locally is very strong. Federal libraries throughout the country generally are prepared to share their collections and services with their nonfederal counterparts.

A variety of issues and problems were discussed in the parent-agency meetings. These included organization, budgeting, contractual services, programing areas, and relationships between the parent agency and field libraries, as well as consideration and possible implementation of the contracting-out provisions of the Office of Management and Budget (OMB) Circular A-76, inconsistencies of interpretation of procurement regulations, the delay and revision of the personnel classification schedules, and the present level of the use of automation. During the course of the project, an advisory committee with individuals representing major government agencies met five times to react to the various draft chapters, the interpretation of the data, and the formulation of the recommendations.

Of special importance to this study are the statistics and information on federal library collections and services. These include the number of volumes and titles, the number of service contracts including interlibrary lending and borrowing, and activities in the area of cooperation and automation. FLC's "Survey of Federal Libraries, FY 1978" (unpublished) provides the basic data on federal library collections, services, and expenditures. Federal libraries are located throughout the United States and in most areas of the world. They serve the Senate, the House of Representatives, courts of the judicial branch, the office of the president, 11 civilian and 3 military departments, and 43 other federal organizations including 42 independent agencies. A total of 2,142 libraries of all types and in all locations were identified for inclusion in the survey. Responses were received from 1,389 libraries. In addition, substantial data was supplied for another 491 libraries by parent agencies, headquarters libraries, and system headquarters. As a result, significant data is included in the survey for 1,880 libraries representing 88 percent of the survey universe. Of the libraries participating in the survey, 1,858 reported collection holdings in excess of 190,000,000 items, expenditures of over half a billion dollars, and an estimated total of almost 60,000,000 individual service contacts (circulation, information transactions, interlibrary loans, and direct patron service). The number of titles totaled 70,871,924, of which 58 percent was print material and 37 percent microforms. Most of the microforms (83 percent) were of documents or reports. National libraries held more than two-fifths of the total items and less than 20 percent of the total titles. Current periodical subscriptions totaled 597,183 at the end of FY 1978. Of these, more than one-third were held by national libraries. In FY 1978, 49,128 new periodical titles were added. Circulation was highest in general, patient, and school libraries (66 to 84 percent). In national, academic, science, medical, and other special libraries, circulation represented between 56 and 59 percent of service contacts. The percent of interlibrary transactions to total service contacts varies from 2 percent for federal libraries overall to 9 percent for medical libraries. In general libraries located on military bases and in patient libraries in Veterans Administration hospitals, interlibrary transactions represented less than 1 percent of the service contacts; however, in special, medical, system (agency), headquarters, and national libraries, interlibrary transactions represented 3 to 8 percent of the service contacts. A check of interlibrary activity for FY 1981 for the Library of Congress, National Library of Medicine (NLM), National Agricultural Library (NAL), and Veterans Administration (VA) reveals a slight decrease for the first two libraries and a modest increase for NAL and the VA medical and hospital libraries. LC and NLM accounted for 44 percent of all materials loaned. NAL is a net lender for journals and reports. Information transactions made up more than one-fifth of total service contacts. The volume was highest in general, special, science, and national libraries. General libraries reported the highest number of reference and directional transactions, science libraries the highest total volume of on-line reference services. National libraries were responsible for about 20 percent of the reference transactions. Photocopies for patrons made up an estimated 6 percent of all service contacts. There was a substantial level of activity by presidential libraries providing, most frequently, manuscript pages. In addition to providing photocopies for library patrons, 27 percent of federal libraries reported providing photocopies in lieu of original materials in interlibrary loan while 34 percent reported that they had received photocopies in interlibrary borrowing.

Data collected in the survey indicated that 25 percent of all federal library respondents reported participation in networks or other cooperative arrangements. In addition to interlibrary lending/borrowing, they participated in shared cataloging, technical processing services, centralized procurement, and so forth. Through FLC, a number of federal libraries have access to the Online Computer Library Center (OCLC) for cataloging data and locations of materials needed in interlibrary loan. Other resource-sharing arrangements include the Regional Medical Library Network supported by NLM, which channels borrowing for all medical libraries throughout the country, and agency resource sharing networks such as those in the U.S. Department of Agriculture (USDA), the Environmental Protection Agency (EPA), the National Oceanic and Atmospheric Administration (NOAA), and VA.

CONCLUSIONS AND RECOMMENDATIONS

Federal libraries represent a diverse universe, a microcosm of the nation's libraries—academic, scientific, technical, other special libraries, general, and school. Cooperation among them is voluntary, in many cases even in the same agency of government. Because federal libraries in the field are basically supported by the field agency, they tend to be independent in funding and services. Parent agencies influence them only to the extent that they provide services or additional funding. In fact, few governmental departments or agencies designate a single authority for coordinating or supporting library facilities within the organization. In most cases federal libraries are responsible only to the specific office or agency that they serve. Some facilities providing library resources are not designated libraries because of the limitation of staffing and clientele served. As a result, there is limited planning, coordination, and cooperation.

Federal Data Base

If the resources of federal libraries are to be shared more effectively among federal and nonfederal libraries, then a more deliberate and planned approach is needed. The development and utilization of a federal data base would provide the opportunity for such sharing on a relatively equal basis. The data base of federal collection holdings can become a reality if the perceived need is agreed on by the major federal agencies. A federal data base could include the OCLC tapes that contain over 3 million logical records input by federal libraries that utilize OCLC's cataloging service. Current monthly level of input is over 60,000 records. The identification of federal documents input by the Government Printing Office (GPO) would also be included. In addition, the data base would include federal library and information services in-house tapes, as well as those prepared by the National Technical Information Service (NTIS) to identify technical reports emanating from federal scientific and technical activities. Merging these tapes could provide a data base of federal library holdings that would serve as a logical first point of reference for federal libraries. The OCLC data base does present some problems for federal libraries that could be alleviated by the development of a federal data base. Two examples are the lack of subject-searching capability for the OCLC data base and the lack of inclusion of local call numbers as part of the on-line data base. Both of these elements could be considered in the development of a federal bibliographic data base. With these added elements, provision of interlibrary lending on a timely basis would improve immeasurably and staff costs for searching and fulfillment would be appreciably reduced. Such a data base would provide easy identification of titles held by others, provide subject-searching capability, and possibly reduce the heavy reliance of federal libraries, especially in the Washington, D.C., area, on LC's collections by providing alternate sources for interlibrary lending. It would enhance the coordination of efforts towards cooperative collection development and in-depth reference service. The development and utilization of a federal data base would also lessen federal library reliance on nonfederal libraries.

The projected federal data base would not provide a shared cataloging function— OCLC, the Research Libraries Information Network (RLIN), and the Washington Library Network (WLN) provide that service effectively. Rather, it would serve as an efficient reference and interlibrary loan tool, because as a subset of the larger data bases, it would be more easily searchable and timely. For example, a federal library union list of serials might start from the data input into OCLC by federal libraries. It would provide an estimated format and could be expanded and updated on a phased and systematic basis. A federal data base could also provide off-line products such as special purpose computer output microfilm (COM) listings, or other products required by individual libraries or groups of libraries. The federal data base would not only be important to federal libraries; it would serve as a major resource for nonfederal libraries as well. By continuing to participate in nonfederal services such as OCLC, RLIN, and WLN, federal libraries will continue their contribution to the growth of those bibliographic data bases. The federal data base would serve as an additional resource, not a replacement, and its development would be evolutionary.

In the area of services, federal libraries have been willing to share their resources through interlibrary lending, the provision of reference and information services, including information retrieval services, and the distribution and delivery of resources both generated and collected by federal agencies. LC, NLM, NAL, GPO, and NTIS all provide data and information about these resources in a variety of formats and in a variety of delivery modes. At present, bibliographic information and document availability of government publications is the primary responsibility of GPO and NTIS.

The problem of accessibility by the public to federal library resources would benefit from this development. If federal documents are entered into the GPO and/or NTIS files on a timely basis, then information about most government publications would be widely available through the federal data base for anyone with access to GPO's data base through OCLC and the NTIS data base through commercial sources such as Systems Development Corporation, Bibliographic Retrieval Services, and Lockheed. In-house use by students, researchers, and scholars of federal library collections has always been honored. Experience indicates that use by the general public, especially of specialized libraries with unique resources, will always be limited. But by declaring as a matter of principle that information about and access to federal publications and federal library collections is easily available, federal libraries will be expressing the spirit of the ideal of resource sharing by all public libraries for users.

Federal Library and Information Services Network

There is a need to develop on a planned basis and within a realistic time frame, perhaps five years, a federal library and information services network. Such a network should be based on existing strengths and organization—it should not be a "reinvention of the wheel" but a full-service network based on user needs and not a technology-driven (dominated) network. Service is the goal and technology is one of the mechanisms. The most important element is the human factor. This, of course, is not meant to diminish the important and vital role of information technology (automation and communication) in a federal network. To achieve more effective resource sharing requires greater sharing and/or interfacing of automated systems. As was noted earlier, in the area of shared cataloging and access to information retrieval data-bases, federal libraries have participated in cooperative activity through FLC/FEDLINK and with commercial services. Not very much has been accomplished in the areas of acquisitions, circulation, serials, and union lists between and among federal agencies. In fact, many agencies have not achieved coordinated automated systems between libraries in their own agencies. The development of prototype systems for governmentwide applications is essential. The technology exists in most cases or will be available shortly. (NLM and NOAA are developing systems presently.) The time for planning, priority setting, scheduling, and implementation is long overdue.

The network must not only serve the needs of the federal establishment, but should play a major role in the developing nationwide library and information services network. A nationwide network will be pluralistic and voluntary; it must be user sensitive, not process oriented, using the latest in technology as its tools. Some of the current pieces or elements in this developing nationwide network are such utility/service centers, national and state libraries, and regional organizations as OCLC, RLIN, WLN, LC, NLM, and NAL, and the many state (e.g., ILLINET, NYSILL) and multistate (e.g., AMIGOS, SOLINET) agencies.

Properly planned and operated, a federal library and information services activity could serve as a model for a nationwide library and information services network. It would be involved in developing standards, protocols, common responsibilities, governmentwide information technology applications, planning and evaluation, suggestions for research, and so forth. The development of a coordinated cooperative federal network will provide the opportunity to identify and resolve many problems that would be of importance and interest to nationwide network development. The activities and actions of a federal library and information services network, as a publicly funded agency, would be scrutinized by the library community as a whole and would serve as an experiment and an example in the areas of services, resource sharing, and even governance. The federal library community could provide leadership to the nation's library community—a responsibility it has previously exercised with caution and hesitation, and in the view of some, not at all.

To improve the coordination of resources and services among federal libraries and information centers and with and between federal and nonfederal libraries to meet local, state, and national needs, and to work toward the integration of federal libraries in the developing nationwide library and information services network, requires a belief in and a support of the philosophy of cooperation and the sharing of resources and services. It requires an understanding of and a commitment to the concept of interdependence for our information needs.

ACADEMIC LIBRARY BUILDINGS IN 1981

Bette-Lee Fox

Associate Editor, *Library Journal*

Shiri Rosenthal

Assistant Editor, *Library Journal*

Library Journal's annual survey of academic construction and remodeling projects found that academic library building and renovation projects totaled 34 in 1981, led by two major ones: California Polytechnic at San Luis Obispo and Indiana University's Fine Arts Library (at $11.5 million and $10.5 million respectively). Two medical libraries and one law library are included.

Identification of building projects was aided by a questionnaire mailed to every academic library listed in the *American Library Directory* (R. R. Bowker). The notes accompanying the questionnaires indicate at least four solar-powered projects, one triangular building, and a library owned and operated health center. These notes, which appear as references at the bottom of Table 4, are denoted in the tables by a superscript numeral following the community or institution name.

Note: Adapted from *Library Journal*, December 1, 1981.

TABLE 1 ACADEMIC LIBRARIES, 1971-1981

	1971	1972	1973	1974	1975	1976	1977	1978-1979	1980	1981
New Libraries	33	17	17	21	18	15	6	38	14	19
Additions	6	2	1	9	2	5	5	8	2	0
Additions plus Renovation	10	3	3	10	5	8	7	22	11	11
TOTALS	49	22	21	40	25	28	18	66	27	30
Combined Additions and Addition plus Renovation	16	5	4	19	7	13	12	30	13	11
Percentage of Combined A and A & R	32.65	22.72	19.04	47.50	28.00	46.42	66.63	45.45	48.15	36.66

ACADEMIC LIBRARY BUILDINGS IN 1981 / 363

TABLE 2 NEW LIBRARIES

Name of Institution	Project Cost	Gross Area	Assignable	Non-Assignable	Sq. Ft. Cost	Building Cost	Equipment Cost	Book Capacity	Seating Capacity	Architect
California Polytechnic State Univ., San Luis Obispo	$11,540,000	203,605	157,875	45,730	$50.63	$9,040,000	$123,202	800,000	2,500	Marquis
Indiana Univ., Fine Arts Lib., Bloomington	10,500,000	106,000	23,042	82,958	99.06	10,387,000	152,000	83,000	220	Pei
Univ. of Michigan, Dearborn	10,200,000	114,899	73,775	41,124	65.93	8,626,000	1,574,000	350,000	1,200	Sherman
Gallaudet Coll., Washington, D.C.[1]	9,800,000	93,137	79,368	13,769	86.00	8,000,000	1,800,000	100,000	500	King
Southwest Missouri State Univ., Springfield	6,585,097	116,643	93,315	23,328	56.46	5,829,976	600,285	335,000	1,767	Hellmuth
Univ. of Wisconsin-Stout, Menomonie	5,672,000	125,000	87,000	38,000	39.35	4,917,556	332,300	388,875	1,063	Durrant
Southwestern Baptist Theological Seminary, Fort Worth, Tex.	5,600,000	100,000	78,200	21,800	66.00	4,200,000	1,000,000	535,000	1,000	Geren
Gettysburg Coll., Pa.	4,959,000	73,000	61,300	9,700	68.00	4,300,000	329,000	420,000	800	Hugh
Babson Coll., Wellesley, Mass.	4,700,000	60,000	48,000	12,000	57.50	3,850,000	500,000	200,000	500	Arrowstreet
Univ. of Minnesota, St. Paul	4,030,000	81,515	51,761	29,754	42.95	3,500,000	530,000	16,469	579	Bentz
Pennsylvania State Univ. (Delaware Cty Campus), Media	2,788,112	50,178	36,307	13,871	49.60	2,488,112	300,000	50,000	350	Geddes
Univ. of California, Bechtel Engineering Ctr., Berkeley	2,764,316	22,000	24,451	549	114.55	2,457,150	258,500	120,000	253	Matsumoto
Western Theological Seminary, Holland, Mich.	2,699,400	33,075	26,712	6,363	67.42	2,230,000	256,000	130,000	160	Droppers
Sheridan Coll., Wy.[2]	1,788,506	39,344	n/a	n/a	37.00	1,455,640	332,966	100,000	175	Drake
Univ. of California, Medical Ctr. Lib., San Diego	1,089,000	10,245	7,100	3,145	99.76	1,022,000	67,000	23,000	100	Bird
SUNY at Buffalo, Music Library (Amherst Campus)	846,322	n/a	9,817	n/a	70.00	748,422	117,900	132,000	90	Ulrich
Ringling Sch. of Art & Design,[3] Sarasota, Fla.	700,000	4,520	n/a	n/a	n/a	660,000	40,000	20,000	75	Shaw
New Mexico State Univ., Las Cruces	400,000	5,014	4,686	328	79.77	333,000	67,000	3,817	72	not reported
Univ. of Utah Law Lib., Salt Lake City[3a]	n/a	47,383	36,500	10,883	66.73	3,133,590	n/a	283,841	433	Fowler

364 / LIBRARY RESEARCH AND STATISTICS

TABLE 3   ADDITION AND RENOVATION

Name of Institution		Project Cost	Gross Area	Assignable	Non-Assignable	Sq. Ft. Cost	Building Cost	Equipment Cost	Book Capacity	Seating Capacity	Architect
Indiana Univ., Pa.	Total	$7,701,252	157,444	142,767	14,677	$45.70	$6,078,285	$807,000	800,000	1,500	Burt...
	New	7,028,811	119,244	107,319	10,925		5,449,844	763,000	650,000	1,200	
	Renovated	672,441	38,200	35,448	2,758	16.45	628,441	44,000	150,000	300	
Virginia Polytechnic Institute & State Univ., Blacksburg	Total	5,554,000	240,000	200,000	40,000	23.14	5,054,000	500,000	1,600,000	2,000	VVKR...
	New	4,554,000	120,000	100,000	20,000	37.95	4,054,000	500,000	600,000	1,200	
	Renovated	1,000,000	120,000	100,000	20,000	10.00	1,000,000	0	1,000,000	800	
St. Joseph's Univ., Philadelphia, Pa.	Total	2,900,000	66,000	53,000	13,000	70.00	1,900,000	209,000	350,000	600	Sabatino...
	New	2,100,000	41,000	31,000	10,000	51.00	1,891,000	209,000			
	Renovated	800,000	25,000	22,000	3,000	19.00					
North Dakota State Univ., Fargo	Total	2,703,928	97,149	84,500	12,649	34.07	2,320,991	229,295	170,000	137	Koehnlein...
	New		42,429	34,800	7,629	16.00	1,445,471		378,000	700	
	Renovated		54,720	49,700	5,020		875,520				
Wheaton Coll., Norton, Mass.	Total	2,555,018	80,415	53,775	26,640	30.03	2,415,018	140,000	350,000	350	Mitchell...
	New	1,669,414	24,375	18,750	5,625	63.57	1,549,414	120,000	250,000	150	
	Renovated	885,604	56,040	35,025	21,015	15.45	865,604	20,000	100,000	200	
Eastern New Mexico[4] Univ., Portales	Total	2,400,000	93,330	72,000	21,330	59.17	17,376	400,000	300,000	750	Holt...
	New										
	Renovated										
Converse Coll., Spartanburg, S.C.	Total	1,881,673	40,000			86.24	1,724,746	156,927	225,000	288	Cain...
	New		20,000								
	Renovated		20,000								
Princeton Univ.,[5] Geology Lib., N.J.	Total	1,800,000	17,816	14,937	2,679		1,500,000	150,000	102,000	80	Mitchell...
	New		13,709	10,830	2,879				100,000	60	
	Renovated		4,107	4,107	0				2,000	20	
Concordia Teachers[6] Coll., Seward, Neb.	Total	1,665,000	52,500	42,578	9,922	40.00	1,420,000	200,000	250,000	400	Henningson...
	New	1,620,000	35,500	29,110	6,390	3.00		200,000	250,000	400	
	Renovated	45,000	17,000	13,468	3,532						
Siena Heights Coll., Adrian, Mich.	Total	1,180,000		21,757		55.00	1,100,000	80,000	150,000	250	Diehl...
	New	1,080,000		15,000		72.00	1,000,000	80,000	100,000	50	
	Renovated	100,000		6,757		15.00	100,000		50,000	200	
Ohio State Univ., Columbus	Total	1,170,000	8,572					1,043	62,100	110	Swearingen...
	New		2,223						21,300	9	
	Renovated		6,349						40,800	101	

TABLE 4 RENOVATION ONLY

Name of Institution	Project Cost	Gross Area	Assignable	Non-Assignable	Sq. Ft. Cost	Building Cost	Equipment Cost	Book Capacity	Seating Capacity	Architect
Univ. of North Carolina, Chapel Hill	$5,660,000	291,000	229,000	62,000	n/a	$5,260,000	$400,000	2,000,000	n/a	Polier....
Marquette Univ., Science Lib., Milwaukee, Wisc.	1,319,000	n/a	29,570	n/a	$38.28	1,132,000	187,000	160,000	550	Architects III
Univ. of the South, Sewanee,[7] Tenn.	500,000	31,192	24,708	6,484	8.92	278,220	220,000	150,000	180	Architect....
Univ. of California, Biomedical[8] Lib., Irvine	97,000	4,015	4,015	0	17.43	70,000	12,000	12,000	40	Woollett...
West Virginia Sch. of Osteopathic[9] Medicine, Lewisburg	49,396	2,920	1,940	980	n/a	46,358	3,038	0	34	Vernon....
Monmouth Coll., West Long Branch,[10] N.J.	40,000	1,125	n/a	n/a	n/a	25,000	15,000	21,000	0	not reported

REFERENCES FOR TABLES 2–4

1. Includes instruction & educational technology spaces: 2400 sq. ft. TV studio; special accommodations for the hearing impaired.
2. Houses instruction technology dept. & learning skills center.
3. Occupies less than one quarter Library Studio complex.
3a. Equipment cost undetermined, therefore project cost unavailable.
4. No breakdown in contract for cost of new area & remodeling.
5. Also houses 185,000 maps.
6. Includes 50,000 nonprint titles.
7. Designed to accommodate Sch. of Theology library; provides for new university archives; triples present storage space, user & exhibit rooms.
8. Technical processing functions moved to lower floor.
9. Houses study area. AV rooms, office, reference & current periodical display—no books.
10. Shelving only.

PUBLIC LIBRARY BUILDINGS IN 1981

Bette-Lee Fox
Associate Editor, *Library Journal*

Shiri Rosenthal
Assistant Editor, *Library Journal*

Public library building maintained and slightly bettered its dollar value, but a good many more dollars went into additions and renovations as opposed to wholly new construction. The figures for funding sources (federal, state, local, gift) are only a close approximation; as in past years, it has been impossible to get complete information from the survey responses. However, there is an expected dip in federal funding, down some $4 million, and an increase in gift and local funds.

The notes accompanying the questionnaires indicate at least four solar-powered projects, one triangular building, and a library owned and operated health center. These notes, which appear as references at the bottom of Table 4, are denoted in the tables by a superscript numeral following the community or institution name. The codes in Tables 1-4 mean the following: B—branch library, BS—branch and system headquarters, M—main library, MS—main and system headquarters, S—system headquarters, SC—school district, NA—not available.

Note: Adapted from *Library Journal*, December 1, 1981.

TABLE 1 NEW PUBLIC LIBRARY BUILDINGS CONSTRUCTED DURING YEAR ENDING JUNE 30, 1981

Community	Pop. in M	Code	Project Cost	Gross Sq. Ft.	Const. Cost	Sq. Ft. Cost	Equip. Cost	Site Cost	Other Costs	Vols.	Reader Seats	Fed. Funds	State Funds	Local Funds	Gift Funds	Architect
CALIFORNIA																
Anaheim	30	B	$1,515,586	18,000	$1,240,000	$67.22	$116,086	owned	$159,500	90,000	122	$988,178	$411,511	$115,887	0	Blurock
Bakersfield	31	B	534,862	7,465	441,970	59.21	48,771	n/a	44,121	40,000	78	441,970	0	92,892	0	not reported
Cathedral City	15	B	435,000	3,700	185,400	50.00	37,000	$69,000	143,600	15,000	65	385,000	0	150,000	0	Outcault
El Toro[1]	45	B	1,667,442	10,000	1,156,031	115.60	220,000	189,000	102,411	70,000	64	124,837	0	1,353,605	$189,000	Brooks
Highgrove	4	B	200,000	1,600	200,000	125.00	0	leased	n/a	12,000	20	200,000	0	0	0	Porta-Structures Ind.
Moorpark	10	B	184,600	2,400	145,600	60.66	0	owned	39,000	20,000	21	0	0	184,000	0	Wilson
San Bernardino	25	B	596,929	7,500	483,843	64.57	20,070	38,172	54,844	20,000	68	594,337	0	2,592	0	Villanueva
CONNECTICUT																
Hamden	50	MS	3,341,046	63,328	2,879,345	52.76	146,500	owned	279,839	150,000	180	1,566,000	72,000	1,691,525	11,521	Franzoni
FLORIDA																
Daytona Beach	258	B	2,316,601	39,442	2,056,692	52.14	196,577	owned	63,332	108,871	254	2,316,601	0	0	0	Faust
Homestead	n/a	B	995,811	16,000	778,029	48.63	148,640	owned	69,142	75,000	100	0	0	995,811	0	Silvers
Miami	55	B	1,382,000	16,000	961,000	60.06	160,000	135,000	126,000	60,000	100	0	0	1,382,000	0	Reed, G. F.
Miami	n/a	B	735,654	11,000	577,163	52.47	140,587	owned	17,904	45,000	97	0	0	735,654	0	Arthur
Miami	n/a	B	697,103	14,000	453,182	32.37	109,748	83,000	51,176	65,900	100	0	0	697,103	0	Gili
GEORGIA																
Jasper	11	B	500,000	7,480	394,395	52.73	59,303	owned	46,302	29,734	66	200,000	250,000	42,000	8,000	Frye
Statesboro	39	MS	1,242,809	21,000	964,628	45.94	126,281	96,000	55,900	150,000	100	0	250,000	846,000	146,809	Holland
Thomaston	25	B	699,383	7,200	555,610	79.00	41,549	62,000	40,224	35,000	60	0	212,500	0	486,883	Searbrough
INDIANA																
Connersville	27	B	1,400,000	21,522	1,051,597	48.00	213,978	owned	134,425	95,000	140	0	n/a	1,400,000	0	Pecsok
Tipton	17	M	1,602,084	20,000	1,248,084	59.43	129,000	owned	225,000	90,000	75	0	0	1,592,084	0	Pecsok
IOWA																
Elliott	5	B	53,224	4,050	45,930	11.34	4,894	2,400	n/a	n/a	22	0	5,000	3,800	45,424	not reported
Fairbank	3	M	66,864	3,000	61,126	23.88	5,738	n/a	0	5,690	40	0	0	0	49,864	not reported
Iowa City[2]	65	M	4,032,391	47,000	2,835,797	60.34	826,443	owned	334,151	275,000	264	66,783	0	3,960,608	5,000	Hansen
KANSAS																
Osawatomie	6	M	270,286	6,800	199,254	39.75	28,492	27,687	14,853	40,000	22	0	0	250,000	20,286	Skidmore
KENTUCKY																
Carrollton	9	B	366,965	6,000	290,254	48.37	26,855	25,548	24,307	3,000	35	0	23,500	131,965	1,847	Coblin
LOUISIANA																
Larose	9	B	109,387	2,440	97,917	40.13	3,338	leased	8,528	12,700	20	100,986	0	5,459	3,338	Gossen
MARYLAND																
Joppa	10	B	1,191,600	14,000	755,700	53.98	80,000	66,000	289,900	40,000	50	0	0	1,191,600	0	Baxter
Whiteford	4	B	71,800	720	46,300	64.31	5,000	18,000	2,500	5,000	6	0	0	71,800	0	Baxter

TABLE 1   NEW PUBLIC LIBRARY BUILDINGS CONSTRUCTED DURING YEAR ENDING JUNE 30, 1981 (cont.)

Community	Pop. in M	Code	Project Cost	Gross Sq. Ft.	Const. Cost	Sq. Ft. Cost	Equip. Cost	Site Cost	Other Costs	Vols.	Reader Seats	Fed. Funds	State Funds	Local Funds	Gift Funds	Architect
MASSACHUSETTS																
Seekonk[3]	12	M	700,000	14,870	528,300	35.53	80,000	owned	91,700	60,000	99	700,000	0	0	0	Providence
MICHIGAN																
Detroit	72	B	1,811,119	20,220	1,583,373	78.31	110,000	owned	117,746	60,000	90	0	0	1,811,119	0	Sims
MINNESOTA																
Duluth[4]	95	M	6,857,415	79,060	5,372,798	67.96	738,807	59,800	686,010	300,000	363	5,000,000	0	773,099	1,084,316	Birkerts
Minneapolis	13	B	299,953	4,096	240,866	58.81	39,323	0	19,764	12,400	35	0	0	300,000	0	Lindberg
MISSISSIPPI																
Carrollton	9	MS	119,657	2,542	93,535	36.80	10,826	7,538	7,758	10,000	24	0	0	119,657	0	Godfrey
Leakesville	1	B	125,200	2,700	89,683	33.22	19,516	7,550	8,451	10,625	20	0	62,600	62,300	300	Reed, M.
NEBRASKA																
Curtis	4	B	85,000	2,200	72,000	36.37	8,000	owned	5,000	12,000	20	0	0	0	85,000	Hudler
NEW JERSEY																
Bridgewater	112	BS	3,126,655	46,200	2,677,337	57.95	288,022	owned	172,858	250,000	220	0	7,262	3,119,393	0	Bouman
Chester	7	M	610,512	7,500	492,584	65.67	80,995	owned	36,636	40,000	80	0	0	539,730	70,485	Nadaskay
Rockaway Township	20	M	1,457,107	22,000	1,252,600	56.90	125,007	owned	79,500	60,000	84	0	0	1,457,107	0	Hessburger
NEW YORK																
Bronx[5]	29	B	2,545,172	20,000	2,222,200	111.11	172,348	90,624	60,000	40,000	110	1,984,200	0	388,624	0	Diadone
Clifton Park	36	M	433,116	4,320	246,953	57.17	26,617	92,769	66,777	24,100	31	0	0	170,000	263,116	Feibes
Martinsburg	1	M	94,000	3,750	86,500	23.00	0	owned	7,500	6,000	60	0	10,000	0	84,000	Orsdell
NORTH CAROLINA																
Kenansville	41	MS	208,033	5,800	192,010	33.10	8,900	owned	16,783	50,000	35	0	27,600	160,433	20,000	Grier
OHIO																
Dublin	6	B	527,652	7,348	411,404	56.00	43,417	owned	72,831	22,942	69	0	0	527,256	0	Kellam
Mendon	3	B	132,000	1,200	120,000	100.00	7,000	5,000	0	10,000	12	88,000	0	10,000	22,000	Anderson
Reynoldsburg	25	B	765,561	9,000	494,217	54.92	48,303	136,400	86,641	n/a	n/a	0	0	765,561	0	Feinknopf
Richfield	20	B	679,000	6,660	543,200	81.56	53,800	leased	82,000	20,000	50	0	0	614,000	65,000	Pearce Office
PENNSYLVANIA																
Allentown	30	M	400,000	5,400	300,000	55.55	38,000	owned	62,000	45,000	24	0	0	0	400,000	Seibert
Elkins Park	16	B	1,083,378	12,700	842,600	66.35	49,778	owned	191,000	47,000	90	0	0	999,500	83,878	Hayes
SOUTH CAROLINA																
Columbia	26	B	183,692	3,030	137,000	45.21	37,102	owned	9,590	26,246	29	122,000	0	24,940	36,752	Drafts
Pageland	8	B	202,000	3,600	136,800	38.00	18,000	6,000	13,000	10,000	30	0	0	152,800	50,000	Boykin
Pendleton	5	B	90,000	1,800	66,000	36.66	9,000	15,000	0	10,000	10	0	0	4,000	86,000	Bankes

368 / LIBRARY RESEARCH AND STATISTICS

TENNESSEE													
Franklin	58	MS	922,272	15,000	742,979	49.52	79,292	50,000	50,000	75,000	112	0	0	842,100	80,172	Robinson...
Maryville	78	M	1,589,983	22,519	1,204,991	53.51	140,508	owned	244,484	90,000	163	800,000	0	283,184	506,799	Community Tectonics
Sweetwater	10	M	310,781	6,000	207,500	35.00	23,328	32,583	47,370	20,000	48	176,500	0	54,506	79,755	Woodard...
TEXAS																
Carrizo Springs[6]	12	M	161,000	4,310	157,000	36.42	4,000	owned	0	30,000	40	0	0	0	161,000	Alexander
Dallas	40	B	1,625,066	10,502	1,090,770	103.86	81,410	344,834	76,343	50,000	115	0	0	1,625,066	0	Odum
Hempstead	70	B	974,466	9,634	763,294	79.23	106,013	66,328	75,234	50,000	80	0	0	974,466	0	Harper...
Mesquite	19	M	210,391	5,820	190,463	35.66	9,928	10,000	n/a	25,000	34	200,391	0	0	0	Keese...
	20	B	910,694	9,960	780,204	78.33	74,500	owned	55,990	50,000	84	0	0	910,694	0	Fisher & Spillman...
VIRGINIA																
Fairfax	n/a	B	42,000	297	42,000	141.00	n/a	owned	0	10,000	0	0	0	42,000	0	Porta-Structures Ind.
Midlothian	26	B	730,335	8,000	653,811	87.50	76,524	owned	0	25,000	0	0	0	730,335	0	Griffey...
Sandston	15	B	539,670	6,233	436,160	86.58	51,980	owned	51,530	30,000	63	0	0	539,670	0	Lee...
WASHINGTON																
Arlington[7]	10	B	448,000	6,000	n/a	90.75	n/a	owned	0	31,000	31	300,000	0	144,500	3,500	Ridenaur
Key Center	12	B	369,761	4,066	279,435	68.72	25,000	30,000	35,326	13,000	28	335,945	0	32,400	1,416	Austin
Manchester	6	B	35,500	1,400	35,500	25.36	n/a	leased	0	15,000	16	23,500	0	7,000	5,000	not reported
Poulsbo	24	B	301,750	4,750	230,860	48.00	25,400	owned	45,490	22,000	46	0	0	211,250	7,500	Fraser
Seattle	30	B	1,234,500	9,000	753,036	83.67	91,222	234,572	155,670	30,000	90	1,234,500	0	0	0	Henningson...
WEST VIRGINIA																
Grafton	17	M	627,415	8,600	524,257	60.96	27,196	39,151	36,541	25,000	24	150,000	250,425	140,000	86,720	Bryan...
Huntington	107	MS	4,086,614	54,000	3,070,065	56.85	457,691	260,223	298,635	180,000	239	0	1,309,980	2,776,634	0	Dean...
Milton	11	B	783,395	7,000	588,053	84.01	62,837	82,388	50,167	29,600	52	0	190,020	593,375	0	Dean...
Union	13	M	360,000	5,000	287,127	57.43	37,969	14,318	20,586	26,000	30	0	316,250	8,000	35,750	Bryan...
WISCONSIN																
Appleton	60	MS	4,225,000	74,100	2,842,063	38.35	887,236	owned	495,701	328,000	260	0	0	4,225,000	0	Miller
Eagle River	5	M	468,722	7,200	443,022	61.53	46,500	52,494	25,700	30,000	45	0	0	35,722	433,000	Reinke...
Kenosha[8]	78	BS	1,362,688	19,320	1,061,295	54.93	202,293	owned	99,100	80,000	97	0	0	1,342,688	20,000	O'Donnell...
WYOMING																
Laramie[9]	30	M	1,864,304	27,624	1,183,748	42.85	259,023	250,000	171,532	130,000	150	100,000	20,600	1,325,000	418,704	Malone...
VIRGIN ISLANDS																
St. Croix	10	B	75,000	170	75,000	382.35	0	owned	0	5,000	0	70,000	0	5,000	0	Porta-Structures Ind.

PUBLIC LIBRARY BUILDINGS IN 1981 / 369

TABLE 2 PUBLIC LIBRARY BUILDINGS ADDITIONS, REMODELINGS, AND RENOVATIONS

Community	Pop. in M	Code	Project Cost	Gross Sq. Ft.	Const. Cost	Sq. Ft. Cost	Equip. Cost	Site Cost	Other Costs	Vols.	Reader Seats	Fed. Funds	State Funds	Local Funds	Gift Funds	Architect
CALIFORNIA																
Ojai[10]	11	B	363,000	5,106	250,000	48.96	40,000	25,000	48,000	75,000	60	0	0	313,000	50,000	Fisher & Wilde
San Jose[11]	16	B	558,400	6,900	507,500	73.55	16,000	owned	34,900	24,000	35	0	0	438,400	0	Baltan
COLORADO																
Colorado Springs	17	B	80,729	6,240	70,933	13.45	6,556	owned	3,240	17,000	0	0	0	80,729	0	Englund
Norwood	1	MS	14,464	910	11,624	12.77	2,840	owned	0	2,000	12	0	79	11,800	2,585	not reported
CONNECTICUT																
Fairfield	56	M	2,870,000	49,600	2,133,143	43.00	470,160	owned	266,696	187,000	230	0	100,000	2,750,000	20,000	Lyons
Greenwich	47	B	946,235	8,865	702,687	79.26	11,659	owned	126,956	40,000	38	0	110,790	56,415	779,030	von Brock
Middlebury	6	M	245,000	3,000	200,000	67.00	22,000	owned	23,000	40,000	74	0	58,500	0	186,500	Moore
Southbury	14	M	850,000	10,000	700,000	66.66	90,000	owned	60,000	80,000	125	100,000	0	750,000	0	Hartford
FLORIDA																
Beverly Hills	7	B	33,000	1,360	26,000	24.00	5,000	owned	2,000	800	14	0	0	28,000	5,000	Kalinski
Port St. Lucie	27	BS	130,279	3,000	98,184	32.38	30,371	owned	8,524	27,000	28	0	0	97,279	37,000	J. Scott
INDIANA																
Clinton	1	MS	82,461	5,400	77,074	14.27	n/a	owned	5,388	25,000	50	0	0	82,461	0	Marsh, Inc.
Danville	5	MS	452,937	7,600	359,288	47.27	39,561	owned	54,088	60,000	80	0	0	452,937	0	Porter
Fort Wayne	287	M	4,302,089	74,551	2,767,742	37.12	609,208	517,000	408,589	504,121	221	0	0	4,302,089	0	Jankowski
Huntington	20	M	52,000	1,500	39,723	26.48	10,159	owned	2,118	4,000	34	0	0	52,000	0	Stevens
Merrillville	184	MS	6,206,554	82,000	5,336,109	65.07	365,914	owned	504,531	425,000	225	0	0	6,206,554	0	Perkins
IOWA																
Dubuque	62	M	3,209,150	53,410	2,395,038	44.84	353,467	owned	460,645	260,000	204	29,150	0	3,180,000	0	Durrant
Lakota	1	M	24,064	825	15,009	18.19	8,844	owned	211	9,000	21	0	0	11,777	12,287	not reported
Swaledale	1	M	15,940	640	13,763	21.50	2,092	owned	85	3,500	30	1,000	0	7,440	7,500	Eddy
Waterloo[12]	75	M	4,026,765	60,000	3,018,037	50.30	352,759	325,000	330,969	250,000	332	0	0	4,009,265	17,500	Flinn
Wyoming	1	M	23,370	2,120	10,970	10.36	1,400	11,000	0	11,000	34	5,000	0	3,500	14,870	not reported
KANSAS																
Stockton	7	M	23,200	2,790	23,200	80.30	0	owned	0	11,000	40	7,000	0	14,500	2,200	not reported
LOUISIANA																
Shreveport	242	MS	5,599,961	80,000	3,454,408	43.18	341,634	1,500,000	303,919	400,000	300	0	0	2,799,961	2,800,000	Walker
MARYLAND																
Friendsville	2	B	1,650	1,244	1,100	.88	550	n/a	0	3,500	16	0	0	1,450	200	not reported
North Beach[13]	6	B	308,000	5,400	301,984	55.92	6,016	owned	0	n/a	16	0	0	308,000	0	not reported
St. Michaels[14]	7	B	4,421	1,500	2,391	1.59	30	leased	2,000	7,000	20	0	0	0	4,421	not reported
MASSACHUSETTS																
Westborough	14	M	1,185,685	20,076	988,046	49.22	88,655	owned	108,984	78,400	97	0	0	1,179,985	5,700	Nault
MICHIGAN																
Deckerville[15]	5	M	44,009	1,558	36,256	28.25	5,053	owned	2,704	10,000	16	10,000	0	23,009	11,000	Harman
Hartland[16]	21	M	1,065,290	12,500	860,965	68.88	107,642	owned	96,683	45,000	84	0	0	1,065,290	12,128	Merritt

PUBLIC LIBRARY BUILDINGS IN 1981 / 371

MISSISSIPPI																
Coldwater[17]	2	B	10,522	890	10,522	11.82	0	owned	31,040	4,325	8	0	10,522	0	not reported	
Jackson	40	B	415,308	6,900	326,768	17.36	57,500	owned	0	57,000	60	0	215,308	0	Godfrey	
Oakland	2	M	3,890	480	3,890	8.10	0	owned	0	10,000	15	200,000	3,890	0	not reported	
Ruleville	2	B	188,732	4,246	146,586	34.52	30,223	owned	11,923	17,500	20	94,366	90,998	3,368	Weilenman	
NEBRASKA																
Ord	3	M	45,000	2,400	45,000	187.50	0	owned	0	3,000	0	19,000	11,000	15,000	not reported	
NEVADA																
Zephyr Cove	5	B	135,442	1,080	121,339	125.40	4,041	owned	10,062	n/a	n/a	0	14,103	121,339	Nopp	
NEW HAMPSHIRE																
Chester	2	M	110,000	4,050	90,000	22.00	35,000	owned	0	11,000	24	0	0	110,000	Moody, G.	
Rye	5	M	37,781	1,050	23,451	22.33	12,128	owned	2,202	5,140	20	0	20,000	8,781	Tambling	
Tamworth	2	M	87,135	2,346	76,500	32.60	250	owned	10,385	12,500	16	0	10,000	77,135	WM	
NEW YORK																
Brooklyn	44	B	785,708	15,942	734,708	46.09	51,000	owned	0	38,000	0	0	785,708	0	Dept. of Gen. Services	
Burnt Hills[18]	12	M	37,209	1,600	37,209	23.26	0	owned	0	30,000	30	5,000	7,500	24,709	not reported	
Greece	15	B	30,000	1,050	15,000	14.30	15,000	leased	0	5,000	8	30,000	0	0	not reported	
Patchogue	46	B	1,900,000	48,000	1,122,632	23.39	216,122	owned	231,265	270,000	144	0	1,900,000	0	Gibbons	
Schenectady[19]	12	B	116,828	3,200	48,907	15.28	11,713	owned	1,000	20,000	28	0	116,828	0	Verrigni	
NORTH CAROLINA																
Morganton	73	M	520,000	19,000	387,000	21.00	60,000	owned	63,000	100,000	100	225,000	285,000	0	Grier	
Weaverville	20	B	191,757	7,500	141,250	25.57	3,507	owned	12,000	18,000	31	61,000	64,260	61,497	Weigman	
Wilmington	103	MS	3,172,154	75,000	2,029,066	33.82	292,031	owned	258,684	180,000	205	2,495,000	690,357	39,585	Jeffries	
Wilson	63	M	903,537	22,332	767,191	40.46	71,974	owned	64,372	80,000	158	451,161	451,161	1,215	Phillips	
OHIO																
Girard	35	M	139,821	3,248	89,980	27.70	16,849	owned	8,462	35,000	60	4,266	130,105	5,450	D'Orazio	
Lakewood[20]	62	MS	783,723	11,945	635,205	53.18	69,529	owned	78,989	36,900	40	20,000	763,723	0	Geary	
North Baltimore	10	M	272,000	3,100	213,532	68.88	33,744	owned	24,724	75,000	80	0	269,000	3,000	Hinkle	
OKLAHOMA																
Yukon	40	MS	500,000	8,250	450,000	60.61	10,570	owned	0	46,690	37	0	350,000	150,000	RGDC	
RHODE ISLAND																
Providence[21]	73	M	747,025	5,204	405,953	78.01	67,279	owned	273,793	50,000	32	18,000	55,000	674,025	Platner	
VERMONT																
Barre	17		15,000	1,400	15,000	10.71	0	owned	0	7,000	20	11,000	0	4,000	not reported	
WASHINGTON																
Langley[22]	8	B	36,000	648	36,000	57.00	5,500	owned	0	10,000	25	0	0	36,000	Boyd	
Mount Vernon	13	M	171,657	2,104	138,992	66.06	18,604	owned	14,061	10,000	39	0	171,657	0	Klein	
WEST VIRGINIA																
Bluefield	74	MS	145,791	2,200	134,400	61.09	0	owned	11,391	60,000	60	100,000	29,791	16,000	Zando	
Martinsburg	47	MS	848,000	8,700	545,605	62.47	256,395	owned	46,000	160,000	200	431,250	0	70,000	Bailey	
Shinnston	5	B	30,393	2,704	27,825	10.29	0	leased	2,568	9,750	18	20,000	3,334	7,059	King	
WISCONSIN																
Hartland	6	M	1,222,500	6,300	938,000	44.19	24,441	owned	0	34,000	50	0	1,222,500	0	R. Horn	
Tomah[23]	7	M	434,366	10,360	325,833	31.45	72,140	owned	36,393	40,000	97	15,550	304,979	113,837	Potter	

TABLE 3 CANADA—PUBLIC LIBRARY BUILDINGS

Community	Pop. in M	Code	Project Cost	Gross Sq. Ft.	Const. Cost	Sq. Ft. Cost	Equip. Cost	Site Cost	Other Costs	Vols.	Reader Seats	Fed. Funds	Prov. Funds	Local Funds	Gift Funds	Architect
ALBERTA																
Camrose	12	M	960,734	12,400	753,234	55.00	90,000	88,000	29,500	38,500	54	0	300,000	629,599	31,135	McIntosh
Drumheller	13	B	1,666,938	23,287	1,289,935	55.39	18,821	255,905	105,366	n/a	20	0	0	425,000	0	Melathopoulos
Edson[24]	9	M	968,217	6,000	860,516	83.00	45,000	owned	62,701	25,000	45	285,00	322,500	212,500	148,217	McIntosh
Vermilion	18	B	403,927	8,058	347,289	48.00	37,621	owned	18,819	30,000	28	0	175,941	198,345	29,443	Groves
MANITOBA																
Ste. Rose du Lac	2	M	110,250	3,552	100,000	31.00	4,000	5,000	1,250	20,000	37	20,750	60,000	7,500	22,000	Lawsmen
Winkler	5	M	217,292	3,400	188,474	55.43	28,818	leased	0	13,000	25	0	50,000	139,589	27,703	Peters

TABLE 4 PUBLIC LIBRARY BUILDINGS—NOT PREVIOUSLY REPORTED

Community	Pop. in M	Code	Project Cost	Gross Sq. Ft.	Const. Cost	Sq. Ft. Cost	Equip. Cost	Site Cost	Other Costs	Vols.	Reader Seats	Fed. Funds	State Funds	Local Funds	Gift Funds	Architect
Golden, CO (1978)	40	M	2,111,175	37,660	1,781,000	47.29	189,822	owned	140,353	450,000		0	1,563,068	0	392,326	Johnson
Essex, CT[25] (1980)	5	M	419,852	4,108	288,086	70.13	39,518	42,500	49,748	26,000	35	0	0	60,100	359,752	Galliher
Putnam, CT (1979)	9	M	291,479	2,500	264,796	105.92	9,479	owned	17,204	15,000	50	282,000	9,479	0	0	Hartford
Jacksonville, FL (1979)	65	B	1,506,455	24,800	1,089,505	43.93	147,378	189,829	79,743	100,000	137	273,755	100,000	1,132,700	0	Pappas
Chicago, IL (1979)	2	B	111,162	8,140	41,162	5.05	60,000	leased	10,000	33,000	48	0	0	111,162	0	not reported

Flossmoor, IL (1980)	8	B	32,669	2,524	24,119	9.56	6,693	owned	1,857	10,000	26	0	32,669	0	Buchsbaum
Matteson, IL (1980)	9	M	17,342	8,000	6,783	0.85	10,080	leased	479	23,000	36	13,362	3,980	0	Millies
Neegas, IL (1979)	2	M	5,440	640	5,040	7.87	400	owned		6,000	8	0	5,265	175	not reported
Oak Forest, IL (1979)	26	M	830,130	20,000	585,680	29.28	104,070	45,000	95,380			0	827,398	2,732	Pavlecic
Lehigh, IA (1979)	1	M	10,000	900	2,000	2.22	6,000	owned	2,000	5,000	35	0	0	10,000	not reported
Woodward, IA (1979)	1	M	3,409		945	n/a	2,464	leased	0			0	3,409	0	not reported
St. Cloud, MN (1979)	260	MS	3,161,787	59,118	2,319,357	39.23	412,901	182,500	247,029	180,000	237	367,179	2,789,608	5,000	InterDesign & Traynor
Clinton, MS (1979)	12	B	221,742	3,300	171,246	51.89	19,413	20,000	11,083	49,375		0	110,871	0	Cooke
Stonewall, MS (1978)	2	B	6,800	1,500	3,129	2.00	3,671	owned	0	5,000	18	0	6,800	0	None
Phoenix, MO (1979)	10	B	17,000	2,000	2,200	1.10	13,400	leased	1,400	15,000	2	0	17,000	0	not reported
Wood River, NB (1979)	1	M	18,012	n/a	15,050	n/a	2,949	owned	13	n/a	7	806	0	17,206	Opp
Fairport, NY (1979)	24	M	99,559	18,000	0	0	92,084	leased	7,475	60,000	116	0	99,559	0	not reported
North Salem, NY[26] (1980)	4	M	311,639	3,615	255,514	70.68	25,247	leased	30,878	18,000	32	0	0	311,639	Faesy
Rochester, NY[27] (1979)	14	B	15,000	5,212	15,000	2.88	0	leased	0	10,000	15	6,500	8,500	0	not reported
Columbus, OH (1979)	33	B	111,685	7,500	79,701	10.63	24,526	leased	7,458	45,000	68	0	111,685	0	not reported
Lower Burrell, PA (1979)	16	B	64,447	2,700	44,198	16.36	11,875	6,405	1,969	15,000	24	18,280	46,167	0	not reported
Chattanooga, TN (1979)	88	B	83,521	7,800	6,040	0.77	67,899	leased	9,582	35,000	70	0	41,760	41,761	not reported
Tacoma, WA (1980)	10	B	626,517	5,000	420,250	84.05	70,851	70,192	65,224	10,000	40	0	0	626,517	Forbes

TABLE 4 PUBLIC LIBRARY BUILDINGS—NOT PREVIOUSLY REPORTED (cont.)

Community	Pop. in M	Code	Project Cost	Gross Sq. Ft.	Const. Cost	Sq. Ft. Cost	Equip. Cost	Site Cost	Other Costs	Vols.	Reader Seats	Fed. Funds	State Funds	Local Funds	Gift Funds	Architect
Toppenish, WA[28] (1980)	27	M	4,800,000	6,000	4,416,000	75.00	(incl)	owned	384,000	27,000	60	4,800,000	0	0	0	Doudna....
Victoria, BC	180	MS	601,732	50,000	303,182	6.06	211,559	leased	86,991	200,000		0	400,000	201,732	0	Wade....

REFERENCES

1. First solar constructed library.
2. Includes three government and public cable TV channels; state of the art AV facilities.
3. Built adjacent to former landfill.
4. CLSI automated circulation system, public access terminals; government documents depository; regional reference center.
5. Concrete, brick, granite facade; center atrium with skylight, coffered concrete ceiling.
6. Design based on old Fort McIntosh barracks, Laredo.
7. Earth-sheltered building using passive solar energy.
7a. Library system will own and operate Phase II (health center) upon completion in 1982.
8. Earth-sheltered design passively collects heat through skylights and windows.
9. Active solar retrofit design; gas, coal convertible boiler; carefully controlled fenestration, insulation. Art donated by local artists.
10. Community raised more than $50,000.
11. Passive energy systems; high intensity metal halide provides more light, expends less power.
12. Former post office and federal building.
13. Housed on second floor of firehouse; also serves as community center.
14. Staffed entirely by volunteers.
15. One-hundred-year-old historical landmark.
16. Children's train donated by Jaycees; landscaping by local high school students.
17. Former teacher's home.
18. Boy Scouts moved furniture, planted shrubs, and painted flagpole.
19. Remodeling done by employees funded under CETA.
20. Elevator for the handicapped and elderly.
21. Won 1980 ALA/AIA Award for Excellence in Architecture.
22. Fully funded by donations; completed with volunteer labor; access for handicapped.
23. Listed in *National Register of Historic Places*.
24. Triangular building.
25. Local monies from sale of old building; no government funds used.
26. No gift over $10,000; sold one sq. ft. for $54.98; residents come to see their sq. ft.
27. Storefront replacement for burned out library.
28. Complex of Museum, Winter Lodge, Media Center, Restaurant, Theater, Gift Shop, and Library Yakima Indians.

TABLE 5 SIX-YEAR COST SUMMARY—PUBLIC LIBRARY BUILDINGS

	Fiscal 1976	Fiscal 1977	Fiscal 1978	Fiscal 1979	Fiscal 1980	Fiscal 1981
Number of new bldgs.	187	142	135	168	94	74
Number of ARR's (1)	90	69	85	112	63	59
Sq. ft., new bldgs.	1,817,272	2,100,016	1,355,130	2,898,585	1,587,199	984,148
Sq. ft. ARR's	980,338	585,635	663,915	912,567	472,626	791,324
New bldgs:						
Construction cost	$66,374,466	$85,986,538	$54,508,361	$96,010,260	$75,691,743	$54,662,187
Equipment cost	8,212,051	10,727,160	7,433,541	13,336,842	9,178,724	7,677,461
Site cost	5,266,693	8,401,254	5,508,018	3,233,751	3,056,691	2,499,379
Other costs	7,858,816	9,442,938	6,712,240	8,523,617	9,315,474	6,255,903
Total—Project cost	87,712,026	114,557,890	74,162,160	121,109,470	97,242,632	$73,004,866
ARR's—Project cost	36,966,911	17,144,009	18,891,111	29,930,142	19,664,731	46,755,932
New & ARR Project cost	$124,678,937	$131,701,899	$93,053,271	$151,039,142	$116,907,363	$119,760,798
Fund Sources:						
Federal, new bldgs.	$23,030,416	$19,226,511	$13,304,652	$63,354,045	$27,034,338	$18,269,728
Federal, ARR's	4,323,509	1,149,718	4,046,901	18,414,336	4,253,080	3,973,877
Federal, total	$27,353,925	$20,376,229	$17,351,553	$81,768,381	$31,387,418	$22,243,605
State, new bldgs.	$5,241,537	$5,757,047	$5,803,920	$13,897,410	$1,289,677	$3,419,248
State, ARR's	2,264,815	1,381,725	2,658,733	1,404,067	3,082,351	1,142,485
State, total	$7,506,352	$7,138,772	$8,462,653	$15,301,477	$4,372,028	$4,561,733
Local, new bldgs.	$50,501,926	$82,266,956	$47,193,528	$73,994,629	$60,511,471	$44,744,494
Local, ARR's	26,900,408	13,286,234	10,371,229	9,854,905	8,741,907	36,202,565
Local, total	$77,402,334	$95,553,190	$57,564,757	83,849,534	$69,253,378	$80,947,059
Gift, new bldgs.	$8,938,147	$7,307,376	$7,860,060	$11,398,318	$5,332,456	$5,157,135
Gift, ARR's	3,478,179	1,326,332	1,658,467	1,352,053	3,560,915	5,509,921
Gift, total	$12,416,326	$8,633,708	$9,518,527	$12,750,371	$8,893,371	$10,667,056
Total funds used	$124,678,937	$131,701,899	$92,897,490	$193,669,763	$113,906,195	$118,419,453

(1) Additions, Remodelings and Renovations

TWO-YEAR COLLEGE LEARNING RESOURCE CENTER BUILDINGS IN 1981

D. Joleen Bock
Dean of Library Services, University of Guam

Since the last survey (*LJ*, December 1, 1979), Learning Resource Center (LRC) building activity has increased in two-year institutions. Reported projects include 28 new and 20 remodeled LRC buildings. This is in keeping with increased enrollments, as reflected in the following statistics from the 1981 *Community, Junior and Technical College Directory:*

	Number of Colleges		Enrollment	
Fall	Public	Independent	Public	Independent
1978	1,047	187	3,159,456	144,502
1979	1,044	186	4,334,344	153,528
1980	1,049	182	4,666,286	159,645

Public institution enrollments were up 47.7 percent. Private institutions, although decreasing in number by five, reported a 10.4 percent enrollment increase. Not reported is an additional four million noncredit enrollments. These enrollment increases mean not only a need for new and remodeled facilities, but also for increased services. Of the 9 LRC components identified, 16 of the 28 new institutions provide at least 6 of those services (see Table 1).

Seating in new buildings ranged from a low of 2.8 percent of full-time equivalent (FTE) at Pikes Peak to a high of 37.7 percent at Tomlinson College, Tennessee, with an average of 12.45 percent.

Square foot costs for new buildings ranged from a low of $35.02 at the Elkhorn Campus of Metropolitan Technical College, Nebraska to a high of $100 in Nassau

TABLE 1 FACILITIES IN 28 NEW LRCs BUILT JULY 1, 1979–JUNE 30, 1981

Services	Number of Colleges
Library	27
AV distribution	27
Graphic/photographic production	18
Audio/video production	23
Reprographic production	16
Audio/video learning lab	17
Learning assistance center	18
Career information center	10
CAI terminals	8

Note: Adapted from *Library Journal*, December 1, 1981.

TABLE 2 PUBLIC CATALOG FORMATS

Book & card	New River (Va.)
Computer terminal	Mission (Cal.)
Computer terminal plus card	Pikes Peak (Co.)
	Miles (Mont.)
	Olive Harvey (Chicago)
Microfiche	Cuyahoga (Ohio) Eastern Campus
	Dallas County (Tex.) Richland College
	Metropolitan Tech (Neb.) Elkhorn and Ft. Omaha Campuses
	Oscar Rose (Okla.)
Microfiche plus card	Gateway (Wis.)–Kenosha Campus
	Pensacola (Fla.)–Warrington Campus
Film	Oakland (Mich.) Highland Lakes Campus
Film plus card	Pima (Ariz.) East Campus

County, New York. For remodeled buildings, the low was $24.14 in Houston to a high of $150.50 at Kanai Peninsula, Alaska, with a central tendency of $55.

Mississippi County (Arizona) reported a solar heated campus.

The other change that related to new facilities was the number of colleges reporting public catalogs in either a card *plus* other format, or solely in another format (see Table 2).

TABLE 3 TWO-YEAR COLLEGE LRC NEW BUILDING CONSTRUCTION JULY 1, 1979–JUNE 30, 1981

College	FTE	Gross Area	Total ASF	Sq. Ft. Cost	Furn. & Equip. Cost	Seats	Percent of FTE	Key to Facilities
ARIZONA								
South Mountain	800	N/A	N/A	N/A	N/A	N/A	N/A	ABG
Mississippi Co.	N/A	450	375	N/A	20,000	50	N/A	ABDEFG
East Campus	1,527	3,096	2,728	61.00	N/A	52	3	A
CALIFORNIA								
L.A. Trade Tech	19,433	82,338	61,516	64.78	961,900	766	4	ABCDEFGHI
Mission	4,000	6,000	N/A	N/A	N/A	400	10	ABCDEFGHI
COLORADO								
Pikes Peak	4,250	26,500	N/A	N/A	N/A	120	3	ABCDEFGHI
FLORIDA								
Manatee	3,600	40,725	N/A	N/A	1,600,000	595	17	ABCDEFG
Pensacola Warrington	1,800	10,100	9,900	48.00	42,000	100	6	ABDEFGH
GEORGIA								
Clayton	2,142	56,440	46,280	38.00	106,000	800	37	ABCDEGI
Dekalb No. Campus	1,793	21,965	20,994	46.00	89,295	307	17	ABCDEFGHI
ILLINOIS								
Chicago Olive-Harvey	4,432	N/A	N/A	N/A	1,500,000	200	5	ABCD
Thornton	2,685	36,000	24,000	N/A	N/A	518	19	ABCD
MICHIGAN								
Oakland Highland Lakes	1,610	N/A	11,000	N/A	91,000	100	6	ABDG
Wayne County Downtown Ctr.	N/A	N/A	12,238	65.28 (incl. site development)	N/A	N/A	N/A	ABCDE
MONTANA								
Miles	451	9,000	9,000	45.00	30,000	60	13	ABCDEFG

TABLE 3   TWO-YEAR COLLEGE LRC NEW BUILDING
CONSTRUCTION JULY 1, 1979–JUNE 30, 1981   (cont.)

College	FTE	Gross Area	Total ASF	Sq. Ft. Cost	Furn. & Equip. Cost	Seats	Percent of FTE	Key to Facilities
NEBRASKA								
Metro. Tech Elkhorn Campus	10,760	7,200	6,950	35.62	N/A	90	8	ABDFGH
NEW YORK								
Nassau	N/A	139,000	107,000	100.00	937,000	N/A		ABF
NORTH CAROLINA								
Albemarle	1,000	9,789	8,811	45.83	22,183	75	8	ABDEFG
Beaufort	1,477	20,787	20,000	62.50	26,341	180	12	ABCDF
Cleveland	1,856	15,250	14,250	44.68	181,000	200	11	ABCDG
Craven	1,229	29,430	21,832	49.78	63,428	N/A	N/A	ABCDFH
Randolph	2,011	27,742	27,000	36.00	100,000	407	20	ABCDEFG
OHIO								
Cuyahoga Eastern Campus	1,902	N/A	50,000	N/A	N/A	N/A	N/A	ABCDEFGHI
OREGON								
Umpqua	2,508	13,344	5,332	88.00	54,000	130	N/A	BDEFGI
TENNESSEE								
Tomlinson	265	7,350	N/A	N/A	N/A	100	38	ABC
TEXAS								
Angelina College	N/A	18,500	N/A	52.00	N/A	255	N/A	ABCDEH
VIRGINIA								
Frederick Campus New River	1,584	43,910	15,150	44.00	165,000	210	13	ABCDF
WISCONSIN								
Elkhorn Campus	N/A	3,600	3,600	N/A	10,000	40	N/A	ABEGH

Key to Facilities: A = Library; B = AV Distribution; C = Graphic/photographic Production; D = Audio/Video Production; E = Reprographic Production; F = Audio/Video Learning Laboratory; G = Learning Assistance Center; H = Career Information Center; I = CAI Terminals

TABLE 4   TWO-YEAR COLLEGE LRC REMODELED BUILDING
CONSTRUCTION JULY 1, 1979–JUNE 30, 1981

College	FTE	Gross Area	Total ASF	Sq. Ft. Cost	Furn. & Equip Cost	Seats	Percent of FTE	Key to facilities
ALASKA								
Kenai Peninsula	441	3,400	3,400	$150.00	35,000	30	N/A	A
ARIZONA								
Coll. of Ganado	96	1,350	1,350	N/A	44,640	N/A	N/A	BD
CONNECTICUT								
Gr. Hartford	2,874	Added	1,300	ASF	25,000	44	N/A	AF
FLORIDA								
Brevard	9,600	43,567	35,000	51.38	65,000	130	N/A	ABD
Daytona Beach	3,875	16,000	15,000	60.00	N/A	N/A	N/A	ABCDEF
Tallahassee	2,494	12,143	11,069	69.91	151,625	338	N/A	ABCDEFGI
MISSISSIPPI								
Hinds	5,522	N/A	23,400 (add.) 14,900 (renov.)	31.50	172,927	558	10	ABCDEFGHI
Pearl River	N/A	2,300	2,000	25.00	50,000	60	N/A	FGH
MISSOURI								
Hannibal La Grange	N/A	N/A	N/A	N/A	N/A	N/A	N/A	AB

TABLE 4 TWO-YEAR COLLEGE LRC REMODELED BUILDING CONSTRUCTION JULY 1, 1979–JUNE 30, 1981 (cont.)

College	FTE	Gross Area	Total ASF	Sq. Ft. Cost	Furn. & Equip Cost	Seats	Percent of FTE	Key to facilities
NEBRASKA								
Ft. Omaha Campus	1,111	4,770	4,256	39.49	N/A	99	9	ABDFGH
NORTH CAROLINA								
Cent. Carolina	3,462	4,000	4,000	57.75	18,175	75		ABCDEFG
OKLAHOMA								
Oscar Rose	5,400	24,000	20,000	52.00	150,000	400		ABCDEGH
OREGON								
SW Oregon	550	2,100	4,014	61.14	3,000	N/A		AC
TEXAS								
Dallas County Richmond Coll.	10,398	13,305	7,983	61.00	68,425	N/A	N/A	ABCDEF
Houston	N/A	16,825	14,579	24.14	0	50	N/A	ABCDFH
Navarro	1,318	9,500	9,500	42.00	N/A	175	N/A	ABFG
VIRGINIA								
Tidewater	N/A	18,600	17,000	96.00	50,000	300		ABCDEFGHI
WISCONSIN								
Gateway Kenosha Campus	5,000	5,000	5,000	N/A	30,000	96		ABEFGH

Key to Facilities: A = Library; B = AV Distribution; C = Graphic/photographic Production; D = Audio/Video Production; E = Reprographic Production; F = Audio/Video Learning Laboratory; G = Learning Assistance Center; H = Career Information Center; I = CAI Terminals

Book Trade Research and Statistics

STANDARD ADDRESS NUMBER (SAN)

Emery I. Koltay

Director, ISBN and SAN Agency, R. R. Bowker Company

PURPOSE

SAN stands for Standard Address Number. It is a unique identification code for addresses of organizations that are involved in or served by the book industry, and that engage in repeated transactions with other members within this group. For purposes of this standard, the book industry includes book publishers, book wholesalers, book distributors, book retailers, college bookstores, libraries, library binders, and serial vendors. Schools, school systems, technical institutes, colleges, and universities are not members of this industry, but are served by it and therefore included in the SAN system.

The purpose of SAN is to facilitate communications among these organizations, of which there are several hundreds of thousands, that engage in a large volume of separate transactions with one another. These transactions include purchases of books by book dealers, wholesalers, schools, colleges, and libraries from publishers and wholesalers; payments for all such purchases; and other communications between participants. The objective of this standard is to establish an identification code system by assigning each address within the industry a discrete code to be used for positive identification for all book and serial buying and selling transactions.

Many organizations have similar names and multiple addresses, making identification of the correct contact point difficult and subject to error. In many cases, the physical movement of materials takes place between addresses that differ from the addresses to be used for the financial transactions. In such instances, there is ample opportunity for confusion and errors. Without identification by SAN, a complex record-keeping system would have to be instituted to avoid introducing errors. In addition, it is expected that problems with the current numbering system such as errors in billing, shipping, payments, and returns, will be significantly reduced by using the SAN system. SAN will also eliminate one step in the order fulfillment process: the "look up procedure" used to assign account numbers. Presently a store or library dealing with fifty different publishers is assigned a different account number by each of the suppliers. SAN solves this problem. If a publisher indicates its SAN on its stationery and ordering documents, vendors to whom it sends transactions do not have to look up the account number, but can proceed immediately to process orders by SAN.

Libraries are involved in many of the same transactions as are book dealers, such as ordering and paying for books, charging and paying for various services to other libraries. Keeping records of transactions, whether these involve buying, selling, lending, or donations, entails similar operations that require a SAN. Having the SAN on all stationery will speed up order fulfillment and eliminate errors in shipping, billing, and crediting; this, in turns, means savings in both time and money.

HISTORY

Development of the Standard Address Number began in 1968 when Russell Reynolds, general manager of the National Association of College Bookstores (NACS), approached the R. R. Bowker Company and suggested that a "Standard Account Number" system be implemented in the book industry. The first draft of a standard was prepared by an American National Standards Institute (ANSI) Committee Z39 subcommittee, which was co-chaired by Russell Reynolds and Emery Koltay. After Z39 members proposed changes, the current version of the standard was approved by NACS on December 17, 1979.

The chairperson of the ANSI Z39 Subcommittee 30, which developed the approved standard, was Herbert W. Bell, former senior vice president of McGraw-Hill Book Company. The subcommittee comprised the following representatives from publishing companies, distributors, wholesalers, libraries, national cooperative on-line systems, schools, and school systems: Herbert W. Bell (chair), McGraw-Hill Book Company; Richard E. Bates, Holt, Rinehart and Winston; Thomas G. Brady, The Baker & Taylor Companies; Paul J. Fasana, New York Public Library; Emery I. Koltay, R. R. Bowker Company; Joann McGreevey, New York University Book Centers; Pauline F. Micciche, OCLC, Inc.; Sandra K. Paul, SKP Associates; David Gray Remington, Library of Congress; Frank Sanders, Hammond Public School System; and Peter P. Chirimbes (alternate), Stamford Board of Education.

FORMAT

SAN consists of six digits plus a seventh modulus-eleven check digit; a hyphen follows the third digit (XXX-XXXX) to facilitate transcription. The hyphen is to be used in print form, but need not be entered or retained in computer systems. Printed on documents, the Standard Address Number should be preceded by the identifier "SAN" to avoid confusion with other numerical codes (SAN XXX-XXXX).

Check Digit Calculation

The check digit is based on Modulus 11, and can be derived as follows:

Example

1. Write the digits of the basic number.
   2 3 4 5 6 7
2. Write the constant weighting factors associated with each position by the basic number.
   7 6 5 4 3 2
3. Multiply each digit by its associated weighting factor.
   14 18 20 20 18 14
4. Add the products of the multiplications.
   $14 + 18 + 20 + 20 + 18 + 14 = 104$
5. Divide the sum by Modulus 11 to find the remainder.
   $104 \div 11 = 9$ plus a remainder of 5
6. Subtract the remainder from the Modulus 11 to generate the required check digit. If there is no remainder, generate a check digit of zero. If the check digit is 10, generate a check digit of X to represent 10, since the use of 10 would require an extra digit.
   $11 - 5 = 6$

7. Append the check digit to create the standard seven-digit Standard Address Number. SAN 234-5676

SAN ASSIGNMENT

The R. R. Bowker Company accepted responsibility for being the central administrative agency for SAN, and in that capacity assigns SANs to identify uniquely the addresses of organizations. No SANs can be reassigned; in the event that an organization should cease to exist, for example, its SAN would cease to be in circulation entirely. If an organization using SAN should move or change its name with no change in ownership, its SAN would remain the same, and only the name or address would be updated to reflect the change.

The current schedule (Phase I) calls for assignment of SANs to bookstores and wholesalers listed in the *American Book Trade Directory* (*ABTD*) and to libraries listed in the *American Library Directory* (*ALD*). R. R. Bowker Company has mailed SAN assignments to these organizations. SAN was also assigned to all publishers listed in *Publishers and Distributors in the United States*. Phase II of SAN assignment will be devoted to schools, school systems, school libraries, and the like. The file for the latter group was scheduled to be developed in 1981/1982, with completion of SAN assignment projected for 1982.

Approximately 280,000 SANs will be assigned, as follows:

Publishers, library binders	20,000
Bookstores, wholesalers, serials vendors	25,000
Libraries: Phase I, in ALD	30,000
Phase II, including school libraries	85,000
Schools and school systems	100,000
Colleges, universities, business schools, technical institutes	5,000
Subtotal	265,000
Quantity to be set aside for uncontrolled use	100,000
Total	365,000
Total available	1,000,000
Total available for expansion and multiple assignments	635,000

A block of SANs was allocated for uncontrolled (decentralized) use, ranging from SAN 900-000C to SAN 999-999C ("C" stands for check digit). The agency will provide at the request of the user a log book containing computer printouts of SANs that may be used to assign SANs to accounts pertaining to organizations that are not related to the book industry. These SANs are for local control only, and not for communication between users.

An organization receiving a SAN should complete and return the updating form, confirming receipt of the SAN and that all the locations have been correctly numbered. SAN should be used in all transactions; it is recommended that the SAN be imprinted on stationery, letterheads, order and invoice forms, checks, and all other documents used in executing various book transactions. The SAN should always be printed on a separate line above the name and address of the organization, preferably in the upper left-hand corner of the stationery to avoid confusion with other numerical codes pertaining to the organization, such as telephone number, zip code, and the like.

Mailings were sent to bookstores in January and March of 1980 and in January and March of 1981. Similar mailings are scheduled each year. Bookstores that did not receive a SAN assignment, or those needing additional SANs for additional addresses should send requests for SAN to: Editor, American Book Trade Directory/American Library Directory, Jaques Cattell Press, 2216 South Industrial Park, Box 25001, Tempe, AZ 85282 (telephone 602-967-8885). Publishers' requests for SAN should be sent to the ISBN/SAN Agency at R. R. Bowker Company, 1180 Avenue of the Americas, New York, NY 10036.

SAN FUNCTIONS AND SUFFIXES

The SAN is strictly a Standard Address Number, becoming functional only in applications determined by the user; these may include activities such as purchasing, billing, shipping, receiving, paying, crediting, and refunding. Every department that has an independent function within an organization could have a SAN for its own identification. Users may choose to assign a suffix (a separate field) to its own SAN strictly for internal use. Faculty members ordering books through a library acquisitions department, for example, may not have their own separate SAN, but may be assigned a suffix by the library. There is no standardized provision for placement of suffixes. Existing numbering systems do have suffixes to take care of the "subset" type addresses. The SAN does not standardize this part of the address. For the implementation of SAN, it is suggested that wherever applicable the four-position suffix be used. This four-position suffix makes available 10,000 numbers, ranging from 0000 to 9999, and will accommodate all existing subset numbering presently in use.

For example, there are various ways to incorporate SAN in an order fulfillment system. Firms just beginning to assign account numbers to their customers will have no conversion problems and will simply use SAN as the numbering system. Firms that already have an existing number system can convert either on a step-by-step basis by adopting SANs whenever orders or payments are processed on the account, or by converting the whole file by using the SAN listing provided by the SAN agency. Using the step-by-step conversion, firms may adopt SANs as customers provide them on their forms, orders, payments, and returns.

For additional information or suggestions, please write to Emery I. Koltay, Director, ISBN and SAN Agency, R. R. Bowker Company, 1180 Avenue of the Americas, New York, NY 10036 (telephone 212-764-3384).

BOOK TITLE OUTPUT AND AVERAGE PRICES, 1981 PRELIMINARY FIGURES

Chandler B. Grannis

Contributing Editor, *Publishers Weekly*

A strong overall level of title output in all areas of American book publishing and a continuing rise in retail prices are indicated in preliminary figures for the year 1981, based on R. R. Bowker Company computations. The preliminary figures cover 1981 books listed from January through December. The final figures, due to appear in *PW* in late summer, will cover, in addition, 1981 books that have been listed in the first half of 1982.

Note: Adapted from *Publishers Weekly*, March 12, 1982, where the article was entitled "1981 Title Output and Average Prices: Preliminary Figures."

The preliminary count of 1981 title output and price averages, given here, includes a far more comprehensive number of mass market paperback publications than has been possible to report for a number of years. This improvement has been brought about by using the listings in Bowker's *Paperbound Books in Print* (*PBIP*) in place of the very scanty mass market paperback listings in the *Weekly Record*—the source of other, fully comprehensive title and price data. (*Weekly Record* is based mainly on records from the Library of Congress, which does not catalogue most mass market paperbound books.)

In using *PBIP* as the data base for mass market paperback output statistics, Bowker's data services division has analyzed the 474 subject headings in the *PBIP* Subject Index and has carefully grouped them according to the 23 Dewey classification-based categories used in *Weekly Record*.

PBIP entries from the following publishers and imprints have been used in making the mass market computations: Ace, Avon, Ballantine, Bantam, Berkley, DAW (New American Library), Dell, Fawcett, NAL, Pinnacle, Playboy Paperbacks, Pocket Books, Popular Library, Warner Books, Washington Square Press (Pocket Books), and Zebra Books.

The *Weekly Record* data (also prepared by the data services division) account for all the other information provided in the tables with this article.

Table 1, showing U.S. title output for all kinds and classes of books, suggests a probable total of between 45,000 and 50,000 titles for 1981. A major part of the apparent increase will be due to the improved reporting of mass market paperbacks. The actual figure will not be known until *PW*'s final report for 1981 is issued in the late summer. Note that the headings on this table should be read with special attention.

Table 2 initiates the mass market paperback count based on *PBIP*. Comparable counts have not been made for earlier years, so 1981 will become the base year for future comparisons of output in this area. With about 300 titles still to be classified for addition to the 1981 totals, the final mass market total for the year will doubtless exceed 4000, including originals and reprints but not reissues.

Table 3 continues *PW*'s reports of other paperbacks (trade and some paperbound monographs), with a likely total of over 11,000 when the final count is in.

Table 4, translations into English, and Table 5, imported books, suggest some declines in 1981, but this cannot be certain until the year's final computations are completed.

Tables 6–10 present average per-volume prices. Readers may notice that throughout this report "preliminary" data are given only for 1981. For prior years, "final" figures are offered: these may be considered more comparable from year to year than those called "preliminary."

Table 6, hardcover prices at all levels, shows steady increases in the totals from year to year, with stronger shifts in some categories.

Table 7 shows what the average per-volume prices in each of the broad Dewey groups are when prices of $81 or higher are eliminated from the calculations. Refinements of this table are under discussion at Bowker.

Table 8, based on *PBIP* listings, show per-volume averages for 1981 mass market paperbacks in all but one very small category.

Table 9, trade paperbacks, suggests a fairly high rise in the per-volume price average: over 12%.

Table 10 continues *PW*'s long-standing manual count of the per-volume prices of novels, biographies and history books advertised in the Fall Announcement issues of the magazine. Indicated increases, 1980–81, are: Novels, average 7.5%, median 17.4%; Biographies, average 6.1%, median 13%; History, average 2.5%, median 2.7%.

TABLE 1 AMERICAN BOOK TITLE PRODUCTION—1979, 1980, AND 1981*
(From Weekly Record Listings of Domestic and Imported Hardbound and Paperbound Books)†

Categories with Dewey Decimal Numbers	1979 titles (final) New Books	1979 titles (final) New Editions	1979 titles (final) Totals	1980 titles (final) New Books	1980 titles (final) New Editions	1980 titles (final) Totals	1981 titles (preliminary) New Books	1981 titles (preliminary) New Editions	1981 titles (preliminary) Totals	All hard- & paperbound Totals
Agriculture (630–639; 712–719)	432	106	538	382	79	461	327	59	386	391
Art (700–711; 720–779)	1,718	303	2,021	1,437	254	1,691	1,126	201	1,327	1,334
†Biography	1,557	485	2,042	1,399	492	1,891	1,153	364	1,517	1,589
Business (650–659)	1,057	305	1,362	935	250	1,185	874	270	1,144	1,156
Education (370–379)	952	169	1,121	876	135	1,011	801	130	931	946
Fiction	2,313	951	3,264	1,918	917	2,835	1,697	628	2,325	5,107
General Works (000–099)	1,248	223	1,471	1,428	215	1,643	1,211	205	1,416	1,493
History (900–909; 930–999)	1,546	614	2,160	1,569	651	2,220	1,422	424	1,846	1,891
Home Economics (640–649)	767	130	897	767	112	879	674	133	807	816
Juveniles	2,704	348	3,052	2,585	274	2,859	2,376	191	2,567	2,780
Language (400–499)	435	125	560	433	96	529	361	98	459	477
Law (340–349)	873	345	1,218	816	286	1,102	851	258	1,109	1,113
Literature (800–810; 813–820; 823–899)	1,298	451	1,749	1,317	369	1,686	1,171	212	1,383	1,426
Medicine (610–619)	2,609	648	3,257	2,667	625	3,292	2,568	541	3,109	3,142
Music (780–789)	219	170	389	236	121	357	244	94	338	338
Philosophy, Psychology (100–199)	1,082	295	1,377	1,097	332	1,429	949	224	1,173	1,250
Poetry, Drama (811; 812; 821; 822)	1,084	277	1,361	962	217	1,179	853	117	970	996
Religion (200–299)	1,861	464	2,325	1,635	420	2,055	1,570	326	1,896	1,913
Science (500–599)	2,563	593	3,156	2,551	556	3,109	2,291	522	2,813	2,863
Sociology, Economics (300–339; 350–369; 380–399)	6,422	1,293	7,715	5,876	1,276	7,152	5,452	1,013	6,465	6,610
Sports, Recreation (790–799)	931	191	1,122	808	163	971	771	148	919	1,064
Technology (600–609; 620–629; 660–699)	1,922	469	2,391	1,923	414	2,337	1,759	376	2,135	2,246
Travel (910–919)	519	115	634	413	91	504	307	83	390	401
Total	**36,112**	**9,070**	**45,182**	**34,030**	**8,347**	**42,377**	**30,808**	**6,617**	**37,425**	**41,538**

*Titles listed in Bowker's *Weekly Record* are the source of all 1979 and 1980 figures above; these figures, however, reflected a considerable undercount of mass market paperbacks. *Weekly Record* is also the source of the preliminary hardbound and trade paperbound totals for 1981. Those figures are combined with the new mass market count (from *Paperbound Books in Print*, Table 2) to form the preliminary 1981 total of all hardbound and all paperbound (mass market and trade) titles thus far recorded and given in the right-hand column above.
†1981 figures also include mass market data from *Paperbound Books in Print*.
‡Includes biographies placed in other classes by the Library of Congress.

TABLE 2 MASS MARKET PAPERBOUND TITLES*
(From *Paperbound Books in Print*)

Categories	1981 Titles Preliminary
Agriculture	5
Art	7
Biography	72
Business	12
Education	9
Fiction	2,782
General works	77
History	45
Home Economics	99
Juveniles	223
Language	18
Law	4
Literature	43
Medicine	33
Music	—
Philosophy, Psychology	77
Poetry, Drama	16
Religion	26
Science	17
Sociology, Economics	50
Sports, Recreation	145
Technology	11
Travel	4
Total	**3,775**

*For Table 2, the 474 subject headings used to classify titles in the Subject Index to *Paperbound Books in Print* were carefully analyzed and grouped according to the 23 Dewey classification-based categories used in the tabulations made from *Weekly Record*. New books and new editions are here combined in a single figure for each category; no breakdown is available at this time.

TABLE 3 PAPERBACKS OTHER THAN MASS MARKET— 1979, 1980, AND 1981
(From *Weekly Record* Listings of Domestic and Imported Books)

Categories	1979 titles (final) New Bks.	New Eds.	Totals	1980 titles (final) New Bks.	New Eds.	Totals	1981 titles (preliminary) New Bks.	New Eds.	Totals
Fiction	256	125	381	271	156	427	240	121	361
Nonfiction	8,671	1,905	10,576	8,535	1,857	10,392	7,832	1,784	9,916
Total	**8,927**	**2,030**	**10,957**	**8,806**	**2,013**	**10,819**	**8,072**	**1,905**	**10,277**

TABLE 4 ENGLISH TRANSLATIONS—
1978, 1979, 1980, AND 1981
(From *Weekly Record* Listings of Domestic and Imported Hardbound and Paperbound Books)

Original Language	1978 Titles (Final)	1979 Titles (Final)	1980 Titles (Final)	1981 Titles (Prelim.)
French	286	315	228	220
German	237	300	228	247
Italian	62	60	62	59
Oriental	70	75	51	61
Russian	102	159	106	81
Scandinavian	34	35	38	31
Spanish	60	61	40	49
Other	494	655	600	538
Total	1,345	1,660	1,353	1,286

TABLE 5 BOOK IMPORTS—1979, 1980, AND 1981
(From *Weekly Record* Listings of Domestic and Imported Hardbound and Paperbound Books)

Categories	1979 New Books	1979 New Editions	1979 Totals	1980 New Books	1980 New Editions	1980 Totals	1981 New Books	1981 New Editions	1981 Totals
Agriculture	107	10	117	94	10	104	63	2	65
Art	206	24	230	148	9	157	111	13	124
Biography	156	17	173	113	13	126	74	5	79
Business	61	18	79	62	12	74	41	5	46
Education	162	7	169	124	9	133	89	4	93
Fiction	62	9	71	63	8	71	51	5	56
General Works	139	11	150	125	7	132	97	7	104
History	271	28	299	267	29	296	162	24	186
Home Economics	48	3	51	38	2	40	9	0	9
Juveniles	42	1	43	54	4	58	30	2	32
Language	122	15	137	123	12	134	69	6	75
Law	75	16	91	92	20	112	73	9	82
Literature	178	16	194	173	10	183	118	6	124
Medicine	475	65	540	596	75	671	410	45	455
Music	25	9	34	33	2	35	26	2	28
Philosophy, Psychology	142	10	152	203	15	218	140	8	148
Poetry, Drama	129	10	139	109	11	120	92	5	97
Religion	129	7	136	85	9	94	68	5	73
Science	829	61	890	991	78	1,069	704	48	752
Sociology, Economics	1,168	68	1,236	1,000	50	1,050	800	35	835
Sports, Recreation	115	10	125	79	6	85	49	3	52
Technology	282	46	328	329	44	373	247	36	283
Travel	67	7	74	51	4	55	29	3	32
Total	4,990	468	5,458	4,951	439	5,390	3,552	278	3,830

TABLE 6 AVERAGE PER-VOLUME PRICES OF HARDCOVER BOOKS—1977, 1978, 1979, 1980, AND 1981
(From *Weekly Record* listings of Domestic and Imported Books)

Categories with Dewey Decimal Numbers	1977 vols. (final) Average prices	1978 vols. (final) Total volumes	1978 Average prices	1979 vols. (final) Total volumes	1979 Average prices	1980 vols. (final) Total Volumes	1980 Average Prices	1981 vols. (preliminary) Total volumes	1981 Total prices	1981 Average prices
Agriculture (630–639; 712–719)	$16.24	416	$17.24	419	$20.94	360	$27.55	313	$ 10,094.08	$32.25
Art (700–711; 720–779)	21.24	1,017	21.11	1,399	21.95	1,132	27.70	857	27,578.82	32.18
*Biography	15.34	1,574	15.76	1,675	17.52	1,508	19.77	1,144	25,286.46	22.10
Business (650–659)	18.00	956	19.27	1,077	23.11	898	22.45	876	18,413.30	21.02
Education (370–379)	12.95	657	13.86	706	15.10	626	17.01	555	10,249.09	18.47
Fiction	10.09	2,254	11.27	2,027	11.99	2,100	12.46	1,740	23,283.38	13.38
General Works (000–099)	30.99	1,140	25.51	989	28.56	1,190	29.84	1,105	36,942.05	33.43
History (900–909; 930–999)	17.12	1,661	17.20	1,685	19.79	1,743	22.78	1,371	31,051.55	22.65
Home Economics (640–649)	11.16	495	11.27	552	11.95	517	13.31	446	6,969.08	15.63
Juveniles	6.65	2,961	6.58	3,002	7.14	2,742	8.16	2,370	19,641.58	8.29
Language (400–499)	14.96	256	16.67	356	18.25	318	22.16	258	5,970.58	23.14
Law (340–349)	25.04	713	24.26	891	29.44	759	33.25	843	27,827.18	33.01
Literature (800–810; 813–820; 823–899)	15.78	1,354	17.98	1,290	17.64	1,266	18.70	1,006	19,444.71	19.33
Medicine (610–619)	24.00	2,199	25.01	2,554	29.27	2,596	34.28	2,442	87,493.28	35.83
Music (780–789)	20.13	361	24.68	289	18.93	273	21.79	232	5,797.21	24.99
Philosophy, Psychology (100–199)	14.43	968	14.75	1,024	17.98	1,045	21.70	820	18,097.95	22.07
Poetry, Drama (811; 812; 821; 822)	13.63	878	14.86	868	15.83	753	17.85	572	11,362.65	19.86
Religion (200–299)	12.26	1,077	13.04	1,286	14.83	1,109	17.61	932	15,817.27	16.97
Science (500–599)	24.88	2,331	26.20	2,525	30.59	2,481	37.45	2,273	91,522.68	40.27
Sociology, Economics (300–339; 350–369; 380–399)	29.88	4,663	29.66	5,656	43.57†	5,138	31.76	4,649	127,985.84	27.53
Sports, Recreation (790–799)	12.28	732	12.96	750	13.88	644	15.92	587	10,962.40	18.68
Technology (600–609; 620–629; 660–699)	23.61	1,384	22.64	1,838	27.82	1,742	33.64	1,496	54,351.03	36.33
Travel (910–919)	18.44	250	17.12	342	15.02	253	16.80	190	3,695.66	19.45
†Total	$19.22	30,297	$19.30	33,200	$23.96	31,234	$24.64†	27,077	$689,837.83	$25.48

*Dewey Decimal Numbers omitted because biographies counted here come from many Dewey classifications.
†See Table 7.

TABLE 7 AVERAGE PER-VOLUME PRICES OF HARDCOVER BOOKS, ELIMINATING ALL VOLUMES PRICED AT $81 OR MORE— 1977, 1978, 1979, 1980, AND 1981*

Dewey Classifications	1977 (final)	1978 (final)	1979 (final)	1980 (final)	1981 (prelim.)
General Works (000–099)	$22.45	$20.34	$21.06	$23.34	$25.15
Philos., Psychol. (100–199)	14.17	15.10	17.50	20.18	21.61
Religion (200–299)	11.98	13.29	13.01	15.55	16.58
Soc., Econ.; Law; Ed. (300–399)	16.04	16.95	18.69	21.07	23.35
Language (400–499)	14.55	17.01	18.07	20.14	20.65
Science (500–599)	23.78	25.21	27.77	32.67	33.97
Tech.; Med.; Agr.; Home Ec.; Bus. (600–699)	—	—	—	26.05	27.49
Art; Music; Sports, Rec. (700–799)	—	—	—	20.61	23.04
Gen. Lit.; Poetry, Drama (800–899)	—	—	—	17.78	18.53
History; Travel (900–999)	—	—	—	19.62	20.70
All Classifications (000–999)	**$17.32**	**$18.01**	**$19.63**	**$22.48**	**$24.33**

*Compare classifications with Table 6.

TABLE 8 AVERAGE PER-VOLUME PRICES OF MASS MARKET PAPERBACKS 1981*
(From *Paperbound Books in Print* Listings)

	Total Vols.	Total Prices	Average Prices		Total Vols.	Total Prices	Average Prices
Agriculture	5	$ 12.70	$2.54	Music	—	—	—
Art	7	38.45	5.49	Philosophy,			
Biography	72	275.30	3.82	Psychology	77	218.35	2.83
Business	12	55.60	4.63	Poetry, Drama	16	51.45	3.21
Education	9	35.65	3.96	Religion	26	70.20	2.70
Fiction	2,782	6,879.15	2.47	Science	17	75.65	4.45
General Works	77	279.30	3.62	Sociology,			
History	45	158.90	3.53	Economics	50	171.65	3.43
Home Economics	99	430.35	4.34	Sports,			
Juveniles	223	400.20	1.79	Recreation	145	441.85	3.04
Language	18	61.50	3.41	Technology	11	46.20	4.20
Law	4	12.35	3.08	Travel	4	12.90	3.22
Literature	43	146.90	3.41				
Medicine	33	120.85	3.66	**Total**	**3,775**	**$9,995.45**	**$2.65**

*Comparable figures for earlier years are not available. See also Table 2.

TABLE 9 AVERAGE PER-VOLUME PRICES OF TRADE PAPERBACKS—1977, 1978, 1979, 1980, 1981
(From Weekly Record Listings of Domestic and Imported Books)

Categories	1977 volumes (final) Average prices	1978 volumes (final) Total volumes	1978 Average prices	1979 volumes (final) Total volumes	1979 Average prices	1980 volumes (final) Total volumes	1980 Average prices	1981 volumes (preliminary) Total volumes	1981 Total prices	1981 Average prices
Agriculture	$ 5.01	139	$ 5.86	117	$ 6.80	104	$ 8.54	72	$ 710.50	$ 9.87
Art	6.27	471	6.81	634	8.33	563	9.09	469	5,045.67	10.76
Biography	4.91	286	4.72	314	5.64	363	6.57	355	2,527.85	7.12
Business	7.09	280	7.99	277	8.94	285	9.90	260	2,629.11	10.11
Education	5.72	410	6.68	404	6.91	382	8.42	373	3,579.36	9.60
Fiction	4.20	353	4.63	388	4.42	432	5.71	367	2,185.60	5.96
General Works	6.18	342	6.67	480	6.47	544	8.00	470	5,004.98	10.65
History	5.81	368	5.99	474	6.67	478	7.57	476	4,331.71	9.10
Home Economics	4.77	365	4.98	337	5.48	360	6.33	355	2,524.21	7.11
Juveniles	2.68	340	2.82	413	3.23	460	3.50	466	1,563.62	3.36
Language	7.79	203	6.18	205	7.53	215	8.59	200	1,708.09	8.54
Law	10.66	361	10.97	361	11.68	317	11.33	284	3,581.96	12.61
Literature	5.18	458	5.48	447	6.50	424	7.26	385	3,127.62	8.12
Medicine	7.63	556	8.31	667	9.55	682	11.46	652	8,002.56	12.27
Music	6.36	81	6.91	97	9.17	83	9.36	102	1,011.34	9.92
Philosophy, Psychology	5.57	379	6.60	340	6.56	382	7.57	344	3,245.67	9.44
Poetry, Drama	4.71	428	4.62	504	4.21	442	5.09	404	2,404.28	5.95
Religion	3.68	1,093	4.22	1,038	4.59	937	6.15	949	6,325.67	6.67
Science	8.81	550	9.49	614	11.48	630	13.46	503	7,634.16	15.18
Sociology, Economics	6.03	1,764	6.52	2,036	8.07	2,016	9.75	1,765	20,807.61	11.79
Sports, Recreation	4.87	413	5.42	360	6.12	326	7.11	328	2,527.20	7.70
Technology	7.97	518	7.55	556	9.24	601	13.52	640	8,904.37	13.91
Travel	5.21	164	6.02	294	5.97	247	6.73	201	1,672.09	8.32
Total	**$ 5.93**	**10,322**	**$ 6.31**	**11,357**	**$ 7.21**	**11,279**	**$ 8.60**	**10,920**	**$101,055.23**	**$ 9.70**

TABLE 10 AVERAGE AND MEDIAN PRICES, THREE CATEGORIES
PW FALL ANNOUNCEMENT ADS, 1972–1981

Novels, Except Mystery, Western, SF, Gothic: Average & Median Prices	Avg.	Med.	Biography, Memoirs, Letters: Average & Median Prices	Avg.	Med.	History, Including Pictorial, but Not Art Books: Average & Median Prices	Avg.	Med.
1981—243 vols./45 pubs.	$12.61	$13.50	1981—116 vols./54 pubs.	$18.09	$16.95	1981—188 vols./70 pubs.	$20.35	$19.00
1980—317 vols./42 pubs.	$11.73	$11.50	1980—130 vols./56 pubs.	$17.05	$15.00	1980—154 vols./57 pubs.	$19.85	$18.50
1979—291 vols./43 pubs.	$10.42	$ 9.95	1979—160 vols./67 pubs.	$15.92	$13.95	1979—219 vols./67 pubs.	$16.88	$15.95
1978—282 vols./43 pubs.	$ 9.63	$ 8.95	1978—213 vols./73 pubs.	$13.54	$12.95	1978—207 vols./85 pubs.	$15.59	$15.00
1977—233 vols./37 pubs.	$ 9.18	$ 8.95	1977—169 vols./62 pubs.	$13.12	$12.50	1977—241 vols./72 pubs.	$15.83	$15.00
1976—174 vols./34 pubs.	$ 8.74	$ 8.95	1976—130 vols./61 pubs.	$12.87	$11.95	1976—151 vols./63 pubs.	$13.96	$14.95
1975—150 vols./35 pubs.	$ 8.51	$ 7.95	1975—128 vols./53 pubs.	$12.50	$10.95	1975—178 vols./74 pubs.	$15.32	$13.95
1974—212 vols./38 pubs.	$ 7.68	$ 7.95	1974—190 vols./80 pubs.	$12.31	$10.95	1974—219 vols./74 pubs.	$12.91	$12.50
1973—225 vols./40 pubs.	$ 7.34	$ 6.95	1973—190 vols./78 pubs.	$10.67	$ 8.95	1973—228 vols./73 pubs.	$13.38	$12.50
1972—171 vols./37 pubs.	$ 6.95	$ 6.95	1972—170 vols./61 pubs.	$10.12	$ 8.95	1972—262 vols./89 pubs.	$12.30	$12.30

BOOK SALES STATISTICS: HIGHLIGHTS FROM AAP ANNUAL SURVEY, 1980

Chandler B. Grannis

The annual statistical report of the Association of American Publishers (AAP) indicated that book publishers' 1980 sales receipts increased approximately 11.2 percent over 1979 receipts. The overall sales figures are part of a 128-page paperbound volume, *AAP 1980 Industry Statistics*, prepared by Touche, Ross & Company, financial consultants. The reported dollar total of 1980 sales by book publishers is $7,039,400,000.

Comparable data for 1981 are not scheduled for release by AAP until late spring 1982. As this volume of the *Bowker Annual* went to press, some early reports were available that suggested trends similar to those of 1980, with continued dollar sales increases in most divisions of book publishing and smaller increases or actual decreases of unit sales in several categories.

One ongoing indicator of industry sales figures is the monthly table, "Estimated Publishers' Net Sales," compiled by John P. Dessauer for the Book Industry Study Group (BISG) and appearing in the *BISG Bulletin*. The sales table in the January 1982 issue of the *BISG Bulletin* covered the period from January through September 1981. Estimates for the nine months suggest a 10.6 percent dollar sales increase over the same period of 1980, but indicate only a .1 percent rise in total unit sales. The most significant decline in unit sales occurred in the bibles and related books category, with other unit decreases occurring in the university press, elhi, and book club categories.

It should be noted that data in the medical and college text categories are still under review at the Bureau of the Census, as the "medical professional" sales reported to the 1977 census seem to have included a substantial amount of textbooks not included in the sales reported to the 1972 census in this category. To "reestablish comparability," some 35 percent of the sales classified in the AAP report as medical-professional (see Table 1) may have to be included in the college textbook category. Readers should make due allowance for this possibility in evaluating the estimates in the table.

The sales estimates in the table are based on the final report of the 1977 Census of Manufacturers for Standard Industry Classification 2731—the book publishing classification. The report was completed in the spring of 1980. AAP's 1978 figures, which were based on the earlier census report, have therefore been adjusted somewhat.

It is also noted that the census data does not cover most university presses or other institutionally sponsored and not-for-profit publishing, nor does it cover audiovisual and other media materials that are included in the AAP study. The AAP figures omit Sunday school materials and "certain pamphlets." The "other sales" item in Table 1 includes only sheet sales (except those to prebinders) and miscellaneous merchandise sales. Finally, it is noted AAP estimates "include domestic sales and export sales only and do not cover indigenous activities of publishers' foreign subsidiaries."

TABLE 1 ESTIMATED BOOK PUBLISHING INDUSTRY SALES 1972, 1977, 1979, and 1980
(Millions of Dollars)

	1972 $	1977 $	1977 % Change from 1972	1979 $	1979 % Change from 1977	1979 % Change from 1972	1980 $	1980 % Change from 1979	1980 % Change from 1972
Trade (Total)	444.8	887.2	99.5	1086.2	4.8	144.2	1271.3	17.0	185.8
Adult hardbound	251.5	501.3	99.3	586.0	16.9	133.0	695.9	14.4	176.7
Adult paperbound	82.4	223.7	171.5	292.9	9.8	255.5	364.6	24.5	342.5
Juvenile hardbound	106.5	136.1	27.8	151.5	4.3	42.3	168.5	11.2	58.2
Juvenile paperbound	4.4	26.1	493.2	33.5	−12.3	661.4	42.3	26.4	861.4
Religious (Total)	117.5	250.6	113.3	295.4	7.2	151.4	351.4	19.0	199.0
Bibles, testaments, hymnals and prayerbooks	61.6	116.3	88.8	138.9	3.2	125.5	168.3	21.2	173.2
Other religious	55.9	134.3	140.3	156.5	11.0	180.0	183.1	17.0	227.5
Professional (Total)	381.0	698.2	83.3	885.1	10.0	132.3	999.1	12.9	162.2
Technical and scientific	131.8	249.3	89.2	301.1	8.5	128.5	334.8	11.2	154.0
Business and other professional	192.2	286.3	49.0	370.0	11.0	92.5	424.4	14.7	120.8
Medical	57.0	162.6	185.3	214.0	10.4	275.4	239.9	12.1	320.9
Book clubs	240.5	406.7	69.1	501.7	8.3	108.6	538.3	7.3	123.8
Mail order publications	198.9	396.4	99.3	485.8	10.3	144.2	566.9	16.7	185.0
Mass market paperback Rack-sized	250.0	487.7	95.1	603.2	10.8	141.3	653.3	8.3	161.3
University presses	41.4	56.1	35.5	68.0	9.3	64.3	80.7	18.7	94.9
Elementary and secondary text	497.6	755.9	51.9	930.1	11.6	86.9	940.3	1.1	89.0
College text	375.3	649.7	73.1	825.8	12.1	120.0	952.7	15.4	153.9
Standardized tests	26.5	44.6	68.3	61.6	18.6	132.5	67.2	9.1	153.6
Subscription reference	278.9	294.4	5.6	383.5	12.4	37.5	384.7	0.3	37.9
AV and other media (Total)	116.2	151.3	30.2	146.3	−3.2	25.9	166.7	13.9	43.5
Elhi	101.2	131.4	29.8	129.6	−0.7	28.1	147.9	14.1	46.1
College	9.2	11.6	26.1	7.8	−36.5	−15.2	8.7	16.1	−5.4
Other	5.8	8.3	43.1	8.9	4.2	53.5	10.1	13.4	74.1
Other sales	49.2	63.4	28.9	59.7	15.0	21.3	66.8	11.9	35.8
Total	3017.8	5142.2	70.4	6332.2	9.3	109.8	7039.4	11.2	133.3

Source: From *AAP 1980 Industry Statistics*, New York: Association of American Publishers, 1981.

U.S. CONSUMER EXPENDITURES ON BOOKS IN 1980

John P. Dessauer
Book Industry Statistician

Expenditures on book purchases by U.S. consumers climbed to an encouraging $8.2 billion in 1980—an increase of 12.5% over 1979 and an improved performance over the prior year, when the gain had only been 9.6%. Even more importantly, units purchased increased by 3.0%, to nearly 1.7 billion, compared to a growth of only 1.7% in 1979.

These findings emerge from the estimates appearing in "Book Industry Trends 1981," recently released by the Book Industry Study Group. This year's version of my annual estimates and forecast of industry sales includes revisions of earlier years' data, notably of some of the 1979 figures cited in this article.

As illustrated in Table 1, nearly all book categories showed strong gains in 1980, with trade books leading the way. Adult trade paperbacks achieved a growth of 29.9% in dollars and 21.5% in units, while hardbound books posted increases of 18.8% in dollars and 17.2% in units. Children's paperbacks, which have been on a rollercoaster ride since they were first introduced a dozen years ago, had an up year, with gains of 53.7% in dollars and 32.2% in units. Mail order publications, though not performing as impressively as they have during some other recent years, did well, with increases of 15.9% in dollars and 12.1% in units.

University presses showed unusual strength, advancing 15.7% in dollars and 14.5% in units, with paperbound books contributing the major share of growth. College textbooks recorded a respectable 16.1% increase in dollars and 5.1% in units, with paperbacks again the major factor. Even mass market paperbacks achieved a slight unit gain of 1.3%, along with a dollar increase of 12.5%. Professional books, on the other hand, while posting gains in dollars, fell behind in units, as did book clubs, school textbooks, and religious books. Declines in both dollars and units were shown by subscription reference books.

The market analysis in Table 2 shows that the retail sectors, general retailers, and college stores achieved the best gains. General retailers, a category that embraces bookstores as well as mass market outlets, recorded a 19.1% growth in dollars and 8.0% in units, while college stores achieved increases of 16.7% in dollars and 4.4% in units. On the other hand, the direct-to-consumer market was a disappointment in 1980, showing only a 6.6% dollar increase and a 1.5% unit loss. Libraries performed as well as could be expected, given their budget constraints, while the expenditures of schools reflected the many problems and difficulties sustained by that sector during the year. Remainder and special sales, included in the "Other" category, were adequate, posting a 15.5% dollar and 3.4% unit growth.

As in past years, our present analysis attempts to gain some insight into the impact of recent book price inflation by comparing per-unit expenditure dollars for 1980 and 1979. (See the last three columns of Table 1.) Here we find that the 1980 increase in the average consumer expenditure was 9.2%, well below the 13.9% increase in the Consumer Price Index for the year. Of course some book categories increased by substantially more

Note: Adapted from *Publishers Weekly*, November 20, 1981, where the article was entitled "Book Sales in 1980: Well Up over 1979."

TABLE 1 U.S. CONSUMER EXPENDITURES ON BOOKS, 1980 & 1979
Millions of Dollars and Units

	1980 Dollars	1980 Units	1979 Dollars	1979 Units	% Change Dollars	% Change Units	Dollars per Unit 1980	Dollars per Unit 1979	% Change
Trade	1984	389	1629	327	21.8	19.0	5.10	4.98	2.3
Adult Hardbound	1161	152	977	130	18.8	17.2	7.65	7.54	1.4
Adult Paperbound	479	116	368	96	29.9	21.5	4.11	3.85	6.9
Juvenile Hardbound	251	64	222	59	12.8	9.6	3.89	3.78	2.9
Juvenile Paperbound	94	56	61	43	53.7	32.2	1.66	1.43	16.2
Religious	516	99	480	108	7.6	−8.1	5.19	4.43	17.0
Hardbound	346	37	332	41	4.2	−9.5	9.34	8.11	15.2
Paperbound	170	62	148	67	15.2	−7.2	2.73	2.20	24.1
Professional	998	52	868	53	15.0	−1.4	19.26	16.51	16.6
Hardbound	796	29	686	29	16.0	0.2	27.16	23.46	15.7
Paperbound	202	22	182	23	11.4	−3.4	8.98	7.79	15.2
Book Clubs	524	211	493	221	6.4	−4.7	2.48	2.22	11.6
Hardbound	404	66	368	64	9.8	3.3	6.08	5.72	6.2
Paperbound	119	144	124	157	−3.7	−8.0	.83	.79	4.5
Mail Order Publications	578	51	499	46	15.9	12.1	11.24	10.87	3.3
Mass Market Paperback	1208	534	1073	527	12.5	1.3	2.26	2.04	11.0
University Press	82	9	71	8	15.7	14.5	9.05	8.96	1.0
Hardbound	60	4	54	4	12.3	7.2	15.12	14.41	4.9
Paperbound	22	5	17	4	26.4	21.1	4.30	4.12	4.4
Elhi Text	936	251	913	261	2.6	−4.6	3.73	3.49	6.8
Hardbound	504	95	504	100	−0.1	−4.5	5.28	5.05	4.6
Paperbound	432	155	409	161	5.8	−3.8	2.78	2.53	9.9
College Text	1075	96	926	92	16.1	5.1	11.14	10.08	10.5
Hardbound	805	63	716	60	12.5	3.5	12.86	11.83	8.6
Paperbound	270	34	210	31	28.6	8.0	7.97	6.70	19.0
Subscription Reference	322	0	356	1	−9.7	−15.4	328.37	307.33	6.8
Total	8224	1694	7308	1644	12.5	3.0	4.85	4.44	9.2

Source: *Book Industry Trends—1981.*
Note: Dollars and unit data have been rounded to millions. Change percentages, however, are based on unrounded data. Some subtotals and totals may not add exactly due to rounding.

TABLE 2 CHANNELS OF U.S. BOOK DISTRIBUTION
1980 & 1979
Estimated Consumer Expenditures—Millions
of Dollars and Units

	1980		1979		% Change	
	Dollars	Units	Dollars	Units	Dollars	Units
General Retailers	3028	736	2542	682	19.1	8.0
College Stores	1437	197	1231	189	16.7	4.4
Libraries and Institutions	660	73	605	72	9.2	1.8
Schools	1222	308	1177	319	3.8	−3.5
Direct to Consumer	1769	315	1659	320	6.6	−1.5
Other	108	63	93	61	15.5	3.4
Total	**8224**	**1694**	**7308**	**1644**	**12.5**	**3.0**

Source: *Book Industry Trends—1981.*
Note: Dollars and unit data have been rounded to millions. Change percentages, however, are based on unrounded data. Some subtotals and totals may not add exactly due to rounding.

than the overall average—religious, professional, mass market paperback and paperbound college textbooks, among them—while a number of categories showed below-average gains. Bearing in mind that these are sales-weighted averages (based on *purchases* rather than on a mere comparison of cover prices from year to year) we note that the lowest increase was posted by adult trade hardbound books, while the highest was recorded by religious paperbacks.

In general, then, 1980 was a better year for the industry than 1979 had been, even granting the disappointments in the school and direct-to-consumer markets. Judging from our observations thus far of 1981, furthermore, last year's trends continue to prevail in most categories.

PRICES OF U.S. AND FOREIGN PUBLISHED MATERIALS

Nelson A. Piper

*Assistant University Librarian, Collections, The General Library,
University of California, Davis, Davis, CA 95616*
916-752-2110

The upward trend in the cost of library materials has continued in 1981, and the rate of increase in the price indexes for periodicals and serial services has continued to outstrip the rate of increase for monographic materials. The rise in cost of library materials published abroad has been mitigated by the sharp rise in value of the U.S. dollar in the international money market.

The cost of library materials in the U.S. marketplace (see Tables 1–8) repeats

TABLE 1 U.S. PERIODICALS: AVERAGE PRICES AND PRICE INDEXES, 1978–1981*
(Index Base: 1977 = 100)

Subject Area	1977 Average Price	1978 Average Price	1978 Index	1979 Average Price	1979 Index	1980 Average Price	1980 Index	1981 Average Price	1981 Index
U.S. periodicals (based on the total group of titles included in the indexes which follow)									
Agriculture	$24.59	$27.58	112.2	$30.37	123.5	$34.54	140.5	$39.13	159.1
Business and economics	11.58	12.48	107.8	14.16	122.3	15.24	131.6	17.24	148.9
Chemistry and physics	18.62	21.09	113.3	22.97	123.4	25.42	136.5	28.88	155.1
Children's periodicals	93.76	108.22	115.4	118.33	126.2	137.45	146.6	156.30	166.7
Education	5.82	6.34	108.9	6.70	115.1	7.85	134.9	8.56	147.1
Engineering	17.54	19.49	111.1	21.61	123.2	23.45	133.7	25.18	143.6
Fine and applied arts	35.77	39.77	111.2	42.95	120.1	49.15	137.4	54.55	152.5
General interest periodicals	13.72	14.82	108.0	17.42	127.0	18.67	136.1	20.51	149.5
History	16.19	17.26	106.6	18.28	112.9	19.87	122.7	21.83	134.8
Home economics	12.64	13.71	108.5	14.67	116.1	15.77	124.8	17.96	142.1
Industrial arts	18.73	21.67	115.7	23.21	123.9	24.63	131.5	27.34	146.0
Journalism and communications	14.37	15.48	107.7	17.65	122.8	20.70	144.1	22.62	157.4
Labor and industrial relations	16.97	19.95	117.6	23.86	140.6	27.34	161.1	29.80	175.6
Law	11.24	13.24	117.8	15.74	140.0	18.84	167.6	21.68	192.9
Library Science	17.36	18.74	107.9	20.98	120.9	23.00	132.5	24.80	142.9
Literature and language	16.97	19.34	114.0	20.82	122.7	23.25	137.0	28.47	167.8
Math, botany, geology, and general science	11.82	12.84	108.6	13.84	117.1	15.30	129.4	17.30	146.4
Medicine	47.13	54.16	114.9	58.84	124.8	67.54	143.3	75.62	160.4
Philosophy and religion	51.31	57.06	111.2	63.31	123.4	73.37	143.0	86.38	168.3
Physical education and recreation	10.89	11.66	107.1	13.25	121.7	14.73	135.3	15.40	141.4
Political science	10.00	10.79	107.9	12.27	122.7	13.83	138.3	15.42	154.2
Psychology	14.83	15.62	105.3	17.47	117.8	19.30	130.1	22.69	153.0
Sociology and anthropology	31.74	34.21	107.8	38.10	120.0	41.95	132.2	47.27	148.9
Zoology	19.68	21.58	109.7	23.70	120.4	27.56	140.0	31.37	159.4
	33.69	37.05	110.0	40.15	119.2	44.58	132.3	48.32	143.4
Total number of periodicals	3,218	3,255		3,314		3,358		3,425	

*Compiled by Norman B. Brown and Jane Phillips. For further comments see *Library Journal*, July 1981, "Price Indexes for 1981: U.S. Periodicals and Serial Services," by Norman B. Brown and Jane Phillips. Note that this table uses a one-year (1977) rather than a three-year (1977–1979) base, conforming to the practice of the Bureau of Labor Statistics and making these price indexes comparable to the consumer price indexes. For average prices for years prior to 1978, see previous editions of the *Bowker Annual*.

TABLE 2 U.S. SERIAL SERVICES: AVERAGE PRICES AND PRICE INDEXES, 1978–1981*
(Index Base: 1977 = 100)

	1977 Average Price	1978 Average Price	1978 Index	1979 Average Price	1979 Index	1980 Average Price	1980 Index	1981 Average Price	1981 Index
Business	$216.28	$222.45	102.9	$249.05	115.2	$294.00	135.9	$343.29	158.7
General and humanities	90.44	94.88	104.9	118.83	131.4	124.28	137.4	142.04	157.1
Law	126.74	137.91	108.8	158.65	125.2	184.38	145.5	212.85	167.9
Science and technology	141.16	160.61	113.8	173.96	123.2	191.35	135.6	214.01	151.6
Social sciences (excluding business and law)	145.50	153.94	105.8	169.55	116.5	190.07	130.6	215.12	147.8
Soviet translations	175.41	187.44	106.9	201.89	115.1	229.68	130.9	253.79	144.7
U.S. documents	62.88	72.52	115.3	75.87	120.7	78.87	125.4	84.48	134.4
"Wilson Index"	438.00	467.17	106.7	487.75	111.4	541.92	123.7	600.58	137.1
Combined (excluding "Wilson Index")	$142.27	$153.95	108.2	$171.06	120.2	$194.21	136.5	$219.75	154.5
Total number of services	1,432	1,426		1,450		1,470		1,477	

*Compiled by Norman B. Brown and Jane Phillips. For further comments see *Library Journal*, July 1981, "Price Indexes for 1981: U.S. Periodicals and Serial Services," by Norman B. Brown and Jane Phillips. Note that this table uses a one-year (1977) rather than a three-year (1977–1979) base, conforming to the practice of the Bureau of Labor Statistics and making these price indexes comparable to the consumer price indexes. For average prices for years prior to 1978, see previous editions of the *Bowker Annual*.

Note: The definition of a serial service has been taken from the *American National Standard Criteria for Price Indexes for Library Materials* (ANSI Z39.20–1974).

its 1980 pattern of serial prices increasing much more sharply than the cost of books. The changes in the indexes for U.S. serial publications and hardcover books are noted below:

	Index Change	Percent Change
Periodicals	18.6	13.3
Serial services	18.0	13.2
Hardcover books	4.4	3.4

Detailed price information by subject class is available for the first time in 1981 for mass market paperbacks (Table 4). The table will become an operational price index when comparable figures become available in 1982. The 12.8% rate of increase for higher priced paperbacks (Table 5) almost matches the rate of increase for domestic serials.

Libraries using the several U.S. price indexes, or other indexes, should be careful not to be mislead by overall, or general, rates of increases in price indexes. The rates of increase for the specific subject classes within each index must be analyzed with an individual library's purchasing pattern clearly in mind. Moreover, the capacity of a single component of an index to skew the general rate of change of an index must be understood by all users. The effect of a 14.2-point (13.3%) drop in the 1981 index for books in sociology and economics on the U.S. hardcover books index (Table 3) shows clearly how an unusual drop in a major component of an index can skew the general rate of increase. When the 4,649 sociology and economics books (17.2% of the total) are deleted from the U.S. hardcover production of 27,007 volumes, the general rate of increase for the index rises to 7.8% rather than 3.5%. Higher than average variations in the rates of increase for hardcover books are illustrated by 28.9- and 11.4-point increases in the indexes for books in agriculture and technology. Significant higher than average price increases for periodicals include a 25.3% rise in the price indexes for journals in both labor relations and economics and medicine. It is also important to note again that preliminary cost increase data should be used with care. The 1981 *Bowker Annual* article on price indexes (see pp. 340–353) reported that the final increase for hardcover monographs in 1979 was 24% rather than the preliminary figure of 13.4%. The 1980 preliminary and final unit cost figures reveal that the average unit cost of hardcover books increased from $23.57 to $24.64, a difference of $1.07 per volume.[1]

It must be noted that the U.S. non-print media index (Table 6) is now primarily based on listings from the *School Library Journal*, the previous source, *Previews*, having ceased publication. As expected, the cost trend for nonprint media is up, the only exception being the index for multimedia kits, which declined by 81.1 points (49.3%). The compiler indicates that the wide variation from the past years' figures is partially caused by the necessity of employing a new source for the price information.

The price indexes for U.S. library microfilm (Table 7) and selected U.S. daily newspapers (Table 8) recorded significant price increases for the period from 1978 to 1981. The cost increase that will most affect library budgets is the 10 percent per year rise in the average subscription cost of newspapers.

The usefulness to U.S. libraries of international price increase information (Tables 9–14) has substantially improved this year. Preliminary book production and price information for 1981 is available for British books for the first time because of the cooperation of the British Library Association. Book price information for German books still remains out-of-date by one full year. For the first time, however, German book price information is available for hardcover (bound volumes) and scholarly paperbacks

TABLE 3 U.S. HARDCOVER BOOKS: AVERAGE PRICES AND PRICE INDEXES, 1977–1981*
(Index Base: 1977 = 100)

Categories with Dewey Decimal Numbers	1977 Average Price	1978 (Final) Vols.	1978 Average Price	1978 Index	1979 (Final) Vols.	1979 Average Price	1979 Index	1980 (Final) Vols.	1980 Average Price	1980 Index	1981 (Prelim.) Vols.	1981 Average Price	1981 Index
Agriculture (630–639; 712–719)	$16.24	416	$17.24	106.2	419	$20.94	128.9	360	$27.55	169.6	313	$32.25	198.5
Art (700–711; 720–779)	21.24	1,017	21.11	99.4	1,399	21.95	103.3	1,132	27.70	130.4	857	32.18	151.5
Biography[1]	15.34	1,574	15.76	102.7	1,675	17.52	114.2	1,508	19.77	128.9	1,144	22.10	144.1
Business (650–659)	18.00	956	19.27	107.0	1,077	23.11	128.4	898	22.45	124.7	876	21.02	116.8
Education (370–379)	12.95	657	13.86	111.7	706	15.10	116.6	626	17.01	131.4	555	18.47	142.7
Fiction	10.09	2,254	11.27	82.3	2,027	11.99	118.8	2,100	12.46	123.5	1,740	13.38	132.6
General Works (000–099)	30.99	1,140	25.51	100.5	989	28.56	92.2	1,190	29.84	96.3	1,105	33.43	107.9
History (900–909; 930–999)	17.12	1,661	17.20	101.0	1,685	19.79	115.6	1,743	22.78	133.1	1,371	22.65	132.3
Home Economics (640–649)	11.16	495	11.27	98.9	552	11.95	107.1	517	13.31	119.3	446	15.63	140.1
Juveniles	6.65	2,961	6.58	111.4	3,002	7.14	107.4	2,742	8.16	122.7	2,370	8.29	124.7
Language (400–499)	14.96	256	16.67	96.9	356	18.25	122.0	318	22.16	148.2	258	23.14	154.7
Law (340–349)	25.04	713	24.26		891	29.44	117.6	759	33.25	132.8	843	33.01	131.8
Literature (800–810; 813–820; 823–89)	15.78	1,354	17.98	113.9	1,290	17.64	111.8	1,266	18.70	118.5	1,006	19.33	122.6

Category												
Medicine (610–619)	24.00	2,199	25.01	104.2	2,554	29.27	122.0	2,596	34.28	142.8	2,442	35.83	107.6
Music (780–789)	20.13	361	24.68	122.6	289	18.93	94.0	273	21.79	108.2	232	24.99	124.1
Philosophy, Psychology (100–199)	14.43	968	14.75	102.2	1,024	17.98	124.6	1,045	21.70	150.4	820	22.07	153.1
Poetry, Drama (811; 812; 821; 822)	13.63	878	14.86	109.0	868	15.83	116.1	753	17.85	130.1	572	19.86	145.7
Religion (200–299)	12.26	1,077	13.04	106.4	1,286	14.83	121.0	1,109	17.61	143.6	932	16.97	138.3
Science (500–599)	24.88	2,331	26.20	105.3	2,525	30.59	123.0	2,481	37.45	150.5	2,273	40.27	161.8
Sociology, Economics (300–339; 350–369; 380–399)	29.88	4,663	29.66	99.3	5,656	43.57	145.8	5,138	31.76	106.3	4,649	27.53	92.1
Sports, Recreation (790–799)	12.28	732	12.96	105.5	750	13.88	113.0	644	15.92	129.6	587	18.68	152.1
Technology (600–609; 620–629; 660–699)	23.61	1,384	22.64	95.9	1,838	27.82	117.8	1,742	33.64	142.5	1,496	36.33	153.9
Travel (910–919)	18.44	250	17.12	92.8	342	15.02	81.4	253	16.80	91.1	190	19.45	105.4
Total	$19.22	30,297	$19.30	100.4	33,200	$23.96	124.7	31,234	$24.64	128.2	27,077	$25.48	132.6

*Price indexes in Tables 3 and 5 are based on the books recorded in the R. R. Bowker Company's *Weekly Record* (cumulated in the *American Book Publishing Record*. The 1981 preliminary figures include items listed during 1981 with an imprint date of 1981; 1980 final data includes items listed between January 1980 and June 1981 with an imprint date of 1980; 1979 final data includes items listed between January 1979 and June 1980 with an imprint date of 1979; 1978 final cata includes items listed between January 1978 and June 1979 with an imprint date of 1978; 1977 includes items listed between January 1977 and June 1978 with an imprint date of 1977. (See "Book Title Output and Average Prices, 1981 Preliminary Figures" by Chandler B. Grannis, earlier in this section.— Ed.)

¹Includes biographies placed in other classes by the Library of Congress.

TABLE 4 AVERAGE PER VOLUME PRICES, U.S. MASS
MARKET PAPERBACKS, 1981*

	Total Volumes	Total Prices	Average Prices
Agriculture	5	$12.70	$2.54
Art	7	38.45	5.49
Biography	72	275.30	3.82
Business	12	55.60	4.63
Education	9	35.65	3.96
Fiction	2,782	6,879.15	2.47
General works	77	279.30	3.62
History	45	158.90	3.53
Home economics	99	430.35	4.34
Juvenile	223	400.20	1.79
Language	18	61.50	3.41
Law	4	12.35	3.08
Literature	43	146.90	3.41
Medicine	33	120.85	3.66
Music	—	—	—
Philosophy, psychology	77	218.35	2.83
Poetry, drama	16	51.45	3.21
Religion	26	70.20	2.70
Science	17	75.65	4.45
Sociology, economics	50	171.65	3.43
Sports, recreation	145	441.85	3.04
Technology	11	46.20	4.20
Travel	4	12.90	3.22
Total	3,775	$9,995.45	$2.65

*Average prices of mass market paperbacks published in 1981 shown in this table are based on listings of 1981 mass market titles in *Paperbound Books in Print*. Comparable figures for earlier years are not available. See also Table 2.

(Table 13) and paperback books (Table 12) as well as the combined hardcover/paperback index (Table 11), which was previously the only price index available for German books. The new hardcover/scholarly paperback index will give libraries accurate price information for the German books that U.S. libraries are much more likely to buy.

The price increases for British books by major categories (Table 9) rose by only 2.2% in 1981 after increasing sharply by 15.6% in 1980. In most subject classes, British adult nonfiction books (Table 10) recorded significant price index increases in both 1980 and 1981. The exceptions in 1980 to the significant increases were religious books, with a 15.7% decrease, and general science and medicine, with increases of only 1.8% and 1.9% respectively. In 1981 the exceptions were general works and language titles, which registered price decreases of 25.2% and 12.4% respectively. Users of the 1981 price increase information need to remember that the figures are preliminary and therefore subject to change.

The price indexes for the three categories of German books all recorded moderate price increases in 1980. The combined index for both hardcover and paperback books (Table 11) increased by 7.4 points (6.8%). The new separate indexes for paperback books (Table 12) and hardcover and scholarly paperbacks (Table 13) registered gains of 7.3 points (6.7%) and 6.6 points (6.0%) respectively. As mentioned earlier in this article, attention to the relationship between a library's purchasing pattern and

TABLE 5 U.S. TRADE (HIGHER PRICED) PAPERBACK BOOKS: AVERAGE PRICES AND PRICE INDEXES, 1977–1981
(Index Base: 1977 = 100)*

	1977	1978 (Final)			1979 (Final)			1980 (Final)			1981 (Prelim.)		
	Average Price	No. of Books	Average Price	Index	No. of Books	Average Price	Index	No. of Books	Average Price	Index	No. of Books	Average Price	Index
Agriculture	$5.01	139	$5.86	117.0	117	$6.80	135.7	104	$8.54	170.5	72	$9.87	197.0
Art	6.27	471	6.81	108.6	634	8.33	132.8	563	9.09	145.0	469	10.76	171.6
Biography	4.91	286	4.72	96.1	314	5.64	114.9	363	6.57	133.8	355	7.12	145.0
Business	7.09	280	7.99	112.7	277	8.94	126.1	285	9.90	139.6	260	10.11	142.6
Education	5.72	410	6.68	116.8	404	6.91	120.8	382	8.42	147.2	373	9.60	167.8
Fiction	4.20	353	4.63	110.2	388	4.42	105.2	432	5.71	136.0	367	5.96	141.9
General works	6.18	342	6.67	107.9	480	6.47	104.7	544	8.00	129.4	470	10.65	172.3
History	5.81	368	5.99	103.1	474	6.67	114.8	478	7.57	130.3	476	9.10	156.6
Home economics	4.77	365	4.98	104.4	337	5.48	114.9	360	6.33	132.7	355	7.11	149.1
Juveniles	2.68	340	2.82	105.2	413	3.23	120.5	460	3.50	130.6	466	3.36	125.4
Language	7.79	203	6.18	79.3	205	7.53	96.7	215	8.59	110.3	200	8.54	109.6
Law	10.66	361	10.97	102.9	361	11.68	109.6	317	11.33	106.3	284	12.61	118.3
Literature	5.18	458	5.48	105.8	447	6.50	125.5	424	7.26	140.2	385	8.12	156.8
Medicine	7.63	556	8.31	108.9	667	9.55	125.2	682	11.46	150.2	652	12.27	160.8
Music	6.36	81	6.91	108.6	97	9.17	144.2	83	9.36	147.2	102	9.92	158.0
Philosophy, psychology	5.57	379	6.60	118.5	340	6.56	117.8	382	7.57	135.9	344	9.44	169.5
Poetry, drama	4.71	428	4.62	98.1	504	4.21	89.4	442	5.09	108.1	404	5.95	126.3
Religion	3.68	1,093	4.22	114.7	1,038	4.59	124.7	937	6.15	167.1	949	6.67	180.4
Science	8.81	550	9.49	107.7	614	11.48	130.3	630	13.46	152.8	503	15.18	172.3
Sociology, economics	6.03	1,764	6.52	108.1	2,036	8.07	133.8	2,016	9.75	161.7	1,765	11.79	195.5
Sports, recreation	4.87	413	5.42	111.3	360	6.12	125.7	326	7.11	146.0	328	7.70	158.1
Technology	7.97	518	7.55	94.7	556	9.24	115.9	601	13.52	169.6	640	13.91	174.5
Travel	5.21	164	6.02	115.5	294	5.97	114.6	247	6.73	129.2	201	8.32	159.1
Total	$5.93	10,322	$6.31	106.4	11,357	$7.21	121.6	11,279	$8.60	145.0	10,420	$9.70	163.6

*See footnote to Table 3.

TABLE 6 U.S. NONPRINT MEDIA: AVERAGE PRICES AND PRICE INDEXES, 1972–1981*
(Index Base, 1972 = 100)

Category	1972 Average Quantity	1972 Index	1977 Average Quantity	1977 Index	1978 Average Quantity	1978 Index	1979 Average Quantity	1979 Index	1980 Average Quantity	1980 Index	1981 Average Quantity	1981 Index
16mm Films												
Average rental cost per minute	$ 1.15	100	$ 1.23	107	$ 1.22	106.1	$ 1.35	117.3	$ 1.41	122.6	$ 1.65	143.4
Average color purchase cost per minute	11.95	100	13.95	116.7	12.56	105.1	13.62	113.9	12.03	100.6	16.09	134.7
Average cost of color film	241.39	100	308.85	127.9	350.42	145.1	328.24	135.9	279.09	115.6	343.79	142.4
Average length per film (min.)	20.2	—	22.14	—	27.9	—	24.1	—	23.2	—	21.4	—
Videocassettes												
Average purchase cost per minute	—	—	—	—	—	—	—	—	7.58	100.0	14.87	196.1
Average purchase cost	—	—	—	—	—	—	—	—	271.93	100.0	322.54	118.6
Filmstrips												
Average cost of filmstrip	12.95	100	18.60	143.6	17.43	134.6	21.42	165.4	21.74	167.8	25.40	196.1
Average cost of filmstrip set (cassette)	37.56	100	76.26	203.0	62.31	165.9	65.97	175.6	67.39	179.4	71.12	189.3
Average number of filmstrips per set	2.9	—	4.1	—	3.6	—	3.08	—	3.1	—	2.8	—
Average number of frames per filmstrip	63.3	—	64.2	—	58.0	—	71.8	—	67.9	—	71.4	—
Multimedia Kits												
Average cost per kit	51.33	100	93.65	182.4	117.38	228.7	85.70	166.9	92.71	180.6	46.99	91.5
Sound Recordings												
Average cost per disc	6.10	100	6.72	110.2	7.06	115.8	7.21	118.2	7.75	127.0	9.00	147.5
Average cost per cassette	7.81	100	10.63	136.1	12.57	161.1	12.58	161.1	9.34	119.5	12.48	159.7

*Compiled by David B. Walch from selected issues of *School Library Journal*. The price information from *School Library Journal* is also compared with and supplemented by new title listings from major publishers' catalogs.

TABLE 7   U.S. LIBRARY MICROFILM: AVERAGE RATES AND INDEX VALUES, 1969–1981*

Negative Microfilm[1] (35mm per exposure)	1969	1972	1975	1978	1981
Average rate	$ .0493	$ .0621	$ .0707	$ .0836	$ .09982
Index value	100.0	125.9	143.4	169.7	202.47
Change in index	0	+25.9	+17.3	+26.3	+32.8

Positive Microfilm[2] (35mm per foot)					
Average rate	$ .0960	$ .0839	$ .1190	$ .1612	$ .2021
Index value	100.0	87.4	123.9	168.0	210.5
Change in index	0	−12.6	+36.6	+44.0	+42.5

*Compiled by Imre T. Jármy, National Preservation Program Office, The Library of Congress, consultant to the Library Materials Price Index Committee, Resources Section, Resources and Technical Services Division, American Library Association, from data secured by correspondence and by telephone interviews with the staff of the 50 indexed libraries. These institutions are listed in the "Library Microfilm Rates" articles in the following issues of *Library Resources & Technical Services:* Winter 1967 (11:1), Summer 1969 (13:3), Summer 1970 (14:3), Winter 1974 (18:1), Fall 1977 (21:4), and Summer 1979 (23:3); in the *Newspaper and Gazette Report,* April 1978 (6:1); and in the *National Preservation Report,* April 1979 (1:1). The rates listed parallel those listed in the 9th edition of the *Directory of Library Reprographic Services: A World Guide* (Microform Review, Westport, Connecticut, 1981). The complete list will be published in a pertinent journal of American librarianship. The title of the journal was not available at press time.

[1]Includes 49 selected libraries for 1969; 48 for 1972; 46 for 1975; and 48 for 1978.
[2]Includes 22 selected libraries for 1969; 20 for 1972; 19 for 1975; and 19 for 1978.

TABLE 8   SELECTED U.S. DAILY NEWSPAPERS: AVERAGE SUBSCRIPTION RATES AND INDEX VALUES, 1969–1981*

Year	Average Rate	Index Value	Change in index
1969	$34.1592	100.0	0
1972	42.7647	125.2	+25.2
1975	58.4120	171.0	+45.8
1978	76.4391	223.8	+52.8
1981	98.5521	288.5	+64.7

*Compiled by Imre T. Jármy, National Preservation Program Office, The Library of Congress, consultant to the Library Materials Price Index Committee, Resource Section, Resources and Technical Services Division, American Library Association from data secured by correspondence and by telephone interviews with the circulation managers and publishers of the indexed newspapers and, when necessary, by examining the year's end edition of individual issues. Data was compiled for the 133 titles surveyed in the continental United States, and Alaska and Hawaii. The complete list will be published in a pertinent journal of American librarianship. The title of the journal was not available at press time.

TABLE 9 BRITISH BOOKS BY MAJOR CATEGORIES: AVERAGE PRICES AND PRICE INDEXES, 1979–81*
(Index Base: 1977 = 100)†

	1977	1979			1980			1981 (preliminary)		
	Average Price £ p	No. of Books	Average Price £ p	Index	No. of Books	Average Price £ p	Index	No. of Books	Average Price £ p	Index
Adult fiction	2.55	4,039	3.20	125.5	5,628	3.68	144.3	1,299	4.21	165.1
Adult nonfiction[1]	6.40	25,038	7.70	120.3	37,340	8.83	138.0	6,665	9.27	144.8
Reference books[2]	7.30	2,326	9.15	125.3	3,818	11.32	155.1	85	14.15	193.8
Children's fiction	1.44	1,441	1.86	129.2	1,822	1.99	138.2	387	2.21	153.5
Children's nonfiction	1.19	1,242	1.37	115.1	1,916	1.81	152.1	383	2.03	170.6
All categories combined	5.49	31,760	6.62	120.6	46,706	7.65	139.3	8,819	7.82	142.4

*Data compiled by Dennis E. Smith from the *Library Association Record*, March 1980, and prepublication information for 1981 from the Library Association.
†The index year 1977 has been adopted to conform to the year used in the U.S. Government's Consumer Price Index.
[1] See Table 10 for breakdown by Dewey Classes.
[2] Reference books are included in the total for nonfiction.

Information note: The average annual market exchange rate for 1981 was 2.0240 U.S. dollars per pound sterling as reported by the Bureau of Statistics, International Monetary Fund, in its periodical *International Finance Statistics*.

TABLE 10 BRITISH ADULT NONFICTION BOOKS: AVERAGE PRICES AND PRICE INDEXES, 1979–1981*
(Index Base: 1977 = 100)†

Classes	1977 Average Price £ p	1979 No. of Books	1979 Average Price £ p	1979 Index	1980 No. of Books	1980 Average Price £ p	1980 Index	1981 (preliminary) No. of Books	1981 Average Price £ p	1981 Index
000	8.18	986	12.70	155.3	1,282	14.39	175.9	190	10.77	131.7
100	5.61	716	7.45	132.8	987	8.70	155.1	185	9.98	177.9
200	3.18	1,035	4.60	144.7	1,499	3.88	122.0	291	5.05	158.8
300	6.28	7,114	7.03	111.9	10,517	8.95	142.5	1,718	8.62	137.3
400	3.63	781	2.74	75.5	881	4.11	113.2	220	3.60	99.2
500	10.95	2,163	13.78	125.8	3,142	14.03	128.1	571	15.52	141.7
600	7.94	4,965	9.99	125.8	8,626	10.18	128.2	1,357	12.27	154.5
700	5.57	2,516	6.19	111.1	3,686	8.27	148.5	745	8.98	161.2
800	3.44	2,581	4.78	139.0	3,188	4.99	145.1	697	6.24	181.4
900	4.54	2,581	4.91	108.1	3,532	5.83	128.4	694	7.82	172.2

*Data compiled by Dennis E. Smith from the *Library Association Record*, March 1980, and prepublication information for 1981 from the Library Association.
†The index year 1977 has been adopted to conform to the year used in the U.S. Government's Consumer Price Index.

000 General works; Bibliographies; Librarianship
100 Philosophy; Psychology; Occultism, etc.
200 Not subdivided
300 Social Science; Politics; Economics; Law; Public Administration; Social Welfare; Education; Social Customs, etc.
400 Language; School Readers
500 General Science; Mathematics; Astronomy; Physics; Chemistry; Geology; Meteorology; Pre-history; Anthropology; General Biology; Botany; Zoology
600 Medicine; Public Safety; Engineering/Technology; Agriculture; Domestic Economy; Business Management; Printing & Book Trade; Manufactures; Building
700 Architecture; Fine Arts; Photography; Music; Entertainment; Sports, Amusements
800 General and Foreign Literature; English Literature
900 Geography; Travel; Biography; History

TABLE 11 GERMAN BOOKS: AVERAGE PRICES AND PRICE INDEXES, 1978–1981*
(Index Base: 1977 = 100)†

	1977 Average Price	1978 Average Price	1978 Index	1979 Average Price	1979 Index	1980 Average Price	1980 Index
General, library science, college level textbooks	DM68.47	DM61.93	90.4	DM67.57	98.7	DM75.23	109.9
Religion, theology	23.31	24.57	105.9	26.08	112.4	24.06	103.7
Philosophy, psychology	26.67	27.28	102.3	24.43	91.6	27.81	104.3
Law, administration	33.92	36.92	108.8	46.28	136.4	47.04	138.7
Social sciences, economics, statistics	25.97	29.13	112.2	31.73	122.2	32.98	127.0
Political and military science	22.91	21.64	94.5	27.44	119.8	25.50	111.3
Literature and linguistics	27.79	29.43	105.9	27.03	97.3	27.71	99.7
Belles lettres	6.57	7.44	113.2	7.47	113.7	7.20	109.6
Juveniles	9.07	9.26	102.1	7.85	86.5	10.29	113.5
Education	16.50	17.54	106.3	17.96	108.8	18.20	110.3
School textbooks	10.88	11.44	105.1	11.51	105.8	11.58	106.4
Fine arts	49.70	46.81	94.2	49.09	98.8	51.76	104.1
Music, dance, theatre, film, radio	28.04	28.76	102.6	25.84	92.2	26.38	94.1
History, folklore	38.79	39.75	102.5	37.29	96.1	39.78	102.6
Geography, anthropology, travel	32.20	27.46	85.3	30.49	94.7	31.14	96.7
Medicine	50.29	50.82	101.1	58.10	115.5	59.91	119.1
Natural sciences	93.45	97.02	103.8	101.75	108.9	99.60	106.6
Mathematics	29.98	30.22	104.3	34.82	120.2	36.48	125.9
Technology	42.45	57.85	136.3	55.13	129.9	62.40	147.0
Touring guides and directories	21.78	34.56	158.7	30.09	138.2	31.02	142.4
Home economics and agriculture	25.10	21.75	86.7	22.36	89.1	24.09	96.0
Sports and recreation	18.99	20.13	106.0	19.01	100.1	20.26	106.7
Miscellaneous	11.30	7.96	70.4	8.39	74.2	13.60	120.4
Total	DM21.87	DM23.28	106.4	DM23.62	108.0	DM25.23	115.4

*This is a combined index for numbered paperback books (Taschenbücher) and for bound volumes and scholarly paperbacks (andere Titel). The indexes are tentative and based on average prices unadjusted for title production. Figures for 1980 were compiled by Dennis E. Smith from *Buch und Buchhandel in Zahlen*, Frankfurt, 1981.

†The index year 1977 has been adopted to conform to the year used in the U.S. Government's Consumer Price Index.

Information note: The average annual market exchange rate for 1980 was 1.9590 Deutsche Marks per U.S. dollar as reported by the Bureau of Statistics, International Monetary Fund in its periodical *International Finance Statistics.*

TABLE 12 GERMAN PAPERBACK BOOKS: AVERAGE PRICES AND PRICE INDEX, 1978–1980*
(Index Base: 1977 = 100)†

	1977 Average Price	1978 Average Price	1978 Index	1979 Average Price	1979 Index	1980 Average Price	1980 Index
General, library science, college level textbooks	DM6.47	DM5.68	87.8	DM5.01	77.4	DM8.71	134.6
Religion, theology	7.03	7.55	107.4	7.84	111.5	7.29	103.7
Philosophy, psychology	8.06	8.41	104.3	8.99	111.5	9.44	117.1
Law, administration	8.95	9.03	100.9	10.58	118.2	13.41	149.8
Social sciences, economics, statistics	10.02	10.36	103.4	10.27	102.5	10.75	107.3
Political and military science	8.24	8.84	107.3	8.85	107.4	9.34	113.3
Literature and linguistics	8.36	9.48	113.4	9.01	107.8	10.21	122.1
Belles lettres	4.89	5.14	105.1	5.75	117.6	5.70	116.6
Juvenile	4.77	4.97	104.2	5.16	108.2	5.51	115.5
Education	10.88	11.21	103.0	11.01	101.2	11.63	106.9
School textbooks	2.52	5.02	199.2	3.62	143.7	3.12	123.8
Fine arts	10.28	9.19	89.4	8.80	85.6	11.77	114.5
Music, dance, theater, film, radio	8.11	8.56	105.5	7.47	92.1	8.60	106.0
History, folklore	8.35	8.39	100.5	9.01	107.9	9.22	110.4
Geography, anthropology, travel	6.82	8.42	123.5	7.74	113.5	9.09	133.3
Medicine	10.42	10.14	97.3	10.96	105.2	12.15	116.6
Natural sciences	10.85	11.26	103.8	13.49	124.3	12.31	113.5
Mathematics	15.00	12.38	82.5	15.32	102.1	16.21	108.1
Technology	20.63	10.16	49.2	26.04	126.2	28.22	136.8
Touring guides and directories	7.11	7.36	103.5	7.69	108.2	10.46	147.1
Home economics and agriculture	6.77	6.63	97.9	6.89	101.8	7.38	109.0
Sports and recreation	6.81	7.21	105.9	7.83	115.0	7.69	112.9
Miscellaneous	5.00	2.80	56.0	5.90	118.0	8.87	177.4
Total	DM6.69	DM6.64	99.3	DM7.27	108.7	DM7.76	116.0

*Indexes are tentative and based on average prices unadjusted for title production for numbered paperback books (Taschenbücher). Figures for 1980 were compiled by Dennis E. Smith from *Buch und Buchhandel in Zahlen*, Frankfurt, 1981.
†The index year 1977 has been adopted to conform to the year used in the U.S. Government's Consumer Price Index.

TABLE 13 GERMAN HARDCOVER AND SCHOLARLY PAPERBACK BOOKS: AVERAGE PRICES AND PRICE INDEXES, 1978–1980*
(Index Base: 1977 = 100)†

	1977 Average Price	1978 Average Price	1978 Index	1979 Average Price	1979 Index	1980 Average Price	1980 Index
General, library science, college level textbooks	DM82.28	DM73.24	89.0	DM80.56	97.9	DM86.93	105.7
Religion, theology	27.67	28.77	104.0	29.97	108.3	28.63	103.5
Philosophy, psychology	40.38	39.41	97.6	33.55	83.1	38.14	94.5
Law, administration	37.50	39.82	106.2	50.46	134.6	50.79	135.4
Social sciences, economics, statistics	32.20	35.55	110.4	40.38	125.4	39.71	123.3
Political and military science	27.85	27.95	100.4	34.36	123.4	32.52	116.8
Literature and linguistics	40.90	39.23	95.9	36.62	89.5	36.06	88.2
Belle lettres	7.48	8.49	113.5	8.75	117.0	8.20	109.6
Juvenile	12.86	12.37	96.2	9.60	74.7	12.69	98.7
Education	18.19	18.66	102.6	19.28	106.0	19.40	106.7
School textbooks	10.98	11.58	105.5	11.60	105.6	11.79	107.4
Fine arts	58.51	54.99	94.0	56.96	97.4	63.70	108.9
Music, dance, theater, film, radio	37.89	41.31	109.0	37.00	97.7	38.73	102.2
History, folklore	49.82	52.72	105.8	49.92	100.2	53.43	107.2
Geography, anthropology, travel	34.76	29.74	85.6	33.10	95.2	34.05	98.0
Medicine	61.55	60.86	98.9	69.13	112.3	68.47	111.2
Natural sciences	131.28	115.90	88.3	122.87	93.6	118.89	90.6
Mathematics	32.83	36.84	112.2	39.10	119.1	41.55	126.6
Technology	45.39	62.51	137.7	59.25	130.5	67.79	149.4
Touring guides and directories	22.94	38.35	167.2	32.42	141.3	34.08	148.6
Home economics and agriculture	31.49	28.57	90.7	28.78	91.4	31.38	99.7
Sports and recreation	24.55	26.00	105.9	25.96	105.7	28.51	116.1
Miscellaneous	11.71	11.21	95.7	9.05	77.3	14.32	122.3
Total	DM27.68	DM30.54	110.3	DM30.37	109.7	DM32.18	116.3

*Indexes are tentative and based on prices unadjusted for title production for bound volumes and scholarly paperback books (andere Titel). Figures for 1980 were compiled by Dennis E. Smith from *Buch und Buchhandel in Zahlen*, Frankfurt, 1981.
†The index year 1977 has been adopted to conform to the year used in the U.S. Government's Consumer Price Index.

TABLE 14 LATIN AMERICAN BOOKS: NUMBER OF COPIES AND AVERAGE COST FY 1980 AND 1981*

	Number of Books FY 1980	Number of Books FY 1981	Average Cost FY 1980	Average Cost FY 1981	%(+ or −) over 1980
Argentina	3,638	4,025	12.37[1]	12.49[2]	+1
Bolivia	1,495	1,552	9.27[1]	12.64[2]	+36.4
Brazil	8,432	8,341	7.79[1]	8.63[2]	+10.8
Chile	1,454	1,040	13.44[1]	15.24[2]	+13.4
Colombia	2,216	2,122	10.42[1]	12.67[2]	+21.6
Costa Rica	147	73	8.87	7.67	−15.6
Cuba	—	225	—	9.73	[2]
Dominican Republic	163	600	9.88	10.10	+22.2
Ecuador	744	659	6.69	7.51	+12.3
El Salvador	159	109	7.97	10.36	+30.0
Guatemala	389	246	3.31	8.78	+165.3
Guyana	10	190	2.60	5.74	+120.0
Haiti	170	293	6.48	8.75	+19.6
Honduras	192	194	5.03	7.89	+56.8
Jamaica	94	294	3.45	4.42	+28.3
Mexico	4,195	3,975	7.26[1]	9.34[2]	+28.7
Nicaragua	154	323	8.68	8.34	−4.1
Panama	12	40	9.41[1]	5.69[2]	−65.3
Paraguay	354	281	8.86[1]	12.71[2]	+43.5
Peru	2,609	2,923	6.09[1]	7.67	+26.3
Puerto Rico	458	390	5.71	8.82	+54.8
Surinam	—	139	—	8.58	[2]
Trinidad	1	159	17.00	7.72	−120.2
Uruguay	1,923	1,921	9.56[1]	10.13[1]	+10.5
Venezuela	1,440	835	10.57	10.50	−.6
Other Caribbean	1,273	871	5.57	4.70	−18.5

*Compiled by Peter J. de la Garza, Seminars on the Acquisition of Latin American Library Materials (SALALM), Acquisition Committee, from reports on the number and cost of current monographs purchased by the libraries of Cornell University, University of Florida, University of Illinois, Library of Congress, University of Minnesota, New York Public Library, University of Texas, Tulane University, and University of Wisconsin.
[1] Includes some binding costs.
[2] Data insufficient for meaningful comparison.

specific price index increases must be kept in mind. As an example, the index for hardcover and paperback books published in technology in Germany in 1980 increased by 18.9 points, or 14.4%, well over the overall average increase of 6.0% for this category.

The wide range of price increases and the prices paid by nine U.S. libraries for Latin American books (Table 14) is still evident in the price information reported for 1981. The low was a decrease of 120% (Trinidad) and the high was an increase of 165.3% (Guatemala). Although there are wide variations in the cost of Latin American books, the cost of books from 18 of the 26 countries included in the table increased substantially. The compiler believes that a major reason for the increases reported is that the more successful vendors handling Latin American books have begun to incorporate a service charge into the cost of the materials supplied.

Library budgets are still being stretched to the limit by double-digit inflation, especially where periodical subscriptions and serial services are concerned. The problem of adjusting to inflation is compounded by the inability of governing bodies to grant their libraries adequate cost-increase allowances because of the almost worldwide recession.

In spite of the bleak picture just noted, U.S. libraries that expend significant portions of their book budget for materials published in foreign countries benefited substantially in 1981 from the rise in value of the dollar against the value of other currencies. A comparison of the value of the currencies of a representative group of other countries with the U.S. dollar at the beginning and close of 1981 illustrates the dramatic gain of U.S. purchasing power abroad during 1981.[2]

Country	Jan. 7, 1981	Dec. 30, 1981	% Change
France	.228	.182	21.9
Germany	.529	.45	15.1
Great Britain	2.43	1.94	20.2
Japan	.00505	.0046	8.9
Netherlands	.483	.4110	14.5

When libraries plan future budgets for library materials, they should keep in mind that the trend noted above can easily be reversed; therefore library materials budgets still need to be carefully allocated. For just this purpose, the ALA/RTSD/RS Library Materials Price Index Committee has sponsored the preparation and publication of the tables that accompany this article.

The price indexes were designed to measure the rate of price changes of newly published materials against those of earlier years. They reflect price trends at the national level and are useful for comparing with local purchasing patterns. The price indexes reflect retail prices and not the cost to a particular library, and they were never intended to be a substitute for information that a library might collect about its own purchases. The prices on which the indexes are based do not include discounts, vendor service charges, or other service charges. These variables naturally affect the average price for library materials paid by a particular library; however, as recent studies have shown, this does not necessarily mean that the rate of increase in prices paid by a particular library is significantly different from the rate of increase shown by the price indexes. The Library Materials Price Index Committee is very interested in pursuing correlations of individual library's prices with national prices and would like to be informed of any studies undertaken.

This year there were two significant changes in the price tables that should be noted by the user. First, in anticipation of the revision to be introduced by the American National Standards Institute (ANSI Z39), the three-year base period on which the price indexes have been calculated has been changed to a one-year base period. Second, the base year has been changed to 1977. These two changes will make it easier to compare library materials prices with the U.S. Government Consumer Price Index, which also has a one-year base of 1977. It is expected that conversion to the 1977 base will be completed for all tables in this article with the 1983 edition of the *Bowker Annual*.

As ever, users are cautioned to use the indexes with care and to note the particulars of each index. They need to be aware, for example, of the categories of "preliminary" and "final" in the U.S. and British book price tables. For a more accurate picture, users should compare similar categories only and not make the mistake of comparing preliminary figures with final figures.

In addition to the indexes presented here, there are at least two other published price indexes. The two indexes are: "Price Indexes, Foreign and Domestic Music," which appears in the *Music Library Association Notes*, and "Price Index for Legal Publications," which appears in the *Law Library Journal*. When appropriate, timely updates of several of the Library Materials Price Index Committee's sponsored indexes are published in the *RTSD Newsletter*.

The current members of the Library Materials Price Index Committee are Nelson A. Piper, chairperson; Mary Elizabeth Clack; Peter Graham; Beth Shapiro; and Dennis E. Smith. Consultants to the committee are Noreen G. Alldredge, Norman B. Brown, Imre Jarmy, Jane Phillips, Davis B. Walch, and Sally F. Williams.

NOTES

1. Chandler B. Grannis, "Domestic Statistical Update, Final 1980 Figures," in *Publishers Weekly* (September 25, 1981), pp. 32–35.
2. *Foreign Checks Drafts and Remittance Orders.* Bank of America, Foreign Exchange Trading Section, January 7 and December 30, 1981.

NUMBER OF BOOK OUTLETS IN THE UNITED STATES AND CANADA

The *American Book Trade Directory* has been published by the R. R. Bowker Company since 1915. Revised annually, it features lists of booksellers, publishers, wholesalers, periodicals, reference tools, and other information about the U.S. book market as well as markets in Great Britain and Canada. The data provided in Tables 1 and 2 for the United States and Canada, the most current available, are from the 1981 edition of the directory.

The 19,545 stores of various types shown in Table 1 are located in approximately 6,283 cities in the United States, Canada, and regions administered by the United States. All "general" bookstores are assumed to carry hardbound (trade) books, paperbacks, and children's books; special effort has been made to apply this category only to bookstores for which this term can properly be applied. All "college" stores are assumed to carry

TABLE 1 BOOKSTORES IN THE UNITED STATES (AND CANADA)*

Antiquarian	993 (61)	Museum store and art gallery	228 (11)
Mail order—antiquarian	594 (15)	Newsdealer	129 (7)
College	2,703 (133)	Office supply	48 (2)
Department store	1,201 (106)	Paperback**	754 (34)
Drugstore	22 (3)	Religious	2,576 (154)
Educational	98 (13)	Remainder	18 (2)
Exporter-importer	28 (1)	Rental	4 (0)
Foreign language	94 (25)	Science-technology	61 (8)
General	5,409 (1,010)	Special***	1,400 (173)
Gift shop	95 (10)	Stationer	148 (19)
Juvenile	133 (17)	Used	494 (16)
Law	63 (3)	Total listed in the United States	17,709
Mail order (general)	313 (9)		
Medical	102 (4)	Total listed in Canada	1,836

*In Tables 1 and 2, the Canadian figure for each category is in parentheses following the U.S. figure.

**This figure does not include paperback departments of general bookstores, department stores, stationers, drugstores, or wholesalers handling paperbacks.

***This indicates stores specializing in subjects other than those specifically given in the list.

TABLE 2 WHOLESALERS IN THE UNITED STATES (AND CANADA)

General wholesalers	533 (86)	Total listed in the United States	996
Paperback wholesalers	463 (40)	Total listed in Canada	126

college-level textbooks. The term "educational" is used for outlets handling school textbooks up to and including the high school level. The category "mail order" has been confined to those outlets that sell general trade books by mail and are not book clubs; all others operating by mail have been classified according to the kinds of books carried. The term "antiquarian" covers dealers in old and rare books. Stores handling only secondhand books are classified by the category "used." The category "paperbacks" represents stores with stock consisting of more than an 80% holding of paperbound books. Other stores with paperback departments are listed under the major classification ("general," "department store," "stationers," etc.), with the fact that paperbacks are carried given in the entry. A bookstore that specializes in a subject to the extent of 50% of its stock has that subject designated as its major category.

BOOK REVIEW MEDIA STATISTICS

NUMBER OF BOOKS REVIEWED BY MAJOR BOOK-REVIEWING PUBLICATIONS, 1980 AND 1981

	Adult 1980	Adult 1981	Juvenile 1980	Juvenile 1981	Young Adult 1980	Young Adult 1981	Total 1980	Total 1981
Booklist[1]	3,267	3,022	1,244	1,270	1,283	1,139	6,149	5,872
Bulletin of the Center for Children's Books	—	—	460	480	405	408	865	888
Choice[2]	6,551	6,462	—	—	—	—	6,551	6,462
Horn Book	51	50	324	292	117	98	492	440
Kirkus Services	3,971	3,996	915	903	—	—	4,886	4,899
Library Journal	6,130	5,878	—	—	—	—	6,130	5,878
New York Review of Books	600	400	—	—	—	—	600	400
New York Times Sunday Book Review	2,000	2,000[3]	300	224	—	—	2,300	2,224
Publishers Weekly[4]	4,400	4,346	550	560	—	—	4,950	4,906
School Library Journal	—	—	2,245	2,291	357	306	2,602	2,597
Washington Post Book World	1,727	1,910	116	102	—	—	1,843	2,012

[1] All figures are for a 12-month period from September 1 to August 31, e.g., 1981 figures are for September 1, 1980–August 31, 1981. Totals include reference and subscription books. In addition, Booklist publishes reviews of nonprint materials: 1,216 in 1980; 1,501 in 1981.

[2] All figures are for a 12-month period beginning in September and ending in July/August, e.g., 1981 figures are for September 1980–July/August 1981. Totals do not include nonprint materials, of which 116 were reviewed in 1981.

[3] Includes paperbacks reviewed in "New and Noteworthy" column.

[4] Includes reviews of paperback originals and reprints.

Part 5
International Reports and Statistics

International Reports

FRANKFURT BOOK FAIR, 1981

Herbert R. Lottman
International Correspondent, *Publishers Weekly*

The 33rd Frankfurt Book Fair, October 14-19, was a time of stocktaking, with gloomy economic reports coming in from most parts of the industrial world. It seemed that no significant publishing country was entirely immune from the effects—or the delayed aftereffects—of the leveling out of business curves, and some of the movement in the aisles this time was created by publishing executives looking for new jobs. But what one may not have expected, and what one found this time, was that there was a silver lining behind nearly every cloud. Most companies, except a few of the largest, seemed to be adapting to the new situation without scars. Adversity had caused them to look for new roads to success. Americans and other trade leaders who could offer books that might guarantee an end to the sluggish behavior of the publishing economies of smaller countries found they were selling well. It seemed there was nothing like a potential best-seller to cure everybody's ailments. This may have been why the refrain of this 33rd fair was: "Things are bad. We're doing fine."

Once again, and despite universal cost-consciousness, records for participation were broken. There were 5482 imprints represented (from 85 countries), up from last year's 5302. Not only were there more West German exhibitors, but more foreigners too: 4017 this time, up from the 3886 in 1980, and more publishers had shifted to individual booths. In fact the increased number of individual exhibits covered an area reduced by a few thousand square feet because of fairground reconstruction; space was found by refusing stand expansion and by cutting existing exhibition areas wherever possible.

"A funny thing happens when the subject of the Frankfurt Book Fair comes up," remarked Simon Michael Bessie of Harper & Row, a fair veteran. "Some say, 'I go there because it's a business obligation.' But others say, 'I go because the experience of all those books is a delight.' Every time we see a new book fair get under way in another country, the need for Frankfurt becomes more obvious. Despite its problems of size and cost, this is the one we couldn't miss." First-timer Stuart Applebaum, director of publicity and public relations at Bantam, was happily surprised to find that the fair wasn't just "an ABA convention without T-shirts," but an event in which people could get excited about the contents of the books they happened to be selling. And Frankfurt was also the place to introduce new faces (say the new team at Bantam), to prove one's resilience (so Fritz Molden of Vienna gave his usual posh party), or to put down rumors (so Hachette brought a record 110 persons to the fair during the very week its owners were negotiating with the French government to guarantee the group's independence of that Socialist government).

Note: Adapted from *Publishers Weekly*, November 20, 1981, where the article was entitled "The Frankfurt Book Fair 1981: At Frankfurt, Dark Clouds on the International Book Scene—And Some Silver Linings."

The Combined Book Exhibit prepared a list of the American imprints—and there were dozens and dozens—represented on its own stand and on the stand of exporter Feffer & Simons (which houses many of the Frankfurt regulars, including Bantam; Braziller; Crown; Dell and Delacorte; Farrar, Straus & Giroux; St. Martin's; and Viking), World Wide Media (big in paperback sales), Ruth Gottstein's Independent Publishers Services (which shows and negotiates for West Coast and West Coast-type imprints), and Academia (which was celebrating its 15th fair with its largest exhibit ever, including 16 small presses showing for the first time to test the possibilities). Many large U.S. trade houses, such as Doubleday; Holt, Rinehart and Winston; Harper & Row; Houghton Mifflin; William Morrow; Random House; Simon & Schuster; and the Times-Mirror group, continued to run individual exhibition areas.

What newcomers might have learned in Frankfurt—and oldtimers already knew—was that the annual fall event was the ideal place to take the measure of one's foreign publishing partners, and few lost that opportunity. They could have learned, for instance, that business was bad all over. But it wasn't as bad in Germany, Japan, the Netherlands or Norway as in other key book countries. Of course pessimism was being expressed, caution exercised, in those lucky countries too, but to paraphrase a celebrated U.S. Supreme Court dictum: "The publishers were crying before they were hurt." And when a few influential trade publishers cry, the whole world seems to sob—because trade publishers are the most articulate of the profession. But dozens of rocks of Gibraltar, in the form of scientific, technical and medical publishers, were proof that certain kinds of publishing continue to thrive and, in such areas as primary journals, even to grow. When an Elsevier tries to sell off its trade publishing interests for X dollars, that's news; when it invests 10 times that amount in the information industry in the same territories, the story continues to circulate as "Elsevier is divesting itself of overseas interests." Yet in the Geneva-bank atmosphere of the book fair's Messehaus West, sci-tech publishers, such as Elsevier and Wiley and Springer-Verlag and Thieme, were keeping their heads while all about them....

It was also true that the solid West German book trade, so long a model for related industries, was beginning to feel the strain. Inflation was running at a higher rate than it had since 1974 (but this higher rate was still only 6.6 percent in the 12 months ending in September). Publishers were trimming costs to anticipate the end of the expanding market. As it happened, Bertelsmann began trimming earlier than most, betting that the business cycle was going to affect books sooner or later; this involved reducing lists and winding down smaller imprints. And then there was the cash crisis at Fritz Molden, for complicated reasons not fully understood outside of Germany but involving the firm's paperback and club backers. Many houses didn't seem to be suffering at all, however, and paperback and serial rights were bringing in more revenue than ever, balancing the loss of hardcover sales.

In Japan, books were definitely down, but the giant companies coped because their popular magazine divisions were thriving. To keep turnover up, Japanese publishers were prepared to offer a good deal for Anglo-American blockbusters, but *not* for middlelist. Thus Carl Sagan's *Contact* was sold by the Japan Uni agency to Shincho-Sha (a company generally considered to be hurting) for $120,000, which is claimed as a record. The same agency sold the Silhouette series (150 titles to start) to Sanrio for $300,000 (Harlequin is already on the scene with its own company). "Thank God for the Japanese!" a Western publisher was heard to exclaim. "When we're down they're up." Still, Tom Mori of Tokyo's Tuttle-Mori agency told *PW* that 235 *new* magazines were launched in his country last year and book returns were running at 40 percent, with sales growing only 10 percent a year for the past five and inflation at 7 percent for the past three. Yet while publishers were cutting lists, they were putting more and more money into the big books, so Mori was getting good advances for list leaders, science fiction, and thrillers. Indeed, good stories, and authors with a reputation for strong story lines, were still selling nearly everywhere.

"Never so many books—never so little to read," a Frankfurt daily summed up the world situation as seen from the fairgrounds—the point being that more copies of fewer titles were being published, and there was little worth reading among these titles. But even proven best-sellers were getting smaller advances in the international marketplace, buyers having in mind recent fairs when bidding hysteria temporarily displaced common sense. "It's the decline of hype," Alfredo Machado of Brazil's Distribuidora Récord observed. "Even bugs eventually develop an immunity to insecticides." And it still seemed possible to make money by selling not from the top of the list but from one's entire list. A publisher who spent a lot of time at his stand still could have a "fantastic" fair (the expression is from Putnam's Peter Israel). His foreign counterparts had to line up to talk to Farrar, Straus & Giroux's Roger W. Straus, Jr. Seymour Lawrence was selling an author like Jim Harrison, not title by title but as an "oeuvre," to foreign publishers who wished to import a "contemporary Hemingway" for their catalogues.

STILL SOME 'BIG BOOKS'

Still, the big-book habit died hard. Fairgoers continued to spend a certain amount of time at each encounter in the aisles, at each party, interrogating each other about the big ones. Among titles most talked about was Simon & Schuster's *Lace*, a first novel by Shirley Conran (author of the nonfiction *The Superwoman Handbook*), agented by Morton Janklow, for world rights in which S&S and Pocket Books had paid $750,000. Penguin and Sidgwick & Jackson, publishers of the author's earlier book, together paid £105,000 for *Lace*, and rights were sold at Frankfurt to Spain's Argos Vergara, Italy's Mondadori, the Netherlands' Luitingh, Finland's Werner Söderström. Holt, Rinehart and Winston was offering—on the basis of a short synopsis that publishers had to scan with a Holt person standing by—*The Vatican Connection*, described as a name-naming exposé of the movement of forged securities from the United States to the Vatican; to maintain suspense, Holt's Patricia Breinin was seeking to coordinate international release for October 1982 (during the fair the first sale was by agent Michelle Lapautre to France's André Balland; indeed, Lapautre was having her best fair ever as French publishers sought a cure for their economic woes in surefire American titles).

The people who had brought the world *Princess Daisy*, Crown, had the Ebert-Hotchstein *Traditions* and Alexandra Penney's *How to Make Love to a Man*, while Crown's Allan Eady was doing an 18-minute video presentation of James Michener's *USA* (the home office had promised Eady a pair of "expensive shoes" if he sold to three countries at Frankfurt, two pairs if he sold to five, etc.; on the last day of the fair Eady was seen in sneakers). As usual, many big deals weren't the kind that make best-seller lists, e.g., Italy's Giunti was selling the "Marco Polo" TV series tie-in slowly but steadily around the world, offering a startling *Quetzalcoatl* by Mexico's President José López Portillo, releasing the introductory volume to the multivolume illustrated catalogue of Leningrad's Hermitage Museum (coproduced with Harcourt Brace Jovanovich, Belser and Weber).

When Wolf Jobst Siedler of the brand-new social science imprint Severin und Siedler visited Lev Kopelev shortly after the Russian writer's arrival in Germany at the home of Kopelev's host Heinrich Böll, Kopelev showed him a biography of Heinrich Heine that he had been working on in Moscow for the past 10 years. The manuscript had been smuggled out of the Soviet Union before Kopelev himself got out last year. Before dinner was over that night at Böll's, contract terms had been agreed on; Severin and Siedler published in early October and sold 16,000 copies in a week; Siedler told *PW* he expects to sell 100,000 copies. Kopelev was a celebrity at this year's Frankfurt fair, and Siedler was negotiating translation contracts with publishing friends everywhere.

Each year the fair is the site of unusual selling efforts combined with cultural happenings. Thus the hard-to-approach Doris Lessing agreed to a quick tour of Germany—the highlight, an appearance in Frankfurt for S. Fischer Verlag, timed with publication of their translation of *Briefing for a Descent into Hell.* The annual German book trade peace prize went to the aforementioned Lev Kopelev at a televised ceremony in Frankfurt's historic Paulskirche; book fair authorities had softened the Eastern bloc's unhappiness at the choice by assurances that the gestures had no political significance, and so the Soviets and their allies limited their reaction to a boycott of the award ceremony.

For most book traders, the fair begins at least a day earlier than its official opening, and many events and trade meetings are scheduled prior to its inauguration, to allow a concentration of attention that is not possible after the opening gun. Thus at 11 A.M. on October 13, and in Mainz, 25 miles from the fairgrounds, the Stuttgart-Zurich house of Belser presented the first finished volume of its ongoing program of Vatican Library facsimiles, the *Codex Benedictus* (*PW*, Jan. 16, 1981). The setting was the Gutenberg Museum, which commemorates the pioneer efforts of a Mainz boy, Johann Gutenberg, and shows his Bible.

The Netherlands' Unieboek took a salon in a hotel near the fair to present its second Poortvliet-Huygen *Gnomes* book to the contented publishers of the first *Gnomes* and other interested parties (guests included Abrams's Paul Gottlieb and Ballantine's Marc Jaffe). Ken Follett, with an assist from Albert Zuckerman and Sue Rapp of Writers House, booked a room at the Frankfurter Hof to hand gift-wrapped photocopies of the manuscript of Follett's next novel (which may be called "The Man from St. Petersburg") to 18 publishers, committed or potential; each of them also got a glass of champagne and a 1-oz. jar of Russian caviar. The companies represented (with their presidents or editors-in-chief getting to eat the caviar) included Morrow and NAL, Corgi, Sweden's Bonnier, Norway's Cappelen, Denmark's Gyldendal, Unieboek of the Netherlands, Mexico's Diana, and Brazil's Récord.

GERMANY COMES TO NEW YORK

Ernst Klett Verlag staged its annual meeting of educational publishers from around the world—a 20-year tradition—in a hotel across the street from the fair, this time to talk about educational journals. The International Group of Scientific, Technical and Medical Publishers (STM) as usual called its general assembly for the day before the fair. Members at this 13th annual event discussed common—and persistent—concerns, such as piracy and other threats to copyright, the effects of new technology, and marketing strategies. STM has been battling with the UNESCO bureaucracy to combat the notion that copyright is a barrier to the free flow of books; at Frankfurt John Wiley's W. Bradford Wiley suggested it was up to publishers to see that their respective governments keep an eye on UNESCO.

Leadership echelons of the International Publishers Association (IPA) met during the fair; Geoffrey King of Australia was confirmed as vice-president of that organization for Southeast Asia and the South Pacific. IPA's Interamerican group met to discuss piracy in the region (in Santo Domingo primarily, but increasingly in Peru); the IPA copyright committee also talked about that region and Asia (in Pakistan, piracy was being blamed for having destroyed the country's book market; in Malaysia, the threat was growing).

Just before the fair, the German book trade association's exhibition arm announced a bold new venture: the organizers of the book fair will do a "Frankfurt Fair" in New York, utilizing Frankfurt-type stands to present the production of German publishers; up to 180 German publishers will be present to talk about rights as well as book sales. Even a literary agents center is planned, like the one in the middle of the Frankfurt fair's Hall 5, to facilitate what the organizers hope will be the main business in New York. But rights and co-publishing negotiations will run concurrently with trade and institutional sales and a strong effort at cultural promotion. "It's a fair for people as well as for books," Frankfurt fair director Peter Weidhaas explained. He thinks there is an increasing need to improve human and political as well as business relations; during the hectic Frankfurt week there is little opportunity for Americans and Germans to sit down together. The fair's Ulrich Bechler was recently in New York for a feasibility study, and before he left he booked the Sheraton Centre's Albert hall for four days in early March 1983. The event is planned as a one-shot—at least until first results can be assessed.

The Nobel prize for literature has been announced during the run of recent Frankfurt fairs. Among publishers of literature there is always a certain amount of suspense and an exchange of guesses. The name of Elias Canetti began circulating at Frankfurt on opening day, and soon after the prize was announced proud publisher Carl Hanser had a rack of books and a poster ready. Then the press tracked down Roger W. Straus, Jr., who showed his upcoming FSG catalogue announcing Canetti's memoir of his beginnings as a writer. Werner Mark Linz told *PW* he had acquired Canetti at Seabury Press and took the author with him when he established the former Seabury imprint Continuum as a separate publishing house (*PW*, Jan. 25, 1980); seven major Canetti titles are on the Continuum list. By happy chance Hanser threw its annual dinner the night of the Nobel award.

D. M. Thomas was in town for another Hanser-sponsored reception for the publishers of *The White Hotel* (Viking and Pocket Books, Gollancz and Penguin, Albin Michel, Argos Vergara, Unieboek, Sperling & Kupfer, with agents Peter Fritz, Erich Linder, Andrew Nurnberg, Donine Mouche, Lennart Sane). There was the traditional Saturday night Reader's Digest party (for everyone but Americans) in the gracious decor of the Hessischer Hof, and the new Friday night tradition of giant Bertelsmann, where Americans mingled with their foreign counterparts—800 guests in all—in the grand ballroom of the Intercontinental. The annual reception for 2000 fair participants sponsored by the fair management was held this time in the restored Old Opera.

On the fairgrounds itself was another new facility: a large and well-endowed Booksellers Center (not to be confused with the preexisting International Booksellers Center), offering free typewriters, free telephones, refreshments at lower-than-usual prices, free lockers, conference booths and conversation corners, and a message board; the fair also hired a boat docked near City Hall for booksellers to meet for beer (with jazz on Saturday night). Both amenities were the result of increasing demands on the part of German booksellers for a greater role in the annual fair, which they felt was not as responsive to their needs as it could have been.

And as it happened, there is a new power lineup in the German book trade organization (the Börsenverein): its president is a bookseller now, his board dominated by members of that trade, and they are getting satisfaction not only during the fair but also in other year-round services. At Frankfurt, the chief activity of German booksellers is to find out about publishers' programs, to discuss discounts and other policies, and to meet each other. The fair thinks it provides a special excitement as well.

Next year's Frankfurt Book Fair, from October 6 to 11, 1982, will come with a theme. "Yesterday's Religion in Today's World." It is intended to cover all faiths, and lacks of faith. Themes are a biennial event; the next one after that, for 1984, has also been announced: "George Orwell."

IFLA CONFERENCE AND COUNCIL MEETING, 1981: AN AMERICAN PERSPECTIVE

Jane Wilson
Former International Relations Officer, American Library Association

The forty-seventh General Conference and Council of the International Federation of Library Associations and Institutions (IFLA) was held in Leipzig, German Democratic Republic, from August 17–22, 1981. Approximately 900 delegates were in attendance from 64 countries. The largest delegation was from the Federal Republic of Germany, including West Berlin, and numbered approximately 100. As has become the custom in recent years, the second largest delegation was that of the United States, which numbered approximately 80. The Conference convened in the Seminar and Lecture Hall buildings of the Karl Marx University, while the opening sessions and council meetings were held in the Leipzig Opera House. A wide variety of sleeping accommodations were available, ranging from the deluxe Hotel Merkur, where no East German marks were accepted, to the Jenny Marx Student Hostel.

OPENING SESSION

The conference was officially opened on Monday morning, August 17, and speakers included Gotthard Ruckl, President of the Library Association of the German Democratic Republic and Chairman of the National Preparatory Committee; Else Granheim, President of IFLA; Yves Courrier, representative of the director general of UNESCO; and Hans Joachim Hoffmann, Minister of Culture. During his address, the minister of culture read a message from Herr Willi Stoph, Chairman of the GDR Council of Ministers and Patron of the Conference, which included the statement that "you have come together when more than ever everything depends upon banning the dangers of an atomic holocaust and on strengthening international security. From this very spot the librarians may be encouraged to make their contributions to maintaining peace, stopping the arms race as well as to military detente and disarmament." Similar statements, as well as references to the neutron bomb, often appeared in the greetings and remarks of various socialist delegates throughout the week.

FIRST PLENARY SESSION AND OTHER PROGRAM SESSIONS

The first of several plenary sessions on the general conference theme "National Institutions and Professional Organizations of Librarianship" followed the opening session. Speakers and their topics included Gotthard Ruckl, "Role and Activities of the Library Association of the GDR"; Lucile M. de Jimenez, "National and Regional Cooperation with Regard to Libraries in Latin America"; D. Oertel, "Library Planning and Central Library Services in the Federal Republic of Germany"; V. V. Serov (not present), "The System of Librarianship Management in the USSR"; and immediate past ALA president Peggy Sullivan, "Local and Regional Library Associations: Views beyond National Library Associations' Boundaries."

Later in the week IFLA board member Jean Lowrie chaired the plenary session "Library Associations on the Move," with speakers from Mexico, Norway, Poland, and the United States. Josephine Fang delivered the paper "The Characteristics of

National Professional Associations in the Library/Information Fields in the U.S." This was followed by a session entitled "National Library Planning on the Move," at which National Commission on Libraries and Information Science (NCLIS) Executive Director Toni Carbo Bearman was the featured speaker.

Many American librarians also presented papers in other meetings on the congress theme. These included David Bender ("Serving the Needs of the Biological Sciences Librarian"), Susan Crawford ("The Role of the Library in a National Professional Organization"), Shirley Echelman ("The Role of the Medical Library Association in Education, Standards, and Other Support Services for Members"), Beverly Lynch ("The Role of Professional Associations in the Development of Academic Library Standards"), and Robert Wedgeworth ("Public Library Associations in the USA" and "Management and Technology in Library Associations"). Two showings of the film *Libraries and the Pursuit of Happiness* were arranged for Thursday, August 20. Peggy Sullivan introduced the film at both showings.

IFLA COUNCIL MEETING

The first IFLA Council Meeting, on Monday afternoon, August 17, was chaired by President Granheim. The secretary general and the treasurer both gave brief presentations, since their reports appear in *IFLA Journal* 7, no. 2 (1981). In her presentation, Secretary General Margreet Wijnstroom pointed out that IFLA now has 121 association members in "good standing," of which 75 had a delegate present at Leipzig. (IFLA has a total membership of 1,005, but the bulk of these are institutional members.) Names of both association and institutional members who were more than two years in arrears were read aloud; however, it was indicated that, at its meeting on August 13, the IFLA Executive Board decided not to recommend exclusion from IFLA, but rather to give these members one more opportunity to pay their dues. In the meantime, they will not receive any of the benefits of membership. In her report, IFLA Treasurer Marie-Louise Boussuat noted that in 1980 IFLA had a deficit of Dfl 40,000; however, IFLA received a subsidy of Dfl 27,000 from the Canadian International Development Agency (CIDA) that greatly reduced the deficit. IFLA currently receives more than 50 percent of its income from dues and one quarter of the budget goes to support membership services (*IFLA Journal*, various mailings, etc.). At present, 12 percent of the dues are in arrearage. Rutherford Rogers, chairperson of the IFLA Program Management Committee, reported that financial support for both Universal Bibliographic Control (UBC) and Universal Availability of Publications (UAP) is falling, and that the future of both programs is in jeopardy.

One of the main items of business at this council meeting was the election to fill vacancies on the IFLA Executive Board. There were three candidates for the two vacancies: Hans-Peter Geh, Director, Württembergische Landesbibliothek, Stuttgart; Ljudmila A. Gvishiani, Director, All-Union State Library of Foreign Literature, Moscow; and Adolfo Rodriguez, Coordinator, Academico Bibliotecario, U.N.A.M., Mexico City. Of the 1,191 votes cast, Geh received 534, Gvishiani 351, and Rodriguez 306. Voting delegates also approved an increase in dues for national association members from developing countries (a country that has a gross domestic product per capita of less than U.S. $2,000) from Dfl 200 to Dfl 300, as well as a proposal allowing association members from developed countries facing a dues increase of more than 50 percent to divide the increase into three equal parts and increase their dues by one-third for each of the next three years. (Dues for these countries are based on the country's national assessment to UNESCO.) Also approved was a new personal affiliation for retired librarians (Dfl 80); a continuation of the present term of four years for the IFLA presidency (at the 1979 council meeting the British Library Association asked the board to consider a two-year term); and a proposal to permit the term of an elected member of a standing committee to lapse if the member is absent without explanation from all standing committee meetings at two successive IFLA Congresses.

IFLA SECTION ACTIVITIES

During the week, the 24 IFLA sections, as well as the round tables, held both program and business meetings. In Spring 1981, IFLA-style "elections" were held to fill the vacancies for the various section standing committees. Again, anyone who received two or more nominations was "elected" to the standing committee since in no instance were there more nominees than vacancies on the committee. The International Relations Officer of the American Library Association (ALA) assisted many of the U.S. nominees in locating the necessary seconds.

Following a week of considerable politicking in some of the IFLA sections, elections for new officers of the standing committees were held at the last meeting of each section standing committee. The following librarians from the United States now serve on IFLA section standing committees (those who were elected as section officers are so designated and the term of office for each standing committee member is given in parentheses):

Section of Administrative Libraries: H. P. von Pfeil, Washington, D.C. (1979–1983)

Section on Bibliography: Guy A. Marco, Consultant, Washington, D.C. (1979–1983); Frances Hinton, Chief, Processing Division, Free Library of Philadelphia, Philadelphia, Pa. (1979–1983)

Section of Biological and Medical Sciences Libraries: Irwin Pizer, Director, Library of the Health Sciences, University of Illinois at the Medical Center, Chicago, Ill., *Chair of Section, Chair, Special Libraries Division, and Member IFLA Professional Board* (1979–1983); Ursula Poland, Librarian, Albany Medical College, Albany, N.Y. (1981–1985)

Section on Cataloguing: Lucia J. Rather, Director for Cataloging, Processing Services Department, Library of Congress, Washington, D.C. (1981–1985)

Section of Children's Libraries: Margaret N. Coughlan, Children's Literature Center, Library of Congress, Washington, D.C. (1981–1985)

Section on Classification and Subject Cataloguing: Richard Holley, Assistant Director for Technical Services, University Libraries, University of Utah, Salt Lake City, Utah (1981–1985)

Section on Conservation: Norman J. Shaffer, Chief, Photoduplication Service, Library of Congress, Washington, D.C. (1981–1985)

Section on Exchange and Acquisition: Nathan Einhorn, Chief, Gifts and Exchange Section, Library of Congress, Washington, D.C. (1981–1985); Leona L. Wise, Gifts and Exchange Librarian, University of Southern California, Los Angeles, Calif. (1981–1985)

Section of Geography and Map Libraries: David Carrington, Library of Congress, Washington, D.C., *Secretary of the Standing Committee* (1981–1985); Gary W. North, Assistant Division Chief, U.S. Geological Survey, Reston, Va. (1981–1985); William Roselle, Director of Libraries, University of Wisconsin-Milwaukee, Wis. (1979-1983); John A. Wolter, Chief, Geography and Map Division, Library of Congress, Washington, D.C. (1979-1983)

Section on Information Technology: Henriette D. Avram, Director for Processing Systems, Networks, and Automation Planning, Library of Congress, Washington, D.C., *Chair of Section, Chair, IFLA Professional Board,* and *ex officio Member IFLA Executive Board* (1981-1985); Frederick Kilgour, Vice Chairman, Board of Trustees, OCLC, Dublin, Ohio (1981-1985)

Section on Interlending: Beth A. Hamilton, Senior Information Scientist, Triodyne, Wilmette, Ill. (1979-1983)

Section on Library Buildings and Equipment: Roscoe Rouse, Director of Libraries, Oklahoma State University, Stillwater, Okla. (1979-1983)

Section on Library Schools and Other Training Aspects: Josephine R. Fang, Professor, Graduate School of Library and Information Science, Simmons College, Boston, Mass. (1981-1985); Donald L. Roberts, Music Librarian, Northwestern University, Evanston, Ill. (1981-1985)

Section of Library Services to Hospital Patients and Handicapped Readers: Frank K. Cylke, Director, National Library Services for the Blind and Physically Handicapped, Library of Congress, Washington, D.C. (1981-1985); Peter Hanke, Director, Talking Books, American Foundation for the Blind, New York, N.Y. (1981-1985); Bruce E. Massis, Library Director, Jewish Guild for the Blind, New York, N.Y. (1981-1985)

Section on Library Theory and Research: Esther Dyer, Assistant Professor, Graduate School of Library and Information Studies, Rutgers University, New Brunswick, N.J. (1979-1983); Jane P. Franck, Director of Library, Columbia University Teachers College, New York, N.Y. (1981-1985)

Section of National Libraries: William J. Welsh, Deputy Librarian of Congress, Washington, D.C. (1979-1983)

Section on Official Publications: Bernadine A. Hoduski, U.S. Congress, Joint Committee on Printing, Washington, D.C., *Chair of Section* (1981-1985); Luciana Marulli-Koenig, Bibliographer, United Nations Library, New York, N.Y. (1981-1985)

Section of Parliamentary Libraries: Gilbert Gude, Director, Congressional Research Service, Washington, D.C. (1981-1985)

Section of Public Libraries: Peggy Sullivan, Dean, College of Professional Studies, Northern Illinois University, De Kalb, Ill. (1981-1985)

Section on Rare and Precious Books and Documents: William J. Matheson, Chief, Rare Book and Special Collection Division, Library of Congress, Washington, D.C. (1981-1985)

Section of School Libraries: Linda Beeler, Head Librarian, Thornridge High School Library, Dolton, Ill. (1981-1985); Clara O. Jackson, School of Library Science, Kent State University, Kent, Ohio (1981-1985); Jean Lowrie, Professor, School of Librarianship, Western Michigan University, Kalamazoo, Mich., *IFLA Executive Board Member* (1979-1983)

Section of Science and Technology: Pat Molholt, Associate Director of Libraries, Rensselaer Polytechnic Institute, Troy, N.Y. (1981-1985); Russell Shank, University Librarian, University of California at Los Angeles, Los Angeles, Calif. (1981-1985)

Section on Serial Publications: Mary E. Sauer, Assistant Director for Processing Systems, Networks, and Automation Planning, Library of Congress, Washington, D.C. (1981–1985)

Section of Social Science Libraries: David Bender, Executive Director, Special Libraries Association, New York, N.Y., *Secretary of the Standing Committee* (1981–1985); Vivian Hewitt, Librarian, Carnegie Endowment for International Peace, Shotwell Library, New York, N.Y. (1981–1985)

Section on Statistics: Patricia Bielke, Associate Professor, Ball State University, Muncie, Ind. (1979–1983); Bill J. Corbin, Assistant Chairman, Peabody College Department of Library Science, Vanderbilt University, Nashville, Tenn. (1981–1985); Thomas P. Slavens, Professor, School of Library Science, University of Michigan, Ann Arbor, Mich. (1979–1983); Alphonse F. Trezza, Director, Intergovernmental Library Cooperative Project, Library of Congress, Washington, D.C. (1981–1985)

Section of University Libraries and Other General Research Libraries: Richard Dougherty, Director of Libraries, University of Michigan, Ann Arbor, Mich. (1981–1985); Beverly Lynch, University Librarian, University of Illinois at Chicago Circle Library, Chicago, Ill. (1981–1985); Peter Spyers-Duran, Director, Library, California State University, Long Beach, Calif. (1981–1985)

ALA ACTIVITY ON BEHALF OF U.S. INSTITUTIONAL MEMBERS OF IFLA AND THE CAUCUS OF U.S. ASSOCIATION AND INSTITUTIONAL MEMBERS OF IFLA

As agreed at the first ALA International Relations Committee–sponsored meeting of U.S. institutional members of IFLA, the ALA International Relations Officer (IRO) serves as coordinator to ensure that the votes of all U.S. institutional members are cast at the IFLA council meetings. Therefore, on June 1, 1981, a memorandum was distributed by the IRO to U.S. institutional members of IFLA to request that they either notify the IRO of the name of their authorized voting member in Leipzig, or send their signed membership certificate to ALA so that their proxy vote could be assigned to another institutional member who would be present in Leipzig. This matter was discussed further at the International Relations Committee (IRC) meeting of the institutional members of IFLA held during the ALA Annual Conference in San Francisco.

At the initiative of the IRO, arrangements were made for a caucus or "national preparatory meeting" of U.S. institutional members of IFLA at Leipzig. A memorandum was sent to all institutional and association members of IFLA on July 28 to inform them of the meeting and again to solicit proxy votes.

The caucus was held on Sunday evening, August 16, in Lecture Room 14 at Karl Marx University. Most U.S. voting delegates were present for the discussion, which was chaired by U.S. IFLA board member Jean Lowrie.

Although almost a tenth of the conference attendees were from the United States, it would appear that only 25 U.S. institutional members of IFLA had a voting delegate present at Leipzig. The IRO received 12 valid proxies, which were assigned accordingly. Despite the efforts of ALA, the U.S. institutional member vote at Leipzig appeared to number only 37. There are approximately 122 U.S. institutional members of IFLA at the present time, more than a tenth of the total institutional membership of IFLA. Thus, if the United States wishes to be a strong force in IFLA affairs, it will be necessary to continue to urge greater participation in IFLA on the part of the U.S. institutional members.

FINAL COUNCIL MEETING

The second council meeting was held on Saturday morning, August 22. One of the main items for discussion was the *IFLA Draft Medium-Term Programme 1981-1985*, which was presented by the chairman of the IFLA Professional Board, but which had already been mailed to the membership in June 1981. The 40-page document briefly describes the proposed activities of the federation for the next four years. Chapter 1 summarizes IFLA's plan as a whole, while Chapter 2 describes the functions and objectives of IFLA's divisions, sections, and round tables and lists the projects and studies they intend to carry out in the next four years. Chapter 3 is concerned with IFLA's major professional programs, UAP, UBC, and the International Machine Readable Cataloging (MARC) program, and with its international offices that support these programs. The medium-term program was accepted with little discussion from the floor, and the study of this document is a must for those wishing to know what IFLA is doing.

The customary reports were given by chairpersons of the IFLA divisions on their conference activities, and by heads of the sections that constitute the division. It was also announced that Henriette Avram will serve for the next two years as chairperson of the IFLA Professional Board and will thus be an ex officio member of the IFLA Executive Board. Various resolutions and statements were received from the IFLA divisions and sections, as was a report on the IFLA/UNESCO presession seminar for librarians from developing countries, "Library Work with Children and Young People."

As is customary, oral invitations were presented for several future IFLA meetings. At present, the schedule of meetings is as follows:

1982: Montreal, August 22-28. Conference. Theme: Networks. Pre- and postconference seminars: Cataloguing in Publication (Ottawa, August 16-19); Canadian Library Buildings (Toronto, August 16-20); and Education for Research and Research for Education (for Third World Colleagues) (Montreal, August 16-20).

1983: Munich, August 21-27. Conference and Council Meeting. Presession, University Libraries in Developing Countries.

1984: Nairobi, Kenya, August 19-25. Conference (tentative).

1985: New York, August 18-24. Conference and Council Meeting.

1986: Tokyo, Japan, October. Conference.

1987: United Kingdom. Conference and Council Meeting.

1988: Invitation received from Australia. Conference.

PRECONFERENCE AND MEETINGS OF THE IFLA SECTION ON STATISTICS, 1981

Katherine H. Packer

Dean, Faculty of Library Science,
University of Toronto

As part of the 1981 annual conference of the International Federation of Library Associations and Institutions (IFLA), the IFLA Section on Statistics sponsored a preconference meeting, "Library Statistics for Developing Countries" (August 14–15), and held two meetings of the standing committee (August 16 and 20) and two open meetings (both August 18). This article reports on highlights of the preconference and open meetings, incorporating discussion of the standing committee meetings as appropriate.

PRECONFERENCE MEETING

The purpose of the preconference was to discuss two main topics. The first was the establishment of a clearinghouse on library statistics, primarily to assist developing countries in setting up their own procedures for collecting and reporting library statistics. The second was a proposal for a project to "survey for evaluation and performance" UNESCO library statistics. Both these projects had been the subject of resolutions put forward by the Section on Statistics at the Manila Conference in 1980. The text of the resolutions (as reported in *IFLA Journal* 6 [1980]4: 401) is as follows:

> I. At an open meeting of the Standing Committee on Statistics in Manila representatives of all IFLA regional groups presented problems which require the aid of a clearinghouse. Therefore be it resolved that the Section on Statistics, in consultation with regional groups, inquire as to the feasibility of a 3-year pilot program to establish a clearinghouse for data gathering and reporting instruments for national library statistics.

> II. The Section on Statistics in cooperation with UNESCO proposes to perform a survey for evaluation and performances of UNESCO library statistics. Therefore be it resolved that this description of the project submitted to IFLA in Spring 1980 be accepted as the first statement of the project.

Ms. L. Martinez de Jimenez (representing the Section on Regional Activities, Latin America and the Caribbean) and Mr. J. A. Dosunmu (Nigeria) spoke in support of the clearinghouse concept.

Clearinghouse for National Library Statistics

The clearinghouse would be designed to serve the following purposes:

1. To serve as a resource center on the mechanics of the collection and analysis of library data for national statistical reporting as well as for UNESCO
2. To develop a collection of examples of instruments used by countries already reporting to UNESCO, as well as reference tools and manuals relevant to the purpose
3. To maintain a list of consultants, by language and region, to advise on the development of a national system of library data collection and analysis

4. To offer seminars on the procedures for collecting and reporting library data for national library statistics

Problems of language, lack of dependability of postal communication, and the cost implications of objectives three and four were identified as obstacles to implementing the resolution. The advantage of locating the clearinghouse in a European country with a well-established library statistics system of its own was considered, and the meeting ultimately recommended setting up one clearinghouse to ensure identical interpretation of the statistical data to be collected. There was also considerable debate over the size of the budget that would be required and should be sought from the Professional Board.

The UNESCO Project

The other issue dealt with was the UNESCO project, described as an investigation to ascertain ways to improve the collection of UNESCO library statistics for international comparability and regional development.

Peter Liebenow had prepared a paper on this subject but, as he was unable to attend the conference, his paper was presented by the chairman. Mr. Liebenow recommended that the UNESCO questionnaire used to gather national library statistics should be expanded to cover many more specific materials, but that in addition to the detailed questionnaire there should also be a greatly simplified version, a basic questionnaire. This questionnaire would not depend on exact counts but on estimates and ranges. Mr. K. Hochgesand confirmed the difficulty UNESCO has had in obtaining responses to its questionnaire, pointing out, however, that many of the countries that failed to cooperate had well-developed systems for collecting their own national statistics. Mr. Dosunmu was put on a task force to work on the basic questionnaire.

The purpose of the UNESCO project was redefined as follows: to identify the means by which IFLA might collaborate with UNESCO to support and assist UNESCO in carrying out its mandate to collect library statistics. The Lenin State Library volunteered to provide personnel for the UNESCO project.

OPEN MEETINGS

The two open meetings, which ran consecutively on the afternoon of Tuesday, August 18, 1981, dealt with the establishment and organization of national library statistics and with the role of professional organizations and national institutions in the establishment, organization, and updating of national library statistics. Papers were presented by: Mr. J. A. Dosunmu, National Library of Nigeria, Lagos, Nigeria; Ms. O. Diakonova, Lenin State Library of the USSR, Moscow, USSR; Mr. P. Gruber, Deutsches Bibliotheksinstitut, Berlin, West Germany; Mr. B. R. Praal, Technische Hogeschool, Eindhoven, The Netherlands; Mr. G. Thirion, Bibliothèque Interuniversitaire, Nancy, France; and Mr. M. Velinsky, Státne Knihovna CSR, Praha, CSSR.

PLANS FOR THE 1982 CONFERENCE

Under "new business," the standing committee discussed the possibility of holding a preconference at the Montreal Conference in 1982. A proposed topic for the meeting was the collection of statistics on network operations that may cross national boundaries. The possibility of dealing with the question of updating the statistics of book production and periodicals in a manner similar to that done for library statistics during the 1981 preconference was also raised. The standing committee declared itself ready to participate in a joint working group; however, the need for official invitation from the International Organization for Standardization (ISO) as well as the cooperation of the International Publishers Association (IPA) was stressed in the discussion that ensued.

STANDING COMMITTEE MEMBERSHIP

The Standing Committee of the Section on Statistics now has the following members:

Continuing (elected 1979-1983): Ms. P. Beilke (U.S.A.), Mr. D. W. Halliwell (Canada), Mr. P. Liebenow (Fed. Rep. of Germany), Mr. K. W. Neubauer (Fed. Rep. of Germany), Mr. T. Nielsen (Denmark), Mr. T. P. Slavens (U.S.A.)

Reelected in the 1981 elections: Ms. O. Diakonova (USSR), Ms. K. H. Packer (Canada), Mr. B. R. Praal (Netherlands), Mr. A. Trezza (U.S.A.), Mr. S. F. Vedi (Norway), Mr. M. Velinsky (Czech. SSR)

New members added to the committee in the 1981 elections: Ms. M. P. Pontes de Carvalho (Brazil), Mr. B. Corbin (U.S.A.), Mr. J. A. Dosunmu (Nigeria), Mr. A. Jopkiewicz (Poland), Mr. J. P. Rompas (Indonesia), Ms. S. Smiddy (U.K.), Mr. G. Thirion (France)

Not all of the above were able to attend the Leipzig conference.

As a result of elections held at the Leipzig Conference, Mr. K. W. Neubauer was returned to office as chairman and Mr. T. Nielsen was reelected secretary.

LIBRARY SERVICES IN ISRAEL

Shmuel Sever

*Director of the Library, University of Haifa,
Mount Carmel, Haifa 31 999, Israel*

Though geographically situated at the crossroads of Europe, Asia, and Africa, in a sociocultural sense Israel is essentially a Western country of a rather heterogenous and multicolored nature that stems from the country's markedly pluralistic demographic structure. Israel has been populated over the past century largely by immigrants from varying cultural backgrounds: idealistic Jews from Western Europe, North and South America; close-knit, traditional Jewish communities from Yemen and Cochin; devoutly religious Hassidim from Eastern Europe; Jews fleeing from the Nazi persecution and, later, Holocaust survivors; some 800,000 Jewish refugees from Arab countries—to mention only a few. The Arab community of the country is almost equally multifarious: the rural population, preserving the traditional Arab way of life; Arabs, both Moslem and Christian, living in urban centers; Bedouin tribes, some already settled, others retaining their old, nomadic way of life; Druzes, with their separate religious and cultural entity, living in their villages; and several other smaller groups, such as the Tserkese and the Kurds.

Recognizing the importance of social and cultural integration in a country populated by people from varying cultural backgrounds, Israel has devoted a great share of its limited resources over the years to the attainment of this goal. Another important goal, no less consistently pursued, has been building a viable and self-supporting economy, in spite of the country's almost total lack of natural resources. However, the overriding consideration in all policymaking and planning has been military defense, because the country has had to fight four wars during one generation.

LIBRARY DEVELOPMENT

In keeping with the country's general Western character, the cultural level of Israelis is comparable to Western standards: The literacy rate of the Jewish population was 93.6 percent in 1980 and 90.7 percent in 1970 and of the non-Jewish population, 81.1 percent in 1980 and 63.9 percent in 1970 (as compared with 27 percent in the Arab world in the 1970s). Almost half (47.6 percent) of the Jews and almost a third (29.5 percent) of the non-Jews have at least partial secondary education. The average Israeli devotes a considerable amount of time to reading: 52.6 percent of the population reads at least one book per month; 29.5 percent reads four or more books per month; 82.2 percent reads a newspaper at least once a week. However, if the cultural level and consequently the information needs of Israelis tally with those prevalent in the Western world, their expectations from the library seem to differ: Inconsistent with the high percentage of active readers, only 24 percent of the population is registered at public libraries. Understanding this phenomenon requires a look at the relatively short history of librarianship in the country.

Israeli librarianship has undergone conceptual changes in conjunction with the different ways in which the library's role in society has been perceived, variously central or marginal to society. When libraries were regarded as potential cultural and social centers of the community, reader-centered library models were adopted and librarians were seen—and, more important, saw themselves—as professionals with sociocultural roles who could, and should, take initiatives. However, at times when the role of the library was perceived mainly as catering to the learned elite, a book-centered library model was adopted, librarians came to be regarded as "mere clerks," and any initiative for improvement or development had to come from outside the profession.

The beginnings of modern Israeli librarianship were part of the efforts made by the pioneers who arrived in Palestine during the period following World War I to rebuild their ancestral homeland and to restructure the cultural and social patterns of the Jewish people. Hugo Bergmann, who became national librarian in 1920, tried to build a modern model of Israeli librarianship based on the Jewish learned tradition, which attributed great importance to learning and reading and within the framework of which there developed a proto-public library—Beit ha-Midrash (House of Learning). Beit ha-Midrash, which served as the cultural center of every Jewish community from the Middle Ages onward, and the general attitude of love of books and learning made the Jewish tradition hospitable to library development as well as compatible with the American model of the library as an agency of education and culture, a model Bergmann also adopted for implementation in Israel.

Pre-state Israel was well on its way to reader-centered library services with a strong commitment to society when, in the mid-thirties, the trend changed. The Jewish refugees fleeing from the persecution in Germany and central Europe introduced into the country the German approach to librarianship and libraries. The German library model of scholarly libraries run by scholars and staffed by clerks, on the one hand, and popular libraries run by technically trained personnel with little claim or inclination to leadership, on the other hand, was all the more quickly accepted by the Jewish community since it was compatible with another facet of the Jewish learned tradition, which stressed the centrality of books to culture, but did not necessarily equate access to information or reading material with libraries. Moreover, the Central-European library tradition was also compatible with the socialist library tradition brought by immigrants from Eastern Europe, since it favored books and reading, but only as means for educating people in the socialist vein, and therefore regarded private ownership of books as the ideal and libraries as second-best substitutes only. Thus, during the thirties and forties libraries came to be considered institutes aimed at fulfilling the information needs of the intelligentsia and the scholarly community centered at the universities, and an attitude of indifference developed toward public libraries and their potential role in society.

Further library development was arrested for a considerable length of time. Since Israeli society was book centered but not library conscious, no pressure was forthcoming for improved library services even where such services were sorely needed, as in new rural settlements and development towns. Public library workers, inadequately trained and thus lacking professional decision-making abilities and initiatives, did not call for improvement of services.

The professional leadership of the time—the librarians at the Jewish National and University Library (JNUL)—were expected to extend services to the scholars of the Hebrew University. JNUL's center of gravity shifted from reader orientation toward the conservation of the book and attention to bibliographic minutiae. The academic librarians did not consider public libraries in need of improvement and did not take measures to initiate any changes in the public library scene.

This trend changed in the 1960s, due to intervention from outside the profession. C. I. Golan, an official of the ministry of education who recognized the importance of library services available to all and not only to elites, managed to start a process of gradual upgrading of public library services. At his insistence the Danish library model, based on a library law and central government participation in financing without interference with local needs, was adopted by the ministry of education. The reader was once more placed at the center of library services; local authorities were encouraged to establish libraries, especially in new rural settlements and development towns, and the Library Law of 1975 provided for the establishment and further development of public libraries.

THE LIBRARY SYSTEM

Israel's "inverted pyramid" library system, in which the research libraries hold most of the national information reservoir and bear the brunt of library services to the entire population, includes the national library, seven academic libraries, 556 public libraries, and approximately 400 special and 500 school libraries.

Jewish National and University Library

JNUL in Jerusalem serves a dual purpose as the national library of Israel and of the Jewish people throughout the world and as the central library of the Hebrew University. Since its founding in 1884, JNUL has been collecting material about Israel, Palestine, Jews, and Judaism; material that is written in Hebrew script or the Jewish language; and any material written by Jews all over the world. Priority is given to acquiring Hebrew and Jewish manuscripts, incunabula, and rare books. Israeli publications are collected by means of the Legal Deposit Law. JNUL's 1,200,000-volume collection includes one of the finest Judaica collections in the world as well as an excellent collection on Arabic and Islamic subjects.

JNUL publishes *Kiryat Sefer*, an annotated bibliography of books on Judaism published in Israel and books about Jews, Judaism, and Israel published all over the world; and the *Index of Articles on Jewish Studies*.

Academic Libraries

In Israel there are eight accredited universities, but only seven of them maintain full-fledged library services. (The Open University has only a very small library and its staff and students are dependent on the other university libraries in the country.) The academic library collections of the country total some four and a half million books, with collection sizes at the individual institutions ranging between 270,000 and 950,000 volumes. Steady growth of the collections in spite of severe budgetary restraints has been ensured with the establishment of the University Grants Committee (1975) and later its Sub-committee for Libraries, so that available funds are dispensed without interfering with matters of academic freedom. Nevertheless, in the absence of formal acquisition policies in most of the academic libraries, collection development is dictated by faculty demand, an ad-hoc process often resulting in gaps in the collection. This problem is further aggravated by a fragmentation of the collection and services among a central and numerous departmental libraries, although lately this trend has started to change because of economic pressures and initiatives taken outside the profession. (For example, at the Hebrew University until recently there were some 70 departmental libraries, 25 of which were united into one library at the end of 1981.)

All academic libraries traditionally provide public library services to the community at large. Moreover, academic libraries fulfill national roles as well; for example, the Technion (Technical Institute of Israel) extends information services to the country's scientific and research institutions and industrial companies; the Hebrew University houses the *Israel Union List of Serials;* the Haifa University Library prepares one of Israel's main bibliographic tools, the computer-based annual *Index to Hebrew Periodicals*, as well as other computer-based bibliographic tools, and as of January 1981 provides MARC (Machine Readable Cataloging) based automated cataloging services to other universities.

Special Libraries

Israel's some 400 special libraries are linked to research institutions, hospitals, professional associations, government agencies, and industrial plants. Having developed close ties through interlibrary loan arrangements, the constant demand for up-to-date information necessitated an agency to foster further cooperation and coordination in scientific and technological information services. Again, the initiative for such an agency came from outside the profession: With the advent of government policy for industrialization in the early 1960s, the National Council for Research and Development established the Center of Scientific and Technological Information (COSTI).

Public Libraries

The measures taken by the ministry of education in the 1960s and the Library Law of 1975 have made Israeli public libraries more of a reality felt in everyday life, but, as mentioned above, they can hardly be considered active cultural centers of the community as only a relatively small percentage of the population uses their services.

Moreover, since the bloom of public libraries in the 1960s and the beginning of the 1970s, the process of development and improvement has slowed down somewhat, mainly because of lack of financing and perhaps as a result of an almost imperceptible change in government attitude since 1977: Out of 779 settlements, 556 have library services but only 42 library systems with 169 branches are recognized by the ministry of education, since such recognition means government financing. Thus, while in the 1960s and the early 1970s government funding for the recognized libraries averaged some 50 percent of their budgets, in 1981 it amounted to only about 17 percent.

Despite the fact that the public does not expect public libraries to provide more than the most rudimentary information in science, economy, and technology, public libraries strive to improve their services beyond providing the expected fiction collection. A new program of nonacademic training for public librarians (at Oranim Teachers' Training College) now provides them with a broader cultural background and more of the social and theoretical aspects of librarianship. In addition, academic libraries try to support the public library system; for example, the public libraries of the southern region are aided by the library of the Ben Gurion University, and the same role is fulfilled by the Haifa University Library in the north. They provide direct service to citizens, "adopt" the public libraries of their region and advise them in the organization of their collections, provide bibliographic services, and donate books to them.

The Center for Public Libraries, founded in 1965, is another agent for the aid of public libraries, providing such centralized services as central cataloging, centralized book acquisition, and book processing for libraries. The center also publishes bibliographies, reference books, and a periodical devoted to librarianship, *Yad la-Kore*.

Kibbutz Libraries

The kibbutz (collective settlement) population has access to the highest proportion of library books per capita in Israel; 84,000 people (3.4 percent of the entire population) have at their disposal 1,883,000 volumes. Some 37 percent of kibbutz residents are active readers and some 77 percent use kibbutz libraries. Until the late 1960s books were scattered throughout the settlements in small, often disorganized collections, but since then serious attempts have been made to apply some method to kibbutz libraries.

Arab Libraries

In towns of mixed Jewish and Arab population, the public libraries serve both Jewish and Arab readers, and Arab students and teachers make use of the Arabic collections at the university libraries. However, the general public in purely Arab settlements still has little access to libraries, although in the past few years the government has made efforts to encourage library development in the Arab sector as part of the general effort toward raising the educational level of the Arab population. (The literacy rate of non-Jewish males was 64.1 percent in 1948 as compared with 91.5 percent today, and that of non-Jewish females was 21 percent in 1948 as compared with 70.4 percent today.) Moreover, as a result of the educated Israeli Arabs' growing older and more influential politically, they are increasingly aware of the potential role of libraries.

School Libraries

In most Israeli schools there is some kind of a book collection, usually numbering a few hundred to a few thousand volumes, and in the more progressive schools children are taught to use books as information sources. Until recently collections were kept in classrooms in closed cabinets for circulation only, and no attempt was made to teach library use. Beginning in the 1970s there was increasing awareness that the lack of school libraries affects educational performance and that public libraries can replace them only in part. Efforts are being made to organize libraries in schools and to integrate library-use instruction into general education. However, the collections and services of school libraries are still rather limited and further improvement is urgently needed.

RECENT DEVELOPMENTS

The Israeli library system still has a long way to go, although there has been undeniable progress toward the gradual upgrading of the importance of libraries, both as providers of information and as sociocultural agencies. In the past decade, patterns of reader-oriented services began to emerge in Israeli libraries, although the problems facing them today have become more complicated: In addition to the as yet unresolved or only partly resolved problems of old, described above, libraries are becoming less and less self-sufficient as both the flood of publication and the constant pressure on library budgets make it impossible for any library to satisfy the information needs of its users exclusively from its own resources. True, these problems are hardly unique, and solutions found elsewhere should be applicable to the Israeli scene. However, Israeli libraries seem to be less than favorably inclined to opt for the most common solution to the problem—interlibrary cooperation and networking.

The minimal demands for information do not justify school and public library involvement in joint working arrangements and in this sector the possible solution is regional planning of library services, so that each library can utilize its resources to maximum advantage. Unfortunately, this trend has been diminishing in the recent past. The situation at the universities is entirely different: As the bulk of the nation's library resources is to be found in research (mainly university, but also larger special) libraries, which provide a variety of services to the academic community and even to the general public, the need for cooperation has been felt in this sector for some time.

The fact that the trend toward library networks and related ventures was slow to reach the Israeli library scene can be attributed to a combination of attitudes and circumstances. The weakness of the library profession, the librarians' lack of professional attitudes and their inability to exert substantial influence on library developments, lack of collection development policies, managerial weaknesses, and the prevailing fragmentation at the libraries could hardly prove hospitable to initiatives toward the development of a library network in the country. The possibility of networking was nevertheless brought to the fore, but again outside intervention was needed. Thus for the past two years the Israeli library scene has been concerned with the various issues related to library networks: Should Israeli academic libraries embark on a comprehensive networking project, or should they start with a bibliographic utility, aimed at fulfilling the needs of the university library community until the international networking scene stabilizes? (There is little doubt that networks are about to undergo considerable structural, technological, and economic changes with the advent of microcomputers and new storing techniques, such as videodiscs.) Should Israel adopt patterns, programs, and technologies developed elsewhere or develop local programs based on experience gained in libraries abroad? What library functions could and should be handled cooperatively and to what extent? With such questions to be resolved, it seems that the next few years will be crucial to the library scene in Israel and considerable change is to be expected.

BIBLIOGRAPHY

Central Bureau of Statistics (Israel). *Standard of Education of the Population (June 1954)*. Special Series No. 66. Jerusalem: Central Bureau of Statistics, 1958.

Central Bureau of Statistics (Israel). *Statistical Abstract of Israel, no. 32 (1981)*. Jerusalem: Central Bureau of Statistics, 1981.

Central Bureau of Statistics and the Ministry of Education and Culture, Culture and Arts Division (Israel). *Reading and Other Leisure Activities of the Jewish Population Ages 14 and Over, 1969-1979*. Special Series No. 654. Jerusalem: Central Bureau of Statistics, 1981.

Council for Higher Education, Grants Committee. *Survey of University Libraries for the Year 1978/9*. Jerusalem: Council for Higher Education, 1981.

Sever, S. "The Arab Library in Israel." *Library Quarterly* 49, no. 2 (1979): 163-181.

Sever, S. "Integration of Immigrants and Libraries in Israel, 1948-1960." *Library Research* 1, no. 1 (Spring 1979): 67-82.

Sever, S. "Library Education in Israel." *Journal of Education for Librarianship* 21, no. 3 (Winter 1981): 208-234.

NETWORK DEVELOPMENT IN CANADA: AN OVERVIEW

Laurent G. Denis

Professor, Faculty of Library Science, University of Toronto

A decade of consolidation and reappraisal for libraries in Canada is to be expected in the 1980s. Any substantial expansion of library service is unlikely in the foreseeable future in view of the retrenchment now being practiced by all levels of government. Cost-effectiveness is already becoming a household word and is soon to be a way of life, or death, in libraries and information agencies. Much effort will be expended in marshaling whatever resources are available toward the achievement of the greatest professional, social, and political benefits. Although libraries have benefited from the general prosperity of the recent past, they have never been allowed to luxuriate in vast stores of riches. The new financial restraints will, therefore, neither astound us nor paralyze us completely. We are made of sterner stuff! In competing for limited resources, however, libraries must pay more attention to planning, to the setting and implementing of goals and objectives, and to the role they must play in the information-rich postindustrial society. It will be necessary to manage in a no-growth situation and to revise the skills that were developed for the management of incremental budgets. Our ability to reorient our strategic directions so as to serve our community adequately, in spite of declining financial support, will be crucial.

Canada is in the forefront of the development of Telidon, the Canadian version of the new videotext technology, and a number of studies are underway in an attempt to assess the impact of these and many other technological developments on traditional, and perhaps not so traditional, library service. Technology is changing the publishing world, which is the principal source of our raw materials for service. Will publishing continue to change, and how? Will the new technology render us obsolete, making us a profession of custodians of the past, or will we adapt to the situation while maintaining our unique role as mediator between the object to be read and the reader, between the information resources and the information seeker? It does appear that books will continue to be produced, read, and handled. Who can deal with masses of books and throngs of readers better than librarians? Some years ago it was thought that documentalists would replace librarians. Where are the documentalists now? For a time we were threatened with displacement by computers. Now some information specialists are sounding our death toll. Librarians are sold short every time. The prophets of our doom pay too little heed to our resilience, to our ability to absorb change and to create order out of chaos. The present decade will sharpen our political awareness and will force us to assure the place of the library in the information world surrounding us.

Canada is a vast country, yet a mere 10 percent of its territory accommodates permanent settlement and its population density ranks among the lowest in the world. At the same time, Canada is one of the most industrialized and urbanized countries in the world. The sparse population of our country and the vastness of its land mass are factors that make library service difficult; yet its urbanization and industrialization facilitate the delivery of service. Politically, Canada is a federation of ten provinces, with each province having its own autonomous governing structure, and two territories under the central jurisdiction. Since each of the ten provinces has exclusive responsibility for the establishment of municipalities and for education, the political structure directly affects academic and public libraries. Because of the various provincial jurisdictions and funding bodies that are involved, library development is necessarily fragmented and the establishment of networks is difficult. Cooperative efforts, however, are increasing, and these are the key to the future of library and information service in Canada.

Perhaps the most basic and common cooperative system is the regional public library service. Regional libraries exist, and have existed in some cases for many years, in all the provinces. These systems may be mandated and provincewide, as in Ontario, or they may be voluntary, covering only a portion of a province, as in British Columbia. The services rendered by regional libraries vary in nature and in quality even as their financial support and their mission vary. At present there are no multiprovince and no nationwide public library systems. The National Library of Canada continues to explore ways to increase cooperation among library and information agencies, since it needs the resources of many other libraries in order to fulfill its mandate of acquiring, preserving, and making available the nation's literary heritage. Acting on the recommendations dating from 1976 of a task group on the Canadian union catalog, and following far-ranging expressions of informed opinion, the National Librarian proposed in 1979 a five-year plan for the National Library that focused not only on the development and promotion of bibliographical standards and the sharing of bibliographical and information resources, but also on the development of communication links between national, regional, provincial, and international centers. Implementing such a five-year decentralized network plan may well be the National Library's most important accomplishment. To this end, and as the first stage of a wider network index, an inventory of library processing data bases produced and used by universities and other degree-granting institutions was published in 1981. To support the technical development of communication standards, the Computer/Communications Protocols for Bibliographic Data Interchange task group has been appointed. Its aim is to make Canadian systems and data bases, including Dortmunder Bibliothekssystem (DOBIS), accessible to libraries everywhere in Canada. The work done in developing DOBIS capabilities for federal libraries is of considerable interest to other libraries, including the Library of Congress, and will be a key factor in the development of the decentralized Canadian library network.

DOBIS, which is the system adopted by a consortium of Ontario's community colleges, is compatible with Machine Readable Cataloging (MARC). The Ontario community colleges have developed Computer Output Microfiche (COM) and catalog cards from the DOBIS system, and are planning to use the system for interlibrary loan and for the control of periodicals. The Provincial Library of Nova Scotia, which provides a variety of services to public libraries of that province, is about to enter into an agreement with the National Library for the introduction of DOBIS into its operations. A recent study recommended to the British Columbia Union Catalogue's executive committee that its proposed British Columbia Library Network replicate the National Library DOBIS system in order to provide a full range of computer-based services to the libraries of British Columbia. Clearly, DOBIS is in a position to play a significant role as a computerized integrated library management system in a Canadian network, should a national network ever materialize.

In an effort to facilitate access to the library resources of the country, the National Library has enhanced its document delivery system by expanding the Library Delivery Service to sixty libraries and by connecting it to the transit system used by the Quebec universities for their interlibrary loans. Another popular resource-sharing service is the provision to public libraries, by the National Library, of collections of books in some 26 languages other than English and French. The scientific resource library for Canada, the Canada Institute for Scientific and Technical Information (CISTI), which was formerly the National Science Library, offers services to the scientific research and industrial communities. In addition to its backup collection of serials and monographs, CISTI provides a computer-based selective dissemination of information (SDI) service, an on-line retrospective data base service (CAN/OLE), and a computerized union list, now in its ninth edition, of all scientific serials held in Canada.

Barring unforeseen negative developments, another sophisticated system has the potential of becoming an unofficial national bibliographic network. The University of Toronto Library Automation System (UTLAS) supplies computer-based systems, services, and products in both English and French to numerous Canadian school, public, college, and university libraries, and recently has entered the U.S. and Japanese markets. More than six hundred individual libraries from the Atlantic to the Pacific receive products and services from UTLAS; more and more libraries and information agencies are finding it advantageous to plug into this system. At the time of writing, UTLAS operations at the University of Toronto are undergoing a comprehensive review to determine the nature and extent of the university's involvement with UTLAS. The need for costly additional space for UTLAS and its large, unforeseen deficit in 1980–1981 instigated the review, although the university assures us that UTLAS operations will not be curtailed or terminated. In addition to the foregoing, La Centrale des Bibliothèques, a consortium of college libraries, is unique in providing a wide range of service in French only to college, school, public, and special libraries in Quebec and other parts of Canada.

Apart from the rather modest regional public library networks and the two large systems, UTLAS and DOBIS, there are a number of cooperative ventures operating at provincial or regional levels. In the past decade, a number of informal groups have provided forums for discussion and other modes of information exchange and cooperation. Among these groups are the Ontario Universities Library Cooperative System (OULCS), the Tri-University Libraries of British Columbia (TRIUL), the Council of Prairie University Libraries (COPUL), the Library Subcommittee of the Conference of Rectors and Principals of Quebec Universities, and the Association of Atlantic Universities Librarians Committee.

A more formal consortium of 21 university, public, special, and government libraries in Quebec and Ontario (UNICAT/TELECAT) disbanded in 1980 after operating for several years. The dissolution of this group indicates that cooperative efforts per se are not enough. Escalating costs, rapidly evolving technology, and sharing in the decision-making process are concerns that cannot be ignored in networking. As elsewhere, there are no simple solutions to the library problems of Canada and certainly no easy answer to the problems involved in networking.

In June 1981, the Canadian Library Association published *Project Progress: A Study of Canadian Public Libraries*. This report is the result of years of planning and fund raising. Its declared purpose is "to supply a base of practical information that public library planners and decision-makers would find useful in understanding and dealing with the current and future status of the public library service in Canada." It remains to be seen whether *Project Progress* will have any real impact on the development of public libraries in Canada, but certainly many of its findings and recommendations will provide trustees and librarians with much food for thought. Marketing approaches to service delivery and competition from private-sector information services are two of the factors library planners must integrate into their blueprints for the future. It was discovered that there was not proper utilization of personnel in libraries, and that administrators, librarians, technicians, and clerical staff performed many of the same tasks. The report found that libraries suffer from insufficient job description and from lack of a clear understanding of responsibilities perceived by professional and clerical staff. This situation makes it extremely difficult to consider the librarian's work professional.

Another study, not yet completed, will also have a strong impact on the public libraries of Ontario. The ongoing "Public Library Program Review," sponsored by the provincial government, may recommend revisions in the present legislative, financial, structural, and organizational arrangements for Ontario libraries. Sentiments expressed at many public meetings, and opinions contained in hundreds of briefs, indicate that library boards want strong policy direction from the government. The consultative process of gathering information and collecting views or comments for the review is over. The next eight months will be devoted to analyzing the mass of information and developing recommendations. By the time it is completed, the review will represent the efforts of many individuals and groups over a two-year period and will have cost between $500,000 and $750,000.

An important library event in 1982 in Canada will be the IFLA General Conference to be held in Montreal from August 22–28. North America has already hosted two such conferences: the first in Toronto in 1967 at the invitation of the Canadian Library Association, and the second in Washington, D.C., in 1974 at the invitation of the American Library Association. At the invitation of the Association pour l'avancement des sciences et des techniques de la documentation (ASTED), the Montreal Conference will have as its theme "Networks." Twelve hundred delegates from 100 countries are expected to attend. This discussion of networking by such a large number of influential library and information specialists from around the world should prove to be most beneficial for the library situation in Canada.

International Statistics

U.S. BOOK EXPORTS AND IMPORTS AND INTERNATIONAL TITLE OUTPUT

Chandler B. Grannis

Contributing Editor, *Publishers Weekly*

Useful, but credible only as far as they go, may be one way to characterize the annual foreign trade figures compiled by the U.S. Bureau of Census.

The figures for 1980, released in the Spring-Summer number of *Printing and Publishing*, issued by the Department of Commerce, indicate a 16.5% increase over 1979 in the dollar value of U.S. book exports that were recorded (Table 1), and a rise of 14.1% in the value of recorded book imports (Table 2). The 1980 dollar totals given in the census report are $511,622,823 for total exports and $306,510,936 for total imports.

The figures fall short by unknown, and possibly significant, amounts, as they do every year, because of certain limits on the shipments that are counted. Export data exclude shipments valued under $500 "and low-valued exports by mail"; and import data exclude shipments valued under $250 "and low-valued nondutiable imports by mail." The $500 minimum limit became effective in April 1980; previously, for some years, the export limit had been $250. The import limit continues unchanged.

These criteria are applied to all industries, but obviously lead to unrealistic results when applied to the book industry or any other in which possibly thousands of small shipments are common in foreign trade.

Another limiting aspect of the census compilations is the fact that over half of all exports are reported in a single category of miscellaneous books and over 80% of all imports are lumped together as "other books," as will be seen in the two tables. Still another flaw is the lack of any figures at all in some categories of unit sales (numbers of copies).

At a time when many publishers are looking to foreign markets for opportunities to expand sales, the census data, as compiled under existing laws and regulations, provide too little helpful analysis.

Canada remains the largest market for U.S. book exports, increasing about 7.4% in 1980 over 1979 in dollars recorded. The 1979 and 1980 data are not clearly comparable, however, because of the 1980 change in minimum shipments counted. This is further suggested by the fact that the Canadian share of U.S. book exports appears to have been about 44% of the total in 1979 and only about 37% in 1980.

As far as trade with countries other than Canada is concerned, additional figures presented by *Printing and Publishing* show the recorded dollar exports to and imports from certain selected countries (Table 3). This tabulation is interesting for a number of reasons—for example, the sharp differences in increases and declines in trade with the various countries.

Note: Adapted from *Publishers Weekly*, September 18, 1981, where the article was entitled "U.S. Export-Import Figures and International Title Output."

TABLE 1 U.S. BOOK EXPORTS 1978–1980
Shipments Valued at $500 or More Only

	TO ALL COUNTRIES: Dollar Values				TO CANADA ONLY: Dollar Values			TO ALL COUNTRIES: Units		
	1978	1979	1980	% Change 1979–80	1978	1979	1980	1978	1979	1980	% Change 1979–80
Bibles, Testaments & Other Religious Books (2703020)	$20,728,789	$23,943,939	$31,867,260	+33.1	$6,313,640	$6,399,153	$6,848,742	42,153,722	39,090,837	43,501,521	+11.3
Dictionaries & Thesauruses (2703040)	3,965,864	5,735,680	6,018,536	+ 4.9	914,692	1,273,275	1,312,839	1,040,744	1,562,092	1,726,792	+10.5
Encyclopedias (2703060)	32,294,083	29,878,607	27,944,503	− 6.5	6,231,693	9,199,365	9,340,069	9,875,858	6,840,325	6,462,048	− 5.9
Textbooks, Workbooks & Standardized Tests (2703070)	70,297,302	83,550,838	99,657,783	+19.3	33,387,418	38,064,696	37,395,796				
Technical Scientific & Professional Books (2703080)	49,479,329	51,577,922	53,927,278	+ 4.6	9,843,843	12,385,527	11,816,779	16,024,867	14,846,886	15,807,469	+ 6.5
Books Not Elsewhere Classified & Pamphlets (2704000)	187,450,445	237,891,882	284,159,654	+19.4	87,244,510	107,881,787	121,136,963	157,759,062	180,163,203	199,852,375	+10.8
Children's Picture & Painting Books (7375200)	6,404,411	6,666,452	8,049,807	+20.7	2,562,161	2,914,796	3,451,007				
Total Domestic Merchandise, Omitting Shipments Under $500	$370,620,223	$439,245,220	$511,622,823	+16.5	$148,597,956	$178,118,599	$191,302,195				+10.1

Source: Extracted from U.S. Department of Commerce, *Printing and Publishing*, issues of April 1978, April 1979, and Spring-Summer 1980; hitherto unpublished data supplied to *PW* by *P&P* editors.

TABLE 2 U.S. BOOK IMPORTS 1978–1980
Shipments Valued at $500 or More Only

	Dollar Values			% Change 1979–80	Units			% Change 1979–80
	1978	1979	1980		1978	1979	1980	
Bibles and Prayerbooks (2702520)	$ 8,781,188	$ 6,082,482	$ 5,912,777	− 2.8	3,995,295	3,388,872	1,513,528	−55.3
Books, Foreign Language (2702540)	25,177,094	25,456,683	30,100,817	+18.2	14,507,863	17,373,156	17,953,146	+ 3.3
Books Not Specially Provided For, wholly or in part the work of an author who is a U.S. national or domiciliary (2701560)	4,678,542	3,454,528	4,152,073	+20.1	2,244,604	1,228,169	1,148,225	− 6.5
Other Books (2702580)	191,808,521	229,713,246	257,041,783	+11.9	159,326,315	183,092,783	196,199,815	+ 7.2
Toy Books and Coloring Books (7375200)	1,880,580	3,978,548	9,303,476	+133.8	—	—	—	
Total Imports, Omitting Shipments Under $250	**$232,325,925**	**$268,685,497**	**$306,510,936**	**+14.1**	—	—	—	**+ 5.7**

Source: Extracted from U.S. Department of Commerce, *Printing and Publishing*, issues of April 1978, April 1979, and Spring-Summer 1980; hitherto unpublished data supplied to *PW* by *P&P* editors.

TABLE 3   U.S. BOOK EXPORTS & IMPORTS, PRINCIPAL COUNTRIES, 1980

	Dollars 1980	% Change 1979–80		Dollars 1980	% Change 1979–80
US Exports (Over $500 only)			**US Imports (Over $250 only)**		
Canada	191,302,195	+ 7.4	United Kingdom	103,523,333	+ 3.6
United Kingdom	94,263,582	+47.6	Canada	39,853,726	+68.7
Australia	39,024,372	− 4.1	Japan	37,077,225	+16.1
Japan	20,308,722	− 5.9	Italy	16,738,435	−30.1
Mexico	14,670,693	+34.0	Germany, Federal Republic of	17,219,894	+37.0
Brazil	13,097,906	+38.0	Hong Kong	17,573,296	+64.1
Netherlands	11,109,413	+14.4	Spain	14,769,385	− 5.8
Germany, Federal Republic of	8,479,082	+ 6.8	Netherlands	9,379,176	+18.0
Philippines	8,237,132	+18.6	Switzerland	7,271,942	+17.4
New Zealand	6,783,066	+ 1.5	Mexico	8,021,906	+70.7
All other countries	104,346,660	+25.3	All other countries	35,082,618	+12.9
Total, all countries	**$511,622,823**	**+16.5**	**Total, all countries**	**$306,510,936**	**+14.1**

Source: Extracted from U.S. Department of Commerce, *Printing and Publishing*, Spring-Summer 1981, Table S-5; data from Bureau of the Census.

Note: U.S. export data do not include individual shipments valued under $500 and do not include individual shipments valued under $250 and low-valued, nondutiable imports by mail.

TABLE 4   TITLE OUTPUT, PRINCIPAL BOOK-PRODUCING COUNTRIES

	1976	1977	1978		1976	1977	1978
AFRICA				**EUROPE**			
Egypt	1,486			Austria	6,336	6,800	6,439
Nigeria			1,175	Belgium	6,414	5,964	9,012
				Bulgaria	3,813	4,088	4,234
NORTH AMERICA				Czechoslovakia	9,457	9,568	9,588
Canada	6,241	7,878	13,190	Denmark	6,783	8,021	9,415
Cuba	726	1,039		Finland	4,589	3,679	3,367
Mexico	4,851			France	29,371	31,673	21,225
U.S.A.*	84,542	87,780	87,569	Germany (E.)	5,792	5,844	5,680
SOUTH AMERICA				Germany (W.)	44,477	48,736	50,950
Argentina	6,719	5,285	4,627	Greece	3,935	4,981	
Brazil	20,025			Hungary	9,393	9,048	9,579
Peru	925	910	968	Italy	9,463	10,116	10,679
ASIA				Netherlands	12,557	13,111	13,393
Bangladesh			1,229	Norway	5,723	4,823	4,407
China			12,493	Poland	11,418	11,552	11,849
Hong Kong	1,494	1,735		Portugal	5,668	6,122	6,274
India	15,802	12,885	12,932	Romania	6,556	7,218	7,562
Indonesia	2,667	2,265		Spain	24,584	24,896	
Iran		3,027		Sweden	7,988	6,009	5,256
Iraq	1,588	1,758	1,618	Switzerland	9,989	9,894	9,453
Israel		2,214		United Kingdom	34,340	36,196	38,766
Japan	36,066	40,905	43,973	Yugoslavia	9,054	10,418	10,509
Rep. Korea	13,334	13,081	16,364				
Malaysia	1,302	1,341	1,328	**OCEANIA**			
Pakistan	1,081	1,331	1,317	Australia	2,325	3,077	
Philippines	1,616	1,753		New Zealand	1,835	1,939	2,079
Singapore	1,203	1,207	1,306				
Sri Lanka	1,140	1,201	1,405	**U.S.S.R.**	84,304	85,395	
Thailand	2,578	3,390		Byeloruss S.S.R.	2,489	2,330	2,618
Turkey	6,320	6,830		Ukraine S.S.R.	9,110	8,430	
Vietnam		1,504					

Sources: UNESCO *Statistical Yearbook 1980*, Table 8.1 (New York: Unipub, 1981); for U.S. figures, R. R. Bowker Co. data services, and University Microfilms.

*Includes books and pamphlets issued through U.S. Government Printing Office (in 1976, 16,931; in 1977, est. 15,000; in 1978, 14,814); also university theses (in 1976, 34,709; in 1977, est. 31,000; in 1978, 31,629). NOT included in the U.S. figures are publications of state and local governments, publications of numerous institutions, and many reports, proceedings, lab manuals, and workbooks.

TABLE 5 OUTPUT OF CHILDREN'S BOOKS BY PRINCIPAL PRODUCERS BY NUMBER OF TITLES AND COPIES

	Titles		Copies (000)	
	Books Only	Total (40+) Books & Pamphlets	Books Only	Total Books & Pamphlets
AFRICA				
Egypt/1976	28	56	1,279	4,001
Nigeria/1978	9	84	—	—
AMERICAS				
Argentina/1978	—	344	—	—
Brazil/1978	2,275	2,421	27,710	36,863
Canada/1978	267	267	—	—
Cuba/1977	70	72	3,999	4,004
United States/1978	2,911	2,911	105,700	105,700
ASIA				
Iran/1977	173	173	—	—
Israel/1977	166	231	—	2,348
Japan/1978	2,339	2,893	—	—
Jordan/1976	47	49	832	833
Korea Rep./1978	952	1,028	4,052	4,132
Malaysia/1978	47	152	166	566
Pakistan/1977	183	183	—	—
Singapore/1978	42	99	184	687
Vietnam/1977	52	76	3,385	5,182
EUROPE				
Austria/1978	142	210	—	—
Belgium/1978	—	1,345	—	—
Bulgaria/1978	—	—	6,237	10,042
Cyprus/1977	7	42	21	45
Czechoslovakia/1978	366	595	8,388	16,266
Denmark/1978	—	1,041	—	—
Finland/1978	76	194	—	—
Germany (E.)/1978	412	707	10,459	17,676
Germany (W.)/1978	1,770	2,636	—	—
Greece/1977	154	194	—	—
Hungary/1978	285	330	11,451	13,238
Iceland/1977	66	112	—	—
Italy/1978	364	578	12,125	15,511
Netherlands/1978	1,760	—	—	—
Norway/1978	227	335	—	—
Poland/1978	219	315	9,550	21,611
Romania/1978	148	178	3,617	5,152
Spain/1977	763	1,801	8,717	25,153
Sweden/1978	—	465	—	—
Switzerland/1978	—	416	—	—
United Kingdom/1978	2,330	2,813	—	—
Yugoslavia/1978	239	315	2,114	3,136
OCEANIA				
Australia/1977	75	111	—	—
New Zealand/1977	11	43	—	—
U.S.S.R./1977	1,833	3,249	148,313	516,192
Byelorussia/1978	67	115	5,377	9,053
Ukraine/1977	208	316	16,826	46,163

Source: Excerpted from UNESCO Statistical Yearbook, 1980, Table 8.9.

TABLE 6 TRANSLATIONS, ACCORDING TO ORIGINAL LANGUAGE
(Top 20 Languages)

Language	1973	1974	1975
English	18,350	20,411	19,020
Russian	5,113	4,824	6,563
French	5,993	5,785	5,298
German	4,277	4,753	4,338
Italian	1,136	1,182	1,046
Swedish	1,006	1,178	1,043
Spanish	1,368	768	935
Hungarian	578	747	696
Polish	626	349	676
Czech	598	657	515
Danish	604	656	512
Romanian	492	115	480
Classical Greek	424	478	478
Latin	374	430	443
Dutch	383	429	329
Serbo-Croatian	499	540	307
Bulgarian	221	131	247
Ukrainian	134	138	229
Norwegian	297	269	224
Chinese	184	188	209
Subtotal top 20 languages	42,657	44,028	43,588
Total All Languages	47,038	47,822	47,775

Source: Excerpted from UNESCO Statistical Yearbook, 1980, Table 8.11.

UNESCO annually provides figures, necessarily delayed, on worldwide book output. Table 4 presents title output of principal book-producing countries for 1976, 1977, and 1978, extracted from the *UNESCO Statistical Yearbook 1980* (available from Unipub, 345 Park Avenue South, New York, NY 10010; 212-686-4707). Figures for the People's Republic of China are given here for the first time; but there are still no data reported from Taiwan, and some countries are not included because their information was not available to UNESCO for any of the years cited.

Tables 5 and 6 present data compiled from two additional sections of the UNESCO report. Table 5 gives numbers of titles and copies of children's books from principal producing countries, and Table 6 gives numbers of translations from 20 languages for the years noted on the table.

BRITISH BOOK PRODUCTION, 1981

In 1981, publishers in Britain issued a total of 43,083 titles, of which 33,696 were new books and 9,387 reprints and new editions. The output of new books and new editions according to category is given in detail in Table 1. The figures have been compiled from the book lists that have appeared week by week in *The Bookseller*.

The 1981 total represents a decline of 5,075 or 10.5 percent from last year's record total of 48,158 (Table 2). But even after this fall of nearly 10 percent in new books, and nearly 13 percent in new editions, the new total remains substantially higher than in any year except 1980.

Just as there was no obvious explanation for last year's leap, so there is no clear reason for 1981's diminution. The proportion of English-language imported books handled through British distributors remained as constant as it has been for several years. It is possible to speculate that some publishers decided that the best way to maintain turnover when print runs and sales were falling was *not* to print more and more titles. More positively, it is possible that the better 1981 business that some publishers' financial results have revealed in recent months made such desperate measures unnecessary. One immediate comment was: "Good Lord, the publishers must be going sane."

The figures in Table 3 show decreases in every category. Fiction remains the largest section, and although it has fallen back by 398 or 7.7 percent, it is still nearly 200 up on 1979. Children's books, down 551 or nearly 16 percent to 2,934, are however back below their 1979 level.

Note: Adapted from *The Bookseller* (12 Dyott Street, London WC1A 1DR, England), January 2, 1982, where the article was entitled "Welcome Fall in UK Publishers Output."

TABLE 1 BOOK TITLE OUTPUT, 1981

	December, 1981				January–December, 1981			
Classification	Total	Reprints and New Editions	Trans.	Limited Editions	Total	Reprints and New Editions	Trans.	Limited Editions
Aeronautics	7	1	—	—	237	35	—	—
Agriculture and forestry	36	8	1	—	451	79	4	1
Architecture	27	4	1	—	347	69	9	1
Art	95	12	—	2	1,383	238	92	7
Astronomy	3	2	—	—	120	35	1	—
Bibliography and library economy	76	11	—	—	788	138	2	—
Biography	87	20	4	—	1,243	302	48	4
Chemistry and physics	70	9	—	—	682	115	19	—
Children's books	160	37	3	1	2,934	496	97	1
Commerce	107	15	—	1	1,213	312	4	1
Customs, costumes, folklore	16	2	1	—	158	37	6	—
Domestic science	65	31	—	—	695	181	13	2
Education	70	6	1	—	1,040	194	6	—
Engineering	144	24	1	—	1,488	239	29	1
Entertainment	47	8	—	—	630	117	12	—
Fiction	292	132	6	—	4,747	1,837	118	5
General	49	11	1	—	557	96	5	—
Geography and archaeology	43	20	1	—	476	102	9	—
Geology and meteorology	29	2	—	—	340	41	5	—
History	148	25	4	—	1,432	347	50	2
Humour	10	2	—	—	171	24	1	—
Industry	55	11	—	—	492	96	1	—
Language	42	8	—	—	657	136	10	—
Law and public administration	130	28	2	—	1,399	304	9	—
Literature	95	20	6	—	1,151	190	54	5
Mathematics	76	14	2	—	726	138	8	—
Medical science	277	41	5	—	2,838	497	27	—
Military science	8	3	1	—	113	28	1	—
Music	27	5	—	—	365	97	12	1

TABLE 1 BOOK TITLE OUTPUT, 1981 (cont.)

Classification	December, 1981				January–December, 1981			
	Total	Reprints and New Editions	Trans.	Limited Editions	Total	Reprints and New Editions	Trans.	Limited Editions
Natural sciences	105	11	1	1	1,234	190	14	1
Occultism	16	2	—	—	251	59	19	—
Philosophy	29	2	3	—	431	111	49	—
Photography	11	1	—	—	237	27	—	1
Plays	10	5	4	—	256	102	51	2
Poetry	50	4	4	4	620	70	61	38
Political science and economy	269	57	3	—	3,764	868	79	—
Psychology	57	3	—	—	725	121	14	—
Religion and theology	85	28	5	—	1,363	274	138	3
School textbooks	145	18	—	—	1,991	261	16	—
Science, general	4	1	—	—	55	12	1	—
Sociology	82	7	1	—	1,031	149	19	—
Sports and outdoor games	38	9	—	—	511	87	15	—
Stockbreeding	17	—	—	—	264	69	2	—
Trade	44	7	—	—	536	141	3	1
Travel and guidebooks	43	9	—	—	677	279	8	1
Wireless and television	25	3	—	—	264	47	3	—
Total	3,321	679	61	9	43,083	9,387	1,144	78

Note: This table shows the books recorded in December and the total for January–December with the numbers of new editions, translations, and limited editions.

TABLE 2   COMPARISON OF BOOK PRODUCTION BY SUBJECT, 1980 AND 1981

	1980	1981	+ or −
Art	1,408	1,383	−25
Biography	1,360	1,243	−117
Chemistry and physics	824	682	−142
Children's books	3,485	2,934	−551
Commerce	1,440	1,213	−227
Education	1,258	1,040	−218
Engineering	1,594	1,488	−106
Fiction	5,145	4,747	−398
History	1,587	1,432	−155
Industry	688	492	−196
Law and public administration	1,548	1,399	−149
Literature	1,185	1,151	−34
Medical science	3,323	2,838	−485
Natural sciences	1,278	1,234	−44
Political science	4,269	3,764	−505
Religion	1,725	1,363	−362
School textbooks	2,317	1,991	−326
Sociology	1,195	1,031	−164
Travel and guidebooks	716	677	−39
Totals	48,158	43,083	−5,075
New Editions	10,776	9,387	−1,389

TABLE 3 TITLE OUTPUT, 1947-1981

Year	Total	Reprints and New Editions
1947	13,046	2,441
1948	14,686	3,924
1949	17,034	5,110
1950	17,072	5,334
1951	18,066	4,938
1952	18,741	5,428
1953	18,257	5,523
1954	18,188	4,846
1955	19,962	5,770
1956	19,107	5,302
1957	20,719	5,921
1958	22,143	5,971
1959	20,690	5,522
1960	23,783	4,989
1961	24,893	6,406
1962	25,079	6,104
1963	26,023	5,656
1964	26,154	5,260
1965	26,358	5,313
1966	28,883	5,919
1967	29,619	7,060
1968	31,470	8,778
1969	32,393	9,106
1970	33,489	9,977
1971	32,538	8,975
1972	33,140	8,486
1973	35,254	9,556
1974	32,194	7,852
1975	35,608	8,361
1976	34,434	8,227
1977	36,322	8,638
1978	38,766	9,236
1979	41,940	9,086
1980	48,158	10,776
1981	43,083	9,387

Part 6
Reference Information

Bibliographies

THE LIBRARIAN'S BOOKSHELF

Jo-Ann Michalak
*Librarian, School of Library Service,
Columbia University Libraries, New York*

This bibliography is intended as a buying and reading guide for individual librarians and library collections. A few of the titles listed are core titles that any staff development collection might contain, but most are recently published titles with an emphasis on continuing education. Bibliographic tools that most libraries are likely to have for day-to-day operations have been excluded from this list.

BOOKS
General Works

The ALA Yearbook: A Review of Library Events, 1980. Chicago: American Library Association, 1981. $55.

ALA World Encyclopedia of Library and Information Services, ed. by Robert Wedgeworth. Chicago: American Library Association, 1980. $95.

Advances in Librarianship. ed. by Michael Harris. New York: Academic Press, 1970– . Vol. 11, 1981. $30.

American Library Association. Headquarters Library. *A.L.A. Publications Checklist, 1981.* Chicago, 1981. $6.

American Library Directory, 1981. 34th ed. New York: R. R. Bowker, 1981. $67.50.

American Library Laws. 4th ed. Chicago: American Library Association, 1974. $50. 1st supplement, 1973–1974. 1975. o.p. 2nd supplement, 1975–1976. 1977. $15. 3rd supplement, 1977–1978. 1980. $15.

Bowker Annual of Library and Book Trade Information 1982. 27th ed. New York: R. R. Bowker, 1982. $35.

Directory of Special Libraries and Information Centers. 6th ed. Detroit: Gale Research Co., 1981. Vols. 1–3. Vol. 1 $175; Vol. 2 $140; Vol. 3 $150.

Encyclopedia of Library and Information Science. New York: Marcel Dekker, 1968–1981. Vols. 1–33. $55 per vol.

Fang, Josephine Riss, and Songe, Alice H. *International Guide to Library, Archival, and Information Science Associations.* 2nd ed. New York: R. R. Bowker, 1980. $32.50.

Libraries in the Political Process, ed. by E. J. Josey. Phoenix, AZ: Oryx Press, 1980. $18.95.

Vaillancourt, Pauline M. *International Directory of Acronyms in Library, Information and Computer Sciences.* New York: R. R. Bowker, 1980. $45.

Administration

Bailey, Martha. *Supervisory and Middle Managers in Libraries.* Metuchen, NJ: Scarecrow, 1981. $12.

Boss, Richard W. *Grant Money and How to Get It: A Handbook for Librarians.* New York: R. R. Bowker, 1980. $19.95.

Breivik, Patricia, and Gibson, E. Burr. *Funding Alternatives for Libraries.* Chicago: American Library Association, 1979. $10.

Chen, Ching-Chih. *Library Management Without Bias*. Greenwich, CT: JAI Press, 1981. $34.50.

——. *Zero-Base Budgeting in Library Management: A Manual for Librarians*. Phoenix, AZ: Oryx Press, 1980. $25.

Current Concepts in Library Management. Littleton, CO: Libraries Unlimited, 1979. $25.

De Hart, Florence E. *Librarian's Psychological Commitments: Human Relations in Librarianship*. Westport, CT: Greenwood Press, 1979. $19.95.

Edsall, Marian S. *Library Promotion Handbook*. Phoenix, AZ: Oryx Press, 1980. $18.50.

Garvey, Mona. *Library Public Relations*. New York: H. W. Wilson, 1980. $14.

Lancaster, F. W. *The Measurement and Evaluation of Library Services*. Washington, DC: Information Resources Press, 1977. $29.95.

Lee, Sul H. *Emerging Trends in Library Organization: What Influences Change*. Ann Arbor, MI: Pierian Press, 1978. $14.95.

Martin, Murray S. *Issues in Personnel Management*. Greenwich, CT: JAI Press, 1981. $36.50.

O'Reilly, Robert C. and Marjorie I. *Librarians and Labor Relations: Employment Under Union Contracts*. Westport, CT: Greenwood, 1981. $25.

Personnel Administration in Libraries, ed. by Sheila Creth and Frederick Duda. New York: Neal-Schuman, 1981. $19.95.

Personnel Policies and Procedures in Libraries, ed. by Nancy Van Zant. New York: Neal-Schuman, 1980. $19.95.

Reeves, William Joseph. *Librarians as Professionals: The Occupation's Impact on Library Work Arrangements*. Lexington, MA: Lexington Books, 1980. $19.95.

Rizzo, John. *Management for Librarians*. Westport, CT: Greenwood Press, 1980. $35.

Sherman, Steve. *ABC's of Library Promotion*. 2nd ed. Metuchen, NJ: Scarecrow Press, 1980. $12.

Stueart, Robert. *Library Management*. 2nd ed. Littleton, CO: Libraries Unlimited, 1981. $25.

Archives, Conservation, and Manuscripts

Banks, Paul Noble. *A Selective Bibliography on the Conservation of Research Libraries Materials*. Chicago: Newberry Library, 1981. $10.

College and University Archives: Selected Readings. Chicago: Society of American Archivists, 1979. $11.

Gracy, David B. *An Introduction to Archives and Manuscripts*. New York: Special Libraries Association, 1981. $7.25.

Kemp, Edward C. *Manuscript Solicitation for Libraries, Special Collections, Museums, and Archives*. Littleton, CO: Libraries Unlimited, 1978. $20.

McWilliams, Jerry. *The Preservation and Restoration of Sound Recordings*. Nashville, TN: American Association for State and Local History, 1979. $8.95.

Morrow, Carolyn Clark. *A Conservation Bibliography for Librarians, Archivists, and Administrators*. Troy, NY: Whitston Publishing Co., 1979. $18.50.

Preservation of Library Materials, ed. by Joyce R. Russell. New York: Special Libraries Association, 1980. $9.50.

Society of American Archivists. Basic Manual Series, unnumbered series. $4.00 for members, $5.00 for nonmembers. (Most recent title is Hickerson, H. Thomas. *Archives and Manuscripts: An Introduction to Automated Access*. Chicago: SAA, 1981).

Swartzburg, Susan. *Preserving Library Materials: A Manual*. Metuchen, NJ: Scarecrow Press, 1980. $12.50.

Thompson, Enid T. *Local History Collections: A Manual for Librarians*. Nashville, TN: American Association for State and Local History, 1978. $5.75.

Young, Laura S. *Bookbinding and Conservation by Hand.* New York: R. R. Bowker, 1981. $35.

Audiovisual

Audio-Visual Equipment Directory 1981/82. 27th ed. Fairfax, VA: National Audio-Visual Association, 1981. $21.

Audiovisual Market Place, 1982: A Multimedia Guide, 12th ed. New York: R. R. Bowker, 1982. $37.50.

Boyle, Deirdre, ed. *Expanding Media.* Phoenix, AZ: Oryx Press, 1977. $17.50.

Cabeceiras, James. *The Multimedia Library: Materials Selection and Use.* New York: Academic Press, 1978. $14.

Educational Media Yearbook 1981, ed. by James W. Brown. Littleton, CO: Libraries Unlimited, 1981. $30.

Sive, Mary Robinson, *Selecting Instructional Media: A Guide to Audiovisual and Other Instructional Media Lists.* Littleton, CO: Libraries Unlimited, 1978. $18.50.

Spirt, Diana L. *Library Media Manual.* New York: H. W. Wilson, 1979. $6.

Video Involvement for Libraries, ed. by Susan Spaeth Cherry. Chicago: ALA, 1981. $6.

Automation and Information Retrieval

Annual Review of Information Science and Technology. Washington, DC: American Society for Information Science. White Plains, NY: Knowledge Industry Publications. Vols. 3–5 (1968–1970) and Vols. 7–11 (1972–1976). $35 per vol. Vols. 12–16 (1977–1981). $42.50 per vol.

Bahr, Alice H. *Automated Library Circulation Systems, 1981–1982.* 2nd ed. White Plains, NY: Knowledge Industry Publications, 1981. $24.50.

Boss, Richard, W. *The Library Manager's Guide to Automation.* White Plains, NY: Knowledge Industry, 1979. $29.50.

Clinic on Library Applications of Data Processing. University of Illinois Proceedings. Champaign, IL: University of Illinois, Grad. School of Lib. Science, Publications Office, 1963–1980 vol. $9.

Corbin, John. *Developing Computer and Network Based Library Systems.* Phoenix, AZ: Oryx Press, 1981. $22.50.

Fedida, Sam, and Malik, Rex. *The Viewdata Revolution.* New York: Wiley, 1980. $38.95.

Gough, Chet, and Srikantaiah, Taverekere. *Systems Analysis in Libraries: A Question and Answer Approach.* Hamden, CT: Shoe String, 1978. $11.50.

Grosch, Audrey N. *Minicomputers in Libraries 1981–82.* White Plains, NY: Knowledge Industry Publications, 1981. $34.50.

Hoover, Ryan, ed. *Library and Information Manager's Guide to Online Services.* White Plains, NY: Knowledge Industry, 1980. $29.95.

International On-Line Information Meeting. 1st–4th (1977–1980). Oxford: Learned Information. $30.

Kent, Allen, and Galvin, Thomas J., eds. *The On-Line Revolution in Libraries.* New York: Marcel Dekker, 1978. $36.75.

King, Donald W. *Key Papers in the Design and Evaluation of Information Systems* (American Society for Information Science). White Plains, NY: Knowledge Industry Publications, 1978. $25.

Professional Librarian's Reader in Library Automation and Technology, ed. by Susan K. Martin. New York: Knowledge Industry, 1980. $24.50.

Rorvig, Mark E. *Microcomputers and Libraries: A Guide to Technology, Products and Applications.* White Plains, NY: Knowledge Industry, 1981. $27.50.

Buildings, Furniture, Equipment

Bahr, Alice H. *Book Theft and Library Security Systems, 1981–82.* White Plains, NY: Knowledge Industry Publications, 1981. $24.50.

Brooks, James, and Draper, James. *Interior Designs for Libraries.* Chicago:

American Library Association, 1979. pap. $12.50.

Cohen, Aaron, and Cohen, Elaine. *Designing and Space Planning for Libraries: A Behavioral Guide.* New York: R. R. Bowker, 1979. $24.95.

Hannigan, Jane A., and Estes, Glenn E. *Media Center Facilities Design.* Chicago: American Library Association, 1978. $12.

Lushington, Nolan, and Mills, Willis N., Jr. *Libraries Designed for Users.* Hamden, CT: Library Professional Publications, 1980. $22.50.

Mason, Ellsworth. *Mason on Library Buildings.* Metuchen, NJ: Scarecrow, 1980. $25.

Novak, Gloria, ed. *Running Out of Space—What Are the Alternatives?* Chicago: American Library Association, 1978. $15.

Pierce, William S. *Furnishing the Library Interior.* New York: Marcel Dekker, 1980. $39.75.

Pollett, Dorothy, and Haskell, Peter C. *Sign Systems for Libraries.* New York: R. R. Bowker, 1979. $24.95.

Reynolds, Linda, and Barrett, S. *Library Signs and Guiding: A Practical Guide to Design and Production.* Hamden, CT: Shoe String, 1981. $32.50.

Sourcebook of Library Technology: A Cumulative Edition of Library Technology Reports 1965-1979. Chicago: American Library Association, 1980. $75. $40 with current subscription to *Library Technology Reports.* On microfiche.

Children's and Young Adults' Services and Materials

The Arbuthnot Lectures, 1970-79. Association for Library Service to Children, American Library Association. Chicago: American Library Association, 1980. $12.50.

Braverman, Miriam. *Youth, Society and the Public Library.* Chicago: American Library Association, 1979. $15.

Briggs, Nancy E. *Children's Literature through Storytelling and Drama.* 2nd ed. Dubuque, IA: W. C. Brown, 1979. $4.95.

Campbell, Patricia J. *Sex Education Books for Young Adults, 1892-1979.* New York: R. R. Bowker, 1979. $15.95.

Celebrating Children's Books: Essays on Children's Literature in Honor of Zena Sutherland, ed. by Betsy Hearne and Marilyn Kaye. New York: Lothrop, Lee & Shepard Books, 1981. $11.95.

Children and Books. 6th ed. Glenview, IL: Scott, Foresman, 1981. $19.95.

Children's Media Market Place. New York: Neal-Schuman, 1981. $24.95.

deWitt, Dorothy. *Children's Faces Looking Up.* Chicago: American Library Association, 1979. $11.

Donelson, Kenneth L., and Nilsen, Alleen Pace. *Literature for Today's Young Adults.* Glenview, IL: Scott, Foresman, 1980. $12.95.

Dreyer, Sharon. *The Bookfinder: A Guide to Children's Literature about the Needs and Problems of Youth.* Circle Pines, MN: American Guidance Service, 1977-1981. 2 vols. $69.50.

Foster, Joan, ed. *Reader in Children's Librarianship.* Englewood, CO: Information Handling Services, 1978. $22.

Haviland, Virginia, ed. *Children's Literature: A Guide to Reference Sources.* Washington, DC: Library of Congress, 1966. $5.45. 1st supplement, 1972. $5.50. 2nd supplement, 1978. $7.75. 3rd supplement, 1980. $12.00.

Illustrators of Children's Books 1967-1976, comp. by Lee Kingman, Grace Allen Hogarth, and Harriet Quimby. Boston: The Horn Book, 1978. $35.

Meacham, Mary. *Information Sources in Children's Literature: A Practical Reference Guide for Children's Librarians, Elementary School Teachers, and Students of Children's Literature.* Westport, CT: Greenwood Press, 1978. $18.95.

Rogers, JoAnn V., ed. *Libraries and Young Adults.* Littleton, CO: Libraries Unlimited, 1979. $17.50.

Vandergrift, Kay E. *Child and Story: The Literary Connection.* New York: Neal-Schuman, 1981. $14.95.

Wilson, June B. *The Story Experience.* Metuchen, NJ: Scarecrow Press, 1979. $10.

Young Adult Literature: Background and Criticism, ed. by Millicent Lenz and Ramona Mahood. Chicago: American Library Association, 1980. $30.

College and University Libraries

Academic Librarianship: Yesterday, Today and Tomorrow, ed. by Robert Stueart. New York: Neal-Schuman, 1981. $19.95.

Association of College and Research Libraries. *New Horizons for Academic Libraries.* Papers Presented at the ACRL 1978 National Conference. Detroit: Gale 1979. $50.

Bender, David R. *Learning Resources and the Instructional Program in Community Colleges.* Hamden, CT: Shoe String, 1980. $19.50.

Cline, Hugh. *Building Library Collections: Policies and Practices in Academic Libraries.* Toronto: Lexington Books, 1981. $15.95.

College Librarianship, ed. by William Miller and D. S. Rockwood. Metuchen, NJ: Scarecrow, 1981. $15.

Johnson, Edward R. *Organization Development for Academic Libraries.* Westport, CT: Greenwood Press, 1980. $19.95.

Kent, Allen, ed. *Use of Library Materials: The University of Pittsburgh Study.* New York: Marcel Dekker, 1979. $29.75.

McClure, Charles R. *Information for Academic Library Decision Making.* Westport, CT: Greenwood, 1980. $23.95.

Martin, Murray S. *Budgetary Control in Academic Libraries.* Greenwich, CT: JAI Press, 1978. $32.50.

Osburn, Charles. *Academic Research and Library Resources: Changing Patterns in America.* Westport, CT: Greenwood Press, 1979. $18.95.

SPEC Kits. Washington, DC: Association of Research Libraries. 1973– . Nos. 1– . $7.50 for members, $15 for nonmembers. (Recent kits have been on such topics as Affirmation Action Programs, AACR2 Implementation Studies, and Preparing for Emergencies and Disasters.)

Wilkinson, Billy R. *Reader in Undergraduate Libraries.* Englewood, CO: Information Handling Services, 1978. $22.

Comparative and International Librarianship

Amadi, Adolphe A. *African Libraries: Western Tradition and Colonial Brainwashing.* Metuchen, NJ: Scarecrow, 1981. $14.

Avicenne, Paul, ed. *Bibliographical Services throughout the World, 1970–1974.* New York: Unipub, 1978, $22.50.

Benge, Ronald. *Cultural Crisis and Libraries in the Third World.* Hamden, CT: Shoe String, 1979. $17.50.

Huq, A. A. Abdul, and Aman, Mohammed M. *Librarianship and the Third World: An Annotated Bibliography of Selected Literature on Developing Nations, 1960–1975.* New York: Garland, 1977. $37.

Penna, C. V., Foskett, D. J., and Sewell, P. H. *National Library and Information Services: A Handbook for Planners.* London: Butterworths, 1977. $16.95.

Copyright

Henry, Nicholas, ed. *Copyright, Congress and Technology: The Public Record.* Phoenix, AZ: Oryx Press, 1978. Vols. 1–5, $95.

Johnston, Donald. *Copyright Handbook.* 2nd ed. New York: R. R. Bowker, 1982. $24.95.

Miller, Jerome K. *U.S. Copyright Documents: An Annotated Collection for Use* by *Educators and Librarians*. Littleton, CO: Libraries Unlimited, 1981. $25.

Education for Librarianship

Bramley, Gerald. *History of Library Education*. 2nd. ed. Hamden, CT: Shoe String, 1980. $13.50.

Conant, Ralph Wendell. *The Conant Report: A Study of the Education of Librarians*. Cambridge, MA: MIT Press, 1980. $20.

Conroy, Barbara. *Library Staff Development Profile Pages: A Guide and Workbook for Library Self Assessment and Planning*. Available from the author, Box 502, Tabernash, CO, 1979. $12.

Financial Assistance for Library Education: Academic Year 1982-83. Chicago: American Library Association, 1981. 75¢.

Morehead, Joe. *Theory and Practice in Library Education*. Littleton, CO: Libraries Unlimited, 1980. $25.

Information and Society

Compaine, Benjamin. *The Book Industry in Transition*. White Plains, NY: Knowledge Industry Publications, 1978. $24.95.

Directory of Fee Based Information Services: 1980/81, ed. by Kelly Warnken. Woodstock, NY: Information Alternative, 1978. $6.95.

The Federal Role in the Federal System: The Dynamics of Growth. Federal Involvement in Libraries. Washington, DC: Advisory Commission on Intergovernmental relations. 1980. $2.50.

The Future of the Printed Word: The Impact and Implications of the New Communications Technology. Westport, CT: Greenwood Press, 1980. $25.

Giuliano, Vincent, et al. *Into the Information Age: A Perspective for Federal Action on Information*. Chicago: American Library Association, 1979. pap. $8.

An Information Agenda for the 1980s: Proceedings of a Colloquium June 17-18, 1980, ed. by Carlton Rochell. Chicago: American Library Association, 1981. $7.50.

Information Industry Association. *Membership Directory, 1981-82*. Bethesda, MD: Information Industry Association, 1981. $21.

Information Industry Market Place, 1982. An International Directory of Information Products and Services. New York: R. R. Bowker, 1981. $37.50.

Machlup, Fritz, and Leeson, Kenneth. *Information through the Printed Word*. 3 vols. New York: Praeger, 1978. $85.85.

Rowley, J. E. *The Dissemination of Information*. London: Andre Deutsch, 1978. $19.25.

Warnken, Kelly. *The Information Brokers: How to Start and Operate Your Own Fee-Based Service*. New York: R. R. Bowker, 1981. $24.95.

White House Conference on Library and Information Services, Washington, D.C., 1979. *Information for the 1980's: Final Report*. Washington, DC: U.S. Government Printing Office, 1980.

Intellectual Freedom

Bosmajian, Haig A. *Censorship, Libraries and the Law*. New York: Neal-Schuman, 1981. $14.95.

Library History

Dictionary of American Library Biography. Littleton, CO: Libraries Unlimited, 1978. $85.

Garrison, Dee. *Apostles of Culture*. New York: Macmillan Information, 1979. $14.50.

Goldstein, Harold, ed. *Milestones to the Present: Papers from Library History Seminar V*. Syracuse, NY: Gaylord, 1978. $15.

Hamlin, Arthur T. *The University Library in the United States: Its Origins and Development*. Philadelphia: University of Pennsylvania Press, 1981. $25.

Harris, Michael H., and Davis, Donald G., Jr. *American Library History: A Bibliography.* Austin, TX: University of Texas Press, 1978. $20.

Thomison, Dennis. *A History of the American Library Association, 1876-1972.* Chicago: American Library Association, 1978. $15.

Weibel, Kathleen, and Heim, Kathleen M. *The Role of Women in Librarianship 1876-1976: The Entry, Advancement, and Struggle for Equalization in One Profession.* Phoenix, AZ: Oryx Press, 1979. $19.50.

Winckler, Paul A. *Reader in the History of Books and Printing.* Englewood, CO: Information Handling Services, 1978. $24.

Materials Selection

American Library Association. Collection Development Committee. *Guidelines for Collection Development,* ed. by David L. Perkins. Chicago: American Library Association, 1979. $5.

Bonk, Wallace John, and Magrill, Rose Mary. *Building Library Collections.* 5th ed. Metuchen, NJ: Scarecrow Press, 1979. $12.50.

Collection Development in Libraries: A Treatise, ed. by Robert D. Stueart and George B. Miller, Jr. Greenwich, CT: JAI Press, 1980. 2 vols. $60.

Evans, G. Edward. *Developing Library Collections.* Littleton, CO: Libraries Unlimited, 1979. $19.50.

Gardner, Richard K. *Collections: Their Origin, Selection and Development.* New York: McGraw-Hill, 1981. $15.95.

Katz, William A. *Collection Development: The Selection of Materials for Libraries.* New York: Holt, 1980. $15.95.

Miller, Shirley. *The Vertical File and Its Satellites.* 2nd ed. Littleton, CO: Libraries Unlimited, 1979. $17.50.

Microforms and Computer Output Microforms

Bahr, Alice H. *Microforms: The Librarians' View, 1978-79.* 2nd ed. White Plains, NY: Knowledge Industry Publications, 1978. $24.50.

Catalog Use Committee, Reference and Adult Services Division, American Library Association. *Commercial COM Catalogs: How to Choose, When to Buy.* Chicago, 1978. $2.50.

Gabriel, Michael R. *The Microform Revolution in Libraries.* Greenwich, CT: JAI Press, 1980. $32.50.

Saffady, William. *Computer-Output Microfilm: Its Library Applications.* Chicago: American Library Association, 1978. $11.

――――. *Micrographics.* Littleton, CO: Libraries Unlimited, 1978. $22.50.

Teague, Sydney. *Microform Librarianship.* 2nd ed. Boston: Butterworths, 1979. $19.95.

Networks and Interlibrary Cooperation

Giuliano, Vincent. *A New Governance Structure for OCLC: Principles and Recommendations.* Metuchen, NJ: Scarecrow Press, 1978. $10.

Kent, Allen. *The Structure and Governance of Library Networks.* New York: Marcel Dekker, 1979. $43.75.

Markuson, Barbara and Woolls, Blanche, eds. *Networks for Networkers: Critical Issues in Cooperative Library Development.* New York: Neal-Schuman, 1980. $17.95.

Martin, Susan K. *Library Networks, 1981-82.* 4th ed. White Plains, NY: Knowledge Industry Publications, 1981. $29.50.

Maruskin, Albert F. *OCLC: Its Governance, Function, Financing, and Technology.* New York: Marcel Dekker, 1980. $22.75.

OCLC: A Bibliography. Columbus, OH: OCLC, Inc., 1979.

Rouse, William and S. H. *Management of Library Networks: Policy Analyses, Implementation, and Control.* New York: Wiley, 1980. $28.95.

Periodicals and Serials

Brown, Clara D. *Serials: Past, Present, Future.* 2nd rev. ed. Birmingham: Ebsco Industries Inc., 1980. $19.50.

Davinson, Donald. *The Periodicals Collection.* 2nd ed. Boulder, CO: Westview, $26.75.

Marshall, Joan K., comp. *Serials for Libraries.* Santa Barbara, CA: ABC-Clio, 1980. $52.50.

Osborn, Andrew D. *Serial Publications: Their Place and Treatment in Libraries.* 3rd ed. Chicago: American Library Association, 1980. $20.

Public Libraries

Book Reading and Library Usage: A Study of Habits and Perceptions. Conducted for ALA. Princeton, NJ: The Gallup Organization, 1978. Available from ALA. $25.

Geddes, Andrew. *Fiscal Responsibility and the Small Public Library.* Small Libraries Publications No. 3. Chicago: American Library Association, 1978. $1.

Getz, Malcolm. *Public Libraries: An Economic View.* Baltimore, MD: Johns Hopkins, 1980. $12.50.

Hanna, Patricia B. *People Make It Happen: The Possibilities of Outreach in Every Phase of Public Library Service.* Metuchen, NJ: Scarecrow Press, 1978. $10.

Jenkins, Harold R. *Management of a Public Library.* Greenwich, CT: JAI Press, 1980. $32.50.

Local Public Library Administration, completely revised by Ellen Altman. 2nd ed. Chicago: American Library Association, 1980. $20.

Palmour, Vernon E. *Planning Process for Public Libraries.* Chicago: American Library Association, 1980. $12.

Public Library Association. *The Public Library Mission Statement and Its Imperatives for Service.* Chicago: American Library Association, 1979. $2.

Role of the Humanities in the Public Library, ed. by R. Broadus. Chicago: American Library Association, 1980. $20.

Sinclair, Dorothy. *Administration of the Small Public Library.* Chicago: American Library Association, 1979. $12.

Wheeler and Goldhor's Practical Administration of Public Libraries, completely revised by Carlton Rochell. New York: Harper & Row, 1981. $27.50.

Reference Services

Fjallbrant, Nancy, and Stevenson, Malcolm. *User Education in Libraries.* Hamden, CT: Shoe String, 1978. $12.50.

Jahoda, Gerald. *Librarian and Reference Queries: A Systematic Approach.* New York: Academic Press, 1980. $12.

Katz, William A. *An Introduction to Reference Work.* 3rd rev. ed. New York: McGraw-Hill, 1978, 2 vols. Vol. 1, $14.95. Vol. 2, $13.95.

———, and Tarr, Andrea. *Reference and Information Services: A Reader.* Metuchen, NJ: Scarecrow Press, 1978. $15.

Library Orientation Series. 1–12; 1972–1981. 1 o.p.; 2–12 $14.95. Recent vols. have been on Reform and Renewal in Higher Education: Implementation for Library Administration; Library Instruction and Faculty Development; Directions for the Decade: Library Instruction for the 1980s.

Lockwood, Deborah. *Library Instruction: A Bibliography.* Westport, CT: Greenwood Press, 1979. $16.50.

Lubans, John. *Progress in Educating the Library User.* New York: R. R. Bowker, 1978. $16.95.

Morehead, Joe. *Introduction to United States Public Documents.* 2nd ed. Littleton, CO: Libraries Unlimited, 1978. $22.50.

Morgan, Candace, ed. *The Purposes of Reference Measurement.* Chicago: American Library Association, 1978. $2.

Online Searching: An Introduction. Woburn, MA: Butterworths, 1980. $31.95.

Reference and Online Services Handbook: Guidelines, Policies and Procedures for Libraries, ed. by Bill Katz. New York: Neal-Schuman, 1981. $19.95.

Renford, Beverly. *Bibliographic Instruction: A Handbook.* New York: Neal-Schuman, 1980. $14.95.

Sheehy, Eugene, P. *Guide to Reference Books.* 9th ed. Chicago: American Library Association, 1976. $30. 1st supplement, 1980. $15.

Watson, Peter G., ed. *Charging for Computer-Based Reference Services.* Chicago: American Library Association, 1978. $4.

Research

Busha, Charles H. *Research Methods in Librarianship: Techniques and Interpretation.* New York: Academic Press, 1980. $19.50.

Carpenter, Ray L. *Statistical Methods for Librarians.* Chicago: American Library Association, 1978. $14.

Chen, Ching-Chih, ed. *Quantitative Measurement and Dynamic Library Service.* Phoenix, AZ: Oryx Press, 1978. $19.50.

Library Science Research Reader and Bibliographic Guide, ed. by Charles H. Busha. Littleton, CO: Libraries Unlimited, 1981. $22.50.

School Libraries

Bell, Irene. *Basic Media Skills through Games.* Littleton, CO: Libraries Unlimited, 1979. $17.50.

Billings, Rolland G., and Goldman, Errol. *Professional Negotiations for Media/Library Professionals: District and School.* Washington, DC: Association for Educational Communication and Technology, 1980. $8.50.

Cole, John Y., ed. *Television, the Book, and the Classroom.* Washington, DC: Library of Congress, 1978. $4.95.

Davies, Ruth Ann. *School Library Media Program: Instructional Force for Excellence.* 3rd ed. New York: R. R. Bowker, 1979. $16.95.

Galvin, T. J. *Excellence in School Media Programs.* Chicago: American Library Association, 1980. $12.50.

Hart, Thomas L., ed. *Instruction in School Media Use.* Chicago: American Library Association, 1978. $9.

Hicks, Warren. *Managing the Building-level School Media Program.* Chicago: American Library Association, 1981.

Martin, Betty, and Carson, Ben. *The Principal's Handbook on the School Library Media Center.* Syracuse, NY: Gaylord Professional Publications, 1978. $8.95.

Schmid, William T. *Media Center Management: A Practical Guide.* New York: Hastings House, 1980. $16.95.

Taggart, Dorothy. *Management and Administration of the School Library Media Program.* New York: Library Professional Publications, 1980. $16.50.

Taylor, Mary M. *School Library and Media Center Acquisitions: Policies and Procedures.* Phoenix, AZ: Oryx Press, 1981. $17.50.

Thomason, Nevada Wallis. *The Library Media Specialist in Curriculum Development.* Metuchen, NJ: Scarecrow, 1981. $15.

Services for Special Groups

Bell, Lorna J. *The Large Print Book and its User.* Phoenix, AZ: Oryx Press, 1980. $33.

Books for the Gifted Child, ed. by Barbara H. Baskin and Karen H. Harris. New York: R. R. Bowker, 1980. $17.95.

Clendening, Corinne P. and Davies, Ruth Ann. *Creating Programs for the Gifted: A Guide for Teachers, Librarians, and Students.* New York: R. R. Bowker, 1980. $24.95.

Cylke, Frank K. *Library Service for the Blind and Physically Handicapped: An International Approach.* New York: K. G. Saur, 1978. $19.50.

Graves, Michael, et al. *Easy Reading: Book Series and Periodicals for the Less Able Reader.* Newark, DE: International Reading Association, 1979. $4.50.

High/Low Handbook: Books, Materials and Services for the Teenage Problem Reader, ed. by Ellen V. LiBretto. New York: Bowker, 1981. $19.95.

Jail Library Service: A Guide for Librarians and Jail Administrators, ed. by Linda Bayley and others. Chicago: American Library Association, 1981. $14.

Jones, Edward V., III. *Reading Instruction for the Adult Illiterate.* Chicago: American Library Association, 1981. $12.50.

Marshall, Margaret Richardson. *Libraries and the Handicapped Child.* Boulder, CO: Westview Press, 1981. $26.25.

Meeting the Needs of the Handicapped: A Resource for Teachers and Librarians, ed. by Carol H. Thomas and James L. Thomas. Phoenix, AZ: Oryx Press, 1980. $18.50.

Pearlman, Della. *No Choice: Library Services for the Mentally Handicapped.* Phoenix, AZ: Oryx Press, 1981. $15.

Rubin, Rhea Joyce, ed. *Bibliotherapy Sourcebook.* Phoenix, AZ: Oryx Press, 1978. $19.50.

———. *Using Bibliotherapy: A Guide to Theory and Technique.* Phoenix, AZ: Oryx Press, 1978. $17.95.

Schauder, Donald E., and Gram, Malcolm. *Libraries for the Blind: An International Study of Policies and Practices.* Steverage, Herts., England: Peter Peregrinas, 1979. $21.50.

Velleman, Ruth A. *Serving Physically Disabled People: An Information Handbook for All Libraries.* New York: R. R. Bowker, 1979. $17.50.

Wright, Keith. *Library and Information Services for Handicapped Individuals.* Littleton, CO: Libraries Unlimited, 1979. $17.50.

Special Libraries

Larsgaard, Mary. *Map Librarianship.* Littleton, CO: Libraries Unlimited, 1978. $18.50.

Ristow, Walter W. *The Emergence of Maps in Libraries.* Hamden, CT: Shoe String, 1980. $27.50.

Special Librarianship: A New Reader. Metuchen, NJ: Scarecrow, 1980. $27.50.

Van Halm, Johan. *The Development of Special Libraries as an International Phenomenon.* New York: Special Libraries Association, 1978. $19.50.

State Libraries

The ASLA Report on Interlibrary Cooperation. Chicago: Association of State Library Agencies (ALA), 1980. $15.

The State Library Agencies: A Survey Project Report, 1981, comp. and ed. by Ann B. Walker. Chicago: Association of Specialized and Cooperative Library Agencies, 1981. $25.

Technical Services

Bernhardt, Frances Simonsen. *Introduction to Library Technical Services.* New York: H. W. Wilson, 1979. $15.

Technical Services: Acquisitions

Grieder, Ted. *Acquisitions: Where, What and How.* Westport, CT: Greenwood Press, 1978. $22.50.

Technical Services: Cataloging and Classification

American Library Association. Filing Committee. *ALA Filing Rules.* Chicago: American Library Association, 1980. $4.

Berman, Sanford. *Joy of Cataloging: Essays, Letters, Reviews and Other Explosions.* Phoenix, AZ: Oryx Press, 1981. $22.50.

The Card Catalog—Current Issues, Readings and Selected Bibliography. Metuchen, NJ: Scarecrow, 1981. $16.

Chan, Lois Mai. *Cataloging and Classification: An Introduction.* New York: McGraw-Hill, 1981. $18.95.

———. *Immroth's Guide to the Library of Congress Classification.* Littleton, CO: Libraries Unlimited, 1980. $27.50.

———. *Library of Congress Subject Headings: Principles and Applications.* Littleton, CO: Libraries Unlimited, 1978. $22.50.

Clack, Doris Hargrett. *The Making of a Code: Issues underlying AACR2.* Chicago: American Library Association, 1980. $15.

Closing the Catalog, ed. by Kaye Gapen. Phoenix, AZ: Oryx Press, 1980. $18.50.

Dewey, Melvil. *Abridged Dewey Decimal Classification and Relative Index.* 11th ed. New York: Forest Press, 1979. $27.

Gorman, Michael. *Concise AACR2.* Chicago: American Library Association, 1981. $7.50.

Gorman, Michael, and Winkler, Paul W., eds. *Anglo-American Cataloging Rules.* 2nd ed. Chicago: American Library Association, 1978. $20.

Lehnus, Donald J. *Book Numbers: History, Principles and Application.* Chicago: American Library Association, 1981. $7.50.

Malinconico, S. Michael, and Fasana, Paul. *The Future of the Catalog: The Library's Choices.* White Plains, NY: Knowledge Industry, 1979. $24.50.

Manheimer, Martha L. *OCLC: An Introduction to Searching and Input.* New York: Neal-Schuman, 1979. $9.95.

Rather, John Carson. *Library of Congress Filing Rules.* Washington, DC: Library of Congress, 1980.

Smith, Lynn S. *A Practical Approach to Serials Cataloging.* Greenwich, CT: JAI Press, 1978. $37.50.

Wellisch, Hans H. *Indexing and Abstracting: A Guide to International Sources.* Santa Barbara, CA: ABC-Clio, 1980. $32.50.

Wynar, Bohdan, et al. *Introduction to Cataloging and Classification.* 6th ed. Metuchen, NJ: Libraries Unlimited, 1980. $25.

PERIODICALS

The journals listed below are titles that might normally be purchased as part of a continuing education program in a library or as subscriptions for individual librarians. Titles used primarily for selection have been excluded.

ALA Washington Newsletter
American Libraries
American Society for Information Science Journal
CABLIS (Current Awareness for Librarianship and Information Scientists)
Cataloging and Classification Quarterly
Collection Management
College and Research Libraries
Conservation Administration News
Drexel Library Quarterly
IFLA Journal
International Library Review
Journal of Academic Librarianship
Journal of Education for Librarianship
Journal of Library Administration
Journal of Library Automation
Journal of Library History, Philosophy, and Comparative Librarianship
Library Journal
Library of Congress Information Bulletin
Library Quarterly
Library Research
Library Resources and Technical Services
Library Trends
Newsletter on Intellectual Freedom
OnLine
Online Review
Public Library Quarterly
RQ
RSR (Reference Services Review)
School Library Journal
School Media Quarterly
Serials Librarian
Serials Review
Special Libraries
Top of the News

UNESCO Journal of Information Science, Librarianship, and Archives Administration

VOYA: Voice of Youth Advocates

Wilson Library Bulletin

BASIC PUBLICATIONS FOR THE PUBLISHER AND THE BOOK TRADE

Jean R. Peters

Librarian, R. R. Bowker Company

BIBLIOGRAPHIES OF BOOKS ABOUT BOOKS AND THE BOOK TRADE

These six books contain extensive bibliographies.

Gottlieb, Robin. *Publishing Children's Books in America, 1919-1976: An Annotated Bibliography.* New York: Children's Book Council, 1978. $15.

Lee, Marshall. *Bookmaking: The Illustrated Guide to Design/Production/Editing.* New York: R. R. Bowker, 1980. $32.50. Bibliography is divided into four parts: Part I covers books and includes a general bibliography as well as extensive coverage of books on all technical aspects of bookmaking; Part 2 lists periodicals; Part 3 lists films, filmstrips, etc.; Part 4 lists other sources.

Lehmann-Haupt, Hellmut, Wroth, Lawrence C., and Silver, Rollo. *The Book in America.* 2nd ed. New York: R. R. Bowker, 1951, o.p. Bibliography covers cultural history, bibliography, printing and bookmaking, book illustration, bookselling, and publishing.

Melcher, Daniel, and Larrick, Nancy. *Printing and Promotion Handbook.* 3rd ed. New York: McGraw-Hill, 1966. $24.95. Bibliography covers general reference, advertising, artwork, book publishing, color, copyright, copywriting, direct mail, displays, editing and proofreading, layout and design, lettering, magazine publishing, newspaper publishing, packaging, paper, photography, printing, publicity, radio and TV, shipping, typography, and visual aids.

The Reader's Adviser: A Layman's Guide to Literature. 12th ed. 3 vols. New York: R. R. Bowker, 1974-1977. $75 (3-vol. set); $29.95 (ea. vol.). Vol. 1. *The Best in American and British Fiction, Poetry, Essays, Literary Biography, Bibliography, and Reference,* edited by Sarah L. Prakken. 1974. Chapters "Books about Books" and "Bibliography" cover history of publishing and bookselling, practice of publishing, bookmaking, rare book collecting, trade and specialized bibliographies, book selection tools, best books, etc. Vol. 2. *The Best in American and British Drama and World Literature in English Translation,* edited by F. J. Sypher. 1977. Vol. 3. *The Best in the Reference Literature of the World,* edited by Jack A. Clarke. 1977.

Tanselle, G. Thomas. *Guide to the Study of United States Imprints.* 2 vols. Cambridge, Mass.: Belknap Press of Harvard University Press, 1971. $60. Includes sections on general studies of American printing and publishing as well as studies of individual printers and publishers.

TRADE BIBLIOGRAPHIES

American Book Publishing Record Cumulative, 1876-1949: An American Na-

tional Bibliography. 15 vols. New York: R. R. Bowker, 1980. $1,975.

American Book Publishing Record Cumulative, 1950–1977: An American National Bibliography. 15 vols. New York: R. R. Bowker, 1979. $1,975.

American Book Publishing Record Five-Year Cumulatives. New York: R. R. Bowker, 1960–1964 Cumulative. 5 vols. $150. 1965–1969 Cumulative. 5 vols. $150. 1970–1974 Cumulative. 4 vols. $150. 1975–1979 Cumulative. 5 vols. $175. Annual vols.: 1978, $53; 1979, $53; 1980, $59; 1981, $68.

Book Publishers Directory: An Information Service Covering New and Established, Private and Special Interest, Avant-Garde and Alternative, Organization and Association, Government and Institution Presses, edited by Elizabeth Geiser and Annie Brewer. Detroit: Gale, 1981. $160. Supplement, 1980. $68.

Books in Print. 4 vols. New York: R. R. Bowker, ann. $129.50.

Books in Print Supplement. New York: R. R. Bowker, ann. $67.50.

Books in Series in the United States. 3rd ed. New York: R. R. Bowker, 1980. $175.

British Books in Print: The Reference Catalog of Current Literature. New York: R. R. Bowker, 1981. $140 (plus duty where applicable).

Canadian Books in Print, edited by Martha Pluscauskas. Toronto: University of Toronto Press, ann. $40.

Canadian Books in Print: Subject Index, edited by Martha Pluscauskas. Toronto: University of Toronto Press, ann. $35.

Cumulative Book Index. New York: H. W. Wilson. Monthly with bound semiannual and larger cumulations. Service basis.

El-Hi Textbooks in Print. New York: R. R. Bowker, ann. $41.

Forthcoming Books. New York: R. R. Bowker. $55 a year. $12.50 single copy. Bimonthly supplement to *Books in Print.*

Large Type Books in Print. New York: R. R. Bowker, 1980. $19.95.

Paperbound Books in Print. New York: R. R. Bowker. 2 vols. $43.

Publishers' Trade List Annual. New York: R. R. Bowker, ann. 5 vols. $62.50.

Robert, Reginald, and Burgess, M. R. *Cumulative Paperback Index, 1939–59.* Detroit: Gale, 1973. $38.

Small Press Record of Books in Print, edited by Len Fulton. Paradise, Calif.: Dustbooks, 1981. $21.95.

Subject Guide to Books in Print. 3 vols. New York: R. R. Bowker, ann. $89.50.

Subject Guide to Forthcoming Books. New York: R. R. Bowker. $39.50 a year. $79.50 in combination with *Forthcoming Books.*

Turner, Mary C., ed. *Libros en Venta.* Supplement, 1978. New York: R. R. Bowker, 1980. $42.50. A Spanish-language "Books in Print/Subject Guide."

BOOK PUBLISHING

Education and Practice

Association of American University Presses. *One Book—Five Ways: The Publishing Procedures of Five University Presses.* Los Altos, Calif.: William Kaufmann, 1978. $18.75. pap. $10.75.

Bailey, Herbert S., Jr. *The Art and Science of Book Publishing.* Austin: University of Texas Press, 1980. pap. $7.95.

Bodian, Nat G. *Book Marketing Handbook: Tips and Techniques for the Sale and Promotion of Scientific, Technical, Professional, and Scholarly Books and Journals.* New York: R. R. Bowker, 1980. $45.

Bohne, Harald, and Van Ierssel, Harry. *Publishing: The Creative Business.* Toronto: Association of Canadian Publishers, 1973. pap. $7.50.

Crutchley, Brooke. *To Be a Printer.* New York: Cambridge University Press, 1980. $19.95.

Dessauer, John P. *Book Publishing: What It Is, What It Does.* New York: R. R. Bowker, 1981. $23.95. pap. $13.95.

Glaister, Geoffrey. *Glaister's Glossary of the Book: Terms Used in Paper-Making, Printing, Bookbinding, and Publishing.* 2nd ed., completely rev. Berkeley: University of California Press, 1979. $75.

Grannis, Chandler B. *Getting into Book Publishing.* New York: R. R. Bowker, 1979. Pamphlet, one free; in bulk 75¢ each.

Grannis, Chandler B., ed. *What Happens in Book Publishing.* 2nd ed. New York: Columbia University Press, 1967. $22.50.

Greenfeld, Howard. *Books: From Writer to Reader.* New York: Crown, 1976. $8.95. pap. $4.95.

Hackett, Alice Payne, and Burke, Henry James. *Eighty Years of Best Sellers, 1895-1975.* New York: R. R. Bowker, 1977. $18.95.

Peters, Jean, ed. *Bookman's Glossary.* 5th ed. New York: R. R. Bowker, 1975. $12.50.

Smith, Datus C., Jr. *A Guide to Book Publishing.* New York: R. R. Bowker, 1966. $14.25.

To Be a Publisher: A Handbook on Some Principles and Programs in Publishing Education. Prepared by the Association of American Publishers Education for Publishing Program. New York: Association of American Publishers, 1979. $10.

Analysis, Statistics, Surveys

ANSI Standards Committee Z-39. *American National Standard for Compiling Book Publishing Statistics, Z-39.8.* New York: American National Standards Institute. 1978. $4.

Altbach, Philip G., and McVey, Sheila, eds. *Perspectives on Publishing.* Lexington, Mass.: Lexington Books, 1976. $24.95.

Altbach, Philip G., and Rathgeber, Eva-Marie. *Publishing in the Third World: Trend Report and Bibliography.* New York: Praeger, 1980. $22.50.

Arthur Andersen & Co. *Book Distribution in the U.S.: Issues and Perspectives.* New York: Book Industry Study Group, 1982. $49.

Association of American Publishers 1980 Industry Statistics. New York: Association of American Publishers, 1981. Nonmemb. $220.

Benjamin, Curtis G. *A Candid Critique of Book Publishing.* New York: R. R. Bowker, 1977. $16.50.

Book Industry Trends, 1981. Five sections in looseleaf format with binder: *Book Industry Markets, 1976-1985,* by John P. Dessauer; *Economic Trends and the Book Industry,* by E. Wayne Nordberg; *Trends in Textbook Markets,* by J. Kendrick Noble, Jr.; *The Book Industry, 1981,* by Paul D. Doebler; *Publishing and Marketing Books in Canada,* by Peter H. Neuman. New York: Book Industry Study Group, 1981. $995; $600 to libraries; price includes annual subscription to *BISG Bulletin. Book Industry Trends, 1979* and *Book Industry Trends, 1980* still available.

Bowker Annual of Library and Book Trade Information. New York: R. R. Bowker, ann. $45.

Bowker Lectures on Book Publishing. New York: R. R. Bowker, 1957. o.p.

Bowker Lectures on Book Publishing, New Series. New York: R. R. Bowker. 9 vols. 1973-1981. $3 each. No. 1. Pilpel, Harriet F. *Obscenity and the Constitution.* 1973. No. 2. Ringer, Barbara A. *The Demonology of Copyright.* 1974. No. 3. Henne, Frances E. *The Library World and the Publishing of Children's Books.* 1975. No. 4. Vaughan, Samuel S. *Medium Rare: A Look at the Book and Its People.* 1976. No. 5. Bailey, Herbert S. *The Traditional Book in the Electronic*

Age. 1977. No. 6. Mayer, Peter. *The Spirit of the Enterprise.* 1978. No. 7. De Gennaro, Richard. *Research Libraries Enter the Information Age.* 1979. No. 8. Dystel, Oscar. *Mass Market Publishing: More Observations, Speculations and Provocations.* 1980. No. 9. Giroux, Robert. *The Education of an Editor.* 1981.

The Business of Publishing: A PW Anthology. New York: R. R. Bowker, 1976. $18.50.

Cheney, O. H. *Economic Survey of the Book Industry, 1930-31.* The Cheney Report. Reprinted. New York: R. R. Bowker, 1960. o.p.

Compaine, Benjamin. *The Book Industry in Transition: An Economic Study of Book Distribution and Marketing.* White Plains, N.Y.: Knowledge Industry Publications, 1978. $24.95.

Coser, Lewis, A., Kadushin, Charles, and Powell, Walter W. *Books: The Culture and Commerce of Publishing.* New York: Basic Books, 1981. $19.

Fitzgerald, Frances. *America Revised: History Schoolbooks in the Twentieth Century.* Boston: Little, Brown, 1979. $11.95.

Gedin, Per. *Literature in the Marketplace.* Translated by George Bisset. Woodstock, N.Y.: Overlook, 1977. $12.95.

Kujoth, Jean Spealman. *Book Publishing: Inside Views.* Metuchen, N.J.: Scarecrow, 1971. $15.50.

Machlup, Fritz, and Leeson, Kenneth W. *Information through the Printed Word: The Dissemination of Scholarly, Scientific, and Intellectual Knowledge.* 4 vols. Vol. 1. *Book Publishing.* Vol. 2. *Journals.* Vol. 3. *Libraries.* Vol. 4. *Books, Journals, and Bibliographic Records.* New York: Praeger, 1978. Vol. 1, $28.95; Vol. 2, $30.95; Vol. 3, $25.95; Vol. 4, $29.95.

Smith, Roger H., ed. *The American Reading Public: A Symposium.* New York: R. R. Bowker, 1964. o.p.

Whiteside, Thomas. *The Blockbuster Complex.* Middletown, Conn.: Wesleyan University Press. Distributed by Columbia University Press, 1981. $12.95.

Yankelovich, Skelly, and White, Inc. *The 1978 Consumer Research Study on Reading and Book Purchasing.* New York: Book Industry Study Group, 1978. Apply for price scale.

History

Briggs, Asa, ed. *Essays in the History of Publishing: In Celebration of the 250th Anniversary of the House of Longman, 1724-1974.* New York: Longman, 1974. $15.

Cerf, Bennett. *At Random: The Reminiscences of Bennett Cerf.* New York: Random House, 1977. $12.95.

Haydn, Hiram. *Words & Faces.* New York: Harcourt Brace Jovanovich, 1974. $8.95.

Hodges, Sheila. *Golancz: The Story of a Publishing House.* London: Golancz, 1978. £7.50.

Kurian, George. *Directory of American Book Publishing: From Founding Fathers to Today's Conglomerates.* New York: Monarch, 1975. $25.

Lehmann-Haupt, Hellmut. *The Book in America.* 2nd ed. New York: R. R. Bowker, 1951. o.p.

Madison, Charles. *Jewish Publishing in America.* New York: Hebrew Publishing Co., 1976. $11.95.

Morpurgo, J. E. *Allen Lane: King Penguin.* New York: Methuen, 1979. $25.

Mott, Frank Luther. *Golden Multitudes: The Story of Best Sellers in the United States (1662-1945).* Reprint ed. New York: R. R. Bowker, 1960. o.p.

O'Brien, Geoffrey. *Hardboiled America: The Lurid Years of Paperbacks.* New York: Van Nostrand Reinhold, 1981. $16.95.

Regnery, Henry. *Memoirs of a Dissident Publisher.* New York: Harcourt Brace Jovanovich, 1979. $12.95.

Schick, Frank L. *The Paperbound Book in America: The History of Paperbacks and Their European Background.* New York: R. R. Bowker, 1958. o.p.

Schreuders, Piet. *Paperbacks U.S.A.: A Graphic History, 1939-1959.* Translated from the Dutch by Josh Pachter. San Diego: Blue Dolphin Enterprises, 1981. $10.95.

Stern, Madeleine B. *Books and Book People in 19th-Century America.* New York: R. R. Bowker, 1978. $28.50.

――――. *Publishers for Mass Entertainment in Nineteenth Century America.* Boston: G. K. Hall, 1980. $25.

Tebbel, John. *A History of Book Publishing in the United States.* 4 vols. Vol. 1. *The Creation of an Industry, 1630-1865.* Vol. 2. *The Expansion of an Industry, 1865-1919.* Vol. 3. *The Golden Age between Two Wars, 1920-1940.* Vol. 4. *The Great Change, 1940-1980.* New York: R. R. Bowker, 1972, 1975, 1978, 1981. $37.50 each.

SCHOLARLY BOOKS

Gaskell, Philip. *From Writer to Reader: Studies in Editorial Method.* New York: Oxford University Press, 1978. $29.50.

Harman, Eleanor, and Montagnes, Ian, eds. *The Thesis and the Book.* Toronto: University of Toronto Press, 1976. $10. pap. $6.

Horne, David. *Boards and Buckram: Writings from "Scholarly Books in America," 1962-1969.* Hanover, N.H.: University Press of New England, 1980. Distributed by American University Press Services, Inc., New York. $10.

Nemeyer, Carol A. *Scholarly Reprint Publishing in the United States.* New York: R. R. Bowker, 1972. o.p.

Scholarly Communication: The Report of the National Enquiry. Baltimore: Johns Hopkins University Press, 1979. $12.95. pap. $4.95.

EDITORS, AGENTS, AUTHORS

Appelbaum, Judith, and Evans, Nancy. *How to Get Happily Published.* New York: Harper & Row, 1978. $11.95.

Berg, A. Scott. *Max Perkins: Editor of Genius.* New York: Pocket Books. pap. $2.95.

Commins, Dorothy Berliner. *What Is an Editor? Saxe Commins at Work.* Chicago: University of Chicago Press, 1978. $10.

Henderson, Bill, ed. *The Art of Literary Publishing: Editors on Their Craft.* Yonkers, N.Y.: Pushcart, 1980. $15.

Madison, Charles. *Irving to Irving: Author-Publisher Relations: 1800-1974.* New York: R. R. Bowker, 1974. $15.95.

Mitchell, Burroughs. *The Education of an Editor.* Garden City, N.Y.: Doubleday, 1980. $8.95.

Reynolds, Paul R. *The Middle Man: The Adventures of a Literary Agent.* New York: Morrow, 1972. $6.95.

Strauss, Helen M. *A Talent for Luck.* New York: Random House, 1979. $12.95.

Unseld, Siegfried. *The Author and His Publisher.* Chicago: University of Chicago Press, 1980. $12.50.

Watson, Graham. *Book Society: Reminiscences of a Literary Agent.* New York: Atheneum, 1980. $10.95.

BOOK DESIGN AND PRODUCTION

Grannis, Chandler B. *The Heritage of the Graphic Arts.* New York: R. R. Bowker, 1972. $24.95.

Lee, Marshall. *Bookmaking: The Illustrated Guide to Design and Production.* 2nd ed. New York: R. R. Bowker, 1979. $32.50.

Rice, Stanley. *Book Design: Systematic Aspects.* New York: R. R. Bowker, 1978. $18.95.

――――. *Book Design: Text Format Models.* New York: R. R. Bowker, 1978. $18.95.

Strauss, Victor. *The Printing Industry: An Introduction to Its Many Branches, Processes and Products.* New York: R. R. Bowker, 1967. $32.50.

White, Jan. *Editing by Design.* 2nd ed. New York: R. R. Bowker, 1982. pap. $24.95.

Wilson, Adrian. *The Design of Books.* Layton, Utah: Peregrine Smith, 1974. pap. $9.95.

BOOKSELLING

Anderson, Charles B., ed. *Bookselling in America and the World: A Souvenir Book Celebrating the 75th Anniversary of the American Booksellers Association.* New York: Times Books, 1975. $9.50.

Bliven, Bruce. *Book Traveller.* New York: Dodd, Mead, 1975. $4.95.

Manual on Bookselling: How to Open and Run Your Own Bookstore. 3rd ed. New York: American Booksellers Association, 1980. Distributed by Harmony Books. $15.95. pap. $8.95.

CENSORSHIP

de Grazia, Edward, comp. *Censorship Landmarks.* New York: R. R. Bowker, 1969. $29.50.

Ernst, Morris L., and Schwartz, Alan U. *Censorship.* New York: Macmillan, 1964. $6.95.

Haight, Anne Lyon. *Banned Books.* 4th ed., updated and enlarged by Chandler B. Grannis. New York: R. R. Bowker, 1978. $14.95.

Hentoff, Nat. *The First Freedom: The Tumultuous History of Free Speech in America.* New York: Delacorte, 1980. $9.95.

Jenkinson, Edward B. *Censors in the Classroom: The Mind Benders.* Carbondale, Ill.: Southern Illinois University Press, 1979. $13.95.

Moon, Eric, ed. *Book Selection and Censorship in the Sixties.* New York: R. R. Bowker, 1969. $18.95.

COPYRIGHT

Bogsch, Arpad. *The Law of Copyright under the Universal Convention.* 3rd ed. New York: R. R. Bowker, 1969. o.p.

Cambridge Research Institute. *Omnibus Copyright Revision: Comparative Analysis of the Issues.* Washington, D.C.: American Society for Information Science, 1973. $48.

Copyright Revision Act of 1976: Law, Explanation, Committee Reports. Chicago: Commerce Clearing House, 1976. $12.50.

Johnston, Donald F. *Copyright Handbook.* 2nd ed. New York: R. R. Bowker, 1982. $24.95.

Wittenberg, Philip. *Protection of Literary Property.* Boston: The Writer, Inc., 1978. $12.95.

BOOK TRADE DIRECTORIES AND YEARBOOKS

American and Canadian

American Book Trade Directory, 1981. 27th ed. New York: R. R. Bowker, ann. $69.95.

Chernofsky, Jacob L., ed. *AB Bookman's Yearbook.* 2 vols. Clifton, N.J.: AB Bookman's Weekly, ann. $10; free to subscribers to *AB Bookman's Weekly.*

Congrat-Butlar, Stefan, ed. *Translation & Translators: An International Directory and Guide.* New York: R. R. Bowker, 1979. $35.

Kim, Ung Chon. *Policies of Publishers.* Metuchen, N.J.: Scarecrow, 1978. pap. $10.

Literary Market Place, 1982, with Names & Numbers. New York: R. R. Bowker, ann. $35. The business directory of American book publishing.

Publishers, Distributors, & Wholesalers of the United States: A Directory. New York: R. R. Bowker, 1981. pap. $24.95.

U.S. Book Publishing Yearbook and Directory, 1981/82. White Plains, N.Y.:

Knowledge Industry Publications, 1981. $60.

Foreign and International

International ISBN Publishers Directory. New York: R. R. Bowker, 1981. $95.

International Literary Market Place 1982-83. New York: R. R. Bowker, 1981. $50.

Publishers' International Directory. New York: K. G. Saur. Distributed by Shoestring Press, 1979. $140.

Taubert, Sigfred, ed. *The Book Trade of the World.* Vol. I. Europe and International Sections. Vol. II. U.S.A., Canada, Central and South America, Australia and New Zealand. Vol. III. Africa, Asia. New York: R. R. Bowker. Vol. I, 1972, $70; Vol. II, 1976, $70; Vol. III, 1980, $70.

UNESCO Statistical Yearbook, 1980. New York: Unipub, 1981. $104.

Who Distributes What and Where: An International Directory of Publishers, Imprints, Agents, and Distributors. New York: R. R. Bowker, 1981. $44.

Newspapers and Periodicals

Directory of Newspapers and Periodicals. Philadelphia: N. W. Ayer, ann. $68.

Editor and Publisher International Year Book. New York: Editor and Publisher, ann. $35.

Irregular Serials and Annuals: An International Directory. New York: R. R. Bowker, 1981. $75.

Magazine Industry Market Place: The Directory of American Periodical Publishing. New York: R. R. Bowker, 1981. $37.50.

New Serial Titles 1950-1970. New York: R. R. Bowker, 1973. 4 vols. o.p. Available on microfilm, $100; or xerographic reprint, $250.

New Serial Titles 1950-1970, Subject Guide. New York: R. R. Bowker, 1975. 2 vols. $138.50.

Sources of Serials: An International Publisher and Corporate Author Directory to Ulrich's and Irregular Serials. New York: R. R. Bowker, 1981. $65.

Ulrich's International Periodicals Directory. 20th ed. New York: R. R. Bowker, 1981. $78.

Working Press of the Nation: Newspapers, Magazines, Radio and TV, and Internal Publications. Chicago: National Research Bureau, ann. 5 vols. $205.

EDITING

Barzun, Jacques. *Simple and Direct: A Rhetoric for Writers.* New York: Harper & Row, 1976. $11.95.

Bernstein, Theodore. *The Careful Writer.* New York: Atheneum, 1965. $14.95. pap. $8.95.

Fowler, H. W. *Directory of Modern English Usage.* 2nd rev. ed. New York: Oxford University Press, 1965. $12.50.

Jordan, Lewis. *The New York Times Manual of Style and Usage.* New York: Times Books, 1976. $10.

A Manual of Style. 12th rev. ed. Chicago: University of Chicago Press, 1969. $20.

Skillin, Marjorie E., and Gay, Robert M. *Words into Type.* Rev. ed. Englewood Cliffs, N.J.: Prentice-Hall, 1974. $18.95.

Strunk, William, Jr., and White, E. B. *Elements of Style.* 3rd ed. New York: Macmillan, 1978. $4.95. pap. $1.95.

Zinsser, William. *On Writing Well: An Informal Guide to Writing Nonfiction.* 2nd ed. New York: Harper & Row, 1980. $8.95.

PERIODICALS

AB Bookman's Weekly (weekly including yearbook). Clifton, N.J.: AB Bookman's Weekly. $50.

American Book Publishing Record (monthly). New York: R. R. Bowker. $38.50.

The American Bookseller (monthly). New York: American Booksellers Association. $12.

BP Report: On the Business of Book Publishing (weekly). White Plains, N.Y.: Knowledge Industry Publications. $195.

Printing and Publishing: Quarterly Industry Report. Washington, D.C.: U.S. Department of Commerce. $7.50.

Publishers Weekly. New York: R. R. Bowker. $51.

Scholarly Publishing: A Journal for Authors & Publishers (quarterly). Toronto: University of Toronto Press. $25.

Weekly Record. New York: R. R. Bowker. $32.50. A weekly listing of current American book publications, providing complete cataloging information.

For a list of periodicals reviewing books, see *Literary Market Place.*

DISTINGUISHED BOOKS

LITERARY PRIZES, 1981

ASCAP-Deems Taylor Awards. *Offered by:* American Society of Composers, Authors, and Publishers. *Winners:* Thomas Delong for *The Mighty Music Box* (Amber Crest Books); Peter Kivy for *The Corded Shell* (Princeton University Press); William Lee for *Stan Kenton/Artistry in Rhythm* (Creative Press of Los Angeles); Drew Page for *Drew's Blues* (Louisiana State University Press); George Perle for *The Operas of Alban Berg* (University of California Press); Charles Rosen for *Sonata Forms* (Norton).

Academy of American Poets Fellowship Award. For distinguished poetic achievement. *Winner:* Richard Hugo.

Jane Addams Children's Book Award. For a book promoting the cause of peace, social justice, and world community. *Offered by:* Women's International League for Peace and Freedom and the Jane Addams Peace Association. *Winner:* Florence Meiman for *First Woman in Congress: Jeanette Rankin* (Dell/Yearling).

American Academy and Institute of Arts and Letters Awards in Literature. *Winners:* Louise Glück, Gail Godwin, Howard Frank Mosher, James Salter, Elizabeth Sewell, William Stafford, Hilma Wolitzer, Jay Wright; John Guare (award of merit medal for drama).

American Academy in Rome Fellowship in Creative Writing. *Offered by:* American Academy and Institute of Arts and Letters. *Winner:* Edward Field.

American Book Awards. *Winners:* (national medal for literature) Kenneth Burke; (autobiography/biography—hardcover) Justin Kaplan for *Walt Whitman* (Simon & Schuster); (autobiography/biography—paperback) Deirdre Bair for *Samuel Beckett* (Harcourt); (fiction—hardcover) Wright Morris for *Plains Song* (Harper & Row); (fiction—paperback) John Cheever for *The Stories of John Cheever* (Ballantine); (first novel) Ann Arensberg for *Sister Wolf* (Knopf); (general nonfiction—hardcover) Maxine Hong Kingston for *China Men* (Knopf); (general nonfiction—paperback) Jane Kramer for *The Last Cowboy* (Pocket); (history—hardcover) John Boswell for *Christianity, Social Tolerance and Homosexuality* (University of Chicago Press); (history—paperback) Leon Litwack for *Been in the Storm So Long: Aftermath of Slavery* (Vintage); (poetry) Lisel Mueller for *The Need to Hold Still* (Louisiana State University Press); (science—hardcover) Stephen Jay Gould for *The Panda's Thumb* (Norton); (science—paperback) Lewis Thomas for *The Medusa and the Snail* (Bantam); (translation) Francis Steegmuller for *The Letters of Gustave Flaubert* by Gustave Flaubert (Belknap Press/Harvard University Press) and John E. Woods for *Evening Edged in Gold* by Arno Schmitt (Harcourt); (book design/pictorial) R. D. Scudellari, designer, for *In China* by Eve Arnold (Knopf); (book design/typographical) Richard Hendel, designer, for *Saul Bellow, Drumlin Woodchuck* by Mark Harris (University of Georgia Press); (book illustration/collected art) *The Lost Museum* by Robert Adams (Viking/Studio); (jacket design-hardcover) R. D. Scudellari, designer, for *In China* by Eve Arnold (Knopf); (cover design—

paperback) Quist-Souratin, designer, for *Fiorucci: The Book* by Eve Babitz (Harlan Quist).

American Book Awards—Children's Books. *Winners:* (fiction—hardcover) Betsy Byars for *The Night Swimmers* (Delacorte); (fiction—paperback) Beverly Cleary for *Ramona and Her Mother* (Dell/Yearling); (nonfiction—hardcover) Alison Cragin Herzig and Jane Lawrence Mail for *Oh, Boy! Babies!* (Little, Brown).

American Institute of Physics/United States Steel Foundation Writing Award. *Winner:* Eric Chaisson for *Cosmic Dawn: The Origins of Matter and Life* (Atlantic-Little, Brown).

American-Scandinavian Foundation/PEN Translation Prizes. *Winners:* (fiction) Kathleen Osgood Dana for excerpts from *Here Beneath the Northern Star* by Vainö Linna (unpublished); (poetry) Lucia Moberg for song lyrics by Birger Sjöberg (unpublished).

Joseph L. Andrews Bibliographical Award. *Offered by:* American Association of Law Libraries. *Winner:* Dorothy P. Wells for *Child Abuse: An Annotated Bibliography* (Scarecrow Press).

Association of Jewish Libraries Book Awards. For outstanding contributions in the field of Jewish literature for children. *Winners:* Leonard Everett Fisher for *A Russian Farewell* (Four Winds); (body of work award) Sadie Rose Weilerstein.

Aviation/Space Writers Association Awards. *Winners:* (technical and historical reference) Peter M. Bowers for *Curtiss Aircraft, 1907-1947* (Putnam); (training) Richard L. Collins for *Tips to Fly By* (Delacorte/Eleanor Friede).

Bancroft Prizes—$4,000 each. For books of exceptional merit and distinction in American history, American diplomacy, and the international relations of the United States. *Offered by:* Columbia University. *Winners:* Ronald Steal for *Walter Lippmann and the American Century* (Atlantic-Little, Brown); Jean Strouse for *Alice James: A Biography* (Houghton).

Banta Award. *Winner:* Margot Peters for *Bernard Shaw and the Actresses* (Doubleday).

Alice Hunt Bartlett Award (Great Britain). *Winner:* John Whitworth for *Unhistorical Fragments* (Secker & Warburg).

Mildred L. Batchelder Award—citation. Intended to encourage the translation and publication in the United States of outstanding books originally written in languages other than English. *Offered by:* ALA Association for Library Service to Children. *Winners:* William Morrow Company for *The Winter When Time Was Frozen* by Els Pelgrom.

Beefeater Club Prizes for Literature. *Winners:* Godfrey Hodgson for *All Things to All Men: The False Promise of the Modern American Presidency* (Simon & Schuster); Richard Kenin for *Return to Albion: Americans in England 1760-1940* (Holt Rinehart/National Portrait Gallery, Smithsonian Institution).

Before Columbus Book Awards. *Winners:* Helen Adams, Miguel Algarin, Alta, Toni Cade Bambara, Peter Blue Cloud, Rose Drachler, Susan Howe, Alan Lau, Lionel Mitchell, Nicholas Mohr, Lawrence P. Neal, Frank Sandford, Ben Santos.

Curtis G. Benjamin Award for Creative Publishing. *Winner:* Arthur J. Rosenthal.

Benson Silver Medal (Great Britain). *Winner:* Odysseus Elytis.

Gerard and Ella Berman Award. For a book of Jewish history. *Offered by:* Jewish Book Council of the National Jewish Welfare Board. *Winner:* Mark R. Cohen for *Jewish Self-Government in Medieval Egypt* (Princeton University Press).

Biennale of Illustrations Bratislava Grand Prix (Czechoslovakia). *Winner:* Roald

Als, illustrator, for *Kristoffers Rejse* (Borgen, Denmark).

Irma Simonton Black Award. *Winner:* William Steig for *Gorky Rises* (Farrar Straus).

James Tait Black Memorial Prizes (Great Britain). *Winners:* (biography) Robert B. Martin for *Tennyson: The Unquiet Heart* (Oxford University Press/ Faber); (novel) J. M. Coetzee for *Waiting for the Barbarians* (Secker & Warburg).

Bologna Children's Book Fair Prizes (Italy). *Winners:* (graphics/children) *Yok-Yok* series by Fallimard (France) and Etienne Delessert (Switzerland); (graphics/young adults) *Insecte* by La Noria (France); (budding critics) Jerry Partridge for *Mr. Squint* by World's Work (Great Britain).

Booker McConnell Award (Great Britain). *Winner:* Salman Rushdie for *Midnight's Children* (Jonathan Cape).

Books in Canada Award for First Novels. *Winner:* W. D. Valgardson for *Gentle Sinners* (Oberon).

Boston Globe-Horn Book Awards. *Winners:* (fiction) Lynn Hall for *The Leaving* (Scribners); (nonfiction) Kathryn Lasky for *The Weaver's Gift* (Warne); (illustration) Maurice Sendak for *Outside Over There* (Harper & Row).

Brandeis University Creative Arts Award in Fiction. *Winner:* Bernard Malamud.

British Fantasy Awards. *Winners:* (novel) Ramsey Campbell for *To Wake the Dead* (Millington); (short fiction) Robert Aickman for *Stains* (New Terrors); (small press) Airgedlamh; (artist) Dave Carson; (for outstanding contribution to the genre) Stephen King.

British National Book Awards. *Winners:* (fiction) A. N. Wilson for *The Healing Art* (Secker & Warburg); (genre fiction) Ruth Rendell for *The Lake of Darkness* (Hutchinson); (creative nonfiction) Richard Jenkyns for *The Victorians and Ancient Greece* (Basil Blackwell).

John Nicholas Brown Prize. *Offered by:* Mediaeval Academy of America. *Winner:* Madeline Harrison Caviness for *The Early Stained Glass of Canterbury Cathedral, c. 1175-1220* (Princeton University Press).

John Burroughs Medal. *Winner:* Mary Durant and Michael Harwood for *On the Road with John James Audubon* (Dodd, Mead).

Witter Bynner Foundation Prize for Poetry. *Offered by:* American Academy and Institute of Arts and Letters. *Winner:* Allen Grossman.

Caldecott Medal. For the most outstanding picture book for children. *Offered by:* ALA Association for Library Service to Children. *Contributed by:* Daniel Melcher. *Winner:* Arnold Lobel for *Fables* (Harper & Row).

John W. Campbell Memorial Award. *Winner:* Gregory Benford for *Timescape* (Simon & Schuster/ Pocket).

Canada Council Translation Prizes. *Winners:* (French into English) Larry Shouldice for *Contemporary Quebec Criticism* (University of Toronto Press); (English into French) Yvan Steenhout for *Construire Sa Maison en Bois Rustique* (Editions de l'Homme).

Canadian Authors Association Literary Awards. *Winners:* (drama) Ted Galay for *After Baba's Funeral* and *Sweet and Sour Pickles* (Playwrights Canada); (fiction) Hugh MacLennan for *Voices in Time* (Macmillan/ Canada); (nonfiction) Pierre Berton for *The Invasion of Canada: 1812-13* (McClelland & Stewart); (poetry); Leona Gom for *Land of the Peace* (Thistledown Press).

Canadian Library Association/ Association of Children's Librarians Book of the Year Award. *Winner:* Donn Kushner for *The Violin Maker's Gift* (Macmillan/ Canada).

Melville Cane Award. *Offered by:* Poetry Society of America. *Winner:* Paul H. Fry for *The Poet's Calling in the English Ode* (Yale University Press).

Carey-Thomas Awards. For a distinguished project of book publishing.

Offered by: R. R. Bowker. *Winner:* Avon Books for the Bard imprint; (honor citations) Schocken Books for the Holocaust Library; Abbeville Press for *The Vatican Frescoes of Michaelangelo* (limited edition).

Carnegie Medal. For the outstanding book for children written in English and first published in the United Kingdom. *Offered by:* British Library Association. *Winner:* Peter Dickinson for *City of Gold* (Gollancz).

Chicago Women in Publishing Book Awards. *Winners:* (trade) Albert Whitman & Co. for *My Mother Lost Her Job Today* by Judy Delton, Ann Fay, and Irene Trivas; (trade) University of Chicago Press for *Homemakers: The Forgotten Workers* by Rae André, T. David Brent, and Julie Wines; (educational) University of Chicago Press for *Women—Sex and Sexuality* by Catharine R. Stimpson and Ethel Spector Person.

Children's Book Guild Nonfiction Award. *Winner:* Milton Meltzer.

Child Study Children's Book Committee at Bank Street College Award. *Winner:* Maureen Crane Wartski for *A Boat to Nowhere* (Westminster Press).

Christopher Awards. For books distinguished for thier "affirmation of the highest values of the human spirit." *Winners:* (adult books) Italo Calvino for *Italian Folktales*, translated by George Martin (Harcourt Brace Jovanovich); Ann Cornelisen for *Strangers and Pilgrims* (Holt, Rinehart and Winston); Torey L. Hayden for *One Child* (Putnam); John Fowles and Frank Horvat for *The Tree* (Little, Brown); Livia E. Bitton Jackson for *Elli* (Times Books); Joseph P. Lash for *Helen and Teacher* (Merloyd Book/Delacorte Press/Seymour Lawrence); Anne Morrow Lindbergh for *War Within and Without* (Harcourt Brace Jovanovich); Richard P. McBrien for *Catholicism* (Winston Press); (children's books) Avi for *Encounter at Easton* (Pantheon); Pamela Bullard and Judith Stoia for *The Hardest Lesson* (Little, Brown); Corinne Gerson for *Son for a Day* (Atheneum); Milton Meltzer for *All Times, All Peoples* (Harper & Row); Peter Spier for *People* (Doubleday).

Frank and Ethel S. Cohen Award. For an outstanding book dealing with an aspect of Jewish thought originally written in English by a U.S. or Canadian resident. *Offered by:* Jewish Book Council of the National Jewish Welfare Board. *Winner:* Isador Twersky for *Introduction to the Code of Maimonides* (Yale University Press).

Common Wealth Awards for Distinguished Service in Literature. *Winners:* Nadine Gordimer and Milan Kundera.

Commonwealth Poetry Prize (Great Britain). For a first published book by a poet who comes from a Commonwealth country other than Great Britain. *Winner:* Philip Salom (Australia) for *The Silent Piano* (Freemantle Arts Centre Press).

Thomas Cook Travel Awards (Great Britain). *Winners:* (travel book) Gavin Young for *Slow Boats to China* (Hutchinson); (guide book) Evelyne Garside for *China Companion* (Deutsch).

Duff Cooper Memorial Prize. *Winner:* Victoria Glendinning for *Edith Sitwell: A Unicorn Among Lions* (Weidenfeld & Nicolson).

Alice Fay diCastagnola Award. *Offered by:* Poetry Society of America. *Winner:* Carolyn Forché for *The Country Between Us* (Harper & Row).

English-Speaking Union Literary Award. *Winner:* Salman Rushdie for *Midnight's Children* (Knopf/Jonathan Cape).

William and Janice Epstein Award. To encourage fictional writing on Jewish themes. *Offered by:* Jewish Book Council of the National Jewish Welfare Board. *Winner:* Johanna Kaplan for *O My America!* (Harper & Row).

Christopher Ewart-Biggs Memorial Prize (Great Britain). *Winners:* Brian Friel for *Translations* (Faber & Faber); Robert Kee for *Ireland: A History* (Weidenfeld & Nicolson).

Eleanor Farjeon Award (Great Britain). For distinguished service to children's books. *Offered by:* Children's Book Circle. *Winners:* Virginia Allen Jensen and Margaret Marshall.

Dorothy Canfield Fisher Children's Book Award. For a book selected by children of Vermont. *Offered by:* Vermont State PTA and Vermont State Department of Libraries. *Winner:* James Howe and Deborah Howe for *Bunnicula* (Atheneum).

William (Zev) Frank Memorial Award for Children's Literature. *Winner:* Leonard Everett Fisher for *A Russian Farewell* (Four Winds Press).

R. T. French Company Tastemaker Awards. *Winners:* (best cookbook and natural foods/special diet) Craig Claiborne with Pierre Franey for *Craig Claiborne's Gourmet Diet* (Times Books); (basic and/or general) Tom Margittai and Paul Kovi for *The Four Seasons* (Simon & Schuster); (American regional and international) Nika Hazelton for *American Home Cooking* (Viking Press); (specialty) Jean Anderson and Ruth Buchan for *Half a Can of Tomato Paste and Other Culinary Dilemmas* (Harper & Row); (single subject) Maida Heatter for *Maida Heatter's Book of Great Chocolate Desserts* (Knopf); (meat, fish, and dairy) Sheryl London and Mel London for *The Fish-Lovers' Cookbook* (Rodale Press); (original softcover—American regional and international) Anne Willan for *LaVarenne's Basic French Cookery* (HP Books); (original softcover—specialty) Colin Tudge for *Future Food* (Harmony Books); (original softcover—single subject) Walter Hall and Nancy Hall for *The Wild Palate* (Rodale Press).

Friends of Literature Awards. *Winners:* (Chicago Foundation for Literature Award) Arthur Weinberg and Lila Weinberg for *Clarence Darrow: A Sentimental Rebel* (Putnam); (Cliff Dwellers Arts Foundation Award) Stuart Dybek for *Childhood and Other Neighborhoods* (Viking); (Vicki Penziner Matson Memorial Award) Jean Auel for *The Clan of the Cave Bear* (Crown).

Georgia Children's Book Award. *Winner:* Katherine Paterson for *The Great Gilly Hopkins* (Crowell).

German Peace Prize. *Winner:* Lev Kopelev (USSR).

Goethe House-PEN Translation Prize. *Winner:* John Brownjohn for *A German Love Story* by Rolf Hochhuth (Little, Brown).

Governor General's Literary Awards (Canada). *Winners:* (books in English—fiction) George Bowering for *Burning Water* (Musson/General Publishing); (nonfiction) Jeffrey Simpson for *Discipline of Power* (Person Library); (poetry) Stephen Scobie for *McAlmon's Chinese Opera* (Quadrant); (books in French—fiction) Pierre Turgeon for *La Première Personne* (Quinze); (nonfiction) Maurice Champagne-Gilbert for *La Famille et l'Homme à Délivrer du Pouvoir* (Lemeac); (poetry) Michel Van Schendel for *De l'Oeil et de l'Écoute* (Hexagone).

Grand Prix du Roman (France). *Winner:* Jean Raspail for *Moi, Antoine de Tounens, Roi de Patagonie* (Albin Michel).

Great Lakes Colleges Association New Writers Award. *Winners:* (fiction) Mary Hedin for *Fly Away Home* (University of Iowa Press); (poetry) Jorie Graham for *Hybrids of Plants and of Ghosts* (Princeton University Press).

Kate Greenaway Medal (Great Britain). *Offered by:* British Library Association. *Winner:* Quentin Blake for *Mr. Magnolia* (Jonathan Cape).

Guardian Fiction Award (Great Britain). *Winner:* John Banville for *Kepler* (Secker & Warburg).

Calouste Gulbenkian-PEN Translation Prize. *Winner:* Gregory Rabassa for *Avalovara* by Osman Lins (Knopf).

Hugh M. Hefner First Amendment Award. *Winner:* Frank Rowe for *The Enemy Among Us: A Story of Witch-Hunting in the McCarthy Era* (Cougar Books).

Heinemann Award (Great Britain). *Winners:* Robert B. Martin for *Tennyson: The Unquiet Heart* (Oxford University Press/Faber); Dick Davis for *Seeing the World* (Anvil Press).

Ernest Hemingway Foundation Award. For the best first book of fiction by an American writer. *Offered by:* PEN. *Winner:* Joan Silber for *Household Words* (Viking).

David Higham Prize for Fiction (Great Britain). *Winner:* Christopher Hope for *A Separate Development* (Routledge & Kegan Paul).

Winifred Holby Prize (Great Britain). *Winner:* Elsa Joubert for *Poppie* (Hodder & Stoughton).

Amelia Francis Howard-Gibbon Illustrator's Award. *Offered by:* Canadian Library Association, Canadian Association of Children's Librarians. *Winner:* Douglas Tait for *The Trouble with Princesses* by Christie Harris (McClelland & Stewart).

Iowa School of Letters Award for Short Fiction. *Winner:* Annabel Thomas for *The Phototropic Woman* (University of Iowa Press).

International Book Award. *Winners:* Rene Entiemble; (special distinction award) Sigfred Taubert.

International Reading Association Literacy Award. *Winner:* Ethiopian Coordinating Committee for the National Literacy Campaign.

Joseph Henry Jackson Award. *Offered by:* San Francisco Foundation. *Winner:* Stefanie Marlis for *The Single Feather* (*Ms.* magazine).

Jewish Chronicle/H. H. Wingate Book Awards (Great Britain). *Winners:* (fiction) Mordechai Richler for *Joshua Then and Now* (Macmillan); (nonfiction) Jerry White for *Rothschild Buildings* (Routledge & Kegan Paul).

Leon Jolson Award. For the best book on the Holocaust. *Offered by:* Jewish Book Council of the National Jewish Welfare Board. *Winner:* Randolph L. Braham for *The Politics of Genocide: The Holocaust in Hungary* (Columbia University Press).

Juniper Prize. *Winner:* David Brendan Hopes for *The Glacier's Daughters* (University of Massachusetts Press).

Janet Heidinger Kafka Prize in Fiction by an American Woman. *Winner:* Anne Tyler for *Morgan's Passing* (Knopf).

Sue Kaufman Prize for First Fiction. *Offered by:* American Academy and Institute of Arts and Letters. *Winner:* Tom Lorenz for *Guys Like Us* (Viking).

Robert F. Kennedy Book Awards. *Winner:* William H. Chafe for *Civilities and Civil Rights: Greensboro, North Carolina, and the Black Struggle for Freedom* (Oxford University Press).

Irwin Kerlan Award. For achievement in children's literature. *Offered by:* Kerlan Collection, University of Minnesota. *Winner:* Tomie De Paola.

Robert Kirsch Award. For a body of work. *Offered by:* Los Angeles Times. *Winner:* Wright Norris.

Lamont Poetry Selection Award. *Offered by:* Academy of American Poets. *Winner:* Carolyn Forche for *The Country Between Us* (Harper & Row).

Locus Awards. *Winners:* (anthology) Edward L. Ferman, ed., *The Magazine of Fantasy & Science Fiction: A 30-Year Retrospective* (Doubleday); (artist) Michael Whelan; (fantasy novel) Robert Silverberg for *Lord Valentine's Castle* (Harper & Row); (first novel) Robert L. Forward for *Dragon's Egg* (Del Rey); (magazine) *The Magazine of Fantasy & Science Fiction;* (novelette) Thomas M. Disch for *The Brave Little Toaster* (*Fantasy & Science Fiction*, August), (novella) George R. R. Martin for *Night-*

flyers (*Analog*, April); (publisher) Ballantine/Del Rey; (related nonfiction book) Isaac Asimov for *In Joy Still Felt* (Doubleday); (science fiction novel) Joan D. Vinge for *The Snow Queen* (Dial); (short story) Clifford D. Simak for "Grotto of the Dancing Deer" (*Analog*, April); (single author collection) John Varley for *The Barbie Murders* (Berkley).

Logos Bookstores Religious Book Awards. *Winners:* (most significant author of the year) Richard Foster for *Celebration of Discipline* and *The Freedom of Simplicity* (Harper & Row); (inspirational book) Richard Foster for *The Freedom of Simplicity* (Harper & Row); (scholarly book) Donald Guthie for *New Testament Theology* (Inter-Varsity) and Madeleine L'Engle for *Walking on Water* (Harold Shaw); (consistent excellence in publishing content) Inter-Varsity; (best new religious publisher) Crossways Books.

Russell Loines Award for Poetry. *Offered by:* American Academy and Institute of Arts and Letters. *Winner:* Ben Belitt.

Los Angeles Times Book Prizes. *Winners:* (fiction) D. M. Thomas for *The White Hotel* (Viking); (current interest) Jacobo Timerman for *Prisoner Without a Name, Cell Without a Number* (Knopf); (biography) David McCullough for *Mornings on Horseback* (Simon & Schuster); (poetry) Ntozake Shange for *Three Pieces* (St. Martin's); (history) Ray Billington (posthumously) for *Land of Savagery/Land of Promise* (Norton).

James Russell Lowell Prize. *Offered by:* Modern Language Association of America. *Winner:* Benjamin Bennett for *Modern Drama and German Classicism: Renaissance from Lessing to Brecht* (Cornell University Press).

Lucky Book Club Four-Leaf Clover Award. *Winner:* Nancy K. Robinson.

Howard R. Marraro Prize. *Winner:* Richard A. Goldthwaite for *The Building of Renaissance Florence* (Johns Hopkins University Press).

Lenore Marshall Poetry Prize. For an outstanding book of poems published in the United States. *Offered by: Saturday Review* and New Hope Foundation. *Winner:* Sterling A. Brown for *The Collected Poems of Sterling A. Brown* (Harper & Row).

Frederic G. Melcher Book Award. For the most significant contribution to religious liberalism. *Offered by:* Unitarian/Universalist General Assembly. *Winner:* John Boswell for *Christianity, Social Tolerance and Homosexuality* (University of Chicago Press).

MIND Book of the Year (Great Britain). *Winner:* Sheila MacLeod for *The Art of Starvation* (Virago).

Mitchell Prize for the History of Art. For the author of an outstanding book on art history. *Winner:* John Pope-Hennessey for *Luca della Robbia* (Cornell University Press).

Charles Rufus Morey Book Award. *Offered by:* College Art Association. *Winner:* Fred Licht for *Goya* (Universe Books).

Mother Goose Award (Great Britain). *Winner:* Juan Wijngaard, illustrator, for *Green Finger House* by Rosemary Harris (Eel Pie).

Frank Luther Mott-Kappa Tau Alpha Research Award. For the best book in journalism. *Winner:* Ronald Steal for *Walter Lippmann and the American Century* (Atlantic-Little, Brown).

Mystery Writers of America—Edgar Allen Poe Awards. *Winners:* (novel) Dick Francis for *Whip Hand* (Harper & Row); (first novel) K. Nolte Smith for *The Watcher* (Coward, McCann & Geoghegan); (short story) Clark Howard for "The Horn Man" (Ellery Queen's Mystery Magazine); (original softcover novel) Bill Granger for *Public Murders* (Jove); (fact crime book) Fred Harwell for *A True Deliverance* (Knopf); (critical/biographical study) John Reilly for *Twentieth Century Crime and Mystery Writers* (St. Martin's); (children's mystery) Joan Lowery Nixon for *The Seance* (Harcourt Brace Jovanovich).

National Arts Club Gold Medal of Honor for Literature. *Winner:* Leon Edel.

National Book Critics Circle Awards. *Winners:* (fiction) John Updike for *Rabbit is Rich* (Knopf); (general nonfiction) Stephen Jay Gould for *The Mismeasure of Man* (Norton); (poetry) A. R. Ammons for *A Coast of Trees* (Norton); (criticism) Virgil Thomson for *A Virgil Thomson Reader* (Houghton Mifflin).

National Council of Teachers of English Award for Excellence in Poetry for Children. *Winner:* Eve Merriam.

National Historical Society Book Prize. *Winner:* Charles Royster for *A Revolutionary People at War: The Continental Army and American Character* (Norton).

National Jewish Book Awards. *Offered by:* Jewish Book Council of the National Jewish Welfare Board. *Winners:* (poetry) Louis Simpson for *Caviar at the Funeral* (Franklin Watts); (visual arts) Yeshiva University Museum for "Purim: The Face and the Mask"; (Yiddish literature) Hyman Bass for *Pathways in Yiddish Literature* (I. L. Peretz Publishing House); (children's book) Leonard Everett Fisher for *A Russian Farewell* (Four Winds Press).

N.C. Award in Literature. *Winner:* Glen Rounds.

Nebula Awards. For excellence in the field of science fiction. *Offered by:* Science Fiction Writers of America. *Winners:* (grand master award) Fritz Leiber; (novel) Gregory Benford for *Timescape* (Simon & Schuster); (novella) Suzy McKee Charnas for *The Unicorn Tapestry* (Pocket Books); (novelette) Howard Waldrup for *The Ugly Chicken* (Doubleday); (short story) Clifford D. Simak for "Grotto of the Dancing Deer" (Analog).

Nene Award. *Winner:* Alfred Slote for *My Robot Buddy* (Lippincott).

New Hampshire Library Association Great Stone Face Award. *Winner:* Judy Blume for *Tales of a Fourth Grade Nothing* (Dutton).

New Jersey Library Association Garden State Children's Book Awards. *Winners:* (easy to read) Arnold Lobel for *Grasshopper on the Road* (Harper & Row); (younger fiction) Katherine Paterson for *The Great Gilly Hopkins* (Crowell); (younger nonfiction) Millicent Selsam for *Tyrannosaurus Rex* (Harper & Row).

New York Academy of Sciences Children's Science Book Awards. *Winners:* (younger category) Vicki Cobb and Kathy Darling (authors) and Martha Weston (illustrator) for *Bet You Can't!* (Lothrop, Lee & Shepherd); (older category) Jan Adkins for *Moving Heavy Things* (Houghton Mifflin/Clarion).

New York Times Best Illustrated Children's Books. *Winners:* Suekichi Akaba for *The Crane Wife*, retold by Sumiko Yagawa (Morrow); Stephen Gammell for *Where the Buffaloes Begin* by Olaf Baker (Warne); Warwick Hutton for *The Nose Tree*, adapted from an old German story (Atheneum/Margaret K. McElderry); Anita Lobel for *On Market Street* by Arnold Lobel (Greenwillow); Nancy Winslow Parker for *My Mom Travels a Lot* by Caroline Feller Bauer (Warne); Robert Andrew Parker for *Flight: A Panorama of Aviation* by Melvin B. Zisfein (Pantheon); Marcia Sewall for *The Story of Old Mrs. Brubeck: And How She Looked for Trouble and Where She Found Him* by Lore Segal (Pantheon); Maurice Sendak for *Outside Over There* by Maurice Sendak (Harper & Row/Ursula Nordstrom); Chris Van Allsburg for *Jumanji* by Chris Van Allsburg (Houghton Mifflin); Paul O. Zelinsky for *The Maid and the Mouse and the Odd-Shaped House: A Story in Rhyme*, adapted by Paul O. Zelinsky (Dodd, Mead).

New Zealand Book Awards. *Winner:* (fiction) Maurice Shadbolt for *The*

Lovelock Version (Hodder & Stoughton).

Newbery Medal. For the most distinguished contribution to literature for children. *Donor:* ALA Library Service to Children. *Medal contributed by:* Daniel Melcher. *Winner:* Katherine Paterson for *Jacob I Have Loved* (Crowell).

Nobel Prize for Literature. For high achievement in the field of literature. *Winner:* Elias Canetti.

Noma Award for Publishing in Africa (Japan). *Winner:* Felix C. Adi for *Health Education for the Community* (Nwamife Publishers, Enugu, Nigeria).

George Orwell Award. For distinguished contributions to honesty and clarity in public language. *Offered by:* National Council of Teachers of English. *Winner:* Dwight Bolinger for *Language—The Loaded Weapon* (Longmans, Great Britain).

Helen Keating Ott Award. *Winner:* Phyllis Anderson Wood.

Pan-American International Literary Award. *Winner:* Barbara Revell Ely for *Gypsum Throne* (Pan-American Publishing Company).

Pegasus Prize for Literature. *Winner:* Tidiane Dem for *Masseni* (Louisiana State University Press).

PEN American Center and PEN South PEN/Faulkner Award. *Winner:* Walter Abish for *How German Is It* (New Directions).

PEN Awards. *Winners:* (translation prize) John E. Woods for *Evening Edged in Gold* by Arno Schmidt (Harcourt Brace Jovanovich/Helen and Kurt Wolff); (writing awards for prisoners) Tony Menninger; (nonfiction) William Williams and Richard C. Stanin; (poetry) D. L. Adamson.

James D. Phelan Literary Award. *Offered by:* San Francisco Foundation. *Winner:* David Jonathan Shields for *Emile Coué's Unlikely Cure* (*Ms.* magazine).

Phi Beta Kappa Book Awards. *Winners:* (Ralph Waldo Emerson Award) George Frederickson for *White Supremacy: A Comparative Study in American and South African History* (Oxford University Press); (Christian Gauss Award) Robert Bernard Martin for *Tennyson: The Unquiet Heart* (Oxford University Press); (science award) Eric Chaisson for *Cosmic Dawn: The Origins of Matter and Life* (Atlantic-Little, Brown).

Renato Poggioli Award. *Offered by:* PEN American Center. *Winner:* W. S. DiPiero for *The Ellipse* by Leonardo Sinisgalli (in progress).

Prix Femina (France). *Winner:* Catherine Hermary-Vieille for *Le Grand Vizir de la Nuit* (Gallimard).

Prix Goncourt (France). *Winner:* Lucien Bodard for *Anne Marie* (Grasset).

Prix Interallié (France). *Winner:* Louis Nucera for *Le Chemin de la Lanterne* (Grasset).

Prix Medicis (France). *Winner:* François-Olivier Rousseau for *L'Enfant d'Edouard* (Gallimard).

Prix Medicis Etranger (France). *Winner:* David Shahar for *Day of the Countess* (Gallimard).

Prix de Meilleur Livre Etranger (France). *Winner:* Anthony Burgess for *Earthly Powers* (Simon & Schuster).

Prix Renaudot (France). *Winner:* Michel de Castillo for *La Nuit du Décret* (Editions du Seuil).

PSP Awards. *Offered by:* Professional and Scholarly Publishing Division, AAP. *Winners:* (R. R. Hawkins Award) Stephan Thernstron, Ann Orlov, and Oscar Handlin for *The Harvard Encyclopedia of American Ethnic Groups* (Harvard University Press); (architecture and urban planning) Henry F. Arnold for *Trees in Urban Design* (Van Nostrand Reinhold); (business and management) Samuel A. Culbert and John J. McDonough for *The Invisible War: Pursuing Self-Interest at Work* (John Wiley & Sons); (design and production)

Michael Coe and Richard Diehl for *In the Land of the Olmec* (University of Texas Press); (health science) Alexander A. Yabriv for *Interferon and Nonspecific Resistance* (Human Sciences Press); (humanities) Roy H. Copperud for *American Usage and Style: The Consensus* (Van Nostrand Reinhold); (life sciences) Avery A. Sandberg for *The Chromosomes in Human Cancer and Leukemia* (Elsevier-North Holland); (most creative and innovative new project) Ben Eisenman for *Prognosis of Surgical Disease* (W. B. Saunders); (technology) Hans S. Rauschenback for *Solar Cell Array Design Handbook* (Van Nostrand Reinhold); (outstanding new journal) Yonah Alexander, ed., *Political Communication and Persuasion: An International Journal* (Crane, Russak & Co.).

Pulitzer Prizes. *Offered by:* Trustees of Columbia University on the recommendations of the Advisory Board on Pulitzer Prizes. *Winners:* (fiction) John Kennedy Toole for *A Confederacy of Dunces* (Louisiana State University Press); (general nonfiction) Carl E. Schorske for *Fin-de-Siecle Vienna: Politics and Culture* (Knopf); (history) Lawrence A. Cremin for *American Education: The National Experience, 1783–1876* (Harper & Row); (biography) Robert K. Massie for *Peter the Great: His Life and World* (Knopf); (poetry) James Schuyler for *The Morning of the Poem* (Farrar, Straus & Giroux).

Regina Medal. For distinguished contribution to children's literature. *Offered by:* Catholic Library Association. *Winner:* Theodore Seuss Geisel.

John Llewelyn Rhys Memorial Prize. (Great Britain). For a memorable book by a British Commonwealth writer under 30. *Offered by:* John Llewelyn Rhys Memorial Trust/National Book League. *Winner:* A. N. Wilson for *The Laird of Abbotsford* (Oxford University Press).

Richard and Hilda Rosenthal Foundation Award. For a work of fiction that is a considerable literary achievement though not necessarily a commercial success. *Offered by:* American Academy and Institute of Arts and Letters. *Winners:* Jerome Charyn for *Darlin' Bill* (Arbor House).

Delmore Schwartz Memorial Poetry Award. *Winner:* Constance Urdang.

Shelley Memorial Award. *Offered by:* Poetry Society of America. *Winner:* Robert Creeley.

Kenneth B. Smilen/Present Tense Literary Awards. *Winners.* (fiction) Johanna Kaplan for *O My America* (Harper & Row); (history) Salo Baron for *Byzantines, Mamelukes and Maghribians* (Columbia University Press); (Jewish religious thought) Isador Twersky for *Introduction to the Code of Maimonides* (Yale University Press); (social and political analysis) Amos Elon for *Flight into Egypt* (Doubleday); (translation) Shlomo Noble and Joshua Fishman for *History of the Yiddish Language* by Max Weinrich (University of Chicago Press); (biography/autobiography) Samuel Pisar for *Of Blood and Hope* (Little, Brown); (children's book) Isaac Bashevis Singer for *The Power of Light* (Farrar, Straus & Giroux).

W. H. Smith Literary Award. To the author of a book written in English and published in the United Kingdom that makes the most significant contribution to literature. *Offered by:* W. H. Smith & Sons Ltd. *Winner:* Isabel Colegate for *The Shooting Party* (Hamish Hamilton).

John Ben Snow Prize. *Winner:* Isabel Thompson Kelsay for *Joseph Brant: Man of Two Worlds* (Syracuse University Press).

Society of Children's Book Writers/Golden Kite Awards. *Winners:* (fiction) Patricia MacLachlan for *Arthur, For the Very First Time* (Harper & Row); (nonfiction) Dorothy Hinshaw Patent for *The Lives of Spiders* (Holiday House).

Society of Colonial Wars Award. *Winner:* James Thomas Flexner for *Lord of the Mohawks: A Biography of Sir William Johnson* (Columbia University Press).

Society of Midland Authors Award. *Winners:* (biography) Arthur Weinberg and Lila Weinberg for *Clarence Darrow: A Sentimental Rebel* (Putnam); (fiction) Stuart Dybek for *Childhood and Other Neighborhoods* (Viking); (history) Lyle Coehler for *A Search for Power: The Weaker Sex in 17-Century New England* (University of Illinois Press); (poetry) Ted Kooser for *Sure Signs: New and Selected Poems* (University of Pittsburgh Press); Robert Siegal for *In a Pig's Eye* (University Presses of Florida); (politics and economics) David Broder for *Changing of the Guard: Power and Leadership in America* (Simon & Schuster); (psychology and sociology) Studs Terkel for *Dreams Lost and Found* (Pantheon); (children's book) Patricia Calvert for *The Snowbird* (Scribners).

Southern California Council on Literature for Children and Young People Awards. *Winners:* (notable book of fiction) John Reynolds Gardiner for *Stone Fox* (Crowell); (distinguished body of work) Sonia Levitin; (for service on behalf of children and literature) Miriam Cox (posthumously).

Texan Bluebonnet Award. *Winner:* Beverly Cleary for *Ramona and Her Father* (Morrow).

Texas Institute of Letters Awards. *Winners:* (for a career in Texas letters) Tom Lea; (fiction) Laura Furman for *The Glass House* (Viking); (nonfiction) Michael Mewshaw for *Life for Death* (Doubleday); (poetry) Naomi Shihab Nye for *Different Ways to Pray* (Breitenbush); (friends of Dallas Public Library Award) Alan Tennant for *The Guadalupe Mountains of Texas* (University of Texas Press).

Theatre Library Association Award. For the outstanding book on recorded performance, including motion pictures and television. *Winners:* Kevin Brownlow and John Kobal for *Hollywood: The Pioneers.*

Universe Literary Prize (Great Britain). *Winner:* Morris West for *The Clowns of God* (Hodder & Stoughton).

University of Southern Mississippi Silver Medallion. *Winner:* Beverly Cleary.

Irita Van Doren Award. For outstanding contributions to the cause of books and reading. *Offered by:* American Booksellers Association, Publishers Ad Club, and Publishers Publicity Association. *Winner: New York Times Book Review.*

Harold D. Vursell Memorial Award. *Offered by:* American Academy and Institute of Arts and Letters. *Winner:* Edward Hoagland.

Western Writers of America Spur Awards. *Winners:* (novel) Jeanne Williams for *The Valiant Women* (Pocket Books); (nonfiction) Stan Hoig for *The Peace Chiefs of the Cheyennes* (University of Oklahoma Press); (children's book) Suzanne Hilton for *Getting There: Frontier Travel Without Power* (Westminster Press).

Whitbread Literary Awards (Great Britain). *Winners:* (novel) Maurice Leitch for *Silver City* (Secker & Warburg); (biography) Nigel Hamilton for *Monty: The Making of a General* (Hamish Hamilton); (first novel) William Boyd for *A Good Man in Africa* (Hamish Hamilton); (children's book) Jane Gardam for *The Hollow Land* (Julia MacRae).

William Allen White Children's Book Award. *Winner:* Katherine Paterson for *The Great Gilly Hopkins* (Crowell).

Walt Whitman Award. To an unpublished poet. *Offered by:* Academy of American Poets and the Copernicus Society of America. *Winner:* Alberto Rios for *One Night in a Familiar Room* (Sheepmeadow Press).

Nero Wolfe Award for Mystery Fiction. *Winner:* Amanda Cross for *Death in a Tenured Position* (Dutton).

World Science Fiction Convention Awards. *Winners:* (John W. Campbell Award) Somtow Sucharitkul; (Gandulf Award) C. L. Moore; *Hugo Awards:* (nonfiction) Carl Sagan for *Cosmos* (Random House); (novel) Joan D. Vinge for *The Snow Queen* (Dial Press); (novelette) Gordon R. Dickson for *The Cloak and the Staff* (Analog, August 1980); (novella) Gordon R. Dickson for *Lost Dorsai* (Destinies); (short story) Clifford D. Simak for "Grotto of the Dancing Deer" (Analog).

Yale Series of Younger Poets Award. *Winner:* David Wojahn for *Icehouse Lights* (Yale University Press).

Young Hoosier Book Award. *Winner:* Jonah Kalb for *The Goof That Won the Pennant* (Houghton Mifflin).

Morton Dauwen Zabel Award. For a poet of progressive, original, and experimental tendencies. *Offered by:* American Academy and Institute of Arts and Letters. *Winner:* Guy Davenport.

NOTABLE BOOKS OF 1981

This is the thirty-fifth year in which this list of distinguished books has been issued by the Notable Books Council of the Reference and Adult Services Division of the American Library Association.

Allen, Gay Wilson. *Waldo Emerson.* Viking.

Ashbery, John. *Shadow Train.* Viking.

Atwood, Margaret. *Two-headed Poems.* Simon and Schuster.

Berke, Roberta. *Bounds Out of Bounds: A Compass for Recent American and British Poetry.* Oxford University Press.

Bowen, Elizabeth. *The Collected Stories of Elizabeth Bowen.* Knopf.

Brent, Peter. *Charles Darwin: A Man of Enlarged Curiosity.* Harper.

Carpenter, Humphrey. *W. H. Auden: A Biography.* Houghton.

Carver, Raymond. *What We Talk About When We Talk About Love.* Knopf.

Fallows, James. *National Defense.* Random.

Garside, Roger. *Coming Alive: China after Mao.* McGraw.

Goodfield, June. *An Imagined World: A Story of Scientific Discovery.* Harper.

Gordimer, Nadine. *July's People.* Viking.

Gould, Stephan Jay. *The Mismeasure of Man.* Norton.

Halberstam, David. *The Breaks of the Game.* Knopf.

Hampl, Patricia. *A Romantic Education.* Houghton.

Hughes, Robert. *The Shock of the New.* Knopf.

Johanson, Donald C., and Maitland A. Edey. *Lucy: The Beginnings of Humankind.* Simon and Schuster.

McCullough, David. *Mornings on Horseback.* Simon and Schuster.

Malone, Dumas. *The Sage of Monticello* (*Jefferson and His Time*, volume 6). Little, Brown.

Mariani, Paul. *William Carlos Williams: A New World Naked.* McGraw.

Mooney, Ted. *Easy Travel to Other Planets: A Novel.* Farrar, Straus & Giroux.

Neely, Richard. *How Courts Govern America.* Yale University Press.

Nijinska, Bronislava. *Bronislava Nijinska: Early Memoirs.* Edited and translated by

Irina Nijinska and Jean Rawlinson. Holt, Rinehart & Winston.

O'Connor, Frank. *Collected Stories.* Knopf.

Peters, F. E. *Ours: The Making and Unmaking of a Jesuit.* Marek.

Plante, David. *The Country.* Atheneum.

Plath, Sylvia. *The Collected Poems.* Edited by Ted Hughes. Harper.

Pond, Elizabeth. *From the Yaroslavsky Station: Russia Perceived.* Universe.

Robinson, Marilynne. *Housekeeping.* Farrar, Strauss & Giroux.

Santoli, Al. *Everything We Had: An Oral History of the Vietnam War by Thirty-three American Soldiers Who Fought It.* Random.

Sato, Hiroaki, and Burton Watson, eds. *From the Country of Eight Islands: An Anthology of Japanese Poetry.* University of Washington Press.

Schwartz-Nobel, Loretta. *Starving in the Shadow of Plenty.* Putnam.

Smith, Adam. *Paper Money.* Summit.

Spence, Jonathan D. *The Gate of Heavenly Peace: The Chinese and Their Revolution, 1895-1980.* Viking.

Spencer, Elizabeth. *The Stories of Elizabeth Spencer.* Doubleday.

Stratton, Joanna L. *Pioneer Women: Voices from the Kansas Frontier.* Simon and Schuster.

Timerman, Jacobo. *Prisoner without a Name, Cell without a Number.* Knopf.

Totman, Conrad. *Japan before Perry: A Short History.* University of California Press.

Tuchman, Barbara. *Practicing History: Selected Essays.* Knopf.

Updike, John. *Rabbit Is Rich.* Knopf.

Wilford, John Noble. *The Mapmakers.* Knopf.

Woods, Donald. *Asking for Trouble: Autobiography of a Banned Journalist.* Atheneum.

BEST YOUNG ADULT BOOKS OF 1981

Each year a committee of the Young Adult Services Division of the American Library Association compiles a list of best books for young adults selected on the basis of young adult appeal. These titles must meet acceptable standards of library merit and provide a variety of subjects for different tastes and a broad range of reading levels. *School Library Journal* (*SLJ*) also provides a list of best books for young adults. This year the list was compiled by *SLJ*'s young adult review committee, which is chaired by Ron Brown, young adult specialist at Boston Public Library, and made up of public and school librarians in the Greater Boston Area. The *SLJ* list was published in the December 1981 issue of the journal. The following list combines the titles selected for both lists. The notation ALA or *SLJ* following the price indicates the source of titles chosen.

Alexander, Lloyd. *Westmark.* Elsevier-Dutton. $9.95. ALA.

Attanasio, A. A. *Radix.* Morrow. $14.95; pap. $8.95. *SLJ*.

Attenborough, David. *Life on Earth: A Natural History.* Little, Brown. $19.95. *SLJ*.

Bauer, Steve. *Satyrday.* Putnam. $11.95. ALA.

Bell, Ruth, and others. *Changing Bodies, Changing Lives.* Random. $14.95. ALA, *SLJ*.

Blume, Judy. *Tiger Eyes.* Bradbury, dist. by Elsevier-Dutton. $9.95. ALA.

Booher, Dianna Daniels. *Rape: What Would You Do If . . . ?* Messner. $9.79. ALA.

Bradshaw, Gillian. *Kingdom of Summer.* Simon & Schuster. $12.95. SLJ.

Bridgers, Sue Ellen. *Notes for Another Life.* Knopf, dist. by Random. $8.95. ALA.

Bykov, Vasil. *Pack of Wolves.* Crowell. $10.10. ALA.

Chester, Deborah. *The Sign of the Owl.* Scholastic/Four Winds. $9.95. ALA.

Childress, Alice. *Rainbow Jordan.* Coward, McCann. $8.95. ALA.

Dickens, Charles, and Leon Garfield. *The Mystery of Edwin Drood.* Pantheon. $12.95. SLJ.

Dolan, Edward F. *Adolf Hitler: A Portrait of Tyranny.* Dodd. $8.95. ALA.

Duncan, Lois. *Stranger with My Face.* Little, Brown. $8.95. ALA.

Eckert, Allan W. *Song of the Wild.* Little, Brown. $10.95. ALA.

Freddi, Chris. *Pork and Others.* Knopf. $10.95. SLJ.

Grace, Fran. *Branigan's Dog.* Bradbury, dist. by Elsevier-Dutton. $9.95. ALA.

Griffiths, Paul. *A Guide to Electronic Music.* Thames & Hudson, dist. by Norton. $6.95. SLJ.

Guy, David. *Football Dreams.* Seaview, dist. by Harper. $10.95. ALA.

Hentoff, Nat. *Does This School Have Capital Punishment?* Delacorte. $8.95. ALA.

Herbert, Frank. *God Emperor of Dune.* Putnam. $12.95. SLJ.

Herring, Robert. *Hub.* Viking. $12.95. ALA.

Hoover, H. M. *Another Heaven, Another Earth.* Viking. $10.95. ALA.

Hughes, Monica. *The Keeper of the Isis Light.* Atheneum. $8.95. ALA.

Jacobs, Anita. *Where Has Deedie Wooster Been All These Years?* Delacorte. $9.95. ALA.

Jaffe, Rona. *Mazes & Monsters.* Delacorte. $13.95. ALA, SLJ.

Janeczko, Paul, comp. and ed. *Don't Forget to Fly.* Bradbury. $9.95. ALA.

Jones, Diana Wynne. *The Homeward Bounders.* Greenwillow. $8.95. ALA.

Kerr, M. E. *Little Little.* Harper. $8.95. ALA.

Klein, Kenneth. *Getting Better: A Medical Student's Story.* Little, Brown. $12.95. SLJ.

Knowles, John. *Peace Breaks Out.* Holt. $9.95. ALA.

Koehn, Ilse. *Tilla.* Greenwillow. $8.95. ALA.

Krementz, Jill. *How It Feels When a Parent Dies.* Knopf, dist. by Random. $9.95. ALA.

Kullman, Harry. *The Battle Horse.* Bradbury. $8.95. ALA.

Lawson, Don. *The United States in the Vietnam War.* Crowell. $8.79. ALA.

Levoy, Myron. *A Shadow like a Leopard.* Harper. $8.95. ALA.

Lubin, Leonard. *The Elegant Beast.* Viking. $10.95. SLJ.

Mann, Peggy, and Gizelle Hersh. *Gizelle Saves the Children.* Everest. $12.95. ALA.

Marzollo, Jean. *Halfway Down Paddy Lane.* Dial. $9.95. ALA.

Mayhar, Ardath. *Soul-Singer of Tyrnos.* Atheneum. $9.95. ALA.

Mazer, Harry. *I Love You, Stupid!* Crowell. $9.95. ALA.

McCracken, Mary. *City Kid.* Little, Brown. $11.95. SLJ.

Mebane, Mary E. *Mary.* Viking. $12.95. SLJ.

Murphy, Barbara Beasley, and Judie Wolkoff. *Ace Hits the Big Time.* Delacorte. $10.95. ALA.

Myers, Walter Dean. *Hoops.* Delacorte. $10.95. ALA.

⸻. *The Legend of Tarik.* Viking. $9.95. ALA.

Namioka, Lensey. *Village of the Vampire Cat.* Delacorte. $9.95. ALA.

Patterson, Francine, and Eugene Linden. *The Education of Koko.* Holt. $15.95. *SLJ.*

Peck, Richard. *Close Enough to Touch.* Delacorte. $10.95. ALA.

Peterson, P. J. *Would You Settle for Improbable?* Delacorte. $8.95. ALA.

Preston, Don, and Sue Preston. *Crazy Fox Remembers.* Prentice-Hall. $10.95. *SLJ.*

Reader, Dennis J. *Coming Back Alive.* Random. $8.95. ALA.

Robeson, Susan. *The Whole World in His Hands.* Citadel Press. $17.95. *SLJ.*

Santoli, Al. *Everything We Had: An Oral History of the Vietnam War by Thirty-three Soldiers Who Fought It.* Random. $12.95. ALA, *SLJ.*

Schwartz, Lynne Sharon. *Balancing Acts.* Harper. $9.95. *SLJ.*

Senn, Steve. *A Circle in the Sea.* Atheneum. $11.95. ALA.

Sheldon, Mary. *Perhaps I'll Dream of Darkness.* Random. $11.50. ALA.

Skurzynski, Gloria. *Manwolf.* Houghton/Clarion. $9.95. ALA.

Snyder, Zilpha Keatley. *A Fabulous Creature.* Atheneum. $9.95. ALA.

Strasser, Todd. *Friends till the End.* Delacorte. $8.95. ALA.

Stratton, Joanna L. *Pioneer Women: Voices from the Kansas Frontier.* Simon & Schuster. $16.95. *SLJ.*

Swanson, Walter S. J. *Deepwood.* Little, Brown. $12.95. ALA.

Taylor, Mildred. *Let the Circle Be Unbroken.* Dial. $11.95. ALA.

Wallin, Luke. *The Redneck Poacher's Son.* Bradbury, dist. by Elsevier-Dutton. $9.95. ALA.

Wilhelm, Kate. *A Sense of Shadow.* Houghton. $9.95. *SLJ.*

Yolen, Jane. *The Gift of Sarah Baker.* Viking. $9.95. ALA.

BEST CHILDREN'S BOOKS OF 1981

A list of notable children's books is selected each year by the Notable Children's Books Committee of the Association for Library Service to Children of the American Library Association (ALA). The committee is aided by suggestions from school and public children's librarians throughout the United States. The book review editors of *School Library Journal* (*SLJ*) also compile a list each year, with full annotations, of best books for children. The following list is a combination of ALA's Notable Children's Books of 1981 and *SLJ*'s selection of "Best Books 1981," published in the December 1981 issue of *SLJ*. The source of each selection is indicated by the notation ALA or *SLJ* following each entry. [See the article "Literary Prizes" for Newbery, Caldecott, and other award winners—*Ed.*]

Adler, David A. *A Picture Book of Jewish Holidays.* Illus. by Linda Heller. Holiday House. $8.95. ALA.

Aesop's Fables. Illus. by Heidi Holder. Viking. $12.95. ALA.

Ahlberg, Janet and Allan. *Funnybones.* Greenwillow. $8.95. *SLJ.*

———. *Peek-a-Boo!* Viking. $10.95. ALA.

Alexander, Lloyd. *Westmark.* Dutton. $9.95. ALA, *SLJ.*

Allard, Harry. *The Stupids Die.* Illus. by James Marshall. Houghton. $7.95. *SLJ.*

Anno, Mitsumasa and Masaichiro. *Anno's Magical ABC: An Anamorphic Alphabet.* Philomel. $16.95. ALA.

Azarian, Mary. *A Farmer's Alphabet.* Godine. $6.95. ALA.

Baker, Olaf. *Where the Buffaloes Begin.* Illus. by Stephen Gammell. Warne. $8.95. ALA.

Barton, Byron. *Building a House.* Greenwillow. $7.95. ALA.

Baylor, Byrd, and Peter Parnall. *Desert Voices.* Scribners. ALA.

Bluestone, Naomi. *"So You Want to Be a Doctor?": The Realities of Pursuing Medicine as a Career.* Lothrop. $12.95. *SLJ.*

Bonners, Susan. *A Penguin Year.* Delacorte. $9.95. ALA.

Brittain, Bill. *Devil's Donkey.* Illus. by Andrew Glass. Harper. $8.95. ALA, *SLJ.*

Byars, Betsy. *The Cybil War.* Illus. by Gail Owens. Viking. $8.95. ALA.

Bykov, Vasil. *Pack of Wolves.* Trans. by Lynn Solotaroff. Crowell. $10.50. *SLJ.*

Cameron, Ann. *The Stories Julian Tells.* Illus. by Ann Strugnell. Pantheon. $7.95. ALA.

Childress, Alice. *Rainbow Jordan.* Coward. $8.95. *SLJ.*

Cleary, Beverly. *Ramona Quimby, Age 8.* Illus. by Alan Tiegreen. Morrow. $7.95. ALA, *SLJ.*

Cobb, Vicki. *How to Really Fool Yourself: Illusions For All Your Senses.* Illus. by Leslie Morrill. Lippincott. $8.89. ALA.

Cohen, Barbara. *Yussel's Prayer: A Yom Kippur Story.* Illus. by Michael J. Deraney. Lothrop. $7.95. ALA.

Cole, Joanna. *A Horse's Body.* Photography by Jerome Wexler. Morrow. $6.95. ALA, *SLJ.*

———. *A Snake's Body.* Photography by Jerome Wexler. Morrow. $6.95. ALA, *SLJ.*

Cunningham, Julia. *The Silent Voice.* Dutton. $10.75. ALA.

Curtis, Patricia. *Cindy, a Hearing Ear Dog.* Dutton. ALA.

de Paola, Tomie. *Fin M'Coul, the Giant of Knockmany Hill.* Holiday House. $10.95. ALA.

Diop, Birago. *Mother Crocodile.* Trans. and adapted by Rosa Guy. Illus. by John Steptoe. Delacorte. $10.95. ALA.

Donnelly, Elfie. *So Long, Grandpa.* Trans. by Anthea Bell. Crown. $7.95. ALA, *SLJ.*

Fisher, Leonard Everett. *The Seven Days of Creation.* Adapted from the Bible. Holiday House. $11.95. ALA.

———. *The Friendly Beasts: An Old English Carol.* Illus. by Tomie de Paola. Putnam. $9.95. ALA.

Fritz, Jean. *Traitor: The Case of Benedict Arnold.* Illus. by John André. Putnam. $9.95. ALA, *SLJ.*

Giblin, James Cross. *The Skyscraper Book.* Illus. by Anthony Kramer, photography by David Anderson. Crowell. $8.89. ALA.

Goor, Ron and Nancy. *Shadows: Here, There, and Everywhere.* Crowell. $7.89. ALA.

Greenfield, Eloise, and Tom Feelings. *Daydreamers.* Dial. $9.95. ALA.

Greenwald, Sheila. *Give Us a Great Big Smile, Rosy Cole.* Atlantic/Little, Brown. ALA.

Haddad, Helen R. *Potato Printing.* Crowell. $8.89. ALA.

Hamilton, Virginia. *The Gathering.* Greenwillow. $8.95. ALA.

Hautzig, Deborah. *Second Star to the Right.* Greenwillow. $7.95. *SLJ.*

Hautzig, Esther. *A Gift for Mama.* Illus. by Donna Diamond. Viking. $8.95. ALA.

Heide, Florence Parry. *Treehorn's Treasure.* Illus. by Edward Gorey. Holiday House. $7.95. ALA, *SLJ.*

Highwater, Jamake. *Moonsong Lullaby.* Photography by Marcia Keegan. Lothrop. $8.95. ALA.

Hill, Eric. *Spot's First Walk.* Putnam. ALA.

Hoban, Tana. *Take Another Look.* Greenwillow. $7.95. ALA.

Howe, James. *The Hospital Book.* Photography by Mal Warshaw. Crown. $10.95. ALA, *SLJ.*

Hughes, Ted. *Under the North Star.* Illus. by Leonard Baskin. Viking. $14.95. ALA.

Isenbart, Hans-Heinrich. *A Duckling Is Born.* Putnam. ALA.

Janeczko, Paul. *Don't Forget to Fly.* Bradbury. $9.95. *SLJ.*

Jaquith, Priscilla. *Bo Rabbit Smart for True: Folktales from the Gullah.* Illus. by Ed Young. Philomel. $9.95. ALA.

Kalan, Robert. *Jump, Frog, Jump!* Illus. by Byron Barton. Greenwillow. $8.95. *SLJ.*

Keller, Beverly. *The Sea Watch.* Four Winds. $7.95. ALA.

Kennedy, Richard. *Song of the Horse.* Illus. by Marcia Sewall. Dutton. $9.50. ALA.

Kerr, M. E. *Little Little.* Harper. $8.95. ALA, *SLJ.*

Krementz, Jill. *How It Feels When a Parent Dies.* Knopf. $9.95. ALA, *SLJ.*

Kullman, Harry. *The Battle Horse.* Trans. by George Blecher and Lone Thygesen-Blecher. Bradbury. $8.95. ALA, *SLJ.*

Lasky, Kathryn. *The Night Journey.* Illus. by Trina Schart Hyman. Warne. $8.95. ALA.

———. *The Weaver's Gift.* Photography by Christopher G. Knight. Warne. $8.95. ALA.

Lauber, Patricia. *Seeds Pop! Stick! Glide!* Photography by Jerome Wexler. Crown. $9.95. ALA, *SLJ.*

Lawson, Don. *The United States in the Vietnam War.* Crowell. $8.95. *SLJ.*

Lindgren, Barbro. *The Wild Baby.* Adapted from Swedish by Jack Prelutsky, illus. by Eva Eriksson. Greenwillow. $7.95. *SLJ.*

Lobel, Arnold. *On Market Street.* Illus. by Anita Lobel. Greenwillow. $8.95. ALA.

———. *Uncle Elephant.* Harper. $6.95. ALA, *SLJ.*

Lowry, Lois. *Anastasia Again!* Houghton. $7.95. ALA.

Maestro, Betsy and Giulio. *Traffic: A Book of Opposites.* Crown. $8.95. ALA.

Major, Kevin. *Far from Shore.* Delacorte. $9.95. *SLJ.*

Modell, Frank. *One Zillion Valentines.* Illus. by author. Greenwillow. $8.95. *SLJ.*

Moeri, Louise. *Save Queen of Sheba.* Dutton. $9.25. ALA.

Nostlinger, Christine. *Luke and Angela.* Trans. by Anthea Bell. Harcourt. $8.95. ALA, *SLJ.*

Ormerod, Jan. *Sunshine.* Lothrop. $7.95. ALA.

Otsuka, Yuzo. *Suho and the White Horse: A Legend of Mongolia.* Adapted from translation by Ann Herring, illus. by Suekichi Akaba. Viking. $10.95. ALA.

Rabe, Berniece. *The Balancing Girl.* Illus. by Lillian Hoban. Dutton. $10.25. ALA.

Rice, Eve. *Benny Bakes a Cake.* Greenwillow. $8.95. ALA, *SLJ.*

Riskind, Mary. *Apple Is My Sign.* Houghton. $7.95. ALA.

Rodowsky, Colby. *The Gathering Room.* Farrar. $9.95. ALA, *SLJ.*

Rounds, Glen. *Mr. Yowder and the Train Robbers.* Holiday House. ALA.

Salassi, Otto R. *On the Ropes.* Greenwillow. $8.95. *SLJ.*

Sandin, Joan. *The Long Way to a New Land.* Harper. $7.89. ALA.

Sargent, Sarah. *Secret Lies.* Crown. $8.95. ALA.

Sarnoff, Jane, and Reynolds Ruffins. *Words: A Book About the Origins of Everyday Words and Phrases.* Scribners. $9.95. ALA.

Sattler, Helen Roney. *Dinosaurs of North America.* Illus. by Anthony Rao. Lothrop. $10.95. ALA.

Schlee, Ann. *The Vandal.* Crown. $8.95. *SLJ.*

Scott, Jack Denton. *The Book of the Pig.* Photographs by Ozzie Sweet. Putnam. $8.95. ALA, *SLJ.*

———. *Moose.* Photographs by Ozzie Sweet. Putnam. $9.95. ALA.

Sendak, Maurice. *Outside Over There.* Harper. $12.95. ALA.

Shannon, George. *The Piney Woods Peddler.* Illus. by Nancy Tafuri. Greenwillow. $7.95. ALA.

Siegal, Aranka. *Upon the Head of the Goat: A Childhood in Hungary, 1939–1944.* Farrar. $9.95. ALA, *SLJ.*

Silverstein, Shel. *A Light in the Attic.* Illus. by author. Harper. $10.95. ALA, *SLJ.*

Simon, Hilda. *The Magic of Color.* Lothrop. $8.95. ALA.

Sleator, William. *The Green Futures of Tycho.* Dutton. $9.95. *SLJ.*

Slepian, Jan. *Lester's Turn.* Macmillan. $8.95. ALA.

Smith, Doris Buchanan. *Last Was Lloyd.* Viking. $8.95. *SLJ.*

Stevenson, James. *The Wish Card Ran Out!* Illus. by author. Greenwillow. $7.95. *SLJ.*

Stolz, Mary. *What Time of Night Is It?* Harper. $9.89. ALA.

Taylor, Mildred D. *Let the Circle Be Unbroken.* Dial. $11.95. ALA.

Turkle, Brinton. *Do Not Open.* Dutton. $11.50. ALA, *SLJ.*

Udry, Janice May. *Thump and Plunk.* Illus. by Ann Schweninger. Harper. $7.95. *SLJ.*

Van Allsburg, Chris. *Jumanji.* Illus. by author. Houghton. $9.95. ALA, *SLJ.*

Van Leeuwen, Jean. *More Tales of Oliver Pig.* Illus. by Arnold Lobel. Dial. $5.99. ALA.

Westall, Robert. *The Scarecrows.* Greenwillow. $8.95. *SLJ.*

Willard, Nancy. *A Visit to William Blake's Inn: Poems for Innocent and Experienced Travelers.* Illus. by Alice and Martin Provensen. Harcourt. $10.95. ALA.

Wiseman, David. *Jeremy Visick.* Houghton. $7.95. ALA, *SLJ.*

Yagawa, Sumiko. *The Crane Wife.* Trans. by Katherine Paterson, illus. by Suekichi Akaba. Morrow. $8.95. ALA.

Yates, Elizabeth. *My Diary—My World.* Westminster. $12.95. ALA.

Zelinsky, Paul O. *The Maid and the Mouse and the Odd-shaped House.* Dodd. $9.95. *SLJ.*

Zisfein, Melvin B. *Flight: A Panorama of Aviation.* Illus. by Robert Andrew Parker. Pantheon. $17.99. ALA.

BEST SELLERS OF 1981: HARDCOVER FICTION AND NONFICTION

Daisy Maryles
Senior Editor, *Publishers Weekly*

A look at the 1981 hardcover best sellers and their sales figures shows the following:

Veteran best-selling novelists dominated the top of the fiction lists this year, but a handful of newcomers made impressive showings.

The number 1 fiction best seller set a new record for the most expensive novel, yet.

Unit sales for the top 25 fiction best sellers slipped from 1980, with 21 of 25 books selling more than 100,000 copies; in 1980, 24 did.

Diet books, cookbooks and books on money matters continued to spark nonfiction best sellers.

Unit sales for nonfiction best sellers topped 1980's figures significantly, with more than 10 books showng sales of 100,000+ copies that were not among the top 25 list.

The books on *PW*'s annual best seller lists, including runners-up, are based on sales figures supplied by publishers. These figures, according to the respective firms, reflect only 1981 U.S. trade sales—that is, sales to bookstores, wholesalers and libraries only. Not included are book club, overseas and direct mail transactions. Some books appear in the listings without accompanying sales figures. These were submitted to *PW* in confidence, for use only in placing the titles in their correct positions on a specific list.

"Sales" as used on these lists refers to books shipped and billed in calendar year 1981. Returns made in 1981, publishers claim, are reflected in their numbers. In many cases, however, the 1981 sales figures include books still on bookstore and wholesaler shelves and/or books on the way back to the publisher warehouses as well as books already stacking up on returns piles. Obtaining *accurate* final net sales would not now be possible as publishers do not yet have a complete accounting of post-Christmas returns.

Since the two national bookstore chains—B. Dalton and Waldenbooks—have their own end-of-the-year bestseller lists, based on actual sales to customers as registered on the chains' computers, *PW* thought it might be interesting to compare its annual best seller list with these two retailers' lists. [See Bookselling & Marketing in *Publishers Weekly*, March 12, 1982.]

THE FICTION BEST SELLERS

The top-selling fiction in 1981 was James Clavell's *Noble House*, which won the prized position after impressive sales of 488,905 last year. These numbers are even more remarkable considering the hefty $19.95 cover price commanded by the title, a record

Note: Adapted from *Publishers Weekly*, March 12, 1982, where the article was entitled "The Year's Bestselling Books: Hardcover Top Sellers."

dollar price for a work of fiction. Neither the cost of the book nor its length (1,200 pages) daunted Clavell fans—many won over anew by the highly successful television miniseries based on his previous bestseller *Shogun*. Back in 1975, when that title was first published in hardcover, it ranked number 9 on *PW*'s end of the year best seller list with sales around 100,000. Still on *PW*'s weekly chart, *Noble House* placed 33 out of 51 weeks on our list in 1981, 15 times in the lead position. The book also set two other hardcover records—a 250,000 first printing was the largest ever for Delacorte, and Waldenbooks' 35,000-copy initial order marked a record purchase for the company.

A much-heralded novel, *The Hotel New Hampshire* by John Irving, was eagerly awaited by many readers of *The World According to Garp*. E. P. Dutton sold 372,000 copies of Irving's latest book in 1981, making it the number 2 fiction seller. *Garp*, published in 1978, made it to number 14 on that year's annual list with sales of 105,000 copies. Its paperback edition had 2,755,000 copies in print in 1979, its first year in mass market life.

Stephen King's status as the bestselling author in the horror-suspense category remains unchallenged. *Cujo* achieved the number 3 spot with sales of 350,000 in 1981, showing King's popularity gaining more hardcover fans with each title. He took the number 4 spot in 1980 for *Firestarter* (a 285,000-copy seller) and the number 6 in 1979 with *The Stand* (175,000 copies).

While Colleen McCullough did not equal her earlier success (*The Thorn Birds* sold 590,000 and placed number 2 for 1977), *An Indecent Obsession* gained the number 4 spot with a much more than respectable sales figure of 297,006. It was the top-selling fiction title nationally during the last month of 1981—the height of the bookselling season.

The number 5 spot is claimed by Martin Cruz Smith for sales of 273,000 copies of *Gorky Park* in 1981. The author is a newcomer to these annual lists but not to the world of books. Smith has 25 paperback originals under his belt (including westerns, spy stories and Nick Carter books) as well as three hardcover novels. He hit the big time with this suspense novel set in Moscow and the U.S., featuring a Russian police detective, and also won the enviable distinction of having the year's longest running hardcover fiction bestseller on *PW*'s weekly charts—37 appearances in 1981.

Police detectives—of the American sort—figured in another top-15 bestseller. Joseph Wambaugh's *The Glitter Dome* gathered enough sales to place it in the number 9 spot. Wambaugh is no newcomer to *PW*'s charts. In 1975, *The Choirboys* took the number 5 spot with sales of 135,000, and in 1977, *The Black Marble* was a runner-up with 100,000.

Other newcomers to our annual lists are Kit Williams, Frank Herbert and Andrew M. Greeley. Williams's *Masquerade* took this year's number 6 position with sales of 245,000 books. An illustrated fantasy (previously a bestseller in England), it contains clues to the whereabouts of a buried treasure. Schocken took a gamble on the book earlier turned down by several publishers and got itself a first-ever position on the end-of-the-year charts. *God Emperor of Dune* sold 165,793 copies in 1981, making it the number 12 bestselling novel for the year and one of the few science fiction titles ever to reach the list of annual top sellers. First novelist Father Andrew M. Greeley scored high with his inside look at the Catholic church; *The Cardinal Sins* made the 13th spot with 1981 sales of 143,000 books.

The rest of the novelists making up the top-15 consist of writers with proven track records. In the number 7 spot is Harold Robbins's *Goodbye, Janette* with sales of 202,000 copies. A veteran of best seller lists, Robbins made his first appearance on *PW*'s annual lists in 1961 for *The Carpetbaggers* (number 5 for 105,000 sales in that calendar year) and his most recent one for *Memories of Another Day* (sales of 187,000 in 1979 gave it the number 4 position). Lawrence Sanders's latest, *The Third Deadly Sin*, takes the number 8 slot with sales of 187,383. Last year, his book *The Tenth Commandment* was number 15 with sales of 129,000 copies. Cynthia Freeman also was among the 1980 top sellers with *Come Pour the Wine* in the number 11 spot. In 1981, she moved up a notch with *No Time for Tears*. Howard Fast's fictional Lavetta family continues to hold reader interest, as evidenced by sales of the fourth volume in the saga of this California clan. *The Legacy* enjoyed sales of 160,000 during 1981, enough to give it the number 12 position. The previous three volumes—*The Immigrants*, *Second Generation* and *The Establishment*—made it to the runners-up lists. Taking the number 14 position is Paul Erdman with 134,000 copies sold of *The Last Days of America*. Erdman's initial appearance on these charts was in 1973 with his first novel, *The Billion Dollar Sure Thing* (number 9 after a 90,000-copy sale). Travis McGee stars in his 19th John D. MacDonald thriller, *Free Fall in Crimson*, which rounds out the top-15 list with 129,000 sold in 1981. In the last six years, MacDonald has been a runner-up four times, most recently in 1979 for *The Green Ripper* (sales that year were reported to be 98,547 copies).

THE FICTION RUNNERS-UP

The second tier of 1981 fiction best sellers includes Irwin Shaw, Morris West and John Updike; a first novel by Bette Bao Lord, covering the years 1892–1972 in China; Bantam's first hardcover fiction published without a simultaneous paperback edition; a short work of fiction by this year's bestselling novelist, first published in 1963 in *Ladies Home Journal;* and the critically-acclaimed sleeper of last year, *The White Hotel*.

In ranked order, the 10 fiction runners-up are: *Remembrances* by Danielle Steel (Delacorte, published 10/23/81; 127,571 copies sold in 1981); *Spring Moon* by Bette Bao Lord (Harper & Row, published 10/28/81; 121,907 copies sold in 1981); *Bread Upon the Water* by Irwin Shaw (Delacorte, published 8/28/81; 115,287 copies sold in 1981); *Clowns of God* by Morris West (Morrow, published 6/5/81); *Red Dragon* by Thomas Harris (Putnam, published 11/16/81; 101,349 copies sold in 1981); *Night Probe!* by Clive Cussler (Bantam, published 8/3/81; 101,000 copies sold); *Rabbit Is Rich* by John Updike (Knopf, published 10/7/81; 97,000 copies sold); *The White Hotel* by D. M. Thomas (Viking, published 3/26/81; 95,000 copies sold); *The Children's Story* by James Clavell (Delacorte, published 9/3/81; 94,773 copies sold); *Tar Baby* by Toni Morrison (Knopf, published 3/30/81; 92,000 copies sold).

THE NONFICTION BEST SELLERS

Diet books, cookbooks and books on money matters were very popular in 1981—11 of the 25 top sellers dealt with just these subjects. Customers also warmed to books dispensing other kinds of advice—words of wisdom from Miss Piggy and Dear Abby and tips on how women can please men sexually. A few tell-alls, essays from a popular, folksy philosopher, and a sharp, witty history of American architecture were also crowd pleasers.

Leading the nonfiction top sellers was one of the more controversial diet programs that may or may not have slimmed the body, but certainly fattened the pockets of the author. Judy Mazel's *The Beverly Hills Diet* sold 756,360 books in 1981. It perched atop *PW*'s weekly hardcover nonfiction list 18 times. Mazel's diet regimen was first popular with a number of Hollywood personalities, but its thesis that monitoring enzymes is more important than watching calories and portion sizes found a much larger audience.

The number 3 bestseller of the year, *Richard Simmons' Never-Say-Diet Book*, also had its first success in Beverly Hills where the author runs a salad bar and exercise studio. The book sold 570,000 copies in 1981 and the trade paperback edition has climbed to the top spot on *PW*'s weekly list.

The third bestseller appealing to the diet-conscious is *Weight Watcher's 365-Day Menu Cookbook*. Reported sales in 1981 are 230,000, making it the number 8 best selling nonfiction this year.

A 1981 top seller that didn't make any appearances on our weekly list in 1981 (or even 1982) is *Better Homes and Gardens New Cookbook*. It sold 465,111 copies in 1981, enough to secure the number 6 position. (One theory explaining why these books are not generally reported as best sellers holds that they are generally categorized as backlist.) According to the publisher, the ninth edition of this perennial best seller (the first new edition since 1964) has been completely revised—65 percent to 75 percent of the recipes are new with many international recipes added.

Sandwiched between these books are new titles from veteran best selling writers as well as a stellar repeat performance from one of 1980's lead titles. A new James Herriot book delights fans, publisher and booksellers, and the Yorkshire veterinarian's latest, *The Lord God Made Them All*, had sales of 613,102, giving it the number 2 spot for the year. Though his early books also hit the annual charts, this outsold all previous titles.

The new work from a bestselling backlist author/illustrator, Shel Silverstein's *A Light in the Attic* was reported by booksellers during the weeks before Christmas as the fastest-selling book in both the adult and children's sections. Written for all ages, the year's number 4 bestseller broke out of its category, and by the end of 1981, it had sold 544,868 copies.

Carl Sagan makes a reappearance in 1981; sales of 487,000 copies make *Cosmos* the year's number 5 nonfiction best seller (it was number 2 in 1980). Previous Sagan books also ranked in *PW*'s end of the year lists and the author's nonfiction triumphs make him a prime candidate for success in the fiction genre. At least that is the expectation of Simon & Schuster, which paid him $2 million for hardcover and paperback rights to a yet-uncompleted work of fiction. The sum was thought to be the largest ever paid for a work not yet in manuscript. Sagan's *Cosmos* is the longest-running nonfiction best seller on *PW*'s weekly 1981 lists—it was on 50 times during the year.

Everyone's favorite muppet, Miss Piggy, charmed enough fans to take the number 7 spot with 1981 sales for *Miss Piggy's Guide to Life* amounting to 237,000 copies. Getting what you want on your own terms is the subject of the year's number 9 best selling nonfiction, *You Can Negotiate Anything* by Herb Cohen. Sales for 1981 were 205,000 copies. It was also the third longest-running nonfiction title (39 weeks) on *PW*'s weekly charts. Advice of yet another type was available in *How to Make Love to a Man*, which sold 196,196 copies, enough to give it the number 12 position on the year-end list.

The nonfiction sleeper and a welcomed end-of-the-year surprise to booksellers was *A Few Minutes with Andy Rooney*, which sold 200,000 copies in 1981 and eased into the number 10 spot for the year. Rooney's national prominence had grown with his appearances on "60 Minutes."

Gail Sheehy's newest book, *Pathfinders*, number 11 on *PW*'s annual list, is about how people navigate through the crises of adult life and find paths to well-being. Her previous best seller, *Passages*, examined midlife crises and made 1976's number 4 position with reported sales of over 350,000 copies. Its publisher Morrow had another top seller in 1981, for in the 13th slot is *The Walk West*, Peter and Barbara Jenkins's sequel to *A Walk Across America*.

The final two nonfiction best sellers are from Simon & Schuster: *Elizabeth Taylor: The Last Star* by Kitty Kelley in the number 14 spot with sales of 169,000 and *The Eagle's Gift* by Carlos Castaneda, number 15 with sales of 169,000 books in 1981. The former follows Taylor from a 10-year-old protégée on the MGM lot to her role as a senator's wife. Castaneda's previous *The Second Ring of Power* was number 8 in 1977 with sales of 173,000.

THE NONFICTION RUNNERS-UP

As noted earlier, a much wider spread of nonfiction titles achieved sales of 100,000 or more in 1981 than ever before; at least 12 titles are claimed by publishers to have U.S. domestic unit sales in the six figures. Last year, this was true only seven titles.

Books that did make the runners-up group of 10 include two more cookbooks—both Betty Crocker products; four titles on business and money; a provocative biography of The King of Rock & Roll (it fetched a cool $1 million from Avon for paperback rights, reported to be the highest price paid for reprint rights to a biography); the first collection of Abigail Van Buren letters in 19 years; and a book that posits that women still fear responsibility for their own lives.

In ranked order, the 10 nonfiction runners-up are: *Theory Z: How American Business Can Meet the Japanese Challenge* by William Ouchi (Addison-Wesley; published 3/21/81); *The Best of Dear Abby* by Abigail Van Buren (Andrews and McMeel; published 10/8/81; 155,000 copies sold in 1981); *Betty Crocker's International Cookbook* (Random House; 9/26/80; 153,000); *The Cinderella Complex: Women's Fear of Independence* by Colette Dowling (Summit Books; June 1981; 145,000); *Money Dynamics for the 1980's* by Venita Van Caspel (Reston/Prentice-Hall; October 1980; 142,000); *Betty Crocker's Microwave Cook Book* (Random House; September 1981; 135,000); *Elvis* by Albert Goldman (McGraw-Hill; 11/8/81; 134,000); *Paper Money* by Adam Smith (Summit Books; 1/27/81; 128,000); *From Bauhaus to Our House* by Tom Wolfe (Farrar, Straus & Giroux; 10/26/81; 127,000); and *William E. Donoghue's Complete Money Guide* by William E. Donoghue with Thomas Tilling (Harper & Row; 1/28/81; 126,000).

PUBLISHERS WEEKLY HARDCOVER TOP SELLERS

Fiction

1. *Noble House* by James Clavell (published April 30, 1981) Delacorte
2. *The Hotel New Hampshire* by John Irving (September 30, 1981) A Henry Robbins Book/Dutton
3. *Cujo* by Stephen King (September 8, 1981) Viking
4. *An Indecent Obsession* by Colleen McCullough (October 28, 1981) Harper & Row
5. *Gorky Park* by Martin Cruz Smith (April 3, 1981) Random House
6. *Masquerade* by Kit Williams (October 3, 1980) Schocken Books
7. *Goodbye, Janette* by Harold Robbins (June 1981) Simon & Schuster
8. *The Third Deadly Sin* by Lawrence Sanders (August 4, 1981) Putnam
9. *The Glitter Dome* by Joseph Wambaugh (June 15, 1981) Perigord Press/Morrow
10. *No Times for Tears* by Cynthia Freeman (December 1, 1981) Arbor House

11. *God Emperor of Dune* by Frank Herbert (May 6, 1981) Putnam
12. *The Legacy* by Howard Fast (September 28, 1981) Houghton Mifflin
13. *The Cardinal Sins* by Andrew M. Greeley (June 1981) Warner/Bernard Geis
14. *The Last Days of America* by Paul Erdman (August 1981) Simon & Schuster
15. *Free Fall in Crimson* by John D. MacDonald (April 29, 1981) Harper & Row

Nonfiction
1. *The Beverly Hills Diet* by Judy Mazel (April 29, 1981) Macmillan
2. *The Lord God Made Them All* by James Herriot (June 19, 1981) St. Martin's
3. *Richard Simmons' Never-Say-Diet Book* by Richard Simmons (October 20, 1980) Warner
4. *A Light in the Attic* by Shel Silverstein (October 7, 1981) Harper & Row
5. *Cosmos* by Carl Sagan (October 24, 1980) Random House
6. *Better Homes & Gardens New Cookbook* (August 1981) Meredith
7. *Miss Piggy's Guide to Life* by Miss Piggy as told to Henry Beard (May 15, 1980) Knopf
8. *Weight Watchers® 365-Day Menu Cookbook* (October 1981) NAL Books
9. *You Can Negotiate Anything* by Herb Cohen (November 15, 1980) Lyle Stuart
10. *A Few Minutes with Andy Rooney* by Andrew A. Rooney (October 28, 1981) Atheneum
11. *Pathfinders* by Gail Sheehy (October 13, 1981) Morrow
12. *How to Make Love to a Man* by Alexandra Penney (May 22, 1981) Clarkson N. Potter
13. *The Walk West* by Peter and Barbara Jenkins (November 20, 1981) Morrow
14. *Elizabeth Taylor: The Last Star* by Kitty Kelley (October 2, 1981) Simon & Schuster
15. *The Eagle's Gift* by Carlos Castaneda (May 11, 1981) Simon & Schuster

Part 7
Directory of Organizations

Directory of Library and Related Organizations

NATIONAL LIBRARY AND INFORMATION-INDUSTRY ASSOCIATIONS, UNITED STATES AND CANADA

AMERICAN ASSOCIATION OF LAW LIBRARIES
53 W. Jackson Blvd., Chicago, IL 60604
312-939-4764

OBJECT

"To promote librarianship, to develop and increase the usefulness of law libraries, to cultivate the science of law librarianship and to foster a spirit of cooperation among members of the profession." Established 1906. Memb. 2,850. Dues (Active) $65.; (Inst.) $65; (Assoc.) $65 & $125; (Student) $10. Year. June 1 to May 31.

MEMBERSHIP

Persons officially connected with a law library or with a law section of a state or general library, separately maintained; and institutions. Associate membership available for others.

OFFICERS (JUNE 1981-JUNE 1982)

Pres. Roger F. Jacobs, U.S. Supreme Court, Law Lib., One First St. N.E., Washington, DC 20543; *V.P./Pres.-Elect.* Leah F. Chanin, Walter F. George School of Law, Mercer Univ., 1021 Georgia Ave., Macon, GA 31207; *Secy.* Shirley R. Bysiewicz, Univ. of Connecticut, School of Law Lib., 1800 Asylum Ave., West Hartford, CT 06117; *Treas.* Joyce Malden, Municipal Reference Lib., 1004 City Hall, Chicago, IL 60602; *Past Pres.* Francis Gates, Attorney at Law, Box 12303, San Francisco, CA 94112.

EXECUTIVE BOARD

Officers; Sue Dyer; Carol C. West; Anthony P. Grech; Marcia Koslov; Betty W. Taylor; Sarah K. Wiant.

COMMITTEE CHAIRPERSONS (1981-1982)

Certification Board, Edgar J. Bellefontaine, Social Law Lib., 1200 Court House, Boston, MA 02108.

CONELL. Margaret C. Shediac, Howard, Prim, Rice, Nemerovsky, Canady & Pollak, The Hartford Bldg., 650 California St., San Francisco, CA 94108.

Constitution and Bylaws. Robert L. Oakley, Boston Univ., Pappas Law Lib., 765 Commonwealth Ave., Boston, MA 02215.

Copyright. Laura Nell Gasaway, Univ. of Oklahoma Law Lib., 300 Timberdell, Norman, OK 73019.

Education. Elizabeth Slusser Kelly, School of Law Lib., Southern Illinois Univ., Carbondale, IL 62901.

Elections. Rita Dermody, Continental Bank, Law Lib., Information Services Div., 231 S. LaSalle St., Chicago, IL 60693.

Exchange of Duplicates. Margaret A. Lundahl, Isham, Lincoln & Beale, One 1st National Plaza, 42nd fl., Chicago, IL 60603.

Foreign, Comparative, and International Law. Claire M. Germain, Law School Lib., Duke Univ., Durham, NC 27706.
Index to Foreign Legal Periodicals. Robert C. Berring, Univ. of Washington, 1100 N.E Campus Pkwy., JB20, Seattle, WA 98105.
Indexing of Periodical Literature. Marlene McGuirl, American British Law Div., Lib. of Congress, Law Lib., 10 First St. N.E., Washington, DC 20540.
Joseph L. Andrews Bibliographic Award. S. Alan Holoch, Univ. of Southern California, Law Center, University Park, Los Angeles, CA 90007.
Law Library Journal. Kenneth Zick, Wake Forest Univ., School of Law Lib., Winston-Salem, NC 27109.
Legislation & Legal Developments. Peggy Richter, American Bar Assn., Governmental Relations Office, 1800 M St. N.W., Washington, DC 20036.
Membership. Mark Estes, Holme, Roberts & Owen, 1700 Broadway, Denver, CO 80290.
Memorials. George Skinner, Univ. of Arkansas, School of Law Lib., Fayetteville, AR 72701.
Nominations. Anne H. Butler, Alston, Miller & Gaines, 1200 Citizens & Southern National Bank Bldg., 35 Broad St., Atlanta, GA 30335.
Placement. Larry B. Wenger, Univ. of Virginia, Law Lib., North Grounds, Charlottesville, VA 22901.
Public Relations. Donald G. Ziegenfuss, Carlton, Fields, Ward, Emmanuel, Smith & Cutler, Exchange National Bank Bldg., Box 3239, Tampa, FL 33601
Recruitment. Judith G. Gecas, Univ. of Chicago, Law Lib., 1121 E. 60th St., Chicago, IL 60637.
Relations with Publishers & Dealers. Carl A. Yirka, Law Lib., Northwestern Univ., 357 E. Chicago Ave., Chicago, IL 60611.
Scholarships & Grants. Dennis J. Stone, Gonzaga Univ., School of Law, 600 E. Sharp, Box 3538, Spokane, WA 99220.

Standards. Reynold J. Kosek, Mercer Univ., Walter F. George School of Law, 1021 Georgia Ave., Macon, GA 31201.
Statistics. David Thomas, Brigham Young Univ., Law Lib., Provo, UT 84601.

SPECIAL-INTEREST SECTION CHAIRPERSONS

Academic Law Libraries. Dan J. Freehling, Cornell Law School, Myron Taylor Hall, Ithaca, NY 14850.
Automation & Scientific Development. Jenni Parrish, Univ. of Pittsburgh, School of Law Lib., 404 Law Bldg., 3900 Forbes Ave., Pittsburgh, PA 15260.
Contemporary Social Problems. Diane C. Reynolds, Los Angeles County Law Lib., 301 W. First St., Los Angeles, CA 90012.
Government Documents. Colleen Pauwels, Indiana Univ., School of Law, Law Bldg., Bloomington, IN 47405.
Micrographics & Audio-Visual. James R. Fox, The Dickinson School of Law, Sheely-Lee Law Lib., 150 S. College St., Carlisle, PA 17013.
On-Line Bibliographic Services. Gregory Koster, Pace Univ., School of Law, 78 N. Broadway, White Plains, NY 10603.
Private Law Libraries. Victoria M. Ward, Morgan, Lewis & Bockius, 1800 M St. N.E., Washington, DC 20036.
Readers' Services. Carol B. Allred, Salmon P. Chase College of Law, Northern Kentucky Univ., 1401 Dixie Hwy., Covington, KY 41011.
State, Court & County Law Libraries. O. James Werner, San Diego County Law Lib., 1105 Front St., San Diego, CA 92101.
Technical Services. Margaret Axtmann, National Center for State Courts, 300 Newport Ave., Williamsburg, VA 23185.

REPRESENTATIVES

ABA (*American Bar Association*). Dan Henke.
American Correctional Association. E. Ann Puckett.

American Library Association. Judith Wright.
American Library Association. Adult Services Committee, Inter-Library Loan Code Revision Committee. Randall Peterson.
American National Standards Institute. Committee PH-5. Larry Wenger.
American National Standards Institute. Committee Z-39. Robert Oakley.
American Society for Information Science. Signe Larson.
Association of American Law Schools. Earl Borgeson.
British-Irish Association of Law Libraries. Muriel Anderson.
CLENE. Dan J. Freehling.
Canadian Association of Law Libraries. Lillian McPherson.
Council of National Library and Information Associations. Jane Hammond; Bill Jepson.
Council of National Library and Information Associations. Ad Hoc Committee on Copyright. Laura N. Gasaway.
International Association of Law Libraries. Arno Liivak.
Library of Congress. Terry Martin.
Special Libraries Association. Sally Wiant.
U.S. Copyright Office. Laura N. Gasaway.

AMERICAN LIBRARY ASSOCIATION
Executive Director, Robert Wedgeworth
50 E. Huron St., Chicago, IL 60611
312-944-6780

OBJECT

The American Library Association is an organization for librarians and libraries with the overarching objective of promoting and improving library service and librarianship. Memb. (Indiv.) 34,642; (Inst.) 3,312. Dues (Indiv.) 1st year, $25; 2nd and 3rd years, $35; 4th year and beyond, $50; (Nonsalaried Libns.) $15; (Trustee & Assoc. Membs.) $20; (Student) $10; (Foreign Indiv.) $30; (Inst.) $50 & up (depending upon operating expenses of institution.)

MEMBERSHIP

Any person, library, or other organization interested in library service and librarians.

OFFICERS

Pres. Elizabeth W. Stone, School of Lib. & Info. Science, Catholic Univ. of America, Washington, DC 20064; *V.P./Pres.-Elect.* Carol A. Nemeyer, Lib. of Congress, Washington, DC 20540; *Treas.* Herbert Biblo, 5225 S. Blackstone Ave., Chicago, IL 60615; *Exec. Dir. (Ex officio)* Robert Wedgeworth.

Address general correspondence to the executive director.

EXECUTIVE BOARD

Officers; *Immediate Past Pres.* Peggy A. Sullivan (1982); Connie R. Dunlap (1982); Grace P. Slocum (1982); E. J. Josey (1983); Ella G. Yates-Edwards (1983); Jane Anne Hannigan (1984); Brooke E. Sheldon (1984); Judith R. Farley (1985); Regina Minudri (1985).

ENDOWMENT TRUSTEES

William V. Jackson (1983); John Juergensmeyer (1984); John E. Velde (1982).

DIVISIONS

See the separate entries that follow: American Assn. of School Libns.; American Lib. Trustee Assn.; Assn. for Lib. Service to Children; Assn. of College and Research Libs.; Assn. of Specialized and

Cooperative Lib. Agencies; Lib. Admin. and Management Assn.; Lib. and Info. Technology Assn.; Public Lib. Assn.; Reference and Adult Services Div.; Resources and Technical Services Div.; Young Adult Services Div.

PUBLICATIONS

American Libraries (11 per year; memb.).
ALA Handbook of Organization 1981-1982 and Membership Directory (ann.).
ALA Yearbook (ann.; $55).
Booklist (22 issues; $40).
Choice (11 issues; $60).

ROUND TABLE CHAIRPERSONS

(ALA staff liaison is given in parentheses.)
Exhibits. Leedom Kettell, Gaylord Bros., Box 4901, Syracuse, NY 13221 (Chris J. Hoy).
Federal Librarians. Beth Yeates, 10201 Grosvenor Place, Apt. 513, Rockville, MD 20852 (Anne A. Heanue).
Government Documents. Jeanne Isacco, Cuyahoga County Lib. System, 4510 Memphis Ave., Cleveland, OH 44144 (Bill Drewett).
Intellectual Freedom. Bruce A. Shuman, Grad. School of Lib. & Info. Studies, Queens College, Flushing, NY 11367 (Sheldon Liebman).
International Relations. Hans Panofsky, Curator of Africana, Northwestern Univ. Lib., Evanston, IL 60201.
Junior Members. Judy Sessions, Gelman Lib., George Washington Univ., Washington, DC 20052 (Patricia Scarry).
Library History. Doris Cruger Dale, Dept. of Curriculum, Instruction and Media, Southern Illinois Univ., Carbondale, IL 62901 (Joel M. Lee).
Library Instruction. Janet Gilligan, International Communication Agency, 1717 H St. N.W., Rm. 736, Washington, DC 20547 (Jeniece Guy).
Library Research. Charles Curran, College of Libnsp. Univ. of South Carolina, Columbia, SC 29208 (Mary Jo Lynch).
Map and Geography. Charles A. Seavey, Government Publications & Maps Dept., General Lib., Univ. of New Mexico, Albuquerque, NM 87131 (Celeste Lavelli).
Social Responsibilities. Barbara J. Pruett, 2734 Ordway St. N.W., Apt. 1, Washington, DC 20008 (Jean Coleman).
Staff Organizations. Kenneth Miller, Jr., Detroit Public Lib., Detroit, MI 48202 (John Katzenberger).

COMMITTEE CHAIRPERSONS

Accreditation (Standing). Kenneth E. Beasley, Univ. of Texas at El Paso, El Paso, TX 79968 (Elinor Yungmeyer).
"American Libraries," Editorial Advisory Committee for (Standing). Ellis Hodgin, Dir., Robert Scott Small Lib., College of Charleston, 66 George St., Charleston, SC 29401 (Arthur Plotnik).
Awards (Standing). Janice Feye-Stukas, Office of Public Libs., 301 Hanover Bldg., 480 Cedar St., St. Paul, MN 55101 (to be appointed).
Chapter Relations (Standing). Hannah McCauley, Lib. Dir., Ohio Univ., Lancaster Branch, Lancaster, OH 43130 (Patricia Scarry).
Conference Program (Standing). Suzanne LeBarron, Lib. Development 10B41, Cultural Education Center, Empire State Plaza, Albany, NY 12230 (Ruth R. Frame).
Constitution and Bylaws (Standing). Frances V. Sedney, Harford County Lib., 100 Pennsylvania Ave., Bel Air, MD 21014 (Miriam L. Hornback).
Council Orientation (Special). Grace Slocum, Cecil County Lib., 135 E. Main St., Elkton, MD 21921 (Miriam L. Hornback).
Equal Rights Amendment (Task Force). Kay Cassell, Dir., Public Lib., 338 Main St., Huntington, NY 11743; Alice B. Ihrig, 9322 S. 53rd Ave., Oak Lawn, IL 60453 (Patricia Scarry).
Instruction in the Use of Libraries

(*Standing*). Joseph A. Boisse, Samuel Paley Lib., Temple Univ., Philadelphia, PA 19122 (Andrew M. Hansen).
Intellectual Freedom (*Standing, Council*). J. Dennis Day, Dir., Public Lib., 209 E. Fifth St. S., Salt Lake City, UT 84111 (Judith F. Krug).
International Relations (*Standing, Council*). Russell Shank, Univ. Libn., Univ. of California, Los Angeles, CA 90024.
Legislation (*Standing, Council*). Peter J. Paulson, State Lib., Cultural Education Center, Empire State Plaza, Albany, NY 12230 (Eileen D. Cooke).
Library Education (*Standing, Council*). Evelyn H. Daniel, School of Info. Studies, Syracuse Univ., Syracuse, NY 13210 (Margaret Myers).
Library Personnel Resources, Office for (*Standing, Advisory*). Patricia Pond, School of Lib. & Info. Science, Univ. of Pittsburgh, PA 15260 (Margaret Myers).
Mediation, Arbitration, and Inquiry, Staff Committee on (*Standing*). Robert Wedgeworth, ALA Headquarters, 50 E. Huron St., Chicago, IL 60611.
Membership (*Standing*). Kenneth E. Vance, 415 Manor Ave., Ann Arbor, MI 48105 (Patricia Scarry).
National Library Week (*Standing*). Carole Cushmore, R. R. Bowker Co., 1180 Ave. of the Americas, New York, NY 10036 (Peggy Barber).
Organization (*Standing, Council*). Donald Wright, Public Lib., 1703 Orrington Ave., Evanston, IL 60201 (Ruth R. Frame).
Outreach Services, Office for Library (*Standing, Advisory*). William D. Cunningham, College of Lib. & Info. Services, Univ. of Maryland, College Park, MD 20742 (Jean Coleman).
Planning (*Standing, Council*). Patricia Senn Breivik, Auraria Library, Lawrence at 11 St., Denver, CO 80204 (Ruth R. Frame).
Professional Ethics (*Standing, Council*). Page Ackerman, 310 20 St., Santa Monica, CA 90402 (Judith F. Krug).

Program Evaluation and Support (*Standing, Council*). F. William Summers, Dean, College of Libnshp., Univ. of South Carolina, Columbia, SC 29208 (Sheldon I. Landman).
Publishing (*Standing, Council*). Helen Lloyd Snoke, School of Lib. Science, Univ. of Michigan, Ann Arbor, MI 48109 (Donald E. Stewart).
Reference and Subscription Books Review (*Standing*). Robert M. Pierson, Grad. School of Lib. & Info. Science, Catholic Univ. of America, Washington, DC 20064 (Helen K. Wright).
Research (*Standing*). Charles Davis, Dean, Grad. School of Lib. & Info. Science, Univ. of Illinois, 410 David Kinley Hall, 1401 W. Gregory Dr., Urbana, IL 61801 (Mary Jo Lynch).
Resolutions (*Standing, Council*). Barbara J. Ford, Documents Libn., Univ. of Illinois–Chicago Circle, Box 8198, Chicago, IL 60680 (Miriam L. Hornback).
Standards (*Standing*). Jasper G. Schad, Box 68, Wichita State Univ., Wichita, KS 67208 (Ruth R. Frame).
Women in Librarianship, Status of (*Standing, Council*). Kathleen Heim, Grad. School of Lib. Science, Univ. of Illinois–Champaign, 410 David Kinley Hall, 1407 W. Gregory Dr., Urbana, IL 61801 (Margaret Myers).

JOINT COMMITTEE CHAIRPERSONS

American Correctional Association— ASCLA Committee on Institution Libraries. Connie House, Box 6164, Arlington, VA 22206.
American Federation of Labor/Congress of Industrial Organizations–ALA, Library Service to Labor Groups, RASD. ALA Chpn. Ginnie Cooper, Alameda County Lib., 3121 Diablo Ave., Hayward, CA 94545; AFL/CIO Co-Chpn. Jim Auerback, AFL/CIO, 815 16 St. N.W., Rm. 407, Washington, DC 20006.
Anglo-American Cataloguing Rules Common Revision Fund. ALA Rep Donald E. Stewart, ALA Headquarters; CLA

Rep. Laurie Bowes, Canadian Lib. Assn., 151 Sparks St., Ottawa, Ont. K1P 5E3 Canada; (British) Lib. Assn. Rep. Joel C. Dowling, c/o Lib. Assn., 7 Ridgmount St., London, WC 1E 7AE, England.

Anglo-American Cataloguing Rules, Joint Steering Committee for Revision of. ALA Chpn. Frances Hinton, 105 W. Walnut Lane, Philadelphia, PA 19144.

Association for Educational Communications and Technology—AASL, AASL Chpn. Marie V. Haley, Community School Dist., Sioux City, IA 51105; AECT Chpn. Dianne de Cordova, 8 Patton Place, Dumont, NJ 07628.

Association of American Publishers— ALA. AAP Chpn. Martin P. Levin, The Times Mirror Co., 280 Park Ave., New York, NY 10017.

Association of American Publishers— RTSD. ALA Chpn. Edna Laughrey, Acquisitions Dept., Univ. of Michigan Lib., Ann Arbor, MI 48109; AAP Chpn. Thomas Houston, New York Academy of Sciences, 2 E. 63 St., New York, NY 10021.

Children's Book Council—ALA. ALA Co-Chpn. Bertha M. Cheatham, School Library Journal, R. R. Bowker, 1180 Ave. of Americas, New York, NY 10036.

Society of American Archivists—ALA Joint Committee on Library-Archives Relationships. Chpn. Ellen Dunlap, Research Libn., Human Resources Center, Univ. of Texas, Austin, TX 78712.

U.S. National Park Service—ALSC Joint Committee. ALSC Co-Chpn. Elizabeth Watson, Public Lib., Fitchburg, MA 01420; *U.S.* National Park Service Co-Chpn. Patricia M. Stanek, Cowpens Memorial Battlefield, Chesnee, SC 29323.

AMERICAN LIBRARY ASSOCIATION
AMERICAN ASSOCIATION OF SCHOOL LIBRARIANS
Executive Director, Alice E. Fite
Program Officer, Ruth E. Feathers
50 E. Huron St., Chicago, IL 60611
312-944-6780

OBJECT

The American Association of School Librarians is interested in the general improvement and extension of library media services for children and young people. AASL has specific responsibility for planning programs of study and service for the improvement and extension of library media services in elementary and secondary schools as a means of strengthening the educational program; evaluation, selection, interpretation, and utilization of media as they are used in the context of the school program; stimulation of continuous study and research in the library field and to establish criteria of evaluation; synthesis of the activities of all units of the American Library Association in areas of mutual concern; representation and interpretation of the need for the function of school libraries to other educational and lay groups; stimulation of professional growth, improvement of the status of school librarians, and encouragement of participation by members in appropriate type-of-activity divisions; and conduct activities and projects beyond the scope of type-of-activity divisions, after specific approval by the ALA Council. Established in 1951 as a separate division of ALA. Memb. 7,000.

MEMBERSHIP

Open to all libraries, school library media specialists, interested individuals and business firms with requisite membership in the ALA.

OFFICERS

Pres. Betty Buckingham, Alternate Program Sec., State Dept. of Public Institutions, Grimes State Office Bldg., Des Moines, IA 50319; *1st V.P./Pres.-Elect.* Dorothy W. Blake, Atlanta Public Schools, 2930 Forest Hill Dr. S.W., Atlanta, GA 30315; *2nd V.P.* Lucille C. Thomas; *Rec. Secy.* Rosa L. Presberry; *Past Pres.* D. Philip Baker; *Exec. Dir.* Alice E. Fite.

BOARD OF DIRECTORS

Regional Dirs. Bernice L. Yesner, Region I (1982); Judith M. King, Region II (1983); Richard J. Sorensen, Region III (1984); Ruth A. Moline, Region IV (1982); Thomas L. Hart, Region V (1984); Lotsee P. Smith, Region VI (1983); Genevieve K. Craig, Region VII (1982); *Regional Dirs. from Affiliate Assembly.* Dale W. Brown (1982); Carolyn L. Cain (1983); Jim Weigel (1982); *NPSS Chpn.* James P. Godfrey; *SS Chpn.* Elizabeth B. Day; *Ex officio Ed. School Library Media Quarterly.* Jack R. Luskay.

PUBLICATION

School Library Media Quarterly (q.; memb.; nonmemb. $15). *Ed.* Jack R. Luskay, School of Lib. Science, Clarion State College, Clarion, PA 16214.

SECTION COMMITTEES— CHAIRPERSONS

Nonpublic Schools Section (NPSS)

Executive. James P. Godfrey, 315 King St., 3K, Port Chester, NY 10573.
Bylaws. Stephen L. Mathews, Currier Lib., Foxcroft School, Middleburg, VA 22117.
International and Domestic Exchanges (*Ad Hoc*). Walter A. Frankel, The Hulbert Taft Jr. Lib., The Taft School, Watertown, CT 06795.
Library Instruction (*Ad Hoc*). Dianne C. Langlois, Choate Rosemary Hall, Wallingford, CT 06492.
Nominating—1982 Election. Mark Hillsamer, The Ellison Lib., St. Albans School, Massachusetts & Wisconsin Aves. N.W., Washington, DC 20016.
Program—Philadelphia, 1982. Jeanette M. Smith, Forsyth Country Day School, 5501 Shallowford Rd., Lewisville, NC 27027.

Supervisors Section (SS)

Executive. Elizabeth B. Day, Coord. of Lib. Services, Santa Barbara County Schools, 4400 Cathedral Oaks Rd., Box 6307, Santa Barbara, CA 93111.
Bylaws. William Morris, 1336 E. Lawrence Lane, Phoenix, AZ 85020.
Nominating—1982 Election. Wanna Ernst, 16 Brisbane Dr., Charleston, SC 29407.
Publications (*Ad Hoc*). Mary Oppman, 7740 Oak Ave., Gary, IN 46403.
Program—Philadelphia, 1982. Elfrieda McCauley, Coord. of Media Services, Greenwich Public Schools, Havemeyer Bldg., 290 Greenwich Ave., Greenwich, CT 06830.
Critical Issues Facing School Library Media Supervisors (*Discussion Group*). Constance J. Champlin, 2051 N. 54 St., Omaha, NE 68104.

AASL COMMITTEE CHAIRPERSONS

Program Coordinating. D. Philip Baker, Stamford Public Schools, 195 Hillandale Ave., Stamford, CT 06902.

Unit Group I—Organizational Maintenance

Unit Head. Marie V. Haley, Sioux City Community Schools, 1221 Pierce St., Sioux City, IA 51105.
Bylaws. Jean D. Battey, Dept. of Education, State Office Bldg., Montpelier, VT 05602.
Conference Program Planning—Philadelphia, 1982. Patricia L. Meier, 2230½ Ripley, Davenport, IA 52803.
Local Arrangements—Philadelphia, 1982. Alice P. Bartz, 646 Pine Tree Rd., Jenkintown, PA 19046.
Nominating—1982 Election. Marie V. Haley, Sioux City Community Schools, 1221 Pierce St., Sioux City, IA 51105.

Resolutions. Lucille C. Thomas, 1184 Union St., Brooklyn, NY 11225.

Unit Group II—Organizational Relationships

Unit Head. Diane A. Ball, 2410 Fairmont Ave., Dayton, OH 45419.

American Association of School Administrators (*Liaison*). Dale W. Brown, 3801 W. Braddock Rd., Alexandria, VA 22303.

American University Press Services, Inc. (*Advisory*). Eileen Losey, Cranbrook Educational Community, Cranbrook Processing Center, 1000 Vaughn Rd., Box 801, Bloomfield Hills, MI 48013.

Association for Educational Communications and Technology (Joint). Marie V. Haley, Sioux City Community Schools, 1221 Pierce St., Sioux City, IA 51105.

Association for Supervision and Curriculum Development (*Liaison*). To be announced.

International Reading Association (*Liaison*). Virginia Mathews, 17 Overshore Dr. W., Hamden, CT 06514.

National Association of Elementary School Principals (*Liaison*). To be announced.

National Association of Secondary School Principals (*Liaison*). To be announced.

National Congress of Parents and Teachers (*Liaison*). Doris Masek, 6815 N. Algonquin Ave., Chicago, IL 60646.

National Council for the Social Studies (*Liaison*). To be announced.

National Council of Teachers of English (*Liaison*). To be announced.

National Council of Teachers of Mathematics (*Liaison*). To be announced.

Unit Group III—Media Personal Development

Unit Head. Jill M. Sienola, 253 College St. S.W., Apt. 3-A, Valley City, ND 58072.

Library Education. Leah Hiland, Dept. of Library Science, Univ. of Northern Iowa, Cedar Falls, IA 50613.

Networking—Interconnection of Learning Resources. Donald C. Adcock, School Dist. No. 41, 793 N. Main St., Glen Ellyn, IL 60137.

Professional Development. Retta B. Patrick, Rte. 1, Box 74 C-1, Roland, AR 72135.

Research. Milbrey L. Jones, 201 Eye St. S.W., Apt. 819, Washington, DC 20024.

Video Communications. Joan E. Griffis, 4752 S.W. 39 Dr., Portland, OR 97221.

Unit Group IV—Media Program Development

Unit Head. Wanna M. Ernst, 16 Brisbane Dr., Charleston, SC 29407.

Early Childhood Education. Chow Loy Tom, 2101 E. Harvard Ave., Apt. 405, Denver, CO 80210.

Elementary School Materials Selection (*Ad Hoc*). Helen E. Williams, 9883 Good Luck Rd., Lanham, MD 20801.

Evaluation of School Media Programs. Nancy R. Motomatsu, Washington State Superintendent of Instruction, 7510 Armstrong St. S.W., Tumwater, WA 98504.

Facilities, Media Center. Rebecca T. Bingham, Dir. of Lib. Media Services, Burrett Center, 4409 Preston Hwy., Louisville, KY 40213.

Library Media Skills Instruction (*Ad Hoc*). Elaine Stratton, WRITE-ON Office, Highland Community Schools, 1800 Lindenthal, Box 149, Highland, IL 62249.

School Faculty Materials Selection (*Ad Hoc*). Joan Myers, Dir. of Libs., School Dist. of Philadelphia, 21 St., S. of the Pkwy., Philadelphia, PA 19103.

School Library Media Services to Children with Special Needs. Jeannine L. Laughlin, School of Lib. Science, Univ. of Southern Mississippi, Box 5146, Southern Sta., Hattiesburg, MS 39401.

Secondary School Materials Selection (*Ad Hoc*). Agnes M. Milstead, 321 S. 13, Laramie, WY 82070.

Standards Program and Implementation. Elsie L. Brumback, 201 Annandale Dr., Cary, NC 27511.

Student Involvement in the Media Center Program. Doris W. Cox, Homestead

Apts. #314, 808 W. Riverside, Muncie, IN 47303.

Vocational/Technical Materials Selection (Ad Hoc). Myran L. Slick, R.D. 2, Box 226, Holsopple, PA 15935.

Unit Group V—Public Information

Unit Head. David A. Russell, College of Education, Univ. of Wyoming, Laramie, WY 82071.

AASL Distinguished Library Service Award for School Administrators. Joanne Troutner, 3002 Roanoke Circle, Lafayette, IN 47905.

Intellectual Freedom Representation and Information. JoAnn G. Davison, Filman School, 5407 Roland Ave., Baltimore, MD 21210.

International Relations. Lucille C. Thomas, 1184 Union St., Brooklyn, NY 11225.

Legislation. Jane H. Love, 11253 Crystal Run, Hickory Ridge, Columbia, MD 21044.

President's Award Selection. AASL/ Baker & Taylor. Shirley Woods, 2455 Beacon, Fullerton, CA 92635.

School Library Media Program of the Year Award Selection, AASL/ Encyclopaedia Britannica. Marilyn Goodrich, 11902 W. 143 Terr., Olathe, KS 66062.

School Library Media Program of the Year Review, AASL/Encyclopaedia Britannica (Ad Hoc). Michael G. deRuvo, 44 E. 57 St., New York, NY 10022.

COMMITTEES (SPECIAL)

Alternate Membership (Ad Hoc). Valerie J. Downes, 4170 Marine Dr., Chicago, IL 60613.

AASL General Conference—Houston, 1982. Albert H. Saley, R.D. 1, Box 111, Blairstown, NJ 07028.

Publications Advisory. Helen Lloyd Snoke, School of Lib. Science, Univ. of Michigan, 580 Union Dr., Ann Arbor, MI 48109.

Resource Development. Antionette Negro, 1022 Stedwick Rd., Apt. 302, Gaithersburg, MD 20760.

REPRESENTATIVES

ALA Legislation Assembly. Jane H. Love.

ALA Membership Promotion Task Force. Anne C. Ansley.

Associated Organizations for Professionals in Education. Leah Hiland.

Education U.S.A. Advisory Board. Alice E. Fite.

Educational Media Council. Alice E. Fite.

Freedom to Read Foundation. JoAnn G. Davison.

Library Education Assembly. Leah Hiland.

RTSD/ CCS/ AASL Cataloging of Children's Materials. Winifred E. Duncan.

AFFILIATE ASSEMBLY

The Affiliate Assembly is composed of the representatives and delegates of the organizations affiliated with the American Association of School Librarians. The specific purpose of this assembly is to provide a channel for communication for reporting concerns of the affiliate organizations and their membership and for reporting the actions of the American Association of School Librarians to the affiliates.

Executive Committee

Ruth F. Fitzgerald, 4151 Louis Dr., Flint, MI 48507.

Bylaws

Noreen Michaud, 312 Park Rd., West Hartford, CT 06119.

Nominating Committee—1982 Election

Jill Seinola, 253 College St. S.W., Apt. 3-A, Valley City, ND 58072.

Organizational Review

Hugh Durbin, 4240 Fairoaks Dr., Columbus, OH 43214.

Affiliates

Region I. Connecticut Educational Media Assn.; Massachusetts Assn. for Educational Media; Maine Educational Media Assn.; New England Educational Media Assn.; Rhode Island Educational Media Assn.; Vermont Educational Media Assn.

Region II. Delaware Learning Resources Assn.; District of Columbia Assn. of School Libns.; Maryland Educational Media Organization; Educational Media Assn. of New Jersey; Pennsylvania School Libns. Assn.; School Lib. Media Sec., New York Lib. Assn.

Region III. Assn. for Indiana Media Educators; Illinois Assn. for Media in Education; Iowa Educational Media Assn.; Michigan Assn. for Media in Education; Minnesota Educational Media Organization; Missouri Assn. of School Libns.; Ohio Educational Lib. Media Assn.; Wisconsin School Lib. Media Assn.; School Div., Michigan Lib. Assn.

Region IV. Mountain Plains Lib. Assn., Children's & School Sec.; Colorado Educational Media Assn.; Kansas Assn. of School Libns.; Nebraska Educational Media Assn.; North Dakota Assn. of School Libns.; South Dakota School Lib./Media Assn.; Wyoming School Lib. Media Assn.

Region V. Alabama Instructional Media Assn.; Children & School Libns. Div., Alabama Lib. Assn.; Florida Assn. for Media in Education, Inc.; Georgia Lib. Media Dept.; School and Children's Sec., Georgia Lib. Assn.; Kentucky School Media Dept.; North Carolina Assn. of School Libns.; School & Children's Sec., Southeastern Lib. Assn.; South Carolina Assn. of School Libns.; School Lib. Sec., Tennessee Education Assn.; Virginia Educational Media Assn.

Region VI. Louisiana Assn. of School Libns.; School Libs., Children, Young Adult Services, New Mexico Lib. Assn.; Oklahoma Assn. of School Lib. Media Specialists; School Libs. Div., Arizona State Lib. Assn.; School Libs. Div., Arkansas Lib. Assn.; Texas Assn. of School Libs.

Region VII. AASL-Alaska; California Media & Lib. Educators Assn.; Hawaii Assn. of School Libs.; Oregon Educational Media Assn.; School Lib. Div., Idaho Lib. Assn.; School Lib./Media Div., Montana Lib. Assn.; Washington State Assn. of School Libns.

AMERICAN LIBRARY ASSOCIATION
AMERICAN LIBRARY TRUSTEE ASSOCIATION
ALTA Program Officer, Sharon L. Jordan
50 E. Huron St., Chicago, IL 60611
312-944-6780

OBJECT

The development of effective library service for all people in all types of communities and in all types of libraries; it follows that its members are concerned as policymakers with organizational patterns of service, with the development of competent personnel, the provision of adequate financing, the passage of suitable legislation, and the encouragement of citizen support for libraries. Open to all interested persons and organizations.

Organized 1890. Became an ALA division 1961. Memb. 1,710. (For dues and membership year, see ALA entry).

OFFICERS (1981-1982)

Pres. Nancy Stiegemeyer, 215 Camellia Dr., Cape Girardeau, MO 63701; *1st V.P./Pres.-Elect.* M. Don Surratt, 3717 N. Pine Grove, Chicago, IL 60613; *2nd V.P.* Barbara Cooper; *Secy.* Herbert Davis; *Council Rep./Parliamentarian.* Jean M. Coleman.

BOARD OF DIRECTORS

Officers; *Council Administrators,* Jeanne Davies (1982); Marlys Mlady (1982); Gloria Glaser (1982); Fran Bobzin (1982); Jo Anne Thorbeck (1982). *Reg. V.Ps.* Kay Vowvalidis (1983); Schuyler Mott (1983); Athalie Solloway (1982); Allan Kahn (1982); Dina Butcher (1982); Nell Henry (1983); Mildred King (1983); Lila Milford (1983); Arthur Kirschenbaum (1982); Eugene Harple (1983). *Past Pres.* Jeanne Davies; *Past Pres. Ex officio.* Robert Rohlf (1982); Ed. *The Alta President's Newsletter.* Nancy Stiegemeyer.

PUBLICATION

The Alta President's Newsletter. Ed. Nancy Stiegemeyer, 215 Camellia Dr., Cape Girardeau, MO 63701.

COMMITTEE CHAIRPERSONS

Action Development. Charles Reid, 620 West Dr., Paramus, NJ 07652.

ATLA Foundation Committee. Herbert Davis, Box 108, Brooklandville, MD 21022.

Awards. Lila Milford, 1225 Northwood Ct., Marion, IN 46952.

Budget. M. Don Surratt, 3717 N. Pine Grove, Chicago, IL 60613.

Conference Program and Evaluation. Fran Bobzin, 1043 23 St. W. Des Moines, IA 50265.

Education of Trustees. Jerome Brill, 38 McElroy St., West Islip, NY 11795; Robert Manley, 816 Union Blvd., West Islip, NY 11795.

Task Force on Identity. Eugene Harple, 74 Gladstone Ave., West Islip, NY 11795.

Intellectual Freedom. Norma J. Buzan, 3057 Betsy Ross Dr., Bloomfield Hills, MI 48013.

Legislation. Deborah Miller, 840 Rosedale, La., Hoffman Estates, IL 60195.

Task Force on Liaison with Leagues of Municipalities. Norma L. Mihalevich, Box 287, Crocker, MO 65452.

Task Force on Literacy Programs. Marguerite W. Yates, 190 Windemere Rd., Lockport, NY 14094.

Task Force on Membership. Betty Simpson, 208 E. 2 St., Mackinaw, IL 61755.

Nominating. James A. Hess, 91 Farms Rd. Circle, East Brunswick, NJ 08816.

Task Force on Personnel Policies and Practices. Peter Cannici, 212 Howard Ave., Passaic, NJ 07055.

Publications. James A. Hess, 91 Farms Rd. Circle, East Brunswick, NJ 08816.

Publicity. Joanne C. Wisener, 860 19 Place, Yuma, AZ 85364.

Task Force on Serving the Unserved. Vacant.

Speakers Bureau. Mary Janowski, 505 Maple St., Oakdale, LA 71463; Mardy Dane, 21380 Edgecliff Dr., Euclid, OH 44123.

State Associations. Barbara Cooper, 936 Intracoastal Dr., Ft. Lauderdale, FL 33304.

Jury on Trustee Citations. Virginia Young, 10 E. Parkway Dr., Columbia, MO 65201; Minnie-Lou Lynch, 404 E. 6 St., Oakdale, LA 71463.

AMERICAN LIBRARY ASSOCIATION
ASSOCIATION FOR LIBRARY SERVICE TO CHILDREN

Executive Director, Mary Jane Anderson
50 E. Huron St., Chicago, IL 60611
312-944-6780

OBJECT

"Interested in the improvement and extension of library services to children in all types of libraries. Responsible for the evaluation and selection of book and nonbook materials for, and the improvement of techniques of, library services to children from preschool through the eighth grade or junior high school age, when such materials or techniques are intended for use in more than one type of library." Founded 1900. Memb. 4,978. (For information on dues see ALA entry.)

MEMBERSHIP

Open to anyone interested in library services to children.

OFFICERS (JULY 1981-JULY 1982)

Pres. Helen Mullen, Office of Work with Children, Free Lib. of Philadelphia, Logan Sq., Philadelphia, PA 19103; *V.P.* Margaret M. Kimmel, School of Lib. and Info. Science, Univ. of Pittsburgh, 135 N. Bellafield, Pittsburgh, PA 19103; *Exec. Dir.* Mary Jane Anderson, ALSC/ALA, 50 E. Huron St., Chicago, IL 60611; *Past Pres.* Amy Kellman, 211 Castlegate Rd., Pittsburgh, PA 15221. (Address general correspondence to the executive director.)

DIRECTORS

Officers; Margaret Bush (ALA Councillor); Adele Fasick; Carolyn Field; Suzanne Glazer; Caroline W. Heilmann; Elizabeth Huntoon; Harriet Quimby; Linda Silver; Mary R. Somerville.

PUBLICATIONS

Top of the News (q.; memb.; $15 nonmemb.).

COMMITTEE CHAIRPERSONS

Priority Group I—Child Advocacy

Coord. Marilyn Iarusso, Office of Children's Services, New York Public Lib., 8 E. 40 St., New York, NY 10016.
Boy Scouts of America (Advisory). Andrea L. Hynes, 7208 Lircon Dr. S.W., Tacoma, WA 98498.
Legislation. Susan Collier, 76 Whitman Dr., New Providence, NJ 07974.
Mass Media (Liaison with). Elizabeth Huntoon, 2046 Clifton, Chicago, IL 60624.
Organizations Serving the Child (Liaison with). Effie Lee Morris, 66 Cleary Ct., Apt. 1009, San Francisco, CA 94109.
U.S. National Park Service/ALS (Joint). Elizabeth Watson, Fitchburg Public Lib., 610 Main St., Fitchburg, MA 01420.

Priority Group II—Evaluation of Media

Coord. Gertrude B. Herman, 1425 Skyline Dr., Madison, WI 53705.
Mildred L. Batchelder Award Selection—1982. Zena B. Sutherland, 1418 E. 57 St., Chicago, IL 60637.
Mildred L. Batchelder Award Selection—1983. Patricia J. Cianciola, 4206 Wabaningo Rd., Okemos, MI 48864.
Caldecott Award. Marilyn B. Iarusso, Office of Children's Services, New York Public Lib., 8 E. 40 St., New York, NY 10016.
Film Evaluation. Susan Harloe, 1825 N. Edison, Stockton, CA 95204.
Filmstrip Evaluation. Hannah Zeiger, 167 Pond Brook Rd., Chestnut Hill, MA 02167.
"Multimedia Approach to Children's Literature" Revision (Ad Hoc). Lynne R. Pickens, 1481 Hampton Ct., Decatur, GA 30033.
Newbery Award. Margaret N. Coughlan, Children's Literature Center, Lib. of Congress, Washington, DC 20540.
Notable Children's Books. Marilyn Kaye, College of Libnshp., Univ. of South Carolina, Columbia, SC 29208.
Print and Poster Evaluation. Alma L. Mehn, 4009 Jay Lane S., Rolling Meadows, IL 60008.
Recording Evaluation. Sharon Gunn, 2678 Briarlake Woods Way, Atlanta, GA 30345.
Selection of Foreign Children's Books. Grace Ruth, 859 42 Ave., San Francisco, CA 94121.
Toys, Games and Realia Evaluation. Darrell Hildebrant, Veteran's Memorial Lib., 520 Ave. A E., Bismarck, ND 58501.
Laura Ingalls Wilder Award—1983. Spencer Shaw, School of Libnshp.,

Suzzalo Lib., FM-30, Univ. of Washington, Seattle, WA 98195.

Priority Group III—People Power

Coord. Betty J. Peltola, 4109 N. Ardmore, Milwaukee, WI 53211.

Arbuthnot Honor Lecture. Margaret K. McElderry, Atheneum Publishers, 597 Fifth Ave., New York, NY 10017.

Continuing Education. Lois Winkel, 1113 Hill St., Greensboro, NC 27408.

Managing Children's Services (Discussion Group). Mary Somerville, 1010 La Fontenay Ct., Louisville, KY 40223.

Media Evaluation: The Group Process, Implementation (Ad Hoc). Bridget L. Lamont, Illinois State Lib., Development Group, Centennial Bldg., Rm. 011, Springfield, IL 62756.

Melcher Scholarship. Deborah Weilerstein, Arlington County Dept. of Libs., 1015 N. Quincy St., Arlington, VA 22201.

Charles Scribner Award Selection. Mary Ann Paulin, 1205 Joliet, Marquette, MI 49855.

State and Regional Leadership (Discussion Group). Margo Daniels, 7400 Old Dominion Dr., McLean, VA 22101.

Teachers of Children's Literature (Discussion Group). Ramona Mahood, Brisler Lib., Rm. 201, Dept. of Lib. Science, Memphis State Univ., Memphis, TN 38152; Bernice Yesner, 16 Sunbrook Rd., Woodbridge, CT 06525.

Priority Group IV—Social Responsibilities

Coord. Kathleen S. Reif, 1020 St. Albans Rd., Baltimore, MD 21239.

Children with Special Needs (Library Services to). Eliza T. Dresang, Media Services, Metropolitan School Dist., 545 W. Dayton St., Madison, WI 53703.

Disadvantaged Child (Library Services to the, Discussion Group). Brenda V. Johnson, D.C. Public Lib., Washington, DC 20001.

Intellectual Freedom. Neel Parikh, 2136 Byron St., Berkeley, CA 94702.

International Relations. Barbara Barstow, 13412 Sprecher, Cleveland, OH 44135.

Preschool Services and Parent Education. Jill Locke, Farmington Community Lib., 32737 W. 12 Mile Rd., Farmington Hills, MI 48018.

Program Support Publications (Ad Hoc). Beth Babikow, Baltimore County Public Lib., 320 York Rd., Towson, MD 21204.

Social Issues in Relation to Library Materials and Services for Children (Discussion Group). Anitra T. Steele, Mid-Continent Public Lib., 15616 E. 24 Hwy., Independence, MO 64050.

Priority Group V—Planning, Research, and Development

Coord. Margaret Poarch, South Hills Apts., 23 South St., Geneseo, NY 14454.

Collection of Children's Books for Adult Research (Discussion Group). Henrietta Smith, 1202 N.W. Second St., Delray Beach, FL 33444.

Local Arrangements—Philadelphia 1982. Carole D. Fiore, 24 Yorktown Ct., Blue Bell, PA 19422.

Membership. Nancy Bush, 101 Foreman Rd., Mobile, AL 36608.

Nominating—1982. Ann L. Kalkhoff, 220 Berkeley Place, Apt. 1D, Brooklyn, NY 11217.

Organization and Bylaws. Martha Barnes, 15 W. 84 St., New York, NY 10024.

Program Evaluation and Support. Amy Kellman, 211 Castlegate Rd., Pittsburgh, PA 15221.

Publications. Blanche Woolls, 270 Tennyson, Pittsburgh, PA 15213.

Regional Activities Planning. L. Gayle Cole, 8512 Charing Cross, Dallas, TX 75238.

Research and Development. Ellin Greene, Univ. of Chicago, Grad. Lib. School, 1100 E. 57 St., Chicago, IL 60637.

Special Collections (National Planning of). Jane M. Bingham, 1653 Riverside, Rochester, MI 48063.

"Top of the News" (*Joint ALSC/YASD Editorial*). Audrey Eaglen, Cuyahoga County Public Lib., 4510 Memphis Ave., Cleveland, OH 44144.

REPRESENTATIVES

ALA Appointments. Margaret M. Kimmel.
ALA Budget Assembly. Margaret M. Kimmel.
ALA Legislative Assembly. Susan Collier.
ALA Library Education Assembly. Lois Winkel.
ALA Los Angeles Conference (1983) Conference Program. Margaret Kimmel.
ALA Philadelphia 1982 Program. Helen Mullen.
ALA Membership Promotion Task Force. Nancy Bush.
Caroline M. Hewins Scholarship. Priscilla Moulton.
International Board on Books for Young People, U.S. Section, Executive Board. Helen Mullen; Mary Jane Anderson; Barbara Barstow.
RTSD/CCS Cataloging of Children's Materials. Helen P. Gregory; Marilyn Karrenbrock.

LIAISON WITH OTHER NATIONAL ORGANIZATIONS

American Association for Gifted Children. Naomi Noyes.
American National Red Cross. Red Cross Youth. Barbara Shumer.
Big Brothers and Big Sisters of America. Helen Mullen.
Boys Clubs of America. Jane Kunstler.
Camp Fire Girls. Anitra Steele.
Child Welfare League of America. Ethel Ambrose.
Children's Defense Fund. Effie Lee Morris.
Children's Theatre Association. Amy E. Spaulding.
Day Care and Child Development Council of America. Margaret Bush.
Girls Clubs of America. Karen Breen.
National Association for the Education of Young Children. Jeanette Studley.
National Story League. Linda Hansford.
Parents Without Partners. To be announced.
Puppeteers of America. Darrell Hildebrandt.
Salvation Army. Margaret Malm.
Society of American Magicians. Marion Peck.

AMERICAN LIBRARY ASSOCIATION
ASSOCIATION OF COLLEGE AND RESEARCH LIBRARIES
Executive Director, Julie A. Carroll Virgo
50 E. Huron St., Chicago, IL 60611
312-944-6780

OBJECT

"Represents research and special libraries and libraries in institutions of postsecondary education, including those of community and junior colleges, colleges, and universities." Founded 1938. Memb. 9,000. (For information on dues, see ALA entry.)

OFFICERS (JULY 1981-JULY 1982)

Pres. David C. Weber, Stanford Univ., Stanford, CA 94305; *V.P./Pres.-Elect.* Carla J. Stoffle, Univ. of Wisconsin–Parkside, Kenosha, WI 53141; *Past Pres.* Millicent D. Abell, Univ. of California at San Diego, La Jolla, CA 92093.

BOARD OF DIRECTORS

Officers; section chairs and vice-chairs; *Dirs.-at-Large.* Joyce Ball (1982); George M. Bailey (1983); Imogene I. Book (1984); Sara Lou Whildin (1984); Barbara Collinsworth (1985); Betty L. Hacker (1985);

Willis M. Hubbard (1985); Donald F. Jay (1983).

PUBLICATIONS

ACRL Nonprint Media Publications (occasional). *Ed.* Jean W. Farrington, 221 Martroy Lane, Wallingford, PA 19086.
ACRL Publications in Librarianship (occasional). *Ed.* Joe W. Kraus, Illinois State Univ., Normal, IL 61761.
Choice (11 per year; $60); *Choice Reviews on Cards* ($135). *Ed.* Jay M. Poole, 100 Riverview Center, Middletown, CT 06457.
College & Research Libraries (6 per year; memb.; nonmemb. $35). *Ed.* C. James Schmidt, Research Library Group, Jordan Quad, Stanford, CA 94305.
College & Research Libraries (11 per year; memb.; nonmemb.; $10). *Ed.* George M. Eberhart, ACRL Headquarters.

SECTION CHAIRPERSONS

Anthropology. David R. McDonald, Green Lib., Stanford Univ., Stanford, CA 94035.
Art. John C. Larsen, Northern Illinois Univ., DeKalb, IL 60115.
Asian and African. Donald F. Jay, New York Public Lib., New York, NY 10018.
Bibliographic Instruction. Shelley E. Phipps, 4001 S. Jamie Dr., Tucson, AZ 85706.
College Libraries. Sherrie S. Bergman, Wheaton College, Norton, MA 02766.
Community and Junior College Libraries. Marcia J. Myers, Univ. of Tennessee Lib., Knoxville, TN 37916.
Education and Behavioral Science. Ann Knight Randall, 167 Eighth St., Providence, RI 02906.
Law and Political Science. Donald J. Dunn, Western New England College, 1215 Wilbraham Rd., Springfield, MA 01119.
Rare Books and Manuscripts. Alexandra Mason, Univ. of Kansas, Lawrence, KS 66095.
Science and Technology. Charles R. Long, New York Botanical Garden, Bronx, NY 10458.
Slavic and East European. Lubomyr R. Wynar, Kent State Univ., Kent, OH 44242.
University Libraries. Joan I. Gotwals, Univ. of Pennsylvania, Philadelphia, PA 19104.
Western European Specialists. Mary Jane Parrine, Stanford Univ. Libraries, Stanford, CA 94305.

Discussion Groups

Audiovisual. David B. Walch, California Polytechnic Univ., San Luis Obispo, CA 94307.
Black Studies Librarianship. Jeff Jackson, Afro-American Collection, Hillman Lib., Univ. of Pittsburgh, Pittsburgh, PA 15260; Wendell Wray.
Cinema Librarians. To be announced.
Librarians of Library Science Collections. Sally A. Davis, Univ. of Wisconsin, Madison, WI 53706.
Metropolitan Academic and Research Libraries. To be announced.
Personnel Officers of Research Libraries. Carolyn J. Henderson, Stanford Univ. Libs., Stanford, CA 94305.
Staff Development in Academic Research Libraries. Barbara von Wahlde, Univ. of Michigan, Ann Arbor, MI 48109.
Undergraduate Librarians. Marc Gittelsohn, Univ. of California, San Diego, La Jolla, CA 92093.

COMMITTEE CHAIRPERSONS

ACRL Academic or Research Librarian of the Year Award. Pearce S. Grove, Research Div., National Endowment for the Humanities, 806 15 St. N.W., Washington, DC 20506.
"ACRL Activity Model for 1990" (Ad Hoc). David Kaser, Indiana Univ., Bloomington, IN 47405.
"ACRL Nonprint Media Publications" Editorial Bd. Jean W. Farrington, 221 Martroy Lane, Wallingford, PA 19086.
"ACRL Publications in Librarianship" Editorial Bd. Joe W. Kraus, Illinois State Univ., Normal, IL 61761.

Academic Status. D. Kaye Gapen, Iowa State Univ., Ames, IA 50011.
Appointments (1982) and Nominations (1983). P. Grady Morein, 525 S. Runnymead, Evansville, IN 47714.
Audiovisual. Morell D. Boone, 1011 W. Cross, Ypsilanti, MI 48197.
Budget and Finance. Richard J. Talbot, Univ. of Massachusetts, Amherst, MA 01002.
Chapters Council. George M. Bailey, 2129 Villa Maria Rd., Claremont, CA 91711.
"Choice" Editorial Bd. William Miller, Michigan State Univ., East Lansing, MI 48823.
"College & Research Libraries" Editorial Bd. C. James Schmidt, Research Libs. Group, Jordan Quad, Stanford, CA 94305.
"College & Research Libraries News" Editorial Bd. Jay K. Lucker, Massachusetts Institute of Technology, Cambridge, MA 02139.
Conference Program Planning—Philadelphia, 1982. David C. Weber, Stanford Univ., Stanford, CA 94305.
Conference Program Planning—Los Angeles, 1983. Carla J. Stoffle, Univ. of Wisconsin–Parkside, Kenosha, WI 53141.
Constitution and Bylaws. Mary W. George, Princeton Univ. Lib., Princeton, NJ 08544.
Continuing Education. Robert Goehlert, Indiana Univ., Bloomington, IN 47401.
Copyright Committee (Ad Hoc). Meredith Butler, State Univ. of New York–Albany, Albany, NY 12222.
Legislation. Keith W. Russell, Council on Lib. Resources, One Dupont Circle, #620, Washington, DC 20036.
Membership. O. Gene Norman, 2417 Morton St., Terre Haute, IN 47802.
Planning. Carla J. Stoffle, Univ. of Wisconsin–Parkside, Kenosha, WI 53141.
Publications. Lawrence J. M. Wilt, Univ. of Maryland–Baltimore, Baltimore, MD 21228.
Standards and Accreditation. Patricia Ann Sacks, Muhlenberg and Cedar Crest Colleges, Allentown, PA 18104.
College Library Standards (Ad Hoc). To be announced.
Supplemental Funds. Carlton C. Rochell, New York Univ., New York, NY 10012.

REPRESENTATIVES

American Association for the Advancement of Science. Thomas G. Kirk.
American Council on Education. Russell Shank.
ALA Committee on Appointments. Carla J. Stoffle.
ALA Conference Program Planning Committee (Philadelphia, 1982). David C. Weber.
ALA Conference Program Planning Committee (Los Angeles, 1983). Carla J. Stoffle.
ALA Legislation Assembly. Keith W. Russell.
ALA Membership Promotion Task Force. O. Gene Norman.
ALA Planning and Budget Assembly. Carla J. Stoffle.
ALA Resources and Technical Services Division. Committee on Cataloging: Description and Access. LeRoy D. Ortopan.
ALA Standing Committee on Library Education (SCOLE). D. Kaye Gapen; Robert Goehlert; Pat Tegler.
Association for Asian Studies, Committee on East Asian Libraries. Warren Tsuneishi.
Freedom to Read Foundation. Tom G. Watson.
LC Cataloging in Publication Advisory Group. Richard C. Pollard.

AMERICAN LIBRARY ASSOCIATION
ASSOCIATION OF SPECIALIZED AND COOPERATIVE LIBRARY AGENCIES
Executive Director, Sandra M. Cooper
50 E. Huron St., Chicago, IL 60611
312-944-6780

OBJECT

To represent state library agencies, specialized library agencies, and multitype library cooperatives. Within the interest of these types of library organizations, the Association of Specialized and Cooperative Library Agencies has specific responsibility for:

1. Development and evaluation of goals and plans for state library agencies, specialized library agencies, and multitype library cooperatives to facilitate the implementation, improvement, and extension of library activities designed to foster improved user services, coordinating such activities with other appropriate ALA units.
2. Representation and interpretation of the role, functions, and services of state library agencies, specialized library agencies, and multitype library cooperatives within and outside the profession, including contact with national organizations and government agencies.
3. Development of policies, studies, and activities in matters affecting state library agencies, specialized library agencies, and multitype library cooperatives relating to (a) state and local library legislation, (b) state grants-in-aid and appropriations, and (c) relationships among state, federal, regional, and local governments, coordinating such activities with other appropriate ALA units.
4. Establishment, evaluation, and promotion of standards and service guidlines relating to the concerns of this association.
5. Identifying the interests and needs of all persons, encouraging the creation of services to meet these needs within the areas of concern of the association, and promoting the use of these services provided by state library agencies, specialized library agencies, and multitype library cooperatives.
6. Stimulating the professional growth and promoting the specialized training and continuing education of library personnel at all levels in the areas of concern of this association and encouraging membership participation in appropriate type-of-activity divisions within ALA.
7. Assisting in the coordination of activities of other units within ALA that have a bearing on the concerns of this association.
8. Granting recognition for outstanding library service within the areas of concern of this association.
9. Acting as a clearinghouse for the exchange of information and encouraging the development of materials, publications, and research within the areas of concern of this association.

BOARD OF DIRECTORS

Pres. Anne Marie F. Falsone, Asst. Commissioner of Education, State Lib., 1362 Lincoln St., Denver, CO 80203; *V.P./Pres.-Elect.* Nancy L. Wareham, Exec. Dir., Cleveland Area Metropolitan Lib. System, 11000 Euclid Ave., Rm. 309, Cleveland, OH 44106; *Past Pres.* Carmela M. Ruby, Direccion de Bibliotecas, Aptdo. Postal 24-441, Mexico 7, D.F.; *Div. Councillor.* Barratt Wilkins (1985). *Dirs.-at-Large.* Catherine D. Cook (1982); Marcia Lowell (1983); S. Stephen Prine, Jr. (1983); Lorraine D. Schaeffer (1982). *Sec. Reps.* Dallas M. Bagby, HCLS Chpn. (1982); Donna O. Dziedzic, LSBPH Chpn.

(1982); Keith C. Wright, LSDS Chpn. (1982); Barbara A. Webb, LSIES Chpn. (1982); Richard T. Miller, Jr., LSPS Chpn. (1982); Barbara M. Robinson, MLCS Chpn. (1982); Leslie M. Berman, SLAS Chpn. (1982). *Ex officio* (Nonvoting). *Interface Ed.* Edward Seidenberg; *Planning, Organization, and Bylaws Committee Chpn.* Patricia H. Smith; *Exec. Dir.* Sandra M. Cooper.

PUBLICATION

Interface (q.; memb.; no subscriptions). *Ed.* Edward Seidenberg, State Lib., Box 12927, Capitol Sta., Austin, TX 78711.

COMMITTEES

American Correctional Association— ASCLA Committee on Institutional Libraries (Joint). Connie House, Box 6164, Arlington, VA 22206.

Awards. Blanche Woolls, 240 Tennyson Ave., Pittsburgh, PA 15213.

Awards—Exceptional Achievement Award Jury. JoAn S. Segal, Interim Exec. Dir., BCR, Inc., 245 Columbine St., #212, Denver, CO 80206.

Bibliotherapy. Barbara F. Allen, 8338 St. Helena Hwy., Napa, CA 94558.

Budget and Finance. Nancy L. Wareham, Exec. Dir., Cleveland Area Metropolitan Lib. System, 11000 Euclid Ave., Rm. 309, Cleveland, OH 44106.

Conference Program. Ann M. Walker, Battelle Columbus Laboratories, 505 King Ave., Columbus, OH 43201.

Continuing Education. Dottie R. Hiebing, Public Lib. Consultant, Continuing Education, Div. for Lib. Services, 125 S. Webster, Madison, WI 53702.

"Interface" Advisory. Alphonse F. Trezza, 3292 Blue Heron Dr., Falls Church, VA 22042.

International Year of Disabled Persons (Ad Hoc). Phyllis I. Dalton, 850 E. Desert Inn Rd., No. 1101, Las Vegas, NV 89109.

Legislation. Barbara F. Weaver, State Libn., State Lib., CN 520, Trenton, NJ 08625.

Membership Promotion. Marnie M. Warner, Trial Court Office of the Chief Administrator of Justice, 300 Court House, Boston, MA 02108.

Nominating. Ruth M. Katz, Assoc. Dir., Joyner Lib., East Carolina Univ., Greenville, NC 27834.

Planning, Organization, and Bylaws. Patricia H. Smith, Mgr., Planning & Management Dept., State Lib., Box 12927, Capitol Sta., Austin, TX 78711.

Publications. Sally B. Roberts, V.P., Yankee Book Peddler, Box 307, Contoocook, NH 03229.

Research. Rosemary Du Mont, School of Lib. Science, Univ. of Oklahoma, 401 W. Brooks St., Rm. 116, Norman, OK 73019.

Standards Review. Susan B. Madden, Coord. of Young Adult Services, King County Lib. System, 300 Eighth Ave. N., Seattle, WA 98109.

Guidelines for Library Service to Small Residential Institutions (Ad Hoc, Subcommittee). R. Brantley Cagle, Jr.

Standards Review for Library Service to the Blind and Physically Handicapped (Ad Hoc, Subcommittee). To be announced.

Standards for the Library Functions at the State Level (Ad Hoc, Subcommittee). To be announced.

REPRESENTATIVES

ALA Government Documents Round Table (GODORT). Cynthia R. Ansell (1983).

ALA International Relations Committee. To be announced.

ALA Legislation Assembly. Barbara F. Weaver (1982).

ALA Library Education Assembly. Dottie R. Hiebing (1982).

ALA Membership Promotion Task Force. Marnie M. Warner (1982).

ALA/LAMA/BES Committees for Facilities for Specialized Library Services. To be announced.

ALA/RASD Interlibrary Loan Committee. Danuta A. Nitecki (1982).

American Correctional Association (ACA). Connie House.

Association for Radio Reading Services, Inc. Barbara Wilson (1983).
Chief Officers of State Library Agencies (COSLA). Exec. Dir., Sandra M. Cooper.
Freedom to Read Foundation. William A. Murray, Jr. (1983).
Interagency Council on Library Resources for Nursing. Frederick Pattison.

SECTION CHAIRPERSONS

Health Care Libraries Section (HCLS). Dallas M. Bagby, Libn., St. Boniface General Hospital, 409 Tache Ave., Winnipeg, Man., R2H 2A6 Canada.

Library Service to the Blind and Physically Handicapped (LSBPH). Donna O. Dziedzic, 2124 N. Sedgewick, Chicago, IL 60614.
Library Service to the Impaired Elderly Section. Barbara A. Webb, Assoc. Dir. of Lib. Operations, Fairfax County Public Lib., 5502 Port Royal Rd., Springfield, VA 22151.
Library Service to Prisoners Section (LSPS). Richard T. Miller, Jr., Coord. for Development of Special Lib. Services, State Lib., Box 387, Jefferson City, MO 65102.

AMERICAN LIBRARY ASSOCIATION
LIBRARY ADMINISTRATION AND MANAGEMENT ASSOCIATION
Executive Director, Roger H. Parent
50 E. Huron St., Chicago, IL 60611
312-944-6780

OBJECT

"The Library Administration and Management Association provides an organizational framework for encouraging the study of administrative theory, for improving the practice of administration in libraries, and for identifying and fostering administrative skill. Toward these ends, the division is responsible for all elements of general administration which are common to more than one type of library. These may include organizational structure, financial administration, personnel management and training, buildings and equipment, and public relations. LAMA meets this responsibility in the following ways:

1. Study and review of activities assigned to the division with due regard for changing developments in these activities.

2. Initiating and overseeing activities and projects appropriate to the division, including activities involving bibliography compilation, publication, study, and review of professional literature within the scope of the division.

3. Synthesis of those activities of other ALA units which have a bearing upon the responsibilities or work of the division.

4. Representation and interpretation of library administrative activities in contacts outside the library profession.

5. Aiding the professional development of librarians engaged in administration and encouragement of their participation in appropriate type-of-library divisions.

6. Planning and development of those programs of study and research in library administrative problems which are most needed by the profession." Established 1957.

OFFICERS

Pres. Carolyn Snyder, Indiana Univ. Libs., Bloomington, IN 47405; *V.P./Pres.-Elect.* David Smith; *Past Pres.* Mary Hall; *Exec. Dir.* Roger H. Parent. (Address correspondence to the executive director.)

BOARD OF DIRECTORS

Officers; Gerard McCabe; Joseph Matthews; Joseph Boisse; Ann Beltran; Florence Stiles; Susanne Henderson. *Dirs.-at-Large:* Gary Strong; Ronald Leach; *Councillor:* Dale Canelas; *Ex officio.* Sec. v.-chpns.; exec. dir.; Nancy McAdams, Org.; *LAMA Newsletter* ed.

PUBLICATIONS

LAMA Newsletter (q.; memb.) *Ed.* Ross G. Stephen, Franklin Moore Lib., Rider College, 2083 Lawrenceville Rd., Lawrenceville, NJ 08648.

COMMITTEE CHAIRPERSONS

Membership. Patricia M. Paine, Fairfax County Public Lib., Springfield, VA 22151.
Nominating. Donald Wright, Evanston Public Lib., 1703 Orrington Ave., Evanston, IL 60201.
Organization. Nancy R. McAdams, Univ. of Texas, Austin, TX 78712.
Orientation. Stella Bentley, Indiana Univ. Libs., Bloomington, IN 47405.
Program. Mary Hall, Prince George's County Memorial Lib., 6432 Adelphi Rd., Hyattsville, MD 20782.
Publications. Ross Stephen, Franklin Moore Lib., Rider College, 2083 Lawrenceville Rd., Lawrenceville, NJ 08648.
Budget and Finance. John Heyeck, Research Libs. Group, Inc., Jordan Quadrangle, Stanford, CA 94305.
Subcommittee on Extra-Conference Programs. Maurine Pastine, San Jose State Univ., San Jose, CA 95192.
Subcommittee for 1982 Philadelphia LAMA Business/Program (Ad Hoc). Carolyn Snyder, Indiana Univ. Libs., Bloomington, IN 47405.
Small Libraries Publications. Kay Cassell, Huntington Public Lib., 338 Main St., Huntington, NY 11743.

DISCUSSION GROUP CHAIRPERSONS

Middle Management. Rebecca Riley, 3000 N. Sheridan Rd., Chicago, IL 60657; Matthew Simon, Queens College Lib., Flushing, NY 11367.
Racism Sexism Awareness. Honoré Francois, Prince George's County Memorial Lib., 6532 Adelphi Rd., Hyattsville, MD 20782.
Women Administrators. Charlene Hurt, Washburn Univ., Mabee Lib., Topeka, KS 66621; E. Jean Orr, Miracle Valley Regional Lib. System, Headquarters, 700 Fifth St., Moundsville, WV 26041.
Fund Raising. Pamela Bonnell, 1317 Regal Dr., Apt. 521, Richardson, TX 75080.
Asst.-to-the-Dir. Bart Lessin, Central Michigan Univ. Lib., Mt. Pleasant, MI 48859

SECTION CHAIRPERSONS

Buildings and Equipment Section. Gerard McCabe, Virginia Commonwealth Univ. Lib., 901 Park Ave., Richmond, VA 23284.
Circulation Services Section. Joseph Matthews, 213 Hill St., Grass Valley, CA 95945.
Library Organization and Management Section. Joseph Boisse, 917 S. 48 St., Philadelphia, PA 19143.
Personnel Administration Section. Ann Beltran, 1511 Pickwick Place, Bloomington, IN 47401.
Public Relations Section. Florence Stiles, State Lib. Commission of Iowa, Historical Bldg., Des Moines, IA 50319.
Statistics Section. Susanne Henderson, 5937 S. Second St., Arlington, VA 22204.
Catalog Form, Function, and Use Committee. Mary Frances Collins, Ernest Di Mattia, Jr.
ALA Poster Session Committee. Elizabeth Salzer.
Library Education Assembly. Lotsee Smith.
Medical Library Association. Ching-Chih Chen.

AMERICAN LIBRARY ASSOCIATION
LIBRARY AND INFORMATION TECHNOLOGY ASSOCIATION
Executive Director, Donald P. Hammer
50 E. Huron St., Chicago, IL 60611
312-944-6780

OBJECT

"The Library and Information Technology Association provides its members and, to a lesser extent, the information dissemination field as a whole, with a forum for discussion, an environment for learning, and a program for action on all phases of the development and application of automated and technological systems in the library and information sciences. Since its activities and interests are derived as responses to the needs and demands of its members, its program is flexible, varied, and encompasses many aspects of the field. Its primary concern is the design, development, and implementation of technological systems in the library and information science fields. Within that general precept, the interests of the division include such varied activities as systems development, electronic data processing, mechanized information retrieval, operations research, standards development, telecommunications, networks and collaborative efforts, management techniques, information technology and other aspects of audiovisual and video cable communications activities, and hardware applications related to all of these areas. Although it has no facilities to carry out research, it attempts to encourage its members in that activity.

Information about all of these activities is disseminated through the division's publishing program, seminars and institutes, exhibits, conference programs, and committee work. The division provides an advisory and consultative function when called upon to do so.

It regards continuing education as one of its major responsibilities and through the above channels it attempts to inform its members of current activities and trends, and it also provides retrospective information for those new to the field."

OFFICERS

Pres. Brigitte L. Kenney, INFOCON, Inc., 400 Plateau Pkwy., Golden, CO 80401; *V.P./ Pres.-Elect.* Carolyn M. Gray, Lib. Support Biblio-Techniques, 12415 N.W. Haskell Ct., #10, Portland, OR 97229; *Past Pres.* S. Michael Malinconico, Assoc. Dir. for Technical and Computer Services, Public Lib., Branch Libs., 455 Fifth Ave., New York, NY 10016.

DIRECTORS

Officers; Hugh Atkinson (1984); Jay B. Clark (1982); Nancy L. Eaton (1983); Anne T. Meyer (1982); Arlene Farber Sirkin (1982); one to be announced. *Councillor.* Bonnie K. Juergens (1985); *Ex officio. Bylaws and Organization Committee Chpn.* Heike Kordish (1982); *Publications Committee Chpn.* Charles Husbands (1982); *Exec. Dir.* Donald P. Hammer.

PUBLICATIONS

Information Technology and Libraries (*ITAL*, formerly *JOLA*) (q.; memb.; non-memb. $20). *Ed.* Brian Aveney, Blackwell North American, 10300 S.W. Allen Blvd., Beaverton, OR 97005. For information or to send manuscripts, contact the editor.

LITA Newsletter (3 issues.; memb.). *Ed.* Patricia Barkalow, Pasadena Public Lib., 285 E. Walnut, Pasadena, CA 91101.

COMMITTEE CHAIRPERSONS

Awards. Hank Epstein, Pres., Information Transform Industries, 1992 Lemnos Dr., Costa Mesa, CA 92626.

Bylaws and Organization. Heike Kordish, Columbia Univ. Libs., 322 Butler Lib., New York, NY 10027.

Education. James Benson, Grad. School of Lib. Science, Univ. of Alabama, Box 6242, University, AL 35486.

Goals and Long-Range Planning. George L. Abbott, B101 Bird Lib., Syracuse Univ., Syracuse, NY 13210.

JOLA Editorial Board. Brian Aveney, Blackwell North American, 10300 S.W. Allen Blvd., Beaverton, OR 97005.

Legislation and Regulation. Lynne Bradley, Lib. Video Network, 1811 Woodlawn Dr., Baltimore, MD 21207.

Membership. Blanche E. Woolls, 270 Tennyson Ave., Pittsburgh, PA 15213.

Nominating. Mary A. Madden, 956 Myrtle St. N.E., Atlanta, GA 30309.

Program Planning. Sue Tyner, Asst. Univ. Libn. for Technical Services, Univ. of Arizona Lib., Tucson, AZ 85721.

Publications. Charles Husbands, Systems Libn., OSPR Widener 88, Harvard Univ. Lib., Cambridge, MA 02138.

Representation in Machine-Readable Form of Bibliographic Information,
RTSD/LITA/RASD (MARBI). Gretchen Redfield, 10 Emerson, No. 502, Denver, CO 80218.

Telecommunications. Joan M. Maier, Chief, Lib. Services, Lib., Rm. 51, National Oceanic and Atmospheric Admin., 325 Broadway, Boulder, CO 80303.

DISCUSSION GROUP CHAIRPERSON

Library and Information Technology. Patricia H. Earnest, 2775 Mesa Verde Dr. E., Apt. U-216, Costa Mesa, CA 92626.

SECTION CHAIRPERSONS

Audio-Visual Section (AVS). Anne T. Meyer, Dept. Head, Carnegie Lib., Allegheny Regional Branch, Allegheny Sq., Pittsburgh, PA 15212.

Information Science and Automation Section (ISAS). Jay B. Clark, Computer Access Network, Public Lib., 500 McKinney, Houston, TX 77002.

Video and Cable Communications Section (VCCS). Arlene Farber Sirkin, 108 Ninth St. S.E., Washington, DC 20003.

AMERICAN LIBRARY ASSOCIATION
PUBLIC LIBRARY ASSOCIATION
Executive Director, Shirley Mills-Fischer
50 E. Huron St., Chicago, IL 60611
312-944-6780

OBJECT

To advance the development, effectiveness, and financial support of public library service to the American people; to speak for the library profession at the national level on matters pertaining to public libraries; and to enrich the professional competence and opportunities of public librarians. In order to accomplish this mission, the Public Library Association has adopted the following goals:

1. Conducting and sponsoring research about how the public library can respond to changing social needs and technological developments.

2. Developing and disseminating materials useful to public libraries in interpreting public library services and needs.

3. Conducting continuing education for public librarians by programming at national and regional conferences, by publications such as the newsletter, and by other delivery methods.

4. Establishing, evaluating, and promoting goals, guidelines, and standards for public libraries.

5. Maintaining liaison with relevant national agencies and organizations engaged in public administration and

human services such as National Association of Counties, Municipal League, Commission on Post-Secondary Education.
6. Maintaining liaison with other divisions and units of ALA and other library organizations such as the Association of American Library Schools and the Urban Libraries Council.
7. Define the role of the public library in service to a wide range of user and potential user groups.
8. Promoting and interpreting the public library to a changing society through legislative programs and other appropriate means.
9. Identifying legislation to improve and to equalize support of public libraries. Organized 1951. Memb. 5,000.

MEMBERSHIP

Open to all ALA members interested in the improvement and expansion of public library services to all ages in various types of communities.

OFFICERS (1981-1982)

Pres. Agnes M. Griffen, Montgomery County Dept. of Public Libs., Rockville, MD 20850; V.P. Donald J. Sager, 6964 N. Tonty, Chicago, IL 60646; Past Pres. Robert H. Rohlf, Hennepin County Lib., Edina, MN 55435.

BOARD OF DIRECTORS (1981-1982)

Officers; Nina S. Ladof; Jerome G. Pennington; Kathleen E. Mehaffey; Patricia Woodrum; Nancy Doyle Bolt; Mildred K. Smock; Sec. Reps. AEPS Pres. Susan K. Schmidt; AFLS Pres. Nathalie G. McMahon; CIS Pres. Dorothy S. Puryear; MLS Pres. Annalee M. Bundy; PLSS Pres. Patrick M. O'Brien; SMLS Pres. Adelle McCarty; Ex officio. PLA-ALA Membership Rep. Mathew Kubiak; Past Pres. ALTA. Jeanne Davies; Councillor. Judith A. Dresher; Exec. Dir. Shirley Mills-Fischer.

PUBLICATIONS

Public Libraries (q.; memb.; nonmemb. $10.00). Ed. Kenneth D. Shearer, Jr., 1205 LeClair St., Chapel Hill, NC 27514.
Public Library Reporter (occas.). Ed. varies. Standing orders or single order available from Order Dept., ALA, 50 E. Huron St., Chicago, IL 60611.

SECTION HEADS

Alternative Education Programs (AEPS). Susan K. Schmidt.
Armed Forces Librarians (AFLS). Nathalie G. McMahon.
Community Information (CIS). Dorothy S. Puryear.
Metropolitan Libraries (MLS). Annalee M. Bundy.
Public Library Systems (PLSS). Patrick M. O'Brien.

COMMITTEE AND TASK FORCE CHAIRPERSONS

Audiovisual. Larry Pepper, Rolling Prairie Lib. System, 345 W. Eldorado St., Decatur, IL 62322.
Bylaws. Leon L. Drolet, Suburban Audio Visual Service, 920 Barnsdale Rd., La Grange Park, IL 60525.
Cataloging Needs of Public Libraries. Joyce A. Wyngaarden, Chattahoochee Valley Regional Lib., 1120 Bradley Dr., Columbus, GA 31995.
Children, Service to. Ethel N. Ambrose, Stockton-San Joaquin County Public Lib., 605 N. El Dorado St., Stockton, CA 95209.
Conference Program Coordinating. Gary M. Shirk, Univ. of Minnesota Libs., Minneapolis, MN 55455.
Division Program—Philadelphia, 1982. Yolanda J. Cuesta, California State Lib., Box 2037, Sacramento, CA 95809.
Division Program—Los Angeles, 1983. Linda F. Crismond, Los Angeles County Public Lib., Box 111, Los Angeles, CA 90053.
Education of Public Librarians. Suzanne Mahmoodi, OPLIC, 301 Hanover Bldg., 480 Cedar St., St. Paul, MN 55101.

Goals, Guidelines, and Standards for Public Libraries. Donald J. Napoli, South Bend Public Lib., 122 W. Wayne St., South Bend, IN 46601.

Legislation. Nettie Barcroft Taylor, State Dept. of Educ., Lib. Development Div., Baltimore, MD 21201.

Membership. Matthew Kubiak, West Florida Regional Lib., 200 W. Gregory, Pensacola, FL 32501.

Allie Beth Martin Award. Betty W. Bender, Spokane Public Lib., W. 906 Main Ave., Spokane, WA 99201.

Multilingual Library Service. To be announced.

National Conference (1983). Charles W. Robinson, Baltimore County Public Lib., 320 York Rd., Towson, MD 21204.

National Conference (1983) Evaluation. Henry E. Bates, Jr., Milwaukee Public Lib., 814 W. Wisconsin Ave., Milwaukee, WI 53233.

National Conference (1983) Exhibits. Milton E. Dutcher, Baltimore County Public Lib., Randallstown Area Branch, 8604 Liberty Rd., Randallstown, MD 21133.

National Conference (1983) Local Arrangements. Anna A. Curry, Enoch Pratt Free Lib., 400 Cathedral St., Baltimore, MD 21201.

National Conference (1983) Program Committee. Robert H. Rohlf, Hennepin County Lib., Edina, MN 55435.

National Conference (1983) Public Relations. John D. Christenson, Traverse des Sioux Lib. System, Box 3446, Mankato, MN 56001.

National Conference (1983) Registration. Betty M. Ragsdale, Blue Ridge Regional Lib., Box 3085, Martinsville, VA 24112.

Nominating—1982. Helen A. Knievel, Yankton Community Lib., 515 Walnut, Yankton, SD 57078.

Nominating—1983. William W. Sannwald, City Libn., City of San Diego, 202 C St., Mail Sta. 99B, San Diego, CA 92101.

Organization. David Snider, Casa Grande Public Lib., 405 E. Sixth St., Casa Grande, AZ 85222.

Orientation. Kathleen E. Mehaffey, Downers Grove Public Lib., 1050 Curtiss, Downers Grove, IL 60515.

Planning. Travis E. Tyer, Great River Lib. System, 515 York St., Quincy, IL 62301.

Preconference—Philadelphia, 1982. Joseph Eisner, Plain Edge Public Lib., 1060 Hicksville Rd., Massapequa, NY 11758.

Public Library Principles (Task Force). Ronald A. Dubberly, Seattle Public Lib., 1000 Fourth Ave., Seattle, WA 98104.

Publications. Betty J. Turock, Rutgers Univ., Grad. School of Lib. and Info. Studies, 4 Huntington, New Brunswick, NJ 08903.

"Public Libraries" Editorial Board. Travis E. Tyer, Great River Lib. System, 515 York St., Quincy, IL 62301.

Research. John C. Shirk, Center for Community Education, College of Education, Texas A & M Univ., College Sta., TX 77843.

State and Regional Affiliates (Task Force). To be announced.

AMERICAN LIBRARY ASSOCIATION
REFERENCE AND ADULT SERVICES DIVISION

Executive Director, Andrew M. Hansen
50 E. Huron St., Chicago, IL 60611
312-944-6780

OBJECT

The Reference and Adult Services Division is responsible for stimulating and supporting in every type of library the delivery of reference/information services to all groups, regardless of age, and of general library services and materials to adults. This involves facilitating the development and conduct of direct service to library users, the development of programs and guidelines for service to meet the needs of these users, and assisting libraries in reaching potential users. The specific responsibilities of RASD are:

1. Conduct of activities and projects within the division's areas of responsibility.
2. Encouragement of the development of librarians engaged in these activities, and stimulation of participation by members of appropriate type-of-library divisions.
3. Synthesis of the activities of all units within the American Library Association that have a bearing on the type of activities represented by the division.
4. Representation and interpretation of the division's activities in contacts outside the profession.
5. Planning and development of programs of study and research in these areas for the total profession.
6. Continuous study and review of the division's activities.

Formed by merger of Adult Services Division and Reference Services Division, 1972. Memb. 5,496. (For information on dues, see ALA entry.)

OFFICERS (1981-1982)

Pres. Geraldine B. King, Ramsey County Public Lib., St. Paul, MN 55113; *V.P./ Pres.-Elect.* Danuta A. Nitecki, Univ. of Illinois, Urbana, IL 61801. *Secy.* Mary U. Hardin, Oklahoma Dept. of Libs., Oklahoma City, OK 73105.

DIRECTORS

Officers; Charles A. Bunge; Susan DiMattia; Sharon Anne Hogan; David F. Kohl; Tina Roose; Margaret L. Thrasher; *Councilor.* Ruth M. Katz; *Past Pres.* H. Joanne Harrar; *Ex officio, History Sec. Chpn.* Tom J. Muth; *Machine-Assisted Reference Sec.* Pamela C. Sieving; *Ed. RASD Update,* Della L. Giblon; *Ed. RQ,* Helen B. Josephine; *Council of State and Regional Groups Chpn.* Glenda S. Neely, Univ. of Louisville, Louisville, KY 40208; *Exec. Dir.* Andrew M. Hansen. (Address general correspondence to the executive director.)

PUBLICATIONS

RQ (q.; memb.; nonmemb. $20). *Ed.* Helen B. Josephine, Box 246, Berkeley, CA 94701.

RASD Update (bi-mo.; memb.; nonmemb. $6). *Ed.* Della L. Giblon, Leon County Public Lib., 1940 N. Monroe St., Suite 81, Tallahassee, FL 32303.

SECTION CHAIRPERSONS

History. Tom J. Muth, Topeka Public Lib., 1515 W. 10, Topeka, KS 66604.

Machine-Assisted Reference (MARS). Pamela C. Sieving, 1163 S. Lyman, Oak Park, IL 60304.

COMMITTEE CHAIRPERSON

Adult Library Materials. Della L. Giblon, Leon County Public Lib., 1940 N. Monroe St., Suite 81, Tallahassee, FL 32303.

Adults, Services to. Neysa Eberhard, Newton Public Lib., 720 North Oak, Newton, KS 67114.

AFL/CIO-ALA Library Service to Labor Groups. Ginnie Cooper, Alameda County Lib., 3121 Diablo Ave., Hayward, CA 94545.

Aging Population, Library Service to. Nancy Clave Bolin, Cambridge M H & D Center, Rte. 35, Cambridge, OH 43725.

Bibliography. Anne K. Beaubine, 413 Grad. Lib., Univ. of Michigan, Ann Arbor, MI 48109.

Business Reference Services. Susan S. DiMattia, 44 Chatham Rd., Stamford, CT 06903.

Catalog Use. Linda Arret, Lib. of Congress, Washington, DC 20003.

Conference Program—Philadelphia 1982. Jo Bell Whitlatch, San Jose State

Univ. Lib., 250 Fourth St., San Jose, CA 95192.
Cooperative Reference Services. Ellen Zabel Hahn, General Reading Rms. Div., Lib. of Congress, Washington, DC 20540.
Dartmouth Medal. James Rettig, Univ. of Dayton Lib., Dayton, OH 45469.
Facts on File Award. Phyllis Massar, Ferguson Lib., Stamford, CT 06901.
Interlibrary Loan. Noelen P. Martin, Pattee Lib., Pennsylvania State Univ., University Park, PA 16802.
Legislation. Virginia E. Parker, Port Washington Public Lib., Port Washington, NY 11050.
Membership. Judith A. Tuttle, Memorial Lib., Univ. of Wisconsin, Madison, WI 53706.
Isadore Gilbert Mudge Citation. Virginia Phillips, Perry-Castaneda Lib., Univ. of Texas, Austin, TX 78712.
Nominating. Thomas M. Gaughan, Bard College Lib., Annandale-on-Hudson, NY 12504.
Notable Books Council. Janet Fletcher, 10 Sheridan Sq., New York, NY 10014.
Organization. David F. Kohl, Undergrad. Library, University of Illinois, Urbana, IL 61801.
Planning. Florence E. Blakely, Perkins Lib., Duke Univ., Durham, NC 27706.
Professional Development. Elaine M. Albright, Lincoln Trail Lib. System, Champaign, IL 61820.
Publications. Linda Beaupré, Perry-Casteneda Lib., Univ. of Texas, Austin, TX 78712.
Reference Sources. Deborah C. Masters, State Univ. of New York Lib., Albany, NY 12222.
Reference Tools Advisory. Sandra Leach, Univ. of Tennessee Lib., Knoxville, TN 37916.
RQ Editorial Advisory Board. Helen B. Josephine, Box 246, Berkeley, CA 94701.
John Sessions Memorial Award. Frances M. Jones, Hennepin County Lib., Brooklyn Park, MN 55443.
Spanish-Speaking, Library Services to. Fabio Restrepo. Texas Woman's Univ. Lib., Denton, TX 76204.
Standards and Guidelines. Lawrence J. Corbus, Geauga County Lib., Chardon, OH 44024.
Wilson Indexes. Larry Earl Bone, Mercy College Lib., Dobbs Ferry, NY 10522.

DISCUSSION GROUP CHAIRPERSONS

Adult Materials and Services. Catherine Smith, 388 Pattie Dr., Berea, OH 44017.
Interlibrary Loan. Mary Jackson, Interlibrary Loan, Univ. of Pennsylvania Libs., Philadelphia, PA 19104.
Library Service to an Aging Population. Allan Kleiman, Service to the Aging/SAGE Program Brooklyn Public Lib., Brooklyn, NY 11229.
Multilingual Services and Materials. William E. McElwain, Foreign Language Sec., Chicago Public Lib., Chicago, IL 60602.
Reference Service in Large Research Libraries. Peter Malanchuk, Univ. of Florida Lib., Gainesville, FL 32611.
Reference Services in Medium-sized Research Libraries. Sandra Leach, Univ. of Tennessee Lib., Knoxville, TN 37916.
Women's Materials and Women Library Users. Pat Simon, New City Lib., New City, NY 10956.

REPRESENTATIVES

ALA Legislation Assembly. Virginia E. Parker, Port Washington Public Lib., Port Washington, NY 11050.
ALA Legislation Committee (Ad Hoc Copyright Subcommittee). Mary U. Hardin, Oklahoma Dept. of Libs., 200 N.E. 18 St., Oklahoma City, OK 73105.
ALA Library Instruction Round Table. Bruce T. Sajdak, Smith College Lib., Northampton, MA 01063.
ALA Membership Promotion Task Force. Judith A. Tuttle, Univ. of Wisconsin Lib., Madison, WI 53705.
Coalition of Adult Education Organization. Eleanore R. Ficke, 11310 Fairway

Ct., Reston, VA 22090; Andrew M. Hansen, ALA, 50 E. Huron St., Chicago, IL 60611.

Freedom to Read Foundation. Deborah Ellis Dennis, Univ. of Maryland Libs., College Park, MD 20742.

AMERICAN LIBRARY ASSOCIATION
RESOURCES AND TECHNICAL SERVICES DIVISION
Executive Director, William I. Bunnell
50 E. Huron St., Chicago, IL 60611
312-944-6780

OBJECT

"Responsible for the following activities: acquisition, identification, cataloging, classification, reproduction, and preservation of library materials; the development and coordination of the country's library resources; and those areas of selection and evaluation involved in the acquisition of library materials and pertinent to the development of library resources. Any member of the American Library Association may elect membership in this division according to the provisions of the bylaws." Established 1957. Memb. 6,351. (For information on dues, see ALA entry.)

OFFICERS (JUNE 1981-JUNE 1982)

Pres. Charlotta C. Hensley, 1385 Edinboro Dr., Boulder, CO 80303; *V.P.* Norman J. Shaffer, 11505 Soward Dr., Silver Spring, MD 20902; *Chpn. Council of Regional Groups.* David Gray Remington, 115-B E St. S.E., Washington, DC 20003; *Past Pres.* Karen Horny, 1915 Sherman Ave., Evanston, IL 60201. (Address correspondence to the executive director.)

DIRECTORS

Officers; section chairpersons; RTSD Planning Committee Chpn.; *LRTS Ed.*; *RTSD Newsletter Ed.*; Doris H. Clack, 1115 Frazier Ave., Tallahassee, FL 32304 (Council of Regional Groups V. Chpn.); Joseph Howard, Asst. Libn. for Processing Services, Lib. of Congress, Washington, DC 20540 (Lib. of Congress liaison); Suzanne Massonneau, Bailey/Howe Lib., Univ. of Vermont, Burlington, VT 05401; Robin N. Downes, Univ. of Houston Lib., 4800 Calhoune Blvd., Central Campus, Houston, TX 77004; Edward Swanson, 1065 Portland Ave., St. Paul, MN 55104 (parliamentarian).

PUBLICATIONS

Library Resources & Technical Services (q.; memb. or $15). *Ed.* Elizabeth Tate, 11415 Farmland Dr., Rockville, MD 20852.

RTSD Newsletter (bi-mo.; memb. or *LRTS* subscription, or $8 yearly). *Ed.* Arnold Hirshon, Box 9184, Duke Sta., Durham, NC 27706.

SECTION CHAIRPERSONS

Cataloging and Classification. D. Kaye Gapen, Dean of Libs., Amelia Gayle Gorgas Lib., Univ. of Alabama, Box S, University, AL 35486.

Preservation of Library Materials. Pamela Darling, ARL/OMS Preservation Project, 516 Butler Lib., Columbia Univ., New York, NY 10027.

Reproduction of Library Materials. R. Grey Cole, Univ. of Mississippi Lib., University, MS 38677.

Resources. William J. Myrick, The City Univ. of New York, Office of Academic Affairs, 535 E. 80 St., New York, NY 10021.

Serials. John R. James, Head, Serials Div., Univ. of Washington, Seattle, WA 98195.

COMMITTEE CHAIRPERSONS

Association of American Publishers/ RTSD Joint Committee. Edna Laughrey, Acquisitions Dept., Univ. of Michigan Lib., Ann Arbor, MI 48109; Tom Houston, New York Academy of Sciences, 2 E. 63 St., New York, NY 10021.

Audiovisual. Nancy B. Olson, 642 S. Hunt St., Lake Crystal, MN 52055.

Commercial Technical Services Committee. Mary Fischer Ghikas, Chicago Public Lib., 425 N. Michigan Ave., Chicago, IL 60611.

Conference Program. Charlotta C. Hensley, 1385 Edinboro Dr., Boulder, CO 80303.

Duplicates Exchange Union. Christina L. Feick, Serials Div., Princeton Univ. Lib., Princeton, NJ 08544.

Education. Lois N. Upham, School of Lib. Service, Univ. of Southern Mississippi, Southern Sta., Box 5146, Hattiesburg, MS 39401.

International Relations. E. Dale Cluff, Dir. of Lib. Services, Southern Illinois Univ., Carbondale, IL 62901.

Membership. Murray S. Martin, Univ. Libn., Wessell Lib., Tufts Univ., Medford, MA 02155.

Nominating. Don Lanier, 613 Ball Ave., DeKalb, IL 60115.

Organization and Bylaws. Karen Horny, 1915 Sherman Ave., Evanston, IL 60201.

Piercy Award Jury. Julieann V. Nilson, 411 E. University, Bloomington, IN 47401.

Planning and Research. Susan H. Vita, 3711 Taylor St., Chevy Chase, MD 20815.

Preservation Microfilming. Francis F. Spreitzer, 4415 W. 62 St., Los Angeles, CA 90043.

Program Evaluation and Support. Norman J. Shaffer, 11505 Soward Dr., Silver Spring, MD 20902.

Representation in Machine-Readable Form of Bibliographic Information, RTSD/LITA/RASD (MARBI). Gretchen Redfield, 10 Emerson, #502, Denver, CO 80218.

Representation in Machine-Readable Form of Bibliographic Information (MARBI), Character Set Task Force (Ad Hoc). Charles Payne, 5807 Blackstone, Chicago, IL 60637.

Technical Services Costs. Barry B. Baker, 325 Snapfinger Dr., Athens, GA 30605.

REPRESENTATIVES

ALA Freedom to Read Foundation. Paul Cors.

ALA Government Documents Round Table. Gail M. Nichols.

ALA Legislation Assembly. Ann H. Eastman. William A. Gosling, Alternate.

ALA Library and Information Technology Association. Two to be announced.

ALA Membership Promotion Task Force. Murray S. Martin.

American National Standards Institute, Inc. (ANSI), Standards Committee Z39 on Library Work, Documentation and Related Publishing Practices. Susan H. Vita; Janice E. Anderson, Alternate.

CONSER Advisory Group. Jean Cook.

Joint Advisory Committee on Nonbook Materials. To be announced.

Joint Steering Committee for Revision of AACR. Frances Hinton.

Universal Serials and Book Exchange Inc. Alfred Lane.

National Conservation Advisory Council. Pamela W. Darling.

AMERICAN LIBRARY ASSOCIATION
YOUNG ADULT SERVICES DIVISION
Executive Director, Evelyn Shaevel
50 E. Huron St., Chicago, IL 60611
312-944-6780

OBJECT

"Interested in the improvement and extension of services to young people in all types of libraries; has specific responsibility for the evaluation, selection, interrelation and use of books and nonbook materials for young adults except when such materials are intended for only one type of library." Established 1957. Memb. 3,000. (For information on dues, see ALA entry.)

MEMBERSHIP

Open to anyone interested in library services to young adults.

OFFICERS (JULY 1981-JULY 1982)

Pres. Evie Wilson, 8602 Champlain Ct., Apt. 85, Tampa, FL 33614; *V.P.* Barbara Newmark, 11 Lake St., White Plains, NY 10603; *Past Pres.* Audrey Eaglen, Cuyahoga County Public Lib., 4510 Memphis Ave., Cleveland, OH 44144; *Division Councillor.* Bruce Daniels, Dept. of State Lib. Services, 95 Davis St., Providence, RI 02908.

DIRECTORS

Thomas Wm. Downen; Joan Atkinson; Jack Forman; Patty Campbell; Lydia LaFleur; Suzanne Sullivan.

COMMITTEE CHAIRPERSONS

Atlanta Bibliographies. Co-Chpn., Joni Bodart, 713 Woodland, Denton, TX 76204; Co-Chpn., Juanita Pace Suttle, Atlanta Public Lib., 3571 Martin Luther King Jr. Dr. S.W., Atlanta, GA 30331.

Best Books for Young Adults. Larry Rakow, 1585 Maple Rd., Cleveland Heights, OH 44131.

Education. Gerald Hodges, Univ. of North Carolina, Greensboro, NC 27412.

High-Interest, Low-Literacy Level Materials Evaluation. Ellin Chu, Monroe County Lib. System, 115 South Ave., Rochester, NY 14604.

Ideas and Activities. Jack Forman, 5708 Baltimore Dr., #396, La Mesa, CA 92041.

Intellectual Freedom. Judith F. Kurman, Rte. 2, Box 326, Apt. D, Jackson, OH 45640.

Leadership Training. Barbara L. Newmark, 11 Lake St., White Plains, NY 10603.

Legislation Committee. Eleanor K. Pourron, Arlington County Public Lib., 1015 Quincy St., Arlington, VA 22201.

Library of Congress, YASD Advisory Committee to the Collection and Development Section and the National Library Service for the Blind and Physically Handicapped of the Library of Congress. Leila C. Shapior, Rockville Lib., 99 Maryland Ave., Rockville, MD 20850.

Media Selection and Usage. Jan Freeman, 3802 W. Bertona, Seattle, WA 98199.

Membership Promotion. Jo Ann Kingston, 614 Bedford Place, Grand Blanc, MI 48439.

National Organization Serving the Young Adult Liaison. Linda Miller, Blue Island Public Lib., 2433 York St., Blue Island, IL 60406.

Nominating 1982. Bruce E. Daniels, Dept. of State Lib. Services, 95 Davis St., Providence, RI 02908.

Organization and Bylaws. Roberta Gellert, Lewis Rd., Irvington, NY 10533.

Outstanding Nonfiction for the College Bound. Penelope S. Jeffrey, 4733 Morningside Dr., Cleveland, OH 44109.

Program and Budget Development. Barbara L. Newmark, 11 Lake St., White Plains, NY 10603.

Program Planning Clearinghouse. Julia M. Losinski, Prince George's County Memorial Lib., 6532 Adelphia Rd., Hyattsville, MD 20782.
Publications. Patsy Perritt, 225 Middleton Lib., LSU Grad. School of Lib. Science, Baton Rouge, LA 70803.
Publishers Liaison. Tony Ieisner, Quality Books, Inc., 400 Anthony Trail, Northbrook, IL 60062.
Research. Janet Stroud, 1833 Summit Dr., West Lafayette, IN 47906.
Selected Films for Young Adults. Donna Rae Meyers, 23691 Delmere Dr., No. 226C, North Olmstead, OH 44070.

Spanish Speaking Youth Committee, Library Service to. John W. Cunningham, 979 N. Fifth St., Philadelphia, PA 19123.
Television. Sylvie Green, Dallas Public Lib., 1954 Commerce St., Dallas, TX 75201.
Top of the News Editorial. Audrey Eaglen, Cuyahoga County Public Lib., 4510 Memphis Ave., Cleveland, OH 44144.
Young Adults with Special Needs. Marilyn McCray, 509 Foster Rd., Huntington, WV 25701.
Youth Participation. Jana Varlejs, 101A Hill St., Highland Park, NJ 08904.

AMERICAN MERCHANT MARINE LIBRARY ASSOCIATION
(Affiliated with United Seamen's Service)
Executive Director, Mace Mavroleon
One World Trade Center, Suite 2601, New York, NY 10048

OBJECT

Provides ship and shore library service for American-flag merchant vessels, the Military Sealift Command, the Coast Guard, and other waterborne operations of the U.S. government.

OFFICERS

Chmn. of the Bd. Thomas J. Smith; *Pres./Treas.* James J. Hayes; *Secy.* Franklin K. Riley, Jr.

TRUSTEES

Edith Augenti; Ralph R. Bagley; George O. Cole; H. A. Downing; John I. Dugan; Charles Francis; Arthur Friedberg; Robert E. Hart; Thomas A. King; George F. Lowman; Carolyn McKinley; Frank X. McNerney; Thomas J. Patterson, Jr.; Andrew Rich; George J. Ryan; S. Fraser Sammis; Adrian P. Spidle; Jeannette Spidle; Philip Steinberg; Samuel Thompson; Paul E. Trimble; Edward Turner; C. E. Whitcomb.

AMERICAN SOCIETY FOR INFORMATION SCIENCE
Executive Director, Samuel B. Beatty
1010 16 St. N.W., Washington, DC 20036
202-659-3644

OBJECT

"The American Society for Information Science provides a forum for the discussion, publication, and critical analysis of work dealing with the design, management, and use of information systems and technology." Memb. (Indiv.) 4,432; (Student) 480; (Inst.) 111. Dues (Indiv.) $55; (Student) $15; (Inst.) $300; (Sustaining Sponsor) $600.

OFFICERS

Pres. Ruth Tighe, Government of Northern Mariana Islands, Dept. of Education, Saipan, GM 96950; *Pres.-Elect.* Charles Davis, Univ. of Illinois, Champaign/Urbana, Champaign, IL 61820; Treas. Frank Slater, Univ. of Pittsburgh, G-33 Hillman Lib., Pittsburgh, PA 15260; Past Pres. Mary C. Berger, Cuadra Assocs., 1523 Sixth St., Santa Monica, CA 90401. (Address correspondence to the executive director.)

BOARD OF DIRECTORS

Officers; *Chapter Assembly Dir.* Joe Ann Clifton; *SIG Cabinet Dir.* George Abbott; *Dirs.-at-Large.* Ching Chih Chen; Ward Shaw; Carol Johnson; Darlene Myers; Edmond J. Sawyer; Julie Carroll Virgo.

PUBLICATIONS

Note: Unless otherwise indicated, publications are available from Knowledge Industry Publications, 2 Corporate Park Dr., White Plains, NY 10604.

Annual Review of Information Science and Technology (vol. 3, 1968–vol. 10, 1975, $35 each, memb. $28; vol. 11, 1976–vol. 16, 1981, $42.50 each, memb. $34).

Bulletin of the American Society for Information Science (6 per year, memb. or $35 domestic, $42.50 foreign). Available directly from ASIS.

Collective Index to the Journal of the American Society for Information Science (vol. 1, 1950–vol. 25, 1974, $60 each, memb. $42). Available from John Wiley & Sons, 605 Third Ave., New York, NY 10016.

Computer-Readable Data Bases: A Directory and Data Sourcebook 1979 ($95, memb. $76).

Cumulative Index to the Annual Review of Information Science and Technology (vols. 1–10, $35 each, memb. $28).

Journal of the American Society for Information Science; formerly *American Documentation* (bi-mo.; memb. or $55 domestic, $60 foreign). Available from John Wiley & Sons, 605 Third Ave., New York, NY 10016.

Key Papers in the Design and Evaluation of Information Systems. Ed. Donald W. King ($25, memb. $20).

Library and Reference Facilities in the Area of the District of Columbia (10th ed., 1979, $19.50, memb. $15.60).

Proceedings of the ASIS Annual Meetings (vol. 5, 1968–vol. 9, 1972, $15 each, memb. $12; vol. 10, 1973–vol. 16, 1979, $19.50 each, memb. $15.60).

COMMITTEE CHAIRPERSONS

Awards and Honors. Mauro Pittaro, Engineering Information, Inc., 345 E. 47 St., New York, NY 10017.

Budget and Finance. Frank Slater, Univ. of Pittsburgh, G-33 Hillman Lib., Pittsburgh, PA 15260.

Conferences and Meetings. Edward J. Kazlauskas, School of Lib. and Info. Management, Univ. of Southern California, Los Angeles, CA 90007.

Constitution and Bylaws. Harley Baade, Shell Oil Co., Box 2463, Rm. 901, One Shell Plaza, Houston, TX 77001.

Education. Ruth Katz, Joyner Lib., East Carolina Univ., Greenville, NC 27834.

Executive. Ruth Tighe, Government of Northern Mariana Islands, Dept. of Education, Saipan, GM 96950.

International Relations. Baja el-Hadidy, Catholic Univ. of America, Washington, DC 20004.

Marketing. Patricia Earnest, 2775 Mesa Verde Dr., Costa Mesa, CA 92626.

Membership. Gerard O. Platau, Chemical Abstracts Service, Box 3012, Columbus, OH 43210.

Nominations. Mary C. Berger, Cuadra Associates, 1523 Sixth St., Santa Monica, CA 90401.

Professionalism. Pamela Cibbarelli, Cibbarelli Associates, 18652 Florida, Huntington Beach, CA 92648.

Public Affairs. Dennis McDonald, 3508 Valley Dr., Alexandria, VA 22302.

Publications. Bonnie C. Carroll, Dept. of Energy, Technical Info. Center, Box 62, Oak Ridge, TN 37830.

Research. Manfred Kochin, Mental Health Research Institute, Univ. of Michigan, Ann Arbor, MI 48104.

Standards. David Liston, King Research, 6000 Executive Blvd., Rockville, MD 20852.

AMERICAN THEOLOGICAL LIBRARY ASSOCIATION
Executive Secretary, Al Hurd
1421 Ramblewood Dr., East Lansing, MI 48823

OBJECT

"To bring its members into closer working relationships with each other, to support theological and religious librarianship, to improve theological libraries, and to interpret the role of such libraries in theological education, developing and implementing standards of library service, promoting research and experimental projects, encouraging cooperative programs that make resources more available, publishing and disseminating literature and research tools and aids, cooperating with organizations having similar aims and otherwise supporting and aiding theological education." Founded 1947. Memb. (Inst.) 150; (Indiv.) 460. Dues (Inst.) $50-$300, based on total library expenditure; (Indiv.) $10-$55, based on salary scale. Year. May 1-April 30.

ATLA is a member of the Council of National Library and Information Associations.

MEMBERSHIP

Persons engaged in professional library or bibliographical work in theological or religious fields and others who are interested in the work of theological librarianship.

OFFICERS (JUNE 1981-JUNE 1982)

Pres. Jerry Campbell, Perkins School of Theology, Southern Methodist Univ., Dallas, TX 75275; *Pres./V.P.-Elect.* Robert Dvorak, Gordon-Conwell Theological Seminary, South Hamilton, MA 01982; *Treas.* Robert A. Olsen, Jr., Libn., Brite Divinity School, Texas Christian Univ., Ft. Worth, TX 76129; *Newsletter Ed.* Donn Michael Farris, Divinity School Lib., Duke Univ., Durham, NC 27706.

BOARD OF DIRECTORS

John Baker-Batsel; James Dunkly; Roberta Hamburger; Dorothy Ruth Parks; Harriet V. Leonard; Richard D. Spoor; Stephen L. Peterson; *ATS Rep.* David Schuller.

PUBLICATIONS

Newsletter (q.; memb. or $6).
Proceedings (ann.; memb. or $10).
Religion Index One (formerly *Index to Religious Periodical Literature*, 1949-date).
Religion Index Two: Multi-Author Works.

COMMITTEE CHAIRPERSONS

ATLA Newsletter. Donn Michael Farris, Ed., Divinity School Lib., Duke Univ., Durham, NC 27706.
ATLA Representative to ANSI Z39. Warren Kissinger, 6309 Queen's Chapel Rd., Hyattsville, MD 20782.
ATLA Representative to the Council of National Library and Information Associations. James Irvine, Princeton Theological Seminary, Box 111, Princeton, NJ 08540.
ATLA Representative to the Universal Serials and Book Exchange. USBE liaison now assigned to Library Materials Exchange Committee.
Annual Conferences. Lawrence Hill, St. Vincent College, Latrobe, PA 15650.
Archivist. Gerald W. Gillette, Presbyterian Historical Society, 425 Lombard St., Philadelphia, PA 19147.
Bibliographic Systems. Elizabeth Flynn, Graduate Theological Union, 2400 Ridge Rd., Berkeley, CA 94709.
Clearinghouse on Personnel. Office of the Exec. Secy.
Collection Evaluation and Development. Donald Vorp, McCormick Theological Seminary, 1100 E. 55 St., Chicago, IL 60615.
Contacts with Foundations. John Baker-Batsel, Grad. Theological Union Lib., 2451 Ridge Rd., Berkeley, CA 94709.

Library Consultation Service. John B. Trotti, Union Theological Seminary, 3401 Brook Rd., Richmond, VA 23227.
Library Materials Exchange (formerly Periodical Exchange). Roger Williams, Nazarene Bible College, Box 15749, Colorado Springs, CO 80935.
Membership. Kay Stockdale, Historical Foundation of the Presbyterian/Reformed Churches, Box 847, Montreat, NC 28757.
Microtext Reproduction Board. Charles Willard, Exec. Secy., Princeton Theological Seminary, Princeton, NJ 08540; Maria Grossmann, Andover-Harvard Lib., 45 Francis Ave., Cambridge, MA 02138.
Nominating. Rosalyn Lewis, United Methodist Publishing House, 201 Eighth Ave. S., Nashville, TN 37202.
Periodical Indexing Board. R. Grant Bracewell, Emmanual College Lib., 75 Queen's Pk., Toronto, Ont. M5S 1K7, Canada.
Publication. Earle Hilgert, McCormick Theological Seminary, 1100 E. 55 St., Chicago, IL 60615.
Reader Services. Sara Mobley, Pitts Theological Lib., Emory Univ., Atlanta, GA 30322.
Relationships with Learned Societies. Andrew Scrimgeour, Iliff School of Theology Lib., 2201 S. University, Denver, CO 80210.
Statistician and Liaison with ALA Statistics Coordinating Committee. David Green, Grad. Theological Union, 2451 Ridge Rd., Berkeley, CA 94709.
Systems and Standards. Doralyn Hickey, Reporter, School of Lib. & Info. Sciences, North Texas State Univ., Denton, TX 76203.

ART LIBRARIES SOCIETY OF NORTH AMERICA (ARLIS/NA)
Executive Secretary, Pamela J. Parry
3775 Bear Creek Circle, Tucson, AZ 85715
602-749-9112

OBJECT

"To promote art librarianship, particularly by acting as a forum for the interchange of information and materials on the visual arts." Established 1972. Memb. 1,100. Dues (Inst.) $60; (Indiv.) $35; (Business Affiliate) $60; (Student) $20; (Retired/Unemployed) $25; (Sustaining) $150; (Sponsor) $500. Year. Jan.–Dec. 31.

MEMBERSHIP

Open and encouraged for all those interested in visual librarianship, whether they be professional librarians, students, library assistants, art book publishers, art book dealers, art historians, archivists, architects, slide and photograph curators, or retired associates in these fields.

OFFICERS (FEB. 1982–FEB. 1983)

Chpn. Caroline Backlund, National Gallery of Art Lib., Washington, DC 20565; *Past Chpn.* Karen Muller, Art Institute of Chicago, Michigan at Adams, Chicago, IL 60603; *Secy.* Barbara Sevy, Philadelphia Museum of Art Lib., Box 7646, Philadelphia, PA 19101. (Address correspondence to the executive secretary.)

COMMITTEES

(Direct correspondence to headquarters.)
Archives.
Cataloging Advisory.
Conference.
Fund Raising.
International Relations.

Membership.
Gerd Muehsam Award.
Nominating.
Publications.
Standards.
Wittenborn Awards.

EXECUTIVE BOARD

The chairperson, past chairperson, chairperson-elect, secretary, treasurer, and four regional representatives (East, Midwest, West, and Canada).

PUBLICATIONS

Art Documentation (bi-mo.; memb.).
Directory of Members (ann.; memb.).
Occasional Papers (price varies).

Miscellaneous others (request current list from headquarters).

CHAPTERS

Allegheny; Arizona; DC-Maryland-Virginia; Delaware Valley; Kansas-Missouri; Kentucky-Tennessee; Michigan; Mid-States; New England; New Jersey; New York; Northern California; Northwest; Ohio; Southeast; Southern California; Texas; Twin Cities; Western New York.

ASSOCIATED INFORMATION MANAGERS
Executive Director, Rita Lombardo
316 Pennsylvania Ave. S.E., Suite 400, Washington, DC 20003
202-544-2892

OBJECT

To serve the management and career needs of information executives and managers who are responsible for the information functions of their organizations. To advance the implementation of information management as a management function.

MEMBERSHIP

Information executives and managers in industry, government, academia, or individual consultants concerned with information management. Employees of firms that market information products and/or services are also eligible for membership.

BOARD OF DIRECTORS

James G. Kollegger, Pres., Environmental Info. Center, Inc.; Sarah T. Kadec, Deputy Dir., Office of Admin., Exec. Office of the President, the White House; Herbert R. Brinberg, Pres., Aspen Systems Corp.; Morton Meltzer, Info. Mgr., Martin Marietta Corp.; Rhoda R. Mancher, Deputy Asst. Attorney General, Office of Litigation and Management Systems, Dept. of Justice. (Address all correspondence to the executive director.)

PUBLICATIONS

AIM Network (bi-weekly). Newsletter.
AIM Membership Roster. Annual directory.
Who's Who in Information Management. Annual directory.
Marketing Yourself in Your Organization, by Morton Meltzer.
Partners in Fact: Information Managers/Information Company Executives Talk. Transcript of a dialogue at 1981 National Information Conference.

ASSOCIATION OF ACADEMIC HEALTH SCIENCES LIBRARY DIRECTORS
Secretary, Peter Stangl, Director, Lane Library, Stanford University Medical Center, Stanford, CA 94305

OBJECT

"To promote, in cooperation with educational institutions, other educational associations, government agencies, and other non-profit organizations, the common interests of academic health sciences libraries located in the United States and elsewhere, through publications, research, and discussion of problems of mutual interest and concern, and to advance the efficient and effective operation of academic health sciences libraries for the benefit of faculty, students, administrators, and practitioners."

MEMBERSHIP

Regular membership is available to nonprofit educational institutions operating a school of health sciences that has full or provisional accreditation by the Association of American Medical Colleges. Annual dues $50. Regular members shall be represented by the chief administrative officer of the member institution's health sciences library.

Associate membership (and nonvoting representation) is available to organizations having an interest in the purposes and activities of the association.

OFFICERS (JUNE 1981-JUNE 1982)

Pres. Virginia H. Holtz, Middleton Health Sciences Lib., 1305 Linden Dr., Madison, WI 53706; *Pres.-Elect.* Richard Lyders, Texas Medical Center Lib., Houston Academy of Medicine, Jesse H. Jones Lib. Bldg., Houston, TX 77030; *Past Pres.* C. Robin LeSueur, Countway Lib. of Medicine, Harvard Univ., 10 Shattuck St., Boston, MA 02115; *Secy.-Treas.* Elizabeth J. Sawyers, Health Sciences Lib., Ohio State Univ., 376 W. Tenth Ave., Columbus, OH 43210.

BOARD OF DIRECTORS (JUNE 1981-JUNE 1982)

Officers; Nelson J. Gilman, Norris Medical Lib., Univ. of Southern California, 2025 Zonal Ave., Los Angeles, CA 90033; Samuel Hitt, Health Sciences Lib., Univ. of North Carolina, Chapel Hill, NC 27514; Gloria Werner, UCLA Biomedical Lib., Center for Health Sciences, Univ. of California, Los Angeles, CA 90024.

COMMITTEE CHAIRPERSONS

Audit Committee. Ralph Arcari.
Bylaws Committee. Priscilla Mayden.
Committee on Information Control and Technology. James Morgan.
Committee on the Development of Standards and Guidelines. Jean Miller.
Medical Education Committee. Jo Ann Bell.
Newsletter Advisory Committee. Richard Fredericksen.
Nominating Committee. Rachael Goldstein.
Program Committee. Jane Port.
Statistics: Annual Statistics of Medical Libraries in the U.S. and Canada. Editorial Board. Richard Lyders.

MEETINGS

An annual business meeting is held in conjunction with the annual meeting of the Medical Library Association in June. Annual membership meeting and program is held in conjunction with the annual meeting of the Association of American Medical Colleges in October.

ASSOCIATION OF AMERICAN LIBRARY SCHOOLS
Executive Secretary, Janet Phillips
471 Park Lane, State College, PA 16801
814-238-0254

OBJECT

"To advance education for librarianship." Founded 1915. Memb. 790. Dues (Inst.) $125; (Assoc. Inst.) $75; (Indiv.) $25; (Assoc. Indiv.) $20. Year. Sept. 1981–1982.

MEMBERSHIP

Any library school with a program accredited by the ALA Committee on Accreditation may become an institutional member; any educator who is employed full time for a full academic year in a library school with an accredited program may become a personal member.

Any school that offers a graduate degree in librarianship or a cognate field but whose program is not accredited by the ALA Committee on Accreditation may become an associate institutional member; any part-time faculty member or doctoral student of a library school with an accredited program or any full-time faculty member employed for a full academic year at other schools that offer graduate degrees in librarianship or cognate fields may become an associate personal member.

OFFICERS (FEB. 1982-JAN. 1983)

Pres. F. William Summers, College of Libnshp., Univ. of South Carolina, Columbia, SC 29208; *Past Pres.* Harold Goldstein, Lib. School, Florida State Univ., Tallahassee, FL 32306. (Address correspondence to the executive secretary.)

DIRECTORS

Jane B. Robbins-Carter (Wisconsin-Madison); Marcy Murphy (Indiana); Shirley Fitzgibbons (Indiana).

PUBLICATION

Journal of Education for Librarianship (5 per year; $18).

COMMITTEE CHAIRPERSONS

Conference. Ronald Blazek, Assoc. Prof., School of Lib. Science, Florida State Univ., Tallahassee, FL 32306.

Continuing Education. Joan C. Durrance, School of Lib. Science, Univ. of Michigan, Ann Arbor, MI 48109.

Editorial Board. Charles D. Patterson, School of Lib. and Info. Science, Louisiana State Univ., Baton Rouge, LA 70803.

Legislation. Genevieve Casey, Div. of Lib. Science, Wayne State Univ., Detroit, MI 48202.

Nominating. Barbara Immroth, Grad. School of Lib. and Info. Science, Univ. of Texas, Austin, TX 78712.

Research. Charles McClure, School of Lib. Science, Univ. of Oklahoma, Norman, OK 73019.

REPRESENTATIVES

ALA SCOLE. Jane B. Robbins-Carter (Wisconsin-Madison).

Council of Communication Societies. Guy Garrision (Drexel).

IFLA. F. William Summers (South Carolina); Josephine Fang (Simmons).

Organization of American States. Margaret Goggin (Denver).

ASSOCIATION OF JEWISH LIBRARIES
c/o National Foundation for Jewish Culture
122 E. 42 St., Rm. 408, New York, NY 10017

OBJECT

"To promote and improve library services and professional standards in all Jewish libraries and collections of Judaica; to serve as a center of dissemination of Jewish library information and guidance; to encourage the establishment of Jewish libraries and collections of Judaica; to promote publication of literature which will be of assistance to Jewish librarianship; to encourage people to enter the field of librarianship." Organized 1966 from the merger of the Jewish Librarians Association and the Jewish Library Association. Memb. 600. Dues (Inst.) $18; (Student/retired) $10. Year. Calendar.

OFFICERS (JUNE 1980-JUNE 1982)

Pres. Barbara Y. Leff, Stephen S. Wise Temple, 15500 Stephen S. Wise Dr., Los Angeles, CA 90024; *Treas.* Mary G. Brand, Rabbi Alexander S. Gross Hebrew Academy Jr.-Sr. Lib., 2842 Pine Tree Dr., 6, Miami Beach, FL 33140; *Corres. Secy.* Edith Lubetski, Hedi Steinberg Lib., Yeshiva Univ., 245 Lexington Ave., New York, NY 10016; *Rec. Secy.* Linda P. Lerman, Boston Theological Inst., 151 North St., C, Newton, MA 02160.

PUBLICATIONS

AJL *Bulletin* (bienn.) *Ed.* Irene S. Levin, 48 Georgia St., Valley Stream, NY 11580.
Membership Kit.
Newsletter (4 per year).
Proceedings.

DIVISIONS

Research and Special Libraries. Edith Degani, Jewish Theological Seminary of America, 3080 Broadway, New York, NY 10027.
Synagogue School and Center Libraries. Rita C. Frischer, Sinai Temple Lib., 10400 Wilshire Blvd., Los Angeles, CA 90024.

ASSOCIATION OF RESEARCH LIBRARIES
Executive Director, Shirley Echelman
1527 New Hampshire Ave. N.W., Washington, DC 20036
202-232-2466

OBJECT

"To initiate and develop plans for strengthening research library resources and services in support of higher education and research." Established 1932 by the chief librarians of 43 research libraries. Memb. (Inst.) 113. Dues (ann.) $3,300. Year. Jan.-Dec.

MEMBERSHIP

Membership is institutional.

OFFICERS (OCT. 1981-OCT. 1982)

Pres. Millicent D. Abell, Libn., Univ. of California, San Diego Lib., La Jolla, CA 92037; *V.P.* James F. Govan, Dir., Univ. of North Carolina Libs., Chapel Hill, NC 27515; *Past Pres.* Jay K. Lucker, Dir., Massachusetts Institute of Technology Libs., Cambridge, MA 02139.

BOARD OF DIRECTORS

Sterling J. Albrecht, Brigham Young Univ. Lib.; Charles Churchwell, Washington Univ. Libs.; Donald Koepp, Princeton Univ. Lib.; Eldred Smith, Univ. of Minnesota Libs.; William J. Studer, Ohio State Univ. Libs.; Richard J. Talbot, Univ. of Massachusetts Libs.; Anne Woodsworth, York Univ. Libs.

PUBLICATIONS

ARL Annual Salary Survey (ann.; memb. or $10).

ARL Library Statistics (ann.; memb. or $10).

ARL Minutes (s. ann.; memb. or $12.50 each).

ARL Newsletter (approx. 6 per year; memb. or $15).

76 United Statesiana. Seventy-six works of American scholarship relating to America as published during two centuries from the Revolutionary era of the United States through the nation's bicentennial year. Ed. by Edward C. Lathem ($7.50; $5.75 paper to nonmembs.).

13 Colonial Americana. Ed. by Edward C. Lathem ($7.50).

(The above two titles are distributed by the Univ. of Virginia Press.)

Our Cultural Heritage: Whence Salvation? Louis B. Wright; *The Uses of the Past,* Gordan N. Ray; remarks to the 89th membership meeting of the association ($3).

Cumulated ARL University Library Statistics, 1962–63 through 1978–79. Compiled by Kendon Stubbs and David Buxton ($15.00).

The ARL Library Index and Quantitative Relationships in the ARL, Kendon Stubbs ($5.00).

COMMITTEE CHAIRPERSONS

African Acquisitions. Hans Panofsky, Northwestern Univ. Lib., Evanston, IL 60210.

ARL/CRL Joint Committee on Expanded Access to Journal Collections. John P. McDonald, Univ. of Connecticut Lib., Storrs, CT 06268.

Federal Relations. Carlton C. Rochell, New York Univ. Libs., New York, NY 10003.

Membership Committee on Nonuniversity Libraries. Roy L. Kidman, Univ. of Southern California Libs., Los Angeles, CA 90007.

ARL Statistics. Richard J. Talbot, Univ. of Massachusetts Libs., Amherst, MA 01002.

Center for Chinese Research Materials. Philip McNiff, Boston Public Lib., Boston, MA 02117.

East Asian Acquisitions. Warren Tsuneishi, Lib. of Congress, Washington, DC 20540.

Interlibrary Loan. Kenneth G. Peterson, Southern Illinois Univ. Lib., Carbondale, IL 62901.

Latin American Acquisitions. Carl W. Deal, Univ. of Illinois Lib., Urbana, IL 61803.

Middle Eastern Acquisitions. David Partington, Harvard Univ. Lib., Cambridge, MA 02138.

Nominations. ARL Vice-President.

Office of Management Studies. Irene Hoadley, Texas A & M Univ. Lib., College Station, TX 77843.

Preservation of Research Library Materials. David Stam, New York Public Lib., New York, NY 10018.

South Asia Acquisitions. Louis Jacob, Lib. of Congress, Washington, DC 20540.

Southeast Asia Acquisitions. Charles Bryant, Yale Univ. Lib., New Haven, CT 06520.

Western European Acquisitions. Howard Sullivan, Wayne State Univ. Lib., Detroit, MI 48202.

TASK FORCE CHAIRPERSONS

Bibliographic Control. James Govan, Univ. of North Carolina Libs., Chapel Hill, NC 27515.

Library Education. Margot B. McBurney, Queen's Univ. Lib., Kingston, Ont. K7L 5C4, Canada.

Collection Development. Joseph H. Treyz, Univ. of Wisconsin Libs., Madison, WI 53706.

National Library Network Development. William J. Studer, Ohio State Univ. Libs., Columbus, OH 43210.

ARL MEMBERSHIP IN 1981

Nonuniversity Libraries

Boston Public Lib.; Center for Research Libs.; John Crerar Lib.; Lib. of Congress; Linda Hall Lib.; National Agricultural Lib.; National Lib. of Canada; National Lib. of Medicine; New York Public Lib.; New York State Lib.; Newberry Lib.; Smithsonian Institution Libs.

University Libraries

Alabama; Alberta; Arizona; Arizona State; Boston; Brigham Young; British Columbia; Brown; California (Berkeley); California (Davis); California (Irvine); California (Los Angeles); California (Riverside); California (San Diego); California (Santa Barbara); Case Western Reserve; Chicago; Cincinnati; Colorado; Colorado State; Columbia; Connecticut; Cornell; Dartmouth; Duke; Emory; Florida; Florida State; Georgetown; Georgia; Guelph; Harvard; Hawaii; Houston; Howard; Illinois; Indiana; Iowa; Iowa State; Johns Hopkins; Kansas; Kent State; Kentucky; Louisiana State; McGill; McMaster; Manitoba; Maryland; Massachusetts; Massachusetts Institute of Technology; Miami; Michigan; Michigan State; Minnesota; Missouri; Nebraska; New Mexico; New York; North Carolina; Northwestern; Notre Dame; Ohio State; Oklahoma; Oklahoma State; Oregon; Pennsylvania; Pennsylvania State; Pittsburgh; Princeton; Purdue; Queen's (Kingston, Canada); Rice; Rochester; Rutgers; Saskatchewan; South Carolina; Southern California; Southern Illinois; Stanford; SUNY (Albany); SUNY (Buffalo); SUNY (Stony Brook); Syracuse; Temple; Tennessee; Texas; Texas A&M; Toronto; Tulane; Utah; Vanderbilt; Virginia; Virginia Polytechnic; Washington; Washington (St. Louis); Washington State; Wayne State; Western Ontario; Wisconsin; Yale; York.

ASSOCIATION OF VISUAL SCIENCE LIBRARIANS
c/o F. Eleanor Warner, Head Librarian,
New England College of Optometry,
420 Beacon St., Boston, MA 02115

OBJECT

"To foster collective and individual acquisition and dissemination of visual science information, to improve services for all persons seeking such information, and to develop standards for libraries to which members are attached." Founded 1968. Memb. (U.S.) 37; (foreign) 13. Annual meeting held in December in connection with the American Academy of Optometry; Philadelphia, Pennsylvania (1982); Houston, Texas (1983); St. Louis, Missouri (1984).

OFFICERS

Chpn. F. Eleanor Warner, Head Libn., New England College of Optometry, 420 Beacon St., Boston, MA 02115; *Chpn.-Elect.* Pat Carlson, Libn., Southern California College of Optometry, 2001 Associated Rd., Fullerton, CA 92631.

PUBLICATIONS

PhD Theses in Physiological Optics (irreg.).
Union List of Vision-Related Serials (irreg.).
Standards for Vision Science Libraries.
Opening Day Book Collection—Visual Science.

BETA PHI MU
(International Library Science Honor Society)
Executive Secretary, Blanche Woolls
School of Library and Information Science
University of Pittsburgh, Pittsburgh, PA 15260

OBJECT

"To recognize high scholarship in the study of librarianship, and to sponsor appropriate professional and scholarly projects." Founded at the University of Illinois in 1948. Memb. 18,000.

MEMBERSHIP

Open to graduates of library school programs accredited by the American Library Association who fulfill the following requirements: complete the course requirements leading to a fifth-year or other advanced degree in librarianship with a scholastic average of A—(e.g., 4.75 where A equals 5 points, 3.75 where A equals 4 points, etc.)—this provision shall also apply to planned programs of advanced study beyond the fifth year that do not culminate in a degree but that require full-time study for one or more academic years; receive a letter of recommendation from their respective library schools attesting to their demonstrated fitness of successful professional careers. Former graduates of accredited library schools are also eligible on the same basis.

OFFICERS

Pres. Robert D. Stueart, Dean, Grad. School of Lib. and Info. Science, Simmons College, Boston, MA 02115; *V.P./Pres.-Elect.* H. Joanne Harrar, Dir. of Libs., Univ. of Maryland, College Park, MD 20742; *Past Pres.* Mary Alice Hunt, Assoc. Prof., School of Lib. Science, Florida State Univ., Tallahassee, FL 32306; *Treas.* Marilyn P. Whitmore, Univ. Archivist, Hillman Lib., Univ. of Pittsburgh, Pittsburgh, PA 15260; *Exec. Secy.* Blanche Woolls, Prof., School of Lib. and Info. Science, Univ. of Pittsburgh, Pittsburgh, PA 15260; *Admin. Secy.* Mary Y. Tomaino, School of Lib. and Info. Science, Univ. of Pittsburgh, Pittsburgh, PA 15260.

DIRECTORS

Marion L. Mullen, 124 Pattison St., Syracuse, NY 13203 (Pi Lambda Sigma Chapter-Syracuse Univ./1982); Elizabeth Snapp, The Lib., Texas Woman's Univ., Denton, TX 76204 (Beta Lambda Chapter-Texas Woman's Univ. and North Texas State Univ./1982); Carol Penka, 200 Main Lib., Univ. of Illinois, Urbana, IL 61801 (Alpha Chapter-Univ. of Illinois/1983); Mary Jane Kahao, Grad. School of Lib. Science Lib., Louisiana State Univ., Baton Rouge, LA 70803 (Beta Zeta Chapter-Louisiana State Univ./1983); David L. Searcy, 703 Durant Place N.E., Apt. 1, Atlanta, GA 30308 (Zeta Chapter-Atlanta Univ./1984); Dorothy M. Shields, Asst. Prof., School of Lib. and Info. Sciences, Brigham Young Univ., Provo, UT 84602 (Beta Theta Chapter-Brigham Young Univ./1984). *Directors-at-Large.* Diane Thompson, Coord. of Children's Services, Pierce County Lib., Tacoma, WA 98402 (1982); Edward Holley, Dean, Grad. School of Lib. Science, Univ. of North Carolina, Chapel Hill, NC 27514 (1984).

PUBLICATIONS

Newsletter (bienn.).

Beta Phi Mu sponsors a modern Chapbook series. These small volumes, issued in limited editions, are intended to create a beautiful combination of text and format in the interest of the graphic arts and are available to members only. In January 1980, the 14th in the Chapbook series was published by the society, *A Book for a Sixpence: The Circulating Library in America*, by David Kaser.

CHAPTERS

Alpha. Univ. of Illinois, Grad. School of Lib. and Info. Science, Urbana, IL 61801; *Beta.* Univ. of Southern California, School of Lib. Science, University Park, Los Angeles, CA 90007; *Gamma.* Florida State Univ., School of Lib. Science, Tallahassee, FL 32306; *Delta* (Inactive). Loughborough College of Further Education, School of Libnshp., Loughborough, England; *Epsilon.* Univ. of North Carolina, School of Lib. Science, Chapel Hill, NC 27514; *Zeta.* Atlanta Univ., School of Lib. & Info. Studies, Atlanta, GA 30314; *Theta.* Pratt Institute, Grad. School of Lib. & Info. Science, Brooklyn, NY 11205; *Iota.* Catholic Univ. of America, School of Lib. & Info. Science, Washington, DC 20064, and Univ. of Maryland, College of Lib. & Info. Services, College Park, MD 20742; *Kappa.* Western Michigan Univ., School of Libnshp., Kalamazoo, MI 49008; *Lambda.* Univ. of Oklahoma, School of Lib. Science, Norman, OK 73019; *Mu.* Univ. of Michigan, School of Lib. Science, Ann Arbor, MI 48109; *Nu.* Columbia Univ., School of Lib. Service, New York, NY 10027; *Xi.* Univ. of Hawaii, Grad. School of Lib. Studies, Honolulu, HI 96822; *Omicron.* Rutgers Univ., Grad. School of Lib. & Info. Studies, New Brunswick, NJ 08903; *Pi.* Univ. of Pittsburgh, School of Lib. & Info. Science, Pittsburgh, PA 15260; *Rho.* Kent State Univ., School of Lib. Science, Kent, OH 44242; *Sigma.* Drexel Univ., School of Lib. & Info. Science, Philadelphia, PA 19104; *Tau.* State Univ. of New York at Geneseo, School of Lib. & Info. Science, College of Arts and Science, Geneseo, NY 14454; *Upsilon.* Univ. of Kentucky, College of Lib. Science, Lexington, KY 40506; *Phi.* Univ. of Denver, Grad. School of Libnshp. and Info. Mgmt., Denver, CO 80208; *Pi Lambda Sigma.* Syracuse Univ., School of Info. Studies, Syracuse, NY 13210; *Chi.* Indiana Univ. School of Lib. & Info. Science, Bloomington, IN 47401; *Psi.* Univ. of Missouri, Columbia, School of Lib. & Info. Science, Columbia, MO 65211; *Omega.* San Jose State Univ., Div. of Lib. Science, San Jose, CA 95192; *Beta Alpha.* Queens College, City College of New York, Grad. School of Lib. & Info. Studies, Flushing, NY 11367; *Beta Beta.* Simmons College, Grad. School of Lib. & Info. Science, Boston, MA 02115; *Beta Delta.* State Univ. of New York-Buffalo, School of Info. & Lib. Studies, Buffalo, NY 14260; *Beta Epsilon.* Emporia State Univ., School of Lib. Science, Emporia, KS 66801; *Beta Zeta.* Louisiana State Univ., Grad. School of Lib. Science, Baton Rouge, LA 70803; *Beta Eta.* Univ. of Texas at Austin, Grad. School of Lib. and Info. Science, Austin, TX 78712; *Beta Theta.* Brigham Young Univ., School of Lib. & Info. Science, Provo, UT 84602; *Beta Iota.* Univ. of Rhode Island, Grad. Lib. School, Kingston, RI 02881; *Beta Kappa.* Univ. of Alabama, Grad. School of Lib. Service, University, AL 35486; *Beta Lambda.* North Texas State Univ., School of Lib. & Info. Science, Denton, TX 76203, and Texas Woman's Univ., School of Lib. Science, Denton, TX 76204; *Beta Mu.* Long Island Univ., Palmer Grad. Lib. School, C. W. Post Center, Greenvale, NY 11548; *Beta Nu.* St. John's Univ., Div. of Lib. & Info. Science, Jamaica, NY 11439; *Beta Xi.* North Carolina Central Univ., School of Lib. Science, Durham, NC 27707; *Beta Omicron.* Univ. of Tennessee, Knoxville, Grad. School of Lib. & Info. Science, Knoxville, TN 37916; *Beta Pi.* Univ. of Arizona, Grad. Lib. School, Tucson, AZ 85721; *Beta Rho.* Univ. of Wisconsin-Milwaukee, School of Lib. Science, Milwaukee, WI 53201; *Beta Sigma.* Clarion State College, School of Lib. Science, Clarion, PA 16214; *Beta Tau.* Wayne State Univ., Div. of Lib. Science, Detroit, MI 48202; *Beta Upsilon.* Alabama A&M Univ., School of Lib. Media, Normal, AL 35762; *Beta Phi.* Univ. of South Florida, Grad. Dept. of Lib., Media & Info. Studies, Tampa, FL 33620.

BIBLIOGRAPHICAL SOCIETY OF AMERICA
Executive Director, Deirdre C. Stam
Box 397, Grand Central Sta., New York, NY 10017

OBJECT

"To promote bibliographical research and to issue bibliographical publications." Organized 1904. Memb. 1,400. Dues. $20. Year. Calendar.

OFFICERS (JAN. 1980-JAN. 1982)

Pres. Marcus A. McCorison, American Antiquarian Society, Salisbury St. & Park Ave., Worcester, MA 01609; *1st V.P.* G. Thomas Tanselle, Guggenheim Memorial Foundation, 90 Park Ave., New York, NY 10016; *2nd V.P.* William B. Todd, Parlin Hall 110, Univ. of Texas, Austin, TX 78712; *Treas.* Frank S. Streeter, 141 E. 72 St., New York, NY 10021; *Secy.* James M. Wells, Newberry Lib., 60 W. Walton Place, Chicago, IL 60610.

COUNCIL

Officers; Katharine Pantzer; Charles A. Ryscamp; P. W. Filby; William B. Todd; Andrew B. Myers; Lola L. Szladits.

PUBLICATION

Papers (q.; memb.). *Eds.* John Lancaster and Ruth Martimer, Box 467, Williamsburg, MA 01096. *Book Review Ed.* Kenneth Carpenter, Baker Lib., Harvard Univ., Cambridge, MA 02163.

COMMITTEE CHAIRPERSON

Publications. G. Thomas Tanselle, Guggenheim Memorial Foundation, 90 Park Ave., New York, NY 10016.

CANADIAN ASSOCIATION FOR INFORMATION SCIENCE (ASSOCIATION CANADIENNE DES SCIENCES DE L'INFORMATION)
Secretariat/Secrétariat, Box 776, Sta. G, Calgary, Alta. T3A 2G6, Canada

OBJECT

Brings together individuals and organizations concerned with the production, manipulation, storage, retrieval, and dissemination of information with emphasis on the application of modern technologies in these areas. CAIS is dedicated to enhancing the activity of the information transfer process, utilizing the vehicles of research, development, application, and education, and serves as a forum for dialogue and exchange of ideas concerned with the theory and practice of all factors involved in the communication of information. Dues (Inst.) $75; (Regular) $25; (Student) $10.

MEMBERSHIP

Institutions and all individuals interested in information science and who are involved in the gathering, the organization, and the dissemination of information (computer scientists, documentalists, information scientists, librarians, journalists, sociologists, psychologists, linguists, administrators, etc.) can become members of the Canadian Association for Information Science.

OFFICERS

Pres. Margaret Telfer; *V.P.* Ellen Pearson; *Secy.* Ron MacKinnon; *Treas.* Monique Lecavalier.

DIRECTORS

P. Lemoy, C. Bregaint; *Past Pres.* F. Matthews.

PUBLICATIONS

CAIS Bulletin (irreg.; free with membership).
The Canadian Conference of Information Science: Proceedings (ann.; ninth ann., 1981, $16.50).
The Canadian Journal of Information Science (ann.; nonmemb. $12).

CANADIAN LIBRARY ASSOCIATION
Executive Director, Paul Kitchen
151 Sparks St., Ottawa, Ont. K1P 5E3, Canada
613-232-9625

OBJECT

To develop high standards of librarianship and of library and information service. CLA develops standards for public, university, school, and college libraries and library technician programs; offers library school scholarships and book awards; carries on international liaison with other library associations; and makes representation to government and official commissions. Founded in Hamilton in 1946, CLA is a nonprofit voluntary organization governed by an elected council and board of directors. Memb. (Indiv.) 4,100; (Inst.) 1,000. Dues (Indiv.) $45.00 & $70.00, depending on salary; (Inst.) $45.00 & $70.00, depending on budget. Year. July 1–June 30.

MEMBERSHIP

Open to individuals, institutions, and groups interested in librarianship and in library and information services.

OFFICERS (1981-1982)

Pres. Marianne Scott, Dir. of Libs., McGill Univ. Libs., Montreal, P.Q. H3A 1Y1; *1st V.P./Pres.-Elect.* Pearce Penney, Chief Provincial Libn., Nfld. Public Lib. Services, St. John's, Nfld. A1B 3A3; *2nd V.P.* Beth Barlow, Head of Info. Services, Saskatoon Public Lib., Saskatoon, Sask. S7K 0J6; *Treas.* Vivienne Monty, Government and Business Lib., York Univ., Downsview, Ont. M3J 2R6; *Past Pres.* Alan MacDonald, Dir. of Libs., Univ. of Calgary, Calgary, Alta. T2N 1N4. (Address general correspondence to the executive director.)

BOARD OF DIRECTORS

Officers, division presidents.

COUNCIL

Officers; division presidents; councillors, including representatives of ASTED and provincial/regional library associations.

COUNCILLORS-AT-LARGE

To June 30, 1982: Sheila Laidlaw, Patricia Cavill.

To June 30, 1983: Marie Zielinska, Gordon Ray.

To June 30, 1984: Madge Mac Gown, Donald Mills.

PUBLICATIONS

Canadian Library Journal (6 issues; memb. or nonmemb. subscribers, Canada $15, U.S. $17 [Can.], international $20 [Can.]).

CM: Canadian Materials for Schools and Libraries (4 per year, $20).

DIVISION CHAIRPERSONS

Canadian Association of College and University Libraries. Michael Angel, Publications Services Coord., Univ. of Manitoba, Winnipeg, Man. R3N 0T9.

Canadian Association of Public Libraries. Diane MacQuarrie, Halifax City Regional Lib., Halifax, N.S. B3J 1E9.

Canadian Association of Special Libraries and Information Services. Patricia Dye, Head, Business Dept., Metropolitan Toronto Public Lib., Toronto, Ont. M4W 2G8.

Canadian Library Trustees Association. Athalie Solloway, Richmond, B.C. V7A 1W2.

Canadian School Library Association. Lorne MacRae, Coord., Media Services, Calgary Bd. of Educ., Calgary, Alta. T2W 2G4.

ASSOCIATION REPRESENTATIVES

Association pour l'Avancement des Sciences et des Techniques de la Documentation (ASTED). Lise Brousseau, Dir.-Gen. ASTED, 360 rue Le Moyne, Montreal, P.Q. H2Y 1Y3.

Atlantic Provinces Library Association. Barbara Eddy, Education Libn., Memorial Univ., St. John's, Nfld. A1C 5S7.

British Columbia Library Association. Maureen Willison, Greater Vancouver Lib. Federation, Vancouver, B.C. V5L 3X3.

Library Association of Alberta. Heather-Belle Dowling, County of Strathcona Municipal Lib., Sherwood Park, Alta. T8A 3J4.

Manitoba Library Association. Doreen Shanks, Head, Education Lib., Univ. of Manitoba, Winnipeg, Man. R3T 0V2.

Ontario Library Association. Jennifer Arbuckle, Deputy Dir., Etobicoke Public Lib., Etobicoke, Ont. M9C 4V5.

Quebec Library Association. Anne Galler, Coord., Lib. Studies Program, Concordia Univ., Montreal, P.Q. H4B 1R6.

Saskatchewan Library Association. Bryan Foran, Libn., Info. Services, Saskatoon, Sask. S7K 0J6.

CATHOLIC LIBRARY ASSOCIATION
Executive Director, Matthew R. Wilt
461 W. Lancaster Ave., Haverford, PA 19041
215-649-5250

OBJECT

"The promotion and encouragement of Catholic literature and library work through cooperation, publications, education and information." Founded 1921. Memb. 3,280. Dues $20–$500. Year. July 1981–June 1982.

OFFICERS (APRIL 1981–APRIL 1983)

Pres. Kelly Fitzpatrick, Mt. St. Mary's College, Emmitsburg, MD 21727; *V.P.* Sister M. Dennis Lynch, SHCJ, Rosemont College, Rosemont, PA 19010; *Past Pres.* Sister Franz Lang, OP, Barry College Lib., Miami, FL 33161. (Address general correspondence to the executive director.)

EXECUTIVE BOARD

Officers; Mary A. Grant, St. John's Univ., Jamaica, NY 11439; Brother Emmett Corry, OSF, St. John's Univ., Jamaica, NY 11439; Sister Teresa Rigel, CSJ, Red Cloud Indian School, Pine Ridge, SD 57770; Irma C. Godfrey, 6247 Westway Place, St. Louis, MO 63109; Sister Chrysantha Rudnik, CSSF, Felician College, Chicago, IL 60659; Gayle E.

Salvatore, Brother Martin H.S., New Orleans, LA 70122.

PUBLICATIONS

Catholic Library World (10 issues; memb. or $30).
The Catholic Periodical and Literature Index (subscription).

COMMITTEE CHAIRPERSONS

Advisory Council. Sister M. Dennis Lynch, Rosemont College, Rosemont, PA 19010.
Catholic Library World Editorial. Sister Marie Melton, RSM, St. John's Univ., Jamaica, NY 11439.
The Catholic Periodical and Literature Index. Sister Therese Marie Gaudreau, SND, Trinity College, Washington, DC 20017.
Constitution and Bylaws. Sister Margaret Huyck, CSJ, Lib. Consultant, New Orleans, LA 70122.
Continuing Education. Sister Kathryn Dobbs, CSFN, Holy Family College, Philadelphia, PA 19114.
Elections. Sister Rose Anthony Moos, CSJ, Sacred Heart Convent, Salina, KS 67401.
Finance. Arnold M. Rzepecki, Sacred Heart Seminary College, Detroit, MI 48206.
Membership. Membership Development Committee.
Nominations. Sister Mary Arthur Hoagland, IHM, Office of the Superintendent of Schools, Philadelphia, PA 19103.
Program Coordinator. John T. Corrigan, CFX, CLA Headquarters, 461 W. Lancaster Ave., Haverford, PA 19041.
Public Relations. Sister Mary Margaret Cribben, RSM, Villanova College, Villanova, PA 19085.
Publications. Brother Emmett Corry, OSF, St. John's Univ., Jamaica, NY 11439.
Regina Medal. Sister Rita Ann Bert, OSF, Oak Lawn Public Lib., Oak Lawn, IL 60453.
Scholarship. Rev. Joseph P. Browne, CSC, Univ. of Portland, Portland, OR 97203.

ORGANIZATIONS TO WHICH CLA HAS REPRESENTATION

Catholic Press Association. John T. Corrigan, CFX, CLA Headquarters, 461 W. Lancaster Ave., Haverford, PA 19041.
Continuing Library Education Network Exchange (CLENE). Sister Kathryn Dobbs, CSFN, Holy Family College, Philadelphia, PA 19114.
Council of National Library and Information Association (CNLIA). Matthew R. Wilt, Exec. Dir., CLA Headquarters, 461 W. Lancaster Ave., Haverford, PA 19041; Brother Emmett Corry, OSF, St. John's Univ., Jamaica, NY 11439.
Special Libraries Association. Mary-Jo DiMuccio, Sunnyvale Public Lib., Sunnyvale, CA 94087.

OTHER REPRESENTED ORGANIZATIONS

AASL Standards Committee.
American National Standards Committee: Library and Information Science and Related Publishing Practices (ANSC Z39).
Catholic Health Association.
National Catholic Educational Association.
Universal Serials and Book Exchange (USBE).

SECTION CHAIRPERSONS

Archives. Sister Martin Joseph Jones, SSMN, State Univ. College at Buffalo, Buffalo, NY 14222.
Children's Libraries. Sister Barbara Anne Kilpatrick, RSM, St. Vincent de Paul School, Nashville, TN 37208.
College, University, Seminary Libraries. Brother Paul J. Ostendorf, FSC, 27 Grove St., Minneapolis, MN 55401.
High School Libraries. Sister Jean

Bostley, SSJ, St. Joseph Central H.S., Pittsfield, MA 01201.
Library Education. Sister M. Lauretta McCusker, OP, Rosary College, River Forest, IL 60305.
Parish/Community Libraries. Sister Mary Agnes Sullivan, OP, St. Agnes Convent, Memphis, TN 38117.
Public Libraries. Margaret Long, Public Lib. of Cincinnati, Cincinnati, OH 45202.

ROUND TABLE CHAIRPERSON

Cataloging and Classification Round Table. Tina-Karen Weiner, La Salle College, Philadelphia, PA 19141.

CHIEF OFFICERS OF STATE LIBRARY AGENCIES
Marcia Lowell, State Librarian, Oregon State Library,
State Library Building, Salem, OR 97310

OBJECT

The object of COSLA is to provide "a means for cooperative action among its state and territorial members to strengthen the work of the respective state and territorial agencies. Its purpose is to provide a continuing mechanism for dealing with the problems faced by the heads of these agencies which are responsible for state and territorial library development."

MEMBERSHIP

The Chief Officers of State Library Agencies is an independent organization of the men and women who head the state and territorial agencies responsible for library development. Its membership consists solely of the top library officers of the 50 states and one territory, variously designated as state librarian, director, commissioner, or executive secretary.

OFFICERS (NOV. 1980-NOV. 1982)

Chpn. Patricia Klinck, State Libn., Vermont Dept. of Libs., c/o State Office Bldg., Montpelier, VT 05602; *V. Chpn.* Robert L. Clark, State Libn., Dept. of Libs., 200 N. East 18, Oklahoma City, OK 73105; *Secy.* Marcia Lowell, State Libn., Oregon State Lib., Salem, OR 97310; *Treas.* Cliff Lange, State Libn., New Mexico State Lib., Box 1629, Santa Fe, NM 87501; *ALA Affiliation.* Sandra Cooper, ALA, Exec. Secy. ASCLA.

DIRECTORS

Officers; immediate past chpn.: William G. Asp, Dir., Dept. of Educ., Office of Public Libs. and Interlibrary Cooperation, 301 Hanover Bldg., 480 Cedar St., St. Paul, MN 55101; two elected members: Barbara Weaver, Dir., State Dept. of Educ., Div. of State Lib. and History, 185 W. State St., Trenton, NJ 08625; Barratt Wilkins, State Libn., State Lib. of Florida, R. A. Gray Bldg., Tallahassee, FL 32301.

COMMITTEE CHAIRPERSONS

Continuing Education. Barry Porter, Dir., State Lib. Commission, Iowa.
Legislation. Bill Asp, Dir., Office of Public Libs. & Interlibrary Cooperation, Minnesota.
Liaison with ALA and Other National Library-Related Organizations. Ray Ewick, Dir., Indiana State Lib.
Liaison with Library of Congress. John Kopischke, Dir., Nebraska Lib. Commission.
Liaison with Library of Congress, Division for Blind and Physically Handicapped. Russell Davis, Utah State Lib. Commission.
Liaison with National Commission on Libraries and Information Science. Elliot Shelkrot, Pennsylvania State Lib.
Liaison with U.S. Department of Education. Barratt Wilkins, State Libn., Florida State Lib.

Liaison with National Center for Education Statistics. Barratt Wilkins, State Libn., Florida State Lib.
Network Development. Tony Miele, Dir., Alabama Public Lib. Service.
Statewide Planning and Organization Committee. Sylvia Short, State Libn., Delaware Div. of Libs.
Outlaying State/Territorial Library Agencies. Ruth Itamura, State Libn., Hawaii Office of Lib. Service.

CHINESE-AMERICAN LIBRARIANS ASSOCIATION
Executive Director, Tze-chung Li
Rosary College Graduate School of Library Science
River Forest, IL 60305

OBJECT

"(1) To enhance communication among Chinese-American librarians as well as between Chinese-American librarians and other librarians; (2) to serve as a forum for discussion of mutual problems and professional concerns among Chinese-American librarians; (3) to promote Sino-American librarianship and library services; and (4) to provide a vehicle whereby Chinese-American librarians may cooperate with other associations and organizations having similar or allied interest."

MEMBERSHIP

Membership is open to everyone who is interested in the association's goals and activities. Memb. 360. Dues (Regular) $15; (Student and Nonsalaried) $7.50; (Inst.) $45; (Permanent) $150.

OFFICERS (JUNE 1981-JUNE 1982)

Pres. David T. Liu, Dir., Pharr Memorial Lib., Pharr, TX 78577; *V.P./Pres.-Elect.* Bessie Hahn, Dir. of Lib. Services, Brandeis Univ., Waltham, MA 02254; *Treas.* Sally C. Tseng, Libn., Univ. of California, Irvine, CA 92713; *Secy.* William W. Wan, Libn., Texas Woman's Univ., Denton, TX 76201; *Exec. Dir.* Tze-chung Li, Rosary College Grad. School of Lib. Science, River Forest, IL 60305.

PUBLICATIONS

Directory of Chinese American Librarians in the United States, 1976 ($5; memb. $2.50).
Journal of Library and Information Science (2 per year; memb. or $15).
Membership Directory, 1981 (free).
Newsletter (3 per year; memb.).

COMMITTEE CHAIRPERSONS

Annual Program. Bessie Hahn, Brandeis Univ., Waltham, MA 02154.
Awards. William Wan, Texas Woman's Univ., Denton, TX 76201.
Membership. Amy Wilson, Univ. Microfilms, Ann Arbor, MI 48104.
Nominating. Lee-hsia Ting, Western Illinois Univ., Macomb, IL 61455.
Publications. Chiou-sen Chen, Rutgers Univ., New Brunswick, NJ 08903.
Foundation. Bessie Hahn, Brandeis Univ., Waltham, MA 02154.

CHAPTER CHAIRPERSONS

California. Cecilia Chen, California State Univ., Dominguez Hills, CA 90630.
Mid-Atlantic. Alana W. Ho, George Mason Univ., Fairfax, VA 22030.
Mid-West. Kuang-liang Hsu, Ball State Univ., Muncie, IN 47360.
Northwest. Norma Yueh, Ramapo College, Mahwah, NJ 07430.

Southwest. Cecilia Tung, Texas Instruments, Garland, TX 75042.

JOURNAL OFFICERS

Margaret Fung, National Taiwan Normal Univ., Taipei, Taiwan; Chen-ku Wang, National Central Lib., Taipei, Taiwan; John Yung-hsiang Lai, Harvard-Yenching Lib., Cambridge, MA 02138.

DISTINGUISHED SERVICE AWARDS

The first distinguished service award was presented to Dr. Ernst Wolff on June 30, 1980.

CHURCH AND SYNAGOGUE LIBRARY ASSOCIATION
Executive Secretary, Dorothy J. Rodda
Box 1130, Bryn Mawr, PA 19010

OBJECT

"To act as a unifying core for the many existing church and synagogue libraries; to provide the opportunity for a mutual sharing of practices and problems; to inspire and encourage a sense of purpose and mission among church and synagogue librarians; to study and guide the development of church and synagogue librarianship toward recognition as a formal branch of the library profession." Founded 1967. Memb. 1,400. Dues (Contributing) $100; (Inst.) $75; (Affiliated) $35; (Church or Synagogue) $20; (Indiv.) $10. Year. July 1981–June 1982.

OFFICERS (JULY 1981–JUNE 1982)

Pres. Elsie E. Lehman, 1051 College Ave., Harrisonburg, VA 22801; *1st V.P./Pres.-Elect.* Anita Dalton, 41 Aberdeen Rd. N., Galt, Cambridge, Ont., N1S 2X1 Canada; *2nd V.P.* Smith D. Gooch, 3507 Monte Vista N.E., Albuquerque, NM 87106; *Treas.* Patricia W. Tabler, Box 116, Keedysville, MD 21756; *Past Pres.* Robert Dvorak, Gordon-Conwell Theological Seminary, South Hamilton, MA 01982. *Publns. Dir. and Bulletin Ed.* William H. Gentz, 300 E. 34 St., Apt. 9C, New York, NY 10016.

EXECUTIVE BOARD

Officers; committee chairpersons.

PUBLICATIONS

Church and Synagogue Libraries (bi-mo.; memb. or $15, Can. $18). *Ed.* William H. Gentz. Book reviews, ads, $130 for full-page, camera-ready ad, one-time rate.

CSLA Guide No. 1. Setting Up a Library: How to Begin or Begin Again ($2.50).

CSLA Guide No. 2, rev. 2nd ed. *Promotion Planning All Year 'Round* ($4.50).

CSLA Guide No. 3, rev. ed. *Workshop Planning* ($6.50).

CSLA Guide No. 4, rev. ed. *Selecting Library Materials* ($2.50).

CSLA Guide No. 5. Cataloging Books Step by Step ($2.50).

CSLA Guide No. 6. Standards for Church and Synagogue Libraries ($3.75).

CSLA Guide No. 7. Classifying Church or Synagogue Library Materials ($2.50).

CSLA Guide No. 8. Subject Headings for Church or Synagogue Libraries ($3.50).

CSLA Guide No. 9. A Policy and Procedure Manual for Church and Synagogue Libraries ($3.75).

CSLA Guide No. 10. Archives in the Church or Synagogue Library ($4.50).

Church and Synagogue Library Resources: Annotated Bibliography ($2.50).

A Basic Book List for Church Libraries: Annotated Bibliography ($1.75).

Helping Children Through Books: Annotated Bibliography ($3.75).

The Family Uses the Library. Leaflet (5¢; $3.75/100).

The Teacher and the Library—Partners in Religious Education. Leaflet (10¢; $7/100).

Promotion and Publicity for a Congregational Library. Sound slide set ($75; rental fee $10).

COMMITTEE CHAIRPERSONS

Awards. Eileen McEwen.
Chapters. Fay W. Grosse.
Continuing Education. Joyce L. White.
Finance. Robert Dvorak.
Library Services. Judith Stromdahl.
Membership. Lois Seyfrit.
Nominations and Elections. Evelyn R. Ling.
Public Relations. Maryann J. Dotts.
Sites. Sherry D. Fleet.

CONTINUING LIBRARY EDUCATION NETWORK AND EXCHANGE (CLENE), INC.

Executive Director, Eleanore R. Ficke
620 Michigan Ave. N.E., Washington, DC 20064
202-635-5825

OBJECT

The basic missions of CLENE, Inc., are (1) to provide equal access to continuing education opportunities, available in sufficient quantity and quality over a substantial period of time to ensure library and information science personnel and organizations the competency to deliver quality library and information services to all; (2) to create an awareness and a sense of need for continuing education of library personnel on the part of employers and individuals as a means of responding to societal and technological change. Founded 1975. Memb. 390. Dues (Indiv.) $15; (Inst. Assoc.) $35–$100; (State Agency) $750–$3,000 according to population. Year. Twelve months from date of entry.

MEMBERSHIP

CLENE, Inc., welcomes as members institutions—libraries, information centers, data banks, schools and departments of library, media, and information science—any organization concerned with continuing education; professional associations in library, media, information science, and allied disciplines; local, state, regional and national associations; individuals; state library and educational agencies; consortia.

OFFICERS (JUNE 1981–JUNE 1982)

Pres. Janet L. Blumberg, Chief, Consultant Services Div., Washington State Lib. AJ-11, Olympia, WA 98504; *Pres.-Elect.* Alphonse F. Trezza, Dir., Intergovernmental Library Cooperation Project, 3292 Blue Heron Dr., Falls Church, VA 22042; *Secy.* Mary Frances Hoban, Mgr., Professional Development, Special Libs. Assn., 235 Park Ave. S., New York, NY 10003; *Treas.* Dottie Hiebing, Public Lib. Consultant-Continuing Education, Div. for Lib. Services, 125 S. Webster St., Box 7841, Madison, WI 53707; *Past Pres.* Suzanne H. Mahmoodi, Continuing Education and Library Research Specialist, OPLIC, 301 Hanover Bldg., 480 Cedar St., St. Paul, MN 55101.

BOARD OF DIRECTORS

Officers; Ann Armbrister, Assoc. Dir. for Lib. Services, AMIGOS Bibliographic Council, Inc., 11300 N. Central Expressway, Suite 321, Dallas, TX 75243; Charles A. Bolles, State Libn., Idaho State Lib., 325 W. State, Boise, ID 83702; Joan C. Durrance, Coord. of Continuing Education, School of Lib. Science, Univ. of Michigan, Ann Arbor, MI 48109; Judith J. Field, Flint Public Lib., 1026 E. Kearsley St., Flint, MI 48502; Donald Haynes, State Libn., Virginia State Lib., Richmond, VA 23219; Margaret Myers, Dir., Office for Lib. Personnel Resources, American Lib. Assn., 50 E. Huron St., Chicago, IL 60611; Sandra S. Stephan, Specialist in Staff Development and Continuing Education, Div. of Lib. Development and Services, Maryland State Dept. of Educ., 200 W. Baltimore St., Baltimore, MD 21201; Sharon A. Sullivan, Personnel Libn., Ohio

State Univ. Libs., 1858 Neil Ave. Mall, Columbus, OH 43210; Dan Tonkery, Assoc. Univ. Libn., Univ. of California, Univ. Research Lib., 405 Hilgard Ave., Los Angeles, CA 90024; Susan S. Whittle, Public Lib. Consultant, State Lib. of Florida, R. A. Gray Bldg., Tallahassee, FL 32301.

PUBLICATIONS

CLENExchange (6/year). Newsletter $6 (nonmemb.).
Continuing Education Communicator (mo.). $10 (Indiv.); $15 (Institutional nonmemb.).
Directory of Continuing Education Opportunities (1979). $22.80.
Model Continuing Education Recognition System in Library and Information Science 1979. $29.80.
Proceedings of CLENE Assembly I: Self-Assessment (January 1976). $4.25 (memb.); $5 (nonmemb.).
Who's Who in Continuing Education: Human Resources in Continuing Library, Information, Media Education (1979). $30.

Concept Papers

#1 *Developing CE Learning Materials.* Sheldon and Woolls (1977). $4.25 (memb.); $5 (nonmemb.).
#2 *Guide to Planning and Teaching CE Courses.* Washtien (1975). $4.25 (memb.); $5 (nonmemb.).
#3 *Planning & Evaluating Library Training Programs.* Sheldon (1976). $4.25 (memb.); $5 (nonmemb.).
#4 *Helping Adults to Learn.* Knox (1976) (out of print).
#5 *Continuing Library Education: Needs Assessment & Model Programs.* Virgo, Dunkel, Angione (1977). $10.20 (memb.); $12 (nonmemb.).
#6 *Recognition for Your Continuing Education Accomplishments.* James Nelson (June 1979).
Annotated Bibliography of Recent Continuing Education Literature (1976). $4.25 (memb.); $5 (nonmemb.).
Continuing Education Resource Book (1977). $2.55 (memb.); $3 (nonmemb.).
Continuing Education Planning Inventory: A Self-Evaluation Checklist (1977). $1.70 (memb.); $2 (nonmemb.).
Guidelines for Relevant Groups Involved in Home Study Programs (1977). $4.25 (memb.); $5 (nonmemb.).

For more information or to order publications, write to CLENE, Inc., 620 Michigan Ave. N.E., Washington, DC 20064.

COMMITTEES

Assembly Planning Committee.
By-laws Committee.
Finance Committee.
Long-range Planning Task Force.
Membership Promotion Committee.
Membership Services Committee.
Nominating Committee.
Publications Committee.
Research and Development Committee.
Tellers Committee.
Voluntary Recognition Service Committee.

COUNCIL OF NATIONAL LIBRARY AND INFORMATION ASSOCIATIONS, INC.
461 W. Lancaster Ave., Haverford, PA 19041
215-649-5251

OBJECT

To provide a central agency for cooperation among library associations and other professional organizations of the United States and Canada in promoting matters of common interest.

MEMBERSHIP

Open to national library associations and organizations with related interests of the United States and Canada. American Assn. of Law Libs.; American Lib. Assn.; American Society of Indexers; American

Theological Lib. Assn.; Art Libs. Society/ North America; Assn. of Christian Libs., Inc.; Assn. of Jewish Libs.; Catholic Lib. Assn.; Church and Synagogue Lib. Assn.; Council of Planning Libns.; Lib. Binding Institute; Lib. Public Relations Council; Lutheran Lib. Assn.; Medical Lib. Assn.; Music Lib. Assn.; National Federation of Abstracting and Indexing Services; Society of American Archivists; Special Libs. Assn.; Theatre Lib. Assn.

OFFICERS (JULY 1981-JUNE 1982)

Chpn. John T. Corrigan, CFX, Catholic Lib. Assn., 461 W. Lancaster Ave., Haverford, PA 19041; *V. Chpn.* David Bender, Exec. Dir., Special Libs. Assn., 235 Park Ave. S., New York, NY 10003; *Past Chpn.* Richard M. Buck, PARC, New York Public Lib., 111 Amsterdam Ave., New York, NY 10023; *Secy.-Treas.* Erich Meyerhoff, Cornell Univ., Medical College Lib., 1300 York Ave., New York, NY 10021. (Address correspondence to chairperson at 461 W. Lancaster Ave., Haverford, PA 19041.)

DIRECTORS

Robert DeCandido, New York Public Lib., Research Lib., Fifth Ave. & 42 St., New York, NY 10018 (July 1980-June 1983); James Irvine, Princeton Theological Seminary, Box 111, Princeton, NJ 08540 (July 1981-1984); Vivian Hewitt, Carnegie Endowment for International Peace, 30 Rockefeller Plaza, New York, NY 10020 (July 1979-June 1982).

COUNCIL OF PLANNING LIBRARIANS, PUBLICATIONS OFFICE
1313 E. 60 St., Chicago, IL 60637

OBJECT

To provide a special interest group in the field of city and regional planning for libraries and librarians, faculty, professional planners, university, government, and private planning organizations; to provide an opportunity for exchange among those interested in problems of library organization and research and in the dissemination of information about city and regional planning; to sponsor programs of service to the planning profession and librarianship; to advise on library organization for new planning programs; to aid and support administrators, faculty, and librarians in their efforts to educate the public and their appointed or elected representatives to the necessity for strong library programs in support of planning. Founded 1960. Memb. 200. Dues. $35 (Inst.); $10 (Indiv.). Year. July 1-June 30.

MEMBERSHIP

Open to any individual or institution that supports the purpose of the council upon written application and payment of dues to the treasurer.

OFFICERS (1981-1982)

Pres. Katharina Richter, Tucson Planning Department, Box 27210, Tucson, AZ 85726; *Vice Pres./ Pres.-Elect.* Gretchen Beal, Knoxville/Knox County Metropolitan Planning Commission, City/County Bldg., Suite 403, Knoxville, TN 37902; *Secy.* Rona Gregory, Rotch Lib. of Architecture & Planning, M.I.T., 77 Massachusetts Ave., Cambridge, MA 02139; *Treas.* Jon Greene, Architecture & Planning Library, Univ. of California, Los Angeles, CA 90024; *Member-at-Large.* Olya Tymciurak, City of Tucson, Planning Dept. Lib., Box 27210, Tucson, AZ 85726; *Editor, Publications Program.* James Hecimovich, 1313 E. 60 St., Chicago, IL 60637.

PUBLICATIONS

CPL Bibliographies (approx. 30 bibliographies published per year). May be purchased on standing order subscription or by individual issue. Subscription rates on request.

#40. *Voluntary Interlocal Cooperation: An Annotated Bibliography*. Betty Walter Honadle (18 pp., $5).

#41. *The Psychological and Social Implications of the Entrance of Women into the Work Force: An Annotated Bibliography of Source Material*. Robert Slater, et al. (72 pp., $13).

#42. *Land Use and Planning Implications of Wood Energy Development: A Bibliography*. Edward Goldstein and Meir Gross (27 pp., $6).

#43. *Earth-Sheltered Housing: An Annotated Bibliography and Directory*. Pauline A. Keehn (61 pp., $11).

#44. *Local Planning in California: A Bibliography of Reference Materials for Practitioners*. M. Kay Mowery and J. Laurence Mintier (43 pp., $8).

#45. *Nontraditional Job Training for Women: A Bibliography and a Resource Directory for Employment and Training Planners*. Katherine Paramore (17 pp., $5).

#46. *Urban Design: A Comprehensive Reference*. Hamid Shirvani (80 pp., $12).

#47. *Solar Access and Land Use Planning: A Bibliography*. Charles Vidich (7 pp., $4).

#48. *Mobility, Residential Location, and Urban Change: A Partially Annotated Bibliography*. Gary T. Johnson (28 pp., $6).

#49. *Citizen Coproduction of Public Services: An Annotated Bibliography*. Stephen L. Percy and Paula C. Baker (14 pp., $4).

COUNCIL ON LIBRARY RESOURCES, INC.
Secretary-Treasurer, Mary Agnes Thompson,
One Dupont Circle, Suite 620, Washington, DC 20036
202-296-4757

OBJECT

A private operating foundation, the council seeks to assist in finding solutions to the problems of libraries, particularly academic and research libraries. In pursuit of this aim, the council makes grants to and contracts with other organizations and individuals. The Ford Foundation established CLR in 1956 and has since contributed $31.5 million to its support. CLR receives support from other foundations as well; the Andrew W. Mellon Foundation and the Carnegie Corporation of New York granted $1.5 million to CLR in 1977. The council's current program interests include establishment of a computerized system of national bibliographic control, library management and institutional development, professional education, library resources and their preservation, and analysis and planning.

MEMBERSHIP

The council's board of directors is limited to 20.

OFFICERS

Chpn. Whitney North Seymour, Sr.; *V. Chpn.* Louis B. Wright; *Pres.* Warren J. Haas; *Secy.-Treas.* Mary Agnes Thompson. (Address correspondence to headquarters.)

PUBLICATIONS

Annual Report.
CLR Recent Developments.

EDUCATIONAL FILM LIBRARY ASSOCIATION
Executive Director, Nadine Covert
43 W. 61 St., New York, NY 10023
212-246-4533

OBJECT

"To promote the production, distribution and utilization of educational films and other audio-visual materials." Incorporated 1943. Memb. 1,800. Dues (Inst.) $85–$180; (Commercial Organizations) $200; (Indiv.) $35. Year. July–June.

OFFICERS

Pres. Stephen Hess (1979–1982), Dir., Educational Media Center, Univ. of Utah, 207 Milton Bennion Hall, Salt Lake City, UT 84112; *Pres.-Elect.* Clifford Ehlinger (1980–83), Dir., Div. of Media, Grant Wood Area Education Agency, 4401 Sixth St. S.W., Cedar Rapids, IA 52404; *Treas.* Nadine Covert (*Ex officio*), Exec. Dir., EFLA, 43 W. 61 St., New York, NY 10023; *Secy.* Angie Leclercq (1980–83), Head, Undergraduate Lib., Univ. of Tennessee, 1015 Volunteer Blvd., Knoxville, TN 37916.

BOARD OF DIRECTORS

Officers; Helen Cyr (1979–82), Audio Visual Dept., Enoch Pratt Free Lib., 400 Cathedral St., Baltimore, MD 21201; Frances Dean (1979–82), Dir., Instructional Materials Div., Montgomery County Public Schools, 850 Hungerford Dr., c/o Mrs. Peffiford, Rm. 55, Rockville, MD 20850; Catherine Egan (1981–84), Audiovisual Services, Pennsylvania State Univ., Foxhill Rd,. University Park, PA 16802; Lillian Katz (1981–84), Port Washington Public Lib., 245 Main St., Port Washington, NY 11050; Lilly Loo (1980–83), Los Angeles County Lib., 6518 Mills Ave., Huntington Park, CA 90255; Elfrieda McCauley (1981–84), Coord., Media Services, Greenwich Public Schools, Box 292, Havemeyer Bldg., Greenwich, CT 06830.

PUBLICATIONS

EFLA Bulletin (q.). *Ed.* Margann Chach.
EFLA Evaluations (5 per year). *Ed.* Judith Trojan.
American Film Festival Program Guide (ann.).
Sightlines (q.). *Ed.* Nadine Covert.
Write for list of other books and pamphlets.

FEDERAL LIBRARY COMMITTEE
Library of Congress, Washington, DC 20540
202-287-6055

OBJECT

"For the purpose of concentrating the intellectual resources present in the federal library and library related information community: To achieve better utilization of library resources and facilities; to provide more effective planning, development, and operation of federal libraries; to promote an optimum exchange of experience, skill, and resources; to promote more effective service to the nation at large. Secretariat efforts and the work groups are organized to: Consider policies and problems relating to federal libraries; evaluate existing federal library programs and resources; determine priorities among library issues requiring attention; examine the organization and policies for acquiring, preserving, and making information available; study the need for a potential of technological innovation in library practices; and study library budgeting and staffing problems, including the recruiting, education, training, and remuneration of librarians." Founded 1965. Memb. (Federal Libs.) 2,600; (Federal Libns.) 4,000. Year. Oct. 1–Sept. 30.

MEMBERSHIP

Libn. of Congress, Dir. of the National Agricultural Lib., Dir. of the National Lib. of Medicine, representatives from each of the other executive departments, and delegates from the National Aeronautics and Space Admin., the National Science Foundation, the Smithsonian Institution, the U.S. Supreme Court, International Communication Agency, the Veterans Admin., and the Office of Presidential Libs. Six members will be selected on a rotation basis by the permanent members of the committee from independent agencies, boards, committees, and commissions. These rotating members will serve two-year terms. Ten regional members shall be selected on a rotating basis by the permanent members of the committee to represent federal libraries following the geographic pattern developed by the Federal Regional Councils. These rotating regional members will serve two-year terms. The ten regional members, one from each of the ten federal regions, shall be voting members. In addition to the permanent representative from DOD, one nonvoting member shall be selected from each of the three services (U.S. Army, U.S. Navy, U.S. Air Force). These service members, who will serve for two years, will be selected by the permanent Department of Defense member from a slate provided by the Federal Library Committee. The membership in each service shall be rotated equitably among the special service, technical, and academic and school libraries in that service. DOD shall continue to have one voting member in the committee. The DOD representative may poll the three service members for their opinions before reaching a decision concerning the vote. A representative of the Office of Management and Budget, designated by the budget director and others appointed by the chairperson, will meet with the committee as observers.

OFFICERS

Chpn. Carol Nemeyer, Assoc. Libn. for National Programs, Lib. of Congress, Washington, DC 20540. *Exec. Dir.* James P. Riley.

PUBLICATIONS

Annual Report (Oct.).
FLC Newsletter (irreg.).

FEDLINK NETWORK OFFICE
Federal Library Committee, Library of Congress, Washington, DC 20540
202-287-6454

OBJECT

The Federal Library and Information Network (FEDLINK) is an FLC operating cooperative program, established to minimize costs and enhance services through the use of on-line data base services for shared cataloging, interlibrary loan, acquisitions, and information retrieval. FEDLINK was established to:

1. Expedite and facilitate on-line data base services among federal libraries and information centers.
2. Develop plans for the expansion of such services to federal libraries and information centers.
3. Promote cooperation and utilization of the full potential of networks and technologies to institutions and pro-

vide for formal relationships between library and information networks and the FEDLINK membership.
4. To serve as the major federal library and information cooperative system in the emerging national library and information service network.
5. Promote education, research, and training in network services and new library and information technology for the benefit of federal libraries and information centers.

MEMBERSHIP

FEDLINK membership is nationwide and is made up of over 400 libraries, information centers, and systems that participate in automated systems and services sponsored and coordinated by FLC.

OFFICERS

Dir. James P. Riley; *Coord.* Lucinda Leonard.

INFORMATION INDUSTRY ASSOCIATION
President, Paul G. Zurkowski
316 Pennsylvania Ave. S.E., Suite 400, Washington, DC 20003
202-544-1969

MEMBERSHIP

For details on membership and dues, write to the association headquarters. Memb. Over 150.

STAFF

Pres. Paul G. Zurkowski; *V.P., Government Relations.* Robert S. Willard; *Mgr., Finance and Admin.* Frank Martins; *Mgr., Marketing and Publications.* Fred Rosenau; *Mgr., Meetings.* Karen MacArthur.

BOARD OF DIRECTORS

Chpn. Thomas A. Grogan, McGraw-Hill; *V. Chpn.* Roy K. Campbell, Dun & Bradstreet; *Secy.* Paul G. Zurkowski, Info. Industry Assn.; *Treas.* Norman M. Wellen, Business International Corp.; *Past Chpn.* Robert F. Asleson, Info. Handling Services; William A. Beltz, Bureau of National Affairs; J. Christopher Burns, Washington Post Co.; William L. Dunn, Dow Jones Info. Services; Elizabeth B. Eddison, Warner-Eddison Assocs.; Andrew P. Garvin, FIND/SVP; James G. Kollegger, Environment Info. Center, Inc.; Robert November, The New York Times Info. Group; Jerome S. Rubin; William J. Senter, Xerox Publishing Group; Roger K. Summit, Lockheed Info. Systems; Loene Trubkin, Data Courier, Inc.

Board Committee Chairpersons

Executive. Thomas A. Grogan
Financial Planning. Norman M. Wellen.
Membership. Roy K. Campbell.
Long-Range Planning. J. Christopher Burns.

PUBLICATIONS

The Business of Information Report (1982).
Information Sources (5th ed., 1981–1982).
Planning Product Innovation (1981).
Understanding U.S. Information Policy (1982).

LUTHERAN CHURCH LIBRARY ASSOCIATION
122 W. Franklin Ave., Minneapolis, MN 55404
612-870-3623
Executive Secretary, E. T. (Wilma) Jensen
(Home address: 3620 Fairlawn Dr., Minnetonka, MN 55404
612-473-5965)

OBJECT

"To promote the growth of church libraries by publishing a quarterly journal, *Lutheran Libraries;* furnishing booklists; assisting member libraries with technical problems; providing meetings for mutual encouragement, assistance, and exchange of ideas among members." Founded 1958. Memb. 1,800. Dues. $15, $25, $100, $500, $1,000. Year. Jan.–Jan.

OFFICERS (JAN. 1981–JAN. 1983)

Pres. Esther Damkoehler, Libn., Hope Lutheran Lib., Milwaukee, WI (7822 Eagle St., Wauwatosa, WI 53213); *V.P.* Marlys Johnson, 4709 Oregon Ave. N., Minneapolis, MN 55428; *Secy.* Vivian Thoreson, American Lutheran Church Women, 422 S. Fifth St., Minneapolis, MN 55415; *Treas.* Mrs. G. Frank (Jane) Johnson, 2930 S. Hwy. 101, Wayzata, MN 55391. (Address correspondence to the executive secretary.)

EXECUTIVE BOARD

Ruby Forlan; Elaine Hanson; Mary Jordan; Charles Mann; Solveig Bartz; Daniel Brumm.

ADVISORY BOARD

Chpn. Gary Klammer; Rev. Rolf Aaseng; Mrs. H. O. Egertson; Mrs. Donald Gauerke; Mrs. Harold Groff; Rev. James Gunther; Rev. A. B. Hanson; Malvin Lundeen; Mary Egdahl; Rev. A. C. Paul; Don Rosenberg; Stanley Sandberg; Les Schmidt; Aron Valleskey.

PUBLICATION

Lutheran Libraries (q.; memb., nonmemb. $8). *Ed.* Erwin E. John, 6450 Warren St., Minneapolis, MN 55435.

COMMITTEE CHAIRPERSONS

Budget. Rev. Carl Manfred, Normandale Lutheran Church, 6100 Normandale Rd., Minneapolis, MN 55436.

Finance. Mrs. Lloyd (Betty) LeDell, Libn., Grace Lutheran of Deephaven, 15800 Sunset Rd., Minnetonka, MN 55343.

Library Services Board. Mrs. Forrest (Juanita) Carpenter, Libn., Rte. 1, Prior Lake, MN 55372.

Publications Board. Rev. Carl Weller, Augsburg Publishing House, 426 S. Fifth St., Minneapolis, MN 55415.

MEDICAL LIBRARY ASSOCIATION
Interim Executive Director, Ann E. Kerker
919 N. Michigan Ave., Chicago, IL 60611
312-266-2456

OBJECT

Founded in 1898 and incorporated in 1934, its major purpose is to foster medical and allied scientific libraries, to promote the educational and professional growth of health sciences librarians, and to exchange medical literature among the members. Through its programs and publications, MLA encourages professional development of its membership, whose foremost concern is for the dissemination of health sciences information for those in research, education, and patient care. Memb. (Inst.) 1,350. (Indiv.) 3,680. Dues (Inst.) Subscriptions up to 199 $75, 200–299 $100, 300–599 $125, 600–999 $150, 1,000+ $175; (Indiv.) $45. Year. From month of payment.

MEMBERSHIP

Open to those working in or interested in medical libraries.

OFFICERS

Pres. Charles C. Sargent, Texas Tech Univ. Health Sciences Center, Lib. of the Health Sciences, Lubbock, TX 79430; *Past Pres.* Gertrude Lamb, Hartford Hospital, Health Science Libs., Hartford, CT 06115; *Pres.-Elect.* Nancy M. Lorenzi, Univ. of Cincinnati, Medical Center Libs., Cincinnati, OH 45267.

DIRECTORS

Naomi C. Broering; Arlee May; Eloise C. Foster; Lucretia McClure; Jana Bradley; Judith Messerle; Ruth W. Wender.

PUBLICATIONS

Bulletin (q.; $45).
Index to Audiovisual Serials in the Health Sciences (4 per year; $18).
Current Catalog Proof Sheets (Option A, w., $45); (Option B, mo., $39).
MLA News (mo.; $15/year).
Vital Notes (3 per year; $20).

STANDING COMMITTEE CHAIRPERSONS

Audiovisual Standards and Practices Committee. Carmel C. Bush, TALON Regional Medical Lib. Program, 5323 Harry Hines Blvd., Dallas, TX 75235.
"Bulletin" Consulting Editors Panel. Gloria Werner, Biomedical Lib., Center for the Health Sciences, Univ. of California, Los Angeles, CA 90024.
By-laws Committee. Jacqueline L. Picciano, American Journal of Nursing Co., 10 Columbus Circle, New York, NY 10019.
Certification and Recertification Appeals Panel. Lucretia McClure, Univ. of Rochester, School of Medicine/Dentistry, Edward G. Miner Lib., 601 Elmwood Ave., Rochester, NY 14642.
Certification Eligibility Committee. Virginia L. Algermissen, Texas A&M Univ. Medical Sciences Lib., Box HJ, College Station, TX 77843.
Certification Examination Review Committee. Susan L. Gullion, Biomedical Lib., Center for the Health Sciences, Univ. of California, Los Angeles, CA 90024.
Committee on Committees. Nancy M. Lorenzi, Univ. of Cincinnati, Medical Center Lib., Cincinnati, OH 45267.
Continuing Education Committee. Martha Jane K. Zachert, Univ. of South Carolina, College of Libnshp., Columbia, SC 29208.
Copyright Committee. Albert M. Berkowitz, National Lib. of Medicine, 8600 Rockville Pike, Bethesda, MD 20209.
Editorial Committee for the Bulletin. James Shedlock, Wayne State Univ., Shiffman Medical Lib., 4325 Brush St., Detroit, MI 48201.
Editorial Committee for the MLA News. Lynda Sanford, Business, Science & Technology Div., Chicago Public Lib., 425 N. Michigan Ave., Chicago, IL 60611.
Elections Committee. Nancy M. Lorenzi, Univ. of Cincinnati, Medical Center Lib., Cincinnati, OH 45267.
Exchange Committee. Joan S. Zenan, Health Sciences Lib., Columbia Univ., 701 W. 168 St., New York, NY 10032.
Executive Committee. Charles C. Sargent, Texas Tech Univ. Health Sciences Center, Lib. of the Health Sciences, Lubbock, TX 79430.
Finance. Lucretia McClure, Univ. of Rochester, School of Medicine/Dentistry, Edward G. Miner Lib., 601 Elmwood Ave., Rochester, NY 14642.
Health Sciences Library Technicians Committee. Karen J. Graves, Univ. of

Tennessee Center for Health Sciences Lib., 800 Madison Ave., Memphis, TN 38163.
Honors and Awards Committee. Julia G. Pfau, Lister Hill Lib. of the Health Sciences, Univ. of Alabama in Birmingham, University Sta., Birmingham, AL 35294.
Janet Doe Lectureship Subcommittee. Martha Jane K. Zachert, Univ. of South Carolina, College of Libnshp., Columbia, SC 29208.
Eliot Prize Subcommittee. Elizabeth B. Davis, Biology Lib., Univ. of Illinois, 101 Burrill Hall, Urbana, IL 61801.
ISI Award. Cecile Quintal, Medical Center Lib., North Campus, Univ. of New Mexico, Albuquerque, NM 87131.
Gottlieb Prize Subcommittee. Julia G. Pfau, Univ. of Alabama in Birmingham, Lister Hill Lib. of the Health Sciences, Univ. Sta., Birmingham, AL 35294.
Rittenhouse Award Subcommittee. Carolyn E. Lipscomb, Univ. of North Carolina, Health Sciences Lib., Chapel Hill, NC 27514.
Hospital Library Standards and Practices Committee. Rosalind F. Dudden, Lib. and Media Resources Dept., Mercy Medical Center, 1619 Milwaukee St., Denver, CO 80206.
Interlibrary Loan and Resource Sharing Standards and Practices Committee. Patricia A. Jones, Lib. of the American Hospital Assn., 840 N. Lake Shore Dr., Chicago, IL 60611.
International Cooperation Committee. Sally Perterson, Iowa State Univ., Veterinary Medical Lib., Ames, IA 50011.
Legislation. Raymond A. Palmer, Wright State Univ., School of Medicine, Health Sciences Lib., Dayton, OH 45435.
Library Standards and Practices Committee. Glenn L. Brudvig, Univ. of Minnesota Bio-Medical Lib., Diehl Hall, 505 Essex St. S.E., Minneapolis, MN 55455.
MLA/NLM Liaison Committee. Arlee May, New England Regional Medical Lib. Service, Framcos A. Countway Lib. of Medicine, 10 Shattuck St., Boston, MA 02115.
Membership Committee. Rosanne Labree, Harvard Medical School, Countway Lib. of Medicine, 10 Shattuck St., Boston, MA 02115.
1982 National Program Committee. Alison Bunting, Biomedical Lib., Univ. of California at Los Angeles, Center for the Health Sciences, Los Angeles, CA 90024.
1983 National Program Committee. Richard Lyders, Texas Medical Center Lib., 1133 M. D. Anderson Blvd., Houston, TX 77030.
1984 National Program Committee. Charles R. Bandy, Medical Center Lib., Univ. of Colorado, 4200 E. Ninth Ave., Denver, CO 80220.
Nominating Committee. Nancy M. Lorenzi, Univ. of Cincinnati, Medical Center Libs., Cincinnati, OH 45267.
Oral History Committee. Nancy Whitten Zinn, The Lib., Univ. of California, San Francisco, CA 94143.
Program and Convention Committee. Jeanne G. Mueller, School of Medicine Lib., Indiana Univ., 1100 W. Michigan Ave., Indianapolis, IN 46223.
Publication Panel. Virginia H. Holtz, W. S. Middleton Health Sciences Lib., Univ. of Wisconsin, 1305 Linden Dr., Madison, WI 53706.
Publishing and Information Industries Relations Committee. Joseph E. Jensen, Medical and Chirurgical Faculty Lib., 1211 Cathedral St., Baltimore, MD 21201.
Recertification Committee. Julie Blume, Rte. 1, Box 232, Baham, NC 27503.
Research and Evaluation Committee. Erika Love, Univ. of New Mexico, Medical Center Lib., Albuquerque, NM 87109.
Scholarship and Grants Committee. Sally Pollak, Univ. of Texas Health Sciences Center at San Antonio, 7703 Floyd Curl Dr., San Antonio, TX 78284.
Status and Economic Interests of Health Sciences Library Personnel Committee. Toby G. Port, St. Elizabeth's Hospital,

Health Science Lib., Washington, DC 20032.

Surveys and Statistics Committee. Faith Van Toll, Wayne State Univ., KOMRML Shiffman Medical Lib., 4325 Brush St., Detroit, MI 48201.

"Vital Notes" Participatory Panel. Donald L. Potts, Medical Lib. Center of New York, New York, NY 10029.

Ad Hoc Committees

Ad Hoc Committee to Examine the Certification and Recertification Process. Beatrix Robinow, McMaster Univ., 1200 Main St. W., Hamilton, Ont., L8S 4J9, Canada.

Ad Hoc Committee on Consumer Health Information. Ellen Gartenfeld, Mount Auburn Hospital, 330 Mount Auburn St., Cambridge, MA 02138.

Ad Hoc Committee for the International Exchange and Redistribution of Library Materials. Janis Sharp, Personnel Libn., Houston Academy of Medicine, Texas Medical Center Lib., Jesse H. Jones Lib. Bldg., Houston, TX 77030.

MLA/HeSCA Joint Committee to Develop Guidelines for Audiovisual Facilities in Health Sciences Libraries. Gloria Holland, Veterans Admin. Medical Center (14A), 700 S. 19 St., Birmingham, AL 35233.

Study Group on MLA's Role in the Educational Process for Health Sciences Librarians. Phyllis S. Mirsky, Reference Sec., National Lib. of Medicine, 8600 Rockville Pike, Bethesda, MD 20209.

MUSIC LIBRARY ASSOCIATION
2017 Walnut St., Philadelphia, PA 19103
215-569-3948

OBJECT

"To promote the establishment, growth, and use of music libraries; to encourage the collection of music and musical literature in libraries; to further studies in musical bibliography; to increase efficiency in music library service and administration." Founded 1931. Memb. about 1,700. Dues (Inst.) $31; (Indiv.) $24; (Student) $12. Year. Sept. 1-Aug. 31.

OFFICERS

Pres. Donald W. Krummel, Grad. Lib. School, Univ. of Illinois, Urbana, IL 61801; *V.P./Pres.-Elect.* Mary W. Davidson, Music Lib., Wellesley College, Wellesley, MA 02181; *Secy.* George R. Hill, Music Dept., Baruch College/CUNY, 17 Lexington Ave., New York, NY 10010; *Treas.* Harold J. Diamond, Music Lib., Lehman College/CUNY, Bedford Park Blvd. W., Bronx, NY 10468; *Ed. of "Notes."* William McClellan, Music Lib., Music Bldg., Univ. of Illinois, Urbana, IL 61801.

DIRECTORS

Officers; Olga Buth; Margaret F. Lospinuso; Charles W. Simpson; Gillian Anderson; Neil M. Ratliff; Annie Thompson.

PUBLICATIONS

Music Cataloging Bulletin (mo.; $12).

MLA Index Series (irreg.; price varies according to size).

MLA Newsletter (q.; free to memb.).

MLA Technical Reports (irreg.; price varies according to size).

Notes (q.; inst. subscription $31; nonmemb. subscription $21).

COMMITTEE CHAIRPERSONS

Administration. Brenda C. Goldman, Music Lib., Tufts Univ., Medford, MA 02155.
Audio-Visual. Philip Youngholm, Connecticut College Lib., New London, CT 06320.
Automation. Garrett H. Bowles, Music Lib., Univ. of California at San Diego, La Jolla, CA 92093.
Awards. Jon W. Newsom, Music Div., Lib. of Congress, Washington, DC 20540.
Basic Music Collection. Pauline S. Bayne, Music Lib., Univ. of Tennessee, Knoxville, TN 37916.
Cataloging. Judith Kaufman, Music Lib., State Univ. of New York, Stony Brook, NY 11794.
Conservation. Jean Geil, Music Lib., Univ. of Illinois, Urbana, IL 61801.
Constitutional Revision. Geraldine Ostrove, Lib., New England Conservatory of Music, Boston, MA 02115.
Education. Kathryn P. Logan, Music Lib., Univ. of North Carolina, Chapel Hill, NC 27514.
Legislation. Carolyn O. Hunter, 5472 Bradford Court, Alexandria, VA 22311.
Microforms. Stuart Milligan, Sibley Music Lib., Eastman School of Music, Rochester, NY 14604.
Public Library. Donna Mendro, Dallas Public Lib., Dallas, TX 75201.
Publications. Suzanne T. Perlongo, Music Sec., Div. for the Blind and Physically Handicapped, Lib. of Congress, Washington, DC 20542.

NATIONAL LIBRARIANS ASSOCIATION
Executive Director, Peter Dollard
Box 586, Alma, MI 48801
517-463-7227

OBJECT

"To promote librarianship, to develop and increase the usefulness of libraries, to cultivate the science of librarianship, to protect the interest of professionally qualified librarians, and to perform other functions necessary for the betterment of the profession of librarianship. It functions as an association of librarians, rather than as an association of libraries." Established 1975. Memb. 550. Dues. $15 per year; $25 for 2 years; (Students and Retired and Unemployed Librarians) $7.50. Year. July 1–June 30.

MEMBERSHIP

Any person interested in librarianship and libraries who holds a graduate degree in library science may become a member upon election by the executive board and payment of the annual dues. The executive board may authorize exceptions to the degree requirements to applicants who present evidence of outstanding contributions to the profession. Student membership is available to those graduate students enrolled full time at any accredited library school.

OFFICERS (JULY 1, 1981–JUNE 30, 1982)

Pres. Ellis Hodgin, Univ. of Baltimore Lib.; *Immed. Past Pres.* Norman Tanis, California State Univ. at Northridge, Northridge, CA 91330. (Address all correspondence to the executive director.)

PUBLICATION

NLA Newsletter: The National Librarian (q.; 1 year $15, 2 years $28, 3 years $39).

COMMITTEE CHAIRPERSONS

Certification Standards. David Perkins, California State Univ., Northridge, CA 91330.

Professional Education. John Colson, 813 Somonauk St., Sycamore, IL 60178.

Professional Welfare. Julio A. Martinez, San Diego State Univ. Lib., San Diego, CA 92181.

NATIONAL MICROGRAPHICS ASSOCIATION
Executive Director, O. Gordon Banks
8719 Colesville Rd., Silver Spring, MD 20910
301-587-8202

OBJECT

The National Micrographics Association (NMA) is the trade and professional association that represents the manufacturers, vendors, and professional users of micrographic equipment and software. The purpose of the association is to promote the lawful interests of the micrographic industry in the direction of good business ethics; the liberal discussion of subjects pertaining to the industry and its relationship to other information management technologies, technological improvement, and research; standardization; the methods of manufacturing and marketing; and the education of the consumer in the use of information management systems. Founded 1943. Memb. 10,000. Dues. (Indiv.) $60. Year. July 1, 1981–June 30, 1982.

OFFICERS

Pres. John C. Marken, Bell & Howell–Micro Photo Div., Drawer E, Old Mansfield Rd., Wooster, OH 44691; *V.P.* William J. McGlone, Jr., Microfilm Products Div., 3M Co., 3M Center–Bldg. 220-9E, St. Paul, MN 55144; *Treas.* John P. Luke, Marketing Research & Admin., BSMD–Eastman Kodak Co., 343 State St., Rochester, NY 14650. (Address general correspondence to the executive director.)

PUBLICATION

Journal of Micrographics (mo.; memb. and subscriptions). *Ed.* Ellen T. Meyer. Book reviews included; product review included. Ads accepted.

SOCIETY OF AMERICAN ARCHIVISTS
330 S. Wells St., Suite 810, Chicago, IL 60606
Executive Director, Ann Morgan Campbell
312-922-0140

OBJECT

"To promote sound principles of archival economy and to facilitate cooperation among archivists and archival agencies." Founded 1936. Memb. 3,800. Dues (Indiv.) $45–$75, graduated according to salary; (Student) $30 with a two-year maximum on student membership; (Inst.) $50; (Sustaining) $100.

OFFICERS (1981-1982)

Pres. Edward Weldon, Office of the Deputy Archivist, National Archives & Records Service, Washington, DC 20408;

V.P. J. Frank Cook, B134 Memorial Lib., Univ. of Wisconsin–Madison, Madison, WI 53706; *Treas.* Paul H. McCarthy, Univ. of Alaska, Box 80687, College Sta., Fairbanks, AK 99708.

COUNCIL

Lynn A. Bonfield; Shonnie Finnegan; Meyer H. Fishbein; Robert S. Gordon; Sue E. Holbert; William L. Joyce; Richard Lytle; Virginia C. Purdy.

STAFF

Exec. Dir. Ann Morgan Campbell; *Dir. Administrative Services.* Joyce E. Gianatasio; *Membership Asst.* Bernice Brack; *Bookkeeper.* Andrea Giannattasio; *Publns. Asst.* Suzanne Fulton; *Program Officer.* Mary Lynn Ritzenthaler; *Newsletter Ed./Program Officer.* Deborah Risteen; *Program Asst.* Linda Ziemer.

PUBLICATIONS

The American Archivist (q.; $30). *Managing Ed.* Deborah Risteen, 330 S. Wells, Suite 810, Chicago, IL 60606. Book reviews and related correspondence should be addressed to the editor. Rates for B/W ads: full-page, $200; half-page, $125; outside back cover, $300; half-page minimum insertion; 10% discount for four consecutive insertions; 15% agency commission.

SAA Newsletter. (6 per year; memb.) *Ed.* Deborah Risteen, SAA, 330 S. Wells, Suite 810, Chicago, IL 60606. Rates for B/W ads: full-page, $300; half-page, $175; quarter-page, $90; eighth-page, $50.

PROFESSIONAL AFFINITY GROUPS (PAGs) AND CHAIRS

Acquisition. Carolyn Wallace, Univ. of North Carolina, 024-A Wilson Lib., Chapel Hill, NC 27514.

Aural & Graphic Records. Gerald J. Munoff, Kentucky Dept. of Lib. and Archives, Box 537, Frankfort, KY 40602.

Business Archives. Linda Edgerly, 103 W. 75 St., Apt. 3B, New York, NY 10023.

Conservation. Howard P. Lowell, 1310 Franklin St., #202, Denver, CO 80218.

College & University Archives. Helen W. Slotkin, Massachusetts Institute of Technology, 14N-118, Cambridge, MA 02139.

Description. Victoria Irons Walch, 9927 Capperton Dr., Oakton, VA 22124.

Government Records. Charles H. Lesser, South Carolina Dept. of Archives & History, Box 11669, Capitol Sta., Columbia, SC 29211.

Manuscript Repositories. Clifton H. Jones, DeGolyer Lib., Southern Methodist Univ., Dallas, TX 75275.

Oral History. Marjorie Fletcher, American College Archives & Oral History Center, 270 Bryn Mawr Ave., Bryn Mawr, PA 19010.

Reference, Access, Outreach. Alexia Helsley, South Carolina Dept. of Archives & History, Box 11669, Capitol Sta., Columbia, SC 29211.

Religious. Sister M. Felicitas Power, Box 10490, Baltimore, MD 21209.

Theme Collections. Olha Della Cava, Columbia Univ. Libs., 535 W. 114 St., New York, NY 10027.

SPECIAL LIBRARIES ASSOCIATION
Executive Director, David R. Bender
235 Park Ave. S., New York, NY 10003
212-477-9250

OBJECT

"To provide an association of individuals and organizations having a professional, scientific or technical interest in library and information science, especially as these are applied in the recording, retrieval and dissemination of knowledge and information in areas such as the physical, biological, technical and social sciences and the humanities; and to promote and improve the communication, dissemination and use of such information and knowledge for the benefit of libraries or other educational organizations." Organized 1909. Memb. 11,500. Dues. (Sustaining) $250; (Indiv.) $55; (Student) $12. Year. Jan.–Dec. and July–June.

OFFICERS (JUNE 1981-JUNE 1982)

Pres. George H. Ginader, 45 S. Main St., Cranbury, NJ 08512; *Pres.-Elect.* Janet Rigney, Council on Foreign Relations, Lib., 58 E. 68 St., New York, NY 10021; *Div. Cabinet Chpn.* Julie H. Bichteler, Univ. of Texas at Austin, Grad. School of Lib. Science, Box 7576, University Sta., Austin, TX 78712; *Div. Cabinet Chpn.-Elect.* Valerie Noble, The Upjohn Co., Business Lib. 88-0, Kalamazoo, MI 49001; *Chapter Cabinet Chpn.* Jane I. Dysart, Royal Bank of Canada, Lib., Royal Bank Plaza, Toronto, Ont., M5J 2J5, Canada; *Chapter Cabinet Chpn.- Elect.* Vivian J. Arterbery, Rand Corp., Lib., 1700 Main St., Santa Monica, CA 90406; *Treas.* Dorothy Kasman, Coopers & Lybrand, 1251 Ave. of the Americas, New York, NY 10020; *Past Pres.* James B. Dodd, Georgia Institute of Technology, Price Gilbert Memorial Lib., Atlanta, GA 30332.

DIRECTORS

Jack Leister (1979–82); Mary Vasilakis (1979–82); Jacqueline J. Desoer (1980–83); Ruth S. Smith (1980–83); Charles K. Bauer (1981–84); M. Elizabeth Moore (1981–84).

PUBLICATIONS

Special Libraries (q.) and *SpeciaList* (mo.). Cannot be ordered separately ($36 for both; add $5 postage outside the U.S., including Canada). *Ed.* Nancy M. Viggiano.

COMMITTEE CHAIRPERSONS

Awards. Joseph M. Dagnese, Purdue Univ. Libs., Stewart Center, West Lafayette, IN 47907.

Consultation Service. Robert B. Lane, U.S. Air Force, Air Univ. Lib., Maxwell AFB, AL 36112.

Copyright Law Implementation. Efren W. Gonzalez, Bristol-Myers Products, 1350 Liberty Ave., Hillside, NJ 07207.

Education. Miriam H. Tees, McGill Univ., Grad. School of Lib. Science, 3459 McTavish St., Montreal, P.Q. H3A 1Y1, Canada.

Government Information Services. Susan B. Roumfort, New Jersey State Lib., 185 W. State St., Trenton, NJ 08625.

Networking. James K. Webster, SUNY–Buffalo, Science & Engineering Lib., 223 Capen Hall, Buffalo, NY 14260.

Nominating. Vivian D. Hewitt, Carnegie Endowment for International Peace, 30 Rockefeller Plaza, New York, NY 10020.

Positive Action Program for Minority Groups. Thomasina Jones, Institute for Defense Analyses, Technical Info. Services, 400 Army-Navy Dr., Arlington, VA 22202.

Publications. David E. King, Standard Educational Corporation, 200 W. Monroe St., Chicago, IL 60606.

Publisher Relations. John Patton, 28 Station Plaza S., Apt. 3K, Great Neck, NY 11021.

Research. Mark Baer, Hewlett Packard Co., 1501 Page Mill Rd., Palo Alto, CA 94304.

Scholarship. Ron Coplen, Harcourt Brace Jovanovich, 757 Third Ave., New York, NY 10017.

Standards. Audrey N. Grosch, Univ. of Minnesota, S-34 Wilson Lib., Lib. Systems Dept., Minneapolis, MN 55455.

Statistics. Beth Ansley, Georgia Power Co., 270 Peachtree St. N.W., Lib., 13th fl., Atlanta, GA 30302.

Student Relations Officer. Linda C.

Smith, Univ. of Illinois, Grad. School of Lib. Science, 410 David Kinley Hall, Urbana, IL 61801.
H. W. Wilson Co. Award. Ronald R. Sommer, Head, Reader's Services, Univ. of Tennessee, Center for Health Sciences, Lib., 800 Madison Ave., Memphis, TN 38163.

THEATRE LIBRARY ASSOCIATION
Secretary-Treasurer, Richard M. Buck
111 Amsterdam Ave., New York, NY 10023

OBJECT

"To further the interests of collecting, preserving, and using theatre, cinema, and performing arts materials in libraries, museums, and private collections." Founded 1937. Memb. 500. Dues. (Indiv.) $15; (Inst.) $20. Year. Jan. 1–Dec. 31, 1982.

OFFICERS (1981-1982)

Pres. Louis A. Rachow, Hampden-Edwin Booth Theatre Collection and Lib., The Players, 16 Gramercy Pk., New York, NY 10003; *V.P.* Don B. Wilmeth, Chairman, Dept. of Theatre Arts, Brown Univ., Providence, RI 02912; *Secy.-Treas.* Richard M. Buck, Asst. to the Chief, Performing Arts Research Center, New York Public Lib. at Lincoln Center, 111 Amsterdam Ave., New York, NY 10023; *Rec. Secy.* Brigitte Kueppers, Archivist, Shubert Archive, Lyceum Theatre, 149 W. 45 St., New York, NY 10036. (Address correspondence, except *Broadside*, to the secretary-treasurer. Address *Broadside* correspondence to Ginine Cocuzza, 413 W. 22 St., #4A, New York, NY 10011.)

EXECUTIVE BOARD

Officers; William Appleton; Mary Ashe; Laraine Correll; Babette Craven; Geraldine Duclow; Robert C. Eason, Jr.; Mary Ann Jensen; Margaret Mahard; Frank C. P. McGlinn; Lee Ash; Sally Thomas Pavett; *Ex officio.* Ginine Cocuzza; Barbara Naomi Cohen; Dorothy L. Swerdlove; *Honorary.* Rosamond Gilder.

COMMITTEE CHAIRPERSONS

Awards. Don B. Wilmeth.
Nominations. Mary Ann Jensen.
Program and Special Events. Richard M. Buck.
Publications. Louis A. Rachow.

PUBLICATIONS

Broadside (q.; memb.).
Performing Arts Resources (ann.; memb.).

UNIVERSAL SERIALS AND BOOK EXCHANGE, INC.
Executive Director, Alice Dulany Ball
3335 V St. N.E., Washington, DC 20018
202-529-2555

OBJECT

"To promote the distribution and interchange of books, periodicals, and other scholarly materials among libraries and other educational and scientific institutions of the United States, and between them and libraries and institutions of other countries." Organized 1948. Memb. year—libraries: Jan. 1–Dec. 31 or July 1–June 30. Memb. year—associations: Jan. 1–Dec. 31.

MEMBERSHIP

Membership in USBE is open to any library that serves a constituency and is an institution or part of an institution or organization. The USBE corporation includes a representative from each member library and from each of a group of sponsoring organizations listed below.

BOARD OF DIRECTORS

Pres. H. Joanne Harrar, Dir. of Libs., Univ. of Maryland, College Park, MD 20742; *V.P./Pres.-Elect.* Juanita S. Doares, Assoc. Dir., Collection Management and Development, New York Public Lib., New York, NY 10017; *Secy.* Virginia Boucher, Head, Interlibrary Cooperation, Univ. of Colorado, Boulder, CO 80309; *Treas.* Murray S. Martin, Libn., Wessell Lib., Tufts Univ., Medford, MA 02155; *Past Pres.* Margaret A. Otto, Libn. of the College, Dartmouth College, Hanover, NH 03755.

MEMBERS OF THE BOARD

Executive director; Helen Citron, Assoc. Dir. of Libs., Georgia Institute of Technology; Richard DeGennaro, Dir. of Libs., Univ. of Pennsylvania, Philadelphia, PA 19104; Anne C. Edmonds, Libn., Mount Holyoke College, South Hadley, MA 01075; Susan K. Martin, Dir., Milton S. Eisenhower Lib., Johns Hopkins Univ., Baltimore, MD 21218; Ryburn M. Ross, Asst. Univ. Libn. for Technical and Automated Services, Cornell Univ. Libs., Ithaca, NY 14853; Joyce Veenstra, Head, Serials Cataloging, Columbia Univ. Libs., New York, NY 10027.

SPONSORING MEMBERS

Alabama Lib. Assn.; Alaska Lib. Assn.; American Assn. of Law Libs.; American Council of Learned Societies; American Society for Info. Science; American Lib. Assn.; American Theological Lib. Assn.; Arizona State Lib. Assn.; Assn. of American Lib. Schools; Assn. of Jewish Libs.; Assn. of Research Libs.; Assn. of Special Libs. of the Philippines; Associazione Italiana Biblioteche; British Columbia Lib. Assn.; California Lib. Assn.; Catholic Lib. Assn.; Colorado Lib. Assn.; District of Columbia Lib. Assn.; Ethiopian Lib. Assn.; Federal Lib. Committee; Federation of Indian Lib. Assns.; Florida Lib. Assn.; Idaho Lib. Assn.; Interamerican Assn. of Agricultural Libns. and Documentalists; Jordan Lib. Assn.; Kenya Lib. Assn.; Lib. of Congress; Maryland Lib. Assn.; Medical Lib. Assn.; Michigan Lib. Assn.; Music Lib. Assn.; National Academy of Sciences; National Agricultural Lib.; Natonal Lib. of Medicine; New Jersey Lib. Assn.; North Carolina Lib. Assn.; Pennsylvania Lib. Assn.; Philippine Lib. Assn.; Smithsonian Institution; Social Science Research Council; South African Lib. Assn.; Southeastern Lib. Assn.; Special Libs. Assn.; Special Libs. Assn. of Japan; Theatre Lib. Assn.; Uganda Lib. Assn.; Vereinigung Österreichischer Bibliothekare.

STATE, PROVINCIAL, AND REGIONAL LIBRARY ASSOCIATIONS

The associations in this section are organized under three headings: United States, Canada, and Regional Associations. Both the United States and Canada are represented under Regional Associations. Unless otherwise specified, correspondence is to be addressed to the secretary or executive secretary named in the library association entry.

UNITED STATES

Alabama

Memb. 1,082. Founded 1904. Term of Office. Apr. 1981–Apr. 1982. Publication. *The Alabama Librarian* (9 per year). *Ed.* Joe Acker, Carl Elliott Regional Library, 20 E. 18 St., Jasper 35501.
Pres. Julia Rotenberry, 249 Highland St. N., Montevallo 35115; *1st V.P./ Pres.-Elect.* Jane McRae, 4608 Scenic View Dr., Bessemer 35020; *2nd V.P.* Joan Atkinson, G.S.L.S., Box 6242, University 35486; *Secy.* Sally Webb, 1340 32 St. S., Birmingham 35205; *Treas.* Pat Moore, 613 Winwood Dr., Birmingham 35226; *ALA Chapter Councillor.* James Ramer, Dean, Graduate School of Library Service, Univ. of Alabama, Box 6242, University 35486.
Address correspondence to the executive secretary, Alabama Lib. Assn., Box BY, University 35486.

Alaska

Memb. (Indiv.) 276; (Inst.) 27. Term of Office. Mar. 1981–Mar. 1982. Publications. *Sourdough* (q.); *Newspoke* (bi-mo.).
Pres. Molly Bynum, Box 8722, Anchorage 99508; *V.P./ Pres. Elect.* To be announced; *Secy.* Ila Jean Reiersen, Anchorage Municipal Libs., 427 F St., Anchorage 99501; *Treas.* Errol Locker, 217 E. 11 St., Anchorage 99501.

Arizona

Memb. 1,050. Term of Office. Oct. 1, 1981–Oct. 1, 1982. Publication. *ASLA Newsletter* (mo.). *Ed.* Mitzi Rinehart, Maricopa County Lib., 3375 W. Durango, Phoenix 85009.
Pres. Maggie Nation, Flagstaff Public Lib., 11 W. Cherry, Flagstaff 86001; *Pres.-Elect.* Sandra Steffey Lobeck, Yuma Elementary School Dist., 450 Sixth St., Yuma 85364; *Secy.* Shirley Wayland, Phoenix Public Lib., 12 E. McDowell, Phoenix 85004; *Treas.* Marge Goble, 6418 W. Colter St., Glendale 85301.

Arkansas

Memb. 1,150. Term of Office. Oct. 1981–Sept. 1982. Publication. *Arkansas Libraries* (q.).
Pres. Jo Wise, N.L.R. Public Schools, Box 687, North Little Rock 72116; *Exec. Dir.* Ruth Williams, Box 2275, Little Rock 72203.

California

Memb. (Indiv.) 3,050; (Inst.) 178; (Business) 70. Term of Office. Jan. 1–Dec. 31, 1982. Publication. *The CLA Newsletter* (mo.).
Pres. Carol Aronoff, Santa Monica Public Lib., 1343 Sixth St., Santa Monica 90401; *V.P./ Pres.-Elect.* Josephine R. Terry, County Libn., Butte County Lib., 1820 Mitchell Ave., Oroville 95965; *Treas.* Wm. F. McCoy, Univ. of California Lib., Davis 95616; *ALA Chapter Councillor.* Gilbert W. McNamee, San Francisco Public Lib., Business Branch, 530 Kearny St., San Francisco 94108.
Address correspondence to Stefan B. Moses, Exec. Dir., California Lib. Assn., 717 K St., Suite 300, Sacramento 95814.

Colorado

Term of Office. Nov. 1981–Oct. 1982. Publication. *Colorado Libraries* (q.). *Ed.* Terry Hubbard, Colorado State Univ. Libs., Fort Collins 80523; *Adv. Mgr.* Richard Beeler, Colorado State Univ. Libs., Fort Collins 80523.
Pres. David Price, Aurora Public Lib., Admin. Services, 1470 S. Havana, Aurora 80012; *Exec. Secy.* Milinda Walker, 3920 S. Truckee Ct., Aurora 80013.

Connecticut

Memb. 1,000. Term of Office. July 1, 1981–July 1, 1982. Publications. *CLA MEMO* (10 per year). *Ed.* Joyce Reid, Windsor Public Lib., 323 Broad St., Windsor 06095; *Connecticut Libraries*(q.). *Ed.* Gretchen Swackhammer, 74C River Bend Rd., Stratford 06497. *Adv. Mgr.*

Andy Bacon, North Haven Lib., 17 Elm St., North Haven 06473.
Pres. Vince Juliano, Waterford Public Lib., 49 Rope Ferry Rd., Waterford 06385; *V.P./Pres.-Elect.* Leslie Berman, Connecticut State Lib., 231 Capitol Ave., Hartford 06115; *Treas.* Carol Hutchinson, Fairfield Public Lib., 1080 Old Post Rd., Fairfield 06430; *Secy.* Jeanne Simpson, Connecticut Lib. Assn., State Lib., Rm. L-216, 231 Capitol Ave., Hartford 06115.

Delaware

Memb. (Indiv.) 224; (Inst.) 22. Term of Office. May 1981–May 1982. Publication. *DLA Bulletin.* (4 per year).
Pres. Dick Humphreys; *V.P./Pres.-Elect.* Judy Roberts, Cape Henlopen H.S., Cape Henlopen 19958; *Secy.* Emily McNatt Dreshfield, 7 Cartier Ct., Drummond Ridge, Newark 19711; *Treas.* Anthony Grillo, Dupont Technical Lib., 2010 Delaware Ave., Wilmington 19806.
Address correspondence to the Delaware Lib. Assn., Box 1843, Wilmington 19899.

District of Columbia

Memb. 980. Term of Office. May 1981–May 1982. Publication. *Intercom* (mo.) *Co-Eds.* Mary Feldman, U.S. Dept. of Transportation, Lib. Services Div., 400 Seventh St. S.W., Washington, DC 20540; Jacque-Lynn Schulman, Pergamon Press, International, 1340 Old Chain Bridge Rd., McLean, VA 22101.
Pres. Martha Bowman, George Washington Univ. Lib., 2130 H St. N.W., Washington, DC 20052; *Pres.-Elect.* Judith Sessions, Mount Vernon College Lib., 2100 Foxhall Rd. N.W., Washington, DC 20007; *Treas.* Betty Bogart, Bogart-Brociner Assoc., Inc., 47 Williams Dr., Annapolis, MD 21401; *Secy.* Susan M. Fifer, National Geographic Lib., 17 & M Sts. N.W., Washington, DC 20036.

Florida

Memb. (Indiv.) 800; (In-state Inst.) 50; (Out-of-state Inst.) 30. Term of Office. July 1, 1981–June 30, 1982.
Pres. Ada M. Seltzer, Univ. of South Florida Medical Center Lib., 12901 N. 30 St., Tampa 33612; *V.P./Pres.-Elect.* Harold Goldstein, 1911 Angels Hollow, Tallahassee 32308; *Secy.* Judith Williams, Jacksonville Public Lib., 122 N. Ocean St., Jacksonville 32202; *Treas.* Thomas L. Reitz, 1333 Gunnison Ave., Orlando 32804.

Georgia

Memb. 800. Term of Office. Oct. 1981–Oct. 1983. Publication. *Georgia Librarian* (q.). *Ed.* Wanda J. Calhoun, Augusta Regional Lib., Augusta 30902.
Pres. Charles E. Beard, Dir. of Libs., West Georgia College, Carrollton 30117; *1st V.P.* Jane R. Morgan, Materials Specialist, Fulton County Schools, 786 Cleveland Ave. S.W., Atlanta 30315; *2nd V.P.* Sara June McDavid, Mgr., Memb. Services, Solinet, 400 Colony Sq., 1201 Peachtree St., Atlanta 30361; *Treas.* Gayle McKinney, Online Search Services Coord., Reference Dept., Pullen Lib., Georgia State Univ., University Plaza, Atlanta 30303; *Sec.* Virginia L. Rutherford, Coord., Southern Forestry Info. Network, Science Lib., Univ. of Georgia, Athens 30602; *Exec. Sec.* Ann W. Morton, Box 833, Tucker 30084.

Hawaii

Memb. 483. Term of Office. Mar. 1981–Mar. 1982. Publications. *Hawaii Library Association Journal* (bienn.); *Hawaii Library Association Newsletter* (4 per year); *HLA Membership Directory* (ann.); *Directory of Libraries & Information Sources in Hawaii & the Pacific Islands* (irreg.); *Index to Periodicals of Hawaii; Hawaii Legends Index.*
Pres. Stella Watanabe, Chief Libn., Hickam AFB, Honolulu; *V.P./Pres.-Elect*, Edna Hurd, Elementary Libn., Kamehameha Schools; *Secy.* Ann Takahashi, Reference Libn., HM/Univ. of Hawaii Lib.; *Treas.* Rex Frandsen, Libn., Archivist, BYU-HC, Laie 96762.

Idaho

Memb. 364. Term of Office. June 1, 1981–May 31, 1982. Publication. *The Idaho Librarian* (q.). *Ed.* Doug Birdsall.
Pres. Sam Sayre, Idaho State Univ. Lib., Pocatello 83209; *Pres.-Elect.* John Hartung, Kootenai County Dist. Lib., Coeur d'Alene 83814; *Secy.* Chris Ellis, Pocatello Public Lib., Pocatello 83201.

Illinois

Memb. 3,300. Term of Office. Jan. 1982–Dec. 1982. Publication. *ILA Reporter* (4 per year).
Pres. Clayton Highum; *V.P./Pres.-Elect.* Judith Drescher; *Treas.* Lawrence Kinports; *Exec. Dir.* Judith Coate Burnison. *Exec. Office* 425 N. Michigan Ave., Suite 1304, Chicago, 60611.

Indiana

Memb. (Life) 59; (Indiv.) 1,500, (Inst.) 240. Term of Office. Nov. 1981–Oct. 1982. Publication. *Focus on Indiana Libraries* (10 per year). *Ed.* Elbert L. Watson; *Indiana Libraries* (4 per year).
Pres. David Bucore, Anderson & Stony Creek Township Public Lib., 32 W. 10 St., Anderson 46016; *V.P./Pres.-Elect.* Robert Y. Coward, Franklin College Lib., Franklin 46131; *Secy.* Betty C. Martin, Vigo County Public Lib., One Liberty Sq., Terre Haute 47807; *Treas.* Leslie R. Galbraith, Christian Theological Seminary, 1000 W. 42 St., Indianapolis 46208; *Exec. Dir.* Elbert L. Watson, Indiana Lib. Assn., 1100 W. 42 St., Indianapolis 46208.

Address correspondence to the executive director.

Iowa

Memb. 1,579. Term of Office. Jan. 1982–Jan. 1983. Publication. *The Catalyst* (bi-mo.). *Ed.* Naomi Stovall, 921 Insurance Exchange Bldg., Des Moines 50309.
Pres. Elizabeth Martin, Assoc. Professor and Dept. Head, Dept. of Lib. Science, Univ. of Northern Iowa, Cedar Falls 50613.

Kansas

Memb. 1,000. Term of Office. July 1981–June 1982. Publications. *KLA Newsletter* (q.); *KLA Membership Directory* (ann.).
Pres. Virginia Quiring, Kansas State Univ. Libs., Manhattan 66506; *V.P./Pres.-Elect.* Richard Rademacher, Wichita Public Lib., 223 S. Main, Wichita 67202; *Secy.* Rebecca Hinton, Topeka Public Lib., 1515 W. 10, Topeka 66604; *Treas.* Rowena Olsen, McPherson College Lib., McPherson 67460.

Kentucky

Memb. 962. Term of Office. Jan. 1981–Dec. 1982. Publication. *Kentucky Libraries* (q.).
Pres. Betty Delius, Dir., Bellarmine College, Louisville 40205; *V.P.* Margaret Trevathian, Libn., Calloway County, Public Lib., Murray 42071; *Secy.* Sara Chumbler, Libn., Don T. Cooper Elementary School, Paducah 42001.

Louisiana

Memb. (Indiv.) 1,260; (Inst.) 82. Term of Office. July 1981–July 1982. Publication. *LLA Bulletin* (q.).
Pres. Ben Brady, Box 131, Baton Rouge 70821; *1st V.P./Pres.-Elect.* Dolores Owen, 218 Antigua Dr., Lafayette 70503; *2nd V.P.* Lyle Johnson, Drawer 1509, Crowley 70526; *Secy.* Florence Jumonville, 7911 Birch St., New Orleans 70118; *Parliamentarian.* Richard Reid, McNeese State Univ., Frazar Memorial Lib., Lake Charles 70609; *Exec. Dir.* Chris Thomas, Box 131, Baton Rouge 70821.

Address correspondence to the executive director.

Maine

Memb. 700. Term of Office. (*Pres.* & *V.P.*). Spring 1980–Spring 1982. Publication. *Downeast Libraries* (4 per year); *Monthly Memo* (12 per year).
Pres. Claire Lambert, Jesup Memorial Lib., 355 Main St., Bar Harbor 04609; *V.P.* Schuyler Mott, Paris Hill, Paris 04271; *Secy.* Richard Sibley, Waterville

Public Lib., Waterville 04901; *Treas.* Jonathan Burns, Portland Public Lib., 5 Monument Sq., Portland 04101.
Address correspondence to Maine Lib. Assn., c/o Maine Municipal Assn., Local Government Center, Community Dr., Augusta 04330.

Maryland

Memb. Approx. 900. Term of Office. June 1, 1981–June 1, 1982.
Pres. Sandra S. Stephan, Maryland State Dept. of Educ., Div. of Lib. Development and Services, 200 W. Baltimore St., Baltimore 21201; *1st V.P.* Jo Ann Pinder, Cooperating Libs. of Central Maryland, 115 W. Franklin St., Baltimore 21201; *2nd V.P.* Micki Freeny, Prince George's County Public Lib., 11731 Old Gunpowder Rd., Beltsville 20705; *Treas.* George Sands, Caroline County Public Lib., 100 Market St., Denton 21629.

Massachusetts

Memb. (Indiv.) 1,000; (Inst.) 200. Term of Office. July 1981–June 1983. Publication. *Bay State Librarian* (3 per year). *Co-Eds.* Gary Sorkin, Bd. of Lib. Commissioners, 648 Beacon St., Boston 02215; Robin Robinson-Sorkin, Lowell City Lib., Lowell 01852.
Pres. Robert Maier, Bedford Public Lib., Bedford 01730; *V.P.* Constance Clancy, South Hadley Public Lib., South Hadley 01075; *Rec. Secy.* Anne Reynolds, Wellesley Free Lib., Wellesley 02181; *Treas.* Claudia Morner, Cape Cod Community College, West Barnstable 02668; *Exec. Secy.* Pat Demit, Box 7, Nahant 01908.
Address correspondence to the executive secretary.

Michigan

Memb. (Indiv.) 2,200; (Inst.) 150. Term of Office. Nov. 1, 1981–Oct. 31, 1982. Publication. *Michigan Librarian Newsletter* (10 per year).
Pres. Patricia Olsen, Avon Township Public Lib., 210 University Dr., Rochester 48063.

Minnesota

Memb. 950. Term of Office. (*Pres.* & *V.P.*). Nov. 1, 1981–Oct. 31, 1982; (*Secy.*) Nov. 1, 1980–Oct. 31, 1982; (*Treas.*) Nov. 1, 1981–Oct. 31, 1983. Publication. *MLA Newsletter* (12 per year).
Pres. Mary Wagner, Dept. of Lib. Science, College of St. Catherine, 2004 Randolph Ave., St. Paul 55105; *V.P./Pres.-Elect.* Marlys O'Brien, Box 84, Kitchigami Regional Lib., Pine River 56474; *Treas.* Janet E. Snesrud, 160 Wilson Lib., Univ. of Minnesota, Minneapolis 55455; *Exec. Dir.* Adele Panzer Morris, 16491 Fishing Ave., Rosemount 55068.
Address correspondence to the executive director.

Mississippi

Memb. 1,000. Term of Office. Jan. 1982–Dec. 1982. Publication. *Mississippi Libraries* (q.).
Pres. Jack Mulkey, Jackson Metropolitan Library System, 301 N. State St., Jackson 39201; *V.P./Pres.-Elect.* Myra Jo Wilson, Delta State Univ., Box 3263, Cleveland 38733; *Secy.* Harriet DeCell, Box 960, Yazoo City 39194; *Treas.* Frieda Quon, Box 336, Moorhead 38761; *Exec. Secy.* Kay V. Mitchell, Box 4710, Jackson 39216.
Address correspondence to the executive secretary.

Missouri

Memb. 1,242. Term of Office. Sept. 30, 1981–Sept. 30, 1982. Publication. *Missouri Library Association Newsletter* (6 per year).
Pres. Sallie Henderson, Dir., Scenic Regional Lib., 11 S. Washington, Union 63084; *V.P./Pres.-Elect.* Paul White, Kinderhook Regional Lib., 104 E. Commercial, Lebanon 65536; *Treas.* Sheila Merrill, St. Louis Regional Lib Network, 13550 Conway Rd., St. Louis 63141;

Secy. Pat Kern, Ozark Regional Lib., 327 N. Main St., Ironton 63650.

Montana

Memb. 560. Term of Office. June 1, 1981–May 31, 1982. Publication. *MLA President's Newsletter* (4–6 per year).

Pres. Erling Oelz, Mansfield Lib., Univ. of Montana, Missoula 59812; *V.P./Pres.-Elect.* Karen Everett, Box 66, Shepherd 59079; *Secy.* Barbara Rudio, City-County Lib. of Missoula, Missoula 59801.

Nebraska

Memb. 760. Term of Office. Oct. 1981–Oct. 1982. Publication. *NLA Quarterly.*

Pres. Verne Haselwood, 9919 Pasadena, Omaha 68124; *V.P./Pres.-Elect.* Ruth Boettcher, 2635 Worthington, Lincoln 68502; *Secy.* Gale Kosalka, 5003 Sunset Dr., Ralston 68127; *Treas.* Morel Fry, Nebraska Lib. Commission, 1420 P St., Lincoln 68508; *Exec. Secy.* Ray Means, Dir., Alumni Memorial Lib., Creighton Univ., 2500 California St., Omaha 68178.

Address correspondence to the executive secretary.

Nevada

Memb. 300. Term of Office. Jan. 1, 1982–Dec. 31, 1982. Publication. *Highroller* (4 per year).

Pres. Dean A. Allen, So. Nevada Vo-Tech. Ctr. Lib., 5710 Mountain Vista, Las Vegas 89120; *V.P./Pres.-Elect.* To be announced; *Exec. Secy.* To be announced; *Treas.* Wendy Muchmore, Washoe County Lib., Box 2151, Reno 89505.

New Hampshire

Memb. 318. Term of Office. May 1981–May 1982. Publication. *NHLA Newsletter* (bi-mo.).

Pres. Carol Nelson, 43 Lyndon St., Concord 03301; *1st V.P.* Vacant; *2nd V.P.* John Courtney, Concord Public Lib., 35 Green St., Concord 03301; *Secy.* Carol Sykes, Laconia Public Lib., Box 598, Laconia 03246; *Treas.* Barry Hennessey, Dimond Lib., Univ. of New Hampshire, Durham 03824.

New Jersey

Memb. 1,600. Term of Office. May 1981–May 1982. Publication. *New Jersey Libraries* (q.).

Pres. June Adams, Dir., Somerset County Lib., Box 6700, Bridgewater 08807; *V.P./Pres.-Elect.* Dorothy E. Johnson, Asst. Dir., Bloomfield Public Lib., 90 Broad St., Bloomfield 07003; *2nd V.P.* Silva Barsumyan, Dir., Union City Public Lib., 324 43 St., Union City 07087; *Past Pres.* Dorothy Jones, Dir., East Orange Public Lib., 21 S. Arlington, East Orange 07018; *Rec. Secy.* Sara Eggers, Dir., Old Bridge Public Lib., 1 Old Bridge Plaza, Old Bridge 08857; *Corres. Secy.* Rose Marie LiBrizzi, Jersey City Public Lib., 472 Jersey Ave., Jersey City 07302; *Treas.* Rowland Bennett, Dir., Maplewood Memorial Lib., 51 Baker St., Maplewood 07040; *Exec. Dir.* Abagail Studdiford, New Jersey Lib. Assn., 116 W. State St., Trenton 08608.

Address correspondence to the executive director.

New Mexico

Memb. 661. Term of Office. Apr. 1981–Apr. 1982. Publication. *New Mexico Library Association Newsletter.* Ed. Laurel Drew, Albuquerque Public Lib., 501 Copper N.W., Albuquerque 87102.

Pres. Jeanne N. Winkles, Lovington Public Lib., 103 N. First St., Lovington 88260; *1st V.P./Pres.-Elect.* Benjamin T. Wakashige, Box 682, Zuni 87327; *2nd V.P.* Linda Erickson, Sandia Labs Lib., 1001 Santa Ana S.E., Albuquerque 87123; *Secy.* Barbara J. Hutchinson, New Mexico State Univ. Lib., Box 3475, Las Cruces 88003; *Treas.* Eleanor A. Noble, Univ. of Albuquerque, 4401 Roxbury N.E., Albuquerque 87111.

New York

Memb. 3,500. Term of Office. Oct. 1981–Nov. 1982. Publication. *NYLA Bulletin* (10 per year). *Ed.* Diana J. Dean.

Pres. Linda Bretz, Monroe County Lib. System, 115 South Ave., Rochester 14604; *1st V.P.* Gerald R. Shields, Asst. Dean, School of Info. and Lib. Studies, S.U.N.Y. Buffalo, Buffalo 14260; *2nd V.P.* Richard D. Johnson, Dir. of Libs., James A. Milne Lib., State Univ. College, Oneonta 13820; *Exec. Dir.* Nancy W. Lian, CAE, New York Lib. Assn., 15 Park Row, Suite 434, New York City 10038.

Address correspondence to the executive director.

North Carolina

Memb. 2,500. Term of Office. Oct. 1981–Oct. 1983. Publication. *North Carolina Libraries* (q.). *Ed.* Jonathan A. Lindsey, Carlyle Campbell Lib., Meredith College, Raleigh 27611.

Pres. Mertys W. Bell, Dean of Learning Resources, Guilford Technical Institute, Box 309, Jamestown 27282; *1st V.P./ Pres.-Elect.* Leland Park, Davidson College Lib., Davidson 28036; *2nd V.P.* Carol Southerland, Box 1046, Elizabethtown 28337; *Secy.* Mary Jo Godwin, Edgecombe County Memorial Lib., 909 Main St., Tarboro 27886; *Treas.* W. Robert Pollard, Head of Reference, D. H. Hill Lib., North Carolina State Univ., Raleigh 27607; *Dir.* Gwendolyn Jackson, Morehead City Elementary School, 1108 Bridges St., Morehead City 28557; *Dir.* Kay Murray, 1303 Willow Dr., Chapel Hill 27514.

North Dakota

Memb. (Indiv.) 350; (Inst.) 30. Term of Office. (*Pres.,V.P.*, and *Pres.-Elect.*). Oct. 1981–Oct. 1983. Publication. *The Good Stuff* (q.). *Ed.* Janet Crawford, Mandan Public Lib., Mandan 58554.

Pres. Ron Rudser, Minot State College Lib., Minot 58701; *V.P./ Pres.-Elect.* Jerry Kaup, Dir., Minot Public Lib., Minot 58701; *Secy.* Connie Strand, Harley French Medical Lib., Univ. of North Dakota Lib., Grand Forks 58202; *Treas.* Cheryl Bailey, Mary College Lib., Bismarck 58501.

Ohio

Memb. (Indiv.) 1859; (Inst.) 187. Term of Office. Oct. 1981–Oct. 1982. Publications. *Ohio Library Association Bulletin* (3 per year); *Ohio Libraries: Newsletter of the Ohio Library Association* (9 per year).

Pres. John Wallach, Dayton Montgomery County Public Lib., Dayton 45402; *V.P./Pres.-Elect.* Wallace White, Piqua 45356; *Secy.* Linda Harfst, OVAL, Wellston 45692; *Exec. Dir.* A. Chapman Parsons, 40 S. Third St., Suite 409, Columbus 43215.

Address correspondence to the executive director.

Oklahoma

Memb. (Indiv.) 550; (Inst.) 12. Term of Office. Jan. 1, 1981–June 30, 1982. Publication. *Oklahoma Librarian* (bi-mo.).

Pres. John Walker, Linscheid Lib., East Central Univ., Box W-2, Ada 74820; *V.P./Pres.-Elect.* Mary Sherman, Pioneer Multi-County Lib. System, 225 N. Webster, Norman 73069; *Secy.* Evelyn Healey, Norman High School, 911 W. Main, Norman 73069; *Treas.* Ray Lau, Northwestern Oklahoma State Univ., Alva 73717; *Exec. Secy.* Dorothy Gaither, 1747 W. Virgin, Tulsa, 74127.

Address correspondence to the executive secretary.

Oregon

Memb. (Indiv.) 675; (Inst.) 50. Term of Office. April 1981–April 1982. Publication. *Oregon Library News* (mo.). *Ed.* Hardin Smith, Jackson County Lib. System, 413 W. Main St., Medford 97501.

Pres. Carol Ventgen, Coos Bay Public Lib., 525 W. Anderson, Coos Bay 97420; *V.P./Pres.-Elect.* Martin Stephenson, Corvallis Public Lib., 645 N.W. Monroe, Corvallis 97330; *Secy.* Darcy Dauble, 802 O Ave., La Grande, 97850; *Treas.* Janet Irwin, Lib. Assn. of Portland, 801 S.W. Tenth Ave., Portland 97205.

Pennsylvania

Memb. 2,000. Term of Office. Oct. 1981–Oct. 1982. Publication. *PLA Bulletin* (mo.).

Pres. Ivy Bayard, Tyler School of Art, Beech & Penrose Aves., Philadelphia 19126; *Exec. Dir.* Nancy L. Blundon, Pennsylvania Lib. Assn., 100 Woodland Rd., Pittsburgh 15232.

Puerto Rico

Memb. 300. Term of Office. April 1980–March 1982. Publications. *Boletín* (s. ann.); *Cuadernos Bibliotecológicos* (irreg.); *Informa* (mo.); *Cuadernos Bibliograficos* (irreg.).

Pres. Jorge Encarnación; *V.P.* Luisa Vigo Cepeda; *Secy.* Leticia P. Encarnación.

Address correspondence to the Sociedad de Bibliotecarios de Puerto Rico, Apdo. 22898, U.P.R. Sta., Rio Piedras 00931.

Rhode Island

Memb. (Indiv.) 560; (Inst.) 33. Term of Office. Nov. 1981–Oct. 1982. Publication. *Rhode Island Library Association Bulletin* (mo.). *Ed.* Deborah Barchi.

Pres. Anne T. Parent, Cranston Public Lib., Cranston 02905; *V.P.* Howard Boksenbaum, Barrington Public Lib., Barrington 02806; *Secy.* Frances Farrell, Providence Public Lib., Providence 02903; *Treas.* Catherine Mello Alves, Fuller Branch, East Providence Public Lib., East Providence 02914; *Mem.-at-Large.* Samuel Streit, John Hay Lib., Brown Univ., Providence 02912; *N.E.L.A. Councillor.* Constance E. Lachowicz, South Kingstown Public Lib. System, Peace Dale 02883; *ALA Councillor.* Margaret A. Bush, Providence Public Lib., Providence 02903.

St. Croix

Memb. 29. Term of Office. Apr. 1981–May 1982. Publications. *SCLA Newsletter* (q.); *Studies in Virgin Islands Librarianship* (irreg.).

Pres. Carole Gooden; *V.P.* Sylvia Trout; *Secy.* Helen Laurence; *Treas.* Nolia Milligan; *Bd. Membs.* Jane Kelley, Mary S. Bandyk.

South Carolina

Memb. 834. Term of Office. Oct. 1981–Oct. 1982. Publication. *The South Carolina Librarian* (s. ann.). *Ed.* Laurance Mitlin, Dacus Lib., Winthrop College, Rock Hill 29733; *News and Views of South Carolina Library Association* (bi-mo.). *Ed.* John Sukovich, Wessels Lib., Newberry College, Newberry 29108.

Pres. Gerda M. Belknap, Richland County Public Lib., Columbia 29201; *V.P./Pres.-Elect.* H. Paul Dove, Francis Marion College, Florence 29501; *2nd V.P.* Susan Roberts, Univ. of South Carolina–Aiken, Aiken 29801; *Treas.* Donna Nance, Thomas Cooper Lib., Univ. of South Carolina, Columbia 29208; *Secy.* Sarah McMaster, Fairfield County Lib., Winnsboro 29180; *Exec. Secy.* Louise Whitmore, Box 25, Edisto Island 29438.

South Dakota

Memb. (Indiv.) 427; (Inst.) 69. Term of Office. Oct. 1981–Oct. 1982. Publications. *Book Mark* (bi-mo.); *Newsletter. Ed.* Phil Brown, H. M. Briggs Lib., South Dakota State Univ., Brookings 57006.

Pres. Jeri Drew, Box 572, Chamberlain 57325; *Pres.-Elect.* Carol Davis, 1040 Second St., Sturgis 57785; *Secy.* Pat Engebretson, Public Lib., Belle Fourche 57717; *Treas.* Sandra Norlin, Brookings Public Lib., Brookings 57006.

Tennessee

Memb. 1,285. Term of Office. May 1981–May 1982. Publication. *Tennessee Librarian* (q.).

Pres. Ruth Ann Vaden, Trustee, Reelfoot Regional Lib. Center, Martin 38237; *Pres.-Elect.* Diane N. Baird, Regional Coord., Tennessee State Lib. and Archives, Nashville 37219; *Treas.* Edith A. Craddock, Asst. Dir., Highland Rim Regional Lib., Murfreesboro 37130; *Exec. Secy.* Betty Nance, Box 120085, Nashville 37212.

Texas

Term of Office. Apr. 1981-Apr. 1982.
Pres. Leroy R. Johnson, Program Dir., Instructional Services, Ft. Worth ISD, 3210 W. Lancaster, Ft. Worth 76107; *Pres.-Elect.* Elizabeth Crabb, Dir., N.E. Texas Lib. System, 15523 El Estado, Dallas 75248; *Continuing Exec. Dir.* Jerre Hetherington, TLA Office, 8989 Westherimer, Suite 108, Houston 77063.

Utah

Memb. 650. Term of Office. (*Pres & V.P.*) Mar. 1981-Mar. 1982. Publications. *Utah Libraries* (bienn.); *ULA Newsletter* (irreg.).
Pres./1st V.P. Blaine Hall, Brigham Young Univ., Provo 84602; *2nd V.P.* Paul Mogren, Univ. of Utah Lib.; *Exec. Secy.* Gerald A. Buttars, Utah State Lib. Commission, 2150 S. 300 W., Salt Lake City 84115; *ALA Chapter Councillor.* Nathan Smith, Lib. School, Brigham Young Univ., Provo 84602.

Vermont

Memb. 500. Term of Office. Jan. 1982-Dec. 1982. Publication. *VLA News* (q.).
Pres. Maxie Ewins, Fletcher Free Lib., Burlington 05401; *V.P.* To be announced; *Secy.* Ann Turner, Libn., Norwich Univ., Northfield, 05663; *Treas.* Marjorie Zunder, Head, Technical Processes, Vermont Dept. of Libs., Montpelier 05602.

Virginia

Memb. 1,075. Term of Office. Dec. 1981-Nov. 1982. Publication. *Virginia Librarian Newsletter* (6 per year).
Pres. H. Gordon Bechanan, Newman Lib., Virginia Polytechnic Institute and State Univ., Blacksburg 24061; *V.P./Pres.-Elect.* Dean Burgess, Portsmouth Public Lib., 601 Court St., Portsmouth 23704; *Secy.* Fran Freimarck, Pamunkey Regional Lib., Box 119, Hanover 23069; *Treas.* Rene Perez-Lopez, Norfolk Public Lib., 301 E. City Hall Ave., Norfolk 23510.

Washington

Memb. (Indiv.) 1,000; (Inst.) 31. Term of Office. Aug. 1981-July 1983. Publications. *Highlights* (bi-mo.); *Password* (bi-mo.).
Pres. Anthony M. Wilson, Highline College Lib., Midway 98031; *1st V.P./Pres.-Elect.* Anne Haley, Walla Walla Public Lib., Walla Walla 99362; *2nd V.P.* Karen Eichhorn, Tacoma Public Lib., Mottet Branch, Tacoma 98404; *Secy.* Michael Schuyler, Kitsap Regional Lib., Bremerton 98310; *Treas.* June Perrin, Spokane Public Lib., Spokane 99207; *Legislative Consultant.* Melanie Stewart, Box 1075, Olympia 98507; *Corresponding Secy.* Marjorie Burns, 1232 143 Ave. S.E., Bellevue 98007.
Address correspondence to the corresponding secretary.

West Virginia

Memb. (Indiv.) 1,100; (Inst.) 42. Term of Office. Dec. 1981-Nov. 1982. Publication. *West Virginia Libraries* (q.).
Pres. Ellen Wilkerson, Box 436, Hamlin 25523; *1st V.P./Pres.-Elect.* Karen Goff, Reference Lib., West Virginia Lib. Commission, Science and Cultural Center, Charleston 25305; *2nd V.P.* Maureen Conley, West Virgina Univ., Medical Center Lib., Morgantown 26505; *Treas.* Dave Childers, West Virginia Lib. Commission, Science and Cultural Center, Charleston 25305; *ALA Councillor.* Jo Ellen Flagg, Kanawha County Public Lib., 123 Capitol St., Charleston 25301.

Wisconsin

Memb. 2,000. Term of Office. Jan. 1982-Dec. 1982. Publication. *WLA Newsletter* (bi-mo.).
Pres. Vida Stanton, Univ. of Milwaukee, School of Lib. Science, Mitchell Hall, Milwaukee 53201; *V.P.* Daniel Bradbury, Janesville Public Lib., 316 S. Main St., Janesville 53545.

Wyoming

Memb. (Indiv.) 434; (Inst.) 17; (Subscribers) 21. Term of Office. Apr. 1981-

572 / DIRECTORY OF LIBRARY AND RELATED ORGANIZATIONS

Apr. 1982. Publication. *Wyoming Library Roundup* (q.). *Ed.* Linn Rounds, Wyoming State Lib., Cheyenne 82002.
Pres. William J. Heuer, Fremont County Lib., 451 N. Second St., Lander 82520; *V.P.* Linda Goolsby, 1228 Ritter, Rawlins 82301; *Exec. Secy.* Lucie P. Osborn, Laramie County Lib. System, 2800 Central Ave., Cheyenne 82001.

CANADA

Alberta

Memb. (Indiv.) 309; (Inst.) 79; (Trustee) 36. Term of Office. May 1981–May 1982. Publication. *Letter of the L.A.A.* (mo.).
Pres. B. J. Busch, Head, Humanities & Social Science Lib., Rutherford Lib. North, Univ. of Alberta, Edmonton T6G 2J4; *1st V.P./Pres.-Elect.* John Gishler, Head, Social Science Dept., Calgary Public Lib., 616 MacLeod Trail S.E., Calgary T2G 2M2; *2nd V.P.* Ingrid Langhammer, Documents Libn., Legislature Lib., 216 Legislative Bldg., Edmonton; *Treas.* Ann Austin, Varsity Branch, Calgary Public Lib., 4616 Varsity Dr. N.W., Calgary T3A 2L9.
Address correspondence to the president, Box 1357, Edmonton T5J 2N2.

British Columbia

Memb. 584. Term of Office. Apr. 1, 1981–Mar. 31, 1982. Publication. *The Reporter* (6 per year). *Ed.* John Black.
Pres. Maureen Willison; *V.P.* Harry Newsom; *Secy.* Judy Capes; *Treas.* Paul Cook.
Address correspondence to BCLA, Box 46378 Sta. G., Vancouver V6R 4G6.

Manitoba

Memb. 300. Term of Office. Sept. 1981–Sept. 1982. Publication. *Manitoba Library Association Bulletin* (q.).
Pres. Doreen Shanks, Education Lib., Univ. of Manitoba, Winnipeg R3T 2N2; *1st V.P.* Vacant; *2nd V.P.* Paul Nielsen, Legislative Lib., Provincial Archives Bldg., 300 Vaughan St., Winnipeg R3C 1T6; *Secy.* Carol Budnick, Reference Services & Collection Development, Elizabeth Dafoe Lib., Univ. of Manitoba, Winnipeg R3T 2N2; *Treas.* H. Drake, St. Paul's Lib., Univ. of Manitoba, Winnipeg R3T 2M6; *Past Pres.* W. F. Birdsall, 54 Village Crescent Rd., Bedford, N.S. B4A 1J2.
Address correspondence to Manitoba Library Assoc., c/o E. MacMillan, 6 Fermor Ave., Winnipeg R2M 0Y2.

Ontario

Memb. 2,200. Term of Office. Oct. 31, 1981–Nov. 6, 1982. Publications. *Focus* (bi-mo.); *Expression* (3 per year); *The Reviewing Librarian* (q.); *The Revolting Librarian* (q.).
Pres. Barbara J. Smith; *1st V.P.* Beth Miller; *2nd V.P.* Eva Martin; *Past Pres.* Jean Orpwood; *Treas.* George Court; *Exec. Dir.* Diane Wheatley.
Address correspondence to Ontario Lib. Assn., Suite 402, 73 Richmond St. W., Toronto M5H 1Z4.

Quebec

Memb. (Indiv.) 160; (Inst.) 67; (Commercial) 6. Term of Office. May 1981–May 1982. Publication. *ABQ/QLA Bulletin*.
Pres. Anne Galler, Concordia Univ., Lib. Sci. Programme, 7141 Sherbrooke St. W., Rm. VL125, Montreal H4B 1R6; *V.P.* Donna Duncan, McGill Univ., McLennan Lib., 3459 McTavish St., Montreal H3A 1Y1; *Treas.* Françoise Brais, Editions Héritage, 300 rue Arran, St. Lambert; *English Secy.* Sharon Huffman, Reginald J. P. Dawson Lib., 1967 Graham Blvd., Mount Royal H3R 1G9; *French Secy.* Agnès Lassonde, 1680 Barré St., St. Laurent H4L 4M9.

Saskatchewan

Memb. 230. Term of Office. (*Pres.*, *1st V.P./Pres.-Elect.*, *Past Pres.*) July 1, 1981–June 30, 1982; (*2nd V.P.*, *Secy.*, *Treas.*) July 1, 1981–June 30, 1983. Publication. *Saskatchewan Library Forum* (5 per year).

Pres. Kenneth P. Sagal, Lib., Saskatchewan Technical Institute, Box 1420 W., Moose Jaw S6H 4R4; *1st V.P./Pres.-Elect.* Alan Ball, BCD Lib. and Automation Consultants, 2268 Osler, Regina S4P 1W8; *2nd V.P.* Bryan Foran, Frances Morrison Lib., 311 23 St. E., Saskatoon S7K 0J6; *Past Pres.* Karen Labuik, Wapiti Regional Lib., 145 12 St. E., Prince Albert S6V 1B7; *Secy.* Linda Fritz, Native Law Center Lib., Univ. of Saskatchewan, 410 Cumberland Ave., Saskatoon S7N 1M6; *Treas.* Catherine Macauley, Regina Public Lib., 2311 12 Ave., Regina S4P 0N3.

Address correspondence to the secretary.

REGIONAL

Atlantic Provinces: N.B., Nfld., N.S., P.E.I.

Memb. (Indiv.) 310; (Inst.) 185. Term of Office. May 1981–Apr. 1982. Publication. *APLA Bulletin* (bi-mo.).

Pres. Ann Neville; *Pres.-Elect.* To be announced; *V.P. Nova Scotia.* Iain Bates; *V.P. Prince Edward Island.* Pam Forsyth; *V.P. Newfoundland.* Barbara Eddy; *V.P. New Brunswick.* Claude Potvin; *Secy.* Susan Whiteside; *Treas.* Betty Sutherland.

Address correspondence to Atlantic Provinces Lib. Assn., c/o School of Lib. Service, Dalhousie Univ., Halifax B3H 4H8, N.S.

Middle Atlantic: Del., Md., N.J., Pa., W.Va.

Term of Office. Jan. 1981–July 1982.

Pres. Jane E. Hukill, Brandywine College Lib., Box 7139, Concord Pike, Wilmington, DE 19803; *V.P.* Nicholas Winowich, Kanawha County Public Lib., 123 Capitol St., Charleston, WV 25301; *Secy.-Treas.* Richard Parsons, Baltimore County Public Lib., 320 York Rd., Towson, MD 21204.

Midwest: Ill., Ind., Mich., Minn., Ohio, Wis.

Term of Office. Oct. 1979–Oct. 1983.

Pres. Robert H. Donahugh, Dir., Public Lib. of Youngstown and Mahoning County, 305 Wick Ave., Youngstown, OH 44503; *V.P.* Walter D. Morrill, Box 287, Duggan Lib., Hanover College, Hanover, IN 47243; *Secy.* Joseph Kimbrough, Dir., Minneapolis Public Lib. & Info. Center, 300 Nicollet Mall, Minneapolis, MN 55401; *Treas.* Frances Pletz, Michigan Lib. Assn., 226 W. Washtenaw, Lansing, MI 48933.

Address correspondence to the president, Midwest Federation of Lib. Assns.

Mountain Plains: Colo., Kans., Nebr., Nev., N. Dak., S. Dak., Utah, Wyo.

Publication. *MPLA Newsletter* (bi-mo.).

Pres. Dorothy Middleton, East High School, 2800 E. Pershing Blvd., Cheyenne, WY 82001; *V.P./Pres.-Elect.* To be announced; *Secy.* To be elected; *Exec. Secy.* Joe Edelen, Head, Technical Services, I. D. Weeks Lib., Univ. of South Dakota, Vermillion, SD 57069.

New England: Conn., Mass., Maine, N.H., R.I., Vt.

Term of Office. Oct. 1981–Sept. 1982. Publications. *NELA Newsletter* (6 per year). *Ed.* Brenda Claflin, Faxon Lib., 1073 New Britain Ave., West Hartford, CT 06110; *A Guide to Newspaper Indexes in New England; The Genealogists' Handbook for New England Research.*

Pres. Stanley Brown, Dartmouth College Lib., Hanover, NH 03755; *V.P./Pres.-Elect.* Peggy M. Abramo, Fairfield Public Lib., 1080 Old Post Rd., Fairfield, CT 06430; *Treas.* David S. Ferriero, Humanities Libn., Massachusetts Institute of Technology, Cambridge, MA 02139; *Secy.* Janice F. Sieburth, Univ. of Rhode Island Lib., Kingston, RI 02881; *Dir.* Denis Lorenz, West Hartford Public Lib., West Hartford, CT 06119; Diane R. Tebbetts,

Univ. of New Hampshire Lib., Durham, NH 03824; *Past. Pres.* Norma Creaghe, Assoc. Dir., Northridge Lib., California State Univ., Northridge, CA 91330; *Exec. Secy.* Exofficio. Ronald B. Hunte, CAE, New England Lib. Assn., 292 Great Rd., Acton, MA 01720.

Address correspondence to the executive secretary.

Pacific Northwest: Alaska, Idaho, Mont., Oreg., Wash., Alta., B.C.

Memb. 950 (Active); 320 (Subscribers). Term of Office. (*Pres./1st V.P.*) Oct. 1981-1982. Publication. *PNLA Quarterly.*

Pres. Joy Scudamore, Greater Vancouver Lib. Federation, 3206 W. 32 Ave., Vancouver, B.C. V6L 2C3; *1st V.P.* Richard Moore, Southern Oregon State College, 1250 Siskiyou Blvd., Ashland, OR 97520; *2nd V.P.* Linda Ayers, King County Lib. System, 300 Eighth Ave. N., Seattle, WA 98109; *Secy.* Audrey Kolb, Alaska State Lib./Northern Region, 1215 Cowles, Fairbanks, AK 99701; *Treas.* Sharon West, Lib., Univ. of Alaska, Fairbanks, AK 99701.

Southeastern: Ala., Fla., Ga., Ky., Miss., N.C., S.C., Tenn., Va., W.Va.

Memb. 2,900. Term of Office. Nov. 1980-Nov. 1982. Publication. *The Southeastern Librarian* (q.).

Pres. Paul H. Spence, Pres., Mervyn Sterne Lib., Univ. of Alabama, Birmingham, AL 35294; *V.P./Pres.-Elect.* Barratt Wilkins, State Libn., State Lib. of Florida, Tallahassee, FL 32304; *Secy.* Joseph F. Boykin, Dir. Robert M. Cooper Lib., Clemson Univ., Clemson, SC 29631; *Treas.* Annette L. Phinazee, Dean, School of Lib. Science, North Carolina Central Univ., Durham, NC 27709; *Exec. Secy.* Ann W. Morton, Box 987, Tucker, GA 30084.

Address correspondence to the executive secretary.

Southwestern: Ariz., Ark., La., N.Mex., Okla., Tex.

Memb. (Indiv.) 825; (Inst.) 207. Term of Office. Oct. 1980-Nov. 1982. Publication. *SWLA Newsletter* (bi-mo.).

Pres. Robert L. Clark, Jr., Dir., Oklahoma Dept. of Libs., 200 N.E. 18 St., Oklahoma City, OK 73150; *Pres.-Elect.* Dorlyn Hickey, Dept. of Lib. Science, North Texas State Univ., Denton, TX 76204; *Rep.-at-Large.* Pat Woodrum, Dir., Tulsa City-County Lib., 400 Civic Center, Tulsa, OK 74103; *Exec. Dir.* Susan K. Schmidt, Box 23713, TWU Sta., Denton, TX 76204.

STATE LIBRARY AGENCIES

The state library administrative agency in each of the states has the latest information on state plans for the use of federal funds under the Library Services and Construction Act. The directors, addresses, and telephone numbers of the state agencies are listed below.

Alabama

Anthony W. Miele, Dir., Alabama Public Lib. Service, 6030 Monticello Dr., Montgomery 36130. Tel: 205-277-7330.

Alaska

Richard B. Engen, Dir., Lib. & Museums, Dept. of Educ., Pouch G., State Office Bldg., Juneau 99811. Tel: 907-465-2910.

Arizona

Sharon G. Womack, Acting Dir., Dept. of Lib., Archives and Public Records, 3rd fl. Capitol, Phoenix 85007. Tel: 602-255-4035.

Arkansas

John A. Murphy, Jr., State Libn., Arkansas State Lib., One Capitol Mall, Little Rock 72201. Tel: 501-371-1526.

California

Gary E. Strong, State Libn., California State Lib., Box 2037, Sacramento 95809. Tel. 916-445-2585 or 4027.

Colorado

Anne Marie Falsone, Deputy State Libn., Colorado State Lib., 1326 Lincoln St., Denver 80203. Tel: 303-866-3695.

Connecticut

Clarence R. Walters, State Libn., Connecticut State Lib., 231 Capitol Ave., Hartford 06115. Tel: 203-566-4192 or 4301.

Delaware

Sylvia Short, Dir., Delaware Div. of Libs., Dept. of Community Affairs and Economic Development, Box 639, Dover 19901. Tel: 302-736-4748.

District of Columbia

Hardy R. Franklin, Dir., Dist. of Columbia Public Lib., 901 G St., N.W., Washington 20001. Tel: 202-727-1101.

Florida

Barratt Wilkins, State Libn., State Lib. of Florida, R.A. Gray Bldg., Tallahassee 32304. Tel: 904-487-2651.

Georgia

Joe B. Forsee, Dir., Div. of Public Lib. Services, 156 Trinity Ave., S.W., Atlanta 30303. Tel: 404-656-2461.

Hawaii

Ruth S. Itamura, Asst. Superintendent/State Libn., Div. of Lib. Services, Dept. of Educ., Box 2360, Honolulu 96804. Tel: 808-548-2431 (through overseas operator 8-556-0220).

Idaho

Charles M. Bolles, State Libn., Idaho State Lib., 325 W. State St., Boise 83702. Tel: 208-334-2150.

Illinois

Kathryn J. Gesterfield, Dir., Illinois State Lib., Centennial Memorial Bldg., Springfield 62756. Tel: 217-782-2994.

Indiana

C. Ray Ewick, Dir., Indiana State Lib., 140 N. Senate Ave., Indianapolis 46204. Tel: 317-232-3692.

Iowa

Barry L. Porter, Dir., State Lib. Commission of Iowa, Historical Bldg., Des Moines 50319. Tel: 515-281-4105.

Kansas

Marty Tucker, State Libn., Kansas State Lib., 3rd fl., State Capitol, Topeka 66612. Tel: 913-296-3296.

Kentucky

James A. Nelson, State Libn., Kentucky Dept. of Lib. and Archives, Box 537, Frankfort 40602. Tel: 502-564-7910.

Louisiana

Thomas F. Jaques, State Libn., Louisiana State Lib., Box 131, Baton Rouge 70821. Tel: 504-342-4923.

Maine

J. Gary Nichols, State Libn., Maine State Lib., Cultural Bldg., State House Sta. 64, Augusta 04333. Tel: 207-289-3561.

Maryland

Nettie B. Taylor, Asst. State Superintendent for Libs., Div. of Lib. Development and Services, State Dept. of Educ., 200 W. Baltimore St., Baltimore 21201. Tel: 301-659-2000.

Massachusetts

Roland Piggford, Dir., Massachusetts Bd. of Lib. Commissioners, 648 Beacon St., Boston 02215. Tel: 617-267-9400.

Michigan

Francis X. Scannell, State Libn., Michigan State Lib., Box 30007, Lansing 48909. Tel: 517-373-1580.

Minnesota

William Asp, Dir., Lib. Div., Dept. of Educ., 301 Hanover Bldg., 480 Cedar St., St. Paul 55101. Tel: 612-296-2821.

Mississippi

David M. Woodburn, Dir., Mississippi Lib. Commission, 1100 State Office Bldg., Box 3260, Jackson 39207. Tel: 601-354-6369.

Missouri

Charles O'Halloran, State Libn., Missouri State Lib., Box 387, Jefferson City 65102. Tel: 314-751-2751.

Montana

Alma Jacobs, State Libn., Montana State Lib., 930 E. Lyndale Ave., Helena 59601. Tel: 406-449-3004.

Nebraska

John L. Kopischke, Dir., Nebraska Lib. Commission, Lincoln 68509. Tel: 402-471-2045.

Nevada

Joseph J. Anderson, State Libn., Nevada State Lib., Capitol Complex, Carson City 89710. Tel: 702-885-5130.

New Hampshire

Shirley Adamovich, State Libn., New Hampshire State Lib., 20 Park St., Concord 03301. Tel: 603-271-2392.

New Jersey

Barbara F. Weaver, Asst. Commissioner of Educ./State Libn., Div. of State Lib. Archives and History, 185 W. State St., Trenton 08625. Tel: 609-292-6200.

New Mexico

Clifford E. Lange, Dir., New Mexico State Lib., 300 Don Gaspar St., Santa Fe 87503. Tel: 505-827-2033.

New York

Joseph F. Shubert, State Libn./Asst. Commissioner for Libs., Room 10C34, C.E.C., Empire State Plaza, Albany 12230. Tel: 518-474-5930.

North Carolina

David Neil McKay, Dir./State Libn., Dept. of Cultural Resources, Div. of State Lib., 109 E. Jones St., Raleigh 27611. Tel. 919-733-2570.

North Dakota

Ruth Mahan, State Libn., North Dakota State Lib., Highway 83 N., Bismarck 58505. Tel: 701-224-2492.

Ohio

Richard M. Cheski, Dir., State Lib. of Ohio, 65 S. Front St., Columbus 43215. Tel: 614-462-6842.

Oklahoma

Robert L. Clark, Jr., Dir., Oklahoma Dept. of Libs., 200 N.E. 18 St., Oklahoma City 73105. Tel: 405-521-2502.

Oregon

Marcia Lowell, State Libn., Oregon State Lib. Bldg., Salem 97310. Tel: 503-378-4367.

Pennsylvania

Elliot L. Shelkrot, State Libn., State Lib. of Pennsylvania, Box 1601, Harrisburg 17105. Tel: 717-787-2646.

Rhode Island

Fay Lipkowitz, Dir., Dept. of State Lib. Services, 95 Davis St., Providence 02908. Tel: 401-277-2726.

South Carolina

Betty E. Callaham, State Libn., South Carolina State Lib., 1500 Senate St., Box 11469, Columbia 29211. 803-758-3181.

South Dakota

Clarence Coffindaffer, State Libn., South Dakota State Lib., State Lib. Bldg., Pierre 57501. Tel: 605-773-3131.

Tennessee

Kathryn C. Culbertson, State Libn. and Archivist, Tennessee State Lib. and Archives, 403 Seventh Ave. N., Nashville 37219. Tel: 615-741-2451.

Texas

Dorman H. Winfrey, Dir.-Libn., Texas State Lib., Box 12927, Capitol Sta., Austin 78711. Tel: 512-475-2166.

Utah

Russell L. Davis, Dir., Utah State Lib., 2150 S. 300 West, Suite 16, Salt Lake City 84115. Tel: 801-533-5875.

Vermont

Patricia E. Klinck, State Libn., State of Vermont, Dept. of Libs., c/o State Office Bldg. Post Office, Montpelier 05602. Tel: 802-828-3261 ext. 3265.

Virginia

Donald R. Haynes, State Libn., Virginia State Lib., Richmond 23219. Tel: 804-786-2332.

Washington

Roderick G. Swartz, State Libn., Washington State Lib., Olympia 98504. Tel: 206-753-5592.

West Virginia

Frederic J. Glazer, Exec. Secy., Science and Cultural Center, West Virginia Lib. Commission, Charleston 25305. Tel: 304-348-2041.

Wisconsin

Leslyn Shires, Asst. Superintendent, Div. for Library Services, Dept. of Public Instruction, 125 S. Webster St., Madison 53702. Tel: 608-266-2205.

Wyoming

Wayne H. Johnson, State Libn., Wyoming State Lib., Barnett Bldg., Cheyenne 82002. Tel: 307-777-7281.

American Samoa

Sailautusi Avegalio, Federal Grants Mgr., Dept. of Educ., Box 1329, Pago Pago 96799. Tel: 633-5237 (through overseas operator).

Guam

Magdalena S. Taitano, Libn., Nieves M. Flores Memorial Lib., Box 652, Agana 96910. Tel: 472-6417 (through overseas operator).

Northern Mariana Islands

Augustine C. Castro, Dir. of Lib. Services, Commonwealth of the Northern Mariana Islands, Saipan 96950. Tel: 6534 (through overseas operator).

Pacific Islands (Trust Territory of)

Harold Crouch, Chief of Federal Programs, Dept. of Educ., Saipan, Mariana Islands 96950.

Puerto Rico

Blanca N. Rivera de Ponce, Dir., Public Lib. Div., Dept. of Educ., Apartado 859, Hato Rey 00919. Tel: 809-753-9191 or 754-0750 (through overseas operator at 472-6620).

Virgin Islands

Henry C. Chang, Dir., Libs. and Museums, Dept. of Conservation and Cultural Affairs, Government of the Virgin Islands, Box 390, Charlotte Amalie, St. Thomas 00801. Tel: 809-774-3407 (through overseas operator at 472-6620).

STATE SCHOOL LIBRARY MEDIA ASSOCIATIONS

Alabama

Alabama Lib. Assn., Div. of Children's and School Libns. Memb. 311. Term of Office. Apr. 1981–Apr. 1982. Publication. *ALACS*.

Chpn. Ruth H. Johnson, 108 Wheeler Ave., Sheffield 35660; *Chpn.-Elect.* Betty Ruth Goodwyn, Rt. 1, Box 405U, Helena 35080; *Secy.* Bettye Johnson, 4254 Lawnwood Dr., Montgomery 36108.

Alaska

[See entry under State, Provincial, and Regional Library Associations.—*Ed.*]

Arizona

School Lib. Div., Arizona State Lib. Assn. Memb. 400. Term of Office. Sept. 1981–Sept. 1982. Publication. *ASLA Newsletter*.

Pres. Marguerite Pasquale, 934 N. Venice Ave., Tucson 85711; *Pres.-Elect.* Bettie Herron, Rte. 3, Box 864, Cottonwood 86326; *Secy.* Caryl Major, 3213 W. Sunnyside Ave., Phoenix 85029; *Treas.* Jerry Wilson, 4148 N. 23 Dr., Phoenix 85015.

Arkansas

School Lib. Div., Arkansas Lib. Assn. Memb. 294. Term of Office. Jan. 1982–Dec. 1982.

Chpn. Jody Charter, Instructional Resources Dept., Univ. of Arkansas, Fayetteville 72701.

California

California Media and Lib. Educators Assn. (CMLEA), Suite 204, 1575 Old Bayshore Hwy., Burlingame 94010. Tel. 415-692-2350. Job Hotline. 415-697-8832. Memb. 1,500. Term of Office. June 1981–May 1982. Publication. *CMLEA Journal* (ann.).

Pres. Marian D. Copeland, Coord. IMC, Rialto Unified School Dist., 182 E. Walnut Ave., Rialto 92376; *Pres.-Elect.* Jay Monfort, Media Services Mgr., Santa Clara County Superintendent of Schools, 100 Skyport Dr., San Jose 95110; *Past Pres.* Curtis May, Dir. of Lib. Services, San Mateo County Office of Education, 333 Main St., Redwood City 94063; *Secy.* Barbara Hamm, Lib., Wm. S. Hart Union H.S. Dist., Canyon High School, 24823 Walnut St., Newhall 91321; *Treas.* Mel Nickerson, Coord., Instructional Media, California State College, Stanislaus, 800 Monte Vista Ave., Turlock 95380.

Colorado

Colorado Educational Media Assn. Memb. 680. Term of Office. Feb. 1981–Feb. 1982. Publication. *The Medium* (mo.).

Pres. Robert Card, Colorado Springs Schools, 1036 N. Franklin, Colorado Springs 80903; *Exec. Secy.* Terry Walljasper, Colorado Educational Media Assoc., Box 22814, Wellshire Sta., Denver 80222.

STATE SCHOOL LIBRARY MEDIA ASSOCIATIONS / 579

Connecticut

Connecticut Educational Media Assn. Term of Office. May 1981–May 1982. Officers to be elected. Address correspondence to Administrative Secy., Anne Weimann, 25 Elmwood Ave., Trumbull 06611. Tel. 203-372-2260.

Delaware

Delaware School Lib. Media Assn. Memb. 116. Term of Office. Nov. 1980–Nov. 1981. Publication. *DSLMA Newsletter.*

Pres. Alice J. Thornton, Ogletown Middle School, Chestnut Hill Rd., Newark 19713; *V.P.* Vacant; *Secy.* Mary Lou Hess, Murdoch & Walsh, P. A. 300 Delaware Ave., Wilmington 19899; *Treas.* Patricia Robertson, Conrad Jr. H.S., Jackson Ave. & Boxwood Rd., Wilmington 19804.

District of Columbia

D.C. Assn. of School Libns. Memb. 150. Term of Office. Aug. 1981–Aug. 1982. Publication. *Newsletter* (3 per year).

Pres. Gwendolyn Cogdell, Jefferson Jr. H.S., Eight & H Sts. S.W., Washington 20024; *V.P./Pres.-Elect.* Vacant; *Secy.* Delesta Cross, Seaton School, Tenth St. & Rhode Island Ave. N.W., Washington 20001; *Treas.* Patricia Copelin, Brookland School, Michigan Ave. and Randolph St. N.E., Washington 20017; *Immediate Past Pres.* Janice Spencer, Shepherd Elementary School, 14 St. & Kalmia Rd. N.W., Washington 20012.

Florida

Florida Assn. for Media in Education, Inc. Memb. 1,400. Term of Office. Oct. 1981–Oct. 1982. Publication. *Florida Media Quarterly* (q.).

Pres. Ron Slawson, 4720 N.W. 16 Place, Gainesville 32601; *V.P.* Shirley Aaron, 101 Cherry St., Havana 32333; *Pres.-Elect.* Winona Jones, 6410 118 Ave. N., Largo 33543; *Secy.* Nancy H Young, 8310 N.W. 4 Place, Gainesville 32601; *Treas.* Henrietta Smith, 1202 N.W. 2 St., Delray Beach 33444.

Georgia

School and Children's Lib. Div. of the Georgia Lib. Assn. Term of Office. Nov. 1981–Nov. 1983.

Chpn. Beth Johnson, Head, Children's Dept., Ida Williams Branch, Atlanta Public Lib., 269 Buckhead Ave. N.E., Atlanta 30309.

Hawaii

Hawaii Assn. of School Libns. Memb. 225. Term of Office. June 1, 1981–May 31, 1982. Publications. *The Golden Key* (ann.); *HASL Newsletter* (q.), c/o HASL, Box 23019, Honolulu 96822.

Pres. Ruth Petrowski; *1st V.P.* Harry Uyehara; *2nd V.P.* Grace Tom; *Rec. Sec.* Roberta Kaneshiro; *Corres. Secy.* Mary Bauckham; *Treas.* Lorna Sakado; *Dirs.* Linda Victor; May Chun.

Idaho

School Libs. Div. of the Idaho Lib. Assn. Term of Office. May 1981–May 1982. Publication. Column in *The Idaho Librarian* (q.).

Chpn. Vera Kenyon, Libn., Wilder Public Schools, Wilder 83676; *Chpn. Elect.* Vaughn Overlie, Libn., Genessee Public Schools, Genessee 83832.

Illinois

Illinois Assn. for Media in Education (IAME). (Formerly Illinois Assn. of School Libns.) Memb. 750. Term of Office. Jan. 1981–Dec. 1981. Publication. *IAME News for You* (q.). *Ed.* Charles Rusiewski, 207 E. Chester, Nashville 62263.

Pres. Jerry R. Wicks, 1411 S. 8 St., St. Charles 60174.

Indiana

Assn. for Indiana Media Educators. Memb. 950. Term of Office. (*Pres.*) Apr. 30, 1981–Apr. 30, 1982. Publication. *Indiana Media Journal.*

Pres. Robert Little, Dept. of Lib. Science, Indiana State Univ., Terre Haute 47809; *Exec. Secy.* Lawrence Reck, School of Education, Indiana State Univ., Terre Haute 47809.

Iowa

Iowa Educational Media Assn. Memb. 500. Term of Office. Apr. 1981–Apr. 1982. Publication. *Iowa Media Message* (q.). *Ed.* Donald Rieck, 121 Pearson Hall, Iowa State Univ., Ames 50011.
Pres. Eleanor Blanks, 635-46 St., Des Moines 50312; *Pres.-Elect.* Charles Ruebling, 804 Gaskill, Ames 50010; *Secy.* Linda Waddle, Cedar Falls H.S., Tenth and Division Sts., Cedar Falls 50613; *Treas.* Marjean Wegner, 7019 N.W. Beaver, Des Moines 50323.

Kansas

Kansas Assn. of School Libns. Memb. 800. Term of Office. July 1981–June 1982. Publication. *KASL Newsletter* (s. ann.).
Pres. Aileen Graham, 446 Edgerton, Manhattan 66502; *V.P.* Martha Dirks, 332 N. 10, WaKeeney 67672; *Treas.* Ramona Haney, 1717 Parkwood, Garden City 67846; *Secy.* Jo Ann Coy, 360 S. Third, Clearwater 67026.

Kentucky

Kentucky School Media Assn. Memb. 625. Term of Office. Oct. 1981–Oct. 1982. Publication. *KSMA Newsletter.*
Pres. James R. Connor, Rte. 12, Box 7, London 40741; *Pres.-Elect.* Jean Ross, Rte. 1, Benton 42025; *Secy.* Joyce Munsey, 48 Deerfield Lane, Somerset 42501; *Treas.* Sharon Dunn, 1205 Meadowridge Trail, Prospect 40059.

Louisiana

Louisiana Assn. of School Libns., c/o Louisiana Lib. Assn., Box 131, Baton Rouge 70821. Memb. 350. Term of Office. July 1, 1981–June 30, 1982.
Pres. Vivian W. Hurst, 404 Parent St., New Roads 70760; *1st V.P./Pres.-Elect.* Genevieve Wheeler, 12987 N. Lake Carmel Dr., New Orleans 70128; *2nd V.P.* Kathleen Simms, 250 Clara Dr., Baton Rouge 70808; *Secy.* Kathryn Derveloy, Rte. 2, Box 491, Springfield 70462; *Treas.* Marvene Dearman, 1471 Chevelle Dr., Baton Rouge 70806.

Maine

Maine Educational Media Assn. Memb. 200. Term of Office. Oct. 1981–Sept. 1983. Publication. *Mediacy* (q.).
Pres. Jeff Small, Media Center, Univ. of Maine at Presque Isle, Presque Isle 04769; *Pres.-Elect.* Edna Mae Bayliss, Maranacook Community School, Readfield 04355; *V.P.* Jean Labrecque, Bonny Eagle H.S., R.F.D. 1, West Buxton 04093; *Secy.* Thomas Peterson, Windham H.S., R.F.D. 1, South Windham 04082; *Treas.* Christine Taylor, Warsaw Junior H.S., School St., Pittsfield 04967.

Maryland

Maryland Educational Media Organization. Memb. 760. Term of Office. Oct. 1981–Oct. 1982. Publication. *MEMO-Random* (newsletter, q.).
Pres. Walker Jung, 1942 Sunberry Rd., Dundalk 21222; *Pres.-Elect.* Margaret Denman, Box 056, Westminster 21157; *Secy.* Penny Alexander, Dundalk Community College, 7200 Sollers Point Rd., Dundalk 21222; *Treas.* Jean Smith, Potomac Senior H.S., 5211 Boydell Ave., Oxen Hill 20745; *Past Pres.* Harry Bock, Prince Georges County Public School, Palmer Park Service, 8437 Landover Rd., Landover 20785.

Massachusetts

Massachusetts Assn. for Educational Media. Memb. 630. Term of Office. June 1, 1981–May 31, 1982. Publication. *Media Forum* (q.).
Pres. Marion S. Dubrawski, 21 Gladstone St., East Boston 02128; *Pres.-Elect.* Edna Kotomski, 28 Strathmore Rd., Worcester 01604; *Secy.* Connie Schlotterbeck, 5 Valley View Rd., Wayland 01778; *Treas.* Stephen W. Scharl, 6 Hillside Apts., Palmer 01069.

Michigan

Michigan Assn. for Media in Education (MAME), Bureau of School Services, Univ. of Michigan, 401 S. Fourth St., Ann Arbor 48109. Memb. 900. Term of Office. One year. Publication. *Media Spectrum* (q.).

Pres. Margaret Grazier, 18300 Parkside, Detroit 48221; *Past Pres.* Ruth Fitzgerald, 4151 Louis Dr., Flint 48507; *Treas.* Robert Nordin, 13481 Haddon St., Fenton 48430; *Secy.* Jeannine Cronkhite, 19182 Lancashire, Detroit 48223.

Minnesota

Minnesota Educational Media Organization. Memb. 1,200. Term of Office. May 1981–May 1982. Publication. *Minnesota Media*.

Pres. Donald E. Overlie, Owatonna H.S., Owatonna 55060; *Secy.* Mick Briscoe, 500 E. Third St., Morris 56267. *Past Pres.* Saundra S. Hustad, 590 N. Owasso Blvd., St. Paul 55112.

Mississippi

Mississippi Assn. of Media Educators. Memb. 70. Term of Office. Mar. 1981–Mar. 1982. Publication. *MAME* (newsletter, bi-ann.).

Pres. Joan P. Haynie, Mississippi ETV, Drawer 1101, Jackson 39205; *Pres.-Elect.* Joseph L. Ellison, Media Center, Jackson State Univ., Jackson 39217; *V.P.* William A. Hughes, Media Center, Mississippi State Univ., Box 1802, Mississippi State 39762; *Secy.* Glenda Lester, Jackson Prep. School, Box 4940, Jackson 39216; *Treas.* Jayne Sargent, 6370 White Stone Rd., Jackson 39206.

Missouri

Missouri Assn. of School Libns. Memb. 600. Term of Office. Sept. 1, 1981–Aug. 31, 1982. Publication. *MASL Newsletter* (4 per year). *Ed.* Mary Reinert, Rte. 3, Nevada 64772.

Pres. Lora Smith, Rte. 3, Box 597, West Plains 65775.

Address correspondence to the president.

Montana

Montana School Lib. Media, Div. of Montana Lib. Assn. Memb. 170. Term of Office. May 1981–May 1982. Publication. *Newsletter* (q.).

Chpn. Avis R. Anderson, Dawson County H.S., Box 701, Glendive 59330.

Address general correspondence to MSL/MA, c/o Montana Lib. Assn., Montana State Lib., 930 E. Lyndale Ave., Helena 59601.

Nebraska

Nebraska Educational Media Assn. Memb. 400. Term of Office. July 1, 1981–June 30, 1982. Publication. *NEMA Newsletter* (4 per year). *Ed.* Cliff Lowell, Box 485, Holdrege 68949.

Pres. Steve Davis, Kearney Senior H.S., 38 St. & Sixth Ave., Kearney 68847; *Pres.-Elect.* Bruce Hough, Center for Instr. Tech., Creighton Univ., 2500 California St., Omaha 68178.

Nevada

Nevada Assn. of School Libns. Memb. 55. Term of Office. Jan. 1, 1982–Dec. 31, 1983.

Chpn. Merilyn Grosshans, Las Vegas H.S., 315 S. Seventh St., Las Vegas 89101.

New Hampshire

New Hampshire Educational Media Assn. Memb. 150. Term of Office. June 1981–June 1982. Publication. *Online* (irreg.).

Pres. Barbara Broderick, Oyster River H.S., Durham 03824; *Pres.-Elect.* Shelley Lochhead, Hopkinton H.S., Hopkinton 03229; *Treas.* Jane McKersie, Pelham H.S., Marsh Road, Pelham 03076; *Rec. Secy.* Sandy Guest, Sunapee Junior-Senior H.S., Sunapee 03782; *Corres. Secy.* Marcia Burch, Jr. H.S., Claremont 03743.

New Jersey

Educational Media Assn. of New Jersey (EMAnj). (Organized Apr. 1977 through merger of New Jersey School Media Assn. and New Jersey Assn. of Educational Communication Technology.) Memb. 1,200. Term of Office. May 1981-Apr. 1982. Publications. *Signal Tab* (newsletter, mo.); *Emanations* (journal, q.).

Pres. Ethel Kutteroff, R.R. 3, M56, Chester 07930; *Pres.-Elect.* Mary Jane McNally, 249 Belleville Ave., Apt. 43A, Bloomfield 07003; *V.P.* Elsie Brainard, 100B Cedar Lane, Highland Park 08904; *Rec. Secy.* Dawn Ganss, 1973 Duncan Dr., Scotch Plains 07076; *Corres. Secy.* Alice Domineske, 14 Hinsdale Lane, Willingboro 08046; *Treas.* Rosemary Skeele, 22 Winding Way, Parsippany 07054.

New Mexico

New Mexico Library Assn., School Libraries, Young Adult Services Div. Memb. 270. Term of Office. Apr. 1981-Apr. 1982.

Chpn. Flomitchel Starkey, Box 1437, Roswell 88201.

New York

School Lib. Media Sec., New York Lib. Assn., 15 Park Row, Suite 434, New York 10038. Memb. 875. Term of Office. Nov. 1981-Nov. 1982. Publications. Participates in *NYLA Bulletin* (mo. except July and Aug.); *SLMS Gram* (s. ann.).

Pres. Mary Joan Egan, Lib. Media Dir., Burnt Hills Ballston Lake Central School Dist., Ballston Lake 12019; *1st V.P./Pres.-Elect.* Margaret Jonson, Dir. of Libs., Albany City Schools, Albany 12234; *2nd V.P.* Mercedes Rowe, Dist. Lib. Media Coord., Bronx Dist. 11, Bronx; *Secy.* Barbara Riley, Lib. Media Specialist, Elliot R. Hughes Lib., New Hartford Central Schools, New Hartford 13413; *Treas.* Barbara Jones, Project Dir., School Lib. System, BOCES, Mexico 13114; *SLMS Publications.* Mercedes Rowe, Dist. Lib. Media Coord., Bronx Dist. 11, Bronx.

North Carolina

North Carolina Assn. of School Libns. Memb. 900. Term of Office. Oct. 1981- Oct. 1983.

Chpn. Paula M. Fennell, Consultant, Div. of Educational Media, State Dept. of Public Instruction, Raleigh 27611; *Chpn.-Elect.* Judie Davie, Dept. of Lib. Science/Educational Technology, Univ. of North Carolina at Greensboro, Greensboro 27402; *Secy.-Treas.* Connie Hull, Media Coord., Tarboro H.S., Tarboro 27886.

North Dakota

North Dakota Lib. Assn., School Sec. Memb. 85. Term of Office. One year. Publication. *The Good Stuff* (q.).

Pres. Connie Cahill, Harvey 58341; *Secy.* Marilyn Johnson, Crosby 58730.

Ohio

Ohio Educational Lib. Media Assn. Memb. 1,700. Term of Office. Oct. 1981- Oct. 1982. Publication. *Ohio Media Spectrum* (q.).

Pres. Ralph Carder, Fairborn City Schools, 312 Whittier Ave., Fairborn 45324; *1st V.P.* Ann Tepe, Beverly Elementary School, Fifth St., Beverly 45715; *2nd V.P.* Anne Hyland, Northeastern Local, 1414 Bowman, Springfield 45502; *Secy.* Joyce Watson, Barberton H.S., 489 Hopocan & Newell, Barberton 44203; *Treas.* William Beuther, Cuyahoga Community College West, 11000 Pleasant Valley, Parma 44130.

Oklahoma

Oklahoma Assn. of School Lib. Media Specialists. Memb. 150. Term of Office. July 1, 1981-June 30, 1982. Publications. *School Library News* column in *Oklahoma Librarian* (q.); "Library Resources" section in *Oklahoma Educator* (mo.).

Chpn. Letty Rains, Jefferson School, Norman 73071; *Chpn.-Elect.* Marcella Petty, Checotah Elementary School, Checotah 74426; *Secy.* Janet Lanier, Lincoln

Elementary School, Norman 73071; *Treas.* Betty Fry, Clinton H.S., Clinton 73601.

Oregon

Oregon Educational Media Assn. Memb. 800. Term of Office. Oct. 1, 1981–Sept. 30, 1982. Publication. *Interchange.*

Pres. Ruth Stiehl, Oregon State Univ., 1809 Balboa St., Eugene 97401; *Pres.-Elect.* Jim Heath, I.M.C. Director, Douglas County ESD, 1871 N.E. Stephens, Roseburg 97470; *Exec. Secy.* Sherry Hevland, 16695 S.W. Rosa, Beaverton 97005.

Pennsylvania

Pennsylvania School Libns. Assn. Memb. 1,300. Term of Office. July 1, 1980–June 30, 1982. Publications. *Learning and Media* (4 per year); *027.8* (4 per year).

Pres. Sue A. Walker, 6065 Parkridge Dr., East Petersburg 17520; *V.P./Pres.-Elect.* Anna Harkins, 5630 Glen Hill Dr., Bethel Park 15102; *Secy.* Linda Cook, R.D. 1, Box 170, Guys Mills 16327; *Treas.* Roberta Ireland, 307 S. Corl St., State College 16801; *Past Pres.* Celeste DiCarlo, 327 Ridge Point Circle, A-23, Bridgeville 15017.

Rhode Island

Rhode Island Educational Media Assn. Memb. 300. Term of Office. June 1981–June 1983. Publications. *RIEMA Newsletter* (9 per year); *Media News* (2 per year). Address correspondence c/o RIEMA, 5 Whitwell Place, Newport 02840.

Pres. James Kenny; *Pres.-Elect.* To be announced; *Secy.* To be announced; *Treas.* To be announced.

South Carolina

South Carolina Assn. of School Libns. Memb. 600. Term of Office. Apr. 1981–Apr. 1982. Publication. *Media Messenger* (5 per year).

Pres. Juanita Brantley, 114 Poole Lane, Clemson 29631; *V.P./Pres.-Elect.* Drucilla Reeves, 1500 Bradley Dr., Columbia 29204.

South Dakota

South Dakota School Lib. Media Assn., Sec. of the South Dakota Lib. Assn. and South Dakota Education Assn. Term of Office. Oct. 1981–Oct. 1982.

Pres. Ray Novak, Baltic Schools, Baltic 57003; *Pres.-Elect.* Kathy Brill, Lead H.S., Lead 57754; *Secy.* Kitty Brewer, Madison Senior H.S., Madison 57042; *Treas.* Jean Hirning, West Jr. High, Rapid City 57701.

Tennessee

Tennessee Education Assn., School Lib. Sec., 598 James Robertson Pkwy., Nashville 37219. Term of Office. June 1981–June 1982.

Chpn. Elberta Davis, 3735 Freemile Cove, Memphis 38311.

Texas

Texas Assn. of School Libns. Memb. 1,800. Term of Office. Apr. 1981–Apr. 1982. Publication. *Media Matters* (2 per year).

Chpn. Pam Johnson, Box 26, Rio Vista 76093; *Chpn.-Elect.* Carol Bramlett, 3205 41 St. Lubbock 79413; *Secy.* Dorothy Smith, 6108 Mountainclimb Dr., Austin 78731; *Treas.* Ann Bennett, 6011 Prospect, Dallas 75206; *Councillor.* Jo Ann Bell, Arapaho Bldg., 1300 Cypress, Richardson 75080.

Utah

Utah Lib. Assn., School Sec. Memb. 130. Term of Office. Mar. 1981–Mar. 1982. Publications. *Horsefeathers* (newsletter, mo.); *Utah Libraries* (journal, q.).

Chpn. Mary Jensen, Provo H.S., 1125 N. University, Provo 84601; *Vice-Chpn.* Carol Buchmiller, Lincoln School, 1090 Roberta, Salt Lake City 84111; *Secy.-Treas.* Marion Karpisek, Salt Lake Dist. Media Center, 440 E. First S., Salt Lake City 84111.

Vermont

Vermont Educational Media Assn. Memb. 135. Term of Office. May 1981–May 1982. Publication. *VEMA News* (q.).
Pres. Pat Mraz, Champlain Valley Union H.S., Hinesburg 05461; *V.P./Pres.-Elect/Proj. Dir.* Judith Davison, St. Albans Elementary School, St. Albans 05478; *Secy.* Tom Karlin, Randolph Union H.S., Randolph 05060; *Treas.* Richard Hurd, Barre City School, Barre 05641.

Virginia

Virginia Educational Media Assn. (VEMA). Term of Office. Nov. 1981–Nov. 1982.
Pres. Jane Bosley, Supv., Lib. Services, Loudoun County Schools, 30 W. North St., Leesburg 22075.

Washington

Washington Lib. Media Assn. Memb. 700. Term of Office. Jan. 1, 1982–Dec. 31, 1982. Publication. *The Medium* (q.); *The Newsletter* (irreg.).
Pres. Dave Wager, 12907 63 N.E., Kirkland 98033; *Pres.-Elect.* Cathy McLeod, 2205 N. Walnut St., Ellensburg 98926; *V.P.* Alice Barnard, 4556 52 N.E., Seattle 98105; *Secy.* Karen Benson, Box 511, Deer Park 99006; *Treas.* Bruce Eyer, 212 S. 29 Ave., Yakima 98902.

West Virginia

School Libns. Dept., West Virginia Education Assn. Memb. 6. Term of Office. Nov. 1979–Nov. 1981. Publication. *Newsletter WVSL* (ann.).
Pres. Marilyn Jean Moellendick, 3315 Smith St., Parkersburg 26101; *Pres.-Elect.* Barbara G. Ball, 1010 Kilgore Ave., Culloden 25510; *Secy.-Treas.* Linda Adkins, Box 33, Comfort 25049.

Wisconsin

Wisconsin School Lib. Media Assn., Div. of Wisconsin Lib. Assn. Term of Office. Jan. 1982–Dec. 1982. Publication. *WLA Newsletter* (6 per year). *Ed.* Bonnie Lynne Robinson.
Pres. Carol Stanke, Maplewood Jr. H.S., 1600 Midway Rd., Menasha 54952; *V.P./Pres.-Elect.* Vonna Pitel, Cedarburg H.S., W63N611 Evergreen Blvd., Cedarburg 53012; *Secy.* Gloria Barclay, Arrowhead H.S., Hartland 53029; *Financial Adviser.* Kathy Tessmer, Rm. 4262, Helen C. White Bldg., Univ. of Wisconsin–Madison, Madison 53706.

Wyoming

Wyoming School Lib. Media Assn. Memb. 25. Term of Office. May 1981–Apr. 1982.
Chpn. Carolyn Harrington, Rte. 2, Worland Way 82401; *Vice-Chpn.* Landra Ranzabeck, Green River H.S., Green River 82935; *Secy.* Vickie Hoff, 511½ 13 St., Rawlins 82301.

STATE SUPERVISORS OF SCHOOL LIBRARY MEDIA SERVICES

Alabama

W. Raymond Jones and Hallie A. Jordan, Educational Specialists, Lib. Media Services, 111 Coliseum Blvd., Montgomery 36193. Tel: 205-832-5810.

Alaska

Patricia C. Wilson, Alaska State Lib., Pouch G, Juneau 99811. Tel: 907-465-2919.

Arizona

Mary Choncoff, Libn. and Learning Resources Coord., ESEA IV-B, State Dept. of Educ., 1535 W. Jefferson, Phoenix 85007. Tel: 602-255-5271.

Arkansas

Betty J. Morgan, Specialist, Lib. Services, State Dept. of Educ., Arch Ford Bldg., Capitol Grounds, Little Rock 72201. Tel: 501-371-1861.

California

Gerald W. Hamrin, ESEA Title IV-B Program Administrator, State Dept. of Educ., 721 Capitol Mall, Sacramento 95814. Tel: 916-445-7458.

Colorado

Boyd Dressler, Consultant, ESEA Title IV, State Dept. of Educ., 201 E. Colfax, Denver 80203. Tel: 303-866-5714.

Connecticut

Robert G. Hale, Sr., Instructional Television Consultant, Betty B. Billman, Lib. Media Consultant, Elizabeth M. Glass, Computer Technology Consultant, Dorothy W. Headspeth, Info. Specialist, and Brenda H. White, Lib. Media Consultant, Learning Resources and Technology Unit, State Dept. of Educ., Box 2219, Hartford 06115. Tel: 203-566-5409.

Delaware

Richard L. Krueger, Supv., Lib. Media Services, and ESEA Title IV-B and C, State Dept. of Public Instruction, John G. Townsend Bldg., Box 1402, Dover 19901. Tel: 302-736-4667.

District of Columbia

Position vacant. Write to Dept. of Lib. Science, Public Schools of the District of Columbia, 801 Seventh St. S.W., Washington 20024. Tel: 202-724-4952.

Florida

Sandra W. Ulm, Administrator, School Lib. Media Services, State Dept. of Educ., Knott Bldg., Tallahassee 32301. Tel: 904-488-0095.

Georgia

Nancy P. Hove, Coord., Media Field Services, State Dept. of Educ., 156 Trinity Ave. S.W., Atlanta 30303. Tel: 404-656-2418.

Hawaii

Patsy Izumo, Dir., Multimedia Services Branch, State Dept. of Educ., 641 18 Ave., Honolulu 96816. Tel: 808-732-5535.

Idaho

Rudy H. Leverett, Coord., Educational Media Services, State Dept. of Educ., Len B. Jordan Bldg., 650 State St., Boise 83720. Tel: 208-334-2281.

Illinois

Marie Rose Sivak, Program Consultant, Lib. Media Services, State Bd. of Educ., 100 N. First St., Springfield 62777. Tel: 217-782-3810.

Indiana

Phyllis Land, Dir., Div. of Instructional Media, State Dept. of Public Instruction, Indianapolis 46204. Tel: 317-927-0296.

Iowa

Betty Jo Buckingham, Consultant, Education Media, State Dept. of Public Instruction, Des Moines 50319. Tel: 515-281-3707.

Kansas

June Saine Level, Lib. Media Consultant, Educational Assistance Sec., Kansas State Dept. of Educ., 110 E. 10 St., Topeka 66612. Tel: 913-296-3434.

Kentucky

Judy L. Cooper, Program Mgr. for School Media Services, State Dept. of Educ., 1830 Capital Plaza Tower, Frankfort 40601. Tel: 502-564-2672.

Louisiana
James S. Cookston, State Supv. of School Lib., State Dept. of Educ., Rm. 602, Education Bldg., Box 44064, Baton Rouge 70804. Tel: 504-342-3399.

Maine
John W. Boynton, Coord., Media Services, Maine State Lib., LMA Bldg., State House Sta. 64, Augusta 04333. Tel: 207-289-2956.

Maryland
Paula Montgomery, Chief, School Media Services Branch, Div. of Lib. Development and Services, State Dept. of Educ., 200 W. Baltimore St., Baltimore 21201. Tel: 301-796-8300, ext. 264.

Massachusetts
Raymond L. Gehling, Jr., Coord., Lib. and Learning Resources, ESEA Title IV-B, Curriculum Services, Dept. of Educ., 31 St. James Ave., Boston 02116. Tel: 617-727-5742.

Michigan
Francis Scannell, State Dept. of Educ., State Lib. Services, Box 30007, Lansing 48909. Tel: 517-374-9630.

Minnesota
Robert H. Miller, Supv., Educational Media Unit, State Dept. of Educ., Capitol Square Bldg., St. Paul 55101. Tel: 612-296-6114.

Mississippi
John Barlow, State Dept. of Educ., Educational Media Services, Box 771, Jackson 39205. Tel: 601-354-6864.

Missouri
Jo Albers, Lib. Supv., Dept. of Elementary and Secondary Educ., Box 480, Jefferson City 65102. Tel: 314-751-4445.

Montana
Sheila Cates, Lib. Media Consultant, Office of Public Instruction, Helena 59620. Tel: 406-449-3126.

Nebraska
Jack Baillie, Administrator of Special Services, State Dept. of Educ., Box 94987, 301 Centennial Mall S., Lincoln 68509. Tel: 402-471-2481.

Nevada
William F. Arensdorf, Chpn., Instructional Materials and Equipment, State Dept. of Educ., Capitol Complex, Carson City 89710. Tel: 702-885-3121.

New Hampshire
Reginald A. Comeau, Consultant, Educ. Media Services, Libs. and Learning Resources, Div. of Instruction, 64 N. Main St., Concord 03301. Tel: 603-271-2401.

New Jersey
Anne Voss, Coord., School and College Media Services, State Dept. of Educ., Trenton 08625. Tel: 609-292-6256.

New Mexico
Dolores Dietz, Coord., ESEA Title IV-B, Libs. and Learning Resources, State Dept. of Educ., Santa Fe 87503. Tel: 505-827-5441.

New York
Beatrice Griggs, Administrator, Bur. of School Libs., and Coord., ESEA Title IV-B, Bur. of School Libs., State Educ. Dept., Albany 12234. Tel: 518-474-2468.

North Carolina
Elsie L. Brumback, Dir., Div. of Educational Media, State Dept. of Public Instruction. Raleigh 27611. Tel: 919-733-3193.

North Dakota
Patricia Herbel, Coord., Lib. Services and Elementary Curriculum, Dept. of Public Instruction, Bismarck 58505. Tel: 701-224-2281.

Ohio
Theresa M. Fredericka, Lib. Media Consultant, State Dept. of Educ., 65 S.

Front St., Rm. 1005, Columbus 43215. Tel: 614-466-2761.

Oklahoma

Carla Kitzmiller, Clarice Roads, and Barbara Spriestersbach, Coords., Lib. and Learning Resources Div., State Dept. of Educ., Oklahoma City 73105. Tel: 405-521-2956.

Oregon

Lyle Wirtanen, Consultant, School Lib. Resources, ESEA Title IV-B, State Dept. of Educ., Salem 97310. Tel: 503-378-5600.

Pennsylvania

Elliot L. Shelkrot, State Libn. and Acting Dir., Div. of School Lib. Media and Educational Resource Services, State Dept. of Educ., Box 911, 333 Market St., Harrisburg 17108. Tel: 717-787-2646.

Rhode Island

Rita Stein, Consultant, Lib. and Learning Resources, State Dept. of Educ., 235 Promenade St., Providence 02908. Tel: 401-277-2617.

South Carolina

Margaret W. Ehrhardt, Lib./Media Consultant, State Dept. of Educ., Rutledge Bldg., Rm. 803, Columbia 29201. Tel: 803-758-2652.

South Dakota

James O. Hansen, State Superintendent, Div. of Elementary and Secondary Education, Richard F. Kneip Bldg., Pierre 57501. Tel: 605-773-3243.

Tennessee

Christine Brown, Dir., School Lib. Resources, 115 Cordell Hull Bldg., Nashville 37219. Tel: 615-741-1896.

Texas

Mary R. Boyvey, Learning Resources Program Dir., Instructional Resources Div., Texas Education Agency, Austin 78701. Tel: 512-475-2478.

Utah

Leroy R. Lindeman, Administrator, Curriculum and Instruction Div., State Office of Educ., 250 E. Fifth S., Salt Lake City 84111. Tel: 801-533-5550.

Kenneth Neal, Media Production Coord., Curriculum and Instruction Div., State Office of Educ., 250 E. Fifth S., Salt Lake City 84111. Tel: 801-533-5573.

Robert Nohavec, Instructional Design and Media Management Specialist, Curriculum and Instruction Div., State Office of Educ., 250 E. Fifth S., Salt Lake City 84111. Tel: 801-533-5572.

Dorothy Wardrop, Coord., Curriculum Development, Curriculum and Instruction Div., State Office of Educ., 250 E. Fifth S., Salt Lake City 84111. Tel: 801-533-5572.

Vermont

Jean D. Battey, School Lib. Media Coord., ESEA Title IV-B, Div. of Federal Assistance, State Dept. of Educ., Montpelier 05602. Tel: 802-828-3124.

Virginia

Mary Stuart Mason, Supv., School Libs. and Textbooks, State Dept. of Educ., Box 6Q, Richmond 23216. Tel: 804-225-2855.

Washington

Nancy Motomatsu, Supv., Learning Resources Services, Office of State Superintendent of Public Instruction. 7510 Armstrong St. S.W., FG-11, Tumwater 98504. Tel: 206-753-6723.

West Virginia

Carolyn R. Skidmore, Coord., and Susannah G. Dunn, Supv., Libs. and Learning Resources, 1900 Washington St., Rm. 346, Charleston 25305. Tel: 304-348-3925.

Wisconsin

Dianne McAfee Williams, Dir., Bur. of Instructional Media Programs, State Dept. of Public Instruction, Box 7841, Madison 53707. Tel: 608-266-1965.

Wyoming

Jack Prince, Coord., Instructional Resources, State Dept. of Educ., Hathaway Bldg., Cheyenne 82002. Tel: 307-777-6252.

American Samoa

Emma S. Fung Chen Pen, Program Dir., Office of Lib. Services, Dept. of Educ., Box 1329, Pago Pago 96799.

Pacific Islands (Trust Territory of)

Tomokichy Aisek, Supv., Lib. Services, Dept. of Educ., Truk, Caroline Islands 96942.

Augustine Castro, Dir., Lib. Services, Dept. of Educ., Saipan, Mariana Islands 96950.

Tamar Jordan, Supv., Lib. Services, Dept. of Educ., Majuor, Marshall Islands 96960.

Puerto Rico

Blanca N. Rivera de Ponce, Dir., Public Lib. Div., Dept. of Educ., Hato Rey 00919. Tel: 809-753-9191; 754-0750.

Virgin Islands

Beulah Harrigan, Acting Dir., L.S.I.M. Dept. of Educ., St. Thomas 00801.

INTERNATIONAL LIBRARY ASSOCIATIONS

INTER-AMERICAN ASSOCIATION OF AGRICULTURAL LIBRARIANS AND DOCUMENTALISTS
IICA-CIDIA, Turrialba, Costa Rica

OBJECT

"To serve as liaison among the agricultural librarians and documentalists of the Americas and other parts of the world; to promote the exchange of information and experiences through technical publications and meetings; to promote the improvement of library services in the field of agriculture and related sciences; to encourage the improvement of the professional level of the librarians and documentalists in the field of agriculture in Latin America."

OFFICERS

Pres. Orlando Arboleda, Info. Specialist, IICA-CIDIA, San José, Costa Rica; *V.P.* Ubaldino Dantas Machado, EMBRAPA/DID, Brasilia, Brazil; *Exec. Secy.* Ana Maria Paz de Erickson, IICA-CIDIA, 7170 Turrialba, Costa Rica. (Address correspondence to the executive secretary.)

PUBLICATIONS

Boletín Informativo (q.).
Boletin Especial (irreg.).
Revista AIBDA (2 per year).
Páginas de Contenido: Ciencias de la Información (3 per year).
Proceedings. Tercera Reunión Interamericana de Bibliotecarios y Documentalistas Agrícolas, Buenos Aires, Argentina, April 10–14, 1972 (U.S. price: $10 including postage). Out of print. Available in Microfiche. (Price U.S. $10).
Proceedings. Cuarta Reunión Interamericana de Bibliotecarios y Documentalistas Agrícolas, Mexico, D.F., April 8–11, 1975 (U.S. price: Memb. $5 including postage; nonmemb. $10 including postage).
Proceedings. Quinta Reunión Interamericana de Bibliotecarios y Documentalistas Agrícolas, San José, Costa Rica, April 10–14, 1978 (U.S. price: Memb. $10 plus postage; nonmemb. $15 plus postage).

INTERNATIONAL ASSOCIATION OF AGRICULTURAL LIBRARIANS AND DOCUMENTALISTS
MAFF, Central Veterinary Laboratory,
New Haw, Weybridge, Surrey KT15 3NB, England

OBJECT

"The Association shall, internationally and nationally, promote agricultural library science and documentation as well as the professional interest of agricultural librarians and documentalists." Founded 1955. Memb. 525. Dues (Inst.) $26; (Indiv.) $13.

OFFICERS

Pres. P. Aries, France; *V.Ps.* H. Haendler, Germany; M. S. Malugani, Costa Rica; *Secy.-Treas.* D. E. Gray, UK; *Ed.* R. Farley, USA.

EXECUTIVE COMMITTEE

H. Buntrock, Luxembourg; S. Contour, France; G. de Bruyn, Netherlands; A. L. Geisendorf, Switzerland; K. Harada, Italy; F. C. Hirst, UK; M. J. MacIntosh, Canada; J. C. Sisan, Philippines; A. T. Yaikova, USSR; representatives of National Assns. of Agricultural Libns. and Documentalists.

PUBLICATION

Quarterly Bulletin of the IAALD (memb.).

AMERICAN MEMBERSHIP

By individuals or institutions.

INTERNATIONAL ASSOCIATION OF LAW LIBRARIES
Vanderbilt Law Library, Nashville, TN 37203, USA

OBJECT

"To promote on a cooperative, non-profit, and fraternal basis the work of individuals, libraries, and other institutions and agencies concerned with the acquisition and bibliographic processing of legal materials collected on a multinational basis, and to facilitate the research and other uses of such materials on a worldwide basis." Founded 1959. Memb. over 600 in 64 countries.

OFFICERS (1980-1983)

Pres. Igor I. Kavass, Vanderbilt Univ., Law School Lib., Nashville, TN 37203, USA; *1st V.P.* Klaus Menzinger, Bibliothek für Rechtswissenschaft der Universität Freiburg, D-7800 Freiburg, Fed. Rep. of Germany; *2nd V.P.* Ivan Sipkov, Lib. of Congress, Washington, DC 20540, USA; *Secy.* Adolf Sprudzs, Law School Lib., Univ. of Chicago, 1121 E. 60 St., Chicago, IL 60637, USA; *Treas.* Arno Liivak, Rutgers Univ., Law Lib., Camden, NJ 08102, USA.

BOARD MEMBERS (1980-1983)

Officers: Robert F. Brian, Australia; Myrna Feliciano, Philippines; Eric Gaskell; Belgium; Lajos Nagy, Hungary; Fernando de Trazegnies, Peru; Yoshiro Tsuno, Japan; Christian Wiktor, Canada; Shaikha Zakaria, Malaysia.

SERVICES

1. The dissemination of professional information through the *International*

Journal of Law Libraries through continuous contacts with the affiliated national groups of law librarians and through work within other international organizations, such as IFLA and FID.
2. Continuing education through the one-week IALL Seminars in International Law Librarianship annually.
3. The preparation of special literature for law librarians, such as the *European Law Libraries Guide*, and of introductions to basic foreign legal literature.
4. Direct personal contacts and exchanges between IALL members.

IALL REPRESENTATIVES

A liaison between the law librarians of their regions and the IALL administration is being appointed for every country or major area.

PUBLICATION

International Journal of Law Libraries (formerly *IALL Bulletin*) (3 per year). Ed.-in-Chief. Arno Liivak, Rutgers Univ. Law Lib., Camden, NJ 08102, USA; Assoc. Ed.-in-Chief. Ivan Sipkov, Law Lib., Lib. of Congress, Washington, DC 20540, USA.

INTERNATIONAL ASSOCIATION OF METROPOLITAN CITY LIBRARIES
c/o P. J. Th. Schoots, Director, Gemeentebibliothek Rotterdam, Nieŭwe Markt 1, NL-3001 Rotterdam, Netherlands

OBJECT

"The Association was founded to assist the worldwide flow of information and knowledge by promoting practical collaboration in the exchange of books, exhibitions, staff, and information." Memb. 97.

OFFICERS

Pres. Pieter J. van Swigchem, Openbare Bibliothek, Bilderdijkstraat 1-7, The Hague, Netherlands; *Secy.-Treas.* Piet J. Th. Schoots, Gemeentebibliothek, Nieŭwe Markt 1, NL-3001 Rotterdam, Netherlands; *Past Pres.* Juergen Eyssen, Stadtbibliothek Hildesheimer Str. 12, D-3000 Hannover 1, Fed. Rep. of Germany. (Address correspondence to the secretary-treasurer.)

PROGRAM

A research team and correspondents are engaged in drawing up a practical code of recommended practice in international city library cooperation and in formulating objectives, standards, and performance measures for metropolitan city libraries.

PUBLICATIONS

Review of the Three Year Research and Exchange Programme 1968-1971.
Annual International Statistics of City Libraries (INTAMEL).

INTERNATIONAL ASSOCIATION OF MUSIC LIBRARIES, ARCHIVES AND DOCUMENTATION CENTRES (IAML)
Musikaliska akademiens bibliotek
Box 16 326, S-103 26, Stockholm, Sweden

OBJECT

To promote the activities of music libraries, archives, and documentation centers and to strengthen the cooperation among them, to promote the availability of all publications and documents relating to music and further their bibliographical control, to encourage the development of standards in all areas that concern the association, and to support the protection and preservation of musical documents of the past and the present. Memb. 1,800.

OFFICERS (AUG. 1980-MAY 1983)

Pres. Brian Redfern, School of Libnshp., Polytechnic of North London, 207-225 Essex Rd., London N1 3PN, England; *Past Pres.* Barry S. Brook, City Univ. of New York, 33 W. 42 St., New York, NY 10036, USA; *V.P.s.* Maria Calderisi, National Lib., Music Div., Ottawa K1A 0N4, Canada; Janos Kárpáti, Lib. of the Liszt Ferenc Academy of Music, Box 206, H-1391 Budapest, Hungary; Nanna Schiødt, Svanevaenget 20, DK-2100 København Ø, Denmark; Heinz Werner, Berliner Stadtbibliothek, Breite Strasse 32-34, DDR-102 Berlin, German Democratic Rep.; *Secy.-Gen.* Anders Lonn, Musikaliska akademiens bibliotek, Box 16 326, S-103 26, Stockholm, Sweden; *Treas.* Wolfgang Rehm, Heinrich-Schütz Allee 29, D-3500 Kassel, Fed. Rep. of Germany.

PUBLICATION

Fontes Artis Musicae (4 per year, memb.).

COMMISSION CHAIRPERSONS

Bibliographical Research. Maria Calderisi, National Lib., Music Div., Ottawa K1A 0N4, Canada.
Broadcasting Music Libraries. Lucas van Dijck, Nederlandse Omroep Stichting, P.O.B. 10, NL-1200 JB Hilversum, Netherlands.
Cataloging. Brian Redfern, School of Libnshp., Polytechnic of North London, 207-225 Essex Rd., London N1 3PN, England.
Education and Training. Don L. Roberts, Music Lib., Northwestern Univ., Evanston, IL 60201, USA.
International Inventory of Musical Sources. Kurt von Fischer, Laubholzstr. 46, CH-8703 Erlebach ZH, Switzerland.
International Repertory of Music Literature. Barry S. Brook, RILM Center, City Univ. of New York, 33 W. 42 St., New York, NY 10036, USA.
International Repertory of Musical Iconography. Barry S. Brook, Research Center for Musical Iconography, City Univ. of New York, 33 W. 42 St., New York, NY 10036, USA.
Libraries in Music Teaching Institutions. Anthony Hodges, Royal Northern College of Music, 124 Oxford Rd., Manchester M13 9RD, England.
Music Information Centers. James Murdoch, Australia Music Centre, Box N9, Sydney NSW 2000, Australia.
Public Music Libraries. Eric Cooper, London Borough of Enfield, Music Dept., Town Hall, Green Lanes, Palmers Green, London N13 4XD, England.
Record Libraries, Claes Cnattingius, Sveriges Riksradio, Grammofonarkivet, S-10510 Stockholm, Sweden.
Research Music Libraries. Richard Andrewes, Pendelbury Lib., Univ. Music School, West Road, Cambridge CB3 9DP, England.

US BRANCH

Pres. Geraldine Ostrove, New England Conservatory of Music, Spaulding Lib., 33 Gainsborough St., Boston, MA 02115; *Secy.-Treas.* Don L. Roberts, Music Lib., Northwestern Univ., Evanston, IL 60201.

UK BRANCH

Pres. John May, 5 Hotham Rd., London SW15 1QN; *Gen. Secy.* Susan M. Clegg, Birmingham School of Music, Paradise Circus, Birmingham B3 3HG; *Hon. Treas.* Pam Thompson, Royal College of Music Lib., Prince Consort Rd., London SW7 2BS.

PUBLICATION

BRIO. Ed. Clifford Bartlett, BBC Music Lib., Yalding House, London W1N 6AJ (2 per year; memb.).

INTERNATIONAL ASSOCIATION OF ORIENTALIST LIBRARIANS (IAOL)

OBJECT

"To promote better communication among Orientalist librarians and libraries, and others in related fields, throughout the world; to provide a forum for the discussion of problems of common interest; to improve international cooperation among institutions holding research resources for Oriental Studies." The term Orient here specifies the Middle East, East Asia, and the South and Southeast Asia regions.

Founded in 1967 at the 27th International Congress of Orientalists in Ann Arbor, Michigan. Affiliated with the International Federation of Library Associations and Institutions (IFLA).

OFFICERS

Pres. Serafin D. Quiason; *Secy.-Treas.* Rosa M. Vallejo, Rm. 405, The National Lib. Building, T. M. Kalaw St., Manila, Philippines 2801; *Ed.* Eloise Van Niel, 3888 Monterey Dr., Honolulu, HI 96816.

PUBLICATION

International Association of Orientalist Librarians Bulletin (s. ann., memb.).

INTERNATIONAL ASSOCIATION OF SOUND ARCHIVES
c/o Helen Harrison, Media Librarian, Open University Library, Walton Hall, Milton Keynes, MK7 6AA, England

OBJECT

IASA is a UNESCO-affiliated organization established in 1969 to function as a medium for international cooperation between archives and other institutions that preserve recorded sound documents. This association is involved with the preservation, organization, and use of sound recordings; techniques of recording and methods of reproducing sound; the international exchange of literature and information; and in all subjects relating to the professional work of sound archives.

MEMBERSHIP

Open to all categories of archives, institutions, and individuals who preserve sound recordings or have a serious interest in the purposes or welfare of IASA.

OFFICERS (1981–1984)

Pres. David G. Lance, Keeper of the Dept. of Sound Records, Imperial War Museum, Lambeth Rd., London SE1 6HZ, England; *V.Ps.* Peter Burgis, National Lib. of Australia, Sound Recordings Lib., Canberra City, A.C.T. 2600, Australia; Dietrich Schüller, Phonogrammarchiv der Österreichischen Akademie der Wissenshaften, Liebiggasse 5, A-1010 Vienna, Austria; Rolf Schuursma, Erasmus Universiteit, Universiteitsbibliotheek, Burg. Oudlaan 50, NL-3062 PA Rotterdam, Netherlands; *Ed.* Ann Briegleb, Music Dept. Univ. of California, Los Angeles CA 90024, USA; *Secy.* Helen P. Harrison, Media Libn., Open Univ. Lib., Walton Hall, Milton Keynes MK7 6AA, England; *Treas.* Ulf Scharlau, Süddeutscher Rundfunk, Schallarchiv/Bandaustausch, Neckarstr. 230, D-7000 Stuttgart 1, Fed. Rep. of Germany.

PUBLICATIONS

An Archive Approach to Oral History.
Directory of IASA Member Archives.
Phonographic Bulletin (3 per year; memb. or subscription).

INTERNATIONAL COUNCIL ON ARCHIVES
Secretariat, 60 r. des Francs-Burgeois
F-75003 Paris, France

OBJECT

"To establish, maintain, and strengthen relations among archivists of all lands, and among all professional and other agencies or institutions concerned with the custody, organization, or administration of archives, public or private, wheresoever located." Established 1948. Memb. 690 (representing 109 countries). Dues (Indiv.) $25; (Inst.) $50; (Archives Assns.) $50 or $100 (Central Archives Directorates) $200 minimum, computed on the basis of GNP and GNO per capita.

OFFICERS

Pres. Alfred W. Mabbs; *V.P.s* Dagfinn Mannsåker; Ms. Soemartini; *Exec. Secy.* C. Kesckeméti; *Treas.* Alfred Wagner. (Address all correspondence to the executive secretary.)

PUBLICATIONS

Archivium (ann.; memb. or subscription to Verlag Dokumentation München, Possenbacker Str. 2, Postfach 71 1009, D-8 Munich 71, Fed. Rep. of Germany).

ICA Bulletin (s. ann.; memb., or U.S. $5).

Microfilm Bulletin (subscriptions to Centro Nacional de Microfilm, Serrano 15, Madrid 6, Spain).

ADPA—Archives and Automation (ann. 250 FB or U.S. $9.00 memb.; subscriptions to M. Jean Pieyns, Archives de l'Etat, rue Pouplin, 8, B-4000 Liege, Belgium).

Guides to the Sources of the History of Nations (Latin American Series, 10 vols. pub.; African Series, 9 vols. pub.; Asian Series, 3 vols. pub.).

Archival Handbooks (8 vols. pub.).

INTERNATIONAL FEDERATION FOR DOCUMENTATION
Box 30115, 2500 GC The Hague, Netherlands

OBJECT

To group internationally organizations and individuals interested in the problems of documentation and to coordinate their efforts; to promote the study, organization, and practice of documentation in all its forms, and to contribute to the creation of an international network of information systems.

PROGRAM

The program of the federation includes activities for which the following committees have been established: Central Classification Committee (for UDC); Research on the Theoretical Basis of Information; Linguistics in Documentation; Information for Industry; Education and Training; Classification Research; Terminology of Information and Documentation; Patent Information and Documentation; Social Sciences Documentation; Informetrics. It also includes the BSO Panel (Broad System of Ordering).

OFFICERS

Pres. Ricardo A. Gietz, CAICYT, Moreno 431/33, 1091 Buenos Aires, Argentina; *V.P.s* S. Fujiwara, Dept. of Chemistry, Chiba Univ., Yoyoi-cho 1-3, Chiba, Japan; M. W. Hill, Science Reference Lib., British Lib., 25 Southhampton Bldgs., Chancery La., London, England; A. I. Mikhailov, VINITI, Baltijskaja ul. 14, Moscow A219, USSR, *Treas.* Herbert S. White, Grad. Lib. School, Indiana

Univ., Bloomington, IN 47405, USA; *Councillors.* Margarita Almada de Ascencio, Mexico City, Mexico; M. Brandreth, Ottawa, Canada; Emilia Currás, Madrid, Spain; I. Essaid, Baghdad, Iraq; C. Keren, Tel-Aviv, Israel; A. van der Laan, The Hague, Netherlands; P. Lázár, Budapest, Hungary; E.-J. Frhr. von Ledebur, Bonn, Fed. Rep. of Germany; S. S. Ljungberg, Södertälje, Sweden; Raimundo N. Fialho Mussi, Brasília, Brazil; V. Stefánik, Bratislava, Czechoslovakia; Mu'azu H. Wali, Lagos, Nigeria; *Belgian Member.* Monique Jucquois-Delpierre, La Hulpe, Belgium; *Secy.-Gen.* K. R. Brown, The Hague, Netherlands; *Pres., FID/CLA.* A. L. Carvalho de Miranda, Brasília, Brazil; *Pres., FID/CAO.* B. L. Burton, Hong Kong; *Pres., FID/CAF.* Canute P. M. Khamala, Nairobi, Kenya. (Address correspondence to the secretary-general.)

PUBLICATIONS

FID News Bulletin (mo.) with supplements on document reproduction (q.). *Newsletter on Education and Training Programmes for Information Personnel* (q.). *International Forum on Information and Documentation* (q.). *R & D Projects in Documentation and Librarianship* (bi-mo.). *FID Directory* (bienn.). *FID Publications* (ann.). *FID Annual Report* (ann.). Proceedings of congresses; Universal Decimal Classification editions; manuals; directories; bibliographies on information science, documentation, reproduction, mechanization, linguistics, training, and classification.

MEMBERSHIP

Approved by the FID Council; ratification by the FID General Assembly.

AMERICAN MEMBERSHIP

National Academy of Sciences–National Research Council.

INTERNATIONAL FEDERATION OF FILM ARCHIVES
Secretariat, Coudenberg 70, B-1000 Brussels, Belgium

OBJECT

"To facilitate communication and cooperation between its members, and to promote the exchange of films and information; to maintain a code of archive practice calculated to satisfy all national film industries, and to encourage industries to assist in the work of the Federation's members; to advise its members on all matters of interest to them, especially the preservation and study of films; to give every possible assistance and encouragement to new film archives and to those interested in creating them." Founded in Paris, 1938. 69 members in 50 countries.

EXECUTIVE COMMITTEE (JUNE 1981–JUNE 1983)

Pres. Wolfgang Klaue, DDR; *V.Ps.* Eileen Bowser, USA; David Francis, UK; Raymond Borde, France; *Secy.-Gen.* Robert Daudelin, Canada; *Treas.* Jan de Vaal, Netherlands. (Address correspondence to B. Van der Elst, executive secretary, at headquarters address.)

COMMITTEE MEMBERS

Todor Andreykov, Bulgaria; Guido Cincotti, Italy; M. Gonzalez-Casanova, Mexico; Eva Orbanz, Fed. Rep. of Germany; Anna-Lena Wibom, Sweden.

PUBLICATIONS

Film Preservation (available in English or French).
The Preservation and Restoration of Colour and Sound in Films.
Film Cataloging.
Study on the Usage of Computers for Film Cataloging.
Handbook for Film Archives (available in English or French).
International Directory to Film & TV Documentation Sources.
International Index to Film and Television Periodicals (cards service).
International Index to Film Periodicals (cumulative volumes).
Preservation of Film Posters.
Guidelines for Describing Unpublished Script Materials.
Annual Bibliography of FIAF Members' Publications.
Proceedings of the FIAF Symposiums: 1977: L'Influence du Cinema Sovietique Muet Sur le Cinema Mondial/The Influence of Silent Soviet Cinema on World Cinema; 1978: *Cinema 1900-1906;* 1980: *Problems of Selection in Film Archives.*

INTERNATIONAL FEDERATION OF LIBRARY ASSOCIATIONS AND INSTITUTIONS (IFLA)
c/o The Royal Library, Box 95312,
2509 CH The Hague, Netherlands

OBJECT

"To promote international understanding, cooperation, discussion, research, and development in all fields of library activity, including bibliography, information services, and the education of library personnel, and to provide a body through which librarianship can be represented in matters of international interest." Founded 1927. Memb. (Lib. Assns.) 155; (Inst.) 762; (Aff.) 101; in 115 countries.

OFFICERS AND EXECUTIVE BOARD

Pres. Else Granheim, Dir., Norwegian Directorate for Public and School Libs., Oslo, Norway; *1st V.P.* Ljudmila Gvishiani, Dir., State Lib. of Foreign Literature, Moscow, USSR; *2nd V.P.* Hans-Peter Geh, Dir., Württembergische Landesbibliothek, Stuttgart, Fed. Rep. of Germany; *Treas.* Marie-Louise Bossuat, Dir., Bibliographical Center of the National Lib., Paris, France; *Exec. Bd.* G. Rückl, Dir., Central Lib. Institute, Berlin, DDR; E. R. S. Fifoot, Pres., Three Rivers Books, Ltd., Oxford, UK; Jean Lowrie, Prof., School of Libnshp., Western Michigan Univ., Kalamazoo, Mich., USA; J. S. Soosai, Rubber Research Institute of Malaysia, Kuala Lumpur, Malaysia; *Ex officio Members.* Henriette Avram, Chairman, Professional Bd., Dir. for Processing Systems, Networks, and Automation Planning, Lib. of Congress, Washington, D.C., USA; Rutherford D. Rogers, Chairman, Programme Management Committee, Dir., Yale Univ. Lib., New Haven, Conn., USA; *Secy.-Gen.* Margareet Wijnstroom, IFLA Headquarters; *Dir., IFLA International Office for Universal Bibliographic Control.* D. Anderson, c/o Reference Div., British Lib., London, UK; *Dir., IFLA Office for International Lending.* M. B. Line, c/o British Lib. Lending Div., Boston Spa, Wetherby, West Yorkshire, UK; *Publications Officer.* W. R. H. Koops, Univ. Libn., Groningen, Netherlands; *Professional Coord.* A. L. van Wesemael, IFLA headquarters.

PUBLICATIONS

IFLA Annual.
IFLA Journal (q.).

IFLA Directory (ann.).
IFLA Publications Series.
International Cataloguing (q.).

AMERICAN MEMBERSHIP

American Lib. Assn.; Art Libs. Society of North America; Assn. of American Lib. Schools; Assn. of Research Libs.; International Assn. of Law Libs.; International Assn. of Orientalist Libns.; International Assn. of School Libns.; Special Libs. Assn. *Institutional Members:* There are 134 libraries and related institutions that are institutional members or affiliates of IFLA in the United States (out of a total of 903), and 37 Personal Affiliates (out of a total of 87).

INTERNATIONAL INSTITUTE FOR CHILDREN'S LITERATURE AND READING RESEARCH
Mayerhofg. 6, A-1040 Vienna, Austria

OBJECT

"To create an international center of work and coordination; to take over the tasks of a documentations center of juvenile literature and reading education; to mediate between the individual countries and circles dealing with children's books and reading." Established Apr. 7, 1965. Dues. Austrian schillings 250 (with a subscription to *Bookbird*); Austrian schillings 270 (with a subscription to *Bookbird* and *Jugend und Buch*).

PROGRAM

Promotion of international research in field and collection and evaluation of results of such research; international bibliography of technical literature on juvenile reading; meetings and exhibitions; compilation and publication of recommendation lists; advisory service; concrete studies on juvenile literature; collaboration with publishers; reading research.

OFFICERS

Pres. Adolf März; *Hon. Pres.* Josef Stummvoll; *V.P.* Otwald Kropatsch; *Dir.* Lucia Binder; *V.-Dir.* Viktor Böhm. (Address all inquiries to director at headquarters address.)

PUBLICATIONS

Bookbird (q.; memb. or Austrian schillings 250 [approx. $14]).
Jugend und Buch (memb. or Austrian shillings 120 [approx. $7]).
Schriften zur Jugendlektüre (series of books and brochures dealing with questions on juvenile literature and literary education in German).

INTERNATIONAL ORGANIZATION FOR STANDARDIZATION
ISO Central Secretariat
1 r. de Varembé, Case postale 56, CH-1211 Geneva 20, Switzerland

OBJECT

To promote the development of standards in the world in order to facilitate the international exchange of goods and services and to develop mutual cooperation in the spheres of intellectual, scientific, technological, and economic activity.

OFFICERS

Pres. Henri-Durand, France; *V.P.* Jan Ollner, Canada; *Secy.-Gen.* Olle Sturen, Sweden.

TECHNICAL WORK

The technical work of ISO is carried out by over 160 technical committees. These include:

TC 46—Documentation (Secretariat, DIN Deutsches Institut für Normung, 4-10, Burggrafenstr., Postfach 1107, D-1000 Berlin 30, Germany). Scope: Standardization of practices relating to libraries, documentation and information centers, indexing and abstracting services, archives, information science, and publishing.

TC 37—Terminology (Principles & Coordination) (Secretariat, Osterreichisches Normungsinstitut, Leopoldgasse 4, A-1020 Vienna, Austria). Scope: Standardization of methods for setting up and coordinating national and international standardized terminologies.

TC 97—Computers & Information Processing (Secretariat, American National Standards Institute ANSI, 1430 Broadway, New York, NY 10018, USA). Scope: Standardization in the area of computers and associated information processing systems and peripheral equipment, devices, and media related thereto.

PUBLICATIONS

Catalogue (ann.).
Memento (ann.).
Bulletin (mo.).
Liaisons.
Member Bodies.

FOREIGN LIBRARY ASSOCIATIONS

The following list of regional and national foreign library associations is a selective one. For a more complete list with detailed information, see *International Guide to Library, Archival, and Information Science Associations* by Josephine Riss Fang and Alice H. Songe (R. R. Bowker, 1980). The *Guide* also provides information on international associations, some of which are described in detail in the article "International Library Associations" that appears earlier in Part 7 of this volume. A more complete list of foreign and international library associations also can be found in *International Literary Market Place* (R. R. Bowker), an annual publication.

REGIONAL

Africa

International Assn. for the Development of Documentation, Libs. and Archives in Africa, Secy. E. K. W. Dadzie, Box 375, Dakar, Senegal.

Standing Conference of African Lib. Schools, c/o School of Libns., Archivists and Documentalists, Univ. of Dakar, B. P. 3252, Dakar, Senegal.

Standing Conference of African Univ. Libs., Eastern Area (SCAULEA), c/o Univ. Libn., Univ. of Nairobi, Kenya.

Standing Conference of African Univ. Libs., Western Area (SCAULWA), c/o M. Jean Aboghe-Obyan, Bibliotheque Universitaire, Univ. Omar Bongo, Libreville, Gabon.

Standing Conference of East African Libns., c/o Tanzania Lib. Assn., Box 2645, Dar-es-Salaam, Tanzania.

The Americas

Assn. of Caribbean Univ., Research and Institutional Libs. (Asociación de Bibliotecas Universitarias, de Investigación e Institucionales del Caribe), Gen. Secy. Oneida R. Ortiz, Apdo. Postal S. Estación de la Universidad, San Juan, PR 00931.

Latin American Assn. of Schools of Lib. and Info. Science (Asociación Latinoamericana de Escuelas de Bibliotecologia y Ciencias de la Información), Colegio de Bibliotecologia, Universidad Nacional Autónoma de México, México 20, D.F., Mexico.

Seminar on the Acquisition of Latin American Lib. Materials, SALALM Secretariat, Memorial Lib., Univ. of Wisconsin-Madison, Madison, WI 53706.

Asia

Congress of Southeast Asian Libns. (CONSAL), Chpn. Patricia Lim, c/o Singapore Lib. Assn., National Lib., Stamford Rd., Singapore 6, Republic of Singapore.

British Commonwealth of Nations

Commonwealth Lib. Assn., Exec. Secy., Box 534, Kingston 10, Jamaica.

Standing Conference on Lib. Materials on Africa (SCOLMA), c/o Secy. P. M. Larby, Institute of Commonwealth Studies, 27 Russell Sq., London WC1B 5DS, England.

Europe

LIBER (Ligue des Bibliothèques Européennes de Recherche), Assn. of European Research Libs., c/o R. Mathys, Zentralbibliothek Zürich, Zahringerplatz 6, Postfach 8025, Zürich, Switzerland.

Scandinavian Assn. of Research Libns. (Nordiska Vetenskapliga Bibliotekarieförbundet), c/o Avdelingsbibliotekar Per Morten Bryhn, Universitetsbiblioteket, Drammensveien 42, N-Oslo 2, Norway.

NATIONAL

Afghanistan

Afghan Lib. Assn. (Anjuman Kitab-Khana-I), Exec. Secy. Eidi M. Khoursand, Box 3142, Kabul.

Argentina

Argentine Assn. of Scientific and Technical Libs. and Info. Centers (Asociación Argentina de Bibliotecas y Centros de Información Científicos y Técnicos), Santa Fe 1145, Buenos Aires. Exec. Secy. Olga E. Veronelli.

Australia

Australian School Lib. Assn., c/o Secy., Box 80, Balmain N.S.W. 2041.

Lib. Assn. of Australia, Exec. Dir. Susan Acutt, 473 Elizabeth St., Surry Hills, N.S.W.

Lib. Automated Systems Info. Exchange (LASIE), Pres. Dorothy Peake, Box 602, Lane Cove 2066, N.S.W.

State Libns.' Council of Australia, Chpn. W. L. Brown, State Lib. of Tasmania, 91 Murray St., Hobart, Tasmania 7000.

Austria

Assn. of Austrian Libns. (Vereinigung Österreichischer Bibliothekare—VÖB), Pres. Franz Kroller, c/o Österreichische Nationalbibliothek, Josefsplatz 1, A-1014 Vienna.

Assn. of Austrian Public Libs. and Libns. (Verband Österreichischer Volksbüchereien und Volksbibliothekare), Exec. Secy. Rudolf Müller, Langegasse 37, A-1080 Vienna.

Austrian Society for Documentation and Info. (Österreichische Gesellschaft für Dokumentation und Information—ÖGDI), Exec. Secy. Bruno Hofer, c/o ON, Österreichisches Normungsinstitut, Leopoldsgasse 4, POB 130, A-1027 Vienna.

Belgium

Assn. of Libns. and Documentalists of the State Institute of Social Studies (Association des Bibliothécaires—Documentalistes de l'Institute d'Etudes Sociales de l'Etat), Secy. Claire Gerard, 26 r. de l'Abbaye, B-1050 Brussels.

Assn. of Theological Libns. (Vereniging van Religieus-Wetenschappelijke Bibliothécarissen), Minderbroederstr. 5, B-3800 St. Truiden. Exec. Secy. K. Van de Casteele, Elsbos 16, B-2520 Edegem.

Belgian Assn. for Documentation (Association Belge de Documentation-ABD/Belgische Vereniging voor Documentatie-BVD), PB 110, 1040 Brussels 26. Pres. De Backer Roger.

Belgian Assn. of Archivists and Libns. (Association des Archivistes et Bibliothécaires de Belgique/Vereniging van Archivarissen en Bibliothecarissen van België), Exec. Secy. T. Verschaffel, Bibliothèque Royale Albert I, 4 bd. de l'Empereur, B-1000 Brussels.

National Assn. of French-Speaking Libns. (Association nationale des Bibliothécaires d'Expression française), Exec. Secy. Ch. Massaux, Bibliothèque Central de la Ville de Bruxelles, Palais du Midi, av. de Stalingrad 55A, 1000 Brussels.

Flemish Assn. of Libns., Archivists, and Documentalists (Vlaamse Vereniging voor Bibliotheek, Archief, en Documentatiewezen—VVBAD), Pres. E. Heidbuchel; Secy. F. Franssens; Goudbloemstraat 10, 2000 Antwerpen.

Bolivia

Bolivian Lib. Assn. (Asociación Boliviana de Bibliotecarios), Pres. Efraín Virreira Sánchez, Casilla 992, Cochabamba.

Brazil

Assn. of Brazilian Archivists (Associação dos Arquivis tas Brasileiros), Praça de Botafogo, 186, Sala B-217, Rio do Janeiro.

Brazilian Federation of Lib. Assns. (Federação Brasileira de Associações de Bibliotecários), c/o Pres. Elizabeth Maria Ramos de Carvalho, rua Humberto de Campos 366, ap. 1302, 22430 Rio de Janeiro, R.J.

Bulgaria

Lib. Sec. at the Trade Union of the Workers in the Polygraphic Industry and Cultural Institutions (Bibliotečna Sekcjica pri Zentralnija Komitet na Profsăjuza na Rabotnicite ot Poligrafičeskata Promišlenost i Kulturnite Instituti), Pres. Nikola Červenkov, Zdanov Str. 6, Sofia.

Canada

ASTED, Inc. (Association pour l'avancement des sciences et des techniques de la documentation), Dir.-Gen. Lise Brousseau, 360 rue LeMoyne, Montréal, P.Q. H2Y 1Y3.

Bibliographical Society of Canada (La Société Bibliographique du Canada), Secy.-Treas. Marion D. Cameron, Box 1878, Guelph, Ont. N1H 7A1.

Canadian Assn. for Info. Science (L'Association Canadienne des Sciences de l'Information), Pres. Margaret Telfer, Box 776, Sta. G, Calgary, Alta. T3A 2G6.

Canadian Assn. of Lib. Schools (Association Canadienne des Écoles des Bibliothécaires), Pres. Lois Bewley, School of Libnshp., Univ. of British Columbia, Vancouver, B.C. V6T 1WS.

Canadian Council of Lib. Schools (Conseil Canadien des Écoles Bibliothéconomie) (CCLS/CCEB), Pres. Katherine Packer, Dean, Faculty of Lib. Science, Univ. of Toronto, Toronto, Ont.

Canadian Lib. Assn., Exec. Dir. Paul Kitchen, 151 Sparks St., Ottawa, Ont. K1P 5E3. (For detailed information on the Canadian Lib. Assn. and its divisions, see "National Library and Information Industry Associations, U.S. and Canada"; for information on the library associations of the provinces of Canada, see "State, Provincial, and Regional Library Associations.")

Chile

Chilean Lib. Assn (Colegio de Bibliotecarios de Chile), Pres. Ursula Schadlich

Schonhals; Secy. Gen. Eliana Bazán del Campo, Casilla 3741, Santiago.

China, People's Republic of

China Society of Lib. Science (CSLS) (Zhongguo Tushuguan Xuehui), Secy.-Gen. Tan Xiangjin, 7 Wenjinjie Beijing (Peking).

Chinese Science and Technology Info. Assn. (Zhongguo Kexue Jishu Qingbao Xuehui), Dir. Wu Heng Heping Li, Beijing (Peking).

Colombia

Colombian Academy of Libns. (Colegio Colombiano de Bibliotecarios—CCB), Apdo. Aéreo 1307, Medellin.

Colombian Assn. of Libns. (Asociación Colombiana de Bibliotecarios—ASCOLBI), Apdo. Aéreo 30993, Bogotá, D.E.

Costa Rica

Assn. of Costa Rican Libns. (Asociación Costarricense de Bibliotecarios), Apdo. Postal 3308, San José.

Cyprus

Lib. Assn. of Cyprus (Kypriakos Synthesmos Vivliothicarion), c/o Pedagogical Academy, Box 1039, Nikosia.

Czechoslovakia

Assn. of Slovak Libns. and Documentalists (Zväz slovenských knihovníkov a informatikov), Pres. Vít Rak; Exec. Secy. Štefan Kimlička, Michalská 1, 885 17 Bratislava.

Central Lib. Council of the Czechoslovak Socialist Republic (Ústřední knihovnická rada ČSR), Jiří Kábrt, CSc., c/o Ministry of Culture of the ČSR, Valdštejnská 30, Prague 1-Malá Strana.

Denmark

The Archives Society (Arkivforeningen), Exec. Secy. Margit Mogensen, Rigsarkivet, Rigsdagsgården 9, DK-1218 Copenhagen K.

Assn. of Danish School Libs. (Danmarks Skolebiblioteksforening), Exec. Secy. Niels Jacobsen. Vejlemosevej 21, DK-2840 Holte.

Danish Assn. of Music Libs., Danish Sec. of AIBM (Dansk Musikbiblioteksforening, Dansk sektion of AIBM), c/o Secy., Irlandsvej 90, DK-2300 Copenhagen K.

Danish Lib. Assn. (Danmarks Biblioteksforening), Pres. K. J. Mortensen, Trekronergade 15, DK-2500 Valby-Copenhagen.

Danish Research Lib. Assn. (Danmarks Forskningsbiblioteksforening), Pres. Mette Stockmarr, c/o Rigsbibliotekarembedet, Christians Brygge 8, DK-1219 Copenhagen K.

Dominican Republic

Dominican Lib. Assn. (Asociación Dominicana de Bibliotecarios—ASODOBI), c/o Biblioteca Nacional, Plaza de la Cultura, Santo Domingo, Pres. Prospero J. Mella Chavier; Secy. Gen. Hipólito González C.

Ecuador

Ecuadorian Lib. Assn. (Asociación Ecuatoriana de Bibliotecarios—AEB), Exec. Secy. Elizabeth Carrion, Casa de la Cultura Ecuatoriana, Casilla 87, Quito.

Egypt

See United Arab Republic.

El Salvador

El Salvador Lib. Assn. (Asociación de Bibliotecarios de El Salvador), c/o Secy.-Gen. Edgar Antonio Pérez Borja, Urbanización Gerardo Barrios Polígono, "B" No. 5, San Salvador, C.A.

Ethiopia

Ethiopian Lib. Assn. (ELA) (Ye Ethiopia Betemetsahft Serategnot Mahber), Exec. Secy. Asrat Tilahun, Box 30530, Addis Ababa.

Finland

Assn. of Research and Univ. Libns. (Tieteellisten Kirjastojen Virkailijat-Vetenskapliga Bibliotekens Tjänstemannaforening R.Y.), Exec. Secy. Anneli Arjasto, c/o Museovirasto, Neryanderinkatu 13, 00100 Helsinki 10.

Finnish Libns. Assn. (Kirjastonhoitajaliitto-Bibliotekarieförbundet r.y.), Exec. Secy. Anna-Maija Hintikka, Temppelikatu 1 A 12, SF-00100 Helsinki 10.

Finnish Lib. Assn. (Suomen Kirjastoseura-Finlands Biblioteksförening), Exec. Secy. Hilkka M. Kauppi, Museokatu 18, SF-00100 Helsinki 10.

Finnish Society for Information Services (Tietopalveluseura-Samfundet för Informationstjänst i Finland), c/o Ritva Launo, Pres., The State Alcohol Monopoly of Finland (ALKO), Helsinki.

France

Assn. of French Archivists (Association des archivistes français, Pres. M. Charnier; Exec. Secys. Mme Rey-Courtel and Mlle. Etienne, 60 r. des Francs-Bourgeois, F-75141 Paris, CEDEX 03.

Assn. of France Info. Scientists and Special Libns. (Association Française des Documentalistes et des Bibliotécaires Spécialisés—ADBS), Exec. Secy. Y. Rosenfeld, 5, av. Franco russe, 75007 Paris.

Assn. of French Libns. (Association des Bibliothécaires Français), Exec. Secy. Jean-Marc Léri, 65 r. de Richelieu, F-75002 Paris.

Assn. of French Theological Libs. (Association des Bibliothèques ecclésiastiques de France), Exec. Secy. Paul-Marie Guillaume, 6 r. du Regard, F-75006 Paris.

German Democratic Republic

Lib. Assn. of the German Democratic Republic (Bibliotheksverband der Deutschen Demokratischen Republik), Exec. Secy. c/o Hermann-Matern-Str. 57, DDR-1040 Berlin.

Germany, Federal Republic of

Assn. of German Archivists (Verein Deutscher Archivare—VDA), Chpn. Eckhart Franz, Hessisches Staatsarchiv, Schloss, D-6100 Darmstadt.

Assn. of German Libns. (Verein Deutscher Bibliothekare e.V.—VDB), Pres. Ltd. Bibliothekarsdirektor Jürgen Hering; Secy. Robert K. Jopp, Postfach 506, Hoäzgartenstrasse 16, Universitätsbibliothek Stuttgart, D-7000 Stuttgart 1.

Assn. of Graduated Libns. at Academic Libs. (Verein der Diplom-Bibliothekare an Wissenschaftlichen Bibliotheken), Chpn. Ingeborg Sobottke, Universitätsbibliothek Bochum, Universitätsstr. 150, 463 Bochum Querenbrug.

Assn. of Libns. at Public Libs. (Verein der Bibliothekare an Öffentlichen Bibliotheken), Secy. Frau Jaenisch, Roonstr. 57, 2800 Bremen 1.

Assn. of Libs. in the Federal State of North Rhine-Westphalia (Verband der Bibliotheken des Landes Nordrhein-Westfalen), Chpn. Severin Corsten, Direktor der Universitäts- und Stadtbibliothek Köln, Universitätsstr. 33, 5000 Köln 41.

Assn. of Special Libs. (Arbeitsgemeinschaft der Spezialbibliotheken), Chpn. Jobst Tehnzen, Universitätsbibliothek der Technischen Universität und Technischen Informationsbibliothek, Welfengarten 1B, 3000 Hannover 1.

German Assn. for Documentation (Deutsche Gesellschaft für Dokumentation, e.V.—DGD), Exec. Secy. Jürgen Scheele, Westendstr. 19, D-6000 Frankfurt am Main 1.

German Lib. Assn. (Deutscher Bibliotheksverband), Secy. Victoria Scherzberg, Bundesallee 184/185, 1000 Berlin 31.

Working Group of Univ. Libs. (Arbeitsgemeinschaft der Hochschulbibliotheken), Chpn. H. Sontag, c/o Universitätsbibliothek der Technischen Universität Berlin, Strasse des 17. Juni 135, D-1000 Berlin 12.

Working Group of Art Libs. (Arbeitsgemeinschaft der Kunstbibliotheken), Exec. Secy. Albert Schug, Kunst- und

Museumsbibiliothek der Stadt Köln, Kattenbug 18-24, D-5000 Köln 1.

Ghana
Ghana Lib. Assn., Exec. Secy. P. Amonoo, box 4105, Accra, Ghana.

Greece
Greek Lib. Assn. (Enosis Ellenon Bibliothakarion), Box 2118, Athens-124.

Guatemala
Lib. Assn. of Guatemala (Asociación Bibliotecológica Guatemalteca), c/o Dir., Biblioteca Nacional de Guatemala, 5a Av. 7-26, Zona 1, Guatemala, C.A.

Guyana
Guyana Lib. Assn. (GLA), Exec. Secy. Pamela Dos Ramos, c/o 76/77 Main St., Box 110, Georgetown.

Honduras
Assn. of Libns. and Archivists of Honduras (Asociación de Bibliotecarios y Archivistas de Honduras), Secy.-Gen. Juan Angel Ayes R., 3 Av. 4y5C., no. 416, Comayagüela, DC, Tegucigalpa.

Hong Kong
Hong Kong Lib. Assn., Pres. R. W. Frenier, c/o Lib., Univ. of Hong Kong, Pofulam Rd., Hong Kong.

Hungary
Assn. of Hungarian Libns. (Magyar Könyvtárosok Egyesülete), Secy. D. Kovács, Box 244, H-1368, Budapest.

Info. Science Society (Tájékoztatási Tudományos Társaság—MTESZ/TTT), c/o Pál Gágyor, Kossuth ter 6-8, Budapest 1055.

Iceland
Icelandic Lib. Assn. (Bókavarðaféiag Íslands), Pres. Th. Thorvaldsóttir, Box 7050, 127 Reykjavík.

India
Indian Assn. of Special Libs. and Info. Centres (IASLIC), Exec. Secy. S. M. Ganguly, P-291. CIT Scheme 6M, Kankurgachi Calcutta 700 054.

Indian Lib. Assn. (ILA), Pres. P. B. Mangla; Secy. O. P. Trikha, Delhi Public Lib., S. P. Mukerji Marg, Delhi 110006.

Punjab Lib. Assn., 233 Model Town, Jullundur City-3.

Indonesia
Indonesian Lib. Assn. (Ikatan Pustakawan Indonesia—IPI), Pres. Mastini Hardjo Prakoso; Secy. Soemarno HS, Jalan Merdeka Selatan 11, Jakarta-Pusat.

Iran
Iranian Lib. Assn., Exec. Secy. M. Niknam Vazifeh, Box 11-1391, Tehran.

Iraq
Iraqi Lib. Assn., Exec. Secy. N. Kamal-al-Deen, Box 4081, Baghdad-Adhamya.

Ireland, Republic of
Irish Assn. of School Libns. (Cumann Leabharlannaithe Scoile—CLS), Headquarters: The Lib., Univ. College, Dublin 4. Exec. Secy. Sister Mary Columban, Loreto Convent, Foxrock Co., Dublin.

Lib. Assn. of Ireland (Cumann Leabharlann Na h-Éireann), Pres. S. Bohan; Hon. Secy. N. Hardiman, Thomas Prior House, Merrion Rd., Dublin 4.

Israel
Israel Lib. Assn. (ILA) (Irgun Safrane Israel), Secy. R. Porath, Box 7067, Jerusalem.

Italy
Federation of Italian Public Libs. (Federazione Italiana delle Biblioteche Popolari—FIBP), c/o La Società Umanitaria, Via Davario 7, Cap. N., 1-20122 Milan.

Italian Libs. Assn. (Associazione Italiana Biblioteche—AIB), Secy. A. M. Caproni, c/o Istituto di Patologia del Libro, Via Milano 76, 00184 Rome.

National Assn. for Public and Academic Libs. (Ente Nazionale per le Biblioteche Popolari e Scholastiche), Via Michele Mercati 4, I-00197 Rome.

National Assn. of Italian Archivists (Associazione Nazionale Archivistica Italiana—ANAI), Secy. Antonio Dentoni-Litta, Via di Ponziano 15, 00152 Rome.

Ivory Coast

Assn. for the Development of Documentation, Libs., and Archives of the Ivory Coast (Association pour le Développement de la Documentation, des Bibliothèques et Archives de las Côte d'Ivoire), c/o Bibliothèque Nationale, B.P. 20915 Abidjan.

Jamaica

Jamaica Lib. Assn. (JLA), Secy. A. Chambers, Box 58, Kingston 5.

Japan

Japan Documentation Society (Nippon Dokumentêsyon Kyôkai—NIPDOK), Exec. Secy. Tsunetaka Ueda, Sasaki Bldg., 5-7 Koisikawa 2-chome, Bunkyô-ku, Tokyo, 112.

Japan Lib. Assn. (JLA) (Nippon Tosho-kan Kyôkai), Secy.-Gen. Hitoshi Kurihara, 1-10, Taishido 1-chome, Setagaya-ku, Tokyo 154.

Japan Special Lib. Assn. (Senmon Toshokan Kyôgikai—SENTOKYO), Exec. Secy. Yasunosuke Morita, c/o National Diet Lib., 1-10-1 Nagata-cho, Chiyoda-ku, Tokyo 100.

Jordan

Jordan Lib. Assn. (JLA), Pres. Anwar Akroush; Secy. Medhat Mar'ei; Treas. Butros Hashweh, Box 6289, Amman.

Korea, Democratic People's Republic of

Lib. Assn. of the Democratic People's Republic of Korea, Secy. Li Geug, Central Lib., Box 109, Pyongyang.

Korea, Republic of

Korean Lib. Assn. (Hanguk Tosogwan Hyophoe), Exec. Secy. Dae Kwon Park, 100, 1-Ka, Hoehyun-Dong, Chung-Ku, Box 2041, Seoul.

Laos

Laos Lib. Assn. (Association des Bibliothécaires Laotiens), Direction de la Bibliothèque Nationale, Ministry of Education, Box 704, Vientiane.

Lebanon

Lebanese Lib. Assn. (LLA), V.P. L. Hanhan, Saab Medical Lib., AUB, Beirut.

Malaysia

Lib. Assn. of Malaysia (Persatuan Perpustakaan Malaysia—PPM), Secy. Noor Aini Osman, Box 2545, Kuala Lumpur.

Mauritania

Mauritanian Assn. of Libns., Archivists, and Documentalists (Association Mauritanienne des Bibliothécaires, des Archivistes et des Documentalistes—AMBAD), c/o Pres. Oumar Diouwara, Dir., National Lib., Nouakchott.

Mexico

Assn. of Libns. of Higher Education and Research Institutions (Asociación de Bibliotecarios de Instituciónes de Enseñanza Superior e Investigación—ABIESI), Pres. Elsa Barberena, Apdo. Postal 5-611, México 5, D.F.

Mexican Assn. of Libns. (Asociación Mexicana de Bibliotecarios, A.C.), Pres. Ana Mari Magaloni de Bustamante, Apdo. 27-102, México 7, D.F.

Netherlands

Assn. of Archivists in the Netherlands (Vereniging van Archivarissen in Nederlan—VAN), Exec. Secy. A. Koolen, Postbus 897, 8901 BR Leeuwarden.

Assn. of Theological Libns. (Vereniging

voor het Theologisch Bibliothecariaat), Exec. Secy. R. T. M. Van Dijk, Postbus 289, 6500 AG Nijmegen.

Assn. of Univ. Libs. and the Royal Lib. (UKB-Samenwerkingsverband van de Universiteits- en Hogeschoolbibliotheken en de Koninklijke Bibliotheek), Exec. Secy. J. L. M. van Dijk, c/o Bibliotheek Rijksuniversiteit Limburg, Postbus 616, 6200 MD Maastricht.

Dutch Lib. Assn. (Nederlandse Vereniging van Bibliothecarissen, Documentalisten en Literatuuronderzoekers—NVB), p/a Mw. H.J. Krikke-Scholten, Nolweg 13 d, 4209 AW Schelluinen.

Netherlands Assn. of Business Archivists (Nederlandse Vereniging van Bedrijfsarchivarissen—NVBA), Secy. C. L. Groenland, Aalsburg 25 26-6602 WD Wijchen.

New Zealand

New Zealand Lib. Assn. (NZLA), Pres. D. Brown; Exec. Officer H. Stephen-Smith, 20 Brandon St., Box 12-212, Wellington 1.

Nicaragua

Assn. of Univ. and Special Libs. of Nicaragua (Asociación de Bibliotecas Universitarias 6 Especializadas de Nicaragua—ABUEN), Secy. Cecilie Aguilar Briceño, Biblioteca Central, Universidad Nacional Autónoma de Nicaragua, Apdo. No. 68, León.

Nigeria

Nigerian Lib. Assn. (NLA), c/o Hon. Secy. E. O. Ejiko, P.M.B. 12655, Lagos.

Norway

Assn. of Archivists (Arkivarforeningen), Secy.-Treas. Atle Steinar Nilsen, Postboks 10, Kringsjå, Oslo 8.

Assn. of Norwegian Research Libns. (Norske Forskningebibliotekarers Forening—NFF), Secy. G. Langland, Malerhaugveien 20, Oslo 6.

Norwegian Lib. Assn. (Norsk Bibliothekforening—NBF), Secy.-Treas. G. Langland, Malerhaugveien 20, Oslo 6.

Pakistan

Pakistan Lib. Assn. (PLA), Exec. Secy. A. H. Siddiqui, c/o Pakistan Institute of Development Economics, Univ. Campus, Box 1091, Islamabad.

Society for the Promotion and Improvement of Libs. (SPIL), Pres. Hakim Mohammed Said, Al-Majeed, Hamdard Centre, Nazimabad, Karachi-18.

Panama

Panama Assn. of Libns. (Asociación Panameña de Bibliotecarios), c/o Apdo. 2444, Panama, Republic of Panama.

Papua New Guinea

Papua New Guinea Lib. Assn. (PNGLA), Secy. Rhonda Eva, Box 5368, Boroko, PNG.

Paraguay

Paraguayan Assn. of Univ. Libns. (Asociación de Bibliotecarios Universitarios del Paraguay—ABUP), c/o Yoshiko M. de Freundorfer, Head, Escuela de Bibliotecologia, Universidad Nacional de Asunción, Asunción.

Peru

Assn. of Peruvian Archivists (Asociación Peruana de Archiveros), Archivo General de la Nación, C. Manuel Cuadros s/n., Palacio de Justicia, Apdo, 3124, Lima 100.

Assn. of Peruvian Libns. (Asociación Peruana de Bibliotecarios), Exec. Secy. Amparo Geraldino de Orban, Apdo. 3760, Lima.

Lib. Group for the Integration of Socio-Economic Info. (Agrupación de Bibliotecas para la Integración de la Información Socio-Económica—ABIISE), Dir. Isabel Olivera Rivarola, Apdo. 2874, Lima 100.

Philippines

Assn. of Special Libs. of the Philippines (ASLP), Pres. Susima Lazo Gonzales, Box 4118, Manila.

Philippine Lib. Assn. Inc. (PLAI), Pres. Filomena M. Tann, c/o National Lib., Teodoro M. Kalaw St., Manila.

Poland

Polish Libns. Assn. (Stowarzyszenie Bibliotekarzy, Polskich—SBP), Pres. Stefan Kubów; Gen. Secy. Władysława Wasilewska, ul. Konopczyńskiego 5/7, 00953 Warsaw.

Portugal

Portuguese Assn. of Libns., Archivists, and Documentalists (Associação Portuguesa de Bibliotecários, Arquivistas e Documentalistas—BAD), Exec. Secy. Maria Constança Pereira, Rua Ocidental ao Campo Grande 83, 1700 Lisboa.

Rhodesia

See Zimbabwe.

Romania, Socialist Republic of

Assn. of Libns. in the Socialist Republic of Romania (Asociatia Bibliotecarilor din Republica Socialista Romania/Association des Bibliothécaires de la République Socialiste de Roumanie), Pres. G. Botez, Biblioteca Centrala de Stat, Strada Ion Ghica 4, 7001 8 Bucharest.

Scotland

See United Kingdom.

Senegal

Senegal Assn. for the Development of Documentation, Libs., Archives, and Museums (Commission des Bibliothèques de l'ASDBAM, Association Sénégalaise pour le Développement de la Documentation, des Bibliothèques, des Archives et des Musées), Gen. Secy. R. Ba, B.P. 375, Dakar.

Sierra Leone

Sierra Leone Lib. Assn. (SLLA), c/o Secy. F. Thorpe, Sierra Leone Lib. Bd., Rokell St., Freetown.

Singapore

Congress of Southeast Asian Libns. (CONSAL), Chpn. Mrs. Hedwig Anuar, c/o National Lib., Stamford Rd., Singapore 0617.

Lib. Assn. of Singapore (LAS), Hon. Secy., c/o National Lib., Stamford Rd., Singapore 0617.

South Africa

South African Indian Lib. Assn. (SAILA), c/o Secy., SAILA, 7 Ascot St., Durban.

Spain

National Assn. of Libns., Archivists, and Archeologists (Asociación Nacional de Bibliotecarios, Archiveros, Arqueólogus y Documentalists), Exec. Secy. C. Iniguez, Paseo de Calvo Sotelo 22, Apdo. 14281, Madrid 1.

Sri Lanka (Ceylon)

Sri Lanka Lib. Assn. (SLLA), Exec. Secy. N.A.T. de Silva, c/o Univ. of Colombo, Race Course, Reid Ave., Colombo 7.

Sudan

Sudan Lib. Assn. (SLA), Exec. Secy. Mohamed Omar, Box 1361, Khartoum.

Sweden

Assn. of Special Research Libs. (Sveriges Vetenskapliga Specialbiblioteks Förening—SVSF), Pres. W. Odelberg; Secy. Ingrid Björkman, c/o Statens Psykologisk-Pedagogiska Bibliothek, Box 23099, 10435 Stockholm.

Swedish Assn. of Archivists (Svenska Arkivasamfundet), Rijksarkivet, Fack, S-100, 26 Stockholm.

Swedish Assn. of Univ. and Research Libs. (Svenska Bibliotekariesamfundet—SBS), c/o Secy. Birgit Nilsson, Libn., Sveriges Lantbruks-universitets bibliotek, Ultunabiblioteket, S-750 07 Uppsala 7.

Swedish Lib. Assn. (Sveriges Allmänna Biblioteksförening—SAB), Pres. B. Martinsson, Box 1706, S-221 01 Lund.

Swedish Society for Technical Documentation (Tekniska Litteratursällskapet—TLS), Secy. Birgitta Levin, Box 5073, S-10242 Stockholm 5.

Union of Univ. and Research Libs. (Vetenskapliga Bibliotekens Tjänstemannaförening—VBT), Pres. Bo Strenström, Box 36 S-13101, Nacka.

Switzerland

Assn. of Swiss Archivists (Vereinigung Schweizerischer Archivare—VSA), c/o Pres. Walter Lendi, Staatsarchivar, Staatsarchiv St. Gallen, Regierungsgebäude, CH-9901, St. Gallen.

Assn. of Swiss Libns. (Vereinigung Schweizerischer Bibliothekare/Association des Bibliothécaires Suisses/Associazione dei Bibliotecari Svizzeri—VSB/ABS), Exec. Secy. W. Treichler, Hallwylstrasse 15, CH-3003 Bern.

Swiss Assn. of Documentation (Schweizerische Vereinigung für Dokumentation/Association Suisse de Documentation—SVD/ASD). Secy.-Treas. W. Bruderer, BID GD PTT 3030 Berne.

Tanzania

Tanzania Lib. Assn., Exec. Secy. T. E. Mlaki, Box 2645, Dar-es-Salaam.

Trinidad and Tobago

Lib. Assn. of Trinidad and Tobago (LATT), Secy. L. Marcelle, Box 1177, Port of Spain, Trinidad.

Tunisia

Tunisian Assn. of Documentalists, Libns., and Archivists (Association Tunisienne des Documentalistes, Bibliothécaires et Archivistes), Exec. Secy. Rudha Tlili, 43 rue de la Liberté, Le Bardo.

Turkey

Turkish Libns. Assn. (Türk Kütüphaneciler Derneği—TKD), Exec. Secy. Nejat Sefercioglu, Necatibey Caddesi 19/22, P.K. 175, Yenisehir, Ankara.

Uganda

Uganda Lib. Assn. (ULA), Chpn. P. Birungi; Secy. J.N. Kiyimba, Box 5894, Kampala.

Uganda Schools Lib. Assn. (USLA), Exec. Secy. J. W. Nabembezi, Box 7014, Kampala.

Union of Soviet Socialist Republics

USSR Lib. Council, Pres. N. S. Kartashov, Lenin State Lib., 3 Prospect Kalinina, 101 000 Moscow.

United Arab Republic

Egyptian Lib. and Archives Assn. (ELAA), Exec. Secy. Ahmed M. Mansour, c/o Lib. of Fine Arts, 24 El-Matbâa, Al-Ahlia, Boulaq, Cairo.

Egyptian School Lib. Assn. (ESLA), Exec. Secy. M. Alabasiri, 35 Algalaa St., Cairo.

United Kingdom

ASLIB (Association of Special Libraries and Information Bureaux), Dir. Dr. D. A. Lewis, 3 Belgrave Sq., London SW1X8PL.

Assn. of British Theological and Philosophical Libs. (ABTAPL), Hon. Secy. Mary Elliott, King's College Lib., Strand, London WC2R 2LS.

Bibliographical Society, Hon. Secy. M. M. Foot, The Rooms of the British Academy, Burlington House, Piccadilly, London W1V 0NS.

British and Irish Assn. Of Law Libns. (BIALL), Hon. Secy. D. M. Blake, Libn., Harding Law Lib., Univ. of Birmingham, Box 363, Birmingham B15 2TT.

The Lib. Assn., Exec. Secy. Keith

Lawrey, 7 Ridgmount St., London WC1E 7AE.
 Private Libs. Assn. (PLA), Exec. Secy. Frank Broomhead, Ravelston, South View Rd., Pinner, Middlesex.
 School Lib. Assn. (SLA), Chpn. Colin Pidgeon, Victoria House, 29-31 George St., Oxford OX1 2AY.
 Scottish Lib. Assn. (SLA), Hon. Secy. Robert Craig, Dept. of Libnshp., Univ. of Strathclyde, Livingstone Tower, Glasgow G1 1XH.
 Society of Archivists (SA), Exec. Secy. C. M. Short, South Yorkshire County Record Office, Cultural Activities Centre, 56 Ellin St., Sheffield S1 4PL.
 The Standing Conference of National and Univ. Libs. (SCONUL), Exec. Secy. A. J. Loveday, Secretariat and Registered Office, 102 Euston St., London NW1 2HA.
 Welsh Lib. Assn., Exec. Secy., c/o Dyfed Cultural Services, Public Lib., St. Peter's St., Carmarthen, Dyfed, South Wales.

Uruguay

 Lib. and Archive Science Assn. of Uruguay (Agrupación Bibliotecológica del Uruguay—ABU), Pres. Luis Alberto Musso, Cerro Largo 1666, Montevideo.

Venezuela

 Assn. of Venezuelan Libns. and Archivists (Colegio de Bibliotecólogos y Archivólogos de Venezuela—COL-BAV), Exec. Secy. M. Hermoso, Apdo. 6283, Caracas 101.

Wales

 See United Kingdom.

Yugoslavia

 Croatian Lib. Assn. (Hrvatsko bibliotekarsko društvo—HBD), Pres. Vera Mudri-Škunca; Exec. Secy. Nada Gomerćić, National and Univ. Lib., Marulicev trg 21, YU-41000 Zagreb.
 Lib. Assn. of Bosnia and Herzegovina (Društvo Bibliotekara Bosne i Hercegovine—DB BiH), Exec. Secy. Fahrudin Kalender, Obala 42, YU-71000 Sarajevo.
 Society of Libns. in Slovenia (Društvo Bibliotekarjev Slovenije—DBS), Exec. Secy. Ana Martelanc, Turjaška 1, YU-61000 Ljubljana.
 Union of Lib. Workers of Serbia (Savez Bibliotečkih Radnika Srbije), Exec. Secy. Branka Popović, Skerlićeva 1, YU-11000 Belgrade.
 Union of Librarians Association of Macedonia (Sojuz na društvata na bibliotekarite na SR Makedonija), Bul. "Goce Delčev" br. 6, Box 566, YU-91000 Skopje.
 Union of Libns. Assns. of Yugoslavia (Sveza Društev Bibliotekarjev Jugoslavije), Exec. Secy. Božika Zdraković, Ramiz Sadiku b b, YU-38000 Priština.

Zaire

 Zairian Assn. of Archivists, Libns., and Documentalists (Association Zairoise des Archivistes, Bibliothecaires, et Documentalistes—AZABDO), Exec. Secy. Mulamba Mukunya, Box 805, Kinshasa XI.

Zambia

 Zambia Lib. Assn. (ZLA), Box 32839, Lusaka.

Zimbabwe

 Zimbabwe Lib. Assn.—ZLA, Hon. Secy. B. L. B. Mushonga, Box 3133, Salisbury.

Directory of Book Trade and Related Organizations

BOOK TRADE ASSOCIATIONS, UNITED STATES AND CANADA

For more extensive information on the associations listed in this section, see the annual issues of the *Literary Market Place* (Bowker).

Advertising Typographers Assn. of America, Inc., 461 Eighth Ave., New York, NY 10001. 212-594-0685.

American Booksellers Assn., Inc., 122 E. 42 St., New York, NY 10168. 212-867-9060. *Pres.* Joan Ripley; *Exec. Dir.* G. Royce Smith.

American Institute of Graphic Arts, 1059 Third Ave., near 63 St., New York, NY 10021. 212-752-0813. *Pres.* David Brown; *Exec. Dir.* Caroline W Hightower.

American Medical Publishers Assn. *Pres.* G. James Gallagher, Williams & Wilkins Co., Baltimore, MD 21202. 301-528-4211; *Secy.-Treas.* Mercedes Bierman, Wiley Medical, John Wiley & Sons, Inc., 605 Third Ave., New York, NY 10158. 212-867-9800.

American Printing History Assn., Box 4922, Grand Central Sta., New York, NY 10163. *Pres. & Ed., APHA Newsletter.* Catherine T. Brody, New York City Technical College Lib., 300 Jay St., Brooklyn, NY 11201. 212-643-3802; *V.P.s* Jack Golden, Philip Grushkin, E. H. "Pat" Taylor; *Secy.* Jean Peters; *Treas.* Philip Sperling; *Ed., Printing History.* Susan Thompson. (Address correspondence to APHA, Box 4922, except Newsletter matters, which go directly to Catherine Brody.)

American Society for Information Science (ASIS), 1010 16 St. N.W., Washington, DC 20036. 202-659-3644.

American Society of Indexers, 235 Park Ave. S., 8 fl., New York, NY 10003. *Pres.* John J. Regazzi, H. W. Wilson Co., 950 University Ave., Bronx, NY 10452. 212-588-8400.

American Society of Journalists & Authors, 1501 Broadway, Suite 1907, New York, NY 10036. *Pres.* Sally Wendkos Olds; *Exec. V.P.* Dodi Schultz; *V.P.s* John H. Ingersoll, Ruth Winter; *Secy.* Evelyn Kaye; *Treas.* Richard Blodgett. 212-997-0947.

American Society of Magazine Photographers (ASMP), 205 Lexington Ave., New York, NY 10016. 212-889-9144. *Dir.* Stuart Kahan.

American Society of Picture Professionals, Inc., Box 5283, Grand Central Sta., New York, NY 10017. *Pres.* Roberta Groves, 212-682-6626; *Secy.* Alice Lundoff, 212-888-3595.

American Translators Assn., 109 Croton Ave., Ossining, NY 10562. 914-941-1500. *Pres.* Ben Teague; *Staff Administrator.* Rosemary Malia.

Antiquarian Booksellers Assn. of America, Inc., 50 Rockefeller Plaza, New York, NY 10020. 212-757-9395. *Pres.* John H. Jenkins; *V.P.* Elisabeth Woodburn;

BOOK TRADE ASSOCIATIONS, UNITED STATES AND CANADA / 609

Secy. Louis Weinstein; *Treas.* Harvey W. Brewer; *Admin. Asst.* Janice M. Farina.

Assn. of American Publishers, One Park Ave., New York, NY 10016. 212-689-8920. *Pres.* Townsend Hoopes; *V.P.s* Thomas D. McKee, Donald A. Eklund; *Dirs.* Phyllis Ball, Gregory V. Gore, Parker B. Ladd, Mary E. McNulty, Saundra L. Smith; *Washington Office.* 1707 L St. N.W., Washington, DC 20336. 202-293-2585; *V.P.* Richard P. Kleeman; *Staff Dirs.* Roy H. Millenson, Diane G. Rennert, Carol A. Risher; *Chpn.* Martin P. Levin, Times Mirror; *V. Chpn.* Alexander Burke, McGraw-Hill; *Secy.* Peter Israel, The Putnam Publishing Group; *Treas.* George Grune, Reader's Digest.

Assn. of American Univ. Presses, One Park Ave., New York, NY 10016. 212-889-6040. *Pres.* Donald R. Ellegood; *Dir.*, Univ. of Washington Press; *Exec. Dir.* Richard Koffler.

Assn. of Book Travelers, c/o *Pres.* Lou Cohen, 31 Omaha Ave., Rockaway, NJ 07866; *Treas.* Eddie Ponger, Holt, Rinehart & Winston, Inc., *Secy.* Vickie Brooks, Cerebrus Group.

Assn. of Canadian Publishers, 70 The Esplanade E., Toronto, Ont., M5E 1R2, Canada. 416-361-1408. *Pres.* Malcolm Lester; *V.P.* Ellen Godfrey; *Treas.* Harry Van Ierssel; *Exec. Dir.* Phyllis Yaffe.

Assn. of Jewish Book Publishers, House of Living Judaism, 838 Fifth Ave., New York, NY 10021. *Pres.* Sol Scharfstein, Pres., Ktav Publishing House, 75 Varick St., New York, NY 10013. 212-966-6980. (Address correspondence to the president.)

Bibliographical Society of America. *See* the preceding section, Directory of Organizations, under National Library & Information-Industry Associations, United States and Canada, for detailed information.

Book Industry Study Group, Inc., 160 Fifth Ave., New York, NY 10010. 212-929-1393. *Chpn.* DeWitt C. Baker; *V. Chpn.* Howard Willets, Jr.; *Treas.* George Q. Nichols; *Secy.* Hendrik Edelman; *Managing Agent.* SKP Associates.

Book League of New York. *Pres.* Alfred H. Lane, Columbia Univ. Lib., New York, NY 10027. 212-280-3532; *Treas.* A. C. Frasca, Jr., Freshet Press Inc., 90 Hamilton Rd., Rockville Centre, NY 11570. 506-766-3011.

Book Manufacturers Institute, 111 Prospect St., Stamford, CT 06901. 203-324-9670. *Pres.* Robert R. Hackford, Maple Vail Book Manufacturing Group, 187 Clinton St., Binghamton, NY 13902; *Exec. V.P.* Douglas E. Horner.

Book Publicists of Southern California, Suite 503, 6430 Sunset Blvd., Hollywood, CA 90028. 213-461-3921. *Pres.* Irwin Zucker; *V.P.* Sol Marshall; *Secy.* Ginny Benson; *Treas.* Steven Jay Rubin.

Book Week Headquarters. Children's Book Council, Inc., 67 Irving Place, New York, NY 10003. 212-254-2666. *Exec. Dir.* John Donovan; *Chpn. 1982.* Margaret Frith, G. P. Putnam's Sons, 200 Madison Ave., New York, NY 10016. 212-576-8900.

The Bookbinders' Guild of New York, c/o *Secy.* Thomas Snyder, Dikeman Laminating, 181 Sargeant Ave., Clifton, NJ 07013. 201-473-5696; *Pres.* Alice Sanchez Claypool, The Book Press, 757 Third Ave., New York, NY 10017; *V.P.* Sam Green, Murray Printing Co., 60 E. 42 St., New York, NY 10165; *Treas.* Gene Sanchez, William Morrow & Co., 105 Madison Ave., New York, NY 10016; *Asst. Secy.* Joel Moss, A. Horowitz & Son, Box 1308, 300 Fairfield Ave., Fairfield, NJ 07006.

Bookbuilders of Boston, Inc., c/o *Pres.* Richard N. Darcy, Arcata Book Group, 275 Hancock St., North Quincy, MA 02171. 617-328-3700; *1st V.P.* Richard O. Sales, Houghton Mifflin Co., One Beacon St., Boston, MA 02107. 617-725-5580.

Bookbuilders of Southern California, 5225 Wilshire Blvd., Suite 316, Los Angeles, CA 90036. *Pres.* Larry J. Cooke, Arcata Book Group, 7120 Hayvenhurst, Van Nuys, CA 91406; *V.P.* Nancy Sjoberg, The Del Mar Associates, 1228½ Camino Del Mar, Del Mar, CA 92014; *Secy.* Judi Tigchelaar, Arcata Book Group, 7120 Hayvenhurst, Van Nuys, CA 91406.

Bookbuilders West, 170 Ninth St., San Francisco, CA 94103. *Pres.* Bill Cartwright, Arcata Book Group, 985 University Ave., Los Gatos, CA 95030. 408-395-6131; *V.P.* Sharon Hawkes, Annual Reviews, Inc., 4139 El Camino Way, Palo Alto, CA 94306. 415-493-4400; *Secy.* Laura Argento, W. H. Freeman & Company, 660 Market St., San Francisco, CA 94104. 415-391-5870; *Treas.* Bill Ketron, Arcata Book Group, 985 University Ave., Los Gatos, CA 95030. 408-395-6131.

Canadian Book Publishers' Council, 45 Charles St. E., Suite 701, Toronto, Ont., M4Y 1S2, Canada. 416-964-7231. *Pres.* Rachel Mansfield, McGraw-Hill Ryerson Ltd., *2nd V.P.* Geoffrey Dean, John Wiley & Sons Canada Ltd.; *Exec. Dir.* Jacqueline Hushion; *Member Organizations.* The School Group, The College Group, The Trade Group, The Paperback Group.

Canadian Booksellers Assn., 49 Laing St., Toronto, Ont. M4L 2N4, Canada. *Exec. Dir.* Bernard E. Rath; *Convention Mgr.* Irene Read.

Chicago Book Clinic, 410 S. Michigan Ave., Suite 433, Chicago, IL 60605. 312-663-9860. *Pres.* Stuart J. Murphy, Ligature Publishing Services, Inc.; *Exec. V.P.* Trudi Jenny, Follett Publishing Co.; *Treas.* Richard G. Young, Synthegraphics Corp.

Chicago Publishers Assn., c/o *Pres.* Robert J. R. Follett, Follett Publishing Co., 1010 W. Washington Blvd., Chicago, IL 60607. 312-666-4300.

The Children's Book Council, 67 Irving Pl., New York, NY 10003. 212-254-2666. *Exec. Dir.* John Donovan; *Assoc. Dir.* Paula Quint; *Asst. Dirs.* Christine Stawicki, Peter Dews; *Pres.* Phyllis Fogelman, V.P. & Ed.-in-Chief, Books for Young Readers, The Dial Press, 245 E. 47 St., New York, NY 10017. 212-832-7300.

Christian Booksellers Assn., Box 200, 2620 Venetucci Blvd., Colorado Springs, CO 80901. 303-576-7880. *Exec. V.P.* John T. Bass.

Connecticut Book Publishers Assn., c/o *Pres.* Alex M. Yudkin, Associated Booksellers, 147 McKinley Ave., Bridgeport, CT 06606; *V.P.* Richard Dunn; *Treas.* John Atkin.

The Copyright Society of the U.S.A., New York Univ. School of Law, 40 Washington Sq. S., New York, NY 10012. 212-598-2280/2210. *Pres.* Stanley Rothenberg; *Secy.* Jerold Couture; *Exec. Dir.* Alan Latman; *Asst.* Kate McKay.

Council on Interracial Books for Children, Inc., 1841 Broadway, New York, NY 10023. 212-757-5339. *Dir.* Bradford Chambers; *Pres.* Beryle Banfield; *V.P.s* Albert V. Schwartz, Frieda Zames, Irma Garcia, Marylou Byler; *Managing Ed., Interracial Books for Children Bulletin.* Ruth Charnes; *Book Review Coord.* Lyla Hoffman; *Dir., CIBC Racism & Sexism Resource Center for Educators.* Robert B. Moore; *Secy.* Elsa Velasquez.

Edition Bookbinders of New York, Inc., Box 124, Fort Lee, NJ 07024. 201-947-7289. *Pres.* Martin Blumberg, American Book-Stratford Press; *Exec. Secy.* Morton Windman; *Treas.* Sam Goldman, Publishers Book Bindery; *V.P.* Robert G. Luburg, Tapley-Rutter Co.

Educational Paperback Assn., c/o *Pres.* John Michel, Florida Educational Paperbacks, 5405 Boran Place, Tampa, FL 33610.

Evangelical Christian Publishers Assn., Box 1568, West Chester, PA 19380. *Exec. Dir.* C. E. (Ted) Andrew.

Fourth Avenue Booksellers, *Perm. Secy.* Stanley Gilman, Box 456, New York, NY 10276.

Graphic Artists Guild, 30 E. 20 St., Rm. 405, New York, NY 10003. 212-777-7353. *Pres.* Diane Dillon.

Guild of Book Workers, 663 Fifth Ave., New York, NY 10022. 212-757-6454. *Pres.* Caroline F. Schimmel.

Information Industry Assn. *See* "National Library and Information-Industry Associations" earlier in Part 7—*Ed.*

International Assn. of Book Publishing Consultants, c/o Joseph Marks, 485 Fifth Ave., New York, NY 10017. 212-867-6341.

International Assn. of Printing House Craftsmen, Inc., 7599 Kenwood Rd., Cincinnati, OH 45236. 513-891-0611. *Pres.* Richard L. Elke; *Exec. V.P.* John A. Davies.

International Copyright Information Center (INCINC), Assn. of American Publishers, 1707 L St. N.W., Suite 480, Washington, DC 20036. 202-293-2585. *Dir.* Carol A. Risher.

International Standard Book Numbering Agency (ISBN) and Standard Address Number Agency (SAN), 1180 Ave. of the Americas, New York, NY 10036. 212-764-3384. *Exec. Dir.* Emery I. Koltay; *Officers.* Beatrice Jacobson, Leigh C. Yuster, Gary Ink, Frank Zirpolo.

JWB Jewish Book Council, 15 E. 26 St., New York, NY 10010. 212-532-4949. *Pres.* Robert Gordis.

Library Binding Institute, 50 Congress St., Suite 633, Boston, MA 02109. 617-227-7450. *Exec. Dir.* Dudley A. Weiss; *Public Relations Dir.* Beverly Adamonis.

Magazine & Paperback Marketing Institute (MPMI), 344 Main St., Suite 205, Mt. Kisco, NY 10549. 914-666-6788. *Exec. V.P.* Woodford Bankson, Jr.

Metropolitan Lithographers Assn., 123 E. 62 St., New York, NY 10021. 212-759-0966. *Pres.* Ralph Mazzocco; *Exec. Dir.* Albert N. Greco.

Midwest Book Travelers Assn., c/o *Pres.* Paul Dimmitt, Wybel Assocs.; *V.P.* Ted Heinecken, Heinecken Assocs.; *Secy.* Peter Muehr, Grosset & Dunlap; *Treas.* Robert Rainer, Rainer Assocs.; *Bd. of Dirs.* Robert Gurney, Harper & Row; Wm. S. Holland, Hayden Book Co.; John Strohmayer, Holt, Rinehart & Winston.

Minnesota Book Publishers Roundtable, c/o *Pres.* Susan Stan, Lerner Publications Co., 241 First Ave. N., Minneapolis, MN 55401; *V.P.* Norton Stillman, Nodin Press, Inc., 519 N. Third St., Minneapolis, MN 55401; *Secy.-Treas.* Beverly Kaemmer, Univ. of Minnesota Press, 2037 University Ave. S.E., Minneapolis, MN 55455.

National Assn. of College Stores, 528 E. Lorain St., Oberlin, OH 44074. 216-775-7777. *Pres.* John Marcus, Matthews Medical Bookstores, 11559 Rock Island Court, Maryland Heights, MO 63043; *Exec. Dir.* Garis Distelhorst.

National Council of Churches of Christ in the U.S.A., Div. of Education and Ministry, 475 Riverside Dr., New York, NY 10115. 212-870-2271/2272.

National Micrographics Assn. For detailed information, *see* National Library and Information-Industry Associations, United States and Canada, earlier in Part 7—*Ed.*

New England Small Press Assn. (NESPA), 45 Hillcrest Place, Amherst, MA 01002. *Dirs.* William R. Darling, Diana Kruchkow.

New Mexico Book League, 8632 Horacio Pl. N.E., Albuquerque, NM 87111. 505-299-8940. *Exec. Dir.* Dwight A. Myers; *Pres.* Ruth Wuori; *V.P.* Drew Harrington; *Treas.* Frank N. Skinner; *Ed.* Carol A. Myers.

New York Rights & Permissions Group, c/o *Chpn.* Dorothy McKittrick Harris, Reader's Digest General Books, 750 Third Ave., New York, NY 10017. 212-972-3762.

New York State Small Press Assn., c/o The Promise of Learnings, Inc., Box 1264, Radio City Sta., New York, NY 10019. 212-586-4235. *Exec. Dir.* Janey Tannenbaum; *Gen. Mgr.* Jim Mele.

Northern California Booksellers Assn., c/o *Pres.* Andy Ross, Cody's Books, Berkeley, CA.

Periodical & Book Assn. of America, Inc., 888 Seventh Ave., New York, NY 10019. 212-307-6182.

Periodical Distributors of Canada. *Pres.* Gerald Benjamin, 425 Guy St., Montreal, P.Q. H3J 1T1, Canada. 514-931-4221; *Secy.* Jim Neill, 120 Sinnott Rd., Scarborough, Ont., Canada. 416-752-8720.

Philadelphia Book Clinic, *Secy.-Treas.* Thomas Colaiezzi, Lea & Febiger, 600 Washington Sq., Philadelphia, PA 19106. 215-925-8700.

Pi Beta Alpha (formerly Professional Bookmen of America, Inc.), 1215 Farwell Dr., Madison, WI 53704. *Pres.* Clyde W. Cooper, Sr.; *Exec. Sec.* Charles L. Schmalbach.

Printing Industries of Metropolitan New York, Inc., 461 Eighth Ave., New York, NY 10001. 212-279-2100. *Pres.* James J. Conner III; *Dir., Communications.* Howard A. McMurchie; *Dir., Government Affairs.* Stuart L. Lituin; *Dir., Industry Activities.* Gary L. Miller.

Proofreaders Club of New York, c/o *Pres.* Allan Treshan, 38-15 149 St., Flushing, NY 11354. 212-461-8509.

Publishers' Ad Club, c/o *Secy.* Caroline Barnett, Denhard and Stewart, 122 E. 42 St., New York, NY 10017. 212-986-1900; *Pres.* Peter Minichiello, Pocket Books, 1230 Ave. of the Americas, New York, NY 10020. 212-246-2121; *V.P.* Susan Ball, William Morrow & Co., 105 Madison Ave., New York, NY 10016. 212-889-3050; *Treas.* Polly Scarvalone, The New York Review of Books, 250 W. 57 St., New York, NY 10019. 212-757-8070.

Publishers' Alliance, c/o Thomas Horton & Daughters, 2662 S. Newtown Dr., Sun Lakes, AZ 85224.

Publishers' Library Marketing Group, *Pres.* Marjorie Naughton, Clarion Books, 52 Vanderbilt Ave., New York, NY 10017. 212-972-1192; *V.P.* Mark McCrackin, Bantam Books, 666 Fifth Ave., NY 10103. 212-765-6500, ext. 356; *Treas.* Sherri Zolt, Dell Publishing Co., 245 E. 47 St., New York, NY 10017. 212-832-7300, ext. 406.

Publishers' Publicity Assn., c/o *Pres.* Diane Glynn, Berkeley Books, 200 Madison Ave., New York, NY 10016. 212-686-9820; *V.P.* Jill Danzig, Pantheon Books, 201 E. 50 St., New York, NY 10022. 212-751-2600; *Secy.* Seldon Sutton, Little, Brown & Co.; *Treas.* Julia Knickerbocker, Simon & Schuster, 1230 Ave. of the Americas, New York, NY 10020. 212-245-6400.

The Religion Publishing Group, c/o Marilyn M. Jensen, Guideposts, 747 Third Ave., New York, NY 10017. 212-754-2227; *Pres.* Eve F. Roshevsky, Doubleday & Co., 245 Park Ave., New York, NY 10017; *Secy.-Treas.* Marilyn M. Jensen.

Research & Engineering Council of the Graphic Arts Industry, Inc., 4351 Garden City Dr., Suite 560, Landover, MD 20785. 301-577-5400. *Pres.* Gilbert Bachman; *1st V.P.-Secy.*, Donald H. Laux; *2nd V.P.-Treas.*, George Kaplan; *Managing Dir.*, Harold A. Molz.

Société de Développement du Livre et du Périodique, 1151 r. Alexandre-DeSève, Montreal, P.Q. H2L 2T7, Canada. 514-524-7528. *Pres.* Claude Trudel; *Directeur General.* Thomas Déri; Association des Editeurs Canadiens, *Pres.* M. René Bonenfant; Association des Libraries du

Québec, *Pres.* Raymond Beaudoin; Société Canadienne Française de Protection du Droit d'Auteur, *Pres.* Pierre Tisseyre; Société des Editeurs de Manuels Scolaires du Québec, *Pres.* Pierre Tisseyre.

Society of Authors' Representatives, Inc., Box 650, Old Chelsea Sta., New York, NY 10113. 212-548-6333. *Pres.* Peter Shepherd; *Exec. Secy.* Susal Bell.

Society of Photographer & Artist Representatives, Inc. (SPAR), Box 845, New York, NY 10022. 212-628-9148. *Pres.* Fran Milsop.

Society of Photographers in Communication. See American Society of Magazine Photographers (ASMP).

Southern California Booksellers Assn., c/o *Pres.* Kim Browning, c/o Dodd's Bookstore, 4818 E. Second St., Long Beach, CA 90803. 213-438-9948; *V.P.* Position vacant; *Secy.* Betty Gaskill, Publisher's Rep., 18560 Van Owen St., Reseda, CA 91335. 213-996-4038; *Treas.* Fran Chaplin, United Book Service, 1235 S. Hipoint St., Los Angeles, CA 90035. 213-276-1904.

Standard Address Number (SAN) Agency. See International Standard Book Numbering Agency.

Technical Assn. of the Pulp & Paper Industry (TAPPI), One Dunwoody Pk., Atlanta, GA 30338. 404-394-6130. *Pres.* Sherwood G. Holt; *V.P.* Terry O. Norris; *Exec. Dir.* Philip E. Nethercut; *Treas.* W. L. Cullison.

West Coast Bookmen's Assn., 27 McNear Dr., San Rafael, CA 94901. *Pres.* Paul Sapak; *Secy.* Frank G. Goodall.

Western Book Publishers Assn., Box 4242, San Francisco, CA 94101.

Women's National Book Assn., c/o *National Pres.* Mary Glen Hearne, Dir., The Nashville Room, Public Lib. of Nashville and Davidson County, Eighth Ave. N. and Union, Nashville, TN 37203. 615-244-4700, ext. 68 (office); *V.P./Pres.-Elect.* Sylvia Cross, 19824 Septo St., Chatsworth, CA 91311. 213-886-8448 (home); *Secy.* Cathy Rentschler, H. W. Wilson Co., 950 University Ave., Bronx, NY 10452. 212-588-8400, ext. 257 (office); *Treas.* Patricia A. Hodge, RSM, Lib. Dir., Trinity College, Colchester Ave., Burlington, VT 05401. 802-864-0337, ext. 343 (office); *Asst. Treas.* Sandra J. Souza, 1606 Stafford Dr., Fall River, MA 02721. 617-678-4179; *Past Pres. and Panel Chair.* Ann Heidbreder Eastman, College of Arts and Science, Virginia Polytechnic Institute and State Univ., Blacksburg, VA 24061. 703-961-6390 (office). NATIONAL COMMITTEE CHAIRS: *Dir., Public Affairs.* Cosette Kies, Dept. of Lib. Science, George Peabody College of Vanderbilt Univ., Nashville, TN 37203. 615-322-8050 (office); *Asst. Secy.* Joan Cunliffe, TABA/AAP, One Park Ave., New York, NY 10016. 212-689-8920; *Ed., The Bookwoman.* Jean K. Crawford, Abington Press, 201 Eighth Ave. S., Nashville, TN 37202. 615-749-6422 (office); *Review Ed., The Bookwoman.* Mary V. Gaver, 300 Virginia Ave., Danville, VA 24541. 804-799-6746; *Membership Chpn.* Anne J. Richter, 55 N. Mountain Ave., A-2, Montclair, NJ 07042. 201-746-5166 (office). November–May; 140 Seaman Ave., Opa-Locka, FL 33054. 305-681-3281; *UN/NGO Rep.* Clare Friedland, 36 E. 36 St., New York, NY 10016. 212-685-6205; *Finance Chpn.* Sandra K. Paul, SKP Associates, 160 Fifth Ave., New York, NY 10010. 212-675-7804 (office). CHAPTER PRESIDENTS: *Binghamton.* L. Jeanette Clarke Lee, 8 Pine St., Binghamton, NY 13901. 607-723-6626; *Boston.* Gaylyn Fullington, 225 Mass. Ave., Apt. 914, Boston, MA 02115. 617-247-2823; *Cleveland.* Billie Joy Reinhart, 2856 Fairfax, Cleveland Heights, OH 44118. 216-371-0459; *Detroit.* Olga Pobutsky, 16815 Parkside, Detroit, MI 48221. 313-683-1389; *Los Angeles.* Doris Dosser, 7009 Enfield Ave., Reseda, CA 91335. 213-345-8962; *Nashville.* Cosette

Kies, 2116 Hobbs Rd., C-1, Nashville, TN 37215. 615-297-7995; *New York.* Barbara J. Meredith, Dir., Center for Publishing, New York Univ., 2 University Place, New York, NY 10003. 212-598-2371; *San Francisco.* Adele Horwitz, Presidio Press, 31 Pamaron Way, Novato, CA 94947. 415-883-1373; *Washington, DC/Baltimore, MD.* Kevin Maricle, Office of the General Counsel, U.S. Copyright Office, Lib. of Congress, Washington, DC 20559. 202-287-8380.

INTERNATIONAL AND FOREIGN BOOK TRADE ASSOCIATIONS

For Canadian book trade associations, see the preceding section on Book Trade Associations, United States and Canada. For a more extensive list of book trade organizations outside the United States and Canada, with more detailed information, consult *International Literary Market Place* (R. R. Bowker). An annual publication, it also provides extensive lists of major bookstores and publishers in each country.

INTERNATIONAL

Antiquarian Booksellers Assn. (International), 154 Buckingham Palace Rd., London SW1W 9TZ, England.

International Booksellers Federation (IBF), Grunangergasse 4, A-1010 Vienna 1, Austria. *Secy.-Gen.* Gerhard Prosser.

International League of Antiquarian Booksellers, c/o *Pres.* Bob de Graaf, Zuideinde 40, NL-2479 Nieuwkoop, Netherlands.

International Publishers Assn., 3 av. de Miremont, CH-1206 Geneva, Switzerland. *Secy.-Gen.* J. Alexis Koutchoumow.

NATIONAL

Argentina

Cámara Argentina de Editores de Libros (Council of Argentine Book Publishers), Talcahuano 374, p. 3, Of. 7, Buenos Aires 1013.

Cámara Argentina de Publicaciones (Argentine Publications Assn.), Reconquista 1011, p. 6, 1003 Buenos Aires. *Pres.* Manuel Rodriguez.

Cámara Argentina del Libro (Argentine Book Assn.), Av. Belgrano 1580, p. 6, 1093 Buenos Aires. *Pres.* Jaime Rodriguez.

Federación Argentina de Librerías, Papelerías y Actividades Afines (Federation of Bookstores, Stationers and Related Activities), Balcarce 179/83, Rosario, Santa Fe. *Pres.* Isaac Kostzer.

Australia

Assn. of Australian Univ. Presses, c/o Univ. of Queensland Press, Box 42, St. Lucia, Qld. 4068. *Pres.* Frank W. Thompson.

Australian Book Publishers Assn., 161 Clarence St., Sydney, N.S.W. 2000.

Australian Booksellers Assn., Box 3254, Sydney, N.S.W. 2001.

Austria

Hauptverband der graphischen Unternehmungen Österreichs (Austrian Graphical Assn.), Grünangergasse 4, A-1010 Vienna 1.

Hauptverband des österreichischen Buchhandels (Austrian Publishers and

Booksellers Assn.), Grünangergasse 4, A-1010 Vienna. *Secy.* Gerhard Prosser.

Osterreichischer Verlegerverband (Assn. of Austrian Publishers), Grünangergasse 4, A-1010 Vienna. *Secy.* Gerhard Prosser.

Verband der Antiquare Österreichs (Austrian Antiquarian Booksellers Assn.), Grünangergasse 4, A-1010 Vienna. *Secy.* Gerhard Prosser.

Belgium

Cercle Belge de la Librairie (Belgian Booksellers Assn.), r. du Luxembourg 5, bte. 1, B-1040 Brussels.

Fédération des Editeurs Belges (Belgian Publishers Assn.), 111 av. du Parc, B-1060 Brussels. *Dir.* J. De Raeymaeker.

Syndicat Belge de la Librairie Ancienne et Moderne (Belgian Assn. of Antiquarian and Modern Booksellers), r. du Chêne 21, B-1000 Brussels.

Vereniging ter Bevordering van het Vlaamse Boekwezen (Assn. for the Promotion of Flemish Books), Frankrijklei 93, B-2000 Antwerp. *Secy.* A. Wouters. Member organizations: Algemene Vlaamse Boekverkopersbond; Uitgeversbond-Vereniging van Uitgevers van Nederlandstalige Boeken at the same address; and Bond-Alleenverkopers van Nederlandstalige Boeken (book importers), De Smethlaan 4, B-1980 Tervuren. *Secy.* J. van den Berg.

Bolivia

Cámara Boliviana del Libro (Bolivian Booksellers Assn.), Box 682, La Paz. *Pres. Lic.* Javier Gisbert.

Brazil

Associação Brasileira de Livreiros Antiquarios (Brazilian Assn. of Antiquarian Booksellers), Rua do Rosario 135–137, Rio de Janeiro.

Associação Brasileira do Livro (Brazilian Booksellers Assn.), Av. 13 de Maio 23, andar 16, Rio de Janeiro. *Dir.* Alberjano Torres.

Cámara Brasileira do Livro (Brazilian Book Assn.), Av. Ipiranga 1267, andar 10, São Paulo. *Secy.* Jose Gorayeb.

Sindicato Nacional dos Editores de Livros (Brazilian Book Publishers Assn.), Av. Rio Branco 37, andar 15, Salas 1503/6 e 1510/12, 20097 Rio de Janeiro. *Exec. Secy.* Maria Helena Geordane.

Bulgaria

Drzavno Obedinenie Bulgarska Kniga (State Bulgarian Book Assn.), pl. Slavejkov 11, Sofia.

Soyuz Knigoizdatelite i Knizharite (Union of Publishers and Booksellers), vu Solum 4, Sofia.

Burma

Burmese Publishers Union, 146 Bogyoke Market, Rangoon.

Chile

Cámara Chilena del Libro, Av. Bulnes 188, Casilla 2787, Santiago. *Secy.* A. Newman.

Colombia

Cámara Colombiana de la Industria Editorial (Colombian Publishers Council), Cr. 7a, No. 17–51, Of. 409–410, Apdo. áereo 8998, Bogotá. *Exec. Secy.* Hipólito Hincapié.

Czechoslovakia

Ministerstvo Kultury CSR, Odbor Knižni Kultury (Ministry of Culture CSR, Dept. for Publishing and Book Trade), Staré Mésto, námesti Perštyně 1, 117 65 Prague 1.

Denmark

Danske Antikvarboghandlerforening (Danish Antiquarian Booksellers Assn.), Silkegade 11, DK-1113 Copenhagen.

Danske Boghandlerforening (Danish Booksellers Assn.) Boghandlernes Hus, Siljangade 6, DK-2300 Copenhagen S. *Secy.* Elisabeth Brodersen.

Danske Forlaeggerforening (Danish Publishers Assn.), Købmagergade 11, DK-1150 Copenhagen K. *Dir.* Erik V. Krustrup.

Ecuador

Sociedad de Libreros del Ecuador (Booksellers Society of Ecuador), C. Bolivar 268 y Venezuela, Of. 501, p. 5, Quito. *Secy.* Eduardo Ruiz G.

Finland

Kirja-ja Paperikauppojen Liittory (Finnish Booksellers and Stationers Assn.), Pieni Roobertinkatu 13 B 26, SF-00130 Helsinki 13. *Secy.* Pentti Kuopio.

Suomen Antikvariaattiyhdistys Finska Antikvariatforeningen (Finnish Antiquarian Booksellers Assn.), P. Makasiininkatu 6, Helsinki 13.

Suomen Kustannusyhdistys (Publishers Assn. of Finland), Merimiehenkatu 12 A6, SF-00150, Helsinki 15. *Secy.-Gen.* Unto Lappi.

France

Cercle de la Librairie (Booksellers Circle), 117 bd. St.-Germain, F-75279 Paris, Cedex 06.

Fédération française des Syndicats de Libraires (French Booksellers Assn.), 259 r. St.-Honoré, F-75001 Paris.

Office de Promotion de l'Edition Française (Promotion Office of French Publishing), 117 bd. St.-Germain, F-75279 Paris, Cedex 06. *Managing Dir.* Gustave Girardot; *Secy.-Gen.* Marc Franconie; *Asst. Dir.* Pierre-Dominique Parent.

Syndicat du Livre Ancien et des Métiers annexes (Assn. of Antiquarian Books), 117 bd. St.-Germain, F-75006, Paris. *Pres.* Pierre Berès.

Syndicat National de l'Edition (French Publishers Assn.), 117 bd. St.-Germain, F-75279 Paris, Cedex 06. *Secy.* Pierre Fredet.

Syndicat National des Importateurs et Exportateurs de Livres (National French Assn. of Book Importers and Exporters), 117 bd. St.-Germain, F-75279 Paris, Cedex 06.

Germany (Democratic Republic of)

Börsenverein der Deutschen Buchhandler zu Leipzig (Assn. of GDR Publishers and Booksellers in Leipzig), Gerichtsweg 26, 7010 Leipzig.

Germany (Federal Republic of)

Börsenverein des deutschen Buchhandels (German Publishers and Booksellers Assn.), Grosser Hirschgraben 17–21, Box 2404, D-6000 Frankfurt am Main 1. *Secy.* Hans-Karl von Kupsch.

Bundeverband der Deutschen Versandbuchhändler e.V. (National Federation of German Mail-Order Booksellers), An der Ringkirche 6, D-6200 Wiesbaden.

Landesverband der Buchhändler und Verleger in Niedersachsen e.V. (Provincial Federation of Booksellers and Publishers in Lower Saxony), Hausmannstr. 2, D-3000 Hannover 1. *Managing Dir.* Wolfgang Grimpe.

Verband Bayerischer Verlage und Buchhandlungen e.V. (Bavarian Publishers & Booksellers Federation), Thierschstr. 17, D-8000 Munich 22. *Secy.* F. Nosske.

Verband deutscher Antiquare e.V. (German Antiquarian Booksellers Assn.), Zum Talblick 2, D-6246 Glashütten im Taunus.

Verband deutscher Bühnenverleger e.V. (Federation of German Theatrical Publishers), Bismarckstr. 17, D-1000 Berlin 12.

Verband Deutscher Buch-, Zeitungs- und Zeitschriften-Grossisten e.V. (Federation of German Wholesalers of Books, Newspapers and Periodicals), Classen-Kappelmann-Str. 24, D-5000 Cologne 41.

Vereinigung Evangelischer Buchhändler (Assn. of Protestant Booksellers), Lehenstr. 31, D-7000 Stuttgart 1.

Ghana

Ghana Booksellers Assn., Box 7869, Accra.

Great Britain

See United Kingdom.

Greece

Syllogos Ekdoton kai Vivliopolon Athinon (Assn. of Publishers and Booksellers Assns. of Athens), Themistocleus 54 Str., Athens 145.

Syllogos Ekdoton Vivliopolon (Greek Publishers Assn.), 22-24 Har. Trikoupi St., Athens.

Hong Kong

Hong Kong Booksellers & Stationers Assn., Man Wah House, Kowloon.

Hungary

Magyar Könyvkiadók és Könyvterjesztök Egyesülése (Hungarian Publishers and Booksellers Assn.), Vörösmarty tér 1,1051 Budapest, *Pres.* György Bernát.

Iceland

Iceland Publishers Assn., Laufasvegi 12, 101 Reykjavik. *Pres.* Oliver Steinn Jóhannesson, Strandgötu 31, 220 Hafnarfjördur. *Gen. Mgr.* Björn Gíslason.

India

All-India Booksellers and Publishers Assn., 17L Connaught Pl., New Delhi 1. *Pres.* Mohan Lal Choudary.

All-India Hindi Publishers Assns., 3625 Subhash Marg, 110 002 New Delhi.

Bombay Booksellers & Publishers Assn., c/o Bhadkamkar Marg, Navjivan Cooperative Housing Society, Bldg. 3, 6th fl., Office 25, Bombay 400 008.

Booksellers & Publishers Assn. of South India, c/o Higginbothams, Ltd., 814, Anna Salai, Mount Rd., Madras 600 002.

Delhi State Booksellers & Publishers Assn., c/o The Students' Stores, Box 1511, 100 006 Delhi. *Pres.* Devendra Sharma.

Federation of Indian Publishers, 18/I-C Institutional Area, New Delhi 110 067. *Pres.* Narendrakumar; *Exec. Secy.* R. K. Dhingra.

Indian Assn. of Univ. Presses, Calcutta Univ. Press, Calcutta. *Secy.* Salil Kumar Chakrabarti.

Indonesia

Ikatan Penerbit Indonesia (IKAPI) (Assn. of Indonesian Book Publishers), Jalan Salemba Tengah 38, Jakarta Pusat. *Pres.* Rachmat M. A. S.

Ireland (Republic of)

CLE/Irish Book Publishers Assn., 55 Dame St., Dublin 2. *Secy.* Hilary Kennedy.

Israel

Book & Printing Center of the Israel Export Institute, Box 29732, 29 Hamered St., 68 125 Tel Aviv. *Dir.* Baruch Schaefer.

Book Publishers Assn. of Israel, Box 20123, 29 Carlebach St., Tel Aviv. *Pres.* Mordechai Bernstein; *Exec. Dir.* Benjamin Sella; *International Promotion and Literary Rights Dept. Dir.* Lorna Soifer.

Italy

Associazione Italiana degli Editori di Musica (Italian Assn. of Music Publishers) Piazza del Liberty 2, I-20121 Milan.

Associazione Italiana Editori (Italian Publishers Assn.), Via delle Erbe 2, I-20121 Milan. *Secy.* Archille Ormezzano.

Associazione Librai Antiquari d'Italia (Antiquarian Booksellers Assn. of Italy), Via Jacopo Nardi 6, I-50132 Florence. *Pres.* Renzo Rizzi.

Associazione Librai Italiani (Italian Booksellers Assn.), Piazza G. G. Belli 2, I-00153 Rome.

Jamaica

Booksellers Assn. of Jamaica, c/o Sangster's Book Stores, Ltd., Box 366, 97 Harbour St., Kingston.

Japan

Antiquarian Booksellers Assn. of Japan, 29 San-ei-cho, Shinjuku-ku, Tokyo 160.

Books-on-Japan-in-English Club, Shin-

nichibo Bldg., 2-1 Sarugaku-cho 1-chome, Chiyoda-ku, Tokyo 101.
Japan Book Imports Assn., Rm. 302, Aizawa Bldg., 20-3 Nihonbashi, 1-chome, Chuoku, Tokyo 103. *Secy.* Mitsuo Shibata.
Japan Book Publishers Assn., 6 Fukuromachi, Shinjuku-ku, Tokyo 162. *Secy.* S. Sasaki.
Japan Booksellers Federation, 1-2 Surugadai, Kanda, Chiyoda-ku, Tokyo 101.
Textbook Publishers Assn. of Japan (Kyokasho Kyokai), 20-2 Honshiocho Shinjuku-ku, Tokyo 160. *Secy.* Masae Kusaka.

Kenya

Kenya Publishers Assn., Box 14681, Nairobi.

Korea (Republic of)

Korean Publishers Assn., 105-2 Sagandong, Chongno-ku, Seoul 110. *Pres.* Young-bin Min; *V.P.s* In-kyu Lim; Daesoo Pyo; *Secy.* Kyung-hoon Lee.

Luxembourg

Confédération du Commerce Luxembourgeois-Groupement Papetiers-Libraires (Confederation of Retailers, Group for Stationers and Booksellers), 23, Centre Allée-Scheffer, Luxembourg. *Pres.* Pierre Ernster; *Secy.* Fernand Kass.

Malaysia

Malaysian Book Publishers Assn., Box 335, Kuala Lumpur 01-02. *Hon. Secy.* J. B. Ho.

Mexico

Instituto Mexicano del Libro A.C. (Mexican Book Institute), Paseo de la Reforma 95, Dept. 1024, México 4 D.F. *Secy.-Gen.* Isabel Ruiz González.

Morocco

Association des Libraires du Maroc (Assn. of Booksellers of Morocco), 67 r. de Foucauld, Casablanca.

Netherlands

Koninklijke Nederlandse Uitgeversbond (Royal Dutch Publishers Assn.), Nieuwe Zijds Voorburgwal 44, 1012 SB Amsterdam. *Secy.* R. M. Vrij; *Managing Dir.* A. Th. Hulskamp.
Nederlandsche Vereeniging van Antiquaren (Antiquarian Booksellers Assn. of the Netherlands), Nieuwe Spiegelstra. 40, 1017-DG Amsterdam. *Pres.* A. Gerits.
Nederlandse Boekverkopersbond (Booksellers Assn. of the Netherlands), Waalsdorperweg 119, 2597-HS The Hague. *Chpn.* H. J. M. Nelissen.
Vereeniging ter bevordering van de belangen des Boekhandels (Dutch Book Trade Assn.), Lassusstraat 9, Box 5475, 1007 AL Amsterdam. *Secy.* M. van Vollenhoven-Nagel.

New Zealand

Book Publishers Assn. of New Zealand, Box 78071, Grey Lynn, Auckland 2. *Pres.* D. J. Heap; *Dir.* Gerard Reid.
Booksellers Assn. of New Zealand, Inc., Box 11-377, Wellington. *Dir.* Kate Fortune.

Nigeria

Nigerian Publishers Assn., c/o P.M.B. 5164, Ibadan.

Norway

Norsk Antikvarbokhandlerforening (Norwegian Antiquarian Booksellers Assn.), Ullevalsveien 1, Oslo 1.
Norske Bokhandlerforening (Norwegian Booksellers Assn.), Øvre Vollgate 15, Oslo 1.
Norsk Bokhandler-Medhjelper-Forening (Norwegian Book Trade Employees Assn.), Øvre Volgate 15, Oslo 1.
Norske Forleggerforening (Norwegian Publishers Assn.), Øvre Vollgate 15, Oslo 1. *Dir.* Tor Solumsmoen.
Norsk Musikkforleggerforening (Norwegian Music Publishers Assn.), Box 1499 Vika, Oslo 1.

Pakistan

Pakistan Publishers and Booksellers Assn., YMCA Bldg., Shahra-e-Quaid-e-Azam, Lahore.

Paraguay

Cámara Paraguaya del Libro (Paraguayan Publishers Assn.), Libreria Internacional S.A., Estrella 721, Asunción.

Peru

Cámara Peruana del Libro (Peruvian Publishers Assn.), Apdo. 10253, Lima 100. *Pres.* Andrés Carbone O.

Philippines

Philippine Book Dealers Assn., c/o Philippine Education Co., Quezon Ave. & Banawe, Metro Manila. *Pres.* Jose C. Benedicto.

Philippine Educational Publishers Assn., 927 Quezon Ave., Quezon City 3008, Metro Manila. *Pres.* Jesus Ernesto R. Sibal.

Poland

Polskie Towarzystwo Wydawców Ksiażek (Polish Publishers Assn.), ul. Mazowiecka 2/4, 00-048 Warsaw.

Stowarzyszenie Ksiegarzy Polskich Zarząd Główny (Assn. of Polish Booksellers), ul. Mokotowska 4/6, 00-641 Warsaw. *Pres.* Tadeusz Hussak.

Portugal

Associação Portuguesa dos Editores e Livreiros (Portuguese Assn. of Publishers and Booksellers), Largo de Andaluz 16, 1, Esq., 1000 Lisboa.

Romania

Centrala editorială (Romanian Publishing Center), Piata Scînteii 1, R-79715 Bucharest. *Gen. Dir.* Gheorghe Trandafir.

Singapore

Singapore Book Publishers Assn., Box 846, Colombo Court Post Office, Singapore 0617. *Secy.* Lena U Wen Lim.

South Africa (Republic of)

Associated Booksellers of Southern Africa, One Meerendal, Nightingale Way, Pinelands 7405. *Secy.* P. G. van Rooyen.

Book Trade Assn. of South Africa, Box 105, Parow 7500.

Book Trade Assn. of South Africa, Box 337, Bergvlei 2012.

South African Publishers Assn., Box 123, Kenwyn 7790. *Secy.* P. G. van Rooyen.

Spain

Federacion de Gremios de Editores de España (Spanish Federation of Publishers Assn.), General Pardiñas, 29-6° Iz., Madrid 1. *Pres.* Juan Salvat; *1st V.P.* Francisco Pérez González; *Secy.-Gen.* Jaime Brull.

Gremi d'Editors de Catalunya (Assn. of Catalonian Publishers), Mallorca, 272-274, Barcelona 37. *Pres.* José Luis Monreal.

Gremio Nacional de Libreros (Assn. of Spanish Booksellers), Fernandez de la Hoz 12, Madrid 4.

Gremi de Libreters de Barcelonia i Catalunya (Assn. of Barcelona and Catalunya Booksellers), c. Mallorca 272-276, Barcelona 37.

Instituto Nacional del Libro Español (Spanish Publishers and Booksellers Institute), Santiago Rusiñol 8-10, Madrid 3. *Dir.* Juan Pedro Cortés Camacho.

Sri Lanka

Booksellers Assn. of Sri Lanka, Box 244, Colombo 2. *Secy.* W. L. Mendis.

Sri Lanka Publishers Assn., 61 Sangaraja Mawatha, Colombo 10. *Secy.-Gen.* Eamon Kariyakarawana.

Sweden

Svenska Antikvariaföreningen, c/o Sigbjörn Ryö, Hantverkargatan 21, S-11221 Stockholm.

Svenska Bokförläggareföreningen (Swedish Publishers Assn.), Stearägen 52,

S-111 34 Stockholm. *Managing Dir.* Jonas Modig.

Svenska Bokhandlareföreningen, Div. of Bok-, Pappers- och Kontorsvaruförbundet (Swedish Booksellers Assn., Div. of the Swedish Federation of Book, Stationery and Office Supplies Dealers), Skeppargatan 27, S-114 52 Stockholm. *Secy.* Per Nordenson.

Svenka Tryckeriföreningen (Swedish Printing Industries Federation), Blasieholmsgatan 4A, Box 16383, S-10327 Stockholm. *Managing Dir.* Per Gålmark.

Switzerland

Schweizerischer Buchhändler-und Verleger-Verband (Swiss German-Language Booksellers and Publishers Assn.), Bellerivestr. 3, CH-8008 Zurich. *Managing Dir.* Peter Oprecht.

Società Editori della Svizzera Italiana (Publishers Assn. for the Italian-Speaking Part of Switzerland), Box 282, Viale Portone 4, CH-6501 Bellinzona.

Société des Libraires et Editeurs de la Suisse Romande (Assn. of Swiss French-Language Booksellers and Publishers), 2 av. Agassiz, CH-1001 Lausanne. *Secy.* Robert Junod.

Vereinigung der Buchantiquare und Kupferstichhändler der Schweiz (Assn. of Swiss Antiquarians and Print Dealers), c/o Markus Krebser, Bälliz 64, CH-3601 Thun.

Thailand

Publishers and Booksellers Assn. of Thailand, c/o *Secy.* Plearnpit Praepanich Praepittaya L.P., 115/10 Soi Asoke, Sukhumvit Rd., Bangkok.

Tunisia

Syndicat des Libraires de Tunisie (Tunisian Booksellers Assn.), 10 av. de France, Tunis.

Turkey

Editòrler Derneği (Publishers Assn.), Ankara Caddesi 60, Istanbul.

United Kingdom

Assn. of Learned and Professional Society Publishers, R. J. Millson, 30 Austenwood Close, Chalfont St., Peter Gerrards Cross, Bucks., SL9 9DE.

Booksellers Assn. of Great Britain & Ireland, 154 Buckingham Palace Rd., London SW1W 9TZ. *Dir.* T. E. Godfram.

Educational Publishers Council, 19 Bedford Sq., London WC1B 3HJ. *Dir.* John R. M. Davies.

National Book League, Book House, 45 East Hill, London SW18 2QZ. *Dir.* Martyn Goff, O.B.E.

National Federation of Retail Newsagents, 2 Bridewell Pl., London EC4V 6AR.

Publishers Assn., 19 Bedford Sq., London WC1B 3HJ. *Secy/Chief Exec.* Clive Bradley.

Uruguay

Asociación de Libreros del Uruguay (Uruguayan Booksellers Assn.), Av. Uruguay 1325, Montevideo.

Cámara Uruguaya del Libro (Uruguayan Publishing Council), Carlos Roxlo 1446, p. 1, Apdo. 2, Montevideo. *Secy.* Arnaldo Medone.

Yugoslavia

Association of Yugoslav Publishers and Booksellers, Kneza Miloša str. 25, Box 883, Belgrade. *Pres.* Branko Juričević.

Zambia

Booksellers Assn. of Zambia, c/o Box 31316, Lusaka.

Zimbabwe

Advertising Media Assn., c/o Associated Chambers of Commerce of Zimbabwe Rhodesia, Box 1934, Salisbury.

Booksellers Assn. of Zimbabwe, Box 1934, Salisbury. *Hon. Secy.* L. Craven.

Calendar, 1982–1983

The list below contains information regarding place and date of association meetings or promotional events that are national or international in scope. Information is as of February 1982. For further details, contact the association directly. Addresses of library and book trade associations are listed in Part 7 of this *Bowker Annual*. For additional information on book trade and promotional events, see the *1982 Exhibits Directory*, published by the Association of American Publishers; *Chase's Calendar of Annual Events*, published by the Apple Tree Press, Box 1012, Flint, MI 49501; *Literary Market Place* and *International Literary Market Place*, published by R. R. Bowker; *Publishers Weekly* "Calendar," appearing in each issue; and *Library Journal*'s "Calendar" feature, appearing in each semimonthly issue.

1982

May

2-7	Association for Educational Communications and Technology	Dallas, TX
3-6	National Micrographics Association	St. Louis, MO
6-7	Association of Research Libraries	Scottsdale, AZ
7-10	Council of Planning Librarians	Dallas, TX
9-11	Book Manufacturers Institute	Williamsburg, VA
9-12	Association of American Publishers	Marco Island, FL
19-24	Warsaw International Book Fair	Warsaw, Poland
5/29-6/1	American Booksellers Association	Anaheim, CA

June

5-10	Special Libraries Association	Detroit, MI
7-10	National Computer Conference (AFIPS)	New York, NY
11-17	American Association of Law Libraries	Detroit, MI
12-17	Medical Library Association	Anaheim, CA
20-23	Association of American University Presses	Spring Lake, NJ
27-29	Church and Synagogue Library Association	Albuquerque, NM

July

10-15	American Library Association	Philadelphia, PA
10-15	Theatre Library Association	Philadelphia, PA
17-20	Canadian Booksellers Association	Toronto, Canada

August

22-25	International Association of Printing House Craftsmen	Lancaster, PA
22-28	International Federation of Library Associations and Institutions (IFLA)	Montreal, Canada

October

3-6	National Association of Printers and Lithographers	Philadelphia, PA
6-11	Frankfurt Book Fair	Frankfurt, Federal Republic of Germany
18-22	American Society for Information Science	Columbus, OH
*	Association of Research Libraries	Washington, DC
*	International Book Fair	Belgrade, Yugoslavia

November

8-11	Information Industry Association	Anaheim, CA
14-20	National Education Association	Washington, DC
18-28	National Council of Teachers of English	Washington, DC
24-27	National Council for Social Studies	Boston, MA

December

27-30	Modern Language Association	Los Angeles, CA

1983

January

7-9	Association of American Library Schools	San Antonio, TX
7-14	American Library Association	San Antonio, TX

March

13-19	Leipzig International Book Fair	Leipzig, German Democratic Republic
*	Brussels International Book Fair	Brussels, Belgium

April

4-7	Catholic Library Association	Washington, DC
6-8	London Book Fair	London, England
24-29	Association for Educational Communications and Technology	Louisville, KY
*	Jerusalem International Book Fair	Jerusalem, Israel

May

2-6	International Reading Association	Anaheim, CA
5-6	Association of Research Libraries	Banff, Alberta, Canada
5/28-6/2	Medical Library Association	Houston, TX

June

4-6	Special Libraries Association	New Orleans, LA
4-7	American Booksellers Association	Dallas, TX
19-21	Church and Synagogue Library Association	Atlanta, GA
26-29	American Association of Law Libraries	Houston, TX
6/26-7/1	American Library Association	Los Angeles, CA
6/26-7/1	Theatre Library Association	Los Angeles, CA

*To be announced.

July
  16-19   Canadian Booksellers Association   Toronto, Canada

August
  *   International Association of Printing House
            Craftsmen   Calgary, Alberta,
                                                       Canada

September
  *   Moscow International Book Fair   Moscow, USSR

October
  12-17   Frankfurt Book Fair   Frankfurt, Federal
                                                       Republic of Germany
  16-20   American Society for Information Science Dallas, TX
  10/31-11/3 Book Manufacturers Institute   Phoenix, AZ
  *   Association of Research Libraries   Washington, DC

December
  27-30   Modern Language Association   New York, NY

*To be announced.

Index

A

AACR 2, see *Anglo-American Cataloguing Rules 2*
AALL, see American Association of Law Libraries
AALS, see Association of American Library Schools
AAP, see Association of American Publishers
AAP Fiche Service, 144
AASL, see American Library Association, American Association of School Librarians
ABA, see American Booksellers Association
ABA Basic Book List, 131
ABA Book Buyer's Handbook, 130
ABA Computer Specifications for Independent Bookstores, 131
ABA Newswire, 131
ACRL, see Association of College and Research Libraries
AECT, see Association for Educational Communications and Technology
AGRICOLA, see Agricultural On-Line Access data base
AGRIS, see International Information System for the Agricultural Sciences and Technology
AHEC, see Area Health Education Centers
AIBDA, see Inter-American Association of Agricultural Librarians and Documentalists
AIC, see American Institute for Conservation
AIM, see Associated Information Managers
AIM-TWX, 53, 54
AJL, see Association of Jewish Libraries
ALA, see American Library Association
ALSC, see American Library Association, Association for Library Service to Children
ALTA, see American Library Association, American Library Trustee Association
AMIGOS, 81

ANSI Committee Z39, see American National Standards Committee Z39
ARL, see Association of Research Libraries
"ARL Academic Leaders of the 1980s: Men and Women of the Executive Suite," 22
ARL Annual Library Survey, 151
ARL Annual Salary Survey 1981, 267
ARL Library Index and Quantitative Relationships in the ARL, 151
ARL Microform Project, 148
ARL Statistics, 237
ARLIS/NA, see Art Libraries Society of North America
ASCLA, see American Library Association, Association of Specialized and Cooperative Agencies
ASIS, see American Society for Information Science
AT&T, antitrust case, 200
  see also Computer Inquiry II
ATLA, see American Theological Library Association
"About Books and Writers with Robert Cromie," 124
Abridged Index Medicus-Teletypewriter Exchange Network, see AIM-TWX
Academic Freedom Group, workshops, 123
Academic Library Management Intern Program, 208
Academic Library Program, 207
Accreditation Manual for Hospitals, 58
Achieving Sexual Maturity, 58
Acquisitions, see Libraries, acquisitions; also subhead acquisitions under types of libraries, e.g., Public Libraries, acquisitions
Action, placement services, 262
Affirmative Action Register, placement services, 261–262
Agricultural On-Line Access data base, 119
Airlie House, research proposals, 305–306
"America, the Library Has Your Number," 124, 125
"America through American Eyes," 142

625

American Association for the Advancement of the Humanities, relations with scholarly community, 150
American Association of Law Libraries, 499–501
  placement services, 253
American Association of School Librarians, see American Library Association, American Association of School Librarians
American Book Awards, 139, 143, 146
American Bookseller, 131
American Booksellers Association, 130–133
  Booksellers School, see Booksellers School
  meetings, 132
  publications, 130–131
  Publisher Planning Committee, 132
American Folklife Center, 109
American Institute for Conservation, 63
American Libraries
  "America's Library Heritage" cover series, 128
  placement services, 253
American Libraries, Consultants Keyword Clearinghouse, 253
American Library Association, 120–130, 501–504
  American Association of School Librarians, 32–33, 504–508
  American Indian Libraries Newsletter, placement services, 253
  American Library Trustee Association, 508–509
  annual conference, 120
  Association for Library Service to Children, 33, 509–512
  workshops, 125
  Association of College and Research Libraries, 512–514
  continuing education courses, 125
  National Conference, 4–5, 9
  placement services, 253
  Association of Specialized and Cooperative Library Agencies, 121, 515–517
  workshops, 125
  Black Caucus, placement services, 254
  Central Production Unit, 128
  Committee on Accreditation, 126–127
  Huron Plaza building, 120
  Intellectual Freedom Committee, 28, 123
  international concerns, 129
  Library Administration and Management Association, 517–518
  member needs, 125
  Library and Information Technology Association, 519–520
  workshops, 125, 126
  new committees, 121
  Office for Library Personnel Resources, salary surveys, 272, 288
  Office for Research, salary surveys, 271
  Office of Intellectual Freedom, 123
  Office of Library Outreach Services, 122
  Minority Concerns Committee, 122
  Operating Agreement, 129–130
  placement services, 253
  Planning Process Discussion Group, 15
  Public Information Office
  programs, 124
  workshops, 126
  Public Library Association, 520–522
  workshops, 126
  publications, 127–128
  Reference and Adult Services Division, 122, 522–525
  continuing education, 126
  standards, 19
  Reference and Subscription Books Committee, 128
  relations with divisions, 32–33
  Resources and Technical Services Division, 525–526
  AACR institutes, 126
  Preservation of Library Materials Section, 62
  salary surveys, 271
  Social Responsibilities Round Table, Rhode Island Affiliate, placement services, 254
  Standing Committee on Library Education, Subcommittee on Training of Library Supportive Staff, 289
  Young Adult Services Division, 33, 257–258
American Library Trustee Association, see American Library Association, American Library Trustee Association
American Merchant Marine Library Association, 528
American National Standards Committee Z39, 133–139
  AAP representation, 142

American Society for Information Science, 528–529
placement services, 254
American Theological Library Association, 530–531
placement services, 254
Anable, Richard, 205
Anglo-American Cataloguing Rules. 2, 101, 106, 114, 126, 148
Anti-Intellectualism in American Life, 40
Arab libraries, Israel, 434
Archives, bibliography, 454–455
see also International Association of Sound Archives; International Council on Archives; International Federation of Film Archives; Library materials, conservation and preservation
Area Health Education Centers, 55
Arndt, Beatrice Simmons, 221
Arntzen, Etta, 208
Art Libraries Society of North America, 531–532
placement services, 254
Artwork donations, tax credit, 188
Associated Information Managers, 532
placement services, 254
Association Canadienne des Sciences de l'Information, *see* Canadian Association for Information Science
Association for Educational Communications and Technology, 33
placement services, 254
Association for Library Service to Children, *see* American Library Association, Association for Library Service to Children
Association of Academic Health Sciences Library Directors, 533
Association of American Library Schools, 534
study of paraprofessional training, 288
Association of American Library Schools Library Education Statistical Report, 271
Association of American Publishers, 139–147
AAP Fiche Service, *see* AAP Fiche Service
Book Distribution Task Force, 142
College Division, 144
public relations program, 144
Copyright Committee, 141
Direct Marketing/Book Club Division, 146
Education for Publishing Program, 142
Freedom to Read Committee, 141
General Publishing Division, 143
Give-a-Book Certificate Program, *see* Give-a-Book Certificate Program
International Division, 145
International Freedom to Publish Committee, 142
Liaison with other associations, 146
Mass Market Paperback Division, 143–144
New Technology Committee, 141
Postal Committee, 141
Professional and Scholarly Publishing Division, 144–145
awards program, *see* PSP Awards Program
publications, 144, 146–147
School Division, 145
Association of College and Research Libraries, *see* American Library Association, Association of College and Research Libraries
Association of Jewish Libraries, 555
Association of Research Libraries, 147–152, 535–537
cooperation with the scholarly community, 150
Office of Management Studies, 151–152
conservation programs, 62
Preservation Committee, 62
publications, 151
Task Force on Bibliographic Control, 148–149
Association of Specialized and Cooperative Library Agencies, *see* American Library Association, Association of Specialized and Cooperative Library Agencies
Association of Visual Science Librarians, 537
Associations, book trade, *see* Book trade associations
Audiovisual materials
bibliography, 455
ESEA support, 222
film prices, 4
off-air taping, 94–95, 183–184
off-air videotaping, 30, 198–199
slow-scan TV, 103–104
telefacsimile, 103–104

Audiovisual materials (Cont.)
    see also Association of Visual Science Librarians; Educational Film Library Association; Library materials; National Medical Audiovisual Center
Authority files, see Bibliographic control, authority files
Authors, see Literary agents and authors
Automated Office: An Introduction to the Technology, 159
Awards, information services, see names of awards, e.g., Knox, William T., Award
Awards, library, 296–301
Awards, literary, 472–483
    see also names of awards, e.g., American Book Awards
Awards, publishers, 146
    see also names of awards, e.g., Benjamin, Curtis G., Award for Creative Publishing

B

BIBLINK, 205
BISAC, see Book Industry Systems Advisory Committee
BISG, see Book Industry Study Group
BSDP, see Council on Library Resources, Bibliographic Service Development Program
Baker, John F., 34
Banks, O. Gordon, 156
Bearman, Toni Carbo, 88
Benjamin, Curtis G., Award for Creative Publishing, 146
Berger, Patricia W., 133
Berkner, Dimi, 265
Best sellers, 419–420, 490–495
    see also Awards, literary; Books, best books
Beta Phi Mu, 538–539
Betamax case, 183
    see also Copyright, off-air taping; Copyright, off-air videotaping
Bibliographic control
    authority files, 81–82, 205–206
    master microforms, 62
    microforms, 110
    standards, 148, 205
Bibliographic data bases, 205–206
    access to, 112
    FLC on-line services, 101–102
    federal, 91, 358–359
    health sciences, 53–55
    linking, 205
    medical libraries, 114
    retrieval services, 119
    systems vendors, 7
    see also Bibliographic control; National Biomedical Serials Holding Database
Bibliographic services, see Council on Library Resources, Bibliographic Service Development Program; Information services; Networks
Bibliographic Services Development Program, 78, 205
Bibliographical Society of America, 540
Bibliographies
    bibliography, 464
    see also Library literature, bibliography; also publications under names of organizations, e.g., Association of American Publishers, publications
Bibliography of Medical Reviews, 1976–1980, 114
Bishop, Sarah G., 233
Black Caucus, see American Library Association, Black Caucus
Bock, D. Joleen, 376
Book design, see Books, design and production
Book exports, 440–445
Book fairs, see Frankfurt Book Fair
Book imports, 387, 440–445
Book Industry Study Group, 392, 394
Book Industry Systems Advisory Committee, formats for computer-to-computer communications, 142
"Book Industry Trends, 1981," 394
Book Preservation Center, 63
Book production, see Books, design and production
Book programs
    Center for the Book, 99–100
    see also Give-a-Book Certificate Program
Book review media
    ALA journals, 127–128
    statistics, 414
Book sales, 37, 392–393
    see also Booksellers; Public libraries, funding
Book stores, 132
    college, AAP concerns, 144
    discount stores, 36
    number of, 413–414

Book trade
  bibliography, 464–465
  directories and yearbooks, bibliography, 469–470
Book trade associations
  foreign, 614–620
  meetings, 621–623
  U.S. and Canada, 608–614
Booklist, 128
Bookmobiles, *see* Public libraries, service outlets
Books
  best books, 483–484
    juvenile, 486–489
    young adult, 484–486
    see also Awards, literary; Best sellers
  consumer expenditures, 394–396
  design and production, bibliography, 468–469
  distribution, *see* Publishing, distribution of books
  incunabula, *see* Incunabula
  international importance, *see* Association of American Publishers, International Division
  prices, 388–389, 391, 396–413, 400–401
    British books, 402, 406–407
    German books, 402–403, 408–410
    Latin American books, 411
    see also Library materials, prices; Paperback books, prices; Periodicals, prices
  sales, *see* Book sales
  title output, 383–391
  translations, 387, 445
  see also Paperback books
"Books Make a Difference," 98–99
Booksellers
  AAP concerns, 143
  continuing education, 131
  invoice prices, 36
Booksellers School, 131
Bookselling, 132–133
  bibliography, 469
  discounts, 35–36
  see also Book stores
Bookstores, *see* Book stores
Boss, Richard W., 265
Branch libraries, *see* Public libraries, service outlets
Branscomb, Lewis M., 25, 99
Brown, Norman H., 3
Bryant, Anita, 41
Buchanan, Sally, 61
Burke, Kenneth, 146

Burke, Theresa M., Employment Agency, employment services, 256
Business of Information Report, 152–153, 154

C

CAIS, *see* Canadian Association for Information Science
CALS, *see* National Agricultural Library, Current Awareness Literature Service
CCC, *see* Copyright Clearance Center
CCRM, *see* Center for Chinese Research Materials
CDS, *see* Library of Congress, Cataloging Distribution Service
CETA, *see* Comprehensive Employment and Training Act
CIP, *see* Cataloging in Publication
CISTI, *see* Canada Institute for Scientific and Technical Information
CKC, *see* American Libraries, Consultants Keyword Clearinghouse
CLA, *see* Canadian Library Association; Catholic Library Association
CLASS, *see* California Library Authority for Systems and Services
CLENE, *see* Continuing Library Education Network and Exchange
CLR, *see* Council on Library Resources
COA, *see* American Library Association, Committee on Accreditation
COG, *see* Metropolitan Washington Council of Governments
COLT, *see* Council on Library/Media Technical Assistants
COM, *see* Computer Output Microforms
CONSER, *see* Conversion of Serials
CONTU, *see* National Commission on New Technological Uses of Copyrighted Works
COPUL, *see* Council of Prairie University Libraries
COSLA, *see* Chief Officers of State Library Agencies
CPL, *see* Council of Planning Librarians
CPU, *see* American Library Association, Central Production Unit
CRIS, *see* National Agricultural Library, Current Research Information System
CSLA, *see* Church and Synagogue Library Association

630 / INDEX

California Library Authority for Systems and Services, 81
California, Proposition 13, see Proposition 13
Call Your Library Campaign, 124
Canada Institute for Scientific and Technical Information, 438
Canadian Association for Information Science (Association Canadienne des Sciences de l'Information), 540–541
Canadian Library Association, 541–542
Canetti, Elias, 421
Careers in Information, 265
Carmel, Michael, 8
Carroll, Mark, 163
Carson, Johnny, 124
Cataloging and classification
  bibliography, 462–463
  catalog formats used, 377
  computerized card catalogs, 31
  cooperative, 101, 104
  LC, 110–111
  on-line, 27, 206
  retrospective, 6–7
  see also Cataloging in Publication; Library of Congress, Cataloging Distribution Service
Cataloging in Publication, 110, 206
  Z39 published standards, 136
Cataloging Machine-Readable Data Files: An Interpretation, 205
Cater, Douglas, 25
Catholic Library Association, 542–544
  placement services, 254
Censorship, see Intellectual freedom
Center for Chinese Research Materials, 151–152
Center for the Book, 98–100, 109
Certification of Public Libraries in the U.S., 265
"Challenge of Change: Critical Choices for Library Decision Makers," 22
Chamberlain, Mary W., 208
"Changes in Information Delivery since 1960 in Health Sciences Libraries," 52–53
Channel 2000, see Online Computer Library Center, computerized home service
Cheap CE: Providing Continuing Education with Limited Resources, 126
Cheatham, Bertha M., 25
Chief Officers of State Library Agencies, 107, 544–545

Child pornography, see Obscenity legislation
Children's books, see Books, best books, juvenile; Publishing statistics, children's books
Childs, Susan, 8
Chinese Academy of Sciences, Institute of Medical Information, 112–113
Chinese-American Librarians Association, 545–546
Choice, 128
Chronicle of Higher Education, placement services, 202
Church and Synagogue Library Association, 546–547
Chute, Adrienne, 212
Civil rights, legislation, 200–201
Clearinghouse for National Library Statistics, 428–429
Cleveland Public Library, Data Research Associates, 7
Cognates, 129
Cohen, Nathan, 212
Cole, John Y., 98
College and university libraries
  acquisitions, 319–320
  additions and renovations, 364–365
  bibliography, 457
  construction, 361–365
  funding, see Library funding, college and university libraries
  future developments, 4–5
  Israel, 433
  personnel
    employment requirements, 19–20
    part time and temporary, 19
    salaries, 266–267, 268, 269
  reference services, see Libraries, reference services
  see also Research libraries; Special libraries
Committee on Production Guidelines for Book Longevity, 207–208
Committee on Scholarly Communication, 150
Communications Act, 1934, revision, 199
Comprehensive Employment and Training Act, 19
Computer Communications Protocols for Bibliographic Data Interchange Task Group, 437
Computer Inquiry II, 200
Computer Output Microforms, 114, 157
  bibliography, 459

Conservation Administration News, 207
Conservation and preservation, *see* Library materials, conservation and preservation
Consultant Training Program, 207
Continuing Library Education Network and Exchange, 547–548
Conversion of Serials, 148, 206
Cooke, Eileen D., 173
Copyright
  bibliography, 457–458, 469
  computer software, 95–96
  five-year review, 184, 198–199
  infringement, 199
  international authorizations to copy, 76–77
  international concerns, 97
  legislation, 95–97
  manufacturing clause, 94, 194
  national information service, 93–94
  off-air taping, 94–95, 183–184
  off-air videotaping, 30, 198–199
  photocopying, 184
  proprietary rights, 198–199
  regulations, 95–96
  user workshops, 74–75
  see also Association of American Publishers, Copyright Committee; U.S., Copyright Office
Copyright Clearance Center, 72–77
  Document Delivery Awareness Program, 73–74
  Large Industry User Assistance Program, 74
  Precoded Permissions Service, 75–76
  publications, 77
Copyright Royalty Tribunal, 93
Council for International Exchange of Scholars, placement services, 262–263
Council of Biology Editors, joint meeting with SSP, 164
Council of National Library and Information Associations, 548–549
Council of Planning Librarians, 549–550
Council of Prairie University Libraries, 438
Council of Scholars, *see* Library of Congress, Council of Scholars
Council on Library/Media Technical Assistants, 289
  placement services, 255
Council on Library Resources, 204–212, 550
  Academic Library Management Intern Program, *see* Academic Library Management Intern Program
  Bibliographic Services Development Program, *see* Bibliographic Services Development Program
  cooperative conservation program, 63–64
  Office of Management Studies, 206–207
    Academic Library Program, *see* Academic Library Program
    Consultant Training Program, *see* Consultant Training Program
    Professional Education and Training for Research Librarianship Program, *see* Professional Education and Training for Research Librarianship Program
"Criteria for Programs to Prepare Library/Media Technical Assistants," 288, 289–290
Cromie, Robert, 124
Crouch, Dora, 206
Cumulated ARL Statistics 1962/63 through 1978/79, 267
Cumulated ARL University Library Statistics, 1962–64 through 1978–79, 151
Curia, Pat, 22

D

DOBIS, *see* Dortmunder Bibliothekssystem
DOD, *see* U.S., Department of Defense
DRA, *see* Cleveland Public Library, Data Research Associates
Dallas Public Library, Specialized Information Service, 46–47
Darling, Louise, 52
Darnton, Robert, 99
Data bases, *see* Bibliographic data bases
Data Research Associates, *see* Cleveland Public Library, Data Research Associates
Daval, Nicola, 147
Dealing with Complaints about Resources, 123
Degrees and Certificates Awarded by U.S. Library Education Programs, 272
Denis, Laurent G., 436
Dessauer, John P., 392, 394
Directory of Fee-Based Information Services, placement services, 264, 265

Disaster Relief Act, 1974, 189
Document Delivery Awareness Program, see Copyright Clearance Center, Document Delivery Awareness Program
Documentary materials, see Library materials, conservation and preservation
Dodd, Sue A., 205
Dortmunder Bibliothekssystem, 437-438

E

ECIA, see Education Consolidation and Improvement Act
EDGAR, see U.S., Department of Education, Education Division General Administrative Requirements
EFLA, see Educational Film Library Association
EIS, see Education Information Service
ESEA, see Elementary and Secondary Education Act
Eckard, Helen M., 329, 344
Economic Recovery Tax Act, 1981, 188, 196
Editing, bibliography, 468, 470
Education, 32
   ESEA school support, 221-225
   instructional materials expenditures, 223, 224
   library services for the aging, 45-47
Education Consolidation and Improvement Act, 173, 178, 179-182
Education for librarianship
   bibliography, 458
   research libraries, 150-151
   see also Librarians, continuing education; Library management, training programs; Library personnel, continuing education; also subheads personnel, continuing education, personnel, training, under types of libraries
Education for publishing
   AAP grants, 145
   see also Association of American Publishers, Education for Publishing Program
Education Information Service, placement services, 262-263
Educational Film Library Association, 551

"Educational Requirements for Academic Librarians in Non-Director Positions," 19
Electronic Library Association, 31
Electronic mail, see Networks, electronic mail service
Elementary and Secondary Education Act
   block grants, 224-225
   Title IV-B, Instructional Materials and School Library Resources, 221-225
Encyclopaedia Britannica, on-line, 8
Engelhard Lecture Series on the Book, 99
Entry-Level Job Clearinghouse, 142
Essays from the New England Academic Librarians' Writing Seminar, 208
"Estimated Publishers' Net Sales," 392
Exhibits
   AAP book exhibit in People's Republic of China, 139
   LC, 111
   NAL, 119
   Z39 materials, 133

F

FAME, see Florida Association for Media in Education
FAUL, see Five Associated University Libraries
FEDLINK Network Office, 552-553
FHWA, see Federal Highway Administration
FIAF, see International Federation of Film Archives
FID, see International Federation for Documentation
FLC, see Federal Library Committee
FoIA, see Freedom of Information Act
Fang, Josephine Riss, 288
Farkas, Eugene M., 117
Federal Health Resources Sharing Committee, Library Subcommittee, 59
Federal Highway Administration, Cooperative Cataloging Project, 104
Federal Information Centers, review, 202
Federal Job Information Directory, 260
Federal libraries, see National libraries, U.S.
Federal Library Committee, 100-105, 551-552
   meetings, 105
   see also Intergovernmental Library Cooperation Project

Federal Research Service, placement services, 262
Fee-Based Information Services: A Study of a Growing Industry, 265
Fellowships, *see* Scholarships
Financing Online Search Services in Publicly Supported Libraries, 306
Five Associated University Libraries, 80–81
Florence Protocol, 184
Florida Association for Media in Education, 27
Fogelstrom, Clarence, 212
Folger Institute of Renaissance and Eighteenth Century Studies, 70–71
Folger Shakespeare Library, 68–72
Folger Theatre Group, 71–72
Foreign library associations, *see* Library associations, foreign
Fox, Bette-Lee, 361, 366
Frankfurt Book Fair, 417–421
  international meeting on book distribution, 142
Frase, Robert W., 133
Freedom of Information Act, 37, 189, 193–194, 201
Freedom of Information Improvement Act, 1981, 193–194
Freedom of speech, *see* Intellectual freedom
Freedom of the press, *see* Intellectual freedom
Freedom to Read Foundation, 123
  see also Intellectual freedom
Friday Memo Special Report, 155
"From Bibliotheque du Roi to World Information Network: The National Library in Historical Perspective," 99

G

GPD, *see* Association of American Publishers, General Publishing Division
Gauri, Kul B., 18
General Concepts of Employment for Library and Information Personnel, 126
German Book Trade peace prize, 420
Give-a-Book Certificate Program, 132, 143
Glazer, Fred, 120
Government publications, access, 37

Grannis, Chandler B., 383, 392, 440
Grant proposals
  HEA evaluation criteria, 240–241
  HEA grants, 233, 241
  NSF grants, 246–247
  OLLT grants, 236–237, 305
Grants, information services
  federal, 346–347
  HEA grants, 233–237
Grants, library
  Bibliographic Service Development Program, 210–211
  block grants, *see* Education Consolidation and Improvement Act
  CLR grants, 210–212
  ECIA grants, 179–182
  HEA grants, 225–227, 228–233, 233–241
  HEA recipients, 239–240
  NLM grants, 116
  Petrel grants, 211–212
  see also Scholarships
Grants, publishers
  AAP School Division, 145
Green, Joseph, 321
Griffin, Robert, 165
Guide to CCC-Participating Document Delivery Services, 74
Guide to the Literature of Art History, 208
"Guidelines for the Training of Library Technicians," 270
"Guidelines Governing the Protection of Privacy and Transborder Flows of Personal Data," 201
Gwinn, Nancy, 62

H

HEA, *see* Higher Education Act
Hanke, Maxine K., 52
Harris, Howard, 205
Harris, Patricia, 205, 237
Harter, Stephen P., 8
Health sciences libraries, *see* Medical libraries
Heim, Kathleen, 22
Henderson, Carol C., 173
Hepatitis Knowledge Base, 114
Higher Education Act
  Title II College and Research Library Assistance and Library Training and Research, 190

Higher Education Act (Cont.)
  Title II-A, College Library Resources, 190, 225, 227
  Title II-B, Library Career Training, 228–233
  Title II-B, Library Research and Demonstration Program, 233–237
  Title II-B, Library Training, Research and Development 190
  Title II-C, Strengthening Research Library Resources, 149, 190, 237–241
    grants for conservation efforts, 64–65
  Title II-D National Periodicals System, 190
Home Country Employment Registry, placement services, 263
Hospital libraries, 58–59
How Libraries Can Resist Censorship, 123
How Public Libraries Serve the Aging, 122
How to Select a Microform Reader or Reader-Printer, 159
Human Genetics Knowledge Base, 114

I

IAALD, see International Association of Agricultural Librarians and Documentalists
IALL, see International Association of Law Libraries
IAML, see International Association of Music Libraries, Archives and Documentation Centers
IAOL, see International Association of Orientalist Librarians
IASA, see International Association of Sound Archives
I&R, see Information and Referral
ICA, see International Council on Archives
IESMP, see Information Exchange System for Minority Personnel
IFC, see American Library Association, Intellectual Freedom Committee
IFLA, see International Federation of Library Associations and Institutions
IFLA Draft Medium-Term Programme, 1981–1985, 427
IIA, see Information Industry Association
ILS, see Integrated Library System
INTAMEL, see International Association of Metropolitan City Libraries
IPA, see International Publishers Association
ISO, see International Organization for Standardization
ISO/TC46, see International Organization for Standardization, Technical Committee, 46
ISS, see International School Services
ISSN, see International Standard Serial Number
IST, see National Science Foundation, Division of Information Science and Technology
IYDP, see International Year for Disabled Persons
Illinois Regional Library Council, disbanded, 18
"Impact of Inflation on Journal Costs," 3
"Increasing Library Productivity," 20
Incunabula, NLM acquisitions, 114
Index of Articles of Jewish Studies, 433
Indexing in Art and Architecture: An Investigation, 206
"Information Agenda for the 1980s," 25
Information and Referral, 46, 47–48
Information Brokering: A State of the Art Report, 265
The Information Brokers: How to Start and Operate Your Own Fee-Based Service, 265
Information centers, federal, see Federal information centers
Information Exchange System for Minority Personnel, 255
Information flow
  international, 100
  legislation, 201–202
  NCLIS concerns, 90
Information Industry Association, 152–156
  annual conference, 153–156
  Business of Operations Council, 154–155
  Future Technology and Innovation Council, 155
  government information concerns, 197
  new council structure, 154–156
Information industry associations, 499–563
Information policy legislation, see Legislation affecting information industry
Information Professional: Survey of an Emerging Field, 265

Information Science and Technology Act, 202
Information science research
  grant recipients, 243–245, 246
  HEA grants, 233–237
  NSF support, 242–247
Information services
  access, 121–122
  bibliography, 153–154, 455, 458
  costs, 353
  expenditures, 347–348
  funding, 345–347, 352, 353
  government competition, 197–198
  health sciences, 53–55
  international, 202
  legislation, see Legislation affecting information industry
  NAL, 117–118
  NCES survey, 344–355
  on-line, 53–55, 306
  personnel, 345
    continuing education, 229, 231–232
    employment opportunities, 264–265
    training workshops, 119
  retrieval services, shared, 102
  telephone companies, 200
  UN, 118
  user needs of the aging, 47–48
  videotext services, 306
  see also Associated Information Managers; Canadian Association for Information Science; FEDLINK Network Office; Information Industry Association; Library services and programs
Information Sources, 1982–1983, 154
Information technology
  HEA grants, 233–237
  NSF support, 242–247
  see also American Library Association, Library and Information Technology Association; American Society for Information Science; Association of American Publishers, New Technology Committee; National Micrographics Association
Integrated Library System, 115
Intellectual freedom, 28–30, 36–37
  ALA concerns, 123–124
  bibliography, 458, 469
  survey, 38–42
  see also American Library Association, Intellectual Freedom Committee; American Library Association, Office of Intellectual Freedom; Association of American Publishers, Freedom to Read Committee; Association of American Publishers, International Freedom to Publish Committee; Obscenity legislation; School library/media services, censorship problems
"Intellectual Freedom in the 80s: The Impact of Conservatism," 28
Intelligence agents, identity disclosure, 195, 201
Inter-American Association of Agricultural Librarians and Documentalists, 588
Intergovernmental Library Cooperation Project, 90–91, 356–360
Interlibrary loan, 13, 334–335, 337
International Association of Agricultural Librarians and Documentalists, 589
International Association of Law Libraries, 589–590
International Association of Metropolitan City Libraries, 590
International Association of Music Libraries, Archives and Documentation Centers, 590–591
International Association of Orientalist Librarians, 592
International Association of School Librarianship, placement services, 263
International Association of Sound Archives, 592
International Council on Archives, 593
  CLR support, 209–210
International Federation for Documentation, 593–594
International Federation of Film Archives, 594–595
International Federation of Library Associations and Institutions, 422–427, 595–596
  ALA participation, 129
  CLR support, 209
  General Council and Conference, 1983, 439
  Statistics Section, 428–430
  U.S. institutional members, 426–427
International Federation of Scientific Editors Association, meeting with SSP, 164
International Flow of Information: A Trans-Pacific Perspective, 100

International Group of Scientific, Technical and Medical Publishers, general assembly, 420
International Information System for the Agricultural Sciences and Technology, 118
International Institute for Children's Literature and Reading Research, 596
International library associations, *see* Library associations, international
International Meeting on Book Distribution, Frankfurt, 142
International Organization for Standardization, 596–597
   Technical Committee 46, 133, 137–139
International Publishers Association, meeting, 420
International School Services, placement services, 263
International Standard Serial Number, assigned to Z39, 136
International Year for Disabled Persons, 121
Irvine, Betty Jo, 22
Island Trees Union Free School Board, 28–29, 37

J

JNUL, *see* Jewish National and University Library
Jewish National and University Library, 432–433
Jones, J. Morris, Award, 127, 307
Jones, Milbrey L., 338
Junior colleges, *see* Two-year college libraries
Juvenile books, *see* Books, best books, juvenile

K

Kacena, Carolyn, 22
Kaiser, John R., 19–20
Kanawha County, West Virginia, 40–41
Kaplan, Gary N., 265
Kibbutz libraries, 434
Kiryat Sefer, 433
Kister, Kenneth F., 8
Kittel, Dorothy, 212
Klassen, Robert, 212
Klett, Ernst, Verlag, meeting of educational publishers, 420

Knachel, Philip A., 68
Knowledge Base Research Program, 114
Knowledge: Its Creation, Distribution and Economic Significance, 308
Knox, William T., award, 155
Koltay, Emery I., 380
Kronenfeldt, Michael R., 3
Krug, Judith F., 38
Kurzweil reading machines, 14

L

LAMA, *see* American Library Association, Library Administration and Management Association
LC, *see* Library of Congress
LDCH, see *Library Data Collection Handbook*
LIBGIS, *see* Library General Information Survey
LITA, *see* American Library Association, Library and Information Technology Association
LORCOST Project, *see* "Levels of Output Related to Cost of Operation of Scientific and Technical Libraries
LSCA, *see* Library Services and Construction Act
LTR, see *Library Technology Reports*
Learmont, Carol L., 20, 273
Legislation affecting information industry, 184–185, 195–203
   NCLIS concerns, 89–90
Legislation affecting libraries, 122–123, 149–150, 173–189, 190–191
   LC, 108
   NCLIS concerns, 89–90
   tax laws, 188–189
   see also Library Services and Construction Act; Omnibus Budget Reconciliation Act, 1981
Legislation affecting publishing, 189–195
Legislation Day, 122
"Levels of Output Related to Cost of Operation of Scientific and Technical Libraries," 307
Levin, Martin P., 137
"Librarian as Scholar," 19
Librarians
   accreditation, *see* Library schools, accredited
   certification requirements, 265

see also Library directors, certification
continuing education, 19
    see also Library personnel, continuing education; Research libraries, personnel, continuing education
demand and supply, 280
employment, 20-22
    non-library, 20, 264-265
employment qualifications, 19
free-lance jobs, 264
international exchanges, 263-264
Israel, 431-432
job-lines, 251-253
overseas job opportunities, 262-264
placement sources, 251-266
salaries, 20-22, 273-287
training in service for the aging, 48-49
see also Library personnel
Librarian's Register, 260-261
Libraries
    accreditation, see American Library Association, Committee on Accreditation; Library Schools, accredited
    acquisitions
        automated, 7
        bibliography, 462
        LC, 109-110
        shared services, 102, 104
        see also subhead acquisitions under types of libraries
    additions and renovations, see subhead additions and renovations under types of libraries
    automated circulation systems, 6
    budgets, 18-19
    buildings, equipment, furniture, 338, 376
        bibliography, 455-456
    circulation statistics, 337
    collection management, 208
    computerized functions, 5-9, 354-355
        bibliography, 455
        microcomputers, 7-8, 31, 117
        minicomputers, 102
        small libraries, 8-9
        see also Cataloging and classification; Libraries, automated circulation systems; Library cooperation, computer support; Networks
    conservation efforts, 64-65
    construction
        Folger Shakespeare Library, 70
        see also College and university libraries, construction; Public libraries, construction

cooperation, see Library cooperation
copying of copyrighted material, see Photocopying
federal, see National libraries, U.S.
fees and fines, 117
funding, see Library funding
history, bibliography, 458-459
hours open, 338
interlibrary loan, see Interlibrary loan
national, see National libraries
number of, U.S. and Canada, 314-315
photocopying, see Photocopying
presidential, see Presidential libraries
reference services
    bibliography, 460-461
    on-line, 8
    see also American Library Association, Reference and Adult Services Division; also subhead reference services under types of libraries
surveys, see Library surveys
system directors, see Library directors
technical services
    bibliography, 462-463
    see also American Library Association, Resources and Technical Services Division
user surveys, see U.S., population served by libraries
see also types of libraries, e.g., Public libraries
Libraries and Literacy, 122
"Libraries and the Pursuit of Happiness," 33
Library administration, see Library management
Library Administration and Management Association, see American Library Association, Library Administration and Management Association
Library agencies, state, see State library agencies
Library and Information Technology Association, see American Library Association, Library and Information Technology Association
Library associations, 32-33
    Canada, provincial, 572-573
        see also Canadian Library Association
    conservation concerns, 62-63
    foreign, 597-607
    international, 588-597
    meetings, 621-623
    national, 499-563

Library associations (Cont.)
  placement services, 253–256
  regional
    foreign, 597–598
    U.S. and Canada, 573–574
  state, 563–572
  state and regional, placement services, 257
  see also Information industry associations
Library Awareness Idea Search, 124
Library Bill of Rights, 123
Library buildings, see Libraries, buldings, equipment, furniture
Library consultants, 21, 24
  automation/management services, 102
  CLR support, 207
Library cooperation
  bibliography, 459–460
  Canada, 437–438
  computer support, 348, 351, 354–355
  conservation efforts, 63–64
  expenditures, 352, 353
  federal/nonfederal libraries, 91
  funding, 352
  hospital libraries, 58–59
  intergovernmental libraries, 103, 356–360
  international, 118
  Israel, 435
  Metropolitan Washington Library Council, 82–87
  network resource sharing, 18
  organizations, 344–355
  state and federal, 118–119
  see also Cataloging and classification, cooperative; Information services; Intergovernmental Library Cooperation Project; Libraries, acquisitions, shared services; Library materials, cooperative purchasing; Library Services and Construction Act, Title III Interlibrary Cooperation; Networks
Library Data Collection Handbook, 307
Library directors
  certification, 20
  salaries, 269
  sex and salaries, 22
"Library Education and Personnel Utilization," 288
Library funding, 9
  college and university libraries, HEA, 225–227
  cutbacks, 26–28
  federal, 174, 175–177, 180–181, 323, 333
  LC, 108–109, 198
  public libraries, 10–11, 306–307, 323, 328, 332, 333
    book sales, 12
    data base services, 13
    fund-raising projects, 11–12
  research libraries, HEA support, 237–241
  state, 323, 333
  see also Library materials, conservation and preservation, funding
Library General Information Survey, 309–310
Library Journal Special Report #21: Metcalf, Downs, Kaser & Shera at Eastern Illinois, 15
Library legislation, see Legislation affecting libraries
Library literature,
  bibliography, 453, 457
  periodicals and serials, bibliography, 460, 463–464
  placement services, 251
  see also publications under names of associations
Library management, 14–15
  ARL/OMS programs, 207
  bibliography, 453–454
  special libraries, 167
  training programs, 208–209
  see also American Library Association, Library Administration and Management Association; Library directors
Library materials
  bibliography, 67, 84, 459
  conservation and preservation, 22–23, 61–68, 207–208
    bibliography, 454–455
    education and training, 65–66
    funding, 67–68
    information catalog, 64
    NAL collections, 118
    Research and development, 66
    see also Library of Congress, Preservation Research and Testing Office
  cooperative purchasing, 84
  nonprint media, prices, 399, 404
  prices, 3–4, 396–413
  see also Audiovisual materials; Libraries, buildings, equipment, furniture; Microforms; Periodicals

Library of Congress, 106-111
　American Folklore Center, see American Folklife Center
　cataloging, 110
　Cataloging Distribution Service, 110-111
　Cataloging in Publication Division, see Cataloging in Publication
　Center for the Book, see Center for the Book
　collections, 110
　cooperative meeting with NLC, 111
　Council of Scholars, 106-107
　funding, see Library funding, LC
　James Madison Memorial Building, 107
　job opportunities, 261
　National Library Service for the Blind and Physically Handicapped, 108, 178
　Network Advisory Committee, 78
　Network Development Office, 110
　Preservation Research and Testing Office, 61, 66
　Processing Services, 110
　publications, 111
　Restoration Office, 61
　see also Intergovernmental Library Cooperation Project
Library personnel
　budget problems, 18-19
　continuing education, 83-84, 104, 125-126, 229, 231-232
　　ACRL courses, 125
　　see also Continuing Library Education Network and Exchange; Librarians, continuing education
　discrimination in employment, 22
　　see also Library directors, sex and salaries
　obituaries, 25
　paraprofessionals, training, 288-291
　　see also Library technical assistants
　personnel changes, 23-24
　placements, 274, 279
　retired personnel, 24
　salaries, 266-273, 307-308
　　see also Library schools, faculty salaries
　sex and salaries, see Library directors, sex and salaries
　supportive staff, see under subhead paraprofessionals, above
　trainee programs, 229
　training programs, 208-209

　volunteers, 21-22, 350
　see also Librarians; also subhead personnel under types of libraries
Library photocopying, see Photocopying, libraries
Library planning, see Library research and development
Library Research, 4
Library research and development, 305-308
　bibliography, 461
　Canada, 437-438
　conservation, 66
　HEA grants, 233-237
　reporting publications, 308
Library schools
　accredited, 291-294
　directors, 267
　faculty salaries, 271-272
　job hunting seminars, 258-259
　placement services, 257-260
　placements, 20, 273-287
　　see also Librarians, employment; Librarians, placement sources
　see also Association of American Library Schools
Library Services and Construction Act, 179, 212-220
　funding of conservation programs, 63
　Title I Public Library Services, 190, 213-218
　Title II Public Library Construction, 190, 218
　Title III Interlibrary Cooperation, 190, 218-220
　Title IV Older Readers Service, 48, 50
Library services and programs, 13-14
　access, 43-45
　effectiveness, 307
　federal libraries, 357-358
　Folger Library, 71-72
　funding, 175-189
　hospital libraries, 58
　international, CLR support, 209-210
　Israel, 430-436
　LC, 108-109
　Metropolitan Washington Library Council, 83-84
　outreach programs, 13-14
　public awareness, 124-125
　standards, 4
　see also Information services; Library Services and Construction Act

Library services for children and young adults
  bibliography, 456–457
  see also American Library Association, Association for Library Service to Children; American Library Association, Young Adult Services Division
Library services for rural patrons, see Library services for special groups
Library services for special groups, 14, 122
  bibliography, 461–462
Library services for the aging, 13, 43–52
  employment information, 47
  LSCA support, 216
  management issues, 48–49
  use of older adults, 50
Library services for the blind, 14
  access to information, 121
  see also Kurzweil reading machines; Library services for the handicapped
Library services for the deaf, 14
Library services for the disadvantaged
  LSCA support, 216, 217
  see also Library services and programs, outreach programs
Library services for the handicapped, 14
  access to information, 121
  LSCA support, 215–216
  see also Library of Congress, National Library Service for the Blind and Physically Handicapped
Library services for the institutionalized, 14
  LSCA support, 214–215
Library Services to persons of limited English-speaking ability, LSCA support, 213–214
Library Standards for Adult Correctional Institutions, 122
Library statistics, 309–312
  ARL program, 151
  college and university libraries, 268, 269
  ECIA funding, 180–181
  federal funding, 174, 176–177
  federal libraries, 357
  national, 428–429
    see also Clearinghouse for National Library Statistics
  personnel, 349, 350
  placements, 276–277, 279, 280, 281, 282–283
  public libraries, 321–328, 329–338
  salaries, 266–273, 274, 275, 282–283, 284, 285, 286, 307–308
  school library/media services, 270
  status of legislation, 186–187
  two-year college libraries, 376–379
  UNESCO, 428
  see also Elementary and Secondary Education Act; Higher Education Act; Information services, funding; Intellectual freedom, survey; International Federation of Library Associations and Institutions, Statistical Section; Libraries, construction; Libraries, number of, U.S. and Canada; Library cooperation, funding; Library Services and Construction Act; Library surveys; National Center for Education Statistics; Networks, NCES survey; Public libraries, construction; Public libraries, expenditures; Public libraries, funding; School library/media services, NCES survey; UNESCO, library statistics; U.S., population served by libraries
"Library Statistics for Developing Countries," 428
Library surveys
  ALA, 208, 271, 272, 288
  computerized operations, 310–311
  federal libraries, 103
  government libraries, 356–360
  health sciences libraries, 57
  LC, 108
  library school placements, 273–287
  NCES, 309–312
  public library personnel, 267, 269
  salary surveys, 266–273
  school library/media services personnel, 270
  services for the aging, 45–46
  special libraries, 270
  state library agencies, 270
  see also *ARL Annual Library Survey*; Library General Information Survey; Library statistics; Networks, NCES survey; School library/media services, NCES survey
Library technical assistants, 289–290
  training programs, 289
  see also Library personnel, paraprofessionals
Library Technology Reports, 128
"Library's Responsibility to the Aging," 122

Limiting What Students Shall Read, 38, 42
Linked Systems Project, 205, 206
Linking the Bibliographic Utilities: Benefits and Costs, 205
Lippe, Jane, 139
Lister Hill National Center for Biomedical Communications, 114–115
   Electronic Document Storage and Retrieval Program, 115
   see also Hepatitis Knowledge Base; Human Genetics Knowledge Base; Integrated Library System; Knowledge Base Research Program; Peptic Ulcer Knowledge Base
Literary agents and authors, bibliography, 468
Literary awards, *see* Awards, literary
Lottman, Herbert, 417
Lufkin, J. M., 163
Lundberg, Susan O., 4
Lutheran Church Library Association, 554
Lynch, Beverly, 9
Lynch, Mary Jo, 305

M

MEDLARS, 53, 54, 113
MEDLINE, 53, 54, 112
   charges, 113
MED77, available on-line, 113
MLA, *see* Medical Library Association; Music Library Association
MLAA, *see* Medical Library Assistance Act
MSC, *see* Mutual Support Corporation
MURL, *see* Public Libraries, MURL programs
McClung, James W., 106
Machlup, Fritz, 308
Madison, James, Memorial Building, *see* Library of Congress, James Madison Memorial Building
Major Urban Resource Libraries, *see* Public libraries, MURL programs
Manual of Procedures for Evaluation Visits and Self-Study, 127
Manual on Bookselling, 131
Manuscript donations, tax credit, 108, 188
Manuscripts, *see* Archives
Maranjian, Lorig, 265
Margolis, Esther, 139
Martin, Susan K., 78
Marton, Victor W., 93
Maryles, Daisy, 490
Massachusetts, Proposition 2½, *see* Proposition 2½
Matheson, Nina, 55
"Media Evaluation: The Group Process," 125
Medical libraries, 52–60
   computerized functions, 54–55
   federal, 59
   funding, 182–183
   personnel, continuing education, 56–57
   regional, 56
   see also Association of Academic Health Sciences Library Directors; Hospital libraries; Medical Library Assistance Act; Medical Library Association; Medical school libraries; National Library of Medicine
Medical Library Assistance Act, 55–56
   funding of NLM grants, 116
Medical Library Association, 554–557
   placement services, 255
Medical Literature Analysis and Retrieval System, *see* MEDLARS
Medical publications, *see* Technical, scholarly, and medical books
Medical school libraries, 57–58
Mehnert, Robert B., 112
Melady, Thomas, 9
Memphis Public Library, salary survey, 267
Mergers and acquisitions, *see* Publishers, mergers and acquisitions
Metropolitan Washington Council of Governments, 83
Metropolitan Washington Library Council, 82–87
Michalak, Jo-Ann, 453
Michigan Library Consortium, 17
Microcomputers, *see* Libraries, computerized functions
Microforms, 110, 148
   access, 206
   bibliography, 459
   NAL, 118
   prices, 405
   standards, 157
   see also ARL Microform Project; Computer Output Microforms; Library materials; National Micrographics Association
"Mid-Career Assessment and Strategies for Advancement in the 90s," 19

Midwest Health Science Library Network, 56
Minorities, see American Library Association, Office of Library Outreach Services, Minority Concerns Committee; Library personnel, discrimination in employment; National Commission on Libraries and Information Science, Task Force on Library and Information Services to Cultural Minorities
Missouri Network Corporation, 17
Molholt, Pat, 206
Morrow, Carolyn Clark, 63
Moscow Book Fair Reception in Exile, 3rd, 142
Music Library Association, 557–558
  placement services, 255
Mutual Support Corporation, 80
Myers, Margaret, 251, 266

N

NAC, see Library of Congress, Network Advisory Committee
NAFS, see Name Authority File Service
NAL, see National Agricultural Library
NCAC, see National Conservation Advisory Council
NCES, see National Center for Education Statistics
NCLIS, see National Commission on Libraries and Information Science
NCLIS/SLA Task Force on the Role of the Special Library in Nationwide Networking, 166
NEDCC, see Northeast Document Conservation Center
NEH, see National Endowment for the Humanities
NELINET, 80
NHPRC, see National Historical Publications and Records Commission
NLA, see National Librarians Association
NLC, see National Library of Canada
NLM, see National Library of Medicine
NLS/BPH, see Library of Congress, National Library Service for the Blind and Physically Handicapped
NLW, see National Library Week
NMA, see National Micrographics Association
NMAC, see National Medical Audiovisual Center
NOAA Automated Library and Information System, 104
NSF, see National Science Foundation
NUC, see National Union Catalog
Name Authority File Service, 206
National Agricultural Library, 117–119
  Current Awareness Literature Service, 118
  Current Research Information System, 118
  Regional Document Delivery System, 117–118
  reorganized, 117
National Archives and Records Service, budget cuts, 179
National Biomedical Serials Holdings Database, 113–114
National Center for Education Statistics, 309
  federal library survey, 103
  library surveys, 272
  funding, 311
  networks and cooperative library organizations survey, 344–355
  public library surveys, 329–338
  publications program, 311
  school library/media centers, 338–343
National Commission on Libraries and Information Science, 88–92
  appointments, 185
  meetings, 92
  Task Force on Community Information and Referral Services, 89
  Task Force on Library and Information Services to Cultural Minorities, 89–90
  Task Force on Public/Private Sector Relations, 90–91
  Task Force on the Role of the Special Library in Nationwide Networks and Cooperative Programs, 91–92
  see also Intergovernmental Library Cooperation Project
National Commission on New Technological Uses of Copyrighted Works, 95
National Conservation Advisory Council, 62
National Endowment for the Arts, funding, 179
National Endowment for the Humanities
  funding, 179
  funds conservation programs, 64

National Historical Publications and Records Commission, funding, 182
National Information Conference and Exposition, 5th, 155
National Librarians Association, 558–559
National libraries
  Canada, 437–438
  U.S.
    acquisitions, 357–358
    employment, 260–261
    funding, 178
    interlibrary cooperation, 356–360
    networks, *see* Networks, national
    public access, 359
    see also Federal Library Committee; *also* names of national libraries, e.g., Library of Congress
National Library and Information Services Act (proposed), 89
National Library of Canada, 437, 438
  cooperative meeting with LC, 111
National Library of Medicine, 112–116
  Regional Medical Library Network, 55
  reconfiguration, 113
  see also Lister Hill National Center for Biomedical Communications; National Medical Audiovisual Center; Toxicology Information Program
National Library of Medicine Act, 112
National Library of Medicine Classification: A Scheme for the Shelf Arrangement of Books in the Field of Medicine and Its Related Sciences, 114
National Library Week, 15, 124, 125
National Medal for Literature, 146
National Medical Audiovisual Center, 115
National Micrographics Association, 156–162
  Current Awareness Service, 162
  Institute, seminars, 161
  meetings, 161
  publications, 157–159
  Resource Center, 161–162
  see also Information technology
National Oceanic and Atmospheric Administration, *see* NOAA Automated Library and Information System
National Periodicals Center, 197
National Periodicals System Corporation, 149
National Preservation Program, 61–62

National Registry for Librarians, placement services, 255
National Science Foundation, Division of Information Science and Technology
  grants, 242–247
  Information Impact Program, 242
  Information Science Program, 242
  Information Technology Program, 242
National Survey of Library Services to the Aging, 44, 50
National Survey of Salaries and Wages in Public Schools, 270
National Union Catalog, Pre-1956 Imprints, 99, 106
  Supplement, 110
National Writers Union (proposed), 35
National Year of Disabled Persons, 122
Neff, Evaline, 212
Network Advisory Committee, AAP membership, 142
Networks, 16–18, 78–82
  bibliography, 459–460
  Canada, 436–439
  educational programs, 91
  electronic mail service, 8, 118, 166
  federal, 91, 360
  financial problems, 79–80, 81
  NCES survey, 344–355
  national, 110, 147–148
    see also Networks, federal, *above*
  regional, 16–17, 80–81
    see also names of networks, e.g., SOLINET; National Library of Medicine, Regional Medical Library Network
  SLA concerns, 166
  state, 5, 17–18
  see also Bibliographic data bases; Information services; Online Computer Library Center; *also* names of other networks
New Career Options for Librarians, 265
New England Document Conservation Center, *see* Northeast Document Conservation Center
New England Library Information Network, *see* NELINET
New Learning for Older Americans, 45–46
Newberry Library, conservation programs, 64
Newspapers
  subscription rates, 405
  vacancy notices, 251

1980-81 Administrative Compensation Survey Report, 267
Nobel Prize for Literature, 421
Northeast Document Conservation Center, 23, 63
Nyren, Karl, 3

O

OCLC, *see* Online Computer Library Center
OCTANET, 56
OIRA, *see* U.S., Office of Management and Budget, Office of Information and Regulatory Affairs
OLLT, *see* U.S., Department of Education, Office of Libraries and Learning Technology
OLOS, *see* American Library Association, Office of Library Outreach Services
OLPR, *see* American Library Association, Office for Library Personnel Resources
OMB, *see* U.S., Office of Management and Budget
OMS, *see* Association of Research Libraries, Office of Management Studies
OULCS, *see* Ontario Universities Library Cooperative System
Obscenity legislation, 29–30, 194
Office of Information and Regulatory Affairs, *see* U.S., Office of Management and Regulatory Affairs
Office of Management and Budget, *see* U.S., Office of Management and Budget
O'Hara, Molly, 19
Olsgaard, Jane Kinch, 19
Olsgaard, John N., 19
Omnibus Budget Reconciliation Act, 1981, 116, 122, 174–175, 179, 180–181, 182–183, 185, 188, 190–191, 196, 221
  Title, V-D-2, 190–191
"On the Nature of Relations among Libraries," 18
Online Computer Library Center, 78–79
  computerized home service, 16, 31
  regional network relations, 16–17
  system malfunctions, 16
  university library members, 16
"Online Encyclopedias: The Potential," 8

Online, Inc., placement services, 255
Ontario Universities Library Cooperative System, 438
Output Measures for Public Libraries: A Manual of Standardized Procedures, 307
Owens, Janice, 28

P

PETREL, *see* Professional Education and Training for Research Librarianship program
PLA, *see* American Library Association, Public Library Association
PLMS, *see* American Library Association, Resources and Technical Services Division, Preservation of Library Materials Section
PSP, *see* Association of American Publishers, Professional and Scholarly Publishing Division
PSP Awards Program, 145, 146
Packer, Katherine H., 428
Pagel, Doris, 288
"Paper for Book Longevity," 99
Paperback books, 36
  marketing, 143–144
  prices, 389–390, 402, 403
    German books, 409
  title output, 384, 386
  see also Association of American Publishers, Mass Market Paperback Division
Paperbound Books in Print, 384
Paperwork Reduction Act, 19, 201
Pay Equity: Comparable Worth Action Guide, 272
Pay Rates in the Public Sector, 271
Peptic Ulcer Knowledge Base, 114
Performax Systems International of Minneapolis, 15
Periodicals
  access, 149
  book trade, bibliography, 470, 470–471
  prices, 3–4, 397
  see also Library literature, periodicals and serials; Library materials; Newspapers; Serial publications
Peters, Jean R., 464
Peterson, Toni, 206
Phillips, Beth, 225
Phillips, Jane, 3

"Philosophy of Scrounge," 12
Photocopying
  five-year copyright review, 184, 198–199
  industrial firms, 74
  libraries, 94
  publishers permissions, 74–75, 75–76
  royalties, 72–73
  see also Copyright Clearance Center
Pico v. *The Island Trees* (NY) *Union Free School Board*, 28–29
Piper, Nelson A., 396
"Placements and Salaries 1980: Holding the Line," 20
Planning for a Nationwide System of Library Statistics, 309
Planning Process for Public Libraries, 14–15, 126
Pornography, see Obscenity legislation
Postal rates, 188, 191
  classification, 191–192
Postal service legislation, 192
  see also U.S., Postal Service
Postal Service Act, 1979, 192
Preservation and conservation, see Library materials, conservation and preservation
Preservation Education Directory, 126
Presidential libraries, 3
Price, Douglas S., 88
"Price Increases for 1981: U.S. Periodicals and Serial Publications," 3
"Price Index for Nonprint Media," 4
Printing and Publishing, 440
Privacy Protection Study Commission, 200
Prizes, see Awards; Grants, information services; Grants, library; Information technology, HEA grants; Scholarships
Professional Education and Training for Research Librarianship program, 208, 306, 307
Project Progress: A Study of Canadian Public Libraries, 439
Proposition 13, survey of results, 27
Proposition 2½, 26
Public libraries
  acquisitions, 317–318, 332, 334
  additions and renovations, 370–371
  bibliography, 460
  Canada, construction, 372
  circulation statistics, 326, 328, 334
  construction, 366–375
  LSCA support, 218
  see also Library Services and Construction Act
  expenditures, 322, 324, 325, 329–338
  fees and fines, 12–13
  funding, see Library funding, public libraries
  future developments, 4
  interlibrary loan, see Interlibrary loan
  Israel, 433–434
  see also Kibbutz libraries
  MURL programs, 216, 218
  personnel, 327, 329, 331, 332
  salaries, 324–325
  workloads, 328
  priorities, 11
  public relations, 15–16
  reference services, 326
  see also Libraries, reference services
  service outlets, 326, 329, 330
  services and programs, see Library services and programs
  statistics, see Library statistics, public libraries; *also* subheads circulation, expenditures, personnel, reference services under Public libraries, *above*
  system mergers, 11
  see also American Library Association, Public Library Association; Research libraries
Public Library Association, see American Library Association, Public Library Association
"Public Library Computerized Support of School Proficiency Testing Program," 31
Public Sector/Private Sector Interaction in Providing Information Services, 90
Publishers
  backlists, see Thor Power Tool decision
  CCC participation, 75–76
  discount structures, 35–36
  employee ownership, 35
  inventory accounting, 192–193
  mergers and acquisitions, 34–35
  personnel changes, 34
  sales, see Book sales
  statistics, see Publishing statistics
  warehouse sales, 4
  see also American Booksellers Association, Publisher Planning Commit-

Publishers (Cont.)
tee; Association of American Publishers
Publishers associations, CCC Participation Program, 75
Publishing
  bibliography, 465-468
  distribution of books, 396
    see also Association of American Publishers, Book Distribution Task Force
  legislation, see Legislation affecting publishing
Publishing Education Information Service, 142-143
Publishing statistics
  British, 446-450
  children's books, 444
  consumer expenditures, 394-396
  exports, see Book exports
  imports, see Book imports
  sales, see Book sales
  title output, 383-391
    British, 446-450
    international, 440-445
    see also Paperback books, title output

R

RASD, see American Library Association, Reference and Adult Services Division
RFPs, see Requests for Proposals
RLG, see Research Libraries Group
RLIN, see Research Libraries Information Network
RML, see Medical libraries, regional; National Library of Medicine, Regional Medical Library Network
RSS, see Regional Support System
RTSD, see American Library Association, Resources and Technical Services Division
Racial, Ethnic, and Sexual Composition of Library Staff in Public and Academic Libraries, 272
Rainwater, Robert, 208
"Read More about It," 98
"Readership Characteristics and Attitudes: Service to Blind and Physically Handicapped Library Users," 108
"Reading and Successful Living: The Family-School Partnership," 99
Reference and Adult Services Division, see American Library Association, Reference and Adult Services Division
Reference services, see Libraries, reference services
Reforma, placement services, 255
Regional library associations, see Library associations, state and regional
Regional Medical Network, see National Library of Medicine, Regional Medical Library Network
Regional networks, see Networks, regional
Regional Support System, 80
"Rely on Your Textbook," advertising program, 144
"Report of the AALS Task Force on Education of Non-Clerical Support Staff," 288-290
Requests for Proposals, 305, 307
Requirements for Certification, 1981, 265
Research in Information Science, 246
Research in librarianship, see Library research and development
Research libraries, 9-10
  funding, see Library funding, research libraries
  personnel
    continuing education, 150
    training, 208, 306
Research Libraries Group, 80
  preservation concerns, 62
  Reconfigured Data Base, 79
  reference services, see Libraries, reference services
  see also Association of Research Libraries; College and university libraries; Public libraries
Research Libraries Information Network, 16, 78-79
Resource sharing, see Cataloging and classification, cooperative; Information services; Interlibrary loan; Libraries, acquisitions; Library cooperation; Networks
Resources and Technical Services Division, see American Library Association, Resources and Technical Services Division
Responsibilities of the American Book Community, 100
"Responsiveness: Key to Developing Li-

brary Awareness; Awareness: Key to Meeting Fiscal Challenges," 124
Retrieval services, *see* Information services, retrieval services
Rhodes, Sarah N., 242
Right to Read, *see* Intellectual freedom
Riley, James P., 100
Riordan, Virginia, 72
Robinson, Barbara M., 82
Rochester Institute of Technology, Book Testing Laboratory, 66
"Rooted in America," 99
Rosenau, Fred S., 152
Rosenberg, Jane A., 204
Rosenthal, Arthur J., 146
Rosenthal, Sheri, 361, 366
Rosenzweig, Robert, 9
Rural library patrons, *see* Library services for special groups

S

SAA, *see* Society of American Archivists
SAN, *see* Standard Address Number
SCOLE, *see* American Library Association, Standing Committee on Library Education
SIS, *see* Dallas Public Library, Specialized Information Service
SLA, *see* Special Libraries Association
SOLINET, 80
  Regional Support Services scrapped, 16
SSP, *see* Society for Scholarly Publishing
STM, *see* International Group of Scientific, Technical and Medical Publishers
"Salaries of Municipal Officials for 1980," 267, 269
Salary Survey of Special Libraries in Metropolitan Washington: 1981, 270
Schick, Frank L., 309
Scholarly publications, *see* Technical, scholarly, and medical books
Scholarships, 294-296, 296-301
  HEA, 228-229, 230-231
School library/media associations, state, 578-584
School library/media services
  acquisitions, 342
  bibliography, 461
  buildings, equipment, furniture, 339
  censorship problems, 28-30
  ESEA expenditures, 223
  ESEA support, 221-225
  expenditures, 340-342
  job opportunities, 262
  Israel, 434-435
  NCES survey, 338-343
  personnel, 340
    salaries, 270
  reference services, *see* Libraries, reference services
  state, 578-584
  state supervisors, 584-588
  statistics, *see* Library statistics, school library/media services; *also* subheads acquisitions, expenditures, personnel, *above*
  see also American Library Association, American Association of School Librarians
Sellen, Betty-Carol, 265
Serial publications
  prices, 398
  see also Library literature, periodicals and serials; Periodicals
Serving Physically Disabled People: An Information Handbook for All Libraries, 122
Sever, Shmuel, 430
"Sex, Salaries, and Library Support," 22
Shaw, Ralph R., Award for Library Literature, 122
Skeptason, Trish, 212
Skipper, James, 17
Small libraries, *see* Libraries
Smith, G. Royce, 130
So You Want to Be an Information Broker?, 265
Society for Scholarly Publishing, 162-165
  joint meeting with International Federation of Scientific Editors Association, and Council of Biology Editors, 164
Society of American Archivists, 550-560
  placement services, 255-256
  preservation concerns, 62-63
Southeastern Library Network, *see* SOLINET
Special libraries
  bibliography, 462
  Israel, 433
  OCLC relations, 91-92
  personnel, continuing education, 167-168

Special libraries (Cont.)
  reference services, see Libraries, reference services
Special Libraries, 167
Special Libraries Association, 165–169, 560–562
  cooperative action, 168
  Government Relations Committee, 165
  membership services, 169
  placement services, 256
  publications, 167
SpeciaList, 167
Specialized Information Service, see Dallas Public Library, Specialized Information Service
Spivak, Jane, 265
Standard Address Number, 380–383
Standards for Accreditation, 127
Standards for College Libraries, 4
Standards for Libraries at Institutions for the Mentally Retarded, 122
"Star Years LSCA," 120
State library agencies, 574–578
  bibliography, 462
  placement services, 256
  see also American Library Association, Association of Specialized and Cooperative Library Agencies; Chief Officers of State Library Agencies
State library associations, see Library associations, state and regional
State networks, see Networks, state
State of the Book World, 99
State Salary Survey, 271
State school library/media associations, see School library/media associations, state
State school library supervisors, see School library/media services, state supervisors
Statistics of Public Libraries in the U.S. and Canada Serving 100,000 Population or More, 267
Stevens, Frank A., 228
Stone, Elizabeth W., 120
Stubbs, Kendon, 151
Sullivan, Peggy, 120
"Survey of Current Hospital Library Resources," 57
Surveys, library, see Library surveys
Symposium on Educating Library and Information Scientists to Provide Information and Library Services to the Disabled, 121

T

TLA, see Theatre Library Association
TRIUL, see Tri-University Libraries of British Columbia
Tax Reform Act of 1969, 149
Technical, scholarly, and medical books
  AAP concerns, 144–145
  bibliography, 468
Telecommunications
  legislation, 184–185, 199–200
  off-air taping, 30, 94–95, 183–184, 198–199
  see also Audiovisual materials, off-air videotaping; Copyright, off-air taping
Telecommunications Competition and Deregulation Act, 185
"Television, the Book and the Classroom," 98
"Temporary Employment and Academic Librarians," 19
The Textbook in American Society, 100
Textbooks
  AAP Concerns, 145
  college, AAP concerns, 144
Theatre Library Association, 562
Thompson, James A., 3
Thor Power Tool decision, 34, 139–140, 188, 192–193
Toward a National Program for Library and Information Services, 356
"Toward a Work-Force Analysis of the School Library/Media Professional," 270
Toxicology Information Program, 116
Toxicology Information Response Center, 116
Translations, see Books, translations
Trezza, Alphonse F., 90, 356
Tri-University Libraries of British Columbia, 438
Turock, Betty J., 43
"Two Hundred Years of Louisiana Sugar," 119
Two-year college libraries
  additions and renovations, 378–379
  construction, 376–379
  service facilities, 376

U

UAP, see Universal Availability of Publications

INDEX / 649

UBC, see Universal Bibliographic Control
UNESCO, library statistics, 429
USBE, see Universal Serials and Book Exchange
USICA, see U.S., International Communication Agency
USPS, see U.S., Postal Service
UTLAS, see University of Toronto, Automation System
Understanding U.S. Information Policy, 154
United Auto Workers, 35
U.S.
  Congress
    House Committee on Education and Labor, 89
    House Post Office and Civil Service Commission, 192
  Congressional budget, 173-175
  Copyright Office, 93-97
    registrations, 108
  criminal code, 194-195
  Department of Defense, overseas job opportunities, 263
  Department of Education
    Education Division General Administrative Requirements, 228
    Office of Libraries and Learning Technology, 305, 233-237
  International Communication Agency, job opportunities, 263
  Office of Information and Regulatory Affairs, see U.S., Office of Management and Budget, Office of Information and Regulatory Affairs
  Office of Management and Budget, Office of Information and Regulatory Affairs, 91, 201-202
  population served by libraries, 312-313
  Postal Rate Commission, 191, 192
    see also Postal rates
  Postal Service, 191-192
    budget cuts, 192
    nine digit Zip, 192
    see also Association of American Publishers, Postal Committee; Postal rates
U.S. v. *AT&T*, 200
Universal Availability of Publications, financial problems, 423
Universal Bibliographic Control, financial problems, 423
Universal Serials and Book Exchange, 18, 562-563

University of Toronto, Library Automation System, 438
Urban libraries, see Public libraries; Research libraries

V

VALNET, see Veterans Administration Library Network
Van Houten, Stephen, 20, 273
Veterans Administration Library Network, 59
Video Cassett Exchange Program, 31
"Video Literacy in the Computer Age," 99
Videotapes, see Audiovisual materials, off-air taping; Audiovisual materials, off-air videotaping; Copyright, off-air taping; Copyright, off-air videotaping
Voice of Z39, 133

W

WCC, see Western Conservation Congress
WHCOLIS, see White House Conference on Library and Information Science
WHCOLIST, see White House Conference on Library and Information Science, Taskforce
WITS, see Worldwide Information and Trade System
WLN, see Washington Library Network
Waite, David P., 72
Walch, David B., 4
Warnken, Kelly, 265
Washington Library Network, 79-80
Western Conservation Congress, 64
Western States Materials Conservation Congress, 64
What Else You Can Do with a Library Degree, 265
White House Conference on Library and Information Science
  NCLIS activities, 88
  Taskforce
    plenary meeting, Atlanta, 89
    plenary meeting, Detroit, 88-89
Who's Who in Library and Information Services, 129
Willard, Robert S., 195
Willison, Ian, 99
Wilson, Jane, 130, 422
Woellner, Elizabeth H., 265

Women in librarianship, 22
  see also Library personnel, discrimination in employment
"Word to the Wise: Library," 125
"Work and Culture in an Eighteenth-Century Printing Shop," 99
Worldwide Information and Trade System, 197

Y

YASD, see American Library Association, Young Adult Services Division

Yale University Library, conservation trainees, 64
Young adult books, see Books, best books, young adult
Young Adult Services Division, see American Library Association, Young Adult Services Division

Z

Z39, see American National Standards Committee Z39

Directory of U.S. and Canadian Libraries

This directory has been compiled for ready reference. For libraries not listed, see the *American Library Directory* (R. R. Bowker, 1981).

UNITED STATES

Univ. of Alabama
Amelia Gayle Gorgas Lib., Box S,
  University, AL 35486
Tel: 205-348-5298

Alameda County Library
3121 Diablo, Hayward, CA 94545
Tel: 415-881-6337

Annapolis & Anne Arundel County Public Library
5 Harry S. Truman Pkwy., Annapolis,
  MD 21401
Tel: 301-224-7371

Arizona State Univ. Library
Tempe, AZ 85281
Tel: 602-965-3417

Atlanta Public Library
One Margaret Mitchell Sq. N.W., Carnegie
  Way & Forsyth St., Atlanta, GA 30303
Tel: 404-688-4636

Baltimore County Public Library
320 York Rd., Towson, MD 21204
Tel: 301-296-8500

Boston Athenaeum
10½ Beacon St., Boston, MA 02118
Tel: 617-227-0270

Boston Public Library
666 Boylston St., Box 286, Boston, MA 02117
Tel: 617-536-5400

Boston Univ. Libraries
Mugar Memorial Lib., 771 Commonwealth
  Ave., Boston, MA 02215
Tel: 617-353-3710

Brigham Young Univ.
Harold B. Lee Lib., University Hill, Provo,
  UT 84602
Tel: 801-378-2905

Brooklyn Public Library
Grand Army Plaza, Brooklyn, NY 11238
Tel: 212-780-7712

Broward County Libraries
Box 5463, Fort Lauderdale, FL 33310
Tel: 305-972-1100

Brown Univ. Library
Providence, RI 02912
Tel: 401-863-2167

Buffalo and Erie County Public Library
Lafayette Sq., Buffalo, NY 14203
Tel: 716-856-7525

Univ. of California, Berkeley
Univ. Lib., Berkeley, CA 94720
Tel: 415-642-3773

Univ. of California, Davis
General Lib., Davis, CA 95616
Tel: 916-752-2110

Univ. of California, Los Angeles
Univ. Lib., 405 Hilgard Ave., Los Angeles,
  CA 90024
Tel: 213-825-1201

Univ. of California, San Diego
Univ. Libs., Mail Code C-075, La Jolla,
  CA 92093
Tel: 714-452-3336

Univ. of California, Santa Barbara
Campus Lib., Santa Barbara, CA 93106
Tel: 805-961-2741

Carnegie Library of Pittsburgh
4400 Forbes Ave., Pittsburgh, PA 15213
Tel: 412-622-3100

Case Western Reserve
Univ. Libs., 11161 East Blvd., Cleveland,
 OH 44106
Tel: 216-368-3530

Univ. of Chicago
Joseph Regenstein Lib., 1100 E. 57 St.,
 Chicago, IL 60637
Tel: 312-753-2977

Chicago Public Library
425 N. Michigan Ave., Chicago, IL 60611
Tel: 312-269-2900

Univ. of Cincinnati Libraries
Central Lib., University & Woodside,
 Cincinnati, OH 45221
Tel: 513-475-2218

Cincinnati-Hamilton County Public Library
800 Vine St., Cincinnati, OH 45202
Tel: 513-369-6000

Cleveland Public Library
325 Superior Ave., Cleveland, OH 44114
Tel: 216-623-2800

Univ. of Colorado at Boulder
Univ. Libs., Norlin Lib., Campus Box 184,
 Boulder, CO 80309
Tel: 303-492-7511

Cclorado State Univ.
William E. Morgan Lib., Fort Collins, CO
 80523
Tel: 303-491-5911

Columbia Univ. Libraries
535 W. 114 St., New York, NY 10027
Tel: 212-280-2241

Univ. of Connecticut Library
Storrs, CT 06268
Tel: 203-486-2219

Contra Costa Country Library
1750 Oak Park Blvd., Pleasant Hill, CA 94523
Tel: 415-944-3423

Cornell Univ. Libraries
Ithaca, NY 14853
Tel: 607-256-3689

Cuyahoga County Public Library
4510 Memphis Ave., Cleveland, OH 44144
Tel: 216-398-1800

John Crerar Library
35 W. 33 St., Chicago, IL 60616
Tel: 312-225-2526

Dallas Public Library
1954 Commerce, Dallas, TX 75201
Tel: 214-748-9071

Dartmouth College
Baker Memorial Lib., Hanover, NH 03755
Tel: 603-646-2235

Dayton-Montgomery County Public Library
215 E. Third St., Dayton, OH 45402
Tel: 513-224-1651

Denver Public Library
1357 Broadway, Denver, CO 80203
Tel: 303-573-5152, ext. 271

Detroit Public Library
5201 Woodward Ave., Detroit, MI 48202
Tel: 313-833-1000

District of Columbia Public Library
Martin Luther King Memorial Lib., 901 G St.
 N.W., Washington, DC 20001
Tel: 202-727-1101

Duke Univ.
William R. Perkins Lib., Durham, NC 27706
Tel: 919-684-2034

Emory Univ. Libraries
Atlanta, GA 30322
Tel: 404-329-6861

Enoch Pratt Free Library
400 Cathedral St., Baltimore, MD 21201
Tel: 301-396-5430

Fairfax County Public Library
5502 Port Royal Rd., Springfield, VA 22151
Tel: 703-321-9810

Univ. of Florida Libraries
210 Lib. W., Gainesville, FL 32611
Tel: 904-392-0341

Florida State Univ.
Robert Manning Strozier Lib., Tallahassee,
  FL 32306
Tel: 904-644-5211

Fort Worth Public Library
300 Taylor St., Fort Worth, TX 76102
Tel: 817-870-7700

Fresno County Public Library
2420 Mariposa St., Fresno, CA 93721
Tel: 209-488-3191

Georgetown Univ.
Joseph Mark Lauinger Lib., Box 37445,
  Washington, DC 20013
Tel: 202-625-4095

Univ. of Georgia Libraries
Athens, GA 30602
Tel: 404-542-2716

Harvard Univ. Library
Cambridge, MA 02138
Tel: 617-495-3650

Univ. of Hawaii Library
2550 The Mall, Honolulu, HI 96822
Tel: 808-948-7205

Hennepin County Library
York Ave. S. at 70, Edina, MN 55435
Tel: 612-830-4944

Univ. of Houston
M. D. Anderson Memorial Lib., 4800
  Calhoun Blvd., Houston, TX 77004
Tel: 713-749-4241

Houston Public Library
500 McKinney Ave., Houston, TX 77002
Tel: 713-224-5441

Howard Univ. Libraries
Founders Lib., 2400 Sixth St. N.W.,
  Washington, DC 20059
Tel: 202-636-7253

Univ. of Illinois at Urbana-Champaign
University Lib., Wright St., 230 Lib.,
  Urbana, IL 61801
Tel: 217-333-0790

Indiana Univ. Libraries
Tenth St. and Jordan Ave., Bloomington,
  IN 47401
Tel: 812-337-3403

Indianapolis-Marion County Public Library
Box 211, 40 E. Saint Clair St., Indianapolis,
  IN 46206
Tel: 317-269-1700

Univ. of Iowa Libraries
Iowa City, IA 52242
Tel: 319-353-4450

Iowa State Univ. Library
Ames, IA 50011
Tel: 515-294-1442

Jacksonville Public Library System
Haydon Burns Lib., 122 N. Ocean St.,
  Jacksonville, FL 32202
Tel: 904-633-6870

Jefferson Parish Library
Box 7490, 3420 N. Causeway Blvd. at
  Melvil Dewey Dr., Metairie, LA 70010
Tel: 504-834-5850

Johns Hopkins Univ. Libraries
Milton S. Eisenhower Lib., Baltimore,
  MD 21218
Tel: 301-338-8000

Joint Univ. Libraries
See Vanderbilt Univ. Library

Kansas City Public Library
311 E. 12 St., Kansas City, MO 64106
Tel: 816-221-2685

Univ. of Kansas Libraries
Watson Lib., Lawrence, KS 66045
Tel: 913-864-3601

Kent State Univ. Libraries
Kent, OH 44242
Tel: 216-672-2962

Univ. of Kentucky
Margaret I. King Lib., Lexington, KY 40506
Tel: 606-257-3801

King County Library System
300 Eighth Ave. N., Seattle, WA 98109
Tel: 206-344-7465

Library of Congress
Washington, DC 20540
Tel: 202-287-5000

Los Angeles County Public Library System
Box 111, 320 W. Temple St., Los Angeles,
CA 90053
Tel: 213-974-6501

Los Angeles Public Library System
630 W. Fifth St., Los Angeles, CA 90071
Tel: 213-626-7555

Louisiana State Univ. Library
Troy H. Middleton Lib., Baton Rouge,
LA 70803
Tel: 504-388-2217

Louisville Free Public Library
Fourth and York Sts., Louisville, KY 40203
Tel: 502-584-4154

Maricopa County Library
3375 W. Durango, Phoenix, AZ 85009
Tel: 602-269-2535

Univ. of Maryland at College Park
Univ. Libs., College Park, MD 20742
Tel: 301-454-3011

Univ. of Massachusetts at Amherst
Univ. Lib., Amherst, MA 01003
Tel: 413-545-0284

Massachusetts Institute of Technology Libraries
Rm. 14 S-216, Cambridge, MA 02139
Tel: 617-253-5651

Memphis-Shelby County Public Library
1850 Peabody Ave., Memphis, TN 38104
Tel: 901-528-2950

Univ. of Miami
Otto G. Richter Lib., Box 248214,
Memorial Dr., Coral Gables, FL 33124
Tel: 305-284-3551

Miami-Dade Public Library System
One Biscayne Blvd., Miami, FL 33132
Tel: 305-579-5001

Univ. of Michigan
Univ. Libs., Ann Arbor, MI 48109
Tel: 313-764-9356

Michigan State Univ. Library
East Lansing, MI 48824
Tel: 517-355-2344

Milwaukee Public Library
814 W. Wisconsin Ave., Milwaukee,
WI 53233
Tel: 414-278-3000

Minneapolis Public Library
300 Nicollet Mall, Minneapolis, MN 55401
Tel: 612-372-6500

Univ. of Minnesota Libraries
O. Meredith Wilson Lib., 309 19 Ave. S.,
Minneapolis, MN 55455
Tel: 612-373-3097

Univ. of Missouri-Kansas City Libraries
5100 Rockhill Rd., Kansas City, MO 64110
Tel: 816-276-1531

Montgomery County Department of Public Libraries
99 Maryland Ave., Rockville, MD 20850
Tel: 301-279-1401

Nassau Library System
900 Jerusalem Ave., Uniondale, NY 11553
Tel: 516-292-8920

National Agricultural Library
U.S. Dept. of Agriculture, 10301 Baltimore
Blvd., Beltsville, MD 20705
Tel: 301-344-3755

National Library of Medicine
8600 Rockville Pike, Bethesda, MD 20209
Tel: 301-496-4000

Univ. of Nebraska-Lincoln
Univ. Libs., Lincoln, NE 68588
Tel: 402-472-2526

State Univ. of New York at Albany
Univ. Lib., 1400 Washington Ave.,
Albany, NY 12222
Tel: 518-457-8542

State Univ. of New York at Buffalo
Univ. Libs., 432 Capen Hall, Buffalo,
NY 14260
Tel: 716-636-2965

State Univ. of New York at Stony Brook
Frank Melville Jr. Memorial Lib., Stony
  Brook, NY 11794
Tel: 516-246-5650

New York Public Library
Astor, Lenox and Tilden Foundations Lib.,
  Fifth Ave. and 42 St., New York, NY 10018
Tel: 212-930-0800

New York Univ.
Elmer Holmes Bobst Lib., 70 Washington Sq.
  S., New York, NY 10012
Tel: 212-598-2450

Newberry Library
60 W. Walton St., Chicago, IL 60610
Tel: 312-943-9090

Univ. of North Carolina at Greensboro
Walter Clinton Jackson Lib., 1000 Spring
  Garden St., Greensboro, NC 27412
Tel: 919-379-5880

Northwestern Univ. Library
1935 Sheridan Rd., Evanston, IL 60201
Tel: 312-492-7658

Univ. of Notre Dame
221 Memorial Lib., Notre Dame, IN 46556
Tel: 219-283-7317

Ohio State Univ.
William Oxley Thompson Memorial Lib.,
  1858 Neil Ave. Mall, Columbus, OH 43210
Tel: 614-422-6151

Univ. of Oklahoma
William Bennett Bizzell Memorial Lib., 401
  W. Brooks, Norman, OK 73019
Tel: 405-325-2611

Oklahoma State Univ. Library
Stillwater, OK 74078
Tel: 405-624-6313

Omaha Public Library
W. Dale Clark Lib., 215 S. 15 St., Omaha,
  NE 68102
Tel: 402-444-4800

Orange County Public Library
431 City Drive S., Orange, CA 92668
Tel: 714-634-7841

Univ. of Oregon Library
Eugene, OR 97403
Tel: 503-686-3056

Univ. of Pennsylvania Libraries
Van Pelt Lib., 3420 Walnut St.,
  Philadelphia, PA 19104
Tel: 215-243-7091

Pennsylvania State Univ.
Fred Lewis Pattee Lib., University Park,
  PA 16802
Tel: 814-865-0401

Free Library of Philadelphia
Logan Sq., Philadelphia, PA 19103
Tel: 215-686-5322

Phoenix Public Library
12 E. McDowell Rd., Phoenix, AZ 85004
Tel: 602-262-6451

Univ. of Pittsburgh
Hillman Lib., Pittsburgh, PA 15260
Tel: 412-624-4400

**Prince George's County Memorial
  Library System**
6532 Adelphi Rd., Hyattsville, MD 20782
Tel: 301-699-3500

Princeton Univ. Library
Princeton, NJ 08540
Tel: 609-452-3180

Purdue Univ. Libraries
Stewart Center, West Lafayette, IN 47907
Tel: 317-494-2900

Queens Borough Public Library
89-11 Merrick Blvd., Jamaica, NY 11432
Tel: 212-990-0700

Univ. of Rochester
Rush Rhees Lib., Rochester, NY 14627
Tel: 716-275-4461

Rutgers Univ. Libraries
College Ave., New Brunswick, NJ 08901
Tel: 201-932-7505

Sacramento Public Library
7000 Franklin Blvd., Suite 540,
  Sacramento, CA 95823
Tel: 916-440-5926

Saint Louis County Library
1640 S. Lindbergh Blvd., Saint Louis,
  MO 63131
Tel: 314-994-3300

Saint Louis Public Library
1301 Olive St., Saint Louis, MO 63103
Tel: 314-241-2288

San Antonio Public Library
203 S. St. Mary's, San Antonio, TX 78205
Tel: 512-299-7790

San Bernardino County Library
104 W. Fourth St., San Bernardino, CA 92415
Tel: 714-383-1734

San Diego County Public Library
5555 Overland Ave., Bldg. 15, San Diego,
  CA 92123
Tel: 714-565-5100

San Diego Public Library
820 E St., San Diego, CA 92101
Tel: 714-236-5800

San Francisco Public Library
Civic Center, San Francisco, CA 94012
Tel: 415-558-4235

San Jose Public Library
180 W. San Carlos St., San Jose, CA 95113
Tel: 408-277-4822

San Mateo County Public Library
25 Tower Rd., Belmont, CA 94002
Tel: 415-573-2056

Seattle Public Library
1000 Fourth Ave., Seattle, WA 98104
Tel: 206-625-2665

Smithsonian Institution Libraries
Constitution Ave. at Tenth St. N.W.,
  Washington, DC 20560
Tel: 202-381-5496

Univ. of South Carolina
Thomas Cooper Lib., Columbia, SC 29208
Tel: 803-777-3142

Univ. of Southern California
Edward L. Doheny Memorial Lib.,
  University Park, Los Angeles, CA 90007
Tel: 213-743-6050

Stanford Univ. Libraries
Stanford, CA 94305
Tel: 415-497-2016

Syracuse Univ. Libraries
Ernst S. Bird Lib., 222 Waverly Ave.,
  Syracuse, NY 13210
Tel: 315-423-2575

Tampa-Hillsborough County Public
  Library System
900 N. Ashley, Tampa, FL 33602
Tel: 813-223-8947

Temple Univ.
Samuel Paley Lib., Berks and 13 Sts.,
  Philadelphia, PA 19122
Tel: 215-787-8231

Univ. of Tennessee, Knoxville
James D. Hoskins Lib., Knoxville, TN 37916
Tel: 615-974-0111

Univ. of Texas Libraries
Box P, Austin, TX 78712
Tel: 512-471-3811

Texas A & M Univ.
Sterling C. Evans Lib., College Station,
  TX 77843
Tel: 713-845-8160

Tulane Univ. of Louisiana
Howard-Tilton Memorial Lib., New Orleans,
  LA 70118
Tel: 504-865-5131

Tulsa City-County Public Library
400 Civic Center, Tulsa, OK 74103
Tel: 918-581-5221

Univ. of Utah
Marriott Lib., Salt Lake City, UT 84112
Tel: 801-581-8558

Vanderbilt Univ. Library
419 21 Ave. S., Nashville, TN 37203
Tel: 615-322-2834

Univ. of Virginia
Alderman Lib., Charlottesville, VA 22904
Tel: 804-924-3026

Virginia Polytechnic Institute & State Univ.
Univ. Libs., Blacksburg, VA 24061
Tel: 703-961-5593

Univ. of Washington Libraries
FM-25, Seattle, WA 98195
Tel: 206-543-1760

Washington State Univ. Library
Pullman, WA 99164
Tel: 509-335-4557

Washington Univ. Libraries
Skinker and Lindell Blvds., Saint Louis,
   MO 63130
Tel: 314-889-5400

Wayne State Univ. Libraries
Detroit, MI 48202
Tel: 313-557-4020

Univ. of Wisconsin-Milwaukee
Golda Meir Lib., Box 604, 2311 E. Hartford
   Ave., Milwaukee, WI 53201
Tel: 414-963-4785

Yale Univ.
Box 1603A, Yale Sta., 120 High St.,
   New Haven, CT 06520
Tel: 203-436-8335

CANADA

Univ. of Alberta Libraries
Edmonton, Alta. T6G 2J8
Tel: 403-432-3790

Bibliothèque de Québec
37 r. Ste-Angele, Quebec, P.Q. G1R 4G5
Tel: 418-694-6356

Univ. of British Columbia Library
1956 Main Mall, Vancouver, B.C. V6T 1Y3
Tel: 604-228-3871

Etobicoke Public Library
Box 501, Etobicoke, Ont. M9C 4V5
Tel: 416-248-5681

London Public Libraries & Museums
305 Queens Ave., London, Ont. N6B 3L7
Tel: 519-432-7166

McGill Univ. Libraries
3459 McTavish St., Montreal, P.Q.
   H3A 1Y1
Tel: 514-392-4948

McMaster Univ.
1280 Main St. W., Hamilton, Ont. L8S 4L6
Tel: 416-525-9140

**Montreal City Library (Bibliothéque de la
   Ville de Montreal)**
1210 Sherbrooke E., Montreal, P.Q. H2L 1L9
Tel: 514-872-5923

**National Library of Canada (Bibliothéque
   Nationale du Canada)**
395 Wellington St., Ottawa, Ont. K1A 0N4
Tel: 613-995-9481

Queen's Univ. at Kingston
Douglas Lib., Kingston, Ont., K7L 5C4
Tel: 613-547-5950

Regina Public Library
2311 12 Ave., Regina, Sask. S4P 0N3
Tel: 306-569-7615

Saint Catharines Public Library
54 Church St., Saint Catharines, Ont. L2R 7K2
Tel: 416-688-6103

Saskatoon Public Library
311 23 St. E., Saskatoon, Sask. S7K 0J6
Tel: 306-664-9555

Scarborough Public Library
1076 Ellesmere Rd., Scarborough, Ont.
   M1P 4P4
Tel: 416-291-1991

Toronto Public Library
40 Orchard View Blvd., Toronto, Ont.
   M4R 1B9
Tel: 416-484-8015

Univ. of Toronto Libraries
Toronto, Ont., M5S 1A5
Tel: 416-978-2294

Univ. of Western Ontario
Univ. Lib., 1151 Richmond St. N., London,
   Ont. N6A 3K7
Tel: 519-679-6191

Windsor Public Library
850 Ouellette Ave., Windsor, Ont. N9A 4M9
Tel: 519-258-8111